Handbook of
MULTIMEDIA COMPUTING

Handbook of
MULTIMEDIA COMPUTING

Editor-in-Chief

BORKO FURHT

Professor of Computer Science and Engineering
Florida Atlantic University, Boca Raton, Florida

CRC Press
Boca Raton   London   New York   Washington, D.C.

Library of Congress Cataloging-in-Publication Data

Handbook of multimedia computing / Borko Furht, editor-in-chief
      p. cm.
    Includes bibliographical references and index.
    ISBN 0-8493-1825-4 (alk. paper)
    1. Multimedia systems. I. Furht, Borivoje.
QA76.575.H355 1998
006.7—dc21

98-24633
CIP

PREFACE

Multimedia computing has emerged in the last few years as a major area of research. Coupled with high-speed networks, multimedia computer systems have opened a wide range of new applications by combining a variety of information sources, such as voice, graphics, animation, images, audio, and video. Looking at the big picture, multimedia can be viewed as the merging of four industries: computer, communication, broadcasting, and consumer electronics.

The purpose of *The Handbook of Multimedia Computing* is to provide a comprehensive reference on advanced topics in this field. We invited world experts and leading researchers in the field to contribute to this Handbook with their visionary views of the trends in this exciting field. The Handbook is intended for both researchers and practitioners in the field, for scientists and engineers involved in multimedia system design and applications, and for anyone who wants to learn about the field of multimedia computing. The Handbook can also be beneficial as the textbook or reference book for graduate courses in the area of multimedia computing.

This Handbook is complemented by *The Handbook of Internet and Multimedia Systems and Applications,* published by the CRC Press as well.

The Handbook is divided into four parts and comprises of 43 chapters. Part I on "Basic Concepts and Standards," which consists of 9 chapters, introduces basic multimedia terminology, taxonomy and concepts, such as multimedia objects, user interfaces, and standards. Part II on "Multimedia Retrieval and Processing Techniques" comprises 11 chapters, which deal with various aspects of audio, image, and video retrieval, indexing, and processing techniques and systems. Part III on "Multimedia Systems and Techniques," which consists of 16 chapters, covers a variety of critical multimedia issues, such as multimedia synchronization, operating systems for multimedia, multimedia databases, storage organizations, processor architectures, and many others. Finally, Part IV on "Multimedia Communications and Networking," which has 7 chapters, deals with various networking issues including quality of service, resource management, video transport, and others.

I would like to thank all 80 authors who have developed individual chapters for the Handbook. Without their expertise and effort this Handbook would never come true. CRC Press also deserves my sincere recognition for their support throughout the project. Special thanks to Jerry Papke, senior publisher, Suzanne Lassandro, production manager, and Mimi Williams, editor, for their encouragement, assistance, and support.

Borko Furht
Boca Raton, Florida

EDITOR-IN-CHIEF

Borko Furht is a professor of computer science and engineering at Florida Atlantic University (FAU) in Boca Raton, Florida. He is the founder and director of the Multimedia Laboratory at FAU, funded by the National Science Foundation. Before joining FAU, he was a vice president of research and a senior director of development at Modcomp, a computer company of Daimler Benz, Germany, a professor at University of Miami in Coral Gables, Florida, and senior scientist at the Institute "Boris Kidric"-Vinca in Belgrade, Yugoslavia.

Professor Furht received BEEE (Dipl.Eng.), M.Sc. and Ph.D. degrees in electrical and computer engineering from the University of Belgrade. His current research is in multimedia systems, video compression, storage and retrieval, synchronization, and Internet and multimedia applications. He is the author of numerous books and articles in the areas of multimedia, computer architecture, real-time computing, and operating systems. He is a founder and editor-in-chief of the *Journal of Multimedia Tools and Applications* (Kluwer Academic Publishers). He has received several technical and publishing awards, and has consulted for many high-tech companies including IBM, Hewlett-Packard, Xerox, General Electric, JPL, NASA, Honeywell, and RCA. He has also served as a consultant to various colleges and universities. He has given many invited talks, keynote lectures, seminars, and tutorials. He is a senior member of the IEEE and a member of the ACM.

CONTRIBUTORS

Karl Aberer
GMD-IPSI
Darmstadt, Germany

Atsushi Atarashi
NEC Corporation
Kawasaki, Kanagawa, Japan

John Bates
University of Cambridge Computer
Laboratory
Cambridge, United Kingdom

Meera M. Blattner
University of California, Davis, and
Lawrence Livermore National
Laboratory
Livermore, California, USA

Thom Blum
Muscle Fish LLC
Berkeley, California, USA

Joseph Celi
IBM Corporation
Boca Raton, Florida, USA

Shih-Fu Chang
Columbia University
New York, USA

Mark Claypool
Worcester Polytechnic University
Worcester, Massachusetts, USA

Remi Depommier
Siemens Corporate Research
Princeton, New Jersey, USA

Wolfgang Effelsberg
University of Mannheim
Mannheim, Germany

Alexandros Eleftheriadis
Columbia University
New York, USA

James Ford
Dartmouth College
Hanover, New Hampshire, USA

Borko Furht
Florida Atlantic University
Boca Raton, Florida, USA

Shahram Ghandeharizadeh
University of Southern California
Los Angeles, California, USA

William I. Grosky
Wayne State University
Detroit, Michigan, USA

Venkat Gudivada
Dow Jones Markets
Jersey City, New Jersey, USA

Wolfgang A. Halang
FernUniversitat Hagen
Hagen, Germany

Rei Hamikawa
NEC Corporation
Kawasaki, Kanagawa, Japan

Rachelle S. Heller
The George Washington University
Washington, DC 20052

Matthias Hemmje
GMD – German National Research
Darmstadt, Germany

Rune Hjeslvold
Siemens Corporate Research
Princeton, New Jersey, USA

Tsuneo Ikedo
The University of Aizu
Aizuwakamatsu-city, Fukusima, Japan

Muriel Jourdan
Inria Rhone-Alpes
Montbonnot, France

Hari Kalva
Columbia University
New York, USA

Douglas Keislar
Muscle Fish LLC
Berkeley, California, USA

Mark Kessler
Motorola, Inc.
Boynton Beach, Florida, USA

Christoph Kuhmunch
University of Mannheim
Mannheim, Germany

Philip A. Laplante
BCC/NJIT Technology Educational
Center
Pemberton, New Jersey, USA

Nabil Layaida
Inria Rhone-Alpes
Montbonnot, France

John Chung-Mong Lee
Hong Kong University of Science &
Technology
Hong Kong, China

Martin Leissler
GMD – German National Research
Darmstadt, Germany

Karen Lentz
Tufts University
Medford, Massachusetts, USA

Clement H.C. Leung
Victoria University of Technology
Melbourne, Victoria, Australia

Qing Li
Hong Kong Polytechnic University
Hong Kong, China

Victor O. K. Li
The University of Hong Kong
Hong Kong, China

Wanjiun Liao
National Taiwan University
Taipei, Taiwan

Reiner Lichtenecker
FernUniversitat Hagen
Hagen, Germany

Rainer Lienhart
University of Mannheim
Mannheim, Germany

Shih-Ping Liou
Siemens Corporate Research
Princeton, New Jersey, USA

Wei-Ying Ma
Hewlett-Packard Laboratories
Palo Alto, California, USA

Fillia Makedon
Dartmouth College
Hanover, New Hampshire, USA

C. Dianne Martin
The George Washington University
Washington, DC 20052

Antonio Massari
Autoriata per l'"Informatica nella
Publica Administrazione
Roma, Italy

Klara Nahrstedt
University of Illinois at Urbana-
Champaign
Urbana, Illinois, USA

Tatsuo Nakajima
Japan Advanced Institute of Science
and Technology
Ishikawa, Japan

Ryohei Nakatsu
ATR Media Integration &
Communications
Research Laboratories
Kyoto, Japan

Walter Napolitano
Universita de Roma
Roma, Italy

Erich J. Neuhold
GMD-IPSI
Darmstadt, Germany

Hidenori Okuda
NTT Human Interface Laboratories
Kanagawa, Japan

Charles B. Owen
Dartmouth College
Hanover, New Hampshire, USA

Aldo Paradiso
GMD – German National Research
Darmstadt, Germany

Silvia Pfeiffer
University of Mannheim
Mannheim, Germany

B. Prabhakaran
National University of Singapore
Singapore

Roy Rada
Washington State University
Pullman, Washington, USA

D. Raychaudhuri
NEC C&C Research Laboratories
Princeton, New Jersey, USA

A.L. Narasimha Reddy
Texas A&M University
College Station, Texas, USA

Daniel Reininger
NEC C&C Research Laboratories
Princeton, New Jersey, USA

John Riedl
University of Minnesota
Minneapolis, Minnesota, USA

Cecile Roisin
Inria Rhone-Alpes
Montbonnot, France

Lorenzo Saladini
Integra Sistemi srl.
Roma, Italy

Eve M. Schooler
University of Southern California
Los Angeles, California, USA

Henning Schulzrinne
Columbia University
New York, USA

Behzad Shahraray
AT&T Labs – Research
Red Bank, New Jersey, USA

Nalin Sharda
Victoria University of Technology
Melbourne, Victoria, Australia

R. Siracusa
NEC C&C Research Laboratories
Princeton, New Jersey, USA

Fabio Sissini
Universita de Roma
Roma, Italy

Rajesh V. Sonak
Intellinet Technologies
Melbourne, Florida, USA

Alex D. Stoyen
New Jersey Institute of Technology
Newark, New Jersey, USA

Dwi Sutanto
Victoria University of Technology
Melbourne, Victoria, Australia

Heiko Thimm
GMD-IPSI
Darmstadt, Germany

Naoko Tosa
ATR Media Integration &
Communications Laboratories
Kyoto, Japan

Philip K.C. Tse
Victoria University of Technology
Melbourne, Victoria, Australia

Markus Wannemacher
FernUniversitat Hagen
Hagen, Germany

Ray Westwater
Future Ware
Princeton, New Jersey, USA

Erling Wold
Muscle Fish LLC
Berkeley, California, USA

James Wheaton
Muscle Fish LLC
Berkeley, California, USA

Ravi Wijayaratne
Texas A&M University
College Station, Texas, USA

Lars C. Wolf
Darmstadt University of Technology
Darmstadt, Germany

Wei Xiong
Hong Kong University of Science &
Technology
Hong Kong, China

HongJiang Zhang
Hewlett-Packard Laboratories
Palo Alto, California, USA

CONTENTS

PART I   BASIC CONCEPTS AND STANDARDS 1

1   **Multimedia Taxonomy for Design and Evaluation**.......................3
     Rachelle S. Heller and C. Dianne Martin

2   **Multimedia Objects**...17
     Atsushi Atarashi and Rei Hamikawa

3   **Multimedia Data Modeling and Management for Semantic
     Content Retrieval**..43
     Clement H.C. Leung and Dwi Sutanto

4   **Middleware Platforms to Support Multimedia Applications**...........55
     John Bates

5   **DAVIC and Multimedia Standards**...89
     *Hari Kalva, Hidenori Okuda, Shih-Fu Chang, and
     Alexandros Eleftheriadis*

6   **Interactive Multimedia User Interfaces**..................................111
     Meera M. Blattner

7   **Digital Audio Presentation and Compression**...........................135
     Ray Westwater

8   **Image Presentation and Compression**....................................149
     Borko Furht

9   **Video Presentation and Compression**.....................................171
     Borko Furht and Raymond Westwater

PART II MULTIMEDIA RETRIEVAL AND PROCESSING TECHNIQUES 205

10 **Classification, Search, and Retrieval of Audio**..........................207
Erling Wold, Thom Blum, Douglas Keislar, and James Wheaton

11 **Content-Based Image Indexing and Retrieval**.........................227
Wei-Ying Ma and HongJiang Zhang

12 **Content-Based Video Browsing and Retrieval**..........................255
HongJiang Zhang

13 **Indexing for Efficient Spatial Similarity-Based Retrieval in Multimedia Databases**...281
Venkat Gudivada, Rajesh V. Sonak, William I. Grosky, and Karen Lentz

14 **Classification and Characterization of Digital Watermarks for Multimedia Data**..299
James Ford, Fillia Makedon, and Charles B. Owen

15 **Automatic and Dynamic Video Manipulation**...........................317
John Chung-Mong Lee, Qing Li, and Wei Xiong

16 **Multimedia Information Retrieval Using Pictorial Transcripts** 345
Behzad Shahraray

17 **Automatic Trailer Production** 361
Rainer Lienhart, Silvia Pfeiffer, and Wolfgang Effelsberg

18 **Multimedia Archiving, Logging, and Retrieval** 379
Rune Hjeslvold, Shih-Ping Liou, and Remi Depommier

19 **Cross-Modal Information Retrieval** 403
Charles B. Owen and Fillia Makedon

20 **Detection and Recognition of Television Commercials**.................425
Rainer Lienhart, Christoph Kuhmunch, and Wolfgang Effelsberg

PART III MULTIMEDIA SYSTEMS AND TECHNIQUES...445

21 Processor Architectures for Multimedia 447
Borko Furht

22 Authoring Techniques for Temporal Scenarios of Multimedia Documents...469
Muriel Jourdan, Nabil Layaida, and Cecile Roisin

23 Scheduling for Integrated Service in Multimedia Systems............491
A.L. Narasimha Reddy and Ravi Wijayaratne

24 Storage Organizations for Multimedia Data.............................507
Clement H.C. Leung and Philip K.C. Tse

25 Multimedia Synchronization...525
B. Prabhakaran

26 High-Precision Temporal Synchronization in Multimedia Systems...545
Wolfgang A. Halang, Markus Wannemacher, Reiner Lichtenecker, Philip A. Laplante, and Alex D. Stoyen

27 Design and Implementation of Multimedia Servers.....................557
Shahram Ghandeharizadeh

28 Multimedia Database Management Systems.............................579
Karl Aberer, Heiko Thimm, and Erich J. Neuhold

29 Multimedia Support in Java..605
Joseph Celi and Borko Furht

30 Operating System Issues for Continuous Media.........................627
Henning Schulzrinne

31 Hypermedia Techniques for Distributed Systems.......................649
Mark Kessler and Borko Furht

32 Distributed Multimedia Systems..681
Victor O. K. Li and Wanjiun Liao

33 Interactive Movies...**701**
Ryohei Nakatsu and Naoko Tosa

34 Virtual Reality Systems for Browsing Multimedia......................**713**
Antonio Massari, Lorenzo Saladini, Fabio Sisinni, Walter Napolitano,
Matthias Hemmje, Aldo Paradiso, and Martin Leissler

35 Multimedia Virtual Reality Systems......................................**737**
Tsuneo Ikedo

36 Multimedia Education...**751**
Roy Rada

PART IV   MULTIMEDIA COMMUNICATIONS
AND NETWORKING...................................**781**

37 Multimedia Networks...**783**
Nalin Sharda

38 Video Transport in ATM Networks: A System View...................**815**
D. Raychaudhuri, Daniel Reininger, and R. Siracusa

39 Quality of Service in Networked Multimedia Systems.................**839**
Klara Nahrstedt

40 End-to-End Quality in Multimedia Applications.......................**875**
Mark Claypool and John Riedl

41 Resource Management in Multimedia Systems.........................**891**
Lars C. Wolf

**42 A Framework for Building Adaptive Continuous Media
     Applications Using Service Proxies**.....................................**913**
Tatsuo Nakajima

43 Conferencing and Collaborative Computing...........................**935**
Eve M. Schooler

INDEX **963**

I

BASIC CONCEPTS AND STANDARDS

1

MULTIMEDIA TAXONOMY FOR DESIGN AND EVALUATION

Rachelle S. Heller and C. Dianne Martin
The George Washington University
Department of Electrical Engineering and Computer Science
Washington, D.C. 20052

1.	**INTRODUCTION**	4
2.	**USE OF TAXONOMIES**	4
3.	**THE FIRST MEDIA TAXONOMY**	5
	3.1 USEFULNESS OF THE MEDIA TAXONOMY IN DESIGN	8
4.	**AN EVOLVING MULTIMEDIA TAXONOMY**	10
	4.1 USE OF THE MULTIMEDIA TAXONOMY FOR EVALUATION	11
5.	**CONCLUSIONS**	14
	REFERENCES	16

Abstract. This chapter presents a *Multimedia Taxonomy* that can be used in the research, evaluation, and development of multimedia applications. The taxonomy is shown as a three-dimensional categorization framework. The increasingly complex media types (Text, Graphics, Sound, Motion, and Multimedia) make up the first dimension. The expression of each medium in three arbitrary categories (Elaboration, Representation, Abstraction) as well as a General category delineates the second dimension, which moves from the concrete, fully explicated expression of information to the abstract, metaphoric form of information within each medium. The third dimension, media context, is characterized by the six discrete categories of Audience, Discipline, Interactivity, Quality, Usefulness, and Aesthetics. Each of these categories can be further enhanced by a set of specific attributes that can be used by designers and evaluators of multimedia systems during the development process.

1. INTRODUCTION

The polysemeous nature of multimedia can be understood by reviewing the many disciplines that lay claim to multimedia: educational software, computer graphics, human-computer interactions, and communications. Each brings a unique lens to multimedia and each demands a specific focus. For example, educational software looks at the learning opportunities provided by the inclusion of media, computer graphics provide algorithms needed to produce the media, and human-computer interactions focus on the interactivity usually provided with a media presentation.

The challenge, then, is to describe and organize the field of multimedia in a way to include these different disciplines and their respective emphases. To do this, it is necessary to delineate a clear organization or framework that can be used by multimedia producers to help organize the phases of design, development, and evaluation. The Multimedia Taxonomy presented here provides such a framework for designers, developers, and evaluators. It will enable designers to characterize each medium by its form and expression while also considering the combined impact of multimedia. It will enable developers to consider the cost benefit of each medium within the overall product, and it will enable evaluators to frame evaluation questions and to generate evaluation protocols for multimedia products.

2. USE OF TAXONOMIES

What is a taxonomy? A taxonomy is a method of organizing a field. The purpose is to enable practitioners to classify known elements within a conceptual framework as well as to produce a classification schema for defining new elements of the field. Taxonomies are specifically useful in new fields, such as multimedia, to provide a descriptive baseline for the field. Good taxonomies are extensible and grow with a growing field. They can be used to identify areas for growth or reflect a growth area within a field. Additionally, taxonomies bring focus and clarity to a field. The act of placing an element from the field within the taxonomy requires a clear examination of all of the salient features of the element.

Taxonomies are not new to the individual media. They have been developed to characterize aspects of music [1], images [2, 3], and graphics [4]. When developing his music taxonomy, Pope [1] made a strong case for the usefulness of taxonomies to clarify the aspects of rapidly changing fields. While not specifically directed toward computing, the Pope music taxonomy is an attempt to organize the vast world of music into broad types such as church music or jazz based upon compositional characteristics.

Both Messaris [2] and Weidenmann [3] categorized computer-based images based upon their interpretive function. Messaris created a taxonomy of salient features, called representational, and aesthetic appreciation, called interpretive. Thus images that are incorporated within a larger software application can be classified according to their function in the application. For example, images can be central to the application such as a schematic of a factory process or merely decorative such as seen in the borders of a PowerPoint presentation. Similarly, Hunter et al. [4] categorized the use of graphics by their function: to embellish, to reinforce, to elaborate, to summarize, and to compare.

The major impetus for our work on a Media Taxonomy came from our observations of graduate students in their computer science-based studies of interactive multimedia. As they began to design, implement, and evaluate multimedia applications, it became apparent that they had no clear, organized understanding of the field. They could examine individual taxonomies for a specific medium, but they needed a more encompassing framework to understand the complexity of media forms and functions.

3. THE FIRST MEDIA TAXONOMY

The first Media Taxonomy [5] was a two-dimensional representation (see Figure 1). That taxonomy was used as a tool to analyze each individual medium for the purpose of determining storage needs, processing time, or possible cognitive load on the user based upon the intended audience, purpose, and venue for the application. As one moved down the taxonomy by media type, the storage demands would increase dramatically. For example, the storage demands for one minute of full motion video are huge compared to those for a purely textural manuscript. Similarly, as one moved across the taxonomy by media expression, the cognitive demands on the user would increase. Being able to decode an icon or a schematic probably will require more cognitive effort than raw video footage or a straight text narrative.

The categories of media expression, elaboration, representation, and abstraction can be understood as a progression from the concrete to the abstract. The dimension can also be understood as requiring increasing decoding efforts on the part of the media user. In the Elaboration category of media expression we consider any form of each medium in which no information has been edited out. For example, in a text-based presentation, this category would include full narrative or transcripts of proceedings. The Elaboration expression of graphics would include a photograph or scanned realistic image. The Elaboration expression of sound would include an audio narrative or transcript of an event. The Elaboration expression of motion would be raw film footage.

| | **MEDIA EXPRESSION** | | |
MEDIA TYPE	**Elaboration**	**Representation**	**Abstraction**
TEXT	Free text, sentences, paragraphs	Bold, italics bullets, underlines, headlines, subheadings	Shapes, icons
GRAPHICS	Photograph, rendering, scanned images	Blueprint, schematic	Icon, metaphorical images
SOUND	Speech, audio transcript	Intensity, tone, inflection, sound effects	Earcon, mood music
MOTION	Raw film footage	Animation, time-lapsed photography	Animated model, highly edited video, morphed image

Figure 1. The Media Taxonomy [5].

Moving away from the fully elaborated form of information to the second category, Representation, the same content can be expressed in a more abbreviated, stylized mode within each medium. In this case, the developer has more control over the expression of the information and the reader/user must accommodate to the author's ellipsis of information. An outline or a series of bullets can be used for text. A blueprint, schematic, or map might be used for graphics. A sound effect, different tone, intensity, or inflection might be used to represent sound, and an animation or time-altered video might be used for motion.

In the last category, Abstraction, the developer relies on metaphor and culturally common understanding to convey information. Thus, text can be used as a graphic such as a logo or registered trademark, or by using a word to look like its meaning, such as 'hill' written as

Hill.

With graphics, an icon or well-known symbol might be used. For sound, the use of mood music or symbolic "earcons" requires the user to make mental connections based upon familiarity with those sounds. Animated models, morphed images, or highly edited film clips for motion again require the user to fill in the gaps. Using media as an abstraction is not a new idea. Apollinaire, a French poet, wrote a poem called *Rain* that, in fact, looked like rain.

The Media Taxonomy is consistent with existing taxonomies. The various music categories expressed by Pope [1] can be accommodated by the sound category. Both Messaris [2] and Weidenmann [3] categorize images based upon their interpretative function, the recognition of salient features (which Messaris calls representational) or the aesthetic appreciation or understanding of the manipulative content of the image (which Messaris calls interpretation). These two categories are consistent with the Media Taxonomy categories of Elaboration and Abstraction. Furthermore, images are seen to lie along a continuum from concrete to abstract to analogy in much the same way that the Media Taxonomy provides the classifications of Elaboration, Representation, and Abstraction. Additional taxonomies or classification schema, such as that of Arnheim[6], can also be accommodated in the Media Taxonomy. His categories of inference, perception, and metaphor map reasonably well into elaboration, representation, and abstraction.

If we review the Media Taxonomy in light of the media characteristics defined by Arens et al. [7], we can see that the Elaboration category relates well to its descriptor, 'real world.' As we move to the right across the dimension of "media expression," the real worldliness of a particular representation diminishes. Figure 2 shows the definition of media characteristics. Figure 3 shows the Media Taxonomy augmented with the applicable media characteristics: temporal, granularity, and baggage. In the temporal category, we extend the meaning to include how the understanding of content changes with time. For example, Elaboration text is permanent; as we move to the Abstraction expression of text, the temporal aspect shifts to transient. The characteristics of granularity and baggage relate well to the increasing degrees of abstraction represented by the dimension, "media expression." Note that for each medium, the overlay of the media characteristics is the same, suggesting that there is an internal consistency within the taxonomy. The issue of detectability relates more to the medium than to format of the medium and is exactly correlated with the four media shown in the taxonomy. Non-aural media will have a lower detectability, with text being the lowest and graphics rated as medium low. The detectability of sound is medium high and motion has the greatest detectability.

Levin et al. [8] propose a functional classification for images, drawn or photographed, based upon the effect of an image on content recall. They identify the categories as decoration, representation, organization, interpretation, and transformation to describe pictures accompanying text. We can apply the Media Taxonomy to their classification and enhance both taxonomies. For example, they classify an image designed to make the page more attractive without relating to the content as decorative. The Media Taxonomy could be used to classify an image used as a decoration as either *Representational*, in the case of a border design, or *Abstract*, in the case of an icon.

Temporal endurance (permanent, transient): An indication whether the created exhibit varies during the lifetime of the presentation.

Granularity (continuous, discrete):   An indication of whether arbitrarily small variations along any dimensional presentation have meaning in the denotation or not.

Baggage (low, high): A gross measure of the amount of extra information a consumer must process in order to become familiar enough with the substrate to correctly interpret it.

Detectability (low, medlow, medhigh, high): A measure of how intrusive to the consumer the exhibit created by the medium will be.

Medium type (aural, visual): What type of medium is necessary for presenting the created exhibit.

Figure 2. Media characteristics [2].

The connection is even stronger when considering Levin's representation category, in which images serve to tell exactly the same story as the other media. In this case one could consult the Media Taxonomy to insure that all media were at the same level of abstraction. Levin's organizational function, usually relying on maps or other diagrams, is analogous to the Representation category of the Media Taxonomy. It is also interesting to note that Levin et al. have identified a form category, called transformation. In this category, information is recorded in a memorable form, not unlike an icon, and in a form different from the other media presentations.

Similarly, it could be combined with the list of attributes described by Hunter et al. [4] to categorize graphics - embellish, reinforce, elaborate, summarize, and compare. In either case the taxonomy provides a framework for a design space that accommodates any of these cognitive areas.

One purpose for delineating each medium across the three categories is to increase our power of analysis in determining which representation of a particular medium will enable us to transmit information in a way that will increase understanding and retention by the user of the information.   Some readers may question our selection of only four media types. For example, many authors categorize maps differently from graphics. The taxonomy could be extended to include refinements to the media type. In the case of maps, a detailed contour map could be classified as Elaboration while a scaled map showing stores in a mall might be a Representational map, and a cognitive map could be considered Abstraction. In fact, it is the extensibility of this taxonomy that underscores its power.

MEDIA TYPE	MEDIA EXPRESSION		
	Elaboration	Representation	Abstraction
TEXT (Detectability = low)			
Temporal *	permanent	transient	transient
Granularity	continuous	discrete	discrete
Baggage	low	high	high
GRAPHICS (Detectability = medlow)			
Temporal *	permanent	transient	transient
Granularity	continuous	discrete	discrete
Baggage	low	high	high
SOUND (Detectability = medhigh)			
Temporal *	permanent	transient	transient
Granularity	continuous	discrete	discrete
Baggage	low	high	high
MOTION (Detectability = high)			
Temporal *	permanent	transient	transient
Granularity	continuous	discrete	discrete
Baggage	low	high	high

*Note: We change the definition of temporal to include whether meaning changes over time.

Figure 3. Media Taxonomy [5] with media characteristics [7].

3.1 USEFULNESS OF THE MEDIA TAXONOMY IN DESIGN

Once created, the evaluation of the merit of the Media Taxonomy rests in its usability and usefulness to the multimedia practitioner. Could the taxonomy be used by students to design and implement multimedia application? Furthermore, could the Media Taxonomy be used to create and carry out protocols for evaluating such applications?

The taxonomy has been used successfully for the past four years in our multimedia graduate program in computer science. Students in the introductory multimedia course use the taxonomy in the design of their media portfolios. They experiment with various presentation forms of each medium before attempting to combine media into a multimedia application. Students in the advanced research and evaluation course use the taxonomy as part of their evaluation protocols to help determine whether each medium in a multimedia presentation is used effectively.

In the introductory graduate course on multimedia each medium is examined from its scientific, psychological, and technical perspectives [9]. Students are required to develop a portfolio of presentations that use all aspects of each medium to describe some place. The place may be real or imaginary, physical or metaphysical. They focus on one medium at a time to enable them to fully understand the technical creation and interactive presentation of information in each medium before putting together multiple media. Students used the taxonomy to develop examples for their portfolio in each of the single medium formats: text, graphics, sound, and video.

When developing the different expressions of the first media type, Text, in the portfolio the initial inclination of students is to write elaborate descriptions of a place, using paragraph form and narrative style. The taxonomy provides guidance about how to go beyond simple narrative to try outlines, headlines, different fonts and formats, and iconic use of text. One student, writing about Korea, chose to use an illuminated manuscript style to describe his homeland. He experimented with color for the anchoring letters of the paragraphs and used a font that was indicative of Korea. Another student, describing his apartment, followed the style aspect of the taxonomy for text and used the coded descriptions usually found in newspapers 'for rent' listings. Another student, describing the university food court in text, used the idea of abstraction with letters to show the shape of the area. She also used different fonts, colors, and styles to represent the different kinds of food available, such as Chinese, Mexican, deli, grille, etc.

In the sound exercise, one student described the whale sanctuary in Antarctica by using sound as narrative, mood music, sound effects of whales singing, and sound as an earcon when moving from one part of the presentation to another. In the graphics exercise, another student described Jamaica by using a map of Jamaica, a schematic drawing of the roads with major tourist stops, and scanned pictures of the island. He also developed graphical icons as navigation buttons. During the video exercise, a student described a popular local area by shooting video sequences that took on the aspect of someone walking down the main street in the area; close-up shots of the stores, restaurants, and theaters. During his animation sequence, he showed an animated map displaying to the viewer where they were and allowing them to go in any direction to any location.

Another student used video and animation in his Ski School project to show actual footage of different skiing techniques with an animated overlay of how the skis were moving in each lesson. He used the dimensions of the taxonomy to develop his ideas of starting with spectacular long distance skiing shots and then zooming into the ski school where the user could view the lessons in actual time, slow motion, stop action, and with the animated ski overlay.

One challenge that designers face is how to insure that what is said in two media, text and images, for example, represent unique, reinforcing expressions of each medium and not mere duplicates of each other. The taxonomy also offers a structure in which to understand how to put two or more media together more effectively. For example, in the two-media exercise in the portfolio, students are asked to combine animation with one other medium to convey the idea of their place. One student, who was describing the Washington, D.C. Metro system, used an animated map of one of the subway lines with the sounds of the subway in the background.

When using the Media Taxonomy, students were able to hone their computer-based technical skills as well as delve into the psychological and scientific aspects of the different media. Admittedly, design is more an art form than a science, but ways of thinking about media implied by the media categories in the taxonomy can help students find their own 'artistic voice'. The taxonomy has helped students to experiment more fully with the many aspects of each medium by using the three categories in each of their single medium explorations. It provides a framework for both students and professional designers to combine different media more intentionally, using the cognitive impact from one aspect of a particular medium to offset or enhance the cognitive impact of a different aspect of another medium.

4. AN EVOLVING MULTIMEDIA TAXONOMY

As useful as the first Media Taxonomy was, it proved to be incomplete when students wanted to examine the possible interactions between the user and the media. For this reason, the first Media Taxonomy also proved to be incomplete as students tried to use it as the basis for the development of evaluation protocols.

Evaluations, both formative and summative, draw focus on the media expression in the context of content as well as the technology. Evaluations examine issues such as whether the medium is clearly and appropriately expressed within a specific discipline or content area as well as whether the technical delivery is of high quality. Other criteria such as whether the software can be used by the intended audience and how the user might navigate within the software are also appropriate for assessment, as are questions of hardware appropriateness and cognitive accessibility. Evaluations can include experiments, field evaluations, system testing, comparative testing, usability testing, and expert evaluations [10]. They can take the form of observations, interviews, surveys, or electronic capture of data. The first Media Taxonomy needed to be extended to include a third dimension to address these issues.

A first attempt was to use the original Media Taxonomy within existing evaluative protocols. For example, Reeves and Harmon [11] suggest a series of questions whose responses lie on a continuum between two opposite instantiations of an attribute. The questions include such criteria as "the instructions are clear" to "the program is aesthetically pleasing." The match between the first Media Taxonomy and that type of evaluation protocol was incomplete. The items in the evaluation instruments tended to be generic questions relating to appropriateness of content and overall media use, whereas the first Media Taxonomy focused on specific media categories without addressing issues of type of content, intended audience, or interaction between the media. These deficiencies led to the development of a Multimedia Taxonomy (Figure 4), a three-dimensional expansion of the first Media Taxonomy [12].

First, we realized that the two original dimensions, media type and media expressions needed to be expanded. An aspect of using the previous taxonomy for evaluation or analysis of media impact that proved to be difficult was determining how to address the interplay of the various media, especially when two media are presented in different expressions. For example, if we have a screen with sound and images and the sound is elaborative, such as the excerpt from a famous speech, and the image is a representational line drawing of the person speaking, how do we extract the impact of one medium from another? In fact, if the intent of multimedia is the seamless integration of different media, then this becomes almost impossible. This difficulty led to the creation of the fifth Media Type, Multimedia, in addition to the four individual media types of Text, Sound, Graphics, and Motion. Including the complexity of multimedia as well as the four media types prompts the evaluator to structure questions about the cognitive synchronization between the textual message and the visual message of a multimedia application.

The next extension of the Media Taxonomy is reflected in the addition of a General category for the dimension of Media Expression. This became a category for the evaluative questions that spanned the three categories of expression for each medium. For example, general questions of font size are appropriate to the three media expression categories of elaborative, representational, and abstract.

The most significant expansion of the original Media Taxonomy, however, was the addition of a new dimension, context, which is comprised of six discrete categories: *Audience, Discipline, Interactivity, Quality, Usefulness, and Aesthetics*. From each of these categories could be drawn a list of specific attributes. The category of Audience would focus on attributes such as age, gender, cultural background, literacy (both computer and reading) level, and abilities that describe the intended audience for the product. Purpose includes the content area of the material and the overall purpose, such as to educate, entertain, inform, or market. Interactivity might include attributes in the interface such as metaphor, amount of user control, navigation strategy, type of feedback, and level of engagement. The Quality category refers to the technical aspects of the application delivery and might be described by the attributes of clarity of presentation or fidelity of reproduction. Appropriate concerns within this category might include clarity of characters on the screen as well as the technical synchronization between media. The attribute of Usefulness would describe how well the presentation met the intended purpose for the intended audience using such criteria as user satisfaction with content, user satisfaction with interface, and retention of information or knowledge. Finally, the attribute of Aesthetics would include criteria such as screen design, use of color, combination of design elements, and overall appeal.

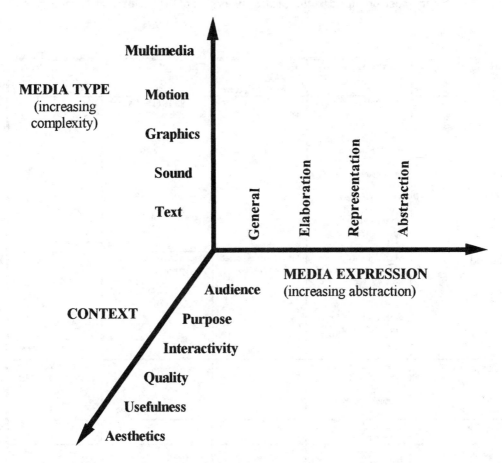

Figure 4. The Multimedia Taxonomy [12].

4.1 USE OF THE MULTIMEDIA TAXONOMY FOR EVALUATION

The Multimedia Taxonomy is best understood in its application. The new media space is 6x4x5, where each cell can be used to address specific aspects of media design or evaluation. For example, the aesthetics category might encompass the following concerns: In the general expression of text, we might ask, is the font size appealing, while in the elaboration expression of text, it is appropriate to ask an aesthetic question concerning the richness of the literary expression on the continuum from dry to poetic. In representational expression of text, we might ask whether the format of the outline is logically well structured and, in considering the abstract expression of text within the aesthetic categories, we could ask if the textual image as an icon is pleasing.

Similarly, when considering questions of *Audience* in the general listing for text we might ask if the instructions are clear, while in elaborative or representational expressions of text we might ask evaluative questions about whether the feedback to the audience is appropriate or if there is a compatibility between the reading level of the audience and the level of expression of the textual description. The *Usefulness* category prompts us to assess the value added by a medium type or expression. The Multimedia Taxonomy elicits questions about sound quality as well as sound impact. Using the attributes within the Quality category as part of an evaluation protocol would prompt the evaluator to ask questions such as whether the motion of the lips is synchronized with the speech. Figure 5 contains a sampling of questions that might be prompted by the Quality dimension of the Multimedia Taxonomy.

MEDIA FORM	GENERAL	MEDIA EXPRESSION ELABORATION	REPRESENTATION	ABSTRACTION
Text	Math functions were correct. It is clear which input device to use. Word choice was unclear/clear. Grammar was correct. Reading characters on screen (very hard to very easy). Spelling was correct (No or Yes)		Font for bold and italics is readable.	
Sound	Sound quality (unclear to clear). Sound speed (too fast/slow to just right). Sound volume (too loud/soft to just right).	Speech is captured without stutters.	Sound effects are recognizable.	
Graphics	Quality of image (low to high) Size of image (too large/small to just right).			Icons are clear. Iconoic metaphor sharp.
Motion	Quality of motion (jerky to smooth).			
Multimedia	Media integration (uncoordinated to coordinated). Media technical synchronization.			

Figure 5. Sample questions from the quality dimension.

While the Multimedia Taxonomy is recent, questions from the student evaluation protocols developed prior to this extension of the taxonomy fit neatly into the new version. For example, under the category of Usefulness, the evaluation protocols contained questions about whether a medium like sound was functional, by asking users to rate the sound on a Likert scale that ranged from annoying to helpful. The protocols also contained open-ended questions about what the user remembered about the sound in the application being evaluated. Thus, the newly expanded Multimedia Taxonomy becomes a floor, not a ceiling, for a series of guidelines that can be used to generate evaluation questions about a multimedia application. Parts of the taxonomy not relevant to the specific product being evaluated can be ignored when developing the evaluation protocol and data-gathering instruments.

Not all of the 120 cells contained within the three-dimensional Multimedia Taxonomy are completed. Some are being examined in detail, while others are still being developed. Aleem [13] examined the relationship between the attribute of interactivity to the media type and expression. He further subdivided the attribute of interactivity into four categories: Passive, Reactive, Proactive, and Directive. With the Passive aspect of interactivity, the user has no control, but instead, all control is embodied in the application (i.e., a PowerPoint presentation). Reactive interactivity provides limited response for the user within a scripted sequence. Proactive interactivity allows the user to play a major role in the design and construction of situations, typically by manipulating values for valuables. Multimedia that have interactivity at the Directive level allow the user to both respond to and initiate actions within the application as well as to tailor aspects of the environment, such as selection of color choice, feedback choice, and so on. Figure 6 identifies examples of media expression within each of these categories for the media types of text and sound. Other categories of the Multimedia Taxonomy require a similar detailed analysis.

Media Expression at Different Levels of Interactivity

MEDIA TYPE	PASSIVE	REACTIVE	PROACTIVE	DIRECTIVE
Text	No user control Sequential presentation	Page turner Linear spacing	Browsing Hypertext Fixed anchors Paths with choices for user	Dialog-based Creative writing Word processing
Graphics	No user control Sequential presentation	Able to make predefined changes to graphics	User initiated changes to graphics (size, shape, color, position)	User created graphics
Sound	No user control Sequential presentation	Able to make predefined changes Adjust volume	Change stations Tracks Fast forward Loop	User created Modify sound
Motion	No user control Sequential presentation	Able to make predefined changes such as path or target of motion	User controlled Start, stop, pause, Forward, reverse	User created Build own animated scenes
Multimedia	No user control Any combination of above types	Any combination of above types	Any combination of above types	Any combination of above types

Figure 6. Examples of media expression within the interactive category
(excerpted from [13], used with permission).

Students have been successful in designing evaluation protocols using the Multimedia Taxonomy as a guideline. Figure 7 represents a sample of the survey comments developed from the formative evaluation of Ada Mentor, an online web site for the study of the Ada programming language. The Multimedia Taxonomy helped pinpoint such problems as too many forms within the web site and the inability for a user to see the entire page. They were able to suggest, on the basis of the evaluation, that the Ada Mentor developers reduce the navigational capabilities and clarify the functionality of navigational icons.

Figure 8 illustrates a part of the summative evaluation developed for a company's multimedia application designed to market cosmetic products to women and men. Using the Multimedia Taxonomy to develop the evaluation protocol, evaluators were able to determine that the sound quality was difficult to hear in a department store setting. Without user controls for the sound, the software application was deemed useful for home settings but less than optimal for public spaces.

Ada Mentor Formative Evaluation Comments for Open Questions

KEYWORD	ACTUAL COMMENTS OF CONCERN	ACTUAL COMMENTS OF PRAISE
Text	Hard to read; could be bigger Too much technical language	Not too wordy.
Navigation	Hard to find exercises Buttons didn't load in some cases Need to move inherent icons Need better button description Trouble getting back to where I was	
Speed	Took forever to load Slow on T1 line Slowness more trouble than it's worth	
Screen Design	Can't see entire page Screen size too small for exercises	Clean setup Easy to look at Nice graphic layout
Interactivity	Not much better than a book Book could have been read anywhere Exercises are not interactive	
Content	Need better explanations Too much technical language Only include security information when necessary Make it more fun	Information on each topic was sufficient
Audience	Get it off the net Show Ada's practical application	Good tutorial for learning Ada First of its kind I've seen Easy to access Potential to be good tutorial

Figure 7. Selected responses to formative evaluation protocol using the taxonomy.

5. CONCLUSIONS

As an organizing principle, the Multimedia Taxonomy presented here can be used to understand both design and content messages. The next step is to review the taxonomy in light of various studies in the psychological and cognitive aspects of understanding of multimedia applications to determine whether this taxonomy can shed light on these areas. Questions such as how we come to understand an image and how that understanding is different from our understanding of text can be answered in part by using the taxonomy. We have presented a few examples of the impact of the Multimedia Taxonomy on the design and implementation of evaluation protocols for multimedia products. More work in this area remains to be done. Finally, however, the Multimedia Taxonomy represents an attempt at the formalism that is needed to provide both a theoretical and practical framework for the new and rapidly growing field of interactive multimedia.

Cosmetic Package Questionnaire

User evaluation: Circle the response that best matches your attitude toward each statement.

#	Item	Low anchor	1	2	3	4	5	High anchor
1.	Screen layouts	Inappropriate	1	2	3	4	5	Appropriate
2.	Screen spacing	Crowded	1	2	3	4	5	Well spaced
3.	Arrangement of information on screens	Confusing	1	2	3	4	5	Clear
4.	Characters on the computer screen	Hard to read	1	2	3	4	5	Easy to read
5.	Colors used for the text	Annoying	1	2	3	4	5	Pleasant
6.	Pictures used for menu options	Unhelpful	1	2	3	4	5	Helpful
7.	Size of pictures used for menu options	Inappropriate	1	2	3	4	5	Appropriate
8.	Quality of pictures used	Poor	1	2	3	4	5	Excellent
9.	Quality of text displayed	Poor	1	2	3	4	5	Excellent
10.	Harmony of text and picture colors	Poor	1	2	3	4	5	Excellent
11.	Pictures used for navigation	Inappropriate	1	2	3	4	5	Appropriate
12.	Animation used	Annoying	1	2	3	4	5	Pleasant
13.	System response time	Too slow	1	2	3	4	5	Fast enough
14.	Learning to use the system	Difficult	1	2	3	4	5	Easy
15.	Discovering new features	Difficult	1	2	3	4	5	Easy
16.	Looking for specific information	Difficult	1	2	3	4	5	Easy
17.	Changing your input	Difficult	1	2	3	4	5	Easy
18.	Feedback provided by the system	Inappropriate	1	2	3	4	5	Appropriate

Figure 8. Summative evaluation protocol using the Taxonomy – selected questions.

REFERENCES

1. Pope, S. J., World Wide Web http://www-mitpress.mit.edu/Computer_music_journal, 1994.
2. Messaris, P., "Visual Literacy: Image, Mind and Reality," Westview Press, San Francisco, 1994.
3. Weidenmann, B., "Codes of instructional pictures," *Comprehension of Graphics*, Schnotz, W. and Kulhavy, R. K. (Ed.), pp. 29-42, 1994.
4. Hunter, R., Crismore, R., and Pearson, P. D., "Visual Displays in Basal Readers and Social Studies Textbooks," *The Psychology of Illustration, Basic Research*, Willows and Houghton (Ed.), Springer, Vol. 1, pp. 116-135, New York, 1987.
5. Heller, R. S. and Martin, C. D., "A Media Taxonomy," *IEEE MultiMedia*, 2 (4), pp. 36-45, 1995.
6. Arnheim, B., *Visual Thinking*, University of California Press, Berkeley, 1969.
7. Arens, Y., Hovy, E., and Vossers, M., "On the Knowledge Underlying Multimedia Presentations," *Intelligent Multimedia Interfaces*, Maybury (Ed.), The MIT Press, Boston, 470-506, 1993.
8. Levin, J. R., Auglin, G. J., and Carney, R. N., "On Empirically Validated Functions of Pictures in Prose," *The Psychology of Illustration, Basic Research*, Willows and Houghton (Eds), Springer, New York, Vol. 1, 51-85, 1987.
9. Heller, R. S., "Creating an Advanced Degree Program in Multimedia," *Proceedings of the ASEE*, New Orleans, pp. 353-356, January 1994.
10. Flagg, R., *Formative Evaluation for Educational Technologies*, Lawrence Erlbaum Associates, 1990.
11. Reeves, T. C. and Harmon, S. W., "Systematic Evaluation Procedures for Instructional Hypermedia/Multimedia," Presented at the Annual Meeting of the AERA, Session 30.05, 1993.
12. Heller, R. S., "Developing Theoretical Frameworks for Designing, Developing and Evaluating Interactive Multimedia," Ed-Media '97 Conference, Calgary, Canada, 1997, and World Wide Web site: http://www.seas.gwu.edu/faculty/sheller2/taxon/index.htm.
13. Aleem, T. A., "A Taxonomy of Multimedia Interactivity," Ph.D. Dissertation in progress, The Union Institute, 1997. Available from WWW site http://www.wrols.com/aleem/interact.html.

2

MULTIMEDIA OBJECTS

Atsushi Atarashi[1] and Rei Hamakawa[2]
NEC Corporation
[1]Human Media Research Laboratories
1-1 Miyazaki 4-Chome, Miyamae-ku,
Kawasaki, KANAGAWA 216-8555, Japan
[2]Personal C&C Group Planning Division
7-1 Shiba 5-Chome, Minato-ku, TOKYO 108-8001, Japan

1. **INTRODUCTION**...18
  1.1 CONCEPTS IN OBJECT-ORIENTED DESIGN 18
  1.2 THE AFFINITY OF THE OBJECT-ORIENTED APPROACH TO MULTIMEDIA APPLICATIONS 18
2. **A CLASS HIERARCHY FOR MULTIMEDIA OBJECTS**.....................19
  2.1 THE BASEOBJECT CLASS 19
  2.2 THE TEMPORALMEDIA CLASS 20
  2.3 CLASSES FOR DISCRETE MEDIA 24
  2.4 CLASSES FOR GUI OBJECTS 24
3. **COMPOSITE MULTIMEDIA OBJECT MODEL BY GIBBS ET AL.**......25
  3.1 MULTIMEDIA OBJECTS AS ACTIVE OBJECTS...25
  3.2 TEMPORAL TRANSFORMATION TO MULTIMEDIA OBJECTS.........................26
  3.3 COMPOSITE MULTIMEDIA OBJECTS 26
4. **OBJECT COMPOSITION AND PLAYBACK MODEL BY HAMAKAWA**....27
  4.1 OBJECT COMPOSITION MODEL..27
  4.2 CONSTRUCTING COMPOSITE OBJECTS...29
  4.3 OBJECT PLAYBACK MODEL 31
5. **MULTIMEDIA OBJECT MODEL IN MHEG**......................................32
  5.1 OVERVIEW OF THE MHEG-5 CLASS HIERARCHY....................................33
  5.2 MECHANISM FOR MHEG-5 EXECUTION 34
  5.3 EXAMPLE 35
6. **NETWORKED MULTIMEDIA OBJECTS IN BERKELEY CONTINUOUS MEDIA TOOLKIT**..36
  6.1 OVERVIEW OF SMT OBJECTS 36
  6.2 INTERACTION AMONG OBJECT OVER THE NETWORK 36
  6.3 THE LOGICAL TIME SYSTEM OBJECTS 37
  6.4 OBJECT FOR MULTIMEDIA DATA DELIVERY...37
  6.5 EXAMPLE 38
7. **CONCLUSION** 39
  REFERENCES 40

Abstract. This chapter describes multimedia objects. For multimedia application designers to take full advantage of the ability of computers to digitally process a variety of multimedia data, the best approach would seem to be the object-oriented approach, with its characteristics of abstraction, modularity, information encapsulation, and compatibility with event-driven programming. We first describe the general concept of multimedia objects, explain the merits of the object-oriented approach to multimedia applications, and then summarize important research activity in the field of multimedia objects.

1. INTRODUCTION

The phrase 'multimedia objects' refers to elements of multimedia data, such as video, audio, animation, images, text, etc. that are used as objects in object-oriented programming.

In the development of multimedia systems, it is often far easier to use an object-oriented approach than to attempt non-object-oriented design. Now that the computer can digitally manipulate a variety of multimedia data, the potential for object-oriented design is significantly enhanced.

In this chapter, we first briefly review object-oriented design and then go on to describe its advantages for application to multimedia.

1.1 CONCEPTS IN OBJECT-ORIENTED DESIGN

Among the many object-oriented programming languages currently in common use (Java [2], C++ [48], Smalltalk [13], etc.), specifications may differ to some extent, but the underlying concepts are essentially the same. The most important concepts are:[1]

Objects In programming, an object is composed of a data structure and an algorithm, i.e., a structure for enclosing a set of data items and a set of operations.[2] An object has both state and behavior: behavior refers to how an object acts or reacts; a state represents the cumulative result of behavior to a given point in time.

Messages Messages are requests sent to objects to get them to perform specific operations.

Classes A class is a specification of the common structure (the concrete representation of state) and behavior of a given set of objects. Objects in the set covered by a given class may be referred to as *instances* of that class, and creating a new object in the set may be referred to as *instantiation*.

Subclasses and inheritance A class can exist in relationship with a subclass below it. With respect to its subclass, this original class exists as a superclass. The objects covered by a subclass *share state* and behavior with those covered by a superclass. The downward sharing of structure and behavior is referred to as *inheritance*.

1.2 THE AFFINITY OF THE OBJECT-ORIENTED APPROACH TO MULTIMEDIA APPLICATIONS

Four fundamental characteristics contribute significantly to the suitability of object-oriented programming to multimedia applications: 1) abstraction; 2) modularity/extensibility; 3) information encapsulation; and 4) compatibility with event-driven programming.

One of the difficulties in designing multimedia applications, beyond the basic requirement of handling a large variety of different media, is the need to be able to deal with an added variety of media formats (MPEG, JPEG, etc.) and hardware. While each of these may differ significantly from each other, they also overlap in many significant areas, and one

---

[1] More detailed explanations can be found in books related to the object-oriented approach [3][7][8][43].

[2] While the term "operation" is often used interchangeably with "method," strictly speaking, a "method" does not represent the actual operation itself but rather a code for implementing an operation.

effective way of economizing on the amount of programming required is to employ inheritance in the form of class hierarchies (i.e., to apply increasing levels of **abstraction**).

Because the requirements placed upon multimedia applications are continually evolving and expanding, it is important to be able to change or add to existing programs easily. The functions of existing media may have to be modified, new media or media formats may have to be added, and new devices may have to be accommodated. The class-hierarchy nature of object-oriented programming allows such changes to be made locally, with minimum disruption to the overall program - **modularity** and **extensibility** increase the ease with which programs can react to changing requirements.

Some multimedia applications may initially require extremely complex mechanisms for controlling media in both spatial and temporal dimensions, and certain hardware connections may require highly individualized programs. At the application programming level, then, it will be extremely helpful if the programmer can be shielded from concerns over the numerous mechanical details of particular media and hardware. One of the strengths of object-oriented programming is its ability to **encapsulate** such particularized **information** into 'black boxes', which the programmer can employ without being concerned over their specific content.

While increasing advances in the power and reach of graphical interfaces have given users important new freedom of action, they have also made application programming a significantly more complex task. No longer bound to a specific order of actions, such as might be found in procedure-oriented interfaces, users may perform actions in whatever order they please, and the program must be capable of reacting to this new unpredictability. Object-oriented programming is particularly well suited to such **event-driven programming** because with it the programmer can simply treat each button or menu item as a separate object with its own individual behavior.

We should note in passing, however, that no design will be useful simply by virtue of the fact that it is object-oriented. Without careful attention to the effective use of class hierarchies, messages, etc., the special strengths of the object-oriented approach can easily be squandered.

2. A CLASS HIERARCHY FOR MULTIMEDIA OBJECTS

This section describes a sample class hierarchy for multimedia objects. Our objectives in presenting the hierarchy are as follows: 1) to demonstrate how we can actually benefit from applying the object-oriented approach to multimedia programming; 2) to clarify what must be considered in designing classes for multimedia objects; and 3) to make it easier to understand subsequent discussions dealing with research activities in the field of multimedia objects.

Please note that the class hierarchy we present here is a very simple one. Detailed issues of implementation, which are very important in real systems, are unnecessary for our purposes here.

2.1 THE BaseObject CLASS

The BaseObject class provides an abstraction of all objects, including temporal media objects as video and audio, discrete media objects as text and images, and GUI objects as buttons and scrollbars. This means that the BaseObject class is the root of the hierarchy and that each subsequent class in the hierarchy inherits the attributes of the BaseObject class (Figure 1).

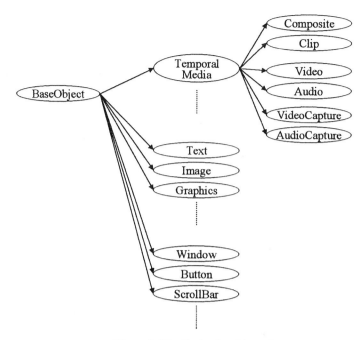

Figure 1. The Basic class hierarchy.

Designing the BaseObject class requires careful attention to the proper level of abstraction. When the level of abstraction has been properly chosen, we are fully able to enjoy the many advantages of the object-oriented approach.

Let us consider, as an example, a multimedia document editor capable of importing various types of multimedia objects into documents. When the designers of the class hierarchy are skillful enough in their object abstraction, it becomes possible for application programmers in control of the editor, on the basis of the methods and instance variables included in the BaseObject class alone, to create an object-importing module for the editor simply as a small piece of code. They need to know none of the details of specific classes of multimedia objects. When the designers of the class hierarchy are not skillful enough in their object abstraction, the application programmers have to use a number of different pieces of code to create the module, each piece being designed to import objects of a specific class. This can be achieved only after a painful process of looking at the class definition and determining how to import objects into documents.

A sample definition for a BaseObject will include instance variables for the dimensions and location of an object, methods to move an object on a display, and so on.

2.2 THE TemporalMedia CLASS

The TemporalMedia class provides an abstraction of all *temporal media*, e.g., video, audio, etc. The most distinctive feature of temporal media is that their content depends on time; conventional discrete media, such as text and images, are independent of time. More specifically, each temporal media has a temporal coordinate, and the content of the media varies according to the time value along that coordinate.

For example, video data is represented as a sequence of frames. Each frame is assigned a time-to-start display and a time-to-finish display on the temporal coordinate assigned to the video data. If we start playing the video, frames are selected and displayed in response to the current value of the temporal coordinate.

A TemporalMedia object is responsible for continually determining, on the basis of the current value on the temporal coordinate, what should be done with any of its data.[3] TemporalMedia objects, then, are *active objects* [52]; i.e., those which spontaneously try to detect situations in which they are required to perform operations.

For example, once you say *start playback* to a TemporalMedia object, you need not send any further messages until you want to stop or suspend playback. It is the responsibility of TemporalMedia objects to find frames or samples for playback, not that of the application programmer or user.

A sample definition of a TemporalMedia class will include information regarding the duration of the data, methods for implementing playback operations, instance variables regarding object internal temporal coordinates, and methods for activating objects.

2.2.1 The Video Class

The Video class is a subclass of the TemporalMedia class. A video object receives video frames from a source, which can be a file, a local process, or a remote process over the network, and it displays them.

Compression is indispensable if we would like to deal with meaningful length of video data. MPEG is the most commonly used compression standard to process video data with a computer [24][31]. There are three MPEG standards, two of which have been finalized: MPEG-1 is intended for intermediate data rates on the order of 1.5 Mbps, whereas MPEG-2 is intended for higher data rates (10Mbps) and has been designed to be able to deal with High Definition TV standards. MPEG-4, which was originally targeted at very low bit rates, focuses on content-based interactivity and "universal access". Other widely used compression schemes include Motion JPEG [38] and H.261 [22][26].

For each compression scheme, there is, in turn, a variety of decompression schemes available (dedicated hardware, i.e., decompression boards, and software [36]). Subclasses for such decompression schemes are located below each of the various compression schemes in the class hierarchy illustrated in Figure 2.

This type of hierarchy has several advantages. First, the application programmers can deal with video objects without being concerned about such details as compression and decompression schemes. They only need to write programs in accord with the definition of the Video class. Secondly, if a new compression scheme becomes available, the class hierarchy designers need only define a new subclass below the appropriate compression scheme class. They do not need to modify the existing class hierarchy in any other way. Similarly, application programmers only need to add a code for the new subclass to the existing programs. They need not modify any part of the existing application programs.

The same principle applies when a new decompression scheme is available. As a matter of fact, real-time MPEG-I video decompression had been expected to require a dedicated hardware board when the MPEG-I standard was defined. But progress in microprocessor technology, including improvements in processor speed and the introduction of multimedia-oriented instruction sets has made it possible for MPEG-I video to be decoded in real-time by software. Similarly, we expect that software-only MPEG-2 decompression will be widely available before long.

---

[3] TemporalMedia objects need to deal with the difference between the playback speed and the originally intended speed. If, for example, the playback speed is faster than that for which they were designed, video objects might need to skip frames. If the playback speed is slower, they might need to wait to play a frame.

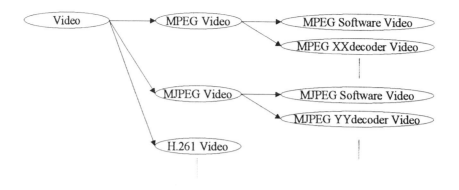

Figure 2. The Video class hierarchy.

2.2.2 The Audio Class

An Audio object receives audio samples from a source and plays them. Formats for uncompressed audio representation include AU(Sparc), WAVE(Windows), AIFF(SGI), etc., while the most common format for compressed audio representation is the MPEG-I Audio format [41][45]. The same sort of hierarchy used to handle video data is necessary for handling audio data.

Since the data size for audio samples is ordinarily much smaller than that for video frames of the same duration, it would seem easier to implement an audio object than a video object. The fact is, however, that considerable effort is required in the implementation of audio objects in order to guarantee playback quality because users are more sensitive to the quality of audio than to the quality of video. If a number of video frames were dropped, users might find it unpleasant but would have little difficulty in following the content of the video. The dropping of an equivalent number of audio samples, however, has the potential to affect a user's understanding far more adversely.

From the viewpoint of implementation, in order to prevent overflow from or underflow to the audio data buffer memory that is connected to the audio playback hardware, audio objects must be activated at regular intervals.

2.2.3 The Composite Class

In general, multimedia applications need to be able to handle a number of temporal objects at the same time. That is to say, while a simple VCR application might require only simultaneous playback of audio and video data, a more useful application would be able to handle other combinations, such as

- playing multiple video objects in a predetermined sequence,
- playing a video object with a selection of audio objects, each of which represents the narration in a different language,
- simultaneously playing two video objects, each of which represents the recording of a scene from a different camera angle,
- etc.

Composite objects serve this purpose. A composite object is a combination of temporal objects. There are two types of composition: spatial and temporal. Spatial composition defines the spatial relationships among the components of a composite object (Figure 3), i.e., the layout of objects in a display.

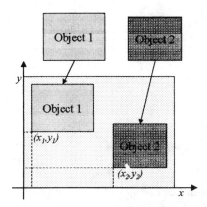

Figure 3. An example of spatial composition.

Temporal composition defines the temporal relationships among the components of a composite object. In other words, temporal composition is the process of placing temporal objects on the temporal coordinate of the new composite object being constructed (Figure 4).

While in a very small number of multimedia object models these two types of composition may be seen to operate together in a unified fashion, in most composition models they function independently of one another. Temporal composition is the key process in creating complex multimedia objects and the most important variations among multimedia object models result from different approaches to temporal composition.

Temporal composition can be further classified into two categories. One is by *absolute* positioning of objects along a temporal coordinate. The other is by *relative* positioning of objects. A typical example of the former has been proposed by Gibbs et al., whereas a typical example of the latter has been proposed by Hamakawa et al. Both of the models will be explained later in this chapter.

A sample definition for a Composite class will include information about components, as well as methods for manipulating components.

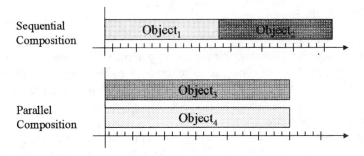

Figure 4. Examples of temporal composition.

2.2.4 The Clip Class

In designing composite objects, we would often like to use only a part of an existing temporal object as a component, or to include as a component an object being played at a different speed than that for which it was originally designed. One obvious approach would be to edit original objects into new objects satisfying the requirements. This would be, however, extremely inefficient in terms of both processing time and storage space.

A better solution is the clip object, a reference to a temporal object, which includes content-range information and a scaling factor for adjusting playing speed (Figure 5).

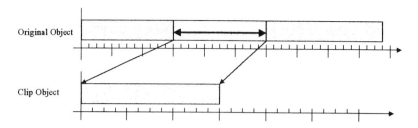

Figure 5. An example of a Clip Object.

2.2.5 Classes for Video/Audio Capturing

These classes define objects for capturing live video data or audio data for sending the data to sinks, which can be local disk files or video/audio objects on the network. These objects are necessary to implement video conferencing systems [51] as well as digital video recording and editing systems.

When designing classes for the objects, care must be taken with regard to the capturing device configuration and the data format.

2.3 CLASSES FOR DISCRETE MEDIA

Even though temporal media objects play primary roles in multimedia applications, they cannot be really useful without discrete media objects. The following is an overview of the classes for discrete media objects:

Text   Text objects contain a large amount of text information. They can be used to hold detailed descriptions of multimedia objects or to hold help messages.

Image   Image objects contain two-dimensional images (or bitmap data). They can be used to implement video browsers. There is a variety of image formats such as JPEG, GIF, and so on. A class hierarchy like the class hierarchy for video objects would be helpful to treat such image objects.

Graphics   Graphics objects are used to draw such graphical objects as lines, rectangles, and ovals.

2.4 CLASSES FOR GUI OBJECTS

GUI objects are responsible for determining the appearance of an application on a display. They are also responsible for receiving users' interaction by keyboard or mouse and for controlling the application. The following are brief descriptions of most often used GUI objects:

Window   A Window object contains a rectangular region for placing objects.

Button   A Button object has a rectangular region to display its graphical view and a 'callback' function attached to it. When the user moves a mouse into the rectangular region of a button and clicks, the callback function attached to it is invoked. Buttons in multimedia applications are typically used to control the temporal behavior of multimedia objects. They are used, for example, to implement PLAY, STOP, etc.

Scrollbar   When an object is too large a region to be displayed at one time, only part of it is displayed. In that case, scrollbars are used to indicate which part of the object is currently being displayed, as well as to access different parts of the object. In multimedia applications, scrollbars are typically used to indicate which part of a multimedia object is being played. Scrollbars are also used for random access of multimedia objects.

Menu   A menu object holds multiple items and lets the user choose one of them. A menu object can be used to choose multimedia data for playback.

Field   A field object is used to contain a few lines of text information. A field object can be used to show a short description of multimedia data or can be used to input keywords for a multimedia data query.

Dialogbox   A dialogbox object is used when an application is not able to continue its execution without asking the user how to proceed. It is typically used to let the user answer yes or no.

3. COMPOSITE MULTIMEDIA OBJECT MODEL BY GIBBS ET AL.

Simon Gibbs et al. have presented a class hierarchy for multimedia objects and a composite multimedia object model based on it [10][12]. This section discusses the most distinctive features of their composite object model.

3.1 MULTIMEDIA OBJECTS AS ACTIVE OBJECTS

In the Gibbs model, multimedia objects are defined as active objects, which produce and/or consume multimedia data values via *ports*. (Multimedia data values are sequences of such data elements as video frames, audio samples, etc.) Multimedia objects may be classified into three categories: **source**, **sink**, and **filter**.

Source   objects have only output ports, and they produce multimedia data values. One example would be an object which records live audio data and outputs a sequence of digital audio samples.

Sink   objects have only input ports, and they consume multimedia data values. One example would be an object, which receives a sequence of video frames and outputs them to a display.

Filter   objects have both input and output ports, and they both produce and consume multimedia data values. Examples include (1) an object, which duplicates its input and then outputs that through two separate output ports, or (2) an object which converts one format to another.

A graphical notation system is used to facilitate representing dataflow relationships between objects and to provide a basis for a visual editor for composing composite objects (Figure 6). Multimedia objects are denoted by circles, to which boxes representing ports are attached. External boxes represent output ports; internal boxes represent input ports. Dataflow is represented by arrows.

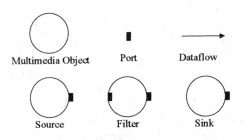

Figure 6. Multimedia objects.

3.2 TEMPORAL TRANSFORMATION TO MULTIMEDIA OBJECTS

The model contains two temporal coordinate systems: *world time* and *object time*. World time is the temporal coordinate common to all multimedia objects in an application, and it dominates their temporal behavior.

Object time is specific to a given multimedia object. Each object can specify: 1) the origin of its object time with respect to world time, 2) its speed for processing multimedia data values, and 3) the orientation of its object time with respect to world time. These specifications are implemented with the following three temporal transformations: they are **Translate, Scale,** and **Invert**.

- ☐ **Translate** shifts the multimedia object in world time.
- ☐ **Scale** scales the overall duration of the object by a given factor.
- ☐ **Invert** flips the orientation of object time back and forth between "forward" and "reverse".

The effect of applying these temporal transformations to a multimedia object is illustrated in Figure 7.

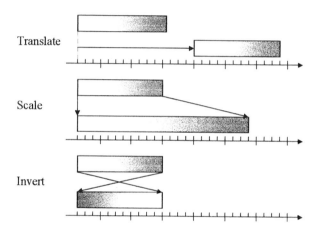

Figure 7. Temporal transformations.

3.3 COMPOSITE MULTIMEDIA OBJECTS

A composite multimedia object contains a set of component multimedia objects and specifications for their temporal and dataflow relationships. Temporal relationships define the synchronization and temporal sequencing of component objects. Dataflow relationships define the connections between the input and output ports of components.

Let us consider the example of creating a new composite object c_1, which performs the following operations:

Presentation of a video object, $video_1$, begins at time t_0. At time t_1, a fade is begun from $video_1$ to a second video object, $video_2$. The transition is completed at time t_2 and at time t_3, $video_2$ is stopped.

The temporal relationships of the component objects of the new composite object can be illustrated with a *composite timeline diagram* as seen in Figure 8.

The dataflow relationships of component objects can be defined with the previously introduced graphical notation, as seen in Figure 9, which illustrates the dataflow relationship for object c_1 for the time interval $[t_1,t_2]$. During the interval, video frame sequences from $video_1$ and $video_2$ are processed by the digital video effect object *dve*, which produces a new sequence of video frames and sends it to the video display object.[4]

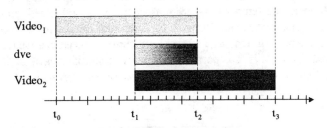

Figure 8. A composite timeline.

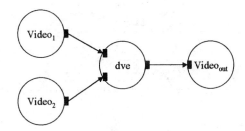

Figure 9. An example of a dataflow relationship.

The implementation of a composite object editor with a graphical user interface has been reported in [28].

4. OBJECT COMPOSITION AND PLAYBACK MODEL BY HAMAKAWA ET AL.

Object composition and playback models (Figure 10) were proposed by Hamakawa et al. and Rekimoto[14][16]. Their object composition model dealt with the static aspects of multimedia objects such as name, duration, etc., while their object playback model dealt with the dynamic aspects of multimedia objects, such as play, stop, etc.

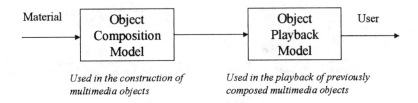

Figure 10. Multimedia object models.

4.1 OBJECT COMPOSITION MODEL
The object composition model proposed by Hamakawa and Rekimoto has three distinctive features:

---

[4] In order to implement dataflow relationships of the type illustrated above, it is also necessary to use *connector* objects as well as port objects.

1. *Temporal glue*

   As in TeX [23], the typesetting system intended for the creation of beautiful books, glue is an object which can stretch or shrink in two-dimensional positional space. This glue can be extended into temporal space, making it "temporal glue," and introduced into multimedia object models (see Figure 11). Each multimedia object will then have glue attributes (normal, stretch, and shrink) in three-dimensional space (2-dimensional position and time). It is also possible to provide a special object, called a *Glue* object, which does not exist as an entity in itself, but which has only glue attributes.

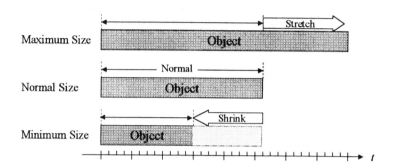

Figure 11. Temporal glue.

2. *Object hierarchy*

   The object composition model employs a hierarchical structure composed of multimedia objects (Figure 12). The complete layout of composite objects, such as the duration of each object, is determined when the highest-ranking composite object is determined. When any multimedia object is edited, the attributes of all related composite objects are automatically recalculated to conform to the change.

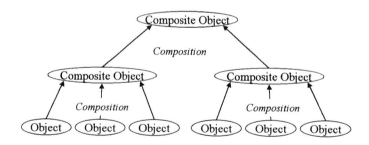

Figure 12. Object hierarchy.

3. *Relative location*

   In one common approach to constructing multimedia objects, the timeline model, individual multimedia objects are located on an absolute timeline scale (see Figure 13). The object composition model differs from the timeline model in that it is unnecessary to decide the precise timeline location for each object. Only the relative locations among objects in time and space need be defined. Once objects are composed, their absolute locations (in both time and space) are calculated automatically.

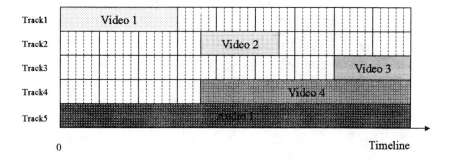

Figure 13. Timeline model.

Each multimedia object has a number of different attributes. Such attributes can be divided into the following three types:

Properties
> General information about multimedia data, such as data type, location, etc.

Hierarchy
> Information about how objects are combined.

Glue Attributes
> Values of temporal glue (i.e., normal, stretch, and shrink sizes), as well as spatial glue attributes.

We may note here that the concepts, which most lend this model its characteristic nature, are the concepts of relative location and temporal glue.

4.2 CONSTRUCTING COMPOSITE OBJECTS

Composite objects are constructed by arranging and modifying multimedia objects along designated dimensions. Control objects used to help in this construction include the following:

Box   This is used to arrange an object group along a designated dimension. There are three types; TBBox, LRBox, SEBox. They correspond, respectively, to an arrangement of Top-Bottom (space), Right-Left (space), and Start-End (time). Figure 14 shows a basic example of Box.

$$Obj_{new} \leftarrow TBBox(Obj_1, Obj_2, \ldots, Obj_N)$$
$$Obj_{new} \leftarrow LRBox(Obj_1, Obj_2, \ldots, Obj_N)$$
$$Obj_{new} \leftarrow SEBox(Obj_1, Obj_2, \ldots, Obj_N)$$

Time-section This is used to create an object, which initially has no attribute values of its own other than representing a given time-section.

$$Obj_{new} \leftarrow Section(Obj, from, to)$$

This value-less object can be referenced to any existing object to create a new object, which contains the attribute values of the specific time-section of the object to which it has been referenced.

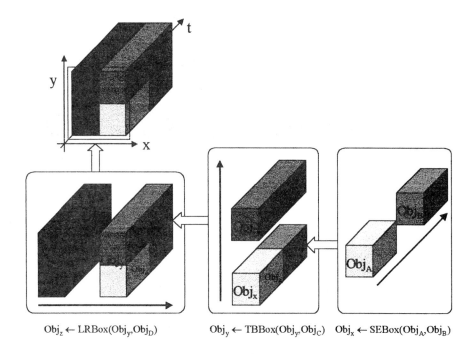

$$\text{Obj}_z \leftarrow \text{LRBox}(\text{Obj}_y, \text{Obj}_D) \qquad \text{Obj}_y \leftarrow \text{TBBox}(\text{Obj}_y, \text{Obj}_C) \quad \text{Obj}_x \leftarrow \text{SEBox}(\text{Obj}_A, \text{Obj}_B)$$

Figure 14. Box example.

Overlay This is used to overlay one object with another object in the time-dimension.

$$\text{Obj}_{new} \leftarrow \text{Overlay}(\text{Obj}_1, \text{Obj}_2, \ldots, \text{Obj}_N)$$

When playing a video object and an audio object simultaneously, the operation is as follows:

$$\text{Obj}_{new} \leftarrow \text{Overlay}(\text{Video Obj, Audio Obj})$$

Loop This is a type of glue used to repeat an original object for a designated length of time.

$$\text{Obj}_{new} \leftarrow \text{Loop}(\text{Obj, normal, shrink, stretch})$$

In this model, because such static media as texts, still pictures, etc. do not contain information regarding the temporal dimension, loop is used to add temporal glue attributes to their other attributes when they are employed with dynamic media (audio, video, etc.) in composite objects.

Position This is used to locate objects on a specific section of an absolute time-scale, as it would be if employed in a timeline model.

$$\text{Obj}_{new} \leftarrow \text{Position}(\text{Obj, StartTime, EndTime})$$

Additionally, the following two methods are provided to facilitate working with objects:

Mark This function serves to mark an object at a certain point in time, and to add to the object a title which indicates some feature of object-content relevant to that point in time.

`Mark(Obj, Time, Title)`

Constraint This function attaches constraints to objects and is used primarily for synchronization, so as, for example, to ensure that a given audio object always ends at the same instant as a given video object, etc.

`Constraint(Condition)`

A constraint may be attached to an object with regard to its start, end, or a point marked on it. For example,

`Constraint(Obj`$_1$`.start=Obj`$_2$`.start),Constraint(Obj`$_1$`.mark`$_1$`=Obj`$_2$`.end)`

4.2.1 Glue Calculation and Determination of the Duration of Each Object

Each of the different objects comprising a composite object has glue attributes, and the composite object itself has glue attributes. This glue attribute of a composite object is determined by the attributes of its component objects. The calculation of glue attributes proceeds from the bottom of the object hierarchy to the top, as shown in Figure 12.

The duration of each object is determined when the highest-ranking composite object has been determined. The duration of the components of a composite object are propagated down the composite object hierarchy. The duration of this highest-ranking composite object is the normal time length of its glue attributes.

A more detailed description of calculation methods is reported in [16].

4.3 OBJECT PLAYBACK MODEL

The object playback model employs two kinds of multimedia classes, the Media class and the Context class. Additionally, a third class, called Viewer is introduced to connect these classes to the screen (Figure 15).

The Media class represents multimedia data. All objects created in the object composition model belong to this class, or its subclasses. (Sound is an example of a Media subclass used to manage digital sound data.)

The Context class keeps track of the playback status of each object, such as "What is the current video data frame?," "What is the current status of audio data?," "Where is data displayed on the window?," etc.

The Viewer class has the information required for display, such as the position coordinates for a window, etc. It also provides convenient interfaces to programmers, such as play, stop, and pause. Viewer is a general management class, implemented to manage both audio and video data. It has no subclasses.

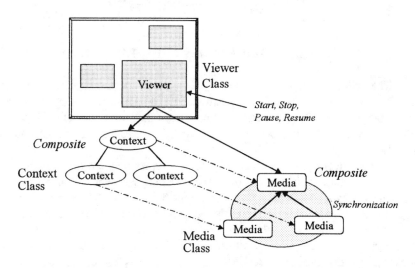

Figure 15. Relationships among three classes.

A Context object is generated whenever a multimedia object is played back. This structure of classes clearly separates multimedia static data from their temporal states. Normally, each media object has a corresponding context object, but it is possible that two or more context objects might share one media object. This means we could playback different portions of the media simultaneously through different windows (Figure 16).

It may be easier to understand these relationships if we think of them in terms of an orchestral performance. Viewer corresponds to the stage upon which the music is performed. Media corresponds to the musical score, the general layout of how the music is to be performed over a period of time. Context corresponds to the conductor, who may interpret the score and conduct it in accord with how he feels it should be played at any given moment.

To implement the above model on a computer, Hamakawa and Rekimoto constructed an audio and video extension library, called *Xavier,*[5] using InterViews [25]. A multimedia presentation system using *Xavier* is reported in [17], and a multimedia editor for *Xavier* is reported in [15].

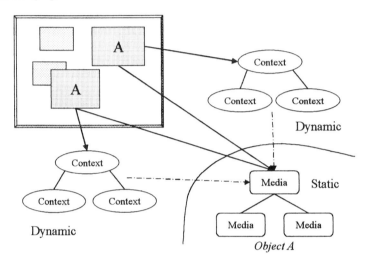

Figure 16. Playback example.

5. MULTIMEDIA OBJECT MODEL IN MHEG

The MHEG (Multimedia and Hypermedia information coding Expert Group), operating jointly for the ISO (the International Organization for Standardization) and the IEC (the International Electrotechnical Commission), has been working to apply the object-oriented approach to the development of a standard format for multimedia and hypermedia interchange.

A multimedia object is essentially useless on its own, and only gains usefulness in the context of a multimedia application; an application-independent format for representing objects is necessary for interchange between applications. The aim of the MHEG standard is to provide the coded final-form representation of multimedia and hypermedia information objects that will be interchanged within or across services and applications. The means of interchange may include storage, local area network, wide area telecommunications, broadcast telecommunications, etc. MHEG provides this format in the form of standard "MHEG objects" (Figure 17).

Note, MHEG is concerned only with the composition of time-based media objects. Encoding format for each multimedia and hypermedia data, or recording format or protocol used upon interchange, etc., are not in the scope of the MHEG standard.

The first MHEG was designed as a generic standard for multimedia and hypermedia interchange [6][20][29][39], whereas the latest MHEG-5 standard intends to provide

---

[5] *Xavier* can be obtained from ftp://intervies.stanford.edu/pub/contrib.

navigation functions for VOD (Video On Demand) systems or Digital TV broadcasting systems [21][49].

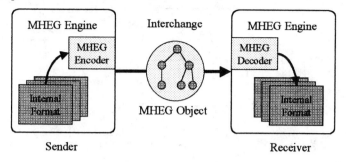

Figure 17. Interchange of MHEG objects.

5.1 OVERVIEW OF THE MHEG-5 CLASS HIERARCHY

The MHEG-5 class hierarchy is briefly shown in Figure 18. All the MHEG-5 classes, except for the Action class and mix-in classes[6] including Interactible, inherit the Root class, which is an abstract class[7] to define the common behavior among MHEG-5 objects. The Group class is an abstract class, which defines functionality for a "set." The following is a brief explanation of the most important MHEG-5 classes.

The classes Application, Scene, and Ingredient are used to define the MHEG-5 application structure (Figure 19):

Application An Application object groups a set of Scene objects and those Ingredient objects which are shared by several Scene objects.

Scene A Scene object contains a set of temporally and spatially composed Ingredient objects. Only one Scene object may be active at a time.

Ingredient The Ingredient class is an abstract class to define the generic behavior of objects which can be part of a Scene object.

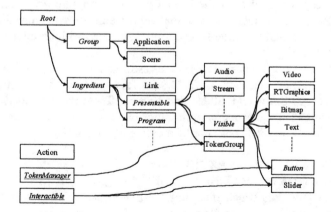

Figure 18. MHEG-5 Class hierarchy.

---

[6] A mix-in class is an abstract class that does not inherit from the Root class.
[7] An abstract class is a class which is never instantiated.

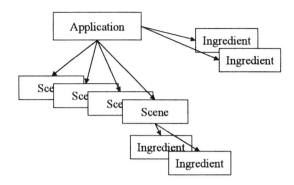

Figure 19. Structure of an MHEG-5 application.

The Subclasses of the Ingredient class are Link, Program, Palette, Font, CursorShape, Variable, and Presentable:

Presentable The Presentable class is an abstract class to define the behavior of objects, which may be presented within a Scene.

Program A Program object is used to call a piece of procedural code from within the MHEG-5 context.

Link Link objects are used to express the behavior of MHEG-5 applications. A Link object consists of a condition and an Action object, which runs when the associated condition evaluates to True.

Action objects are used to describe the link effect in Link objects.

Action An Action object specifies a synchronized set of elementary actions to be applied to one or more objects.

Subclasses of the Presentable class are Audio, Visible, TokenGroup, and Stream:

Visible The Visible class is an abstract class to define the behavior of Presentables, which have a visual representation on the display. The subclasses of the Visible class include Text, Slider, Button, Bitmap, Video, RTgraphics, LineArt, etc.

Stream A Stream object defines the behavior of a composition of continuous media (Video, Audio and RTGraphics) that are presented in synchronization.

The Interactible class is used to define functionality associated with an interaction behavior of Visibles:

Interactable Interactable is an abstract mix-in class to define functionality associated with an interaction behavior of Visibles. Classes, which inherit Interactable, are HyperText, EntryField, Slider, and Button. These interactions enable the user to change the status and/or appearance of the objects, for instance by entering text in an EntryField object or by pressing an Button object.

5.2 MECHANISM FOR MHEG-5 EXECUTION

MHEG-5 objects are executed by MHEG-5 engines. An MHEG-5 engine is a process or a set of processes which interprets MHEG-5 objects encoded according to the MHEG-5 encoding specification. Implementations for MHEG-5 engines might include an ASN.1 decoding function [18][19], processing action objects, processing link objects, creating and managing MHEG-5 objects, etc.

Figure 20 shows the MHEG-5 event-processing mechanism. When the user operates on an Interactable object, or a source, then an event is generated. MHEG-5 engine then examines the LinkCondition of each active Link objects, and if it evaluates to true, then the Action object associated with the LinkCondition is triggered. Then the content of the action object is executed.

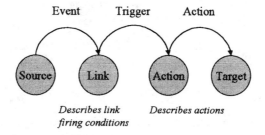

Figure 20. Event Processing Mechanism in MHEG-5.

5.3 EXAMPLE

Let us show a very simple example of MHEG-5 application, which plays back a movie when the user presses the carriage-return (Figure 21).

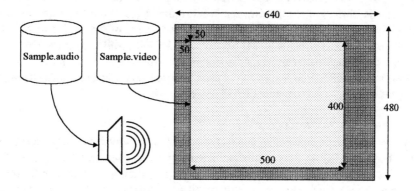

Figure 21. An MHEG example.

This can be accomplished with an MHEG-5 objects as follows:

```
{:Scene("scene" 0)
 :Items(
    {:Stream 10
     :InitiallyActive false
     :Multiplex(
       {:Video 11
        :OrigContent
        :ContentRef("sample.video")
        :OrigBoxSize 500 400
        :OrigPosition 50 50
        :ComponentTag 101
        :Termination freeze
       }
       {:Audio 12
        :OrigContent
        :ContentRef("sample.audio")
        :ComponentTag 102
       }
     )
    {:Link 13
     :InitiallyActive true
     :EventSource 0
     :EventType UserInput
```

```
          :EventData 15            // carriage return
          :LinkEffect(:Run 10)
        }
     )
     :InputEventReg 1
     :SceneCS 640 480
  }
```

6. NETWORKED MULTIMEDIA OBJECTS IN THE BERKELEY CONTINUOUS MEDIA TOOLKIT

With the recent dramatic progress in networking technology, a number of new issues have come to the fore with regard to the implementation of multimedia objects. These include, for example, how to name and locate distributed objects [32], and how to transmit multimedia data over network in real-time [9][44][56].

The Berkeley CMT (Continuous Media Toolkit) tries to address these issues[42][37].[8] It is an extension to the Tcl/Tk toolkit [35] and introduces a mechanism for creating distributed objects, a mechanism for synchronizing distributed objects, and a best-effort protocol for real-time multimedia data transmission on top of the UDP protocol. CMT supports such single media streams as MPEG-I video, MPEG-I audio, Motion JPEG, Sparc audio, etc., as well as such interleaved media streams as MPEG-I System stream. A higher-level data abstraction, called a movie script, is used to synchronize several media streams.

The following is an overview of CMT objects.

6.1 OVERVIEW OF CMT OBJECTS

CMT provides five types of objects: 1) source objects, which read continuous media data that has been input from files, real-time capturing devices, etc., and send that data to destinations objects; 2) destination objects, which receive continuous media data from source objects and play it; 3) filter objects, which receive continuous media data from source objects, modify it, and send the modified data to destination objects. Filter objects, in this sense, act both as source objects and as destination objects; 4) network delivery objects, which implement a best-effort protocol for real-time continuous media data transmission over the Internet; 5) logical Time System (LTS) objects, which synchronize CMT objects.

Creating multimedia applications in CMT is accomplished by creating these CMT objects over the network, by defining dataflow relationships among them, and by defining synchronization relationships with LTS objects.

6.2 INTERACTION AMONG OBJECTS OVER THE NETWORK

The CMT objects are placed in different machines over the network. In general, objects in charge of playback are placed in client machines, whereas objects supplying multimedia data are placed on remote multimedia servers equipped with large storage devices. A more complicated application might use objects on multiple servers, or might introduce other machines dedicated to transforming multimedia data from one format to another. To accomplish multimedia data playback in such a network environment, objects in the client machines need to be able to locate and communicate objects on the servers, and vice versa.

Tcl-DP, a distributed programming package for Tcl, is used to support such interaction among CMT objects.[9] Tcl-DP provides mechanism for creating objects at remote machines and transparently accessing the remote objects as if they were in the local machine.

---

[8] See http://bmrc.berkeley.edu/ for more information on the Berkeley Continuous Media Toolkit.
[9] Tcl-DP was originally developed as a module for CMT, but is now provided as a separate Tcl extension for generally distributed programming.

Tcl-DP also provides a general Remote Procedure Call (RPC) mechanism to facilitate distributed programming [46].

6.3 THE LOGICAL TIME SYSTEM OBJECTS

In Logical Time System (LTS) objects, which define the time coordinates used in the CMT applications, the current clock value is calculated as

$$LTS = (SystemTime - offset) * speed$$

where *SystemTime* and *speed* are the current system clock value and the speed of playback, respectively. Normal playback from the beginning can be achieved by setting the *speed* value to 1 and the *LTS* value to 0. Reverse playback can be accomplished by setting the *speed* value to -1. Setting the *LTS* value to a specific position and the *speed* value to 0 results in the display of still video frames at that position. *Offset* is automatically calculated upon the change of the *LTS* value and/or the *speed* value.

LTS objects are used to synchronize CMT objects. For example, objects in charge of sending frames from files decide which frames to send according to the current LTS value; objects in charge of playback examine the current LTS value to see which frames are to be played and which frames are to be discarded. To be more precise, all the objects participating in the playback of a set of synchronized multimedia data do so in reference to a common LTS.

It might seem possible to achieve synchronization among distributed CMT objects simply by referring to a common LTS at a specific machine, but, in fact, RPC overhead would result in an inaccurate LTS value, making the quality of synchronization extremely poor.

That is why CMT uses a set of synchronized LTS objects. In other words, each object refers to a locally created LTS object, and all the LTS objects are configured to be synchronized among themselves. To achieve this, each LTS object is designed to be able to function as a master LTS object, and to be able to have slave LTS objects. Whenever the status of a master LTS object changes, that change is propagated to all its slave objects. After the change has been propagated, each of the LTS objects refers to the local system clock value to update its LTS value.

6.4 OBJECTS FOR MULTIMEDIA DATA DELIVERY

In order to transmit multimedia data over the Internet, CMT introduces Cyclic-UDP, a best-effort protocol on top of UDP [47]. The key idea in Cyclic-UDP is: 1) to prioritize data from the viewpoint of playback quality before sending, and 2) to give data with higher priority a better chance to be delivered to its destination within the available bandwidth. CMT provides objects to implement these two types of operations.

The prioritization of multimedia data by CMT objects varies according to data type. For media without frame dependency (e.g., Motion JPEG), data are prioritized by calculating the Inverse Binary Order (IBO) for the sequence of the data. Its basic idea is that when the available bandwidth is insufficient to handle the total amount of data to be sent, frames will be evenly dropped along the timeline. Suppose 5 out of 10 frames must be dropped. Rather than simply dropping the first 5 frames, playback quality would be generally better if every other frame were dropped.

For the media with frame dependency, frames are given higher priority if their decoding is initially required by other frames. In case of MPEG, I frames have higher priority than P-frames, which in turn have higher priority than B-frames.

PktSrc (packet source) objects and PktDest (packet destination) objects perform multimedia data delivery over the Internet. A pktSrc object sends prioritized multimedia data packets to a pktDest object using UDP protocol, and re-transmits packets that have not been acknowledged as having been received. PktSrc objects and PktDest objects also keep track of the total amount of data actually sent in order to estimate bandwidth usage as accurate as possible.

6.5 EXAMPLE

Figure 22 illustrates a typical CMT example of Motion JPEG and Sparc audio playback over the Internet.

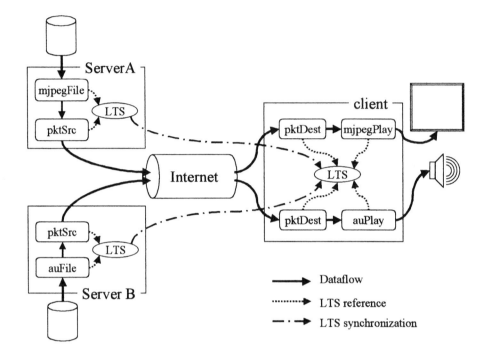

Figure 22. A typical example of video and audio playback with CMT.

This playback can be achieved by executing the following CMT script at the client's side:

```
# create CMT API objects for the client and the servers
set local_cmt [cmt ""]; $local_cmt open -local;
set srvA_cmt [cmt ""]; $srvA_cmt open -host serverA -port
6000
set srvB_cmt [cmt ""]; $srvB_cmt open -host serverB -port
6001

# create local objects
set mp [$local_cmt create mjpegPlay];
set ap [$local_cmt create auPlay];
set mpd [$local_cmt create pktDest];
set apd [$local_cmt create pktDest];
set ltslocal [$local_cmt create lts];

# create objects in server A
set mf [$srvA_cmt create mpegFile];
set mps [$srvA_cmt create pktSrc];
set ltssrvA [$srvA_cmt create lts];

# create objects in server B
set af [$srvB_cmt create auFile];
```

```
set aps [$srvB_cmt create pktSrc];
set ltssrvB [$srvB_cmt create lts];

# define dataflow in server A
$mf conf -filename "........." -lts $ltssrvA -outCmd @$mps.accept
$mps conf -dest [$mpd address]

# define dataflow in server B
$af conf -filename "........." -lts $ltssrvB -outCmd @$aps.accept
$aps conf -dest [$apd address];

# define dataflow in client
$mpd conf -outCmd @$mp.accept; $apd conf -outCmd @$ap.accept;

# LTS synchronization
$ltslocal -addSlave $ltssrvA; $ltslocal -addSlave $ltssrvB;

# start clock
$ltslocal -conf -speed 1.0 -pos 0.0
```

7. CONCLUSION

We have described the basics of multimedia objects and important research activities in the area. Other notable research activities on multimedia objects are those on multimedia object composition and the integration of multimedia objects with multimedia databases.

Much research on the multimedia object composition is based on the interval-based temporal logic proposed by Allen [1]. Allen has shown that there are thirteen binary interval relationships, which can represent any interval relationship. Little et al. extended this interval relationships to *n-ary* and *reverse* temporal relationships [27]. The *n-ary* model is particularly elegant in that it captures an arbitrary number of component objects with a common temporal relationship without requiring many levels of hierarchy, and the *reverse* temporal relationships are useful in providing a basis for reverse playback of composite multimedia objects. Weiss [53][54] has proposed a data model called *algebraic video* for composing, searching, and playing back digital video presentations and has demonstrated a prototype system which can create new video presentations with algebraic combinations of these segments. Buchanan [4][5] has described a *temporal layout* that indicates when events in the multimedia document occur, and introduced TeX's glue, as well as a model similar to the object composition model mentioned earlier in this chapter, to arrive at an "optimal" display for a document.

The integration of multimedia objects with multimedia databases is particularly important because we need to be able to store and retrieve multimedia data as we use it more and more. Gibbs has proposed how to construct composite multimedia objects out of a BLOB (binary large object) stored in databases, and how to create multimedia objects flexibly by applying *interpretation*, *derivation*, and *temporal composition* to a BLOB [11]. Oomoto and Tanaka have proposed a video-object data model and defined several operations, such as *interval projection*, *merge*, *overlap*, etc. for composing new video objects [33]. They also introduced the concept of "interval-inclusion inheritance," which describes how a video object inherits attribute/value pairs from another video object.

As a whole, applying object-oriented design to multimedia systems appears to have been very successful. Recent important interest on multimedia objects would be how we can best design and implement multimedia objects for the most up-to-date multimedia applications.

One such application is interactive TV, including digital TV broadcasting and VOD systems. As previously explained in this chapter, the MHEG-5 object model has been targeted toward such applications. OpenTV has designed an object-oriented operating system, which is supposed to run on set-top-boxes for digital broadcasting [34].

Another important application is the World Wide Web. The Berkeley CMT has been extended to run as a Netscape plug-in which interprets movie scripts and play distributed multimedia data within Web browsers. W3C (World Wide Web Consortium) is working on SMIL (Synchronized Multimedia Integration Language), which allows a set of independent multimedia objects to be integrated into a synchronized multimedia presentation [50].

We believe that the foundations of multimedia object technology have been firmly laid and that the technology is now mature enough to be used in such new applications.

REFERENCES

1. Allen, J.F., "Maintaining Knowledge about Temporal Intervals," Communications of the ACM, Vol. 26. No.11, pp. 832-842, 1983.
2. Arnold, K. and Gosling, J., "The Java Programming Language, Second Edition," Addison-Wesley, 1998.
3. Booch, G., "Object-Oriented Analysis and Design," Second Edition, The Benjamin/ Cummings, 1994.
4. Buchanan M.C. and Zellweger P.T., "Scheduling Multimedia Documents Using Temporal Constraints," Third International Workshop on Network and Operating System Support for Digital Audio and Video, *Lecture Notes in Computer Science*, Springer-Verlag, pp. 237-249, 1992.
5. Buchanan M.C. and Zellweger P.T., "Automatic Temporal Layout Mechanisms," The proceedings of the ACM Multimedia 93, pp. 341-350, 1993.
6. Buford, J.F.K. Ed., "Multimedia Systems," Addison-Wesley, 1994.
7. Champeaux, D. de, Lea, D., and Faure, P., "Object-Oriented System Development," Addison-Wesley, 1993.
8. Coleman, D., *et al.*, "Object-Oriented Development - The Fusion Method," Prentice Hall, 1994.
9. Ferrari, D., Banerjer, A., and Zhang, H., "Network Support for Multimedia - A Discussion of the Tenet Approach," Technical Report TR-92-072, International Computer Science Institute, University of California at Berkeley, 1992.
10. Gibbs, S., "Composite Multimedia and Active Objects," The proceedings of OOPSLA 91 (Conference on Object-Oriented Programming Systems, Languages, and Applications), pp. 87-112.
11. Gibbs, S., Breiteneder, C., and Tsichritzis D.C., "Data Modeling of Time-Based Media," the proceedings of the ACM-SIGMOD 1994, Conference on Management Data, pp. 91-102.
12. Gibbs, S. and Tsichritzis, D.C., "Multimedia Programming – Objects, Environments and Frameworks," Addison-Wesley, 1995.
13. Goldberg, A.J. and Robson, D., "Smalltalk-80: The Language and Its Implementation," Addison-Wesley, Reading, MA, 1983.
14. Hamakawa, R., Sakagami, H., and Rekimoto, J., "Audio and Video Extensions to Graphical User Interface Toolkits," Third International Workshop on Network and Operating System Support for Digital Audio and Video, *Lecture Notes in Computer Science*, Springer-Verlag, pp. 399-404, 1992.
15. Hamakawa, R., et al., "Mbuild – Multimedia Data Builder with Box and Glue," Proc. 1994 International Conference On Multimedia Computing & Systems (ICMCS94), pp. 520-525, Boston, 1994.

16. Hamakawa, R. and Rekimoto, J., "Object Composition and Playback Models for Handling Multimedia Data," Multimedia Systems, Springer-Verlag, Vol. 2 1994, pp. 26-35.

17. Hamakawa, R., Atarashi, A., and Kawagoe, K., "HyperStation: A Platform for Distributed Multimedia Applications," NEC Research and Development, Vol. 35, No. 4, pp. 376-381, October 1994.

18. ISO/IEC, "Specification of Abstract Syntax Notation One (ASN.1)," 2nd ed., IS 8824, 1990.

19. ISO/IEC, "Specification of Basic Encoding Rules for Abstract Syntax Notation One (ASN.1)," 2nd ed., IS 8825, 1990.

20. ISO/IEC, "Information Technology–Coding of Multimedia and Hypermedia Information, Part 1:–MHEG object representation,–Base Notation (ASN.1)," ISO/IEC DIS 13522-1, October 14, 1994.

21. ISO/IEC, "Information Technology–Coding of Multimedia and Hypermedia Information, Part 5: Support for base-level interactive applications," ISO/IEC IS 13522-5, April 15, 1997.

22. ITU, "Video codec for audiovisual services at p*64kb/s," ITU-T Recommendation H.261, 1993.

23. Knuth, D.E., "THE TeX book," Addison-Wesley Publishing Company, 1986.

24. LeGall, D., "MPEG: a video compression standard for multimedia applications," Communications of the ACM, April 1991, Vol. 34, No. 4, pp. 46-58.

25. Linton, M., Vlissides, J., and Calder, P., "Composing user interfaces with *InterViews*," Computer, Feb. 1989, pp. 8-22.

26. Liou, M. "Overview of the px64kbits/s Video Coding Standard," Communications of the ACM, April 1991, Vol. 34, No. 4, pp. 59-63.

27. Little, T. and Ghafoor, A., "Interval-Based Conceptual Models for Time-Dependent Multimedia Data," IEEE Transactions on Knowledge and Data Engineering, Vol.5, No. 4, pp. 551-563, 1993.

28. De Mey, V. and Gibbs, S., "A Multimedia Component Kit," The Proceedings of ACM Multimedia 93, pp. 291-300.

29. Meyer-Boudnik, T. and Effelberg, W., "MHEG Explained," IEEE Multimedia, Spring, pp. 26-38, 1995.

30. Microsoft Corp., "ActiveMovie Streaming Format – Product Information,"

31. Mitchell, J.L., Pennebaker, W.B., Fogg, C.E., and LeGall, D.J., "MPEG Video Compression Standard," Chapman & Hall, 1996.

32. Object Management Group, "The Common Object Request Broker: Architecture and Specification OMG Document Number 91.12.1 Revision 1.1," 1991.

33. Oomoto, E. and Tanaka, K., "OVID: Design and Implementation of a Video-Object Database System," IEEE Transactions Knowledge and Data Engineering, August 1993, pp. 629-643.

34. OpenTV, Inc., URL http://www.opentv.com/.

35. Ousterhout, J., "Tcl and the Tk Toolkit," Addison-Wesley, 1994.

36. Patel, K., Smith, B.C. and Rowe, L.A., "Performance of a Software MPEG Video Decoder," The proceedings of ACM Multimedia 93, pp. 75-82.

37. Patel, K. and Rowe, L.A., "Design and Performance of the Berkeley Continuous Media Toolkit," Proc. SPIE 3020, pp. 194-206.

38. Pennebaker, W.B., "JPEG still image data compression standard," Van Nostrand Reinhold, New York, 1992.

39. Price, R., "MHEG: An Introduction to the future International Standard for Hypermedia Object Interchange," The proceedings of the ACM Multimedia 93, pp. 121-128.

40. DeRose, S.J. and Durand, D.G., "Making Hypermedia Work - A User's Guide to HyTime," Kluwer Academic Publishers, 1994.

41. Van Rossum, G. "FAQ: Audio File Formats," can be obtained from anonymous ftp at ftp://ftp.cwi.nl/pub/audio as files AudioFormats.part[12], 1995.

42. Rowe, L.A., Patel, K., et al., "MPEG Video in Software: Representation, Transmission and Playback," The Proceedings of IS&T/SPIE 1994, International Symposium on Elec. Imaging: Science and Technology.

43. Rumbauch, J., et al., "Object-Oriented Modeling and Design," Prentice Hall, 1991.

44. Schulzrinne, H., Casner, S., Frederick, R., and Jacobson, V., "RTP: A Transport Protocol for Real-Time Applications," RFC189, January 1996.

45. Shlien, S., "Guide to MPEG-1 Audio Standard," IEEE Transactions on Broadcasting, Vol. 40, No. 4, pp. 206-218, 1994.

46. Smith, B., Rowe, L.A. and Yen, S., "Tcl Distributed Programming," Proc. of the 1993 Tcl/TK Workshop, Berkeley, CA, June 1993. http://www.cs.Cornell.EDU/Info/Faculty/bsmith/tcl-dp.ps.Z.

47. Smith, B., "Cyclic-UDP: A Priority-Driven Best-Effort Protocol," NOSSDAV 95, http://www.cs.Cornell.EDU/Info/Faculty/bsmith/nossdav.ps.Z.

48. Stroustrup, B., "The C++ Programming Language, 2nd edition," Addison-Wesley, 1991.

49. Takikawa, K., "Latest trends in Multimedia/Hypermedia encoding technology – MHEG-5," (in Japanese), Advance Imaging Seminar '97, The Institute of Image Electronics Engineers of Japan, April 1997.

50. W3C, "Synchronized Multimedia Integration Language," February 2, 1998, http://www.w3.org/TR/1998/WD-smil-0202.

51. Watabe, K., Sakata, S., et al., "Distributed Desktop Conferencing System with Multiuser Multimedia Interface," IEEE Journal on Selected Areas in Communications, Vol. 9, No. 4, pp. 531-539, 1991.

52. Wegner, P., "Concepts and Paradigms of Object Oriented Programming," OOPS Messenger 1, 1 (Aug. 1990), pp. 7-87.

53. Weiss, R., Duda, A., and Gifford, D.K., "Content-Based Access to Algebraic Video," The Proceedings of the International Conference on Multimedia Computing and Systems, pp. 140-151, 1994.

54. Weiss, R., Duda, A., and Gifford, D.K., "Composition and Search with a Video Algebra," IEEE Multimedia, pp. 12-25, Spring 1995.

55. Woelk, D., Kim, W., and Luther, W., "An Object-Oriented Approach to Multimedia Databases," The proceedings of the ACM-SIGMOD 1986, Conference on Management Data, pp. 311-325.

56. Zhang, L., et al., "RSVP: A New Resource ReSerVation Protocol," IEEE Network Magazine, September 1993.

3

MULTIMEDIA DATA MODELING AND MANAGEMENT FOR SEMANTIC CONTENT RETRIEVAL

Clement H. C. Leung and Dwi Sutanto
Victoria University of Technology
Department of Computer and Mathematical Sciences
Ballarat Road, P.O. Box 14428, MCMC
Melbourne 8001, Victoria, Australia.

1. **THE NEED FOR MULTIMEDIA DATA MODELING** 44
2. **MARKS OF A GOOD DATA MODEL** 44
3. **MODELING OF IMAGE DATA** 46
4. **SIMPLE EXPRESSIVE MODELS: THE TERNARY FACT MODELS** 47
    4.1   THE BASIC MODEL AND DATABASE ORGANIZATION 48
    4.2   DYNAMIC CONCEPT BUILDING AND AUTOMATIC INDEX EXPANSION 49
    4.3   EXAMPLE 50
5. **CONCLUDING REMARKS** 52
    REFERENCES 53

Abstract.   This chapter examines the role and mechanisms of data modeling and management for multimedia systems. The need for effective multimedia data modeling is explained and desirable model characteristics are indicated. Particular attention is focused on the modeling of visual data from which mechanisms for content-based indexing and retrieval of still and moving images may be developed. A good model for visual data is able to induce a high degree of uniformity in the representation of image and video contents, which would facilitate the efficient organization of search indexes. In addition, its semantic richness may be progressively built up through the incorporation of new visual data concepts. A rich data modeling paradigm that exhibits these properties is described, which includes mechanisms for learning new concepts from basic ones as well as incorporates the ability to automatically perform index expansion.

1. THE NEED FOR MULTIMEDIA DATA MODELING

Multimedia is an integration of all forms of computer objects such as text, image, graphics, audio, and video. Multimedia database is a database for storing these different kinds of data, which is structured for efficient indexing, storage, and query retrieval. Due to the nature and characteristics of multimedia data, managing them is very different from managing a traditional database, which deals only with simple data types such as structured fields, text, and strings [1]. Multimedia data objects are generally very much larger in size (hence the need for compression), and they require different methods of presentation, editing, content extraction, and representation. An early method to integrate multimedia data into traditional database systems is by using BLOB (Binary Large Object). BLOB can be used to represent different kinds of media data, while permitting the ordinary database to handle them without incurring major alterations to the database management system. However, not being fully aware of their characteristics, the database management system would not be able to perform any meaningful modification, content extraction, and optimization upon these data [2].

Previous work in multimedia data modeling primarily focuses on object-oriented methodology and its variants [3]. Despite its popularity, a number of issues related to this approach, e.g., synchronization mechanism, relationship between objects, object decomposition and recombination, remain to be resolved [4]. To model multimedia data, it is necessary to consider new features which characterize the data, an example of which is time constraint in video and audio data. Later works take time and space (spatio-temporal model) components into consideration [5,6,7]. Using these models, it is possible to determine whether objects are overlapping, contained in, or disjoint to perform relevant functions to obtain object properties, and to obtain time semantics among objects. However, due to limited success in object recognition technology, objects have to be modeled artificially. Hence, there are comparatively few real world applications adopting this modeling approach.

Although there is little difficulty for humans to recognize and retrieve the contents in an image, this presents severe difficulties for current computers. To automate this procedure, effective techniques for feature representation and data management are required, and images must be suitably organized for rapid retrieval based on their contents. Efficient feature indexing is central to any successful multimedia database system's implementation, and such indexing may be automated in varying degrees. In the case of video data, it is often useful to decompose them into a stream of still images. In this way, it is possible to simplify their modeling by concentrating on still image data and then integrating time constraint into the model. To fully exploit the potential of image databases, it is important to have efficient schemes to structure and represent image data by contents. To do so, it is necessary to first provide an effective scheme for modeling image data.

2. MARKS OF A GOOD DATA MODEL

A good data model must take into account the semantic richness of the underlying information, and should be applicable to a wide range of application domains. This chapter primarily focuses attention on modeling the semantic content of still images, into which video streams may also be decomposed.

There has not been adequate research on the modeling of visual data. In most multimedia applications, image objects are modeled as unknown entities, whereas in image database applications, an image object is often viewed at the pixel level. Most image database systems focus on the technique of retrieving information from raw image data such as color, shape, and texture [8,9]. The unavailability of an image data model will deprive the database of its semantic representation. Hence, querying the database will have to be done at a relatively low level by specifying color components of the picture, drawing shapes, or providing sample textures. It is clear that queries specified in this way will not normally be able to narrow down search results to a certain domain. For example, a query specifying 30% white and 70% blue can result in any images with those color compositions, which can be a white car parked in front of a blue wall, white beach against a blue sky, or a white book on a blue table.

Effective modeling of image data is critical to the success of multimedia databases. In particular, high level content abstraction is natural to the way humans think, and plays a key role in a semantically rich multimedia information system. Design considerations for an effective multimedia data model should ideally include:

- support for semantically rich conceptual contents
- ability to represent diverse aspects of the data to be modeled
- facilities for dynamic concept enrichment and expansion
- incorporation of knowledge of low level data
- isolation of the user from the low level representation and storage levels

Most current approaches to image databases tend to concentrate on low-level attributes. Despite the many attempts made to index and retrieve image content using low level attributes, these have not been widely accepted by the end users. The fact that most commercial image databases still adhere to the text-based approach [16] indicates that this indexing method is a reliable one in comparison with alternative approaches. A key objection to this approach, however, is the amount of time and manual effort required indexing the database [10]. However, as we shall see later in this chapter, it is possible to automate part of the indexing task using knowledge-assisted indexing paradigm.

The international standards community has also recognized the importance of a data modeling and descriptive approach to multimedia data. While the early MPEG (Motion Picture Experts Group) efforts concentrated on the representation of the actual data, MPEG-7 recognizes the need for providing descriptions to the data, focusing on the data contents to facilitate their meaningful search and retrieval. Such an approach is necessary to provide inter-operability. To support a workable content-based descriptive approach, a semantically rich data modeling paradigm is vital.

Increasingly, multimedia applications are required to operate across networks [11]. The main drawback in data delivery is limited bandwidth of the system and, from the user point of view, it will be the time spent to search and retrieve multimedia objects. For example, in video-on-demand applications, users may pose their query based on the title of a movie, actor name, or a specific dialogue of the movie. Assuming the users have seen a preview of the movie but cannot recall its title, it is unlikely that they will pose their query using low-level contents. Although it is possible that they could query the database using a sample image or a segment of the movie, this tends to be much more difficult because they have to provide a sample image or a video clip, and sending these queries over the network will be time consuming. Although not without limitations, modeling multimedia content using text tends to be more efficient in terms of response time and user friendliness.

To balance the semantic richness of free-text natural-language format against search efficiency, a canonical structured approach [12] is necessary (see Figure 1). By using a structured representation, the associated index may be constructed efficiently which will facilitate the search and identification of visual data based on high level concepts.

Figure 1. Representation of semantic content.

3. MODELING OF IMAGE DATA

In a structured database, there are a number of real world entities whose characteristics need to be modeled and represented in the database and, for each entity type of interest, decisions are made concerning which of its characteristics are required. Relational tables are often used to store these characteristics, which are fixed at the design stage. Due to the highly structured format of normalized relations, searching for particular features can be performed quite efficiently using standard file-access techniques. One of the main methods for conventional database design is the entity-relationship model [13,14]. Such a paradigm can be applied to the identification of pictures in certain cases where the contents of pictures do not form the main focus of interrogation. Here, an entire picture may be treated as an entity, and information such as the originator, date, and title may be regarded as properties of the image and entered into a relational database record. With this approach, only limited search of contents is possible using the title field within the structured record. In situations where the picture contents are central to user queries, however, such an approach is inadequate, and different data modeling and design structures have to be used.

When dealing with the subject matter of an image, data characteristics differ from those of conventional databases in several important ways. While conventional databases tend to deal with large classes of similar entities, the number of similar objects of interest within an image tend to be small. Moreover, the aggregate number of such objects across different images do not warrant their being stored together in a separate file, since their number is still relatively insignificant and such a grouping offers no significant performance advantage. The number of object types in images tends to be large compared with a conventional database. If a conventional database design paradigm is adopted for this situation, this would, in some extreme cases, result in a separate file for each image, with the size of each file containing the equivalent of no more than a relatively small number of records. On the either hand, it will not be advantageous to keep these together in a single file consisting of multiple record types, since the searching and indexing of such files will be slow and inefficient. In conventional databases, it is often necessary to represent general k-ary relationships involving k entities. The need to express such complex relationships is generally not critical for image data. While the ability to update data is a key requirement in conventional databases, no updating of values is usually required for image data. However, the ability to add and, to a lesser extent, delete data will offer significant advantages in enhancing retrieval performance.

In order to exploit the performance advantages of structured file processing, it is necessary to use a data model that is able to transform the intrinsic heterogeneous unstructured image contents to a set of homogeneous structured data items. This approach supports rapid searching, while at the same time provides adequate scope for the semantic richness of the images to be accommodated. It is useful to categorize the content of an image into two main types as shown in Figure 2.

Primitive Content	Complex Content
1. basic elements from which the image is constructed 2. features of the image that can be recognized and extracted automatically by the computer 3. extraction based on image processing and pattern recognition algorithms	1. patterns within a picture that are perceived as meaningful by human users 2. cannot normally be automatically identified by the computer 3. extraction via data modeling and description

Figure 2. The two main types of image contents.

Primitive contents may be handled and extracted using image processing and pattern recognition algorithms, while data modeling is concerned with complex contents. Modeling of content data furnishes a fundamental building block for subsequent content-based processing. Figure 3 shows the role of data modeling in complex content extraction.

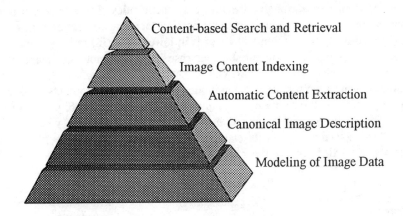

Content-based Search and Retrieval

Image Content Indexing

Automatic Content Extraction

Canonical Image Description

Modeling of Image Data

Figure 3. The role of data modeling.

4. SIMPLE EXPRESSIVE MODELS: THE TERNARY FACT MODELS

A data model for image content must represent both the attributes of individual data objects and the relationships between different data objects. From the data model, a canonical image description may be automatically built, which can capture the content semantics. The canonical description may be used to construct a content-based index using a relational database structure. The database structure can then be indexed and searched rapidly to provide fast image identification and retrieval.

4.1 THE BASIC MODEL AND DATABASE ORGANIZATION

We consider the basic building blocks of an image data model as consisting of *facts*, which may be modified and linked together in different ways to express the subject matter of an image. Conceptually, image facts may be distinguished into four main types as shown in Figure 4. In the case of binary and ternary facts, a *link* signifies the part that specifies the relationship.

Elementary Facts	Modified Facts	Binary Facts	Ternary Facts
Patterns within image that are perceived as meaningful to human users. An elementary fact states the presence of a particular item in the image.	Elementary facts augmented with descriptive properties through the use of modifiers.	Patterns within image linking together exactly two elementary or modified facts together that are perceived as meaningful to human users.	Patterns within image linking together exactly three elementary or modified facts together that are perceived as meaningful to human users.
Examples: book, television, pen	**Examples**: *blue* book, *round* table.	**Example**: blue book on round table	**Example**: woman gives child biscuit

Figure 4. The main fact types in an image.

The facts in the data model may be expressed in a way to facilitate the automatic extraction of image contents from them through adhering to syntactic rules. For example, a possible syntactic convention is: (i) elementary facts and derived facts are represented by words in upper case, (ii) modifiers are represented by words in lower case, (iii) in binary and ternary facts, the link is expressed using an initial upper case letter. Examples of image contents conforming to this convention are: "BICYCLE," "square TABLE," "CAT On yellow CHAIR." From such representation, automatic extraction of contents becomes a straightforward process of classification. The algorithm is illustrated in Figure 5. From the canonical description, no ambiguity should exist in the parsing process, where words in upper case will be placed in the Facts class, those in lower case will be placed in the Modifiers class, and words in initial upper case letters will be identified as links.

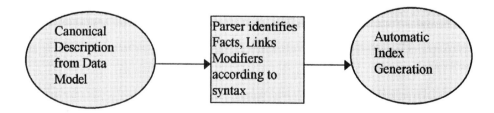

Figure 5. Automatic content extraction.

The main objective of the database structure is to be able to relate the image content, as given in the canonical descriptions, to a frame number. Once the frame numbers are identified, the database task is considered complete. Subsequently, the actual display of the image on the screen or via other forms of image output will be necessary, but this should be relatively mechanical. The canonical descriptions will be placed in index tables for rapid search and identification. In all the tables, the frame number constitutes the unique identifier, and is the only candidate key available. Following are the four basic relational structures constituting the image content index:

T_1 (Fact, Frame#)
T_2 (Fact, Modifier, Frame#)
T_3 (Fact1, Fact2, Link, Frame#)
T_4 (Fact1, Fact2, Fact3, Link, Frame#)

where T_1 corresponds to the Elementary Fact Table, T_2 corresponds to the Modified Fact Table, T_3 corresponds to the Binary Fact Table, and T_4 corresponds to the Ternary Fact Table. To facilitate search, it is possible that a given fact may be stored in more than one table.

4.2 DYNAMIC CONCEPT BUILDING AND AUTOMATIC INDEX EXPANSION

It is possible to expand the content information and index by suitably extending the basic model and restructuring elementary facts into a hierarchy. This extension is assisted by rules to automate the generation of new *derived facts* from elementary facts, from other lower level derived fact(s), or a combination of the two. This extension is depicted in Figure 6.

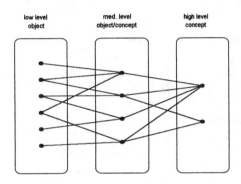

Figure 6. Extended model.

In Figure 6, a dot represents a fact and a line to the left of the fact relates that particular fact with its components. Here, it can be seen that elementary facts are labeled as low level objects, while derived facts are labeled as medium or high level concepts. Apart from the leftmost set, which contains all the elementary facts, the remaining sets contain derived facts. A derived fact is composed of two or more elementary facts or other derived facts from a lower level. From this representation, it is clear that the higher the level of the concept, the less the number of facts in the set. This is an important characteristic that will be advantageous for database search.

The base index, based on *atomic objects*, is entered manually or extracted automatically from the image. Atomic objects are defined as the smallest entity that cannot be decomposed further into components. For example, if a table were regarded as an atomic component, then in the future, a table leg or a table top would not be recognized from the database. Therefore, depending on the application, an indexer will have to predetermine to what extent he/she wants to decompose an image object into an atomic index entry. From the atomic indexes, the system will develop higher level indexes using its knowledge-based subsystem.

It is the task of the rules to perform the creation of the higher level indexes. A rule consists of an IF part, which lists all the conditions that must be satisfied, and a THEN part, which concludes the rule given that the conditions are met. A rule is created by assigning lower level (atomic) objects in the IF part and higher level objects in the THEN part. Boolean AND or OR can be used to define the relationship among the atomic objects in the condition of the rule. The AND part is the necessary condition and the OR part is the optional condition. By validating the rule conditions with existing indexes (which could be elementary facts or derived facts), new index entries may be created automatically. In other words, we build a higher level index from lower level (atomic) indexes that may be directly recognizable from the image. This indexing mechanism will avoid inconsistency in human perception of the image concept when the process is performed manually. On the retrieval side, users can take advantage of the high level indexes to speed up the search and narrow down the search space. We illustrate below how to construct a typical rule to define a high level object "computer."

IF	there exists	
	a monitor	AND
	a CPU	AND
	a keyboard	AND
	a mouse	
THEN	the OBJECT is a computer.	

In turn, we can treat the object "computer" as an intermediate level index item, and use it as a condition for a higher level object description as follows.

IF	there exists	
	a desk	AND
	a computer	AND
	a telephone	AND
THEN	the OBJECT is an office.	

In this way, we have structured the index representations into a hierarchy. Therefore, several atomic index entries will be able to define intermediate indexes and several intermediate index entries will be able to define higher level indexes, and so on. The benefit of this method is the reusability of the rules. Once a rule that defines an object is created, it can be used to define several other higher level objects/concepts.

4.3 EXAMPLE

Suppose that we have four pictures in the database with the following details

Table 1. Elementary Indexes

Frame#1	Frame #2	Frame #3	Frame #4
ribbon	ribbon	ribbon	tree
balloon	balloon	flower	flower
light	light	car	lawn
cake	Xmas tree		
candle	present		
people			

In the database, these objects will be treated as elementary facts (elementary indexes) which will be stored in an elementary fact table. Frame numbers are related to each index indicating to which image an index will point. For example, frame numbers 1, 2, and 3 are related to index entry *ribbon*, as the object ribbon has been indexed in pictures 1, 2, and 3. Suppose that we have created a knowledge-based system containing the following rules.

Rule 1:

IF	there exists		
	a ribbon	AND	[1,2,3]
	a balloon	AND	[1,2]
	a light		[1,2]
THEN	the OBJECT is *a decoration*		[1,2]

Rule 2:

IF	there exists		
	a ribbon	AND	[1,2,3]
	a flower	AND	[3,4]
	a car		[3]
THEN	the OBJECT is *a wedding party*		[3]

Rule 3:

IF	there exists		
	a tree	AND	[4]
	a flower	AND	[3,4]
	lawn		[4]
THEN	the OBJECT is *a garden*		[4]

Rule 4:

IF	there exists		
	a decoration	AND	[1,2]
	a cake	AND	[1]
	a candle	AND	[1]
	people		[1]
THEN	the OBJECT is *a birthday party*		[1]

Rule 5:

IF	there exists		
	a decoration	AND	[1,2]
	a Christmas tree	AND	[2]
	a present	AND	[2]
	a 'Santa'		[2]
THEN	the OBJECT is *a Christmas event*		[2]

Upon the execution of these rules, new index entries will be generated that represent intermediate or high level indexes. These indexes will be stored in different tables corresponding to the level of abstraction or the stage of creation of the index. Frame numbers are represented as extended conditions of the rule, because indexes are bound to frame numbers. To fire the rule, the inference engine requires that the same picture satisfy all of the conditions.

Table 2. Index Hierarchy

Atomic Index Table		Intermediate Index Table		High Level Index Table	
ribbon	1,2,3	decoration	1,2	birthday party	1
balloon	1,2	wedding party	3	Christmas event	2
candles	1	garden	4		
cake	1				
people	1				
Xmas tree	2				
present	2				
light	1,2				
car	3				
flower	3,4				
tree	4				
lawn	4				

Table 2 shows an instance of an index hierarchy. Image retrievals are performed by searching indexes from the higher level to the lower level tables. Searching image in this direction will produce faster results, first, because the number of items in the higher level table is less than the lower ones and, second, because the results are already narrowed down to fewer numbers of possible image results. If the item is not found in the highest level index table, then it will move to the next table, and so on until it reaches the lowest one.

The Ternary Fact Model can also be applied and integrated with other multimedia objects. For example, in retrieving a particular frame sequence in a video clip, one may use the query specification:

> Video (WOMAN Holds KNIFE)
> Audio ("how dare you")

Here, a group of similar consecutive frames may be indexed together, which operate in conjunction with a speech recognition module for audio information identification.

5. CONCLUDING REMARKS

Rapid accumulation of large volumes of multimedia data requires mechanisms for their selective retrieval. A key effort of MPEG-7 is to provide facilities to search and identify multimedia data by content and, to do so, it is necessary to provide standardized descriptions to multimedia contents. Before the inclusion of a meaningful content description, a data modeling paradigm must be adopted. A key purpose of data modeling is to inject some degree of structure and order into a seemingly unstructured situation. In doing so, certain uniformity may be achieved. From this, indexes and database structures may be built, which is essential for the construction of versatile visual information systems [15].

A useable data model need not be complicated, but should capture the main semantics of multimedia data. Although data semantics may be viewed at different levels, the most meaningful appears to be one that corresponds closest to human perception, which should ideally be isolated from any machine level considerations. As it is normally impossible to incorporate all the facts within an image in the description, it is often advantageous to be able to dynamically build up additional index entries from the base descriptions.

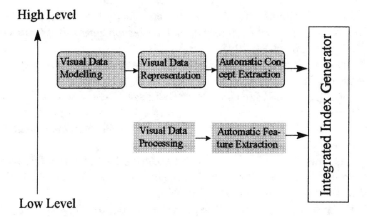

Figure 7. The role of data modeling in the construction of an integrated contents index.

The characteristics of the data modeling paradigm described here directly address high level semantics at the object level, and has the ability to automatically perform index expansion, which would substantially lower the indexing cost for high level contents and, at the same time, would also considerably enhance semantic richness. Such knowledge-assisted image database indexing is able to partially automate the indexing process by generating a higher level index from lower level ones. Furthermore, it should also prove advantageous to automatically incorporate relevant low level image characteristics to assist and complement the content indexing process. Figure 7 indicates such an approach in the construction of an integrated content index.

Hierarchical abstractions of the index structure will not only help to speed up database search, but will also allow the system to be queried using high level concepts, which may be learned by the system through the inclusion of new rules in the knowledge base.

REFERENCES

1. Adjeroh, D. A. and Nwosu, K. C., "Multimedia Database Management – Requirements and Issues," *IEEE Multimedia*, pp. 24-33, July-September 1997.
2. Campbell, S. T., "The Role of Database Systems in the Management of Multimedia Information," *International Workshop on Multi-Media Database Management Systems*, pp. 4-11, 1995.
3. Meghini, C., Rabitti, F., and Thanos, C., "Conceptual Modeling of Multimedia Documents," *IEEE Computer*, pp. 23-29, October 1991.
4. Nwosu, K. C., Thuraisingham, B., and Berra, P. B., "Multimedia Database Systems - A New Frontier," *IEEE Multimedia*, pp. 21-23, July-September 1997.
5. Bimbo, A. D., "Symbolic Description and Visual Querying of Image Sequences Using Spatio-Temporal Logic," *IEEE Transactions on Knowledge and Data Engineering*, 7(4), August 1995.

6.   Hirzalla, N. and Karmouch, A., "A Multimedia Query Specification Language," *International Workshop on Multi-Media Database Management Systems*, pp. 66-73, 1995.

7.   Hibino, S. and Rundensteiner, E. A., "A Visual Query Language for Identifying Temporal Trends in Video Data," *International Workshop on Multi-Media Database Management Systems*, pp. 74-81, 1995.

8.   Gudivada, V. N. and Raghavan, V. V., "Content-Based Image Retrieval Systems," *IEEE Computer*, pp. 18-31, 1995.

9.   Barber, R., et. al., "Ultimedia Manager: Query By Image Content and its Applications," *IEEE Comput. Soc. Press: Digest of Papers, Spring Compcon '94*, pp. 424-429, 1994.

10. Cawkell, A. E., "A Guide To Image Processing And Picture Management," *Gower Publishing Limited*, 106-144, 1994.

11. Adjeroh, D. A. and Lee, M. C., "Synchronization Mechanisms for Distributed Multimedia Presentation Systems," *IEEE International Workshop on Multi-Media Database Management Systems*, pp. 30-37, 1995.

12. Leung, C.H.C. and Zheng, Z.J., "Image Data Modeling for Efficient Content Indexing," *IEEE International Workshop on Multi-Media Database Management Systems*, 143-150, 1995.

13. Teorey, T., "Database Modeling and Design: The Entity Relationship Approach," *Morgan Kaufman*, 1990.

14. Chen, P. P-S., "The Entity-Relationship Model – Towards a Unified View of Data," *ACM Transactions on Database Systems*, 1, 1976.

15. Leung, C. H. C. (Ed.) *Visual Information Systems*. Springer-Verlag Lecture Notes in Computer Science 1306, 1997.

16. Guglielmo, E. J. and Rowe, N., "Natural Language Retrieval of Images Based on Descriptive Captions," *ACM Transactions on Information Systems*, 14, pp. 237-267, 1996.

4

MIDDLEWARE PLATFORMS TO SUPPORT MULTIMEDIA APPLICATIONS

John Bates
University of Cambridge Computer Laboratory
Pembroke Street, Cambridge CB2 3QG
United Kingdom

1. BACKGROUND 56
    1.1 WHAT MAKES AN APPLICATION "MULTIMEDIA"? 56
    1.2 MULTIMEDIA APPLICATION TYPES 58
    1.3 MOTIVATIONS FOR THE DEVELOPMENT OF SUPPORT PLATFORMS...................59
    1.4 PLATFORM DESIGN...61
2. MULTIMEDIA OBJECTS 62
    2.1 OBJECT AUTHORING APPROACHES 62
    2.2 OBJECT RUN-TIME SUPPORT 66
3. MULTIMEDIA DATA MODELING 73
    3.1 MODELING, BROWSING, AND COLLATING 73
    3.2 DATABASE SUPPORT 75
4. SYNCHRONIZATION...76
    4.1 SPECIFYING SYNCHRONIZATION RELATIONSHIPS 76
    4.2 SUPPORTING RUN-TIME SYNCHRONIZATION 76
5. EVENT-DRIVEN PROGRAMMING 77
    5.1 EVENT-BASED AUTHORING 78
    5.2 RUN-TIME EVENT SUPPORT...82
6. CONTROLLING GROUPS OF OBJECTS 83
    6.1 AUTHORING POLICIES FOR CONTROLLING GROUPS.......................................83
    6.2 RUN-TIME SUPPORT FOR GROUPS 85
7. CONCLUSIONS 85
    REFERENCES..86

Abstract. The emphasis of this chapter is on the need to provide *platforms* to support the authoring and run-time management of multimedia applications. Such platforms are required at the *middleware* level, i.e., between the environment (which consists of deployed hardware devices, operating systems, networks, and system services) and the application. The aim is to provide generic environment-independent abstractions for application development. We term the functionality of multimedia applications that can be supported in a generic way *interactive presentation*, the two sub-processes of which can be defined as follows:

- **Presentation** - a process involving any of the following functions: accessing, processing, synchronization, display, and storage of multiple media types.

- **Interaction** - using asynchronous occurrences (events) related to the media presentation to affect the course of the presentation. Human interaction with the media, via the application user interface, may include multi-user collaboration. Events can be generated from analyzing media items, e.g., spotting a pattern in a video. We must also take into account interaction with the environment, e.g., system requests to adjust media resource usage. Monitoring user mobility can generate events that affect presentation, e.g., requiring that an application move its user interface to a user's new physical location.

We stress the importance of supporting interactive presentation within *distributed environments*. In a non-networked, single user environment, people cannot share data, access remote devices, or communicate with other users. Application functionality is thus limited to a subset of that possible in a distributed environment. Distributed applications also need to be constructed more flexibly because of resource sharing and network data transmission. Applications developed, using distributed principles, scale down well to single machines; the reverse is not true.

Experience has shown that monolithic applications, built directly on top of environment-specific abstractions, are not reusable and are unnecessarily time-consuming to build. The platform approach encourages composing and interconnecting distinct components (see Figure 1), each potentially running on separate machines. Although each component can be viewed as a program in its own right, together they represent a multimedia application. Developing an application in this way is more flexible and rapid than developing a monolithic solution.

Our experience has been gained in developing the *IMP* (Interactive Multimedia Presentation) distributed multimedia application support platform [7,8]. In this discussion we take examples from IMP along with other contemporary platforms.

1. BACKGROUND

This section identifies the features that a multimedia application support platform should provide. First, we define exactly what we mean by multimedia in the context of this chapter. Second, we outline some classes of multimedia application with the aim of highlighting the generic support required by all. Third, we summarize the complexities involved in developing applications in modern multimedia environments. Finally, we introduce the platform components studied in this chapter.

1.1 WHAT MAKES AN APPLICATION "MULTIMEDIA"?

A multimedia application involves the interactive presentation of mixed media data items in a multimedia environment. Interactive presentation is the set of processes within an application that can be generalized as the core multimedia activities. It is not limited to display but also encompasses analysis and processing of multimedia data, synchronization in the display of multiple media items, and the ability to support interaction with the data. However, multimedia applications are not necessarily solely concerned with interactive presentation. Individuals who comment on the limited usefulness of multimedia often inaccurately think that a multimedia application is a closed world, the functionality of which is limited to the display of media components and interaction with them. In actual fact, this is often just a subset of the application's functionality. One survey [50] illustrates that multimedia has implications for a wide range of mainstream areas, including *office automation*, *service industry applications* (such as in education, financial services and health), *retail applications* (such as in publishing, travel and property), *domestic applications*, *science, engineering,* and *cultural activities.* Some experienced developers have now worked in many of these areas. One developer [22] details experience gained in developing multimedia applications *in medicine, collaborative working, multimedia mail, multimedia fax, news-on-demand,* and *distance learning.*

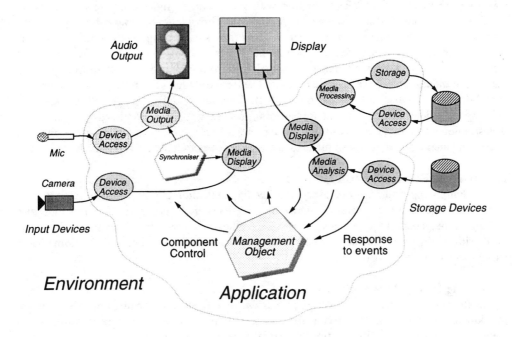

Figure 1. A distributed multimedia application.

We now define what a multimedia environment refers to in the context of this chapter. Due to the recent interest in the integration of audio and video into the workstation environment, a misconception has emerged that multimedia means video and audio. Video and audio is an instance of multimedia, not a definition. A multimedia environment integrates multiple media, both static (e.g., text and pictures) and dynamic (e.g., audio and video). In such an environment an application developer has the choice of using media types appropriate for his/her application. To address the fact that resource availability can vary at run-time and between different environments, dynamic interchangeability is possible. One media combination can be replaced by another, e.g. substituting audio and video for still images with text subtitles. Multimedia environments are often distributed, with multimedia peripherals widely deployed. This means that often applications must be distributed, too, for example, multimedia conferencing. Supporting continuous media in a distributed environment presents further challenges (see below).

Multimedia is no longer isolated to experimental environments. Use of the Internet for multimedia applications is an area of constant development [52]. Additionally, multimedia computing environments are diverging to include the home. Recent work has shown the feasibility of connecting household appliances and consumer electronics to a Home Area Network [24]. Televisions, hi-fi, and central heating systems will no longer be stand-alone components. They will be able to interchange data and be controlled using distributed systems principles, in the same way as multimedia devices connected to a network. This will expand the deployment potential for techniques such as those described in this chapter. It will also enhance the range of input and output devices, e.g., it will be possible to instruct your washing machine to do this week's washing while using your digital watch at work. Also, low resolution video can be relayed to the digital watch showing the current location of a child. When the child moves out of view of one camera, another is selected automatically.

Looking to the future, new media types with potential for interaction and presentation are emerging. Virtual Reality (VR) animation with the option of full-immersion represents an exciting new display medium. Augmented Reality (AR) involves enhancing everyday working with presentation and interaction mechanisms. It is intrinsically bound with computer support for user mobility. An output device, such as the wearable computer [43], allows real-world views to be overlaid with computer-generated information. Various input devices for the tracking of mobile users have been developed. The Active Badge system [25] is an example of a mobile input device, which transmits a signal to allow individuals' locations within a building to be determined. Other examples are ultrasound badges [47] and active floors [1]. It is desirable to be able to use these new media interchangeably in applications. Environments integrating audio, video, text, and pictures are not the limit of multimedia, but the beginning.

1.2 MULTIMEDIA APPLICATION TYPES
Rather than giving a summary of every multimedia application that has been developed, this section describes application areas in which multimedia is an integral part. Platforms must aim to support the general requirements of all these application types. In this section each area is dealt with in isolation, but there is no reason why an application cannot use multimedia in more than one of the ways described.

1.2.1 Time-Driven Presentations
Applications can involve *time-driven presentations* that display multimedia information using the dimension of time as the driving force. The notion of presentation time commences at application start-up. The presentation of media items can be triggered by a certain point in time being reached. Some applications allow interaction or other functionality within specified time slices.

1.2.2 Hypermedia Documents
In a *hypermedia* application, media components represent information nodes. Virtual links between nodes can be navigated by interacting with an information node. Examples are displaying relevant video clips if words in a text document are clicked on, or displaying a text and picture biography about someone if that person is clicked on in a video story.

1.2.3 Conferencing Systems
Conferencing applications provide multimedia-enriched methods of formal or informal meetings between geographically separated colleagues. Text-based conferencing systems have been developed in which users each have a text window to type into and another to see the output of the other user. *Shared drawing* tools allow distributed users to collaborate in visualizing ideas. Each user is presented with a drawing area and a selection of drawing tools. Any drawing strokes made are propagated to every user's display. There has been much recent interest in video conferencing. Such systems allow two or more users to carry out a conversation while seeing and hearing the other conferences. The power of an integrated multimedia environment is that any of these methods of conferencing can be used interchangeably. The selection can be made on appropriateness and resource availability. We are not limited to window-based conferences and, given hardware and systems support, meetings can be conducted using VR, with live video being overlaid onto virtual representations of users.

1.2.4 Multimedia Agents

Multimedia agents apply intelligent heuristics to multimedia filtering. By tailoring them with individual requirements they can perform media processing duties normally undertaken by a human. Examples are automatic filtering of text files, such as mail or news, or looking for movement in a video stream to assist a security guard. Many simple agents can cooperate to compose a more complex application.

1.2.5 Mobile Multimedia

Users of multimedia applications may be mobile. It is not always desirable or adequate to use a portable computer with a wireless network, as it is cumbersome or may not have adequate performance or peripherals, e.g., for video conferencing. If the user is moving between computing equipment then it is beneficial if his/her applications can follow and adapt transparently to the nearest computing hardware. In a distributed multimedia application this involves applications which are aware of user locations and are themselves able to move around a network, re-mapping endpoints, such as cameras, microphones, and user interfaces, onto current user locations. A simple example of mobile multimedia is using a video window to track a user. When the user moves, the image in the window switches to the nearest camera. Another example is for music to be relayed to the nearest speaker as a person moves around a home. A natural progression of mobile multimedia is to support mobility for a cooperating set of users. In a multimedia conference, if a user moves, his/her endpoints must move and connections to the other users involved must be re-established.

1.2.6 Event-Driven Control

It is often desirable to use an event associated with one media item to control another. This is subsumed by all of the above but can be useful in its own right. For example, we may want to specify that when two people are together in an office, a certain audio/video message is played on the nearest workstation.

1.3 MOTIVATIONS FOR THE DEVELOPMENT OF SUPPORT PLATFORMS

The development of multimedia applications directly on top of environment-specific devices and services is a time-consuming and ad hoc process. Platforms to support multimedia applications encourage authoring in a way that reflects the application's function rather than the peculiarities of the environment. This section briefly outlines some of the complexities and introduces how support platforms can assist application development.

1.3.1 Continuous Media and Quality of Service

Due to the continuous and time-dependent nature of media such as audio and video, environment resources can be utilized for undisclosed periods of time. An environment must thus embody the principle of Quality of Service (QoS) [46]. QoS describes the ability to adjust the quality of data presentation in response to resource availability. Environment components embody policies for the allocation of their resources. For instance, if a network, processor, or storage service cannot support the presentation of high quality video at 25 frames per second, then an application must *negotiate* alternative QoS parameters. Resource availability can also change in the event of an application migrating to another computer or computing environment.

1.3.2 Environment Complexity and Evolution

Due to the evolutionary nature of multimedia environments the characteristics and interfaces of components are constantly being re-evaluated and updated. As services evolve it is often desirable to continue to support older services since applications may rely on them. This leads to an environment with many heterogeneous services with different interfaces and different levels of functionality. There is also a wide range of data formats for representation of media items, both standardized and proprietary. This experimental nature within environments means that applications are often developed on a *per application* basis. As an example, Figure 2 shows the system services (such as storage services and live devices) in the Cambridge multimedia environment from the time when IMP was constructed. It had a rich variety of devices, thus yielding a large degree of heterogeneity, including traditional distributed services such as NFS and emerging distributed services including *Pandora* [29] and *MSSA* [35] storage and live components. It also supports the Active Badge system to monitor the location of members of the department.

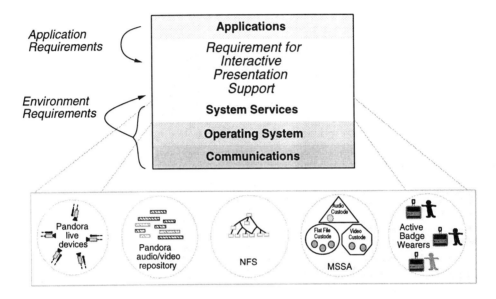

Figure 2. Application support requirements and experimental system services.

Applications are therefore required to manage a complicated range of run-time tasks, which must be specified by the application developer. They may be required to retrieve and display many different medium types, such as text, pictures, video, and audio, each of which may have a different format (encoding). Presentation functions such as processing, synchronization, or analysis of data may be required before display. It is also often a requirement to make applications adaptive [23], so that they can adjust dynamically to different levels of resource availability. They must respond to events, e.g., from devices or the user interface. In summary, application structure tends to reflect management of the underlying system rather than the function of the application.

1.3.3 Motivational Factors
In summary, developing applications without platform support can present long- and short-term software development problems for the following reasons:

- **The complexity involved in application development**: It may be necessary to use the facilities of many heterogeneous components and specify many complicated run-time tasks. This prolongs the application development process leading to inconvenience and increased development costs.
- **The lack of application portability**: Directly referencing a specific interface ties an application to that device or service. This makes applications difficult to port between different environments.
- **The lack of application maintainability**: Within the same environment, if devices or services are changed or their characteristics updated, applications may require time-

consuming updates. The unrepresentative nature of application structure increases maintenance difficulties as the code may be difficult to follow.

- **The lack of application component reusability**: Development on a per application basis leads to a lack of reusable abstractions for long term support.

- .

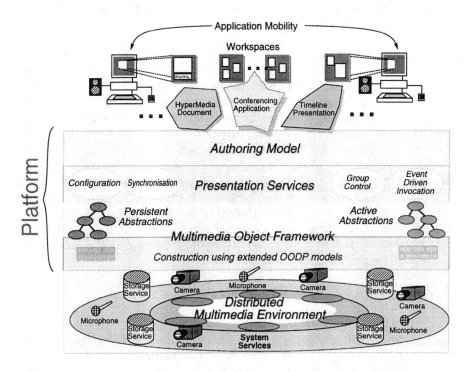

Figure 3. Support platform concepts.

1.4 PLATFORM DESIGN

By developing a platform between the application and the environment (see Figure 3) it is possible to provide a uniform authoring approach to the application developer as well as a set of services to realize authored applications at run-time. This addresses the problems of complexity, portability, and maintainability. To address reusability and speed up application development, platforms provide a component-based method of development. The facilities of the platform must capture the generalized requirements of a wide range of application types.

Figure 3 shows a graphical overview of the concerns of our analysis, which we break down into the following sections:

- Building applications using multimedia objects
- Multimedia data modeling
- Synchronizing the presentation of multiple objects
- Event-driven programming
- Group control of objects

In each section we describe the motivating requirements and discuss platform approaches from the following two angles:

- **Authoring**: Our study of authoring is concerned with the facilities provided to allow an application developer to express the multimedia aspects of his/her application. The platform run-time facilities are represented as abstractions, accessible from within existing programming languages. To assist authoring, some platforms offer a specially designed *script language* for expressing interactive presentation. An entire application does not necessarily have to be written in a script language; a more powerful approach is to invoke scripts from a user program. Also, various high level graphical tools have been developed to provide easy access to multimedia facilities for novice users. Examples are multimedia database browsers, timeline editors, and configuration editors.

- **Run-time Support**: The run-time facilities in a platform are responsible for realizing the associated authoring model. Presentation platforms vary in approach from systems designed for display on a single-user workstation to those designed for use in a multi-user distributed system. At one extreme are *presentation engines* – programs responsible for all aspects of a run-time presentation. This type of approach is designed with a single user platform in mind, since one is master of all resources and problems such as network delay are excluded. On the other extreme are *distributed presentation platforms* which aim to provide the ease of authoring found in single user platforms but take into account issues such as QoS, specialization of service, and extensibility. This type of approach scales down well to cater to single user workstations, whereas monolithic presentation engines do not scale up well. Although some systems, such as *Quicktime* [49], *Macromind Director* [36], and *MHEG* [32], assume presentation using an engine, they also use principles of extensibility and system independence. Presentation platforms for distributed environments are still in the research domain, but this may change through the work of the IMA [30].

2. MULTIMEDIA OBJECTS

Rather than implementing multimedia applications in an ad hoc way, it is desirable to have standard *building blocks* with which to construct applications. Using such objects enables abstraction of system-specific details at an authoring level. From a systems perspective, as new requirements emerge, object technology provides a framework into which new support can be easily added.

2.1 OBJECT AUTHORING APPROACHES

An application developer should be able to express presentation scenarios in an intuitive way. The notion of selecting objects appropriate for a task and configuring them to work together is appealing. This section examines some approaches developed to allow *plug and play* authoring.

2.1.1 Presentation Objects and Configuration

Most approaches center on *presentation objects*. A presentation object is an encapsulation of a presentation function for a particular medium type. Such objects input data, perform the relevant function, and output the data. They typically perform one or more of the following functions:

- **Device access**: *Source* objects can take data from a device (either a live device or a storage service). *Sink* objects can be used for putting data onto storage devices.

- **Monitoring/Analyzing**: Examining the data for particular phenomena, e.g., a word of a text object being clicked on, a certain video frame being presented, or a known face appearing in a video clip.

- **Filtering**: Taking the data and changing it in some way, e.g., dynamic visual effects on video.

- **Displaying**: Displaying the data in a certain style. In some systems, display components associated with the same presentation can be shown within the same *workspace*, i.e., a window into which the display component can be laid out.

- **Synchronizing**: For continuous media, intra-stream synchronization can be performed to remove jitter.

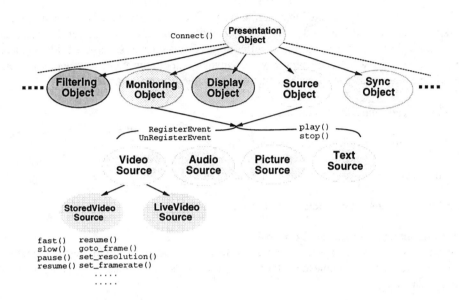

Figure 4. Application developer's view of a presentation object hierarchy.

Presentation objects promote the concept of reuse by defining a series of standard abstractions. The choice of objects can be represented as a class hierarchy. Part of such a class hierarchy is illustrated in Figure 4. In this example all presentation objects are derived from the class `PresentationObject`. Class `StoredVideoSource` is shown to be defined using multiple inheritance and specialization.

Configurations promote the notion of tailorability by allowing the composition of presentation objects. Within a configuration, media data is passed between presentation objects; the output of one presentation object is the input of the next. Mechanisms for specifying configurations are illustrated in Sections 2.1.4 and 2.1.5.

2.1.2 Presentation Object Events

Presentation objects, which actively monitor the data for certain occurrences, are capable of notifying events to inform interested parties of relevant occurrences. One use for this is in monitoring points of presentation; certain classes of video objects can monitor for frame boundaries, e.g., they can report if frame 123 is detected. Another use is in monitoring user interaction, e.g., a display object monitoring for user interaction with areas of the data it is displaying. Application developers should not cut themselves off from the environment and objects can notify them of various system occurrences. An example is a video source object that negotiates use of resources and can report any renegotiation requested by the system.

Event classes, analogous to object classes, define a template for instantiating events. For example, instances of event class `Location(Person, Room, Domain)` inform us when a particular mobile user, wearing an active badge, is seen in a particular room. We may receive an event

```
Location('John.Bates@cl.cam.ac.uk','Meeting Room','cl.cam.ac.uk')
```

which specifies that John has been seen in the Cambridge meeting room.

In order to receive information of this nature, we must first register interest in occurrences of importance to us. To cut down on network traffic and the amount of local event filtering, it is useful to be able to specify to an object offering an event service specific details about our interests. To do this we use *templates*, which involve supplying event parameters as actual values of interest or variables, which can match any value. Examples are:

- Tell me every time John is seen anywhere:

```
Location('John.Bates@cl.cam.ac.uk',L,D)
```

- Tell me when anyone is seen in the meeting room:

```
Location(P, 'Meeting Room', 'cl.cam.ac.uk')
```

2.1.3 Controlling Presentation Objects
At run-time, presentation objects can be controlled dynamically by invoking their methods. With reference to the example class hierarchy, a video source object has methods for the following functions:

- **Presentation control**: Processing functions, such as play, stop, etc.

- **Quality control**: Presentation objects can also be responsible for negotiating resources for themselves. They notify a client if they cannot gain adequate resources. The quality control methods allow the adjusting of resource utilization, e.g., for the video source object set_resolution and set_framerate. Lower resolution and frame rate for a video object implies less network bandwidth and fewer processor cycles to process and display it.

- **Interconnection**: Compatible classes of presentation object can be connected together. Methods are provided to control this process.

- **Event registration**: These methods are used by the system to tell the presentation object the events to monitor for. An event template is passed as a parameter to specify the range of interest.

2.1.4 Configuring by Script Language
Some authoring approaches have involved specification of configurations within a script language. The *VuSystem* at MIT [44] uses an extended TCL to specify configuration; the *Touring Machine* system from Bellcore [10] provides an API with which a *session* can be configured in terms of a user of object communication endpoints. IMP was specifically developed to express interactive presentation using presentation objects. In IMP, the part of the application authored by the user is responsible for creating presentation objects and controlling them in response to run-time events. When an IMP script is instantiated, it creates a *management object* to control run-time presentation.

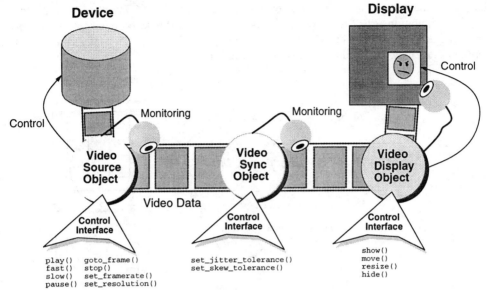

Figure 5. Application developer's view of a configuration.

To specify a configuration of presentation objects, the following syntax is used:

```
SourceObject | PresObject₁ | PresObjectₙ > SinkObject
```

Each `PresObject` is a presentation object class. A presentation object instance for each class is created. The source and optional sink are multimedia database objects (described later in Section 3), used to automatically create the relevant presentation object. The input of each presentation object in the configuration is linked to the output of the object preceding it. In some situations, the system can automatically insert presentation objects into configurations. As an example, to display the video data object `Film` using an object of class `VideoDisplay`, the following statement could be used:

```
Film | VideoDisplay ;
```

For all configurations the system automatically creates a source presentation object to access the source data. In this case it will create a source video object to access the data associated with `Film`. The source and display objects are controlled separately but act on the same data. The system may create other objects and automatically insert them; for example, in this case an object for intra-stream synchronization can be inserted. Such synchronization objects remove jitter before display, thus, in this case, it is inserted in the configuration before the display object. The application developer's view of this example configuration is illustrated in Figure 5.

Objects can be controlled by invoking methods. As an example, the video could be paused and its window moved to a 50 by 50 pixel area in the top left corner of the parent window. Invocations of the following form can be used:

```
Film$Source.pause();
Film$Display.move(0,0);
Film$Display.resize(50,50);
```

In this example the presentation objects are referenced by class. The invocations specify that the `pause` method should be invoked on all objects derived from the class `Source` in the `Film` configuration. Also, the `move` and `resize` methods should be invoked on all objects which are derived from the class `Display`. If there are multiple objects of the same class in a configuration, they can be uniquely specified by index.

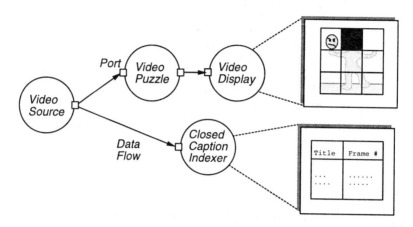

Figure 6. Example from the VuSystem.

2.1.5 Configuring Graphically

Three projects that have investigated graphical configuration are the VuSystem, the *Medusa* system [48], and the University of Geneva's *multimedia framework* [17]. These provide direct manipulation tools to abstract above the level of script-based authoring. The idea is that presentation objects can be selected and appear as a graphic within a drawing space. Compatible objects can then be connected together in a data flow diagram. The underlying model realizes these data flows directly. This approach is very good for prototyping data flow but is limited as it doesn't allow the specification of other activities, such as event handling. Figure 6 shows an example that can be constructed using the VuSystem editor.[1] Filters can be inserted on the fly, such as the square puzzle. Also shown is an object examining the same video and using closed caption subtitles to index it.

2.2 OBJECT RUN-TIME SUPPORT

The overriding motivation of object-based approaches is to effectively manage device and format heterogeneity; however, at their maximum potential they replace the management of complex distributed architectures with uniformly configurable building blocks. As will become apparent in discussing specific implementations, models vary in the facilities they provide.

2.2.1 Active Presentation Objects

Presentation objects (see Figure 7) must be implemented as active objects; that is, objects with their own asynchronous threads of control. This is because, as well as being activated on receipt of a message, they must be able to perform asynchronous processing and send messages. As shown in Figure 7, active presentation objects can be implemented *directly*, e.g., an image processing object, which takes data into its address space, and physically manipulates it. Alternatively they can just provide a consistent interface and *refer* their function to an existing system component, e.g., a source object that controls, and receives events from, a storage service.

---

[1] As demonstrated at the First IEEE International Conference on Multimedia Computing and Systems

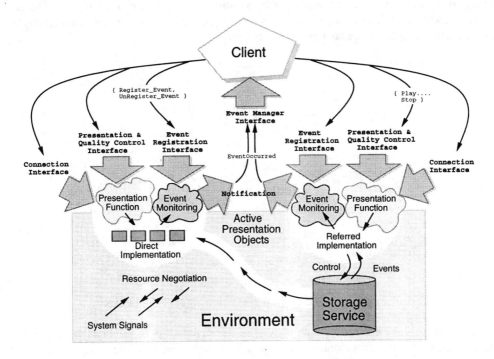

Figure 7. Active presentation object functions.

The autonomous concerns of a typical active presentation object are as follows:

- **Presentation functions**: This involves taking in data from a device or another presentation object, performing some function on it and outputting it, or storing it on a device. In some environments, objects must negotiate a QoS with environment components. If the desired level of service is not obtainable then system events can be notified by the object. Presentation objects must also provide a mechanism through which they can be connected to compatible objects. If connection is implemented directly, this can be via port abstractions or through some form of mutually agreeable shared memory arrangement.

- **Event monitoring**: This involves continuous monitoring to detect whether events associated with the data presentation functions have occurred.

- **Handling invocations**: By invoking methods, clients can initialize and influence at run-time the presentation and event monitoring processes.

- **Event notification**: If events are detected at run-time then they must be notified to relevant clients. Objects must keep a list of interested clients, whom they will notify when the relevant registered event occurs.

The system-specific aspects of building active presentation objects means that an abstraction must be built for every supported device and format combination. The class hierarchy as seen by an application developer must be extended to take this into account. Figure 8 shows how the class hierarchy in Figure 4 can be extended to cater for the different video device and format types within the example environment (see Figure 2). Additional objects to help connect system-dependent features together may be built. Examples are translator objects to convert one format of video to another, thus avoiding having to build totally new format-specific objects. Such components may be inserted by a higher level service transparently to the application developer or may be selected by hand.

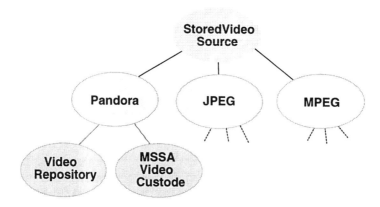

Figure 8. Continuation of the presentation object class hierarchy.

The component of the application authored by the developer must be instantiated at run-time. We term such an instance a *management object*. It must be implemented as an active object since it must control several concurrent management functions, including creating, configuring, and controlling objects and run-time event handling, as well as managing any additional application states.

Presentation objects are created dynamically by *factories*. These can be distributed in sites around an environment and created objects exist at these sites. With reference to Figure 9, the display factory could be on a user workstation and the source factories on the same machine as an associated source device. Mechanisms for configuring objects together differ in implementation. Some systems require an application to be written to bind input and output ports together. Others provide a higher level service to type-check and connect objects together (as shown in Figure 9).

2.2.2 Prototype Presentation Object Systems
This section reviews systems that have used object-oriented paradigms in their presentation support platforms. Some objects are designed to share address spaces and others allow distribution.

Systems designed to run on stand-alone workstations have been designed using objects to manage heterogeneity in formats and devices. The presentation engines of packages, such as *Quicktime, MME* [37] *Macromind Director,* and *MHEG*, use object instances to manage various presentation functions. For example, in Quicktime instances of *components* manage various format and device-dependent functions like compression, decompression, and digitization. Each component is controlled using an interface. A component manager is responsible for keeping track of components and allowing clients to connect to and communicate with component instances. New types can be added to support new format and device types. An image compression manager addresses heterogeneity by providing uniform access to components of the same function. A high level movie toolbox manages editing and playback of Quicktime format movies using the image compression manager interface.

The systems described so far do not explicitly take into account distribution. In a distributed implementation, objects must be able to run in separate address spaces. They should also take into account resource issues, such as QoS.

The *Touring Machine* system developed by Bellcore is a platform developed to support the development of communication-oriented multimedia applications. It uses resource objects to abstract devices such as audio and video switches. These are coordinated by a resource manager. A higher level session object is created for each application instance to manage the process of configuration. It achieves this by communicating with resource managers. This model concentrates on the platforms' communications aspects and does not directly address interaction. The *Distributed Media Control System* (DMCS) [33] developed at University of Massachusetts Lowell provides a similar model but augments the view of logical devices. Sources, sinks, and processing objects such as speech recognizers and special effects objects can be supported as well.

ACME [2] takes the approach of extending a window system server with an ACME server, one of which runs on every workstation. The server is a factory that can manage the creation of logical device objects representing abstractions of physical devices. Many logical devices can be mapped to one physical device. Objects managed by different ACME servers can be connected together by streams. They are typed by medium and format, and only compatible objects can be connected together. A synchronized stream (termed a *rope*) can be created by associating several logical devices into a composite logical device. Each stream has a logical time system (LTS) at the server where it is to be presented. This can be used to ensure the synchronization of ropes (described later). It can also be used for event notification, i.e., notify an event at a certain point in a logical stream. The model takes into account resource reservation by allowing connections to be requested before required. *Tactus* [16] has built on ACME by providing a toolkit of active display objects. These provide a higher level of construction than the original ACME model.

Three similar approaches to implementing active objects are presented in the VuSystem, Medusa, and the Geneva multimedia framework. Objects are represented as programming language level classes and can be manipulated within programs. Objects exchange data by binding to the ports of other objects.

Active presentation objects developed in the IMP system can be distributed and provide all the functionality described in the earlier discussion. An IMP script is instantiated as a management object, which is then responsible for creating and connecting presentation objects. The approach differs from the above in that a service is provided to assist with the process of configuration, as illustrated in Figure 9. The configuration service manages references to distributed object factories within its computing domain. Its other functions are considered further in the section on data modeling (see Section 3). With respect to the discussion so far, the configuration service can create objects without the client needing to know the location of distributed factories. It can also type-check object connections, e.g., disallowing an audio source object from being connected to a video display. This relies on it having access to a repository of class information.

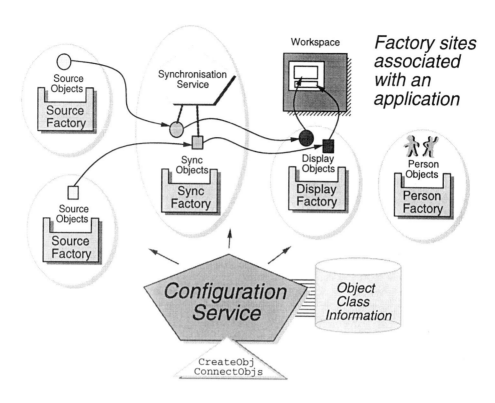

Figure 9. Presentation object factories and a configuration service.

Initial research has illustrated the potential of using active presentation objects as the building blocks of multimedia applications. The work of the *Interactive Multimedia Association* (IMA) [30] is moving toward international standardization of object-based multimedia services. The proposed model is based on CORBA. Configuration involves a client managing object creation, via factories, and connecting objects using stream objects. Various levels of QoS can be requested on streams. Objects also understand registration and notification of events.

2.2.3 Building Active Objects with Extended OODP
Active presentation objects enhance reusability by allowing selections to be made from an existing component library. However, if a new class of abstraction is desirable, it must be developed and added to the class hierarchy. One area of research has been an extension of Object-Oriented Distributed Programming (OODP) to support the construction of active presentation objects.

OODP paradigms use Interface Definition Languages (IDLs) to define the methods that can be invoked on a particular object. Interfaces represent a specification of communication requirements to the underlying architecture. Multimedia has been facilitated by the integration of continuous media into distributed environments. However, stream endpoints and uniform declaration of the event characteristics of an interface are not catered for in current IDL models.

Some research work has focused on developing underlying communications architectures and making features available at an OODP level. Work at Lancaster [15] investigated providing generic object types for building devices and streams. The underlying model is a QoS-based communications architecture enabling stream abstractions of varying bandwidths to be instantiated. Work at Cambridge [38] took a similar approach but allows stream endpoints and quality factors to be specified in an IDL. This allows clients to import an interface with a QoS appropriate to them. Example interfaces and abstractions are shown in Figure 10.

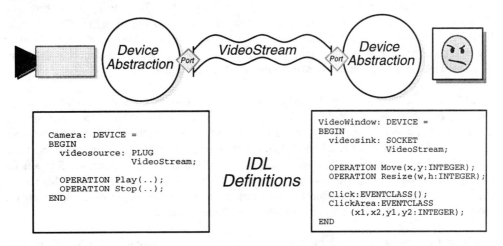

Figure 10. Extending OODP with devices, streams, and events.

Other work has addressed the shortcomings within OODP in supporting events. When building an active object it is desirable to be able to declare typed events in the same way as methods. Current OODP platforms force the object builder into ad hoc approaches in which callback routines must be declared within the client. The event-providing object reference is passed to the client's callback interface and calls back using some agreed method. This is an inelegant way of notification as it relies on some instance-specific agreement between client and server and declaration of functionality in client instead of server. Work at Cambridge [5] has provided an underlying event architecture to support generic registration and notification. An IDL has been extended to support the declaration of events within active object interfaces. Figure 10 shows how event classes can be defined. In this case `VideoWindow` objects can have events of class `Click` and `ClickArea` registered. Libraries are provided to assist in the construction of event services and clients. The server-side library provides the following features: a registration interface, template storage, a programming interface to allow the service to signal events, template matching against stored templates and client notification. The client-side library provides registration using templates, a notification interface and callback of user-specified routines on notification. Support for marshalling and unmarshalling of event instances for transmission over a network is provided in both client and server libraries.

2.2.4 Supporting Mobile Multimedia

This section discusses supporting user mobility within distributed multimedia environments. We have already described how, when a trackable application user (e.g., a user wearing an active badge) moves, this movement can be detected. As a user moves, so an application can follow, reconfiguring where necessary. It is desirable to provide this mobility by default, i.e., without it having to be explicitly programmed. However, it is often beneficial to be able to detect the mobility in order to vary and adapt application behavior in response to changes in conditions following a move.

Teleporting [40] is a technique to support user mobility with the user interface of an application following a mobile user. By clicking a button on their active badge, a user's current session pops up on the nearest workstation. The teleporting system is based on the technology of the X window system. A proxy X server on a user's *base workstation* is able to forward X protocol requests to another server thus providing a level of indirection. The display of X applications can thus move with a mobile user. A simple database provides a mapping between current location and workstation display. Teleporting is a powerful technique, the main advantage being that it makes any existing X application mobile. However, it is tied to the X system and thus limited for multimedia use as it cannot be used with any medium that does not go through X, e.g., audio. Only the display connections follow a user and there is no dynamic reconfiguration at an application level.

Another approach to mobile multimedia is to build multimedia applications using a mobile agent system that supports mobile computation, i.e., freezing a running agent, sending it to another machine and restarting it where it left off. An example is the Migratory Applications work [11] which employs the Obliq mobile agent system so applications can move from one user to another or can be configured to follow users from machine to machine. Support for state saving in Visual Obliq allows applications to take their user interfaces with them when they move. This approach produces monolithic applications for single users in which the mobile agent contains all control functionality and the user interface.

Work at Cambridge extended the IMP platform to support mobile users of distributed, possibly cooperative multimedia applications [6,9]. An application can register interest in the location of the controlling user. If he/she moves then the application is notified and can take appropriate action. The controlling management object can then decide to move itself and any other relevant presentation objects to a location appropriate to the user's new position. Some presentation objects are location-dependent. An example is a user interface object, because the user always wants to see the user interface. As an illustrative scenario consider the multi-user video conference described in Section 1.2.5. Each user has many streams from their video source going to the other participants' video windows. If a user moves, the following stages are initiated. First, the connections to everyone's video windows must be changed to a source at the user's new location. Second, the user interface of the mobile user must pop up at the new location on an appropriate display and the video windows must show the other users by reconnecting to their video sources. To achieve these goals, two technologies for moving the constituent objects of applications were utilized:

- **Lightweight mobility for presentation objects**: Presentation objects must be fast because multimedia processing can be time-consuming. There is often little application-specific state associated with them and they often perform memory-less functions, e.g., processing frames of video. For these reasons, compiled objects, rather than less efficient interpreted mobile agents, were used to implement presentation objects and a lightweight mechanism of moving their state was developed. Communications connection state (e.g., this object is sending video to object X) and registered events (e.g., this object is looking for frame 321 for object Y) are stored by a third party. Stream connections to other objects are broken and current instances are destroyed. Objects of the relevant classes can then be re-instantiated in the new location and the saved state used to set up the connections with the objects to which they were attached. The fact that IMP promotes system-independence in class definitions means that a compatible class should be available even if the hardware/OS platform is different. The presentation objects which were connected to the objects that moved, can be relocated by querying the trader in their domain. Events are also automatically re-registered with objects. Traders maintain forwarding information, useful on occasions when objects have moved from where they were thought to be.

- **Full state migration for management objects**: It was decided that management objects are more complex entities than presentation objects and can benefit from being implemented using a mobile agent system. The rationale here is that the controlling part of the application can follow the user within an administrative domain as well as across domain boundaries, dependent on the application developer's requirements. It is responsible for managing the process of presentation objects migration, where required and, when it moves, takes with it the stored state of any frozen presentation objects. We built management objects using a locally-developed mobile agent system called *the Tube*. Mobile agents can move between Tube landing sites, running on ubiquitously deployed computers. The scheme is enhanced by deploying location databases. Each database can respond to queries about local facilities, e.g., we have a location event which gives us John's location (L), what is the nearest workstation to him with video? (`Workstation(L,W)=>HasVideo(W)`[2]). Using this facility, it is possible to author adaptive applications that can adjust to the conditions on the available equipment.

These mechanisms are in keeping with the desire to keep presentation objects as simple building blocks and management objects as high level controllers.

3. MULTIMEDIA DATA MODELING

Many single-user platforms are simplified by storing all data locally as files. The disadvantage is that no sharing of data is possible. It is possible to store all data as flat files on a centralized server, but this does not take into account the different requirements of individual media. The best solution to storage of media with widely different characteristics is a specialized set of distributed services. As already stated, functional development and the need to maintain old services result in a range of heterogeneous devices and services.

Even with the abstraction of functions provided by presentation objects, an application developer still has to provide source objects with device-specific referencing information. Also adding to the complexity, data items of a particular medium can be of different formats, e.g., video can be encoded as MPEG, JPEG, or Pandora. An application developer is usually concerned only with medium type and should not be burdened with this heterogeneity management.

To avoid the complexity of referencing distributed data items on a per-application basis, a multimedia data model can be used. It should not be necessary for an application developer to know the object's system-specific details. The way in which data objects can be manipulated should be defined by medium type alone, e.g., video, audio, text, or pictures. A data model must take account of both live and stored data. It must be extensible if new formats, devices, or media need to be integrated, e.g., *person* objects representing the wearer of an active badge. It is desirable for it to be integrated with a presentation object model to provide both persistent and active abstractions.

Implementing such a data model creates a repository of *presentable objects*. An application developer can browse such a repository in search of objects for his/her application. A set of tools can be provided for them to edit and tailor the data and associated class information.

3.1 MODELING, BROWSING, AND COLLATING

3.1.1 Multimedia Data Objects
Several approaches have recognized the need to store persistent references to data as modeled data objects. They have integrated this view with an active object hierarchy to provide both persistent and active views of the data. In this way, a data object can be used to instantiate a

---

[2] See Section 5.

source presentation object and thus a configuration. For example in the *ORION* database system [51], every stored multimedia object is an instance of the class "captured object". To manipulate these, active objects with functions such as capture, storage, and presentation are integrated into the database framework.

3.1.2 Tailoring Data Objects for Presentation

It is possible to associate additional presentation information with data objects, to assist with browsing and retrieval and to tailor them for particular presentations.

In the Geneva model [12] a temporal entity type $N[T,Q,D]$ is stored to enable applications to know how to process the data. N and T represent the name and format type. Q represents the quality factor of the stored object, e.g., "Broadcast Quality" for video. D represents a discrete time system, e.g., 30 frames per second.

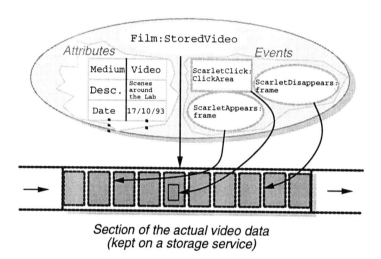

Section of the actual video data
(kept on a storage service)

Figure 11. A tailored data object.

An example IMP video data object, `Film`, is shown in Figure 11. Objects can be annotated with attributes. This allows queries to be composed, for example, to find all video objects that feature "motorcycles" and "John" or "James". IMP also allows the marking of events, i.e., associating event instances with a data object. Rather than registering events within an application program, marking events on objects allows the run-time behavior of data objects to be modeled persistently. For example, in Figure 11, the data object `Film` has marked events `ScarletAppears` that signifies the frame at which our colleague Scarlet appears on screen, `ScarletDisappears` that signifies the frame at which she ceases to be on-screen, and `ScarletClick` that marks the part of the screen she occupies while on it, as a clickable hotspot. If a data object is used in a presentation then marked events are automatically registered on the presentation objects involved. In this way, many different instances of the same data object can be modeled for different presentation requirements.

3.1.3 Storing Data Relationships

The Geneva data model supports the storage of object relationships. An example is storing a video with soundtrack as a related object. Other approaches, including IMP, assume that relationships are expressed externally to the database. It allows related objects to be stored together as a context to which a presentation script is applied.

3.1.4 Data Modeling Tools

The IMP database provides a graphical browser to allow users to retrieve, view and tailor objects from a large repository. Tools can also be built to assist application builders with this object tailoring process. *Graphical event markers* allow an application developer to view particular data objects and, using direct manipulation, mark spatial and temporal events on them. An example is a tool with which the user can play and pause video at particular frames and mark particular image details or frames.

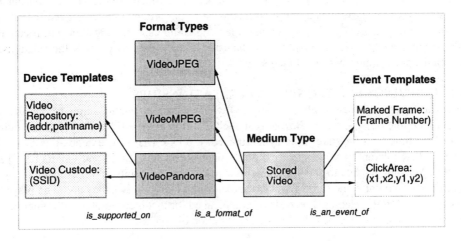

Figure 12. System-dependent database relations.

3.2 DATABASE SUPPORT

The IMP system data modeling facilities allow multimedia data to be manipulated without having to deal with system-specific details. The actual complexities of heterogeneous references must be managed within the platform. The IMP platform database contains a typing scheme representing facilities available in the environment and platform facilities built to manipulate them. The typing scheme makes it easier to model and relate components of a multimedia environment. Examples of typed items are media, formats of media, and devices associated with the generation of media. Templates are types which require parameters to instantiate a particular instance. An example is a source device `VideoRepository` which requires a repository address and a pathname to identify an object in the repository. Relationships can exist between types to form composite type dependencies. Figure 12 illustrates part of such a dependency for stored video data.

Data objects, which are stored in a presentation database, represent instantiations of particular platform database relationships. For example, with reference to Figures 11 and 12, the object `Film` could have been defined as class `StoredVideo_Video_-Pandora_VideoCustode` and a Storage Service Identifier (SSID) provided. This allows it to have events of classes `ClickArea` and `MarkedFrame` marked on it. When instantiating data objects and marking events, platform database information must be consulted to ensure a valid dependency exists.

Only when registering a new data item with the database is it necessary to provide its system-dependent type details. Once these details are provided (maybe with the help of a tool), the user never has to know anything about the object except its name and medium type (e.g., video, audio, or text) to tailor and present it. However, this information is known to the platform, allowing many operations to be performed automatically.

In IMP the configuration service can use database information when creating configurations. Presentation objects can be created with reference to data objects and are thus tailored for the specific system-dependent formats. If events are marked on the data object then the configuration service informs the presentation objects of events for which they must monitor.

4. SYNCHRONIZATION

Due to the differing characteristics of media types, services are often specialized, e.g., a service for the storage and retrieval of video. Problems can arise in the output of media items that are designed to be used together but which are handled differently at the environment level. The term *skew* describes a temporal mismatch in the presentation of related data items. The classic example is that of *lip synching* video and audio captured together, but it can also apply to other media. Synchronization mechanisms allow a user to express the relationship between the presentation of related media items.

4.1 SPECIFYING SYNCHRONIZATION RELATIONSHIPS

Some authoring approaches allow complex synchronization relationships to be defined between multiple objects. In the *Harmony* model [21] it is assumed that if objects are played at the same time then they are to be synchronized. CWI's *CMIF* [13] extends this model by allowing skew tolerances to be specified on an inter-object link. Little and Ghafoor [34] use graphical Petri net models to specify temporal synchronization points in a presentation, e.g., a synchronization point at the start of a video and an audio clip indicates they are to be played in lip sync. The *MODE* system [4] provides a graphical editor that incorporates both timeline and synchronization point specification for the presentation of objects.

In the IMP language, the `sync` declaration is used to specify that a group of objects are to be synchronized in their playback. This is used in conjunction with object sets (described later). For example, to synchronize audio and video tracks:

```
set Movie = union(Film,Soundtrack);
sync Movie;
..
Movie$Source.play();
```

In IMP, the process of synchronization can be tailored dynamically via object methods, e.g., adjusting the acceptable skew threshold. It is useful to be able to express the degree to which media items should be synchronized. The tradeoff is between synchronization system overhead and the fact that skew greater than a few tens of milliseconds between audio and video generates user annoyance.

4.2 SUPPORTING RUN-TIME SYNCHRONIZATION

Several models have been developed to support synchronization on top of multimedia object models. They take a similar approach in having a higher level synchronization service responsible for coordinating lower level objects (as in Figure 13). Usually, if skew exceeds a specified threshold some objects are paused while others are allowed to 'catch up'.

The ACME approach to objects has already been discussed. It supports explicit synchronization in presentation by examining the logical time system of presentation objects. Time stamps for streams are converted to a common scale. Unfortunately the specific format differences are not masked by the objects and the synchronization server has to have information on scheduling various formats. If specified skew is exceeded then streams can be paused, allowing others to catch up.

In MODE a thread within a synchronizer is assigned to monitor each stream. These report to each other when they reach synchronization points. A decision is then made based on the specified skew bound as to how long the first thread should wait for the others and whether some should be speeded up to retain synchronization.

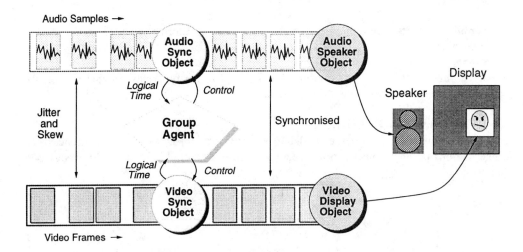

Figure 13. Synchronization using group agents.

Lancaster's *Orchestration* model [15] uses a High Level Orchestrator (HLO) to control Lower Level Orchestrators (LLO). LLOs exist on all presentation object source and sink sites. The HLO and LLOs interact at regular intervals to control skew. Again, this can be achieved by pausing streams that are ahead or skipping in those behind.

The model adopted by the IMP system was developed at Cambridge [42]. The idea is that a synchronization presentation object is added by the system to every configuration of presentation objects involving continuous media. As already described, these provide jitter removal through buffering. A synchronization service is informed of objects that require mutual synchronization, such as related audio and video (for lip sync). In this model, synchronization presentation objects are related together by a *synchronization group agent* (see Figure 13). This agent views logical time values from each synchronization presentation object and adjusts their presentation rate to keep them in sync. The synchronization service is system independent as synchronization presentation objects notify logical time events in a uniform way, regardless of class.

5. EVENT-DRIVEN PROGRAMMING

Recall that the term event can be used to generalize any run-time occurrence including:

- **User interaction**: e.g., using the mouse pointer to click on media objects.

- **Presentation-related occurrences**: i.e., triggered by parts of media items being presented, e.g., frame 123 of a video clip or an agent detecting mail from a particular person.

- **Temporal events**: i.e., notification of the elapsing of a time delay, possibly relative to the occurrence of other events.

- **System events**: i.e., occurrences from the environment, such as an application being informed that it must adjust its resource utilization.

- **Cooperation events**: i.e., events notified from another application context which can be used to update a local state view of what other users are doing.

- **Mobility events**: e.g., those notified by objects monitoring people's active badge movements.

We have already discussed how multimedia objects can notify events. In this section we outline how events can be used to drive presentation.

5.1 EVENT-BASED AUTHORING

Event-based authoring provides a model to specify how object run-time occurrences can trigger actions in other objects. In this section we look at several approaches to event-based authoring.

Figure 14. An example timeline.

5.1.1 Timelines

A timeline represents a temporal coordination in the presentation of objects. Time events are used as triggers for the presentation of objects. Authoring systems that have successfully used this type of model include *Athena Muse* [28], Quicktime, and Macromind Director. Many of these models provide a graphical editor to lay out components on the temporal dimension (as shown in Figure 14).

Basic timelines are restricted as far as interaction is concerned. Some models allow temporal events to specify contexts for interaction. For example, in Macromind Director, at defined points in time a script can be run to monitor for user interaction. In Muse, hypermedia links can be set up between timelines; these are traversed through user interaction. In [27] a new type of media is defined, called *choice*, which allows user interaction for the period it is active on the timeline.

Some systems are specified using an extended timed Petri net model [34]. Nodes in the Petri net represent media object presentation. Nodes can be linked by transitions, indicating a presentation sequence. Several nodes can be presented in parallel and, in order to synchronize between these objects, transitions are used. Transitions implement a wait for related concurrently presenting media objects to finish before proceeding. This model has been extended to support user interaction and to allow rewinding, fast forwarding and pausing of the presentation [18,39].

5.1.2 General Event Triggers

A richer approach is to support multiple types of events. The occurrence of an event within one object can be used to trigger an action on another. Harmony, work at Athens [45], CWI's CMIF, and the Eventor system [19] exhibit this type of event model. In Harmony, presentation objects can detect event occurrences and invoke methods on other objects. Objects are simplified by not being configurable; they only access and display a media item. However, additional complexity is put into objects as they must be able to communicate with any other class of object. To limit this complexity all prototype objects support only the method `play`. Event types supported are `started`, `finished`, and `clicked`. Time offsets can express temporal delays with reference to other events. Sub-objects can be declared for event tailoring, e.g., an area of video or a word of text. These can handle events and send messages in the same way. A graphical editing tool was implemented to express event-driven interactive presentations via direct manipulation. The example shown in Figure 15 synchronizes an audio clip with a video clip; 30 seconds after this, some text is displayed.

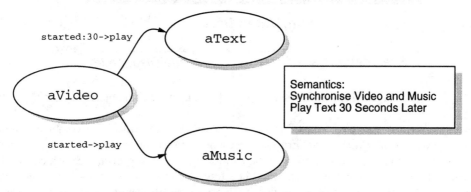

Figure 15. Event-driven presentation in harmony.

5.1.3 Event Rules

The IMP project took a novel approach in using *Event Condition Action* (ECA) rules to express complex multimedia monitoring scenarios [5]. ECA rules have been used successfully in the field of active databases to monitor database state updates. Distributed multimedia environments are more complicated with distributed events and a wide variety of event types. However, using a uniform mechanism of event notification as described in Section 2.2 allows different primitive types to be combined into complex expressions. Event driven rules can be specified, of the form

```
rule <name> <event expression> ; {<list of invocations>}
```

An event expression specifies one or a combination of events which will cause this rule to *fire*. A list of invocations (of the form described in Section 2.1), on any of the objects in the application context, are performed if the rule fires. The rule name represents an event which occurs when the rule fires. It can be incorporated into the event expressions of other rules.

We will illustrate some examples with reference to the example event scenario shown in Figure 16. We can specify that when the event ScarletDisappears, associated with the object Film, occurs, we want to go back to the beginning.

```
rule restart -> Film.ScarletDisappears ;
```

```
{ Film$Source.goto_frame(0); }
```

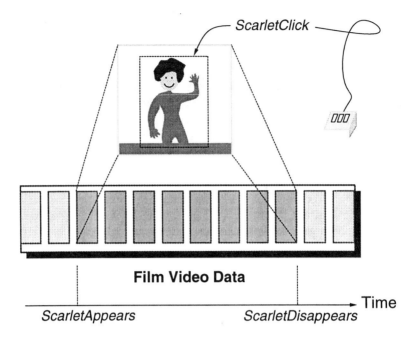

Figure 16. Notification of marked events in the film object.

This example uses a single event to trigger the rule. It is also possible to combine several events into a *composite event expression* using various operators. Composite event expressions provide a generalized way of expressing composite scenarios which would otherwise have to be implemented in an ad hoc way. As an example composite event, with reference to Figure 16, we can specify that in object `Film`, if Scarlet is clicked on between the events which indicate she is on screen, then pause the video and display the text information. Before we illustrate this expression we introduce some composite event operators.

`-> evexpr`: This statement specifies that the expression `evexpr` must occur **after** any previous expressions.

`-> evexpr1 - evexpr2`: This composite event expression is detected if the expression `evexpr1` occurs **after** any previous expressions **without** any intervening occurrences of `evexpr2`.

`evexpr1 | evexpr2`: This expression is detected if either `evexpr1` **or** `evexpr2` is detected. These must be monitored for concurrently since each expression may be temporally complex.

`evexpr1 ^ evexpr2`: This expression is detected if `evexpr1` **and** `evexpr2` have been detected, in any temporal order.

```
The composite rule described above can be specified as follows:
```

```
rule in_position -> Film.ScarletAppears
                 -> Film.Clicked - Film.ScarletDisappears ;
{
  Film$Source.pause();
  Info$Display.show(80,270,250,80);
  Info$Source.play(); }
}
```

In addition to the single arrow (->), the double arrow (=>) can be used. The single arrow indicates interest in only the first relevant occurrence of an event. The double arrow indicates interest in every occurrence of an event. For example, we can modify the above expression to notify us of every click between Scarlet appearing and disappearing as follows:

```
rule in_position2 -> Film.ScarletAppears
                  => Film.Clicked - Film.ScarletDisappears ;
```

Note we are interested in a single instance of Scarlet appearing and multiple instances of the click event without intervening disappear events.

Additionally, the following timer operators are available. They allow authors to specify time windows, within which other events either do or do not occur:

`evexpr<t`: This expression is detected if `evexpr` occurs within time period `t`.

`evexpr>t`: This expression is detected if `evexpr` does not occur within time period `t`.

`evexpr,t`: This expression is detected if `evexpr` has not occurred for time period `t`.

`evexpr1,evexpr2,t`: This expression is detected if `evexpr2` occurs. It is rejected if `evexpr1` does not repeatedly occur within time period `t`.

Within an event expression, parameter matching can be performed. For example, consider an audio-on-demand server that can play many different tracks simultaneously through audio outputs in different offices. Also consider a phone exchange server that can report the telephone number and location of phones that are picked up, put down, or are ringing. We can compose the following expression to automate the pausing of music when the phone rings in a particular room:

```
rule greeting => AudioServer.playing(M,R)
              -> PExchange.phonering(N,R)
              -  (AudioServer.stopped(R) | AudioServer.paused(R)) ;
{
  AudioServer$Source.pause(R);
}
```

The audio server can notify about events when someone starts playing a particular music track in a particular room (variables M and R), and when this process is stopped or paused. Music sessions can be controlled by specifying the location as a parameter. Parameter matching is used to match the location of music playing with the location of the phone ring. Note the double arrow which specifies that we are interested in every time someone is playing music in a room, mirroring the fact that there may be multiple concurrent music sessions. We assume the first phone ring in a room will pause music playing there.

5.2 RUN-TIME EVENT SUPPORT

To implement timeline-based systems simply requires an accurate time source on which to base the initiation of presentation operations. In Quicktime, for example, clock objects can be created to run at certain rates.

In the Harmony model, the responsibility of managing event-driven presentation is shared between objects. Few specific model details are proposed. CWI's *AMF* [14] extends the model by proposing a flexible architecture for presentation. The set of distributed components used at run-time can be dynamically altered. For example, if there is not enough bandwidth for video with audio, then still images and text representing the same information can be used.

The approach investigated in IMP is a service to support the monitoring of composite events, expressed using the language illustrated earlier. Distributed objects notify their events to such a service which updates its state accordingly. If the entire expression is detected, it will notify a specified client. Invocations and application callbacks associated with the firing of an event rule can be performed upon receipt of a notification from the composite event service.

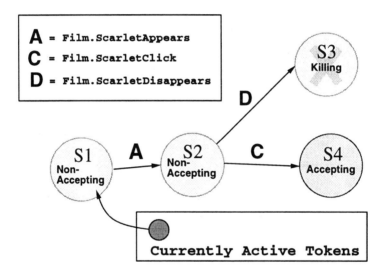

Figure 17. Finite state machine for the `in_position` rule.

Monitoring for event expressions is achieved by constructing non-deterministic finite state machines. As a simple illustration, a finite state machine representing the `in_position` expression is shown in Figure 17. Tokens mark the state of currently active composite detections. If a relevant event occurs, a token moves into a new state. States are either *accepting*, which indicate the expression has been detected, *killing*, which destroy any token on entry, or *non-accepting*. If an expression is concerned with every instance of an event (marked as => transitions in an expression) then multiple tokens may be active inside the same machine, each corresponding to a different event matching sequence. Upon detection of a => link event, tokens split into two, one instance remaining in the current state and one traversing the link.

When attempting to order events from different distributed sources, one must take into account delays such that the order in which one receives events may not be the order in which they occurred. Events must be time-stamped reliably at source to allow the receiver to make sense of their true temporal sequence. The Cambridge event work allows ordering for composite events based on source time stamps. An application may have to wait an unacceptable amount of time due to event source crashes or network delays, so the client can specify how long it is prepared to keep events before consuming them, pending the arrival of potential earlier occurrences. To speed up consumption, event services use regular *heartbeat* events to assure the composite event service that they have no outstanding events to notify.

6. CONTROLLING GROUPS OF OBJECTS

Within an object-based multimedia framework it is often necessary to control groups of objects. This is useful for building:

- **Application-wide policies**: For example, QoS policy definition, such as specifying that if we can't support a certain level of service, then degrade video rather than turn off audio.
- **Cooperative application instances**: Each instance needs to notify events to all other instances of the same application, e.g., shared drawing strokes or video conferencing floor control.

A wide range of groupware toolkits have been built in the context of supporting shared views of data. We are interested in generic features of group support to assist with application development using multimedia objects.

6.1 AUTHORING POLICIES FOR CONTROLLING GROUPS

Cruiser [20] and *Rendezvous* [26] are systems built over the Touring machine platform. Together they provide support for building multi-user applications. Cruiser is a collaborative session management system. Its broadcast facility allows multiple users to join in on new sessions. Rendezvous allows shared applications to be added to a Cruiser session. By using the underlying Touring machine facilities, the users in the session configuration can be implicitly queried and the shared application set up.

Using Lancaster's OODP model extensions for multimedia, groups can be set up both for interfaces and stream connections. For example, a source can connect via streams to a group of sinks. The sinks can be controlled as a group.

Several groupware toolkits have been developed to assist the process of writing cooperative applications. *Groupkit* [41] is an example which simplifies the authoring of conferencing applications. It provides generic plug-in modules to support session joining and notification of conference events.

The *set* mechanism is the authoring construct to support group control in the IMP platform. An invocation performed on a set is propagated to every object in the set. One emerging use for this is in policies for QoS. Imagine scenarios in which the application must degrade its usage of network resources. Policies can be encoded of the form "degrade all source video objects to 50% and cut the frame rate to 10%" and, if that fails, "turn off all audio".

Set operators are of the form {union, intersection, not}. Database attributes can also be used in `select` queries to define sets. An example of a set definition is

```
set jkspeak = intersection(select(medium = audio),
                    union(select(subject = Jean),
                        select(subject = Ken)))
```

which specifies all audio objects in the current context which are of Jean or Ken speaking. The following invocation will stop any such object which is playing:

```
jkspeak$Source.stop();
```

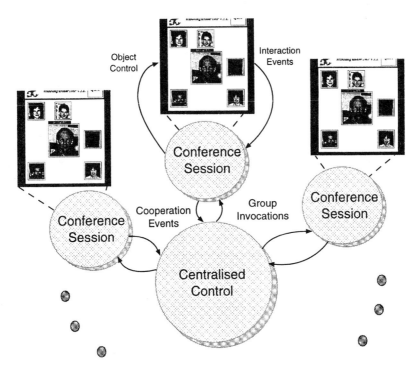

Figure 18. Structure of "Opera Group Meeting."

In IMP, scripts are crafted as part of user applications. We provide an IMP management tools library which can be used within application programs to activate and manage groups of interactive presentations. Rather than performing operations or notifying events to every presentation session individually, invocations and callbacks can be managed on a group basis. This is useful if an application involves communication with management objects on different users' workstations. If, for example, we have an audiovisual conferencing application and a new user must be added, we want to show that new user appearing on every participant's display.

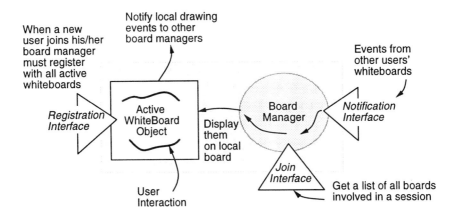

Figure 19. A replicated shared drawing instance.

Event models investigated in the IMP project support both centralized and replicated models of cooperative applications. In a centralized model many interactive presentation workspaces can be managed from a single controlling program. Figure 18 illustrates a centralized conferencing application developed using IMP. In a replicated model each user has a copy of the entire application which interacts with other instances. As an example, the IMP shared whiteboard is shown in Figure 19.

6.2 RUN-TIME SUPPORT FOR GROUPS

It is beneficial if the underlying programming model provides distributed object group support, such as *ISIS* [31] or *ANSA* [3]. These programming models support named object groups, an invocation which is sent to all objects in the group.

7. CONCLUSIONS

Multimedia environments are complex. Building multimedia applications from scratch within an environment can lead to a lack of maintainability, reusability, and portability. A multimedia application can be composed of many sub-components and may involve diverse media manipulation and interaction response. Multimedia applications within distributed environments are not concerned merely with information presentation but also with remote information access and exchange. To address these problems, it is useful to provide a middleware platform with generalized facilities to support a wide range of application types. It is suggested that at the bottom level a platform should provide an object-based framework. Above should be services to realize complex functions, such as synchronization, event-driven presentation, and group control, in terms of multimedia objects. A high level authoring approach must allow flexible and system-independent construction mechanisms.

A component-based approach has been shown to be useful for building multimedia applications. The application developer authors a management object that is responsible for creating and controlling configurations of active presentation objects, e.g., media sources, processors, and sinks. Presentation objects are abstractions designed to fit a wide range of application requirements. Presentation objects can be plugged together in configurations to tailor interactive presentation, e.g., a video source to a video window. Some presentation objects can monitor for events while carrying out their other functions. Clients can register interest, using templates, in ranges of events of interest. Events are notified to the client, if detected. Rules can be set up so management objects can invoke methods in response to event notifications and thus drive presentation. Mobility to allow objects to follow mobile users has been investigated.

Multimedia data modeling involves maintaining a repository of multimedia data objects. Additional information, such as annotations and persistent event registrations, can be stored alongside these items. It is often appropriate to store the physical media data on specialized servers, e.g., a video repository. Under these circumstances, a data object abstracts a system-specific reference. Data objects can be used in conjunction with active presentation objects as an instantiation mechanism for configurations.

Synchronization is required to remove jitter from multimedia streams and to synchronize related tracks, e.g., audio and video. Synchronization can be expressed using Petri net models or simpler group models. To realize synchronization requires a group object that monitors and controls the presentation of disparate streams.

Events generalize run-time occurrences that can be used to invoke actions on objects. Examples of events are instances of user interaction, points of interest in the presentation of media, and system occurrences. Event-driven presentation can be expressed in terms of timelines, event-trigger models, or ECA rules. ECA rules allow primitive events to be combined together in composite event expressions. To realize time events requires an accurate time source. To realize event-trigger models requires that objects understand how to invoke methods on other objects when events are detected. To realize composite events requires a finite-state machine (or similar) approach for monitoring the state-based scenarios.

Group control over objects assists activities such as building application-wide policies and managing interaction between multiple cooperating application instances. Invocations using a group name are propagated to all objects in the group. Support for group protocols can be provided by the underlying system.

In summary, the platform features discussed in this chapter represent general-purpose tools which together can be used to implement a wide range of multimedia applications.

REFERENCES

1. M.D. Addlesee, et al., "The ORL Active Floor," IEEE Personal Communications 4(5), 1997.
2. D. Anderson and G. Homsy, "A Continuous Media I/O Server and its Synchronization Mechanism," Computer 24(10), 1991.
3. Architecture Projects Management Ltd., "Advanced Networked Systems Architecture Testbench Implementation Manual," 1993.
4. G. Blakowski, et al., "Tools for Specifying and Executing Synchronized Multimedia Presentations," 2nd ACM International Workshop on Network and Operating System Support for Digital Audio and Video, Heidelberg, Germany, 1991.
5. J. Bacon, et al. "Using Events to Build Distributed Applications," 2nd IEEE International Workshop on Services for Distributed and Networked Environments, 1995.
6. J. Bacon, et al., "Location-Oriented Multimedia," IEEE Personal Communications 4(5), 1997.
7. J. Bates and J.M. Bacon, "A Development Platform for Multimedia Applications in a Distributed ATM Network Environment," 1st IEEE International Conference on Multimedia Computing and Systems, May 1994.
8. J. Bates and J.M. Bacon, "Supporting Interactive Presentation for Distributed Multimedia Applications," Multimedia Tools and Applications, 1(1), 1995.
9. J. Bates, et al., "A Framework to Support Mobile Users of Multimedia Applications," Mobile Networks and Applications 1(1996).
10. Bellcore Information Networking Research Laboratory, "Touring Machine System," Communications of the ACM, January 1993.
11. K. Bharat and L. Cardelli, "Migratory Applications," ACM Symposium on User Interfaces, Software and Technology," 1995.
12. C. Breiteneder et al., Object Frameworks, chapter "Modeling of Audio/Video Data," University of Geneva, 1992.
13. D. Bulterman, et al., "A Structure for Transportable Dynamic Multimedia Documents," Multimedia for Now and the Future, USENIX, 1991.
14. D. Bulterman, "Specification and Support of Adaptable Networked Multimedia," Multimedia Systems, 1(2), 1993.
15. G. Coulson, "Multimedia Application Support in Open Distributed Systems," Ph.D. Thesis, Department of Computing, Lancaster University, 1993.
16. R. Dannenberg, et al., "Tactus: Toolkit-level Support for Synchronized Interactive Multimedia," Multimedia Systems 1(2), 1993.

17. V. De Mey, et al., Object Frameworks, chapter "Visual Composition and Multimedia," University of Geneva, 1992.
18. C. Djeraba, et al., "Management of Multimedia Scenarios in an Object-Oriented Database System," Multimedia Tools and Applications, 4(2), 1997.
19. R. Eun, et al., "Eventor: An Authoring System for Interactive Multimedia Applications," ACM Multimedia Systems, 2(3), 1994.
20. R. Fish, et al., "Video Informal Communication," Communications of the ACM, January 1993.
21. K. Fujikawa, et al., "Multimedia Presentation System Harmony with Temporal and Active Media," Multimedia for Now and the Future, USENIX, 1991.
22. N. Georganas, "Multimedia Applications Development: Experiences," Multimedia Tools and Applications, 4(3), 1997.
23. J. Gecsei, "Adaptation in Distributed Multimedia Systems," IEEE Multimedia, 4(2), 1997.
24. D. Greaves, "ATM in the Home and the Home Area Network," IEE Colloquium on ATM in Professional and Commercial Applications, May 1997.
25. A. Harter and A. Hopper, "A Distributed Location System for the Active Office," IEEE Network 8(1), 1994.
26. R. D. Hill, et al., "Rendezvous Language," Communications of the ACM, January 1993.
27. N. Hirzalla, et al., "A Temporal Model for Interactive Multimedia Scenarios," 2(3), 1995..
28. M. E. Hodges, et al., "A Construction Set for Multimedia Applications," IEEE Software, January 1989.
29. A. Hopper, "Pandora – An Experimental System for Multimedia Applications," ACM Operating Systems Review 24(2), April 1990.
30. Interactive Multimedia Association, "Multimedia System Services," Technical Report (Version 1.0), 1993.
31. ISIS Distributed Systems Inc., "ISIS Reference Manual," 1994.
32. ISO/IEC, "Coded Representation of Multimedia and Hypermedia Information Objects," Draft Standard, 1993.
33. J. Koegel and A. Syta, "Routing in Hybrid Multimedia Networks," SPIE Conference on Multimedia Communications, September 1992.
34. T.D.C. Little and A. Ghafoor, "Synchronization and Storage Models for Multimedia Objects," IEEE Journal on Selected Areas in Communications 8(3), April 1990.
35. S.L. Lo, "A Modular and Extensible Network Storage Architecture," Ph.D. thesis, University of Cambridge Computer Laboratory, 1993.
36. Macromind Inc., "Director Studio Manual," 1991.
37. Microsoft Corp., "Microsoft Windows Multimedia Programmers Reference," 1991.
38. C. Nicolaou, "An Architecture for Real-time Multimedia Communications Systems," IEEE Journal on Selected Areas in Communications 8(3), April 1990.
39. Prabhakaran and S.V. Raghavan, "Synchronization Models for Multimedia Presentation with User Participation," ACM Multimedia Systems, 2(2), 1994.
40. T. Richardson, et al., "Teleporting in an X Windows System Environment," IEEE Personal Communications, August 1994.
41. M. Roseman and S. Greenberg, "Building Real-time Groupware with Groupkit, A Groupware Toolkit," ACM Transactions on CHI, 3(1), 1995.
42. C.J. Sreenan, "Synchronization Services for Digital Continuous Media," Ph.D. thesis, University of Cambridge Computer Laboratory, 1993.
43. T. Starner, et al., "Augmented Reality Through Wearable Computing," Presence (Special Issue on Augmented Reality), 1997.
44. D. Tennenhouse, et al., "A Software-Oriented Approach to the Design of Media Processing Environments," 1st IEEE International Conference on Multimedia Computing and Systems, 1994.

45. M. Vazirgiannis and C. Mourlas, "An Object-Oriented Model for Interactive Multimedia Presentations," The Computer Journal 36(1), 1993.

46. A. Vogel, et al., "Distributed Multimedia and QoS: A Survey," IEEE Multimedia, 2(2), 1995.

47. A. Ward, et al., "A New Location Technique for the Active Office," IEEE Personal Communications 4(5), 1997.

48. D. Woelk and W. Kim, "Multimedia Information Management in an Object-Oriented Database System," 13th VLDB Conference, 1987.

49. S. Wray, et al., "The Medusa Applications Environment," First International Conference on Multimedia Computing and Systems, May 1994.

50. P. Wayner, "Inside Quicktime," Byte 16(13), 1991.

51. N. Williams and G. Blair, "Distributed Multimedia Application Study," Technical Report MPG-92-11, Department of Computing, Lancaster University, 1992.

52. M. Wynblatt, et al., "Multimedia Meets the Internet: Present and Future," Multimedia Tools and Applications, 5(1), 1997.

ACKNOWLEDGEMENTS

Thanks are due to my colleagues in the Opera group at the University of Cambridge Computer Laboratory, in particular, Jean Bacon. Further gratitude is due to Mark Spiteri and Giles Nelson for their suggested improvements. I also extend my thanks to St Catharine's College, Cambridge and to Michael and Morven Heller for their support in the form of my Fellowship.

5

DAVIC AND MULTIMEDIA STANDARDS

Hari Kalva,[1] Hidenori Okuda,[2] Shih-Fu Chang,[1] and Alexandros Eleftheriadis[1]

[1]*Department of Electrical Engineering, Columbia University, New York, USA*
[2]*Visual Communication Laboratory, NTT Human Interface Laboratories, Kanagawa, Japan*

1. INTRODUCTION 90
2. EVOLUTION OF DAVIC 90
3. THE BASE SPECIFICATION 93
4. DAVIC 1.2 98
5. DAVIC 1.3 102
6. DAVIC 1.4 105
7. DAVIC TECHNOLOGY SUMMARY 106
8. CONCLUSION 106
    REFERENCES 108

Abstract. There are many organizations developing standards for multimedia tools including international authorities such as ISO and ITU-T. Multimedia tools refer to components of multimedia presentations and services. MPEG-2 video, MPEG-4 audio, and ATM are some examples of tools for video, audio, and networking. Most of the current standards (tools) are developed, for the most part, independently by the standards body concerned. It is rather difficult to ensure that the tools developed independently can be combined to facilitate a single multimedia presentation. The Digital Audio Visual Council (DAVIC) plays the role of an integrator by providing specifications that bind the various standards enabling multimedia applications and services. This chapter gives an introduction to DAVIC specifications including, tools, functionalities, applications, and services.

0-8493-1825-4/99/$0.00+$.50
© 1999 by CRC Press LLC

1. INTRODUCTION

A DAVIC tool is a technology that supports a DAVIC functionality. For example, ATM is a tool to transport audio-visual data in the core network. Following a one-functionality one-tool policy, DAVIC selects the best technology available to support its functionalities. DAVIC also develops tools to support the functionality that cannot be achieved by the existing technology.

DAVIC is a consortium of companies, research institutes, and universities, standardizing tools for end-to-end systems to provide audio-visual services [1,2]. DAVIC is a relatively new body founded in 1994. Following an aggressive schedule, DAVIC has released a series of specifications within a short period of three years. The first specification, DAVIC 1.0, was released in December 1995. Subsequent specifications, 1.1, 1.2, and 1.3 were released as extensions to DAVIC 1.0 and specify new tools and extensions to previously specified tools to support new functionalities and applications. DAVIC is continuing its work on extension 1.4 to extend the support for new functionalities.

This chapter is intended to give a comprehensive introduction to DAVIC specifications including, tools, functionalities, applications, and services.

2. EVOLUTION OF DAVIC

DAVIC defines it's purpose "to advance the success of emerging digital audio-visual applications and services, initially of the broadcast and interactive type, by the timely availability of internationally-agreed specifications of open interfaces and protocols that maximize interoperability across countries and applications or services"[1]. The DAVIC concept of *Digital Audio-Visual Applications and Services* includes all applications and services in which there is a significant digital audio-video component. DAVIC started out mainly in response to the industry interest in video on-demand in the early 90s and apparent lack of standards that would ensure interoperability among the various systems and implementations. By the time DAVIC published its first specification in 1995, video on-demand was no longer seen as the *killer application* it was originally thought. However, the development of technologies and standards by DAVIC was the core to support any form of audio-visual services. The nature and scope of DAVIC's work and its ability to quickly respond to industry needs, such as support for Internet services, kept its work relevant.

DAVIC specifies *everything* necessary to support the core audio-visual services it defines; left to right, content provider to the content consumer, and top to bottom, physical layer of the transport to the application layer. Figure 1 shows the DAVIC subsystems and the reference points between the subsystems. Content providers produce content, which is distributed to the consumers by service providers. Delivery system supports the delivery of content to service providers and consumers. DAVIC specifies and/or develops technologies to build these subsystems and defines reference points and interfaces between and also within the subsystems. The conformance points are the reference points and any DAVIC compliant system should be conformant at these points.

2.1 INFORMATION FLOWS AND REFERENCE POINTS
The subsystems were specified in an evolutionary manner with each new set of DAVIC specifications adding functionality to the previous set. To facilitate this evolutionary approach, reference points, interfaces, and information flows were introduced between the subsystems. The information flow between the subsystems is divided into five logical flows based on the nature of the information. Figure 1 shows the information flows and reference

points between the subsystems. Only reference points A1, A9, A10, and A11 are shown in the figure. There are also reference points that are internal to the subsystems.

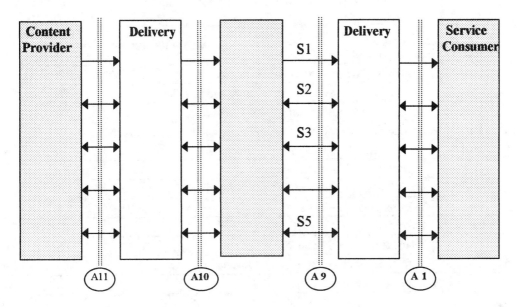

Figure 1. Components of a DAVIC system.

The s1 information flow corresponds to the principal service information, e.g., MPEG-2 transport stream carrying audio and video. The s2 flow corresponds to the application control information, s3 corresponds to session control, s4 to connection management, and s5 corresponds to billing and other management functions. The s1 flow is unidirectional from the service provider to the service consumer (STU) while the other information flows are bi-directional. Future versions of the specification are expected to include a bi-directional s1 flow supporting applications such as video conferencing. The five logical information flows may use a single physical channel or more than one physical channel.

2.2 DAVIC SPECIFICATIONS
As already mentioned, DAVIC specifications are published in different versions with each version specifying new tools to support new functionalities. DAVIC specifications are backward compatible; i.e., a DAVIC 1.2 compliant system will be backward compatible with DAVIC 1.1, 1.0 systems. DAVIC specifications are divided into parts with each part specifying tools or technical specifications (TS) and *guidelines* or technical reports (TR) for subsystems. The parts that are *guidelines* provide implementers of subsystems with information on using the tools that are specified in other parts of the specification. Table 1 lists the 13 parts of a DAVIC specification and their contents.

DAVIC 1.0 specification was the foundation that the subsequent versions were built on. Even though 1.0 was published as a specification, it did not include the tools to support functions such as security, network management, and billing necessary to deploy a commercial service. However, it provided a good basis to develop extensions to the specification. DAVIC 1.0 specified tools for end-to-end systems, from service provider to the service consumer with minimal functionalities. The emphasis was on specifying the tools for access networks. In the next phase DAVIC emphasized service consumer system (set-top box), specifying interfaces and ports to support a range of applications and services, specifically providing support for

Internet access and services. The current efforts in DAVIC are aimed towards convergence of audio-visual and Internet applications.

Table 1. Parts of a DAVIC Specification

Part	Title	Type
Part 1	Description of DAVIC Functionalities	TR
Part 2	System Reference Models and Scenarios	TR
Part 3	Service Provider System Architecture and Interfaces	TR
Part 4	Delivery System Architecture and Interfaces	TR
Part 5	Service Consumer System Architecture and High Level API	TS
Part 6	Management Architecture and Protocol	TS
Part 7	High and Mid Layer Protocols	TS
Part 8	Lower Layer Protocols and Physical Interfaces	TS
Part 9	Information Representation	TS
Part 10	Basic Security for DAVIC	TS
Part 11	Usage Information Protocols	TS
Part 12	Reference Points, Interfaces, and Dynamics	TS
Part 13	Conformance and Interoperability	TR

2.3 INTEROPERABILITY

The key to the success of standardization activity like DAVIC is interoperability; interoperability across countries, applications, and services. To achieve its goal of global deployment of DAVIC systems and services, DAVIC places special emphasis on interoperability. Interoperability promotes global competition and speeds up the deployment of services to consumers. Since the DAVIC specification is made up of a number of independently developed standards, it is important to ensure that these standards work when used together in DAVIC components and systems. The work related to verifying the specification and interoperability is undertaken by the interoperability sub-group. The charter of the interoperability sub-group is to verify that the specification does not have any 'gaps' and to provide guidelines for conformance testing.

To promote implementation and deployment of DAVIC specifications and also to ensure the proper inter-operation of DAVIC subsystems, DAVIC is promoting a series of public interoperability events. The first multi-platform global interoperability event took place at Columbia University in New York in June 1996 [3,5]. Eight organizations from around the world participated in this event, cross-connecting their servers and clients on Columbia's testbed [5]. Even though the implementations were only partial, the interoperability experiments gave valuable feedback to DAVIC to clarify and improve the specification [7]. The feedback from the subsequent interoperability events at the Tokyo Electronics Show [4] and Telecom Interactive were also taken into account in improving the specifications.

2.4 DAVIC AUDIO-VISUAL (AV) SESSION

The notion of an AV session was introduced in DAVIC 1.0. Another important notion introduced by DAVIC was programmable set-top units with downloadable applications. The notion of a session and the technology to support session establishment was taken from DSM-CC, Part 6 of the MPEG-2 specification [8]. The download protocol for application download was added to the DSM-CC specification to support downloadable functionality in DAVIC.

Downloadability and session establishment are the keys to establishing an audio-visual session in a DAVIC system.

An audio-visual session includes server selection, connection setup, session setup, application download, application selection, content selection, and content playback. Figure 2 shows the components involved in establishing a session between a STU and a server. Service providers are connected to the core network and customers (STUs) are usually connected to an access network. Before establishing a session, a client must first be able to locate a service provider. This is done using a level 1 gateway (L1GW). L1GW provides the first point-of-connection for the customer to the service environment. A basic L1GW provides a connection to a single service provider while an enhanced L1GW gives more choices by making many service providers accessible to an end user. When the user selects a service provider, L1GW establishes a connection and drops out. In the figure, connection setup to the service provider 1 is shown. When a connection is initially established, default resources are allocated for a downstream channel and also for an upstream channel, if necessary. Session establishment is completed using DSM-CC session establishment protocols. During session establishment, the DSM-CC-download protocol may be used to download the client application from the server. The entity that provides navigational services allowing choice of applications and services on a service provider system are the level 2 gateway (L2GW). The STU selects a service using L2GW services. Depending on the bandwidth requirements of the service, resources for the established channels are re-provisioned. The user launches the application (e.g., a movie) and interacts with it using DSM-CC user-user primitives. When the user quits, the session is torn down and resources are released.

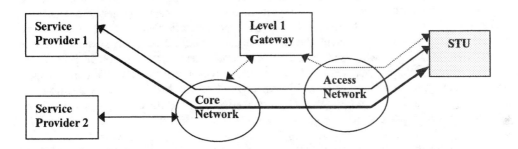

Figure 2. Audio-visual session in a DAVIC system.

3. THE BASE SPECIFICATION

The first set of DAVIC specifications, 1.0 and 1.1, specified the core technologies to facilitate broadband audio-visual and internet services. This section presents the key technologies in these specifications. Subsequent extensions 1.2 and 1.3 added more tools to enable more flexible, scalable, and secure services. These are presented in Sections 4 and 5.

3.1 SERVICE CONSUMER SYSTEM

The service consumer system, popularly referred to as STU or "set top unit" is the main component of any digital audio-visual service. STU is the only part of a DAVIC system an end user sees. STU usually consists of a network interface unit (NIU), an operating system, memory, ports to connect other peripherals, and decoders for media decoding. Figure 3 shows some common modules in a STU along with the reference points specified by DAVIC. An STU is connected to the Service Provider System (SPS) by means of a Delivery System (DS). A NIU provides network connectivity to the STU and contains access network specific hardware. If an NIU is part of an STU, the STU itself becomes network specific and connects to the delivery system at A1 reference point. STUs can be made network independent by separating the NIU from the STU. In this case, STUs connect to the delivery system at A0 reference point. Several interfaces are specified within a STU as shown in Figure 3 but not all of them are defined.

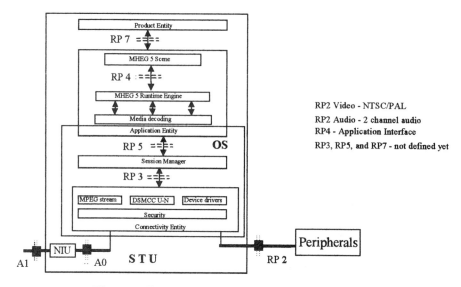

Figure 3. Common modules in a STU.

DAVIC does not specify how a STU should be implemented. Only reference points in a STU are specified and a compliant system should meet these specifications. Furthermore, a DAVIC compliant STU is expected to handle the media types specified in Part 9 [10,11] of the specifications. A DAVIC STU should be able to decode MPEG-2 transport streams with one or more programs. If ATM is used to deliver transport streams, transport stream packets are mapped to ATM cells as specified by the ATM Forum with the restriction that two transport packets be mapped to eight ATM cells. The upper limit on the MPEG-2 video bit rate is 15 Mbps (Main Profile at Main Level). For compressed audio, MPEG-1 audio is specified and MHEG-5 is specified for encoding multimedia objects.

Java is used for the virtual machine (VM) that runs on an STU. Use of Java on a STU enables a range of applications. The core of the VM consists of java.lang, java.util, java.io, iso.mheg5, as defined by ISO/IEC 13522-6 for manipulating MHEG-5 presentations, and DAVIC.dsmcc to enable network access of DSMCC-UU objects. DAVIC.dsmcc contains a subset of DSMCC-UU primitives.

3.1.1 STU Data Port
A data port on a STU is necessary to connect to peripheral devices and also to support data services such as Internet services. The data port should support all the media types specified by DAVIC and also data for Internet services. Based on the type of data that is flowing through it, the data port can be classified as PC data port and multimedia data port. The PC data port is specified to be IEEE 10BaseT Ethernet. The multimedia data port is IEEE 1394-1995. Data services over the multimedia data port are specified in DAVIC 1.2.

3.1.2 Internet Access
In response to the popularity of the Internet, DAVIC specified tools to facilitate Internet services in a DAVIC system; in particular to make it possible to access Internet services via the STU. When a STU is used to access only Internet services, it just acts as a modem with an

Internet Service Provider (ISP) at the other end. A STU also allows more than one PC to access the Internet at the same time. Depending on the delivery system a STU is connected to, IP services can be delivered over an end-to-end ATM network or with ATM terminated in the access network. The two scenarios are shown Figures 4 and 5.

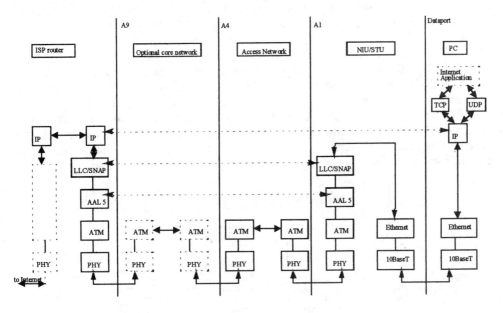

Figure 4. Internet access: upstream – all cases, downstream – ATM end-to-end.

DAVIC Internet access provides the end user with *full* or *client* Internet access using a PC connected to the STU. The different levels of Internet access are defined in [13]. Figure 4 shows the protocol stack for Internet access with upstream traffic for all cases and for end-to-end ATM downstream traffic. Figure 5.a shows the protocol stack used for downstream IP traffic when ATM terminates in the access network. In this case, IP packets are encapsulated in MPEG-2 transport stream packets. For IP over ATM, classical IP over ATM AAL 5 as specified in RFC 1483 and 1577 is used.

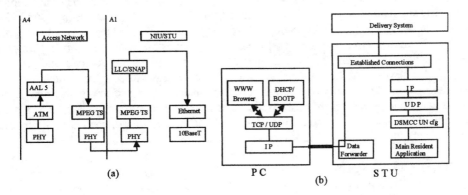

Figure 5. Internet access with ATM terminated in the access network.

For Internet access, ISP is pre-agreed between the network provider and the end user. A PC is connected to the STU data port as shown in Figure 5.b. Connection to the ISP may be pre-established through ATM PVCs or dynamically established using Q.2931 signaling. IP addresses may be pre-assigned or dynamically obtained using protocols such as DHCP. STU contains a data forwarder module, which forwards the IP packets from the data port (PC) to the network element. This module is responsible for LLC/SNAP encapsulation to and from the ISP.

3.1.3 Reference Decoder Model

A Reference Decoder Model (RDM) is specified to enable application developers to develop applications that execute on all STUs. The DAVIC RDM specifies semantic constraints on the content and minimum memory requirements for STUs. A DAVIC compliant STU shall satisfy the constraints of the RDM. By ensuring that their applications can run without violating RDM constraints, application developers can be assured that their applications run on all STUs without having to test their applications on individual STUs. RDM thus is a virtual platform to verify the conformance of DAVIC applications.

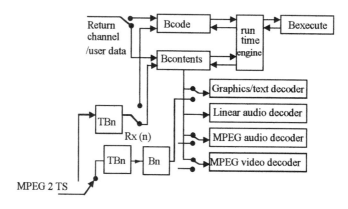

Figure 6. DAVIC Reference Decoder Model.

The DAVIC RDM was developed based on MPEG-2 system decoder model [14]. Figure 6 shows the RDM specified in DAVIC 1.1. This model is an extension of the MPEG-2 Transport System Target Decoder model (T-STD). Only the DAVIC extensions to the T-STD are shown in the figure. The data enters the transport buffer (TB_n) from an MPEG-2 TS. The raw content used by the application is transferred to the content buffer ($B_{contents}$) at a rate $R_x(n)$ specified by the application. The coded MHEG-5 objects are transferred to a code buffer (B_{code}). B_{code} also contains the Java VM bytecode. The run-time engine executes the code in B_{code} by loading it in to the memory ($B_{execute}$) and controls the times at which contents are decoded and removed from $B_{contents}$. Every DAVIC application includes a resource descriptor, which provides information about the memory requirements, resolution and number of colors, the transfer rate $R_x(n)$, and the rate of transfer from TB_n to $B_{contents}$ and B_{code}. This information is used by STUs to determine if they can run the application. Every DAVIC compliant STU shall have a minimum buffer size of 128 KB for B_{code}, 512 KB for $B_{contents}$, and 128 KB for $B_{execute}$.

3.2 DELIVERY SYSTEM

Delivery System is a means to deliver information from a service provider to the service consumer or from content provider to the service provider. The means can be networked or non-networked (CD-ROM, tape etc.). The networked delivery system was specified mainly in DAVIC 1.0 and 1.1 phases. As shown in Figure 1, the service provider and service consumer are connected by a delivery system and so are a content provider and a service provider.

The components of a delivery system are shown in Figure 7. The delivery system is composed of a core network and an access network. The core network is ATM based, and for the access network, several access types are supported. A service provider is usually directly connected to the core network. Access networks are distribution networks in communities. Several access network types are specified by DAVIC to cover existing as well as new access technologies.

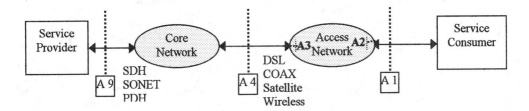

Figure 7. Delivery system.

The existing access networks to provide broadband services are either COAX or twisted-pair telephone lines. DAVIC specified technologies to support audio-visual services over these networks. For COAX, the unidirectional downstream channel is supported by 38 Mbps MPEG-2 transport stream or ATM in 64QAM/8MHz and a bidirectional control channel of up to 3 Mbits/s down and 3 Mbits/s up per QPSK carrier is also supported. ADSL and VDSL are specified to support broadband services over telephone lines. In addition to these networks, wireless networks are also specified. A unidirectional satellite channel of up to 30 Mbps is supported. Two other new wireless access technologies specified are Local Multipoint Distribution System (LMDS) and Multichannel Multipoint Distribution System (MMDS). Both LMDS and MMDS are line-of-sight wireless technologies. MMDS is unidirectional, operates in frequency spectrum below 10 GHz with a bandwidth of 200 MHz, and has a range of up to 50 km. LMDS can be unidirectional or bidirectional, has a shorter range of up to 5 km, and operates in the frequency spectrum above 10 GHz.

Before an audio-visual session is started, a DAVIC system has to establish a connection between a service provider and a STU over the delivery system. Connection establishment is completed using Q.2931 signaling. Once a connection is set up, Session Resource Manager (SRM) and DSMCC session establishment protocols are used to establish a session and allocate default resources for the session. An upstream channel is also established for interactive applications that need a back channel to the service provider. For cabled networks, establishing a back channel is not a problem. However, for Hertzian access networks (satellite/terrestrial broadcast), a wireless back channel is not practical because of transmission delays and equipment cost (e.g., satellite transmitter). To support interactive applications over Hertzian access networks, DAVIC developed technology for the back channel over PSTN/ISDN networks. This form of broadcast, with a back channel over wired networks is called *Interactive Broadcast*.

3.3 SERVICE PROVIDER SYSTEM

SPS provides DAVIC services such as movies on demand. Unlike the SCS components in a DAVIC system, SPS does not have internal reference points. Only an external reference point A9, between SPS and the core network, is specified. The server reference model specified is an object-oriented distributed server model with a collection of well-defined services. Four core services are specified in the server model: service gateway, application service, stream service, and content service. These services are based on DSMCC user-user services and provide the minimal functionality necessary to provide audio-visual services.

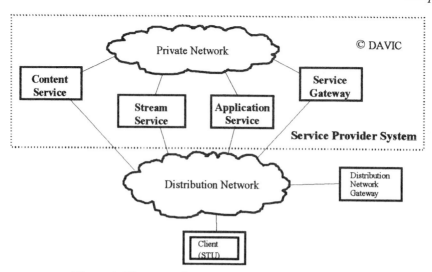

Figure 8. Elements of a service provider system [12].

Figure 8 shows the core elements of a service provider system. Additional services such as file service, directory service, download service, session gateway, etc. are also based on DSMCC services. In addition to the services adopted from DSMCC, DAVIC defines several service interfaces among which are domain, stream, group, and content mainly for access control/management and content loading. Content loading to a service provider domain is done over the A10 interface. This interface, supported by the content service, allows content provider to add/remove/modify titles, applications, and services. Any DAVIC compliant system should support the core services. All the service elements have well-defined interfaces, specified in IDL. Since IDL is part of CORBA [9], one natural way of implementing these services is using CORBA.

Service gateway is the STU's entry point in a server. Services available from a SPS are registered with the service gateway and de-registered when a service is discontinued. The service gateway allows a STU to browse and select service. It is also responsible for session management including resource provisioning and re-provisioning for a session. The application service provides a set of basic functions required by all the services such as directory functions. Additional services are built by adding service-specific functions. The stream service is the primary one and is responsible for storing and delivering media streams. Content service is used by information providers to install new services and content on the server.

4.   DAVIC 1.2

DAVIC 1.2, which was published in December 1996, is a super-set of DAVIC 1.1. This section summarizes the major additions and changes from DAVIC 1.1.

4.1 STU MULTIMEDIA DATAPORT
DAVIC 1.2 specifies three tools for STU data ports: a multimedia data port, a PC data port, and a parallel data port. Among them, only a multimedia data port is normative and the others are informative.

4.1.1 Multimedia Dataport
This interface supports both MPEG and IP traffic. Home electronics appliances (such as camcorders and DVD players) and PCs can be connected. The interface shall be compliant to

IEEE 1394-1995. DAVIC 1.2 defines the supplemental specifications for IP over IEEE 1394, such as MTU size, encapsulation and link fragmentation, Address Resolution Protocol (ARP), and multicast/broadcast mechanisms.

4.1.2 PC Dataport
This interface supports IP traffic only for PCs. The interface shall be compliant to IEEE 10Base-T Ethernet as specified in IEEE 802. Although it was normative in DAVIC 1.1, it is informative in DAVIC 1.2.

4.1.3 Parallel Dataport
Peripheral devices such as printers can be connected to a STU through this interface. The specification shall be compliant to IEEE 1284.

4.2 ATM OVER ADSL
DAVIC 1.2 added the ATM transmission convergence layer specifications over ADSL. This is adopted from the ADSL Forum.

4.3 HIGHER QUALITY AUDIO
In order to augment sound quality, DAVIC 1.2 supports another specification for compressed audio; ATSC A/52 audio, i.e., Dolby AC-3. MPEG-1 audio, which was a unique audio format in DAVIC 1.1, is still normative in DAVIC 1.2. Audio contents can be in either format in accordance with the quality requirement.

4.4 HIGHER QUALITY AUDIO
DAVIC 1.1 supports resolutions less than or equal to ITU-R 601 and the quality of video was bounded by MPEG-2 MP@ML specification. DAVIC 1.2 incorporates MP@HL to support higher resolutions.

4.5 CONTENT PACKAGING
Multimedia content consists of multiple components. Although MHEG-5 specifies their synchronized presentation mechanism at service consumers, it does not specify how to package them for delivery from a content provider to service providers over A10 reference point. DAVIC 1.2 gives the general structure of content packaging and details the metadata. The actual packaging format is specified in DAVIC 1.3.

A content package can contain multiple content items and/or content item elements. A content item element is the smallest content unit and can be shared by more than one content item. A content item is a set of content item elements and corresponds to a complete application. A content item can contain other content items. Metadata are defined to handle the above three-layered structure. Metadata include CosNaming names, physical pathnames, version numbers, copyright information, etc.

4.6 SECURITY TOOLS
DAVIC's approach in specifying solutions is a one-functionality, one-policy tool. However, security requirements greatly depend on the nature of access networks, contents, and business models. Also, each country or region has its own security regulation. Moreover, defining a common cryptographic algorithm may cause a global catastrophe if it is cracked. Therefore, DAVIC specifications allow multiple cryptographic algorithms and provide mechanisms for negotiating their use. DAVIC 1.2 defines a number of security tools as described below.

4.6.1 S1 Scrambling
Contents (video, audio, etc.) are scrambled at the MPEG-2 Transport Stream packet layer. In accordance with ISO/IEC 13818-1, only payloads can be scrambled. Headers and adaptation fields shall not be scrambled to ease handling of TS packets in the network. Also, each TS

packet is independently scrambled toward erroneous conditions. The transport scrambling control field in TS header is used to alternately control words, which are short-life cryptographic keys for de-scrambling. Since DAVIC does not define a common cryptographic algorithm, the scrambling algorithm is identified through the S2 flow or the scrambling descriptor in the Program Map Table.

4.6.2 S2/S3 Authentication

The entities interacting on S2 or S3 flow use a three-way authentication mechanism described in X.509 for mutual authentication. DAVIC 1.2 defines syntax of the authentication messages based on X.511. These messages are encapsulated in DSM-CC User-to-User primitives in the case of S2 authentication. The mode for carrying S3 authentication messages is unclear in the current specifications.

4.6.3 S2/S3 Confidentiality and Integrity

The functions are provided at IP layer below DSM-CC. For confidentiality, the IP Encapsulating Security Payload is used as described in RFC1827. Also, for integrity, the IP Authentication Header is used as in RFC1826. Although DES CBC mode is recommended in RFC1825, DAVIC 1.2 does not specify a particular algorithm. The algorithm can be negotiated using the authentication messages.

4.6.4 S2 Digital Signatures

DAVIC does not define a digital signature mechanism. It is implementation dependent.

4.6.5 S2 Primitives for S1 Security Management

In order to negotiate a scrambling algorithm and/or transfer cryptographic keys for S1 flow, DAVIC 1.2 defines an interface, S1Security. The interface is defined in OMG IDL and the primitives are carried in the same manner as other DSM-CC UU primitives.

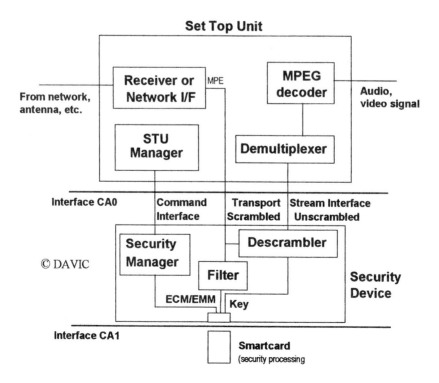

Figure 9. Security interfaces CA0 and CA1 [15].

4.6.6 Secure Download

Secure download is achieved by including a security module, which contains signatures in a downloaded data image. DSM-CC download messages are augmented for security fields.

4.6.7 Parental Control

Parental control is supported by rating the content. However, DAVIC 1.2 has not yet provided technical specifications.

In addition to the above security tools, DAVIC 1.2 enables the use of detachable security devices, which are effective to replace security functionality. DAVIC 1.2 defines two conditional access interfaces CA0 and CA1 in a STU (Figure 9), and at least one of them should be supported.

4.6.8 CA0

This interface resides between a host and a PC-card-based security device. The specification is based on CENELEC/DVB Common Interface Standard EN 50221. Scrambled MPEG streams are fed into the security device and fed back to the host after de-scrambling. The de-scrambler is initialized by a smart card.

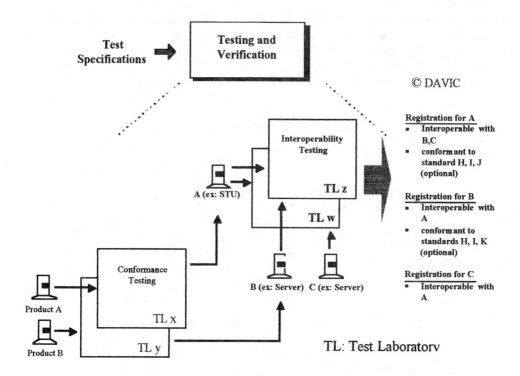

Figure 10. Conformance testing and interoperability testing [15].

4.6.9 CA1

This interface resides between the security device and a smart card. The specification is based on ISO/IEC 7816 parts 1 to 6. The filter in the security device extracts CA messages from MPEG streams. A smart card uses those messages to initialize the de-scrambler.

4.7 CONFORMANCE AND INTEROPERABILITY TESTING

DAVIC 1.2 describes two types of testing; conformance testing and interoperability testing. The objective of conformance testing is to verify that a product conforms to a DAVIC specification. Although it is a pre-requisite to interoperability, it does not guarantee that the product can inter-work with a product developed by a different vendor. On the other hand, interoperability testing verifies interoperability between them, and assures inter-working. The relationship between conformance testing and interoperability testing is depicted in Figure 10.

DAVIC uses ISO/IEC 9646 as conformance testing methodology and defines its own methodology for interoperability testing. DAVIC products are expected to go through these two types of testing procedures. However, it should be noted that DAVIC itself will not be involved in certifying conformance/interoperability of products.

5.   DAVIC 1.3

DAVIC 1.3, which was published in December 1997, is a super-set of DAVIC 1.2. This section summarizes the major additions and changes from DAVIC 1.2.

5.1 DISTRIBUTED SERVER

DAVIC 1.3 added a new reference point, A9*, to allow interoperable interconnection between service elements in a distributed server. Although A9 is exposed to the core network, A9* is an internal service provider system. The distributed server architecture is shown in Figure 11. The physical interfaces at A9*, A10, A11 shall be ATM STM-1, ATM STM-4, DVB Asynchronous Serial Interface, Ethernet 10Base-T or Ethernet 100Base-T.

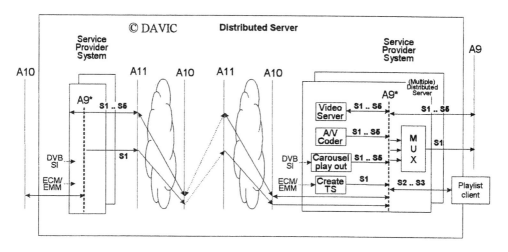

Figure 11. Distributed server architecture [16].

Two MPEG-2 TS packets are mapped over eight ATM cells at A9, regardless of whether PCR exists, as specified in DAVIC 1.0. That is, the AAL-5 encapsulation is "PCR unaware" at A9. However, at the reference points A9*, A10 and A11, the encapsulation should be "PCR aware" to avoid jitter propagation. In other words, a TS packet with PCR shall always be in the last position in an AAL-5 PDU. If the first packet contains PCR, the single packet is encapsulated into an AAL-5 PDU and mapped over five ATM cells.

5.2 PASSBAND UNIDIRECTIONAL PHYSICAL INTERFACE FOR MOBILE RECEPTION

This is a new physical interface to support unidirectional transmission over radio frequency. The interface is based on Coded Orthogonal Frequency Division Multiplex (COFDM) modulation. From the point of channel capacity, two grades, Grade A and Grade B, are defined.

5.3 PHYSICAL SPECIFICATIONS FOR INTERNAL NIUs

DAVIC 1.3 defines two types of internal NIUs; a user-replaceable internal NIU and a manufacturer-replaceable internal NIU. A user replaceable internal NIU can be easily replaced by a user without disassembling the STU. The specifications describe the dimensions of the NIU enclosure, the faceplate and the backplate, the interface bay and emission. On the other hand, a manufacturer replaceable internal NIU is a PCB daughter card and needs disassembling of the STU to replace. The specifications describe the dimensions, the faceplate, the location of connectors, the interface bay, and emission (EMI emission and thermal emission). The A0 connector is DIN 41612 in both NIUs.

5.4 MANAGEMENT ARCHITECTURE AND PROTOCOLS

The management architecture of DAVIC 1.3 is based on TMN architecture [17]. The protocol is SNMP or CMIP as specified in DAVIC 1.0.

5.5 STU/NIU INITIALIZATION

In order to make a STU network-independent, network specific software modules such as signaling with SRC may be stored in a NIU and downloaded to the STU at the initialization stage. STU/NIU initialization messages and flows have been updated to support this function since DAVIC 1.2. The client functionalities are downloaded with Image messages.

5.6 NETWORK GRAPHICS

The specification of uncompressed graphics in DAVIC 1.2 was replaced by that of network graphics in DAVIC 1.3. The format shall be Portable Network Graphics (PNG) as defined by the World Wide Web Consortium.

5.7 OUTLINE FONT FORMAT

DAVIC 1.3 defines the original outline font format called Portable Font Resource (PFR). The specification is described in the normative annex.

5.8 SCALEABLE AUDIO

When the network bandwidth is limited or not guaranteed, scaleable audio is needed. DAVIC 1.3 supports ISO/IEC 13818-3 (MPEG-2 audio) for this functionality.

5.9 TRANSITION EFFECT FOR STILL PICTURES

To support effective presentation of still pictures, transition effects and their parameters are specified. The effects include dissolve, wipes, slide-ins, slide-outs, rolls, and so on.

5.10 EXPANSION OF JAVA APIs

The following APIs were added to the core set of Java APIs, DVB-SI API, MPEG-2 section filter API, MPEG component API, and resource notification API. These APIs give more convenience to application development.

5.11 CONTENT PACKAGING FORMAT AND CONTENT LOADING TOOL SET

A basic file format for content packaging shall be Bento, which was specified by Apple Computer [18]. DAVIC 1.3 defines DAVIC objects in Bento representation. Contents provided by a content provider are loaded on a service provider system over A10 interface.

The specification of the content loading tool set shall be Content Metadata Specification Language (CMSL), which is described in an Annex.

5.12 CONTOURS

DAVIC specifications are sets of tools in nature and do not specify systems. Choice of tools is implementation dependent. The specifications can be used to build different systems with different tools.

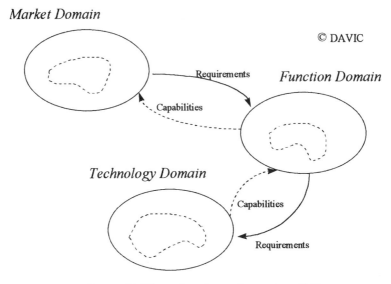

Figure 12. Three domains and a contour [16].

A contour gives a definition of a system. The conceptual picture is shown in Figure 12. Each contour is described in three domains: the market domain, the function domain, and the technology domain. For a particular market segment, a set of market and user requirements is specified in the market domain. This set is mapped into a set of functional requirements in the function domain and then into a set of technical tools in the technology domain. The systems, which claim to be compliant to a particular contour, shall be built using all tools in the last set. DAVIC 1.3 elaborates requirements, functions, and tools for each contour.

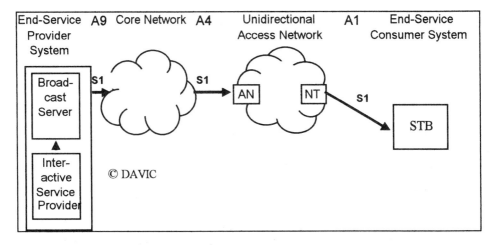

Figure 13. Configuration of enhanced digital broadcast [16].

DAVIC 1.3 specifies two contours; Enhanced Digital Broadcast (EDB) and Interactive Digital Broadcast (IDB). Other contours will be added to the specifications in the future, according to the other market segments. The configuration of EDB is shown in Figure 13. An EDB system does not have a return channel. The interactivity is achieved by the object carousel tool over S1 flow.

The configuration of IDB is shown in Figure 14. An IDB system has a return channel for full service interactions. ISDN, PSTN, or a bidirectional access network is used as an interaction network.

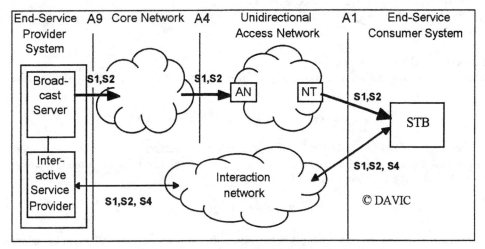

Figure 14. Configuration of interactive digital broadcast [16].

6. DAVIC 1.4

DAVIC 1.4 was published on March 1998. The non-exhaustive list of major work items is shown below together with a brief description.

6.1 TWO-WAY SATELLITE
The previous DAVIC specifications supported unidirectional satellite systems. DAVIC 1.4 supports a two-way satellite. The proposed transmission scheme uses TDM for downstreams and FDM/TDMA for upstreams.

6.2 HOME NETWORK
A network enables functions similar to Local Area Network (LAN) at home. To accommodate this architectural expansion, incorporation of new reference points, A20 and A21, is considered.

6.3 COMMUNICATIVE SERVICES
The interfaces and protocols are considered to provide communicative services such as telephone and video phone.

6.4 ADDITIONAL JAVA APIs
It is proposed to add several Java APIs for enhanced functionality.

6.5 CA1 EXTENSIONS

The following extensions are considered: protection of CA1 interface, support of Impulse Pay Per View (IPPV), support of reporting on a return channel, and support of the transparent mode.

6.6 COPYRIGHT PROTECTION

Tools such as copy control, playback control, and watermarking are considered to protect the right of content creators.

6.7 ENHANCEMENTS TO USAGE METERING

Protocols for collection and transfer of usage data are considered for management operations such as billing.

6.8 ADDITIONAL CONTOURS

Interactive Multimedia contour is considered for more interactive services than EDB or IDB.

7.   DAVIC TECHNOLOGY SUMMARY

The set of specifications published by DAVIC covers a number of technologies to support end-to-end digital audio-visual services. The key technologies and the functionality provided by these technologies are summarized in Table 2.

8. CONCLUSION

Started as a forum to standardize tools for video-on-demand systems, DAVIC quickly adapted to embrace the emerging Internet-based services. However, DAVIC is not meant to provide pure Internet services, but enables a digital audio visual service provider (e.g., a cable operator) to provide Internet services. DAVIC is publishing its specifications at a fast pace to keep up with the rapidly changing technology. Some of the DAVIC tools and subsystems are already commercially available. However, currently there is no system that incorporates all functionalities and tools specified by DAVIC. It may take a few years before fully compliant systems are deployed. One of the reasons for slow deployment of DAVIC systems is their complexity and that verifying interoperability and compliance of an entire system is an extremely difficult task. There are also market-related issues, as deployment of DAVIC-capable networks represents a significant capital investment. Since the DAVIC specifications are a set of tools with well-defined interfaces, they can easily be used in other systems. For example, the current digital TV standard in the U.S. addresses phasing in of digital TV broadcast. However, the same effort is clearly missing for cable TV. The subsystems and tools specified by DAVIC could be valuable for such an effort.

Table 2. Some DAVIC Functionalities and Tools

Functionality	DAVIC Tool
Compressed video	MPEG-2 main profile at main level
Video format	AS transmitted (NTSC, PAL, etc.)
Higher quality video	MPEG-2 high profile at main level
Compressed audio	MPEG-1 audio
Higher quality audio	Dolby AC-3
Linear audio	AIFF
Scalable audio	MPEG-2 audio, layer 2
Still pictures (natural, photographs)	MPEG-2 intra frames
Graphics (still pictures and bitmaps)	PNG
Text coding	HTML 3.2
Content and metadata packaging	Bento
Synchronization mechanism	MPEG-2 presentation time stamps
Multimedia application format	MHEG-5
Virtual Machine	Java
Media encapsulation/multiplexing	MPEG-2 packetized elementary stream and transport stream
Connection management	Q.2931 and UNI 3.1
STU to Server, user interaction operations	DSM-CC
User-Network signaling (session management)	DSM-CC
Network management architecture	TMN
Network management	SNMP and subset of CMIP
STU boot and program download	DSM-CC
TCP	TCP RFC 793
UDP	UDP RFC 768
IP	IP RFC 791
IP over ATM	Classical IP over ATM, RFC 1483
Core network	SONET, SDH, PDH, ATM
Access network	ADSL, VDSL, HFC, FTTC, satellite, MMDS, LMDS, ATM/SDH (FTTH)
Security - authentication	X509, X511 certificate formats
Security – confidentiality and integrity	IP V6
STU multimedia data port	IEEE 1394

REFERENCES

1. The Digital Audio-Visual Council (DAVIC), "Part 1 – Description of DAVIC Functionalities," DAVIC 1.0 Specification, Geneva, Switzerland, 1995.

2. Eleftheriadis, A., "Architecting Video-on-Demand Systems: DAVIC 1.0 and Beyond," Proceedings, International Symposium on Multimedia Communications and Video Coding, Brooklyn, New York, October 1995.

3. Kalva, H., "DAVIC New York Interoperability Experiments: Report and Results," DAVIC Contribution No. DAVIC/TC/SYS/96/09/008, Geneva, Switzerland, 1996.

4. Kasahara, H., "Report of the DAVIC Interoperability Event in Tokyo Electronics Show '96," DAVIC Document, DAVIC/358, Hong Kong, December 1996.

5. Kalva, H., Chang, S.-F., Eleftheriadis, A., "DAVIC and Interoperability Experiments," *Journal on Multimedia Tools and Applications*, Special Issue on Video on Demand, Kluwer Academic Publishers, Vol. 5, No. 2, pp. 119-132, September 1997.

6. Chang, S.-F., Eleftheriadis, A., Anastassiou, D., Jacobs, S., Kalva, H., and Zamora, J., "Columbia's VoD and Multimedia Research Testbed with Heterogeneous Network Support," *Journal on Multimedia Tools and Applications*, Special Issue on Video on Demand, Kluwer Academic Publishers, Vol. 5, No. 2, pp. 171-188, September 1997.

7. Okuda, H, Morinaga, M., Kasahara, H., and Shimamura, K., "An Interoperability Testbed and Test Results for DAVIC 1.0 Specification," *Journal on Multimedia Tools and Applications*, Special Issue on Video on Demand, Kluwer Academic Publishers, Vol. 5, No. 2, pp. 147-160, September 1997.

8. ISO/IEC/SC29/WG11, "Generic Coding of Moving Pictures and Associated Audio (DSM-CC)- ISO/IEC 13818-6," International Standards Organization, 1996.

9. OMG – Object Management Group, "Common Object Request Broker: Architecture and Specification," CORBA Revision 2.0, (OMG CORBA 2.0), July 1995.

10. The Digital Audio-Visual Council (DAVIC), "Part 9 – Information Representation," DAVIC 1.0 Specification, Geneva, Switzerland, January 1996.

11. The Digital Audio-Visual Council (DAVIC), "Part 9 – Information Representation," DAVIC 1.1 Specification, Geneva, Switzerland, November 1996.

12. The Digital Audio-Visual Council (DAVIC), "Part 3 – Service Provider System Architecture and Interfaces," DAVIC 1.1 Specification, Geneva, Switzerland, November 1996.

13. Crocker, D., "To be on the Internet," RFC 1775, IETF, March 1995.

14. ISO/IEC/SC29/WG11, "Generic Coding of Moving Pictures and Associated Audio (MPEG-2 Systems) ISO/IEC 13818-1," International Standards Organization, November 1994.

15. The Digital Audio-Visual Council (DAVIC), "DAVIC 1.2 Specifications," DAVIC 1.2 Specification, Geneva, Switzerland, December 1996.

16. The Digital Audio-Visual Council (DAVIC), "DAVIC 1.3 Specifications," DAVIC 1.3 Specification, Geneva, Switzerland, December 1997.

17. ITU-T, "ITU Recommendation M.3010: Principles for a Telecommunications Management Network."

18. Apple Computer, "Bento Specification," Bento Specification Revision 1.0d5, July 15, 1993.

6

INTERACTIVE MULTIMEDIA USER INTERFACES

Meera M. Blattner
University of California, Davis, and
Lawrence Livermore National Laboratory
Livermore, California 94550

1.	**OVERVIEW**	112
2.	**WINDOW-BASED USER INTERFACES**	113
3.	**MULTIMODALITY**	114
3.1	HUMAN INPUT/OUTPUT MODALITIES	114
3.2	COMPUTER INPUT/OUTPUT MODALITIES	114
4.	**INTERACTIVE INTERFACE TECHNOLOGIES**	116
4.1	PEN TECHNOLOGY	116
4.2	VOICE RECOGNITION AND NATURAL LANGUAGE PROCESSING	117
4.3	NONSPEECH AUDIO INTERFACES	118
4.4	RECOGNITION AND DISPLAY OF FACIAL EXPRESSION, GAZE, AND UNENCUMBERED GESTURE	120
4.5	INTERFACE AGENTS	121
4.6	OTHER TECHNOLOGIES FOR INTERACTIVE INTERFACES	122
5.	**INTEGRATING MEDIA AND MODALITIES**	122
5.1	STEPS IN INTEGRATING MULTIMODAL INPUTS	123
6.	**SOFTWARE ENGINEERING MULTIMEDIA USER INTERFACES**	124
7.	**EXAMPLES OF MULTIMEDIA USER INTERFACES**	125
7.1	INTERFACES FOR PEOPLE WITH SPECIAL NEEDS	125
7.2	OFFICE AND HOME ENVIRONMENTS	127
7.3	INTERFACES FOR MOBILE COMPUTING AND WEARABLE COMPUTERS	127
7.4	THE WORLD-WIDE WEB	128
8.	**CONCLUDING REMARKS**	130
	REFERENCES	131

Abstract. Interactive systems try to take advantage of the human senses to facilitate human-computer communication. New technologies are incorporating audio, gesture, and facial expressions as computer input. The problem of integrating multiple media requires not only the recognition of different input streams, but also techniques for combining pieces from each input into a coherent whole. With the diversity, mobility, and ubiquity of new computers, we will see computers incorporated into our clothing and in our home and office environments—pen and voice will be increasingly important. The design of interfaces for people with special needs such as those with disabilities, children, and those who balk at learning new technologies will become increasingly important, as will software engineering these interfaces. Finally, we examine new directions in interfaces for web design.

1. OVERVIEW

This is a critical time for user-interface designers. Paradigms used in the graphical user interface (GUI) are rapidly being replaced because of new computer technologies. This does not mean that GUIs will disappear entirely; they will remain as placeholders of our past as new technologies surround and overtake them. They are much like the architecture in a city that retains many of its usable old buildings, even retrofitting them with modern conveniences, while new structures surround them.

The topic of interactive multimedia interfaces is so large and unwieldy that this chapter will explore some topics in more depth than others and will not discuss many interesting subjects at all. With new interactive interfaces, the question may arise not only as to what interfaces are, but also where they are located. Interfaces are where two or more entities meet (the entities to which we refer in this chapter are humans and computers). Although interfaces may have physical realizations, such as computer screens or keyboards, they may also consist of devices such as microphones and speakers that capture and transmit sound waves. Virtual-reality interfaces are very complex and require a variety of different sensing devices, such as microphones and earphones, position trackers, touch sensors, and possibly body sensors. The location of an interface may be highly distributed about the environment and the human body itself. We still cannot have an interface without a language or set of conventions that must be used to make user interactions known to computers. To be interpreted by computers, a language must be a formal system structured according to specific rules, such as grammatical rules. We assign meaning or semantics to these rules. In some cases, there may be several levels of communication. We may use computers to transmit information, as with electronic mail (e-mail) messages, rather than sending instructions to computers.

Interactive systems try to take advantage of the human senses—the human *modalities*—to facilitate our communication with one another and with computers. People communicate through voice, touch, gesture, eye contact, facial expression, and a myriad of other capabilities that computers did not have only a short time ago; now, because of rapidly advancing technology, computers are gaining rudimentary modalities. The desire to achieve natural and expressive interaction has given rise to a large number of input devices that transform human expressions, such as gesture, voice, and gaze, to bits and bytes. For this reason, input devices are as important a part of interface design as output devices [1].

There are three primary characteristics of the direction of interface technology:

- Human-like computer-user interactions.
- Diversity of functionality.
- Ubiquity.

In the early years, computers were used for business and scientific applications. Now their functionality has greatly expanded and will continue to do so. Computers manage our money, guide our cars, warn us of dangerous environmental conditions, and schedule our appointments. They provide indispensable assistance for people with a variety of disabilities. How could we access information without the World-Wide Web (WWW, or web)—now routinely used to look up old friends and post photos of family reunions, as well as to find the best airfare and track down a research article.

What is the present state of the art in multimedia interfaces? The answer is not simple; we cannot take a snapshot of today's interfaces and say "this" is now, and "that" is in the future. Technologies of the future are emerging in prototype forms side by side with our current commercially successful computer systems. The future of computing is here now, as well as next year, or five years from now. We know that computers will increase their reach and their roles everywhere throughout our homes, offices, and public places. To provide the ubiquity and diversity required for computing, it is the task of interface designers to make computers usable to the very young and very old, to those who balk at using new technology, to those who do not speak English, to the disabled, and to those who do not read instructions.

Still, high-tech computer applications may require complex interfaces that take very application-specific knowledge and many days to master.

What are these new technologies whose existence compels us to devise new interface paradigms? Here are five we know are changing the way we interact with our computers:

- New interfaces that combine text, graphics, voice, and nonspeech audio as output and provide a whole host of new input devices for speech, pen, sensors, etc. Gestural interfaces will develop new roles. Computers will be customized for users, but particularly for the disabled, children, and other users with special needs.
- Displays may be very large (occupying a wall) or very small (just inches in size), such as palm-tops and wrist-tops; and, of course, there will be a whole range of sizes in between. Speech interfaces may have little or no visual display.
- Computers are increasingly portable, mobile, and networked. Computers will become part of our clothing. We will be in constant communication with the world around us as telephones, computers, and television merge.
- The web and e-mail will be available on all of our communication devices and used routinely for accessing information. New types of browsers will become available. We will become "web-centric" [2]. Information now stored in books, compact discs, magazines, etc., will be on the web.
- The office, home, and public spaces will have their own automated environments to maintain, monitor, and configure inner spaces. These environments will be in constant communication with their users.

2. WINDOW-BASED USER INTERFACES

GUIs are not considered multimedia user interfaces, even though they use many different types of data structures, text, and graphics and may even emit simple sounds, such as beeps. As GUIs have become the dominant paradigm for user interfaces for more than 15 years, it is useful to begin from a description of this platform. GUIs evolved from a research project at Xerox in the 1970s that used the Smalltalk programming language for implementation [3]. *Widgets*—menus, icons, windows, scroll-bars, and a host of other interface objects meant to interact with users—were developed for interfaces. Interfaces were based on the metaphor of a desktop; items could be dragged from one point to another by direct manipulation using a mouse (pointing device). Direct manipulation enables users to click on visual representations, such as icons, and "drag" them or execute a variety of actions on them, for example, moving files to the trash can to throw them out. Users can carry out tasks quickly and easily without remembering commands and object names [4]. The input devices are a keyboard and mouse.

In 1982, Apple Computer, using these concepts, developed a GUI interface for the Lisa Computer, which became a commercial success. This interface was also known as a WIMP (windows, icons, menus, and pointing) interface. GUIs evolved by increments from this beginning. The basic paradigm—and the method of interaction—remains one of using widgets, point and click, and direct manipulation. One of the major advances in GUIs since their original introduction is interface builders. These are tool kits that enable interface designers to quickly assemble new interfaces. Interface builders are essential in the design process to prototype and test designs on prospective users.

The ability to include text, graphics, video, and audio in interfaces during the late 1980s gave rise to interfaces with multiple media. It was necessary to create systems that could be used to assemble content with multimedia interfaces on the part of expert users. AthenaMuse of Project Athena [5] was among the most advanced authoring systems. The ability to include text, graphics, video, and audio was an important step for interface design; each medium appeared in its own window. There were a number of different widgets to manipulate the design, and graphics, video, and audio were coordinated by time lines. Hundreds of ingenious applications used these new interfaces. To find out more about contemporary authoring systems, see the chapter on authoring systems in this book.

If GUIs are such a tremendous success, why are we considering the use of other technologies? Four major arguments for the use of other paradigms are that (1) many new computers are very small and mobile and have interfaces that do not work well in the GUI setting—for example, they may be better suited to a pen and voice than to a keyboard; (2) new tasks and functionalities are arising in expanding computer markets; (3) there is a growing realization that certain tasks can be performed more efficiently or more naturally, i.e., more in accordance with users' cognitive styles, for example, by speaking to a portable computer; and (4) GUIs are based on viewing information through windows, which separate our world into little chunks. The basic look and feel of interfaces in AthenaMuse and the older authoring systems are that each medium is experienced through its own window. Yet the way people interact with the real world is not through windows, but in a more integrated manner. New technologies for interfaces are generally multimedia; that is, they combine and integrate multiple media and modalities.

3. MULTIMODALITY

To understand the evolving nature of interactive user interfaces, we shall first examine the human senses and their impact on our ability to create interfaces in relation to computer inputs/outputs (I/O).

3.1 HUMAN INPUT/OUTPUT MODALITIES

To enable us to design interfaces that have human-like interactions with their users, we must understand how humans communicate with each other. Multimodality is the term used to express the use of multiple senses of humans in their communication with the world around them. The senses can input from the eye (vision), ear (hearing), touch (tactile or haptic), nose (smell or olfactory), tongue (taste or gustatory), and body using balance and motion (kinesthetic). Human outputs can include motions such as hand manipulation, pressure, gesture and other body movements; speech or other sounds made with the mouth; and facial expression and eye gaze. For people with severe motor disabilities, devices are made to sense the electrical pulses of the muscles to effect computer inputs from the human body [6]. How human brains process multimodal input is not well understood. These questions fall largely in the domains of philosophy, psychology, linguistics, and cognitive science [7].

Figure 1 shows that computer outputs become human inputs, and human outputs become computer inputs. There are many more exotic I/O devices not shown in Figure 1 or discussed in this chapter. Inputs to computers may not necessarily be the result of conscious inputs on the part of users. Sensors play an intermediate role in that they can be used to detect sound, motion, temperature, and a variety of other changes of state in the environment. Some experimental systems use *active badges* to track users wearing them. Active badges emit an infrared signal, which is detected by a low-cost network of sensors placed in an environment [8]. Cameras are used as input to a computer that identifies gestures. Sensors were typically used to monitor the state of processes such as those used in scientific experiments, manufacturing, and electrical and mechanical devices such as automobiles and airplanes. However, cameras and sensors will be used more and more to provide computer inputs to user interfaces, particularly in home and office environments.

3.2 COMPUTER INPUT/OUTPUT MODALITIES

3.2.1 Output Modalities

Classifications or taxonomies are created to address problems in human-computer interaction systematically and to address complexity. An example is given below of a taxonomy for computer output modalities and their interaction styles. Bernsen created *generative taxonomy* output modalities [9] that allows combinations of simpler elements to form more complex structures. The elements of the Bernsen taxonomy have four features: linguistic/non-linguistic, analog/non-analog, arbitrary/non-arbitrary, static/ dynamic, plus three media of expression: graphics, sound, and touch used in the taxonomy.

Human ◄──────── Computer		
Input	**Modality**	**Output**
eye	vision	screen/projected images
hand	haptic	force feedback
	tactile	texture
ear	auditory	audio (speaker)
body	kinesthetic	treadmill

Human ──────► Computer		
Input	**Modality**	**Output**
hand/arm movement	haptic/gesture	keyboard mouse/joystick trackball/data glove touchscreen/camera
facial expression	gesture	camera
voice	auditory	microphone
body movement	kinesthetic	position tracker camera
gaze	gesture	eye-tracker/camera
skin/body	EMG	sensors
brain waves	EEG	sensors

Figure 1. Some examples of the relationship between computer and human input/output. An electromyographic signal (EMG) is an electrical signal from muscles and an electroencephalogram (EEG) records voltage fluctuations of the brain. EMGs and EEGs are not generally considered modalities.

Analog representations are iconic in nature; non-arbitrary representations rely on already existing systems with defined meanings; dynamic representations require the passage of time. Hence, there are 2 x 2 x 2 x 3 elements, or the 48 elements of the taxonomy; however, only 28 are possible. The following description of the 28 modalities in the taxonomy may be grouped into six categories with a more intuitive organization as:

1. Language (natural or otherwise).
2. Pictures (in the ordinary sense).
3. Analog representations using sound or touch.
4. Graphs.
5. Representations with a conventionally assigned meaning.
6. Explicitly rendered structuring of information.

Each of the 28 modalities can be placed into one of these categories. Some examples of elements of the taxonomy are:
- Linguistic and non-arbitrary modalities: Some examples are everyday spoken language, written language, text, musical notation, Braille, non-arbitrary tables of information.
- Non-linguistic, analog, and non-arbitrary modalities. Examples are photographs, movies, real-world sounds, sounds generated through visualizations, pie charts, touch sequences, maps, cartoons.
- Non-linguistic and non-analog modalities. Examples are diagrams with geometrical elements, trees, windows, scroll bars, arbitrary lists, arbitrary sounds in sequences.

3.2.2 Input Modalities

The question of computer input modalities has not yet been addressed adequately. Card, Mackinlay, and Robertson [10] proposed a taxonomy to classify input devices within an abstract *design space* according to their expressiveness and how they communicate meaning. The taxonomy classifies input devices by physical properties (the position and force vs linear or rotary), and how they can be composed. There are three composition operators: (1) *merge,* two devices combined so that the resulting input domain is the cross-product of the input domains of the two devices; (2) *layout,* the colocation of two devices on different places of a common panel; and (3) *connect,* composition that occurs when the output domain of one device is mapped only on the input domain of another. The design space itself is considerably more complex, but space does not permit a full explanation of these ideas. Although this is the most comprehensive classification for inputs based on user-manipulated devices, it does not address important input modalities such as temporal and linguistic structures (e.g., voice recognition). Bernsen uses data structures—not devices—as examples. The final goal of taxonomies in the study of computer modalities is to understand how they can be applied to the problem of mapping information and to examine their compatibilities and trade-offs.

4. INTERACTIVE INTERFACE TECHNOLOGIES

In this section we briefly describe six technologies that are found in the new interactive multimedia computers.

4.1 PEN TECHNOLOGY

A pen falls under the general category of a stylus, an instrument for writing, marking, or incising. The terms used are *pen, pen-computing, and pen-based interfaces.* Various technologies are used for pens, from light-emitting pens to simple devices that can use common writing pens as inputs by occluding light from the surface or sensing pressure. There are pen systems that use a camera to detect the shape and position of the markings on surfaces (rather than creating the marks through computer software). Pens can be used only on a flat surface, and the current preferred technology is that of a liquid crystal display (LCD). The notion of pen computing goes back to 1968 and the idea of the DynaBook [11], which envisioned a personal computing system of the future. A DynaBook was seen as a portable computer that would supply users with the tools and applications to solve their own information-processing problems. The technology to make a DynaBook was not available at the time, but it evolved into the Apple Newton, which became available as a commercial product in 1990. Several other ventures that used the concepts of the DynaBook's portability and flexibility failed commercially. Also during 1990, the GO Corporation developed PenPoint [12], the first truly pen-based computing operating system. With the introduction of the PalmPilot in 1996, 30 years after the DynaBook was conceived, it appears that pen interfaces have become accepted and commercially successful. More than one million PalmPilots were sold in the first year and a half after they appeared on the market [13]. There is still a good deal of new research on pen computing in academic laboratories, and we may expect to see more applications with pen interfaces in the near future.

One overriding advantage of pens is that the pen form and shape are suitable to the human hand and have evolved over thousands of years. Pens allow manipulation using the fine muscles and dexterity of the hand to create very sharp and detailed drawings and writing. Anyone who has tried writing with a mouse can testify that fine manipulation is nearly impossible because the gestures are made by the arm rather than the hand. Pens work well as a pointing device in place of a mouse, and they are small, light, and inexpensive [14].

The problem with pen-based computing is the recognition of markings made by pens, which result from inexact inputs. Complex handwriting algorithms are needed to recognize such inputs. Handwriting recognition may employ neural nets, fuzzy logic, or hidden Markoff models. The problem becomes more complex when both writing and graphics are used. Often inputs do not have to be recognized, but merely recorded and transmitted, as in storing jotted notes or sketches. Gesture recognizers have a great potential for error. A recognizer may return a collection of interpretations ranked with respect to probability. Various clever methods have been devised to return alternative choices to users' displays. For example, a tap may indicate that the user would like another choice displayed [15].

The dominant metaphors for pen-based interfaces for personal digital assistants (PDAs) are those of notebooks, calendars, and address books. Pen systems have widgets similar to those of GUIs with a keyboard and mouse—that is, scrollbars, icons, resizing boxes, menus, buttons, and checklists. The notebook metaphor incorporates tables of contents, pages, and tabs for quick access to parts of contents. Our traditional alphabet may not be the best selection of symbols to be used for writing in pen systems because each time the pen is lifted from the surface, the system tries to interpret what is already there as a character. Characters for pen computing are more easily recognized if they consist of a single stroke. The Unistroke alphabet [16] was devised for this purpose, and the PalmPilot adapted Unistrokes in a character set called "Graffiti." See Figure 2 for a subset of the Graffiti alphabet. Graffiti is not strictly a one-stroke alphabet, but close to it. It is also easy to remember and has nearly a 100% recognition rate.

4.2 VOICE RECOGNITION AND NATURAL LANGUAGE PROCESSING

It is easy to confuse a number of related technologies in the area of speech and natural language: *natural language processing, voice or speech recognition,* and *speaker recognition.* Natural language processing requires inputs by voice, keyboard, pen, and/or optical character readers of utterances in a natural language into a computer. The computer then attempts to recognize these utterances semantically, that is assign a meaning to them. Natural-language interfaces have been in use for control systems, database retrieval, and interfaces for the disabled. Recognition depends upon the existence of a grammar or a formal system that defines the structure of sentences in the language. The formal rules define a *syntax* for the language. The syntax allows us to *generate* sentences; the reverse process of identifying the structure or syntax is called *parsing* the sentence. For example, in English we can parse a sentence into nouns, verbs, etc. A grammar for a true natural language may require hundreds of grammatical rules and thousands of words, perhaps as many as 20,000 in English. (This does not include many thousands of terms from technical areas, such as medicine.)

One of the major difficulties with natural-language systems is that people do not speak or write in grammatically correct ways. People speak ambiguously; that is, there may be two different syntactic structures for the same sentence, so it may be assigned different meanings. An example is: the shooting of hunters was heard from afar. This sentence can be interpreted as either that the hunters were shooting or that the hunters were being shot. Meanings are often disambiguated in the context of the utterance in real-world situations. The problem of giving computers a real-world context is very difficult and has been studied in the realm of artificial intelligence. Another problem cited in the literature is the meaning of the sentence when the words, "this," "that," "he," "she," etc., are used (anaphoric reference). The general problem of true natural-language recognition may be intractable; to make language systems work, they are generally restricted to limited vocabularies and simplified syntactic structures, and often made application dependent.

Speech and voice recognition is the technology that enables computers to accept voice inputs. Just as voice inputs may be used in a natural-language interface, so they may be used to execute commands in an artificial language. Speech and natural language I/O do not constitute a new technology, but the performance of speech recognizers has improved steadily. Significant advances in this area now make the use of speech input available in commercial systems.

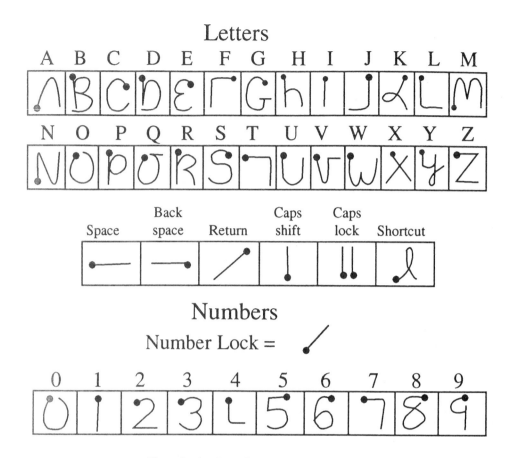

Figure 2. A subset of the Graffiti character set.

The nature of our communication with computers will change dramatically when speech inputs are part of computer interfaces. Four significant dimensions in speech recognition are: (1) is the speech isolated or continuous, (2) is there speaker independence, (3) what is the size of the vocabulary and what are the language constraints, and (4) are there background and acoustic noises? There is another related area of speaker recognition in which the words do not have to be recognized—only the speaker's identity. The ability of a computer to identify speakers has great potential for forensics and security systems. Another technology is being developed to assist users in learning foreign languages and removing accents.

4.3 NONSPEECH AUDIO INTERFACES

Nonspeech audio may be used as an input medium; for example, piano tutors use piano inputs. Sensors may also monitor nonspeech sounds in an environment. Here we are concerned with audio outputs, which are sometimes called auditory displays. Auditory outputs are greatly underutilized as a human-computer communication medium. Some of the benefits of auditory displays are providing an eyes-free interface, alerting, orienting, parallel activities, and time-sequenced relationships [17]. A practical advantage is that sound I/O fits on small devices, but there are disadvantages: sound can be annoying, disturb others in the same room, lack persistence, and interfere with speech communication.

The first use of a nonspeech audio interface found in the literature goes back to the 1950s; work in this area continued sporadically until the 1980s. In the early 1980s there was a flurry of activity in connection with nonspeech auditory displays. The introduction to

Auditory Displays [17] provides an excellent introduction to the field, as well as giving the historical background. Researchers have been slow to examine the use of nonspeech audio, though they have been consistently active in two areas: computer music and interfaces for the blind. The computer music area is very active, fueled by money from the entertainment industry. The goal of creating computer music is quite different from that of providing auditory cues or data display and for this reason research in nonspeech auditory display is considered a different discipline from research in computer music. Auditory displays are to music as graphics are to fine art. The primary goal of music is to create an aesthetic experience (though there can be other objectives, such as music designed for theater), while auditory displays are designed to communicate information. Those working in the area of computer music have expertise in digital signal processing and electronics as well as music. Auditory displays of informational messages are not devoid of aesthetics, and a lack of attention to this important attribute of audio will greatly diminish the quality of auditory experiences for users.

Interfaces for the blind have been focused on speech, generally involving reading text either from printed material or on the computer interface. Recently, displays for blind users have also begun to employ nonspeech auditory cues, primarily for the graphic qualities of textual material, such as indentations and new pages. One system for reading mathematics to the blind uses nonspeech audio to describe equations (number of terms, exponents, etc.) before the equation itself is read vocally [18]. Some of the early experiments with auditory displays have included presenting scientific data to blind users, using tones to translate visual attributes, such as color and shape, into auditory parameters.

The incorporation of audio in interfaces requires capturing sound by recording, generating sound synthetically, or using the musical instrument digital interface (MIDI). Recording can be digital or analog. Digital recordings sample the sound waves at discrete moments of time and assign numbers to the sampled values. MIDI is a communications protocol that allows electronic musical instruments to interact with each other—you might compare MIDI to a score rather than a sound file [19]. MIDI has revolutionized the recording industry by allowing many instruments to be centrally controlled like one electronic orchestra. MIDI can send and receive performance information on any of 16 channels. A multitrack sequencer can be added to edit and play back in real time. One reason for the increased activity in audio is that computers are being equipped with a plethora of tools for generating audio.

The composition of audio messages has been studied since the middle 1980s. An audio message is intended to inform listeners of some event in the environment or computer interface. Audio messages constitute abstract information quite different from that of associating sound for the display of data. An example of an audio message is, "The computer is going down." Sequences of structured musical tones called *earcons* are employed for this purpose [20]. The building blocks of earcons are motives (or motifs), which consist of short sequences of tones that are identified by the musical parameters of pitch, rhythm, and timbre. (Audio has many dimensions or parameters [21]—these three are used to distinguish earcons because they are quickly recognized by listeners.) An earcon may be a motive, or combinations of motives may be used as building blocks to form new earcons. Three different principles found in language and music are used to compound motives to create new earcons: (1) combining motives, that is, linking motives one after the other sequentially; (2) transforming motives, that is, transforming a tonal sequence to another tonal sequence by changing its timbre, pitch, or rhythm; and (3) using hierarchical constructions (called inheriting), in which an earcon is constructed from an increasingly complex chain of related motives.

Multiple auditory messages when generated dynamically can present problems in their presentation; this problem is not as critical in the presentation of multiple visual interfaces. Multiple visual presentations can be placed in different locations, and users can examine each independently. Auditory output has severe restrictions on users' ability to understand simultaneous output. (Imagine listening to multiple voices speaking simultaneously.) An algorithm for managing dynamically generated audio messages to arrange auditory output for maximum clarity in the display is available [22].

4.4 RECOGNITION AND DISPLAY OF FACIAL EXPRESSION, GAZE, AND UNENCUMBERED GESTURE

What could be more human in human-to-human communication than facial expression? The recognition of objects in space is generally considered a problem in the area of computer vision. The automated recognition of facial expression will enable computers to recognize the emotions of users. Although thousands of complex expressions varying in complexity and meaning are possible, the goal of most researchers at the present time is to recognize a basic set of facial expressions, such as joy, fear, anger, surprise, puzzlement, and confusion. Some expressions and body gestures are used to facilitate communication, such as nodding to indicate understanding, while others show emotions or fatigue. A 3D, 500-polygon face with a skin-like surface to represent 26 different facial expressions in interfaces in conjunction with voice and text was developed by Sony to provide information about its products [23].

The recognition of facial expression is a complex science using many different technologies from engineering, mathematics, physiology, and psychology. The facial expressions under investigation are those that are caused by brief movements of the facial muscles, temporarily distorting the shape of the eyes, brows, and lips and causing furrows or folds in the skin. The facial action coding system (FACS) developed in 1978 [24] serves as a basis for the analysis of facial expressions. FACS is a system for describing all visually distinguishable facial movements based on *action units* (AU) involved with simple facial motions. The FACS system does not identify emotions, but rather describes the sets of muscles in the face (the action units) that have moved and how they perform certain actions such as raising the brows, smiling, furrowing the skin between the eyebrows, etc. The task is to identify how a subject's face is moving to identify the action units. This is done by using a wireframe model and/or *optical flow* techniques. Optical flow is used on a face in motion while an expression is generated; motion vectors are estimated at a regular array of points on the scene (the face) [25]. The faces in Figure 3 are shown with vectors obtained from optical flow and pixel-wise facial action. These motion vectors must be identified with action units, and these, in turn, are correlated with emotions or other expressions. Note that this analysis is done in a laboratory while the subject is rigidly positioned and illumination is constant. Even then, the problems are enormous. The interested reader may wish to begin with the *Report to the NSF of the Planning Workshop on Facial Expression Understanding* [26], and continue on to more recent publications.

The recognition of unencumbered gestural interactions is another technology heavily dependent upon techniques developed in computer vision. Not only are the hands identified and their shape recognized, but also hand motions are parsed to interpret meanings. The gestures considered in this description are only for communication—gestures are also used for purposes such as manipulating objects or otherwise interacting with the environment. To interpret gestures, we must know (1) the strokes in a gestural sequence, (2) the hand poses (positions) at stroke extrema, and (3) the strokes' dynamic characteristics. Techniques from artificial intelligence, which are based on inductive learning, are used to set up training sequences to obtain rules for the recognition of gestures [27]. Another technology required in the gesture-recognition process is that of moving-edge detectors, in which video data are analyzed as a time-varying image stream, using techniques from computer vision.

Gaze is very important in our interactions with other people. Lack of eye contact, or eye contact at an unexpected moment, can make us feel uncomfortable. Gaze can help reveal our thoughts and show where our concentration lies. Furthermore, eyes move quickly and without conscious effort. The most reliable eyetrackers use corneal reflection of infrared light, which is then displayed and screen or video recorded. Several other methods can be used that require attaching something to the skin or applying contact lenses to users' eyes. Another newer technology can be used for monitoring eye gaze, which is non-intrusive: the use of a camera to detect and track users' eyes. One such method uses skin color to locate the face area [28]. (Wide ranges of colors are recognized as skin color.) After the face is identified, the eye area, as well as the nose and mouth, can be located to determine the orientation of the head. Once the pupils are found, they can be tracked about their current position by finding the darkest pixel in a small search window and using a neural net for the identification of eye gaze. The system currently requires users' head positions be relatively stable.

Figure 3. Pixel-wise tracking of AU4 (the brows lowered); AU1+4 (inner part of the brow raised and drawn together), and AU1+2 (entire brow raised). Photos courtesy of James Lien.

Moving from the subject of recognition of unencumbered gesture to displays of gestures as computer graphics, we see that an understanding of the semantics of gesture is required, but now the technology has shifted to computer graphics. So far, gestural displays are used primarily for communicating with the deaf, but the creation of animated figures in virtual reality would also use gestural displays. A remarkable display of a free-standing finger-spelling hand to feel and interpret the motion and position of the hand was constructed for the blind and deaf [29].

4.5 INTERFACE AGENTS

One of the genuine innovations in interface technology in the past five years has been the notion of agents. *Software agents* are computer programs that act on behalf of users to perform routine, tedious, and time-consuming tasks. They are also called *autonomous agents* and *intelligent agents*. Software agents know the individual user's preferences and interests; for this very reason, they are proactive and can take the initiative. Another characteristic of agents is that they are continuously running while users go about and do other things. To paraphrase Maes [30]: Our computer environments are getting too complex, and users are from a broad spectrum of society, while the number of tasks to handle are increasing. In former days, the only information on computers was put there by users. Our modern networked computers have changed this situation radically. Consider how many times you have changed your software versions recently. Agents allow the delegation of small tasks to pieces of software. Agents have been constructed as personal filters to help users determine their choice of entertainment, whether topics are on the web that they may want to see, if they have answered their e-mail, and so on.

You may be wondering how these miraculous pieces of software can be developed. One can personalize a software agent by task-specific rules [31]. The personal agent needs to know its users' goals, habits, and preferences. For example, one could include the rule: When the price of XYZ stock falls below $30, buy 100 shares. When the evaluation of the rule is true, the agent acts on users' behalf. Creation of rules for personal agents can be simplified by using a rule template or editor to introduce new rules. Creating rules still entails a certain amount of effort on the part of users. Also, users must remove rules that are no longer current. There are some experimental systems that use agents that learn rules by watching user behavior and detecting patterns [32].

Most agents are not personified or anthropomorphized by representations of humans, animals, or cartoon characters; they work behind the scenes to obtain information and perform their tasks. Because this is an article on interactive multimedia interfaces, however, something should be said about visible representations of agents in the form of humans or creatures. Personified agents have been called *interface agents,* although the terminology has not been standardized. Some of the most interesting work done on interface agents is not new [33]. Interface agents appear in *The Americana Series: A CD-ROM Sampler of United States History*. The guides are a set of prototypical characters, such as settlers, hunters, native Americans, etc., drawn from the period of 1800 to 1850, that appear in the interface to lead users through the historical material with their particular points of view. The guides appear alternately as icons, graphic images with text, and characters represented on video. The guides assume various attitudes while users are browsing for information. When the content is of great interest to guides, they become excited and wave their hands; when the material is of little interest to them, they start doing other things; and when the content is of no interest to them, they fall asleep. Of course, the guides are implemented as hyperlinks to information that is relevant to them. The importance of the information to the guide is judged by the length of the hyperlink. Users can view the individual guides in a series of video clips that makes use of narratives (stories) to emphasize the temporal flow of events. Interface agents must be used with great caution because they can be annoying or insulting to the intelligence.

In order to prevent the suspicion that might arise from the use of characters in an interface, the guides are introduced as storytellers or (stage) actors that are playing the role of guides. The example above is given as an illustration of an excellent use of interface agents. The series incorporates guides into the interface to simplify navigation through a confusing compendium of bits and pieces of American history.

4.6 OTHER TECHNOLOGIES FOR INTERACTIVE INTERFACES

One can hardly understand multimedia interfaces without understanding the role of graphics, animation, and video in creating interfaces. The problems and uses of graphics, animation, and video are presented elsewhere in this book. These are media that have been studied largely for their use in presentations rather than in interactive systems. The use of highly modeled life-like images cannot be done in real time. This problem faces those creating virtual realities, where the quality of images degrades as limits of time constraints on generating images increase. As computers become faster, the problems of creating realism in real time decrease. The difficulty of using video in interactive systems is the rapid retrieval of segments that are needed for constructing stories or other informational displays in real time. The subject of indexing video for rapid retrieval is an interesting technology that is now being widely studied. Material on this topic can be found in other chapters of this book.

5. INTEGRATING MEDIA AND MODALITIES

When people communicate under ordinary circumstances, they speak, gesture, use facial expressions, and gaze. Body language and prosody can reveal hidden meanings while people are communicating with others. Studying the gestural prosody of children when doing arithmetic shows some of these meanings [34]. Irregular writing or long delays in computing answers may indicate problems that a teacher may spot immediately, but computers that only recognize numbers and not gestural prosody may not detect such problems. The goal of today's multimedia/multimodal systems is to allow users the same freedom of expression in communicating with a computer as with another person.

In Section 4 above, we briefly summarized a number of technologies that recognize human modalities and enable users to tap into multiple modalities. These multimodal inputs, as described above, are not integrated. That is, voice and gesture inputs are parsed separately, so that if a voice is saying, "move this red square over here" and a gesture points at a specific location, there is no connection between the spoken command and the location designated by pointing.

We now examine how multimodal inputs from different modalities can be integrated into one expression so that the system understands that the red square is to be moved to the location indicated by the voice and the gesture. As the number of modalities increases, the problem of matching pieces of recognized fragments into one expression grows in complexity.

5.1 STEPS IN INTEGRATING MULTIMODAL INPUTS FROM DIFFERENT MODALITIES INTO ONE EXPRESSION

Step 1: Recognizing input streams from different modalities

In all systems that integrate modalities, there are several steps that the recognition process must go through. The first is the recognition of the expression fragments that are limited to each modality, as in the example of "paint this circle red and put it here." A gesture is made that draws a circle-like object for users. The speech-recognition system now must recognize the words before a meaning is found. The techniques described above for speech recognition are used for identifying words. This most likely results in tokens obtained by the use of hidden Markov models, neural nets, grammars, etc. Similarly, a location indicated by the gesture must be recognized. The inexact nature of pen inputs may also require recognition through the use of a neural net or hidden Markov model. The gesture-recognition process also yields tokens. For this task, some researchers use agents: programs that possess a specific, well-defined competence. Peripheral agents or "micro agents" [35] can be used for recognizing specific input streams. Hierarchies of agents may be organized to perform successively more complex tasks.

Step 2: Integrating multiple expression fragments

To make sense of a very complex process, the material below is oversimplified to reveal the major steps in the integration process. The fragments (tokens) obtained from different input streams must now be integrated to yield a meaningful expression. The problem is to combine the meaning contributed from each of these fragments into a meaningful whole. Often *frames* are used to hold the results of the integration. Frames have been used throughout the artificial intelligence literature. Frames have *slots* that hold information about the expression. Some slots may hold spatial information, while others hold categorical information—an object's attributes (red, round, noisy, etc.). Researchers may complete this integration either by using slots for each input stream and then combining them, or by filling slots directly as information is received and resolving differences as more information is received. As you can well imagine, the time intervals of incoming input streams may make a difference in the interpretation of an expression. For this reason, input streams are usually time-stamped.

Three frame-based systems of integration are PAC-Amodeus [36], Quickset [37], and Jeanie [38]. The PAC-Amodeus platform uses the concept of *fusion* for multimodal integration. It uses three levels of fusion: lexical, syntactic, and semantic. Quickset uses the notion of *unification*: an operation determines the consistency of two pieces of partial information; if they are consistent, it combines them into a single expression. The multimodal interpreter for Jeanie creates frames for each type of input stream, then merges the frames. Context information is retained across input events by merging it with previous interpretation frames.

The interpretation of sequences of tokens from multimodal input streams may be accomplished by parsing; that is, a grammar may be used to describe the expression's syntax. One approach [39] is to employ a grammar in which some tokens are constructed from both word- and gesture-yielding compound tokens. The use of grammars in interpreting multimodal expressions has many advantages. The construction and analysis of language generation and parsing based on grammars is thoroughly understood and forms the foundation of both natural-language understanding and programming languages. The integration of tokens obtained from multiple input streams can be understood from the point of view of when tokens are merged [40]. Tokens can be merged or sequenced at the pre-syntactic, syntactic, or semantic levels.

Another very different technique for merging multiple modalities is to merge them during execution, when speech can be added to an existing graphical user interface. In this method, the processing of inputs, say by a pen, is suspended when users begin an utterance. After the utterance is recognized and interpreted, the pen movements that were made during the utterance are processed retroactively.

6.   SOFTWARE ENGINEERING MULTIMEDIA USER INTERFACES

We have seen that new technologies will enable user interfaces to be capable of advanced forms of communication with humans. A speech-recognition engine may perform with 99% accuracy and a pen input system may also work with remarkable accuracy, but in spite of these advances, how many times have we found ourselves "stuck" in some sequence of operations—unable to terminate a session or move to another operation? New interfaces for navigation systems in automobiles usually require following a map—a dangerous operation for someone driving a car! To be effective, interfaces must be *usable,* which may be characterized by five user-oriented characteristics [41]:

- Ease of learning.
- High speed of user task performance.
- Low user error rate.
- Subjective user satisfaction.
- User retention over time.

Software engineering for multimedia interfaces has the same general methodology as software engineering for any other type of user interface. There is a very large body of literature on the subject of software engineering, quality assurance, and usability. The approach taken here can be found in Hix and Hartson [42]. Experts in software engineering have found that understanding user interactions is neither obvious nor intuitive. Human beings are not predictable in the same sense that chemical reactions are; they continually surprise interface designers by the way they interact with interfaces. The only way to anticipate users' actions is to perform early and continuous empirical testing in which users perform representative tasks.

The need for effective methods for software engineering was realized when the General Accounting Office in 1979 discovered that only 2% of the software contracted for the U.S. government (in dollars) could be used as delivered, another 3% could be used only after extensive reworking, and the other 95% could not be used at all, either because the software did not work or the requirements had changed by the time the software was completed [43]. In 1978 these costs already ran in the hundreds of millions of dollars.

Government and industry began to impose rules and regulations for contracted software to follow software engineering guidelines. A software life cycle was developed, called the Waterfall Method, that moved from step to step in the development process, moving from feasibility, requirements, high-level design, detailed design, coding, unit testing, integration and testing, to maintenance. It made a lot of sense to those searching for a systematic approach to software development. After all, you can't build a house until you have the blueprints. The problem was that the requirements of large and complex systems required many hundreds of pages to document. The developers had little idea of what the final result would be like until the system was realized. The situation was particularly unmanageable with user interfaces. People are unpredictable.

In the late 1980s, two of the techniques developed to modify the inflexible waterfall method were prototyping and a spiral model of software development [44]. The 1990s brought us the concept of user-centered design [45], which is that user interfaces must be designed and developed with repeated interaction with users. User interfaces have their own development cycle. An interesting paradigm shift was accomplished in ten years. Software engineering the user interface was recognized to depend upon user interactions—hence, the examination of the way people interact with machines, rather than an abstract method dependent upon algorithms. We have moved from math and engineering to the social sciences to provide a systematic method for designing and testing user interfaces. A complex user interface requires the skills and expertise of designers, software developers, computer scientists, social scientists, computer engineers, artists, and application specialists.

The *Star life cycle* puts usability evaluation at the center of development activities [42]. There are four points of the star: (1) systems/task/functional user analyses, (2) requirements/usability specifications, (3) design and design representation, and (4) rapid prototyping. The points of the star are not connected or ordered in sequence. Development can be either top down or bottom up and move from any point of the star to any other point, but it always returns to the center of the star to evaluate the usability of the interface. Figure 4 shows the Star life cycle, which occurs within the shaded area.

The multimedia/multimodal interface places even more complex demands upon designers. Early stages of user and task analyses require greater examination than if the interface is a GUI. Inexact inputs, such as speech or handwriting, have their own difficulties that require the incorporation of techniques to handle errors to a much greater extent than in the case of GUIs. As an example, extensive testing was done to examine user *disfluencies*, that is, interruptions in the smooth flow of an otherwise coherent sentence by users [46]. The investigators set up Wizard of Oz experiments, one of which is shown in Figure 5. (A Wizard of Oz experiment provides a simulation of an interface, which is actually operated by a human rather than a computer.) The objective is to save hours of prototyping software and let a simulation mimic the role of the computer for pen and voice inputs for interactions with maps. The experiments showed that the resulting system should incorporate the use of templates to reduce errors caused by disfluencies.

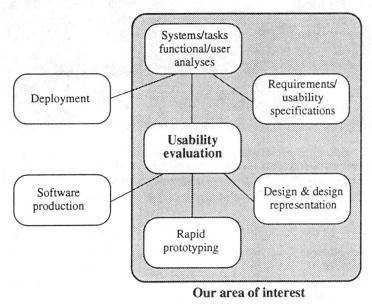

Figure 4. The Star life-cycle for interface development.

7. EXAMPLES OF MULTIMEDIA USER INTERFACES

Interfaces for multimedia/multimodal interactions are best given by examples. The examples cited below show both the diversity of interfaces and the diversity of users now driving our contemporary computing needs. A great deal of work continues with interfaces for scientific visualization, office business applications, programmers, and other applications that use workstations and window-type environments.

7.1 INTERFACES FOR PEOPLE WITH SPECIAL NEEDS

In a survey made in 1989 by the U.S. National Center for Health Statistics, more than 49-million people identified themselves as having a degree of activity limitation because of injury or chronic illness [47]. This number does not include the institutionalized or mentally ill. Statistics on disabilities gathered in Germany show that about 8% of the population is disabled. When those people who cannot read because they have not learned the language or are not sufficiently educated are added, this number rises. Children also are part of this population. They cannot read well until they are about eight years old, but a large portion of our computer software is for children. As computers enter our schools and replace textbooks, we cannot take lightly the problem of shaping computers to children's needs. The aging constitute an increasingly large part of our population, and with aging we find impairments arising in virtually all sensory perceptions and motor activities. People with some kind of limitations on the use of computers range from 20% to 30%. Accommodating those who must make adjustments in their computer use because of disabilities is termed *assistive technology*.

Figure 5. A Wizard-of-Oz experiment conducted at the Oregon Graduate Institute for a pen and voice system design. A test subject selects real estate during a data collection session (right panel), and a programmer assistant provides simulated system response (left panel). Photos courtesy of Sharon Oviatt.

Assistive computer technology is almost entirely multimedia. One modality must often replace another for users who cannot fully use all of their modalities. For example, screen readers are voice output systems that read textual material to those who either cannot see the screen or are unable to read the screen because of dyslexia or another type of inability to read. Specialized interfaces for users with specific disabilities are impractical. We must learn to construct interfaces that may be configured to accommodate different users and environments. Some of these problems are discussed in *Ensuring Access for People with Disabilities to the National Information Infrastructure and Multimedia Computing* [47]. Each limitation in a user's disability may be seen as a limitation on an environment; hence, flexible interfaces are also of benefit to users who are not challenged by disabilities. One solution to provide flexible assignments of information to particular output modalities is a design based on *metawidgets* [48]—interface objects that can shift their representations from one modality to another. Each metawidget contains a repertoire of representations in various sensory modalities (or combinations thereof) and methods for selecting among them. By accounting for user preferences and relevant extra- and intra-system factors, the selection mechanism can determine the optimal representation when the metawidget is displayed. Several prototype systems have been developed using these concepts [7].

Children provide entirely different problems for interface developers. Children like audio, vivid colors, and fantasy, and they have short attention spans. There are limitations on their coordination, their ability to reason and, of course, children under eight years old may not read well. In the next decade we will see computers replacing text books in elementary schools, so the problem of interfaces for children goes beyond computer "baby-sitting" when children are at home. It is recognized that there are three major characteristics that make intrinsically motivating instructional environments [49]: (1) challenge without frustration— move from simple to more complex levels; (2) use appealing fantasies; and (3) encourage exploration and curiosity. Children's software has been available only for the same computer hardware used by adults, perhaps with Nintendo controllers as an exception. Clearly this is an area that needs a great deal of research.

7.2 OFFICE AND HOME ENVIRONMENTS

Home automation is an emerging field for computer research. Major computer companies have created projects to bring various home automation devices to the market. Sensors can check light, temperature, moisture, sound, weight, pollutants, presence of motion, location of objects, and, more generally, detectable changes in the status of the environment. The sensor-acquired information is sent to a control device that can alter the status (as with internal home temperature) or simply inform users of the conditions (as with the external temperature). The more advanced research in interfaces for home automation systems uses the technology of computer vision, such as facial recognition and systems for tracking people [50].

Information sensed from the environment includes:

- Inside conditions: temperature, lights, appliances on/off, audio, intercom, the presence of people in particular rooms.
- Outside conditions: temperature, pollen count, smog, rain, moisture in the garden, pool conditions, external lights.
- Security: person(s) at the door, baby monitor, windows or doors open/closed, car entering/leaving the garage.
- Scheduling devices: interactive timers, home entertainment, calendars, and bulletin boards.

The most advanced homes may have hundreds of sensors linked to control devices that display their state. A central display is seen on a computer terminal, while panels of buttons and lights in locations throughout the home indicate the status of the rooms in which they are located. These devices can be difficult to understand and to set. Although home automation controllers are ingenious, little thought has gone into their communication and interaction with users.

Both speech and nonspeech audio communication may be used to inform inhabitants of the status of control devices [51]. Some sounds are ambient (background) sounds; others notify or are urgent. The nonspeech sounds are based on *earcons*, sequences of tones developed for auditory cues. (See Section 4.3 above.) Another approach to communication with the environment is *auras* [52]. Audio auras are based on three known technologies: active badges, distributed systems, and digital audio delivered via portable wireless headphones. As users walk through a building, active badges trigger audio auras. These auras may take the form of spoken messages or auditory cues. An example is an office whose entrance has information on whether individuals are in or, if not, how long they have been out.

7.3 INTERFACES FOR MOBILE COMPUTING AND WEARABLE COMPUTERS

We are entering a new stage in computer technology in which a personal digital assistant (PDA) can connect to a myriad of services at any time. Multimedia, interactivity, and mobile communications are merging to form a new type of computer environment. PDAs will not only be our personal notebooks; they will be our telephones, and they can transmit our e-mail and search web pages. PDAs have some of these capabilities now, and the next few years will see the technology evolving rapidly. These devices must be usable by a large part of the population, so the interfaces are very important. The success or failure of any particular PDA will depend largely upon its usability.

Why should users wear computers? In the section on home and office environments, we saw that an environment can anticipate the needs of the people who work or reside in that space. We now move into a computer environment in which computers see what users see, hear what users hear, feel what users feel, and have access to the locations of users and to the information they may need at any time. The first wearable computers made their wearers appear grotesque—boxes the size of suitcases were attached to users' backs, while strange projections came from hats and helmets. The scene has changed considerably. Wearable computers are becoming comfortable and convenient [53]. Displays are located in standard prescription eyeglasses and keyboards in belts, and computers are sewn into jackets, as shown in Figure 6. Seven-mm cameras can be placed in glasses so that cameras see what wearers see, and messages can be overlaid through the use of heads-up displays. Voice may be a better mode of communication for wearable computers, when privacy is not an issue. Whenever an object can be uniquely identified, either through computer vision and physical location or other means such as radio frequency identification tags, computation can be assigned to that object via proxy by the wearable computer.

There are already applications of wearable computers for the disabled, such as the recognition of American Sign Language aimed at deaf individuals by cameras in the hat. Applications for the visually impaired are even more promising; they include guidance systems and voice instructions built right into users' clothing. The Media Lab at MIT is looking at inputs such as using wearers' fingers in space as a mouse, tracking users' feet and lips, and using ambient light and head orientation clues. The potential for this technology is very great, but the applications are not entirely obvious as with all very new inventions. One application may be for wearable computers to interact with home and office computers. A limitation on the home automation environment is that sensing devices do not know the identity of the individual they are tracking. A wearable computer would be an easier technology to implement than face recognition—it assumes the role of an active badge, but is considerably more powerful when communicating with the environment.

Figure 6. The M.I.T. Media Lab wearable computer jacket. Photo by Sam Ogden.

7.4 THE WORLD-WIDE WEB

It has been speculated that the web may some day be our only interface [30]. James Foley says, "In 10 years, by far the most prevalent interfaces will be web-centric. The growth of the web will further accelerate both in users and in ubiquity. Not only will we have the obvious GUI-style web interface of today's browsers and tomorrow's integrated desktop/file/system/browser, but we will have interfaces that have been scaled, up and down, to accommodate different bandwidths (from high-speed video on demand to low-speed cellular) and different sizes (from wrist-watch/pager size to wall size). But, beyond that, the web will be everywhere and so too will our interfaces . . . . many more of the interfaces will be of the ubiquitous, imbedded, mobile appliance style as opposed to the explicit GUI style. Multimodal inputs (voice, vision-recognized gestures) and outputs will play more significant roles." [2]

This quotation reveals the importance that leading computer scientists give to the web in our future computing environments. This importance cannot be overestimated. But what is the role of the web now and to the millions of users who interact with it on a daily basis? The primary use for the web at present is to search for, retrieve, and display information—this is a far cry from being a universal interface. The applications to commerce and education are enormous, but we still require word processors, spreadsheets, programming environments, and many other software tools. The web has not produced effective collaborative tools as of this date. The types of interaction on the web are very limited—typing, clicking, and scrolling still constitute the main forms of interaction. Before we examine what is being done to enlarge the functionality of the web, let us examine the generations of the web interface.

The first generation of interfaces for the web depended upon HyperText Markup Language (HTML). Documents in HTML are in the stripped-down ASCII format, and they are marked with *tags,* which are used by browsers for structural information about such things as paragraphs, pages, spacing, etc. (Anyone who has worked with an editor such as LaTex or nroff has used tags.) There is very little format control using HTML, which was basically meant to be used with black-and-white monitors and low-resolution color displays. Web browsers read HTML tags and format the interface. (Unfortunately, different browsers have different appearances.) The design of web pages may be followed in terms of generations [54]. Most first-generation web pages are edge-to-edge text with a scanned picture on the top.

The second generation of web sites began with extensions to Netscape in 1995. More graphics, blinking, and tiled images could now be included. Third-generation sites have sophisticated graphics, audio, and animation. Java and application program interfaces (APIs) provide an object-oriented, independent platform for creating interactive programs that execute in the context of a web browser (*applets*) delivered via the web. The Java programming environment offers capabilities for much more powerful web interfaces, but requires programming skills. Development environments are now available for both novice users and professional designers. Commercial sites compete for excitement to hold potential customers. This is done through animation, color, sound, and beautiful graphics.

In 1992, the *Iris Inventor* 3D toolkit was released by Silicon Graphics, Inc., which set the foundation for a 3D interchange format—the 3D (three-dimension) version of HTML, the format used for the 2D version on the web. Several years later this evolved into the virtual-reality modeling language (VRML 1.0—currently VRML 2.0); it enables users to move through their interfaces as if they were moving through 3D space [55]. (It should be noted that 3D space here does not refer to stereoscopic vision as in head-mounted displays of virtual reality.) Basically, VRML defines most of the commonly used semantics found in today's 3D applications. These may include hierarchical transformations, light sources, viewpoints, geometry, animation, fog, material properties, and texture mapping. One advantage of VRML 2.0 is that it is being designed so it is *composable* and *scaleable*—it is easy to cut and paste from several VRML documents to create a new document, and VRML worlds are being designed to scale with network performance from the 14.4-K modems to multigigabit connections we may expect to have in the future as well as with both powerful and inexpensive machines. (There are still unresolved problems in connection with scalability.) A major problem for most users is having sufficient bandwidth to download their pages quickly. Until users have greater bandwidth, many of the improvements discussed here remain academic.

Multimodal components for the web are being developed at the Carnegie Mellon Interactive Systems laboratories, which are conducting speech, gesture, face-tracking, and handwriting research for use on the web. The Carnegie Mellon researchers created a Java front end to communicate with a multimodal server [56]. Processing multimodal inputs requires a lot of computing power and a lot of space. Also, expertise is required to set up and maintain multimodal interfaces, and different platforms require different software support. The incorporation of multimodal inputs and collaborative tools to the web will change the way the web is used and bring us a step closer to the predictions of James Foley.

8. CONCLUDING REMARKS

In the introduction, three characteristics were given of interactive computer-human interfaces as they are evolving in the commercial world and research labs: (1) human-like computer-user interactions, (2) diversity of functionality, and (3) ubiquity. Although the GUI remains a staple of the office and engineering computing environment, a new world of computing is emerging around us and is moving computers into the hands of nearly everyone, at any time, and any place for very diverse applications. These new computers have interfaces that are small and portable or built into the environment. To make them easily accessible to a broad set of users of all ages and educational backgrounds, as well as those with disabilities, they must be usable, that is, easy to learn and use, reliable, with low error rates. Pens, voices, gestures, and sensors are the primary sources of inputs to this new type of computer. With portable computers, outputs are confined to small screens or audio. *Docking* enables a small computer to metamorphize into a larger machine; however, such large machines may not always be available to a moving user. The technologies of wearable computers and recognition of facial expression are emerging from the research laboratories and will soon be part of interfaces on commercial products. The integration of multimodal inputs is still in the early stages of development, and true integration methods are still being studied in the research laboratories.

Voice and nonspeech audio are important methods of output in the design of small computers, which have little or no screen space available. A new twist to interface displays is the introduction of interface agents, which assist users in navigating their systems. Agents can either work undercover, displaying only the results of their interactions, or they can be represented as figures on screens. Human figures must be treated with caution because anthropomorphism can be annoying and misleading. Merging of video, audio, graphics, and text are largely accomplished by authoring systems, covered in another chapter in this book.

Finally, Section 7.4 touches on interfaces for the web. The web does have a multimedia display based on hypermedia, but web technology is evolving so fast that we cannot properly identify its characteristics. At present, the web is used primarily for searching for and communicating with others. Within the short lifetime of the web, we have seen four or more generations of multimedia interface design. Now web interfaces use graphics, audio, video, and animation. An exciting new type of interface on web interfaces is 3D, where the user can move interactively through a 3D scene. The web's interactive capability is very limited at present; for example, it is not well suited for collaboration, but research laboratories are carrying on the work of giving the web full interactive capabilities.

ACKNOWLEDGMENTS

Meera M. Blattner is also with the Department of Biomathematics, M.D. Anderson Cancer Research Hospital, University of Texas Medical Center, Houston.

This work was performed with partial support of NSF Grant DUE-96-18688 and under the auspices of the U.S. Department of Energy by Lawrence Livermore National Laboratory under Contract No. W-7405-Eng-48.

REFERENCES

1. Blattner, M.M., "In Our Image: Interface Design in the 90's," *IEEE Multimedia,* 1(1), 15–26, 1994.
2. Jacob, R.J.K. and Feiner, S.K., "UIST '007: Where will we be ten years from now?" Excerpt from position statement by J.D. Foley. *Proceeding of the ACM Symposium on User Interface Software and Technology,* Banff, Canada, 115–118, October 14-17, 1997.
3. Miller, L.H. and Johnson, J., "The Xerox Star: An Influential User Interface Design," 70–100, *Human-Computer Interface Design* (Rudiseill, Lewis, Polson, and McKay, Eds.), Morgan Kaufmann Publishers, Inc., San Francisco, CA, 1995.
4. Shneiderman, B. "Direct manipulation: A step beyond programming languages," *IEEE Computer,* 16(8), 57–69, 1983.
5. Hodges, M.E. and Sasnett, R.M., *Multimedia Computing: Case Studies from MIT Project Athena,* Addison-Wesley Publishing Co., Reading, MA, 1993.
6. Lusted, H.H. and Knapp, R.B., "Controlling Computers Through Neural Signals," *Scientific American,* October 1996.
7. Blattner, M.M. and Glinert, E.P., "Multimodal Integration," *IEEE Multimedia,* 4(3), IEEE Press, 14–24, 1996.
8. Want, R., Hopper, A., Falcao, V., and Gibbons, J., "Active Badge Location System," *ACM Transactions on Information Systems,* 10(1), 91–102, 1992.
9. Bernsen, N.O., "The Structure of the Design Space," *in Computers, Communication and Usability: Design Issues, Research, and Methods for Integrated Servers* (Byerly, Bernard, and May, Eds.), North Holland, Amsterdam, 221–244, 1993.
10. Card, S.K., Mackinlay, J.D., and Robertson, G.G., "The Design Space of Input Devices," *Multimedia Interface Design* (Blattner and Dannenberg, Eds.), ACM Press and Addison-Wesley, Reading, MA, 217–232, 1992.
11. Kay, A. and Goldberg, A. "Personal dynamic media," *IEEE Computer,* 10(3), 31–41, March 1977.
12. Carr, R. and Shafer, D., *The Power of Pen Point,* Addison-Wesley Publishing Co., Reading, MA, 1991.
13. Rae-Dupree, J., "PalmPilot hands industry a big lesson," *The Philadelphia Inquirer,* December 4, 1997.
14. Meyer, A., "Pen Computing: A Technology Overview and a Vision," *ACM SIGCHI bulletin,* July 1995. (Also on the Web.)
15. Goldberg, D. and Goodison, A., "Stylus user interfaces for manipulating text," *ACM User Interface Systems and Technology (UIST) '91,* Monterey, CA., 127–135, 1991.
16. Goldberg, D. and Richardson, C., "Touch-Typing With a Stylus," *INTERCH'93 Conference Proceedings,* Amsterdam, 80–87, 1993.
17. Kramer, G., Ed. *Auditory Displays,* Addison-Wesley Santa Fe Institute Series, Reading, MA, 1994.
18. Stevens, R.D., Brewster, S.A., Wright, P.C., and Edwards, A.D.N., *Proceeding of the 2nd International Conference on Auditory Display,* Santa Fe, NM, 1994.
19. *MIDI—Musical Instrument Digital Interface, Detailed Specification,* The International MIDI Association, 5316 W. 57th St., Los Angeles, CA, 1988. Also see the MIDI web site: http://www.eeb.ele.tue.nl/midi/index.html
20. Blattner, M.M., Sumikawa, D.A., and Greenberg, R.M., "Earcons and Icons: Their Structure and Common Design Principles," *Human-Computer Inter.,* 4(1), 11–44, 1989.
21. Cohen, M. and Wenzel, E.M., "The Design of Multidimensional Sound Interfaces," *Virtual Environments and Advanced Interface Design* (Barfield and Furness, Eds.), Oxford University Press, 1995. Also available as Tech. Report 95-1-004, University of Aizu, Japan.
22. Papp III, A.L., *The Presentation of Dynamically Overlapping Auditory Messages in User Interfaces,* Ph.D. dissertation, University of California, Davis; also appeared as Lawrence Livermore National Laboratory Technical Report UCRL-LR-128454, 1997.
23. Takeuchi, A. and Nagao, K., "Communicative Facial Displays as a New Conversational Modality," *Proc. ACM InterCHI 93, Amsterdam,* ACM Press, New York, 187–193, 1993.

24. Ekman, P. and Friesen, W.V., *Facial action coding system: A technique for the measurement of facial movement*, Consulting Psychologists Press, Palo Alto, CA, 1978.
25. Lien, J.J., Zlochower, A.J., Cohen, J.F., Li, C.C., and Kanade, T., "Automatically Recognizing Facial Expression in the Spatio-Temporal Domain," *Workshop on Perceptual User Interfaces*, Banff, Alberta, Canada, 94–97, Oct. 19-21, 1997.
26. Ekman, P., Huang, T.S., and Sejnowski, T.J., *Final Report to NSF of the Planning Workshop on Facial Expression*, 1992.
27. Quek, F.K.H., "Unencumbered Gestural Interaction," *IEEE Multimedia*, 4(3), 36–47, 1996.
28. Stiefelhagen, R., Yang, J., and Waibel, A., "Tracking Eyes and Monitoring Eye-Gaze," *Workshop on Perceptual User Interfaces*, Banff, Alberta, Canada, 98–100, October 19-21, 1997.
29. Jaffe, D.L., "An Overview of Programs and Projects at the Rehabilitation Research and Development Center," *ACM ASSETS '94*, Marina Del Rey, CA, 69–76, October 31-November 1, 1994.
30. Shneiderman, B. and Maes, P., "Direct Manipulation vs Interface Agents," *Interactions*, 4(6), 42–61, November–December 1997.
31. Terveen, L.G. and Murray, L.T., "Helping Users Program Their Personal Agents," *Proceedings of ACM CHI '96, ACM Conference on Human Factors in Computing Systems*, ACM Press, 355–361, April 13-18, 1996.
32. Maes, P., "Agents that Reduce Work and Information Overload," *Communications of the ACM*, 37(7), 55–67, 1994.
33. Laurel, B., Oren, T., and Don, A., "Issues in Multimedia Interface Design: Media Integration and Interface Agents," *Proc. of ACM CHI '90*, Seattle, Wash., ACM Press, 133–139, April 1990.
34. Kimura, T.D., "A Pen-Based Prosodic User Interface for Schoolchildren," *IEEE Multimedia*, 3(4), 48–55, Winter 1996.
35. Cohen, P.R., Cheyer, A., and Wang, M., "An Open Agent Architecture," in *Software Agents—AAAI Spring Symposium*, AAAI Press, Menlo Park, CA, 1–8, 1994.
36. Nigay, L. and Coutaz, J.A., "Generic Platform for Addressing the Multimodal Challenge," *Proc. 1993 ACM Conference on Human Factors in Computer Systems (INTERCHI 93)*, ACM Press, New York, 98–105, 1995.
37. Johnston, M., Cohen, P.R., McGee, D., Oviatt, S.L., Pittman, J.A., and Smith, I., "Unification-based multimodal integration," *Proceedings of the 35th Annual Meeting of the Association for Computational Linguistics*, Madrid, Spain, 1997.
38. Vo, M.T. and Wood, C., "Building an Application Framework for Speech and Pen Input Integration in Multimodal Learning Interfaces," *Proc. of IEEE Inter. Conference on Acoustics, Speech, and Signal Processing*, Atlanta, GA, May 1996.
39. Bellik, Y. and Teil, D. "A multimodal dialogue controller for multimodal user interface management system application: a multimodal window manager," *Proceedings of INTERCHI '93*, ACM Conference on Human-Computer Interaction, Amsterdam, 93–94, April 24-29, 1993.
40. Milota, A., "New Uses of Pen Interaction for Multimodal Interfaces," an unpublished document prepared as partial requirements for a qualifying exam at the University of California at Davis, 1997.
41. Shneiderman, B., *Designing the User Interface*, Addison-Wesley, Reading, MA, 1992.
42. Hix, D. and Hartson, H. R., *Developing User Interfaces*, John Wiley & Sons, Inc., New York, 1993.
43. General Accounting Office, Report to The Congress, Contracting for Computer Software Development—Serious Problems Require Management Attention to Avoid Wasting Additional Millions, November 1979. Available in: IEEE Tutorial: *Software Configuration Management*, IEEE Press, 322–410, 1980.
44. Boehm, B.W., "A Spiral Model of Software Development and Enhancement," *ACM SIGSOFT Software Engineering Notes*, 11(4), 14–24, August 1986.
45. Norman, D.A. and Draper, S.W., *User Centered Design*, Lawrence Erlbaum Associates, Hillsdate, NJ, 1986.

46. Oviatt, S., "User-center modeling for spoken language and multimodal interfaces," *IEEE Multimedia*, 3(4), 26–35, Winter 1996.
47. Glinert, E.P., *Ensuring Access for People with Disabilities to the National Information Infrastructure and Multimedia Computing*, Rensselaer Polytechnic Institute, Troy, NY, 12180-3590, Report No. 96-16, 1996.
48. Glinert, E.P. and Blattner, M.M., "Programming the Multimodal Interface," *Proceedings of ACM Multimedia '93*, Anaheim, CA, 189–198, August 1-3, 1993.
49. Malone, T.W., "Toward a Theory of Intrinsically Motivating Instruction," *Cognitive Science 4*, 333–369, 1981.
50. Wren, C., Azarbayejani, A., Darrell, T., and Pentland, A., "Pfinder: Real-Time Tracking of the Human Body," *IEEE Transactions on Pattern Analysis and Machine Intelligence*, 19(7), 780–785, 1997.
51. Blattner, M., "Responsive Environments," *Workshop on Perceptual User Interfaces*, Banff, Alberta, Canada, 7–9, October 19-21, 1997.
52. Mynatt, E.D., Back, M., Want, R., and Fredrick, R., "Audio Aura: Light-Weight Audio Augmented Reality," *Proceeding of the ACM Symposium on User Interface Software and Technology (UIST)*, Banff, Canada, 211–212, October 14-17, 1997.
53. Starmer, T., and Pentland, A., "First Person Perceptual User Interfaces through Wearable Computing," *Workshop on Perceptual User Interfaces*, Banff, Alberta, Canada, 107–109, October 19-21, 1997.
54. Seigel, D., *Creating Killer Web Sites*, Hayden Books, Indianapolis, IN, 1996.
55. Carey, R. and Bell, G., *The Annotated VRML 97 2.0 Reference Manual*, Addison-Wesley Longman, Reading, MA, 1997.
56. Jing, X., Yang, J., Vo, M., T., and Waibel, A., "Java Front-end for Web-based Multimodal Human-Computer Interaction," *Workshop on Perceptual User Interfaces*, Banff, Alberta, Canada, 78–81, Oct. 19-21, 1997.

7

DIGITAL AUDIO PRESENTATION AND COMPRESSION

Raymond Westwater
Future Ware
475 Wall Street
Princeton, New Jersey 08540
drray@futureware.com

1.	**INTRODUCTION**	136
2.	**REPRESENTATION OF UNCOMPRESSED AUDIO – PCM**	136
3.	**AUDIO COMPRESSION TECHNIQUES**	139
	3.1 LOGARITHMIC CODING	139
	3.2 DIFFERENTIAL PCM COMPRESSION	140
	3.3 LINEAR PREDICTIVE CODING	143
	3.4 TRANSFORM-BASED AUDIO COMPRESSION	144
4.	**CONCLUSIONS**	147
	REFERENCES	147

Abstract. This overview describes the current state of the audio compression art, emphasizing the trade-off between voice-only and music compression. The exposition begins with an introduction to the basics of representing digital audio (pulse code modulation), featuring an introduction to the mathematics of compression. Voice-specific compression includes a discussion of Differential Pulse Code Modulation, Adaptive Differential Pulse Code Modulation, and Linear Predictive Coding. General music compression includes a description of the human auditory model and an overview of wavelet and Discrete Cosine transforms. Finally, a comparison of the techniques is presented.

1. INTRODUCTION

Audio compression has been the subject of continuous research for over thirty years – and remains an important issue in modern multimedia research to this day. As any audiophile is aware, commercial quality digital stereo audio may be represented with a sample rate of 44,100 samples per second, corresponding to a data rate of 176,400 bytes per second. Many digital transmission media are incapable of such high throughput, and those that are may not be sufficiently economical to support a high-quality audio application.

Accordingly, audio compression has branched into two main camps; voice compression and music compression. The voice compression camp generally uses lower sample rates (say 8,000 monaural samples per second) and has developed techniques that predict the behavior of the audio signal based on a model of the human vocal tract. One of the leading technologies of this type is incorporated into the ITU G.723.1 standard.

Music compression generally processes quite high sample rates (32,000 to 48,000 samples per second) and has developed a "psychoacoustic" model of hearing that is used to remove sounds that would be inaudible to the human ear. The compressed data results from applying the psychoacoustic model to the frequency domain representation of the sampled material, not directly to the sampled data as in the voice case. This technology is codified in the ISO MPEG I/II standards.

2. REPRESENTATION OF THE UNCOMPRESSED AUDIO – PCM

Sound is communicated by momentary changes in air pressure. These changes are often periodic, and are modeled as 'waves' of air pressure changes propagating from the point of origin. As our typical audiophile quoted above will further attest, perfect reproduction of these waves by analog means is an expensive and ultimately unattainable goal. As one might imagine, the digital situation has even more tradeoffs and compromises.

Figure 1 is a pictorial illustration of the analog representation of one of the simplest possible audio sounds: a single, pure 1 KHz tone. This tone is the C two octaves above middle C on the piano. The perceived loudness of the tone is a function of the 'sound pressure level' (the total energy under the envelope of the wave), and is expressed in units of decibels (dB). A change in the sound pressure level of 10 decibels corresponds to a perceived doubling in the loudness of the sound; the limit of human hearing is 0 to 10 dB; a difference in sound level of 1 to 3 dB is barely perceptible.

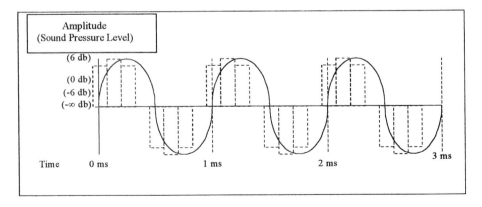

Figure 1. Solid line: an analog signal representing a pure 1000 cycle/sec tone. Dashed boxes: the same signal is quantized to a finite number of discrete levels.

When a sound wave is represented as an analog electrical signal, an amplitude of .7 volts driving a load of 600 ohms is defined to represent a sound pressure level of 0 dB. The perceived loudness of the sound is proportional to the square of the signal amplitude, and we may therefore define the perceived intensity I_P as

$$I_P = 20 * \log\left(\frac{V}{.7}\right) \qquad (1)$$

Digital representation of sound is done by a means known as 'Pulse Code Modulation.' This technique is applied to the continuous electrical signal captured by an analog device (i.e., a microphone). A fixed period is chosen at which the signal is regularly 'sampled' by converting its instantaneous amplitude to an integer value. This process is called analog-to-digital (A/D) conversion. Figure 2 illustrates the conversion between an analog signal and its PCM representation.

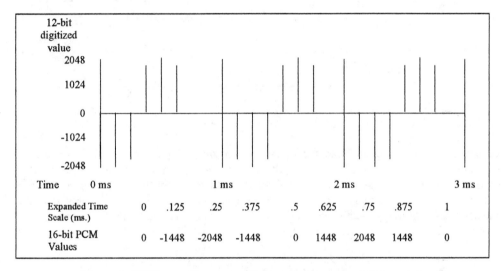

Figure 2. PCM sampling a signal representing a pure 1000 cycle/sec.
Audio tone, sample rate is 8000 samples/sec.

The number of discrete levels in the A/D conversion limits the accuracy of the sample. The process of representing signal information with a reduced number of discrete levels is termed 'quantization.' Typical audio A/D converters use 8 through 16 bits of accuracy in the sampling, resulting in uniform quantization of the voltage levels to 256 through 65536 discrete levels.

Unfortunately, the process of quantization introduces error into the signal. Limiting the number of discrete levels used to represent information clearly reduces the accuracy of the representation. Uniform quantization of audio signals to Q levels introduces an error of up to Q/2 in each sample. The quantization error terms, illustrated in Figure 3, are perceived as 'hiss,' or high-frequency noise. The perceptual intensity I_{SNR} of this noise relative to signal intensity is measured (in decibels) as

$$I_{SNR} = 20 * \log\left(\frac{S}{N}\right) \qquad (2)$$

where

S represents the voltage level representing the signal strength, and
N represents the voltage level representing the noise level.

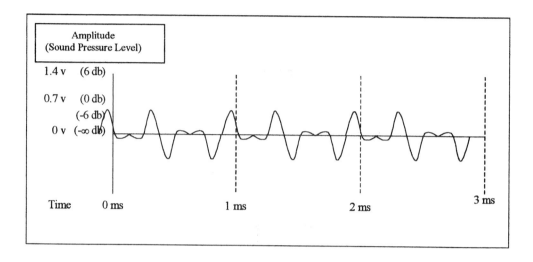

Figure 3. Quantization error.

For typical real-world applications, the signal is often sinusoidal in nature. When performing A/D conversion with n bits of resolution, the largest signal strength that can be represented without clipping has a peak voltage of $2^{n-1}Q$ giving an average (in the R.M.S. sense) voltage of $2^{n-1}Q/2^{.5}$. The quantization error may be expected to be uniformly distributed in the range $[-Q/2, Q/2]$, giving an average voltage of $Q/12^{.5}$. The perceived signal-to-noise ratio in this case will be

$$I_{SNR} = 20*\log\left(\left(2^{n-1}*Q/\sqrt{2}\right)\Big/\left(Q/\sqrt{12}\right)\right)$$
$$= 6.02n + 1.76 \tag{3}$$

For a 16-bit A/D converter, this results in a best-case SNR of 98 dB. Even for an eight-bit A/D converter, the best-case SNR will be an extremely faint 50 dB. However, the dynamic range of the human ear is extremely large (about 120 decibels), and the SNR for lower-intensity signals will be much worse.

PCM-represented data may be used to reproduce the original signal. Samples are played back through a digital-to-analog (D/A) converter. The D/A converter produces an electrical level equivalent to the instantaneous sampled voltage. As illustrated in Figure 4, error is introduced in the reconstructed signal when the instantaneous voltage is held throughout the sample period. While some D/A systems support interpolation or wave-shaping to minimize this kind of error, the process of sampling itself introduces yet another error – a limitation of the frequency range that may be represented by the sampled data points (Nyquist frequency). This type of error is illustrated in Figure 5 and is perceived as a loss in high frequency response.

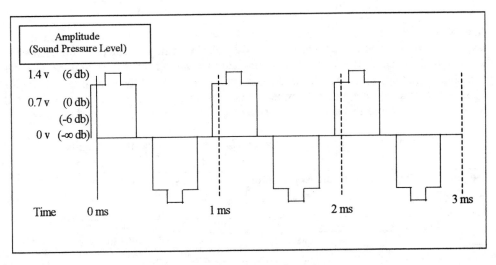

Figure 4. Reproducing a PCM-sampled signal.

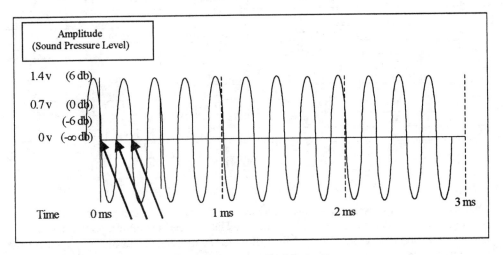

Figure 5. An 8K signal.
If sampled at 8K, every sample point will be 0 (the first three samples are indicated).

3. AUDIO COMPRESSION TECHNIQUES

3.1 LOGARITHMIC CODING

One of the earliest audio compression strategies was developed for carrier systems in the United States and was first implemented in analog circuitry. In analog form, this process is known as "companding," where the signal's dynamic rage is reduced before transmission, and expanded on receipt. In the digital case, this process amounts to a non-uniform choice of quantization intervals.

The μ-law family of compression characteristics is defined as

$$F_\mu(x) = \text{sgn}(x) \frac{\ln(1 + \mu|x|)}{\ln(1 + \mu)} \qquad (4)$$

where x is the input signal amplitude ($1 \geq x \geq -1$), sgn(x) is the polarity of x, and u is a parameter used to define the amount of compression. This family of compression curves has the property that quantization noise is proportional to the sample amplitude, and that changes in amplitude are logarithmic, similar to the perceptual sensitivity of the human ear. A μ value of 255 is in common usage in North America, and results in a logarithmic curve that is well approximated by 17 linear segments, as illustrated in Table 1.

Table 1. 17-Segment Approximation Used in μ255 Logarithmic Coding

Segment Number	Step Size	Input Amplitude Range	Code Range	First Step In	First Decoded Value
1	256	-8159 to -4064	-127 to -112	-8159 to -7903	-8031
2	128	-4063 to -2016	-111 to -96	-4063 to -3935	-3999
3	64	-2015 to -992	-95 to -80	-2015 to -1951	-1983
4	32	-991 to -480	-79 to -64	-991 to -959	-975
5	16	-479 to -224	-63 to -48	-447 to -463	-471
6	8	-223 to -96	-47 to -32	-223 to -215	-219
7	4	-95 to -32	-31 to -16	-95 to -91	-93
8	2	-31 to -2	-15 to -1	-31 to -29	-30
9	1	-1 to 1	0	-1 to 1	0
10	2	2 to 31	1 to 15	1 to 3	2
11	4	32 to 95	16 to 31	31 to 35	33
12	8	96 to 223	32 to 47	95 to 103	99
13	16	224 to 479	48 to 63	223 to 239	231
14	32	480 to 991	64 to 79	479 to 511	495
15	64	992 to 2015	80 to 95	991 to 1055	1023
16	128	2016 to 4063	96 to 111	2015 to 2143	2079
17	256	4064 to 8159	112 to 127	4063 to 4319	4191

Compression-decompression hardware (codecs) based on μ255 companding encode the results of a 14-bit A/D into an eight-bit number. The reduced resolution of the encoding is inaudible to the human ear inasmuch as the difference in encoded values at the high end of the logarithmic scale is no more audible than the difference in encoded values at the low end of the scale.

Table 1 illustrates the conversion between 8-bit μ255-encoded values and their equivalent 14-bit PCM samples values. Note that the step size in the conversion ranges from a low of 1 to a high of 256. This encodes human auditory response in that PCM differences of 1 may be audible at low volumes, but a change of 256 may be required to produce audibly distinguishable tones at high volumes. This early means of compression returns a compression ratio of 14:8, or 1.75:1.

3.2 DIFFERENTIAL PCM COMPRESSION

Differential pulse code modulation takes advantage of the relatively slow change in a typical speech waveform. Most of the energy in speech waveforms is concentrated into the frequency range 75 through 400 cycles per second. These waveforms can be more efficiently represented by the differences in the PCM values, rather than directly by the PCM values themselves.

The maximum difference in PCM values between samples can be estimated by modeling the speech waveform by a sine wave.

$$s(t) = A\sin(2\pi f t) \tag{5}$$

The amplitude A may be taken to be the maximum sampling amplitude, which in the case of 16-bit samples would be 32767. The difference between two PCM samples is then the difference between the sine wave taken at two consecutive sample points.

$$s(t) = A\sin(2\pi f t) - A\sin(2\pi f (t + \Delta t)) \tag{6}$$

where Δt is the time between samples. The maximum difference is found by taking the derivative of (7) and setting the result to 0.

$$ds(t)\big/_{dt} = A2\pi f \cos(2\pi f t) - A2\pi f \cos(2\pi f (t + \Delta t)) \tag{7}$$

The maximum is found at

$$t = -\Delta t\big/_{2} \tag{8}$$

Since the sample rate Δt is small by its definition, we may approximate sin(x) by x, and we rewrite (7) (ignoring sign) as

$$\left| s\left(-\frac{\Delta t}{2} \right) \right| = A2\pi f \Delta t \tag{9}$$

If we assume voice is bounded at 400 cycles per second (f = 400), the sample size is 16 bits (A = 32767), and the sample rate is 8000 (Δt = 1/8000), we find the maximum DPCM value to be

$$\max(s(t)) = \frac{32767 * 2 * \pi * 400}{8000} = 10294 \tag{10}$$

The difference signal can be perfectly represented with 15 bits, leading to a compression ratio of 16/15, or 1.07.

It is possible to introduce quantization into DPCM. With this technique, each sample is quantized to a representative value. While this technique will reduce the number of bits required to represent each difference, the quantization error introduced may compound across samples.

Two solutions are available to bound the error: framing and dithering. If samples are collected into a fixed-size frame, the first sample may be encoded in PCM, while the subsequent samples would be decoded in DPCM. If PCM samples are encoded into DPCM and linearly quantized, the error introduced per sample is, at most,

$$|E_{\Delta t}| = M\!\!\Big/\!\!_N - 1 \qquad\qquad (11)$$

where
$E_{\Delta t}$ is the maximum error introduced at each step,
M is the maximum value a sample may take, and
N is the number of quantization steps.

Then the maximum error that may be introduced in a frame of size F is

$$E_F = (F-1) * |E_{\Delta t}|$$
$$= (F-1) * \left(\frac{M}{N} - 1\right) \qquad\qquad (12)$$

The number of bits required to represent F PCM samples is

$$B_{PCM} = F * \big(\log_2(M) + 1\big) \qquad\qquad (13)$$

and the number of bits required to represent a frame of quantized DPCM samples is

$$B_{DPCM} = \big(\log_2(M) + 1\big) + (F-1) * \log_2(Q) \qquad\qquad (14)$$

where Q is the number of quantized levels. By way of example, a frame of 32 16-bit samples encoded with an 8-bit quantizer will show a compression ratio of (16*32)/(16+8*31), or 1.9:1. However, the maximum error is a large 31*127, or 3937.

Dithering can more closely control the error. This technique adds the accumulated error into the sample value to be represented, creating a dithered value and effectively reducing the accumulated error to 0. The dithered sample value is then quantized, and the error introduced in the representation becomes the new accumulated error value. The maximum error is then constrained to single-step quantization error without impacting the compression ratio. A logarithmic quantizer may be chosen to reduce the background quantizing noise (as in logarithmic coding).

Adaptive DPCM is motivated on three key ideas:
- The range of data values will stay small over a small period of time.
- Error introduced in a data value will not be audible if it is corrected quickly.
- Audio is dominated by lower frequency components.

Several (typically four) sets of quantizers are maintained. Framing is used, typically about 32 samples per frame. Choice of which quantizer set to use is made by examining the dynamic range of the samples that will be encoded into the frame.

The quantizer set is encoded as the initial entry in the frame, and the initial sample value is coded with the full resolution (as in framed DPCM). Subsequent values are lookup indices in the selected dequantizing table. The size of these lookup indices gives the compression, with 4 bits being considered a good trade-off between compression and sound quality. The resulting compression ratio for a frame of 32 16-bit samples with choice of 16 tables would then be $(32*16)/(4+16+31*4)$, or $3.6:1$.

3.3 LINEAR PREDICTIVE CODING

It has been shown that speech samples can be predicted with great accuracy from a linear combination of the previous samples, essentially refining the DPCM strategy by adding prediction variables

$$p_t = \sum_{i=1}^{M} \alpha_{t-i} s_{t-i} \qquad (15)$$

where
M is the number of predictors,
α_i is the ith predictor coefficient,
p_t is the predicted value of the sample, and
s_{t-i} is the ith sample in the past (i.e., $s_{t-i} = s[t - i*\Delta i]$).

A frame of N samples will contain the first M samples represented in PCM, followed by the M prediction coefficients. If the prediction coefficients are sent with the resolution of PCM, the compression ratio will be $N/(2*M)$. Typical compressors use a frame size of 240 samples compressed using 8 coefficients, resulting in a compression ratio of 15 (but rather poor quality, as will be discussed below).

Calculation of the coefficients is done by minimizing the total error introduced in the approximation. The difference between the predicted and actual sample values, $s_t - p_t$, is squared and summed over N-M samples to give the total error E.

$$E = \sum_{t=M+1}^{N} \left(\sum_{i=1}^{M} \alpha_i s_{t-i} - s_t \right)^2 \qquad (16)$$

If we define α_0 to be -1, and differentiate E by each prediction coefficient α_i, i = 1,M, we get

$$\frac{\partial E}{\partial \alpha_i} = 2 \sum_{i=0}^{M} \alpha_i \left(\sum_{t=M+1}^{N} s_{t-i} * s_{t-j} \right) \qquad (17)$$

The M simultaneous equations (17) are set to 0 and solved for α_i. Up to 80% of speech energy is encoded into LPC coefficients, resulting in high compression ratios. These ratios can be improved by quantizing the first M samples. A process known as vector quantization is often used for this purpose. The quantization process described above replaces a single sample with a codebook entry that best approximates the sample, and is known as scalar quantization. Vector quantization replaces a sequence of samples with a codebook entry that best approximates the entire sequence of samples. This process gives almost double the compression ratio with minimal loss in quality.

Commercial compression algorithms use LPC to generate filter coefficients to govern decoder behavior, and use various other techniques to "excite" or drive the decoder. One such technique extracts the dominant periodic signal from the signal.

Modeling the period behavior with a sine wave motivates the technique that is used to extract the dominant frequency. Let the signal be convolved with itself at a phase shift of φ.

$$\int_0^N \sin(t) * \sin(t+\varphi) =$$

$$= \frac{N}{2} * \cos(\varphi) \tag{18}$$

The convolution reaches a maximum value when the phase shift is π. An exhaustive search is performed, convolving the sampled signal with the same signal offset by a phase shift.

$$C_p = \sum_{i=1}^{N-p} s_i * s_{i+p} \tag{19}$$

where
p is the phase shift in sample times being tested,
C_p is the numerical value of the convolution by p sample times, and
S_i is the ith sample value.

The p for which C_p is maximized is taken as ½ the period of the sine wave that best approximates the sampled signal. LPC techniques using codebook lookup and dominant frequency excitation return very good audio quality with compression ratios of about 12:1.

3.4 TRANSFORM-BASED AUDIO COMPRESSION
This family of audio compression algorithms is based on the notion of performing a linear transform to convert the data from sample space to frequency space. Once the data is represented in frequency space, it is quantized and (typically) entropy-coded.

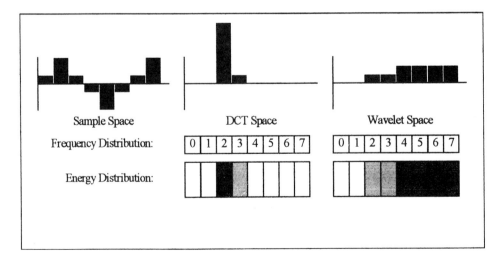

Figure 6. Representing a continuous tone in sample space, DCT space, and wavelet space.

Two of the more popular linear transformations are the Discrete Cosine Transform (DCT) and the wavelet transform (actually, wavelets form a family of transforms). Both of these transforms are orthogonal, which is to say that the transform to encode the data is of precisely the same complexity of the transform that reconstructs the data – i.e., the compression algorithm is symmetric. However, many real-world compression algorithms refine these techniques at the cost of greater compression times.

The DCT is essentially the real version of the Discrete Fourier Transform, transforming N sample points to N frequency points. The DCT is comprised of a large spread of frequencies, and therefore represents pure tones and slowly varying data quite well (i.e., with few data points, as shown in Figure 6). However, as is illustrated in Figure 7, the DCT has trouble representing discontinuous data such as an impulse.

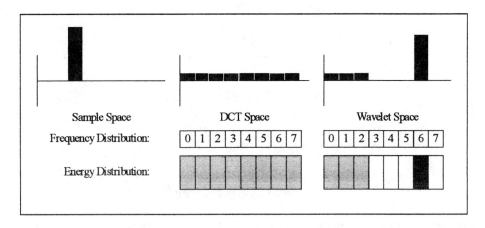

Figure 7. Representing an impulse in sample space, DCT space, and wavelet space.

The wavelet transforms covers fewer frequencies, but shows better time resolution at the higher frequencies. This property makes the wavelet a good candidate for compact representation of data that contains abrupt transitions particularly characteristic of low sample rates. Figure 7 illustrates the superior ability of the wavelet to represent an impulse.

While (hopefully) the transformation of data from sample space to frequency space will concentrate the energy into fewer coefficients, the transformation preserves the energy of the sample space and no real compression is guaranteed. Rather, the process of quantization must be introduced to reduce the number of bits needed to represent the transformed result.

The essential difference between transform-based and LPC-based compression now becomes apparent – while LPC models the behavior of the human throat, transform-based compression models the sensitivity of the human ear. The quantization factors will be used to remove redundant data – i.e., data to which the human ear is insensitive. The choice of quantization factors is essentially an embodiment of a mathematical model of human auditory perception.

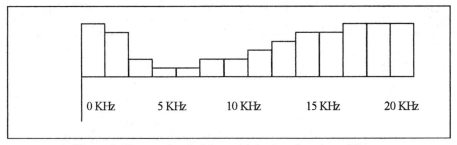

Figure 8. Human threshold sensitivity is a function of frequency.

Unfortunately for these compression algorithms, human auditory perception is quite acute and very sensitive to aliasing errors in reconstruction from compressed data. Generally, the spectrum is subdivided into many bands, relying on the logarithmic sensitivity of the human ear to changes in frequency. As it is well known, octaves in a musical scale are perceived as equal changes in pitch, but physically correspond to a doubling in frequency, as shown in Figure 8. Development of accurate filters to model this behavior is fairly expensive computationally.

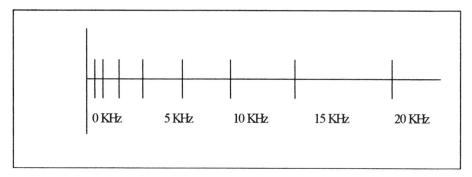

Figure 9. The auditory system is modeled as a collection of bands
of constant relative frequency.

The quantization process is applied to each band individually. Each band is associated with an individual threshold value corresponding to the sensitivity of the human ear at that frequency, as shown in Figure 9. The energy of the band may be linearly quantized, or a logarithmic quantizer may be applied to model the response of the human ear to volume. However, waveforms may contribute energy to several bands. These waveforms must be quantized equally to avoid aliasing, limiting the effective compression expected from this class of algorithm. Typical compression ratios for high-quality audio are about 8:1. An example of audio compression is illustrated in Table 2.

Table 2. Sample Bands, Quantizers, and Quantized Coefficients for Transform-Based Coding

Band	Quantizer	Energy in Band	Quantized Energy	Dequantized Energy
50	100	128	1	100
150	80	160	2	160
250	70	170	2	140
350	60	180	3	180
570	60	200	3	180
700	50	190	3	150
840	50	200	4	200
1000	40	190	4	160

4. CONCLUSIONS

The perfect compression algorithm is waiting to be developed. Compression techniques that generate good quality audio at high compression ratios restrict the content of the audio, or are complex computationally. The trade-off between the techniques described here is summarized in Table 3.

Table 3. Comparison of Popular Audio Compression Strategies

Technique	Expected Compression Ratio	Compression Power	Decompression Power	Comments
Logarithmic Encoding	2:1	286	286	Useful as an encoding scheme; usable with other coding techniques.
ADPCM Compression	4:1	286	286	Very efficient computationally. Best with slow-moving content (speech).
LPC-based Compression	12:1	586/100	386	Speech-specific. Expensive to compress.
Transform-based Compression	8:1	586/300	586/100	Extremely expensive computationally.

REFERENCES

1. J. Bellamy, "Digital Telephony," John Wiley & Sons, 1991.
2. J. Benedetto and M. Frazier, "Wavelets: Mathematics and Applications," CRC Press, 1994.
3. S. Furui, "Digital Speech Processing, Synthesis, and Recognition," Marcel Dekker, 1989.
4. C. B. Rorabaugh, "Digital Filter Designer's Handbook," McGraw-Hill, 1997.
5. M. Vitterli and J. Kovacevic, "Wavelets and Subband Coding," Prentice Hall, 1995.
6. J. Watkinson, "Compression in Video & Audio," Focal Press, 1997.
7. J. Watkinson, "The Art of Digital Audio," Focal Press, 1995.
8. D.Y. Pen, "Digital Audio Compression," Digital Technical Journal, Vol. 5, No. 2, pp. 28-40, 1993.

8

IMAGE PRESENTATION AND COMPRESSION

Borko Furht
Florida Atlantic University
Department of Computer Science and Engineering
Boca Raton, Florida 33431
borko@cse.fau.edu

1.	**IMAGE CONCEPTS AND STRUCTURES**	150
2.	**STORAGE REQUIREMENTS FOR MULTIMEDIA APPLICATIONS**	152
3.	**CLASSIFICATION OF COMPRESSION TECHNIQUES**	153
4.	**JPEG ALGORITHM FOR FULL COLOR STILL-IMAGE COMPRESSION**	155
	4.1 SEQUENTIAL JPEG ENCODER AND DECODER	155
	4.2 COMPRESSION MEASURES	160
	4.3 SEQUENTIAL JPEG ENCODING EXAMPLE	161
	4.4 JPEG COMPRESSION OF COLOR IMAGES	162
	4.5 PROGRESSIVE JPEG COMPRESSION	164
	4.6 INTERACTIVE PROGRESSIVE JPEG	166
	4.7 LOSSLESS JPEG COMPRESSION	169
	4.8 HIERARCHICAL JPEG COMPRESSION	169
5.	**CONCLUSION**	169
	REFERENCES	170

Abstract. This chapter covers the JPEG compression algorithm, which is primarily used for full-color still image applications. First, we describe various image presentations, such as RGB, YUV, and YCbCr, and standard image formats. Then, we describe all components of the JPEG algorithm including discrete cosine transform, quantization, and entropy encoding. We also define both encoder and decoder architectures. The main emphasis is given to the sequential mode of operation, which is the most typical use of JPEG compression. However, the other three modes of operation, progressive, lossless, and hierarchical JPEG, are described as well.

0-8493-1825-4/99/$0.00+$.50

1. IMAGE CONCEPTS AND STRUCTURES

A digital image represents a two-dimensional array of samples, where each sample is called a pixel. Precision determines how many levels of intensity can be represented, and is expressed as the number of bits/sample. According to precision, the images can be classified into

- *Binary images,* represented by 1 bit/sample. Examples include black/white photographs and facsimile images.
- *Computer graphics,* represented by a lower precision, as 4 bits/sample.
- *Grayscale images,* represented by 8 bits/sample.
- *Color images,* represented with 16, 24, or more bits/sample.

According to the trichromatic theory, the sensation of color is produced by selectively exciting three classes of receptors in the eye. In a RGB color representation system, shown in Figure 1, a color is produced by adding three primary colors: red, green, and blue (RGB). The straight line, where R = G = B, specifies the gray values ranging from black to white.

Figure 2 illustrates how a three-sensor RGB color video camera operates and produces colors at a RGB monitor. Lights for sources of different colors are added together to produce the prescribed color.

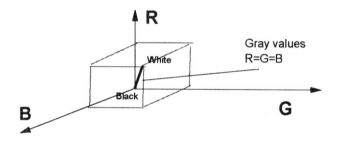

Figure 1. RGB representation of color images.

Another representation of color images, YUV representation describes luminance and chrominance components of an image. The luminance component (Y) provides a grayscale version of the image, while two chrominance components (U and V) give additional information that converts the grayscale image to a color image.

The YUV representation is more natural for image compression. An image represented in RGB color, can be converted into YUV systems using the following transformations:

$$Y = 0.3R + 0.6G + 0.1B$$
$$U = B - U$$
$$V = R - Y$$

where Y is the luminance component, and U and V are two chrominance components. When $R = G = B$, then $Y = R = G = B$, and $U = V = 0$, which represents a grayscale image.

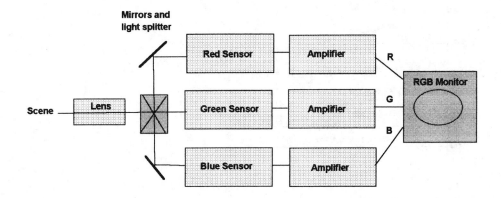

Figure 2. Three-sensor RGB color video camera.

Another color format, referred to as YCbCr, similar to the YUV format, is intensively used for image compression. In YCbCr format, Y is the same as in YUV system; however, U and V are scaled and zero-shifted to produce C_b and C_r, respectively, as follows:

$$C_b = U / 2 + 0.5$$
$$C_r = V / 1.6 + 0.5$$

Resolutions of an image system refer to its capability to reproduce fine detail. Higher resolution requires more complex imaging systems to represent these images in real time. In computer systems, resolution is characterized by number of pixels (for example, VGA has a resolution of 640 H 480 pixels). In video systems, resolution refers to the number of line pairs resolved on the face of the display screen, expressed in cycles per picture height, or cycles per picture width. For example, the NTSC broadcast system in North America and Japan, denoted 525/59.94, has about 483 picture lines. (525 denotes the total number of lines in its rates, and 59.94 is its field rate in Hertz.) The HDTV system will approximately double the number of lines of current broadcast television at approximately the same field rate. The system will have 937 total lines and a frame rate of 65.95 Hz.

Figure 3 compares various image structures, showing the vertical and horizontal pixel counts, and the approximate total number of pixels.

The CCITT has adopted several picture formats for video-based telecommunications: Common Intermediate Format (CIF), Quarter-CIF (QCIF), Small QCIF (SQCIF), 4CIF, and 16CF, which are described in Chapter 9 on video presentation and compression.

The full-motion video is characterized with at least 24 Hz frame rate (or 24 frames/s), up to 30, or even 60 frames/s for HDTV. For animation, acceptable frame rate is in the range 15 to 20 frames/s, while for video telephone it is 5-10 frames/s. Videoconferencing and interactive multimedia applications require a rate of 15-30 frames/s.

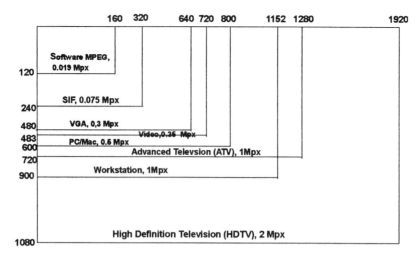

Figure 3. Various image structures.

2. STORAGE REQUIREMENTS FOR MULTIMEDIA APPLICATIONS

Audio, image, and video signals require a vast amount of data for their presentation. Table 1 illustrates the mass storage requirements for various media types, such as text, image, audio, animation, and video.

There are three main reasons why present multimedia systems require data to be compressed. These reasons are related to: (a) large storage requirements of multimedia data; (b) relatively slow storage devices which do not allow playing multimedia data (specifically video) in real time, and (c) the present network's bandwidth, which do not allow real-time video data transmission.

Table 1. Storage Requirements for Various Media Types

	Text	**Image**	**Audio**	**Animation**	**Video**
Object Type	ASCII EBCDIS	Bitmapped graphics Still photos Faxes	Non-coded stream of digitized audio or voice	Synched image and audio stream at 15-20 frames/s	TV analog or digital image with synched streams at 24-30 frames/s
Size and Bandwidth	**2KB per page**	Simple: **64KB per image** Detailed (color) **7.5 MB per image**	Voice/Phone 8 KHz/8 bits (mono) **6-44 KB/s** Audio CD 44.1 kHz/ 16 bit/stereo **176 KB/s**	320x640x16 pixels/frame 16 bit color 16 frames/s **2·5 MB/s**	640x480x24 pixels/frame 24-bit color 30 frames/s **27.7 MB/s**

As an example, a typical multimedia application may require the storage of more than 30 min of video, 2,000 images, and 40 min of stereo sound on each laser disc side. This application would require about 50 GB storage for video, 15 GB storage for images, and 0.4 GB storage for audio, that gives a total of 65.4 GB of storage.

In another example, assuming color video frames with 620x560 pixels and 24 bits per pixels, it would be necessary to save about 1 Mbytes per frame. For a motion video requiring 30 frames/s, it gives a total of 30 Mbytes for 1 second of motion video. Even if there is enough storage available, we won't be able to playback the video in real time due to insufficient speed of storage devices. According to the previous calculation, the required speed of a storage device should be 20 Mbytes/s. However today's technology provides about 1.2 Mbytes/s transfer rate of CD ROMs. Therefore, at the present state of technology of storage devices the only solution is to compress the data before the storage and decompress it before playback.

Modern image and video compression techniques offer a solution to this problem, which reduces these tremendous storage requirements. Advanced compression techniques can compress a typical image ranging from 10:1 to 50:1. Very high compression ratios of up to 1000:1 can be achieved in compressing of video signals.

Figure 4 illustrates storage requirements for a multimedia application consisting of various media types, assuming that the image is compressed by ratio 15:1, audio 6:1, and video and animation by factor 50:1. The total storage requirement for this storage-intensive application becomes about 3 GB, which is feasible.

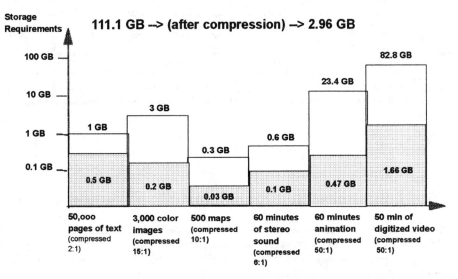

Figure 4. Storage requirements for a multimedia application.
Before compression the application required 111.1 GB of storage and after compression 2.96 GB.

3. CLASSIFICATION OF COMPRESSION TECHNIQUES

Compression of digital data is based on various computational algorithms, which can be implemented either in software or in hardware. Compression techniques are classified into two categories: (a) lossless, and (b) lossy approaches. Lossless techniques are capable of recovering the original representation perfectly. Lossy techniques involve algorithms, which recover the presentation similar to the original one. The lossy techniques provide higher compression ratios, and, therefore, they are more often applied to image and video compression than lossless techniques. The classification schemes for lossless and lossy compression are presented in Figures 5(a) and (b), respectively.

The lossy techniques are classified into: (1) prediction-based techniques, (2) frequency-oriented techniques, (3) importance-oriented techniques, and (4) hybrid techniques. Predictive-based techniques, such as ADPCM, predict subsequent values by observing previous values. Frequency-oriented techniques apply the Discrete Cosine Transform (DCT), or subband coding, which relates to fast Fourier transform. Importance-oriented techniques use other characteristics of images as the basis for compression. For example, DVI technique uses color look-up tables and data filtering.

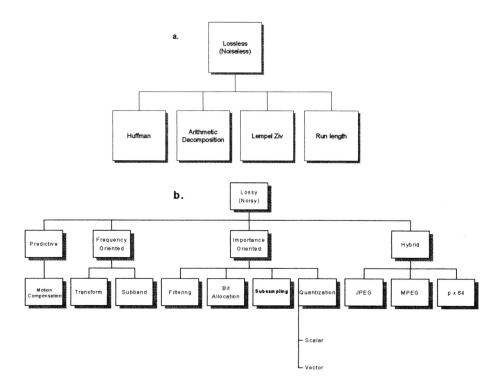

Figure 5. Classification schemes for (a) lossless and (b) lossy compression techniques.

The hybrid compression techniques, such as JPEG, MPEG, and px64, combine several approaches including DCT, quantization, motion estimation, and Huffman coding. Recently, standards for digital multimedia have been established based on these three techniques, as illustrated in Table 2.

Table 2. Multimedia Compression Standards

Short Name	Official Name	Standards Group	Typical Compression Ratios
JPEG	Digital compression and coding of continuous-tone still images	Joint Photographic Experts Group	**15:1** Full color still-frame applications
H.261/H.263 or px64 Kbps	Video encoder/decoder for audio-visual services at px64 Kbps	Specialist Group on Coding for Visual Telephone	**100:1 to 200:1** Video-based telecommunications
MPEG	Coding of moving pictures and associated audio	Moving Pictures Experts Group	**50:1** Motion-intensive applications

4. JPEG ALGORITHM FOR FULL COLOR STILL-IMAGE COMPRESSION

Originally, JPEG standard is targeted for full color still-frame applications, achieving 15:1 average compression ratio [1,2,4,5,6,7]. However, JPEG is also applied in some real-time, full-motion video applications (Motion JPEG-MJPEG). JPEG standard provides four modes of operation:

- *sequential DCT-based encoding,* in which each image component is encoded in a single left-to-right, top-to-bottom scan.
- *progressive DCT-based encoding,* in which the image is encoded in multiple scans, in order to produce a quick, rough decoded image when the transmission time is long.
- *lossless encoding,* in which the image is encoded to guarantee the exact reproduction, and
- *hierarchical encoding,* in which the image is encoded in multiple resolutions.

4.1 SEQUENTIAL JPEG ENCODER AND DECODER
The block diagram of the JPEG sequential encoder and decoder is shown in Figure 6.

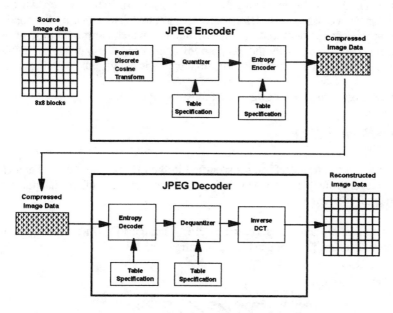

Figure 6. Block diagram of sequential JPEG encoder and decoder.

JPEG Encoder
The original samples, in the range [0, 2^p-1], are shifted to sign in the range [-2^{p-1}-1]. For a grayscale image, where p=8, the original samples in the range [0, 255], are shifted in the range [-128, + 127].

These values are then transformed into the frequency domain using the Forward Discrete Cosine Transform (FDCT) using the following equations:

$$F(u, v) = \frac{C(u)}{2} \bullet \frac{C(v)}{2} \sum_{x=0}^{7} \sum_{y=0}^{7} f(x, y) \cos \frac{(2x+1)u\pi}{16} \cos \frac{(2y+1)v\pi}{16}$$

where

$$C(u) = \tfrac{1}{\sqrt{2}} \; for \; u = 0$$

$$C(u) = 1 \; for \; u > 0$$

$$C(u) = \tfrac{1}{\sqrt{2}} \; for \; v = 0$$

$$C(u) = 1 \; for \; v > 0$$

The transformed 64-point discrete signal is a function of two spatial dimensions x and y, and its components are called spatial frequencies or DCT coefficients.

The F(0,0) coefficient is called the "DC coefficient," and the remaining 63 coefficients are called the "AC coefficients." Several fast DCT algorithms are presented and analyzed in [1].

For a typical 8x8 image block, most of the spatial frequencies have zero or near-zero values, and need not be encoded. This is illustrated in JPEG example, presented later in the chapter. This fact is the foundation for achieving data compression. In the next step, all 64 DCT coefficients are quantized using a 64-element quantization table, specified by the application. The quantization reduces the amplitude of the coefficients, which contribute little or nothing to the quality of the image, with the purpose of increasing the number of zero-value coefficients. Quantization also discards information, which is not visually significant.

The quantization is performed according to the following equation:

$$F_q(u,v) = Round\left\lfloor \frac{F(u,v)}{Q(u,v)} \right\rfloor$$

where $Q(u, v)$ are quantization coefficients specified in the quantization table. Each element $Q(u, v)$ is an integer from 1 to 255, which specifies the step size of the quantizer for its corresponding DCT coefficient.

A set of four quantization tables is specified by JPEG standard [1]. In the JPEG example, a quantization formula is used to produce the quantization tables.

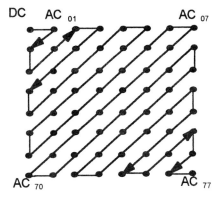

Figure 7. Zig-zag ordering of AC coefficients.

After quantization, the 63 AC coefficients are ordered into the "zig-zag" sequence, as shown in Figure 7. This zig-zag ordering will help to facilitate the next phase, entropy encoding, by placing low-frequency coefficients, which are more likely to be nonzero, before high-frequency coefficients.

This is confirmed by the experiment presented by Pennenbaker and Mitchell [1] and the results are shown in Figure 8. These results show that when the coefficients are ordered zig-zag, the probability of coefficients being zero is an increasing monotonic function of the index. The DC coefficients, which represent the average values of the 64 image samples, are coded using the predictive coding techniques, as illustrated in Figure 9.

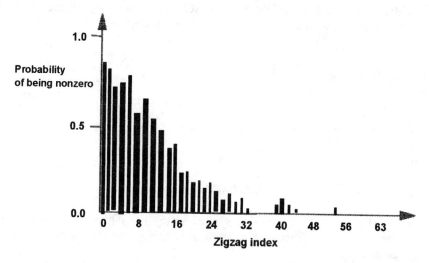

Figure 8. Probability of being nonzero of zig-zag ordered DCT coefficients.

The reason for predictive coding of DC coefficients is that there is usually a strong correlation between the DC coefficients of adjacent 8x8 blocks. As a consequence, the compression ratio will be improved. Finally, the last block in the JPEG encoder is the entropy coding, which provides additional compression by encoding the quantized DCT coefficients into more compact form. The JPEG standard specifies two entropy coding methods: Huffman coding and arithmetic coding [1]. The baseline sequential JPEG encoder uses Huffman coding.

The Huffman coder converts the DCT coefficients after quantization into a compact binary sequence using two steps: (1) forming intermediate symbol sequence, and (2) converting intermediate symbol sequence into binary sequence using Huffman tables.

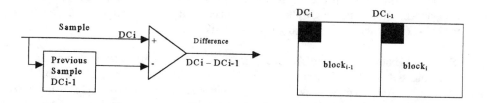

Figure 9. Predictive coding for DC coefficients.

In the intermediate symbol sequence, a pair of symbols represents each AC coefficient:

| Symbol-1 | Symbol-2 |
| (RUNLENGTH, SIZE) | (AMPLITUDE) |

where:

RUNLENGTH is the number of consecutive zero-lined AC coefficients preceding the nonzero AC coefficient. The value of RUNLENGTH is in the range 0 to 15, which requires 4 bits for its representation.

SIZE is the number of bits used to encode AMPLITUDE. The number of bits for AMPLITUDE is in the range of 0 to 10 bits, so there are 4 bits needed to code SIZE.

AMPLITUDE is the amplitude of the nonzero AC coefficient in the range of [+1024 to -1023], which requires 10 bits for its coding. In an example, if the sequence of AC coefficients is

$$\underbrace{0,\ 0,\ 0,\ 0,\ 0,\ 0,}_{6}\ \ 476$$

The symbol representation of the AC coefficient 476 is:

(6, 9) (476)

where: RUNLENGTH = 6, SIZE = 9, and AMPLITUDE = 476.

If RUNLENGTH is greater than 15, then symbol-1 (15,0) is interpreted as the extension symbol with runlength = 16. These can be up to three consecutive (15, 0) extensions. In the following example:

(15, 0) (15, 0) (7, 4) (12)

RUNLENGTH is equal to 16+16+7 = 39, SIZE = 4, and AMPLITUDE = 12. The symbol (0,0) means 'End of block' (EOB) and terminates each 8x8 block. For DC coefficients, the intermediate symbol representation consists of:

| Symbol - 1 | Symbol – 2 |
| (SIZE) | (AMPLITUDE) |

Because DC coefficients are differentially encoded, this range is double the range for AC coefficients, and is [-2048, + 2047].

The second step in Huffman coding is converting the intermediate symbol sequence into binary sequence. In this phase, symbols are replaced with variable length codes, beginning with the DC coefficients, and continuing with AC coefficients.

Each Symbol-1 (both for DC and AC coefficients) is encoded with a Variable-Length Code (VLC), obtained from the Huffman table set specified for each image component. The generation of Huffman tables is discussed by Pennenbaker and Mitchell [1]. Symbol-2 is encoded using a Variable-Length Integer (VLI) code, whose length in bits is given in Table 3.

For example, for an AC coefficient presented as the symbols

(1, 4) (12)

the corresponding binary presentation will be: **(1111101101100),** where (111110110) is VLC obtained from the Huffman table, and (1100) is a Variable-Length Integer (VLI) code for 12.

Table 3. Huffman Coding of Symbols-2

Size	Amplitude range
1	(-1, 1)
2	(-3, -2) (2, 3)
3	(-7..-4) (4..7)
4	(-15..-8) (8..15)
5	(-31..-16) (16..31)
6	(-63..-32) (32..63)
7	(-127..-64) (64..127)
8	(-255..-128) (128..255)
9	(-511..-256) (256..511)
10	(-1023..-512) (512..1023)

JPEG Decoder

In the JPEG sequential decoding, all the steps from the encoding process are inversed and implemented in reverse order, as shown in Figure 6.

First, an entropy decoder (such as Huffman) is implemented on the compressed image data. The binary sequence is converted to s symbol sequence using Huffman tables (VLC coefficients) and VLI decoding, and then the symbols are converted into DCT coefficients. Then, the dequantization is implemented using the following function:

$$F_q(u,v) = F_q(u,v) \times Q(u,v)$$

Then, the Inverse Discrete Cosine Transform (IDCT) is implemented on dequantized coefficients in order to convert the image from frequency domain into spatial domain. The IDCT equation is defined as

$$F(x,y) = \frac{1}{4}\left[\sum_{u=0}^{7}\sum_{v=0}^{7} C(u)\,C(v)\,F(u,v)\,\cos\frac{(2x+1)u\pi}{16}\cos\frac{(2y+1)v\pi}{16}\right.$$

where

$$C(u) = \tfrac{1}{\sqrt{2}}\ for\ u=0$$
$$C(u) = 1\ for\ u>0$$
$$C(v) = \tfrac{1}{\sqrt{2}}\ for\ v=0$$
$$C(v) = 1\ for\ v>0$$

The last step consists of shifting back the decompressed samples in the range $[0, 2^P - 1]$.

4.2 COMPRESSION MEASURES
The basic measure for the performance of a compression algorithm is Compression Ratio (C_r), defined as

$$C_r = \frac{Original\,data\,size}{Compressed\,data\,size}$$

There is a trade-off between the compression ratio and the picture quality. Higher compression ratios may produce lower picture quality. Quality and compression can also vary according to source image characteristics and scene content. One measure for the quality of the picture, proposed by Wallace [2], is the number of bits per pixel in the compressed image (N_b) which is defined as the total number of bits in the compressed image divided by the number of pixels:

$$Nb = \frac{Encoded\_number\_of\_bits}{Number\_of\_pixels}$$

According to this measure, four different picture qualities are defined [2], as shown in Table 4.

Another statistical measure that can be used to evaluate various compression algorithms is the Root Mean Square (RMS) error, calculated as

$$RMS = \tfrac{1}{n}\sqrt{\sum_{i=1}^{n}(X_i - \hat{X}_i)^2}$$

where

X_i - original pixel values

$\hat{X}_i$ - pixel values after decompression

n - total number of pixels in an image

The RMS shows the statistical difference between the original and decompressed images. However, in some cases, the quality of a decompressed image with higher RMS is better than one with lower RMS. In the next two sections, we will calculate these measures in several examples.

Table 4. Picture Quality Characteristics

Nb [bits/pixel]	Picture quality
0.25 – 0.5	Moderate to good quality
0.5 – 0.75	Good to very good quality
0.75-1.0	Excellent quality
1.5-2.0	Usually indistinguishable from the original

4.3 SEQUENTIAL JPEG ENCODING EXAMPLE

In order to illustrate all the steps in baseline sequential JPEG encoding, we present step-by-step results obtained in encoding an 8x8 block of 8-bit samples, as illustrated in Figure 10. The original 8x8 block shown in Figure 10(a) and, after shifting, the obtained block is given in Figure 10(b). After applying the FDCT, the obtained DCT coefficients are given in Figure 10(c). Note that, except for low-frequency coefficients, all the other coefficients are close to zero.

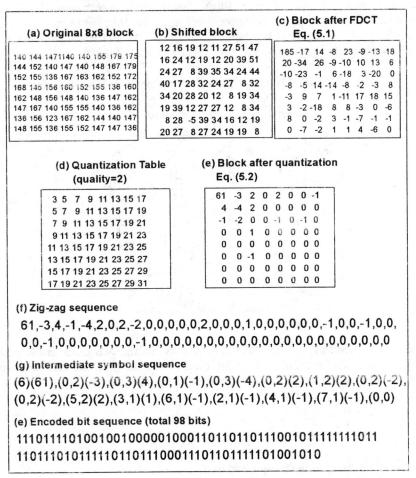

Figure 10. Step-by-step procedure in JPEG sequential encoding of an 8x8 block.

For the generation of the Quantization Table, we used the program proposed by Nelson [3]:

```
for i = 0 to n;
        for j = 0 to n;
                Q[I, j] = 1 + (1 + I + j)* quality;
        end j;
end i;
```

The parameter 'quality' specifies the quality factor and recommended range is from 1 to 25, where quality = 1 gives the best quality, but the lowest compression rate, and quality = 25 gives the worst quality and the highest compression rate. In our example, we used quality = 2, which generates the Quantization Table in Figure 10(d).

After implementing quantization, the obtained quantized coefficients are shown in Figure 10(e). Note that a number of high-frequency AC coefficients are zero.

The zig-zag ordered sequence of quantized coefficients is shown in Figure 10(f), and the intermediate symbol sequence in Figure 10(g). Finally, after implementing Huffman codes, the obtained encoded bit sequence is shown in Figure 10(h). The Huffman table used in this example is proposed in the JPEG standard for luminance AC coefficients (3), and the partial table needed to code the symbols from Figure 11(g) is given in Table 5.

Table 5. Partial Huffman Table for Luminance AC Coefficients

(Runlength, size)	Code word
(0,,0) EOB	1010
(0,1)	00
(0,2)	01
(0,3)	100
(1,2)	11011
(2,1)	11100
(3,1)	111010
(4,1)	111011
(5,2)	11111110111
(6,1)	1111011
(7,1)	11111010

Note that the DC coefficient is treated as being from the first 8x8 block in the image, and therefore, it is coded directly (not using predictive coding as all the remaining DC coefficients). For this block the compression ratio can be calculated as

$$Cr = \frac{64 \times 8}{98} = \frac{512}{98} = 5.22$$

The number of bits/pixel in the compressed form is

$$Nb = \frac{98}{64} = 1.53$$

4.4 JPEG COMPRESSION OF COLOR IMAGES

The described sequential JPEG algorithm can be easily expanded for compression of color images, or, in a general case, for compression of multiple-component images. The JPEG source image model consists of 1 to 255 image components [2,7], called color or spectral bands, as illustrated in Figure 11.

For example, RGB and YUV representations both consist of three color components. Each component may have a different number of pixels in the horizontal (X_l) and vertical (Y_l) axis. Figure 12 illustrates two cases of a color image with three components. In the first case, all three components have the same resolutions, while in the second case they have different resolutions.

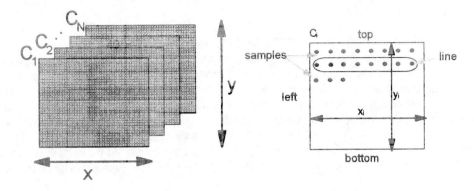

Figure 11. JPEG source image model.

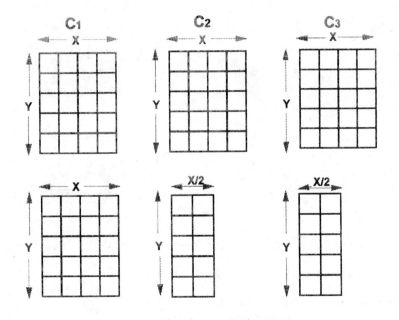

Figure 12. Color image with three components: (a) with same resolutions; (b) with different resolutions.

The color components can be processed in two ways:

- *Non-interleaved data ordering*, in which processing is performed component by component from left-to-right and top-to-bottom. In this mode, for a RGB image with high resolution, the red component will be displayed first, then the green component, and finally the blue component.
- *Interleaved data ordering*, in which different components are combined into so-called Minimum Coded Units (MCUs).

Block diagrams of the encoder and decoder for color JPEG compression are identical to those for grayscale image compression, shown in Figure 7, except the first block into the encoder is a color space conversion block. For example, the first block provides RGB to YUV conversion at the encoder side, and at the decoder side the last block is the inverse color conversion, such as YUV to RGB.

4.5 PROGRESSIVE JPEG COMPRESSION TECHNIQUES

In some applications, an image may have large numbers of pixels and the decompression process, including transmission of the compressed image over the network, may take several minutes. In such applications, there may be a need to produce a rough image quickly, and then improve its quality using multiple scans [1,2,7]. The progressive JPEG mode of operation produces a sequence of scans, each scan coding a subset of DCT coefficients. Therefore, the progressive JPEG encoder must have an additional buffer at the output of the quantizer and before the entropy encoder. The size of the buffer should be large enough to store all DCT coefficients of the image, each of which is 3 bits larger than the original image samples.

Figure 13 illustrates the differences in displaying a decompressed image in the progressive and sequential JPEG.

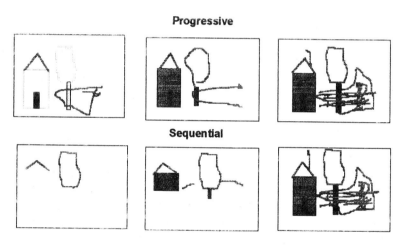

Figure 13. Progressive vs sequential JPEG decoding.

Progressive JPEG compression can be achieved using three algorithms.

(1)   Progressive spectral selection algorithm
(2)   Progressive successive approximation algorithm
(3)   Combined progressive algorithm

In the *progressive spectral selection algorithm*, the DCT coefficients are grouped into several spectral bands. Typically, low-frequency DCT coefficients bands are sent first, and then higher-frequency coefficients. For example, a sequence of four spectral bands may look like this:

> Band 1: DC coefficient only
> Band 2: AC_1 and AC_2 coefficients
> Band 3: AC_3, AC_4, AC_5, AC_6, coefficients
> Band 4: AC_7, ... AC_{63}, coefficients

In the *progressive successive approximation algorithm,* all DCT coefficients are sent first with lower precision, and then refined in later scans. For example, a sequence of three successive approximation bands may be as follows:

> Band 1: All DCT coefficients (divided by four)
> Band 2: All DCT coefficients (divided by two)
> Band 3: All DCT coefficients (full resolution)

Combined progressive algorithm combines both spectral selection and successive approximation algorithms. Figure 14 illustrates an image divided into eight combined scans. For example, in the first scan only DC coefficients divided by two (will lower resolution) will be sent, and so on.

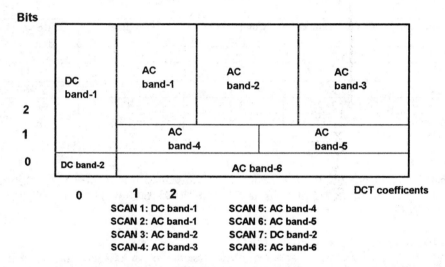

Figure 14. An example of image encoded using the combined progressive JPEG algorithm.

Progressive JPEG Experiment

In this experiment, we implemented both progressive algorithms, spectral selection (SS), and successive approximation (SA) to compress and decompress a 320x200 grayscale image "Cheetah." In both cases, we used four scans, as follows:

	Spectral selection	*Successive approximation*
Scan 1	DC, AC1, AC2	All DCT – divided by 8
Scan 2	AC3-AC9	All DCT – divided by 4
Scan 3	AC10-AC35	All DCT – divided by 2
Scan 4	AC36 – AC63	All DCT – full resolution

The results of the experiments are presented in Tables 6 and 7. Figures 15 and 16 show results of sequential and progressive JPEG compression using Easy/Tech/Codec, respectively. In the case of sequential JPEG, compression ratios obtained are in the range 21 to 52. Assuming an image transmitted over a 64 Kbit/s ISDN network, the following four images are produced using progressive JPEG (Figure 16). The first image of reduced quality appears on the screen very quickly, in 0.9 s. Each subsequent pass improves the image quality and it is obtained after 1.6, 3.6 and 7.0 s, respectively.

Table 6. Progressive Spectral Selection JPEG (Image 'Cheetah': 320x240 pixels → 512,000 bits)

Scan number	Bits transmitted	Compression ratio	Bits/pixel	RMS error
1	29,005	17.65	0.45	19.97
2	37,237	7.73	1.04	13.67
3	71,259	3.72	2.15	7.90
4	32,489	3.01	2.66	4.59
Sequential JPEG	172,117	2.97	2.69	4.59

Table 7. Progressive Successive Approximation JPEG (Image 'Cheetah': 320x240 pixels→ 512,000 bits)

Scan number	Bits transmitted	Compression ratio	Bits/pixel	RMS error
1	26,215	19.53	0.41	22.48
2	34,506	8.43	0.95	12.75
3	63,792	4.11	1.95	7.56
4	95,267	2.33	2.43	4.59
Sequential JPEG	172,117	2.97	2.69	4.59

Note that in both algorithms, the first scan will be transmitted 6 to 7 times faster than the sequential JPEG algorithm (26,215 bits in SA and 29,005 bits in SS vs 172,117 bits in sequential JPEG).

4.6 INTERACTIVE PROGRESSIVE JPEG

We developed an interactive progressive JPEG system for an efficient transmission of complex images. This system is intended for those applications that require a fast transmission of complex, high-quality, high-resolution images through the network with a limited bandwidth. These applications include transmission of medical images, space and earth exploration applications, as well as Internet applications. This technique can also be applied to image archive and browsing systems.

The system operates as follows. Users submit requests for imagery to the remote database via a graphical user interface. Images in the database are stored in compressed form using standard JPEG compression technique using quantization tables, which provide very high quality and low compression rates. Upon an initial request, a DCT image is transmitted and reconstructed at the user site. The DCT image is a version of an image based only on DC coefficients. The transmission of a DCT image, even for very complex images, will take a relatively short time. The user can then isolate specific regions of interest within the image and request additional levels of details through additional scans. In each scan, additional DCT coefficients are transmitted, which improve the quality of the selected region of the image. If all levels of detail are sent, the transmitted image is visually indistinguishable from the original.

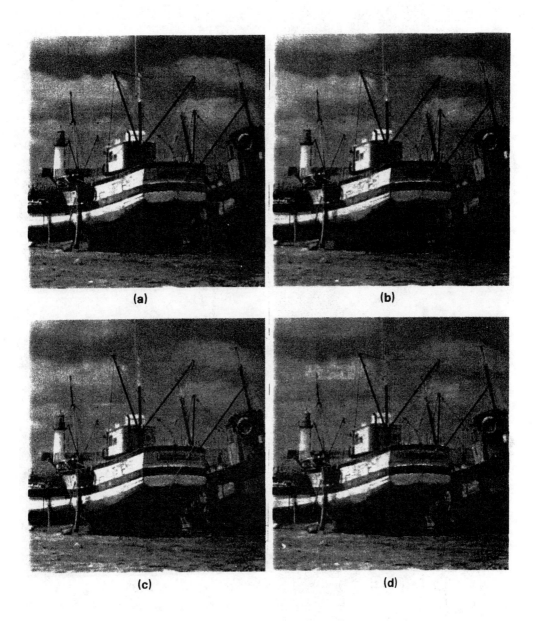

Figure 15. Sequential JPEG results using Easy/Tech Codec (courtesy of Autograph International).
(a) Original image; (b) compression factor 21:1 (low); (c) compression factor 33:1 (medium);
(d) compression factor 52:1 (high).

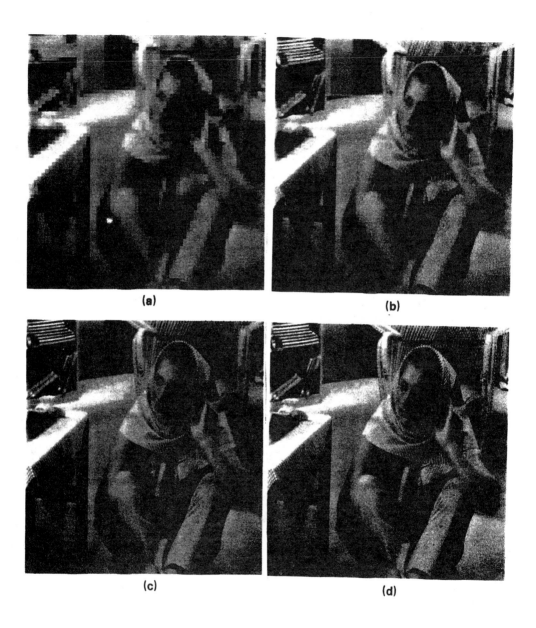

Figure 16. Progressive JPEG results using Easy/Tech Codec (courtesy of Autograph International).
(a) Image after 0.9 s; (b) image after 1.6 s; (c) image after 3.6 s; (d) image after 7.0 s.

4.6 LOSSLESS JPEG COMPRESSION

JPEG standard also supports a lossless mode of operation, by providing a simple predictive compression algorithm, rather than DCT-based technique, which is a lossy one. Figure 17 shows the block diagram of the lossless JPEG encoder, in which a prediction block has replaced the FDCT and the quantization blocks from the baseline sequential DCT-based JPEG.

The predictor block works in a way that a prediction of the sample $\hat{X}$ is calculated on the basis of previous samples A, B and C, and then the difference $\Delta X = X - \hat{X}$ is computed, where X is the actual value of the sample [Figures 18(a) and (b)]. Then, the difference ΔX is coded using the Huffman arithmetic encoder.

Table 8 illustrates several different predictor formulae than can be used for lossless prediction. Lossless JPEG compression typically gives approximately 2:1 compression ratio for moderately complex color images.

4.7 HIERARCHICAL JPEG COMPRESSION

The hierarchical JPEG mode of operation creates a set of compressed images beginning with the small images and then increasing resolution. This process is called down-sampling or pyramidal coding [3,5,8]. After the down-sampling phase, each lower-resolution image is scaled up to the next resolution (up-sampling process), and is used as a prediction for the following stage. Hierarchical JPEG encoder requires significantly more buffer space. However, the benefits are that the encoded image is immediately available at different resolutions.

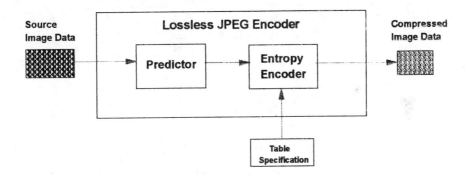

Figure 17. Block diagram of the lossless JPEG encoder.

5. CONCLUSION

In this chapter we presented JPEG compression standard, intended for full-color still-image compression. Several experiments have been performed with the aim of illustrating features and performance of various JPEG techniques, such as sequential, progressive, and lossless techniques. A number of vendors offered software and hardware JPEG implementations, and commercial systems include ALICE 200 from Telephoto, the Super Still-Frame Compression Card from New Medial Graphics, and Optipac 3250 and 5250 JPEG compression accelerator boards from Optivision. LSI Logic has developed L64702 JPEG compressor that can support real-time video applications.

The most popular use of JPEG image compression technology includes its use in photo ID systems telecommunications of images, military image systems, and distributed image management systems.

Nonstandard image compression techniques include vector quantization [8], subband coding and wavelet-based compression, fractal compression, and many other schemes.

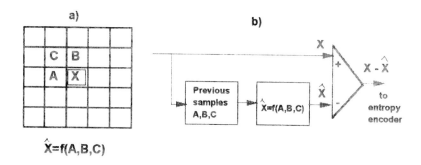

Figure 18.   Lossless JPEG encoding: (a) location of four samples in the predictor,
(b) predictor block diagram.

Table 8. Predictors for Lossless JPEG Compression

Selection value	Predictor formula
0	No prediction
1	X=A
2	X=B
3	X=C
4	X=A+B-C
5	X=A+(B-C)/2
6	X=B+(A-C)/2
7	X=(A+B)/2

REFERENCES

1. W.B. Pennenbaker and J.L. Mitchell, "JPEG Still Image Data Compression Standard," New York, Van Nostrand Reinhold, 1993.
2. G. Wallace, "The JPEG still picture compression standard," *Communications of the ACM*, Vol. 34, pp. 30-44, 1991.
3. M. Nelson, "The Data Compression Book," San Mateo, CA, M&T Books, 1992.
4. R. Steinmetz, "Data Compression in Multimedia Computing – Standards and Systems," Part I and II, *Journal of Multimedia Systems*, Vol. 1, pp. 166-172 and 187-204, 1994.
5. R. Aravind, G. L. Cash, D. C. Duttweller, H-M. Hang, B.G. Haskel, and A. Puri, "Image and Video Coding Standards," *AT&T Technical Journal*, Vol. 72, pp. 67-88, 1993.
6. V. Bhaskaran and K. Konstantinides, "Image and Video Compression Standards – Algorithms and Architectures," Kluwer Academic Publishers, Norwell, MA, 1995.
7. B. Furht, "A Survey of Multimedia Compression Techniques and Standards – Part I: JPEG Standard," *Real-Time Imaging Journal*, Vol. 1, pp. 49-67, 1995.
8. A. Gersho and R.M. Gray, "Vector Quantization and Signal Compression," Kluwer Academic Publishers, Norwell, MA, 1992.

9

VIDEO PRESENTATION AND COMPRESSION

Borko Furht and Raymond Westwater
Florida Atlantic University
Department of Computer Science and Engineering
Boca Raton, Florida 33431
borko@cse.fau.edu

1. **INTRODUCTION**..172
   1.1   VIDEO REPRESENTATION AND FORMATS 172
   1.2   VIDEO INFORMATION UNITS 174
2. **OVERVIEW OF VIDEO COMPRESSION TECHNIQUES** 175
3. **THE H261/H.263 COMPRESSION STANDARD FOR VIDEO TELECOMMUNICATIONS**...177
   3.1   PICTURE FORMATS FOR H.261/H.263 VIDEO CODECS 177
   3.2   THE H.261/H.263 VIDEO ENCODER 178
   3.3   THE H.261/H.263 VIDEO DECODER 180
   3.4   VIDEO DATA STRUCTURE 180
4. **THE MPEG VIDEO COMPRESSION STANDARD**............................181
   4.1   MPEG FRAME STRUCTURE 182
   4.2   MPEG VIDEO ENCODER AND DECODER 183
   4.3   MPEG DATA STREAM 184
   4.4   MOTION ESTIMATION AND COMPENSATION..186
   4.5   MPEG AUDIO ENCODER AND DECODER...194
   4.6   MPEG INTERLEAVED A/V DATA STREAM 195
5. **THE XYZ VIDEO COMPRESSION ALGORITHM**...............................195
   5.1   THE XYZ ENCODER...196
   5.2   THE XYZ DECODER...200
   5.3   COMPARISON WITH MPEG STANDARD 202
6. **CONCLUSIONS** 202
   REFERENCES 203

Abstract. This chapter we first presents various video representations and formats. Then, an overview of video compression techniques is given. Two standards and related techniques are described and evaluated – px64 Kbps (or H.261/H.263) standard for video-based communications and MPEG standard for intensive applications of full-motion video. Both standards use the combination of DCT-based intraframe compression and predictive interframe coding based on motion vector estimation. The techniques for motion vector estimation are analyzed as well. Finally, we also introduce the XYZ video compression technique based on 3D-DCT, which does not require motion vector estimation.

0-8493-1825-4/99/$0.00+$.50
© 1999 by CRC Press LLC

1. INTRODUCTION

This section first describes representation and formats for full-motion video, including computer and television formats. Then, we decompose a video sequence into information units, which are used for video compression and manipulation.

1.1 VIDEO REPRESENTATION AND FORMATS

Video represents a collection of images or frames, where each image (frame) can be represented in one of the formats discussed in the previous chapter. These formats include RGB, YUV, and YCrCb. Continuous motion is produced at a frame rate of 15 frames per second (fps) or higher. Full motion video is typically referred as one at 30 fps, while the traditional movies run at 24 fps. The NTSC television standard in U.S.A. uses 29.97 Hz frequency, which is approximately 30fps, while PAL and SECAM television standards use 25 fps. The new Showscan technology creates movies at 60 fps.

1.1.1 Computer Video Formats

Resolution of an image or video system refers to its capability to reproduce fine detail. Higher resolution requires more complex imaging and video systems for representing these images (video frames) in real time. In computer systems, resolution is characterized by the number of pixels. Table 1 summarizes popular computer video formats and related storage requirements.

Table 1. Characteristics of a Variety of Computer Video Formats

Computer Video Format	Resolution (pixels)	Colors (bits)	Storage Capacity Per Image
CGA - Color Graphics Adapter	320x200	4 (2 bits)	128,000 bits = 16 KB
EGA - Enhanced Graphics Adapter	640x350	16 (4 bits)	896,000 bits= 112 KB
VGA - Video Graphics Adapter	640x480	256 (8 bits)	2,457,600 bits= 307.2 KB
88514/A Display Adapter Mode	1024x768	256 (8 bits)	6,291,456 bits= 786.432 KB
XGA - Extended Graphics Array (a)	640x480	65,000 (24 bits)	6,291,456 bits= 786.432 KB
XGA - Extended Graphics Array (b)	1024x768	256 (8 bits)	6,291,456 bits= 786.432 KB
SVGA - Super VGA	1024x768	65,000 (24 bits)	2.36 MB

Computer video display system architecture typically consists of a frame memory and video controller, which is interfaced to the computer monitor.

1.1.2 Television Formats

In television systems, resolution refers to the number of line pairs resolved on the face of the display screen, expressed in cycles per picture height, or cycles per picture width. For example, the NTSC broadcast system in North America and Japan, referred as 525/59.94, has about 483 lines. The HDTV system doubles the number of lines of current broadcast television at approximately the same field rate. For example, a 1050x960 HDTV system has a total of 960 lines.

Spatial and temporal characteristics of conventional television systems (NTSC, SECAM, and PAL), and high-definition TV (HDTV) are presented in Tables 2 and 3, respectively.

Table 2. Spatial Characteristics of Television Systems

System	Total Lines	Active Lines	Vertical Resolution	Optimal Viewing Distance [m]	Aspect Ratio	Horizontal Resolution	Total Picture Elements
HDTV USA	1050	960	675	2.5	16/9	600	720,000
HDTV Europe	1250	1000	700	2.4	16/9	700	870,000
NTSC	525	484	242	7.0	4/3	330	106,000
PAL	625	575	290	6.0	4/3	425	165,000
SECAM	625	575	290	6.0	4/3	465	180,000

Aspect ratio in Table 2 specifies the geometry of the field and is defined as:

$$Aspect\_Ratio = \frac{Width}{Height}$$

Conventional television systems have the aspect ratio 4/3 = 1.33, while the aspect ratio of HDTV system is 16/9 = 1.78.

The viewing distance (D) determines the angle (h) subtended by the picture height (H), and is defined as:

$$h = \frac{D}{N}$$

Optimal viewing distance for NTSC systems is 7.0 meters, for PAL and SECAM, 6.0 meters, and for HDTV U.S.A. 2.5 meters.

Table 3. Temporal Characteristics of Television Systems

System	Total Channel Width [MHz]	Video Baseband Y [MHz]	Video Baseband R-Y [MHz]	Video Baseband B-Y [MHz]	Scanning Rate Camera [Hz]	Scanning Rate HDTV Display [Hz]	Scanning Rate Convent. Display [Hz]
HDTV U.S.A.	9.0	10.0	5.0	5.0	59.94	59.94	59.94
HDTV Europe	12.0	14.0	7.0	7.0	50	100	50
NTSC	6.0	4.2	1.0	0.6	59.94	NA	59.94
PAL	8.0	5.5	1.8	1.8	50	NA	50
SECAM	8.0	6.0	2.0	2.0	50	NA	50

Television video signals are transmitted through a single television channel. For example, NTSC channel requires 6 MHz frequency, and luminance, chrominance, and sound carriers are separated to avoid interference, as illustrated in Figure 1.

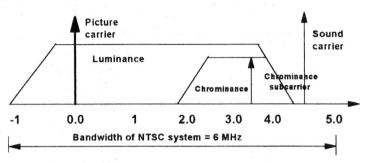

Figure 1. Transmission of TV video signals.

In television systems, combining individual components (RGB or YUV) can create a composite video signal into one signal. During the composition in one signal, chrominance signals can interfere with the luminance, and therefore appropriate modulation methods are used to eliminate this interference. In TV systems, RGB representation provides the highest quality (483 lines per frame in the case of NTSC). S-video includes two components, one chrominance and one luminance, and provides 400 lines per frame, while composite signal, which is a single line, gives 200 lines per frame. RF video signal gives the lowest quality.

1.2 VIDEO INFORMATION UNITS
When the motion video is represented in digital form, it can be decomposed into a time-dependent sequence of individual information units. For example, a motion video sequence can be divided into film, clips, frames, blocks, and pixels, as illustrated in Figure 2.

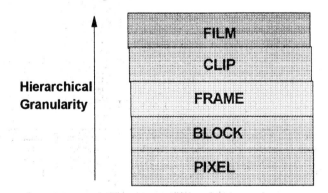

Figure 2. Motion video sequence divided into information units.

A full motion video, or film, consists of a number of clips, which are characterized with a common thread (for example, a camera shot). Each clip consists of a number of frames. Each frame can be divided into blocks. Typical sizes of the blocks, which are used in video processing systems (such as compression, retrieval and indexing, motion estimation, etc.) are 8x8 and 16x16 pixels. Pixels are the smallest pieces of information, which consist of 8, 16, or 24 bits.

2. OVERVIEW OF VIDEO COMPRESSION TECHNIQUES

Most digital images contain a high degree of redundancy, which means that an efficient compression technique can significantly reduce the amount of information needed to store or transmit them. This redundancy can be found between single pixels, between lines, or between frames, when a scene is stationary or slightly moving.

Since about 1989, moving digital video images have been integrated with programs. The difficulty in implementing moving digital video is the tremendous bandwidth required for the encoding of video data. For example, a quarter screen image (320 x 240 pixels) playing on an RGB video screen at full speed of 30 fps requires storage and transmission of 6.9 million bytes per second (MB/s). This data rate is simply prohibitive, and so means of compressing digital video suitable for real-time playback are a necessary step for the widespread introduction of digital motion video applications.

Many digital video compression algorithms have been developed and implemented. The compression ratios of these algorithms vary according to the subjective acceptable level of error, the definition of the word compression, and who is making the claim. Table 4 summarizes video compression algorithms, their typical compression ratios reported in the literature, and their characteristics.

Table 4. Overview of Video Compression Algorithms

Compression Algorithm	Typical Compression Ratio	Characteristics
Intel RTV/Indeo	3:1	A 128X240 data stream is interpolated to 256X240. Color is subsampled 4:1. A simple 16 bit codebook is used without error correction. Frame differencing is used.
Intel PLV	12:1	A native 256X240 stream is encoded using vector quantization and motion compensation. Compression requires specialized equipment.
IBM Photomotion	3:1	An optimal 8-bit color palette is determined, and run-length encoding and frame differencing are used.
Motion JPEG	10:1	Uses 2-D DCT to encode individual frames. Gives good real-time results with inexpensive but special-purpose equipment. This technique supports random-access since no frame differencing is used.
Fractals	10:1	Fractals compress natural scenes well, but require tremendous computing power.
Wavelets	20:1	2-D and 3-D wavelets have been used in the compression of motion video. Wavelet compression is low enough in complexity to compress entire images, and therefore does not suffer from the boundary artifacts seen in DCT-based techniques.
H.261/H263	50:1	Real-time compression and decompression algorithm for video telecommunications. It is based on 2-D DCT with simple motion estimation between frames.
MPEG	30:1	Uses 2-D DCT with motion estimation and interpolation between frames. The MPEG standard is difficult and expensive to compress, but plays back in real time with inexpensive equipment.

An ideal video compression technique should have the following characteristics:

- Will produce levels of compression rivaling MPEG without objectionable artifacts.
- Can be played back in real time with inexpensive hardware support.
- Can degrade easily under network overload or on a slow platform.
- Can be compressed in real time with inexpensive hardware support.

In this chapter, we focus on two well-established standard techniques, MPEG for intensive video applications and H.261/H.263 standard for video telecommunications. We also describe the promising XYZ technique.

Video compression techniques made feasible a number of applications. Four distinct applications of the compressed video can be summarized as: (a) consumer broadcast television, (b) consumer playback, (c) desktop video, and (d) videoconferencing.

Consumer broadcast television, which includes digital video delivery to homes, typically requires a small number of high-quality compressors and a large number of low-cost decompressors. Expected compression ratio is about 50:1.

Consumer playback applications, such as CD-ROM libraries and interactive games, also require a small number of compressors and a large number of low-cost decompressors. The required compression ratio is about 100:1.

Desktop video, which includes systems for authoring and editing video presentations, is a symmetrical application requiring the same number of encoders and decoders. The expected compression ratio is in the range from 5:1 to 50:1.

Videoconferencing applications also require the same number of encoders and decoders, and the expected compression ratio is about 100:1.

Table 5. Applications of the Compressed Video and Current Video Compression Standards

Application	Bandwidth	Standard	Size	Frame Rate [frames/sec]
Analog Videophone	5-10 Kbps	none	170x128	2-5
Low Bit-rate Video Conferencing	26-64 Kbps	H.263	128x96 176x144	15-30
Basic Video Telephony	64-128 Kbps	H.261	176x144 352x288	10-20
Video-conferencing	>= 384 Kbps	H.261	352x288	15-30
Interactive Multimedia	1-2 Mbps	MPEG-1	352x240	15-30
Digital TV - NTSC	3-10 Mbps	MPEG-2	720x480	30
High Definition Television	15-80 Mbps	MPEG-2	1200x800	30-60

Table 5 summarizes applications of the compressed video, by specifying current standards used in various applications, the required bandwidth, and the typical frame sizes and frame rates.

3. Px64 COMPRESSION ALGORITHM FOR VIDEO TELECOMMUNICATIONS

The H.261/263 standard, commonly called px64 Kbps, is optimized to achieve very high compression ratios for full-color, real-time motion video transmission. The px64 compression algorithm combines intraframe and interframe coding to provide fast processing for on-the-fly video compression and decompression. *Intraframe coding* refers to the coding of individual frames, while *interframe coding* is the coding of a frame in reference to the previous or future frames.

The px64 standard is optimized for applications such as video-based telecommunications. Because these applications are usually not motion-intensive, the algorithm uses limited motion search and estimation strategies to achieve higher compression ratios. For standard video communication images, compression ratios of 100:1 to over 2000:1 can be achieved.

The px64 compression standard is intended to cover the entire ISDN channel capacity ($p = 1$, 2,...30). For $p = 1$ to 2, due to limited available bandwidth, only desktop face-to-face visual communications (videophone) can be implemented using this compression algorithm. However, for p >6, more complex pictures are transmitted, and the algorithm is suitable for videoconferencing applications.

3.1 PICTURE FORMATS FOR H.261/H.263 VIDEO CODECS

For the H.261 algorithm two formats are defined: CIF and QCIF, while for the H.263 algorithm three additional formats are specified: SQCIF, 4CIF, and 16CIF.

The Common Intermediate Format (CIF) is a non-interlaced format, based on 352x288 pixels per frame at 30 frames per second. These values represent half the active lines of 625/25 television signal and the picture rate of a 525/30 NTSC signal. Therefore, 625/25 systems need only to perform a picture rate conversion, while NTSC systems need to perform only a line-number conversion.

Color pictures are coded using one luminance and two color-difference components (YCbCr format), specified by the CCIR 601 standard. The Cb and Cr components are subsampled by a factor of two on both horizontal and vertical directions, and have 176x144 pixels per frame. The picture aspect ratio for all five CIF-based formats is 4:3. Table 6 summarizes the picture formats for H.261 and H.263 codecs.

Table 6. Picture Formats for H.261 and H.263 Video Codecs

PICTURE FORMAT	LUMINANCE PIXELS	MAX FRAME RATE [F/S]	VIDEO SOURCE RATE	AVERAGE CODED BIT RATE	H.261 CODEC	H.263 CODEC
SQCIF	128 x 96	30	1.3 Mb/s	26 Kb/s	Optional	Required
QCIF	176 x 144	30	9 Mb/s	64 Kb/s (px64 Kbps)	Required	Required
CIF	352 x 288	30	36 Mb/s	384 Kb/s (px64 Kbps)	Optional	Optional
4CIF	704 x 576	30	438 Mb/s	3-6 Mb/s	Not defined	Optional
16CIF	1408 x 1152	50	2.9 Gb/s	20-60 Mb/s	Not defined	Optional

Example 1: Desktop videophone application

For a desktop videophone application, if we assume $p = 1$, the available ISDN network bandwidth is $B_A = 64$ Kbits/s. If the QCIF format is used, the required number of bits per frame consists of one luminance and two chrominance components:

$$N_b = (144 \times 176 + 72 \times 88) \times 8 \ bits = 300 \ Kbits/frame$$

If the data is transmitted at 10 frames/s, the required bandwidth is:

$$B_r = 300\,Kbits/frame \times 10\,frames/s = 3\,bits/s$$

As a consequence, a video compression algorithm should provide compression ratio of minimum:

$$C_r = \tfrac{B_r}{B_A} = \tfrac{3\,Mbits/s}{64\,Kbits/s} = 47$$

Example 2: Videoconferencing application

If we assume $p = 10$ for a videoconferencing application, the available ISDN network bandwidth becomes $B_r = 640$ Kbits/s. If the CIF format is used, the total number of bits per frame becomes:

$$N_b = (288 \times 352 + 144 \times 176 + 144 \times 176) \times 8\,bits = 1.21\,bits/frame$$

Assuming a frame rate of 30 frames/s, the required bandwidth for the transmission of videoconferencing data becomes:

$$B_r = 1.21\,Mbits/frame \times 30\ frames/s = 36.4\,Mbits/s$$

Therefore, a video compression algorithm should provide compression ratio of minimum:

$$C_r = \tfrac{B_r}{B_a} = \tfrac{36.4\,Mbits/s}{640\,Kbits/s} = 57$$

3.2 THE H.261/H.263 VIDEO ENCODER

The H.261/H.263 video compression algorithm combines intraframe and interframe coding to provide fast processing combines intraframe and interframe coding to provide fast processing for on-the-fly video. The algorithm creates two types of frames:

- DCT-based intraframe compression, which similar to JPEG, uses DCT, quantization, and entropy coding, and
- Predictive interframe coding based on Differential Pulse Code Modulation (DPCM) and motion estimation.

The block diagram of the video encoder is presented in Figure 3.

The H.261/H.263 coding algorithm begins by coding an intraframe block and then sends it to the video multiplex coder. The same frame is then decompressed using the inverse quantizer and inverse DCT, and then stored in the frame memory for interframe coding.

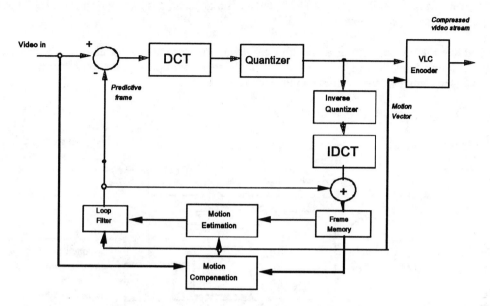

Figure 3. Block diagram of the H.261/H.263 video encoder.

During the interframe coding, the prediction based on the DPCM algorithm is used to compare every macro block of the actual frame with the available macro blocks of the previous frame, as illustrated in Figure 4. To reduce the encoding delay, only the closest previous frame is used for prediction. Then, the difference, created as error terms, is DCT-coded and quantized, and sent to the video multiplex coder with or without the motion vector.

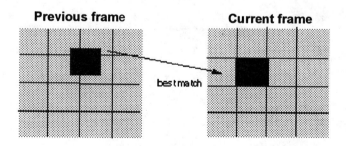

Figure 4. The principle of interframe coding in H.261/263 codecs.

For interframe coding, the frames are encoded using one of the following three techniques:

(i)   DPCM coding with no motion compensation (zero-motion vectors).
(ii)   DPCM coding with non-zero vectors.
(iii)   Blocks are filtered by an optional predefined filter to remove high-frequency noise.

At the final step, variable-length coding (VLC), such as Huffman encoder, is used to produce more compact code. An optional loop filter can be used to minimize the prediction error by smoothing the pixels in the previous frame. At least one in every 132 frames should be an intraframe.

3.3 THE H.261/H.263 VIDEO DECODER

The H.261/H.263 video decoder is shown in Figure 5. It consists of the receiver buffer, VLC decoder, inverse quantizer, inverse DCT, and the motion compensation, which includes frame memory and an optional loop filter [3,4].

In addition to the encoding and decoding of video, the audio data must also be compressed and decompressed. Special buffering and multiplexing/demultiplexing circuitry is required to handle the complexities of combining the video and audio.

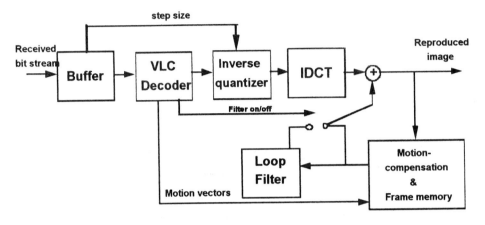

Figure 5. Block diagram of the H.261/H.263 video decoder.

3.4 VIDEO DATA STRUCTURE

According to the H.261 standard, a data stream has a hierarchical structure consisting of Pictures, Groups of Blocks (GOB), Macro Blocks (MB), and Blocks [3,4]. A Macro Block is composed of four (8 x 8) luminance (Y) blocks, and two (8 x 8) chrominance (C_r and C_b) blocks, as illustrated in Figure 6.

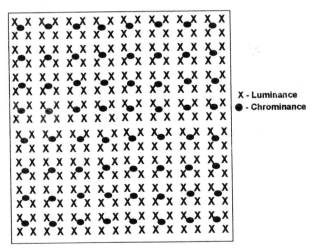

Figure 6. The composition of a Micro Block: MB = 4Y + Cb + Cr.

A Group of Blocks is composed of 3x11 MBs. A CIF Picture contains 12 GOBs, while a QCIF Picture consists of four GOBs. The hierarchical block structure is shown in Figure 7.

Each of the layers contains headers, which carry information about the data that follows. For example, a picture header includes a 20-bit picture start code, video format (CIF or QCIF), frame number, etc. A detailed structure of the headers is given by Liou [3].

A H.261 codec, proposed by Ghanbari [5], expands the existing H.261 codec to operate in ATM networks. A software-based video compression algorithm, called the Popular Video Codec (PVC), proposed by Huang et al. [6], is suitable for real-time systems. The PVC coder simplifies compression and decompression processes of the px64 algorithm by removing the transform and the motion estimation parts, and modifies the quantizer and the entropy coder.

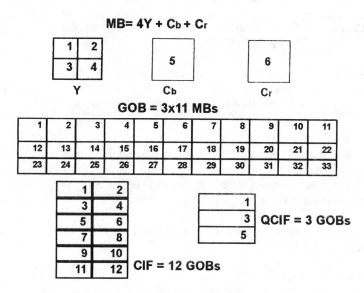

Figure 7. Hierarchical block structure of the p x 64 data stream.

4. THE MPEG VIDEO COMPRESSION STANDARD

The MPEG compression algorithm is intended for compression of full-motion video [8,10]. The compression method uses interframe compression and can achieve compression ratios of 200:1 through storing only the differences between successive frames. The MPEG approach is optimized for motion-intensive video applications, and its specification also includes an algorithm for the compression of audio data at ratios ranging from 5:1 to 10:1.

The MPEG first-phase standard (MPEG-1) is targeted for compression of 320x240 full-motion video at rates of 1 to 1.5 Mb/s in applications, such as interactive multimedia and broadcast television. MPEG-2 standard is intended for higher resolutions, similar to the digital video studio standard, CCIR 601, EDTV, and further leading to HDTV. It specifies compressed bit streams for high-quality digital video at the rate of 2-80 Mb/s. The MPEG-2 standard supports interlaced video formats and a number of features for HDTV.

The MPEG-2 standard also addresses scalable video coding for a variety of applications, which need different image resolutions, such as video communications over ISDN networks using ATM [7,8]. The MPEG-4 standard is intended for compression of full-motion video consisting of small frames and requiring slow refreshments. The data rate required is 9-40 Kbps, and the target applications include interactive multimedia and video telephony. This standard requires the development of new model-based image coding techniques for human interaction and low-bit-rate speech coding techniques [7]. Table 7 illustrates various motion-video formats and corresponding MPEG parameters.

The MPEG algorithm is intended for both asymmetric and symmetric applications. Asymmetric applications are characterized by frequent use of the decompression process, while the compression process is performed once. Examples include movies-on-demand, electronic publishing, and education and training. Symmetric applications require equal use of the compression and decompression processes. Examples include multimedia mail and video-conferencing.

Table 7. Parameters of MPEG Algorithms

FORMAT	VIDEO PARAMETERS	COMPRESSED BIT RATE	
SIF	352 x 240 at 30 Hz	1.2-3 Mbps	→ MPEG-1
CCIR 601	720 x 486 at 30 Hz	5-10 Mbps	
EDTV	960 x 486 at 30 Hz	7-15 Mbps	→ MPEG-2
HDTV	1920 x 1080 at 30 Hz	20-40 Mbps	

When the MPEG standard was conceived, the following features were identified as being import: random access, fast forward/reverse searches, reverse playback, audio-visual synchronization, robustness to errors, editability, format flexibility, and cost-trade-off. These features were described in detail by LeGall [8].

The MPEG standard consists of three parts: synchronization and multiplexing of video and audio; video; and audio.

4.1 MPEG FRAME STRUCTURE
In the MPEG standard, frames in a sequence are coded using three different algorithms, as illustrated in Figure 8.

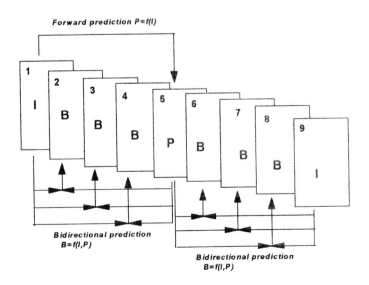

Figure 8. Types of frames in the MPEG standard.

I frames (intra images) are self-contained and coded using a DCT-based technique similar to JPEG. **I** frames are used as random access points to MPEG streams, and they give the lowest compression ratios within MPEG.

P frames (predicted images) are coded using forward predictive coding, where the actual frame is coded with reference to a previous frame (**I** or **P**). This process is similar to H.261 predictive coding, except the previous frame is not always the closest previous, as in H.261 coding (see Figure 4). The compression ratio of **P** frames is significantly higher than of **I** frames.

B frames (bidirectional or interpolated images) are coded using two reference frames, a past and a future frame (which can be **I** or **P** frames). Bidirectional or interpolated coding provides the highest amount of compression.

Note that in Figure 8, the first three **B** frames (2, 3 and 4) are bidirectionally coded using the past frame **I** (frame 1) and the future frame **P** (frame 5). Therefore, the decoding order will differ from the encoding order. The **P** frame 5 must be decoded before **B** frames 2, 3, and 4, and **I** frame 9 before **B** Frames 6, 7, and 8. If the MPEG sequence is transmitted over the network, the actual transmission order should be {1, 5, 2, 3, 4, 9, 6, 7, 8}.

The MPEG application determines a sequence of **I**, **P**, and **B** frames. If there is a need for fast random access, the best resolution would be achieved by coding the whole sequence as **I** frames (MPEG become identical to MJPEG). However, the highest compression ratio can be achieved by incorporating a large number of **B** frames. The following sequence has been proven to be very effective for a number of practical applications [7]:

$$\textbf{(I B B P B B P B B) (I B B P B B P B B)...}$$

In the case of 25 frames/s, random access will be provided through nine still frames (**I** and **P** frames), which is about 360 ms [7]. On the other hand, this sequence will allow a relatively high compression ratio. In an example, if we assume that the compression ratio for **I** frames is 1:10, for **P** frames is 1:40, and for **B** frames is 1:90, an average compression ratio for this MPEG sequence is

$$Cr = \frac{1 \times 10}{9} + \frac{2 \times 40}{9} + \frac{6 \times 90}{9} = 70$$

4.2 MPEG VIDEO ENCODER AND DECODER

The block diagram of the MPEG encoder is given in Figure 9, while the MPEG decoder is shown in Figure 10.

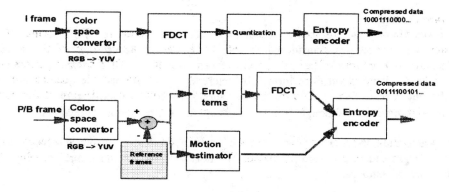

Figure 9. The block diagram of the MPEG encoder.

I frames are created similar to JPEG encoded pictures, while **P** and **B** frames are encoded in terms of previous and future frames. The motion vector is estimated, and the difference between the predicted and actual blocks (error terms) are calculated. The error terms are then DCT encoded and the entropy encoder is used to produce the compact code.

4.3 MPEG DATA STREAM

The MPEG specification defines a "video sequence" composed of a video sequence header and many Group-Of-Pictures (GOP), as illustrated in Figure 11. The video sequence header defines the video format, picture dimensions, aspect ratio, frame rate, and delivered data rate. Supported video formats include CCIR601, HDTV(16:9), and VGA. Supported chroma formats include "4:2:0" (YUV) and "4:4:4" (RGB). A suggested buffer size for the video sequence is also specified, a number intended to buffer jitter caused by differences in decode time.

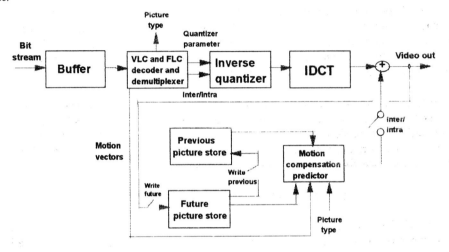

Figure 10. The block diagram of the MPEG decoder

A GOP contains pictures that may be encoded into one of three supported compression formats. The GOP header contains a starting time for the group, and can therefore be used as a point of random access. Each frame within the GOP is numbered, and its number coupled with the GOP start time and the playback frame rate determines its playback time. Each picture is subdivided into "slices" and then into "macroblocks." A macroblock is composed of four 8x8 blocks of luminance data, and typically two 8x8 blocks of chrominance data, one Cr and one Cb.

I Picture Format

The **I** (Intraframe) picture format substantially corresponds to the JPEG format. These pictures are encoded by transformation into DCT space, quantization of the resultant coefficients, and entropy coding of the result. Transformation into DCT space is performed by an 8x8 DCT. Quantization is performed by reference to a user-loadable quantization table modified by a scale factor. This mechanism supports adaptive quantization at the cost of additional complexity – although 30% improvement in compression is claimed [9].

After quantization, the resulting coefficients are reordered in zig-zag order, run-length coded, variable-length coded, and entropy coded. The resulting data stream should roughly show JPEG levels of compression.

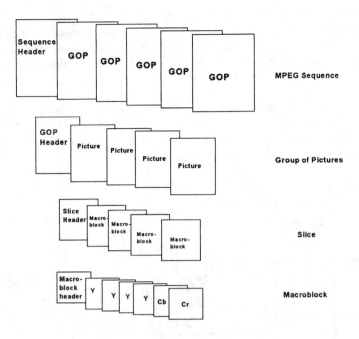

Figure 11. MPEG data stream.

P Picture Format

The **P** (Predicted) picture format introduces the concept of motion compensation. Each macroblock is coded with a vector that predicts its value from an earlier **I** or **P** frame. The decoding process copies the contents of the macroblock-sized data at the address referenced by the vector into the macroblock of the **P** frame currently being decoded. Five bits of resolution are reserved for the magnitude of the vector in each of the x and y directions, meaning that 1024 possible data blocks may be referenced by the predicted macroblock. However, eight possible magnitude ranges may be assigned to those five bits, meaning as many as 8192 macroblocks might have to be evaluated to exhaustively determine the best vector. Each evaluation might require testing as many as 384 pixels, and a further complexity is seen in performing fractional interpolation of pixels (vector motions as small as 1/2 pixel are supported). Finally, the difference between the prediction and the macroblock to be compressed may be encoded in like fashion to **I** frame encoding above.

B Picture Format

The **B** (Bidirectional prediction) picture format is calculated with two vectors. A backward vector references a macroblock-sized region in the previous **I** or **P** frame, the forward vector references a macroblock-sized region in the next **I** or **P** frame. For this reason, **I** and **P** frames are placed in the coded stream before any **B** frames that reference them.

The macroblock-sized regions referenced by the motion compensation vectors are averaged to produce the motion estimate for the macroblock being decoded. As with **P** frames, the error between the prediction and the frame being encoded is compressed and placed in the bitstream. The error factor is decompressed and added to the prediction to form the **B** frame macroblock.

Many demanding technical issues are raised by the MPEG specification. These include fast algorithms for the DCT, fast algorithms for motion vector estimation, algorithms for adaptive quantization, and decompression in environments that allow some errors.

4.4 MOTION ESTIMATION AND COMPENSATION

The coding process for **P** and **B** frames includes the motion estimator, which finds the best matching block in the available reference frames. **P** frames always use forward prediction, while **B** frames always use bidirectional prediction, also called motion-compensated interpolation, as illustrated in Figure 12 [4,12].

B frames can use forward, backward prediction, or interpolation. A block in the current frame (**B** frame) can be predicted by another block from the past reference frame (**B** = **A** → forward prediction), or from the future reference frame (**B** = **C** → backward prediction), or by the average of two blocks (**B** = (**A** + **C**)/2 → interpolation).

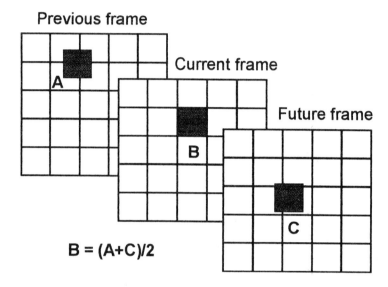

Figure 12. Motion compensated interpolated implemented in MPEG. Each block in the current frame is interpolated using the blocks from a previous and a future frame.

Motion estimation is used to extract the motion information from the video sequence. For every 16 x 16 block of **P** and **B** frames, one or two motion vectors are calculated. One motion vector is calculated for **P** and forward and backward predicted **B** frames, while two motion vectors are calculated for interpolated **B** frames.

The MPEG standard does not specify the motion estimation technique; however, block-matching techniques are likely to be used. In block-matching techniques, the goal is to estimate the motion of a block of size (n x m) in the present frame in relation to the pixels of the previous or the future frames. The block is compared with a corresponding block within a search area of size ($m + 2p$ x $n + 2p$) in the previous (or the future) frame, as illustrated in Figure 13(a). In a typical MPEG system, a match block (or a macroblock) in 16x16 pixels ($n = m = 16$), and the parameter $p = 6$ [Figure 13 (b)].

Many block-matching techniques for motion vector estimation have been developed and evaluated in the literature, such as

      (i)   the exhaustive search (or brute force) algorithm;
      (ii)   the three-step-search algorithm;
      (iii)   the 2-D logarithmic search algorithm;
      (iv)   the conjugate direction search algorithm;

(v)   the parallel hierarchical 1-D search algorithm; and

(vi)   the modified pixel-difference classification, layered structure algorithm.

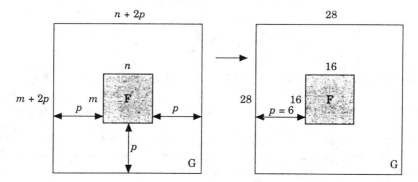

Figure 13. The search area in block-matching techniques for motion vector estimation:
(a) general case, (b) typical case for MPEG: $n = m = 16$, $p = 6$.
F - a macroblock in the current frame; G - search area in a previous (or a future) frame.

4.4.1 Cost Functions

The block matching techniques for motion estimation obtain the motion vector by minimizing a cost function. The following cost functions have been proposed in the literature:

(a)   The Mean-Absolute Difference (MAD), defined as:

$$MAD\,(dx, dy) = \tfrac{1}{mn} \sum_{i=n/2}^{n/2} \sum_{j=-m/2}^{m/2} |\,F(i, j) - G(i + dx, j + dy)\,| \qquad [1]$$

where

F(I, j) represents a (m x n) macroblock from the current frame,

G(I, j) represents the same macroblock from a reference frame (past or future),

(dx, dy) a vector representing the search location.

The search space is specified by $dx = \{\,-p, +p\}$ and $dy = \{-p, +p\}$.

For a typical MPEG system, $m = n = 16$ and $p = 6$, the MAD function becomes:

$$MAD(dx, dy) = \tfrac{1}{256} \sum_{i=-8}^{8} \sum_{j=-8}^{8} |\,F(i, j) - G(i + dx, j + dy)| \qquad [2]$$

and

$$dx = \{-6, 6\}, dy = \{-6, 6\}$$

(b)   The Mean-Squared Difference (MSD) cost function is defined as:

$$MSD\,(dx, dy) = \tfrac{1}{mn} \sum_{i=-n/s}^{n/2} \sum_{i=-m/2}^{m/2} [F(i, j) - G(i + dx, j + dy)]^2 \qquad [3]$$

(c)   The Cross-Correlation Function (CCF) is defined as:

$$CCF(dx,dy) = \frac{\sum_i \sum_j F(i,j)G(i+dx,j+dy)}{\left(\sum_i \sum_j F^2(i,j)\right)^{\frac{1}{2}} \left(\sum_i \sum_j G^2(i+dx,j+dy)\right)^{\frac{1}{2}}} \qquad [4]$$

The mean absolute difference (MAD) cost function is considered a good candidate for video applications, because it is easy to implement in hardware. The other two cost functions, MSD, and CCF, can be more efficient, but are too complex for hardware implementations.

To reduce the computational complexity of MAD, MSD, and CCF cost functions, Gharavi and Mills have proposed a simple block matching criterion, called Pixel Difference Classification (PDC) [13]. The PDC criterion is defined as:

$$PDC(dx,dy) = \sum_i \sum_j T(dx,dy,i,j) \qquad [5]$$

for $(dx, dy) = \{-p, p\}$.

T (dx, dy, I, j) is the binary representation of the pixel difference defined as:

$$T(dx,dy,i,j) = \begin{cases} 1, & |F(i,j) - G(i+dx,j+dy)| \le t; \\ 0, & otherwise \end{cases} \qquad [6]$$

where t is a pre-defined threshold value.

In this way, each pixel in a macroblock is classified as either a matching pixel ($T = 1$) or a mismatching pixel ($T = 0$). The block that maximizes the PDC function is selected as the best matched block.

4.4.2 Motion Vector Estimation Algorithms

The exhaustive search algorithm.
The exhaustive search algorithm is the simplest but computationally most intensive search method that evaluates the cost function at every location in the search area. If MSD cost function is used for estimating the motion vector, it would be necessary to evaluate $(2p + 1)^2$ MSE functions. For $p = 6$, it gives 169 iterations for each macroblock..

The three-step search algorithm.
The three-step search algorithm, proposed by Koga et al. [14] and implemented by Lee et al. [15] first calculated the cost function at the center and eight surrounding locations in the search area. The location that produces the smallest cost function (typically MSD function is used) becomes the center location for the next step, and the search range is reduced by half.

A three-step motion vector estimation algorithm for $p = 6$ is shown in Figure 14.

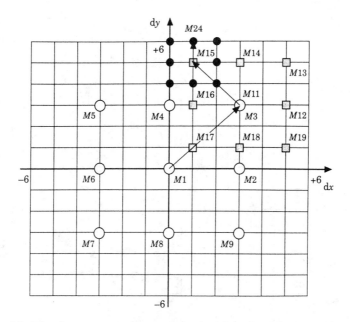

Figure 14. The three-step motion vector estimation algorithm – an example.

Step 1
In the first step, nine values for the cost function MAD (for simplification purposes denoted as M) are calculated: $M_1 = M(0, 0)$, $M_2 = M(3, 0)$, $M_3 = M(3, 3)$, $M_4 = M(0, 3)$, $M_5 = M(-3, 3)$, $M_6 = M(-3, 0)$, $M_7 = M(-3, -3)$, $M_8 = (0, -3)$, $M_9 = M(3, -3)$, as illustrated in Figure 14. Assuming that M_3 gives the smallest cost function, it becomes the center location for the next step.

Step 2
Nine new cost functions are calculated, for M_3 and eight surrounding locations, using a smaller step equal to 2. These nine points are denoted in Figure 14 as $M_{11}, M_{12}, M_{13}...M_{19}$.

Step 3
In the last step, the location with the smallest cost function is selected as a new center location (in the example in Figure 14, this is M_{15}), and nine new cost functions are calculated surrounding this location: $M_{21}, M_{22}, M_{23},...M_{29}$. The smallest value is the final estimate of the motion vector. In the example in Figure 14, it is M_{24}, which gives the motion vector {dx, dy} equal to {1, 6}.

Note that the total number of computations of the cost function is: $9 \times 3 - 2 = 25$, which is much better than 169 in the exhaustive search algorithm.

The 2-D logarithmic search algorithm.
This algorithm, proposed by Jain and Jain [16], uses the MSD cost function and performs a logarithmic 2-D search along a virtual direction of minimum distortion (DMD) on the data within the search area. The modified version of the algorithm, described by Srinivasan and Rao [17], uses the MAD cost function, and can be described using the following steps, as illustrated in Figure 15.

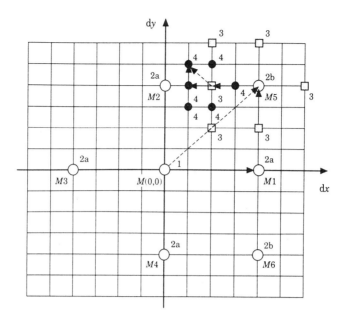

Figure 15. The modified 2-D logarithmic search algorithm.

Step 1

The MAD function is calculated for $dx = dy = 0$, $M(0, 0)$ and compared to the threshold (e.g., the value is 4 out of 255): $M(0, 0) < T$. If this is satisfied, the tested block is unchanged and the search is complete.

Step 2a

The next four cost functions are calculated, $M_1(4, 0)$, $M_2(0, 4)$, $M_3(-4, 0)$, and $M_4(0, -4)$, and their minimum is found and compared to $M(0, 0)$:

$$M' = \min(M_1, M_2, M_3, M_4) < M(0,0).$$

If the minimum $M' > M(0, 0)$, go to step 3; otherwise, this value is compared against the threshold, T. If $M' < T$, the value M' is the minimum and the search ends. Otherwise, the algorithm continues with step 2b.

Step 2b

Assuming in the previous step 2a that the minimum $M' = M_1(4, 0)$, then the next two surrounding positions are calculated: $M_5(4, 4)$, and $M_6(4, -4)$, as indicated in Figure 15. The tests for minimum and threshold are performed again and, if the minimum is found, the procedure is complete. Otherwise, step 3 continues.

Step 3

Assuming that the new minimum location is $M_5(4, 4)$, a similar search procedure (steps 2a and 2b) is continued, except the step is divided by 2. In Figure 15, the new minimum becomes $M(2, 4)$.

Step 4

The step is further reduced by 2, and the final search (steps 2a and 2b) is performed. The minimum (dx, dy) is found. In Figure 15 it is $(1, 5)$.

For $p = 6$, this algorithm requires maximum 19 cost function calculations, as shown in Figure 15.

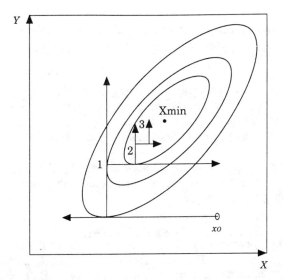

Figure 16. A principle of the conjugate direction search algorithm (one-at-a-time search).

The conjugate direction search algorithm.

This algorithm for motion vector estimation, proposed by Srinivasan and Rao [17], is an adaptation of the traditional iterative conjugate direction search method. This method can be implemented as one-at-a-time search method, as illustrated in Figure 16.

In Figure 16, direction of search is parallel to one of coordinate axes, and each variable is adjusted while the other is fixed. This method has been adapted for motion vector estimation [17], as illustrated in Figure 17. The algorithm consists of the following three steps:

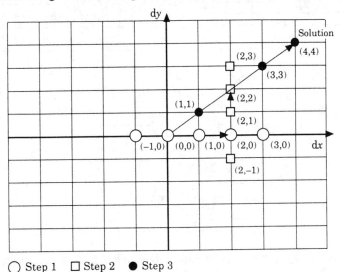

Figure 17. The conjugate direction search method for motion vector estimation.

Step 1

Values of the cost function MAD in the dx direction are calculated until the minimum is found. The calculation is as follows: (a) $M(0, 0)$, $M(1, 0)$, and $M(-1, 0)$. (b) If $M(1, 0)$ is the minimum, $M(2, 0)$ is computed and evaluated, and so on. This step is complete when a minimum in the dx direction is found [in Figure 17, the minimum is $M(2, 0)$].

Step 2
The search now continues in the dy direction by calculating cost functions $M(2, -1)$ and $M(2, 1)$. A minimum in the dy direction is then found at $M(2, 2)$ in Figure 17.

Step 3
The direction of search is now the vector connecting the starting point $(0, 0)$ and the obtained minimum $(2, 2)$. The following cost functions are calculated and evaluated next: $M(1, 1)$ and $M(3, 3)$, and so on, until a minimum in this direction is found. In the example in Figure 17, the minimum is $M(4, 4)$, and the obtained motion vector is d$x = 4$ and d$y = 4$.

It may happen that the dx and dy vectors, obtained in steps 2 and 3, do not constitute a square as given in Figure 17. In that case, the nearest grid points on the direction joining $(0, 0)$ and the obtained minimum point are selected.

The parallel hierarchical 1-D search algorithm (PHODS).
The PHODS algorithm, proposed by Chan *et al.* [18], reduces the number of blocks to be searched. In this algorithm, the 2-D motion vector for each block is represented as two 1-D motion vectors, one in horizontal and one in vertical direction. Both vectors are searched in parallel. The algorithm uses MAD or MSD cost function and can be described using the following steps as illustrated in Figure 18.

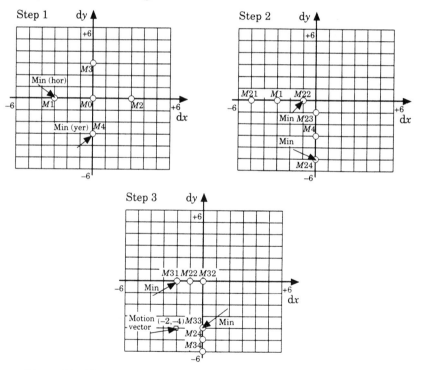

Figure 18. The parallel hierarchical 1-D search algorithm – an example.

Step 1
The cost function is further calculated in the search center (M_0), and in two additional positions in both directions (M_1 and M_2 in horizontal direction, and M_3 and M_4 in vertical direction). The positions with the smallest cost functions in both directions become the search centers in the next step, and the distance between the candidate blocks is reduced. M_1 gives the minimum in horizontal direction, while M_4 in the vertical direction. They are new search centers for the next step.

Step 2

The cost function is further calculated in M_1, M_{21}, and M_{22} horizontal locations and M_4, M_{23} and M_{24} vertical locations. New minimum locations are found as M_{22} in horizontal and M_{24} in vertical direction.

Step 3

In the last step, the search step is further reduced to 1, and the cost function is calculated in horizontal locations M_{22}, M_{31}, and M_{32}, and vertical locations M_{24}, M_{33}, and M_{34}. Assuming the M_{31} is the minimum in horizontal direction and M_{33} in vertical direction, the estimation motion vector becomes $dx = -2$ and $dy = -4$.

The modified pixel-difference classification, layered structure algorithm (MPDC-LSA).
This algorithm, proposed by Chan et al. [18], is a block-matching algorithm based on a modified PDC function, which gives low computational complexity. The algorithm is based on the MPDC criterion, where a block is classified as a matching block if all its pixels are matching pixels with respect to the defined threshold. The MPDC criterion is defined as

$$MPDC \quad (dx, dy) = \begin{cases} 1, & if \quad PDC \quad (dx, dy) = n^2; \\ 0, & otherwise \end{cases} \qquad [7]$$

The search procedure and experimental results are presented by Chan et al. [18].

Using a block-matching motion estimation technique, the best motion vector(s) is found which specifies the space distance between the actual and the reference macroblocks. The macroblock in the current frame is then predicted based on a macroblock in a previous frame (forward prediction), a macroblock in a future frame (backward prediction), or using interpolation between macroblocks in a previous and a future frame. A macroblock in the current frame $F(i, j)$ is predicted using the following expression:

$$F_p(i, j) = G(i \ dx, j + dy) \qquad [8]$$

for $(i, j) = \{-8, 8\}$.

$F_p(i, j)$ is the predicted current macroblock, $G(i, j)$ is the same macroblock in a previous/future frame, and (dx, dy) is the estimated motion vector.

For interpolated frames, a macroblock in the current frame $F(i, j)$ is predicted using the following formula

$$F_p(i, j) = \tfrac{1}{2}[G_1(i + dx_1) + G_2(i + dx_2, j + dy_2)] \qquad [9]$$

for $(i, j) = \{-8, 8\}$,

$G_1(i, j)$ is the same macroblock in a previous frame, (dx_1, dy_1) is the corresponding motion vector, $G_2(i, j)$ is the same macroblock in a future frame, and (dx_2, dy_2) is its corresponding motion vector.

The difference between predicted and actual macroblocks, called the error terms $E(i, j)$, is then calculated using the following expression:

$$E(i,j) = F(i,j) - F_p(i,j) \qquad [10]$$

for *(i, j)* = {-8, 8}.

4.5 MPEG AUDIO ENCODER AND DECODER

The MPEG standard also covers audio compression. MPEG uses the same sampling frequencies as compact disc digital audio (CD-DA) and digital audio tapes (DAT). Besides these two frequencies, 44.1 KHz and 48 KHz, 32 KHz are also supported, all at 16 bits. The audio data on a compact disc, with two channels of audio samples at 44.1 KHz with 16 bits/sample, require a data rate of about 1.4 Mbits/s [19]. Therefore, there is a need to compress audio data as well.

Existing audio compression techniques include μ-law and Adaptive Differential Pulse Code Modulation (ADPCM), which are both of low complexity, low compression ratios, and offer medium audio quality. The MPEG audio compression algorithm is of high complexity, but offers high compression ratios and high audio quality. It can achieve compression ratios ranging from 5:1 to 10:1.

The MPEG audio compression algorithm is comprised of the following three operations:

(i)   The audio signal is first transformed into the frequency domain, and the obtained spectrum is divided into 32 non-interleaved subbands.

(ii)   For each subband, the amplitude of the audio signal is calculated, and the noise level determined by using a "psychoacoustic model." The psychoacoustic model is the key component of the MPEG audio encoder and its function is to analyze the input audio signal and determine where in the spectrum the quantization noise should be masked.

(iii)   Finally, each subband is quantized according to the audibility of quantization noise within that band.

The MPEG audio encoder and decoder are shown in Figure 19 [7,10,11,19].

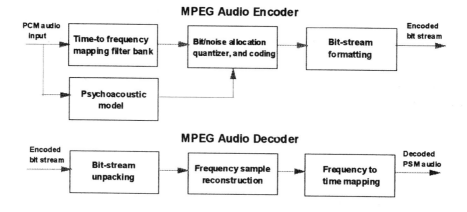

Figure 19. Block diagrams of MPEG audio encoder and decoder.

The input audio stream simultaneously passes through a filter bank and a psychoacoustic model. The filter bank divides the input into multiple subbands, while the psychoacoustic model determines the signal-to-mask ratio of each subband. The bit or noise allocation block uses the signal-to-mask ratios to determine the number of bits for the quantization of the subband signals with the goal to minimize the audibility of the quantization noise. The last block performs entropy (Huffman) encoding and formatting the data. The decoder performs entropy (Huffman) decoding, then reconstructs the quantized subband values, and transforms subband values into a time-domain audio signal.

The MPEG audio standard specifies three layers for compression: layer 1 represents the most basic algorithm and provides the maximum rate of 448 Kbits/s, layers 2 and 3 are enhancements to layer 1 and offer 384 Kbits/s and 320 Kbits/s, respectively. Each successive layer improves the compression performance, but at the cost of the greater encoder and decoder complexity.

A detailed description of audio compression principles and techniques is reported elsewhere [10,11,19].

4.6 MPEG INTERLEAVED A/V DATA STREAM

The MPEG standard specifies a syntax for the interleaved audio and video data streams. An audio data stream consists of frames, which are divided into audio access units. Audio access unit consists of slots, which can be either four bits at the lowest complexity layer (layer 1), or one byte at layers 2 and 3. A frame always consists of a fixed number of samples. Audio access unit specifies the smallest audio sequence of compressed data that can be independently decoded. The playing times of the audio access units of one frame are 8 ms at 48 KHz, 8.7 ms at 44.1 KHz, and 12 ms at 32 KHz [7]. A video data stream consists of six layers, as shown in Table 8.

Table 8. Layers of MPEG Video Stream Syntax

Syntax layer	Functionality
Sequence layer	Context unit
Group of pictures layer	Random access unit: video coding
Picture layer	Primary coding unit
Slide layer	Resynchronization unit
Macroblock layer	Motion compensation unit
Block layer	DCT unit

At the beginning of the *sequence layer* there are two entries: the constant bit rate of a sequence and the storage capacity that is needed for decoding. These parameters define the data buffering requirements. A sequence is divided into a series of GOPs. Each GOP layer has at least one **I** frame at the first frame in GOP, so random access and fast search are enabled. GOPs can be of arbitrary structure (**I, P,** and **B** frames) and length. The GOP layer is the basic unit for editing an MPEG video stream.

The *picture layer* contains a whole picture (or a frame). This information consists of the type of the frame (**I, P,** or **B**) and the position of the frame in the display order.

The bits corresponding to the DCT coefficients and the motion vectors are contained in the next three layers: *slice, macroblock*, and *block* layers. The block is a (8x8) DCT unit, the macroblock is a (16x16) motion compensation unit, and the slice is a sting of macroblocks of arbitrary length. The slice layer is intended to be used for re-synchronization during a frame decoding when bit errors occur.

5. THE XYZ VIDEO COMPRESSION ALGORITHM

The XYZ motion video compression algorithm relies on a different principle for compression of temporal information than the MPEG and H.261/H.263 standards. While the MPEG and

H.261/H.263 strategies look for motion vectors to represent a frame being compressed, the XYZ strategy more closely resembles the technique adopted by both MPEG and JPEG for intraframe compression.

A continuous tone image can be represented as a two-dimensional array of pixel values in the spatial domain. The Forward Discrete Cosine Transform (FDCT) converts the two-dimensional image from spatial to frequency domain. In spatial representation the energy distribution of pixels is uniform, while in the frequency domain the energy is concentrated into a few low-frequency coefficients.

Pixels in full-motion video are also correlated in the temporal domain, and the FDCT will concentrate the energy of pixels in the temporal domain just as it does in the spatial domain. The XYZ video compression is based on this property.

5.1 THE XYZ ENCODER

The XYZ video compression algorithm is based on the three-dimensional DCT (3D DCT). This algorithm takes a full-motion digital video stream and divides it into groups of 8 frames. Each group of 8 frames is considered as a three-dimensional image, where X and Y are spatial components and Z is the temporal component. Each frame in the image is divided into 8x8 blocks (like JPEG), forming 8x8x8 cubes, as illustrated in Figure 20. Each 8x8x8 cube is then independently encoded using the three blocks of the XYZ video encoder: 3D DCT, Quantizer, and Entropy encoder [WF95]. The block diagram of the XYZ encoder is shown in Figure 21.

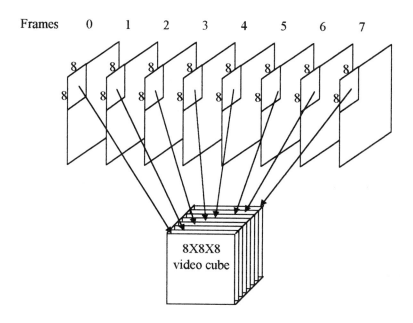

Figure 20. Forming 8x8x8 video cube for XYZ compression.

The original unsigned pixel sample values, typically in the range [0,255], are first shifted to signed integers, say in the range [-128,127]. Then each 8x8x8 cube of 512 pixels is transformed into the frequency domain using the Forward 3D DCT:

$$F(u,v,w) = C(u)C(v)C(w) * \sum_{x=0}^{7}\sum_{y=0}^{7}\sum_{z=0}^{7} f(x,y,z) *$$

$$\frac{\cos((2x+1)u\pi)}{16} \frac{\cos((2y+1)v\pi)}{16} \frac{\cos((2z+1)w\pi)}{16}$$

where:
x,y,z are index pixels in pixel space,
f(x,y,z) is the value of a pixel in pixel space,
u,v,w are index pixels in DCT space,
F(u,v,w) is a transformed pixel value in DCT space, and

$$C(i) = \frac{1}{\sqrt{2}} \quad \text{for i = 0} \qquad C(i) = 1 \quad \text{for i > 0}$$

The transformed 512-point discrete signal is a function in three dimensions, and contains both spatial and temporal information. Most of the energy is contained in few low-frequency coefficients, while the majority of the high-frequency coefficients have zero or near-zero values.

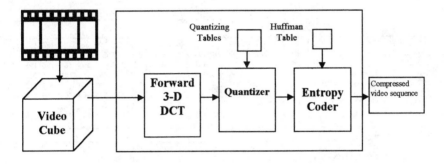

Figure 21. Block diagram of the XYZ encoder.

In the next step, all 512 DCT coefficients are quantized using a 512-element quantization table. Quantization introduces minimum error while increasing the number of zero-value coefficients. Quantization may also be used to discard visual information to which the human eye is not sensitive. Quantizer tables may be predefined, or adaptive quantizers may be developed and transmitted with the compressed data.

Quantization is performed according to the following equation:

$$F_q(u,v,w) = \left\lfloor \frac{F(u,v,w)}{Q(u,v,w)} \right\rfloor$$

where:
F(u,v,w) are the elements before the quantization,
F_q(u,v,w) are the quantized elements, and
Q(u,v,w) are the elements from the quantization table.

Each quantizer Q(u,v,w) is in the range [1,1024]. The result of the quantization operation is a collection of smaller-valued coefficients, a large number of which are 0. These coefficients are then converted into a compact binary sequence using an entropy coder (in this case, a Huffman coder).

The entropy coding operation starts with reordering the coefficients in descending order of expected value. This sequence has the benefit of sequentially collecting the largest number of zero-valued coefficients. The run-lengths of zero coefficients is computed, and the alphabet of symbols to be encoded becomes the run-length of zeros appended to the length of the non-zero coefficient. This binary sequence represents the compressed 8x8x8 block.

Figure 22 illustrates an example of encoding a video cube (eight frames of 8x8 pixels) using the XYZ compression algorithm. Figure 22 shows the original video cube, Figure 23a shows the DCT coefficients after the 3D DCT, and Figure 23b presents the quantized coefficients. Note that the largest quantized coefficient is Fq(0,0,0), which carries the crucial information on the video cube, while the majority of quantized coefficients are zero.

Frame 0

197	195	199	207	209	199	213	217
207	201	201	210	210	200	214	220
224	212	207	213	213	202	216	223
233	230	224	228	229	218	228	230
225	227	233	238	243	233	240	233
205	212	231	243	248	242	250	239
191	198	212	227	234	238	254	252
188	196	202	215	222	224	250	255

Frame 1

182	189	191	189	200	198	186	184
187	192	192	192	201	198	186	185
196	200	196	196	201	198	189	188
225	223	206	206	210	211	205	202
239	235	216	222	224	226	217	210
237	236	221	235	237	241	227	218
227	220	210	225	237	250	243	234
219	209	202	209	224	233	236	236

Frame 2

228	208	206	201	188	186	191	198
229	208	201	199	186	186	191	198
227	208	197	199	186	186	191	198
222	212	207	199	189	195	205	207
221	216	213	201	194	203	212	212
224	221	215	204	201	210	216	216
230	232	223	210	212	221	224	224
226	229	224	213	224	231	238	238

Frame 3

216	212	221	219	209	218	209	207
216	214	223	221	209	214	209	209
216	214	223	221	214	214	209	209
211	213	225	223	218	213	211	205
212	213	226	224	221	213	211	203
217	214	227	223	221	213	209	202
223	220	231	221	215	210	209	200
226	228	234	225	214	209	209	199

Frame 4

208	202	189	193	190	194	201	205
209	204	190	195	189	198	203	208
211	204	193	198	189	198	203	208
212	208	200	202	197	209	207	209
214	211	203	203	202	213	209	209
216	214	204	204	204	211	209	209
220	216	210	208	204	214	209	212
223	216	211	209	207	214	209	211

Frame 5

186	186	186	186	184	182	184	179
186	186	186	187	184	185	185	182
186	186	186	193	184	188	188	186
189	189	189	195	192	196	196	195
191	191	191	196	197	201	199	199
191	191	191	196	200	203	199	199
191	191	191	196	202	203	199	199
191	191	194	196	203	203	199	202

Frame 6

166	165	166	166	166	179	185	196
169	167	170	170	170	179	178	193
169	169	173	173	173	179	174	184
167	169	175	183	183	179	175	178
166	171	176	188	188	179	177	177
166	174	176	188	188	179	180	179
168	174	176	188	188	179	187	183
169	174	178	190	188	179	186	186

Frame 7

183	176	176	179	176	176	175	179
180	174	177	181	178	179	182	182
178	174	174	181	178	181	186	191
176	173	176	173	172	181	186	184
174	173	178	167	167	179	182	179
174	172	178	166	166	178	177	177
174	168	175	166	166	175	170	168
174	168	169	166	166	169	167	161

Figure 22. An example of encoding an 8x8x8 video cube – original pixels in video cube.

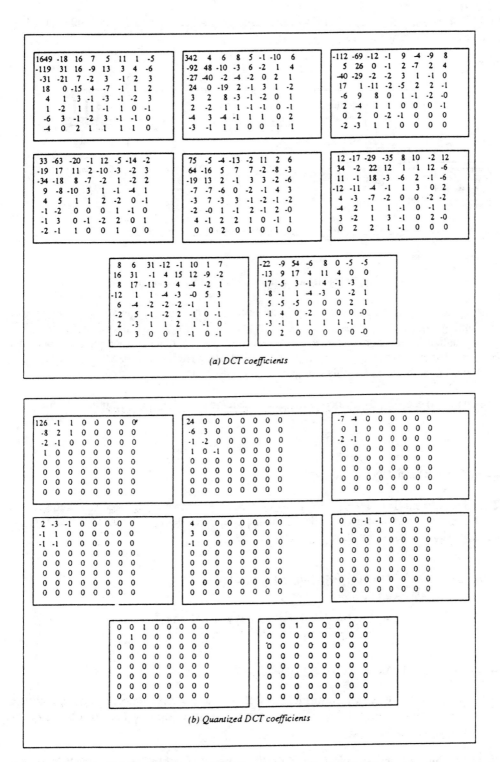

(a) DCT coefficients

(b) Quantized DCT coefficients

Figure 23. An example of encoding an 8x8x8 video cube.
(a) DCT coefficients, after 3-D DCT, and (b) quantized DCT coefficients.

5.2 THE XYZ DECODER

In XYZ decoding, the steps from the encoding process are inverted and implemented in reverse order, as shown in Figure 24.

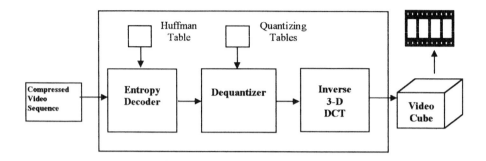

Figure 24. Block diagram of the XYZ decoder.

First the compressed data stream is Huffman-decoded. This data stream is now composed of the coding alphabet symbols of run-length and VLC lengths alternated with the VLC representation of the non-zero coefficient. The decoded data is run-length expanded and converted into a stream of quantized coefficients. These quantized coefficients are resequenced into XYZ video cubes of quantized coefficients.

The quantized coefficients are dequantized according to the following equation:

$$F'(u,v,w) = F_q(u,v,w) * Q(u,v,w)$$

where F'(u,v,w) is a dequantized coefficient.

The three-dimensional inverse DCT (3-D IDCT) is implemented on the dequantized coefficients in order to convert video from the frequency domain into the spatial/temporal domain. The 3-D IDCT equation is defined as

$$f'(x,y,z) = \sum_{u=0}^{7}\sum_{v=0}^{7}\sum_{w=0}^{7} C(u)C(v)C(w) * F'(u,v,w) *$$

$$\frac{\cos((2x+1)u\pi)}{16}\frac{\cos((2y+1)v\pi)}{16}\frac{\cos((2z+1)w\pi)}{16}$$

where f'(x,y,z) is the value of a pixel in pixel space.

After the pixels have been transformed in spatial/temporal representation, they are shifted back to the original range [0,255]. Finally, the video cubes are reorganized into frames of video data ready for playback.

Figure 25 illustrates an example of the XYZ decompression, applied on the same 8x8x8 video cube in Figures 22 and 23.

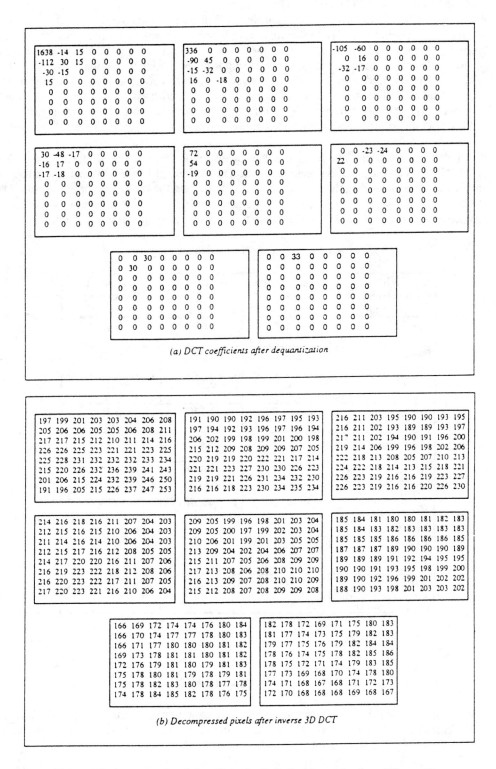

(a) DCT coefficients after dequantization

(b) Decompressed pixels after inverse 3D DCT

Figure 25. An example of decoding the 8x8x8 video cube from Figure 22.
(a) DCT coefficients after dequantization, (b) decompressed pixels after inverse 3-D DCT.

5.3 COMPARISON WITH MPEG STANDARD

We compared the XYZ compression algorithm with the MPEG standard. Motion estimation in MPEG is performed by 2D logarithmic search and by exhaustive search of a region 16 pixels wide. First frame (frame 0) is compressed as I frame using MPEG-recommended quantizer. Frame 7 is compressed as P frame using forward motion prediction. Error terms are calculated and encoded using the DCT. Frames 1 to 6 are compressed as bidirectional B-frames. Motion estimation is done using bidirectional prediction. Four experiments were performed using MPEG: two including error correction with two different search algorithms, and two with no error correction for both search algorithms.

We applied XYZ compression for five sets of quantization tables, referred to as QT1 to QT5 in [20,21,22]. The quantization tables are selected so that QT1 tables contain the smallest coefficients, thus achieving the best quality of the video and the lowest compression ratio. On the other hand, the QT5 tables have the largest coefficients, thus producing the highest compression ratio and the lowest video quality. The results are summarized in Table 9.

Table 9. Comparison of XYZ and MPEG Video Compression Algorithms

Video Compression Technique	Compression Ratio	Normalized RMS Error	Execution Time [min] (8 frames, 320x240)
XYZ (QT1)	34.5	0.079	6.45
XYZ (QT2)	57.7	0.097	6.45
XYZ (QT3)	70.8	0.105	6.45
XYZ (QT4)	101.7	0.120	6.45
XYZ (QT5)	128.1	0.130	6.45
MPEG Logarithmic Search and Error Correction	11.0	0.080	21.35
MPEG Exhaustive Search and Error Correction	15.6	0.080	163.0
MPEG Logarithmic Search and No Error Correction	27.0	0.140	21.35
MPEG Exhaustive Search and No Error Correction	32.9	0.125	163.0

6. CONCLUSIONS

This chapter presented two commonly used video compression standards, px64 Kbps (or H261/263 standard) and MPEG. We also presented the XYZ video compression algorithm, based on 3D-DCT transformation.

The following conclusions can be made [20,21]:

- The XYZ video compression algorithm gives significantly better compression ratios than the MPEG algorithm for the same quality of video. For example, XYZ result 1 and

MPEG result 1 (see Table 9) give similar NRMS errors (0.079 and 0.08, respectively) and reconstructed sequences show similar image quality. However, the XYZ algorithm provides much higher compression ratio (34.5 vs 15.6).

- For similar compression ratios, the XYZ video compression algorithm gives much better quality of the decompressed video than the MPEG algorithm. For example, XYZ result 1 and MPEG result 4 (see Table 9) give similar compression ratios (34.5 and 32.9, respectively), but XYZ algorithm gives much better quality (NRMS error for XYZ is 0.079, while for MPEG it is 0.125).

- The obtained results suggest that XYZ video compression algorithm is faster than the MPEG algorithm (including both compression and decompression).

- The XYZ results 4 and 5 (Table 9) suggest that very high compression ratios (greater than 100) can be achieved using the XYZ video compression algorithm, while the NRMS error is still kept relatively small (in the range from 0.120 to 0.130). In this case, for videos with the fast camera movement the visual artifacts are significant. However, the algorithm gives very good results for videos with little movement, which is the case in videoconferencing applications.

- Finally, the MPEG technique is based on three different algorithms: one for **I**, another for **P**, and the third algorithm for **B** frames. MPEG is also an asymmetrical algorithm, requiring a complex encoder and a simple decoder. On the other hand, the XYZ technique applies only one algorithm to all frames and is a symmetrical algorithm requiring the same complexity for both encoder and decoder. This fact is beneficial for VLSI implementation of the algorithm, which is described in [21].

REFERENCES

1. B. Furht, "A Survey of Multimedia Techniques and Standards, Part I: JPEG Standard," *Real-Time Imaging Journal*, Vol. 1, No. 1, pp. 49-67, 1995.
2. B. Furht, "A Survey of Multimedia Compression Techniques and Standards," Part II: Video Compression," *Real-Time Imaging Journal*, Vol. 1, pp. 319-337, 1995.
3. M. Liou, "Overview of the Px64 Kbits/s Video Coding Standard," *Communications of the ACM*, Vol. 34, No. 4, pp. 59-63, 1991.
4. R. Aravind, G.L. Cash, D.C. Duttweller, H.-M. Hang, and A. Puri, "Image and Video Coding Standards," *AT&T Technical Journal*, Vol. 72, pp. 67-88, 1993.
5. M. Ghanbari, "An Adapted H.261 Two-Layer Video Codec for ATM Networks," *IEEE Transactions on Communications*, Vol. 40, No. 9, pp.1481-1490, 1992.
6. H.-C. Huang, H.-H. Huang, and J.-L. Wu, "Real-Time Software-Based Video Coder for Multimedia Communication Systems," *Journal of Multimedia Systems*, Vol. 1, pp. 110-119, 1993.
7. R. Steinmetz, "Data Compression in Multimedia Computing - Standards and Systems," Part I and II, *Journal of Multimedia Systems*, Vol. 1, pp. 166-172 and 187-204, 1994.
8. G. LeGall, "MPEG: A Video Compression Standard for Multimedia Applications," *Communications of the ACM, Vol.* 34, No. 4, pp. 45-68, 1991.
9. W.B. Pennenbaker and J.L. Mitchell, "JPEG Still Image Data Compression Standard," Van Nostrand Reinhold, New York, 1993.
10. V. Bhaskaran and K. Konstantinides, "Image and Video Compression Standards – Algorithms and Architectures," Kluwer Academic Publishers, Norwell, MA, 1995.
11. J. L. Mitchell, W.B. Pennenbaker, C.E. Fogg, and D.J. LeGall, "MPEG Video Compression Standard," Chapman & Hall, New York, 1996.

12. B. Furht, J. Greenberg, and R. Westwater, "Motion Estimation Algorithms for Video Compression," Kluwer Academic Publishers, Norwel, MA, 1997.

13. H. Gharavi and M. Mills, "Block Matching Motion Estimation Algorithms – New Results," *IEEE Transactions on Circuits Systems*, Vol. 37, pp. 649-651, 1990.

14. J. Koga, K. Iinuma, A. Hirani, Y. Iijima, and T. Ishiguro, "Motion Compensated Interframe Coding for Video Conferencing," Proceedings of the National Telecommunications Conference, pp. G5.3.1-5.3.5, 1981.

15. W. Lee, Y. Kim, R.J. Gove, and C.J. Read, "Media Station 5000: Integrating Video and Audio," *IEEE MultiMedia*, Vol. 1, No. 2, pp. 50-61, 1994.

16. J.R. Jain, and A.K. Jain, "Displacement Measurement and Its Application in Interframe Image Coding," *IEEE Transactions on Communications*, Vol. 29, pp. 1799-1808, 1981.

17. R. Srinivasan and K.R. Rao, "Predictive Coding Based on Efficient Motion Estimation," *IEEE Transactions on Communications*, Vol. 33, pp. 888-896, 1985.

18. E. Chan, A.A. Rodriguez, R. Gandhi, and S. Panchanathan, "Experiments on Block-Matching Techniques for Video Coding," *Journal of Multimedia Systems*, Vol. 2, No. 5, pp. 228-241, 1994.

19. D. Y. Pen, "Digital Audio Compression," *Digital Technical Journal*, Vol. 5, No. 2, pp. 28-40, 1993.

20. R. Westwater and B. Furht, "The XYZ Algorithm for Video Compression of Full-Motion Video," *Real-Time Imaging Journal*, Vol. 2, pp. 19-34, 1996.

21. R. Westwater and B. Furht, "Real-Time Video Compression – Techniques and Algorithms," Kluwer Academic Publishers, Norwell, MA, 1997.

22. R. Westwater and B. Furht, "Three-Dimensional DCT Video Compression Technique Based on Adaptive Quantizers," Second IEEE International Conference on Engineering of Complex Computer Systems, Montreal, Canada, October 1996.

II

MULTIMEDIA RETRIEVAL AND PROCESSING TECHNIQUES

10

CLASSIFICATION, SEARCH, AND RETRIEVAL OF AUDIO

Erling Wold, Thom Blum, Douglas Keislar, and James Wheaton
Muscle Fish LLC
2550 Ninth Street, Suite 207 B
Berkeley, CA 94710, USA
inquiries@musclefish.com

1. **INTRODUCTION** 208
　1.1　OVERVIEW 208
　1.2　RELATED WORK 209
2. **AUDIO FEATURE ANALYSIS AND COMPARISON** 209
　2.1　OVERVIEW 209
　2.2　FRAME-LEVEL FEATURES 210
　2.3　DISTRIBUTION ANALYSIS 213
　2.4　MUSIC ANALYSIS 215
　2.5　SPEECH TO TEXT 217
3. **INDEXING** 217
4. **EXAMPLES** 218
　4.1　LAUGHTER 218
　4.2　FEMALE SPEECH 219
5. **APPLICATIONS** 220
　5.1　AUDIO DATABASES AND FILE SYSTEMS 220
　5.2　SOUND EFFECTS BROWSER 221
　5.3　AUDIO EDITORS 223
　5.4　SURVEILLANCE 223
　5.5　REAL-TIME SEGMENTATION OF AUDIO AND VIDEO 224
　5.6　REAL-TIME CLASSIFICATION OF AUDIO AND VIDEO 224
6. **CONCLUSION** 225
　　　REFERENCES 225

Abstract: Many audio and multimedia applications would benefit if they could interpret the content of audio rather than relying on descriptions or keywords. These applications include multimedia databases and file systems, digital libraries, automatic segmentation or indexing of video (e.g., news or sports footage), surveillance, as well as sound browsers for effects designers and musicians.

0-8493-1825-4/99/$0.00+$.50
© 1999 by CRC Press LLC

This chapter describes an audio analysis, search, and classification engine that reduces sounds to acoustical and perceptual features. This analysis allows the sounds to be classified or queried by their audio content. Queries can based on any one or a combination of the acoustical features, by specifying previously learned classes based on these features, or by selecting or entering reference sounds and asking the engine to retrieve sounds that are similar or dissimilar to them. We present examples of this engine as it would be used in some of the application areas listed.

1. INTRODUCTION

1.1. OVERVIEW

The rapid increase in speed and capacity of computers and networks has allowed the inclusion of audio as a data type in many modern computer applications. Until recently, the audio has been treated as an opaque collection of bytes with only primitive fields attached: name, sampling rate, and so on. Developers and users who are accustomed to searching, scanning and retrieving text data can be frustrated by the inability to look at the content inside an audio object.

For example, multimedia databases or file systems can easily have thousands of audio recordings. These could range from sound effects or music libraries to archives of news footage. Such libraries are often sparsely indexed. Even if someone has assigned keywords or indices to the data, these keywords are highly subjective. They may be useless to another person who is coming to the data from a different perspective or who uses a different taxonomy. To make things worse, audio is hard to browse directly, since it must be auditioned in real time unlike video which can be keyframed. To search for a particular sound or class of sound (e.g., applause or music or a particular person's speech) can be a daunting task.

Here are some typical ways that one might want to access sound:

- Physical attributes: describing a sound in terms of commonly understood acoustical characteristics, such as brightness, pitch, and loudness.
- By example: saying one sound is like another sound or a group of sounds in terms of some characteristics. For example, "like the sound of a herd of elephants." A simpler example would be to say that it belongs to the class of speech sounds or the class of applause sounds, where the system has previously been trained on other sounds in this class. As another example, the user could make a buzzing sound to find bees or electrical hum.
- Subjective features: describing the sounds using personal descriptive language. This requires training the system (in our case, by example) to understand the meaning of these descriptive terms. For example, a user might be looking for a "shimmering" sound.
- Semantic content: text content for speech recordings and the score (events, instruments, and rhythms) for musical recordings.

In a retrieval application, all of the above could be used in combination with traditional keyword and text queries.

To accomplish the above, we develop analyses of sound which compute the instantaneous acoustic characteristics. These characteristics have been chosen based on knowledge of what is psychoacoustically important. Next, we apply statistical and heuristic algorithms to reduce this data to a more compact or more easily compared set of features. Finally, we use several different distance measures to compare these features and thus to compare, classify, and search for sound. Note that this approach is not unique to audio. It has been used in the image retrieval world and, more generally, in the field of pattern recognition for many years. What is unique here are the particular features which are appropriate for audio and the use of these features in audiocentric applications.

1.2. RELATED WORK

Sounds have traditionally been described by their pitch, loudness, and timbre. The first two of these psychological percepts are well understood and can be accurately modeled by measurable acoustic features. Timbre, on the other hand, is an ill-defined attribute that encompasses all the distinctive qualities of a sound other than its pitch and loudness. The effort to discover the components of timbre underlies much of the previous psychoacoustic research that is relevant to content-based audio retrieval [1].

Salient components of timbre include the amplitude envelope, harmonicity, and spectral envelope. The attack portions of a tone are often essential for identifying the timbre. Timbres with similar spectral energy distributions tend to be judged as perceptually similar. However, research has shown that the time-varying spectrum of a single musical instrument tone cannot generally be treated as a "fingerprint" identifying the instrument, because there is too much variation across the instrument's range of pitches and dynamic levels.

In the computer music community, various researchers have discussed or prototyped algorithms capable of extracting audio structure from a sound [2]. The goal was to allow queries such as "find the first occurrence of the note G-sharp." These algorithms were tuned to specific musical constructs and were not appropriate for all sounds.

There are a number of people who have done work which overlaps what we will present here. Feiten and Gnzel looked at audio databases with content analysis using neural nets [3]. Foote developed algorithms for classification and comparison using cepstral coefficients and histogram representations of their probability densities [4]. Fischer et al. at the University of Mannheim have been working in the area of audio content analysis [5]. Scheirer and Slaney developed a music/speech classification system which uses features similar to ours as well as many features designed specifically for this task [6]. They look at a broad range of classifier strategies as well. Many in the field of speaker identification, although focused on this particular task, have used the strategy of feature extraction and statistical comparison. Speech recognition systems can be used to be used to transcribe speech, allowing for text-based queries [7]. Finally, there is our own early work [8-10].

2. AUDIO FEATURE ANALYSIS AND COMPARISON

This section presents techniques for analyzing audio signals in a way that facilitates audio classification and search.

2.1. OVERVIEW

Figure 1 shows an overview of the feature extraction process. For each frame of audio data (25 to 40 msecs), we measure a number of acoustic features of each sound. These are the basis for all the higher-level analyses which follow. The features analyzed here are not the only acoustic features which could be extracted. We have found these features to be of wide utility, but, for specific applications, it may be advantageous to look at other low-level parameters.

Note that each class of features has its own set of useful distance measures. In addition, some distance measures may be more useful in particular applications.

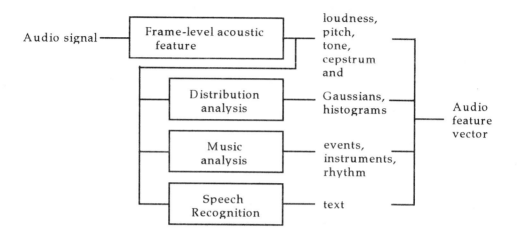

Figure 1. Overview of feature extraction.

2.2. FRAME-LEVEL FEATURES

The following features are currently extracted from each frame of sound, producing, for the entire sound, a time-series *{fj}* where each element is a vector of floating point numbers representing the instantaneous values of the features. For some applications, this is the appropriate level of content description. For example, a melody-matching algorithm would compare the pitch functions of two or more musical selections more or less directly. Similarly, an audio copyright-infringement detection system could be built using correlations of some or all the time functions.

2.2.1. Features

2.2.1.1. Loudness
Loudness is approximated by the square root of the energy of the signal computed from the short-time Fourier transform (STFT) in decibels. The loudness time series is highpass filtered to remove the long-term average volume level. A more accurate loudness estimate would account for the frequency response of the human ear; if desired, the necessary equalization can be added by applying the Fletcher-Munson equal-loudness contours and even more detailed models of loudness summation. The human ear can hear over a 120 decibel range. Our software produces estimates over a 100 decibel range given 16-bit audio recordings.

2.2.1.2. Pitch
The monophonic pitch is estimated from the STFT. For each frame, the frequencies and amplitudes of the spectral peaks are computed using a parabolic interpolation. An approximate greatest-common-divisor algorithm is used to calculate an estimate of the fundamental frequency. The pitch-time series is cleaned up by heuristics which remove harmonic jump and noise errors. We store the pitch as a log frequency. The pitch algorithm also returns a pitch confidence value that can be used to weight the pitch in later calculations. A perfect young human ear can hear frequencies in the 20Hz to 20kHz range. Our software can measure pitches in the range of 50Hz to about 8kHz.

2.2.1.3. Tone (brightness and bandwith)

Brightness is computed as the centroid of the STFT, again stored as a log frequency. It is a measure of the higher-frequency content of the signal. As an example, putting your hand over your mouth as you speak reduces the brightness of the speech sound as well as the loudness. This feature varies over the same range as the pitch, although it can't be less than the pitch estimate at any given instant.

Bandwidth is computed as the magnitude-weighted average of the differences between the spectral components and the centroid. As examples, a single sine wave has a bandwidth of 0 and ideal white noise has an infinite bandwidth.

2.2.1.4. Cepstrum

We compute a vector of Mel-Filtered Cepstral Coefficients (MFCCs) by applying a mel-spaced set of triangular filters to the STFT and following this with the discrete cosine transform. We have an option which can alleviate channel and noise effects using cepstral mean subtraction and other post-filtering techniques.

2.2.1.5. Derivatives

Since the dynamic behavior of a sound is important, the low-level analyzer also computes the instantaneous derivative (time differences) for all of the features above.

2.2.2. Example

Figure 2 shows the time-varying nature of selected acoustic parameters for a recording of a Bulgarian vocalist. At the beginning of the recording, she is holding a long tone with a large vibrato. About halfway through, she switches to a pattern of notes which is repeated two times. Both of these are fairly clear in the pitch and loudness traces. There are clearly correlations between the pitch, loudness, and spectral features. The vowel changes, especially the one at the end of the first held note, are visible in the spectral features.

2.2.3. Distance

Distance measures are necessary for classification and query-by-example. There are several useful distance measures for comparing the frame data of two sounds. A straight least-squared error or correlation measure is appropriate for applications where an exact match is required, e.g., finding a piece of copyrighted audio in an internet broadcast. Given two feature vector time-series $\{f_j\}$ and $\{g_j\}$ of length L from two sounds, the least-squares distance is given as follows. For simplicity, we show the 1-dimensional case. For N dimensions, the distances can be computed separately for each dimension and summed.

$$D = L^{-1} \left(\sum_j (f_j - g_j)^2 \right)^{1/2} \tag{1}$$

The correlation measure is given below. Again, the 1-dimensional case is shown. For N dimensions, the 1-dimensional correlations can be multiplied together.

$$C = L^{-1} \sum_j f_j^* g_j \tag{2}$$

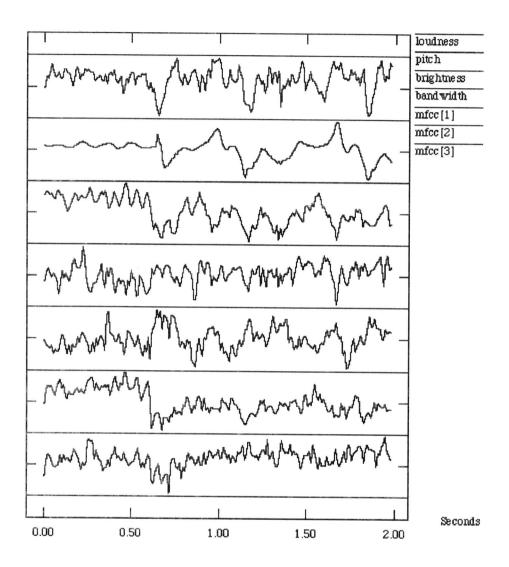

Figure 2: Bulgarian singer.

Both of the above should be normalized by the length of the series. Some policy must be decided upon for series of different lengths. For the correlation measure, the mean is typically removed before the correlation is performed.

In some applications, such as searching for sound effects by example, it is more useful to compare the *shape* of the time function rather than the exact values. This can be accomplished by scaling the time functions in both dimensions to lie in 1×1 square, say, and then comparing these two functions using either of the measures above.

In all these distance measures, it is useful to provide user-controllable weights on the components of the distances. For example, a user might want to consider only the timbral features when doing a comparison.

2.3. DISTRIBUTION ANALYSIS

Once we have a time series of frame values, we can extract higher-level information from it. The first thing we do is a statistical analysis. When determining a general classification for a sound, e.g., speech or music, or when comparing the quality of two sounds, we don't want to compare the above time functions directly. Rather, we would like to compare their statistical properties.

2.3.1. Gaussian model

2.3.1.1. Analysis

In the simplest case, we compute the mean μ and standard deviation σ of the frame-level time series for each parameter, including the parameter derivatives. This is detailed enough to distinguish between many classes of sound and can achieve subjectively reasonable sound-to-sound comparisons. When computing the mean and standard deviation, the frame-level features are weighted by the instantaneous loudness so that the perceptually important sections of the sound are emphasized.

For applications where finer sound distinctions are necessary, such as speaker ID, a simple mean and standard deviation is not enough for satisfactory performance. The Gaussian model can be extended to include Gaussian mixtures. The increase in performance is accompanied by additional costs in storage and computation.

Note that in query applications, it can be useful to directly specify constraints on the values of the N-vector described above. For example, the user could be looking for musical instrument samples in a certain range of pitch. However, it is also possible to query-by-example. In this case, the user trains the system given examples of sounds.

The above analysis makes sense when the input sound is homogeneous in character (statistically stationary). For example, a short sound effect like a door slam or recording of a rain ambience. When analyzing a longer heterogeneous sound recording, for example, a live news broadcast, it is more reasonable to segment the recording and compute a feature vector for each segment. The segmentation can be done arbitrarily, e.g., in overlapping equal-sized windows of a few seconds each where we hope that each window is relatively homogeneous, or it can be done by a scene change analysis which we will describe later.

2.3.1.2. Modeling a class

If the system is presented with several homogeneous sound recordings which are all examples of a single class of sound, this can be interpreted in two ways. The first is to just treat the sounds as if they were parts of one long sound. This is reasonable if the resulting sound is homogeneous. For example, in speaker ID, there may be several recordings of the same speaker, all of which can be treated together.

The second is to treat them as different members of the class. In this case, we can infer something from the variability of the parameters across the different recordings. For example, there may be several samples of oboe tones, each at a different pitch. If one of these is presented to the system as an example of an oboe sound, the system has no *a priori* way of determining that it is the timbre of the sound that determines the class, rather than the particular pitch of this sample. However, if all the samples are presented to the system, the variability of the pitch can be noted across the samples and then used to weight the different parameters in comparison. This information can then be used when comparing new sounds to this class. This variability can be stored in standard deviation portion of the N-vector above, or, if the standard deviation portion of the N-vector is important to the class identity, it can be stored as additional information.

2.3.1.3. Distance

For the single Gaussian model, there are several different useful distance measures. When the two sounds are both homogeneous, an effective and simple measure is the Euclidean distance between the two sounds' N-vectors.

$$D = ||a_0 - a_1||$$

where a_0 and a_1 are the feature vectors for the two sounds being compared.

When one of the feature vectors, say, a_0, represents a class of sound such as the oboe example, the inverse of the standard deviation of its N-vector can be used to weight the distance calculation. If we break the N-vector a into its component mean μ and standard deviation σ, we have the sound-to-class distance given by

$$D = ((\mu_1 - \mu_0)^T R_0^{-1} (\mu_1 - \mu_0))^{1/2} \tag{3}$$

where R_0 is the covariance matrix containing the squared elements of the σ vector down the diagonal. If, as was discussed in the previous section, the variability information was stored as additional information, the distance measure should be modified to be

$$D = ((a_1 - a_0)^T R_0^{-1} (a_1 - a_0))^{1/2} \tag{4}$$

where R_0 now contains this additional variability information.

When a Gaussian mixture has been estimated from the frame data, we need to use a density distance measure such as the joint entropy.

In all these distance measures, the users should be given the ability to apply their own weights to the different elements in the N-dimensional computation based on their *a priori* knowledge of the importance of the different features for the task at hand.

2.3.2. Histogram model

2.3.2.1. Analysis

A Gaussian mixture model can represent the N-dimensional probability density of the frame features with arbitrarily high accuracy. However, another model which, as we shall see, can be useful in certain applications is a histogram model. This simply is a count of the number of frames of the sound in each volume of a particular partitioning of the feature space. Determining useful and efficient partitionings of the space is the difficult part of the computation. We will discuss just one possible partitioning strategy which is useful for discrimination applications, i.e., applications which require the classification of sound or sound segments into one of several classes. When the classes are very broad, e.g., speech and music, it is desirable to find those places in the space which most *distinguish* the different classes.

Our strategy is simple. We build a decision tree by searching for optimal split points along each dimension of the frame feature data. These split points are chosen to maximize the partitioning of the different classes. The algorithm is as follows. Starting with the unpartitioned N-dimensional space and M classes represented by their frame-level feature data, we do a Monte Carlo optimization looking for the dimension d and value v which maximizes a quality of separation metric. If the total number of frames in class i is given by n_i, the total number of frames in all classes by n, the total number of frames in class i which lie above v in dimension d is given by c_i, and the sum of this over all dimensions is c, the quality metric is

$$r_0 = c_i/n_i$$
$$r_1 = (c-c_i)/(n-n_i)$$
$$Q = \Sigma_i \, MAX \, [\, r_0 + (1 - r_1), \, r_1 + (1 - r_0) \,] \qquad (5)$$

After the best split is found, the algorithm is run again on each of the resulting partitions. No split is computed for a partition if it is dominated by features of only one class. When this condition is met, this partition is made a leaf of the decision tree and is given a unique leaf index. We keep track of these leaves, their index numbers, and how many points from each class are in each leaf.

When the process is finished, we have a set of histogram vectors, one for each class of sound. We normalize the histograms so that the nth element of the vector for a particular class of sound contains the number of points from that class in the nth leaf divided by the total number of points in that class. Thus, it is a measure of how densely that class populates all the leaves of the decision tree. How distinct these histogram vectors are from each other is a measure of how well the sound classes can be distinguished given the current set of frame-level features.

2.3.2.2. Distance
Given a target segment of sound, we can use the decision tree to classify the sound. The sound segment is run through the preliminary audio analysis, producing a set of frame data points. Each point is used to traverse the decision tree and will end up in one of the leaves. The total number of points from the segment's data set in each leaf is put into a normalized histogram vector sorted by leaf index as before.

This vector is then compared to the vectors for each class derived in the training process above using the correlation distance. If the two histograms are given by the sequences $\{g_i\}$ and $\{h_i\}$, the similarity is given by

$$S = \Sigma_i \, g_i^* h_i \qquad (6)$$

The target sound is assigned to the class with the highest similarity value.

2.4. MUSIC ANALYSIS
When the audio recording is known or has been classified to be music, one would like to extract music-level information, including rhythms, events such as notes (which might include fields such as pitch, duration, loudness), and instrument identification. The overall

sound of the music is a useful measure as well, but this is handled by the statistical features above.

2.4.1. Rhythm

2.4.1.1. Analysis
Various beat detection and rhythm analysis algorithms have been reported in the literature. Ours is relatively simple, as we do not need a sophisticated analysis, just one which can produce enough features for reasonable comparisons.

To set up the rhythm analysis, another frame-level parameter needs to be computed. Since, for many types of music, the bass instruments are a more reliable indicator of the beat, we produce an alternate version of the loudness feature using a linearly bass-weighted version of the STFT.

The first step is to perform an FFT on the bass-loudness time series. This yields a spectrum whose x-axis measures distances in time, and whose peaks indicate the most frequent separation in time between bass events. The spectrum is normalized so that its maximum value is 1.0.

We search for a peak through the spectrum's frequencies over a search band corresponding to a reasonable maximum and minimum tempo. This way, peaks at very large time separations are interpreted, not as the actual beat of the music, but as a time interval comprising several beats. Similarly, the minimum time separation avoids excessively small time intervals. We compute a parabolic interpolation of the amplitude to arrive at a tempo estimate.

Once the tempo is known, the bass loudness time series is normalized into a rhythm feature vector in two ways. First, it is normalized in value so that it has an average loudness of 1.0, and, secondly, it is downsampled to a rate of 1/6th of beat. For simple rhythms made of duplets and triplets, this will capture the most important sub-beat information. A higher sampling rate would pick up finer subdivisions, but would also tend to pick up rhythmically unimportant details that are due to deviations of the musician's performance from a strictly metronomic, theoretical performance. This normalization makes the rhythm feature vector independent of tempo. This independence allows the system to identify two musical excerpts as having similar rhythms, even if one excerpt has a faster tempo.

2.4.1.2. Distance
The distance between two tempi is trivial, although it should be computed in a log space for perceptual scaling. As explained earlier, rhythm feature vectors are always normalized in time so that their sampling rates are all 1/6 beat, allowing rhythms with different tempos to be meaningfully compared. One problem is that the rhythm feature vectors might be offset from each other. For example, they might be identical except that one starts with an upbeat while the other starts on the downbeat.

To detect such cases, we slide the two rhythm feature vectors past each other, one sample at a time, computing the least-squared distance at each point. We then take the average of the two smallest values of the distance as the overall rhythm distance.

2.4.2. Events
Score-level descriptions of music are typically in the form of events. These events are typically characterized by a starting time, a duration, and a series of parameters such as pitch, loudness, articulation, vibrato, and so on. All of these parameters can vary in time

during the event. MIDI data is widely used as a score-level representation of music in computer environments. It is very limited in terms of the musical concepts it contains, but can be coerced into representing a wide range of music well enough.

Since we already have continuous frame-level data for pitch, loudness, and so on, it is straightforward to convert these into the MIDI values for key number, pitch bend, key velocity, and so on. The major difficulty is determining the event boundaries. If you look at Figure 2, you will see that the note boundaries are not selfevident. The heuristics we follow for extracting musical note events are as follows:

A new event begins when:
  • the loudness increases above a silence threshold

The current event ends when:
  • the loudness decreases below a silence threshold

The current event transitions to a new event when:
  • the loudness increases by a factor above the current average level
  • the pitch changes suddenly
  • the pitch has been changing, then settles into a new steady value
  • the spectrum changes suddenly

2.4.3. Instrument identification
We would like to identify what is the type of the sound source. For musical examples, this would typically be one of the standard musical instruments. Instrument identification is accomplished using the histogram classification system described in section 2.3.2. This requires that the system be trained on all possible instruments.

2.5. SPEECH TO TEXT
When the audio recording is known or has been classified to contain speech, it is very useful to provide a text version of the speech. Since there is a large body of literature on the problem of transcribing speech to text as well as on the problem of searching text in useful ways, we will not discuss it in detail here. Suffice it to say, it is a necessary part of a comprehensive audio-content-based system. It may be useful in a query environment to keep an intermediate, phonetic form of the speech rather than the final text. The advantage of this is that the final text may have mistranscribed a word to a similar sounding word, whereas the intermediate form will have several possible phonetic transcriptions with likelihoods attached and can thus allow for fuzzier matches.

3. INDEXING

When performing a query-by-example in a small database, it is easy to compute the distance measure for all the sounds in the database from the example sound or model and then choose the sounds that match the desired result. For large databases, this can be prohibitively expensive. To speed up the search, we produce an index of the sounds in the database by all the acoustic features. This allows us to quickly retrieve any desired hyper-rectangle of sounds in the database by requesting all the sounds whose feature values fall in a set of desired ranges. Requesting such hyper-rectangles allows a much more efficient search. This technique has the advantage that it can be implemented on top the very efficient index-based search algorithms in existing databases.

As an example, consider a query to retrieve the top M sounds in a class. If the database has M_0 sounds total, we first ask for all the sounds in a hyper-rectangle, which is centered around the mean μ and has volume V such that

$$V/V_0 = M/M_0 \tag{7}$$

where V_0 is the volume of the hyper-rectangle surrounding the entire database. The extent of the hyper-rectangle in each dimension is proportional to the standard deviation of the class in that dimension.

We then compute the distance measure for all the sounds returned and return the closest M sounds. If we didn't retrieve enough sounds that matched the query from this first attempt, we increase the hyper-rectangle volume by the ratio of the number requested to the number found and try again.

Note that the above discussion is a simplification of our current algorithm, which initially asks for bigger volumes to correct for two factors. First, for our distance measure, we really want a hypersphere of volume V, which means we want the hyper-rectangle that circumscribes this sphere and, second, the distribution of sounds in the feature space is not perfectly regular. If we assume some reasonable distribution of the sounds in the database, we can easily compute how much larger V has to be to achieve some desired confidence level that the search will be successful.

4. EXAMPLES

We now show the behavior of some of the above algorithms on a test sound database. These sound files were culled from various sound effects and musical instrument sample libraries. There are a wide variety of sounds represented from animals, machines, musical instruments, speech, and nature. The sounds vary in duration from less than a second to about 15 seconds.

A number of classes were made by running the simple single-Gaussian classification algorithm of Section 2.3.1. on some perceptually similar sets of sounds. These classes were then used to reorder the sounds in the database by their likelihood of membership in the class. The likelihood is a mapping of the distance measure given in Section 2.3.1.3, where a distance of 0 corresponds to a high likelihood and an infinite distance corresponds to a likelihood of 0. The likelihood is normalized so that 1.0 corresponds approximately to the boundary of the original set of sounds which made up the class. The following shows the results of this process for several sound sets. These examples show the character of the process and the fuzzy nature of the retrieval. An interactive demonstration (with sound) is available at the Muscle Fish web site.

4.1. LAUGHTER
For this example, all of the recordings of laughter except two were used in creating the class. Figure 3 shows a plot of the class membership likelihood values (the Y-axis) for all of the sound files in the test database. Each vertical strip along the X-axis is a user-defined category (the directory in which the sound resides). The highest returned likelihoods are for the laughing sounds, including the two that were not included in the original training set, as well as one of the animal recordings. This animal recording is of a chicken coop and has strong similarities in sound to the laughter recordings, consisting of a number of strong sound bursts.

4.2. FEMALE SPEECH

Our test database contains a number of very short recordings of a group of female and male speakers. For this example, the female spoken phrase "tear gas" was used. Figure 4 shows a plot of the likelihood of each of the sound files in the test database to this sound using a default value for the covariance matrix R. The highest likelihoods are for the other female speech recordings, with the male speech recordings following close behind.

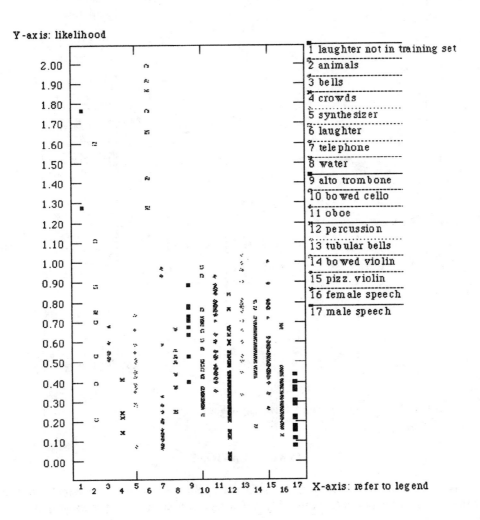

Figure 3: Likelihoods of membership in laughter class.

Y-axis: likelihood

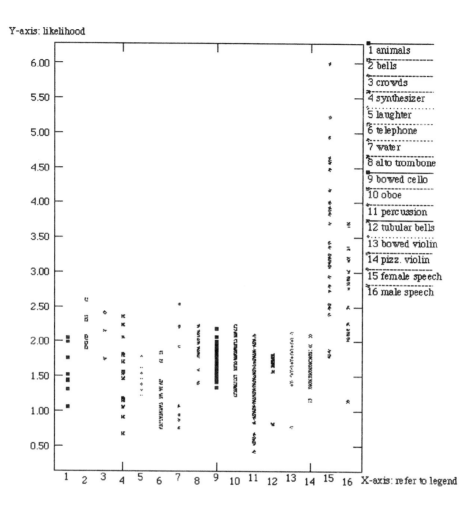

Figure 4: Similarity to female speech.

5. APPLICATIONS

The above technology is relevant to a number of application areas. The examples in this section will show the power this capability can bring to a user or developer working in these areas.

5.1. AUDIO DATABASES AND FILE SYSTEMS

Any audio database or, equivalently, a file system designed to work with large numbers of audio files, benefits from content-based capabilities. Both of these require that the audio data be represented or supplemented by a so-called *metadata* record or object that points to the sound and adds the necessary analysis data.

When a sound is added to the database, the analyses presented in Section 2 are performed and a new database record or object is formed with this supplemental information. Typically, the database would allow the user to add his or her own information to this record. In a multi-user system, each user could have their own copy of the database records to modify for their particular requirements.

Figure 5 shows an example database schema which would be appropriate for a sound effects database. Fields in this record include features such as the sound file's name and properties, some of the acoustic features as computed by system analysis routines, and user-defined keywords and comments. This level of functionality is available commercially in the current INFORMIX-Universal Server. The Bulldog Group's asset management system has similar capabilities.

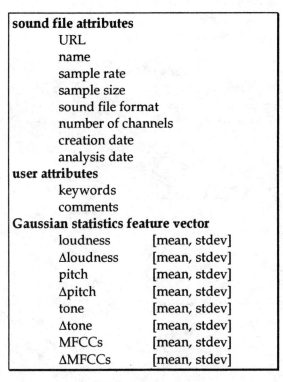

Figure 5: Database record

Any user of the database can form an audio class. Audio classes are formed by presenting a set of sounds to the classification algorithm of the last section. The object returned by the algorithm contains a list of the sounds and the resulting statistical information. This class can be private to the user or could be made available to all users of the database. The kind of classes that would be useful depends on the application area. For example, a user who was doing automatic segmentation of sports and news footage might develop classes that allow the recognition of various audience sounds (applause, cheers, and so on), referee's whistles, close-miked speech, etc.

The database should support the queries that were described in the last section in combination with more standard queries on the keywords, sampling rate, and so on.

5.2. SOUND EFFECTS BROWSER

In this section, we present the **SoundFisher** audio browser. It is a front-end database application written in JAVA which allows a user to search for sounds using combinations of content-based and traditional text queries. In addition, it permits general maintenance of the database's entries through adding, deleting, and editing of sounds and sound record data.

Figure 6 shows the GUI for the application after a search has been performed. This is an artificially complex query, but it serves to illustrate the functionality. The upper portion of the window contains the query itself. The *Search* button initiates a search using the query and the results are then displayed in the *Current Records* window.

A query is formed using a combination of constraints on the various fields in the database schema as well as query-by-example. That shown in Figure 6 is a query to find mid-fidelity sounds in the database in the "animals" or "laughter" categories that are similar to the previously-defined class called "laughter young male".

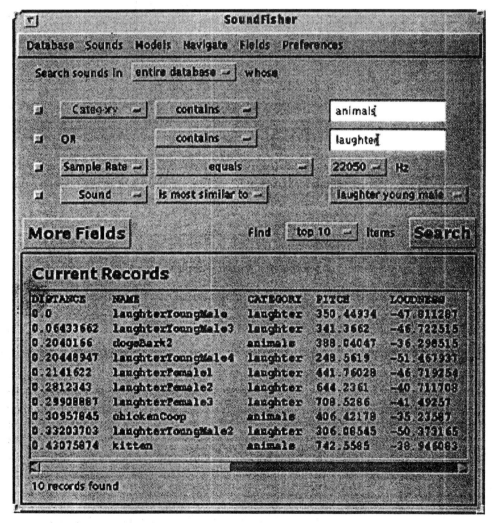

Figure 6. SoundFisher browser.

The topmost element of the query indicates that it is to be applied to the entire database. It could have been applied to the list in the *Current Records* window as well. Below this, there is a set of rows, each of which is a component of the total query. Each component includes the name of the field, a constraint operator appropriate for the data type of that field, and the value to which the operator is applied. Pressing one of the buttons in the row pops up a menu of possibilities. In Figure 6, there is one component which constrains the categories and one which specifies a medium sampling rate. The **OR** subcomponent on the category field is added through a menu item. There are also menu items for adding and deleting query components. The final component specifies the query-by-example. The "laughter young male" class was built using functions available through the *Models* menu, and consists of a single laughter recording.

Although not visible in this figure, many of the query component operators are fuzzy. For example, the user can constrain the pitch to be approximately 100 Hz. This constraint will cause the system to compute the distance between each sound's mean pitch and 100 Hz and use this as part of the query resolution.

There are a number of ways to refine searches through this interface. Any query can be saved (bookmarked) under a name given by the user. These queries can be recalled and modified. The *Navigate* menu contains these commands as well as a history mechanism which remembers all the queries on the current query path. The *Back* and *Forward* commands allow navigation along this path. An entry is made in the path each time the Search button is pressed. It is of course possible to start over from scratch.

5.3. AUDIO EDITORS

Current audio editors operate directly on the samples of the audio waveform. The user can specify locations and values numerically or graphically, but the editor has no knowledge of the audio content. The audio content is accessible only by auditioning the sound, which is tedious when editing long recordings.

A more useful editor would include knowledge of the audio content. Using the techniques presented in this chapter, a variety of sound classes appropriate for the particular application domain would be developed. For example, editing a concert recording would be aided by classes for audience applause, solo instruments, loud and soft ensemble playing, and so on. Using the classes, the editor could have the entire concert recording initially segmented into regions and indexed, allowing quick access to each musical piece and subsections thereof. During the editing process, all the types of queries presented in the preceding sections could be used to navigate through the recording. For example, the editor could ask the system to highlight the first C sharp in the oboe solo section for pitch correction.

A graphical editor with these capabilities would have *Search* or *Find* commands that functioned like the query command of the sound browser of the last section. Since it would often be necessary to build new classes on the fly, there should be commands for classification and analysis or there should be tight integration with a database application such as the audio browser of the previous section.

5.4. SURVEILLANCE

The application of content-based retrieval in surveillance is identical to that of the audio editor except that the identification and classification would be done in real time. Many offices are already equipped with computers that have built-in audio input devices. These could be used to listen for the sounds of people, glass breaking, and so on. Also, there are a number of police jurisdictions using microphones and video cameras to continuously survey areas where there is a high incidence of criminal activity or a low tolerance of such activity. Again, such surveillance could be made more efficient and easier to monitor with the ability to detect sounds associated with criminal activity.

5.5. REAL-TIME SEGMENTATION OF AUDIO AND VIDEO

The audio soundtrack of video as well as audio-only recordings can be automatically indexed and segmented. Segmentation can be accomplished in a number of ways.

Analogous to automatic keyframing in the video world, we can find audio windows which represent each homogeneous section of audio. First, we extract the desired audio features from a short (1-5 seconds) window of the recording. As new sections of audio arrive and are analyzed, they are compared to the first window using the appropriate distance measure. When the distance exceeds a threshold, this window is marked as a new "keyframe."

Alternately, one can look for scene changes by measuring the distance between neighboring windows of audio. When the distance between neighbors exceeds a threshold, this represents a sudden change in the audio sound characteristics.

A trivial segmentation is to look at fixed-size overlapping windows of the raw analysis data as the individual sound segments. Once the segmentation is done, each of these sounds can be classified and thus indexed.

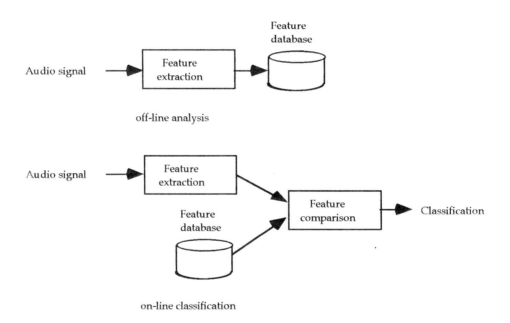

Figure 7: Real-time classification.

5.6. REAL-TIME CLASSIFICATION OF AUDIO AND VIDEO

Figure 7 shows a block diagram of a real-time system capable of classifying audio on the fly. This system has been used at Muscle Fish to create a real-time speech/music classifier. The system is used commercially in the Virage video logging and archival system. An interactive demo is available on the Muscle Fish web site.

6. CONCLUSION

This chapter has outlined some of the main features of an engine for content-based classification and retrieval of audio. The engine analyzes the acoustic features of the audio and extracts higher-level features from them. The analyzed features are relatively straightforward but suffice to describe a relatively large universe of sounds. More analyses could be added to handle specific problem domains.

We have presented examples that show the efficacy and useful fuzzy nature of the search. The results of searches are sometimes surprising in that they cross semantic boundaries, but aurally the results are reasonable.

We have also presented some example applications, including an audio database or file system, an audio browser, a real-time classifier, as well as a content-aware audio editor and surveillance system. We have found that the basic approach presented here works well for a variety of interesting audio applications.

REFERENCES

1. Plomp, R., "Aspects of Tone Sensation: A Psychophysical Study." Academic Press, London, 1976.
2. Foster, S., Schloss, W., and Rockmore, A. J., "Towards an Intelligent Editor of Digital Audio: Signal Processing Methods," *Computer Music Journal* , 6(1), 42-51, 1982.
3. Feiten, B. and Günzel, S., "Automatic Indexing of a Sound Database Using Self-Organizing Neural Nets," *Computer Music Journal*, 18(3), 53-65, Summer 1994.
4. Foote, J., "A Similarity Measure for Automatic Audio Classification," Proceedings of AAAI 1997 Spring Symposium on Intelligent Integration and Use of Text, Image, Video and Audio Corpora, Stanford, California, March 1997.
5. Pfeiffer, S., Fischer, S., and Effelsberg, W., "Automatic audio content analysis," Tech. Rep. TR-96-008, University of Mannheim, D-68131 Mannheim, Germany, April 1996.
6. Scheirer, E. and Slaney, M., "Construction and Evaluation of a Robust Multifeature Speech/Music Discriminator," Proceedings ICASSP-97, Munich, Germany, 1997.
7. Brown, M., Foote, J., Jones, G., Spärck-Jones, and K., Young, S., "Open-Vocabulary Speech Indexing for Voice and Video Mail Retrieval," Proceedings ACM Multimedia 96, Boston, November 1996.
8. Keislar, D., Blum, T., Wheaton, J., and Wold, E., "Audio Databases with Content-Based Retrieval," Proceedings of the International Computer Music Conference 1995, International Computer Music Association, San Francisco, 1995, pp. 199-202.
9. Blum, T., Keislar, D., Wheaton, J., and Wold, E., "Audio Databases with Content-Based Retrieval," in Intelligent Multimedia Information Retrieval, AAAI Press, Menlo Park, California, 113-135, 1997.
10. Wold, E., Blum, T., Keislar, D., and Wheaton, J., "Content-Based Classification, Search and Retrieval of Audio," *IEEE Multimedia*, 3(3), 27-36, Fall 1996.

11

CONTENT-BASED IMAGE INDEXING AND RETRIEVAL

Wei-Ying Ma and HongJiang Zhang
Hewlett-Packard Laboratories
1501 Page Mill Rd, Palo Alto, CA94304

1. **INTRODUCTION**..228
2. **COLOR CONTENT FEATURES** 230
    2.1 COLOR HISTOGRAMS 230
    2.2 COLOR MOMENTS...232
    2.3 COLOR COHERENCE VECTOR 233
    2.4 COLOR CORRELOGRAMS 234
3. **TEXTURE CONTENT FEATURES** 234
    3.1 TAMURA TEXTURE FEATURES 235
    3.2 SIMULTANEOUS AUTO-REGRESSIVE (SAR) TEXTURE FEATURE 236
    3.3 ORIENTATION FEATURES...237
    3.4 GABOR TEXTURE FEATURES 238
    3.5 WAVELET TRANSFORM FEATURES..239
4. **SHAPE AND OTHER FEATURES**..239
    4.1 FOURIER-BASED SHAPE DESCRIPTORS...240
    4.2 TURNING ANGLES...242
    4.3 MOMENT INVARIANTS 242
    4.4 CIRCULARITY, ECCENTRICITY, AND MAJOR AXIS ORIENTATION.............243
    4.5 SPATIAL INFORMATION..243
5. **SIMILARITY MEASURES AND INDEXING SCHEMES** 244
    5.1 SIMILARITY/DISTANCE MEASURES 244
    5.2 INDEXING..245
6. **PERFORMANCE EVALUATION OF IMAGE FEATURES**........................246
    6.1 COMPARISON OF COLOR FEATURES 246
    6.2 COMPARISON OF TECTURE FEATURE..247
7. **LEARNING AND RELEVANCE FEEDBACK** 248
    7.1 RELEVANCE FEEDBACK ARCHITECTURE 249
    7.2 LEARNING THE QUERY VECTOR..249
    7.3 LEARNING THE METRIC 250
    7.4 LEARNING USING A SOCIETY OF MODELS......................................250
8. **CONCLUDING REMARKS: RESEARCH CHALLENGES**...........................251
    REFERENCES 251

Abstract. In the last few years, visual data has become the center of multimedia computing and image analysis researches, and substantial research efforts have been devoted to visual data content analysis and retrieval. This is in response to the need in multimedia applications, especially interactive video and digital libraries, where efficient image indexing, and access tools are essential. In this chapter, we discuss all basic research issues and concepts in content-based image representation and retrieval. We focus our on definitions, extraction algorithms, representation powers, and retrieval performances of image features, in the context of applications. Other key components in visual information systems, such as visual similarity measures, effective indexing schemes, query formation and refinement with relevance feedback, are also covered in great detail.

1. INTRODUCTION

As computer networks improve and digital image libraries become more readily available to homes and offices via the Internet, the issue of rapidly accessing relevant visual information becomes more challenging. This issue has to be resolved before we can take full advantage of visual information in image and video data, though the most important investments have been targeted at the information infrastructure, including networks, servers, coding and compression, and systems architecture, as described in other chapters of this handbook. The fact of the matter is that interacting with image and video data requires much more than just connecting everyone with data banks and delivering data via networks to everyone's home and office. To address this need, research on visual content representation, indexing, and browsing technologies has become a major effort and attracted many researchers aiming at a variety of applications.

To accommodate and access the vast amount of image data, a variety of image database and visual information systems have become available recently [1,2,3]. These systems have been used in a wide variety of applications, including medical image management, visual art archives, multimedia libraries, geographic information systems, CAD/CAM systems, and criminal identifications. By and large, these systems take a keyword or text-based approach for indexing and retrieval of image data. That is, as a database object, each image in the database is associated with a text description, in the form of either keywords or free text. These descriptors may be searched by standard Boolean queries, and retrieval may be based on either exact or probabilistic match of the query text, often enhanced by thesaurus support [1,3,4]. Moreover, topical or semantic hierarchies may be used to classify or describe images using knowledge-based classification or parsing techniques; such hierarchies may then facilitate navigation and browsing within the data.

However, there are several problems inherent in systems that are exclusively text-based [2,5]. First, automatic generation of descriptive keywords or extraction of semantic information to build classification hierarchies for broad varieties of images is beyond the capability of current computer vision and intelligence technologies. Thus, these text descriptors have to be typed in by human operators. Apart from the fact that this is a time-consuming process in indexing a large number of images, it is also often subjective, inaccurate, and incomplete. As a result, such an indexing scheme will not be able to support very broad varieties of user queries, unless users are forced to constrain their query to a given set of templates or a range of key words. Moreover, certain visual properties, such as textures and color patterns, are often difficult, if not impossible, to describe with text in an objective way, at least for general-purpose usage.

The alternative to relying on text-based indexing of images is to work with descriptions based on properties that are inherent in the images themselves [5,6,7]. That is, the natural way to represent and index *visual* content is to base them on the *visual* features of an image: colors, textures, patterns, and shapes, layouts, and locations of objects. For many applications such indexing schemes may be either supplemental or preferable to text, and in other cases, they may be necessary. Furthermore, visual queries may simply be easier to formulate. For example, given a collection of fabric patterns, a fashion designer may want to retrieve specific images based on which color and texture patterns are present. Formulating a query for such a search would involve either selecting or creating one or more representative examples and then searching for images that resemble those examples. In other words, with visual feature-based indexing scheme, search is driven by first establishing one or more sample images and then identifying specific features of those sample images, which need to match images in the database. Since the focus is on those visual features themselves, we refer to such a retrieval scheme as *content-based* image retrieval.

It is understood that content-based retrieval of visual data requires a paradigm that differs significantly from both traditional databases and text-based image understanding systems. First, image content is no longer represented only by textual descriptors; thus, search should be based on *similarity* defined in terms of visual features. Formulating a query for such a search would involve either selecting or creating one or more representative examples and then searching for images which resemble those examples. This is the notion of *query by image example*. Consequently, this paradigm should reject the idea that queries have to be expressed in terms of necessary and sufficient conditions that will determine *exactly* which images one wishes to retrieve. Instead, a query is more like an *information filter* and a good filter should provide only a small number of relevant candidates for the user to examine after a query is submitted. Therefore, it is more important in this paradigm that relevant candidates are not *excluded* than it is that possibly irrelevant candidates be *included*. This implies that the functionality that supports interactivity between the user and the database through a *visual interface* is as significant as the ability to support image-based queries. Such interactivity enhances the user's ability to *define* queries, *evaluate* retrieval results, and *refine* queries on the basis of those evaluations.

Figure 1 illustrates a system architecture that supports this approach to content-based image retrieval. At the heart of this architecture is a meta-data database where image features are stored. These content meta-data are extracted for both data entry and query interpretation and compared for similarity during retrieval. The user interface then supports the "closing of the loop," which relates the formulation of queries to the browsing of retrieved data. This architecture also illustrated the key issues in developing content-based image retrieval algorithms and systems as follows:

- selection, and computation of image and object features that provide useful query expressiveness;
- retrieval methods based on similarity, as opposed to exact matching, and effective indexing schemes compatible with similarity based search; and
- a user interface that supports the visual expression of queries, and allows navigation of retrieval results and query refinement with relevance feedback.

Figure 1: Functional elements of content-based image retrieval systems.

In this chapter, we discuss the major research issues and methods for image content representation and content-based retrieval. We first define and discuss a set of image features for content representation in Sections 2, 3, and 4. These features include colors, textures, and shapes, layouts, and locations of objects. We also discuss similarity measures and efficient indexing schemes for content-based image retrieval in Section 5. The evaluation results of these features in term of retrieval performance are then presented in Section 6. Schemes for query formation and refinement with relevance feedback are discussed in Section 7. Finally, Section 8 concludes the chapter by offering a brief view of current research issues in content-based image retrieval.

It is worth mentioning that there are two ways in which the content-based retrieval paradigm may be approached: *model-based* and *general-purpose* approach. The model-based approach is similar in nature to the classical artificial intelligence approach to scene analysis, where some *a priori* knowledge of the image structure or content exists. On the other hand, the general-purpose approach makes no assumptions at all about the nature of the images being searched. Clearly, the model-based approach is most effective when the model supports a rich collection of assumptions regarding the nature of the images being searched. A successful example of this approach has been in fingerprint databases, where each image contains one type of object and can be modeled and compared based on a well-defined feature vector. The general-purpose approach requires multiple features for representing different properties of an image, and different instances of those features should be compared for similarity. In this chapter, we shall concentrate on the features and approaches that have been demonstrated to be most effective for the general-purpose approach. In the next chapter, both general-purpose and model-based approaches to video content analysis and browsing will be discussed.

2. COLOR CONTENT FEATURES

Color information is the most intensively used feature for image retrieval because of its strong correlation with the underlying image objects or scenes. Compared to other low-level visual information, color is more robust with respect to scaling, orientation, perspective, and occlusion of images.

There are several common issues associated with the design of color features for image retrieval. First, it is essential to select a proper color space for representing color content of images. Second, we need to choose a color quantization scheme to reduce the dimensions of a color feature. Last, but not least, we need to determine appropriate similarity/distance measures for comparing images based on their color features. In this section, we introduce a number of color features commonly used for image retrieval, including color histograms, color moments, color coherence vectors (CCV), and color correlograms. A detailed performance comparison of these features will be presented in Section 6.

2.1 COLOR HISTOGRAMS

Color histogram is a very popular color feature that has been widely used in many image retrieval systems [5,6,8,9,10]. Color histogram is effective in characterizing the global distribution of colors in an image, without requiring knowledge of how an image is composed of component objects. Such a feature is especially useful for representing color content of textured images and other images that are not particularly amenable to segmentation. Obviously, we can define the histogram of an image in one of many different color coordinates or spaces. A commonly used one is the RGB space because most digital images are acquired and represented in this space. However, due to the fact that RGB space is not perceptually uniform, histograms defined in color spaces such as HSV (Hue, Saturation, and Value), CIE $L^*u^*v^*$, and CIE $L^*a^*b^*$ tend to be more appropriate for calculating color similarities between images, due to their perceptual uniformity.

Let (r, g, b) represent the color in RGB space and (h, s, v) be the color in HSV space. The color transform from RGB space to HSV space can be accomplished through the following equations:

$$v = \max(r, g, b)$$

$$s = [v - \min(r, g, b)]/v$$

$$h = \begin{cases} 5 + b' & \text{if } r = \max(r, g, b) \text{ and } g = \min(r, g, b) \\ 1 - g' & \text{if } r = \max(r, g, b) \text{ and } g \neq \min(r, g, b) \\ 1 + r' & \text{if } g = \max(r, g, b) \text{ and } b = \min(r, g, b) \\ 3 - b' & \text{if } g = \max(r, g, b) \text{ and } b \neq \min(r, g, b) \\ 3 + g' & \text{if } b = \max(r, g, b) \text{ and } r = \min(r, g, b) \\ 5 - r' & \text{otherwise} \end{cases} \tag{1}$$

$$r' = [v - r]/[v - \min(r, g, b)]$$

$$g' = [v - g]/[v - \min(r, g, b)]$$

$$b' = [v - b]/[v - \min(r, g, b)]$$

where $r, g, b \in [0 \ldots 1]$, $h \in [0 \ldots 6]$, and $s, v \in [0 \ldots 1]$. The transform from RGB space to CIE L*u*v* or CIE L*a*b* spaces can be found in [11].

Different methods of computing color distance in the HSV space have been proposed in different image retrieval systems [9,12]. In [12], the following equation was used to measure the color similarity:

$$a(i, j) = 1 - \frac{1}{\sqrt{5}} \left[(v_i - v_j)^2 + (s_i \cos(h_i) - s_j \cos(h_j))^2 + (s_i \sin(h_i) - s_j \sin(h_j))^2 \right]^{1/2} \tag{2}$$

where (h_i, s_i, v_i) and (h_j, s_j, v_j) are the index of two HSV colors. This color similarity measure implies that the color distance can be computed using the Euclidean distance in a cylindrical HSV space, where h and s are angular and radial coordinates on a disk at height v (see Figure 2(a)). The coordinate of color in this space is represented as $(s\cos h, s\sin h, v)$. In [9], this cylindrical space is further modified by making the radius of disk (spanned by the angular h and radial s) proportional to the height v (see Figure 2(b)), so that it becomes a cone and the coordinate of color in this new space is $(sv\cos h, sv\sin h, v)$. This modification makes the differences of hue and saturation less distinguishable when value v is small.

To define discrete color histograms, we need to quantize a given color space into a finite number of color cells, each of them corresponding to a histogram bin. The color histogram of an image is then constructed by counting the number of pixels that fall in each of these cells. There are many different approaches to color quantization, including vector quantization, clustering, and neural networks [5,13]. An advantage of cluster-based color quantization approaches is that, if we apply it to all or at least representative images of a database, the clustering process will take into account the color distributions of images over the entire database. This process will minimize the likelihood of histogram bins in which no or very few pixels fall, thus resulting in a very efficient color quantization for images in the database. If images are originally represented in RGB color space, a color look-up table, which maps each RGB color into another quantized color space such as HSV, can be generated in advance. In this way, computing color histograms of images in a selected color space can be speeded up significantly by simply using this color look-up table.

As a result of color quantization, two images with almost the same color distribution, but off by one color bin will result in a very low similarity between them if we compare their histograms using, for instance, L-1 distance measure, as described later in Section 5. To overcome this problem, we need to take into account similarities between similar but not identical colors. One approach is to use the quadratic distance measure as in [14]. Another approach is to apply a smoothing filter to histograms of images such that pixels in a given color bin also contribute with a certain weight to the count in its neighboring bins; thus, similarities between similar but not identical colors will be taken into account in the comparison of two histograms.

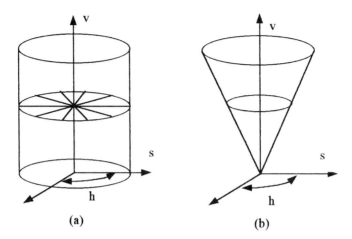

Figure 2.   (a) The HSV color cylinder. (b) The HSV color cone.

The selection of number of color cells and quantization approaches depend on performance and speed requirements of applications [15]. The greater the number of cells, the more discrimination power a color histogram has. However, histograms with a large number of bins will not only increase the computation load in comparing histograms, but also is less desirable in building efficient indexes for image databases [5, 8]. Furthermore, a very fine quantization does not necessarily improve retrieval performance in applications, especially when a low missing rate is the main concern and reasonable false matches can be tolerated [8, 15, 16]. Another effective way to reduce the number of bins of histograms in indexing images is to select only the largest bins (in terms of pixel counts) as the representation of a histogram. This is based on the fact that a small number of dominant color bins tend to capture the majority of pixels of an image. Therefore, as long as these dominant color bins of the query and data images are appropriately matched, similarity may be computed over this reduced histogram representation. Experiments have shown that such reduction does not degrade the performance of histogram matching. In fact, it may even enhance it, since small histogram bins are likely to be noisy, thus distorting the intersection computations. Two effective indexing schemes based on dominant color histogram bins can be found in [8, 16].

Figure 3 shows an example of using color histograms for image retrieval. The histogram consists of sixty-four colors in HSV space. As can be seen, the retrieved images match the query example very well in terms of color content, indicating the effectiveness of color histogram as a feature representation.

2.2 COLOR MOMENTS

Color moments of an image are a very simple yet very effective feature for color-based image retrieval. It does not require color quantization to compute this feature. The mathematical foundation of this feature is that any color distribution of images can be characterized by its moments. Furthermore, as most of the color distribution information can be captured by the low-order moments, using only the first order (mean color), the second- and the third-order moments (color variance and skewness) is a good approximation and has been proved to be efficient and effective in representing color distributions of images [10]. Mathematically, the first three moments are defined as:

$$\mu_i = \frac{1}{N} \sum_{j=1}^{N} p_{ij} \tag{3.1}$$

$$\sigma_i = \left(\frac{1}{N} \sum_{j=1}^{N} (p_{ij} - \mu_i)^2\right)^{\frac{1}{2}} \tag{3.2}$$

$$s_i = \left(\frac{1}{N} \sum_{j=1}^{N} (p_{ij} - \mu_i)^3\right)^{\frac{1}{3}} \tag{3.3}$$

where p_{ij} is the value of the i-th color component of the j-th image pixel. We need only 3×3 = 9 (three moments for each color components) numbers to represent the color content of each image and it is obviously a very compact representation compared to other color features. To overcome the shortcoming of having low discrimination power if used alone, color moments can be used as the first pass to narrow down the search space before other sophisticated color features are used in retrieval.

Figure 3. An example of image retrieval based on color histograms.
The first image is the query example.

2.3 COLOR COHERENCE VECTOR

Because color histograms and moments lack information about spatial distribution of colors in an image, they cannot distinguish, for example, an image with a single large yellow region from that with a large number of scattered yellow pixels. To overcome this shortcoming, color coherence vectors (CCV) have been proposed to incorporate spatial information into color histogram representation [17]. By classifying each pixel in an image based on whether or not it belongs to a large uniformly colored region, e.g., a region with area larger than 1% of the image, the CCV partitions each histogram bin into two; one representing coherent pixels and the other representing incoherent pixel. Let α_i denote the number of coherent pixels of the ith color bin of an image and β_i the number of incoherent pixels. Then, the CCV of the image is defined as $<(\alpha_1, \beta_1), (\alpha_2, \beta_2), ..., (\alpha_N, \beta_N)>$. Note that $<\alpha_1+\beta_1, \alpha_2+\beta_2, ..., \alpha_N+\beta_N>$ is the color histogram of the image. With this additional distinguishing power, color coherence vectors have been shown to provide better retrieval result than color histograms.

The CCV feature can be smoothed based on the same strategy used in color histograms in order to take into account the similarities between similar but not identical colors. However, the smoothing should be conducted only within the bins with the same spatial property.

2.4 COLOR CORRELOGRAMS

Color correlogram features are another approach proposed for representing color distribution of images [18]. This feature characterizes not only color distributions of pixels in term of percentages of a given color, but also the spatial correlation of pairs of colors in term of correlation changes with distance between a pair of colors in an image. It has shown to provide better retrieval performance compared to color histograms and CCVs, when one is looking for images with spatially coherent colors.

Let I and $I_{c(i)}$ represent the entire image pixels and the set of pixels whose colors are $c(i)$. Then, the color correlogram is defined as

$$\gamma_{i,j}^{(k)} = \Pr_{p_1 \in I_{c(i)}, p_2 \in I} \left[p_2 \in I_{c(j)} \middle| \, |p_1 - p_2| = k \right] \tag{4}$$

where $i, j \in \{1, 2, ..., N\}$, $k \in \{1, 2, ..., d\}$, and $|p_1 - p_2|$ is the distance between pixels p_1 and p_2. This feature can be considered as a table indexed by color pairs, where the kth entry for $<i, j>$ represents the probability of finding a pixel of color $c(j)$ at a distance k from a pixel of color $c(i)$ in the image. Because the size of the color correlogram will be very large ($O(N^2 d)$) if we consider all possible combinations of color pairs, a simplified version of this feature called color autocorrelogram is often used instead. This feature captures only spatial correlation between identical colors and thus reduces the dimension to $O(Nd)$.

3. TEXTURE CONTENT FEATURES

Texture is another type of basic low-level image feature that has also been used intensively for content-based image retrieval. Texture is an innate property of virtually all object surfaces, such as papers, clouds, woods, and fabrics, et al. An image can be considered a mosaic of different texture regions, and the texture associated with each of these regions can be used as a representation of the region and used for image search and retrieval. Therefore, a typical texture-based query could be that a user provide a region of interest with certain type of texture, such as a vegetation patch outlined in a satellite image. Figure 4 shows an example of using texture feature for browsing large aerial photographs based on texture similarities [19].

Due to the usefulness of texture features in pattern recognition and computer vision, texture analysis research has a long history. Statistic algorithms for texture analysis range from using random field models to multi-resolution filtering techniques such as wavelet transform. In this section, we introduce a number of texture features which have been used frequently and proved to be effective in content-based image retrieval systems, which include Tamura features, simultaneous auto-regressive (SAR) models, orientation features, Gabor texture features, and wavelet transform features. A detailed comparison of their retrieval performances is presented in Section 6.

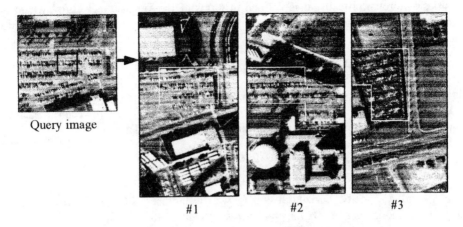

Query image

#1   #2   #3

Figure 4. An example of browsing large aerial photographs using texture features.
Both the query image and retrieved regions are from the parking lots areas.

3.1 TAMURA TEXTURE FEATURES

The Tamura features are designed based on the psychological studies in human visual perceptions of textures. They correspond to the properties of a texture which are readily perceived such as coarseness, contrast, directionality, linelikeness, regularity, and roughness [20]. Such a characteristic of Tumura features make them, especially the first three features, very attractive and used intensively in image retrieval systems [e.g., 5,7]. In this subsection, we discuss in detail the definition and calculation of coarseness, contrast, and directionality.

Coarseness: the procedure to compute the coarseness feature can be summarized in the following steps.

Step 1: Compute the moving average in windows of size $2^k \times 2^{\kappa}$ at each pixel (x, y), i.e.,

$$A_k(x, y) = \sum_{i=x-2^{k-1}}^{x+2^{k-1}-1} \sum_{j=y-2^{k-1}}^{y+2^{k-1}-1} g(i, j) \Big/ 2^{2k} \tag{5}$$

where $k = 0, 1, \ldots, 5$ and $g(i, j)$ is the pixel intensity at (i, j).

Step 2: At each pixel, compute the difference between pairs of non-overlapping moving averages in the horizontal and vertical directions, i.e.,

$$\left. \begin{aligned} E_{k,h}(x, y) &= \left| A_k(x+2^{k-1}, y) - A_k(x-2^{k-1}, y) \right| \\ E_{k,v}(x, y) &= \left| A_k(x, y+2^{k-1}) - A_k(x, y-2^{k-1}) \right| \end{aligned} \right\} \tag{6}$$

Step 3: At each pixel, the value of k that maximizes E in either direction is used to set the best size:

$$S_{best}(x, y) = 2^k \tag{7}$$

Step 4: The coarseness is computed by averaging S_{best} over the entire image, i.e.,

$$F_{crs} = \frac{1}{m \times n} \sum_{i=1}^{m} \sum_{j=1}^{n} S_{best}(i, j) \tag{8}$$

Instead of taking the average of $S_{best,}$, an improved version of the coarseness feature can be obtained by using a histogram to characterize the distribution of S_{best}. This modification makes the feature capable of dealing with an image or region which has multiple texture properties, and thus more useful to image retrieval applications.

Contrast: The contrast is computed based on the statistical distribution of pixel intensities. More specifically, it is defined in terms of the kurtosis $\alpha_4 = \mu_4/\sigma^4$, where μ_4 is the fourth moment about the mean, and σ^2 the variance. The formula for the measure of contrast is as follows:

$$F_{con} = \frac{\sigma}{\alpha_4^{1/4}} \tag{9}$$

This value provides a global measure of the contrast over an entire image or region.

Directionality: To compute the directionality measure, the gradient vector at each pixel is computed. The magnitude and angle of this vector are defined as

$$|\Delta G| = \left(|\Delta_H| + |\Delta_V|\right)/2$$
$$\theta = \tan^{-1}\left(\Delta_V/\Delta_H\right) + \pi/2 \tag{10}$$

where Δ_H and Δ_V are the horizontal and vertical differences obtained by convoluting the image with the following two 3x3 operators, respectively,

$$\begin{matrix} -1 & 0 & 1 \\ -1 & 0 & 1 \\ -1 & 0 & 1 \end{matrix} \qquad\qquad \begin{matrix} 1 & 1 & 1 \\ 0 & 0 & 0 \\ -1 & -1 & -1 \end{matrix}$$

Once the gradients have been computed at all pixels, a histogram of θ values, denoted as H_D, is constructed by first quantizing θ and counting the pixels with the corresponding magnitude $|\Delta G|$ larger than a threshold. This histogram will exhibit strong peaks for highly directional images and will be relatively flat for images without strong orientation. The entire histogram may then be summarized by an overall directionality measure based on the sharpness of the peaks as follows:

$$F_{dir} = \sum_{p}^{n_p} \sum_{\phi \in w_p} \left(\phi - \phi_p\right)^2 H_D(\phi) \tag{11}$$

In this sum p ranges over n_p peaks; and for each peak p, W_p is the set of bins distributed over it, while ϕ_p is the bin in which it assumes its highest value. The only peaks included in this sum must have predefined ratios between the peak and its surrounding valleys.

3.2 SIMULTANEOUS AUTO-REGRESSIVE (SAR) TEXTURE FEATURE

During the past twenty years a considerable amount of research has been conducted in modeling texture using random field models. In particular, Markov random field (MRF) models have been very successful. The SAR model is an instance of such MRF models with the advantage of requiring fewer parameters.

In the SAR model, the pixel intensities are treated as random variables and each pixel is described in terms of its neighboring pixels. Let s be a pixel location, its intensity $g(s)$ can be estimated as a linear combination of the neighboring pixel values and an additive noise term $\varepsilon(s)$, i.e.,

$$g(s) = \mu + \sum_{r \in D} \theta(r) g(s+r) + \varepsilon(s) \tag{12}$$

where μ is a bias value which depends on the mean of the entire image and D defines the neighbor set. Figure 5 shows a common way of choosing the second-order neighborhood. $\theta(r)$ is a set of model parameters which define the weights associated with each of the neighboring pixel values. $\varepsilon(s)$ is an independent Gaussian random variable with zero mean and variance σ^2. The parameters θ and the standard deviation σ can be used to measure the texture property. For example, a higher σ implies a finer granularity or less coarseness and higher values for $\theta(0, 1)$ and $\theta(0, -1)$ indicate that the texture is vertically oriented. The least square error (LSE) technique or the maximum likelihood estimation (MLE) method is usually used to estimate the parameters of SAR model.

$$
\begin{matrix}
(-1,1) & (0,1) & (1,1) \\
(-1,0) & (0,0) & (1,0) \\
(-1,-1) & (0,-1) & (1,-1)
\end{matrix}
$$

Figure 5. The second-order neighborhood of the pixel at $(0, 0)$

The rotation-invariant SAR (RISAR) model has been used to derive rotation-invariant SAR features for image representation. This model is established as follows:

$$
g(s) = \mu + \sum_{i=1}^{p} \theta_i x_i(s) + \varepsilon(s) \tag{13}
$$

where p is the number of circles which are used to describe the neighborhood, and $x(s)$ can be computed as

$$
x_i(s) = \frac{1}{8i} \sum_{r \in N_i} w_i(r) g(s+r) \tag{14}
$$

where N_i is the set of pixels that is used for interpolating the points on the ith circle around s; $w_i(r)$ are the pre-computed weights which indicate the contribution of the pixel r to the ith circle. Note that the computation of this model becomes expensive when p gets larger. Experimental results have indicated that $p = 2$ appears to be a reasonable choice.

In order to define an appropriate SAR model, one has to determine the size of the neighborhood. However, a fixed size neighborhood does not represent all texture variations very well. As a result, the multi-resolution simultaneous auto-regressive (MRSAR) model has been proposed to enable such multi-scale texture analysis [21]. The MRSAR model tries to account for the variability of texture primitives by defining the SAR or RISAR model at different resolutions of Gaussian pyramid. In [22, 23, 24] the comparison of the MRSAR features with other texture features such as principal component analysis of textures, Wold model features, and wavelet transform features using Brodatz texture images have been made. The results indicate that the MRSAR feature is very powerful in discriminating texture patterns. Furthermore, using four pyramid layers appears to be sufficient for yielding high classification accuracy [25].

3.3 ORIENTATION FEATURES

For some time, orientation has been recognized as an important feature for texture recognition and classification, especially after the physiological experiments suggested the existence of orientation selective mechanisms in the human visual system. A good example of using orientation features for quick sorting of images has been reported in [26].

Several orientation-finding algorithms have been proposed in the literature using directional filters in the spatial domain [27, 28] and in the Fourier domain [29]. On the other hand, the orientation features often become part of many existing texture features, such as the Tamura directionality and the Wold features [22].

The edge histogram can be considered as a simple way of characterizing the orientation property. Given an image, the edge detector can be applied to detect local image edges and a pre-defined threshold is further used to remove the weak edges. The edge histogram can be computed by grouping the remaining edge pixels falling into an edge orientation and counting the number of pixels in each direction.

3.4 GABOR TEXTURE FEATURES

The use of Gabor filters in extracting image features has been motivated by several factors. These filters have been shown to be optimal in the sense of minimizing the joint uncertainty in space and frequency [30], and they are often considered orientation and scale tunable edge and line (bar) detectors. There have been many approaches proposed to characterize textures of images based on the output of these filters [31, 32]. However, in this chapter we only introduce the approach proposed in [24], which uses the statistics of filter responses to characterize the underlying texture information.

A two-dimensional Gabor function $g(x, y)$ is defined as

$$g(x, y) = \frac{1}{2\pi\sigma_x\sigma_y} \exp\left[-\frac{1}{2}\left(\frac{x^2}{\sigma_x^2} + \frac{y^2}{\sigma_y^2}\right) + 2\pi jWx\right] \tag{15}$$

Figure 6 shows 3-D profiles of the real and imaginary components of a Gabor function. Let $g(x, y)$ be the mother Gabor wavelet, then a bank of self-similar Gabor filters (sometimes, referred to as Gabor wavelets) can be obtained by appropriate dilations and rotations of $g(x, y)$ through the generating function

$$\begin{aligned}
g_{mn}(x, y) &= a^{-m}g(x', y') \\
x' &= a^{-m}(x\cos\theta + y\sin\theta) \\
y' &= a^{-m}(-x\sin\theta + y\cos\theta)
\end{aligned} \right\} \tag{16}$$

where $a > 1$, $\theta = n\pi/K$, $n = 0, 1, ..., K\text{-}1$, and $m = 0, 1, ..., S\text{-}1$. K and S are the number of orientations and scales. The scale factor a^{-m} is meant to ensure that energy is independent of m. The nonorthogonality of the Gabor wavelets implies that there is redundant information in the filtered images, and a filter design strategy which reduces this redundancy has been described in [24].

Given an image $I(x, y)$, its Gabor transform is defined as

$$W_{mn}(x, y) = \int I(x, y)g_{mn}^*(x - x_1, y - y_1)dx_1 dy_1 \tag{17}$$

where * indicates the complex conjugate. Assumed that local texture regions are spatially homogeneous, and the mean μ_{mn} and the standard deviation σ_{mn} of the magnitude of the transform coefficients $W_{mn}(x, y)$, an be used to construct the texture feature. For example, if the filter bank consists of four scales and six orientations, then the resulting Gabor texture feature can be written as

$$f = [\eta_{00}, \sigma_{00}, \eta_{01}, \sigma_{01}, ..., \eta_{35}, \sigma_{35}] \tag{18}$$

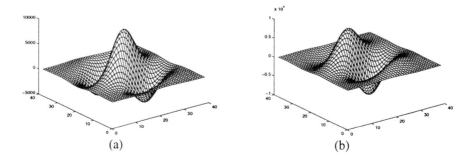

(a) (b)

Figure 6: 3-D profiles of the Gabor function: (a) shows the real (even) component and (b) shows the imaginary (odd) component.

3.5 WAVELET TRANSFORM FEATURES

Similar to the Gabor filters, the wavelet transform [33, 34] is another multi-resolution approach that has been used quite frequently for texture analysis and classification [35, 36]. Wavelet transforms refer to the decomposition of a signal with a family of basic functions $\psi_{mn}(x)$ obtained through translation and dilation of a mother wavelet $\psi(x)$, i.e.,

$$\psi_{mn}(x) = 2^{-m/2}\psi(2^{-m}x - n) \tag{19}$$

where m and n are integers. Thus, a signal $f(x)$ can be represented as

$$f(x) = \sum_{m,n} c_{mn}\psi_{mn}(x) \tag{20}$$

The computation of 2-D wavelet transforms involves recursive filtering and sub-sampling; and at each level, it decomposes a 2-D signal into four sub-bands, which are often referred to as LL, LH, HL, and HH according to their frequency characteristics. Two types of wavelet transforms have been used for texture analysis, which include the pyramid-structured wavelet transform (PWT) and the tree-structured wavelet transform (TWT) (see Figure 7). The PWT recursively decomposes the LL band. However, for some textures the most important information often appears in the middle frequency channels, further decomposition just in the lower frequency band may not be sufficient for analyzing the texture. As a result, the TWT has been utilized to overcome such drawbacks. The key difference between TWT and PWT is that the decomposition no longer simply performs on the LL band recursively. Instead, it can be applied to other bands such as LH, HL, or HH if the decomposition is needed.

A simple wavelet transform feature of an image can be constructed using the mean and standard deviation of the energy distribution corresponding to each of the sub-bands at each decomposition level. For three-level decomposition, PWT results in a feature vector of 3x4x2 components. As for TWT, the feature will depend on how sub-bands at each level are decomposed. A fixed decomposition tree can be obtained by sequentially decomposing the LL, LH, and HL bands, resulting in a feature vector of 52x2 components. Note that in this example, the feature obtained by PWT can be considered a subset of feature by TWT. Furthermore, according to the comparison of different wavelet transform features conducted in [37], the particular choice of wavelet filter is not very critical for texture analysis purpose.

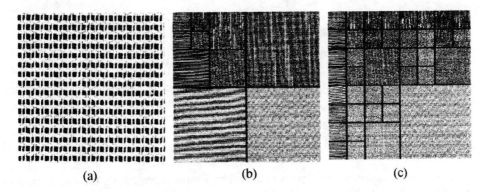

(a) (b) (c)

Figure 7: Wavelet decomposition: (a) original image, (b) traditional pyramid-structured wavelet transform, and (c) tree-structured wavelet transform.

4. SHAPE AND OTHER FEATURES

Shapes of objects or regions of interest are another important feature for content representation and thus content-based image retrieval. In contrast with low-level color and texture features, shape features need good segmentation algorithms as a first step to detect object/region boundaries. Over the past few decades, many approaches to the characterization of shape have been proposed in the literature, two of which can be categorized as boundary-based and region-based. Boundary-based shape features include rectilinear shapes [38], polygonal approximation [39,40,41], finite element models [42], and Fourier-based shape descriptors [43,44,45]. Statistical moments [46,47] is an effective region-based shape feature. However, due to the fact that robust and accurate image segmentation is difficult to achieve, the use of shape features for image retrieval has been limited to special applications where objects or regions are readily available. Furthermore, shape similarity is still a difficult problem that remains to be resolved, due to the requirement that a good shape-representation feature for an object should be invariant to translation, rotation, and scaling since human visual perception tends to be robust against such variations in object recognition. In this section, we briefly describe some of these shape features that have been used in image retrieval applications.

4.1 FOURIER-BASED SHAPE DESCRIPTORS

The basic idea of Fourier shape descriptors is to use the Fourier transform of the boundary of an object as its shape representation. Let us consider the contour of a 2-D object as a closed sequence of successive boundary pixel coordinates (x_s, y_s), where $0 \le s \le N-1$ and N is the total number of pixels on the boundary. Then, from these boundary coordinates, three types of contour representations can be derived: curvature function, centroid distance, and complex coordinate functions.

The curvature at a point along the contour is defined as the rate of change in tangent direction of a contour, as a function of arc length. Let $K(s)$ denote the curvature function, which can be expressed in formula as

$$K(s) = \frac{d}{ds}\theta(s) \tag{21}$$

where $\theta(s)$ is the tangent angle function of the contour, defined as

$$\left. \begin{aligned} \theta(s) &= \tan^{-1}\left(\frac{y'_s}{x'_s}\right) \\ y'_s &= \frac{dy_s}{ds} \\ x'_s &= \frac{dx_s}{ds} \end{aligned} \right\} \tag{22}$$

The centroid distance function is defined as the distance of boundary pixels from the centroid (x_c, y_c) of the object

$$R(s) = \sqrt{(x_s - x_c)^2 + (y_s - y_c)^2} \tag{23}$$

The complex coordinate function is obtained by simply representing the coordinates of the boundary pixels as complex numbers

$$Z(s) = (x_s - x_c) + j(y_s - y_c) \tag{24}$$

Fourier transform of such a contour representation generates a set of complex coefficients. These coefficients represent the shape of an object in the frequency domain, with lower frequency describing the general shape property and higher frequency denoting the shape details. Shape descriptors can be extracted from these transform coefficients. In order to achieve rotation invariance, we use only the amplitude information of the coefficients and discard the phase component. This allows the encoding of the contour to begin at any point along the contour. Scale invariance is achieved by dividing the amplitude of the coefficients by the amplitude of DC component or the first non-zero coefficient. Note that translation invariance is obtained directly from the contour representation.

For curvature and centroid distance functions, we only need to consider the positive frequency axes because these functions are real and, therefore, their Fourier transforms exhibit symmetry, i.e., $|F_{-i}| = |F_i|$. The shape descriptor corresponding to the curvature is

$$f_K = \left[|F_1|, |F_2|, ..., |F_{M/2}|\right]$$

(24)

where F_i denotes the ith component of Fourier transform coefficients. Similarly, the shape descriptor corresponding to the centroid distance is

$$f_R = \left[\frac{|F_1|}{|F_0|}, \frac{|F_2|}{|F_0|}, ..., \frac{|F_{M/2}|}{|F_0|}\right]$$

(25)

For complex coordinate function, both negative and positive frequency components are used. The DC coefficient is dependent on the position of a shape, and, therefore, is discarded. The first non-zero frequency component is used to normalize the other transform coefficients. The shape descriptor corresponding to complex coordinate is

$$f_Z = \left[\frac{|F_{-(M/2-1)}|}{|F_1|}, ..., \frac{|F_{-1}|}{|F_1|}, \frac{|F_2|}{|F_1|}, ..., \frac{|F_{M/2}|}{|F_1|}\right]$$

(26)

In order to ensure that the resulting shape features of all objects in a database have the same length, the boundary function $((x_s, y_s), 0 \le s \le N\text{-}1)$ of each object is re-sampled to M samples before performing the Fourier transform. For example, M can be set to $2^n = 64$ so that the transformation can be conducted efficiently using fast Fourier transform.

Figure 8 shows an example of using the Fourier-based shape descriptors for image retrieval, where shapes of the query object and objects in the retrieval images are outlined.

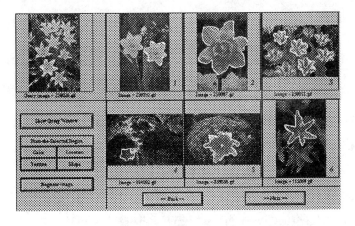

Figure 8. Image retrieval based on the shape similarity.

4.2 TURNING ANGLES

The $\theta(s)$ defined in (22) has also been used as a shape representation [41]. It is called turning function or turning angle which measures the angle of the counterclockwise tangents as a function of the arc-length s according to reference points on the object's contour. One major problem with this representation is that it is variant to the rotation of the object and the choice of reference point. If we shift the reference point along object's boundary by an amount t, then the new turning function becomes $\theta(s+t)$. If we rotate the object by angle ω, then the new function becomes $\theta(s)+\omega$.

In order to measure the shape similarity between objects A and B using their turning functions, one needs to find the minimum distance over all possible shifts t and rotations ω, i.e.,

$$d_p(A,B) = \left(\min_{\omega \in R, t \in [0,1]} \int_0^1 \left| \theta_A(s+t) - \theta_B(s) + \omega \right|^P ds \right)^{\frac{1}{p}} \tag{27}$$

where we assume that each object has been re-scaled so that the total perimeter length is 1. This distance is invariant under translation, rotation, and change of scale.

4.3 MOMENT INVARIANTS

Moment invariant is derived from region-based moments of objects or regions. Let us consider the case that object R is represented as a binary image; then central moments of order $p+q$ for the shape of object R is defined as

$$\mu_{p,q} = \sum_{(x,y) \in R} (x - x_c)^P (y - y_c)^q \tag{28}$$

where (x_c, y_c) is the center of object. This central moment can be normalized for scale invariance [11]:

$$\eta_{p,q} = \frac{\mu_{p,q}}{\mu_{0,0}^\gamma}, \quad \gamma = \frac{p+q+2}{2} \tag{29}$$

Based on these moments, a set of moment invariants with respect to translation, rotation, and scale differences was first derived by Hu [46]:

$$\begin{aligned}
\phi_1 &= \mu_{2,0} + \mu_{0,2} \\
\phi_2 &= (\mu_{2,0} - \mu_{0,2})^2 + 4\mu_{1,1}^2 \\
\phi_3 &= (\mu_{3,0} - 3\mu_{1,2})^2 + (\mu_{0,3} - 3\mu_{2,1})^2 \\
\phi_4 &= (\mu_{3,0} + \mu_{1,2})^2 + (\mu_{0,3} + \mu_{2,1})^2 \\
\phi_5 &= (\mu_{3,0} - 3\mu_{1,2})(\mu_{3,0} + \mu_{1,2})\left[(\mu_{3,0} + \mu_{1,2})^2 - 3(\mu_{0,3} + \mu_{2,1})^2\right] \\
&\quad + (\mu_{0,3} - 3\mu_{2,1})(\mu_{0,3} + \mu_{2,1})\left[(\mu_{0,3} + \mu_{2,1})^2 - 3(\mu_{3,0} + \mu_{1,2})^2\right] \\
\phi_6 &= (\mu_{2,0} - \mu_{0,2})\left[(\mu_{3,0} + \mu_{1,2})^2 - (\mu_{0,3} + \mu_{2,1})^2\right] + 4\mu_{1,1}(\mu_{3,0} + \mu_{1,2})(\mu_{0,3} + \mu_{2,1}) \\
\phi_7 &= (3\mu_{2,1} - \mu_{0,3})(\mu_{3,0} + \mu_{1,2})\left[(\mu_{3,0} + \mu_{1,2})^2 - 3(\mu_{0,3} + \mu_{2,1})^2\right] \\
&\quad + (\mu_{3,0} - 3\mu_{2,1})(\mu_{0,3} + \mu_{2,1})\left[(\mu_{0,3} + \mu_{2,1})^2 - 3(\mu_{3,0} + \mu_{1,2})^2\right]
\end{aligned} \tag{30}$$

Many improved versions of moments invariant have been proposed, including a fast method of computing the moments for binary images based on the discrete version of Green's theorem [48].

4.4 CIRCULARITY, ECCENTRICITY, AND MAJOR AXIS ORIENTATION

Apart from the set of moment invariants, the QBIC image retrieval system [5] also uses circularity, eccentricity, and major axis orientation as shape features. Circularity is computed as

$$\alpha = \frac{4\pi S}{P^2} \tag{31}$$

where S is the size and P is the perimeter of an object. This value ranges between 0 (which would correspond to a perfect line segment) and 1 (which would correspond to a perfect circle).

The second order covariance matrix of an object is computed using the pixels contained in the object. From this covariance matrix, the major axis orientation is the direction of the largest eigenvector, and the eccentricity is defined as the ratio of the smallest eigenvalue to the largest eigenvalue.

Although it is not too difficult to compute shape features, the problem of the shape similarity measures that correspond to human perception still remains to be resolved. Also, to fully utilize the shape information in content-based image retrieval, a general and robust image segmentation algorithm needs to be developed. Some recent works on designing an image segmentation algorithm that is particularly useful for processing a large and diverse collection of images can be found in [49].

4.5. SPATIAL INFORMATION

The spatial location of objects or regions in an image or the spatial relationship between multiple objects is another important aspect of image content and is very useful information for searching images. For example, the regions of blue sky and ocean may have similar color histograms, but if we impose the constraint on the spatial location as "regions from the upper-half of image," then we can distinguish the sky from the ocean. Another example of spatial query could be "finding all images having a house to the right of a mountain." In such case, the spatial relationship between the house and the mountain should be used to filter out irrelevant images.

There have been a few spatial query methods proposed in the literature, including 2-D strings [50], spatial quad-tree [51], and symbolic image [52]. The 2-D strings are constructed by projecting an image along the x and y directions. The problem of spatial query then becomes a problem of 2-D subsequence matching. In [52], the spatial similarity is measured based on the assumption that images have been segmented into meaningful objects, each object being associated with its centroid and a symbolic name. All these methods assume that the individual objects can be matched exactly based on certain properties, and thus, they have concentrated only on the matching algorithms of spatial relationships of objects. However, this is usually not the case in most image database applications, where each region is represented by a set of image features and an exact match between features is not a reasonable assumption. In addition, there is the fact that reliable segmentation of objects or regions is often not feasible except in very limited applications.

To avoid the problem of lacking reliable segmentation of regions and at the same time provide some basic information about regional structure in an image, a trade-off solution is to pre-divide the entire image into sub-blocks (often with certain overlap) and represent each sub-block with image features extracted from the sub-block [16, 53, 54]. Such a scheme of spatial division of images supports matches based on simple spatial relation in addition to image features, such as color histograms or texture descriptors of each sub-block. For example, with this scheme one can pose a query "find images with blue sky over golf course." In this case, the similarity between two images should be the (weighted) sum of similarities of corresponding sub-blocks that meet the spatial constraints. However, only limited successes have been achieved with such spatial division schemes since most natural images are not spatially constrained to regular sub-blocks. Therefore, searching images based on multiple region properties and spatial similarity remains a difficult research problem in content-based image retrieval.

5. SIMILARITY MEASURES AND INDEXING SCHEMES

5.1 SIMILARITY/DISTANCE MEASURES

A key feature of the content-based image retrieval paradigm is that searching of images is based on visual similarity between a query and candidate image in a database, as opposed to exact matching. Therefore, in addition to extracting most representative visual features, the choice of appropriate similarity/distance measures will significantly affect retrieval performances of an image retrieval system.

For image features whose dimensions are independent and of equal importance, the distance between feature vectors $X^{(1)}$ and $X^{(2)}$ can be computed based on the L_1-distance or the L_2-distance (also called Euclidean distance). The L_1-distance is defined as

$$D_1 = \sum_{i=1}^{N} \left| X_i^{(1)} - X_i^{(2)} \right| \tag{32}$$

and the L_2-distance is given by

$$D_2 = \sum_{i=1}^{N} (X_i^{(1)} - X_i^{(2)})^2 \tag{33}$$

L_1-distance is commonly used to calculate distance between histograms. Another popular distance measure between color histograms is the so-called *histogram intersection*. Let I and Q be two histograms, each containing N bins. The intersection of these two histograms is defined to be

$$\sum_{j=1}^{N} \min(I_j, Q_j) \tag{34}$$

This value is the number of pixels that are common to both histograms, and may be normalized by the number of pixels in one of the two histograms so that it always ranges between 0 and 1. That is,

$$S(I,Q) = \sum_{j=1}^{N} \min(I_j, Q_j) \Big/ \sum_{j=1}^{N} Q_j \tag{35}$$

For color histogram-based image retrieval, a quadratic form of distance measure has been shown to lead to perceptually more desirable results than Euclidean distance and histogram intersection method because it computes the cross similarity between colors. The quadratic distance metric between two histograms is given by

$$D = (Q - I)^t A (Q - I) \tag{36}$$

The key idea of this color histogram measure is that it takes into account similarities between similar but not identical colors by introducing color similarity matrix $A = [a_{ij}]$, where a_{ij} denotes the similarity between color bins i and j. The color similarity matrix A should be defined from color psychology studies [14]. Equivalently, one can apply a convolution to histograms so that the resultant count of each color bin has a contribution from its neighboring color bins with certain weights, which is defined by the same matrix $[a_{ij}]$. In this way, similarities between different colors are taken into account in the process of calculating color histograms of images, and Euclidean distance or histogram intersection can be applied directly. The advantage of pre-smoothing histograms is that it requires less computation in the retrieval process.

When dimensions of a feature vector have inter-dependence and different importance, the Mahalanobis distance metric is commonly used to compute distance measure. The Mahalanobis distance is defined as follows:

$$D_{mahal} = (X^{(1)} - X^{(2)})^t C^{-1} (X^{(1)} - X^{(2)})$$ (37)

where C is the covariance matrix of the feature vectors. This distance is commonly used in comparing SAR features.

The Mahalanobis distance can be simplified if we can assume independence of the feature dimensions. In that case it is necessary to compute only a variance of each feature component, c_i. The simplified Mahalanobis distance is defined as follows:

$$D_s = \sum_{i=1}^{N} \frac{(X_i^{(1)} - X_i^{(2)})^2}{c_i}$$ (38)

Choosing an appropriate similarity/distance measure for a given image feature is important to ensure satisfactory retrieval. What is more important and certainly also more difficult is to choose appropriate weights for different features or feature components when multiple features or a multiple dimensional are used in a query.

5.2 INDEXING

Another important research issue in content-based image retrieval is effective indexing and fast searching, because the feature vectors of images tend to have high dimensionality and therefore are not well-suited for traditional indexing structures. Many researchers have proposed the use of Karhunen-Loeve (KL) transform to reduce the dimensions of the feature space. Although the KL transform has some nice properties such as identifying the most important sub-space, one should be careful in its use as the feature properties that are important for identifying the pattern similarity might be destroyed during blind dimensionality reduction [55].

On the other hand, there have been a number of approaches proposed to index multi-dimensional data, examples of which include R-tree (particularly, R*-tree [56]), linear quad-trees, k-d-B tree [57], and grid files [58]. All these indexing schemes provide reasonable performance for a small number of dimensions (up to 20), but for a big number of dimensions their performance deteriorates, a phenomenon known as the "dimensionality curse." Furthermore, these indexing schemes assume that the underlying feature comparison is based on the Euclidean distance, which is not necessarily true for many image retrieval applications.

One attempt to solve the indexing problems is the hierarchical indexing scheme based on the Self-Organization Map (SOM) proposed in [13]. The advantage of this approach apart from indexing is that it also provides user a useful browsing tool to view the representative images of each type. This indexing scheme was further applied in [59] to create a texture thesaurus for indexing a database of large aerial photographs.

For image retrieval based on color histograms, an efficient indexing scheme for quadratic form distance functions has been proposed in [60]. This approach uses a pre-filtering scheme to reduce the search space before the quadratic form distance measure is computed. Their experimental results indicated that this pre-filtering method easily outperforms the naïve histogram comparison method. Another indexing and fast searching scheme for color histogram-based image retrieval is the incremental histogram intersection [8].

6. PERFORMANCE EVALUATION OF IMAGE FEATURES

A very basic issue in designing an image retrieval system is to select the most effective image features to represent image contents in a database. Such a selection requires a comprehensive evaluation of retrieval performance of image features. This section gives a detailed comparison of retrieval performances of a set of commonly used color and texture features. This comparison is based on a data set of 20,000 color images obtained from Corel photo galleries and texture images digitized from Brodatz album [61]. There is a large diversity and heterogeneity in contents of these images, which ensures the validity and objectivity of the performance evaluation. For simplicity, all features are extracted from entire images in the database, without considering the issue of spatial segmentation and spatial similarity.

The retrieval performance of image features is measured by the *recall vs. scope*. Let R_1, $R_2, ..., R_t$ be the top t retrieved images based on the query image Q, and each of them labeled according to their relevance to Q. The recall r at a scope s is then defined as

$$r(s) = \left| \left\{ R_i \middle| \text{ relevant}(R_i) = \text{true, } 1 \le i \le s \right\} \right|, \ s \le t \tag{39}$$

where $|\{\}|$ is the number of elements which are relevant. This measure is simpler than the conventional *recall vs. precision*, and is effective in evaluating the performance of features.

6.1 COMPARISON OF COLOR FEATURES

This subsection presents the comparison of retrieval performances of four basic color features: color histograms, color moments, color coherence vector, and color autocorrelgram.

Color Histograms: Our retrieval performance evaluation of color histograms has focused on relative performance of histograms defined in different color spaces. The color spaces are: CIE L*u*v*, CIE L*a*b*, original HSV and its two variations (HSV cylinder and cone as discussed in Section 2.1.1). The RGB space is not considered because it is not very useful for measuring perceptual color similarities. The experimental results have indicated that the HSV color spaces (original and cylinder) provide the best retrieval performance for color histograms.

Color Coherence Vector: Since CCV is basically a refinement of color histogram, not surprisingly, the HSV spaces give the best retrieval performance compared to other color spaces. Because CCV has additional capability to distinguish the spatial coherence, in theory they should provide better retrieval performance than color histograms. However, looking through our test results, it is found that the CCV only enhances the retrieval performance significantly for those images which have either mostly uniform color or mostly texture regions. It is also noticed that L_1 distance performs better than L_2 distance for CCVs and color histograms.

Color Moments: In contrast with color histograms, retrieval performances of color moment defined in both L*u*v* and L*a*b* color spaces are superior to those in HSV space. Using additional third-order moment improves the retrieval performance overall compared to using only the mean and standard deviation. However, this third-order moment sometimes makes the feature representation more sensitive to image scene changes so that it actually decreases the performance in many cases. Although the color moment feature has a much smaller dimension than color histogram, in our experiments, its retrieval performance is almost as good as color histogram.

Color Autocorrelogram: In this case, we focused on the retrieval performance of color autocorrelogram in relation to other color features. Table 1 provides a comparison of feature computation time and feature dimension. Figure 9 shows the performance comparison in terms of recall vs. scope. It is shown that the color autocorrelogram provides the best retrieval result, but is also the most computational expensive color feature with the highest feature dimensionality.

Table 1. Feature Computation Time and Feature Vector Length of Various Color Features Based on 64- Color Quantization

Feature	Computation time	Dimension
Color histogram	0.13 sec	64
Color moments	0.55 sec	6
CCV	0.41 sec	128
Color autocorrelogram	46.0 sec	256

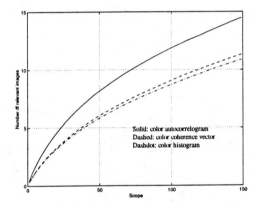

Figure 9. Comparison of color autocorrelogram, color coherence vector, and color histogram features based on 64 L*u*v* colors. The graph shows the number of relevant images retrieved at various scopes.

6.2 COMPARISON OF TEXTURE FEATURE

This subsection presents the comparison of retrieval performances of all texture features discussed in Section 3. Figure 10(a) shows the retrieval performance comparison based on the number of relevant images retrieved at various scopes from the Corel image database. The features, with performance ordered from the best to the worst, are MRSAR (based on the image-dependent covariance), Gabor feature, TWT feature, PWT feature, MRSAR (based on the global covariance), modified Tamura features, coarseness histogram, directionality, edge histogram, and traditional Tamura features. Note that the coarseness histogram and directionality are also part of the modified Tamura feature set.

In this experiment, two types of Mahalanobis distances are used to compare MRSAR features. The best performance is achieved by the use of image-dependent covariance matrix. This matrix is associated with the covariance of model parameters in the image and thus needs to be stored along with the MRSAR feature. If a global covariance matrix is used instead in order to reduce the storage and search complexity, the performance of MRSAR feature drops behind the PWT feature.

The modified Tamura features refer to the change of coarseness feature from a single average value to a histogram representation. As shown in Figure 10(a), the retrieval performance of the modified Tamura features increases significantly.   Furthermore, the experimental results indicate that the coarseness histogram (which characterizes image scale distribution) outperforms the directionality and edge histogram (both represent image orientation distributions).

In addition to the Corel image database, the Brodatz texture album has also been used to evaluate the performance of texture features. This database has been widely used for evaluations of texture classification and analysis algorithm and thus is a very appropriate data set for the benchmark of retrieval performance of texture features. The database currently contains 116 such images, and each of them is divided into 16 non-overlapping sub-images, resulting in a database of 1856 images. In the experiment, each query image will have another 15 similar (or same class) images which we would like to retrieve as the top matches. Figure 10(b) shows the average percentage of retrieving all 15 correct images at various scopes using different texture features.   The result is basically consistent with the previous experiment except that now the performance of the Gabor feature is about the same as that of MRSAR, and the rank of original Tamura feature set moves upward. The latter change indicates that the original Tamura feature set is more effective in representing homogenous texture images since images in the Brodatz texture database have higher spatial texture homogeneity than those in the Corel image database.

A comparison of feature computation time and feature dimension is provided in Table 2.

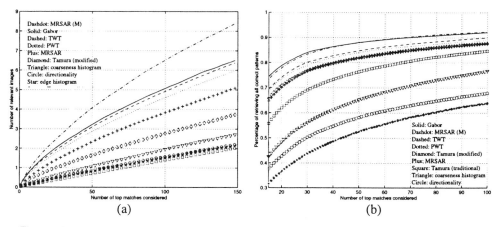

(a)   (b)

Figure 10. Retrieval performance of different texture features according to the number of relevant images retrieved at various scopes: (a) based on 20,000 Corel images, (b) based on Brodatz album.

Table 2. Feature Computation Time and Feature Vector Length of Various Texture Features

Feature	Computation time	Dimension
MRSAR	0.94 sec	15 + (15x15)
Gabor	16.75 sec	48
TWT	1.02 sec	104
PWT	0.64 sec	24
Coarseness	2.16 sec	10
Directionality	0.26 sec	8
Edge histogram	3.44 sec	8

7. LEARNING AND RELEVANCE FEEDBACK

As discussed earlier, content-based image retrieval is more like an *information filter* process and a good filter should provide a high percentage of relevant candidates for the user to examine after a query is submitted. In typical applications, a number of top candidates ordered based on the similarities of certain feature vectors to the query are retrieved. However, the similarity measures, such as color histograms, in general do not necessarily match the *human perception semantics and subjectivity*. In addition, each type of image feature tends to capture only one of many aspects of image similarity and it is difficult to require a user to specify clearly exactly which aspect or what combination of these aspects he/she wants to apply in defining a query. To address these problems, interactive relevance feedback techniques have been proposed to incorporate human perception subjectivity into the retrieval process and to provide users abilities to *evaluate* retrieval results and automatically *refine* queries on the basis of those evaluations [62, 63, 64]. In this section, we briefly discuss the framework of relevance feedback and some relevance feedback techniques.

7.1 RELEVANCE FEEDBACK ARCHITECTURE

Relevance feedback is the process of automatically refining an existing query using the information fedback by the user about the relevance of previously retrieved results. Before we describe the various existing approaches, it is worth looking at the model of image feature-based image retrieval and distinguish different levels of feature representations.

Figure 11 illustrates the different levels of feature representations in image retrieval. Normally, each image is represented by multiple features, each feature has multiple representations, and each representation consists of multiple components. The retrieval process is conducted based on the use of three levels of weights associated with features of the query and images in a database. By choosing the first-level weights, $W_{O,F}$, we can decide what image features are important for a search, such as color vs. texture. With the second-level weights, $W_{F,R}$, we can choose the appropriate representation for each feature, such as color histogram vs. color moments. Finally, by choosing the third-level weights, $W_{R,R}$, we can select proper similarity/distance measures and enhance or diminish the importance of different dimensions. Based on this model, the key issue in relevance feedback algorithms is how to adjust the weights of various levels to accommodate the user's need and perception subjectivity [63]. It should be pointed out that, in practice, the boundaries between the levels are often blurred or ignored since the weights at the different levels will affect one another.

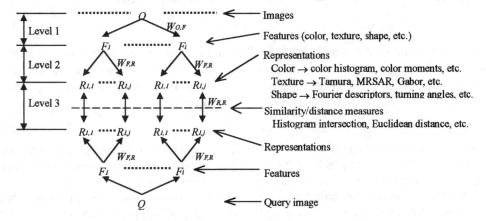

Figure 11. Different levels of feature representations in the image retrieval model.

7.2 LEARNING THE QUERY VECTOR

The relevance feedback techniques used in textual document retrieval for query refinement can be adopted for image retrieval. However, before applying these techniques, we need to convert the feature vector into a new presentation that is similar to the weight vector used in the document retrieval systems. One such conversion scheme was proposed in [63]. That is, based on user's feedback, an original query Q can be modified as

$$\alpha \cdot f(Q) + \beta \left(\frac{1}{|A^+|} \sum_{i=1}^{|A^+|} f(A_i^+) \right) - \gamma \left(\frac{1}{|A^-|} \sum_{i=1}^{|A^-|} f(A_i^-) \right) \tag{40}$$

where $f(Q)$ denotes the weight vector; α, β, and γ are suitable constants; $A^+ = \{A_1^+, ..., A_{|A^+|}^+\}$ and $A^- = \{A_1^-, ..., A_{|A^-|}^-\}$ represent the set of positive (relevant) and negative (irrelevant) examples. This technique can be referred to as *learning the query vector*.

Huang, et al., [64] used a similar relevance feedback scheme to improve the retrieval performance of color correlogram, except that the negative examples were not used in the query refinement.

7.3 LEARNING THE METRIC

Another relevance feedback approach, proposed by Huang, et al. [64], is to modify the weighted metric for computing the distance between feature vectors. The basic idea is to enhance the importance of those dimensions of a feature that help retrieve the relevant images and reduce the importance of those dimensions that hinder this process. Let us consider one weighted metric defined as

$$D = \sum_{j \in [N]} \omega_j \cdot \left| X_j^{(1)} - X_j^{(2)} \right| \tag{41}$$

When a retrieval image of a query is labeled as a positive example, the feature components that contribute more similarity to the query image can be considered more important, while the components with less contribution can be considered to be less important. The following simple rule can be used to update the weights based on positive examples:

$$\omega_i = \omega_i \cdot (1 + \overline{\delta} - \delta_i), \quad \delta = \left| f(Q) - f(A_j^+) \right| \tag{42}$$

where $\overline{\delta}$ is the mean of δ. On the other hand, if an image is labeled as a negative example, the feature components that contribute more quantities to δ can be considered to be more important and the components with less contributions can be considered to be less important. The rule for updating the weights based on negative examples is

$$\omega_i = \omega_i \cdot (1 - \overline{\delta} + \delta_i) \tag{43}$$

This technique can be referred as *learning the metric*. It is worth noticing that the above two relevance feedback techniques perform the weight adjustments at the representation and (mostly) the component level according to the model illustrated in Figure 11.

Instead of updating the individual components of a distance metric, we can begin with a set of pre-defined distance metrics and use the relevance feedback to automatically select the best one in the retrieval process. A simple algorithm that fulfills this idea was described in ImageRover system [65]. This algorithm automatically selects appropriate L_m Minkowski distance metrics which minimize the mean distance between the relevant images specified by the user.

7.4 LEARNING USING A SOCIETY OF MODELS

The learning approach proposed by Minka and Picard [62] is essentially focused on the feature and representation levels. The key idea behind this approach is that each feature model has its own strength in representing a certain aspect of image content and, thus, the best way for effective content-based retrieval is to utilize "a society of models." This approach uses a learning scheme to dynamically determine which model or combination of models is best for subsequent retrieval, based on the user's inputs or feedback to the initial classification of objects or regions of images in the learning process. In other words, the system has the capability to learn the user's subjectivity in terms of the best feature or feature set for representing a particular class of object.

8. CONCLUDING REMARKS: RESEARCH CHALLENGES

In this chapter, we discussed a variety of existing techniques for content-based image retrieval, including visual content feature extraction, representation and indexing, query formation and refinement, and retrieval tools. A detailed description of a set of widely used image features is provided, together with a comprehensive comparison of performances of the color and texture features. These comparison results provide a benchmark for selecting image features when designing an image retrieval system. Despite significant efforts devoted to research of these techniques, the current automated solutions for content analysis and retrieval still depend heavily, if not totally, on use of low-level visual features. On the other hand, the current low-level feature-based content representation and retrieval algorithms and tools have already improved our productivity in image and video retrieval. Though they are far less than satisfactory, we believe these tools also provide a bridge to more intelligent and automated solutions.

As discussed, content-based image retrieval is more like an *information filter* process and a good filter should provide a high percentage of relevant candidates for the user to examine after a query is submitted. It is known that the visual information content of images is not explicit and the visual similarity measures, such as color histograms, in general, do not necessarily match the human perception of visual semantics. As a result, the retrieval results of low-level feature-based retrieval approaches in general are not very satisfactory and often not predicable. Hence, an important problem is how to refine a query based on user's relevance assessment and feedback to retrieve more relevant candidates. We need new interactive relevance feedback techniques to incorporate human perception into the retrieval process and to automatically refine queries on the basis of those evaluations. We have briefly discussed three schemes addressing this problem in this chapter, which have limited successes. However, this problem remains unsolved in general and more research efforts are needed.

In general, each type of image feature tends to capture only one of many aspects of image similarity and it is difficult to require a user to clearly specify exactly which aspect or what combination of these aspects he/she wants to apply in defining a query. Therefore, it is important to identify salient features for a given image and to apply the appropriate similarity metric. In addition, an effective search of relevant images often requires a combination of different visual features, which makes selection of appropriate similarity metrics even more difficult. So far, no effective algorithm has been developed to address these problems.

Indexing is another critical component in visual information systems of large scales, which has been only very briefly discussed in this chapter. Given the high dimensionality of features and interactive nature of the query process in content-based image retrieval, efficient indexing is definitely another very challenging research topic.

REFERENCES

1. S. K. Chang and A. Hsu, "Image Information Systems: Where Do We Go From Here," *IEEE Transactions on Knowledge and Data Engineering*, October 1992,Vol. 4,No. 5, pp. 431-442.
2. R. Jain, A. Pentland, and D. Petkovic (editors), *Workshop Report: NSF-ARPA Workshop on Visual Information Management Systems*, Cambridge, MA, June 1995.
3. A. E. Cawkill, "The British Library's Picture Research Projects: Image, Word, and Retrieval," *Advanced Imaging*,Vol. 8, No. 10, October 1993, pp. 38-40.
4. S. Al-Hawamdeh, et al., "Nearest Neighbour Searching in a Picture Archive System," *International Conference on Multimedia Information Systems '91*, Singapore, January 1991, pp. 17-33.
5. Niblack, et al., "The QBIC project: querying images by content using color, texture, and shape," *Proc. of SPIE, Storage and Retrieval for Image and Video Databases*, Vol. 1908, February 1993, San Jose, pp. 173-187.
6. B. Furht, S. W. Smoliar, and H. J. Zhang, *Image and Video Processing in Multimedia Systems*, Kluwer Academic Publishers, 1995.
7. A. Pentland, R.W. Picard, and S. Sclaroff, "Photobook: Content-Based Manipulation of Image Databases," *Proc. Storage and Retrieval for Image and Video Databases II*, Vol. 2185, San Jose, CA, February, 1994.
8. M. J. Swain and D. H. Ballard, "Color indexing," *International Journal of Computer Vision*, Vol. 7, No. 1, pp. 11-32, 1991.
9. S. Belongie, et al., "Recognition of images in large databases using a learning framework," *Technical Report* 97-939, U.C. Berkeley CS Division, 1997
10. M. Stricker and M. Orengo, "Similarity of color images," SPIE Storage and Retrieval for Image and Video Databases III, Vol. 2185, pp. 381-392, Feb. 1995.
11. A. K. Jain, *Fundamentals of Digital Image Processing*, Englewood Cliffs, Prentice Hall, 1989.
12. J. R. Smith and S. F. Chang, "VisualSEEk: a fully automated content-based image query system," *ACM Multimedia 96*, Boston, MA, Nov. 1996.
13. H. J. Zhang and D. Zhong, "A Scheme for visual feature-based image indexing," Proc. of SPIE conf. on Storage and Retrieval for Image and Video Databases III, pp. 36-46, San Jose, Feb. 1995.
14. M. Ioka, "A method of defining the similarity of image on the basis of color information," *Technical Report* RT-0030, IBM Research, November 1989.
15. H. J. Zhang, et al., "Image retrieval based on color features: An evaluation study," *SPIE Conf. on Digital Storage and Archival*, Pennsylvania, Oct. 25-27, 1995.
16. Y. Gong, H. J. Zhang, and T. C. Chua, "An image database system with content capturing and fast image indexing abilities," *Proc. IEEE International Conference on Multimedia Computing and Systems*, Boston, 14-19 May 1994, pp. 121-130.
17. G. Pass and R. Zabih, "Histogram refinement for content-based image retrieval," *IEEE Workshop on Applications of Computer Vision*, pp. 96-102, 1996.
18. J. Huang, et al., "Image indexing using color correlogram," *IEEE Int. Conf. on Computer Vision and Pattern Recognition*, pp. 762-768, Puerto Rico, June 1997.
19. B. S. Manjunath and W. Y. Ma, "Browsing large satellite and aerial photographs," *IEEE Int. Conf. on Image Processing*, Vol. 2, pp. 765-768, Lausanne, Switzerland, Sep. 1996.
20. H. Tamura, S. Mori, and T. Yamawaki, "Texture features corresponding to visual perception," *IEEE Trans. On Systems, Man, and Cybernetics*, Vol. Smc-8, No. 6, June 1978.
21. J. Mao and A. K. Jain, "Texture classification and segmentation using multiresolution simultaneous autoregressive models," Pattern Recognition, Vol. 25, No. 2, pp. 173-188, 1992.
22. F. Liu and R. W. Picard, "Periodicity, directionality, and randomness: Wold features for image modeling and retrieval," *MIT Media Lab Technical Report*, No. 320.

23. R. W. Picard, T. Kabir, and F. Liu, "Real-time recognition with the entire Brodatz texture database," *Proc. IEEE Int. Conf. on Computer Vision and Pattern Recognition*, pp. 638-639, New York, June 1993.

24. B. S. Manjunath and W. Y. Ma, "Texture features for browsing and retrieval of image data," *IEEE Trans. on Pattern Analysis and Machine Intelligence*, Vol. 18, No. 8, pp. 837-842, Aug. 1996.

25. A. Kankanhalli, H. J. Zhang, and C. Y. Low, "Using texture for image retrieval," *Third Int. Conf. on Automation, Robotics and Computer Vision*, pp. 935-939, Singapore, Nov. 1994.

26. M. M. Gorkani and R. W. Picard, "Texture orientation for sorting photos "at a glance," Proc. of Int. Conf. on Pattern Recognition, Vol. 1, pp. 459-464, 1994.

27. W. T. Freeman and E. H. Adelson, "The design and use of steerable filters," IEEE Trans. on Pattern Analysis and Machine Intelligence, 13(9), pp. 891-906, Sep. 1991.

28. R. Rao and B. G. Schunck, "Computing oriented texture fields," CVGIP Graphical Models and Image Processing, 53(2), pp. 157-185, 1991.

29. S. Chaudhuri, et al., "A Fourier domain directional filtering method for analysis of collagen alignment in ligaments," *IEEE Trans. on Biomedical Engineering*, 34(7), pp. 509-517, 1987.

30. J. G. Daugman, "Complete discrete 2D Gabor transforms by neural networks for image analysis and compression," IEEE Trans. ASSP, Vol. 36, pp. 1169-1179, July 1998.

31. A. C. Bovic, M. Clark, and W. S. Geisler, "Multichannel texture analysis using localized spatial filters," *IEEE Trans. Pattern Analysis and Machine Intelligence*, Vol. 12, pp. 55-73, January 1990.

32. A. K. Jain and F. Farroknia, "Unsupervised texture segmentation using Gabor filters," *Pattern Recognition*, 24(12), pp. 1167-1186, 1991.

33. I. Daubechies, "The wavelet transform, time-frequency localization and signal analysis," *IEEE Trans. Information Theory*, Vol. 36, pp. 961-1005, September 1990.

34. S. G. Mallat, "A theory for multiresolution signal decomposition: the wavelet representation," *IEEE Trans. Pattern Analysis and Machine Intelligence*, Vol. 11, pp. 674-693, July 1989.

35. T. Chang and C.-C. Jay Kuo, "Texture analysis and classification with tree-structured wavelet transform," *IEEE Trans. on Image Processing*, Vol. 2, No. 4, pp. 429-441, October 1993.

36. A. Laine and J. Fan, "Texture classification by wavelet packet signatures," *IEEE Trans. Pattern Analysis and Machine Intelligence*, Vol. 15, No. 11, pp. 1186-1191, Nov. 1993.

37. W. Y. Ma and B. S. Manjunath, "A comparison of wavelet features for texture annotation," *Proc. of IEEE Int. Conf. on Image Processing*, Vol. II, pp. 256-259, Washington D.C., Oct. 1995.

38. H. V. Jagadish, "A retrieval technique for similar shapes," *Proc. of Int. Conf. on Management of Data, SIGMOID '91*, Denver, CO, pp. 208-217, May 1991.

39. W. I. Grosky and R. Mehrotra, "Index based object recognition in pictorial data management," *CVGIP*, Vol. 52, No. 3, pp. 416-436, 1990.

40. J. E. Gary and R. Mehrotra, "Shape similarity-based retrieval in image database systems," *Proc. of SPIE, Image Storage and Retrieval Systems*, Vol. 1662, pp. 2-8, 1992.

41. E. M. Arkin et al., "An efficiently computable metric for comparing polygonal shapes," *IEEE Trans. Pattern analysis and Machine Intelligence*, Vol. 13, No. 3, pp. 209-226, 1991.

42. S. Sclaroff and A. Pentland, "Modal matching for correspondence and recognition," *IEEE Trans. on Pattern Analysis and Machine Intelligence*, Vol. 17, No. 6, pp. 545-561, June 1995.

43. K. Arbter, et al., "Application of affine-invariant Fourier descriptors to recognition of 3D objects," *IEEE Trans. Pattern Anal. Machine Intell.*, Vol. 12, pp. 640-647, 1990.

44. E. Persoon and K. Fu, "Shape discrimination using Fourier descriptors," *IEEE Trans. Syst., Man, and Cybern.*, Vol. 7, pp. 170-179, 1977.

45. H. Kauppinen, T. Seppnäen, and M. Pietikäinen, "An experimental comparison of autoregressive and Fourier-based descriptors in 2D shape classification," *IEEE Trans. Pattern Anal. Machine Intell.*, Vol. 17, No. 2, pp. 201-207, 1995.

46. M. K. Hu, "Visual pattern recognition by moment invariants," in J. K. Aggarwal, R. O. Duda, and A. Rosenfeld, *Computer Methods in Image Analysis*, IEEE Computer Society, Los Angeles, CA, 1977.

47. D. Tegolo, "Shape analysis for image retrieval," *Proc. of SPIE, Storage and Retrieval for Image and Video Databases -II*, No. 2185, San Jose, CA, pp. 59-69, February 1994.

48. L. Yang and F. Algregtsen, "Fast computation of invariant geimetric moments: A new method giving correct results," *Proc. IEEE Int. Conf. on Image Processing*, 1994.

49. W. Y. Ma and B. S. Manjunath, "Edge flow: a framework of boundary detection and image segmentation," *IEEE Int. Conf. on Computer Vision and Pattern Recognition*, pp. 744-749, Puerto Rico, June 1997.

50. S.-K. Chang, Q. Y. Shi, and C. Y. Yan, "Iconic indexing by 2-D strings," *IEEE Trans. Pattern Anal. Machine Intell.*, 9(3), pp. 413-428, May 1987.

51. H. Samet, "The quadtree and related hierarchical data structures," *ACM Computing Surveys*, 16(2): 187-260, 1984.

52. V. N. Gudivada and V. V. Raghavan, "Design and evaluation of algorithms for image retrieval by spatial similarity," *ACM Trans. on Information Systems*, Vol. 13, No. 2, pp. 115-144, April 1995.

53. C. Faloutsos, et al., "Efficient and Effective Querying by Image Content," *Journal of Intelligent Information Systems*, Nov. 3, pp. 231-262, 1994.

54. M. Stricker and M. Orengo, "Color indexing with weak spatial constraint," *Proc. SPIE Conf. on Visual Communications*, 1996.

55. W. J. Krzanowski, *Recent Advances in Descriptive Multivariate Analysis*, Chapter 2, Oxford Science Publications, 1995.

56. N. Beckmann, et al., "The R*-tree: An efficient robust access method for points and rectangles," *ACM SIGMOD Int. Conf. on Management of Data*, Atlantic City, May 1990.

57. J. T. Robinson, "The k-d-B-tree: a search structure for large multidimensional dynamic indexes," *Proc. of SIGMOD Conference*, Ann Arbor, April 1981.

58. J. Nievergelt, H. Hinterberger, and K. C. Sevcik, "The grid file: an adaptable symmetric multikey file structure," *ACM Trans. on Database Systems*, pp. 38-71, March 1984.

59. W. Y. Ma and B. S. Manjunath, "Image indexing using a texture dictionary," *Proc. of SPIE Conf. on Image Storage and Archiving System*, Vol. 2606, pp. 288-298, Philadelphia, Pennsylvania, Oct. 1995.

60. J. Hafner, et al., "Efficient color histogram indexing for quadratic form distance functions," *IEEE Trans. on Pattern Analysis and Machine Intelligence*, Vol. 17, No. 7, pp. 729-736, July 1995.

61. P. Brodatz, "Textures: A photographic album for artists & designers," Dover, NY, 1966.

62. T. P. Minka and R. W. Picard, "Interactive learning using a "society of models," *IEEE Int. Conf. on Computer Vision and Pattern Recognition*, pp. 447-452, 1996.

63. Y. Rui, et al., "A relevance feedback architecture in content-based multimedia information retrieval systems," *Proc. of IEEE Workshop on Content-based Access of Image and Video Libraries*, 1997.

64. J. Huang, S. R. Kumar, and M. Metra, "Combining supervised learning with color correlograms for content-based image retrieval," *Proc. of ACM Multimedia'95*, pp. 325-334, Nov. 1997.

65. S. Sclaroff, L. Taycher, and M. L. Cascia, "ImageRover: a content-based image browser for the World Wide Web," Boston University CS Dept. *Technical Report* 97-005.

Acknowlededgments

Figure 4 is extracted from "A texture thesaurus for browsing large aerial photographs," by W.Y. Ma and B.S. Manjunath, which appeared in *Journal of the American Society for Information Sciences*, Vol. 49, No. 7, pp. 633-648, 1998.

Figure 6 is extracted from "Texture-based pattern retrieval from image databases," by W.Y. Ma and B.S. Manjunath, which appeared in *Journal of Multimedia Tools and Applications*, Vol. 2, No. 1, pp. 35-51, January 1996.

Figure 7 is extracted from "A comparison of wavelet transform features for texture image annotation," by W.Y. Ma and B.S. Manjunath, which appeared in *the Proceedings of IEEE Int. Conference on Image Processing*, Vol. II, pp. 256-259, Washington D.C., October 1995, © 1995 IEEE.

12

CONTENT-BASED VIDEO BROWSING
AND RETRIEVAL

HongJiang Zhang
Hewlett-Packard Laboratories
1501 Page Mill Rd, Palo Alto, CA 94304

1. **INTRODUCTION**..256
2. **VIDEO PARSING**..257
   2.1   SHOT DETECTION: THE NATURE OF THE PROBLEM...258
   2.2   SHOT DETECTION: ALGORITHMS 258
   2.3   SHOT DETECTION: ALGORITHMS FOR COMPRESSED VIDEO 261
   2.4   SCENE DETECTION..262
   2.5   CAMERA WORK AND OBJECT MOTION ANALYSIS 263
3. **VIDEO ABSTRACTION**...264
   3.1   KEY-FRAME EXTRACTION 264
   3.2   VIDEO ICON...266
   3.3   VIDEO SUMMARY 267
4. **VIDEO CONTENT REPRESENTATION AND INDEXING** 268
   4.1   STRUCTURED VIDEO CONTENT REPRESENTATION...268
   4.2   CONTENT REPRESENTATION PRIMITIVES FOR A SHOT 269
   4.3   OBJECT-BASED SHOT REPRESENTATION SCHEME 270
   4.4   SHOT CLUSTERING FOR INDEXING AND BROWSING...272
5. **RETRIEVAL AND BROWSING SCHEMES** 273
   5.1   SHOT SIMILARITY..273
   5.2   BROWSING SCHEMES 274
6. **CONCLUDING REMARKS**..277
   REFERENCES 277

Abstract: This chapter extends the discussions on image retrieval techniques to video data, which introduces the third dimension of visual content presentation – time. We discuss in detail video structure parsing algorithms, video abstraction techniques, video content representation schemes, and video retrieval, and browsing tools.

1. INTRODUCTION

As introduced in the last chapter, access and interact with image and video data requests much more than just connecting everyone with data banks and delivering data via networks to everyone's home and office. What also is needed are visual information management systems with content-based retrieval capability. To develop means for quick relevance assessment of video documents is even more critical considering the great amount of video data available. However, when we look at managing of video data, the conventional tools for indexing and retrieval are even more preliminary, although more and more computers are equipped with video capturing, compression, and playing functions. For example, selection of a video clip in current video information systems or World Wide Web sites of video collections rarely involves anything more than key-words search or category browsing and any browsing of the video itself is limited to the lowest level of VCR-like control and display window. The fundamental need to change this situation is similar to that of image databases: video data should be structured and indexed. When it is possible, the human production of text-based content-descriptive data of video has the similar shortcoming as text-based indexing of image data: subjective, inaccurate, and incomplete. Moreover, the manual production of video content description is even more time consuming -- and thus more costly – and is almost impossible to generate it for the vast amount of video data available.

Content-based image retrieval technologies can be extended to video retrieval; however, such an extension is not straightforward. Considering a video clip, a sequence of image frames, indexing each of them as a still image not only will introduce extremely high redundancy, but will also be impossible given the number of frames in a video of even just one minute. Furthermore, such a scheme will destroy or miss the story structure that makes video distinct from still images. The fact is that video is a structured media in which actions and events in a time and space comprise stories or convey particular visual information. That is, a video program should be viewed more like a document than just a nonstructured sequence of frames. Thus, the indexing of video should also be analog to text document indexing, where a structure analysis is performed to decompose a document into paragraphs, sentences, and words, before the index is built. In other words, we need to identify *structures* of video, decompose video into basic *components*, and then build indexes based on the structures information, in addition to individual image frames [1].

Moreover, content-based *browsing* is another significant issue for quick relevance assessment of video source material, considering the large amount of data of video [1,2]. By browsing, we mean an informal but quick access of content which may lack any specific goal or focus. How can we spend only a few minutes viewing an hour of video and still have a fairly correct perception of its contents? Or, how can we map an entire segment to some small number of representative images? Browsing is a means that may be more suitable to address those needs. The task of browsing is actually also very intimately related to and needed for retrieval of video. Unlike image retrieval where retrieval results can be easily presented as thumb nails for examining, viewing retrieval results of video require more sophisticated browsing tools, given the temporal nature and vast amount of data. Furthermore, browsing of retrieval results is the best way to provide feedback for a given query, thus, serving as an aid to *formulating queries*, making it easier for the user to "just ask around" in the process of figuring out the most appropriate query to pose. To achieve content-based browsing, we need to have a representation to present information landscape or structure of video in a more abstracted or summarized manner.

Therefore, current video indexing schemes involve three primary processes: *video parsing, content analysis* (feature extraction), and *abstraction*, which are significantly different and more complicated than those involved in image content indexing [1,2,3]. Parsing is the process of temporal structure segmentation that involves the detection of temporal boundaries and identification of meaningful segments of video and thus extracts structural information of video. Content feature extraction process is similar to that of image feature extraction, but extended to extraction of features that describe object motions, events, and actions in video sequences. Abstraction is the process to extract or construct a subset of video data from the original video such as key-frames or key-sequences as entries for shots, scenes, or stories. The outcome of the abstraction process forms the basis for content-based video browsing; key-frames, for instance, enable browsing with a content-based hierarchical viewer.

Based on the content features or meta-data resulting from these three processes, indexes of video can built based on these content meta-data through, for instance, a clustering process which classifies sequences or shots into different visual categories or indexing structure. Again, similar to that in image database systems, schemes and tools are needed to utilize the indices and content meta-data to query, search, and browse large video databases to locate desired video clips. These processes are illustrated by Figure 1. It should be pointed out that the content analysis and the abstraction processes are somewhat parallel such that the abstraction process of a video clip involves content analyses based on extracted motion and image features.

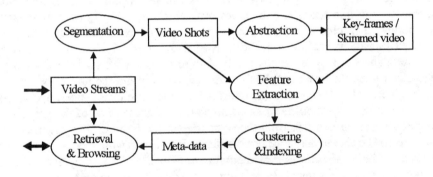

Figure 1. Process diagram for video content analysis and retrieval.

In this chapter, we discuss in detail algorithms for the three video indexing processes outlined above as well as schemes and tools for video browsing and retrieval. Section 2 focuses on video parsing algorithms, including shots and scene segmentation. Section 3 presents three video abstraction schemes: key-frames, video icons, and video summary. These are followed by a detailed discussion on video content representation schemes using visual features, especially object and motion properties in Section 4. Section 5 describes schemes for content-based video retrieval and browsing. Finally, Section 6 concludes the chapter by offering a brief view of current research issues in content-based video retrieval and browsing.

2. VIDEO PARSING

When text is indexed, a document is first divided into smaller components such as sections, paragraphs, sentences, phrases, words, letters, and numerals, and indices can then be built on these components. Similarly, a long video sequence has to be organized into smaller and more manageable components to identify index entries. These components should be categorized in a hierarchy similar to storyboards used in film-making [4]. The top level consists of sequences or stories, which are composed of a set of scenes. Scenes are further partitioned into shots. Each shot contains a sequence of frames recorded contiguously representing a continuous action in time or space. Decomposing a long video sequence into the meaningful components as described is the task of video parsing or temporal partitioning.

However, the current state-of-the art algorithms for temporal partitioning are still limited to shot detection, while scene detection algorithms have only limited success [5,6,7]. Part of the problem is that scenes and stories in video are only constructed logical layers based more on semantics, and there is no universal definition or rigid structure for scenes and stories. In contrast, shots are an actual physical most-basic layer in video and boundaries are determined by editing points or where the camera is switched on or off. Analog to words or sentences in text documents, or shots are a good choice as the basic unit for video content indexing. As illustrated in more detail in the next several sections, shot based analysis, classification, and grouping form the basis for content-based video indexing, browsing and retrieval. In this section, our discussions are focused on algorithms for partitioning video into shots, while algorithms for partitioning of scenes and stories will be briefly discussed.

2.1 SHOT DETECTION: THE NATURE OF THE PROBLEM

Shot detection is the process of detecting boundaries between two consecutive shots, so that a sequence of frames belonging to a shot will be grouped together. There are a number of different types of transitions or boundaries between shots. The simplest transition is a cut, an abrupt shot change which occurs between two consecutive frames. More sophisticated transitions include fades, dissolves, and wipes, etc. [4]. A fade is a slow change in brightness of images usually resulting in or starting with a solid black frame. A dissolve occurs when the images of the first shot get dimmer and the images of the second shot get brighter, with frames within the transition showing one image superimposed on the other. A wipe occurs when pixels from the second shot replace those of the first shot in a regular pattern such as in a line from the right edge of the frames. A robust partitioning algorithm should be able to detect all these different boundaries with good accuracy. In the following, a number of algorithms for temporal partitioning of video using video data either in its original format or in compressed domain representations are presented.

The basis of detecting shot boundaries is the fact that consecutive frames on either side of a boundary generally display a significant change in content. Therefore, what is required is some suitable quantitative measure that can quantitatively determine the difference between such a pair of frames. Then, if that difference exceeds a given threshold, it may be interpreted as indicating a shot boundary. Hence, establishing suitable metrics is the key issue in automatic partitioning. The optimal metrics for automatic video partitioning should be able to detect the following three different factors of image change: shot change, either abrupt or gradual; motions, introduced both by camera operation and object motion; and luminosity changes and noise.

2.2 SHOT DETECTION: ALGORITHMS

The major difference among automatic video partitioning algorithms is the difference metrics used to quantitatively measure changes between consecutive frames and schemes to apply the metrics. Difference metrics used in partitioning video can be divided into two major types: those based local pixel feature comparison, such as pixel values and edges, and those based on global features such as histograms and statistic distributions of pixel-to-pixel change. These types of metrics may be implemented with a variety of different modifications to accommodate the idiosyncrasies of different video sources and have been successfully used in shot boundary detection.

2.2.1 PIXEL OR BLOCK COMPARISON ALGORITHMS

A simple way to detect a qualitative change between a pair of frames is to compare the spatially corresponding pixels in the two frames to determine how many have changed. This approach is known as *pair-wise pixel comparison* [8,9]. The major problem with this metric is its sensitivity to camera movement. For instance, in the case of camera panning, a large number of objects will move in the same direction across successive frames; this means that a large number of pixels will be judged as changed even if the pan entails a shift of only a few pixels. To overcome this problem, instead of comparing individual pixels, we can compare corresponding *regions* (blocks) in two successive frames. One of such comparison algorithms is to apply motion compensation at each block [10]. That is, each frame is divided into a small number of non-overlap blocks. Block matching within a given search window is then performed to generate a motion vector and match value, normalized to range from zero to one with zero representing a perfect match. Then, the difference between two frames can be defined as

$$D_M = \sum_{i=1}^{K} c_i R_i \qquad (1)$$

where i is the block number in a frame, K the total number of blocks, R_i the match value for block i, and c_i a set of predetermined weight coefficient for each block. A cut is declared if D_m exceeds a given threshold.

2.2.2 HISTOGRAM COMPARISON ALGORITHMS

The most popular metric for cut detection is the difference between histograms of two consecutive frames. The assumption is that two frames having an unchanging background and objects will show little difference in their respective histograms. The histogram comparison algorithm should be less sensitive to object motion than the pair-wise pixel comparison algorithm, since it ignores the spatial changes in a frame [9].

Similar to the case of histogram-based image retrieval, there are many ways to compare histograms of two consecutive video frames, and a popular one is χ^2-test formula. A shot boundary is declared if the overall difference histogram is larger than a given threshold T. To be more robust to noise, it is proposed to divide each frame into a number of regions of same size, e.g., 16 regions. That is, instead of comparing global histogram, histograms for corresponding regions in two frames are compared and the 8 largest differences are discarded to reduce the effects of object motion and noise [8].

There have been many variations of the above two types of algorithms, as well as algorithms using other image features such as edge distribution [11], and reasonable detection accuracy has been achieved. However, applying these algorithms in detecting progressive shot changes is still far less reliable than detecting abrupt cut.

2.2.3 GRADUAL TRANSTION DETECTION ALGORITHMS

Cuts are the simplest shot boundary and are relatively easy to detect using the difference metrics described above. However, more sophisticated shots boundaries such as dissolve, wipe, fade-in, and fade-out are much more difficult to detect since they involve much more gradual changes between consecutive frames than does a sharp cut. Furthermore, changes resulting from camera operations may be of the same order as that from gradual transitions, which further complicates the detection. Figure 2 shows five frames from a typical dissolve: the last frame of the current shot just before the dissolve begins, three frames within the dissolve, and the frame in the following shot immediately after the dissolve. The actual dissolve occurs across about 30 frames, resulting in small changes between every two consecutive frames in the dissolve. This sequence illustrates that gradual transitions will downgrade the power of a simple difference metric and a single threshold for camera break detection algorithms. In this subsection, we discuss three partition algorithms that are capable of detecting gradual transitions with acceptable accuracy while achieving very high accuracy in detecting sharp cuts. They are: *twin comparison, statistic analysis of pixel change distribution,* and *editing effect modeling.*

Figure 2. An example of dissolve sequences.

The *twin-comparison* algorithm was the first published algorithm to detect gradual shot changes [9]. This algorithm uses two comparisons: one looks at the difference between consecutive frames to detect sharp cut, and the other looks at *accumulated difference* over a sequence of frames to detection gradual transitions. This algorithm also applies a global motion analysis to filter out sequences of frames involving global or large moving objects, which may confuse the gradual transition detection. Experiments show the twin comparison algorithm is very effective and achieves a very high level of accuracy.

Another algorithm for detecting both cuts and gradual transitions is derived based on statistics of distributions of pixel value changes between two consecutive frames [12]. It is assumed that the inter-frame pixel value changes results from a combination of resources: first, a small amplitude additive zero-central Gaussian noise, modeling camera, tape and digitization noises; second, changes of pixels resulting from object or camera operation and lighting within a given shot; and third, changes caused by cuts and gradual transitions. According to analytical models for each of these changes, cuts can be found by looking at the number of pixels whose change of value between two consecutive frames falls in the range $\{128, 255\}$, whereas dissolves and fades can be identified by the number of pixels whose change of value between two consecutive frames falls in the range $\{7, 40\}$ for 8 bits coded grey-level images. However, changes of pixel value resulting from wipes are also in the range of $\{128, 255\}$; thus, wipes may not be detected reliably. This algorithm is not designed to detect cuts or transitions based upon only two consecutive frames, but upon incorporating a temporal filtering over a sequence of consecutive frames. Also, histogram equalization needs to be applied to frames for wipe and cut detection, which slows down the detecting process.

Hampapur, et al., have studied the *editing model fitting* algorithm for detecting different types of gradual transitions. The algorithm detects the editing effect by fitting sequences of inter-frame changes into editing models, one for a given type of transition [13]. However, the potential problem with such model-based algorithms is that as more and more different types of editing effects (which will still fall in mainly three basic classes: dissolve, wipe, and fade) become available, it is hard to model each of them. Furthermore, transition sequences may not follow any particular editing model, due possibly to noises and/or a combination of editing effects. Such problems may exit in other detection algorithms as well, although this particular algorithm may be more limited.

There have been many variations of the algorithms discussed, as well as algorithms using other image features such as edge distribution. Several comparison studies of various shot change detection algorithms have been presented [14,15]. It is interesting to observe that histogram based algorithms outperform others in both accuracy and speed based the experiments carried out by Boreczky and Rowe [15]. In summary, automatic shot detection can be reliably achieved by software only methods at real-time video rate using today's PCs or workstations. However, the algorithms developed so far are still far from a perfect detection rate, due mainly to the large variety of contents, editing effects, and lighting changes in video. Also, detecting progressive shot changes is still far less reliable than detecting abrupt cuts. Robustness of shot boundary detection in the presence of important object motion calls for a motion detector [9].

2.3 SHOT DETECTION: ALGORITHMS FOR COMPRESSED VIDEO

Due to the fact that JPEG, MPEG, and H.26X [2] have become industrial standards, more and more video data have been and will continue to be stored and distributed in one of these compressed formats. It would therefore be advantageous for the analysis tools to operate directly on compressed representations, saving on the computational cost of decompression. More important, the compressed domain representation of video defined by these standards, namely DCT (Discrete Cosine Transform) coefficients and motion vectors, are more effective and readily available features for compressed video partitioning. In this sub-section, we discuss some basic algorithms developed to utilize such content information.

In general, compression of a video frame begins with dividing each color component of the image into a set of 8x8 pixel blocks [2]. The pixels in the blocks are then transformed by the forward DCT (FDCT) into 64 coefficients, which are then quantized and Huffman entropy encoded. The process can then be reversed for decompression. Since the DCT coefficients are mathematically related to the spatial domain and represent the content of each frame, they can be used to detect the difference between two video frames.

Based on this basic idea, the first comparison metric based on DCT for partitioning JPEG compressed videos was developed by Arman, et al. [16] and extended to MPEG by Zhang, et al. [17]. In this algorithm, a subset of the blocks in each frame and a subset of the DCT coefficients for each block were used as a vector representation (V_f) for each frame. The difference metric between frames is then defined by content correlation in terms of a normalized inner product

$$D_{DCTC} = 1 - \left| V_f \bullet V_{f+\varphi} \right| / \left| V_f \right| \left\| V_{f+\varphi} \right| \tag{2}$$

where φ is the number of frames between the two frames being compared.

It has been observed that for detecting shots boundaries, DC components of DCTs of video frames provide sufficient information [18]. Based on the definition of DCT, this is an equivalent to a low-resolution version of frames, averaged over 8x8 non-overlap blocks [2]. Applying this idea makes calculation of (2) much faster while maintaining similar detection accuracy.

Using DC sequences also makes it easy to apply histogram comparison. That is, instead of comparing histograms of pixel values, we compare histograms of DCT-DC coefficients of frames. This algorithm has to be very effective, achieving both high detection accuracy and speed in detecting sharp cuts [18].

The DCT based metrics can be directly applied to JPEG video, where every frame is intra-coded. However, in MPEG, there are three types of frames used: intra (I-) framed, predicated (P-) frames, and bidirectional predicated and interpolated (B) frames. Only the DCT coefficients of I-frames are transformed directly from original images, while P- and B-frames DCT coefficients are ideally only residual errors from motion compensated predication. That is, DCT based metrics can be applied only in comparing I-frames in MPEG video. Since only a small portion of frames in MPEG are I-frames, this significantly reduces the amount of processing required to compute differences. On the other hand, the loss of temporal resolution between I-frames will introduce a large fraction of false positives in video partitioning which have to be handled with subsequent processing [17,18,19].

Apart from pixel value, motion resulting from either moving objects, camera works, or both represents another important visual content in video data. In general, the motion vectors should show continuity between frames within a camera shot and show discontinuity between frames across two shots. Thus, a continuity metric for a field of motion vectors should serve as an alternative criterion for detecting segment boundaries.

Motion data are readily available in MPEG data stream since there is one set of motion vectors associated with each **P**-frame representing the predication from the last or next **I** frame; and there are two sets of motion vectors associated with each **B**-frame, forward and backward. If there is a significant change (discontinuity) in visual content between two frames, either two **B**-frames, a **B**-frame and an **I/P**-frame, or a **P**-frame and an **I**-frame, there will be many macro blocks in the two frames whose residual errors from motion compensation are too high to tolerate. For those macro blocks, MPEG will not apply the motion compensation predication but instead intra-code them using DCT. That is, if there is a shot boundary falling in between two frames, there will a larger number of intra-coded blocks. Based on this observation, we can detect shot boundary by counting the number of inter-coded blocks in **P**- and **B**-frames [17]. That is, if

$$N_{inter} < N_b \qquad (3)$$

is lower than a given threshold, then a shot boundary is declared between the two frames.

Combining the DCT based and motion based metrics into a hybrid algorithm will improve the detection accuracy as well as processing speed in partitioning MPEG compressed video [17]. That is, DCT-DC histograms of every two consecutive **I**-frames are first compared to detect potential cut points. Since the temporal distance between two consecutive **I**-frames is so large, we can assume that if we set the threshold relatively low, all shot boundaries, including gradual transitions, will be detected by looking at the points where there is a high difference value. Of course, this first pass will also generate some false positives. Then, **B**- and **P**-frames between two consecutive **I**-frames, which have detected as potentially containing shot boundaries, will be examined in a second pass using motion. That is, the second pass is applied only to the neighborhood of the potential boundary frames. In this way, both high processing speed and detection accuracy are achieved at the same time.

In summary, experimental evaluations have shown that the shot detection algorithms based on compression domain features perform with at least the same order of accuracy as those using video data in the original format, although the detection of sharp cuts is more reliable than that of gradual transitions. On the other hand, algorithms based on compression features achieve high processing speed, which makes software-only real time video partitioning possible.

2.4 SCENE DETECTION

In media production, the level immediately higher than shots is called *scene* or *sequence*. From the narrative point of view, a scene consists of a series of consecutive shots, because they are shot in the same location or they share some thematic visual content. The process of detecting these video scenes is analogous to paragraphing in text document parsing and requires a higher level content analysis.

Two different kinds of approaches have been proposed for the automatic recognition of sequences of programs: filming rule-based and *a priori* program model based. Aigrain, et al. have used filming rules to detect local (in time) clues of macro-scope change [20]. These rules refer to transition effects, shot repetition, shot setting similarity, apparition of music in the soundtrack, editing rhythm, and camera work. After detection of the local clues, an analysis of their temporal organization is done in order to produce the segmentation and to choose one or two representative shots for each sequence.

Yeung and Yeo have proposed a similar approach to scene or story detection, called *time-constrained clustering* [6,7]. In this approach, both visual similarity and temporal locality of shots are considered in shots grouping and event detection. This is based on the idea that content presented in video programs tends to be localized in time: two visually similar shots occurred next to each other may present a continuing event; if they occurred far apart in time, they may present different contents or belong to different scenes. Use of information of special temporal events, namely, dialogues and fast action shots, is another essential part of this approach.

A priori model-based algorithms utilize certain structure models of special video programs such as news and particular sports [21,22,23]. For those special video programs, the temporal structures are normally very rigid. Thus, if one can identify a few key types of shots, such as anchor-persons in news video, then, the rest of shots can be classified according to the structure models, without sophisticated and often impossible semantic content analysis of the entire video. For example, Zhang, et al. have developed such an approach to automatic parsing and indexing TV news [22]. They recognize specific types of shots, such as anchor-person shots using motion information, and then use the news program model to analyze the succession of shot types and produce a segmentation of news stories. However, the problem of such an approach is that it is often impossible to build *a priori* models when we extend to other application domains. Even for the news video, this approach is not able to classify the segmented news stories into appropriate categories since it does not have the capability to extract the semantic content of each shot.

In summary, general scene detection requires content analysis of a higher level and it should not be expected that this task will be fully automated in near future based on only visual content analysis using current image processing and computer vision techniques. However, fusion of information from image, audio, and close caption or transcript text analysis is a feasible solution and successful examples include the *Informedia* Project [24] and many others [25,26,27].

2.5 CAMERA WORK AND OBJECT MOTION ANALYSIS

Object motion and camera work are another important source of information and can contribute to shot content analysis and classification. It is well known that camera work or framing of shots are elaborately made by directors/camera operators to present certain scenes or objects and to guide viewer's attention [4]. Object motions usually represent human activity and events in video shots. Detection of camera work and object motion need to be performed in the following three processes in video content analysis:

- motion-based partitioning, and filtering false positives resulting from motion in gradual transitions detection, as discussed in the last section;
- selection of key-frames and construction of salient stills for representing video contents, as to be discussed in the Section 3; and
- content representation and motion-based shot retrieval, to be discussed in Section 4.

The scientific problem of camera work analysis resides in the discrimination between camera work-induced apparent motion and object motion-induced apparent motion, followed by analysis to identify particular camera work and to describe object motion. These are classical and unsolved problems in computer vision. However, for our needs in video content analysis and representation, several algorithms can perform with satisfactory accuracy and speed.

Camera work includes panning and tilting (horizontal or vertical rotation of camera); zooming (focal length change), in which camera position does not change; tracking and booming (horizontal and vertical transverse movement of camera); and dollying (horizontal lateral movement of camera) in which position of camera *does* change, as well as combinations of these operations. The specific feature that serves to classify camera work is the *motion field,* as each particular camera work will result in a specific pattern of motion field. Based on this, Zhang, et al. have developed a simple, yet effective approach to camera work analysis has been proposed to distinguish the gradual transition sequences and classify camera pan and zoom operations [9].

A more sophisticated quantitative approach to detecting camera work is to establish a transformation between a point in space and its coordinates in image space [28]. The transformation is then used to derive the pixel coordinate changes when there is a pan or zoom. A simple zoom is caused by a change in the camera's focus length and there is no camera body movement. Camera pan, on the other hand, is caused by rotating the camera about a axis parallel to the image plane. This approach not only detects camera pans, zooms, and combinations, but also describes them quantitatively. The price paid for this information is a significant investment in computation time.

More sophisticated motion detection algorithms for video content parsing also include those based on discrete tomography for camera work identification [29]. The distribution of the angles of edges in 3-D tomography images resulting from video can be matched to camera work models, and camera motion classification and temporal segmentation can be obtained directly. Discrimination between pan and lateral traveling and between zoom and booming can be achieved only through a complete projective model including parallax analysis.

Detecting object motion is far more difficult than detecting camera work and is still a challenging research problem in computer vision [30].

3. VIDEO ABSTRACTION

Video content abstraction is referred to as the process to extract a presentation of visual information about landscape or structure of video, which should be much shorter than the original video. When text documents are indexed, key words or summaries are used as index entries for sentences, paragraphs, chapters, or entire documents. Similarly, in video indexing, we can extract key-frames and key-sequences as entries for shots, scenes, or stories. Apart from browsing, key-frames can also be used in representing video in retrieval; video index may be constructed based on visual features of key-frames, and queries may be directed at key-frames using query by image content techniques. In this section, we discuss three approaches to visual abstraction of video data: key-frames, video icons, and video summaries.

3.1 KEY-FRAME EXTRACTION

Key-frames are still images extracted from original video data that best represent the content of shots in an abstract manner. Key-frames have been frequently used to supplement the text of a video log [31], but identifying them was done manually in the past. The effectiveness of key-frames depends on how well they are chosen from all frames of a sequence. The image frames within a sequence are not all equally descriptive. Certain frames may provide more information about the objects and actions within the shot than other frames. In some prototype systems and commercial products, the first frame of each shot has been used as the only key-frame to represent the shot content. However, while such a representation does reduce the data volume, its representation power is very limited since it often does not give a sufficient clue as to what actions are presented by a shot, except for shots with no change or motion.

Key-frame-based representation views video abstraction as a problem of mapping an entire segment (both static and motion content) to some small number of representative images. The challenge is that the extraction of key-frames needs to be automatic and content-based so that they maintain the important content of the video while removing all redundant information. In theory, semantic primitives of video, such as interesting objects, actions, and events should be used. However, such general semantic analysis is not currently feasible, especially when information from soundtracks and/or closed caption is not available. In practice, we have to rely on low-level image features and other readily available information instead.

An effective approach to key-frame extraction, based on temporal variation of low-level image features such as color histograms and motion information, has been proposed by Zhang, et al. [17,1,32,33]. The key idea of this approach is that the number of key-frames needed to represent a segment should be based on temporal variation of video content in the segment; if there is a large temporal variation of content, there should be more key-frames, and vise versa. That is, after shot segmentation, key-frames in a shot will be selected based on the amount of temporal variation of color histograms and motion in reference to the first frame or the last selected key-frame of the shot. It is reported that this approach achieves real-time processing speed, especially when MEPG compressed video and reasonable accuracy is used according to the user studies [1,33].

In more detail, in this approach, frames in a shot will be compared in terms of color histogram changes against the last key-frame or the first frame of the shot sequentially as they are processed, based on their similarities defined by color histogram. If a significant content change occurs, the current frame will be selected as a new key-frame. Such a process will be iterated until the last frame of the shot is reached. In this way, any significant action in a shot will be captured by a key-frame, while static shots will result in only one key-frame. In addition, information of dominant or global motion resulting from camera operations and large moving objects is added into the selection process according to a set of rules. For a zooming-like (zooming, dollying, and perpendicular motion of large objects) sequence, the first and last frames will usually be selected as key-frames, one presents a global, and the other a more focused view. For a panning-like (panning, tilting, and tracking) sequence, the number of frames to be selected will depend on the scale of panning: ideally, the spatial context covered by each frame should have little overlap, or each frame should capture a different, but sequential part of object activities.

Figure 3 shows an example in which three key-frames from a tilt-up shot were extracted using this approach. One can see clearly that it is a tilt-up sequence, which will not be concluded reliably from any single key-frame. In this respect, extracting three key-frames is a more adequate abstraction than only a single key-frame, which is important for users (especially producers and editors) who want to choose some particular types of shots from stock footages.

Figure 3. Examples of key-frame extracted automatically from a shot.

In this approach, the density of key-frames or the abstraction ratio can be controlled according to the user's need by adjusting the threshold for determining "significant" color histogram changes and the overlap ratio of key-frames in panning sequences [1,33]. However, the exact number of resultant key-frames will be determined *a posteriori* by the actual content of the input video. This fact has been argued to be a disadvantage of this type of key-frame extraction approach [34]. On the other hand, predefining the absolute number of key-frames without knowing the content of the video may not be desirable; assigning two key-frames for a talking head sequence of 30 minutes should still be considered having too much redundancy! In addition, assigning the same number of key-frames to, for instance, two video sequences of same length does not guarantee the same level of visual abstraction since the contents of the two sequences may have different levels of abstraction and/or totally different levels of activities. Therefore, controlling the level of abstraction ratio or key-frame density is a more robust and useful approach.

A compromise to meet the need of having a predefined number of key-frames, while maintaining the content-based selection criteria and constant level of abstraction ratio among a given set of video sequences, is to set up a maximum number of key-frames allowed. In this way, an initial set of key-frames can be selected at a given abstraction ratio using the approach discussed above. Then, if the number of key-frames exceeds the maximum, a post-filtering can be applied to filter out the frames whose similarity to their immediate neighboring two frames are high.

The key-frame extraction approach described above is based on a frame-based representation. That is, each frame is considered the basic unit for content representation. However, if we could further decompose frames into key-objects, then key-frames can be extracted based on the motion or activity of these objects. Below we outline some strategies for key-frames selection based on the motion activity and attributes of key-objects within the shot [35]:

- a key-object enters or leaves the image frame boundaries;
- key-objects participate in occlusion relationship;
- two key-objects are at the closest distance between them;
- mean and extrema of key-object attributes, i.e., color, shape, motion;
- key-frames should have some small amount of background object overlap.

Figure 4 shows 3 key-frames selected from the video sequence according to the criteria outlined above.

(a)   (b)   (c)

Figure 4. Key-frames selected based on moving objects: (a) the horse enters the scene; (b) the horse is in the middle of the scene; (c) the horse leaves the scene.

The discussions in this subsection have been focused on extraction of key-frames, and the criteria have been to ensure that key-frames are extracted for each shot. Therefore, these key-frames represent content of shots and should be referred a key-frames of shots. How to further extract from these frames an even smaller set as the visual abstract of scenes or stories is an even more challenging problem, similar to that of detecting scene or story boundaries. This problem will be further discussed in Subsection 4.4.

3.2 VIDEO ICON

Another abstract presentation scheme for shot content is video icons. This type of presentation is designed mostly for video browsing. There are two major schemes: *3-D icon* and *video mosaic*.

3-D video is a visual icon for a shot constructed based on a key-frame, supplemented with pseudo-depth to present the duration of the shot and, perhaps, arrows and signs for the representation of object and camera motion. This approach has been favored when the emphasis is on building a global structured view of a video document, fitted for quick visual browsing, such as in the IMPACT system [36].

Video mosaicing synthesizes an image representing the global visual contents of a shot from all frames of the shot. Video mosaic images are constructed by mapping successive images into a common frame progressively, using the geometrical transformation parameters between these frames obtained from the motion analysis. As mentioned briefly earlier in this chapter, motion analysis is the critical step in mosaic construction and many sophisticated algorithms have been developed. The resultant mosaic image is not generally rectangular. Such synthesized images have also been termed *salient stills* [37], *micon* (motion icon) [38,39], or *VideoSpaceIcons* [38,40]. The construction of video mosaics has been based mainly on background or dominant motion; however, it can also constructed according to a moving object of interest [30]. The advantage of video mosaics in presenting video content is that it provides an overview of a shot with a single image, rather than a few key-frames. However, video mosaics are effective only in presenting overviews of sequences whose content changes resulted predominantly from motions. Sequences whose content changes result predominantly from lighting changes or effects, or from deformations of objects, will not be effectively represented by video mosaics. In addition, usually only dominant motion and the associated objects in a shot are well presented in video mosaics and it is difficult to construct a mosaic when there are many small moving objects with many different local random motions.

3.3 VIDEO SUMMARY

Video summarization is to meet the request of abstracting an hour of video, for instance, into a 5-minute highlight or summary sequence with a fair perception of the video contents. This is a relatively new research area and requires high level content analysis. A successful approach is to utilize information from multiple sources, including sound, speech, transcript, and image analysis of video. Researchers [e.g., 41] working on documents with textual transcriptions have suggested producing video abstracts by first abstracting the text using classical text skimming techniques and then looking for the corresponding parts in the video.

A successful application of this type of approach has been the *Informedia* project, in which text and visual content information are fused to identify video sequences that highlight the important contents of the video [24]. More specifically, low-level and mid-level visual features, including shot boundary, human face, camera, and object motion and subtitles of video shots are integrated with keywords, spotted from text obtained from closed caption and speech recognition, using the following procedures:

- Keyword selection using the well-known TF-IDF technique to skim audio;
- Sequence characterization by low-level and mid-level visual features;
- Selecting a number of keywords according to the required skimming factor;
- Prioritizing image sequences located in close proximity to each selected keyword:
  1) frames with faces or text;
  2) static frames following camera motion;
  3) frames with camera motion and human faces or text;
  4) frame at the beginning of the scene;
- Composite a skimmed sequence with selected frames.

Experiments using this skimming approach have shown impressive results in generating video summaries on limited types of documentary video which have very clean speech or text (closed caption) contents, such as education video, news, or parliament debates [24]. However, satisfactory results may not be achievable using such a text- or keyword-driven approach to other videos with a soundtrack containing more than just speech, such as home videos. Therefore, extracting a video summary for general video materials remains a challenging research topic.

4. VIDEO CONTENT REPRESENTATION AND INDEXING

After partitioning and abstraction, another key step in video content processing is to identify and compute representation primitives of video content, upon which the content of shots can be classified, indexed, and compared. These content primitives are often also referred as the content meta-data of video. Here again we constrain our discussion to visual representations, although text descriptors included were possibly derived from visual data. Ideally these primitives should be semantic, including constituent object names, appearances, and motions, as well as relationships among objects at different times, which contribute to the story being presented in a video sequence [e.g., 42]. A user can employ such primitives easily to define *interesting* or *significant* events. However, automatic extraction of such primitives is not feasible, like in image indexing as discussed in the last chapter. Instead, we have to build content representation of video based mainly on low-level images features, such as color, texture, and motion statistics of shots, in combination with limited semantic cues resulting from, for instance, anchor-person detection. In this section, we discuss a structured content presentation scheme for video and a set of low-level content primitives of the representation scheme.

4.1 A STRUCTURED VIDEO CONTENT REPRESENTATION

As discussed in Section 3.1, a video program or documents can be decomposed into three structural levels: sequences, scenes, and shots. Therefore, the representation of a video document should have the same structural levels. The structured representation scheme in Figure 5 is a good example that meets the above criterion. Also, although we focus on video content representative based on low-level visual features, this scheme can accommodate high-level semantic features.

Sequence
    Sequence-ID: x (a unique index key of the sequence)
    Scenes: {Scene(1), Scene (2), ... Scene (L)}
    Summary: A
Scene
    Scene-ID: y_l (a unique index key of the scene l)
    Shots: {Shot(1), Shot(2), ... Shot(M)}
    ***Key-frames*: {$KF_l(1)$, $KF_l(2)$, ..., $KF_l(I)$}**
Shot
    Shot-ID: z_m (a unique index key of the shot m)
    Primitives: {$f_s(1), f_s(2), ..., f_s(N)$}
    ***Key-frames*: {$KF_m(1)$, $KF_m(2)$, ..., $KF_m(J)$}**

Figure 5. A structured video content representation scheme: three levels of content descriptors.

Note that the boldly printed items in Figure 5 are primitives based on visual abstractions of a sequence, which are not usually contained explicitly in conventional video representation schemes. These primitives are included to make the representation especially useful in content-based video browsing and in indexing of video contents as discussed later in this section. Also, note that the video summary, A, as part of the sequence representation, could be a set of pointers to highlight the segments extracted by using video summarization approaches presented in Section 3.3. Similarly, key-frames are included in both the scene and shot representation primitives. However, the set of key-frames of a scene should be a *subset* of the key-frames of all shots comprising the scene; thus, $KF_l(i)$ is a set of *pointers* to $KF_m(j)$, i.e., $KF_l(j)$ is a more abstracted set extracted from $KF_m(j)$. If key-frames are not extracted in the level of scene, then the *key-frame* item should be removed from the scene representation.

4.2 CONTENT REPRESENTATION PRIMITIVES FOR A SHOT

Give the representation structure as in Figure 5, the key issue in video content representation then is to use which set of low-level visual features as content primitives. We concentrate our discussions on appropriate features for representing content of shot and assume that a scene can represented by and retrieved based on the content primitives of all of its shots. The features are divided into two groups: those associated with key-frames, and the rest of the shot features. The former is derived only from single key-frames, which capture only representative information at a few sampling points where key-frames are located. The latter is derived from the sequence of frames of a shot, including temporal variation of any given image feature or feature set, and motions associated with the shot or even some objects in the shot. We refer the first group as *key-frames-based* and the other, *shot-based*. Therefore, these two groups constitute a complete set of content primitives for video shots and form the basis for shot based video indexing and retrieval.

Key-frames-based representation of video content uses the same features as those for content based still image retrievals as discussed in the last chapter. These features are extracted from each of the key-frames associated with a shot [1,33]. Apart from the low-level primitives, one can also include high-level semantic features, such as objects, e.g., news-anchor, in a key-frame [22].

Therefore, we can add one more extension for each key-frame of a shot to the representation scheme in Figure 5 as shown in Figure 6.

> *Key-frames:*
> *KF-ID:* **KF$_m$(j)**
> *Primitives:* $\{f_{KF}(1), f_{KF}(2),..., f_{KF}(K)\}$.

Figure 6. Representation scheme for key-frame primitives. An extension to the video representation scheme shown in Figure 5.

Obviously, key-frame-based features alone will be insufficient to support event-based classification and retrieval since they do not capture motion and temporal changes in a shot, which are an essential and unique feature of video. The key-frame-based primitives are defined in response to this requirement. Zhang, et al. [1,33] have proposed a set of shot-based features, including statistical motion measures and the temporal mean and variance of color features over a shot, to provide information about activities, and motion complexity and distribution that might be useful in queries. A more detailed description of this feature set is given below.

Temporal mean and variance: The *temporal mean* and *variance* of mean color over all frames in a shot are used as a quantitative indicator of the shot context and scope of temporal content changes within the shot. They are defined as

$$\mu_T = \frac{1}{T-1}\sum_{t=1}^{T-1}\mu_i(t) \tag{4.1}$$

$$\sigma_T = (\frac{1}{T-1}\sum_{t=1}^{T-1}(\mu_i(t)-\mu_T)^2)^{\frac{1}{2}} \tag{4.2}$$

where $\mu_i(t)$ is the mean color of frame t and T the total number of frames in a shot. This feature can also be calculated from a sub-sampled number of frames in a shot to reduce computation time. The temporal variation defined by (4.2) has been used successfully as an activity measure to classify news video clips into anchorperson shots and news shots [22], which indicates that it is an effective feature to distinguish shots of high-activity level from those of low-activity level. However, the activity representation power of this feature is very limited.

Global motion feature: To enhance representation power, model parameters of global or dominant motion in a shot are another feature vector for representing motion content. This feature captures the general motions in the shot such as camera pan or zoom, and can be used to classify video sequences into static and motion sequences. It can be obtained using motion analysis algorithms presented in Subsection 2.5. The motion models can range from simple translation to complex planar parallax motion. It is found that the affine motion model (only 6 model parameters) provides a good compromise between complexity and stability.

Statistic motion features: This is a feature introduced to describe motion distributions in terms of directions and magnitude. It complements the global motion feature, which is not effective when there is no dominant motion in a shot. It includes *directional distribution of motion, directional average speed,* and *local average speed,* which are all derived from optical flow calculated between consecutive frames [33]. The motion directional distribution is a direction histogram, $h(t)(i)$, which counts the percentage of total motion vectors between two frames, t and $t+1$, that fall in a given direction. That is,

$$h(i)(t) = \frac{N_i(t)}{N_m} \times 100 \tag{5.1}$$

where $N_i(t)$ is the total number of motion vectors falling in direction i between frame t and $t+1$. N_m is the total number of motion vectors and is constant across all frames. Then, the average speed and standard deviation at a given direction i are defined as follows:

$$\overline{s(i)(t)} = \frac{1}{N_i(t)} \sum_{j=1}^{N_i(t)} s_i(i)(t) \tag{5.2}$$

$$\sigma_i(i)(t) = (\frac{1}{N_i(t)} \sum_{j=1}^{N_i(t)} (s_j(i)(t) - \overline{s_j(i)(t)})^2)^{\frac{1}{2}} \tag{5.3}$$

where $s(i)(t)$ is the speed of jth motion vector in direction i between frame t and $t+1$, and $i = 1, ..., M$. M is the total number of directions (histogram bins). There are a total of $3 \times M$ parameters in this feature set. M is usually very low, e.g., 8 or 16 if we choose 45° or 15° direction intervals. To add some locality information into this set of features, we can also calculate them for each uniformly divided block in the frames.

Both the global motion and this set of features may change over frames within a shot; these two feature sets may have to be a time series, with one set of values at a frame. Another simpler way to accommodate temporal changes is to use the temporal average over all frames in a shot, or to use values at a few sampling points, such as points where key-frames are extracted. Experiments have shown that this set of features, obtained at a set of sampling points, are effective in representing motion information of shots and in retrieving shots of similar motion patterns [33,43].

4.3 OBJECT-BASED SHOT REPRESENTATION SCHEME

Often, it is desirable to quantify queries based on particular attributes that involve objects and sub-regions within the viewable frame of video. However, the video frame-based features described in the last subsection sometimes do not provide sufficient resolution for object-based queries. Therefore, to incorporate object-based primitives into video content representation would be greatly advantageous in dealing with these interesting queries about objects and their motions.

Key-frames provide a suitable abstraction and framework for video browsing; however, we could support an even wider range of queries by defining smaller units within the key-frame. We call these smaller units "key-objects" because we used them to represent key regions that participate in distinct actions within the shot [35]. Key-objects do not necessarily correspond to semantic objects. Instead, we seek out regions of coherent motion to avoid the semantic object analysis problem. The criterion is that coherent motion is perceptually and physically motivated, since points of an object exhibit motion coherence and people tend to group regions of similar motion into one semantic object. Thus motion coherence might capture some aspect of objects desirable in retrieval, and is a key attribute of a key-object.

We incorporate our key-objects within the shot-based key-frame representation. In the augmented representation, each shot is represented by a set of key-frames, which are further decomposed into key-objects. Main attributes attached to key-objects are motion, shape, and life cycle, as well as other image features such as color and texture. Life cycle of a key-object is the duration from the time (or relative frame number) when the object appears into a shot (birth) to the time when the object disappears (death). The key-object motions can be modeled as affine. Furthermore, key-object motion can be decomposed into a global component and a local/object-based component to reflect motion relative to the background and other key-objects in the scene. This decomposition can be easily completed with a simple matrix transformation on the affine parameters. Without this distinction, the key-object motion would instead represent motion relative to the image frame. Thus this decomposition provides a more meaningful and effective description for retrieval.

We summarize the object descriptors for video indexing in Figure 7. Apart from object-based motion descriptors, a general description of motion or activities of shots, such features discussed in the last subsection, is also provided in this representation. The shot-based motion feature set complements nicely to the object-based motion features, especially in shots where key-objects cannot be reliably detected.

Shot
Shot-ID:	s_m (a unique index key of the shot m)
Primitives:	$\{f_s(1), f_s(2), ..., f_s(N)\}$
Key-frames:	$\{KF_m(1), KF_m(2), ..., KF_m(J)\}$
Key-objects:	$\{\mathbf{KO_m(1), Ko_m(2), ..., KO_m(K)}\}$ }

Object
Object-ID:	o_m (a unique index key of the object)
Shape:	$\square$ (alpha map of the object)
Life:	$\{F_b, F_d\}$
Primitives:	$\{f_o(1), f_o(2), ..., f_o(O)\}$
Motion:	motion model parameters and/or trajectory

Figure 7. Adding object-based primitives the shot representation scheme shown in Figures 5 and 6.

Several techniques exist for coherent-motion-based key-object extraction, such as the motion segmentation techniques described by Wang and Adelson [30]. The two major components of this algorithm consist of local motion estimation and motion model estimation. This algorithm is similar to other techniques that employ a generic algorithm except it makes several optimizations that improve robustness. It also reduces computations in our analysis procedure because we also use this local motion information to derive a measure of motion activity.

In cases where clear and distinct motion regions exist, we track the region throughout the duration of the shot. These regions and their attributes of shape, color, and texture are cataloged along with the shot descriptors. Furthermore, we use the size of the region to determine a global motion. For example, a large region that includes the peripheral pixels might correspond to the background. This assumption performs fairly well when foreground objects are proportionately smaller than the background.

Figure 8 shows an example of optic-flow calculated between two frame of a video shot, where the moving object, a man riding a horse, can be clearly seen.

Figure 8. Optic-flow corresponding to the frame shown in Figure 4 (a).
The key-object of a man riding a horse is clearly visible.

The object-based representation shown in Figure 7 also provides a unified framework for both video indexing and compression. Using this framework in video coding, we may achieve higher compression ratio and support content-based data access. The major difference from traditional video coding schemes is that a video sequence is first segmented into shots, each shot is then decomposed into objects with extracted content features, and, finally, the encoding module encodes the objects. The emerging video standard, MPEG-4, also incorporates a similar object-based scheme in compression; however, retrieval has not been the focus [44].

There have also been other proposed object-based representation schemes using only trajectories of moving objects as motion features of shots [45,46,47]. However, motion trajectories alone may not be sufficient in representing activities in a shot, and thus, may not achieve good performance in video retrieval.

4.4 SHOT CLUSTERING FOR INDEXING AND BROWSING

Clustering shots into groups or classes, each of which contains similar content, are essential to building an index of shots for content-based retrieval and browsing. It is also a necessary step in detecting scenes in the video parsing process as discussed in Subsection 2.4. For the purpose of clustering, a large number of shots to build an index with different levels of abstractions, called partitioning-clustering methods, are more suitable since they are capable of finding optimal clustering at each level and are more suitable to obtain a good abstraction of data items [48]. An approach of this type was proposed as video shot grouping [5,49]. This approach is flexible because different feature sets, similarity metrics, and iterative clustering algorithms can be applied at different levels.

One implementation of this approach is to use an enhanced K-means clustering algorithm incorporating fuzzy classification, which allow assignment of data items at the boundary of two classes to both of them according to membership function of the data item to all the classes. This is useful especially at higher levels of hierarchical browsing, where users expect all similar data items to be under a smaller number of nodes [5]. The clustering can be based on key-frames and motion features of video shots. Implementation and evaluation of this clustering approach using the Self-Organization method can be found in [5,49]. The advantage of SOM is its good classification performance and learning ability without prior knowledge, which have been shown by many researchers. Another benefit of using SOM is that the similarities among the extracted classes can be seen directly from the two-dimensional map. This will allow horizontal exploring as well as vertical browsing of the video data, which is very useful when we have a large number of classes at lower levels.

5. RETRIEVAL AND BROWSING SCHEMES

Once a collection of video sequences have been parsed into shots and scenes, and the content features of the sequences have been extracted and represented as described in Section 4, then tools for content-based retrieval and browsing of video can be built to utilize the meta-data. Similar to the case of image retrieval, the retrieval process and, especially, browsing process, should be interactive and iterative, with the system accepting feedback. This section discusses similarity measures for video content comparison and schemes for content-based retrieval and browsing of video.

5.1 SHOT SIMILARITY

Compared with the case in feature-based image retrieval, how to combine multiple features to define the content similarity between two video sequences of shots for retrieval is even more challenging since more features, often with different importance, are involved. Also content comparison can be performed based on key-frame-based features, shot-based temporal and motion features, object-based features, or a combination of the three.

When content comparison are performed using key-frame-based content representation scheme, as illustrated by Figures 5 and 6, we can define shot similarity based on the similarities between the two key-frame sets. If two shots are denoted as $\mathcal{S}_i$ and $\mathcal{S}_j$, their key-frame sets as $K_i =\{ f_{i,m} , m= 1, ..., M\}$ and $K_j = \{f_{j,n}\ n = 1, ... , N\}$, then the similarity between the two shots can be defined as

$$\mathbf{S}_k \left(s_i, s_j\right) = \max[s_k (f_{i,1}, f_{j,1}), s_k (f_{i,1}, f_{j,2}), ..., s_k (f_{i,1}, f_{j,N}), ...,$$
$$s_k (f_{i,1}, f_{j,1}), s_k (f_{i,m}, f_{j,2}), ..., s_k (f_{i,m}, f_{j,N})] \tag{6}$$

where s_k is a similarity metric between two images defined by any one or a combination of the image features; and there are totally $M \times N$ similarity values, from which the maximum is selected. This definition assumes that the similarity between two shots can be determined by the pair of key-frames which are most similar, and it will guarantee that if there is a pair of similar key-frames in two shots, they are considered similar.

Another definition of key-frame based shot similarity is:

$$\mathbf{S}_k \left(s_i, s_j\right) = \frac{1}{M} \sum_{m=1}^{M} \max[s_k (f_{i,m}, f_{j,1}), s_k (f_{i,m}, f_{j,2}), ..., s_k (f_{i,m}, f_{j,N})] \tag{7}$$

This definition states that the similarity between two shots is the sum of the most similar pairs of key-frames. When only one pair of frames match, this definition is equivalent to the first one. The key-frame-based similarity measure as defined above can be further combined with the motion feature-based to make the comparison more meaningful for video.

Similarly, when object-based content representation scheme, as illustrated by Figure 7, is used, the matching between the query and candidate shots is based on visual attributes of individual objects and/or their compositions in shots. That is, for queries searching for the presence of one or more objects in a shot, the similarity between the query and the candidate is defined as the similarity between the key-objets. Formally, if two shots have key-object sets as $K_i\{o_{i,m}, m= 1, ..., M\}$ and $K_j\{o_{j,n}, n= 1, ... , N\}$, then the similarity between the two shots can be defined as

$$\mathbf{s}_k\left(s_i, s_j\right) = \frac{1}{M} \sum_{m=1}^{M} \max\left[s_k\left(o_{i,m}, o_{j,1}\right),\ s_k\left(o_{i,m}, o_{j,2}\right),\ ...,\ s_k\left(o_{i,m}, o_{j,N}\right)\right] \qquad (8)$$

where s_k is a similarity metric between two objects.. Similar to (47), this definition states that the similarity between two shots is the sum of similarities of the most similar key-object pairs.

Apart from key-frame or key-object based similarity, shot-based feature set, $\{f_s(1), f_s(2), ..., f_s(N)\}$, as in the representation illustrated in Figure 5, is also used in defined similarity between video sequences, similar to that in the feature-based image retrieval. The overall similarity between two video sequences is often defined as a combination of weighted multi-feature-based similarities. How to weight each similarity based on a particular feature, especially temporal features vs. image features, for a given query is currently left to the user [1,47]. This is often asking too much from the user, especially for naïve ones. As a result, retrieval performance is often limited. Though there have been many research efforts, the research on effective visual feature-based similarity for video retrieval is in an even earlier stage than that for image retrieval, and will need much more progress before we can apply feature-based retrieval schemes to large scale, heterogeneous video databases.

5.2 BROWSING SCHEMES

Interactive browsing of full video contents is probably the most essential feature of new forms of interactive access to digital video. Content-based video browsing tools should support two different nonlinear approaches to accessing video source data: sequential and random access. In addition, these tools should accommodate two levels of granularity, *overview* and *detail*, along with an effective bridge between the two levels. Such browsing tools can be built only by utilizing structure and content features obtained in the video parsing, abstraction, and feature extraction processes as discussed in previous sections.

There are mainly four types of browsing tools built based on different structural and content features of video, as follows:

1. time-line display of frames;
2. light table of video icons;
3. hierarchical browser;
4. graph based story board.

Time-line based browsers have been favored by users in video production and editing systems, for which time-line interfaces are classical. Some browsers rest on a single shot-based image component line [3,17]; but the multidimensional dimension character of video, calling for multi-line representation of the contents, has been stressed by researchers working in the frame of the Muse toolkit [49,51]. This has been systematized in the strata model proposed by Aguierre-Smith and Davenpoprt [52]. Limitation of time-line browsers is that, since it is difficult to zoom out while keeping a good image visibility, the time-scope of what is actually displayed at a given moment on screen is relatively limited.

The light-table kind of video browser is often called a clip window, in which a video sequence is spread in space and represented by video icons which function rather like a light table of slides [17,39]. In other words the display space is traded for time to provide a rapid overview of the content of a long video. The icons are constructed with methods presented in the Subsection 3.2. A window may contain sequentially listed shots or scenes from a video program, a sequence of shots from a scene, or a group of similar or related shots from a stock archive. A user can get a sense of the content of a shot from the icon, especially when salient stills are used. They can also be used to display the results of retrieval operations. A clip window browser can also be constructed hierarchically just like the

Windows file systems used in PC operating systems nowadays. That is, each icon in a clip window can be zoomed in to open another clip window, in which each icon represents the next level and finer segment of video sequences [39].

A first attempt at building hierarchical browsers, called the Video Magnifier [53], simply used successive horizontal lines, each of which offered greater time detail and narrower time scope by selecting images from the video program. To improve the content accessibility of such browsers, the structural content of video obtained in video parsing are utilized [1,32]. As shown in Figure 9, videos are segmented into and accessed as a tree. At the top of the hierarchy, an entire sequence or program is represented by five key-frames, each corresponding to one of the five groups of an equal number of consecutive shots. Any one of these segments may then be subdivided to create the next level (shots in the case shown in Figure 9) of the hierarchy. As we descend through the hierarchy, our attention focuses on smaller groups of shots, single shots, and finally the key-frames of a specific shot, and all frames of a shot. We can also view sequentially any particular segment of video selected from this browser at any level of the hierarchy by launching a video player.

The hierarchical browser shown in Figure 9 is a very powerful tool for fast assessment of content of a video sequence or programs, since it utilizes the structure information of video. To use this browser, a video program or sequence is loaded into the browser either from a list of names specified by retrieval results or a database index. The shots at the high levels are grouped only according to their sequential relations, not their content similarity. Thus, it will not be very convenient when we use it to browse a large collection of video clips, but it will be helpful if similar shots can be grouped together. To achieve this, the browser is further extended to use similarity information between shots or sequences, probably pre-defined or clustered. That is, when a list of video programs or clips are accessed for browsing, the system clusters shots into classes, consisting of shots of similar visual content, using either key-frame and/or shot features.

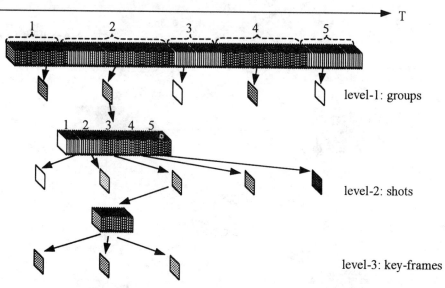

Figure 9. Data structure and browser layout for key-frame-based hierarchical browser.

After such clustering, each class of shots is represented by a key-frame determined by the centroid of the class, which is then displayed at the higher levels of the hierarchical browser. Figure 10 shows the data structure and browser layout for such a hierarchical browser. With this type of browser, the viewer can roughly get a sense of the content of the shots in a class even without moving down to a lower level of the hierarchy [5,33].

An alternative approach to hierarchical browsers is the class based transition graph, proposed by Yeung, et al. [54,6]. By clustering visually similar shots into scenes, a directed graph whose nodes are scenes is constructed, as shown in Figure 11. Cluster A is linked to cluster B if one of the shots in A is immediately followed by a shot in B. The resulting graph is displayed for browsing, each node being represented by a key-frame extracted from one of the shots in the node. This graph can be edited for simplification by a human operator. The drawbacks of this approach lie in the difficulty of the graph layout problem, resulting in poor screen space use, and in the fact that the linear structure of the document is no longer perceptible.

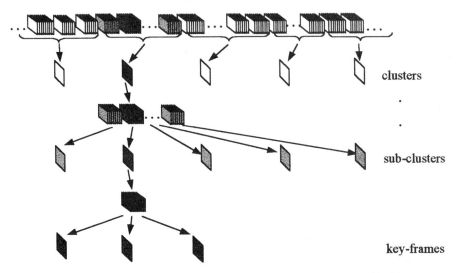

Figure 10. Data structure and browser layout for similarity-based hierarchical browser.

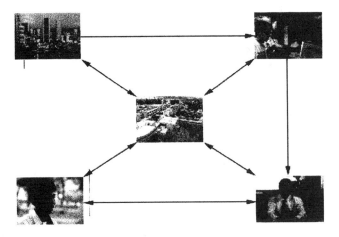

Figure 11. Scene transition viewgraph.

Note that the browsing tools presented in this subsection make use of key-frames as visual icons to present video content and context. That is, we are able to browse the video content down to the key-frame level without necessarily storing the entire video. This is an important advantage of the key-frame-based browsing schemes, particularly if our storage space and/or bandwidth are limited; storage and bandwidth requirement is much lower if we store or download only a small number of key-frames compared to video. Therefore, through the hierarchical browsers, one may browse a large collection of videos before downloading a few interesting ones identified.

6. CONCLUDING REMARKS

In this chapter, we have discussed a variety of existing techniques for video structure parsing, video content representation using visual features, and content-based video retrieval and browsing. Similar to that in image retrieval, the current automated solutions video browsing and retrieval still depend heavily, if not totally, on use of low-level visual features. On the other hand, the current structure parsing, content representation, and browsing algorithms and tools can already increase our productivity in video data browsing, management, and applications significantly more than that for image databases. This is largely due to the fact that conventional video management and browsing tools simple do not support non-linear and content-based access.

In general, each type of image features tends to capture only one of many aspects of image similarity and it is difficult to require a user to specify clearly exactly which aspect or what combination of these aspects he/she wants to apply in defining a query. Therefore, it is important to identify salient features for a given image or shot and to apply the appropriate similarity metric. In addition, effective search of relevant images or video clips often requires a combination of different visual features, which makes selection of appropriate similarity metrics even more difficult. So far, no effective algorithm has been developed that address these problems successfully.

When we strive for visual content analysis and representation, it is worthwhile to point out that information fusion from different sources, such as speech, sound, and text, is as important as visual data itself in understanding and indexing visual data. Keywords and conceptual retrieval techniques are and will always be an important part of visual information systems.

Finally, as we have observed again in the discussions in this chapter, application-oriented approaches are the most successful in visual data representation and retrieval researches. By working on strongly focused applications, the research issues reviewed in this chapter can be addressed in the context of well-defined applications and will facilitate the applications, while achieving general solutions remain long term research topics. One can find detailed presentations of many application specific systems in other chapters of this handbook. On the other hand, one of the most important lessons from the past research is that image and video content analysis, retrieval, and management should not be thought of as a fully automatic process. We should focus on developing video analysis tools to facilitate human users to manage visual data more intelligently and efficiently.

REFERENCES

1. H.J. Zhang, et al., "Video Parsing, Retrieval and Browsing: an Integrated and Content-Based Solution," *Proc. ACM Multimedia'95*, San Francisco, Nov. 5-9, 1995, pp. 15-24.
2. B. Furht, S. W. Smoliar, and H. J. Zhang, *Image and Video Processing in Multimedia Systems*, Kluwer Academic Publishers, Norwell, MA, 1995.

3. P. Aigrain, H.J. Zhang, and D. Petkovic, "Content-Based Representation and Retrieval of Visual Media: A State-of-the-Art Review," *International Journal of Multimedia Tools and Applications*, Kluwer Academic Publishers, Vol. 3, No. 3, 1996.

4. D. Bordwell and K. Thompson, *Film Art: An Introduction*, McGraw-Hill, New York, 1993.

5. D. Zhong, H.J. Zhang, and S.-F. Chang, "Clustering Methods for Video Browsing and Annotation," *Proc. of SPIE Conf. on Storage and Retrieval for Image and Video Databases IV*, San Jose, February 1996.

6. M. M. Yueng, B.-L. Yeo, and B. Liu, "Extracting Story Units from Long Programs for Video Browsing and Navigation," *Proc. of IEEE International Conference on Multimedia Computing and Systems*, June 1996.

7. M. Yeung and B.-L. Yeo, "Video Content Characterization and Compaction for Digital Library Applications," *Proc. of SPIE Conf. on Storage and Retrieval for Image and Video Databases V*, San Jose, CA, February 1997.

8. A. Nagasaka and Y. Tanaka, "Automatic Video Indexing and Full-Search for Video Appearances," in E. Knuth and I.M. Wegener, Editors, *Visual Database Systems*, Elsevier Science Publishers, Vol.II, Amsterdam, 1992, pp. 113-127.

9. H. J. Zhang A., Kankanhalli, and S. W. Smoliar, "Automatic Partitioning of Full-Motion Video," *Multimedia Systems*, ACM-Springer, Vol. 1, No. 1, 1993, pp. 10-28.

10. B. Shahraray, Scene Change Detection and Content-Based Sampling of Video Sequences, *IS\&T/SPIE'95 Digital Video Compression: Algorithm and Technologies*, San Jose, February 1995, Vol. 2419, pp. 2-13.

11. R. Zabih, K. Mai, and J. Miller, A Robust Method for Detecting Cuts and Dissolves in Video Sequences," *Proc. ACM Multimedia '95*, San Francisco, CA, November 1995.

12. P. Aigrain and P. Joly, "The Automatic Real-Time Analysis of Film Editing and Transition Effects and its Applications," *Computers & Graphics*, January-February 1994, Vol.18, No. 1, pp. 93-103.

13. A. Hampapur, R. Jain, and T. E. Weymouth, "Production Model Based Digital Video Segmentation," *Multimedia Tools and Applications*, 1995, Vol. 1, No. 1, pp. 9-46.

14. A. Dailianas, R. Allen, and P. England, "Comparison of Automatic Video Segmentation Algorithms," Proceedings of SPIE Photonics East, Philadelphia, October 1995.

15. J. S. Boreczky and L. A. Rowe, "Comparison of Video Shot Boundary Detection Techniques," *Proc. SPIE Conf. Storage and Retrieval for Video Databases IV*, San Jose, CA, February 1995.

16. F. Arman, A. Hsu, and M. Y. Chiu, "Feature Management for Large Video Databases," *Proc. SPIE Conf. Storage and Retrieval for Image and Video Databases I*, SPIE, Vol. 1908, February 1993, pp. 2-12.

17. H.J. Zhang, et al., "Video Parsing Using Compressed Data," *Proc. SPIE '94 Image and Video Processing II*, San Jose, CA, February 1994, pp. 142-149.

18. B.-L. Yeo and B. Liu, "A Unified Approach to Temporal Segmentation of Motion JPEG and MPEG Compressed Video," *Proc. IEEE International Conf. on Multimedia Computing and Networking*, Washington D.C., May 1995, pp. 81-88.

19. I. S. Sethi and N. Patel, "A Statistical Approach to Scene Change," *Proc. SPIE Conf. Storage and Retrieval for Video Databases III*, San Jose, February 1995.

20. P. Aigrain, P. Joly, and V. Longueville, "Medium-Knowledge-Based Macro-Segmentation of Video into Sequences," Chapter 8, in Intelligent Multimedia Information Retrieval, M. T. Maybury (editor), AAAI/MIT Press, Cambridge, 1997, pp. 159-173.

21. D. Swanberg, C. F. Shu and R. Jain, "Knowledge Guided Parsing in Video Databases," *Proc. of SPIE Conf. on Storage and Retrieval for Image and Video Databases*, San Jose, CA, February 1993.

22. H.J. Zhang, et al., "Automatic Parsing and Indexing of News Video," *Multimedia Systems*, ACM, Vol. 2, No. 6, 1995, pp. 256-265

23. Y. Gong, et al., "Automatic Parsing of TV Soccer Programs," *Proc. Second IEEE International Conference on Multimedia Computing and Systems*, Washington D.C., May 1995, pp. 167-174.

24. A. G. Hauptmann and M. Smith, "Text, Speech and Vision for Video Segmentation: The Informedia Project," Working Notes of IJCAI Workshop on Intelligent Multimedia Information Retrieval, Montreal, August 1995, pp. 17-22.

25. M. G. Brown, et al., "Automatic Content-Based Retrieval of Broadcast News," Proc. of ACM Multimedia '95, San Francisco, CA, November 1995, pp. 35-43.

26. B. Shahraray and D. Gibbon, "Automatic Authoring of Hypermedia Documents of Video Programs," Proc. of ACM Multimedia '95, San Francisco, CA, November 1995, pp. 401-409.

27. A. Merlino, D. Morey, and M. Maybury, "Broadcast Navigation Using Story Segmentation," Proc. of ACM Multimedia '97, Seattle, WA, November 1997, pp. 381-388.

28. Y.T. Tse and R.L. Baker, "Global Zoom/Pan Estimation and Compensation for Video Compression," *Proc. ICASSP '91*, Vol. 4, May 1991.

29. A. Akutsu and Y. Tonomura, Video Tomography: An Efficient Method for Camerawork Extraction and Motion Analysis, Proc. ACM Multimedia Conference, San Francisco, CA, October 1993.

30. J.Y.A. Wang and E. H. Adelson, "Representing Moving Images with Layers," *IEEE Transactions on Image Processing*, 3(5), pp. 625-638, September 1994.

31. B. C. O'Connor, "Selecting Key Frames of Moving Image Documents: A Digital Environment for Analysis and Navigation," *Microcomputers for Information Management*, 8(2), pp. 119-133, 1991.

32. H.J. Zhang, S. W Smoliar, and J. H Wu. "Content-Based Video Browsing Tools," Proc. *IS&T/SPIE Conf. on Multimedia Computing and Networking '95*, San Jose, CA, 1995.

33. H.J. Zhang, et al., "An Integrated System for Content-Based Video Retrieval and Browsing," *Pattern Recognition*, Pergomon Press/Pattern Recognition Society, May 1997.

34. A. Hanjalic and R. L. Langendijk, "A New Key-Frame Allocation Method for Representing Stored Video Streams," *Proc. of 1st Int. Workshop on Image Databases and Multimedia Search*, 1996.

35. H.J. Zhang, J. Y. A. Wang, and Y Altunbasak, "Content-Based Video Retrieval and Compression: A Unified Solution," *Proc. of IEEE Int. Conf. on Image Processing*, Santa Barbara, October 1997.

36. H. Ueda, T. Miyatake, and S. Yoshisawa, "IMPACT: An Interactive Natural-Motion-Picture Dedicated Multimedia Authoring System," *Proceedings of CHI '91*, ACM, 1991, pp. 343-350.

37. L.Teodosio and W. Bender, "Salient Video Stills: Content and Context Preserved," *Proc. ACM Multimedia '93*, Anaheim, CA, August 1993.

38. Y. Tonomura, et al., "VideoMAP and VideoSpaceIcon: Tools for Anatomizing Video Content," *Proc. InterChi '93*, ACM, 1994, pp. 131-136.

39. H.J. Zhang and S. W. Smoliar, "Developing Power Tools for Video Indexing and Retrieval," *Proc. SPIE '94 Storage and Retrieval for Video Databases*, San Jose, CA, February 1994.

40. Y. Taniguchi, A. Akutsu, and Y. Tonomura, "PanoramaExcepts: Extracting and Packing Panoramas for Video Browsing," *Proc. ACM Multimedia Conference*, Seattle, December 1997, pp. 427-436.

41. A. Takeshita, T. Inoue, and K. Tanaka, "Extracting Text Skim Structures for Multimedia Browsing," *Working Notes of IJCAI Workshop on Intelligent Multimedia Information Retrieval*, Montreal, Canada, August 1995, pp. 46-58.

42. M. Davis, "Media Streams: An Iconic Visual Language for Video Annotation," *Proc. of Symposium on Visual Languages*, Bergen, 1993.

43. D. Zhong, *Visual Feature Based Image and Video Indexing and Retrieval*, M.S. Thesis, Institute of Systems Science, National University of Singapore, August 1995.

44. "Description of MPEG-4," ISO/IEC JTC1/SC29 /WG11 N1410, Oct. 1996.

45. S.Y. Lee and H.M. Kao, "Video Indexing – An Approach Based on Moving Object and Track," *Proc. SPIE Conf. Storage and Retrieval for Image and Video Databases*, San Jose, February 1993, pp. 25-36.

46. N. Dimitrova and F. Golshani, "$R_\square$ for Semantic Video Database Retrieval," *Proc. of ACM Multimedia '94*, San Francisco, CA, October 1994, pp. 219-226.

47. S.F. Chang, et al., "VideoQ: A Automated Content Based Video Search System Using Visual Cues," Proc. of ACM Multimedia'97, Seattle, WA, November 1997, pp. 313-324.

48. R. Duda and P. Hart, *Pattern Recognition and Scene Analysis*, John Wiley, New York, 1973.

49. H. J. Zhang and D. Zhong, "A Scheme for Visual Feature-Based Image Indexing," *Proc. of SPIE Conf. on Storage and Retrieval for Image and Video Databases III*, pp. 36-46, San Jose, February 1995.

50. M.E. Hodges, R. M. Sassnett, and M. S. Ackerman, "A Construction Set for Multimedia Applications," *IEEE Software*, January 1989, pp. 37-43.

51. W. E. Mackay and G. Davenport, "Virtual Video Editing in Interactive Multimedia Applications," *Communications of the ACM,* Vol. 32, No. 9, July 1989.

52. T. G. Aguierre-Smith and G. Davenport, "The Stratification System: A Design Environment for Random Access Video," *Proc. 3rd Int. Workshop on Network and Operating System Support for Digital Audio and Video*, La Jolla, CA, November 1992, pp. 250-261.

53. M. Mills, J. Cohen, and Y. Y. Wong, "A Magnifier Tool for Video Data," *Proc. INTERCHI '92*, ACM, May 1992, pp. 93-98.

54. M. M. Yeung, et al., "Video Browsing Using Clustering and Scene Transitions on Compressed Sequences," *Proc. of IS\&T/SPIE '95 Multimedia Computing and Networking*, San Jose, Vol. 2417, February 1995, pp. 399-413.

13

INDEXING FOR EFFICIENT SPATIAL SIMILARITY-BASED RETRIEVAL IN MULTIMEDIA DATABASES

Venkat N. Gudivada,[1] **Rajesh V. Sonak,**[2]
William I. Grosky,[3] **and Karen Lentz**[4]

[1]*Dow Jones Markets, Jersey City, NJ 03711*
[2]*Intellinet Technologies, Melbourne, FL 32904*
[3]*Computer Science Department, Wayne State University, Detroit, MI 48202*
[4]*Electrical Eng. & Computer Science, Tufts University, Medford, MA 02155*

1. **CONTENT-BASED MULTIMEDIA INFORMATION RETRIEVAL**............................282
2. **NOTIONS OF INDEX**..283
3. **REPRESENTATIONS AND ALGORITHMS FOR SPATIAL QUERY PROCESSING**..284
    3.1 SPATIAL REPRESENTATION BASED ON SINGLE DESCRIPTOR...............................284
    3.2 SPATIAL REPRESENTATION BASED ON PAIRWISE RELATIONSHIPS BETWEEN DOMAIN OBJECTS....285
4. **PROPOSED INDEXING SCHEME**..286
    4.1 GENERATING THE $r=aG^B$ CURVE..286
    4.2 BUILDING THE INDEX...286
    4.3 OBJECTED INVERTED LIST AND OTHER DATA STRUCTURES...............................287
    4.4 DETERMINING POV..288
    4.5 MERGING OF CLUSTERS...290
    4.6 SEARCHING THE INDEX...291
5. **EXPERIMENTAL EVALUATION**...291
    5.1 EXPERIMENTAL DATA...292
    5.2 EXPERIMENTAL RESULTS AND DISCUSSION...294
6. **CONCLUSIONS AND FUTURE WORK**...295
    REFERENCES...298

Abstract. In multimedia databases, one major class of user queries requires retrieving database images that are spatially similar to a query image. To rank order the database images with respect to the query, existing spatial similarity algorithms compute the similarity of every database image with the query.

For large multimedia databases, this task is computationally expensive and renders interactive query processing difficult. In this chapter, we propose an indexing scheme that will eliminate non-relevant images to a query before the actual similarity computation. In other words, the indexing scheme serves as a filter and spatial similarity computation is done only on those images that pass through the filter. The central idea of the indexing technique presented here is a mapping from every image to a real number A, done at the time of addition of the image to the database, taking into consideration its similarity to the images already in the database. A tree-based index is incrementally built based on the value of A. Some non-relevant images may pass through the filter (i.e., false positives) but the proposed indexing scheme guarantees that no relevant images are eliminated (i.e., no false negatives). The indexing scheme is robust in the sense that it recognizes translation, scaling, and rotation variant images of the query image as relevant to the query. We demonstrate the effectiveness of the proposed algorithm experimentally.

1. CONTENT-BASED MULTIMEDIA INFORMATION RETRIEVAL

The bulk of the data processed by computers in the near future will be audio-visual in nature. With the proliferation of multimedia computing into the ubiquitous desktop computer, multimedia data will be as common to computers of the near future as text data is to today's computers. Structured data, text, digital ink, graphics, animation, images, audio, and video comprise multimedia data types. Multimedia data management systems are expected to coherently handle these diverse media types and provide content-based access to the data. Content-based multimedia information retrieval (CBMIR) is characterized by the ability of the system to perform retrieval based on textual, visual, auditory, and semantic contents of the media interpreted at suitable levels of abstraction in a transparent way to the system user. Tools and techniques for multimedia data organization, search, retrieval, and presentation comprise the enabling technologies for realizing CBMIR. However, they have not kept pace with our insatiable quest for multimedia data generation. The severity of this problem has been already witnessed in the limitations of tools for searching the World-Wide Web. Advances in CBMIR are essential for developing multimedia database systems, as CBMIR comprises the core component of a multimedia database system.

By studying the retrieval requirements of a number of image retrieval applications, we have identified the following generic query operators to support CBMIR [7]: color, texture, sketch, shape, volume, spatial relationships, topological relationships, browsing, extrinsic attributes, subjective attributes, sequence, keywords, natural language text, and domain concepts. These generic query operators are as fundamental to CBMIR as relational algebra is to relational database management systems (DBMS).

In this chapter, we focus on one query operator – spatial relationships. This operator is required to process a class of queries, referred to as *retrieval by spatial similarity* (RSS). RSS queries are prevalent in applications such as interior design, architectural design, real estate marketing, geographic information systems, medical [10], among others. For example, in real estate marketing, user queries include spatial relationships among various functional units in a house in addition to the attributes such as location, cost, and number of bedrooms.

Spatial similarity algorithms are required to process RSS queries. A spatial similarity algorithm computes the degree to which the spatial relationships among the domain objects in a database image conform to those specified in the query. Algorithms for spatial similarity computation typically compute the similarity of every database image with the query. For large image databases, this task is computationally expensive and renders interactive query processing difficult.

In this chapter, we propose an indexing scheme[1] that will eliminate all non-relevant images to a query before the actual spatial similarity computation. In other words, the indexing scheme serves as a filter, and spatial similarity algorithms are applied to only those images that pass through the filter. Some non-relevant images may pass through the filter (i.e., false positives), but the proposed scheme guarantees that no relevant images are eliminated (i.e., no false negatives). The indexing scheme is robust in the sense that it recognizes the following as relevant to the query image: translation, scaling, and rotation variants of the query; composite variants of the query formed by an arbitrary composition of translation, scaling, and rotation; medium- to large-size sub-images of the query.

The proposed indexing scheme involves mapping every database image to a real number A, and then using this value to generate a balanced tree-based index. We refer to the A value of an image as its *spatial coefficient* (SC). During retrieval, the query image is also mapped to a real number A, and then the index is searched for those images whose spatial coefficient values are close to A. The index is dynamic in the sense that new images can be added to and existing images can be deleted from, the index. We demonstrate the effectiveness of the proposed indexing scheme experimentally.

The remainder of this chapter is organized as follows. In Section 2, we clarify the notion of indexing in the information retrieval area [14], and in relational and object-oriented databases. Section 3 provides an overview of spatial representations, associated similarity algorithms, and related work. The proposed indexing scheme is introduced in Section 4. Experimental evaluation of the scheme is described in Section 5. Section 6 indicates future work and concludes the chapter.

2. NOTIONS OF INDEX

First, we clarify two different notions of indexing that exist in the literature. Information retrieval [14] has traditionally been concerned with automatically managing large collections of textual documents. The term indexing is used to refer to the process of assigning terms or phrases to a document. They are intended to represent the information content of the document and are often referred to as *index terms*. In contrast, the notion of an index in relational and object-oriented DBMS refers to access structures (e.g., B-tree and hash indexes, parent-child links) built on a file(s) of records to facilitate efficient query processing. Indices can only be specified on attributes that have ordered domains.

The notion of an index in the multimedia systems literature is similar to that in information retrieval. Multimedia indexing is primarily concerned with assigning suitable descriptors to media that indicate the information content of the media. This is not a trivial task, for the interpretation of media content is subjective and it is difficult to determine *a priori* what type of descriptors are needed. This is because the type of descriptors needed depends on the domain and the nature of the query. Due to these difficulties, there has not been much research into developing suitable index structures. However, to efficiently process queries in large multimedia databases, access structures based on content descriptors become necessary. From the multimedia database viewpoint, an index should encompass both the assignment of content descriptors to the media and the access structures associated with these content descriptors.

Image retrieval and browsing systems such as Photobook [13] operate without an index. Database images are rank ordered by computing the similarity of the query image with each database image. On the other hand, indexing in the QBIC system [4] is based on multidimensional access structures (MAS) [15]. A multimedia object (say, an image) is represented by an n-dimensional vector and thus constitutes a point in the associated

---

[1] As will be seen in Section 3, the notion of an index in multimedia information retrieval is slightly different from that in traditional database systems.

multidimensional space. For example, the first three components of the vector represent texture, the next sixty-four components represent color, the next two components represent shape, and so on. Finding similar images to a query then involves retrieving those images whose corresponding locations in the n-dimensional space are within some measure of proximity to the point corresponding to the query image. In the context of MAS-based indexing, we make the following observations.

MAS can be used only if the content descriptors have ordered domains. When the number of dimensions is high, MAS degenerates to sequential scanning. It is less likely that a given multimedia application requires all the generic query operators discussed in Section 1. Having a separate but specialized index for each generic query operator reduces the overhead and provides opportunities for query optimization. By its very nature, it is difficult to precisely characterize multimedia data and user queries. Also, multimedia data interpretation can vary from one user to another. Adaptive query reformulation based on user relevance feedback has been successfully used to alleviate these problems [6]. Grouping all features into an n-dimensional vector and using MAS does not facilitate adaptive query reformulation.

3. REPRESENTATIONS AND ALGORITHMS FOR SPATIAL QUERY PROCESSING

Regardless of the application, we can assume that images contain one or more domain objects. A domain object is a semantic entity meaningful in the application. At the pixel level, a domain object is a subset of the image pixels. As an example, in a residential floor plan image, various rooms and functional units constitute the domain objects. Although the notion of domain object is general, what actually are domain objects is domain-dependent. We represent an image I consisting of n domain objects $\{o_1, o_2, \cdots, o_n\}$ as

$I = \{o_i[j], x_i[j], y_i[j]), 1 \le j \le n\}$, where $o_i[j]$ is the name of the jth object, and $x_i[j]$ and $y_i[j]$ are its centroid coordinates. The set of objects in I is denoted $obj(I)$ and is given by $obj(I) = \{o_1, o_2, \cdots, o_n\}$. We use the notation $x[o_i]$ and $y[o_i]$ to denote the x- and y-coordinate of o_i. We assume that no two domain objects in an image have the same centroid coordinates (that is, for $o_i, o_j \in obj(I), i \ne j$, we have that $x[o_i] \ne x[o_j]$ or $y[o_i] \ne y[o_j]$)

To provide context for the proposed indexing scheme, we next present an overview of the work on spatial similarity. There are two major approaches for describing spatial relationships among the domain objects in an image. In the first approach, a single content descriptor or structure is used, while in the second, several content descriptors (e.g., pair-wise spatial relationships) are employed. Although the latter approach is more amenable for indexing, it has several disadvantages that will be discussed later in this section. Algorithms are used to compute spatial similarity in both the approaches. Some algorithms based on the second approach perform logical deduction/reduction before applying a similarity algorithm [16]. Spatial relationship representations based on the first approach include the 2D-string and its variants [2], the spatial orientation graph [5], and the $\theta\mathcal{R}$-string [9]. Studies reported in [1,16] are based on the second approach. Typically associated with a spatial knowledge representation scheme is an algorithm for computing the spatial similarity between images.

3.1 SPATIAL REPRESENTATION BASED ON SINGLE DESCRIPTOR
2D-string and its variants: 2D-string is introduced in [2] as a spatial knowledge representation structure. 2D-string considers domain objects as point objects situated at their center of mass. Algorithms for spatial similarity retrieval based on a 2D-string

representation are given in [2,11,12]. Extensions have been proposed to 2D-string to include the spatial extent of the domain objects [11,12]. With 2D-string representation, it is difficult to recognize rotational variants of an image as spatially similar images.

The spatial orientation graph (Figure 1(a)) and an associated algorithm for spatial similarity is introduced in [5]. The spatial orientation graph is a completely connected, weighted graph. Vertices correspond to the centroids of domain objects and there is an edge connecting every vertex to every other vertex. The weight of an edge is the slope of the edge. The algorithm for spatial similarity based on the spatial orientation graph is robust in that it recognizes translation, scale, and rotation variants, as well as variants obtained by an arbitrary composition of translation, scale, and rotation as similar images.

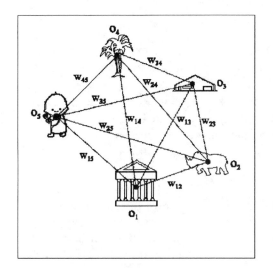

(a) Spatial orientation graph

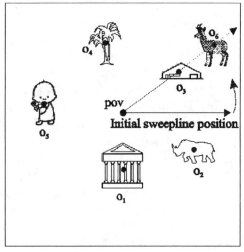

(B) ThetaR-string

Figure 1. Representation of spatial relationships.

$\theta\mathfrak{R}$ -string and an associated algorithm for spatial similarity is introduced in [9]. $\theta\mathfrak{R}$ -string is based on a total ordering of the domain objects induced by a binary relation $< \theta\mathfrak{R}$. As shown in Figure 1(b), a total order is obtained by sweeping the image plane using a radial sweep-line pivoted at a reference point (or *point of view* (*POV*)) and noting the order in which the domain objects are intersected by the line. If more than two objects intersect the line for a given radial position (objects o_3 and o_6 in Figure 1(b)), the Euclidean distance of the domain objects from the *POV* is used to break the tie (e.g., o_6 comes after o_3 in the total ordering). The similarity algorithm associated with $\theta\mathfrak{R}$ -string representation is also robust. The proposed indexing scheme is based on this approach.

None of the above algorithms employ an index in processing user queries. The similarity of the query image with every database image is computed and these values are used to rank order the database images.

3.2 SPATIAL REPRESENTATIONS BASED ON PAIRWISE RELATIONSHIPS BETWEEN DOMAIN OBJECTS

Approaches based on pair-wise spatial relationships differ in terms of whether or not all relationships are exhaustively enumerated and persistently stored. In the approach proposed in [1], spatial relationships are exhaustively represented by a set of ordered triples of the form (o_i, o_j, γ_{ij}); o_i and o_j are the domain objects, and γ_{ij} is the directional relationship (e.g., *north*, *south*) of o_i with respect to o_j. The similarity algorithms based on this approach recognize translation and scale variants, but not rotation variants.

To eliminate exhaustive enumeration and persistent storage of all pair-wise relationships, the notion of *logical reduction* and *deduction* is introduced in [16]. Given a set $\Re$ of spatial relationships and spatial inference rules, the reduction problem is to generate a minimal set of relationships from $\Re$. Only this minimal set is persistently stored. All the original relationships in $\Re$ can be recovered from the minimal set by using a deduction algorithm at query processing time. Algorithms based on this approach recognize translation and scale variants, but not rotation variants.

4. PROPOSED INDEXING SCHEME

Central to the proposed indexing scheme is the generation of a curve of the form $r = a\theta^b$ for every database image; a and b are constants. Later we will show that spatially similar images will have proportionately similar forms in their $r = a\theta^b$ curves. Therefore, the area under the curve can be used to build an index using a balanced tree structure. During query processing, the $r = a\theta^b$ curve for the query image is generated and the area under the curve is used to traverse the index tree to locate potentially relevant images.

4.1 GENERATING THE $r = a\theta^b$ CURVE

To illustrate the generation of the $r = a\theta^b$ curve, consider the image shown in Figure 1(b). The domain objects and their centroid coordinates are shown in columns 2 and 3 of Table 1. The *POV* (point of view) plays a key role in capturing the spatial similarity between two images by insuring that domain object orientations are recorded in both images from the same viewpoint. Assume that the *POV* for Image 1(b) is located at (51.58, 84.44) (more on this in Section 4.4). Column 4 lists the Euclidean distance r_i of the objects from the *POV*. The angle (measured counterclockwise) subtended by the line joining the centroid of a domain object and the *POV* with the initial sweep-line position is shown in column 5. Figure 2 shows the $r = a\theta^b$ curve for the image in Figure 1(b). It is constructed by fitting a curve to the set of (θ_i, r_i) points using non-linear regression techniques. Other forms for the curve are conceivable and remain as a task for future research.

Table 1. Calculation of Points for $r = a\theta^b$ Curve for Image Shown in Figure 1(b)

i	Object (o_i)	(x,y)	Distance (r_i)	θ_i (radians)
1	o_1	(51.58,78.81)	5.63	4.89
2	o_2	(59.1,80.68)	8.40	5.82
3	o_3	(57.69,88.99)	7.61	0.64
4	o_4	(49.70,92.12)	7.90	1.81
5	o_5	(43.13, 85.54)	8.52	3.01
6	o_6	(61.29, 91.80)	12.18	0.64

4.2 BUILDING THE INDEX

The index building scenario proceeds as follows. For the very first image i_1, we choose *POV* arbitrarily, generate $r = a\theta^b$ curve, and compute its spatial coefficient (*SC*). *SC* is computed as the area between the curve and a fixed length l of the x-axis. The selection of a value for l is not critical, and $l \geq 6$ radians gives excellent results. We add i_1 to an empty cluster C_1. We also associate a balanced tree with C_1 and insert i_1 into this tree using its SC value. We denote SC of i_1 as SC_{i_1}. If the second image i_2 to be inserted into the database has at least two objects in common with i_1, i_2 is also added to C_1. Inserting an image into a cluster involves first determining the POV for the image, generating the $r = a\theta^b$ curve, computing SC, and then inserting the image into the tree associated with the cluster using its SC value. How to determine the POV for a new image is discussed in Section 4.4. For inserting an arbitrary image i_k, first we determine whether i_k has at least two objects in common with *some* image in C_1. If so, i_k is inserted into C_1 as we did for the case of i_2; otherwise, we create a new cluster, say C_2 and insert i_k into C_2.

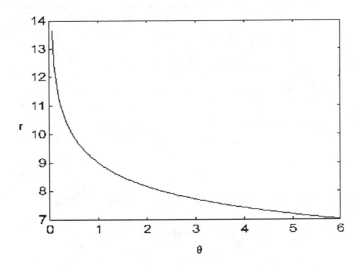

Figure 2. $r = a\theta^b$ curve for image shown in Figure 1(b).

In general, for a new image i_n we first identify its cluster. There are three possibilities: i_n belongs to none of the existing clusters; i_n belongs to only one of the existing clusters; i_n belongs to more than one existing cluster (we refer to these as *potential clusters*). In the first case, i_n is inserted into a new cluster. In the second case, i_n is inserted into its cluster similar to the insertion of i_k into C_1 (also see Section 4.4). The third case is more involved and requires replacing the potential clusters by merging them into a new cluster using i_n as a link. This process is explained in Section 4.5. It should be noted that the clusters form a partition on the database images.

4.3 OBJECT INVERTED LIST AND OTHER DATA STRUCTURES

An inverted list is a data structure which has been used in information retrieval over the years to efficiently implement the Boolean information retrieval model [3,14]. In our context, an inverted list is used to efficiently determine the cluster to which a new image belongs. Let O_{db} denote the set of domain objects in the database images, given by $O_{db} = \{o_1, o_2, \cdots, o_m\}$. We create an inverted list for $o_i, 1 \leq i \leq m$; it is simply a list of image *ids* in which o_i is present. In addition to these image *ids*, other information such as the centroid coordinates of the object in each image is also stored. We also need a data structure shown in Table 2 to efficiently insert an image into a cluster or to merge potential clusters. The values for the first three columns in the table are based on Figure 4. For each image in the database this table keeps track of i_{db}; the cluster to which i_{db} belongs, the image in the cluster based on which the *POV* for i_{db} is determined (referred to as the parent image of i_{db}), and centroid coordinates (after all the transformations discussed in Section 4.4) of two objects in i_{db} used to determine *POV* of i_{db} in conjunction with its parent image. Information shown in Table 3 is also needed. For each cluster, this table maintains: *id* of the very first image of the cluster (also known as the root image of the cluster) and its *POV* coordinates.

Table 2. Data Structure to Facilitate Efficient Merging of Clusters

Image id	Cluster number	Parent image *id*	$o_i(x,y)$	$o_i(x,y)$
i_1	C_1	*null*	(16.7, 14.3)	(21.3, 18.4)
i_2	C_1	i_1	(47.6, 34.9)	(52.4, 41.6)
i_3	C_2	*null*	(67.32, 43.17)	(18.23, 19.63)
i_4	C_1	i_2	...	...
i_5	C_1	i_1	...	...
i_6	C_2	i_3	...	...
i_7	C_2	i_6	...	...
i_8	C_2	i_6	...	...
...	...	...	...	...
...	...	...	...	...

Table 3. Another Data Structure to Facilitate Efficient Merging of Clusters

Cluster number	Root image	*POV* (x,y)
C_1	i_1	(13.7, 17.3)
C_2	i_3	(42.4, 51.6)
...	...	...
C_m	...	...

4.4 DETERMINING *POV*

Assume that we want to insert a new image i_n into the database. Also, assume that using the inverted list data structure, it has been determined that i_n has two objects in common with i_p and i_p is in cluster C_1. Therefore, i_n should also go into cluster C_1. If i_n has two objects in common with several images in C_1, one such image is arbitrarily chosen for the role of i_p. Image i_p is referred to as the *parent image* of i_n. As shown in Figure 3, image i_p has six objects: $o_1, o_2, \cdots o_6$. Let $p_1, p_2, \cdots p_6$ be their respective centroid coordinates. Image i_n has all the objects of i_p. In addition, it has another object o_7. Let $o_1', o_2', \cdots o_6'$ be the objects in i_n corresponding to the objects $o_1, o_2, \cdots o_6$ in i_p. Also, let $p_1', p_2', \cdots p_6'$ be the centroid coordinates of $o_1', o_2', \cdots o_6'$. Assume that the coordinates of the *POV* for i_p are (x_{pov}, y_{pov}) and that the coordinates of p_1, p_2, p_1' and p_2' are $(x_{p_1}, y_{p_1}), (x_{p_2}, y_{p_2}), (x_{p_1'}, y_{p_1'})$, and $(x_{p_2'}, y_{p_2'})$, respectively. We perform the following geometric transformations on all the objects in i_n so that the *POV* of i_p can be used as the *POV* of i_n.

1. Translate image i_n so that p_1 and p_1' coincide. In a homogeneous coordinate system, this translation is given by matrix T:

$$T = \begin{bmatrix} 1 & 0 & x_{p_1} - x_{p_1'} \\ 0 & 1 & y_{p_1} - y_{p_1'} \\ 0 & 0 & 1 \end{bmatrix}$$

Let p_{1t}' and p_{2t}' be the points corresponding to p_1' and p_2' after applying the transformation T.

2. Let $\xrightarrow{p_i p_j}$ denote the vector from point p_i to point p_j. Let the included angle between $\xrightarrow{p_1 p_2}$ and $\xrightarrow{p_1' p_2'}$ be ϕ. Rotate $\xrightarrow{p_1' p_2'}$ about p_{1t}' so that $\xrightarrow{p_1 p_2}$ and $\xrightarrow{p_1' p_2'}$ are parallel and point in the same direction. This rotation transformation is given by matrix R:

$$R = \begin{bmatrix} \cos(\phi) & -\sin(\phi) & 0 \\ \sin(\phi) & \cos(\phi) & 0 \\ 0 & 0 & 1 \end{bmatrix}$$

Let p_{1tr}' and p_{2tr}' be the points corresponding to p_{1t}' and p_{2t}' after applying this transformation R.

3. Let d be the Euclidean distance between p_1 and p_2. Also, let d' be the distance between p_{1tr}' and p_{2tr}'. Scale line segment $p_{1tr}' p_{2tr}'$ so that p_{2tr}' coincides with p_2. This scaling transformation is given by matrix S:

$$S = \begin{bmatrix} \dfrac{d}{d'} & 0 & 0 \\ 0 & \dfrac{d}{d'} & 0 \\ 0 & 0 & 1 \end{bmatrix}$$

Let p_{1trs}' and p_{2trs}' be the points corresponding to p_{1tr}' and p_{2tr}' after applying this transformation.

Note that, after the composite transformation TRS, $p_{1trs}' = p_1$ and $p_{2trs}' = p_2$. TRS is the key to recognize translation, rotation, and scale variants of an image since the variants are transformed to the original image. Now the POV of i_p, (x_{pov}, y_{pov}), can be used as the POV for i_n.

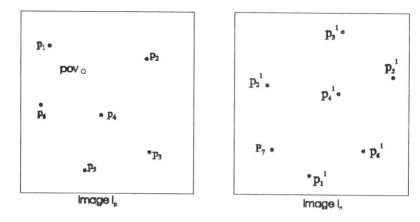

Figure 3. Determining *POV* for a new image.

4.5 MERGING OF CLUSTERS

If a new image i_n to be inserted into the database has two or more potential clusters, the clusters are merged using the new image as a link. For simplicity in presentation, assume that we have two potential clusters as shown in Figure 4. However, the following procedure holds on any number of clusters. The arrow from image i_2 to i_1 in cluster C_1 indicates that i_1 is the parent of i_2 for *POV* determination. This also implies that i_1 and i_2 have at least two objects in common. This information is readily available from Table 2.

Without loss of generality, assume that images i_1 and i_3 are the root images of clusters C_1 and C_2 (this information is available from Table 3); i_1 and i_3 each have two objects in common with i_n. If i_1 or i_3 has more than two objects in common with i_n, we arbitrarily select two objects common to i_1, i_3, and i_n. Next arbitrarily choose *POV* for i_n, generate the curve, compute its spatial coefficient, and insert i_n into a new cluster, say C_3. Since i_n and i_1 have at least two objects in common, we can use the *POV* of i_n for i_1 after applying the *TRS* transformation on i_1. Next i_2 is inserted into the index using i_1 as the parent. Similarly, other images in C_1 are inserted into C_3. By following the same procedure, images in C_2 are inserted into C_3, starting with i_3. Now clusters C_1 and C_2 cease to exist. Tables 2 and 3 are updated to reflect these changes.

On the other hand, it may be the case that i_n does not have two objects in common with the root image of C_1; instead, it has two objects in common with some other image, say i_2 (Figure 4). Now i_2 should be treated as the root image of C_1 and its *POV* is determined based the *POV* of i_n. All images for which i_2 is the parent can then be inserted into C_3 by using the *POV* of i_2 as the *POV* for its children. This is done recursively. Next we find the parent of i_2, denoted *parent* i_2, and determine *parent* $(i_2)'s$ *POV* based on the *POV* of i_2. It should be noted that, in the *TRS* transformation, original coordinates should be used for all objects in *parent* i_2. This process is recursively carried out for the parent and all children of *parent* i_2.

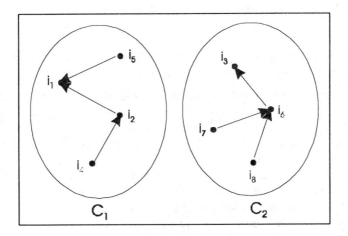

Figure 4. Merging of potential clusters.

4.6 SEARCHING THE INDEX

Using the object inverted lists, the set of images which have two or more objects in common with the query image is determined. Next, the clusters to which these images belong are found using Table 3. If this results in only one cluster, say C_1, *the spatial coefficient* for the query image is computed using the *POV* of C_1 as the *POV* for the query. The index tree associated with C_1 is traversed to retrieve images whose spatial coefficient is equal or close to *SC*. On the other hand, if the query image belongs to more than one cluster, all index trees associated with these clusters are traversed to retrieve spatially similar images. Typically, an index tree is traversed to retrieve those images whose spatial coefficients are in the range $SC \pm \delta$, where δ is a user-specifiable parameter. We refer to $SC \pm \delta$ as the *index search range* of the query image. When $\delta = 0$, the index retrieves database images that have objects in identical spatial locations as the query (this includes variants of the query image). By increasing the value of δ, we can retrieve additional images that have lower spatial similarity with the query. We define the *selectivity of the index search range* as the fraction of database images retrieved. In a typical database, when $\delta = 0$, the selectivity of the index search range is low and increases with the corresponding increase in δ.

5. EXPERIMENTAL EVALUATION

Objectives for the experimental evaluation include testing the hypothesis that spatially similar images have spatial coefficients proportional to their similarity; establishing that variants of an image have the same spatial coefficient as that of the image; and analyzing the behavior of the indexing scheme on sub-images and super-images.

5.1 EXPERIMENTAL DATA

We created 7 spatially similar images as shown in Figure 5. These images are termed as A, B, C, D, E, F, and G. A is the original image with 10 objects. Image B is a translation variant of A ($t_x = 30$ and $t_y = 20$).[2] C is a rotation variant of A obtained by rotating A by $60°$ counterclockwise about the coordinate origin.[3] Image A is scaled about the origin with $s_x = s_y = 2$ to obtain its scale variant image D.[4] Image E is a composite variant of A obtained by first rotating A about the origin by $60°$ counterclockwise and then scaling about the origin with $s_x = s_y = 2$. Image F is a super-image of A since F has all the objects in A plus an additional object (comb). Moreover, the spatial location of one of the objects (brush) in A has been slightly moved in F. Image G is a sub-image of A. G has all the objects in A except two (binoculars and clock). We refer to images A-G as *group 1* images. We have also created images H, I, and J (Figure 6) that are spatially dissimilar to group 1 images. Image H contains only two objects of A and nothing else. Image I has 8 objects in common with A but only 2 (binoculars and clock) have the same centroid location as their counterparts in image A; the centroids for the remaining 6 have been displaced. Additionally, image I has 5 new objects. Image J has all the 10 objects of A, but their spatial locations have been displaced. Images H-J are referred to as *group 2*. The symbol O is used to denote *POV* in Figures 5 and 6.

To study the behavior of the indexing scheme on sub-images, 8 sub-images are created as follows. The first sub-image A_1, is generated from A by removing one object. The second sub-image A_2, is generated from A_1 by removing one object from A_1. The next sub-image A_3, is generated from A_2 by removing one object from A_2. Likewise, we generate sub-images A_4, A_5, A_6, A_7, and A_8. Note that image A_8 has only 2 objects. We refer to image A and its sub-images $A_1, A_2, \cdots, A_8$ as *group 3*. We say that image i_d is an $x\%$ sub-image of i_q, if i_d contains $x\%$ of the domain objects in i_q, in identical spatial locations.

To study the behavior of the indexing scheme on super-images, we created 7 super-images of A as follows. The first super-image A^1 is formed by adding one object to A. The second super-image A^2 is formed by adding one object to A^1. Likewise, remaining super-images A^3, A^4, A^5, A^6, and A^7 are formed. Note that image A^7 has 17 objects. We refer to images $A, A^1, A^2, \cdots A^7$ as *group 4* images. We say that image i_d is an $x\%$ super-image of i_q, if i_d contains all the domain objects in i_q in identical spatial locations; in addition i_d has additional objects equal to $x\%$ of the domain objects in i_q.

---

[2] Parameters t_x and t_y represent the translation displacement along the x- and y-axis, respectively.
[3] The coordinate origin is the left bottom vertex of the rectangle enclosing the image objects.
[4] Parameters s_x and s_y represent scaling factors in the direction of x- and y-axis.

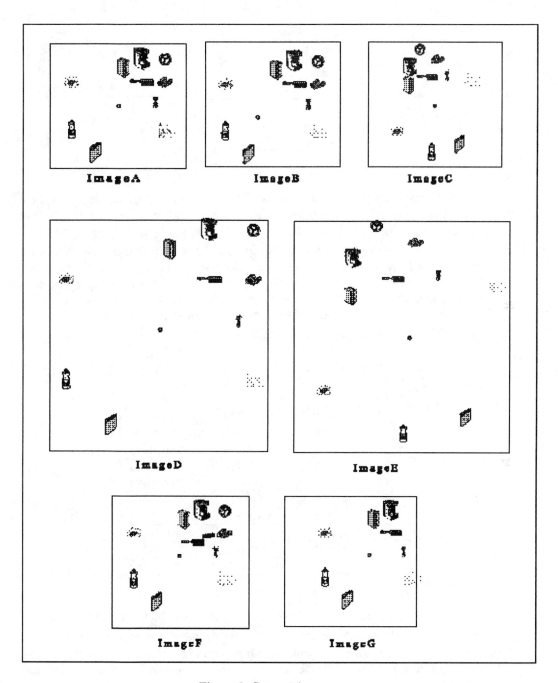

Figure 5. Group 1 images.

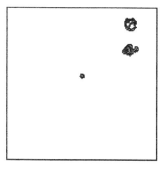 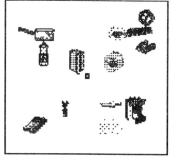 

Image H   Image I   Image J

Figure 6. Group 2 images.

5.2 EXPERIMENTAL RESULTS AND DISCUSSION

Table 4 shows the values of a and b (of $r = a\theta^b$ curve), and spatial coefficient (SC) for images in groups 1 and 2. The corresponding $r = a\theta^b$ curves are shown in Figure 7. The value of l used in computing SC is 300 radians. As can be seen in Figure 7, images A-E have identical forms for their $r = a\theta^b$ curves. Also images F and G have their $r = a\theta^b$ curve forms very similar to those for images A-E. Due to the low resolution of Figure 7, this is not evident. However, Table 4 clearly shows this distinction. This is exactly what is expected, since the indexing scheme recognizes images A-E as variant images and images F and G as spatially similar to images A-E. Since image H is spatially quite different from images A-G, I and J, $r = a\theta^b$ curve is also quite different for H.

Table 4. Values of a, b, and SC for Images in Groups 1 and 2

Image	a	b	SC
A	100.60124	0.068428	41638.679688
B	100.60124	0.068428	41638.679688
C	100.60122	0.068428	41638.679688
D	100.60124	0.068428	41638.679688
E	100.60124	0.068428	41638.679688
F	94.087997	0.095613	44360.472656
G	92.585709	0.109555	46678.203125
H	157.50389	0.445869	415561.81250
I	92.581032	-0.121811	15683.040039
J	123.54713	-0.153578	18091.814453

The values of a, b, and SC for group 3 images are shown in Table 5 and the corresponding $r = a\theta^b$ curves are shown in Figure 8. It is observed that the $r = a\theta^b$ curves for the sub-images differ more and more from that of the original image (i.e., A), as the sub-images become increasingly different from the original image. That is, typically $r = a\theta^b$ curve for the first sub-image is more similar to A than the $r = a\theta^b$ curve for the second sub-image, and so on.

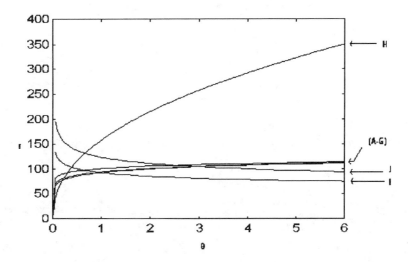

Figure 7. $r = a\theta^b$ curves for images in groups 1 and 2.

The values of a, b, and SC for group 4 images are shown in Table 6 and the corresponding $r = a\theta^b$ curves are shown in Figure 9. As more and more objects are added to the original image (i.e., A) to form its super-images, in general, the curves for the super-images tend to go farther away from that of A. In summary, experimental results conclude that the proposed indexing scheme recognizes variants of an image, as well *as high per cent sub-images* and *low per cent* super-images.

Table 5. Values of a, b, and SC for Group 3 Images

Image	a	b	SC
A	100.601242	0.068428	41638.679688
A_1	104.945389	0.052852	40323.765625
A_2	105.089325	0.054432	40684.441406
A_3	105.643105	0.062384	42480.808594
A_4	106.241501	0.068805	44052.527344
A_5	106.974464	0.075523	45805.027344
A_6	126.999916	0.201048	99750.632813
A_7	122.291901	0.037434	43662.906250
A_8	157.503922	0.445869	415561.96875

6. CONCLUSIONS AND FUTURE WORK

We believe that the scheme proposed in this chapter represents the first comprehensive attempt in providing indexing for efficient spatial similarity based query processing in multimedia retrieval applications. Though the approaches proposed in [1,16] provide indexing, they employ a coarse representation for spatial relationships and fail to retrieve rotational variant images of the query.

The time complexity of searching an index tree is $\Theta(\log n)$, where n is the number of images in the index (since the computation involved is bounded by the height of the tree).

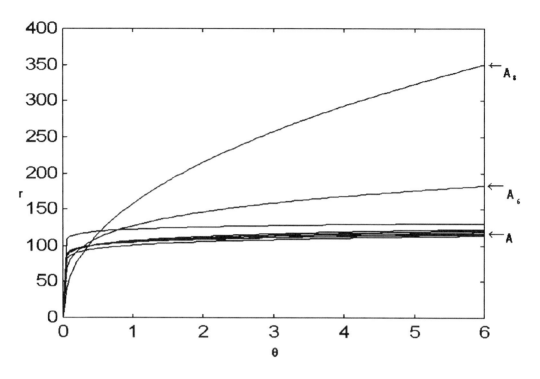

Figure 8. $r = a\theta^b$ curves for group 3 images.

Table 6. Values of a, b, and SC for Group 4 Images

Image	a	b	SC
A	100.601242	0.068428	41638.679688
A^1	104.044426	0.051274	39677.960938
A^2	104.399445	0.055026	40532.023438
A^3	104.652405	0.056577	40931.976563
A^4	103.166489	0.025091	34736.968750
A^5	102.506836	0.026176	34693.007813
A^6	101.574051	0.001589	30599.439453
A^7	99.791512	-0.003281	29379.029297

The number of false positives in the set of images returned by the index can significantly be reduced by making use of the inverted list data structure and manipulating the value of δ. Let n be the number of objects in the query image. We use the notation s_{db}^i, for $0 \le i \le n$, to refer to the database images that contain i number of objects in the query, regardless of their spatial location. Using the inverted list data structure, we can determine s_{db}^n (that is, the set of database images that contain all the objects in the query image). Let S_{index} be the set of database images returned by the index for the query. Note that the size of S_{index} is governed by the value of δ. The set $\left(s_{db}^n \cap S_{index}\right)$ gives database images that are *spatially identical* to the query.[5] We can add to this result the set $\left(s_{db}^{n-1} \cap s_{index}\right)$ to obtain images that are *spatially similar* to the query image. The number of images in the result can be further increased by adding $\left(s_{db}^{n-2} \cap s_{index}\right)$, $\left(s_{db}^{n-3} \cap s_{index}\right)$ and so on, to the result. In other words, $\left(s_{db}^{i} \cap s_{index}\right)$ can be used to control the size of the system output; this can be done automatically by the system in a transparent way to the user. Under this scheme, the cost of searching the inverted list should be added to the cost of searching the index tree.

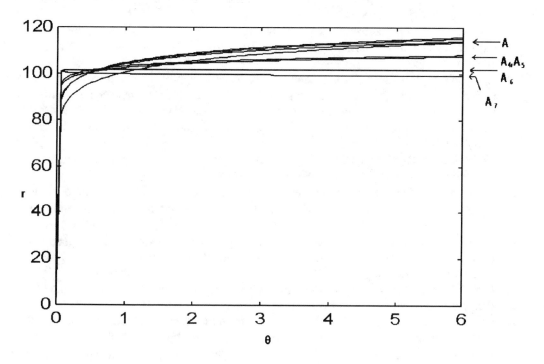

Figure 9. $r = a\theta^{b}$ curves for group 4 images.

How similar the curve of a sub-image is to the curve of the original image depends on both the number of objects removed and which objects are removed from the original image to generate the sub-image. Given a set of n objects, we have $^{n}C_{k}$ number of k-object subsets. The curves corresponding to k-object subsets need not necessarily be identical to each other. The same observation holds for super-images. One of our future research directions is to investigate this aspect to make quantitative statements about curve similarities probabilistically.

If the indexing scheme is used in conjunction with the inverted lists, the *SC* values themselves may be used to rank order database images. In other words, the indexing scheme also plays the role of a spatial similarity algorithm. This aspect merits further investigation. Another future research direction is to extend the indexing scheme to consider the spatial extent of domain objects. We will also experiment with other forms for the curves.

---

[5] Note that database images that are super-images of the query, but are not spatially identical to the query, can still be retrieved.

REFERENCES

1. Chang, C. and Lee, S., "Retrieval of similar pictures on pictorial databases," *Pattern Recognition*, 24(7):675-680, 1991.

2. Chang, S.K., Shi, Q.Y., and Yan, C.W., "Iconic indexing by 2D Strings," *IEEE Transactions on Pattern Analysis and Machine Intelligence*, 9(3):413-428, 1987.

3. Frakes, W. and Baeza-Yates, R. (editors), *Information Retrieval: Data Structures and Algorithms*, Prentice Hall, Englewood Cliffs, NJ, 1992.

4. Flickner, M. et al., "Query by image and video content: The QBIC system," *IEEE Computer*, 28(9):23-32, September 1995.

5. Gudivada, V. and Raghavan, V., "Design and evaluation of algorithms for image retrieval by spatial similarity," *ACM Transactions on Information Systems*, 13(1):115-144, April 1995.

6. Gudivada, V., Raghavan, V., and Seetharaman, G., "An approach to interactive retrieval in face image databases based on semantic attributes," in Third Annual Symposium on Document Analysis and Information Retrieval, Las Vegas, NV, 319-335, April 1994.

7. Gudivada, V. and Raghavan, V., "Content-based image retrieval systems," *IEEE Computer*, 28(9):18-22, 1995.

8. Gudivada, V. and Raghavan, V., "Modeling and retrieving images by content," *Information Processing & Management*, 33(4):427-452, 1997.

9. Gudivada, V., $\theta\Re$-string: "A geometry-based representation for efficient and effective retrieval of images by spatial similarity," To appear in *IEEE Transactions on Knowledge and Data Engineering*.

10. Hou, T.-Y. et al., "A content-based indexing technique using relative geometry features," In Storage and Retrieval for Image and Video Databases, *Proceedings of SPIE '92*, Vol. 1662, pp. 59-68, 1992.

11. Lee, S.Y. and Hsu, F.-J., "2D C-String: A new spatial knowledge representation for image database systems," *Pattern Recognition*, 23(10):1077-1087, 1990.

12. Lee, S.-Y. and Hsu, F.-J., "Spatial reasoning and similarity retrieval of images using 2D C-String knowledge representation," *Pattern Recognition*, 25(3):305-318, 1992.

13. Pentland, A., Picard, R., and Sclaroff, S., "Photobook: Tools for content-based manipulation of image databases," In Storage and Retrieval for Image and Video Databases II, *Proceedings of SPIE '94*, Vol. 2185, pp. 34-46, 1994.

14. Salton, G., *Automatic Text Processing*, Addison-Wesley, Reading, MA, 1989.

15. Samet, H., *Application of Spatial Data Structures: Computer Graphics, Image Processing and GIS*, Addison-Wesley, Reading, MA, 1990.

16. Sistla, P., Yu, C., and Haddad, R., "Reasoning about spatial relationships in picture retrieval systems," *Proceedings of VLDB*, 570-581, Santiago, Chile, 1994.

14

CLASSIFICATION AND CHARACTERIZATION OF DIGITAL WATERMARKS FOR MULTIMEDIA DATA

James Ford, Fillia Makedon, and Charles B. Owen
Dartmouth Experimental Visualization Laboratory
Dartmouth College
6211 Sudikoff Labs, Hanover, NH 03755
{jford,makedon,cowen}@cs.dartmouth.edu

1.	**INTRODUCTION**	300
2.	**RELATED APPROACHES**	301
3.	**MEDIA-SPECIFIC ISSUES**	302
	3.1 CONTINUOUS VS SAMPLED MEDIA	302
	3.2 TEMPORAL VS STATIC MEDIA	302
4.	**INSERTION OF WATERMARKS**	303
	4.1 LINEAR VS NONLINEAR WATERMARKING	303
	4.2 PERCEPTUALLY ENCODED WATERMARKS	304
	4.3 STATISTICALLY ENCODED WATERMARKS	304
	4.4 DOCUMENT DEPENDENCY	305
	4.5 INTERFERENCE	305
5.	**DETECTION OF WATERMARKS**	306
	5.1 KEY AND ORIGINAL MEDIA	306
	5.2 KEY ONLY	307
	5.3 PUBLIC KEY ONLY	307
6.	**INVERTIBILITY**	308
7.	**OTHER ISSUES IN WATERMARKING**	309
	7.1 BENCHMARKS OF RECOVERABILITY	309
	7.2 QUANTIFYING PERCEPTIBILITY AND DEGRADATION	309
8.	**CONCLUSIONS**	310
	REFERENCES	312

0-8493-1825-4/99/$0.00+$.50
© 1999 by CRC Press LLC

Abstract. *Digital watermarking*[1] is the insertion of hidden and encoded information in a media document (e.g., images, video, and audio) for the purpose of copyright protection and proof of ownership. This chapter introduces a formal categorization scheme for digital watermarks based on several fundamental issues in their design, insertion, and detection. These issues—*media type, linearity, document dependency, inter-watermark interference, detection parameters*, and the use of *perceptual* and *statistical encoding*—are discussed in detail and used to categorize more than two dozen watermarking techniques. Our categorization scheme extends some of the properties that have been used previously in the discussion of watermarks and is intended to facilitate objective classifications in the comparison and analysis of watermarking techniques.

1. INTRODUCTION

The growing use of digital storage and transmission for images, audio, and video materials has the potential to cause many copyright problems. Digital materials are extremely easy to copy, and copies can be modified with very simple techniques (e.g., brightness adjustments in images) so that the copying is not detectable using simple file comparisons. Content providers and authors using digital media are concerned that this fact places their intellectual property in jeopardy when it is distributed publicly.

Digital watermarking is an emerging enabling technology that promises to assist in the establishment of intellectual ownership for digital media. Two major approaches exist: perceptible and imperceptible. *Perceptible watermarking systems*, like IBM's "visible watermarking technique" [1,2], add visible but difficult-to-remove patterns to images. *Imperceptible watermarking systems* insert the same kind of robust "information stamps" in forms that are difficult to detect onto various types of media. Watermarks of both types allow owners of digital media to prove the origin of copies and modified copies of their work. The three current applications of this idea are proofs of ownership, traces of distribution paths, and inclusion of "tag information." The latter can include public information like copyright notices or private information like copy prohibition tags, and is "universal" in that it doesn't require a fixed distribution format. The proliferation of the World Wide Web has motivated watermarking research, and new techniques are emerging every few months. For the remainder of this chapter, we consider only the more difficult and newer problem of using imperceptible digital watermarks.

Another distinction of sub-areas is made by Podilchuk and Zeng [3], who use the terms "destination-based" and "source-based" watermarking applications. *Destination-based watermarks* in their definition are those used for tracking different copies of a document after distribution. *Source-based watermarks* are those used for authenticating the source of a particular document; this is useful for detecting changes in media files, such as photographic retouching in a digital image [4]. Most authors use the terms "digital watermarking" to refer exclusively to destination-based systems, and we follow that convention. Source authentication techniques are similar in overall spirit, but they differ in having an intentional susceptibility to distortion that runs counter to the design principles of destination-based watermarks. Because of this difference in design principles, we consider only destination-based approaches when we use the term "watermarking" in this chapter.

---

[1] Some authors prefer the terms "labels" or "digital signatures" for multimedia watermarks, since those terms are not specific to images and do not seem to imply easily perceptible changes in documents. We propose the term "multimedia signatures" to avoid confusion with cryptographic signatures.

The problem of watermarking is conceptually simple: encode an undetectable signal in an existing media document[2] in such a way that it is recoverable only by parties in possession of its "key." All watermarking techniques work by introducing a signal that appears as noise into a media document. In some techniques, this signal only resembles noise as a side effect; in others, the signal is deliberately designed to resemble "natural" noise. Unfortunately, the task of devising watermarks that are robust to compression, common document manipulations, and outright attacks is not easy. The watermark signal should resist degradation, both from ordinary media manipulations and from purposeful efforts to erase it.

Digital watermarks are similar in spirit to traditional paper-based watermarks: both are intended as nearly imperceptible superposing of additional information on a document. The difference is that traditional watermarks are attached to a particular *document*, while digital watermarks are attached to the *information* itself. Traditional watermarks are not transferred by most copies—whether a scribe's copy of an ancient manuscript or a photocopier's copy of a typewritten document on watermarked paper. Digital watermarks, referred to simply as "watermarks" for the remainder of this chapter, are designed to be transferred by copying.

Digital watermarking is a sub-area of steganography, or data hiding, in which secret signals are embedded into public ones. The defining factor is the lack of secrecy concerning the *existence* of the watermark signal (or "covert channel" in the terminology of the cryptographic community). Since the existence of watermarks is not assumed to be secret, ensuring their robustness is as important as hiding them well [5,6] The general intention is to make the watermark *locations* secret, so that they are computationally infeasible to detect, and thus difficult to separate from the data they accompany [7]. Digital watermarking is a very new area, with the earliest work barely a decade old [8,9,10,11,12].

Existing watermarking techniques, despite sharing the same basic goals, exhibit tremendous variety in their design. These differences can make direct comparisons difficult. There are, however, some basic issues that all methods must address. In an attempt to develop a formal method for watermark classification, this chapter presents design considerations based on (a) the choice of media, (b) the insertion process, and (c) the detection process. The next three sections correspond to these three types of design criteria. In addition, more than two dozen watermarking techniques have been selected from the literature and classified under a set of fundamental design criteria. These results are summarized in Table 1.

2. RELATED APPROACHES

The problem of copyright protection is not new, and several different approaches to protecting digital documents have been proposed. Most have centered around proposals in the audio industry to protect digital recordings and cryptographic systems for preventing unauthorized access to documents.

The audio industry has long advocated standards for *copy prevention*. Copy prevention systems like DiscGuard [13] work by attaching a "label" to digital media that is similar to a watermark. Unlike watermarks, copy prevention labels are not mixed with media data and thus are lost in processes like compression and digital-to-analog conversion. Special "compliant" hardware may prevent digital copies from being made if the labels are present, but "non-compliant" hardware can be designed that will not have this restriction.

Other systems, like IBM's "cryptolopes" [14], use cryptography to protect documents and hinder unauthorized use. Each digital document is stored in a protected form for distribution, with executable functions included for extracting or viewing the original data given the correct key. Cryptolopes may allow only a subset of access rights—e.g., previewing

---

[2]The term "media document" is used to denote any self-contained piece of sampled digital information, such as an image, graphically presented or scanned text, or a video or audio segment.

an image but not saving it at full resolution—but once access is granted, a clever user can distribute unprotected copies with no access restrictions.

Watermarks address the limitations of copy prevention and cryptographic-based systems. Since watermarks are embedded directly in the documents they protect, there is no need for special hardware to ensure that watermarks are included in copies, and thus no problem with non-compliant copy devices. For the same reason, watermarks are resistant to conversions to analog form and compression. Watermarks do not need to be removed to make a document useful, as encryption does, and therefore can continue to protect documents after distribution. There is some possibility that watermarks can be made detectable and yet not easily removable using techniques from public-key cryptography; this is covered in Section 5.3.

3. MEDIA-SPECIFIC ISSUES

The nature of the media involved is important in the design of watermarking techniques. A technique that works well for one medium may not necessarily work well for another, although ideally it should be insensitive to specific document formats within its media type. In this section we present two primary media distinctions: digital vs analog and static vs temporal.

Watermarking different media successfully with the same algorithm is extremely difficult because of the differences in how different media are perceived. The degree to which a document transformation affects perceptibility in one medium may not correspond to its affect in any other. Some common transformations, like time expansion with pitch correction in audio or color histogram equalization in images, have no obvious analogy in other media. A watermark designed to survive a set of transformations in one domain may not have the same success in another, where the effects of transformations on perceptibility is different—for example, transformations that would be impossible without ruining the quality of an audio track may result in acceptably small changes when applied to images.

3.1 CONTINUOUS VS SAMPLED MEDIA

Media documents occur in two fundamentally different forms: continuous (analog) and sampled (digital). Normally watermarks are inserted in digital media, but analog counterparts are feasible. Modern digital watermarks are designed with the aim of resistance to common media transformations, including digital-to-analog (D/A) and analog-to-digital (A/D) conversions. If a digital watermark survives a conversion to analog form and back, then an analog counterpart of the digital watermark exists in the analog version. The remainder of this chapter deals exclusively with watermarks of digital media documents, but the ideas apply to analog documents and analog watermarks as well.

All of the systems in Table 1 are intended to operate on sampled (digital) media. All but the systems based on least significant bit encoding [7,12] have an analog counterpart by the survivability argument above: if a digital watermark can survive through a transformation of its document to an analog version and back, then the analog version necessarily contains the watermark in an analog form.

3.2 TEMPORAL VS STATIC MEDIA

Watermarking temporal media—media that change with time, such as audio and video—is a newer and more challenging area of digital watermarking. There are important considerations in designing watermarking algorithms for temporal media that make them more complex than algorithms for static media. For example, since digital video can be viewed as a sequence of static images, it might seem natural to apply image watermarking techniques to each image in the sequence. The problem with this approach is that small changes used to encode a watermark in a single image may become much easier to find when other images in the sequence are available to provide statistical correlations. Furthermore, watermarks in temporal media need to be resistant to additional transformations; for example, interpolation between video frames may eliminate watermarks encoded using image watermarking techniques on each frame.

The majority of the systems in Table 1 are mono-media techniques. Those that claim to be appropriate for all media (e.g., [15,16]), typically have a significant media-specific component. The one exception is the system in [12], which encodes watermarks in the least significant bits of an arbitrary bytestream. Clearly, this scheme will work for any media document, but, as noted above, it does not have an analog counterpart and is susceptible to D/A, A/D conversions and resampling. It is also one of the easiest methods to attack since random bit changes can obliterate the watermark completely.

4. INSERTION OF WATERMARKS

In this section we present an overview of some of the important distinguishing features of watermarks and watermarking techniques: *Linear* vs *nonlinear* watermarking, *Perceptual encoding, Statistical encoding, Document independence,* and *Interference.* Cox and Miller [5] present a similar overview using the categories of *Difficulty to notice, Robustness, Tamper-resistance, Bit rate, Modification and multiple watermarks,* and *Scalability.* We do not evaluate algorithms on any of the latter categories except "Modification and multiple watermarks" (our "interference" property) because only highly subjective classifications would be possible.

4.1 LINEAR VERSUS NONLINEAR WATERMARKING

Watermarking technologies can be divided into linear and nonlinear categories based on how the watermark is inserted. Linear watermarking techniques are those in which the watermark and the watermarked document can be related to the original document using a linear equation. This is a broad class of techniques and includes transform and additive techniques. Nonlinear techniques are less common and can include techniques that use statistical and probabilistic measures to determine how the watermarked document differs from the original. Both classes are described in more detail below.

4.1.1 LINEAR INSERTION OF WATERMARKS

A linear media watermarking technology applies a watermark using a linear operation on the digital media. Linear watermarking techniques can be expressed with the following equation:

$$\mu^* = T^{-1}(\text{diag}(\alpha)\, T\mu + \beta) \tag{1}$$

This equation applies a precalculated watermark $<\alpha, \beta>$, represented as two column vectors, to a finite media object represented by the column vector μ (images and other higher dimensional media can be decomposed into a single dimension through concatenation). The matrix T is an invertible transformation matrix and μ^* is the watermarked media object. Systems have been proposed which use various transformation matrices, including discrete Fourier transforms and discrete cosine transforms. It is also possible for T to be the identity transform, in which case watermark encoding and decoding operate directly on the media data.

The watermark is represented using the column vectors α and β; α is the multiplicative component and β is the additive component. Systems which are only multiplicative in nature will have $\beta = [0, 0, ..., 0]^T$. Systems which are only additive in nature will have $\alpha = [1, 1, ..., 1]^T$.

By a simple algebraic manipulation

$$\mu^* = T^{-1} \, diag(\alpha) \, T\mu + T^{-1}\beta \tag{2}$$

Hence, for any transform-based additive system there is an identical non-transform additive system—it can be created by simply applying the inverse transformation T^{-1} to the additive component:

$$\mu^* = \mu + T^{-1}\beta \tag{3}$$

A specific example of a linear technique from Table 1 is Caronni's "image tags" method [17], in which the pixel intensities of selected regions are adjusted by some small amount.

4.1.2 NONLINEAR INSERTION OF WATERMARKS

Nonlinear watermarking techniques are any that cannot be expressed in the form of Equation 1. An example is encoding information by altering all or some least significant bits, or by perturbing data values in some probabilistic way based on a watermark signal. In the case of images, for example, pixel intensity values can be expected to be closely correlated with their neighbors, so significant deviations introduced by manipulations can be effective in hiding information. By using more than one set of pixels, a binary string can be encoded over an image (see, for an example, Kutter [18]). This idea can also be extended to apply to the coefficients of a document in a transform domain.

Very few techniques use nonlinear insertion; a specific example of a nonlinear technique is least significant bit encoding [12]. The technique is nonlinear because a given byte is replaced only if its least significant bit is "incorrect" for some watermark; otherwise, it is left alone.

4.2 PERCEPTUALLY ENCODED WATERMARKS

Theoretically, watermarks can be inserted using any method and stored using any variation in the original data. In practice, however, there are practical limitations on the range of techniques. The documents that watermarks are used to protect are media files, and watermarks must avoid making large degradations in their quality. In addition, watermarks should avoid making changes only in "imperceptible" data; for if they do, these changes may be lost completely to compression, alteration, or outright attack without any loss in document quality. Small changes in "perceptible" data, such as brightness levels in an image, may result in changes that do not noticeably degrade the quality of the original document and yet are not easy to remove without assistance or large losses in quality. This point illustrates the importance of *perceptual modeling*, an aspect that is also discussed in [5].

Some techniques for watermarking utilize what can be called "perceptual holes"—parts of a media document that are not very perceptible to humans, like high frequencies in images (textures) and some aspects of phase in audio (as used, e.g., in the echo hiding technique [19]).[3] The problem with this approach is that "lossy" compression algorithms are steadily encroaching on this kind of information, and current holes are not guaranteed to be open in the future.

Most of the systems in Table 1 employ some perceptual modeling. Some authors (e.g., [19]) have added perceptual models to existing systems to improve their performance, thereby confirming the importance of such models.

---

[3]Phase in audio is the offset of a waveform in time.

4.3 STATISTICALLY ENCODED WATERMARKS

We call techniques that rely on aggregate measures of a document *statistical* techniques. These measures can be over the entire document, as with perturbations of Fourier components [20,21], or they can be over a small part, as with local pixel brightness adjustments [18,19]. Statistically encoded watermarks are useful for creating watermarks that can be detected without access to an original document (Section 5.2) because they naturally support non-localized and redundant encoding. These features also increase their resistance to compression and other transformations that may result in watermark loss.

About half of the systems included in Table 1 employ some statistical modeling.

4.4 DOCUMENT DEPENDENCY

The choice of position of a digital watermark, whether in space, time, frequency, or elsewhere, is made either dependent on or independent of the document. Perceptual watermarking techniques (Section 4.1) may insert data in locations determined by properties of the document, or by general expectations of perceptual ranges (e.g., human-audible frequencies in an audio recording). Statistical watermarking techniques (Section 4.3) may choose the location of the watermark independently of the specific document by adding a known pattern (e.g., the Patchwork technique [19] or Caronni's image tags [17]) or may alter statistical properties of the document's data. The majority of the systems in Table 1 are what we call *document-dependent*.

	Independent	Dependent
Linear	Scaling first 1000 DCT coefficients	Scaling 1000 largest DCT coefficients [20, 21]
Non-Linear	Least significant bit (LSB) encoding [12]	LSB encoding for the 10% most significant elements

Figure 1. Independence versus linearity. Examples show how two published watermarking algorithms are classified by document independence and linearity. Variations of the algorithms are also shown to illustrate the remaining combinations of these two properties.

Cox and Miller [5] use the term "linear insertion" in images for what is called document-independent encoding; in their case, the term "linear" comes from the fact that the watermarked image is a linear combination of the original data and a watermark signal. Cox and Miller's "non-linear insertion" encoding, which they describe as "shaping the watermark to the spectrum of the image," symmetrically corresponds to our document-dependent encoding. The particular technique of this latter class that they describe [20,21], which scales selected Fourier components, we class as a linear generation method (Section 4.1.1). Figure 1 gives examples of each of the four combinations of the independence and linearity properties. Separating independence and linearity makes classifications easier in some cases, and also distinguishes two fundamentally different ideas: how a watermark is generated and how it is inserted.

4.5 INTERFERENCE

It is possible that multiple watermarks applied to the same media document may interfere with each other. Depending on the encoding method, a watermark may use the same "places" in its host document, whether in space, time, frequency, or elsewhere, as others added before it. If this happens, a common result is that the newest watermark partially or completely obliterates the older ones; we call this "interference."

Ideally one would like watermarks to be completely non-interfering, so that an arbitrary number can be overlaid. In practice, good techniques seem to be able to support up to perhaps five to ten overlaid watermarks before degradation in document quality or actual interference makes adding more infeasible. Interference constrains the usefulness of watermarks by restricting the number of parties that can add their own mark to a document. It can also be a vulnerability: a clever attacker may be able to destroy an existing watermark by inserting a new one encoded with the same technique.

The majority of the systems in Table 1 are non-interfering to the extent that they allow at least a few watermarks to be inserted with the same technique. Since each watermark insertion adds noise to the original document, it is not possible for independently inserted watermarks to be arbitrarily non-interfering; there is a limit to the number of times that watermarks can perturb or replace the original document's information without destroying the original document.

5. DETECTION OF WATERMARKS

Another major criterion of classification is the method by which a watermark is detected. Watermark techniques can be divided into three categories based on their detection requirements and methods: *key and original*, *key only*, and *public key only*. The first two of these are in use in various systems, while the third is proposed here and elsewhere as a potentially useful watermarking technique but has not yet been widely used.

5.1 KEY AND ORIGINAL MEDIA

Techniques which encode a watermark by making small alterations in the original media file often require the original as a baseline for detection (Figure 2). If the changes are small and independent of the data, then, without some way of determining where changes were made, no useful watermark information can be extracted from the watermarked document—even if the method of insertion is known.

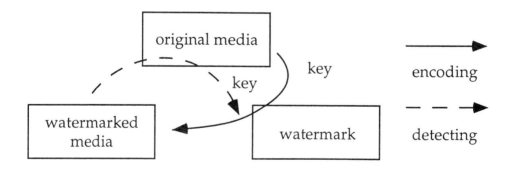

Figure 2. Key and original media detection. Encoding uses the original data (optionally) and a key to generate a watermark, which is combined with the original data to produce a watermarked version. Detection uses the original data to extract a potential watermark from a suspected derivative of the watermarked version; this is then analyzed with the key to determine if it is a valid watermark.

This type of technique, which has been referred to as *cover image escrow* in the image domain [22], has the advantages of being easy to implement and highly resistant to distortion. One disadvantage is that an unmodified copy of each document must be stored, doubling storage requirements. Parties wishing to verify the existence of a watermark need access to the unmodified original document, making verification by anyone other than the original owner or distributor complicated. Another disadvantage is that escrow techniques provide essentially no proof of origin in legal disputes because false originals can easily be "faked" (see Section 6). As a consequence of these drawbacks, only a minority of the systems in Table 1 require the original document for watermark detection.

5.2 KEY ONLY

Storing an unmodified version of every watermarked document and providing it to anyone who wishes to read the watermark is clearly undesirable. A more advanced technique (Figure 3) is to make the watermark readable even *without* access to the unmodified original. For example, in images, pixel luminance statistics might be manipulated in a known pattern [18] and, in audio, a special repeating signal might be superimposed over an audio segment. Changes are sometimes related to the original document, as in Section 5.1, and may be detectable only by statistical measurement (Section 4.3) or may be added independent of the structure of the media document.

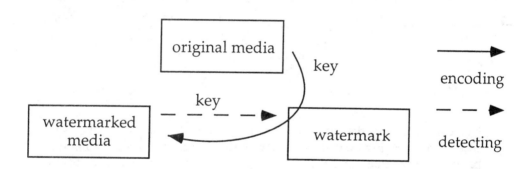

Figure 3. Key only detection. The encoding process uses the original data (optionally) and a key to generate a watermark, which is combined with the original data to make a watermarked version. Detection uses only the key to determine if a document contains a watermark corresponding to that key.

Key-only detection has clear advantages over the original document-based methods described in Section 5.1. It avoids the problems associated with storing extra copies of all watermarked documents; it avoids the legal indefensibility mentioned in Section 6; and it allows the potential for any party supplied with a key to verify a watermark. Its major remaining limitation, which is addressed by the public key watermarks described in Section 5.3, is that users cannot be granted the ability to detect watermarks without giving away a great deal of information about how to eradicate it. The majority of the systems in Table 1 are key-only techniques.

5.3 PUBLIC KEY ONLY

In order to read a watermark, it seems obvious that one must first know something about how or where it is encoded. This is an undesirable situation—it implies that distributing information about how to read a watermark may equate to distributing information about how to destroy it.

A solution to this problem is to use ideas from public key cryptography. In a public key system like RSA, a pair of keys replaces the single key of traditional encryption. Information encrypted with one key can only be decrypted by the other, and knowledge of either key gives no information about its companion.

To apply this idea to digital media, some modifications are necessary (Figure 4). Since traditional encryption transforms data in a completely arbitrary way, ideally using every bit of the data as an input, there is no correlation between the unencrypted and encrypted versions. Unfortunately, this is a problem in this application: adding a small watermark signal in an encrypted set of coefficients may cause large changes in the coefficients (and result in large changes in the original media file). Any changes that are introduced need to result in small changes in the original data, meaning that there must be some correlation between the data and the encoded watermark. As a result, this technique could probably only be used as a tactic for discouraging attacks, not as a completely safe encoding method.

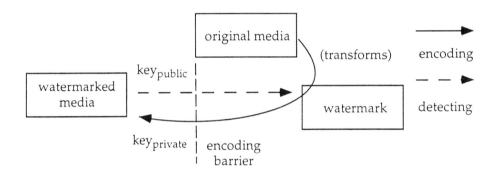

Figure 4. Public key detection. An "encoding barrier" similar to a public key encryption system is used to protect the watermark. Instead of using a symmetric key for both encoding and detecting the watermark, a complementary pair of keys (as in public-key cryptography) might be used to allow detection of watermarks without easy eradication of them.

The idea of asymmetric encoders and detectors is also suggested in [19], [5], and [23]. None of the systems in Table 1 are public-key-only techniques. Hartung and Girod [24] presented the first prototype of such a method that we are aware of, what makes public parts of a private pseudo-noise key for MPEG video. Their approach is similar to encoding two separate watermarks, one public and one private, and does not yet fully protect the "public" part.

6. INVERTIBILITY

An important legal problem for any watermarking system is the degree to which a watermark it encodes can be "trusted." For example, if the odds of a particular watermark pattern occurring by chance are not acceptably small, then the system may suffer from "false positive" detections of watermarks that were not inserted.

The "invertibility problem" presented by [23,25] is a high-level problem with watermark authentication. If a watermark can be encoded with an easily reversible transform and if there are no restrictions on the format of the watermark, then anyone can claim any random noise in any data is a "watermark" by simply computing the inverse of the watermark encoding transform on that noise. Original media-based techniques (Section 5.1) are always vulnerable to inversion attacks because in principle an "original" document can be constructed to match any watermark [26].

Which watermark techniques exhibit this problem? It seems that every one will, but the problem can be minimized (eventually to an acceptable level) by requiring non-random watermark strings and by increasing the complexity of the encoding; this reduces the fraction of combinations in "watermark space" that are legal encoding. Another alternative is to require using an official registry of watermarks if they are to be admitted as legal proofs [23]. As the invertibility problem becomes more widely understood and acknowledged, techniques may develop such that an additional column in our table labeled "Invertible" will be warranted.

7. OTHER ISSUES IN WATERMARKING

The previous four sections have described a number of useful properties for qualitative comparisons of watermarking systems. A more complete classification system should include the ability to make quantitative comparisons as well. Each of the systems listed in the table do report performance statistics from *ad hoc* experiments but comparing these statistics is far from straightforward. We describe here a few possibilities for facilitating quantitative comparisons based on the level of distortion a watermark can survive and the degree to which it perceptibly alters a document.

7.1 BENCHMARKS ON RECOVERABILITY

A good watermarking technique is one that resists attacks; that is, the watermark is still recoverable after the watermarked document is somehow modified. However, attacks can vary in severity from the unintentional to the malicious. One can imagine creating a benchmark set of attacks for testing. Each attack might be labeled as either "unintentional" or "hostile" (it need not be a binary distinction). Researchers and corporations could then report their technique's success under each kind of attack. Potential users of the technology could then make informed decisions based on their needs.

Different benchmark sets would be needed for each media type. We present here some possibilities for image, video, and audio benchmarks. The parameters for these attacks could be standardized, allowing researchers to report relevant data (e.g., false positives, false negatives) which can be compared directly with other techniques.

Images: A standard set of attacks on images might include the following manipulations: rotation, cropping, low-pass filtering, scaling, dithering, resampling, color reduction, JPEG compression, and compositing.

Video: A standard set of attacks on video might include some of the same attacks as on images but should also include manipulations to MPEG data streams due to their ubiquity. Specifically, attacks that involve frame interpolation should be included.

Audio: A standard set of attacks on audio might include low-pass filtering, dynamic compression and expansion, data compression, resampling, time scaling (independent of pitch scaling) and pitch scaling (independent of time scaling), collapsing stereo signals to mono, and mixing.

7.2 QUANTIFYING PERCEPTIBILITY AND DEGRADATION

Another means of providing quantitative data on a watermarking technique is to measure its "perceptual resilience." This can be defined as the loss of quality that would be introduced by whatever transformations are needed to completely erase a watermark. Watermark encoding typically results in potential variations of many parameters of the original document, most of which are not actually modified or are changed less than the maximum possible modification. In order to be absolutely certain of destroying the watermark, an attacker with knowledge of the encoding technique must assume that *all* such parameters were modified [16]. Smaller modifications can be made with a decreasing certainty that a hypothetically present watermark will still be detectable.

If the encoding process places the watermark at the limit of the "perceptual capacity" of the document, that is, the point beyond which the watermark noticeably degrades the document (given some criteria for "noticeable degradation"), then the attacker must degrade the original document's quality in order to remove the watermark. Placing the watermark at the perceptual capacity of the document also guards against the problems associated with improving compression techniques discussed in Section 4.1. In order to successfully place the watermark at the bounds of perceptibility, reliable methods of measuring the perceptual capacity of a document are needed. Some techniques do attempt this (e.g., [27,16]) but there is room for improvement especially for dynamic media where the temporal limits of perception are less well understood.

8. CONCLUSIONS

The trend toward the distribution of digital media documents stimulates research toward the development of methods for protecting copyrights. Digital watermarks are a promising technology toward ensuring that these rights are protected. There have been many approaches to digital watermarks and new ones are introduced regularly. With the wide variety of methods it becomes difficult to adequately compare and contrast them. This chapter has introduced a formal means for categorizing watermarking techniques based on *media, linearity, document dependency, inter-watermark interference, detection parameters*, and the use of *perceptual* and *statistical encoding*. More than two dozen contemporary watermarking methods from the literature have been classified using this system. We hope that this scheme will be useful to encourage further discussion about the fundamental issues underlying digital watermarking.

At the present time, no watermarking system can insert watermarks robust enough to survive all efforts to remove them. Even without such systems, however, watermarking remains useful. Most users of digital content are not sophisticated enough to remove watermarks reliably without expert assistance, and those that are will be required to expend some effort to do so. These factors, coupled with the indicators that visible watermarks can provide, make watermarks a useful technological advance for copyright protection.

Table 1 presents a representative sample of existing watermarking techniques. The first column lists the authors of the technique, reference citations, and a brief description of the technique. The second column lists the media type demonstrated in the cited reference(s). The third column characterizes the method used to detect the presence of a given watermark (Section 5). The fourth and fifth columns indicate whether the technique employs perceptual (Section 4.1) and statistical (Section 4.3) techniques, respectively. The sixth column lists whether the position of the watermark is document-dependent (Section 4.4). The seventh column lists whether the technique does *not* allow for multiple watermarks being encoded in the same document because of the possibility of inter-watermark interference (Section 4.5). The final column lists whether the insertion procedure is linear (Section 4.5) or not.

Table 1. Comparison of Existing Watermarking Systems

System	Media	Detection	Perceptual	Statistical	Dependence	Interference	Linear
Aura 96 [7] *Permutations of cover bits*	Images	Key + Original	No	No	Yes	Yes	No
Bender et al. 96 [19] *Patchwork – Pixel Value Adjustment*	Images	Key	Yes	Yes	No	No	Yes
Bender et al. 96 [19] *Texture Block*	Images	Key	Yes	No	Yes	No	No
Bender et al. 96 [19] *Echo Hiding*	Audio	Key	Yes	No	Yes	Yes	Yes
Bender et al. 96 [19] *Phase Encoding*	Audio	Key	Yes	No	Yes	Yes	No
Boney et al. 96 [27] *Filtered PN Sequences*	Audio	Key + Original	Yes	No	Yes	No	Yes
Brassil et al. 94, 95 [28, 29] *Character/Line Respacing*	Scanned Text	Key	No	Yes	Yes	Yes	Yes
Bruyndonckx et al. [30] *Luminance Modification*	Images	Key	Yes	Yes	Yes	No	No
Caronni 95 [17] *Adjusted Brightness in Rectangles*	Images	Key + Original	Yes	No	Yes	No	Yes
Cox et al. 95, 96 [16,20,21] *Most-Significant DFT Modification*	General	Key + Original	Yes	Yes	Yes	No	Yes
Digimarc PictureMarc [15] *Fourier-Mellin Transform*	Images	Key + Original	Yes	Yes	Yes	No	Yes
Fleet & Heeger 97 [31] *Sine Wave Grid*	Images	Key + Original	Yes	Yes	Yes	Yes	No
Hartung & Girod 96, 97 [32, 33, 34] *Alter DCT Coefficients*	Video	Key	Yes	No	Yes	Yes	Yes
Koch & Zhao 95 [35] JPEG/DCT *Coefficient Manipulation*	Images/ Video	Key	Yes	Yes	No	No	Yes
Kutter et al. 97 [18] *Pixel Value Adjustments*	Images	Key	Yes	Yes	Yes	No	Yes
Langelaar et al. 96, 97 [36, 37, 38] *DCT Modification*	Video	Key	Yes	No	No	Yes	No
Langelaar et al. 96, 97 [36, 37] *Luminance Modification*	Images	Key	Yes	Yes	No	No	Yes
Nikolaidis & Pitas 96 [39] *Pixel Value Modification*	Images	Key	No	Yes	No	No	Yes
Ó Ruanaidh 96 [40] *DFT Phase Modification*	Images	Key	Yes	Yes	Yes	No	Yes
Ó Ruanaidh 97 [41] *Fourier-Mellin Transform*	Images	Key	Yes	Yes	Yes	No	Yes
Piva et al. 97 [42] *DFT Subrange Modification*	Images	Key	Yes	Yes	Yes	No	Yes
Puate & Jordan 96 [43] *Fractal Coding*	Images	Key	No	Yes	Yes	Yes	No

van Schyndel et al. 94 [12] *Least Significant Bit*	General	Key	No	No	No	Yes	No
Swanson et al. 96 [44, 45] *Filtered PN Sequences*	Images	Key + Original	Yes	No	Yes	No	Yes
Swanson et al. 97 [46] *Object-Centered Perceptual Encoding*	Video	Key + Original	Yes	Yes	Yes	Yes	Yes
Smith & Comiskey 96 [22] *Pixel Value Adjustment*	Images	Key	Yes	Yes	Yes	No	Yes
Tao & Dickinson [47] *Alter DCT Coefficients*	Images	Key + Original	Yes	No	Yes	Yes	No
Voyatzis & Pitas 96, 97 [48, 49, 50] *Chaotic Mixing*	Images	Key	No	Yes (97)	No	No	No
Wolfgang & Delp 96 [51] *Pixel Value Adjustment*	Images	Key	Yes	Yes	No	No	Yes

REFERENCES

1. Gladney, H. M., Mintzer, F., and Schiattarella, F., "Safeguarding digital library contents and users: Digital images of treasured antiquities," *D-Lib Magazine*, July/August 1997.
2. Mintzer, F. C., Boyle, L. E., Cazes, A. N., Christian, B. S., Cox, S. C., Giordano, F. P., Gladney, H. M., Lee, J. C., Kelmanson, M. L., Lirani, A. C., Magerlein, K. A., Pavani, A. M. B., and Schiattarella, F., "Toward on-line, worldwide access to Vatican library materials," *IBM Journal of Research & Development*, 40(2), 1996.
3. Podilchuk, C. I. and Zeng, W., "Perceptual watermarking of still images," Electronic Proceedings of the IEEE Signal Processing Society 1997 Workshop on Multimedia Signal Processing, Princeton, New Jersey, June 1997.
4. Zhu, B., Swanson, M. D., and Tewfik, A. H., "A transparent authentication and distortion measurement technique for images," 7th IEEE Digital Signal Processing Workshop, pp. 45-48, 1996.
5. Cox, I. J. and Miller, M. L., "A review of watermarking and the importance of perceptual modeling," Proceedings of Electronic Imaging '97, February 1997.
6. Zhao, J., "Look, it's not there," *Byte*, 401S(7), January 1997.
7. Aura, T., "Practical invisibility in digital communication," Proceedings of the Workshop on Information Hiding, Number 1174 in Lecture Notes in Computer Science, Cambridge, England, May 1996.
8. Holt, L., Maufe, B. G., and Wiener, A., "Encoded marking of a recording signal," U.K. Patent no. GB 2196167A, 1988.
9. Adelson, E. H., "Digital signal encoding and decoding apparatus," US Patent No. 4,939,515, 1990.
10. Tow, R. and Bloomberg, D., "Adaptive scaling for decoding spatially periodic self-clocking glyph shape codes," U.S. Patent No. 5,091,966, February 1992.
11. Tow, R., "Methods and means for embedding machine readable digital data in halftone images," US Patent no. 5,315,098, 1994.
12. Van Schyndel, R. G., Tirkel, A. Z., and Osborne, C. F., "A digital watermark," IEEE International Conference on Image Processing (ICIP'96), Vol. II, pp. 86-90, Los Alamitos, CA, 1994.

13. Sollish, B. D., "Enhanced data hiding system using DiscGuard technology: A proposal to the Data Hiding Subgroup of the Copy Protection Technical Working Group," TTR Technologies, Kfar-Saba, Israel, September 1997.

14. Moeller, M., "'DataBolts' turn content into applets to deliver data without leaving web site," *PC Week*, January 13, 1997.

15. Digimarc Corporation, "Identification/authentication coding method and apparatus," U.S. Patent no. 5,636,292, June 1997.

16. Cox, I. J., and Kilian, J., and Leighton, T., and Shamoon, T., "Secure spread spectrum watermarking for multimedia," Technical Report 95-10, NEC Research Institute, 1995.

17. Caronni, G., "Assuring ownership rights for digital images," H. H. Brueggemann and W. Gerhardt-Haeckl (editors), Proceedings of Reliable IT Systems VIS '95, Germany, 1995.

18. Kutter, M., Jordan, F., and Bossen, F., "Digital signature of color images using amplitude modulation," Proceedings of SPIE Storage and Retrieval for Image and Video Databases, Vol. 3022, pp. 518-526, San Jose, California, 1997.

19. Bender, W., Gruhl, D., Morimoto, N., and Lu, A., "Techniques for data hiding," *IBM Systems Journal*, 35(3&4):313-336, 1996.

20. Cox, I. J., and Kilian, J., and Leighton, T., and Shamoon, T., "A secure, robust watermark for multimedia," Workshop on Information Hiding, Newton Institute, University of Cambridge, May 1996.

21. Cox, I. J., and Kilian, J., and Leighton, T., and Shamoon, T., "Secure spread spectrum watermarking for images, audio, and video," IEEE International Conference on Image Processing (ICIP'96), Vol. III, pp. 243-246.

22. Smith, J. R. and Comiskey, B. O., "Modulation and information hiding in images," Workshop on Information Hiding, Volume 1174 of Springer-Verlag Lecture Notes in Computer Science, Isaac Newton Institute, University of Cambridge, U.K., May 1996.

23. Craver, Scott, Memon, Nasir, Yeo, Boon-Lock, and Yeung, Minerva, "Can invisible watermarks resolve rightful ownerships?," Technical Report RC 20509, IBM Research Division, July 1996.

24. Hartung, Frank and Girod, Bernd, "Fast public-key watermarking of compressed video," IEEE Signal Processing Society 1997 International Conference on Image Processing (ICIP'97), Santa Barbara, California, October 1997.

25. Craver, Scott, Memon, Nasir, Yeo, Boon-Lock, and Yeung, Minerva, "On the invertibility of invisible watermarking techniques," IEEE Signal Processing Society 1997 International Conference on Image Processing (ICIP'97), Santa Barbara, California, October 1997.

26. Zeng, W. and Liu, B., "On resolving rightful ownerships of digital images by invisible watermarks," IEEE Signal Processing Society 1997 International Conference on Image Processing (ICIP'97), Santa Barbara, California, October 1997.

27. Boney, Laurence, Tewfik, Ahmed H., and Hamdy, Khaled N., "Digital watermarks for audio signals," 1996 IEEE Int. Conference on Multimedia Computing and Systems, pp. 473-480, Hiroshima, Japan, 1996.

28. Brassil, J., Low, S., Maxemchuk, N., and O'Gorman, L., "Electronic marking and identification techniques to discourage document copying," Proceedings of Infocom '94, pp. 1278-1287, June 1994.

29. Low, S. H., Maxemchuk, N. F., Brassil, J. T., and O'Gorman, L., "Document marking and identification using both line and word shifting," Infocom '95, Boston, MA, April 1995.

30. Bruyndonckx, O., Quisquater, J.-J., and Macq, B., "Spatial method for copyright labeling of digital images," Nonlinear Signal Processing Workshop, pp. 456-459, Thessaloniki, Greece, 1995.

31. Fleet, D. J. and Heeger, D. J., "Embedding invisible information in color images," IEEE Signal Processing Society 1997 International Conference on Image Processing (ICIP'97), Santa Barbara, California, October 1997.

32. Hartung, F. and Girod, B., "Digital watermarking of raw and compressed video," Proceedings European EOS/SPIE Symposium on Advanced Imaging and Network Technologies, Berlin, Germany, October 1996.

33. Hartung, F. and Girod, B., "Copyright protection in video delivery networks by watermarking of pre-compressed video," S. Fdida and M. Morganti (editors), Multimedia Applications, Services and Techniques - ECMAST '97, Volume 1242 of Springer Lecture Notes in Computer Science, pp. 423-436, Springer, Heidelberg, Germany, 1997.

34. Hartung, F. and Girod, B., "Digital watermarking of MPEG-2 coded video in the bitstream domain," Proceedings of ICASSP 97, Munich, Germany, April 1997.

35. Koch, E. and Zhao, J., "Towards robust and hidden image copyright labeling," Proceedings of 1995 IEEE Workshop on Nonlinear Signal and Image Processing, pp. 452-455, Halkidiki, Greece, June 1995.

36. Langelaar, G. C., Van der Lubbe, J. C. A., and Biemond, J., "Copy protection for multimedia data based on labeling techniques," 17th Symposium on Information Theory in the Benelux, Enschede, The Netherlands, May 1996.

37. Langelaar, G. C., van der Lubbe, J. C. A., and Lagendijk, R. L., "Robust labeling methods for copy protection of images," Proceedings of SPIE Electronic Imaging '97, Storage and Retrieval for Image and Video Databases V, San Jose, California, February 1997.

38. Langelaar, G. C., Lagendijk, R. L., and Biemond, J., "Real-time labeling methods for MPEG compressed video," 18th Symposium on Information Theory in the Benelux, Veldhoven, The Netherlands, May 1997.

39. Nikolaidis, N. and Pitas, I., "Copyright protection of images using robust digital signatures," IEEE International Conference on Acoustics, Speech and Signal Processing (ICASSP-96), Vol. 4, pp. 2168-2171, May 1996.

40. Ó Ruanaidh, J., "Watermarking digital images for copyright protection," Electronic Imaging and the Visual Arts, Florence, Italy, February 1996.

41. Ó Ruanaidh, J. J. K. and Pun, T., "Rotation, translation and scale invariant digital image watermarking," IEEE Signal Processing Society 1997 International Conference on Image Processing (ICIP'97), Santa Barbara, California, October 1997.

42. Piva, A., Barni, M., Bartolini, F., and Cappellini, V., "DCT-based watermark recovering without resorting to the uncorrupted original image," IEEE Signal Processing Society 1997 International Conference on Image Processing (ICIP'97), Santa Barbara, California, October 1997.

43. Puate, J. and Jordan, F., "Using fractal compression scheme to embed a digital signature into an image," Proceedings of SPIE Photonics East '96 Symposium, Boston, MA, 1996.

44. Swanson, M. D., Zhu, Bin, and Tewfik, A. H., "Robust data hiding for images," 7th IEEE Digital Signal Processing Workshop, pp. 37-40, 1996.

45. Swanson, M. D., Zhu, B., and Tewfik, A. H., "Transparent robust image watermarking," 1996 SPIE Conference on Visual Communications and Image Proceedings, Vol. III, pp. 211-214, 1996.

46. Swanson, M. D., Zhu, B., Chau, B., and Tewfik, A. H., "Object-based transparent video watermarking," Electronic Proceedings of the IEEE Signal Processing Society 1997 Workshop on Multimedia Signal Processing, Princeton, New Jersey, June 1997.

47. Tao, B. and Dickinson, B., "Adaptive watermarking in the DCT domain," International Conf. on Acoustics, Speech, and Signal Processing, ICASSP '97, April 1997.

48. Voyatzis, G. and Pitas, I., "Chaotic mixing of digital images and applications to watermarking," European Conference on Multimedia Applications, Services and Techniques (ECMAST'96), Vol. 2, pp. 687-695, Louvain-la-Neuve, Belgium, May 1996.

49. Voyatzis, G. and Pitas, I., "Applications of toral automorphisms in image watermarking," IEEE Signal Processing Society 1996 International Conference on Image Processing (ICIP'96), Vol. II, pp. 237-240, Lausanne, Switzerland, September 1996.

50. Voyatzis, G. and Pitas, I., "Embedding robust logo watermarks in digital images," 13th International Conference on Digital Signal Processing (DSP'97), Vol. 1, pp. 213-216, Santorini, Greece, July 1997.

51. Wolfgang, R. B. and Delp, E. J., "A watermark for digital images," IEEE International Conference on Image Processing (ICIP'96), Lausanne, Switzerland, September 1996.

52. Bender, W., Gruhl, D., and Morimoto, N., "Techniques for data hiding," Proceedings of SPIE, Vol. 2420, February 1995.

53. Berghel, H. and O'Gorman, L., "Protecting ownership rights through digital watermarking," *IEEE Computer*, 29(7):101-103, 1996.

54. Berghel, H., "Watermarking cyberspace," *Communications of the ACM*, 40(11):19-24, November 1997.

55. Bors, A. and Pitas, I., "Embedding parametric digital signatures in images," EUSIPCO-96, Vol. III, pp. 1701-1704, Trieste, Italy, September 1996.

56. Bors, A. and Pitas, I., "Image watermarking using DCT domain constraints," IEEE International Conference on Image Processing (ICIP'96), Vol. III, pp. 231-234, Lausanne, Switzerland, September 1996.

57. Brassil, J., Low, S., Maxemchuk, N., and O'Gorman, L., "Hiding information in document images," CISS '95, 1995.

58. Braudaway, G. W., "Protecting publicly-available images with an invisible image watermark," IEEE Signal Processing Society 1997 International Conference on Image Processing (ICIP'97), Santa Barbara, California, October 1997.

59. Delaigle, J.-F., Boucqueau, J.-M., Quisquater, J.-J., and Macq, B., "Digital images protection techniques in a broadcast framework: An overview," TALISMAN project report, ACTS project AC019, Université Catholique de Louvain Laboratoire de Télécommunications et Télédétection, Brussels, Belgium, 1996.

60. Hsu, C.-T. and Wu, J.-L., "Hidden signatures in images," IEEE Signal Processing Society 1996 International Conference on Image Processing (ICIP'96), Vol. III, pp. 743-746, Lausanne, Switzerland, September 1996.

61. Kundur, D. and Hatzinakos, D., "A robust digital image watermarking scheme using the wavelet-based fusion," IEEE Signal Processing Society 1997 International Conference on Image Processing (ICIP'97), Santa Barbara, California, October 1997.

62. McKenzie, M., "Copyright protection: Understanding your options," *The Seybold Report on Internet Publishing*, 1(4), December 1996.

63. Morris, D. C., "Embedding hidden identification codes in digital objects," US Patent No. 5,530,751, 1996.

64. Paatelma, O. and Borland, R. H., "Method and apparatus for manipulating digital data works," WIPO Patent No. WO 95/20291, 1995.

65. Pitas, I. and Kaskalis, T. H., "Applying signatures on digital images," IEEE Workshop on Nonlinear Image and Signal Processing, pp. 460-463, Neos Marmaras, Greece, June 1995.

66. Pitas, I., "A method for signature casting on digital images," IEEE International Conference on Image Processing (ICIP'96), Vol. III, pp. 215-218, Lausanne, Switzerland, September 1996.

67. Preuss, R. D., Roukos, S. E., Huggins, A. W. F., Gish, H., Bergamo, M. A., and Peterson, P. M., "Embedded signaling," US Patent no. 5,319,735, 1994.

68. Rhoads, G. B., "Identification/authentication coding method and apparatus," WIPO Patent No. WO 95/14289, 1995.

69. Schneider, M. and Chang, S. F., "A robust content based digital signature for image authentication," IEEE International Conference on Image Processing (ICIP'96), 1996.

70. Shivakumar, N. and Garcia-Molina, H., "Building a scalable and accurate copy detection mechanism," Proceedings of the 1st ACM Conference on Digital Libraries (DL'96), Bethesda, Maryland, March 1996.

71. Wu, T. L. and Wu, S. F., "Selective encryption and watermarking of MPEG video," International Conference on Image Science, Systems, and Technology, CISST'97, June 1997.

72. Xia, X.-G., Boncelet, C., and Arce, G., "A multiresolution watermark for digital images," IEEE Signal Processing Society 1997 International Conference on Image Processing (ICIP'97), Santa Barbara, California, October 1997.

73. Yeung, M. M., Mintzer, F. C., Braudaway, G. W., and Rao, A. R., "Digital watermarking for high-quality imaging," Technical Report RC20797, IBM T. J. Watson Research Center, 1997.

15

AUTOMATIC AND DYNAMIC VIDEO MANIPULATION

John Chung-Mong Lee[1], Quing Li[2], and Wei Xiong[3]
[1]Department of Computer Science,
Hong Kong University of Science & Technology
cmlee@cs.ust.hk
[2]Department of Computing,
Hong Kong Polytechnic University
csqli@comp.polyu.edu.hk
[3]Department of Computer Science,
Hong Kong University of Science & Technology
csxwei@cs.ust.hk

1. **INTRODUCTION**..318
2. **AN OVERVIEW OF RELATED WORK**................................320
3. **VCC: VIDEO CLASSIFICATION COMPONENT** 323
    3.1   VIDEO PARTITIONING AND KEY FRAME SELECTION 323
    3.2   KEY FRAME SELECTION AND CLUSTERING................................324
    3.3   AUTOMATIC CAMERA MOTION ANNOTATION 325
4. **CCM: CONCEPTUAL CLUSTERING MECHANISM**................327
    4.1   THE CONCEPTS OF CLUSTERS AND ROLES................................327
    4.2   THE DATA STRUCTURES FOR CLUSTERS AND ROLES................328
5. **INCORPORATION OF VCC AND CCM IN VIMS** 330
    5.1   COUPLING OF VCC AND CCM..330
    5.2   VIDEO DATA PROCESSING BASED ON CONCEPTUAL CLUSTERING................331
    5.3   CONTEXT-DEPENDENT AND CONTEXT-FREE RETRIEVAL FACILITIES 333
    5.4   SOME EXAMPLES..336
6. **AN EXPERIMENTAL PROTOTYPE**................................337
    6.1   ARCHITECTURE AND COMPONENTS OF OUR PROTOTYPE SYSTEM 337
    6.2   SOME FURTHER IMPLEMENTATION ISSUES ON CCM................338
    6.3   CURRENT STATUS..339
7. **SUMMARY AND CONCLUDING REMARKS**................................340
    REFERENCES 341

317

1. INTRODUCTION

With the rapid progress in video technology, more and more information is available as video data. Video cassettes tapes, CD-ROM, and laser discs are used for many purposes such as entertainment, scientific records, education, storage of art images, and so on.

In most places, however, huge piles of videotapes are simply kept for possible future use without good semantic indices. The indexing of semantically meaningful scenes requires someone to preview the whole video and to provide a manually-entered information tag to every significant scene in it, which is not only tedious but also time consuming. As the amount, complexity, and inter-relation of video information grow, the need for automatically analyzing and manipulating video tapes and laser discs becomes evident.

The availability of video data is not synonymous with *accessibility* and *manipulability* of video data, the two most fundamental facilities needed from a video database. The reason for this is twofold. On the one hand, raw video data is not structured. For example, there are few or no temporal tags associated with video data, and traditional approaches do not provide powerful access to the video data from a video database. On the other hand, the conventional object-oriented database (OODB) modeling approach still falls short in providing adequate support for video data management, which is, by nature, changing dynamically and incrementally. Thus, what is desired in an effective video database management system (VDMS) is

- structuring the video data and associating it with a rich set of indices to enable powerful access to the meaningful video segments of the video database, and
- extending the conventional OODB approaches to facilitate dynamic creation, deletion, and management of video data from the database.

With these ideas in mind, we have been developing a full-fledged video information manipulation system (VIMS) that can accommodate semantic analysis and classification as well as efficient management of video data. This system is composed of two fundamental components:
- a Video Classification Component (VCC) for the generation of effective indices necessary for structuring the video data, and
- a Conceptual Clustering Mechanism (CCM) that has advanced object-oriented features and techniques. The former supports video structuring through scene change detection, key frame computation, shot classification using domain knowledge, as well as content-based retrieval through interactive learning, whereas the latter enables users to form, among other things, video programs (or scenes) from existing objects based on semantic features/index terms dynamically and adaptively. By tightly coupling CCM techniques together with VCCs, the VIMS further allows the user to perform annotation-based and content-based retrieval in a well integrated and interleaved manner, which we regard as essential for a versatile video manipulation server. A prototype of VIMS embodying VCC and CCM running on the PC Pentium platform has recently been constructed.

Different from other existing systems, VIMS has the following special objectives:
- extending OODB modeling with CCM facilities, which provides users with flexible and efficient operations [10];
- employing an SQL-like query language, which supports both content-dependent query and content-free queries [12];

- advocating an efficient method for scene change detection [27,28], and an effective method for key frame selection [29];
- using novel approaches to detect image sequences features [11,23,27].

Figure 1 shows the system architecture of our VIMS prototype system. It illustrates the conceptual architecture of the prototype system, in which it is shown that there are two main development components on top of an object-oriented database. One is the Video Classifier Component (VCC) and the other is the Conceptual Clustering Mechanism (CCM). Both are connected to the underlying database and an up-front user interface.

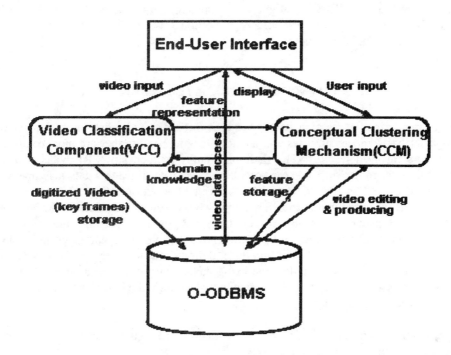

Figure 1. The architecture of VIMS prototype system.

VCC partitions the video into shots, selects key frames for each shot, and extracts image/video features automatically. From key frames, it extracts low level image features, such as color, texture, edge, shape, motion, and wavelet decomposition. The wavelet coefficients of key frames are used to build a basic indexing system that supports direct access to the video data by the end-user. The use of other features is decided by the message from CCM. Examples are shown in section 5.4.

CCM supports end-users in reorganizing the video program dynamically using newly defined attributes. In this way, it is possible that different users can organize video data with different semantics or domain knowledge. This domain knowledge tells what and how features are used or grouped to form meta-level features in the VCC part. The relationship between VCC and CCM is bidirectional since an edited video segment and/or package may lead to an enhanced classification or trigger a reclassification process, possibly using domain knowledge supplied by users. On the other hand, a newly classified result (feature representation) from VCC may allow users to refine domain knowledge and perhaps trigger a classification process again.

The rest of the chapter is organized as follows. In Section 2, we briefly review the related works. In Section 3, we present the VCC portion of VIMS. We first discuss the issues and goals of VCC in trying to structure the raw video data through scene change detection and key frame computing. Then we introduce an efficient method for camera motion annotation as an example of automatic video annotation. In Section 4, we present the CCM portion of VIMS wherein we first discuss the problems with existing database models and then present the CCM model and its fundamental features to overcome those problems. In Section 5, the interaction between VCC and CCM and flexible content-based query is described. An illustration of utilization of CCM applications is presented. Some examples are also given to provide a general picture of how VCC interacts with CCM. In Section 6, we present an experimental prototype of VIMS, highlighting the implementation issues, current status of VCC and CCM, and our ongoing work. Finally, in Section 7, we summarize the scope of the VIMS project and conclude the chapter.

2. AN OVERVIEW OF RELATED WORK

Recently, a large amount of research activity has been focused on video databases. Compared with image databases, video databases are more challenging because they are more complex and have more involved features. The traditional entity relationship (ER) model and/or relational databases are not sufficient for describing video data, since this data may involve complex objects as well as other relationships that cannot be adequately accommodated by relational and ER modeling approaches. That is why object-oriented databases (OODB) are being utilized as a better means due to their increased power of semantic modeling, in particular behavioral modeling and encapsulation, complex object support, type hierarchy and inheritance, and so on [26]. Despite these powerful features, conventional OODB systems are still not sufficient for video data management, particularly with respect to such subjective activities as video editing and production, which form the basis for facilitating the desired video data manipulability.

More specifically, video databases involve more issues to be resolved than text or image databases due to the following special features:

1. Complex objects need to be defined and supported in a video DB since video data can take several different forms, e.g., frames, segments, and programs. These objects are not independent; rather they share some inherent relationships in the form of "is-part-of" (or so-called composition) links.
2. From different points of view, the same image sequence may be given different descriptions. For example, given a specific video sequence, one user may be interested in its attributes, like color/BW or gun fighting/car racing. Another user may be more interested in whether it is an indoor or outdoor scene. However, it is impossible and inefficient to include all possible attributes in a video DB when it is built.
3. Different video scenes may be better described by different features. For example, motion information is important to distinguish a wide-angle playing scene and a wide-angle free throw scene in a basketball video, but color, texture, or other still image features could hardly tell the difference between them because these features do not sufficiently describe whether the athletes (players) are moving or not. On the other hand, motion information is not as important to describe a close-up scene because the movement of a particular player may not be as interesting.
4. The semantic descriptions may be added or deleted dynamically. Suppose, for example, we defined a sequence with several attributes like sound/no-sound, sports type, main

roles, etc. But later on, we may no longer be concerned with certain attributes, say, sound/no-sound, yet need other features for describing the sequence. Unfortunately, the conventional OODBMS are not good at accommodating new classes dynamically.

5. Sharing of attributes (and values) or methods is often needed among video data objects, since meaningful scenes, in particular, may be overlapping or included in other meaningful scenes. For instance, we may describe sequence A as being about U.S. President Bill Clinton's activities. We may also define sequence B as being about Clinton's hobbies. Sequence B is actually a subset of A. Obviously, B will have some attributes that A has, say, they are both color and both outdoor scenes. On the one hand, sharing among values and methods is very common. On the other hand, it is tedious to let users repeatedly input the same information for different objects. However, conventional OODBMS do not support the inheritance of attribute values or methods at the object instance level.

In the following, we briefly examine several existing research efforts to overcome some of the shortcomings of conventional OODB systems, both in terms of video data modeling and video data management.

- E. Oomoto and K. Tanaka [19] proposed a schemeless object-oriented model. Their model allows users to (1) identify an arbitrary video frame sequence (a meaningful scene) as an independent object, (2) describe its contents in a dynamic and incremental way, (3) share descriptional data among video objects, and (4) edit author and abstract video objects. As their model is schemeless, the traditional class hierarchy of the object-oriented approach is not assumed as a database schema.
- W. I. Grosky *et al.* [4] proposed a content-based hypermedia (CBH) model. It is basically an object-oriented schema over non-media objects, which has undergone a transformation. They classified an object-oriented schema into three domains: class hierarchy, nested object hierarchy, and complex object hierarchy. Then they used meta-data classes to build various relations between objects, such as "is-part-of" and "appearing-in."
- R. Jain and A. Hampapur [7] proposed a video model (ViMod) based on studies of the applications of video and the nature of video retrieval requests. The features of their model include content dependence, temporal extent, and labeling. A feature is said to be content independent if the feature is not directly available from the video data. Certain aspects of a video can be specified based on viewing a single frame in temporal intervals, whereas other features like motion can be specified based only on a time interval. The changes that occur in a video can be tracked over the extent of a time interval.

A follow-up challenge in developing any video information management system is the support of efficient and effective video management and access. In this context, we are aware of the following existing research work:

- Hirata and Kato [5] built a query system that uses visual examples, i.e., ART MUSEUM. A user has only to draw a rough sketch to retrieve the original image and all similar images in a database. The system evaluates the similarity between the rough sketch, i.e., visual example, and each part of the image data in the database automatically. This method is quite good from the viewpoint of users; however, there is a question about the system's effectiveness.
- Bimbo *et al.* [REFERENCES1] used Spatio-Temporal Logic to support the retrieval by content of video sequences through visual interaction. Temporal Logic is a language for

the qualitative representation of ordering properties in the execution sequences of temporal systems. In their database, video sequences are stored along with a description of their contents in Spatio-Temporal Logic. Retrieval is supported through a 3D iconic interface.

- Little et al. [15] implemented a system that supports content-based retrieval of video footage. They define a specific data schema composed of movie, scene, and actor relations with a fixed set of attributes. The system requires manual feature extraction, and then fits these features into the data schema. Their data model and virtual video browser do not support queries related to the temporal ordering of scenes.

- Smoliar and Zhang [22] used a frame-based knowledge base method to support retrieval. They used frames to represent both classes (the categories) and instances (the elements categorized). In addition to the common techniques in the frame-based knowledge base, they translated knowledge of a shot's type into knowledge of how to search it for retrieval purposes.

From the above observations, it is clear that meaningful video sequences are often identified and associated with their descriptional data incrementally and dynamically (after the video objects are stored in a video database). Therefore, it is important to have a flexible data structure that can be changed dynamically to accommodate video objects. In [13], we have proposed to advocate a dynamic object conceptual clustering video database model called CCM, which is based on Li and Smith's Conceptual Model for Dynamic Clustering in Object Databases [14]. Among others, this new model facilitates dynamic creation, deletion, and management of *ad hoc* object collections (called "clusters"), with a goal to complement existing object-class power for accommodating generic application dynamics.

Related research works on the video structuring aspect have been at different levels. At the first level, some prototype systems proposed in the literature allow users to access desired images from image databases by directly making use of visual cues [8,18,20]. For example, in [18], Niblack *et al.* reported that the QBIC system developed at IBM allows images to be retrieved by a variety of image content descriptors including color, texture, and shape. However, these prototype systems, even though they address the issues regarding the exploitation of spatial structure in images for effective indexing for retrieval, do not deal with video sequences where the temporal information also has to be considered. At the next level, video data structuring is viewed as segmenting the continuous frame stream into physically discontinuous units, usually called *shots*. In general, these physical units need to be clustered to form more semantically significant units, such as scenes. This so-called *story-based* video structuring has been used in video information browsing systems (e.g., [13,24]). The shots or scenes are described by one or several representative frames, known by the name *key frames* [11,24,34].

Camera breaks are usually characterized by brusque intensity pattern change between consecutive frames at the boundary. Several methods such as pairwise comparison, likelihood comparison, and histogram comparison have been introduced [17,32]. These methods have their merits and limitations. The histogram comparison method is insensitive to image movements since it considers intensity/color distribution – a statistical entity – between consecutive images. But it fails if the intensity/color distributions are similar because it ignores spatial information [9]. Both pairwise comparison and likelihood comparison make use of spatial information but the former is too sensitive to image movements and easily causes false alarms, whereas the latter suffers from computational complexity.

Based on the above observation, we have proposed a sub-sampling method called "Net Comparison" in [28]. It computes only a fraction of the image pixels. It is accurate and fast because it uses both statistical and spatial information in an image and does not have to process the entire image. The size of the base windows (L) depends on the maximum non-(camera)break displacement (δ), which is the largest movement between two images. In [28], we conducted a statistical analysis showing that camera-break detection with a low probability of error requires, in essence, checking only a few, rather than the complete set of base windows (small square regions). The number of the base windows required is also computed on the basis of the analysis. In [27], we improve the algorithm by sub-sampling video data both spatially and temporally. The improved algorithm can efficiently detect both abrupt scene change and gradual transition of scenes.

We want to capture as *complete* a content of a video sequence as we can, using as few key frames as possible. How to find a systematic way to select key frames is a problem. There is some work relating to this subject in the literature. In [25], for each shot, one key frame is selected at a predefined position in the shot. In [16], a representative video cut is selected as the first frame or the first subpart of each extracted cut. In [20], it has been suggested that key frames should be chosen according to color and motion (e.g., panning, zooming, object motion, etc.). In [33,34], a method (*robust*, according to the authors) was mentioned, but little detail was given. In [29], we presented a systematic method for selecting the key frame. The method includes a *Seek and Spread* algorithm and an image similarity measure using wavelets. In [31], the authors proposed a method to classify key frames of different shots using clustering techniques in order to establish semantic links between the shots; however no experimental results were reported.

3. VCC: VIDEO CLASSIFICATION COMPONENT

As depicted in Figure 1, a major component of VIMS is the video classification component (VCC), which works closely with CCM (to be described in Section 4). Basically, VCC has two functions: (1) structuring the video data, and (2) extracting image features from key frames. Video data structuring is viewed as segmenting the continuous frame stream into physically discontinuous units, generally called *shots*, and clustering the shots into semantically significant units using key frames. We propose a sub-sampling method called *Net Comparison* for video segmentation and a method called *Seek and Spread* for key frame selection. We use wavelet decomposition and centered moment for the image similarity measure in key frame selection. Image features extraction, in our system, includes extracting color, texture, edge, shape, and motion information from key frames using generic methods. The features are not extracted until the user specifies some features are needed for classifying some key frames. The user may also input some simple domain knowledge (from CCM) for the features extraction.

3.1 VIDEO PARTITIONING AND KEY FRAME SELECTION

The partitioning process consists of the detection of boundaries between uninterrupted segments (camera shots) that involve screen time, space, or graphic configurations. These boundaries, also known as transitions, can be classified into two categories: gradual and instantaneous. The most common transition is camera breaks.

In addition to existing methods for camera break detection, we propose a method called Net Comparison (NC). It combines the advantage of the robustness of the histogram method and the simplicity of the pairwise method by comparing a statistical quantity – the mean value of intensity – along the predefined net lines. The *sub-sampling* approach compares pixels in predefined regions and inspects only a fraction of the pixels. The *size* of the sub-sampling regions (L) depends on the maximum non-(camera)break displacement (δ), which is the largest movement between two images. The movement may be caused by an object moving or by camera zooming, panning, etc. Obviously, we do not need to consider the movement of any small object in the image, such as bullets or rain drops, which usually have speeds that are very high. So velocity (δ) here means the movement of a sufficiently large region in the image between two consecutive frames. The *number* of sub-sampling regions we use in this method is computed by probability analysis [28]. We compare the method's performance with other existing algorithms and evaluate them on a large set of typical image sequences [28].

For the purpose of comparison, we have implemented four other methods for camera break detection: pairwise, likelihood, global histogram, and local histogram. Many experiments have been conducted on both color and black/white video. The proposed method outperforms the others both in accuracy and in speed in our experiments [28]. This is because the method chooses an analyzed size of sub-sampling regions to make use of spatial information. Actually, pairwise, likelihood and local histogram methods all use spatial information; however, the areas they use are either too small (even one pixel) and therefore too sensitive or too large and thus lose the spatial information. The reason why Net comparison is faster than the others is obviously due to its using only parts of images instead of the entire image.

In addition to sub-sampling the image in space, we also propose a *Step-variable* algorithm that sub-samples the image sequences in time. Instead of comparing every pair of consecutive frames, we compare Frame i with Frame j where $j = i + myStep$. If no significant change is found between the two frames, we move a *half step* forward. The next comparison is between Frame $i + myStep/2$ and Frame $j + myStep/2$. If the significant change is found, we use a binary search method to locate the precise place where the change occurred. That is, we reduce the search step *myStep* by half until the main change is located between two consecutive frames (e.g., Frame u and Frame v). The difference between Frame u and Frame v is further investigated. If the difference is larger than a threshold, a scene change is determined; otherwise, no change is declared. In either case, *myStep* is restored to the initial value (we use 30 frames in our experiments) and Frame $v + 1$ and Frame $v + 1 + myStep$ are compared to start to search the next scene change. More details can be found in [27].

It is easy to understand that our method significantly increases the detection speed without losing the detection precision. To increase the detection of the scene changes, some researchers have also proposed sub-sampling in time [21,30]; however, their methods sacrifice the detection precision because they are using fixed step. In addition, their methods are not necessarily able to locate the gradual transitions, while our step-variable algorithm can prove that both camera breaks and gradual transitions can be detected [27].

3.2 KEY FRAME SELECTION AND CLUSTERING

A continuous video is segmented into shots by partitioning. Each shot is represented by or abstracted into one or some frames, commonly called *key frames*. Key frames can serve two purposes: *browsing* and *computation of indices*. In retrieval by browsing, showing shots using key frames as they are may confuse an untrained user rather than help him/her get the *story* or facilitate the retrieval. Like the table of contents of a book, shots must be organized into several levels of semantic abstraction. We call this *conceptual* or *semantic clustering*.

The unit is a *cluster*, which is a collection of semantically related shots and/or clusters [6, 13]. Now the question raised is how to find clusters and, to a lesser extent, how to choose key frames to represent them.

Basically, there are two issues related to key frame selection. One is the selection algorithm. Another is the image similarity measure or the definition of image distance.

For the selection approach, we propose a novel algorithm called *Seek and Spread*. The main idea is to search a key frame sequentially based on a similarity measure and extend (spread) the representative range of the key frame to the maximum. The image similarity measure is defined by wavelet coefficients that account for both spatial layout and detail content in an image. The coefficients from both the scaling function and wavelet function are used (details are described in [29]).

In the next subsection, we introduce an efficient method for camera motion annotation, which displays an example of image/video features extraction around key frames.

3.3 AUTOMATIC CAMERA MOTION ANNOTATION

After partitioning the video sequences, it is necessary to extract various video/image features for video classification. An important feature in video sequences is the temporal luminance change of successive pictures. The changes generally originate from the motion of objects or the motion of the camera. Camera motion information is a powerful and important cue in video retrieval. Although the estimation of camera motion is important and can be used for many different purposes, there has not been extensive work addressing automatic camera motion extraction, especially in the context of structuring video sequences.

We used a novel approach to estimate the dominant camera motions. The method is based on analyzing the optical flow information in a decomposing manner. The horizontal and vertical optical flows are analyzed separately and different sub-regions of images are computed individually. The method is efficient because only mean values and standard deviations in some sub-regions are used. Each kind of the camera motion is detected based on the prior analyzed patterns. Experiments on many types of typical camera motions are given in [27] to show the effectiveness of the method.

We follow a standard camera model using the camera-centered coordinate system, as shown in Figure 2. A camera projects a 3D world point $P = (X, Y, Z)^t$ to a 2D image point $P = (X, Y)^t$. Let f be the focal length of the camera. If $(u(x, y) v(x, y))^t$ is the observed optical flow at location $P = (X, Y)^t$, we can derive that:

$$u(x,y) = -\frac{xy}{f}\Omega_X + (f + \frac{x^2}{f})\Omega_Y - y\Omega_Z + \frac{f}{Z}T_X - \frac{x}{Z}T_Z - f[\arctan(\frac{x}{f})](1 + \frac{x^2}{f^2})r_{zoom} \quad (1)$$

$$v(x,y) = -(f + \frac{y^2}{f})\Omega_X + \frac{xy}{f}\Omega_Y + x\Omega_Z - \frac{f}{Z}T_Y - \frac{Y}{Z}T_Z - f[\arctan(\frac{y}{f})](1 + \frac{y^2}{f^2})r_{zoom} \quad (2)$$

where $V = (V_X V_Y V_Z)^t$ is the 3D velocity vector of the point whose position vector is $P = (X, Y, Z)^t$, $T = (T_X T_Y T_Z)^t$ is the 3D vector that models the camera translation,

$\Omega = (\Omega_X \Omega_Y \Omega_Z)^t$ is the 3D vector that models the angular velocity of the camera rotation, and r_{zoom} denotes the camera zoom factor (the angular magnification factor).

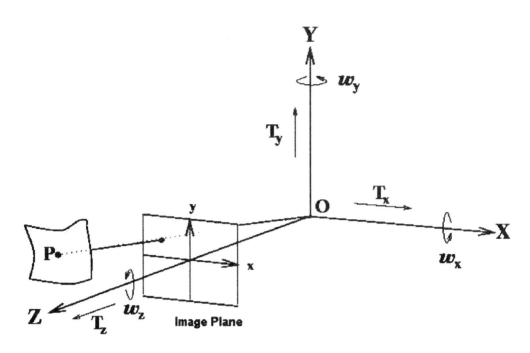

Figure 2. Camera model.

We assume that there is only one type of camera motion in each video segment. The assumption is still applicable if there are two or more camera motions but one of the motions overwhelms the others. Based on this presumption, each type of the camera motion can be analyzed separately and we have merely one non-zero parameter each time. The camera motion is analyzed separately in the x and y directions. An image is divided into 7 non-overlapping sub-regions, $O, X_0, Y_0, I, II, III, IV$, as shown in Figure 3. Optical flow is investigated in different sub-regions. Using this method, we can compute the camera motion and u(x,y) and v(x,y) in some sub-regions.

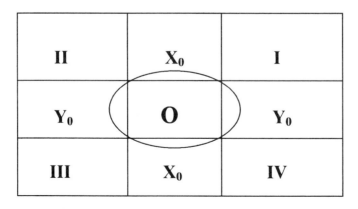

Figure 3. Image sub-regions.

4. CCM: CONCEPTUAL CLUSTERING MECHANISM

In a conventional OODB model, the fundamental concepts are object and class. An object represents an encapsulation of attributes and methods; it has a unique object identifier (Oid) in the OODB. A class is described as a means of gathering all objects that share the same set of attributes and methods. There are two kinds of inter-class relationships captured by a conventional OODB model: one is the subclass ("is-a") relationship and the other is the composition ("is-part-of") relationship. The former facilitates the notion of *inheritance* (i.e., a subclass may inherit the attributes and methods from its superclass as well as from local additional ones), and the latter supports the notions of *existence dependency* and *component sharability* between a composite object and its component objects [13,26]. Both types of inter-class relationships form class hierarchies that are useful for modeling video object relationships and data structure. For example, the composition hierarchy can accommodate the description of the structure of video data. In particular, a video program can be viewed as a composite object consisting of a sequence of frames that are component objects of the video program.

The main problems with the conventional OODB modeling approach are that a class has to be predefined statically and objects of a class must be homogeneous in nature. Hence, such a model does not provide adequate support for those applications involving objects and inter-object relationships that are, by nature, *ad hoc*, irregular, tentative, and evolving (as exemplified by video data objects). Extensions to the conventional OODB models are therefore needed in order to accommodate such advanced applications effectively.

In [14], a basic conceptual clustering mechanism (CCM) that facilitates dynamic creation, deletion, and management of *ad hoc* object collections (called "clusters") was defined, such that this mechanism can effectively accommodate more application dynamics, including various video data manipulations [13]. In this subsection, we describe the concepts as well as proper data structures of the CCM constructs that are suitable for flexible video data manipulation and management.

4.1 THE CONCEPTS OF CLUSTERS AND ROLES

In CCM, a cluster consists of attributes, methods, and a dynamic grouping of existing objects in the database, within which each object is assigned to one or more roles. More precisely, a cluster C_t is a dynamic object that has a tripartite form:

$$C_t = <A, M, X>$$ (3)

where A is a set of cluster attributes, M is a set of cluster methods, and X is a set of the role-player associates:

$$X = \{< R_i : S_i > | 1 \leq i \leq n\}$$ (4)

where R_i is a role, and S_i is a set of the objects that play that role within the cluster. Hence, the objects in S_i are called the "players" of the role R_i, and they are also the "constituents" of the cluster C_t. A role R_i can be described as follows:

$$R_i = < A_p, M_p >$$ (5)

where A_p and M_p are a set of attributes and methods defined by the role R_i; these attributes and methods are applicable to the role players. A role R_i is active if the set of its methods (M_p) is not empty, otherwise it is a passive role. The players of a role may be "homogeneous"/ "heterogeneous."

Clusters do not create or delete objects; they only include or exclude objects of databases. Therefore, they allow the user to form views over existing databases by tailoring at the cluster level without affecting the database itself. This is very useful and important for video data processing, such as video indexing and video production.

Clusters can establish a super-cluster/sub-cluster hierarchy similar to a composite hierarchy of classes. But a cluster may dynamically define its constituent objects and these objects can be of different types (heterogeneous).

Similar to classes that form an "is-a" hierarchy, roles can establish a super-role/sub-role hierarchy. A sub-role may inherit the attributes and methods (if any) of its direct and indirect super-roles. Furthermore, a sub-role can also define new properties and/or overwrite some of the inherited ones. Any objects playing the sub-role should be viewed as players of the super-roles. Examples of clusters and roles in video databases are given in section 4.2.

4.2 THE DATA STRUCTURES FOR CLUSTERS AND ROLES

To better understand the concepts and feasible support of the cluster and role facilities, we describe here suitable data structures that we have recently used as a guideline for implementing such dynamic constructs.

Cluster Tree   A cluster tree can be represented internally as a binary tree with a father pointer in each node. For example, the cluster tree in Figure 4 (a) is expressed as shown in Figure 4 (b). The father pointer is used to quickly search all super-clusters of a specific sub-cluster. The structure of each node in a cluster tree is illustrated in Figure 4 (c). Its type definition may be viewed as a meta-cluster. All application clusters of any user defined are instances of this meta-cluster. All cluster nodes in a cluster tree may be dynamically created, removed, and modified by the user.

Since we cannot forecast how many attributes, methods, and roles a user will define in a cluster, attribute-, method-, and role-lists should be defined as dynamically linked lists. Their structures are illustrated in Figure 5.

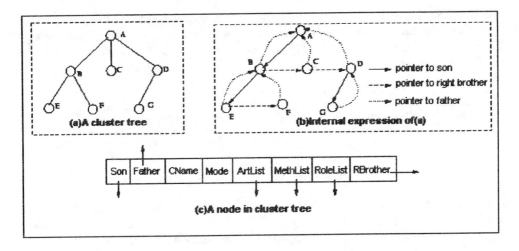

Figure 4. The structure of cluster tree.

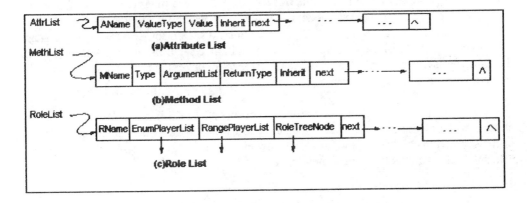

Figure 5. The linked-lists used in cluster node.

In the attribute list (Figure 5 (a)), "ValueType" is char, string, int, float, etc., and "Value" is a union type in order to save storage. "Inherit" indicates whether the attribute is inheritable by its sub-cluster or not. For a method-list (Figure 5 (b)), the "Type" is used to distinguish whether the method is an executable file or a library function. The "ArgumentList" is a linked list that stores the type of these arguments. The "ReturnType" is a type of return value if the method is a library function. "Inherit" determines whether or not a method may be inherited by its sub-clusters. Each role in the role list ((Figure 5 (c)) has a set of players that are also the constituent objects of the cluster. These players may be added and removed dynamically; hence they should also be dynamically linked lists. The players of a role may be of an enumeration and/or range form; thus we employed both "EnumPlayerList" and "RangePlayerList" to express these two types of players. The attributes and methods (if active) in a role are defined by some node of a role tree. Therefore, each role node in a role list has a "RoleTreeNode" pointing to a corresponding node of the role tree.

In the enumeration type of the player-linked list, each node includes an object identifier (Oid) of the EOS. In the range type of player-linked list, each node includes the upper- and lower-limit of the players, which are logically continuous.

<u>Role Tree</u>   Similar to the cluster tree, a role tree is represented as a binary tree with a father pointer. The structure of each node in a role tree is shown in Figure 6. Its type definition may also be viewed as a meta-role. All role nodes in a role tree are also created, deleted, and modified dynamically by the user.

Figure 6. A node in role tree.

In Figure 6, the attribute- and method-lists are the same as those of the cluster node mentioned above (viz. Figure 5 (a),(b)). The "LinkType" indicates the link manner (strong/weak) between a role and its super-role. The deletion of a super-role implies the deletion of its sub-roles if the "LinkType" of those sub-roles is strong. Otherwise, the deletion of a super-role does not imply the deletion of its sub-roles. The "Type" of role node may be active or passive depending on whether or not the role includes methods. The "ReferenceCount" of a role node in a role tree denotes referenced times of the role. When the user adds a new role into a cluster node, the system will search for this role in the role tree and, if it finds it, the "ReferenceCount" is an automated increment. Otherwise, the system adds a new role node whose "ReferenceCount" is initialized into the role tree. Similarly, if the user deletes a role in a cluster node, the "ReferenceCount" of the corresponding role node in the role tree is decreased by one.

The role node in a role tree may be created as independent or dependent of the role of the cluster. In other words, we may first establish the role tree and then establish the cluster tree; or first create the cluster tree and, in the meanwhile, create the role tree. A role node in the role tree is deleted if its ReferenceCount value is zero.

5.   INCORPORATION OF VCC AND CCM IN VIMS

5.1   COUPLING OF VCC WITH CCM

With VCC's partitioning of video sequences and selection of key frames from each shot, VIMS can proceed subsequently to group/cluster the key frames and build indices using predefined low level image features. Currently, we are using wavelet coefficients of each key frame to build the basic indexing. Ideally, there will be multiple levels of indexing (from low-level to semantic-level) and each level of indexing will be organized in terms of original "story semantics." Unfortunately this is not feasibly supported by present techniques. However, with our proposed architecture, it is possible to do so in an incremental fashion toward the direction by, for example, (1) keeping the order of the key frames and adding a temporal tag to each key frame; (2) carefully pruning key frames for story continuity, etc. As mentioned earlier, CCM and VCC interact with each other. VCC provides CCM feature representation and basic indexing. CCM can dynamically introduce new user-defined attributes and more semantics for the video classification and VCC can, therefore, re-classify the video data more objectively and minutely and feed the new feature representation back to CCM. In Subsection 5.2, we illustrate how CCM can be used to support video data processing effectively in a video database context. We will then present some examples in Subsection 5.4.

5.2 VIDEO DATA PROCESSING BASED ON CONCEPTUAL CLUSTERING

First, we consider video indexing. As mentioned before, video classification enables video frames to be decomposed and grouped into segments. We will show that clusters are an efficient means for describing video structure and indices derived from the video classification process of VCC. As an example, suppose *Prog15* is a news program comprised of a sequence of news items, some commercial advertisements, and a weather forecast. Through VCC's classification, *Prog15* is decomposed into segments: *Seg1*, *Seg2*, *Seg3*, and *Seg4*, which represent local news, commercials, international news, and the weather forecast, respectively. Furthermore, *Seg1* (local news) and *Seg3* (international news) are broken into some sub-segments, say, *Sseg11*, *Sseg12*, ..., *Sseg1k*; *Sseg31*, ..., *Sseg3i*, ..., *Sseg3j*, each of which is a news item consisting of a sequence of frames. The structure of the news program *Prog15* is constructed in a cluster tree as shown in Figure 7 (a), with each node a cluster. For nodes *Seg3* and *Sseg3i* (suppose it is a news item about a football game), their clusters' definitions are illustrated in Figure 7 (b). The cluster *Sseg3i* is the sub-cluster of *Seg3*. Obviously, most of the attributes and/or methods of *Seg3* are not inherited by *Sseg3i*. If a sub-cluster inherits some properties from its super-cluster, we must explicitly specify which properties are inherited. For example, we may specify that the attribute "Anchorperson" in *Seg3* is inherited by its sub-clusters.

We define four roles in cluster *Sseg3i*, two of which are active roles as shown in Figure 7 (c). These two active roles denote play- and goal-scoring scenes, respectively. The role *Goal-frames* is a sub-role of the role *Play-frames* as shown in Figure 7 (b). In fact, super-roles and sub-roles also form a tree. Obviously, the attributes of the super-role *Play-frames* may be inherited by its sub-role *Goal-frames*. The method "display" is defined in cluster *Sseg3i*, role *Play-frames* and *Goal-frames*, respectively. Although the names of the methods are the same, the "display" of *Sseg3* may show all frames in this cluster (i.e., *Frame1126..Frame2000*); whereas the "display" of role *Play-frames* displays only the frames of its player (i.e., *Frame1141.. Frame2000*); similarly, "display" of role "goals-frames" displays only the frames of its player (*Frame1200..Frame1240* and *Frame1900..Frame1950*). New attributes and methods may be added dynamically to these two roles for later use (e.g., we may add a method "slow motion" into role *Goal-frames* in order to watch goal-scoring scenes clearly).

Second, let us consider video (re-)production, where clustering techniques again prove to be very effective means for this type of activity. To us, video (re-)production is the creation of a new video program out of a collection of video segments that are pre-existing and/or newly produced.

Assume that we would like to produce a goal-scoring program out of various pre-existing news programs. We may search news programs from video databases and inspect each news program to see whether or not it contains video sequences of a football game. When a cluster representing a football game is retrieved, we extract the frames of scored goals out of this cluster to form a new cluster. A collection of such new clusters forms the program of "goal-scoring" as desired. For example, Figure 8 shows a cluster (*Seg5*) extracted from cluster *Sseg3i* in Figure 7 (c). Users may add a variety of attributes and methods into the new cluster and their roles as desired in later processing phases (e.g., editing).

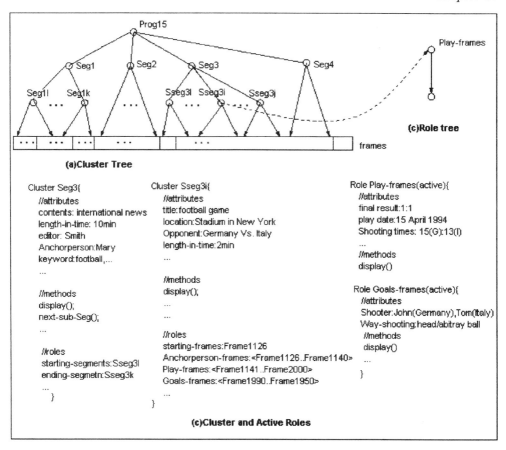

Figure 7. An example of Video Program.

Although we discussed only video re-production that makes use of pre-existing video segments and frames, the same principle should also be applicable to producing video programs that involve newly shot segments. The difference here is that these new video segments need to be classified (into clusters and sub-clusters) by a classifier such as VCC beforehand.

```
Cluster Seg5{
        //attributes
        opponent:  Germany Vs. Italy
        location:   Stadium in New York
        final result:  1:1
        play date:  15 April 1994
        shooter:   John(Germany), Tom(Italy)
```

Figure 8. An example of Video Production.

5.3 CONTEXT-DEPENDENT AND CONTEXT-FREE RETRIEVAL FACILITIES

Annotation-based video retrieval is a natural and effective means for accessing video data when higher level semantics are involved, and is complementary to content-based access. In the context of VIMS, both context-oriented and feature-based meta-data descriptions are organized in a structured yet flexible manner, and an associated set of query language facilities is currently being developed that can facilitate user queries that are either context-free or context-dependent. In this section, we briefly look at such advanced querying facilities. More details can be found in [12].

5.3.1 Navigational Browsing of the Meta-Data

The previously derived video segmentation and key frame descriptions serve as a natural form of "meta data" of VIMS, upon which higher level forms of meta data that are semantically meaningful to the end-users can be constructed through conceptual clustering techniques [13], resulting in so-called cluster- and role-trees [6]. Both the cluster- and role-trees can be naturally used for browsing meta-data of a set of video collections. Browsing the cluster-tree provides the end-user with an overall picture about the structure of a video program, whereas navigating the role-tree offers an introduction to the semantic features recognized/understood by the system, which can be used as high-level indices for feature-oriented search.

To be more specific, traversing the cluster tree downward (from a cluster to its sub-clusters) reveals a less detailed overview of the video program moving into a more detailed one. Similarly, one can traverse the role tree from top to bottom, which corresponds to moving from a more general feature to a more specific one. Hence there exists a "rough" correspondence between the two trees, as intuitively depicted in Figure 9.

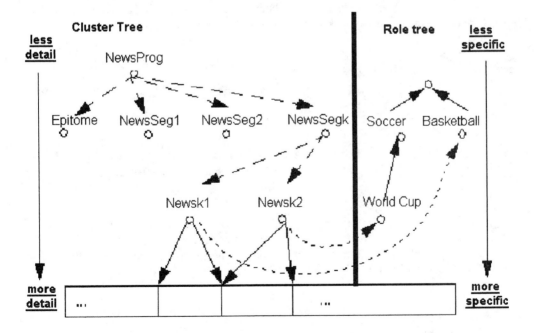

Figure 9. Navigation nodes across the cluster- and role-trees.

For example, starting from the cluster tree node Newsk1, which contains a role called basketball (cf., Figure 9), it is natural to expect that the parent node (i.e., Newsegk) may contain a role that is more general than the role basketball (e.g., Sports). The construction of the role tree nodes in VIMS is indeed "guided" by this philosophy. Such rough correspondence relationships between these two kinds of trees serve as an excellent navigational means that is similar to "relevance feedback" in information retrieval (IR). This technique enables the user to browse among different clusters (i.e., video programs) and different roles (i.e., semantic features) flexibly, as illustrated in Figure 9.

5.3.2   Context-Dependent Retrieval

The cluster tree in VIMS is useful not only for browsing the structure of video programs, but also for delimiting the search scope of user queries. For example, the user can choose to see a video clip at any level of abstraction. Back to the news example, if the user wants to watch all the main news, he can select the tree node in the upper level of the cluster tree. When he wants to see only a portion of a sports news piece (say, about soccer), he can select the node at the bottom and retrieve the video segment there according to an appropriate role (viz. Soccer). Structured querying facilities similar to SQL can be devised naturally to accommodate these kinds of searches. In this way, the user can easily select video objects at different levels of abstraction, and/or retrieve the video data from different search "scopes" or contexts. We consider below a couple of scenarios, using the associated query language facilities called OQL/race [3] for CCM, to retrieve video data based on this approach.

5.3.3   Restriction on the Cluster's Attributes

This type of query allows a cluster (viz., a video program) to be retrieved based on the attribute description of the cluster. For example, suppose we want to retrieve from NewsProg all the sub-clusters (video clips) that are about "sports." Using the OQL/race syntax, the SQL-like query statement may look like the following:

```
Select x
    from NewsProg
    Where       x belongs_to NewsProg AND
        x.category ="sport";
```

Note that the roles of the clusters are not involved in this kind of searching, and it is, therefore, similar to the conventional type of queries in relational databases.

5.3.4   Restriction on the Attributes of Role

In this situation, queries are processed according to certain types of roles in a cluster. For example, suppose the user is interested in viewing all the events that have taken place at the New York Stadium. The following OQL/race query statement may be issued:

```
Select x
    from NewsProg
    Where       x belongs_to NewsProg AND
        x has-role y AND
        y.venue = "New York Stadium".
```

5.3.5   Context-Free Retrieval

Context-sensitive retrieval is very efficient when the user has a clear idea of where to look. Quite often, however, the user may have only very vague idea of what program/clips to select, though she/he may know what semantic features to look for (e.g., any video scene about "horse racing"). In VIMS, this type of retrieval is called a "context-free" search, and is readily supported by the role-tree facilities since, as adumbrated above, roles can be utilized both within a cluster context and/or outside of a cluster context. In the latter case, roles effectively serve as semantic feature indices to the clusters, without which one cannot perform an effective context-free search. For instance, without knowing which particular video programs contain a scene about a bus accident, it is possible for a user to start a probe in VIMS by selecting from the role-tree a node describing a bus-accident, and the system will respond by returning a list of video clusters (programs/scenes/clips) that contain such a role. In other words, backward search from role-tree to cluster-tree is also allowed and supported in VIMS, in addition to the forward search (i.e., from a cluster to its roles).

Furthermore, there are also scenarios where different selection restrictions can be applied. The cases are similar to those of a context-sensitive search. We illustrate the main idea in the following example. Suppose we want to see some video clips about soccer in 1994, but don't know which video programs (clusters) to look for in the whole video library/database. The corresponding OQL/race statement can be used to formulate such a "context-free" query:

>   Select *
>   from [all] x
>   Where x has-role y AND
>   y type_of soccer AND
>   y.year = "1994".

Note that in this type of search, the search path starts from a role (denoted by y in the above example) that satisfies the user's description, relates back to any/all cluster (i.e., x) that contains y as its role, and then displays the video clips of x. Note that the default case is to select only one video cluster, but the user can optionally request to select all the possible video clusters by specifying the keyword all in the from clause.

5.3.6   Combing Annotation-Based and Content-Based Search

Clearly, annotation-based search is efficient for end-users to perform searches based on classified/annotated features, and the result returned from such a search is typically at video-scene or video-clip level. When a finer-grained search is needed (e.g., at individual frame level), and/or when annotated features are inadequate to delimit the frame scope, a content-based search based on image features (such as color, shape, texture, etc.) can be very effective and significant. In the next section, we describe several image analysis algorithms working with such primitive features that serve as a basis for accommodating various content-based searches. Note that the combined use of annotation-based and content-based searches does not have to be fixed in a particular order, but can be in any "interleaved" manner. Sometimes, repeated applications of each of these two search techniques can also be possible and needed.

5.4 SOME EXAMPLES

Continuing the example of the last subsection, the user may define further clusters and roles in CCM; an example would be a role called *Goal-frames*. However, in the initial input from VCC (basic indexing), *Goal-frames* are not discernible from other frames. It is impossible to index all possible features in all frames. In VIMS, our goal is to provide as many generic features extraction methods as possible as part of VCC. These feature extraction modules are executed only when required by CCM. Also, the domain knowledge from CCM (provided by the user) can simplify and focus better on the feature detection. In our *Goal-frames* example, we may notice that one way to specify these frames is to identify all segments containing the penalty areas, or, more simply, the goal post, because when shots take place, the goal post is, in general, in the camera's view. A goal post is composed of two vertical bars and a horizontal bar. Due to viewpoint differences, the horizontal bar is seen as slanted most of the time. On the contrary, no matter what the viewpoint is, the two vertical bars are almost always vertical in the image plane. Thus we model the goal post as (two) vertical bar(s) in the image and then instruct VCC (through CCM) to extract all images containing two vertical bars. Moreover, this detection can use generic edge detection and linking methods that are already implemented in VCC to suit the problem at hand. Here the images are indexed according to user specified semantics that are more application oriented than basic indexing. The idea has been applied to the video tape, "94 World Cup, 50 exciting shots." Figure 10 shows some example images of *Goal-frames* detected.

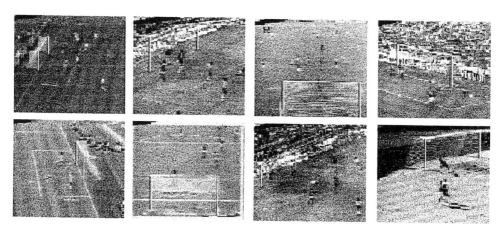

Figure 10. Localization of verticals bars for goal post detection.

In CCM, users usually use only high-level knowledge to define clusters and roles, but, unless they like to extract interesting images manually, they have to instruct VCC how to extract the images in terms of low-level features. A running example is to use color. People may define a role about some indoor scenes. The users may desire in the scene some special object, say a green sofa. They can tell VCC to extract images containing ranged sizes with green color. VCC can apply the color detection algorithm to do the job and thereby generate a semantic cluster of frames of indoor scenes containing a green sofa. Figure 11 shows some results of our experiments in searching for sofas in the images.

These two examples illustrate the natural harmony and power of coupling CCM with VCC, as envisaged in the fundamental design of our VIMS system. It should be noted that the VIMS architecture can facilitate, through user interaction, multi-perspective, semantic-level clustering and, hence, content-based retrieval in almost any situation. We are currently engaged in experimenting with other kinds of features like texture, motion, shape, etc.

Figure 11. Object searching with colors.

6. AN EXPERIMENTAL PROTOTYPE

As part of the research, we have developed an experimental prototype of VIMS. In this section, we give more details about the architecture of our VIMS prototype system. Also we describe some implementation aspects of the CCM. At the end, we report current status of our experimental VIMS prototype.

6.1 ARCHITECTURE AND COMPONENTS OF OUR PROTOTYPE SYSTEM

The current prototype of VIMS embodies a heterogeneous approach and environment in implementing the various components. As shown in Figure 12, the VCC part is implemented in Visual C++ on a Pentium PC equipped with Targa_2000 – a real-time frame grabber. The output of this component is then fed into the video database component, viz., the Video Base that is based on EOS – a persistent object storage manager developed at AT&T Bell Labs to support access to large objects by programs compiled with any C or C++ compiler such as the ones distributed by AT&T, SUN, GNU, and CenterLine [2]. The CCM is built on top of the Video Base and also the Method Base in which methods may be pre-existing video operation commands/functions provided by the VIMS, as well as those appended by the users. These methods can be invoked by roles/clusters, and any one method can be shared by several different roles/clusters. Note that the objects operated by methods of a role are the role's players who are corresponding clusters of component objects. Such objects, in general, are video materials in a video database. Therefore, the role can be viewed as the bridging mechanism between a video base and a method base.

Also shown in Figure 12 is a graphical user interface (GUI) through which the end-users interact with VIMS for video access and management. Among other features, the GUI provides the user with navigational facilities to browse the meta-data involved (i.e., the cluster- and role-trees). A structured query language is also being incorporated to facilitate both "declarative" and "feature-based" access to the video data [3]. Note that multiple clusters can be defined with respect to the same sequence of video data so that *semantic relativism* can be also accommodated.

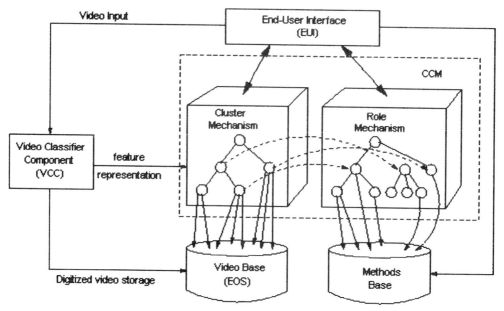

Figure 12. The components of VIMS prototype.

6.2 SOME FURTHER IMPLEMENTATION ISSUES ON CCM

In Section 4.2, we have described suitable data structures for implementing the clusters and roles. We will now discuss some further implementation issues related to operating the cluster hierarchy, role hierarchy, and dynamic execution of methods, respectively. More details can also be found in [6].

6.2.1 The Operations on the Cluster- and Role-Tree

At present, cluster- and role-hierarchies are only tree structures, namely, sub-clusters (sub-roles) and super-clusters (super-roles) are of a single-inheritance relationship. Generally, however, they are sufficient for video data processing because an existing object in a video database can play many different roles that are not in the same role hierarchy; similarly, an object can also participate in a variety of clusters that are not at all related.

In addition to the dynamic creation, deletion, and modification of a node in the cluster- and role-trees, the current prototype provides many basic operations as follows: it displays the structure of the cluster- and role-trees hierarchically; it displays all methods and attributes of a node in the two trees and inheritable ones of this node's ancestor nodes. A cluster node may display all its roles and those of the super-clusters. In these two trees, the user may find specified role- or cluster-nodes and identify their attributes, methods, and member objects. These basic operations (methods) facilitate the creation, deletion, and modification of node in cluster- and role-tree, and addition, removal and modification of attributes, methods, and member objects. For example, when the user adds attributes of role- and cluster-nodes, the system will invoke the method to display all the attributes of this node and inheritable attributes of its super-nodes. Thus the user knows which attributes have been defined or may be inherited to avoid repeating the definition. (Of course, the system can prompt the user if the definition is repeated.)

6.2.2 The Execution of Methods

As the prototype allows the user to include a set of methods into a cluster and a role dynamically, it greatly enhances dynamic characterization of clusters and roles. When including methods into a role or cluster, the user is required to provide the method name, and argument type, along with other details. While the user invokes a method from some role or cluster, the prototype will automatically display all methods (including inheritable methods of ancestor nodes) of this role or cluster to allow the user to choose the ones he/she desires.

The prototype supports two kinds of methods: one involves executable files, the other involves library functions. For the former, the prototype will invoke the method selected by the user through the UNIX system. For the latter, the process is more complex because the name of the function selected by the user is stored in a string as the value of this string, i.e., it is not an identifier-denoted function-name and so the program cannot invoke the function through this value. Fortunately, UNIX's C or C++ provides an interface of dynamic link programming. A Method Base (cf., Figure 12) must be created for a shared object library by a compiler system. Thus our prototype can obtain the address of the function by a string of symbols and then invoke the function by its address. A similar problem exists in passing arguments of function, however the C++ compiler provides only a means of obtaining the address of global variables by a string of symbols so that we cannot find the address of a real-argument by string value if the real-argument is a local variable. This is sufficient in the context of VIMS because the executives of the methods are all video data such as frame, segment, etc., so the prototype system may use Oids of EOS as arguments of invoking methods.

C++ allows the same name to denote different functions (i.e., overloading) so that the name of each function has a suffix in the internal symbol table generated by the C++ compiler. Hence, our prototype must map the method names provided by the user into its internal expressions.

6.2.3   Storage and Re-storage of Cluster- and Role-Trees

In the current prototype, cluster- and role-trees are not stored in EOS to maintain the efficiency of the system. The reason is that the structures of the two trees are rather complex, which imposes some difficulty for the EOS database kernel to operate efficiently.

In order to save memory, the prototype uses generalized lists as a storage structure of the trees. In particular, all information about the tree is converted into a character string by a set of recursive algorithms. The string is then stored in an external file. Restoring cluster- and role-trees involves the creation of the trees and all the related linked lists by reading and converting strings from the corresponding external file.

6.3 CURRENT STATUS

At present, the basic functionality of the CCM component has been implemented and tested, and the VCC component has achieved the following functions:

- detects camera breaks in image sequences (i.e., scene changes);
- selects key frames in video shots;
- builds a table of contents based on key frames for the entire sequence of images;
- allows end-users to index any segment of the image sequence using key frames and/or key words;
- allows end-users to select an object/pattern in a frame manually and track or search for that object/pattern in image sequences based on color and/or edges.

Figure 13 shows some sample indices obtained using VCC from a video sequence together with the computer interface of the control panel for the laser disc player. We are currently engaged in developing further VCC algorithms to classify the various contents of video segments including scenes with moving objects, camera zooming and panning, complex road scenes, fade-outs, noisy scenes, videos with degraded quality, and very dark video images. These classified features will also be fed into VIMS to enhance its efficiency and scope.

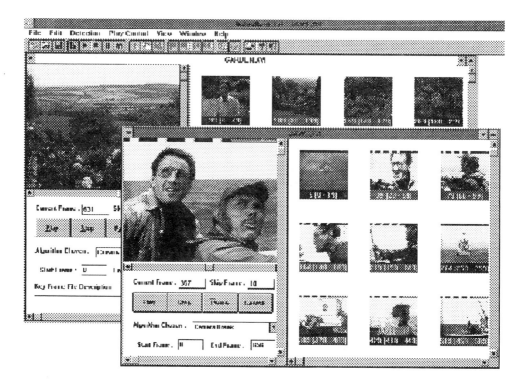

Figure 13. Screen layout of VIMS prototype.

7. SUMMARY AND CONCLUDING REMARKS

We have described the development of an experimental video database system called VIMS. Our research activities concerning the two fundamental components – i) a Video Classification Component (VCC) for the generation of effective indices necessary for structuring the video data and ii) a Conceptual Clustering Mechanism (CCM) having extended object-oriented features and techniques – have been presented.

The CCM portion of VIMS aims at overcoming the shortcomings of traditional relational database technology and conventional object-oriented database (OODB) approaches, especially in handling video data objects. The extension is centered around the notion of a conceptual clustering mechanism (CCM). Such extended clustering facilities allow *ad hoc*, irregular, tentative, and/or evolving video object collections ("clusters") to be dynamically formed, stored, and manipulated; thus various features of video data derived from video classification and/or management can be represented and accommodated in a flexible manner. Further, clusters can impact and interact with the constituents (i.e., video data objects) through the method defined by the active roles within the clusters. The utility of

CCM in various managements of video objects has been discussed. We have also described some of the design and implementation issues of CCM as part of our VIMS prototype system (which has been developed on top of a persistent object storage manager).

The VCC portion of VIMS deals with effective structuring and indexing of the raw video data. Some techniques recently developed, as part of VCC, at our laboratory are presented. We briefly introduced our methods for camera break detection and key frame selection. The relationships between VCC and CCM are discussed. We have also shown how to take advantage of domain knowledge of underlying applications. Experimental results have been provided.

For the current prototype, there are several remaining issues that need to be addressed in subsequent research. For the VCC, we are going to do more experiments for testing and improving our methods. Some other features such as texture, shape, and object motion are to be used in our system. For the CCM, a plan is ongoing to extend the current cluster-/role-tree to be lattices, so that a cluster/role can be derived from multiple super-clusters/super-roles. We will also enrich the current method base to provide richer types of functions/operations for video data processing and management. One problem that must be addressed here is the support of passing arbitrary arguments in order to provide flexible method definitions for the user. Also, a structured query language (extended Object-Oriented version of SQL) is being devised for CCM [3], which is to be ported and developed on top of VIMS. We plan further developments in our VIMS prototype system, emphasizing *accessibility* and *manipulability* – two fundamental functionalities that the end-user would expect from a system like VIMS. Finally, we plan to test and refine our system by applying it to several real-life environments, including TV news room studios, university educational technology centers, and perhaps public libraries.

REFERENCES

1. Bimbo, A., Vicario, E., and Zingoni, D., Sequence retrieval by contents through spatio-temporal indexing, in *Proc. IEEE Symposium on Visual Languages* (Cat. No.93TH0562-9), 1993, 88.
2. Eos, *Eos 2.1 User's Manual*, Technical Report, AT&T Bell Lab, Murray Hill, New Jersey 07974, USA, 1994.
3. Fung, C. W., and Li, Q., Versatile querying facilities for a dynamic object clustering model, in *Proc. Of OOER'95: Object-Oriented and Entity-Relationship Modeling, 14th International Conference*, Gold Coast, Australia, 1995, 77.
4. Grosky, W., Fotouli, F., Sethi, I., and Capatina, B., Object-oriented databases: Definition and research directions, *ACM SIGMOD Record*, 1994, 23.
5. Hirata, K., and Kato, T., Query by visual example, in *Advances in Database Technology EDBT'92, Proc. Third International Conference on Extending Database Technology*, Pirotte, A., Delobel, C., and Gottlob, G., Eds., Vol. 580 of Lecture Notes in Computer Science, Vienna, Austria, 1992, Springer-Verlag, 56.
6. Huang, L. S., Lee, J. C. M., Li, Q., and Xiong, W., An experimental video database management system based on advanced object-oriented techniques, in *Proc. of the SPIE - The International Society for Optical Engineering*, 2670, 1996, 158.
7. Jain, R., and Hampapur, A., Metadata in video databases, *SIGMOD Record*, 23, 1994, 27.

8. Kato, T., Database architecture for content-based image retrieval, in *SPIE Proc. Image Storage and Retrieval Systems*, 1662, 1992, 112.

9. Lee, J. C. M., and Ip, M. C., A robust approach for camera break detection in color video sequence, in *Proc. IAPR Workshop on Machine Vision Application (MVA'94)*, Kawasaki, Japan, 1994, 502.

10. Lee, J. C. M., Li, Q., and Xiong, W., VIMS: A video information manipulation system, *Multimedia Tools and Applications*, 4, 1997, 7.

11. Lee, J. C. M., Xiong, W., Shen, D. G., and Ma, R. H., Video segment indexing through classification and interactive view-based query (invited paper), in *Proc. of Second Asian Conference on Computer Vision*, 2, Singapore, 1995, 524.

12. Li, Q., and Lam, K. M., Context-sensitive and context-free retrieval in a video database system, in *Proc. IAPR TC12 First Int'l Workshop on Image Database and Multi Media Search (IDB-MMS)*, Amsterdam, 1996, 123.

13. Li, Q., and Lee, J. C. M., Dynamic object clustering for video database manipulations, in *Proc. IFIP 2.6 Working Conference on Visual Database Systems*, Lausanne, Switzerland, 1995, 125.

14. Li, Q., and Smith, J., A conceptual model for dynamic clustering in object databases, in *Proc. 18th Intl. Conf. on VLDB*, 1992, 457.

15. Little, T. D. C., Ahanger, E., Folz, R. J., Gibbon, J. F., Reeve, F. W., Schelleng, D. H., and Venkatesh, D., A digital on-demand video service supporting content-based queries, in *Proc. First ACM Intl. Conf. on Multimedia*, 1993, 427.

16. Nagasaka, A., Miyatake, T., and Ueda, H., Video retrieval method using a sequence of representative images in a scene, in *Proc. of IAPR Workshop on Machine Vision Applications*, Kawasaki, Japan, 1994, 79.

17. Nagasaka, A., and Tanaka, Y., Automatic video indexing and full-video search for object appearances, in *IFIP Proc. Visual Database Systems*, II, Knuth, E., and Wegner, L., eds., IFIP, Elsevier Science Publishers B. V. (North-Holland), 1992, 113.

18. Niblack, W., Barber, R., Equitz, W., Flickner, M., Glasman, E., Petkovic, D., Yanker, P., Faloutsos, C., and Taubin,G., The QBIC project: Query images by content using color, texture and shape, in *SPIE Proc. Storage and Retrieval for Image and Video Databases*, 1908, 1993, 173.

19. Oomoto, E., and Tanaka, K., Ovid: Design and implementation of a video-object database system, *IEEE Trans. on Knowledge and Data Engineering*, 5,629, 1994.

20. Pentland, A., Picard, R. W., and Scaroff, S., Photobook: Tools for content-based manipulation of image databases, in *SPIE Proc. Storage and Retrieval for Image and Video Databases II*, 2185, 1994, 34. Longer version available as MIT Media Lab Perceptual Computing Technical Report No.255, 1993.

21. Sethi, I. K. and Patel, N., A statistical approach to scene change detection, in *Proc. of the SPIE - The International Society for Optical Engineering*, 2420, San Jose, CA, 1995, 26. Storage and Retrieval for Image and Applications.

22. Smoliar, S. W., and Zhang, H. J., Content-based video indexing and retrieval, *IEEE Multimedia*, 1, 356, 1994.

23. Sudhir, G. and Lee, J. C. M., Video annotation by motion interpretation using optical flow streams, *Journal of Visual Communication and Image Representation*, 7, 354, 1996.

24. Tonomura, Y., Video handling based on structured information for hypermedia systems, in *Proc. ACM Int'l Conf. on Multimedia Information Systems*, ACM Press, New York, 1991, 333.

25. Ueda, H., Miyataka, T., and Yoshizawa, S., Impact: An interactive natural-motion-picture dedicated multimedia authoring system, in *Proc. Human Factors in Computing Systems CHI'91*, 1991, 343.

26. Bertino, E. and Garza, J. F., Composite object revisited, in *Proc. of ACM SIGMOD Intl. Conf. on Management of Data*, 1989, 337.

27. Xiong, W. and Lee, J. C. M., Efficient scene change detection and camera motion annotation for video classification, *Technical Report HKUST-CS97-16*, HK Univ. of Science & Technology, also submitted to *Computer Vision and Image Understanding* (Special Issue on Computer Vision Applications for Network-Center Computing).

28. Xiong, W., Lee, J. C. M., and Ip, M. C., Net comparison: a fast and effective method for classifying image sequences., in *Proc. of the SPIE - The International Society for Optical Engineering*, 2420, San Jose, CA, 1995, 318. Storage and Retrieval for Image and Video Databases III.

29. Xiong, W., Lee, J. C. M., and Ma, R. H., Automatic video data structuring through shot partitioning and key frame selection, *Machine Vision and Application*, 10, 51, 1997.

30. Yeo, B. L., and Liu, B., Rapid scene analysis on compressed video, *IEEE Transactions on circuits and systems for video technology*, 5, 533, 1995.

31. Yeung, M., Yeo, B. L., Wolf, W., and Liu, B., Video browsing using clustering and scene transitions on compressed sequences, in *Conf. on Multimedia Computing and Networking (1995)*, 2417 of *Proc. of the SPIE - The International Society for Optical Engineering*, 1995, 399.

32. Zhang, H. J., Kankanhalli, A., and Smoliar, S. W., Automatic partitioning of full-motion video, *ACM Multimedia Systems*, 1, 10, 1993.

33. Zhang, H. J., Low, C. Y., Gong, Y. H., and Smoliar, S. W., Video parsing using compressed data, *in Proc. of the SPIE - The International Society for Optical Engineering*, 2182, San Jose, CA, 1994, 142. Image and Video Processing II.

34. Zhang, H. J. and Smoliar, S. W., Developing power tools for video indexing and retrieval, in *SPIE Proc. Storage and Retrieval for Image and Video Databases II*, 2185, 1994, 140.

16

MULTIMEDIA INFORMATION RETRIEVAL USING PICTORIAL TRANSCRIPTS

Behzad Shahraray
AT&T Labs - Research
Multimedia Processing Research Department
Red Bank, New Jersey 07701

1. INTRODUCTION...346
2. CONTENT-BASED SAMPLING OF VIDEO.......................................346
3. TEXT PROCESSING..348
4. AUDIO ENCODING...349
5. AUTOMATED HYPERMEDIA DOCUMENT GENERATION............349
6. SEARCHING AND BROWSING MECHANISMS................................351
7. STREAMING DELIVERY OF MULTIMEDIA INFORMATION.........357
8. CONCLUSIONS...359
   REFERENCES...359

Abstract. This chapter describes a working system for the acquisition and retrieval of multimedia information. The system employs multimedia processing techniques to process the pictorial, textual, and auditory information contained in television broadcasts, to condense and index the information, and populate a digital multimedia library. Visual information contained in the video is condensed by a content-based sampling method. These samples provide a compact representation of the visual information and serve as a pictorial index into the program. Linguistic processing refines the textual information supplied by closed captions and extracts key words and phrases for generating a textual index into the program. Audio and motion video are compressed and indexed based on their temporal relationships with the selected video frames. The extracted information is used to generate a hypermedia rendition of the program suitable for searching, browsing, and selective retrieval. Several searching and browsing mechanisms are provided that allow for the efficient retrieval of multimedia information from several thousand hours of television programs.

1. INTRODUCTION

Advances in media compression algorithms and the availability of high-capacity and cost-effective storage devices have made it feasible to store large volumes of multimedia information in digital form. Multimedia networking systems and protocols that allow for the exchange of multimedia information between computers have enabled remote access to this information. Effective creation and utilization of these large repositories of information involves the application of media processing techniques to organize, condense, and index information.

The creation of such repositories involves the conversion of the constituent media streams into a digital form suitable for storage and manipulation on a digital computer, as well as establishing the spatial and temporal relationship between different media segments. It also involves the processing of multimedia information to extract relevant information about their content and structure that can be utilized to organize and index the information. A large body of work exists in the area of text-based information retrieval. Multimedia indexing and information retrieval has been a very active area of research in the past few years. There are a large number of research papers and many working systems based on this research that have shown promising results. A review, or even a brief mention, of the relevant work in the area of multimedia indexing and information retrieval is beyond the scope of this chapter. Therefore, we will limit our discussion to one system; namely, *Pictorial Transcripts* [1] and the associated media processing algorithms that have been developed and refined over the last few years.

Television and video programs are rich sources of information. Despite their dynamic nature, in comparison to documents consisting of text and still images, they lack the interactivity that is needed to perform efficient searching and browsing. Organizing these programs into a searchable and browsable digital library that is accessible on a communications network would provide a large archive of programs spanning a long period of time that would be available for selective retrieval and browsing.

The Pictorial Transcripts system is an example of how media processing methods can be applied to the automatic generation of a digital multimedia library of television programs. The digital library accumulated over a period of several years currently contains thousands of hours of video programs in a condensed form that can be a searched, browsed, and selectively retrieved over communications networks.

A discussion of the media processing algorithms and the searching and browsing capabilities of the Pictorial Transcripts system are given.

2. CONTENT-BASED SAMPLING OF VIDEO

The bandwidth and storage requirements of digitized video (even in compressed form) presents challenges, in terms of storage and bandwidth requirements, to most multimedia server systems. This problem is addressed by representing the visual content of the program using a small set of still images that are selected by a content-based sampling algorithm [2]. The selection process divides the video into segments with similar visual contents, and uses a single *representative frame* to represent each of the segments. In general, performing this task would require levels of image understanding beyond what is possible, or feasible, with the current state of the art in computer vision and image understanding. However, the structure that has been built into professionally produced video programs can be exploited to achieve acceptable levels of performance. The content-based sampling method is based on detecting the abrupt and gradual transitions between consecutive shots, as well as quantitative measurement of camera motion parameters within individual shots.

The block diagram for the content-based sampling method is shown in Figure 1. Motion compensated block matching generates match and motion estimates between corresponding blocks in consecutive video frames. An order statistic filter combines the block match values into a one dimensional inter-frame match signal representing the likelihood that the consecutive frames belong to the same video segments (shots). This signal is a good indicator of abrupt transitions (i.e., *cuts*) between consecutive video shots. The detection of gradual transitions (e.g., dissolves, fades, digital editing special effects) between shots requires additional processing of the inter-frame match signal over several video frames. This task is performed by temporally filtering the signal with a filter whose coefficients are controlled by a motion analysis module. This enables the detection of gradual transition while considerably reducing the likelihood of false detections resulting from rapid motion. The motion analysis module also serves the purpose of estimating the components of the global motion resulting from camera motion. This camera motion information is used to detect *camera-induced* scene changes. These are changes in the visual contents of the scene that result from limited or continuous camera pan and tilt motions. Such motions are used in professionally produced video programs to achieve such goals as *association* (i.e., bridging the views from two different objects), or *orientation* (i.e., showing a wide area that would not fit in a single image). The camera-induced scene changes further divide individual shots into smaller segments from which representative frames are retained. A decision module employs a finite state machine to keep track of the sequence of events and generate a sample signal indicating the proper points within the video sequence where representative images should be taken. The decision module also serves the task of classifying the scene transition points into a number of categories (e.g., cut, fade, dissolve, camera-induced). This information is utilized to improve the quality of the final presentation when choices need to be made between several representative images.

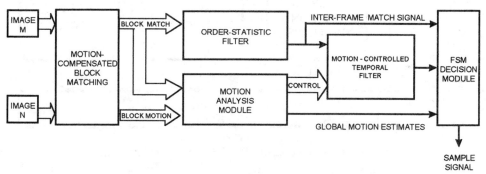

Figure 1. Block diagram of content-based video sampling.

The images obtained by the content-based sampling process provide a compact representation of the visual contents of a video program. This representation can either be used in conjunction with other media, such as text or audio, to create a compact rendition of the program contents, or used as a pictorial index for selective retrieval of segments from the original program. Efficient computational methods have been devised that enable the real-time implementation of the content-based sampling method using only a small fraction of the compute cycles on a personal computer (PC). Additional image processing to compute the degree of similarity between different representative images, as well as spotting the occurrence of predetermined images in the video are also performed. Such information is utilized to refine the final presentation and help create more intelligent searching and browsing mechanisms.

3. TEXT PROCESSING

Textual representation of information enables the representation of non-pictorial information in a compact form that lends itself easily to text-based search. Ideally, such a *transcript* should be generated from the audio track of the program using automatic speech recognition (ASR). Large vocabulary automatic speech recognizers (LVASR) exist for specific domains (e.g., the North American Business News task) that are capable of transcribing speech with an off-line word accuracy as high as 90.5 percent [3,4]. When applied to other tasks for which the existing language and acoustic models do not apply, however, the error rates can be considerably higher. Encouraging results have been obtained by applying such techniques to transcribing television programs [5]. Such transcripts have shown promise for searching and information retrieval tasks. However, the high error rates limit the utility of such automatically generated transcripts for direct use by humans.

Manually entered closed caption text that accompanies most television programs provides a more accurate textual representation of the information contained in the program. This information, that is included for the benefit of hearing-impaired viewers, is encoded in the video signal and is recovered from the video signal during the data acquisition phase (see Figure 2), decoded, and stored in raw form for further processing. This acquisition phase also includes the real-time application of the content-based sampling method, as well as acquisition and compression of the audio and video components.

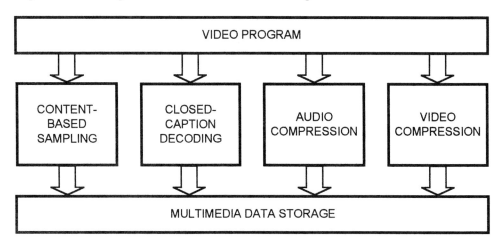

Figure 2. Data acquisition phase of the Pictorial Transcripts system.

The raw closed caption text undergoes lexical and linguistic processing (as shown in Figure 3) to convert it to a form suitable for generating the hypermedia documents. This processing serves several purposes that are briefly outlined here. It converts all of the upper-case text from the closed captions into lower-case while preserving the correct capitalization. The processing also serves to extract key words and key phrases for creating a list of index terms representing the content of the video. Another purpose of the text processing stage is to extract relevant words or phrases that are used to create hyperlinks to other parts of the video or to other multimedia documents. As will be demonstrated later, such links are used to provide supplementary information about topics covered in the program. Currently these tasks rely on phrase databases that have been generated either automatically or manually prior to text processing. The manual entry is very limited and serves the purpose of supplying the processing algorithms with specific information such as uncommon names and specific information about other available documents that can be used to provide supplementary information. The main phrase database is generated automatically by an offline analysis of a large corpus of text from the Associated Press (AP) newswire. Lexical processing also serves the goal of refining the temporal relationship (synchronization) between the images and the textual information. The synchronization information is recorded during the acquisition phase and stored in a Media Correspondence Table (MCT).

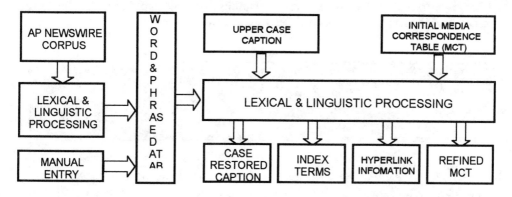

Figure 3. Lexical and linguistic processing of closed caption text.

4. AUDIO ENCODING

While the combination of the images obtained by content-based sampling and the associated text provides the most compact representation of the information content of the video program, audio is added to convey additional information about the video (e.g., music, non-speech sounds). The audio component is essential when the closed caption text is unavailable.

In order to provide a high quality audio stream, a Transform Predictive wideband speech Coder (TPC) [6] is used to compress the 7 kHz bandwidth audio stream to a 16 Kb/s rate. This bit rate can be reliably transmitted (along with the images and the text) over switched telephone networks with modems running at rates of 28.8 Kbs and higher. Digitization and compression of the audio signal is performed in real time during the acquisition phase. The audio signal is segmented on the basis of its temporal relationship with the video segments.

5. AUTOMATED HYPERMEDIA DOCUMENT GENERATION

In the final phase, the information derived by media processing is used to generate a hypermedia rendition of the video program contents in Hypertext Markup Language (HTML) form. The HTML generation process is driven by predetermined templates that are tailored to fit the requirements of different applications. Moreover, the process dynamically adjusts the final presentation based on the availability of different media components (e.g., audio, video) for the given program. The entire process, from media processing to HTML generation, takes place in real time.

Each program is organized into several HTML pages to make it more manageable. Initially, the segmentation of the program into individual pages was based on size, as well as detected commercial boundaries. Eventually the system will be able to take advantage of more advanced text segmentation techniques to perform topic segmentation [7]. In certain cases, the information about the structure of the visual information can be used to segment the program at the story boundaries. In these cases image matching capabilities can be utilized to locate the story boundaries, thereby achieving a more meaningful page segmentation. An example of how image similarity computation can be used to address this problem is given in Section 6.

A segment of a sample HTML page generated by the system is shown in Figure 4. The images extracted by the content-based sampling algorithm are displayed next to the corresponding linguistically processed closed caption text.

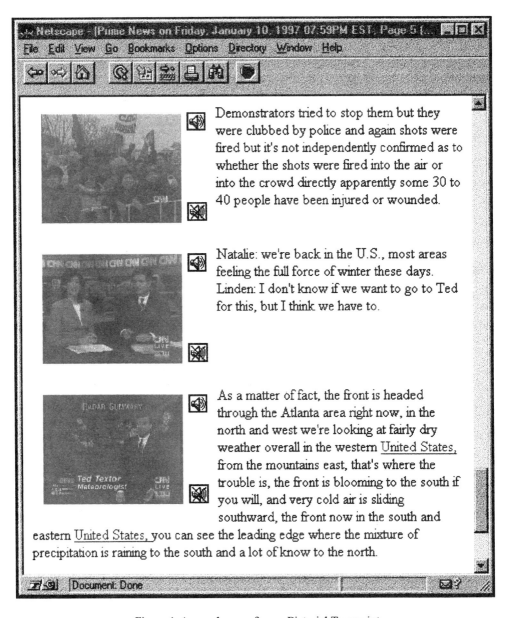

Figure 4. A sample page from a Pictorial Transcript.

Audio icons next to each image in Figure 4 can be used to initiate the replay of the corresponding audio contents. Hence, the compact representation serves as an index into the audio stream associated with the video program. Later in this chapter, we will give an example of how a similar arrangement can be used to initiate selective replay of motion video by selecting the images. Figure 4 also depicts the use of the automated word and phrase spotting to generate links to supplementary information. The two (underlined) occurrences of the phrase "United States" on this page are links to another HTML document with additional information. This link takes the user to a document in a different digital library (i.e., the CIA World Fact Book), a small segment of which is shown in Figure 5.

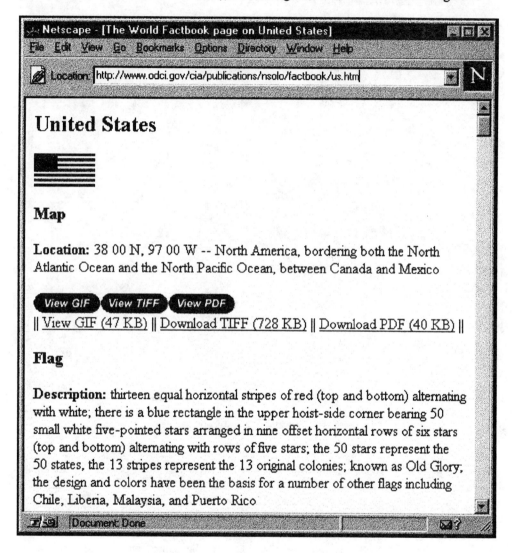

Figure 5. Supplementary information about a topic.

6. SEARCHING AND BROWSING MECHANISMS

The research prototype of the Pictorial Transcripts system currently contains several thousand hours of video programs from several broadcasters, as well as some internal video presentations. Effective utilization of this large digital multimedia library calls for intelligent mechanisms for selective retrieval of information. This is done by organizing the programs into several different categories and providing several searching and browsing mechanisms.

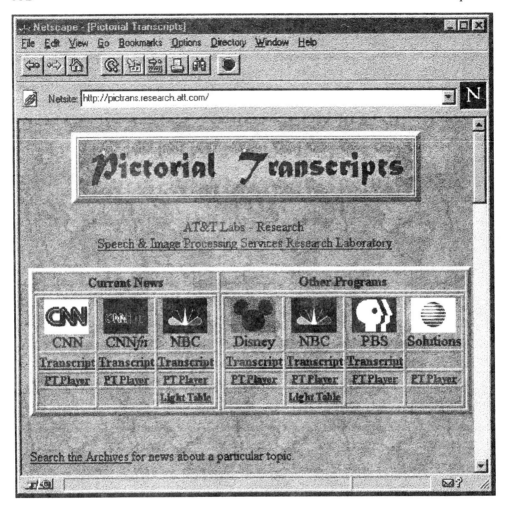

Figure 6. The Pictorial Transcripts home page.

Figure 6 shows a segment of the Pictorial Transcripts home page. This figure shows the organization of programs of the television network. There are several different representations for each program as follows. The "transcript" which gives an HTML presentation of the information in the form that consists of still images, text, and icons for initiating the replay of associated audio. This representation is depicted in Figure 4. The "PT Player" representation provides a real-time replay of the same image, text, and audio information using a streaming player that will be discussed later. The "light-table" rendition of a segment of a video program is depicted in Figure 7. This representation consists of images, or images and audio, and is useful for rapid browsing of the program material based on pictorial information. This representation enables users to quickly browse through the entire program to spot an image of interest. The audio icon can then be used to supply additional information about the program by initiating the replay of audio at the corresponding point.

Figure 7. The light-table presentation of program content for visual searching.

Selecting one of the networks (e.g., CNN) from the home page presents the user with a list of the different programs from the selected network (Figure 8a). For each program, selecting the most recent broadcast takes the user directly to that program. Selecting "previous shows" will give access to the archives of the program through a dynamically generated sequential calendar interface depicted in Figures 8b and 8c.

(a)

(b)

(c)

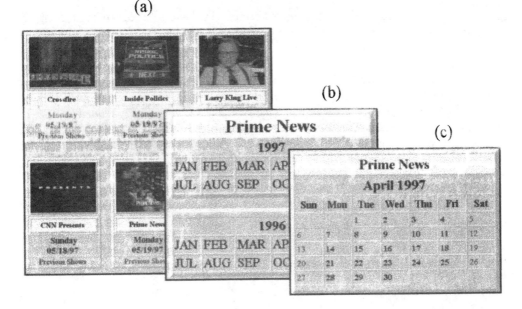

Figure 8. Navigation mechanisms.

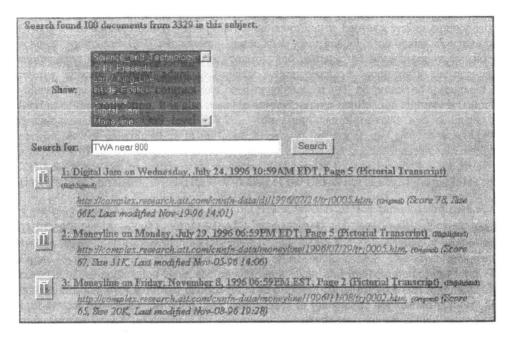

Figure 9. An example of full-text search.

The system provides several searching and browsing mechanisms to facilitate selective retrieval of specified material. One such searching mechanism allows the user to select programs based on full-text search as shown in Figure 9. This interface enables the user to specify one or a combination of programs to be included in the search. A search string specified by the user returns information about relevant video programs that can be selectively retrieved.

Image-based searches can also be performed. In this case, a user-selected image is compared with each of the images within the program (or any other set of programs) to compute a set of similarity measures that select the most similar images. These images serve as links to corresponding points in the program. As it was pointed out in Section 5, in certain cases, this capability can be utilized to segment a news program into story units. For example, for some news programs, the beginning of a new story is always associated with an off-center view of the anchorperson with a small window showing a story-related picture. In these cases the image matching capabilities can be utilized to locate the story boundaries. This is done by using one such image to perform a "query by example" to find all similar images as shown in Figure 10.

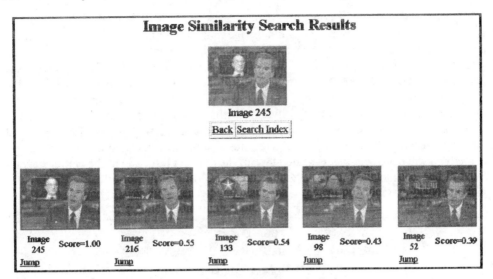

Figure 10. Browsing by image similarity.

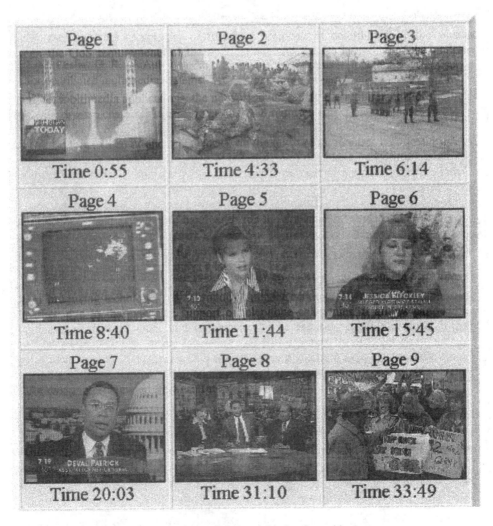

Figure 11. An example of a pictorial index for a video program.

Each video program is organized into pages. Each page provides links to enable navigation to the previous, next, or any other page in the program, as well as an *index page*. The index page enables the selection of the pages using textual and pictorial indices. The pictorial index (Figure 11) consists of a collection of images each of which represents the contents of a single page of the transcript. These images can be clicked to bring up the corresponding page of the transcript. The index page (Figure 12) enables the user to retrieve a given segment of the program by specifying the time. It also presents the user with a set of key words and phrases extracted during the linguistic processing phase of the Pictorial Transcripts generation. Selecting one of these words or phrases results in the generation of a *keyword specific transcript* that is geared toward the efficient browsing of the entire program to access relevant information about the selected keyword.

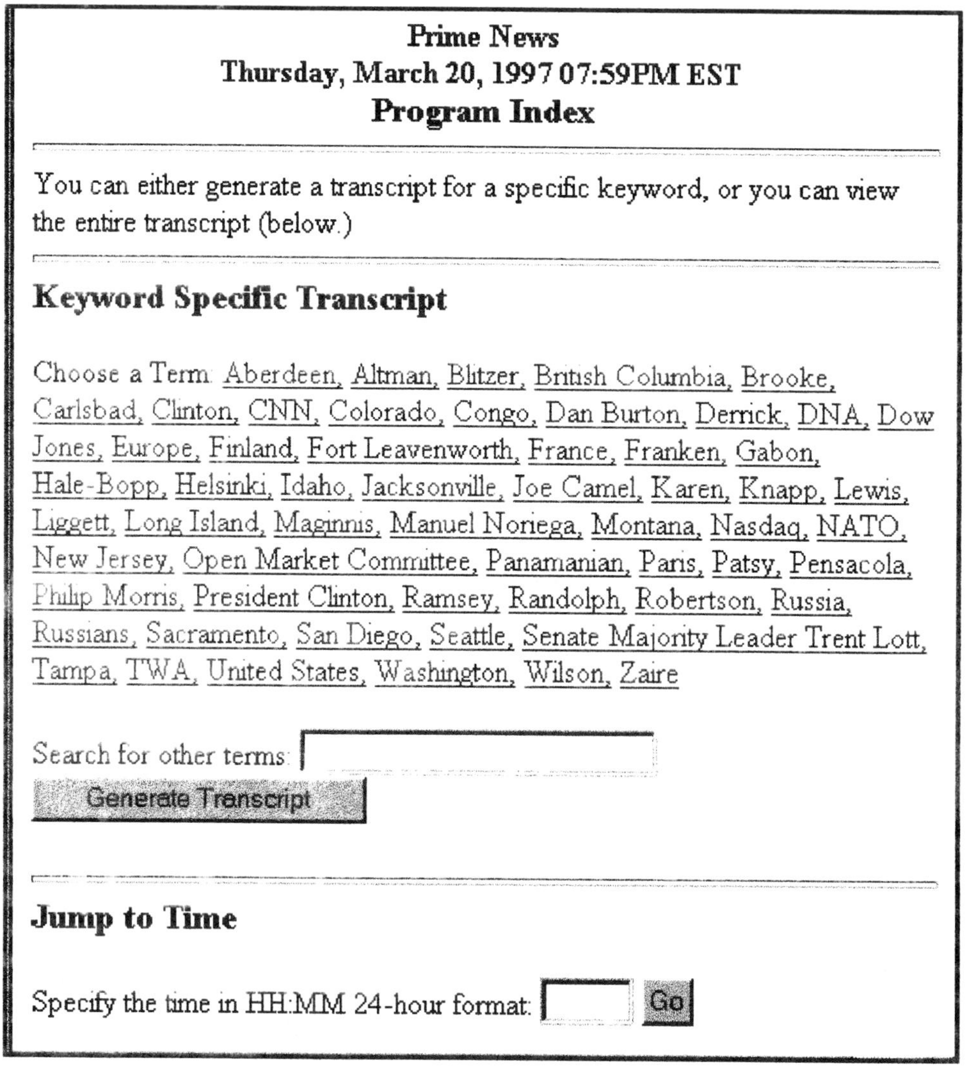

Prime News
Thursday, March 20, 1997 07:59PM EST
Program Index

You can either generate a transcript for a specific keyword, or you can view the entire transcript (below.)

Keyword Specific Transcript

Choose a Term: Aberdeen, Altman, Blitzer, British Columbia, Brooke, Carlsbad, Clinton, CNN, Colorado, Congo, Dan Burton, Derrick, DNA, Dow Jones, Europe, Finland, Fort Leavenworth, France, Franken, Gabon, Hale-Bopp, Helsinki, Idaho, Jacksonville, Joe Camel, Karen, Knapp, Lewis, Liggett, Long Island, Maginnis, Manuel Noriega, Montana, Nasdaq, NATO, New Jersey, Open Market Committee, Panamanian, Paris, Patsy, Pensacola, Philip Morris, President Clinton, Ramsey, Randolph, Robertson, Russia, Russians, Sacramento, San Diego, Seattle, Senate Majority Leader Trent Lott, Tampa, TWA, United States, Washington, Wilson, Zaire

Search for other terms: [   ]

[Generate Transcript]

Jump to Time

Specify the time in HH:MM 24-hour format: [   ] [Go]

Figure 12. An example of the keyword section of an index page.

Added efficiency is achieved by displaying only a subset of the representative images that are likely to correspond to the selected keyword. The association is established based on proximity (i.e., only images which correspond with, or are in close proximity to, the segments of text containing the keyword are retained). The keyword-based browsing capability is achieved by placing navigation controls next to each occurrence of the keyword in the specialized transcript. These controls allow the user to jump to preceding or succeeding occurrences of the word in the transcript. A segment of a keyword specific transcript generated by selecting the phrase "President Clinton" (in Figure 12) is shown in Figure 13. In this case the proximity-based association criterion performs satisfactorily and presents the user with a relevant picture. The forward arrow takes the user to the next occurrence of the phrase, while the backward arrow goes to the previous occurrence.

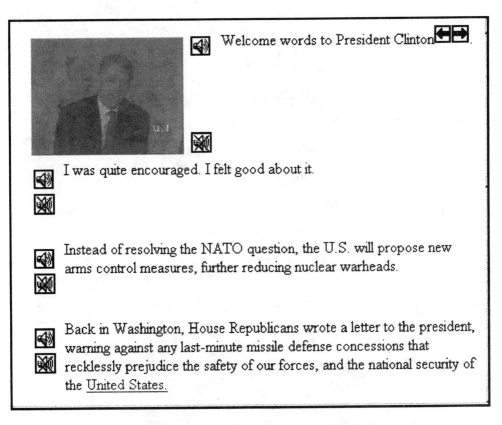

Figure 13. A browsable keyword-specific transcript.

7. STREAMING DELIVERY OF MULTIMEDIA INFORMATION

Representing the information contained in video programs by text and still frames generates a compact presentation with considerably reduced storage and bandwidth requirements. When storage and bandwidth constraints preclude the delivery of continuous media, such as audio and video, this compact presentation can be used to convey the information. In the presence of sufficient bandwidth, this compact representation can serve as an index into the higher bandwidth presentations to allow selective, non-linear access to information. Different combinations of still-frames, text, audio, and video can be used to meet different bandwidth and quality requirements. Two possible implementations are presented here.

Figure 14 shows a streaming player for the Pictorial Transcripts. This player delivers a real-time presentation of the video program using the content-based sampled images, in synchronization with processed closed captioned text and audio. The combination of JPEG compressed images, TPC encoded audio, and Lempel-Ziv compressed text results in sufficiently low bandwidth requirements that allow the delivery of information over a 28.8 Kbs modem connection.

Figure 14. The streaming multimedia player.

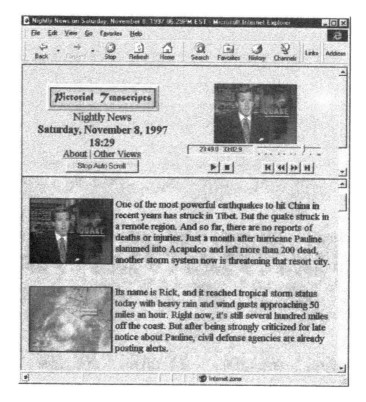

Figure 15. Selective retrieval and streaming delivery of indexed video.

The player provides VCR-type controls for browsing. The forward and backward controls enable non-linear navigation through the program by jumping to the next or previous scene. The slider allows rapid image-based browsing of the program.

Figure 15 shows an implementation that allows selective delivery of MPEG encoded video. The bottom frame contains the low bandwidth representation that can be quickly browsed to find a segment of interest. Once a segment has been identified, selecting the image initiates the streaming delivery of the video in the top frame.

8. CONCLUSIONS

Effective management of large volumes of multimedia information involves the employment of a diverse set of techniques from areas such as image and video processing, speech and audio processing, and text-based information retrieval. The current state of the art in these fields precludes the extraction of high level descriptors that can be used to generate indices based on the information contents. However, experiments indicate that, in specific domains, the levels of understanding currently achievable can go a long way in generating acceptable levels of performance for indexing and selective retrieval of multimedia information.

REFERENCES

1. Shahraray B. and Gibbon D.C., "Automated Authoring of Hypermedia Documents of Video Programs," *Proceedings of the Third ACM Conference on Multimedia*, pp. 401-409. San Francisco, Calif. 1995.

2. Shahraray B., "Scene Change Detection and Content-Based Sampling of Video Sequences," in *Digital Video Compression: Algorithms and Technologies*, Proceedings of SPIE 2419, 1995.

3. Riley M., Ljolje A., Hindle D., and Pereira F., "The AT&T 60,000 Word Speech-to-Text System," *Proceedings of Eurospeech*, 1995.

4. Mohri M. and Riley M., "Weighted Determinization and Minimization for Large Vocabulary Speech Recognition," *Proceedings of Eurospeech*, 1997.

5. Hauptmann A.G. and Witbrock M., "Informedia: News-on-Demand – Multimedia Information Acquisition and Retrieval," in *Intelligent Multimedia Information Retrieval*, Maybury, M. (Ed), AAAI Press / MIT Press, 1997.

6. Chen J.H. and Wang D., "Transform Predictive Coding of Wideband Speech Signals," *Proceedings of IEEE Int. Conf. Acoustics, Speech and Signal Processing ICASSP'96*, pp. 275-278, Atlanta, GA. 1996.

7. Salton G., Singhal A., Buckley C., and Mitra M., "Automatic Text Decomposition Using Text Segments and Text Themes," *Proceedings of the Seventh ACM Conference on Hypertext*, pp. 53-65, Washington, D.C., 1996.

17

AUTOMATIC TRAILER PRODUCTION

Rainer Lienhart, Silvia Pfeiffer, and Wolfgang Effelsberg
University of Mannheim
68131 Mannheim, Germany
{lienhart,pfeiffer,effelsberg}@pi4.informatik.uni-mannheim.de

1. **INTRODUCTION**..362
2. **RELATED WORK**...363
3. **DEFINITIONS**..363
4. **CONCEPTUAL OVERVIEW**..365
5. **VIDEO ANALYSIS FEATURES**..365
    5.1   COLOR HISTOGRAMS AND COLOR COHERENCE VECTORS 366
    5.2   FRONTAL FACE DETECTOR 367
    5.3   DIALOG DETECTION 368
    5.4   TEXT RECOGNITION AND TITLE EXTRACTION 368
    5.5   AUDIO EVENTS..369
6. **VIDEO SEGMENTATION**...369
    6.1   SHORT BOUNDARY DETECTION...369
    6.2   AUDIO CUTS AND AUDIO FEATURE VECTORS 370
    6.3   SHORT CLUSTERING CONCEPT 370
    6.4   SCENE DETERMINATION...371
7. **TRAILER GENERATION**..372
    7.1   CLIP SELECTION 372
    7.2   CLIP ASSEMBLY..373
8. **EXPERIMENTAL RESULTS**...375
9. **POST-EDITING**..376
10. **CONCLUSION AND OUTLOOK**..376
     REFERENCES 376

Abstract. This chapter presents an algorithm for automatic production of a video abstract of a feature film, similar to movie trailers. It selects clips from the original video based on detection of special events like dialogs, shots, explosions, and text occurrences, and general action indicators applied to scenes. An editing model is used to assemble these clips into a movie trailer. Such movie abstracts are useful for multimedia archives, in movie marketing, or for home entertainment.

1. INTRODUCTION

We all know that the abstract of an article is a short summary of a document, often used to pre-select material relevant to the user. The medium of the abstract and the document is the same, namely, text. In the age of multimedia, it would be desirable to use video abstracts in very much the same way: as short clips containing the essence of a longer video, without a break in the presentation medium. However, the state of the art is to use textual abstracts for indexing and searching large video archives. This media break is harmful since it typically leads to considerable loss of information. Unclear, for example, is the level of abstraction desirable for textual description; if we see a famous politician at a dinner table with a group of other politicians, what should the text say? Should it specify the names of the people, give their titles, specify the event, or just describe the scene as if it were a painting, emphasizing colors and geometry? An audio-visual abstract, to be interpreted by a human user, is semantically much richer than a text.

The power of visual abstracts can be helpful in many application contexts. Let us look at some examples.

Multimedia archives. With the advent of multimedia PCs and workstations, the World Wide Web, and standardized video compression techniques, more and more video material is being digitized and archived worldwide. Wherever digital video material is stored, we can use video abstracts for indexing and retrieval. For instance, the on-line abstracts could support journalists when searching old video material, or when producing documentaries. Another example is the Internet movie database IMDb on the Web (http://uk.imdb.com/). It is indexed on the basis of "hand-made" textual information about the movies; sometimes, a short clip, selected at random, is also included. This index could be easily extended by automatically generated video abstracts.

Movie marketing. Trailers are widely used in movie advertising in cinemas and on television. Currently the production of this type of abstract is quite costly and time-consuming. With our system we could produce trailers automatically or at least support a professional trailer producer. In order to tailor a trailer to a specific audience, we would set certain parameters such as the desirable amount of action or violence.

Another possibility would be a digital TV magazine. Instead of reading short textual descriptions of upcoming programs you could view the abstracts without having to get up from your couch (assuming you have an integrated TV set and Web browser). And for digital video-on-demand systems, the content provider could supply video abstracts in an integrated fashion.

Home entertainment. Should you miss an episode of your favorite television series, the abstracting system could perform the task of telling you briefly what happened "in the meantime."

Many more innovative applications can be built around the basic video abstracting technique.

This chapter is structured as follows. Section 2 relates our work to the achievements of others. Section 3 defines the most frequently used basic terms, Section 4 presents the concept of our approach, which is described in detail in the subsequent three sections. The results produced by our fully automated abstracting system are described in Section 8. A scenario of a semi-automatic trailer production process using our work is described in Section 9, and Section 10 concludes the chapter.

2. RELATED WORK

Research is booming in the field of video abstracting. Most systems, e.g., [1][10][17][20][21][23][26][27], work on the image track alone and extract key frames only. However, we regard the audio track as a very important source of information, as do Smith et al. [18] and Taniguchi et al. [19]. In abstracting, we explore the content of the audio track as well as that of the image track. We are also convinced that in order to get a good idea of the content of a video, it is best to watch a short abstract of it. We therefore calculate a moving-images abstract with audio and enlarge this information by the additional extraction of special events. The system presented extracts clips for their content, an approach distinctly different from all other systems, which extract key frames on a shot basis (except for [18],[14], and [22]).

Prerequisite to the construction of a good abstract is the segmentation of the video into larger semantic units, so-called shot clusters or scenes. The proposed shot-clustering algorithm in Section 6 is similar to the time-constrained clustering proposed by Yeung et al. in [22] but uses semantically richer features such as color coherence vectors, audio cuts, and human dialog detection for clustering.

Two other systems are suitable to create abstracts of long videos. The first is called video skimming [18]. It aims mainly at abstracting documentaries and newscasts. Video skimming assumes that a transcript of the video is available. The video and the transcript are then aligned by word spotting. The audio track of the video skim is constructed by using language analysis (such as the *Term Frequency Inverse Document Frequency* measure) to identify important words in the transcript; audio clips around those words are then cut out. Based on detected faces [24], text, and camera operation, video clips for the video skim are selected from the surrounding frames. The second approach is based on the image track only. It does not generate a video abstract, but a static scene graph of thumbnail images on a 2D canvas. The scene graph represents the flow of the story in the form of key frames. It allows an interactive descent into the story by selecting a story unit in the graph [21].

We introduce some new approaches, especially for scene clustering and clip assembly, and a system which explores all video abstracting content extraction techniques developed within the MoCA project [7].

3. DEFINITIONS

A *video abstract* is defined as "a sequence of still or moving images (with or without audio) presenting the content of a video in such a way that the respective target group is rapidly provided with concise information about the content while the essential message of the original is preserved" [8] [14].

A *video trailer* is a special type of abstract. It is a short appetizer and outlook on a broadcast, made to attract the attention of the viewers so that they become interested in the broadcast and impatient to watch the presentation. The demands on a trailer differ from film genre to film genre and depend on the specific objective. For instance, the criteria of clip selection for parts of a trailer in a periodic sitcom usually differ from those for a trailer in a feature film. Often a sitcom trailer includes material of or allusions to previous broadcasts.

The terms *shot* and *scene* appear frequently in this chapter. We use them in the sense common to the research field of automatic video content analysis and digital video libraries. A video is described at four different levels of detail. At the lowest, it consists of a set of frames which — at the next higher level — are grouped into shots according to the cuts performed during video production. Consecutive shots are aggregated into scenes based on their pertinence. All scenes together compose the video (see Figure 1). Note that in this chapter a video comprises both image and audio tracks. Consequently, each frame consists of two parts: image and audio.

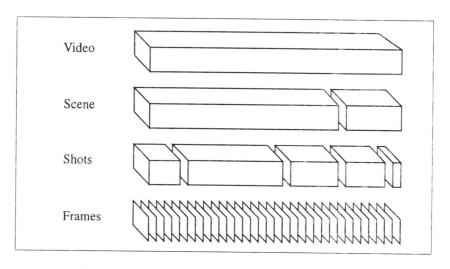

Figure 1: A common hierarchical video structuring model.

The term *frame sequence* is used and it is formally defined as follows. A *frame sequence* FS_i of a video is a sequence of contiguous frames whose length is at least one frame up to a full video. It is specified by the time interval it covers within the video. That is,

$$FS_i = [t_b^i, t_e^i] \text{ with } t_b^i, t_e^i \in \Re^+, t_b^i \leq t_e^i.$$

For a fixed frame rate, the frame sequence FS_i of a video can also be specified via the start and end frames of the sequence, i.e.,

$$FS_i = [f_b^i, f_e^i] \text{ with } f_b^i, f_e^i \in N, f_b^i \leq f_e^i$$

Both representations are used interchangeably based on convenience. The frames are represented in the RGB color space together with the raw audio sample.

A *clip* denotes a frame sequence selected to become an element of an abstract by reason of its specific content. It is extracted from different types of frame sequences such as shots, scenes, and frame sequences of special events. Thus, a clip may be contained within a shot or a scene, but it may also overlap the boundaries of either. A video abstract is then viewed as a collection of clips.

4. CONCEPTUAL OVERVIEW

The definition of a video abstract given above is very general. In practice, the purpose of an abstract can vary widely; for example, viewers of documentaries might want to be as fully informed as possible of all the content of the full-size video, whereas the aim of a Hollywood film trailer is to lure the audience into a movie theater. Thus a documentary abstract should give a good overview of the contents of the entire video, whereas a movie trailer should be entertaining in itself and should not reveal the end of the story.

When we began with our movie trailer project we had to make a basic decision about the type of material used as input. Different types of material can be used to produce a movie trailer: unchanged material from the original movie, revised material, and/or cut-out material that was not used in the final version of the movie. In our project, we use only unchanged material from the original movie. This enables our system to work with any video archive, independent of additional sources of information.

The abstracting algorithm developed can be subdivided into three consecutive steps (see Figure 2). In step 1, *video segmentation and analysis,* the input video is segmented into its shots and scenes. At the same time frame sequences with special events, such as text appearing in the title sequence, close-up shots of the main actors, explosions, gunfire, etc. are determined. In the second step, *clip selection,* those video clips that will become part of the abstract are selected. The third step, the *clip assembly,* assembles the clips into their final form and produces the presentation layout. This implies determining the order of the video clips, the type of transitions between them, and other editing decisions.

We are aware that no fully automatic system can produce an abstract as good in quality as a professional abstractor, for several reasons.

- An automatic system can only use syntactic knowledge from the video and does not understand the semantics.
- A human often has a specific intention in mind which is dificult to match to an automatic system.
- Often material which is not present in the original is used; especially the audio track of a trailer to which a speaker's voice is nearly always added.

Therefore, for a commercial system, a fourth step, *post-editing,* is added in which the multimedia objects (video trailer, clips, images, audio pieces, and text) are presented to a professional video abstract editor for revision of the video abstract.

5. VIDEO ANALYSIS FEATURES

This section describes the features which serve to determine and analyze shots, scenes, and frame sequences containing special events.

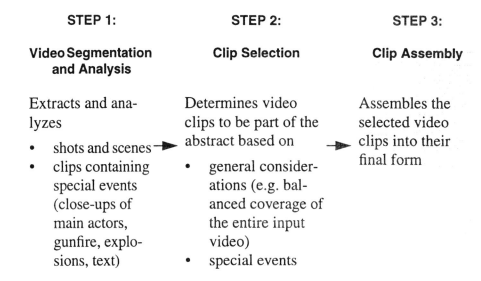

STEP 1:	STEP 2:	STEP 3:
Video Segmentation and Analysis	**Clip Selection**	**Clip Assembly**

Extracts and analyzes

- shots and scenes
- clips containing special events (close-ups of main actors, gunfire, explosions, text)

Determines video clips to be part of the abstract based on

- general considerations (e.g. balanced coverage of the entire input video)
- special events

Assembles the selected video clips into their final form

Figure 2: Overview of the three abstracting steps.

5.1 COLOR HISTOGRAMS AND COLOR COHERENCE VECTORS

The color contents are an important feature of individual frames and frame sequences. They can be viewed as a compact summary. In practice, the color contents are most often measured by *color histograms*. The color histogram H_i of a frame sequence FS_i is defined as the vector $\langle (h_1), ..., (h_n) \rangle$, where h_j specifies the number of pixels of color j normalized by the total number of pixels in FS_i. Typically, only a few of the most significant bits of each RGB color component are used to calculate the color histogram. Two color histograms are compared using the root of the Euclidean distance.

The *color coherence vector* (CCV) [15] is related to the color histogram. However, instead of counting only the number of pixels of a certain color, the color coherence vector additionally distinguishes between coherent and incoherent pixels within each color class j depending on the size of the color region to which they belong. If the region (i.e., the connected 8-neighbor component of that color) is larger than a threshold t_{ccv}, a pixel is regarded as coherent; otherwise, as incoherent. Thus, there are two values associated with each color j:

- α_j, the number of coherent pixels of color j, and
- β_j, the number of incoherent pixels of color j.

Then the color coherence vector CCV_i is defined as the vector $\langle (\alpha_1, \beta_1), ..., (\alpha_n, \beta_n) \rangle$. Before it is calculated, the input image is scaled to 240x160 pixels and smoothed by a Gaussian filter of sigma 1 as proposed in [15]. t_{ccv} is set to 300, and only the two most significant bits of each RGB color component are used. Two CCVs are compared using the Euclidean distance.

5.2 FRONTAL FACE DETECTOR

In many video genres the cast is an essential piece of information. This is particularly true for feature films. Our abstracting system must understand where the main actors appear in the video. We have implemented a face detection algorithm and a method for recognizing the face of the same actor again, even across shot boundaries.

One of the most reliable *face detectors* in digital images was developed by Rowley, Baluja, and Kanade [24]. Their system recognizes about 90% of all upright and frontal faces while rarely identifying non-faces as faces. Therefore, we have recreated their proposed neural network-based frontal face classification system for arbitrary images (e.g., photos, newspapers, and single video frames) as a basis for our frontal face detector in video sequences. To widen the range of detectable faces, our detector also searches for slightly tilted/rotated faces (∓ 30 degree). This is necessary because the faces of the actors in motion pictures are always moving, in contrast to the faces in typical still images such as portrait and sports team photographs which are usually depicted upright. However, this more general face search increases by a factor of three the number of patterns which have to be tested in each image. To speed up processing, the candidate frontal face locations are drastically reduced by an extremely fast pre-filtering step. Only locations whose pixel colors approximate human skin colors [4] and which show some structure (such as nose, mouth, and eyes) in their local neighborhood are passed to the face detector. This pre-filter reduces the number of candidate face locations by 80%. Moreover, only every third frame of the video sequence is investigated.

Each face detected is described by the vector $(t_j^i, x_{pos}, y_{pos}, s, \gamma)$. It specifies the frame t_j^i, in which a face of size s (in pixels) was detected, as well as the x- and y-coordinates (x_{pos}, y_{pos}) of its center and its angle of incline γ.

So far, each detected face is isolated and unrelated to other faces in the video. The next task is to classify frames with similar faces in order to find groups of frames showing the same actors. Such a group of related frames is called a *face-based class*. We are interested only in the main actors and, therefore, consider only faces larger than 30% of the frame size (i.e., faces in close-up shots). In a first step, faces within shots are related to each other according to the similarity of their position and size in neighboring frames, assuming that these features change only slightly from frame to frame. This is especially true for dialog scenes. In addition, we dispose of accidental misclassifications by the face detector by discarding all face-based classes with fewer than three occurrences of a face, and by allowing up to two drop-outs in the face-tracking process. This simple grouping algorithm works very well within shots and is computationally cheap. It does not demand complex face recognition algorithms such as described in [5]. In a second step, face-based classes with similar faces are merged by the eigenface face recognition algorithm [12] in order to obtain the largest possible face-based classes.

The same face recognition algorithm is used to identify and merge face-based classes of the same actor across shots throughout the video, resulting in so-called face-based sets. There is a face-based set for each main actor. It describes where, when, and in what size that actor appears in the video. However, the eigenface face recognition algorithm cannot guarantee that all face groups of the same actors merge together. An actor's face varies too much throughout a video. Thus, our grouping algorithm splits the main actors generally into a few distinguished face-based sets.

5.3 DIALOG DETECTION

It is easy to detect typical shot/reverse-shot dialogs and multi-person dialogs with the frontal face detector. We search for sequences of face-based classes, close together in time, with shot-overlapping face-based classes of the same actor, and cross-over relations between different actors. For example, a male and a female actor could appear in an m-f-m-f sequence.

A sequence of contiguous shots of a minimum length of three shots is denoted as a *dialog frame sequence* if

(1) at least one face-based class is present in each shot no further apart from its neighbor than 1 second, and

(2) the eigenface-based shot-overlapping relations between face-based classes interlink shots by crossings.

The length of the dialog is cut down to the first and last face-based set that has a shot-overlapping relation. An example of a detected dialog is shown in Figure 3.

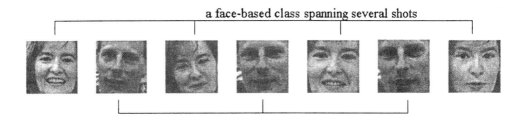

Figure 3: A dialog and their shot-overlapping relation.

5.4 TEXT RECOGNITION AND TITLE EXTRACTION

In the opening sequence of a feature film two important items appear in letters: the title and the names of the main actors. Both pieces of information should be contained in the video abstract as well as be available as a search index over a set of abstracts. The text segmentation and text recognition algorithms for text appearances in digital videos presented in [6] and [9] are deployed to extract the bitmaps of the different text appearances and to translate their content into ASCII for retrieval purposes.

The *text segmentation* step results in a list of character regions per frame and a list of their motion paths throughout the sequence. These motion paths interconnect the regions of same characters over time [6]. In order to be able to extract the bitmaps of the title and the names of main actors, character regions within each frame are clustered into words/text lines based on their horizontal distance and vertical alignment. Next, those clusters that are connected via the motion path of at least one character region are combined into a text line representation over time. For each text line representation, a time-varying (one per frame) bounding box is calculated. The content of the original video framed by the largest bounding box is chosen as the representative bitmap of the text line representation. This method works correctly under the following assumptions:

- the text line is stationary or moving linearly, and
- all characters of a cluster are contained in the segmented character regions within at least one frame.

If these assumptions hold true, the largest bounding box will enclose the text and we can perform a *text recognition* on it. In our experience these assumptions are true for most of the opening sequences in feature films.

Assuming that the *title* distinguishes itself by being centered on the screen and either by the largest size of characters in the opening sequence or, if no such can be found, by the length of the text line, the title bitmap candidate is determined. The font size is largest for short titles, while for longer titles, the font size used decreases with increasing title length.

We do not analyze the closing sequence containing title and credits since — in contrast to TV production — in most movies these are illegibly small in their video version and thus can neither be segmented nor recognized by our algorithms.

5.5 AUDIO EVENTS

Attractiveness to the user is an important criterion in designing abstracts of feature films. Action films often contain *explosions* and *gunfire;* we can recognize these events automatically. The distribution of the audio parameters loudness, frequencies, pitch, fundamental frequency, onset, offset, and frequency transition are calculated for short time-windows of the audio track. For each time-window we compare the distribution of the indicators with a database of known distributions for explosions and gunfire. If the distribution is found in the database, gunfire or an explosion is recognized [13].

6. VIDEO SEGMENTATION

A shot designates a video sequence which was recorded by an uninterrupted camera operation. That means a shot is a frame sequence $S_j = FS_i$ in which the contiguous frames do not differ very much. Several shots are used to build one larger semantic unit in the video. They are then called *scene, act,* or just a *cluster of shots*. The clustering of shots depends on the criterion which stands in the foreground. Here, we only describe an algorithm to determine logical scenes although other approaches, like grouping by same setting, are possible. The scenes are used in Section 7 as the basic unit to determine clips which will become part of the trailer.

6.1 SHOT BOUNDARY DETECTION

Determination of shots implies automatic detection of editing effects such as hard cuts, fades, wipes, or dissolves. Most of the editing effects result in characteristic spatio-temporal changes in subsequent frames of the video stream and can, therefore, be detected automatically. Various methods have been proposed (see [2] for examples). We use the edge change ratio with global motion compensation as proposed by Ramin Zabih et al. [25].

6.2 AUDIO CUTS AND AUDIO FEATURE VECTORS

One way to cluster shots into meaningful units like scenes is to analyze the audio track and group together shots with similar sound. We determine audio cuts, i.e., time instances that delimit time periods with similar sound. Audio cuts are calculated by comparison of the frequency and intensity spectrum of the audio frames of the shots. These parameters are extracted via Fourier transform, where we choose a certain analysis window size (between 100 and 200 ms) and a certain windowing function (usually a Hamming window) as parameters. The resulting complex values are converted into real values by calculation of decibels. Such a collection of real values for a specific analysis window is called an *audio feature vector* x_t.

In order to analyze a frame sequence, consecutive audio feature vectors are calculated on overlapping analysis windows (the overlap usually amounting to 1/4 of the analysis window's size). We calculate a *forecasting vector* for the next time window by exponential smoothing. Forecasting: $F_{t+1} = \alpha x_t + (1 - \alpha)F_t$, where $0 < \alpha < 1$ is called the smoothing constant (here set to 0.2). The forecast is the weighted sum of the last observation and the previous forecast. The forecasting vector therefore contains representative feature values from previous feature vectors. The speed at which the forecasting vector adapts to new feature values is controlled by the smoothing constant. The forecasting vector compares the next feature vector with the afore-analyzed feature vectors by means of Euclidean distance.

The decision about an *audio cut* is based on the difference between a new feature vector and the forecasting vector. We have two difference thresholds: a high threshold which directly determines a cut (because there was a significant difference) and a lower threshold which determines similarity (i.e., the difference is hardly significant). If, however, too many consecutive feature vectors are only similar, we also deduce a cut. After a cut is detected, a completely new forecasting vector is used: $F_t = x_t$.

As calculation of an audio cut refers to about 100 to 200 ms, an audio cut is related to several frames. Therefore, an audio cut is attributed to a frame sequence and denoted by $AC_j = FS_i$.

6.3 SHOT CLUSTERING CONCEPT

First, for each shot S_j, the required feature values $F_k(S_j)$ are determined (possible features have been presented in Section 5). These values are then used to compare and group shots. Therefore, for each feature F_k we must define a metrics d_k, which results in a distance measure of shots such that we can determine the amount of similarity between them. This enables shots to be clustered according to one or several features.

If we choose to cluster shots based only on one feature, F_k, then shots are grouped together based solely on this feature's distance metrics. Shots S_{j_1} and S_{j_2} are grouped together, if $d_k(F_k(S_{j_1}),F_k(S_{j_2})) < threshold_k$.

If we choose to cluster shots based on several features, we first determine separately the distances of each feature and then combine the results by a function. For example, we may determine separately clusters based on each feature and then apply a simple "OR"-function:

If $[d_{k_1}(F_{k_1}(S_{j_1}),F_{k_1}(S_{j_2})) < threshold_{k_1}]$ or $[d_{k_2}(F_{k_3}(S_{j_1}),F_{k_2}(S_{j_2})) < threshold_{k_2}]$, S_{j_1} and S_{j_2}

belong to one cluster.

Another approach would be to define a new metrics, $d_{k_{1,2}}$, interweaving the feature values of F_{k_1} and F_{k}:

We implemented a heuristics to determine shot clusters. It is described in the following paragraph. Other clustering algorithms are of course possible and may be included in our system in the future.

6.4 SCENE DETERMINATION

In order to determine scenes, we had to consider what constitutes a scene and arrived at the following heuristics:

1. Sequential shots with very similar color content usually belong to a common scene, because they share a common background [22]. The color content changes more dramatically at the end of a scene than within it. A change of camera angle usually has no influence on the main background colors.
2. Shot boundaries not accompanied by a (very close) audio cut do not establish a scene boundary, since the audio contents before and after the shot boundary are similar. In different scenes, however, the audio differs significantly. Little change in audio implies that no change of scene has occurred.
3. A third heuristic composes together consecutive shots which are interweaved by a dialog.

Therefore, the algorithm to determine scene boundaries is based on three features: color histograms (See "Color Histograms and Color Coherence Vectors" on page 6.), audio cuts (see "Audio Cuts and Audio Feature Vectors" on page 10.) and dialogs (see "Dialog Detection" on page 8.). The algorithm proceeds as follows:

1. If, for two consecutive shots, S_i and S_{i+1}:

$$\sqrt{CCV_i^2 + CCV_{i+1}^2} < threshold_{CCV},$$ then these shots belong together.

2. If, for a shot boundary between shots, S_i and S_{i+1}, described by the delimiting frame f_i, there is no audio cut $AC_j = [f_b^j, f_e^j]$ such that $b - c \le i \le e + c$, where c is a constant describing the closeness of the audio cut to the shot boundary, then shots S_i and S_{i+1} belong together.

3. If, for a shot boundary between shots, S_i and S_{i+1}, described by the delimiting frame f_i, there is a dialog frame sequence $DFS_j = [f_b^j, f_e^j]$ such that $b \le i \le e$, then shots S_i and S_{i+1} belong together.

For all shots and shot boundaries, the above three steps must be tested in order to determine which of the shot boundaries coincide with scene boundaries.

7. TRAILER GENERATION

We now concentrate on the generation of trailers for movies as a very important type of abstract. A movie trailer is a short appetizer for a movie, made to attract the attention of the viewer. Such a trailer requires the incorporation of eye-catching clips into the abstract. Again we use heuristics over the basic physical parameters of the digital video to select the clips for our trailer:

1. *Important objects and people*: The most important objects and actors appearing in the original movie should also appear in the trailer. Starring actors are especially important since potential viewers often prefer specific actors.
2. *Action*: If the film contains explosions, gunfire, car chases, or violence, some of these should be in the trailer. They attract attention and make viewers curious.
3. *Dialogs*: Short extracts from dialog scenes with a starring actor stimulate the watchers' imagination and often carry important messages.
4. *Title text and title music:* The title text and parts of the title music should be contained in the trailer. Optionally, the names of the main actors from the opening sequence can be shown.

A special feature of our trailer generation technique is that the end of the movie is not revealed; we simply do not include clips from the last 20% of the movie. This guarantees that we don't take away the suspense.

7.1 CLIP SELECTION

The user of our abstracting system can specify a target length not to be exceeded by the movie abstract. When selecting clips the system has to come up with a compromise between the target length and the above-mentioned heuristics. This is done in an iterative way. Initially, all scenes of the first 80% in the movie are in the scene candidate set. All decisions have to be based on physical parameters of the movie because only those can be derived automatically. Thus the challenge is to determine relevant scenes, and a good clip as a subset of frames of each relevant scene, based on computable parameters.

We employ two different mechanisms to select relevant scenes and clips. The first mechanism extracts *special events* and *texts* from the movie, such as gunfire, explosions, cries, close-up shots, dialogs by main actors, and title text. We claim that these events and texts summarize the movie well, and are suited to attract the viewer's attention (see properties (1)-(4) above). The identification of the relevant sequences of frames is based on the algorithms described above, and is fully automatic.

The percentage of special events to be contained in the abstract can be specified as a parameter by the user. In our experiments it was set to 50%. If the total length of special event clips selected by the first mechanism is longer than desired, scenes and clips are chosen uniformly and randomly from the different types of events. The title text, however, will always be contained in the abstract.

The second mechanism adds *filler clips* from different parts of the movie to complete the trailer. To do so, the remaining scenes are divided into several non-overlapping sections of about the same length. We used eight sections in our experiments. The number of clips and their total length within each section are determined. Clips are then selected repeatedly from those sections with the lowest share in the abstract so far, until the target length of the trailer is reached. This mechanism ensures good coverage of all parts of the movie even if special events occur in only some sections.

In general, clips must be much shorter than scenes. So how is a clip extracted from a scene? We have tried two heuristics. With the first one, we pick those shots with the highest amount of action and with the same basic color composition as the average of the movie. More details can be found in [14]. Action is defined through motion, either object motion or camera motion, and the amount of motion in a sequence of frames can easily be computed based on motion vectors or on the edge change ratio. The action criterion is motivated by the fact that action clips are often more interesting and carry more content in a short time than calm clips. The idea behind the color criterion is that colors are an important component for the perception of a movie's mood, hence color composition should be preserved in the trailer.

The second heuristic takes a completely different approach. It uses the results of our MoCA genre recognition project [3]. The basic idea of that project is to compute a large number of audio-visual parameters from an input video and use them to classify the video into a genre such as newscast, soccer, tennis, talk show, music clip, cartoon, feature film, or commercial. The classification is based on *characteristic parameter profiles*, derived beforehand and stored in a database. The results of this project can now be used to select clips for the trailer in a more sophisticated way. Those clips closest in parameter values to the characteristic profile of the entire movie are selected. The advantage of this clip selection process is that it will automatically tailor the selection process to a specific genre provided there is a characteristic parameter profile available.

7.2 CLIP ASSEMBLY

In the assembly stage, the selected video clips and their respective audio tracks are composed into the final form of the abstract. We have experimented with two degrees of freedom in the composition process:

- ordering, and
- edits (types of transition) between the clips.

Ordering. Pryluck et al. showed that the sequencing of clips strongly influences the viewer's perception of their meaning [16]; therefore, ordering of the clips must be done very carefully. We first group the video clips into four classes. The first class or *event class* contains the special events, currently gunfires and explosions. The second class consists of *dialogs*, while the *filler clips* constitute the third class. The extracted *text* (in the form of bitmaps and ASCII text) falls into the fourth class. Within each class the original temporal order is preserved.

Dialogs and event clips are assembled in turn into so-called *edited groups*. The maximum length of an edited group is a quarter of the length of the total share of special events. The gaps between the edited groups are filled with the remaining clips, resulting in a preliminary abstract.

The text occurrences in class four usually show the film title and the names of the main actors.

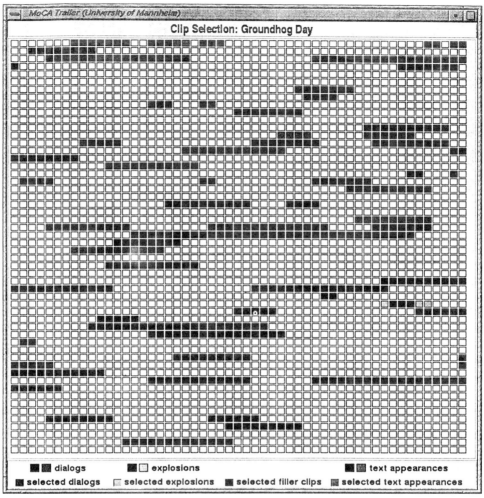

Figure 4: This graph shows the temporal distribution of the detected video and audio events of the movie "Groundhog Day" as well as those chosen during the clips selection process to be part of the trailer. Note, since "Groundhog Day" is not an action movie, there are only two explosions and no gunfire. Each box represents two seconds (2828 in total). Time passes from left to right and top to bottom.

The title bitmap is always added to the trailer, cut to a length of one second. Optionally, the actors' names can be added to the trailer.

Edits. We apply three different types of video edits in the abstract: hard cuts, dissolves, and wipes. Their usage is based on general rules derived from knowledge elicited from professional cutters [11]. This is a research field in its own right. As a preliminary solution we found it reasonable to concatenate special event clips with every other type of clip by means of hard cuts and insert soft cuts (dissolves and wipes) only between calmer clips, such as dialogs. Table 1 shows the possible usage of edits in the different cases. A much more sophisticated approach to automatic video editing of humorous themes can be found in [11].

Table 1: Edits in an Abstract

	Event Clips	**Dialog Clips**	**Other Clips**
Event Clips	hard cut	hard cut	hard cut
Dialog Clips	hard cut	dissolve, wipe, fade	hard cut, dissolve, wipe, fade
Other Clips	hard cut	hard cut, dissolve, wipe, fade	hard cut, dissolve, wipe, fade

Interestingly, audio editing is much more difficult. A first attempt to simply concatenate the sound tracks belonging to the selected clips produced terrible audio when the clips were very short. In dialog scenes it is vital that audio cuts have priority over video cuts so as not to cut a sentence at a meaningless point. The audio track of the abstract is constructed as follows:

- The audio of special event clips is used as it is in the original.
- The audio of dialogs respects audio cuts in the original. The audio of every dialog is cut in length to the length needed to fill the gaps between the audio of the special events (these gaps resulted from filler clips). Dissolves are the primary means of concatenation.
- The entire audio track of the abstract is underlaid by the title music when no other music is present. During dialogs and special events, the title music is reduced in volume.

We are planning to experiment with speaker recognition and speech recognition to be able to use higher-level semantics from the audio stream. The combination of speech recognition and video analysis is especially promising.

8. EXPERIMENTAL RESULTS

In order to evaluate the MoCA video abstracting system, we ran a series of experiments with video sequences recorded from German television. We quickly found that there is no absolute measure of the quality of an abstract; even experienced movie directors told us that making good trailers for a feature film is an art, not a science. It is interesting to observe that the shots extracted by a human for an abstract depend to a large extent on the purpose of the abstract. For example, a trailer for a movie often emphasizes thrill and action without giving away the end, a preview for a documentary on television attempts to capture the essential contents as completely as possible, and a review of last week's soap opera highlights the most important events of the story. We conclude that automatic abstracting should be controlled by a parameter describing the purpose of the abstract.

When we compared the abstracts generated by our system with abstracts actually shown on television, we observed no visual difference in quality (at least within the picture track — the audio track usually contains material which was originally not part of the video). In the case of the reviews for last week's episode of a TV series, the scenes generated by our tool were very similar to those shown on television (see [14]).

For browsing and searching large information archives, many users are now familiar with the popular WWW interfaces. Therefore our abstracting tool can compile its results into an HTML page, including the anchors for playback of the short video clips.

9. POST-EDITING

So far, the video abstracting functions completely automatically. An extension to this approach is a fourth step, where a professional video abstract editor revises the video abstract generated. To do so, the system would transfer the video abstract and all the extracted information to a video editing software such as Adobe Premiere of Ulead MediaStudio. There, the calculated video abstract would be shown on the time line in the editing window and all special events and filler-clips would be listed on a clipboard. On a second clipboard, the original video shots grouped hierachically into scenes would be shown. With such a trailer production supporting system, a professional editor can easily revise the automatically produced video abstract and produce a high-quality trailer in very short time.

10. CONCLUSION AND OUTLOOK

We have presented an algorithm for automatic production of a video trailer of a feature film. It is based first on the segmentation of the input video into larger semantic units, so-called shot clusters or scenes, and, second, on the detection and extraction of semantically rich special events such as dialogs, shots, explosions, and text in the title sequence. Additional video clips, audio pieces, images, and text are added and combined automatically on an HTML-page.

Our initial experiments show promising results. Another directive is to enhance the shot clustering algorithms so that it not only segments a video into scenes but also relates the scenes in their context, thus providing additional information during the clip selection process. Also, the editing model should be improved. So far, only the relationship between the three classes of clips and their original order in the feature film determine the assembly. There should also be an analysis of whether two contiguous clips fit to each other, e.g., regarding color composition or other features.

Our tools will find ready use in large multimedia archives since browsing for video abstracts is a technique far more powerful than the current method of browsing for textual abstracts. Broadcasting stations are sitting on a gold mine of archived video material which is hard to access today. Another application of our technique might be an on-line TV guide on the Web, with short abstracts of upcoming shows, documentaries, and feature films. Just how well the generated abstracts can capture the essentials of all kinds of videos remains to be seen in a larger series of practical experiments.

References

1.   Arman, F., Depommier, R., Hsu, A., and Chiu, M.-Y., "Context-Based Browsing of Video Sequences," *Proc. ACM Int. Conf. Multimedia*, San Francisco, CA, pp. 97-103, Oct. 1994.

2.   Dailianas, A., Allen, R. B., and England, P., "Comparison of Automatic Video Segmentation Algorithms", *Proc.* SPIE 2615, Photonics East 1995: *Integration Issues in Large Commercial Media Delivery Systems*, Andrew G. Tescher; V. Michael Bove, Eds., pp. 2-16, Oct. 1995.

3.   Fischer, S., Lienhart, R., and Effelsberg, W., "Automatic Recognition of Film Genres", *Proc. ACM Multimedia 95*, San Francisco, California, pp. 295-304, Nov. 1995.

4. Hunke. M., "Locating and Tracking of Human Faces with Neural Networks", Master's thesis, University of Karlsruhe, 1994. http://ernie.sfsu.edu/~hunke/.

5. Lawrence, S., Giles, C. L., Tsoi, A. C., and Back, A. D., "Face Recognition: A Convolutional Neural Network Approach", *IEEE Transactions on Neural Networks, Special Issue on Neural Network and Pattern Recognition*, Vol. 8, No. 1, pp. 98-113, Aug. 1997.

6. Lienhart, R., "Automatic Text Recognition for Video Indexing", *Proc. ACM Multimedia 96*, Boston, MA, pp. 11-20, Nov. 1996.

7. Lienhart, R., Pfeiffer, S., and Effelsberg, W., "The MoCA Workbench: Support for Creativity in Movie Content Analysis", *Proc. IEEE Conference on Multimedia Computing & Systems*, Hieroshima, Japan, pp. 314-321, June 1996.

8. Lienhart, R., Pfeiffer, S., and Effelsberg, W., "Video Abstracting", *Communications of the ACM*, pp. 55-62, Dec. 1997.

9. Lienhart, R. and Stuber, F., "Automatic Text Recognition in Digital Videos", in *Image and Video Processing IV 1996*, Proc. SPIE 2666-20, pp. 180-188, Jan. 1996.

10. Mills, M., Cohen, J., and Wong, Y. Y., "A Magnifier Tool for Video Data", *Proc. ACM Computer Human Interface (CHI)*, May 1992.

11. Nack, F. and Parkes, A., "The Application of Video Semantics and Theme Representation in Automated Video Editing", *Multimedia Tools and Applications*, Vol. 4, No. 1, pp. 57-83, Jan. 1997.

12. Pentland, A., Moghaddam, B., and Starner, T., "View-Based and Modular Eigenspaces for Face Recognition", *IEEE Conf. on Computer Vision and Pattern Recognition*, Seattle, WA, July 1994.

13. Pfeiffer, S., Fischer, S., and Effelsberg, W., "Automatic Audio Content Analysis", *Proc. ACM Multimedia 96*, Boston, MA, pp. 21-30, Nov. 1996.

14. Pfeiffer, S., Lienhart, R., Fischer, F., and Effelsberg, W., "Abstracting Digital Movies Automatically", In *Journal of Visual Communication and Image Representation*, Vol. 7, No. 4, pp. 345-353, Dec. 1996.

15. Pass, G., Zabih, R., and Miller, J., "Comparing Images Using Color Coherence Vectors", *Proc. ACM Multimedia 96*, Boston, MA, pp. 65-73, Nov. 1996.

16. Pryluck, C., Teddlie, C., and Sands, R., "Meaning in Film/Video: Order, Time and Ambiguity. *J. Broadcasting* 26 (1982), 685-695.

17. Rorvig. M. E., "A Method for Automatically Abstracting Visual Documents", *Journal of the American Society on Information Science* 44 (1993) 1.

18. Smith, M. and Kanade, T., "Video Skimming for Quick Browsing Based on Audio and Image Characterization", Computer Science *Technical Report, Carnegie Mellon University*, July 1995.

19. Taniguchi, Y., Akutsu, A., Tonomura, Y., and Hamada, H. "An Intuitive and Efficient Access Interface to Real-Time Incoming Video Based on Automatic Indexing", *Proc. ACM Multimedia 1995*, San Francisco, CA, pp. 25-33, Nov. 1995.

20. Tonomura, Y., Akutsu, A., Taniguchi, Y., and Suzuki, G., "Structured Video Computing", *IEEE Multimedia Magazine* 1 (1994), 34-43.

21. Yeung, M., Yeo, B.-L. ,Wolf, W., and Liu, B. "Video Browsing Using Clustering and Scene Transitions on Compressed Sequences", *Multimedia Computing and Networking* 1995, Proc. SPIE 2417, San Jose, CA, pp. 399-414, Jan. 1995.

22. Yeung, M., Yeo, B.-L., and Liu, B., "Extracting Story Units form Long Programs for Video Browsing and Navigation", *Proc. IEEE Multimedia Computing & Systems*, Hiroshima, Japan, pp. 296-305, June 1996.

23. Yeung, M. and Yeo, B.-L., "Video Content Characterization and Compaction for Digital Library Applications", in *Storage and Retrieval of Image and Video Databases 1997*, Proc. SPIE 3022, pp. 45-58, Jan. 1997.
24. Rowley, H. A., Baluja, S., and Kanade, T., "Human Face Recognition in Visual Scenes", *Technical Report Carnegie Mellon Uuniversity*, CMU-CS-95- 158R, School of Computer Science, Nov. 1995.
25. Zabih, R., Miller, J., and Mai, K., "A Feature-Based Algorithm for Detecting and Classifying Scene Breaks", *Proc. ACM Multimedia 95*, San Francisco, CA, pp. 189-200, Nov. 1995.
26. Zhang, H., Smoliar, S. W., and Wu, J. H., "Content-Based Video Browsing Tools", *Multimedia Computing and Networking* 1995, Proc. SPIE 2417, San Jose, CA, pp. 389-398, Jan. 1995.
27. Zhang, H., Low, C. Y., Smoliar, S. W., and Wu, J. H., "Video Parsing, Retrieval and Browsing: An Integrated and Content-Based Solution", *Proc. ACM Multimedia 1995*, San Francisco, CA, pp.15-24, Nov. 1995.

Acknowledgments. Figures 1,2,3, and 4, and Table 1 are extracted from R. Lienhart, S. Pfeiffer, and W. Effelsberg, "Video Abstracting," Communications of the ACM, December 1997, © 1997 Association for Computing Machinery.

18

MULTIMEDIA ARCHIVING, LOGGING, AND RETRIEVAL

Rune Hjelsvold, Shih-Ping Liou, and Rémi Depommier
Siemens Corporate Research
Multimedia and Video Technology Department
Princeton, New Jersey 08540

1. **INTRODUCTION**...380
2. **MULTIMEDIA CONTENT ARCHIVING, LOGGING, AND RETRIEVAL**....................380
    2.1 CHALLENGES FOR CONTENT OWNERS 380
    2.2 EXISTING APPROACHES 382
    2.3 MEETING THE CHALLENGES: THE CARAT APPROACH.............................384
3. **CARAT SYSTEM ARCHITECTURE** 385
    3.1 ARCHIVING 386
    3.2 ACQUISITION, SEARCH, AND MANAGEMENT...386
    3.3 BROADCAST AUTOMATION..386
4. **MULTIMEDIA CONTENT LOGGING** 386
    4.1 STRUCTURED LOGGING..387
    4.2 MULTIMEDIA OBJECTS AS INDICES 388
    4.3 PREPARING MULTIMEDIA CONTENT FOR LOGGING..................................390
    4.4 A HYBRID, STRUCTURED MULTIMEDIA LOGGING APPROACH....................393
5. **MULTIMEDIA CONTENT RETRIEVAL** 395
    5.1 SEMANTIC CONTENT RETRIEVAL..396
    5.2 QUERYING INTER-OBJECT RELATIONSHIPS 396
    5.3 OTHER QUERYING MECHANISMS 397
    5.4 CARD-BASED QUERYING...397
6. **MULTIMEDIA ARCHIVE META-DATA MANAGEMENT** 398
7. **CONCLUSION** 399
    REFERENCES 400

Abstract. Multimedia archiving, logging, and retrieval are challenging tasks for content owners as well as for software developers. This chapter discusses some of these challenges. We will focus on challenges related to the variety of meta-data formats that exist, the efficiency of the logging process, the quality of multimedia information retrieval, and the demand for powerful, but easy-to-use, multimedia query mechanisms. We will also describe a commercially available archiving system, the CARAT system. The CARAT solution offers new ways to meet the challenges in multimedia archiving.

First, it provides a logging approach that offers efficient means for end-users to create content descriptions of high quality and accuracy. Second, it offers a card-based query approach that allows end-users to specify complex queries in an intuitive way. Third, it contains an internal catalog that allows content owners to use CARAT to store content description in any familiar format.

1. INTRODUCTION

Asset management is an important task for content owners who want to capitalize as much as possible on the potential value of their assets. It is also a challenging task because each item may have rich contents and because of the large number of items that need to be managed. Digital media makes this challenge even greater because it is now easier than ever to create multimedia items. As a result, the number of items that need to be managed increases at a high rate. Content owners are aware of the situation and are looking for ways to make it easier to manage the vast amount of information stored in the archive [1].

What users of a media archive are asking for is a system where they can have immediate access to items in the archive by specifying content characteristics or circumstances related to content creation. The approach taken by creators of multimedia content today is usually called *content logging* [2]. Throughout the creation of multimedia content, production teams will make detailed records of each of the items being created. Each record describes the content of the multimedia item as a set of keywords. The descriptions may also contain notes related to the creation process itself that the production team thinks would be important to record. At query time, end-users type in some relevant keywords and specify logical operators or weights associated with the given keywords. The system retrieves the objects satisfying the query specification – possibly sorted by their relevance to the end-user query.

In this chapter we will discuss some of the problems and challenges content owners face in multimedia information management. We will also describe a multimedia archiving system, CARAT, that provides means for content owners to meet these challenges. In Section 2 we discuss these challenges in more detail and describe some of the common methods to deal with them. It also briefly summarizes how CARAT meets the challenges. In Section 3 we present an overview of the CARAT architecture. In Sections 4 and 5 we present the support for content logging and retrieval, respectively. In Section 6 we describe the process of defining and managing the semantics being used in the logging and retrieval process. Section 7 concludes this chapter.

2. MULTIMEDIA CONTENT ARCHIVING, LOGGING, AND RETRIEVAL

Multimedia archives are used to store and manage digitized *media* data. There is, however, also a need to store additional data that describes the multimedia objects in the archive. Such *meta-data* is needed, for instance, to record who the creator (or owner) of the object is, what the title of the object is, where one can find copies of the object, etc. Meta-data might also describe the contents of multimedia objects, for instance, content summaries or indexes. This type of meta-data is crucial for providing effective retrieval mechanisms. All together, proper meta-data management is as important to a multimedia archive as media data management.

2.1 CHALLENGES FOR CONTENT OWNERS

2.1.1 Meta-data Formats

When establishing a media archive, the owner of the archive would have to select the proper way to format meta-data. There are a number of formats that are considered as standard for given communities [3], such as the various MARC formats used by libraries and the CIMI format used by museums. The challenges for the content owner are to select the most appropriate format and to find an archiving system and logging tools that support this format.

2.1.2 Precision and Recall Ratios

It is important for an archive of any kind to offer effective means for retrieving information from the archive. The information retrieval effectiveness is usually measured by precision and recall ratios. Precision is defined by the information retrieval community to be *the proportion of retrieved documents, which are relevant*, while recall is defined to be *the proportion of relevant documents retrieved* [4].

It is not yet feasible to develop generic multimedia archives that can provide fully automatic indexing and retrieval. Thus, the process of manual logging is still a required part of a generic multimedia archive. During manual logging, the human operator will create content-oriented meta-data – i.e., meta-data that describes the content of the multimedia objects in a form that is more appropriate for retrieval than the original media data. In such a system, the effectiveness of the retrieval system depends heavily on the quality of the meta-data. The precision of the retrieval system depends on how accurate the meta-data is; the recall depends on how comprehensive the meta-data is in describing the contents of the multimedia objects.

Many multimedia archives store content-oriented meta-data in the form of free-text documents where retrieval is based on keyword searching. It is well known that pure keyword searching may result in poor precision/recall ratios. MIT Media Lab's Glorianna Davenport, for instance, asks: *"Is there any sign of intelligent life beyond keyword searching?"* [5]. Multimedia archive owners worry about these problems knowing that the content-oriented meta-data they create today may limit precision/recalls.

2.1.3 Efficiency

Generally, only content-oriented meta-data will be used for content-based retrieval. This means that content that has not been described in the content-oriented meta-data will not be visible for querying. This puts a heavy burden on the production team (or any librarian that might be assigned to support the team). Those responsible for content logging would be required not only to accurately record all features that are important to the production team; they will also need to anticipate future use of the object to make sure that *all* relevant features are logged. This becomes particularly important in a large archive having a variety of multimedia objects and end-users. The logging process is usually a time-consuming task because of this. The big challenge for archive owners, in this respect, is to make the logging process more efficient without sacrificing the quality and accuracy of the meta-data.

2.1.4 Query Functionality

Multimedia objects, audio and video objects in particular, may have a complex inherent structure. Content creators usually compose such structures carefully to strengthen the messages they want to convey. A multimedia information retrieval system should be able to retrieve objects from a specification of structural properties in addition to content characteristics. The retrieval system should also provide a variety of retrieval techniques because of the variety and diversity of contents and users. It should, for instance, provide mechanisms for querying the content directly wherever possible (e.g., by free-text searching text documents). In many cases, end-users are not able to precisely characterize the objects they want to retrieve. Therefore, a multimedia retrieval system should provide alternative ways to explore the contents of the archive, for instance, by navigating the information space or by performing similarity queries. An additional challenge is to combine all these mechanisms in a consistent, coherent, and easy-to-use interface. Without such an interface, only experts would be able to utilize advanced query functions.

2.2 EXISTING APPROACHES

2.2.1 Meta-data Formats

Selecting the proper meta-data format is an important issue, especially if there is a need to exchange meta-data between archives. There are several standardization initiatives and development activities addressing issues related to meta-data representation and exchange. The Dublin Core initiative [3] is targeted at defining a core set of elements (currently 15) that will be a standard way to encode information about title, author, date, language, etc. Baldonado et al. [6] describes how such a core set of meta-data elements can be used to translate meta-data between different formats (Dublin Core and USMARC).

Once a meta-data format is selected, the problem is still to find tools and archiving systems that support this format. The Vane tool [7] is a generic video logging tool that can be adapted to a given meta-data model. This is achieved through the use of SGML. The output of a logging session is stored as an SGML document. The document is defined by its DTD (Document Type Definition) that reflects the database meta-data model. The Vane tool adapts the logging interface of the given document to the DTD and is thus dynamically configured. The Vane tool requires a specific DTD that properly represents the meta-data model. A system user will have to define this DTD and implement software that will convert data between the database model and the document model.

2.2.2 Precision and Recall Rates

As noted by Marc Davis [8], keywords are not semantic representations (there is no implicit inheritance between "dog" and "German shepherd"), keywords do not describe relations between concepts ("man," "dog," and "bite" would describe both "man bites dog" and "dog bites man"), and keywords suffer from the vocabulary problem (different keywords are used to describe the same phenomenon). Davis proposes to use a controlled vocabulary to overcome the limitations of regular keywords. Other researchers [9,10,11] argue that there is a need for complex representations of the semantic content of media items. They propose various ways to model semantic relationships between concepts such as "objects," "events," and "roles." The problem here is that semantic models tend to be big and difficult to use and maintain.

Simonnot et al. [12] proposes to aggregate a set of attributes into a *facet*. In a movie, for instance, one facet might be *actor* while director might be another one. If a user is searching for movies in which Clint Eastwood appears, she could query for the name *Clint Eastwood*. Clint Eastwood, however, is also a movie director and the query would also retrieve movies where Clint Eastwood is the director. The user may resolve this ambiguity by explicitly linking the actor's name to the facet *actor* [12].

England et al. [13] and Oomoto et al. [14] describe a similar way to structure the description of a media item. They propose to use tagging schemes where each keyword (in this case also called *attribute*) is tagged with a name. The challenge for a tagging scheme is to define the proper attributes for a multimedia object – especially when used in archives having different types of objects such as news video, movies, classic music concert CDs, etc.

Oomoto et al. [14] propose a schema-less description where the human operator can define any attributes to be used for each multimedia object. The problem here is that, in an archive used by many users, the schema-less approach may create another variant of the vocabulary problem. Attributes that are supposed to represent the same semantic feature may be differently named for different multimedia objects. In addition, a querying user may not know what kind of attributes might be useful when specifying a query.

The traditional logging approach is text-based. Marc Davis [8] describes an iconic language composed of over 3500 iconic primitives organized in a hierarchy to be used for content logging of video. An icon-based logging system also has its limitations. The user would have to learn a new (sign) language. In addition, although icons are adequate for representing real objects, icons are not suited for representing abstract concepts. The problem here is that a system based on icons only will not scale well; as the number of icons increases, the differences among items might become subtle.

2.2.3 Efficiency

Once multimedia information is represented in a digital form, it can be processed by a computer. One way to improve the efficiency of multimedia content archiving is to automate the content logging process by using multimedia content processing systems. Multimedia content processing is a large research area and it is beyond the scope of this chapter to describe the result of this research. In this section, however, we will point to some of the areas that seem promising.

A crucial step in video logging is to segment it into coherent units that have a common content and should be logged as one unit. At the lowest level, this means being able to identify each individual *shot* within a video. (*Shot* refers to a contiguous recording of one or more frames depicting a continuous action in time and space.) It is not uncommon to have videos contain more than ten shots per minute of video. Thus, automatic detection of the shot boundaries would be important in improving the efficiency in video logging.

In the early years, shot transitions were created on a *splicer* and an optical printer, while shot lists were kept on paper records referred to as the *count sheets*. Since 1985, most shot changes have been generated using modern editing machines. Information on each individual shot is retained electronically on an Editing Decision List (EDL), which can be indexed directly into a database. However, for most videos and films that were produced before the invention of such machines, this information, which was recorded on paper, may no longer be accessible. This is certainly true for raw sports films, since cuts are generated by turning on and off the camcorders or film cameras. In either case, cuts will have to be detected from the video through manual or automatic means.

The efforts on cut detection can be traced back to Coll and Choma [15]. The authors performed an extensive experimental study of frame difference signals using four different types of videos: a football game, a drama show, a talk show, and a cartoon. The authors divide each uncompressed video frame into 8x8 blocks, each of which is represented by its average grayscale value. In their study, the average of the magnitudes of the differences between corresponding blocks of consecutive frames is used as the difference metric. Coll and Choma show that a threshold determined experimentally can detect shot changes that match the accuracy of a human observer. More scene change detection algorithms based on uncompressed video can also be found in the computer vision literature [16,17] or elsewhere [18-27].

For digital video that is stored and transmitted in compressed form (for instance, Joint Photographic Experts Group (JPEG), Moving Picture Experts Group (MPEG), or International Telegraph and Telephone Consultative Committee (CCITT) H.261), performing cut detection as well as image processing on compressed video saves unnecessary decompression-compression effort. This idea led to many efforts in pursuing solutions that can process compressed video directly, started by Arman, Hsu, and Chiu [28]. Arman, Hsu, and Chiu developed a scene change detection algorithm for JPEG and movie-JPEG video, where a subset of Discrete Cosine Transform (DCT) coefficients are used to characterize the underlying frame. Unfortunately, full DCT coefficients are difficult or impractical to obtain in MPEG or H.261 video without full scale decoding, because motion vectors are quantities in the spatial domain, while DCT coefficients are quantities in the frequency domain.

Other researchers have proposed the use of motion vectors directly either to filter out scene change frames or to detect scene cuts [29-31]. They are often based on the ratio of number of forward-predicted macro blocks and the total number of macro blocks. This approach is very sensitive to different encoders and types of encoding algorithms since there are no standard criteria in determining whether a certain macro block should be inter-coded (temporarily predicted from a previous reconstructed picture) or intra-coded (like a baseline JPEG picture) during the encoding process.

A few commercial logging tools such as The Executive Producer [2] have built-in shot detection. There is still a lack of good tools to verify and correct the outcome of the automatic shot detection. There is also a need for tools that can detect advanced shot transitions (e.g., wipes and dissolves). Video editing software (for instance, Avid MCXpress [32]) offers a wide selection of transition patterns.

Speech recognition has also been an important area for multimedia content processing research. A speech recognition system can be used to automatically create a transcript of audio and video objects containing speech. This transcript can later be used as input to a manual logging process or used directly in query processing. The Informedia Digital Library Project at CMU has been working on such a solution. The big challenge here is accuracy in the word recognition. The CMU Sphinx-II recognition system has a word recognition error rate around 50% for news videos and documentaries [33]. The technology is constantly improving but still has a long way to go before the automatic transcript is so accurate it can replace some of the manual logging.

2.2.4 Query Functionality

A lot of work has been done on extending query languages and tools for multimedia databases [8,34–41]. Research has also been devoted to navigation in multimedia document bases and to content-based querying (e.g., free-text searching, query by image content, etc.). Existing systems, however, have not been able to that integrate all these features together with ordinary meta-data querying and still provide an easy-to-use interface.

2.3 MEETING THE CHALLENGES: THE CARAT APPROACH

The following subsection will summarize how CARAT meets the challenges described above. We will give more detailed descriptions of the CARAT system and its functionality in later sections.

2.3.1 Meta-data Formats

The CARAT database contains a catalog describing the meta-data format(s) supports. This catalog allows several such formats (e.g., MARC and Dublin Core) to be present at the same time, allowing some objects to be described according to one format while other object descriptions are using other formats. All end-user tools accessing the CARAT archive will retrieve meta-data from the internal CARAT catalog to configure the user interface according to the selected meta-data format. This is further described in Section 6.

2.3.2 Precision and Recall Rates

The flexibility of the internal CARAT catalog allows content owners to specify user domain semantics. CARAT uses the notion *log structure* to describe the log format. Content owners can define as many fields as they want to in the log structure of a certain type of object. Each type of multimedia object may have its special log structure. And multimedia objects can be grouped into special *user domains* where each domain has its own set of log structures. The CARAT catalog gives full support to create controlled vocabularies/thesauri. Each field within a log structure can be associated with one of the available thesauri. Finally, the CARAT system allows images and other multimedia objects to be used as part of the meta-data describing a given object. This is further described in Sections 4.1 and 4.2.

2.3.3 Efficiency

The CARAT system includes software for shot detection and it also provides tools for end-users to manually verify and, if necessary, augment the outcome of the result of automatic preprocessing. This is further described in Sections 4.3 and 4.4.

2.3.4 Query Functionality

The CARAT system provides a query mechanism based on query cards that gives the end-user an easy-to-use mechanism for specifying advanced queries. This is further described in Section 5.

3. CARAT SYSTEM ARCHITECTURE

In the previous section we described some of the challenges we face in developing a multimedia archive. In the remaining sections, we will describe how the CARAT system meets these challenges starting with a summary of the CARAT system architecture.

The CARAT system is highly modular. The system architecture consists of three main modules having components that are interconnected via a high-speed network for media data exchange, as shown in Figure 1. The *archiving* module contains components that are used to store media and meta-data. The *acquisition, search, and management* module contains components used to add, search, and modify media and meta-data. The *automation* module contains components that can be used in a broadcasting environment to schedule and control audio or video broadcasting. These modules will be further described in the following subsections.

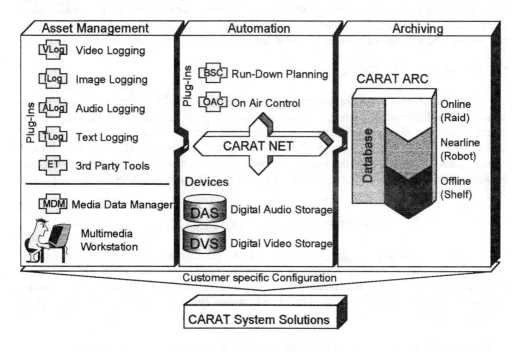

Figure 1. CARAT system architecture.

The CARAT system is also highly configurable. The CARAT database contains configuration information that is used to generate customer-specific system solutions. The configuration functionality is presented in more detail in Section 6.

3.1 ARCHIVING

The archiving module is the main repository for media and meta-data. Meta-data are stored in relational database running on a commercial RDBMS. Media data are stored on a hierarchical storage system that might include online storage provided by a RAID array system and nearline storage provided by a tape robot system. Data migration between the online and the nearline storage is automatically controlled by the archiving module. The archive also offers means for integrating management of data stored in an offline archive (for example, regular video tapes stored on a shelf or photographs stored in a folder in a file cabinet). It is beyond the scope of this chapter to go into further detail about the storage system.

3.2 ACQUISITION, SEARCH, AND MANAGEMENT

This module contains the components that can be used by end-users to manage the contents of the archiving module. One or more multimedia workstations (Pentium-based PCs) with necessary hardware for media-data compression and decompression will give the user the ability to digitize, compose, and replay multimedia objects. The multimedia workstations are connected to the high-speed network transfer multimedia data between the workstation and the archiving module.

The software components in this module are usually provided as plug-ins. It is up to the owner of the archive to decide which components should be included in a given system's configuration. The *Media Data Manager* exists in every CARAT configuration and offers functionality for transferring data between the archive and the workstation. It also gives end-users means for previewing media data and for modifying or enhancing the meta-database structure. The plug-ins for content logging offer means for digitization, processing, logging, retrieval, and presentation of multimedia content. Sections 4 and 5 describe the functionality of these components in more detail. Third party tools, such as non-linear video editing tools may also be added to the suite of tools available to end-users of a CARAT archive.

3.3 BROADCAST AUTOMATION

Radio and television broadcasting is one important market segment for multimedia archives. The *automation* module contains components that can assist broadcasters in the important tasks of planning and controlling broadcasts. The *Run-down Planning* component can be used to create run-down scripts. The On-Air Control controls various playout units and content mixers accordingly to the run-down scripts and also supports manual overriding and modification of the run-down scripts. It is beyond the scope of this chapter to go into detail about broadcast automation.

4. MULTIMEDIA CONTENT LOGGING

The rest of this chapter will focus on the acquisition, search, and management module of the CARAT system. Having all the considerations discussed in Section 2 in mind, CARAT tries to improve multimedia asset management by first improving the logging approach and then by improving the query mechanisms. The goals for improving the logging approach are:

Precision: The logging system should extend the traditional keyword system with means for representing semantics and relations between keywords or items in the log. The system should also allow the users to use familiar terminology.

Quality: The logging system should provide a way to remove or, at least, reduce the problems introduced by typing errors, the vocabulary problem, and having different human operators adhering to different logging conventions.

Media richness: A logging system should not disregard the advantages of an iconic language in certain cases. An improved logging system should allow the user to select the most appropriate media type (keyword, image, or any other type) for content logging.

Time efficiency: The logging system should allow human operators to achieve higher precision and quality goals without sacrificing efficiency. Trivial operations should be optimized or replaced with more efficient ones.

This section discusses how these issues are dealt with in the CARAT system. The precision and quality issues will be addressed in Section 4.1, the media richness will be discussed in Section 4.2, while time efficiency is the main issue in Section 4.3. In Section 4.4, we discuss how the different components are put together in the CARAT system.

4.1 STRUCTURED LOGGING

The main purpose of a logging process is to generate a log record for every media item being imported into the archive. There are several ways to improve the precision and quality of this process by making it more structured. First, the log record itself (i.e., its format) might be structured to represent as much semantic content as possible. Second, the semantic concepts used as parts of log records can be organized into conceptual structures. Third, the logging process might unveil the semantic structure of a media item, if it has such a structure. The following paragraphs will discuss these issues in more detail.

In CARAT, the log records' semantic is extended in ways similar to the tagging and facet approaches mentioned in Section 2.2.2. The log record consists of a number of fields or attributes where some of the fields may represent some semantic description of the content. Assume for instance that a television news story has a log structure as depicted in

Figure 2. This example illustrates how the definition of attributes in a log structure can be used to represent user-domain semantics. Persons, for instance, will be associated with a television news story either as the reporter of this story or as a person that was involved in the event being reported.

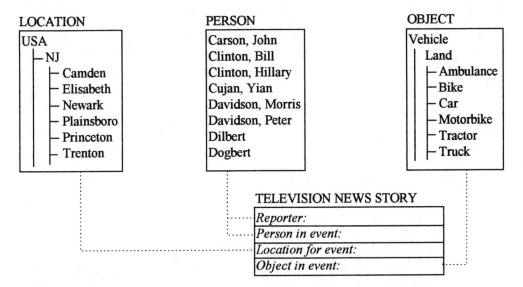

Figure 2. Log record with four attributes and the corresponding value types.

CARAT also supports the use of controlled vocabularies and thesauri. As mentioned before, this will reduce the vocabulary problem and eliminate problems related to misspelling. Vocabularies are especially useful when combined with the log structuring proposed above. In CARAT, each field in a log record may be bound to a specific vocabulary or thesaurus.

Figure 2, for example, shows how the four attributes of the sample television news story log structure are bound to three different thesauri, one for geographical locations, one for persons represented in the database, and one for objects that might be depicted in multimedia objects. The figure also illustrates the fact that several attributes (i.e., *Reporter* and *Person in event*) in the same log structure may bind to the same vocabulary (i.e., *PERSON*). Additionally, of course, vocabularies are shared between log structures so attributes of other log structures may also bind the *PERSON* vocabulary (or any other vocabulary).

The design of a log structure is a challenge in itself. We believe it is important to acknowledge that not all attributes that seem useful to describe one type of media item would be applicable to other types of multimedia objects. For instance, in logging images or video, it might be appropriate to record the season the media items depict (e.g., summer). This attribute is not very useful in describing music items or text books. In addition, more complex media items may define a hierarchical internal structure where each of the layers in the structure has specific semantic. In a broadcast news domain, for instance, the video structure hierarchy may consist of *news*, *news section*, *news story*, and *shot*. In an American football domain, on the other hand, the structure may consist of *game*, *half*, *quarter*, *play*, and *shot* (starting from the top of the hierarchy).

One way to solve this problem would be to use a schema-less approach and let the logging user pick the appropriate attributes on a *per item* basis. We strongly believe that it will be confusing both to the users responsible for logging a media item and for querying users if the set of attributes available for logging is dynamically changing. Thus, in CARAT we chose to make the log structure of a given media item functional dependent on its type. This means, for instance, that all television news stories can be logged and queried by the same set of attributes. At the same time, this set can be totally different from the sets used to log a news shot or a news photo.

As discussed earlier, the description of the content does not depend only on the type of media, it also depends on the domain to which the multimedia object belongs. A news photo, for instance, might be described very differently from pictures in a medical X-ray domain. In CARAT, log structures are grouped together in one or more *user domain*s. Each user domain specifies which types of multimedia objects can be logged in the given domain. It also defines how the hierarchical structure looks for hierarchical multimedia objects, and it defines the log structure for each of the object types in the domain. In Section 6, we will discuss what services CARAT provides to content owners to specify their user domain in the most appropriate way.

The log structure meta-data is used by the CARAT logging tool to set up a proper interface for logging (see Section 4.4). Once a multimedia object has been selected by the end-user from a user domain's collection of multimedia objects, the CARAT tools retrieve the corresponding log structure meta-data and structures the user interface accordingly.

4.2 MULTIMEDIA OBJECTS AS INDICES

CARAT is a multimedia database that manages items of different media types. The types that are supported include:

Audio: Audio objects can be used to represent music, interviews, radio shows, voice mail, etc. Audio objects can be organized into a temporal structure hierarchy.

Video: Video objects can be used to represent movies, television, home video, video conferences, etc. Video objects can be organized into a temporal structure hierarchy.

Image: Image objects can be used to represent photographs, paintings, drawings, etc. Plans exist to make it possible to define hierarchical image regions within images.

Free text and text documents: Free text could be used to represent long portions of text such as transcripts of audio or video items. Plans exist to make it possible to represent texts having a hierarchical structure.

Singular descriptor: Singular descriptor objects can be used to represent text keywords, dates, numeric values, etc.

Dynamic annotation: Dynamic annotation objects can be used to record and store graphical gestures, drawings, and speech from a session where a user annotates other multimedia items.

Unknown type: The unknown type allows CARAT to be open for the future by being able to include objects of a media type not specifically supported (e.g., CAD drawings).

Traditionally, a media archive has been designed to manage the first four media types from the list above while these objects have been logged mainly by free text items or by keywords (singular descriptors). As mentioned earlier, a multimedia database should allow non-text languages to be used to log media items. CARAT offers a powerful and flexible way of doing this by allowing any media type to be used as part of a log record. This would support existing keyword based indexing (using text to describe audio, video, or pictures) and the iconic indexing proposed by Marc Davis [8] (using images to describe video). In addition, it would also allow other useful combinations such as:

1. Images can be used to describe audio objects (for instance including a picture of the cover in the log for music CDs) or text documents (including a picture of the book cover).
2. A keyword (singular descriptor) itself might be logged. In a sports domain, for instance, the owner of the archive might want to represent the age of all athletes (singular descriptor), their major records (singular descriptors), a brief summary of their background (free text), and store a few typical images or videos showing each athlete in action.
3. Video might be used to describe another video object. This can be useful in creating references from a follow-up story to the original story it refers to.
4. Items of one media type might have a reference to an item of another media type that is supposed to represent the same information encoded in a different media. In the news case, for instance, the log record for a news story might refer to an audio-only or text-only version of the same story.

We do not claim that the combinations listed above are useful in all archives or that these combinations are the only ones. The list is intended to illustrate the fact that there are cases where it would be useful to have the opportunity to use one multimedia item to describe another. CARAT supports this functionality by defining all types of descriptive date (even singular values such as keywords and dates) as multimedia objects that can be logged and that can be part of another object's log. The log for a certain object in CARAT contains a collection of references to objects that describes the given object.

By organizing the content descriptions this way, a CARAT archive effectively becomes a hypermedia archive where each object's log record is nothing but a collection of hyperlinks. When we combine this with the typing of attributes described in the previous section we have a hypermedia archive with semantically typed hyperlinks. For instance, a television news story might have two attributes of free text type, *transcript* and *text version*. The former could be a pure transcript of what is being said by the reporter and interviewed persons, while the second contains a text-based summary of the story. The log structure of a news story may contain references to the two text objects constituting the transcript and the text version of the story, respectively. This semantic allows the end-user to decide to read the transcript whenever he or she could not understand what the reporter was saying or to read the text summary before deciding to start video playback.

4.3 PREPARING MULTIMEDIA CONTENT FOR LOGGING

For a multimedia information system to better meet information users' needs, it must capture the semantics and terminology of specific user domains and allow users to retrieve information according to such semantics. A key initial stage in this content preparation process is to capture the structure present in the video, providing a *video table of contents* analogous to the table of contents in a book.

It is a complex process to automatically obtain such video table of contents, even to a reasonable degree of accuracy. First, video frames must be segmented into a set of units called *shots*. Repeating shots are then identified to detect parallel events in a scene and this information is finally used to construct the video table of contents. Since the generation of the table of contents consists of a sequence of dependent steps, even one mistake could create results that are completely useless.

Existing approaches have their limitations. The attribute-based approach requires a human operator to manually index multimedia information, which is very time consuming. On the other hand, the automatic approach is computationally expensive, difficult, and tends to be very domain specific. It is nearly impossible, in practice, to obtain a useful video organization based solely on automatic processing.

What we need is a hybrid approach [42], i.e., automatically segmenting video and creating the video table of contents in a preprocessing step, while providing an easy-to-use interface for verification, correction, and augmentation of the automatically extracted video structure.

This section describes techniques behind such a hybrid approach: cut detection, shot grouping, and video table of content creation.

4.3.1 Cut Detection

Pixel-based (e.g., inter-frame difference) and distribution-based (e.g., statistics) difference metrics respond differently to different types of shots and shot transitions. For example, the former is very sensitive to camera moves but is a very good indicator for shot changes. On the other hand, distribution-based metrics are relatively insensitive to camera and object motion but may be too insensitive in cases where two shots look quite different but have similar distributions. We feel that it is necessary to combine both measures in cut detection.

Unlike existing methods that have no notion of *time series* or *non-stationarity*, CARAT treats a sequence of difference metrics as *non-stationary* time series signals and models the time trend deterministically. The sequences of difference metrics, no matter how they are computed, are just as any economic or statistic data collected over time. In this view, shot changes as well as the 3:2 pull-down process will both create *observation outliers* in time series, while the gradual shot transition and gradual camera moves will produce *innovation outliers*. Fox [43] defines the observation outlier to be the one that is caused by a gross error of observation or recording error and it affects only a *single* observation. Similarly, the innovation outlier is the one that corresponds to the situation in which a single "innovation" is extreme. This type of outlier affects not only the particular observation but also subsequent observations.

There are standard methods [43–45] in the literature that detect both outliers. These standard methods, however, cannot be applied to the cut detection problem directly for the following three reasons. First, most methods require intensive computation, for example, least squares, to estimate time trend and auto-regressive coefficients. This amount of computation is generally not desired. Second, the observation outliers created by slow motion and the 3:2 pull-down process could occur as often as one in every other sample, making the time trend and auto-regressive coefficient estimation an extremely difficult process. Finally, since gradual shot transitions and gradual camera moves are indistinguishable in most cases, location of gradual shot transitions requires not only detection of innovation outliers but also an extra camera motion estimation step.

In CARAT's solution, we use a zero*th*-order auto-regressive model and a piecewise-linear function to model the time trend. With this simplification, samples from both the past and the future must be used in order to improve the robustness of time trend estimation. We also need to discard more than half of the samples, because the observation outliers created by slow motion and the 3:2 pull-down process could occur as often as one in every other sample. Fortunately, these types of observation outliers are least in value, therefore, could be easily identified. After the time trend is removed, the remaining value is tested against a normal distribution $N(0, \sigma)$ in which σ can be estimated recursively or in advance.

To make the cut detection method more robust, we further apply the Kolmogorov-Smirnov test to eliminate false positives. This test is chosen because it does not assume *a priori* knowledge of the underlying distribution function. The traditional Kolmogorov-Smirnov test procedure compares the computed test metric with a preset significance level (normally at 95%). It has been used by some researchers [46] to detect cuts from videos. This use of single pre-selected significance level completely ignores the non-stationary nature of the cut detection problem. We feel that the Kolmogorov-Smirnov test is properly used only if it takes into account the non-stationary nature of the problem. In other words, the significance level should be *automatically adjusted* to different types of video contents.

One way to represent video contents is to use measurement in both the spatial and the temporal domain together. For example, image contrast is a good spatial domain measurement, because the amount of intensity changes across two neighboring frames measures video content in the temporal domain. The adjustment should be made such that,

1. the higher the image contrast is, the more sensitive the cut detection mechanism should be, and
2. the more changes that occur in two consecutive images, the less sensitive the detection mechanism should be.

The traditional Kolmogorov-Smirnov test also cannot differentiate the long shot from the close up of the same scene. To guard against such transitions, we invent a *hierarchical* Kolmogorov-Smirnov test. In this hierarchical Kolmogorov-Smirnov test, each frame is divided into four rectangular regions of equal size and the traditional Kolmogorov-Smirnov test is applied to every pair of regions as well as to the entire image. This test therefore produces five binary numbers that indicate whether there is a change in the entire image as well as in each of the four sub-images.

Finally, instead of directly using these five binary numbers to eliminate false positives we use the test result only in a qualitative sense. The significance of the shot change frame in test result is compared with that of its neighboring frames.

4.3.2 Shot Grouping

Similarity between shots is determined by comparing the representative frame images that represent the shots. Thus, the automatic clustering of shots into visually similar groups requires deciding whether two images are similar. CARAT used color to cluster the shots into initial groups, and then used edge information within each group to refine the clustering results.

The use of color in computing image similarity has found wide use in image retrieval systems, color histograms [47] being especially popular. Note that the ability of the color histogram to detect similarity in the presence of illumination variations is greatly affected by the color space used as well as how the color space is quantized. The normalized histogram bin counts are used as the feature vector to describe the color content of an image.

Figure 3 shows the color histograms of the shots grouped together on the basis of similar color distributions.

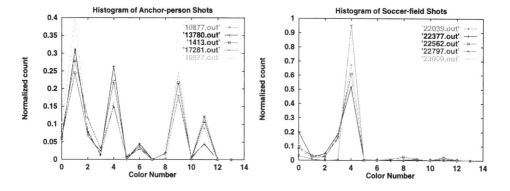

Figure 3. Color histogram of similar images.

Edge information is used as a filter to remove shots that have been incorrectly grouped together based on color. We use a very straightforward global measure of the edge information in an image. Each edge pixel is classified as belonging to one of four cardinal directions based on the sign and relative magnitude of its response to edge operators along x and y directions. The histogram showing pixel counts along each of the four directions is used as a feature vector to describe the edge information in the image.

The clustering algorithm used in CARAT is based on nearest neighbor classification, combined with a threshold criterion. Each cluster is specified by a feature vector, which is the mean of the vectors of its members. When a new shot is available, the city block distance between its color feature vector and the means of the existing clusters is computed. The new shot is grouped into the cluster with the minimum distance from its feature vector, provided the minimum distance is less than a threshold. If an existing cluster is found for the new shot, the mean of the cluster is updated to include the feature vector of the new shot. Otherwise, a new cluster is created with the feature vector of the new shot as its mean. The threshold is selected based on the percentage of the image pixels that need to match in color, in order to call two images similar.

4.3.3   Creation of Video Table of Contents

We have found that a hierarchical tree structure captures the organization of the video adequately and is easy for the user to understand and manipulate directly. The whole video is the root node, which can have a number of child nodes, each corresponding to a separate *story* in the video. Each *story* node may have further children corresponding to sub-plots in the story and the sub-plots may be further sub-divided and so on. A story is a self-contained unit, which deals with a single or related subject(s). Sub-plots are different elements in a story unit or sub-plot unit. The tree structure used to depict the organization of the video has nodes of different types, the node type providing semantic information about its contents. Each node also has a representative icon visible to allow browsing without having to unravel the full structure.

CARAT's algorithm contains two major functions. The main function, `Create-VTOC-from-Merged-List`, modified from the algorithm presented in [48], finds all story units, creates a story node for each story, and calls the second function `Find-structure` to find structure within each story. Each story unit extends to the last re-occurrence of a shot, which occurs within the body of the story. `Find-structure` is a function that takes a segment of shot indices and traverses through the segment to create a node for each shot until it finds one shot that re-occurs later. At this point, it divides the rest of the segment into sub-segments, each of which is lead by the recurring shot as a sub-plot node and recursively calls itself to process each sub-segment. If consecutive shots are found to be similar, they are grouped under a single similar node. The structure produced by `Find-structure` is attached as a child of the story node for which it was called.

4.4 A HYBRID, STRUCTURED MULTIMEDIA LOGGING APPROACH

We have developed a tool, the CARAT logging tool, that implements structured multimedia logging. This tool allows the user to modify the results of automatic organization at both levels. The main steps in the interactive generation of the final organized video can be summarized as follows:

1. Automatic construction of shot list from raw video.
2. Viewing and editing the shot structure to add new shots or merge shots into a single shot.
3. Automatic clustering of shots into groups of visually similar shots.
4. Viewing and editing the clusters generated automatically to create new clusters and modify existing clusters.
5. Automatic generation of tree structure to describe the high level units in the video using the cluster information from the earlier step.
6. Viewing and modifying the tree structure to reorganize the video as well as entering textual description about the video content.

Steps 2, 4, and 6 in the above list require user interaction and, therefore, there is a need for an interface that can provide appropriate functionality. Since these interfaces work with higher level representations of the video, a separate component is also provided to view the raw video accompanied by its audio.

The structured logging interface is shown in Figure 4.

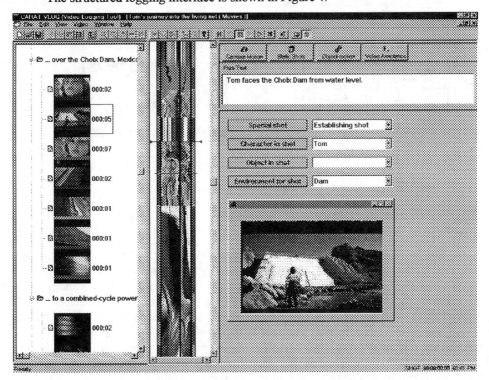

Figure 4. The CARAT video logging interface.

This interface contains four regions. The various components controlling these regions communicate with each other so that changes made using one component produce the appropriate updates in the other interfaces. The region to the left serves a dual purpose. Before the creation of the high level tree structure of the video, it is used to view and alter the automatic clustering of shots based on visual similarity. Once the similarity-based grouping results have been finalized, it is used as an interface to organize the video into a tree structure. It displays the name of the various nodes in the hierarchy, and it displays all representative key frames for all shots in the video. The colored region next to the video table of contents is a graphical scrollbar that shows the pattern of shot transitions. This interface is used to view and modify the shot list. The video stream is represented as a composite image making it easy to visually detect shot boundaries. The results of automatic shot detection are displayed alongside using colored bars, and can be easily altered. This graphic bar is a cross-section image generated directly from the original video. In our implementation, we select one in the horizontal and the other in the vertical direction of the video volume, although we could, in general, select any number of directions.

The process of constructing a cross-section image is illustrated in Figure 5.

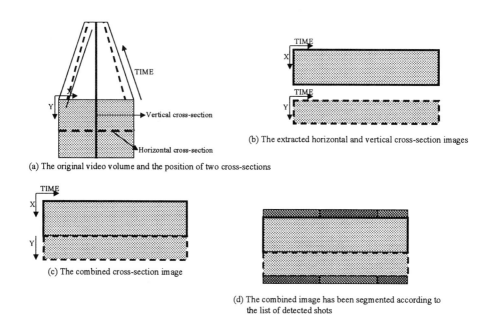

(a) The original video volume and the position of two cross-sections

(b) The extracted horizontal and vertical cross-section images

(c) The combined cross-section image

(d) The combined image has been segmented according to the list of detected shots

Figure 5. The Process of constructing a cross-section image.

The horizontal (vertical) cross-section image is constructed by sampling the middle row (or the middle column) from every image and by collecting all samples over time. To provide a complete view of both cross-section images, we combine them into one image and then segment the image into two bands according to the list of detected shots. This representation provides a level of abstraction, which reveals the continuity of video frames. For example, if there is a missed shot that is the result of a visually abrupt cut or camera break, we see a clear discontinuous pattern as shown in the left picture of Figure 6. For cuts that are associated with gradual shot transitions such as dissolves, we see a blurred discontinuous pattern as shown in the right two pictures of Figure 6.

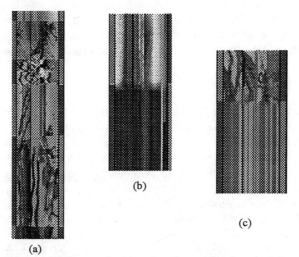

Figure 6. Cross-section images showing abrupt cuts (a) and gradual changes (b,c).

The upper right region shows the free text summary of the selected item in the video table of contents, while the lower right region shows the indexes used to describe the selected node. All indexes in this case are based on text keywords. Each field in this log is associated with one specific object type (such as keywords, locations, and persons) and values can be selected from objects of the corresponding type.

To facilitate the specification of domain-independent and domain-specific knowledge, we have developed a domain modeler that enables the owner of the archive (e.g., the museum or the broadcast station). This tool is used to enter data in the internal catalog of CARAT (see also Section 6) and can be used to specify

1. the types of objects that can be logged,
2. domain specific name for each type of object, and
3. (multimedia) descriptors that constitute a collection of indexes describing the object.

The user interfaces provided by the CARAT logging tool and the querying and browsing tool will be instantiated from the specified domain model.

5. MULTIMEDIA CONTENT RETRIEVAL

It is crucial for a multimedia archive to provide some sort of associative access where items are retrieved based on a specification of their content. This content specification might describe content at a semantically low level, for instance, a *blue sky*. It might also describe higher level semantics such as a *love scene*. The querying user might combine semantics at a different abstraction level, for instance, in querying for a *love scene on a beach under a blue sky*. A multimedia archive should provide mechanisms for combining high-level and low level semantics in a query. It should also provide the means for the user to specify the semantics as precisely as possible.

Complex multimedia objects such as video and text documents often define a structural hierarchy of sub-objects. Objects within such structures will have relationships to the other objects in the structure. In Section 4.1 we described how CARAT is using hyperlinking as the basic approach to implement a log. Thus, the resulting log record defines inter-object relationships. Such relationships represent important aspects of the objects and it should be possible for querying users to include specifications of inter-object relationships when formulating a query.

In Section 5.1 we will describe how semantics can be used to achieve multimedia content retrieval. Section 5.2 will examine the use of inter-object relationships in a query. In Section 5.3, we describe how navigation and similarity retrieval is supported by CARAT. Section 5.4 describes CARAT's card-based approach for specifying queries.

5.1 SEMANTIC CONTENT RETRIEVAL

Most automatic content-indexing query systems fail to take into account the importance of semantics to a content-based query. For instance, assume that a video director is looking for a video shot from the Persian Gulf where a crew of pilots watches a military airplane take off from an American aircraft carrier. This is a difficult query to formulate by image-level features only. It is difficult to formulate this query very precisely even if the system provided a textual description of the content because the querying user would not know what kind of textual description was entered for this shot. For instance, the shot will never show up if the text used the term *battleship*, the ship's real name, USS Enterprise, instead of *aircraft carrier*.

In Section 4.1 we proposed to structure the log by defining specific attributes drawing their values from a controlled vocabulary (thesaurus). This approach will make it possible to define more precise semantics than a regular keyword based system. Figure 7 illustrates how the query mentioned in the previous paragraph could be specified.

Object:	Pilot; Airplane, military
Environment:	Battleship
Location:	Persian Gulf
Event:	Airplane take-off

Figure 7. Specifying a media item's semantic features.

We assume that the following semantic is being used in the domain: *Object* is an attribute used to list a real-world object that can be seen in the shot having *Pilot, Airplane,* and *military* as values defined in the vocabulary; *Environment* is an attribute used to describe features about the physical environment depicted in the shot, such as sea, sky, etc. having *Battleship* as a value defined in the vocabulary; *Location* is an attribute used to specify the geographical location for the shooting of the video having *Persian Gulf* as a value defined in the vocabulary; and *Event* is an attribute used to specify events or types of actions that are recorded on the video having *Airplane take-off* as a value defined in the vocabulary.

CARAT supports semantic querying in the same way it supports semantic logging. The querying will ask the end-user to select what user domain(s) and object type(s) should be used for the query. Once the selection is made, a proper logging card containing the appropriate attributes is created. If the attribute is bound to a specific vocabulary the user will be able to select values only from the corresponding vocabularies.

5.2 QUERYING INTER-OBJECT RELATIONSHIPS

As already mentioned, the use of multimedia objects to log other multimedia objects will result in a set of hyperlinks between media items. Take a television news archive as an example. Assume that information about each story and each shot is stored in the archive and that each shot contains a reference to a transcript of what is being said in the shot. To find all news stories where Bill Clinton mentions the name *Saddam*, the query needs to combine information about video shots and their relationships to news stories and a transcript item.

Figure 8 shows example items from a news archive having the given properties and inter-object relationships. A multimedia archive should provide means to end-users to exploit such relationships when formulating queries.

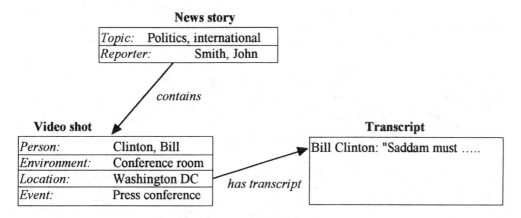

Figure 8. Inter-object relationships.

CARAT provides the card-based approach as a means for the end-user to specify such queries. This approach will be described in Section 5.4.

5.3 OTHER QUERYING MECHANISMS

Querying users may not always be able to express the query so that it retrieves the relevant objects. A digital multimedia archiving system should allow the user to combine traditional queries, with navigation and similarity as additional means for information retrieval. Navigation in CARAT means following the links that are stored in the content description of an object.

The log record for a multimedia item, as defined in CARAT, constitutes a semantic feature vector for the item. Querying now becomes an issue of mapping the feature vector of the query with the feature vector of the items in the database. This has several good side-effects. First, a system using both manual and automatic indexing will have one homogeneous way for indexing and retrieval since automatic indexing also generates feature vectors. The second advantage is that the feature vector facilitates similarity search based on semantic similarity. The similarity between two items can be measured by comparing their respective feature vectors. By using semantic feature vectors, it is even possible to measure similarity between objects of different media types; for instance, the similarity between a television news story and a newspaper article. This is impossible to do based on content-derived indexes since video and text media do not share any features.

5.4 CARD-BASED QUERYING

The CARAT system provides a query mechanism called *card-based querying*. End-users will formulate a query by using one or more query cards. First, the user will select the type of item the card is supposed to retrieve, for instance, a video shot. After selecting the proper media type, the query card will display all attributes defined for items of the given media type within the given domain. The user may now select values for the appropriate attributes by selecting a value for a controlled vocabulary or list of multimedia objects. Figure 9 shows a sample query card. The sample query cards presents the log structure for a video shot in the News domain. As can be seen from the figure, end-users may select attribute values from the controlled vocabularies and/or specify terms that should appear in the object's textual summary. There are three query cards defined on the figure. Only the one that is selected (in this example Query Card 0) is shown. The end-user may select one of the other cards by selecting the corresponding tab on top of the cards. The user can also define inter-card relationships by using the selection box in the lower right corner.

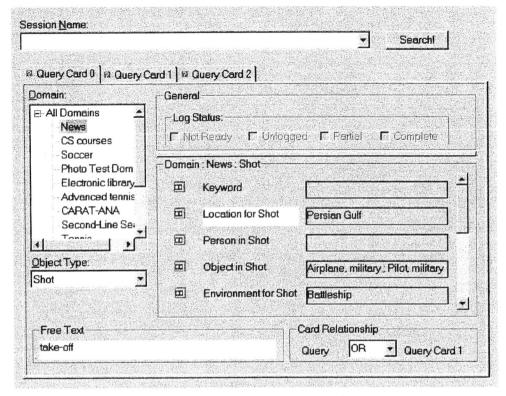

Figure 9. Sample CARAT query card.

To make more complex queries like the one in Figure 8, the user would have to add more query cards. Each query card specifies the properties of individual objects involved in the query (in the example, one query card specifying the news story, one specifying the video shot and one specifying the transcript object). The user would then have to specify the relationships that should exist between the individual objects; a *contains* relationship should be defined between the query cards for the *news story* and the *video shot*, respectively, and a *has transcript* relationship should be defined between the query cards for the *video shot* and the *transcript*, respectively.

When the end-user has specified the attributes of each individual query card and the relationship between the cards, the execution of the query can be invoked. The CARAT system now translates the query from the query card form to the equivalent SQL statement that is then sent to the database. The strength of the query card method is that it provides a consistent way to specify queries for any type of multimedia object and that it provides an easy way to formulate queries specifying inter-object relationships.

6. MULTIMEDIA ARCHIVE META-DATA MANAGEMENT

As mentioned before, CARAT contains an internal catalog. The content of this catalog specifies the individual log structures. This gives content owners a system that can easily be adapted to their specific needs and that can be extended over time as their needs are changing. The most important information stored in the internal catalog is:

Object types: In CARAT the object type is not the same as a media type (see Section 4.2). An object type is always derived from a specific media type, but the content owner may define several object types as being the same media types. For instance, there might exist several textual vocabularies, which would all be of a singular text media type. If the content owner wants to attach an image portrait of all persons represented in the database, he or she might define an object type *PERSON_PORTRAIT* being of media type image to distinguish such images from other images in the database.

Controlled vocabularies: Some of the object types can be defined to be a controlled vocabulary. The individual objects of this type then constitute the "terms" in the vocabulary. The media type of a vocabulary can be of any of the types defined in the database. The *PERSON_PORTRAIT* mentioned above, for instance, can be defined to be a vocabulary of image type objects.

User domains: As mentioned before, a user domain specifies the semantics that will apply to a group of multimedia objects. The CARAT allows several user domains to be defined in the catalog at the same time. A broadcasting station, for instance, may group their media items into a *news domain*, a *sports domain*, an *arts and culture domain*, etc. allowing the media items to be described in a way most suitable for the given domain.

Hierarchical structures: Text, audio, and video objects may have an internal structure. This structure may often be divided into semantic levels. A news video, for instance, may be segmented into individual news stories, which again might be divided into individual shots. The CARAT catalog stores information about individual semantic levels as part of a domain's description. This allows different domains to define different semantics for objects of the same type.

Log structures: A log structure defines what attributes are to be used to describe a multimedia object of a certain type within a specific domain. Each log structure is related to a given object type and a specific semantic level within the object type and it is associated with one user domain. Each attribute within a log structure is associated with a multimedia object type. If this object type is defined to be a controlled vocabulary, end-users will have to select one of the existing objects when selecting values for the corresponding attributes.

CARAT provides a tool, the *Meta Data Modeler*, for database administrators to manage the contents of the internal catalog. Thus, there is no need for the database administrator to know all the details about the internal catalog or to use a database language for modifying it.

7. CONCLUSION

In this chapter, we have discussed some of the challenges for multimedia archive owners. We have specifically looked at challenges related to the variety of existing meta-data formats, the efficiency of the logging process, the quality of multimedia information retrieval, and query mechanisms for multimedia archives. We also described how CARAT dealt with these challenges. The key elements in the CARAT solution are:

- The internal catalog that allows content owners to use CARAT to store content descriptions in any familiar format. Even more, it allows content owners to use different formats for different types of objects. Also, it gives content owners means for changing the format of the content descriptions as time goes and needs change.
- The hybrid, structured multimedia logging approach that offers efficient means for end-users to create content description of high quality and accuracy, which is needed to achieve good precision and recall ratios.
- The card-based query approach that allows end-users to utilize the rich semantic stored in the database. The query approach also gives the end-users an easy way to create complex queries specifying temporal, structural, and/or referential relationships between objects in the database.

Multimedia information management is a demanding task. CARAT is a good step toward making this task easier for multimedia content owners. We are, however, still working on pushing the system even further to be an archiving system that really supports content owners in their day-to-day operation. Especially, we are integrating feedback from end-users to make the system even better adapted to the various configurations. In addition, we are working on the difficult problems of content processing to improve the efficiency of the logging process even more. Last, we are also working on meta-data management problems such as meta-data export and automatic extraction.

ACKNOWLEDGMENTS

We would like to thank Ningping Fan, Kangesh Gunaseelan, and Bernhard Klein for their efforts in implementing the CARAT tools and Candemir Toklu for support on content processing. Also, we would like to thank our business group, Siemens Audio and Video, Vienna, Austria, for their work on the overall CARAT system architecture and the tools for broadcast automation and audio data management.

REFERENCES

1. Bond, B., Minimizing media mayhem: a producer's look at media asset management, *Digital Video*, 10, 54, 1997.
2. Feeley, J., The joy of logging, *Digital Video*, 9, 40, 1997.
3. Dempsey, L. and Heery, R., *A Review of Metadata: A Survey of Current Resource Description Formats*, Ver. 1.0, Project RE1004, DESIRE, Project Deliverable D3.2, Fourth Framework Programme of the European Union, 1997.
4. van Rijsbergen, C. J., *Information Retrieval*, 2nd Edition, Butterworth & Co (Publishers) Ltd., 1979, 10.
5. Davenport, G., Indexes are "out", models are "in", *IEEE Multimedia*, 3, 10, 1996.
6. Baldonado, M., Chang, C.-C. K., Gravano, L., and Paepcke, A., Metadata for digital libraries: architecture and design rationale, in *Proceedings of the 2nd International ACM Conference on Digital Libraries*, Philadelphia, PA, 1997, 47.
7. Carrer, M., Ligresti, L., Ahanger, G., and Little, T. D. C., An annotation engine for supporting video database population, *Multimedia Tools and Applications*, 5, 199, 1997.
8. Davis, M., Media streams: an iconic visual language for video representation, in *Readings in Human-Computer Interaction: Toward the Year 2000*, Baecker, R. M. et al., Eds., 2nd ed., Morgan Kaufmann Publishers, Inc., 1995, 854.
9. Adah, S., Candan, K. S., Chen, S.-S., Erol, K., and Subrahmanian, V. S., The Advanced Video Information System: data structures and query processing, *Multimedia Systems*, 4, 172, 1996.
10. Chakravarthy, A. S., Toward semantic retrieval of pictures and video, in *Proceedings of the RIAO 94, Intelligent Multimedia Information Retrieval Systems and Management*, 1994, 676.
11. Rosengren, P., Applying conceptual models to multimedia information retrieval, in *Proceedings of the RIAO 94, Intelligent Multimedia Information Retrieval Systems and Management*, 1994, 328.
12. Simonnot, B. and Smail, M., Model for interactive retrieval of videos and still images, in Nwosu, K. C., Thuraisingham, B., Berra P. B., Eds., *Multimedia Database Systems: Design and Implementation Strategies*, Kluwer Academic Publishers, 1996, 89.
13. England, P., Allen, R. B., Sullivan, M., and Heybey, A., "I/Browse: the Bellcore video library toolkit", in *Storage and Retrieval for Still Image and Video Databases IV*, SPIE 2670, 1996, 254.
14. Oomoto, E. and Tanaka, K., Design and implementation of a video-object database system, *Transaction on Knowledge and Data Engineering*, 4, 629, 1993.

15. Coll, D. and Choma, G., Image activity characteristics in broadcast television, *IEEE Trans. on Communications*, 26, 1201, 1976.
16. Hsu, Y. Z., Nagel, H.-H., and Pekers, G., New likelihood test methods for change detection in image sequences, *CVGIP*, 26, 73, 1984.
17. Sethi, I., Salari, V., and Vemuri, S., Image sequence segmentation using motion coherence, *First International Conference on Computer Vision*, 1987, 667.
18. Aigrain, P., Joly, P., The automatic real-time analysis of film editing and transition effects and its applications, *Computer and Graphics*, 1, 93, 1994.
19. Dubner, H., International Patent Classification 04N9/79,5/76, *Video Logging System and Method Thereof*, 1993.
20. Gove, R. J., U.S. Patent 5,099,322, Scene Change Detection System and Method, 1992.
21. Hampapur, A., Jain, R., and Weymouth, T., Digital video segmentation, in Proceedings of the ACM Multimedia Conference, 1994, 357.
22. Koga, T., U.S. Patent 5,032,905, Accurate Detection of a Drastic Change Between Successive Pictures, 1991.
23. Nagasaka, A. and Tanaka, Y., Automatic video indexing and full-video search for object appearances, in Visual Database Systems, II, Knuth, E. and Wegner, L. M., Eds., Elsevier Science Publishers B. V., 1992, 113.
24. Otsuji, K., Tonomura, Y., and Ohba, Y., Video browsing using brightness data, in *Visual Communication and Image Processing*, SPIE 1606, 1991, 980.
25. Zhang, H., Kankanhalli, A., and Smoliar, S. W., Automatic parsing of full-motion video, *ACM Multimedia Systems*, 1, 10, 1993.
26. Yeo, B. L. and Liu, B., Rapid scene analysis on compressed video, *IEEE Trans. on Circuits and Systems for Video Technology*, 5, 533, 1995.
27. Ishikawa, H. and Matsumoto, H., European Patent 0-615-245-A2, *Method for Detecting a Scene Change and Image Editing Apparatus*, 1994 filed.
28. Arman, F., Hsu, A., and Chiu, M. Y., IPD 93E7522 U.S., *On the Processing of Encoded Video Sequences*, 1993.
29. Liu, H.-C. H. and Zick, G. L., Scene decomposition of MPEG compressed video, in *Digital Video Compression Algorithms and Technologies*, SPIE 2419, 1995, 26.
30. Meng, J., Juan, Y., and Chang, S. F., Scene change detection in a MPEG compressed video sequence, in *Digital Video Compression Algorithms and Technologies*, SPIE 2419, 1995, 14.
31. Zhang, H., Low, C. Y., and Smoliar, S. W., Video parsing and browsing using compressed data, *Multimedia Tools and Applications*, 1, 89, 1995.
32. Avid Technology, Inc., *Avid MCXpress™ for Windows NT™: Tutorial & Reference Guide*, 1996.
33. Witbrock, M. J. and Hauptmann A.G., Speech recognition for a digital video library, to appear in *Journal of the American Society for Information Science*.
34. Hauglid, J. O., *Searching in Temporal and Bibliographical Data in a Web-based Video Database* (in Norwegian), M.Sc. Thesis, Norwegian University of Science and Technology, 1997.
35. Hibino, S. and Rundensteiner, E. A., A visual multimedia query language for temporal analysis of video data, in Nwosu, K. C., Thuraisingham, B., and Berra, P. B., Eds., *Multimedia Database Systems: Design and Implementation Strategies*, Kluwer Academic Publishers, 1996, 123.
36. Hjelsvold, R., Midtstraum R., and Sandstå, O., Searching and browsing a shared video database, in Nwosu, K. C., Thuraisingham, B., Berra P. B., eds., *Multimedia Database Systems: Design and Implementation Strategies*, Kluwer Academic Publishers, 89, 1996.
37. Hjelsvold, R., Langørgen, S., Midtstraum, R., and Sandstå, O., Integrated video archive tools, in *Proceedings of the ACM Multimedia '95*, November 1995, 283.
38. Hwang, E. J. and Subrahmanian, V. S., Querying video libraries, *Journal of Visual Commmunication and Image Representation*, 1, 44, 1996.

39. Little, T. D. C., Ahanger, G., Folz, R. J., Gibbon, J. F., Reeve, F. W., Schelleng, D. H., and Venkatesh, D., A digital on-demand video service supporting content-based queries, in *Proceedings of the ACM Multimedia Conference*, 1993, 427.

40. Rowe, L. A., Boreczky, J. S., and Eads, C. A., Indexes for user access to large video databases, in *Storage and Retrieval for Image and Video Databases*, SPIE 2185, 1994, 150.

41. Weiss, R., Duda, A., Gifford, D. K., Composition and search with a video algebra, *IEEE Multimedia*, 1, 12, 1995.

42. Das, M. and Liou, S.-P., A new hybrid approach to video organization for content-based indexing, to appear in the *Proceedings of IEEE Multimedia Systems Conference*, 1998.

43. Fox, A. J., Outliers in time series, *Journal of the Royal Statistical Society*, Series B(34), 350, 1972.

44. Abraham, B. and Chuang, A., Outlier detection and time series modeling, *Technometrics*, 2, 241, 1989.

45. Hotta, L. K. and Neves, M. M. C., A brief review of tests for detection of time series outliers, *ESTADISTICA*, 44, 142, 143, 103-148, 1992.

46. Sethi, I. K. and Patel, N., A statistical approach to scene change detection, in *Storage and Retrieval for Image and Video Databases*, SPIE 2420, 1995, 329.

47. Swain, M. J. and Ballard D. H., Indexing via color histograms, in *Proceedings of the Third International Conference on Computer Vision*, 1990, 390.

48. Yeung, M. M. and Yeo, B. L., Time-constrained clustering for segmentation of video into story units, in *Proceedings of the International Conference on Pattern Recognition*, 1996, 375.

19

CROSS-MODAL INFORMATION RETRIEVAL

Charles B. Owen and Fillia Makedon
Dartmouth Experimental Visualization Laboratory
Dartmouth College
6211 Sudikoff Labs, Hanover, NH 03755
{cowen,makedon}@cs.dartmouth.edu

1.   **INTRODUCTION**..404
2.   **CAUSAL MEDIA** 406
3.   **CROSS-MODAL INFORMATION RETRIEVAL**................408
4.   **CMIR APPLICATIONS**..410
    4.1   SPEECH-BASED MEDIA 410
    4.2   SLIDE-AND-LECTURE PRESENTATION SEARCHING................410
    4.3   FUNCTIONAL MAGNETIC RESONANCE IMAGING OF THE BRAIN 411
    4.4   TRANSLATION SYNCHRONIZATION..............................411
5.   **COMPUTED SYNCHRONIZATION APPROACHES** 412
    5.1   INHERENT SYNCHRONIZATION....................................412
    5.2   MANUAL SYNCHRONIZATION 412
    5.3   COMPUTED SYNCHRONIZATION 413
    5.4   MULTIPLE STREAM MEDIA CORRELATION....................413
6.   **AN EXAMPLE SYNCHRONIZATION APPLICATION**..........415
    6.1   BUILDING THE TRANSCRIPTION GRAPH........................415
    6.2   SPEECH FEATURE RECOGNITION 417
    6.3   SYNCHRONIZATION COMPUTATION 417
    6.4   MODIFICATIONS TO THE VITERBI APPROACH................417
    6.5   EDITS..419
    6.6   EXPERIMENTAL RESULTS 420
7.   **A GENERALIZED SOLUTION APPROACH**......................421
    7.1   THE XTRIEVE INFORMATION RETRIEVAL SYSTEM..........421
8.   **CONCLUSION** 421
    REFERENCES 422

Abstract. The increased appearance of large multimedia databases has necessitated the development of new methods that can extract information fast and accurately. This chapter describes a new framework for multimedia information retrieval called Cross-Modal Information Retrieval (CMIR). Traditionally, multimedia information retrieval has been based on searching or indexing technologies designed for a particular medium, such as text retrieval, color histogram analysis of images, or video segmentation.

0-8493-1825-4/99/$0.00+$.50
© 1999 by CRC Press LLC

In practice, however, some media, such as images and audio, are more difficult to search (or query) than others. For a large class of applications, the search can be simplified if queries are applied to a type of "query media" that is easier to search, such as text or pre-indexed content, while results are presented in the *target media* that is more difficult to search. The process of querying one media for results in another is called *Cross-Modal Information Retrieval* (CMIR). A fundamental prerequisite for CMIR is computing the synchronization information between the different (query-target) media streams. Examples of CMIR are presented that include text-to-speech retrieval, image-to-video retrieval, text-to-text retrieval, and a special application to functional magnetic resonance imaging (fMRI).

1. INTRODUCTION

This chapter introduces a new framework for querying multimedia databases, which is based on the idea that some data types are easier to query than others. Given two different data types that can be synchronized in some way, a query of the simpler data type will yield the equivalent information in the more complex data type. For example, if a video clip comes with a text "track" (transcript), the transcript can be searched for a keyword to yield the video frame(s) in which the keyword appears. Searching the transcript is easier than searching for visual cues in the video. This is the idea behind CMIR. To facilitate this type of cross-modal query, the different types of data types must be synchronized.

Information retrieval in multimedia data is often very difficult. Many media, such as audio, images, and video, contain large amounts of redundancy, are suffused with noise, and contain information that is still not well understood computationally. At the same time, other media, such as text, are relatively easy to query. Methods for indexing and searching text have been around for hundreds of years and electronic indexing and querying is a mature technology. Also, some media have annotation information that is easy to comprehend and search. Such an example might be the slides used in a presentation. The order and contents of the slides are known in advance of the presentation and are easy to browse and search. However, finding the corresponding video segment of a presentation that discusses a particular slide is not so simple.

For a large class of multimedia applications, varying degrees of redundancy exist between the component media. Video of human speakers contains mouth motions highly correlated to the speech audio. Closed-captioned video has text information that redundantly presents what is spoken in the audio (and often provides cues to sound effects and music). Any application where a script or transcription exists (court testimony, dramatic productions, or broadcasting, for example) will have a large amount of redundancy between the transcript and the audio. Often this redundancy will represent identical information in more than one potentially heterogeneous media, one of which is easy to query, while the other is difficult. Locating specific content in a text transcript is easy. Locating that same content in speech audio is complicated by all of the problems associated with large vocabulary speech recognition. However, it is often the complicated media result that is desired and more useful.

For such applications it would be advantageous to query the easier media and present the result in the richer media. In court cases an attorney wishes to play back testimony rather than reading it, if possible. This task is typically performed by shuttling videotape to locate the appropriate testimony, even though its exact location in the transcript is known. The querying of one media for results in another is CMIR. The underlying requirement for CMIR is the existence of synchronization information that will allow the location of the desired result in the target media given its location in the query media. This chapter discusses CMIR in the context of several applications, one being *text to speech retrieval*. Text-to-speech retrieval is the process of accessing information in speech audio by querying the corresponding textual transcript of that audio.

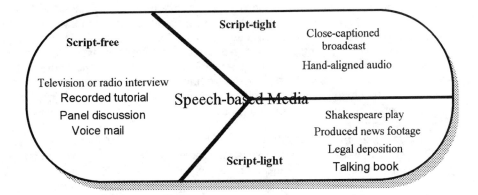

Figure 1. Three classes of speech data (a) script-less data: speech without a corresponding transcript, such as content resulting from interviews or panels. This is the least constrained form of speech-based content. (b) Script-light data: speech which has a corresponding textual transcript associated with it, but no alignment between the transcript and the audio. A surprisingly large amount of material of interest to users exists in this form, including courtroom testimony, news media which is routinely transcribed, and plays or other dramatic presentations. (c) Script-tight data: speech that has a hard alignment to its transcription, such as is the case with any TV program with associated closed-captioning.

In this framework, speech is divided into three categories based on the type of transcript it is associated with: *script-free, script-light,* and *script-tight.* Script-free means that there is no associated transcript with the audio stream in question while script-tight means that there is transcript that is temporally synchronized with the speech audio. Script-light is speech audio that has transcript associated with it, but this transcript is not synchronized with the audio. The efficient retrieval of transcripted speech-based media uses text queries. Script-tight content is the easiest to query since a temporal synchronization between the transcription and the database is already known; script-free is the hardest to query, while, in script-light, the synchronization is either non-existent or very coarse. The CMIR technique provides efficient algorithms to query and retrieve scripted speech media content (script-light content). Figure 1 indicates the division of speech into different categories.

Multiple media stream analysis is a relatively new area. Some early projects included alignment of newly recorded voice audio to degraded voice audio, a technique used for motion picture dubbing. This work is described along with several other unsolved application areas by Chen et al. and by Bloom [1,2]. The ViewStation project included cross-modal retrieval of closed-captioned video, a member of the *script-tight* category [3]. Chen et al. illustrate joint audio-video coding based on audio prediction of lip motion in order to achieve higher compression levels [4,5].

There has been considerable work on methods for searching speech content, an important application area discussed in this chapter. Most applications assume no available transcription data, thereby not partaking of the advantages of cross-modal information retrieval. Of particular interest is work at Cambridge University [6] and the Swiss Federal Institute of Technology [7]. The Informedia project at CMU is heavily based on automatic transcription technologies [8]. A good introduction to speech recognition technologies can be found in Rabiner and Juang [9]. Most previous work on text-to-speech alignment has been concerned with automatic corpora labeling, the accurate temporal location of sound elements such as phonemes in speech audio [10,11]. The process is applied to very short audio segments and is used to generate standard training and testing data. These systems are designed for precise alignment of very short segments of audio, not for entire texts. They are not designed to effectively recover from alignment failures or to scale to hours of content.

The importance of alignment of text to speech audio has been recognized in the Informedia project at CMU, specifically the News-on-demand element of that project [12]. That project seeks to index speech-based audio using automatic transcription. Whenever possible, they have taken advantage of the availability of transcript data. However, the approach to synchronization is to perform automatic transcription on the audio without knowledge of the transcription and align the text transcripts on a word-matching basis, hoping for some minimal recognition performance. The News-on-demand project heavily utilizes closed-captioned digital video, but has observed that the caption content can lag the video by up to 20 seconds.

Two additional applications discussed in this chapter include functional magnetic resonance imagery and translation synchronization. Functional magnetic resonance imagery (fMRI) is the capture of volume imagery of human anatomy in a time series [13]. The techniques briefly described in this chapter are closely related to those described in [14]. Although the alignment of common language content described herein is new, it is closely related to alignment of differing languages. There has been considerable work in this area including work with and without domain knowledge (lexical information) [15,16,17].

A major component of CMIR is *media synchronization*. This should not be confused with the conventional multimedia topic of synchronization [18]. Typically, synchronization in multimedia is concerned with the synchronized presentation of content. Actual synchronization information is either assumed to exist (as in video-audio streams) or will be provided as an element of the authoring process (as in spatio-temporal composition). Gibbs et al. present temporal models for time-based media. These models are primarily concerned with synchronized delivery, but are sufficiently general that they are closely related to the causal media model presented in Section 2 [19].

Section 2 describes the causal media model, a model for time-based and other sequential media that is used throughout this chapter. Section 3 introduces cross-modal information retrieval. Applications of cross-modal information retrieval are described in Section 4. Section 5 describes general issues of synchronization computation with a specific solution example for text-to-speech synchronization in Section 6. Section 7 expands the specific solution to a general solution for a large class of problems. Section 8 describes the Xtrieve information retrieval system, a prototype cross-modal information retrieval system.

2. CAUSAL MEDIA

There are many forms of media. For some media, such as video and audio, the presentation order is determined by the flow of time. Such media are traditionally called time-based media. Other media, such as text, are not considered to be fundamentally time-based at all. An image is a single discrete event and has no fundamental ordering. For synchronization information to exist, however, there must be a distinct ordering that allows indexing to specific points in time or specific points in the media data for non-time-based media. This section describes a simple description for media that has an ordering that may or may not be time-based. Such media is called *causal media*. The notion of causal media is used to create a basis for synchronization. In this case, synchronization is not used as a time-based problem, but as a more general problem using the concept of ordered segments of information.

The literature is replete with models for time-based media and media ordering. Gibbs et al. [19] present models ranging from *binary large objects* (BLOBs) to *timed streams*. BLOBs consider media elements to be amorphous entities that function as black boxes. Time goes in, data comes out. This is a minimalist view of media structure. Timed streams assume media elements to be media data (frames, samples, etc.) combined with a *discrete time system*, a mapping from media element indices to moments in time.

A major goal of media time representations is synchronized presentation. Synchronized presentation assumes the existence of synchronization information between multiple media streams. This data is utilized to present composite media objects in a timed presentation with bounding of timing errors between elements [18,20]. This is unique from the requirements of cross-modal information retrieval. Cross-modal information retrieval requires the existence of synchronization between element indices for retrieval purposes. In most applications this data does not exist *a priori* and must be computed. In addition, this information is often of a finer grain than that required for presentation. Text is typically presented without regard to time, whereas the synchronization between text and speech may exist at the sub-word level.

Gibbs et. al. describe media as being constructed in a hierarchical structure from simple to more complex objects called *media elements* [19]. The smallest media element in digital media is typically the bit. Bits are aggregated into bytes, which may be aggregated into larger groups for integers, floating point values, or characters. Characters may be aggregated into words, then sentences, paragraphs, etc. The same is true for temporal media such as digital video, which may be divided into pixels, scan-lines, frames, camera sequences (cuts), or entire presentations. The inherent hierarchical nature of multimedia data complicates the description of these media for synchronization purposes. In addition, the stored media format may not be a one-to-one mapping with the presented format. Examples include complex media compression and annotation formats such as MPEG [22]. This lack of correspondence will be ignored in this chapter due to the existence of a conversion from one form to the other (decompression or compression).

> **Definition 1**: *Temporal media element.* A temporal media element is a composite media element that produces a disjoint, sequential segmentation such that a specific time is associated with each media element.

Temporal media elements are the basis for time-based media. Examples include frames in a video, samples in digital audio, or even words in speech audio. Although more complex representations exist, time-based media can be described as a simple function of time: $\mu(t)$. Note that this definition does not imply discrete media. Analog audio, a continuous media, can also be partitioned into finite length temporal elements (cycles of a waveform, spoken phonemes or words, or elements between edits).

The use of the parameter t in the presence of segmentation can be confusing. There are two approaches to the definition of the time parameter. The function $\mu(t)$ can be considered to be a continuous function over the domain of t (real values for time or sample points for audio samples or video frames). The models presented herein will assume the domain of t to be the locations of media elements, with $\mu(t)$ mapped to a null set at all other locations. However, this is not a firm requirement and the alternative approach of assuming media elements as a range of t values is equally acceptable.

Time-based media is a large and important category of multimedia. However, many media are not time-based at all, but still have a distinct ordering. The simplest of these is text, an ordered set of letters. Larger groupings of letters also emit orderings, including words, paragraphs, sections, and chapters. Media that exhibit ordering, a more general classification than time-based media, are referred to as causal media.

> **Definition 2**: *Causal media element.* A causal media element is a composite media element that produces a disjoint, sequential segmentation such that a specific index is associated with each media element.

> **Definition 3**: *Causal media.*[1] Causal media is any media composed of causal media elements.

The difference between causal, non-temporal media and temporal media is the lack of a time reference in the former. Of course, just about any causal media could be considered time-based by simply assigning an arbitrary time-line to the ordering index. However, this complicates the meaning of time-based indexing.

---

[1] The term *causal* has been chosen as a more general term than the term *temporal*. Ordering in causal media implies a cause-and-effect relationship between earlier elements and later. Any media which can be segmented into ordered elements is causal in nature.

Any causal media can be represented as a set of causal media elements. Such a set is referred to as a *causal media stream* due to the streaming (sequential presentation) nature of the data. Not all media are causal. An example is hypermedia. Hypermedia is not causal in that the presence of links permits multiple navigation paths through the data. However, at the lowest level, the nodes of hypermedia documents are sequential and causal in nature. At a higher level, a valid ordering of the documents by the navigation mechanism will also emit a causal ordering of the data. Another example is media with no ordering whatsoever. A set of images may have no ordering, yet be related to a video that contains the images. In such a case an arbitrary ordering can be supplied to serve as a causal ordering. This may be as simple as the sequential numbering of elements in an image database.

3. CROSS-MODAL INFORMATION RETRIEVAL

As defined earlier, cross-modal information retrieval is the searching of one media for content in another. The media onto which the query is applied is the *query media*. The media that is the query result is the *target media*. Searching text transcriptions and presenting the results as video segments is an example of cross-modal information retrieval. In this example, the query media is text, the target media is digital video. Text is much easier to search than digital video or audio. Cross-modal information retrieval is not considered to include applications wherein the query media is directly derived from the target media as in most indexing methodologies [21]. While the final result is determined by a cross-modal operation, the process that created the index could be repeated at query time, collapsing the process to a traditional media query. This type of query is quite general and does not have the special characteristics of cross-modal queries in that the two media with intermedia redundancy do not initially exist.

As indicated earlier, the primary mechanism for cross-modal retrieval is *media synchronization*. Given two causal media, a query media μ_q and a target media μ_t, cross-modal retrieval requires, as a minimum, a temporal synchronization τ, a function from the μ_q ordering domain to the μ_t ordering domain. A query result in μ_q is an ordered set of intervals $<<s_1, e_1>, <s_2, e_2>, ..., <s_n, e_n>>$ such that each interval includes a start index s_i and an end index e_i. The ordering indices for target segment i are, then, $\tau(s_i)$ to $\tau(e_i)$. This is a minimum requirement since it is necessary that a relation between the two temporal coordinate systems exists. For some applications this relationship will be an identity relationship $\tau(t) = t$. In such an application, the two media are assumed to exist in an identical causal ordering system, perhaps seconds.

This discussion has assumed a single target media. In many applications multiple target media may exist. An example is a target media of digital video, wherein an associated digital audio sound track will usually exist. A query result is then presented in both media. However, it is possible that there may be two target media with differing synchronization functions or that a final target media synchronization will require composition of multiple synchronization functions. Such an example might include the location of the description of a given projected slide in a recorded presentation.

Presentations often use projected slides to highlight or present important points. These slides can be scanned or, given the popularity of presentation software packages such as PowerPoint, may already exist in electronic form. Slides are often highly condensed summaries of the material in the presentation and are limited in number. They are an ideal browsing media. A user may select slide 13 and wish to know what was said about the slide. A computed or stored synchronization can locate the time when the slide was presented in a video recording of the presentation. This is the first level of synchronization. Given the location in the video, the user may prefer to read a transcript of this portion of the presentation rather than viewing the speaker. A second ordering translation will be used to find the associated period or duration in the transcript. Two temporal synchronization functions are required for this query, with the result determined by the composition of these functions. This process is illustrated in Figure 2.

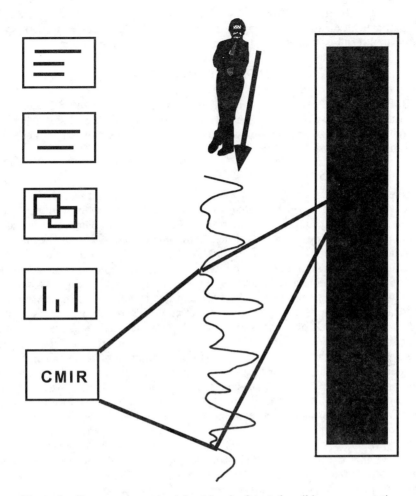

Figure 2. Two step cross-modal retrieval of text describing a presentation slide. Each slide is associated with a temporal period of the presentation audio and video. The period is determined by automatically recording the slide presentation times or correlating to the video of the presentation. Given this period, a location in the transcript for the audio is found. Users can typically read faster than they can listen to audio playback of speech. This second synchronization is computed using the algorithm in Section 6.

Temporal synchronization is the process of obtaining the temporal location of specific information as a result of a query. The result is not only the location of this information in time, but also a duration (period, in the case of causal media elements). Some applications require *spatial synchronization* or *localization*. An example is the location of a speaker's lips in an image sequence. This process requires not only the synchronization of the query to the image sequence temporally, but also the spatial location of the lips in the frames. Temporal synchronization is synchronization at the media element level, while spatial synchronization is at the sub-element level. Some applications are inherently temporally synchronized and require only the computation of spatial results.

Functional magnetic resonance imagery (fMRI) is a non-invasive imaging technology for human anatomy that can be described as a time series. This technique is often spatially based in that the stimulus can be a multimedia stream of data that is correlated with the acquired human anatomy data captured in an identical time frame. Thus, a query into the stimuli media time produces results which are anatomical features that are related to the stimuli. In many cases, the results are perceived activations in the human brain. Spatial synchronization between the stimulus and the brain response permits spatial results. A spatial result is locations within output media frames or data sets.

4. CMIR APPLICATIONS

CMIR is a large category of multimedia data retrieval and several applications of CMIR already exist. However, they have not been previously identified as a specific class. This section describes some existing as well as new applications currently under study and serves to illustrate the scope of the field.

4.1 SPEECH-BASED MEDIA

One of the largest categories of media data is *speech-based media*, i.e., audio that contains speech content. Speech content, is the most common form of human communication. It is being accumulated at alarming rates in massive databases. Broadcasting, interviews, legal proceedings, speeches, panels, and much more will soon become unusable to the common user due to the scale of information. This makes clear the critical importance to develop high quality search tools which locate specific audio content upon user demand.

The general problem of searching speech-based databases necessarily requires large-vocabulary speech recognition tools. Although this technology is improving, it is still far from ideal and may remain so for some time to come. Therefore, it is useful to examine the problem area in search of a constraint that will allow fast and accurate searching of a significant subset of speech content. In this chapter, two subsets of speech-based media are considered, *script-tight* and *script-light* (as defined in an earlier section). Script-tight (speech audio for which a temporally aligned transcription exists) is closed-captioned television broadcasting. Compared to voice recognition technologies, this technique is trivial to implement and as accurate as the captioning. However, closed-caption data is not always sufficient for information retrieval purposes due to the fact that the alignment error may be up to 25 seconds [25].

Script-light is a surprisingly large category of speech-based media, larger than script tight. In this category, a textual transcription exists with no temporal alignment information. Most broadcasting is produced from a script, although only what is aired is closed-captioned. Recordings of dramatic productions are of great interest to researchers in the arts and nearly always have scripts available. Most legal proceedings are recorded and transcribed. Services such as Lexis-Nexis transcribe major political speeches, debates, and proceedings. Closed-captioning often begins as script-light content that is then hand aligned by a human operator. If an automatic method can be devised to perform this alignment, searching is reduced to simple text searches. Once the appropriate content is found in the transcription, the audio becomes immediately available. A computed alignment provides an automatic way to generate the alignment in closed-captioning, something which is currently done by hand. The final category of speech content is referred to as *script-free,* content that can only be searched using large vocabulary speech recognition tools.

4.2 SLIDE-AND-LECTURE PRESENTATION SEARCHING

The second application of CMIR describes mechanisms of retrieving video segments which correspond to a given slide selected from a sequence of slides or overhead transparencies. The user wants to know which video (audio) segment corresponds to a given slide. The traditional *slides-and-lecture* format is a common form of presentation (especially in the sciences) and there are large video libraries of such presentations compiled daily. The usual format consists of a presenter lecturing to an audience while, at the same time, presenting important points with the use of overhead projection of slides or other notes. Slides are often available electronically and have a distinct ordering, though there is no guarantee that they will be presented in exactly that order. Presenters leave slides out or repeat them to return to a point.

If a slide-and-lecture presentation is video-taped, the video provides a time-based representation of the presentation. However, the presentation may be hours long, so finding specific information is difficult. Conventional approaches to video sequence browsing, such as video segmentation, do not help in this application. There are no cuts in the video to cue segmentation, and all images are of a speaker talking and all or part of the associated slide. Browsing for the desired information is very time consuming.

Using conference materials from the DAGS'93 institute [23], for each presentation slide, the audio (video) of the speaker and the associated parts of the conference paper submitted can be presented. Since the slides are compact representations of the material presented, they can be quickly and easily browsed. An average presentation has about 20 slides for 20 minutes of audio. This is an example of cross-modal information retrieval using a browsing interface. The browsing is in the slide set, while the results are presented as text or audio. In earlier interactive multimedia conference proceedings produced by the DEVLAB, the synchronization between the slides and the audio (video) was supplied manually by the editors and producers of the publication. An automatic synchronization mechanism is currently under development at the DEVLAB.

4.3 FUNCTIONAL MAGNETIC RESONANCE IMAGING OF THE BRAIN

A third application of CMIR is magnetic resonance imaging (MRI) in which the functioning of the brain is researched. Researchers at the DEVLAB and the Dartmouth Medical School are applying cross-modal information retrieval techniques to Functional Magnetic Resonance Imaging data sets in order to better understand the human brain [24]. In any given experiment, two media streams are created, one being the stimulus streams presented to the subject being scanned and the other being the subject's responses, as recorded by the fMRI scanner. The goal is to determine which parts of the brain respond to what types of stimuli. More specifically, we wish to precisely classify *spatial and temporal* characteristics of brain activation in the presence of multimedia stimuli (video and audio), thereby providing a valuable tool for the diagnosis and treatment of disease as well as a better understanding of how the brain functions.

fMRI captures image sequences that detail changes in cerebral blood flow, a valuable clue in the search for detailed understanding of the operation of the brain [13]. fMRI is a noninvasive technique; subjects can be imaged repeatedly and large studies can be performed on both diseased and normal subjects. In the analysis of fMRI data, the two streams undergoing correlation are the multimedia subject stimulus $\mu_1(t)$ and the fMRI image sequence $\mu_2(t)$. While both streams in this application are temporal in nature, they are not necessarily aligned. The temporal correction function is a multi-parameter function that performs time warping of the stimulus function to account for hemodynamic response characteristics of the brain.

There are two goals of this research: temporal and spatial localization. The multimedia stimuli is designed to emphasize particular tasks. For many stimuli, a stimulus waveform has been designed into the sequencing (motor skill finger tap sequences are one example; the subject is instructed to tap at specific times). In other cases (memory response, for example), this function is dependent upon subject participation as well as media presentation. The result is a location in the brain that has activity correlated to the stimuli and the hemodynamic response characteristics of that region. As a cross-modal information retrieval application, the stimuli is browsed for specific activation patterns (left motor skills, for example) and locations in the brain and their corresponding data are retrieved. It is hoped that this research can increase knowledge of specific activity within the brain.

4.4 TRANSLATION SYNCHRONIZATION

The last application of CMIR presented in this chapter deals with the synchronization or alignment of different translations of the same text. *Translation alignment* is the alignment of elements of two documents that are assumed to be related to each other through translation. The problem of aligning documents in differing languages is a classic problem and considerable work has been done on it for many years. Several references are provided in Section 1. Many of these techniques could be described using the multiple media stream correlation formulation. However, what is of most interest to this research is a new application area dealing with ancient text translations and the application of the approaches described below.

The new application area is simultaneous translations of an identical document. In such a case, two documents, β_1 and β_2, are translations of an original document α. β_1 and β_2 are in the same language (α probably is not). An alignment between β_1 and β_2 is desired to see how the two translators represent the same original concept. This task is actually rather difficult to do by hand since the translations are often quite fanciful. An example might be two translations of Homer's *Odyssey*. Since this text has been around for thousands of years, there are many translations. Scholars are very interested in comparing these translations.

As a cross-modal information retrieval application, a researcher finds a specific section of one translation. The result is the related section of the second translation, allowing direct comparison. The solution for this problem is based on representing one translation as a media representation graph, as described in Section 7. Word matches at locations in the document are scored in order to compute media element likelihoods. The algorithm of Section 7 is then applied directly. The word match scoring under development is based on a matching criterion derived from matching sets defined in WordNet, a standard lexical database of the English language [25].

5. COMPUTED SYNCHRONIZATION APPROACHES

This section deals with the central issue of synchronization between different media types. In the simplest case, multiple media streams come already synchronized, such as a video recording where the audio is recorded at the same time, yielding a natural synchronization. Another approach is to create the synchronization manually, such as in closed-captioning. However, this does not always warrant the effort. Thus the need for *computed synchronization*. As discussed earlier, the two most common forms of synchronization are temporal and spatial. The major prerequisite of CMIR is *inter-media synchronization*, i.e., the temporal and spatial synchronization between two media streams. This section describes common existing approaches to inter-media synchronization and presents a model for computational approaches that can be applied to a large class of applications. Many means of solving this model exist, including pure statistical approaches such as linear regression (a technique common in the solution of fMRI data synchronization).

5.1 INHERENT SYNCHRONIZATION

Some applications are inherently synchronized, such as is the case with the audio track of a video stream. In such cases, the audio and video are mapped to an identical time-line and synchronization is supplied by the media format. This is typically a result of simultaneous, synchronized acquisition. This form of synchronization is necessary for synchronized delivery and can also be very important in a CMIR system because it allows the retrieval of both media based on a computed synchronization to only one of these media. If text is synchronized to audio, the synchronized video is retrieved "for free."

Closed-caption video can be considered inherently synchronized (the text with the video) from an application point of view, since the synchronization exists in acquisition mechanism, off-air monitoring. However, this synchronization did not always exist and had to be created at some point in time.

5.2 MANUAL SYNCHRONIZATION

Synchronization between media streams is a surprisingly useful tool in many applications. Hence, this synchronization has been an important element of some applications for many years. Since automatic solutions did not exist, manual solutions are supplied. The most common example is closed-captioning of video broadcasts. The captioning is typically based on known script material. However, the alignment between the broadcast and the script is not known. The captioning is, therefore, aligned by hand by an operator. In addition, live broadcasting often requires the generation of a transcript "on-the-fly" by a transcription operator. The quality of live transcription alignments is typically considerably less than that of script alignments due to the increased complexity of the task and the latency of the transcription operator.

5.3 COMPUTED SYNCHRONIZATION

In many cases a synchronization between two media streams does not exist and manual creation of the synchronization would be too costly. What is needed is means of computing a synchronization automatically. *Multiple Media Stream Correlation* is the derivation of temporal and spatial relationships between two or more media streams. Multiple media stream correlation is a general model and has many applications in addition to cross-modal retrieval. Temporal synchronization derives the modification of the timing of one or more of the media streams in order to maximize the correlation. An example is the alignment of two similar audio streams using speed variation techniques to align the voices. In many applications one media will be considered to be on a reference time frame and others temporally adjusted to achieve synchronization to that media. This is particularly the case when one medium is in real time (measured in seconds) and the others are only causal in nature (as in text). Some applications get temporal synchronization for free and are only concerned with spatial synchronization.

Spatial synchronization, the second goal, is the spatial translation of contents at a point in time in order to maximize correlation. This may consist of spatial warping or selection. *Warping* is the adjusting of parameters in order to rearrange a media element temporally or spatially. As an example, some *motion analysis* techniques of image processing attempt to compute the optimal spatial warping of images to cancel the motion from frame to frame. *Selection* wherein all of the unselected components of the media are omitted can be considered to be warping. *Lip Motion Localization* correlates speech audio with motion detection in video: it selects the particular moving components of the image sequence that represent the moving lips. In text-to-speech synchronization, spatial synchronization is concerned with selecting the correct translation option from among the various possibilities presented by possible pauses, noise, and other sounds, and alternative pronunciations. Possible alternative audible representations of a transcription represent a search space. The location of the correct elements of that space at any point in time constitutes spatial synchronization in text-to-speech synchronization. It is common in applications that this information is discarded, but it must necessarily be computed during the synchronization process since temporal synchronization is dependent upon selecting the optimal model for the audible representation.

5.4 MULTIPLE STREAM MEDIA CORRELATION

The multiple media stream correlation model is now derived. The representation of media in this model is continuous causal media (a discrete formulation will be derived later). This is simply a function of a causal ordering variable t: $\mu_i(t)$. The general formulation will assume continuous media and N media streams.

Synchronization is achieved through modification of the temporal ordering variable. In the model, this is denoted by the function $\tau_i(t)$, the temporal synchronization function; hence, stream i under temporal alignment is $\mu_i(\tau_i(t))$. For most applications, the goal of a computational synchronization algorithm is the computation of $\tau_i(t)$. A temporal synchronization function is selected from a set of possible functions T_i for stream i. This set contains all possible valid warpings of the input stream for synchronization. It is commonly implemented using a discrete parameter space, with parameters indicating temporal offsets at discrete times. Continuous functions can use this information to interpolate intermediate offsets. It is unlikely that all streams being synchronized will need to be temporally offset. As an example, for text-to-speech synchronization, only the text stream will require computation of a temporal synchronization function. The audio stream exists in a real time base and is easier to manage without offset. For streams which are not offset, the temporal synchronization function is assumed to be the identity function.

Domain translation is an important element of the model. It is difficult to construct appropriate correlation functions with disparate media parameters. As an example, consider the complexity of directly comparing text, a discrete set of language representations, to audio, a one-dimensional function representing sound pressure. Instead, standard sound units called *phonemes* are compared to a table of estimates of the probability that a given sound is a phoneme. Even when two or more media are the same, they may be too complicated to correlate directly. For this reason, the CMIR model specifies that all media be translated to a common domain for comparison by a correlation function ρ. It might be assumed that domain translation would be simply a function of a single media element. While such a model could be possible, it sacrifices flexibility. Recall that media elements are hierarchical and causal. Higher levels of the hierarchy may exist upon which domain translation may depend. Also, the causal nature of media elements implies that *context* may be critical to translation. Indeed, in applications undertaken in the DEVLAB, this has been found to be the case. Hence, the domain translation function is a function of the temporally offset media stream $\mu_i \circ \tau_i$ and the ordering variable t: $\psi_i(\mu_i \circ \tau_i, t)$.

Example domain translation functions for text-to-speech synchronization are: ψ_1, translation from words to a representation of units of sound and ψ_2, translation from sounds to an estimation of the probability that a sound matches a given sound element. The possible translations for ψ_1 are indicated by the possible pronunciations for a given word and the possible duration of each sound element. ψ_2 is computed using speech feature recognition tools.

The final element of the multiple media stream correlation model is the *correlation function, ρ*. In many uses of multiple media stream correlation, ρ is a derivative of simple statistical correlation. Applications of multiple media stream correlation implemented at the DEVLAB have favored complicated domain translation and simple correlation. In the text-to-speech synchronization application, ρ computes the logarithm of the probability that the selected sound representation in ψ_1 is audible as the current sound. This is simply a multiplication of the probability of that sound unit at that time by the probability that that sound unit is emitted at that time. The logarithm operation is necessary to ensure the result will combine properly using a summation and to avoid numeric underflow.

Combining these elements, the multiple media stream correlation model is presented as Equation 1.

$$\eta = \arg \max_{\tau_i \in T_i, \psi_i \in \Psi_i, i=1...N} \int_{-\infty}^{\infty} \rho\left(\psi_i\left(\mu_i \circ \tau_i, t\right), ..., \psi_N\left(\mu_N \circ \tau_N, t\right)\right) dt \qquad (1)$$

Several models for media stream correlation can be derived from this model. Some of these are described in Owen and Makedon [26]. In particular, Equation 2 is the discrete formulation more commonly used in sampled media applications.

$$\eta = \arg \max_{\tau_i \in T_i, \psi_i \in \Psi_i, i=1...N} \sum_{-\infty}^{\infty} \rho\left(\psi_i\left(\mu_i \circ \tau_i, t\right), ..., \psi_N\left(\mu_N \circ \tau_N, t\right)\right) \qquad (2)$$

It is important to note that the result of this computation is not the maximization of the summation, but, rather, the *functions that achieve this maximization*. This model specifies a structure for defining and selecting functions that maximize the correlation. The resulting functions indicate necessary temporal and spatial correlation. The temporal translation function result τ_i for a media stream i indicates the appropriate temporal synchronization for maximum correlation. The set of domain translation function results indicate the appropriate spatial synchronization for maximum correlation.

6. AN EXAMPLE SYNCHRONIZATION APPLICATION

A general solution algorithm has been developed that supports a large class of applications of multiple media stream correlation, including many cross-modal information retrieval applications. However, rather than presenting that algorithm independently, this section presents a specific example (instance) of that algorithm for *text-to-speech synchronization*. Text-to-speech synchronization is the alignment of two media streams. μ_1 represents the text and μ_2 represents the audio. In this application the text will be aligned to the speech. The alignment is easily inverted to provide speech to transcription retrieval or captioning location information, if necessary (given a location in the audio, provide the written transcription at that point). This application is meant to be more concrete and easier to understand than the general solution for CMIR. Insight into the general solution is provided in the next section.

6.1 BUILDING THE TRANSCRIPTION GRAPH

Ψ_1, the space of all possible representations of text as sound units, is implemented by converting the text to a *media representation graph*. In the text-to-speech retrieval application, the media representation graph is referred to as the *transcription graph,* a directed graph representing the possible state transitions for a speech recognition engine. Each node in this graph corresponds to a unit of sound in speech.

The unit of sound used in this application is the *biphone*. The biphone was chosen because it models speech context. The modeling of speech as sub-word units is a complex field and there are many choices. The most common sub-word speech unit is the *phoneme*. There are several standard phoneme sets including the International Phonemic Alphabet (IPA), Worldbet, and OGIbet. These differ in coverage of sounds, but frequently overlap. This chapter uses the Worldbet language as a standard. As an example, the word "the" can be considered to be the Wordbet phonemes "D ^", where "D" is the "th" sound, as in **thy** and "^" is the "ah" sound as in **above**. Many words have alternate pronunciations. "The" can also be pronounced using the phonemes "D i:", where "i:" is the "ee" sound as in **beet**. It is common in literature to use the term *phone* either interchangeably with phoneme or as a representation of an actual sound rather than a class of sounds.

A problem with phonemic representations is the co-articulatory effect of speech. While phonemes attempt to model physical states of the vocal system, in real speech these states are only reached momentarily. Hence, speech is not well modeled as a series of only phonemes. There are many approaches to accommodating these co-articulatory effects. Glass et al. [27] treat speech as a dynamic process using time warping. However, the most common approach is to consider phonemes in context. This context is typically either a biphone or triphone context. A *triphone* context considers each phoneme in the context of the phonemes proceeding and following it. This is the approach used in the CMU Sphinx-II speech recognition system [28]. *Biphones* are used in the Oregon Graduate Institute speech tools [29]. A biphone models transitions into and out of a context-free phoneme state. Basically, the period of a phoneme is modeled as a beginning (left context), middle (context independent), and end (right context). The beginning is where the phoneme is transitioning from the previous phoneme sound to the new phoneme sound and where the new phoneme is dominant. The middle models the part of the phoneme that is stable. The end models the transition out of the phoneme toward the next phoneme. Biphones have been selected as the contextual sound unit in this work due to the availability of effective tools, the tolerance for a larger sound unit search space inherent in a transcript-driven system, and previous experience with this technology. Future work is planned that will attempt to classify the ramifications of phone, biphone, or triphones as the sound unit in this application.

There are about 50 phonemes. Modeling all biphones would require 50^2 or 2500 possible sound states. This is an unreasonable number. Fortunately, many transition states are not necessary because they are either too short or indistinguishable. Also, many states sound virtually identical. Hence, a subset can be used. In this research, a subset of 536 biphones is used.

The transcription graph is built in a two-step process. The initial step is the conversion of the word sequences to a *phoneme transcription graph*. A phoneme transcription graph models all of the transitions of all possible phonemic translations of the text. The word to phoneme translation is performed using a phonemic dictionary available from CMU that has been translated from OGIbet to Worldbet and to which some additional vocabulary has been added. For words that do not appear in the dictionary, an estimate of the translation is done using the public domain package `english2phoneme`. In implementation, this process builds a transcription graph at a rate of approximately 50 words per second. Experimental text has averaged 24.9 biphones per word, for about 1245 biphones per second. These experiments were done on a 175MHz DEC Alpha processor. It is felt that simple performance improvements could increase this speed considerably, but it should be noted that the time to build the transcription graph on this processor is considerably less than the speech analysis time, which is a bit less than real time and processes approximately 2 words per second. Most of this time is devoted to available speech analysis tools not modified for this application. At the beginning of the graph is an artificial phoneme named ".start." At the end is an artificial phoneme named ".end." Between each word the two artificial phonemes ".pau" and ".garbage" are included. Figure 3 is an example of the phoneme transcription graph. The ".pau" and ".garbage" phonemes model pause and random noise between words. Note that this modeling between words is optional. Speakers may or may not pause between words. Higher level semantics, such as sentence pauses, etc. are not modeled in this application since they are detected automatically by the optional pause/noise detection included in the model.

Once the phoneme transcription graph is built, the phonemes are expanded to biphones. As an example, in Figure 3 the phoneme "^" will expand to the three biphones "9r<^, <^>, ^>n." (Note: in the biphone model used, the phonemes 9r, 3r, and &r are considered to be identical in left context. Likewise, m, n, N, N=, and n= are considered identical in right context. This happens in order to reduce the number of biphones and because they have similar co-articulatory properties.)

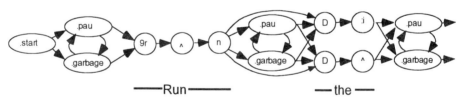

Figure 3. Phoneme transcription graph for the beginning of the sentence "Run the race."

Construction of the transcription graph is linear in time and space. Although the process described could be performed off-line using a buffering strategy, the initial implementations have been entirely in memory and can accommodate even very large texts. The text tests performed averaged 8.3 phonemes per word and 24.9 biphones per word.

Each node in the transcription graph represents a unit of sound. The speech feature recognition engine used in this application computes biphone probabilities for 10 millisecond audio *frames*. Because the duration of any given biphone cannot be known in advance, but is typically greater than 10 milliseconds, each node in the graph is also considered to have an implicit link to itself in order to allow the state to repeat as often as necessary. As an example, saying the word "run" might require 400 milliseconds, or 40 frames. In that time there are 9 biphones. Most will repeat two or more times.

The transcription graph is the fundamental speech modeling tool for text-to-speech synchronization. It is designed to model the possible sounds for the speech. If a path through the graph can be found that matches the sounds of the speech best, the path will represent the synchronization between the text and the speech. Additional features can also be modeled using this graph, as described in a later section.

6.2 SPEECH FEATURE RECOGNITION

Ψ_2 is the conversion of speech audio to sound unit probabilities. In this application, the sound unit is biphones, so speech recognition tools are used that convert audio into a sequence of *biphone probabilities*. This process is beyond the scope of this chapter, but is described in detail in Rabiner [9]. In summary, audio is blocked into finite frames (of 10 millisecond duration) and the probability of any given biphone at that point in time is estimated. In the current implementation 536 biphone probabilities are computed for each audio frame. These vectors are treated as a terrace where each $\psi_2 \in \Psi_2$ is a left-to right path through the terrace. The optimal ψ_2 is a path that is valid in the transcription graph and maximizes the total path probability. Clearly, ψ_1 and ψ_2 must correspond. The OGI CSLU-C toolkit [29] is used in combination with the ImageTcl multimedia algorithm development system [30] for the audio manipulation and speech feature recognition functions of the implementation.

6.3 SYNCHRONIZATION COMPUTATION

The temporal synchronization function τ_1 is derived from the computed optimal path ψ_1 through the transcription graph. In effect, these parameters are computed simultaneously. What is required is the computation of a path $<v_1, v_2, ..., v_m>$ for m frames of audio such that $v_t \in V$, the set of transcription graph vertices. The *best* path is the path such that $P(.end|v_1, v_2, ..., v_m)$ is maximized. This result is equivalent to a maximization of the discrete formulation of multiple media stream correlation, Equation 2. The probability of a given vertex v_t at time t is computed by the speech feature recognition system. Computation of this path can be performed using the Viterbi algorithm that is described in many places [9]. Viterbi's algorithm takes advantage of the fact that for any given time t it is necessary to discover only the highest probability path to a vertex v_t. Any optimal probability path through the transcription graph that includes v_t cannot have a path to v_t of lower probability or the higher probability path could be substituted for the lower probability path and achieve a higher probability solution. This problem can be approached as a shortest path problem by considering a terrace of nodes such that columns of the terrace have n nodes corresponding to each node in the transcription graph. Each of these columns in the graph represents a time frame. The probability of a given vertex at any time is the product of the probability of the sound represented by that vertex biphone and any probability associated with that element of the transcription graph at any point in time. In a simple application, the probability of a node in the transcription graph at any time frame is considered to be a uniform identical distribution if an edge exists in the transcription graph (explicit or implicit) from the previous note to the next node.

Figure 4 is an example of this illustration. At any time other than time zero, the weight of the edge of the third note from the top to the second is the product of the probability of the sound of the phoneme "^" at that time, as measured by the speech feature recognition system and the probability that a transition from "9r" to "^" is possible in the transcription graph. In this example, that probability is 1.0.

Viterbi's algorithm proceeds from left to right in the illustration. Each active node is extended to the next time frame and the best path for each new node that can be reached is computed. In order to prevent numeric underflow, all probabilities are computed as logarithms.

6.4 MODIFICATIONS TO THE VITERBI APPROACH

There are several problems with a pure Viterbi approach. The computational requirement is $O(nm)$, where n is the number of edges in the transcription graph (i.e., on the order of the number of words in this application) and m is the number of time frames. Since the word length and time are closely related, this performance is effectively quadratic. In addition, each possible path must be maintained in memory, leading to a quadratic memory requirement. A common solution to this problem is to apply the *beam search heuristic* [31]. At each frame, step the number of active nodes in the Viterbi search is pruned by elimination of paths with probabilities less than some heuristically determined threshold. A typical approach in speech recognition systems is to base this threshold on a linear multiple of the highest ranking path probability (thresholding probabilities at 90% of the maximum path probability, for example).

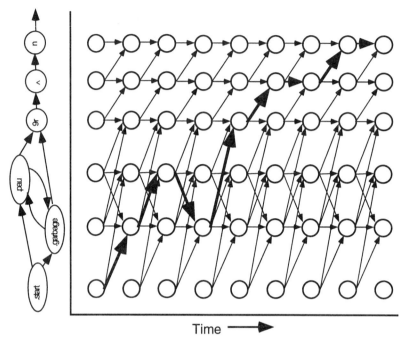

Figure 4. Viterbi search illustration. The bold edges represent a path through the transcription graph such that the subsequent sequence of phonemes are detected with maximum probability: .garbage .pau .garbage 9r ^ ^ n n. Phonemes have been used in this figure rather than biphones for illustrative purposes only.

The conventional Viterbi algorithm with threshold-based path pruning is not ideally suited to this application. Text-to-speech synchronization differs from speech recognition in several ways. Conventional speech recognition is based on a vocabulary model that is very wide and shallow. The width is the number of possible word choices at any moment in time. The depth is the limit of the model context, typically a few words. The text-to-speech transcription graph is very narrow and long. The context is the entire transcription, a much longer language model than most applications and, at any point in the graph, there are a very limited number of branching possibilities.

The conventional linear threshold beam parameter has been found experimentally ineffective in this application. An active candidate path will always end in a node in the transcription graph and only one such path will end in that node. Since nodes correspond to words, the beam search parameter corresponds to search range. Specifically, a beam search parameter bounds the search range from below (larger search ranges are possible if a distant path has higher probability than a closer path). Hence, a larger, fixed pruning parameter is more effective in this application. This has been supported by experimental evidence that suggests that synchronization can be lost in extended periods of noise or other non-speech content if a linear multiple or undersized fixed beam parameter is utilized. Preliminary results seem to indicate a fixed beam parameter of 200 is effective for most material. This parameter corresponds to a search range of approximately 10 words. Given that common errors are single or double word errors, and that word length is probabilistic with words of double the average length having lesser probabilities, a range of plus or minus five seems effective. The beam threshold could be determined by current word length, but it is felt that is not necessary since longer words are actually more likely to synchronize because they are equivalent, in the CMIR model, to concatenated shorter words.

In order to save space, a *synchronization tree* is built that represents only the active nodes in the search process. When nodes are pruned, the tree is recursively pruned of leaves in all but the current frame level. This ensures a computation time of O(bm), where b is the beam width and m is the number of frames. A complex tree structure is not normally required in Viterbi implementations since the amount of context is limited to a relatively small, finite bound. This application utilizes very large context, so a special data structure is necessary to preserve memory.

The beam search heuristic bounds the memory usage to O(bm) due to the limitation of tree width at each level. Since b is a fixed parameter, the algorithm is effectively linear in space usage. Experimental implementation has also demonstrated actual memory usage equal to O(m+b) due to the contraction of the tree to a single path; this is because candidate paths that synchronized differently in the distant past are being pruned. The algorithm tends to select a winning synchronization in the past with a wide range of alternatives for only relatively recent time frames. The time requirements increase when speech is not present and decrease when it is present because, in the first case, the system attempts to match many possible speech paths to noise.

6.5 EDITS

Edits are inconsistencies between the transcription text and the actual audio. There are three classes of edits: deletions, insertions, and substitutions. A major issue in text-to-speech synchronization is the effective handling of edits. Inconsistent transcriptions are quite common. Content in a script is often cut to save time, speakers go "off-script" to fill time, and obvious errors are sometimes made in the reading or performance of a script. Insertion and substitution mechanisms are currently under development. However, deletions are now handled by the system. Deletions seem to be very common in dramatic material.

A deletion is transcription text for which there is no audio. Deletions are modeled in the system using bypass edges. A bypass edge is an edge that allows the model to skip a portion of the transcription graph. An example might be a word bypass, where an edge is placed from the pause/garbage pair before the word to the same pair after the word (actually, 4 edges are utilized). Indeed, this is the lowest level of the bypass mechanism, allowing the deletion of single words in the transcription. Sub-word deletions are typically not required since a truncated or partially audible word will either skip the word or synchronize, depending on the relative percentage and strength of the content.

A general solution to deletions would be bypass edges that accommodate every possible transition, basically a bypass from every word to every following word. This creates a transcription graph of size $O(n^2)$, significantly decreasing performance and increasing memory consumption, not an attractive option. An obvious question is: if all words have bypass edges around them, will that accommodate deletions? The problem is that bypass edges are, by design, from node to node. A 15 word deletion would require the traversal of 15 bypass edges. Since a node must exist between each edge (a .garbage or .pau biphone), 150 milliseconds of audio must match to these nodes. After traversal of the nodes, synchronization will be off by 150 milliseconds and must recover. This is a rather large perceptual error for retrieval purposes, often clipping word beginnings, and limits the synchronization range necessary to return to synchronization.

A compromise between these extreme solutions is a hierarchical structure of bypass edges. Bypass edges are placed around words in groups of 2, 4, 8, ... This structure limits the number of bypass edges that must be traversed when bypassing d words to O(log d). The number of bypass edges is linear in the size of the graph.

An additional heuristic that has been found effective is the sentence bypass. This is a bypass around sentence content. Very little overhead is added for the advantage of almost ideal modeling of sentence deletions, a common way that material is "cut." The sentence bypass prevents the accumulations of word bypass overhead and models dramatic production well.

Several alternatives for insertions and substitutions are being explored. It should be noted that preliminary experiments show that single word insertions or substitutions are not an issue. The vast weight of the surrounding match overcomes substitution match probabilities very easily. Insertions tend to kick the matching out of synchronization for a few words. However, provided the beam depth is larger than the range it affects, typically 2–4 words, the system returns to synchronization.

6.6 EXPERIMENTAL RESULTS

The text-to-speech alignment approach has been implemented and is currently being tested on a variety of materials. The test materials include dramatic presentations of Hamlet and Romeo and Juliet as well as a reading of two works by Sir Arthur Conan Doyle. Legal and political material from CSPAN and Court TV have been tested. It is also planned that material from National Public Radio will be utilized for testing. The criterion for choosing the test material is that it fall in the *speech-light* class, which means that it has an electronic transcription. Dramatic productions of older material, such as Shakespeare, are readily available. Transcriptions of proceedings of the House of Representatives, and of most major national political speeches, are available from Lexis-Nexis, and NPR publishes transcriptions of their news programming.

These are several approaches to testing the implementation. A subjective examination of the results for several hours of audio has been performed and the experience is that the system works very well, matching even noisy audio and audio in the presence of music. In these experiments, the audio, which is played as caption text, is presented to a user who serves as a judge of system performance. Typically failures in synchronization are limited to ranges of only several words. The maximum range for a failure in tested material is 10 words where some background noise advanced the synchronization. Note that synchronization did return in spite of the fact that the error exceeded the minimum beam parameter search range. This is due to the fact that the beam parameter imposes a lower bound on the search range, not a fixed search range.

A quantitative approach to testing the synchronization results is to compare them to results selected by a human operator. This requires hand marking the alignment in a corpus of test materials, a time-consuming activity. At the time of this writing the marking program had just been completed and a 5 minute segment from act 1, scene 2 of the motion picture Hamlet staring Mel Gibson, directed by Franco Zeffirelli, an adaptation of the William Shakespeare play, had been marked by hand. There are 518 words in this segment. This is a particularly difficult test since it begins with a twenty second interval of noise and effects. In addition, it has music over the audio in several places, and is mostly "British English," whereas the speech engine was trained on American English. In several places the dialog is reduced to a whisper. There are three speakers. In the synchronization results for this test the average error between the human operator and the program was 24 milliseconds. The worst case error was 2.27 seconds. The larger errors (in excess of 1 second) are due to matching the start of the words "A" and "The" at the beginning of a sentence following noise. A more useful measure is word distance errors. A word distance error is an error where a word is found to begin more than one word away from its actual location. In this test there were 14 one word distance errors and 2 two word distance errors. In all cases there were very rapidly spoken word groups of short words ("fair are you sir," "we do my Lord"). In all cases, the error was positive, detecting the word early.

A suggested evaluation method is the comparison of computed results to closed-caption data. The closed-caption data provides a complete transcription and is aligned manually with the content. However, observation has shown the alignment to be rather coarse-grained and not likely to be suitable for system evaluation. Indeed, it has been brought into question if closed-caption data is sufficiently aligned for accurate cross-modal information retrieval in applications requiring clear presentation of sentence or phrase results.

7. A GENERALIZED SOLUTION APPROACH

This section describes how the specialized text-to-speech retrieval method can be abstracted to provide a more general method designed to synchronize two media streams, one being considered as the "fixed" stream to which the other needs to be aligned or synchronized. It also gives a brief description of a prototype system called Xtrieve. A spatio-temporal synchronization method has been devised to handle the specific application of text-to-speech synchronization. As this work progressed and the unique characteristics of phoneme to audio matching in a large synchronization model were discovered, it became clear that a general approach to solve a large class of these problems is possible. In this class of applications two (or more) media streams are assumed, wherein one is considered to be in a base time-frame and the other must be matched. The algorithm is based on the construction of a *media representation graph* and the computation of *media element likelihoods*. A beam-search algorithm, which is based on a variation of Viterbi's algorithm, is applied with some specific optimizations and modifications. While the CMIR technique employs ideas similar to the traditional Viterbi solution for speech recognition, it is also very different in the way it applies the Viterbi algorithm to the different types of multiple media stream synchronizations.

As a specific example, for slide presentation synchronization, the media representation graph corresponds to the possible ordering of slides. This graph is more than just a simple set of sequential nodes. To improve matching performance, a slide must appear a minimum amount of time. In this application, 30 frames or 1 second is used. A slide appearing for less than that period is considered to have not appeared. Looping edges allow slides to be presented for any longer period necessary. Edges are supplied which allow slides to be presented in any order, provided the minimum presentation criteria is met. Media element likelihoods are determined by comparison of slides to the video images, wherein all or part of the slide image may appear. A simple co-registration comparison is used for the slides. Each slide is compared to each frame. The requirement of minimum slide duration allows slide transition periods and noise or matching loss to be ignored. The system is still under development and additional results will be presented in future publications.

7.1 THE XTRIEVE INFORMATION RETRIEVAL SYSTEM

A major goal of this research is the development of a cross-modal information retrieval prototype system, the Xtrieve information retrieval system. This system allows for cross-modal information retrieval of a database of material. Several cross-modal pairings based on text are under development, including text-to-audio, text-to-video, and text-to-text.

An important issue in a media retrieval system is *granularity*, the size of retrieved elements. Searching in Xtrieve is based on a simple keyword text retrieval system. In Xtrieve, documents can represent transcripts for long form programming such as plays or complete newscasts. Granularity allows the selection of results to be adjusted to sub-document sizes which are more effective for presentation in continuous media such as video or audio. Retrieval granularity is adjustable to word, sentence, and paragraph levels.

In addition to text searching, Xtrieve supports media browsing, specifically the viewing of image sets and video or audio segments. Inversion of computed synchronization functions allows location of text content from speech audio or location of the appropriate slide from the presentation video.

The goal of this system is to provide user effectiveness testing for retrieval. An ideal retrieval system will return exact content, beginning with initial utterance of the first word and ending with the final word, with minimal clipping of word beginnings or additional content. Results from this system will be reported in future publications.

8. CONCLUSION

This chapter describes cross-modal information retrieval, the process of querying or browsing one media for results in another. Beyond the trivial results of standard synchronized media such as video and audio, cross-modal information retrieval (CMIR) allows for complex and rich queries into media for which general search mechanisms may remain in the future for some time. CMIR improves database queries by moving the multimodal type of queries to a simpler search space which depends on achieving the synchronization of the queried space and the actual target space. The primary component of this technology is the known or computed synchronization between media components. A model for this synchronization is presented which takes into account both spatial and temporal synchronization. This work is based on causal media, a more general class of media than time-based media and a framework which allows discrete media such as text to be placed in the same context as time-based media such as digital audio. While the same theoretical framework underlines the different CMIR applications, not all applications have the same solutions to text-to-speech retrieval. Some media types are too different to produce samples of one type based on the other type. These problems are partly overcome by the Xtrieve system which is described in a future publication.

This work is ongoing at the DEVLAB (the Dartmouth Experimental Visualization lab) and results presented herein will be augmented as more media are analyzed and new application areas are explored. One area of the computed solution approach that is still under development is *enforced interpolation*. With the use of bypass edges in the case of text-to-speech retrieval, for example, the transcription graph allows searching all the way to the end of the text while at the beginning of the audio. We are currently finalizing a method for enforcing a distribution curve on the transcription graph nodes that will weigh the probabilities of nodes relative to their location in the text. The goal is two-fold: to decrease the probability of futile searching of the far future and to encourage interpolation over areas of very poor audio. Additional work in progress includes a mechanism for insertions and substitutions, development of a larger test corpus, and completion of the Xtrieve information retrieval system.

REFERENCES

1. Bloom, P. J., "High-quality digital audio in the entertainment industry: An overview of achievements and challenges," *IEEE ASSP Magazine*, 2(4):2-25, 1985.

2. Chen, T. and Rao, R., "Audio-visual interaction in multimedia," *IEEE Circuits and Devices*, 11(6): 21-26, 1995.

3. Lindblad, C. J., *A programming system for the dynamic manipulation of temporally sensitive data*, Technical Report MIT/LCS/TR-637, Massachusetts Institute of Technology, 1994.

4. Chen, T., Graf, H. P., and Wang, K., "Lip synchronization using speech-assisted video processing," *IEEE Signal Processing Letters*, 2(4):57-59, 1995.

5. Rao, R. R. and Chen, T., "Cross-modal prediction in audio-visual communication," in *Proc. of ICASSP'96*, Volume IV, pp. 2056-2060, Atlanta, GA, 1996.

6. Brown, M. G., Foote, J. T., Jones, G. J. F., Jones, K. S., and Young, S. J., "Video mail retrieval by voice: An overview of the Cambridge/Olivetti retrieval system," *Proc. of the ACM Multimedia'94 Workshop on Multimedia Database Management Systems*, pp. 47-55, San Francisco, CA, 1994.

7. Schäuble, P. and Wechsler, M., "First experiences with a system for content based retrieval of information from speech recordings," *IJCAI Workshop: Intelligent Multimedia Information Retrieval*, 1995.

8. Hauptmann, A. G., Witbrock, M. J., Rudnicky, A. I., and Reed, S., "Speech for multimedia information retrieval," *Proc. of User Interface Software and Technology*, UIST-95, Pittsburgh, PA, 1995.

9. Rabiner, L. and Juang, B-H., *Fundamentals of Speech Recognition*, Signal Processing Series, PTR Prentice Hall, Englewood Cliffs, NJ, 1993.

10. Vostermans, A. and Martens, J. P., "Automatic labeling of corpora for speech synthesis development," *Proc. of IEEE ProRisc '94*, pp. 261-266, 1994.

11. Zue, V. W. and Seneff, S., "Transcription and alignment of the TIMIT database," *The Second Symposium on Advanced Man-Machine Interface through Spoken Language*, Oahu, Hawaii, 1988.

12. Hauptmann, A. G. and Witbrock, M. J., "Informedia news-on-demand: Using speech recognition to create a digital video library," *Proc. of Intelligent Integration and Use of Text, Image, Video, and Audio Corpora*, AIII 1997 Spring Symposium, pp. 120-126, Stanford University, CA, 1997.

13. Bandettini, P. A. and Wong, E. C., "Echo Planar Imaging," chapter in *Echo-Planer Magnetic Resonance Imaging of Human Brain Activation*, Springer-Verlag, 1997.

14. *Institute of Neurology Short Course 1996: Statistical Parametric Mapping and Functional Neuroimaging*, Functional Imaging Laboratory, London, U.K.

15. Bonhomme, P. and Romary, L., "The Lingua parallel concordancing project: Managing multilingual texts for educational purposes," *Proc. of Language Engineering 95*, Montpellier, France, 1995.

16. Church, K. W., "Char_align: A program for aligning parallel texts at the character level," *Proc. of the 31st Annual Meeting of the Association of Computational Linguistics, ACL'93*, Columbus, OH, 1993.

17. Dagan, I., Pereira, F., and Lee, L., "Similarity-based estimation of word cooccurrence probabilities," *Proc. of the 32nd Annual Meeting of the Association of Computational Linguistics, ACL'94*, Las Cruces, NM, 1994.

18. Little, T. D. C. and Ghafoor, A., "Spatio-temporal composition of distributed multimedia objects for value-added networks," *Computer*, 42-50, October 1991.

19. Gibbs, S., Breiteneder, C., and Tsichritzis, D., "Data modeling of time-based media," in *Visual Objects*, Université de Genève, 1993.

20. Hamakawa, R. and Rekimoto, J., "Object composition and playback models for handling multimedia data," *Proceedings of ACM Multimedia'93*, 273-281, Anaheim, CA, August 1993.

21. Bobick, A. F., "Representational frames in video annotation," in *27th Annual Asilomar Conference on Signals, Systems, and Computers*, 1993.

22. La Gall, D., "MPEG: A video compression standard for multimedia applications," *Communications of the ACM*, 34(4):46-58, 1991.

23. Gloor, P. A., Makedon, F., and Matthews, J., *Parellel Computation: Practical Implementation of Algorithms and Machines*. TELOS/Springer-Verlag, Santa Clara, CA, 1993. (CD-ROM).

24. Owen, C. B., "Application of multiple media stream correlation to functional imaging of the brain," *Proc. of the International Conference on Vision, Recognition, Action: Neural Models of Mind and Machine*, Boston, MA, 1997.

25. Miller, G. A., Beckwith, R., Fellbaum, C., Gross, D., and Miller, K., "Introduction to WordNet: An on-line lexical database," CSL Report 43, Princeton University Congnitive Science Laboratory, 1990, revised August 1993.

26. Owen, C. B. and Makedon, F., "Multiple media stream data analysis: Theory and applications," in *Data Highways and Information Flooding, a Challenge for Classification and Data Analysis*, Springer-Verlag, 1997.

27. Glass, J., Goddeau, D., Hetherington, L., McCandless, M., Pao, C., Phillips, M., Polifroni, J., Seneff, S., and Zue, V., "The MIT ATIS system: December 1994 progress report," *Proc. of ARPA Spoken Language Technology Workshop*, Austin, TX, 1995.

28. Ravishankar, M. K., "Efficient algorithms for speech recognition," Technical report, Carnegie Mellon University, 1996.

29. Schalkwyk, J. and Fanty, M., *The CSLU-C Toolkit for Automatic Speech Recognition*, Oregon Graduate Institute Center for Spoken Language Understanding, 1996.

30. Owen, C. B., "The ImageTcl multimedia algorithm development system," *Proc. of the 5th Annual Tcl/Tk Workshop'97*, Boston, MA, 1997.

31. Lowerre, B., "The Harpy Speech Understanding System," Ph.D. Thesis, Carnegie Mellon University, 1976.

20

DETECTION AND RECOGNITION OF TELEVISION COMMERCIALS

Rainer Lienhart, Christoph Kuhmunch, and Wolfgang Effelsberg
University of Mannheim, Praktishe Informatik IV
68131 Mannheim, Germany
{lienhart,kuhmuenc,effelsberg}@pi4.informatik.uni-mannheim.de

1. INTRODUCTION..426
2. TECHNICAL FEATURES OF TV COMMERCIALS.............................426
  2.1 STRUCTURE OF A COMMERCIAL BLOCK......................................426
  2.2 LIST OF TECHNICAL FEATURES 427
3. FEATURE-BASED DETECTION OF COMMERCIALS 428
  3.1 MONOCHROME FRAMES 429
  3.2 SCENE BREAKS...430
  3.3 ACTION..434
  3.4 A FEATURE-BASED COMMERCIAL DETECTION SYSTEM...............436
4. RECOGNITION OF KNOWN COMMERCIALS..................................436
  4.1 FINGERPRINT 438
  4.2 COMPARISON 439
  4.3 RECOGNITION-BASED COMMERCIAL DETECTION 439
5. COMBINING TWO APPROACHES INTO A SELF-LEARNING COMMERCIAL
   DETECTION SYSTEM..441
6. CONCLUSIONS 442
   REFERENCES 443

Abstract. TV commercials are interesting in many respects: advertisers and psychologists explore their influence on human purchasing habits, while parents might want to shield their children from their influence. This chapter describes two methods for detecting and extracting commercials in digital videos. The first method is based on statistics of measurable features and enables the detection of commercial blocks within TV broadcasts. The second method performs detection and recognition of known commercials with high accuracy. Finally, we show how both approaches can be combined into a self-learning system. Our experimental results underline the practicality of the methods.

This chapter is based on "On the Detection and Recognition of Television Commercials" by R. Lienhart et al., which appeared in *The Proceedings of IEEE International Conference on Multimedia Computing and Systems*, June 1997, Ottawa, Canada. © 1997 IEEE.

1. INTRODUCTION

Commercials play an important role in our lives — whether we like it or not. Popular institutions such as TV are mainly sponsored by advertisers or supported by advertising. For companies, commercials are marketing instruments essential to highlighting their products and increasing their sales. These companies generally charge other companies to verify that their TV commercials are actually broadcasted as contracted. Presently, employees/humans must watch TV to carry out such verification. It would be desirable to transfer this task to a computer system. Such a computer system would watch TV and record precisely the spot time and date of broadcasting and the channel identifier. Perhaps companies would also like to observe automatically what their competitors are doing. Marketing companies may be interested in relating the measurable features of the different TV spots to their success in the market. These are all objectives of potential interest to producers and advertising agencies. On the consumer side, parents might want to shield their children from the commercials' influence by interrupting TV during commercial breaks.

A commercial detection system would enable applications such as commercial broadcast logging and commercial-free TV. Some of the possible applications require only the detection of commercials as such whereas others also require recognition of a particular spot. Two different approaches to commercial detection are described: one feature-based and the other recognition-based. The first approach detects only commercial blocks as such, while the latter also allows recognition of known commercials and can even distinguish slightly different versions of the same spot [11].

Section 2 presents the most important technical features of TV commercials and TV commercial blocks, using German television as an example. For all these features, we derive detection indicators in Section 3 and combine them into a complete feature-based commercial detection system. Section 4 presents our second, recognition-based approach. It is capable of commercial detection as well as of commercial recognition. In Section 5 we combine both approaches into a reliable self-learning commercial detection system. Finally, Section 6 concludes the chapter with an outlook on future work.

2. TECHNICAL FEATURES OF TV COMMERCIALS

In this section we lay down the features of commercials. Although the focus is on German television, most of the features are also valid for commercials in general or else an equivalent can be found in other countries. These features ordinarily distinguish commercials from other film genres such as feature films, newscasts, and sportscasts.

2.1 Structure of a Commercial Block

Generally, commercials are grouped into blocks, which are simply a sequence of several consecutive commercials. A typical (German) commercial block contains the following elements (Figure 1):

- a commercial block introduction,
- a sequence of commercials (spots),
- a broadcasting station's advertisements and previews, and
- optionally a film introduction or short repetition of the cast.

A commercial block is always preceded by a transitional sequence leading from the broadcast into the commercial block itself. This limiting sequence of 3 to 5 seconds' length makes the difference in content clear to the viewer and is called *"commercial block introduction"* in German broadcasting. Broadcast stations are required by law to visually distinguish the broadcast

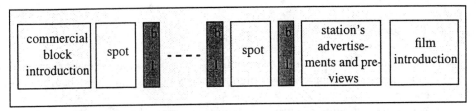

Figure 1.   Structure of a German commercial block.

clearly from the interrupting commercial block (we will address some other legal points later). The introductions change frequently, e.g., in correspondence to the four seasons or special events such as the Olympic Games. On the other hand, the transitional sequence usually never changes during the transmission of a telecast. Once recognized, it can be used for the detection of subsequent insertions of commercial blocks during the same telecast.

A *film introduction* has properties similar to those of a commercial block introduction. It is a short transition back to the program, whose aim is to signal to the observer that the movie is continuing, e.g., by a film title. However, it is often omitted since there exists no pertinent legal regulation. As a substitution in the case of movies, some channels replay the last shots of the movie broadcasted right before the commercial break or superimpose the title of the telecast at the top or bottom together with a phrase such as "continued."

A *broadcasting station's advertisements and previews* announce upcoming or future telecasts on that channel. Typically, they last between 15 and 30 seconds.

The commercial *spots* themselves are video sequences lasting between 5 and 90 seconds. Several are broadcasted consecutively. Individual spots are separated from each other by dark monochrome frames. A particularity of German telecasts is that a stations's screen logo is turned off during commercials and turned on again afterward.

2.2   List of Technical Features

The features of commercial blocks and individual spots can be divided into two groups: those directly measurable and those measurable only indirectly. Directly measurable are low-level features which can easily be detected by the computer, while indirectly measurable features are of a higher level of abstraction and more difficult to compute. Moreover, some features are valid for all commercial blocks and/or spots, while others are valid only for a subset of them.

Directly Measurable Features

1. A directly measurable feature of commercial blocks and spots is their restricted temporal length. Generally, a spot lasts no longer than 30 s and a block no longer

than 6:30 min. The maxima ever observed were 90 s for a spot and 8 min for a block.

2. Two consecutive commercials are separated by a short break of 5 to 12 dark monochrome frames [5][12].

3. The volume of the audio signal is turned up during commercials and turned down afterward.

Indirectly Measurable Features

1. A human observer perceives commercials as full of motion, animation, and action. This sensation is supported by a high frequency of cuts and quick changes in color content.

2. A commercial contains many still images. In particular, the last scene is often a "still" image presenting the product, the company, and/or product name.

3. Special editing habits exist which are frequently used and can be recognized automatically.

4. Often text appears within commercials. The text shows the product or company name and other useful semantic information. It can be identified and evaluated [9][13].

In Section 3 we will show how these features can be computed and how relevant they are for detecting commercials.

Legal Regulations

In Germany the ratio of commercials to other televised material is regulated by law. The regulations differ for private and public TV stations, with the regulations for public TV being more restrictive. The following table summarizes the restrictions for private TV stations.

Table 1. Legal Regulations about Commercials on German Private TV.

Restriction	Value
Maximum share of commercial time	20% of the daily broadcasting time
Maximum share per hour	12 minutes
Minimum distance between two commercial blocks	20 minutes
Commercial block introduction	clearly visible distinction between broadcast and commercial

Additional regulations restrict commercials during movies which is of importance in our case. Movies may not be interrupted more than once every 45 minutes.

3. FEATURE-BASED DETECTION OF COMMERCIALS

In this section we investigate how the technical features of commercials can be measured. We present our computational indicators and analyze experimentally their ability to identify commercial blocks and spots. In general, the features will not simultaneously hold true for each commercial block. Not every commercial spot will end with a still image, containing text or depicting a moving action. Moreover, some feature films may also exhibit features which are typical of commercial spots. Therefore, our feature-based commercial detection system operates in two steps. First, potential commercial block locations within a video sequence are located; then they are analyzed in more detail.

Ten sample video sequences recorded from German television are used to prove the characteristics of the features (Table 2).

Table 2. The sample video set (times in *minutes:seconds* or *minutes:seconds:frame#*).

name	total length	commercial block		commercials		# of spots	avg. spot length
		start	end	start	end		
Aliens 2	22:53	07:57:20	14:54:05	08:00:23	14:21:17	17	00:22
Dancing with Wolves	22:37	07:58:01	14:35:00	08:02:06	14:04:16	17	00:19
Scent of Women	18:33	05:58:23	12:20:06	06:08:01	12:16:04	16	00:21
The Firm	17:40	04:53:06	11:47:10	04:56:08	11:26:21	18	00:20
Black Rain	17:24	05:01:14	12:21:14	05:04:18	11:20:17	18	00:18
Superman	29:20	08:40:00	11:36:00	08:42:19	11:07:21	7	00:16
Sneakers	20:00	04:59:03	12:40:18	05:02:23	11:52:02	16	00:24
Star Trek 4	25:46	10:39:13	19:0:22	10:43:24	18:01:18	16	00:26
Sitcom	21:40	07:57:18	14:01:17	08:00:24	13:03:18	15	00:18
Awakenings	19:59	08:15:07	15:16:10	08:18:03	14:42:14	16	21:24

Whenever parameters (e.g., thresholds) have to be determined for the feature indicators, they are derived from the first five sample videos and validated by the five remaining ones. Note that in all our examples the commercials were embedded in feature films; we have no experience yet with commercials embedded in other genres, such as sports or newscasts.

3.1 Monochrome Frames

In Section 2 we pointed out that individual commercial spots within a commercial block are always separated by several dark monochrome frames. They can be easily identified by calculating the standard intensity deviation σ_I of the pixels in each frame. Here, intensity equals the gray-level of the pixels. For a perfect monochrome frame σ_I should assume zero. In practice, in the presence of noise, a frame is regarded as monochrome if σ_I drops below the small threshold $t_{MF\sigma}$. In order to detect only dark monochrome frames, the average intensity μ_I is also required to be below the small threshold $t_{MF\mu}$. In formulas,

$$MF(I) = \begin{cases} \text{dark monochrome frame} & (\sigma_I \le t_{MF_\sigma}) \wedge (\mu_I \le t_{MF_\mu}) \\ \text{other monochrome frame} & (\sigma_I \le t_{MF_\sigma}) \wedge (\mu_I > t_{MF_\mu}) \\ \text{polychrome frame} & else \end{cases}$$

with $\quad \mu_I = \frac{1}{N} \cdot \sum_{n=1}^{N} I_n \quad$ and $\quad \sigma_I = \sum_{n=1}^{N} (I_n - \mu_I)^2 \quad$.

In the formulas the original image is represented as a list of intensity values I_n, one for each pixel, N pixels in total. In Figure 2 we depict the dark monochrome frame occurrences during a feature film interrupted by a commercial break. Note the large difference in the frequency of such frames during the commercial blocks and during the feature films. We also measured the distribution of the length of such dark-frame sequences. As you can see in Table 3, the length of commercial separation is usually between 0.12 s and 0.4 s. We conclude that any monochrome frame sequence shorter than 0.12 s or longer than 0.4 s is therefore not a commercial separator.

Table 3. Monochrome frame sequence length distribution.

Name	Monochrome frame sequence length distribution used for commercial separation						
	<.12	<.2	0.2	0.24	0.28	<=.4	>.4
Aliens 2	.00	.06	.82	.06	.00	.00	.06
Dancing with the Wolves	.00	.00	.00	.00	.63	.37	.00
Scent of Women	.07	.80	.13	.00	.00	.00	.00
The Firm	.06	.29	.41	.06	.06	.12	.00
Black Rain	.00	.00	.12	.59	.06	.17	.06
Superman	.00	.17	.83	.00	.00	.00	.00
Sneakers	.00	.00	.27	.07	.47	.20	.00
Star Trek 4	.07	.00	.07	.00	.20	.53	.07
Sitcom	.00	.07	.14	.65	.00	.14	.00
Awakenings	.00	.00	.00	.86	.07	.00	.07

On German TV, commercial blocks consisting of at least 4 spots can be reliably detected by the following simple detection scheme. Find each set of at least three monochrome sequences of 0.12 to 0.4s which are no further apart than 60 seconds. 99.98% of the candidate sequences in our test set were part of a commercial block; no block was missed, but 12.7% of the overall length of a commercial block was not detected, i.e., the commercial block introduction, the first and last spot, and the station's advertisements and previews. Thus, while monochrome frame sequences are a strong commercial block indicator, they generally miss a substantial part of a commercial block.

3.2 Scene Breaks

In this subsection we analyze the style and frequency of scene breaks used in commercials and feature films, concentrating exclusively on hard cuts and fades.

Hard Cuts

While watching commercials you may notice the high editing frequency. Since most scene transitions are hard cuts, a high hard-cut frequency can be observed during commercials. Hard cuts are scene breaks which result from splicing two shots together without any transition. They are perceived as an instantaneous change from one shot to another [1]. The difference in color histograms between consecutive frames is an approach for detecting hard-cuts [3]. Thus, we compute a 64-bin color histogram over the entire frame, considering only the two most significant bits of each color band, and normalize it by the number of pixels in the frame.

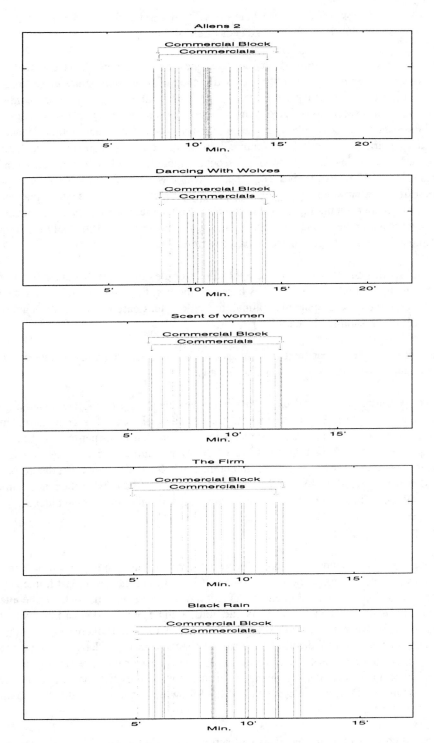

Figure 2. Monochrome frame distribution for the sample video set. To save space only the graphs of the first five sample videos are shown. The other five graphs look similar.

Then, the color histogram difference between two successive frames is calculated. A shot boundary is declared if the difference exceeds threshold $t_{HardCut}$.

However, even within a set of hard cuts, stronger ones can be distinguished from weaker ones. Weak hard cuts are characterized by a low difference of histogram values close to $t_{HardCut}$, while the difference for strong hard cuts is significantly above $t_{HardCut}$. Since commercial blocks consist of a set of non-related spots, we expect strong hard cuts between them. Moreover, they want to give the observer the impression of dynamics and action. Hence, even within a spot, the scene of action changes frequently, resulting again in strong hard cuts. Strong hard cuts are detected by applying a second, higher threshold to the difference in histograms between consecutive frames: $t_{StrongHardcut}$, while weak hard cuts are defined by all histogram differences between $t_{HardCut}$ and $t_{StrongHardcut}$. Figure 3 shows the rate of the weak and strong hard cuts per minute for the video samples. Notice that the weak hard-cut frequency is not as significant as the strong hard-cut frequency for our purpose. Thus, only the frequency of strong hard cuts is further considered as a discriminator.

It is obviously difficult to determine the right values for the thresholds. In our studies so far we have "manually" set all threshold values based on the first five sample videos. In principle it would be preferable to compute the optimal threshold values based on a statistical analysis of the features of the sample video set [18].

The average strong hard-cut frequency, measured in strong hard cuts per minute, is 21.5 for spots and only 3.1 for the rest of our video samples.

To detect potential commercial block locations, we select each connected subgraph of the strong hard-cut graphs in Figure 3 as a potential commercial block. The graph is regarded as disconnected at all locations where it drops below 5 strong hard cuts per minute. Each candidate sequence is rejected if it does not exceed 30 strong hard cuts per minute at least once. Applying this rule to our test video set, all commercial blocks are found. On the average, the detected ranges covered 93.46% of the commercial blocks and 0.07% of the non-commercial block sequences. Thus, strong hard cuts are a good pre-filter for commercial blocks.

Fades

Fades are scene breaks which gradually blend out from a scene into a monochrome frame or blend in from a monochrome frame into a scene [1] [7]. Either the first or last frame is monochrome and exhibits a standard intensity deviation σ_I close to zero. In contrast, the alternate end point shows the scene in full intensity and, thus, assumes a large standard intensity deviation value. In between these two extremes, σ_I is either monotone increasing or monotone decreasing. For nearly all fades the graph can be specified in more detail: during a fade the graph of σ_I plotted against the frame number is either linear or concave. This characteristic temporal behavior of the standard deviation of intensity enables fade patterns to be reliably detected. Thus, our indicator detects a fade if the following conditions hold for a sequence of consecutive σ_I values.

- It consists of linear segments with a minimum correlation of 0.8.
- Each linear segment has a minimum length of 10 frames.
- The gradients of the segments are either decreasing and positive or increasing and negative.

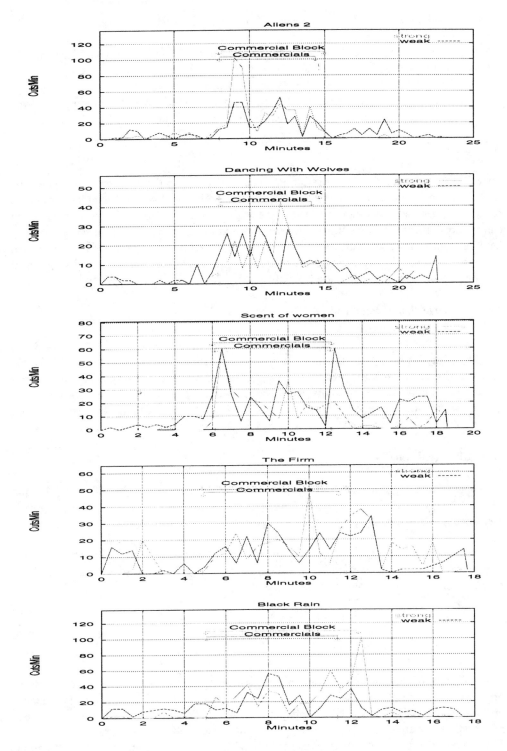

Figure 3. Hard cuts per minute for the sample video set. Notice the difference between "strong" and "weak" hard cuts. To save space only the graphs of the first five sample videos are shown. The other five graphs look similar.

- Either the last or the first σ_l value of the sequence is monochrome.

For our commercial blocks the fade rate was 0.5 fades/minute contrasting to 0.02 fades/minute for our feature film set.

Note that the subsequent features are calculated only for non-monochrome frames, and from scene break to scene break. The scene transition frames are no longer considered.

3.3 Action

Typically spots have a high level of "action." The human perception of action is influenced by many different aspects. The impression of action can be caused by fast-moving objects in the scene, e.g., people running around or fighting with each other. But the impression of action can also result from certain editing and camera control operations [1]. For instance, frequent hard cuts and many zooms also give the impression of action. Moreover, a calm scene with pumping and changing colors is perceived as action. These are many different aspects of "action" which we want to measure (partially) by the following indicators:

- edge change ratio, and
- motion vector length.

Initially, we also investigated the motion energy (= the sum of the pixel differences between consecutive images) since it seemed to be optimally suited to registering all three different aspects, especially change of colors and camera operations. It turned out, however, that the quality of information generated is below that of the other action indicators. Thus, motion energy is no longer considered.

Edge Change Ratio (ECR)

The edge change ratio (ECR) was proposed as a characteristic feature by Zabih, Miller, and Mai [19]. They used the well-known Canny edge detection algorithm [2], although, in principle, any edge detection algorithm could be used.

Let σ_n be the number of edge pixels in frame n and X_n^{in} and X_{n-1}^{out} the number of the entering and exiting edge pixels in frames n and n-1, respectively. Then the edge change ratio ecr_n between frames n-1 and n is defined as

$$ecr_n = max\left(\frac{X_n^{in}}{\sigma_n}, \frac{X_{n-1}^{out}}{\sigma_{n-1}}\right)$$

The advantage of the edge change ratio as a characteristic parameter is that it registers structural changes in the scene such as the entry, exit, and motion of objects as well as fast camera operations. However, it is somewhat independent of variations in color and intensity since it relies only on sharp edges. Consequently, pumping images have no effect on the indicator. Thus, it registers two of the three parts of "action" listed at the beginning of the subsection. Notice that the edge change ratio is only calculated within each shot. It is not used here for detecting scene breaks.

As can be seen from the graphs in Figure 5, the edge change ratio for commercial blocks is very dynamic; it is often much more static for feature films. Thus, a commercial block candidate can be detected by frequent changes of the ECR values above a threshold t_{ECR}. The indicator's extended finite state machine is depicted in Figure 4. When we applied this indicator to our set of test videos, all commercial blocks were detected. On average, the detected ranges covered 96.65% of the commercial blocks and 0.07% of the non-commercial block sequences.

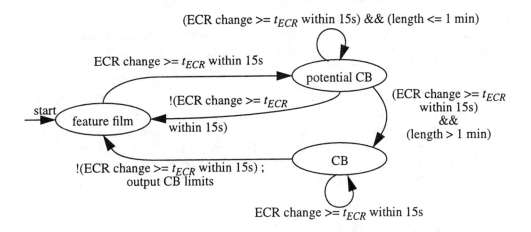

Figure 4. Extended finite state machine of the indicator for dynamic subgraph ranges in action graphs (i.e., in the ECR and in the motion vector length graphs).

Motion Vector Length

An important feature of action is fast object movement. The motion vector length measures object movement by using an algorithm similar to a motion compensation algorithm used by MPEG encoders [4] [6] called "Multiple- Step-Search Method" [17]. Each single frame of the video is divided into so-called macroblocks of 16x16 pixels. The best matching position for each macroblock of a frame is calculated by comparing the block with nine positions on a coarse grid of the nest frame within an area of 16 pixels around the original location. Then, at the position with the lowest difference, the same procedure is applied within an area of 8 pixels around that position. This procedure is applied down to a search area of 0.

The result of the matching operation is a motion vector with the length of the distance between the positions of a block in two consecutive frames. With (x_1, y_1) the position of the macroblock in the first frame and (x_2, y_2) its position in the consecutive frame, the length of the vector for a macroblock i is calculated as follows:

$$MB_i = \begin{cases} \sqrt{20^2 + 20^2} & \text{if position cannot be located} \\ \sqrt{(x_1 - x_2)^2 + (y_1 - y_2)^2} & \text{else} \end{cases}$$

A closer look at Figure 5 shows that a commercial block candidate can also be detected by our indicator for dynamic subgraph ranges. Applying this indicator to our test video set, all commercial blocks are found. On the average, the detected ranges covered 96.43% of the commercial blocks and 0.16% of the non-commercial block sequences.

3.4 A Feature-based Commercial Detection System

Having introduced the characteristic features, we now explain their composition into a system delivering accurate results at reduced computational costs. Our commercial detection system uses the monochrome frame sequence feature and the strong hard cut feature as fast pre-selectors; the accurate, but computationally expensive action detector is utilized to determine the precise limits. We distinguish between the following cases:

- If both pre-selectors indicate a commercial block, i.e., the intersection of their detected candidate ranges is not empty, or only the strong hard cut feature, a commercial block is detected. The action criterion is now used to find its precise limits. If the action criterion at one limit is below the commercial block criterion, the search for the precise limits is performed towards the inner range, otherwise outward from the range.
- If the monochrome frame sequence detector indicates only a commercial block, the range is regarded as a false detection.

Applying this detection system to our test video set, all commercial blocks were selected. On the average, the ranges detected covered 96.85% of the commercial blocks and 0.07% of the non-commercial block sequences. However, computation time is reduced by a magnitude of one in comparison to that required to calculate all features for all frames.

If our objective O1 is to save all commercial block frames while discarding as many feature film frames as possible, the following supplementary rules must be added to the above outline of the feature-based commercial detection algorithm. The detected commercial block ranges are extended by 30 seconds at both ends. If it is our objective O2 to save all feature film frames while discarding as many commercial block frames as possible, the detected commercial block ranges are shortened by 10 seconds at both ends. In practice, these values result in excellent outcomes.

4. RECOGNITION OF KNOWN COMMERCIALS

The feature-based commercial detection system presented so far allows a rough localization of the commercial blocks. However, to determine their precise limits, i.e., down to a single shot, the system would have to be capable of grouping semantically related shots [18]. Additionally, some of the features used may be easily changed in the future, for example, the delimiting monochrome frames between spots can be easily omitted by the television stations.

Furthermore, in other film genres such as sports or in other countries such as the U.S.A., programs are sometimes interrupted by a single commercial without any transition to or from it. Reliable detection of a single commercial is difficult since the feature-based approach expects it to have a minimum length of a commercial block. If the block is too short, features either do not change enough due to averaging, or the change is too short to distinguish it from accidental runaways. A second approach, able to cope with all the stated situations, is described here. It is based on the fact that commercials often run on TV for an extended period of time, and it

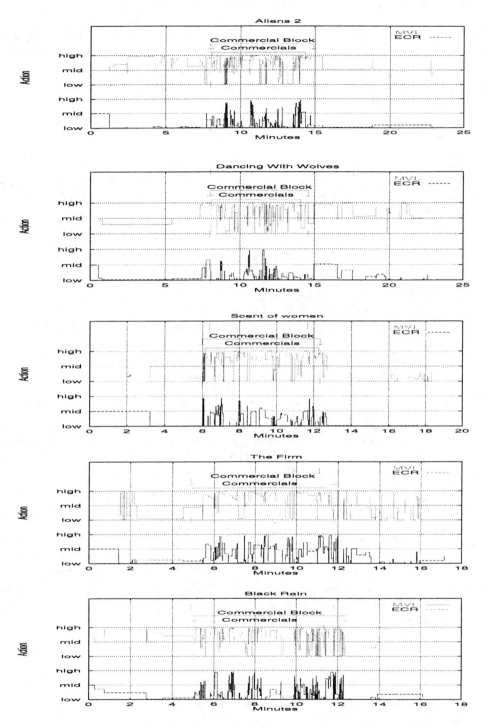

Figure 5. The different indicators for "action" and typical patterns during a commercial block. To save space only the graphs of the first five sample videos are shown. The other five graphs look similar.

is thus possible to store and recognize features of *known* commercials.

Recognition-based detection of commercials depends on a database of an initial set of spots whose recognition in the current program is the aim. Individual spots are stored and compared on the basis of comprehensive fingerprints [10]. Two questions will be investigated in the following. What is a suitable and comprehensive fingerprint for shots, and how should two fingerprints be compared?

4.1 Fingerprint

A commercial spot consists of a sequence of images. Accordingly, we construct a fingerprint of each spot by calculating important features per frame and then represent the spot's fingerprint as a sequence of these features. We call the representation of the value of a feature a *character*, the domain of possible values an *alphabet,* and the sequence of characters a *string* [10].

A feature used for a fingerprint should meet the following requirements:

- It should tolerate small differences between two fingerprints calculated from the same spots, but broadcasted and digitized at different times. The differences are caused by slight inaccuracies in rate and color, or by TV and digitizer artifacts.
- It should be easy/fast to calculate and rely on only a few values, so that computation, storage, and comparison of fingerprints remain inexpensive.
- It should show a strong discriminative power.

As an example we use the following simple feature as a fingerprint: the color coherence vector (CCV) [16]. In our opinion it fulfills the requirements that CCVs are fast to calculate, show strong discriminative power, and tolerate slight color inaccuracies. However, rate inaccuracies (such as dropped frames) must be absorbed by the comparison algorithm.

Color Coherence Vectors

The color coherence vector (CCV) [16] is a refined color histogram technique. However, instead of counting only the number of pixels of a certain color, the color coherence vector also differentiates between pixels of the same color depending on the size of the color region they belong to. If the region (i.e., the connected 8-neighbor component of that color) is larger than t_{ccv}, a pixel is regarded as coherent, otherwise, as incoherent. Thus, in an image there are two values associated with each color j:

- α_j, the number of coherent pixels of color j, and
- β_j , the number of incoherent pixels of color j.

A color coherence vector then is defined as the vector

$$\langle (\alpha_1, \beta_1), ..., (\alpha_n, \beta_n) \rangle$$

Before calculating the color coherence vector we scaled the input image to 240x160 pixels and smoothed the image by a Gaussian filter of sigma 1 as also done by Pass et. al. [16]. t_{ccv}

was set to 25, and the color space used only the two most significant bits of each RGB color component.

4.2 Comparison

Let us now introduce our fingerprint matching algorithm. Given a query string A of length P and a longer subject string B of length N, the *approximate substring matching* finds the substring of B that aligns with A with minimal substitutions, deletions, and insertions of characters [14] [15]. The minimal number of substitutions, deletions, and insertions transforming A into B is called the minimal distance D between A and B. Two fingerprint sequences A and B are regarded as identical if the minimal distance D between query string A and subject string B does not exceed the threshold $t_{stringDist}$, and the difference in length does not exceed 90%, i.e., P/N is greater than or equal to 0.9.

At first glance, use of approximate substring matching rather than approximate string matching seems questionable since we want to identify identical spots; however, in our experiments we noticed that commercials are sometimes slightly shortened at the beginning and/or end, and the distance D should not be increased by this effect. Moreover, the shot boundaries might not be determined down to the precise frame number, but displaced by a few frames. The approximate matching procedure guarantees that sequences recorded with minor rate and color inaccuracies can still be found. In addition, it cannot be expected that the same commercial spot recorded at different times and from different broadcasting stations have identical fingerprints.

Long sequences are more likely to contain erroneous characters, and thus $t_{stringDist}$ is set in relation to the length of the search string A. Several fast approximate substring matching algorithms exist with worst-case time complexity $O(DN)$ requiring only $O(P^2)$ to $O(D^2)$ space. We use the one proposed by Landau and Vishkin [8].

4.3 Recognition-based Commercial Detection

We use the fingerprint and comparison techniques as follows to identify individual spots precisely. A sliding window of length L seconds runs over the video, stepping forward from shot to shot (see Figure 6), each time calculating the CCV fingerprint of the window. At each position the window fingerprint is compared with the first $L + S$ seconds of each spot fingerprint stored in the database. If two are similar (i.e., the minimal distance is below $t_{stringDist}$), the window is temporally expanded to the whole length of the candidate fingerprint in the database and the two are compared (see Figure 7). If a commercial is recognized, the window jumps to the end of that commercial, otherwise it only shifts forward to the next shot.

Recognition-based detection, like feature-based detection, consists of two steps. Step one aims to reduce the computational cost by shortening the fingerprints to be compared at the expense of discrimination power. Therefore, this step can detect only candidate spots. Step two determines whether the candidate is identical to a stored spot. The reason for setting the subject string to length $L + S$ in the first step is to avoid an increase of the approximate distance by frames dropped at the start of the commercial or by slight inaccuracies in the determination of the precise position of shot boundaries, both of which might occur in practice. Therefore, S will always be set as low as possible and should be zero in the ideal case. For our test spots $S = 2$ frames was fine.

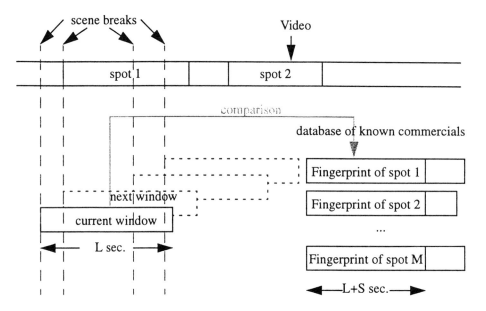

Figure 6. First step of the recognition-based commercial detection system.

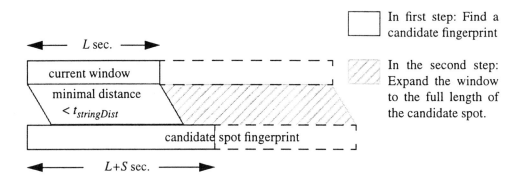

Figure 7. Expansion process in the second step of the recognition-based commercial detection system.

We do not require L to be less than the length of the shortest possible commercial since that would reverse the role of the two fingerprints. However, a computationally optimal value for L is difficult to determine. Two factors affect the computation time:

• First, the cost of finding candidate commercial spot windows. Given an $O(DN)$ comparison algorithm, M as the number of commercials in the database, D_{rel} as the maximum difference expressed in percent, the time needed to compare the fingerprint of the window with one in the database is $O((L*D_{rel}) * (L+S))$, and the time to determine all candidate commercial spots for a window is proportional to $O((L*D_{rel}) * (L+S) * M)$. In the formulas, $(L+S)$ specifies the length of each fingerprint used from the database for comparison,

$L*D_{rel}$ the maximal difference allowed, and M the size of fingerprint database of commercials.

- Second, test whether a candidate is a known commercial or not. It is obvious that the complexity is fixed for any candidate, and the total complexity thus depends on the average number of candidates determined per window position by the first step. This number increases inversely to the length L of the fingerprint. The lower L is, the less discriminate is the window fingerprint. But it is difficult to specify this change in probability by formulas since consecutive CCV values are highly correlated. Thus we determined heuristically good values for L and S by run-time analysis with the video test set.

Experimental Results

We digitized 200 commercial spots from several German TV channels. This set contained a number of new spots in addition to the spots from our sample video set, but recorded from different TV channels and/or at different times. We applied our spot recognition approach to each sample in our video set. All commercials were recognized, none was missed, and none was falsely detected. The localization was also very high. The maximal difference between the precise and detected locations was only 5 frames.

The processing time spent by our recognition system was only 90% of the duration of the video sample in realtime, once the CCV values for the video had been calculated. Therefore, by using a fast assembler implementation of the CCV computation and string comparison, the whole process could be performed in realtime.

5. COMBINING THE TWO APPROACHES INTO A SELF-LEARNING COMMERCIAL DETECTION SYSTEM

In this chapter we describe a commercial detection system that makes use of both formerly described approaches. It is our objective to build a system of the same precision in localization and recognition of spots as the second approach while reducing the computational cost and keeping the system automatically up-to-date, i.e., the database should "learn" new spots autonomously. In the following we assume that our system is always on-line; or, in other words, the system is constantly running, checking all TV channels for commercial blocks.

The two approaches are combined hierarchically. In the first step we use the feature-based approach to reduce the number of candidate commercial areas by means of the "monochrome frame sequence" and "strong hard cut" criteria. Since the feature-based approach is used as a pre-filter, the objective is to miss as few spots as possible. Therefore, we follow the objective O1 as described in Section 3.4. In the second step the recognition-based approach is used to identify the individual spots and determine their exact borders. That way the computationally more expensive CCV calculation and the approximate string comparison must be applied to only a small subset of the video. The scene breaks and thus the hard cuts have to be computed anyway for the recognition-based approach and detection of the monochrome frame sequences is very inexpensive.

Furthermore we try to find unknown spots automatically, i.e., let the system learn new spots autonomously. We assume that our database contains almost every currently broadcasted spot, so if a new commercial is broadcasted for the first time, we can assume that it will usually be surrounded by known spots. If so, the commercial recognition algorithm will find the end of the known spot aired before and the beginning of the known spot aired after the new one, defining the exact position of the unknown spot. After removal of the dark monochrome frames at the head and tail, the new spot can be inserted into the database. Problems will arise in the following cases:

- The unknown spot is either the first or last one in a commercial block. But it is not very likely that a new spot will always be the first or the last in the commercial blocks. It can be assumed that sooner or later the spot will be surrounded by two well-known spots in one of the next commercial blocks and can then be inserted into the database.
- More than one unknown spot is surrounded by known spots, in which case we cannot distinguish between the different spots. The system would assume that the two spots are one — although quite long — and would insert the whole piece into the database. We deal with this case by searching for the appearance of monochrome frame sequences of characteristic length to break the sequence up into the individual spots.

To overcome the problem of erroneously inserted clips we suggest the following. First, we can let the system require confirmation by the user each time a new spot is detected. Second, we can insert the clips only provisionally. The clip will only then be inserted permanently when it is found in other commercial blocks, too. If the clip cannot be detected in other blocks after a certain time, it will be removed automatically.

Finally, the precise borders of the commercial blocks must be determined. Thus, the first 2 minutes of each commercial block are searched for repeatedly appearing sequences of 3 to 5 seconds. If such a sequence can be found in several commercial blocks of the same channel, the sequence is regarded as a commercial block introduction and added to a database labeled "commercial block introduction." Consequently, the commercial block candidates are searched not only for known and new commercials but also for known and new commercial block introductions. This procedure allows precise determination of the beginning of the commercial blocks. Unfortunately, this does not work for the end of a commercial block due to the lack of legal regulations. Thus the end of a commercial block must be determined roughly via the features as described in Section 3.

We have not yet completed any experimental studies with the integrated algorithm, but are planning to do so.

6. CONCLUSIONS

This paper describes two methods for detecting and extracting commercials in digital videos. The first approach is based on the heuristics of measurable features. It uses features fundamental to TV advertising such as high action rate and short shot length. These features cannot be easily changed by the advertising industry. Only the short dark monochrome sequences used as commercial separators have — strictly speaking — nothing to do with the commercial spot itself and can therefore easily be replaced by another separator. This feature must therefore be adjusted to local habits. For instance, on our sample tapes from the U.S. the commercials have been separated by one to three dark monochrome frames, often surrounded by a fast fade.

The performance of the feature-based commercial detection system was quite high: 96.85% of all commercial blocks were selected, while only 0.07% feature film frames were misclassified. The system can be easily adjusted to the local features of commercials in different countries.

The second approach relies on a database of known commercial spots. Due to its design — it recognizes known commercials in advance — it attains high precision. Moreover, the method is also capable of recognizing individual spots. No adjustments for different countries are needed. The performance is very high; all spots were recognized with no false hits at all.

Both approaches have been combined into a reliable self-learning TV commercials detection and recognition system.

So far we have tested only our feature-based detection approach on a limited number of samples. In the upcoming months we will use the system with the parameters derived from the initial set to analyze new video material, in particular, genres other than feature films.

In the near future we will also extend our work into the audio domain and explore the different application domains in which our commercial detection and recognition system might be used.

References

1.   Bordwell, D. and Thompson, K., "Film Art: An Introduction", 4th ed. McGraw-Hill, New York, 1993.
2.   Canny, J., "A Computational Approach to Edge Detection", *IEEE Transactions on Pattern Analysis and Machine Intelligence*, Vol. 8, No. 6, pp. 679-697, November 1986.
3.   Boreczky, J. S. and Rowe, L. A., "Comparison of Video Shot Boundary Detection Techniques", in *Storage and Retrieval for Still Image and Video Databases IV*, Proc. SPIE 2664, pp. 170-179, January 1996.
4.   Clan, E., Rodriguez, A., Gandhi, R., and Panchanathan, S., "Experiments on Block-Matching Techniques for Video Coding", *Multimedia Systems*, 2(5):228-241, December 1994.
5.   Fischer, S., Lienhart, R., and Effelsberg, W., "Automatic Recognition of Film Genres", *Proc. ACM Multimedia 95*, San Francisco, CA, pp. 295-304, November 1995.
6.   Gall, D.L., "MPEG: A Video Compression Standard for Multimedia Applications", *Communications of the ACM*, Vol. 34, No. 4, pp. 47-58, April 1991.
7.   Hampapur, A., Jain, R., and Weymouth, T., "Production Model Based Digital Video Segmentation", *Journal of Multimedia Tools and Applications*, Vol. 1, No. 1, pp. 1-38, March 1995.
8.   Landau, G. M. and Vishkin, U. "Introducing Efficient Parallelism into Approximate String Matching and a New Serial Algorithm", *Symp. on Theory of Computing*, pp. 220-230, 1986.
9.   Lienhart, R., "Automatic Text Recognition for Video Indexing", *Proc. ACM Multimedia 96*, Boston, MA, pp. 11-20, Nov. 1996.
10.   Lienhart, R., Effelsberg, W., and Jain, R., "Towards a Visual Grep: A Systematic Analysis of Various Methods to Compare Video Sequences", in *Storage and Retrieval for Image and Video Databases VI*, Ishwar K. Sethi, Ramesh C. Jain, Editors, Proc. SPIE 3312, pp. 271-282, January 1998.

11. Rainer Lienhart, Christoph Kuhmünch, and Wolfgang Effelsberg. On the Detection and Recognition of Television Commercials. *Proc. IEEE Conf. on Multimedia Computing and Systems*, Ottawa, Canada, pp. 509 - 516, June 1997.

12. Lienhart, R., Pfeiffer, S., and Effelsberg, W., "The MoCA Workbench: Support for Creativity in Movie Content Analysis", *Proc. of the IEEE Conference on Multimedia Computing & Systems*, Hiroshima, Japan, pp. 314-321, June 1996.

13. Lienhart, R. and Stuber, F. "Automatic Text Recognition in Digital Videos", in *Image and Video Processing IV 1996*, Proc. SPIE 2666-20, pp. 180-188, Jan. 1996.

14. Meyers, E. W., "A Sublinear Algorithm for Approximate Keyword Matching", *Algorithmica* 12, 4-5, pp. 345-374, 1994.

15. Ottmann, T. and Widmayer, P., "Algorithms and Data Structures", *BI-Verlag*, Mannheim, 1993 (in German).

16. Pass, G., Zabih, R., and Miller, J., "Comparing Images Using Color Coherence Vectors", *Proc. ACM Multimedia 96*, Boston, MA, pp. 65-73, Nov. 1996.

17. Tekalp, A. M., "Digital Video Processing", Prentice Hall Signal Processing Series, 1995.

18. Therrien, C. W., "Decision, Estimation, and Classification: An Introduction to Pattern Recognition and Related Topics", John Wiley & Sons, Inc. 1989.

19. Zabih, R., Miller, J., and Mai, K., "A Feature-Based Algorithm for Detecting and Classifying Scene Breaks", *Proc. ACM Multimedia 95*, San Francisco, CA, pp. 189-200, Nov. 1995.

III

MULTIMEDIA SYSTEMS AND TECHNIQUES

21

PROCESSOR ARCHITECTURES FOR MULTIMEDIA

Borko Furht
Florida Atlantic University
Department of Computer Science and Engineering
Boca Raton, Florida 33431

1. **INTRODUCTION AND CLASSIFICATION**..448
2. **COMPLEXITY OF MULTIMEDIA FUNCTIONS**...449
3. **DEDICATED MULTIMEDIA PROCESSORS**..452
   3.1   FUNCTION SPECIFIC ARCHITECTURES 453
   3.2   PROGRAMMABLE DEDICATED ARCHITECTURES 454
   3.3   NEW ARCHITECTURAL TRENDS...458
4. **GENERAL-PURPOSE PROCESSORS AND THEIR SUPPORT FOR MULTIMEDIA**..461
   4.1   GENERIC OPERATIONS IN MULTIMEDIA PROCESSING 461
   4.2   INTEL MMX TECHNOLOGY 462
   4.3   SUN'S VISUAL INSTRUCTION SET 463
   4.4   OTHER GENERAL-PURPOSE PROCESSORS...465
5. **PERFORMANCE ANALYSIS**..465
6. **CONCLUSIONS**...466
   REFERENCES 467

Abstract. In this chapter, we present contemporary VLSI processor architectures that support multimedia applications. We classified these processors into two groups: dedicated multimedia processors, which perform dedicated multimedia functions, such as MPEG encoding or decoding, and general-purpose processors that provide support for multimedia. Dedicated multimedia processors use either function-specific architectures with limited flexibility but higher speed and efficiency, or programmable architectures with increased flexibility. Both architectures are exploring parallelism inherent in video and image applications by applying single-instruction, multiple-data (SIMD) or/and very-large-instruction-word (VLIW) concepts. Advanced general-purpose processors provide the support for multimedia by incorporating new multimedia instructions and executing them in parallel by using the SIMD coprocessor approach. A survey of these processor architectures and their performance is presented in this chapter.

447

1. INTRODUCTION AND CLASSIFICATION

During the last few years we have witnessed the process of "poising" for multimedia: from PC and workstation manufacturers (multimedia PCs and workstations), add-in-board vendors (video and audio capture and playback cards), and silicon vendors (compression and graphics chips), to operating systems designers (OS support for multimedia) and software creators (authoring tools and a variety of multimedia applications). The last players to enter this poising game have been microprocessor designers.

In this chapter, we present a survey of processor architectures designed to support multimedia applications. Designs of these architectures range from fully custom to fully programmable dedicated architectures and to general-purpose processor architectures with an extensive support for multimedia. The classification of these architectures is shown in Figure 1.

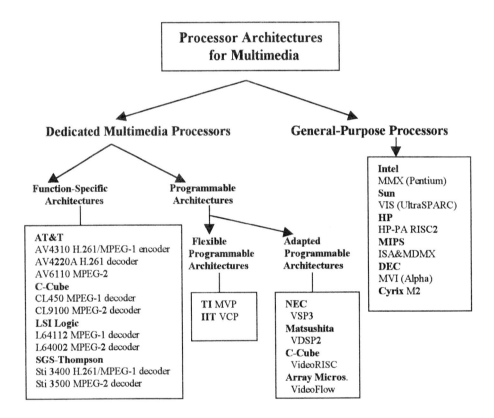

Figure 1. Classification of processor architectures that support multimedia.

Dedicated multimedia processors are typically custom designed architectures intended to perform specific multimedia functions. These functions usually include video and audio compression and decompression, and in this case these processors are referred to as video codecs. In addition to support for compression, some advanced multimedia processors provide support for 2D and 3D graphics applications. Designs of dedicated multimedia processors range from fully custom architectures, referred to as function specific architectures, with minimal programmability, to fully programmable architectures. Furthermore, programmable architectures can be classified into flexible programmable architectures, which provide moderate to high flexibility, and adapted programmable architectures, which provide an increased efficiency and less flexibility [1]. The dedicated multimedia processors use a variety of architectural schemes from multiple functional units and a RISC or DSP (digital signal processor) core processors to multiple processor schemes. Furthermore, the latest dedicated processors use single-instruction-multiple-data (SIMD) and very-long-instruction-word (VLIW) architectures, as well as some hybrid schemes. These architectures are presented in Section 3.

General-purpose (GP) processors provide support for multimedia by including multimedia instructions into the instruction set. Instead of performing specific multimedia functions (such as compression and 2D/3D graphics), GP processors provide instructions specifically created to support generic operations in video processing. For example, these instructions include support for 8-bit data types (pixels), efficient data addressing and I/O instructions, and even instructions to support motion estimation. The latest processors, such as MMX (Intel), VIS (Sun) and MAX-2 (HP), incorporate some types of SIMD architectures, which perform the same operation in parallel on multiple data elements.

2. COMPLEXITY OF MULTIMEDIA FUNCTIONS

In video and signal processing applications, a measure of algorithmic complexity is the total number of operations per second, expressed in MOPS (million operations per second), or GOPS (giga operations per second). This measure incorporates the total number of primitive operations needed to perform specific functions, and includes data load and store operations as well as arithmetic and logic operations on data elements.

For purposes, we present the calculation of the complexity (adapted from [2]) for an MPEG-2 decoder, shown in Figure 2. We assume the encoded bit rate for the input bit sequence is 4 Mbps. Assuming that the average symbol size is 4 bits, the average rate is then 1 million symbols/second.

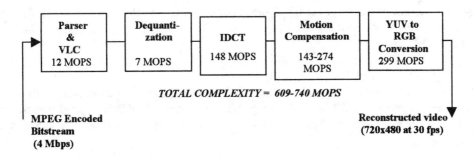

Figure 2. MPEG decoder and the complexity of its blocks.

The input video is 720x480 at 30 fps, encoded in 4:2:0 YUV format. In 4:2:0 format, the Y component contains 720x480 pixels, while U and V components have 320x240 pixels. Total number of 8x8 blocks in each frame is 90x60 = 5,400 (in Y) and 45x30 = 1,350 (in U and V). This gives 8,100 blocks in each frame, and total of a 8,100 x 30 sec = 243,000 blocks per second. The MPEG sequence used for this calculation comprises the group of pictures (GOP) consisting of 1 I-, 4 P-, and 10 B-frames.

Block 1: Bit stream parser and variable length (Huffman) decoder
The decoding of 1 symbols requires the following operations:

- 1 compare, 1 subtract, and 1 shift for grabbing a variable number of bits from data buffer (total 3 operations),
- 1 load, 2 shifts, and 1 mask for searching for a code in a code table (total 4 operations), and
- 1 compare, 1 subtract,1 shift, 1 add, and 1 mask for updating the data buffer (total 5 operations).

This gives total of 12 operations per symbol, and total of 12 x 1 million symbols = 12 MOPS for this block.

Block 2: Dequantization

The dequantization, applied to each non-zero DCT coefficient, requires the following operations:

- 1 load for reading the quantizer scale matrix (total 1 operation),
- 2 integer multiplications and 1 division (by a constant of 8 or 16) for dequantization (total 3 operations), and
- 2 logical, 1 compare, 1 shift, and 1 add for the oddification (total 5 operations).

The total count for one DCT coefficient is 9 operations. Among 1 million symbols, we assume that 80% are coded DCT coefficients. This gives the total complexity of the quantization block: 9 x 800,000 = 7.2 MOPS.

Block 3: Inverse Discrete Cosine Transform (IDCT)

There are many different implementations for the inverse DCT. For illustration purposes we assume the fast inverse DCT algorithm, described in [3], that requires the following operations:

- 464 additions, 80 integer multiplications, and 64 stores for each 8x8 block (total 608 operations per block).

Then, the total complexity of the IDCT block becomes 243,000 blocks x 608 = 147.7 MOPS. Since not every block is coded in a P- or B-frame, this is the maximum complexity for using the fast IDCT.

Block 4: Motion Compensation

The worst-case scenario is that all blocks in a P-frame are motion compensated with 4-pixel interpolation and all blocks in a B-frame are motion compensated with 8-pixel interpolation from two predictor frames. For an 8x8 block in a P-frame, the following operations are required:

- 8x9x2 = 144 load operations for reading blocks with both horizontal and vertical overlapping (total 144 operations),
- 3 additions and 1 shift for interpolating one predictor pixel (total 4x64 = 256 operations), and
- 1 load, 1 addition, 2 compares, 1 assignment, and 1 store for reconstructing the pixel (total 6x64 = 384 operations).

The total number of operations for each block is 784. Because there are 8 P-frames in a one-second sequence, the total complexity for P-frames is: 8 x 8,100 blocks x 784 = 50.8 MOPS.

For each 8x8 block in a B-frame, the following operations are required:

- 2x(8x9x2) = 288 operations for reading blocks from two predictor frames (total 288 operations),
- 3 additions and 1 shift for interpolating one predictor pixel from the first frame (total 4x64 = 256 operations),
- 3 additions and 1 shift for interpolating one predictor pixel from the second frame (total 4x64 = 256 operations),
- 2 additions and 1 shift for forming the final pixel predictors (total 3x64 = 192 operations), and
- 1 load, 1 addition, 2 compares, 1 assignment, and 1 store for reconstructing the pixel with clipping (total 6x64 = 384 operations).

The total number of operations for each block is 1,376. There are total of 20 B-frames in a one-second sequence and, therefore, the total complexity for B-frames is 20 x 8,100 blocks x 1,376 = 222.9 MOPS. Adding complexities for P- and B-frames, the complexity for motion compensation becomes 273.7 MOPS.

The best case scenario for motion compensation is when all P- and B-frame blocks have no pixel interpolation. Then, the total number of operations is 143.1 MOPS.

Block 5: YUV to RGB Color Conversion
The conversion from YUV to RGB color format, based on CCIR-601 standard, can be performed using the following formula:

$$\begin{bmatrix} R \\ G \\ B \end{bmatrix} = \begin{bmatrix} 1.1644 & 0 & 1.5966 \\ 1.1644 & -0.3920 & -0.8132 \\ 1.1644 & 2.0184 & 0 \end{bmatrix} \begin{bmatrix} Y-16 \\ U-128 \\ V-128 \end{bmatrix}$$

$$(1)$$

where Y and U/V are clipped prior to transform to the ranges [16,240] and [16,235], respectively.

The following operations are required for each pixel:

- 1.5 loads for reading YUV (total 1.5 operation per pixel),
- 1.5 subtractions, 2.5 compares, and 3 assignments for YUV clipping (total 7 operations per pixel),
- 2 integer multiplications, 3.25 additions, and 3 shifts for the transformation (total 8.25 operations per pixel),
- 6 compares and 3 assignments for RGB clipping (total 9 operations per pixel), and
- 3 stores for writing RGB (total 3 operations per pixel).

The total number of operations per each pixel is 28.75. In the 4:2:0 YUV format, there are 4 Ys, 1 U, and 1 V for each pixel. The total number of pixels in one second becomes 10.4 million, which gives the total complexity for YUV to RGB color conversation 28.5 x 10.4 million = 299 MOPS.

In summary, the complexity of the analyzed MPEG decoder is in the range from 609.0 to 739.6 MOPS, as indicated in Figure 2.

Table 1 shows complexities of various H.261 and MPEG encoders and decoders reported in the literature. They differ from one to another due to different implementations of DCT and IDCT algorithms, search algorithms for motion estimation, and formulas used for RGB to YUV transformations.

Table 1. MOPS Requirements for a variety of (a) H.261, and (b) MPEG Encoders and Decoders, Reported in the Literature [4,5,6]

H.261 CODECS	Complexity of Encoders [MOPS]	Complexity of Decoders [MOPS]
CIF format at 30 fps Fast implementation of DCT Logarithmic search for motion estimation [5]	968	198
CIF at 15 fps Exhaustive motion estimation algorithm [4]	1,240-1,320	220-315
CIF at 30 fps Exhaustive motion estimation algorithm [4]	2,480-2,640	440-630
CIF at 30 fps Logarithmic search for motion estimation [6]	Total Encoder/Decoder 1,193	Total Encoder/Decoder 1,193

MPEG CODECS [5]	Complexity of Encoders [MOPS]			Complexity of Decoders [MOPS]		
	SIF 352x240	CCIR 601 720x486	HDTV 1440x1152	SIF 352x240	CCIR 601 720x486	HDTV 1440x1152
No B-frames	738	3,020	14,498	96	395	1,898
20% B-frames	847	3,467	16,645	101	415	1,996
50% B-frames	1,011	4,138	19,865	108	446	2,143
70% B-frames	1,120	4,585	22,012	113	466	2,241

MOPS requirements for a variety of multimedia functions are estimated and presented in Figure 3. In the same figure, the current trends in computing power of GP processors, programmable digital signal processors, and programmable video processors are plotted [5],[7]. It can be concluded that it is feasible to implement MPEG-1 or MPEG-2 decoders using GP or DSP processors. However, the encoder requirements, which are more than 1000 MOPS, are still outside of the complexity of GP processors and, therefore, dedicated multimedia processors must be designed.

3. DEDICATED MULTIMEDIA PROCESSORS

In designing dedicated multimedia processors, the selection of architectures depends on the speed requirements of the target function and the constraints on circuit integration, performance, power requirements, and cost. In order to assess and evaluate various architectures, the well-known AT-product is used [1]. Efficiency of an architecture (E) is defined as:

$$E = \frac{1}{Asi \times Tp} \qquad (2)$$

where: Asi is the required silicon area for a specific architecture under evaluation, and
           Tp is the effective processing time for one sample.

A comprehensive evaluation of dedicated multimedia processors can be found in [1]. Dedicated multimedia processors, presented in this section, are based on function specific architectures and programmable architectures.

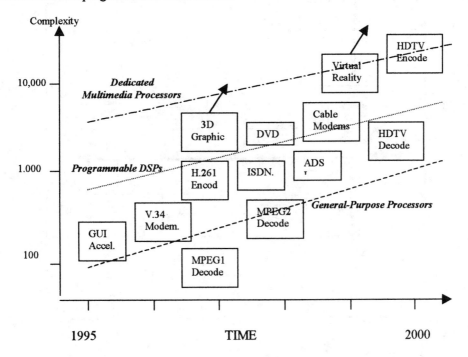

Figure 3. MOPS requirements for various multimedia functions and
the current trends in computing power.

3.1 FUNCTION-SPECIFIC ARCHITECTURES

Function-specific multimedia architectures provide limited, if any, programmability, because they use dedicated architectures for a specific encoding or decoding standard. However, their efficiency and speed are typically better compared to programmable architectures. The silicon area optimization achieved by function-specific architectures allows lower production cost.

Regardless of implementation details, the general design theme for dedicated multimedia processors consists of using

- a DSP or RISC core processor for main control, and
- special hardware accelerators for the DCT, quantization, entropy encoding, and motion estimation.

A block diagram of a typical function-specific architecture for a video encoder is shown in Figure 4. In the first generation of function-specific video processors, each of these functions was implemented in one chip, and a chipset was necessary to create the system for encoding or decoding. However, the next generations of function-specific architectures integrate all these functions in a single VLSI chip.

Some popular commercially available dedicated function specific video processors are listed in Figure 1.

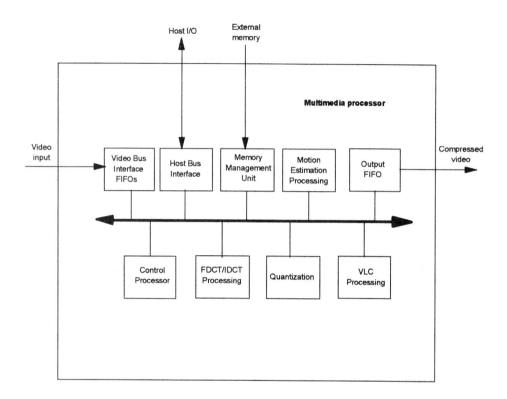

Figure 4. Block diagram of a typical function-specific architecture for a video encoder. The dedicated processors (or functional units) are used for various operations, such as DCT, quantization, variable length coding (VLC), motion estimation, etc.

3.2 PROGRAMMABLE DEDICATED ARCHITECTURES

In contrast to function oriented approach with limited flexibility, programmable architectures enable the processing of different tasks under software control. The main advantage of programmable architectures is the increased flexibility. Changes of architectural requirements, such as changes of algorithms or an extension of the application domain, can be handled by software changes.

On the other hand, programmable architectures incur a higher cost for design and manufacturing, since additional hardware for program control is required. In addition, programmable architectures require software development for the application. Video coding applications require real-time processing of the image data and, therefore, parallelization strategies have to be applied.

Two alternative programmable architectures include: (a) flexible programmable architectures and (b) adapted programmable architectures.

3.2.1 Flexible Programmable Architectures

Flexible programmable architectures, with moderate to high flexibility, are based on coprocessor concept as well as parallel datapaths and deeply pipelined designs. An example of a commercially available video processor, based on flexible programmable architecture, is TI's Multimedia Video Processor (MVP) TMS320C80 [6]. The MVP combines a RISC master processor and four DSP processors in a crossbar-based SIMD shared-memory architecture, as shown in Figure 5.

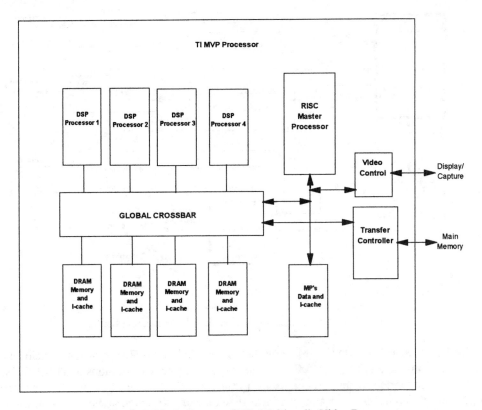

Figure 5. Block diagram of TI's Multimedia Video Processor.

The master processor can be used for control, floating-point operations, audio processing, or 3D graphics transformations. Each DSP performs all the typical operations of a general-purpose DSP and can also perform bit-field and multiple-pixel operations. Each DSP has multiple functional elements (multiplier, ALU, local registers, a barrel shifter, address generators, and a program-control flow unit), all controlled by very long 64-bit instruction words (VLIW concept). The RISC processor, DSP processors, and the memory modules are fully interconnected through the global crossbar network that can be switched at an instruction clock rate of 20 ns. A 50 MHz MVP executes more than 2 GOPS.

The MVP has been integrated into the MediaStation 5000 programmable multimedia system [8]. Its key function in this system is MPEG compression. The data flow in the system during MPEG compression is shown in Figure 6. Video data are captured into the video buffer at a resolution of 320x240. The MVP reads the data from the video buffer and stores it in the main (DRAM) memory. The MVP performs all MPEG compression functions on the data stored in the main memory. Similar operations are performed on the digitized audio samples. Once when the MVP completes the compression of a video or audio frame, the compressed bit stream is sent to the host computer, where the audio and video streams are multiplexed together, synchronized, and stored on a disk or transferred to a network.

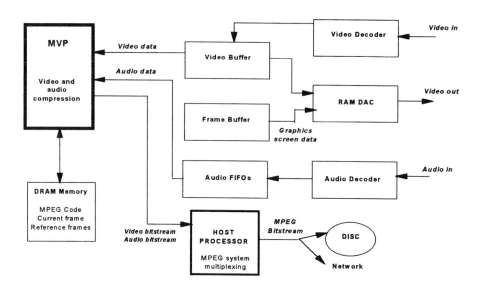

Figure 6. Data flow in the MVP during the MPEG compression [8].

Performance results, reported in [8], show that the MediaStation 5000 system can achieve a real-time compression (30 fps) of MPEG-1 video sequences with resolutions of 320x240 (SIF format). The reported compression times for I frames are 17.7 ms, for P frames 27.3 ms, and for B frames 30.5 ms; for all frame types less than the video frame period of 33 ms. Multiple MVPs are needed for real-time MPEG-2 encoding.

3.2.2 Adapted Programmable Architectures

Adapted programmable architectures provide increased efficiency by adapting the architecture to the specific requirements of video coding applications. These architectures provide dedicated modules for several tasks of the video codec algorithm, such as DCT module or variable length coding [9],[10].

Examples of a commercially available multimedia processor based on adapted programmable architecture are VideoRISC processors (VRP and VRP2) from C-Cube Microsystems. The VRP2 processor consists of a 32-bit RISC processor and two special functional units for variable-length coding and motion estimation, as shown in the block diagram in Figure 7. Specially designed instructions in the RISC processor provide an efficient implementation of the DCT and other video-related operations. The VRP can perform real-time MPEG-1 encoding and decoding; however, the real-time MPEG-2 encoding requires a design consisting of 8 to 13 VRP2 processors.

Table 2, adapted from [5], shows commercially available programmable processors and their features.

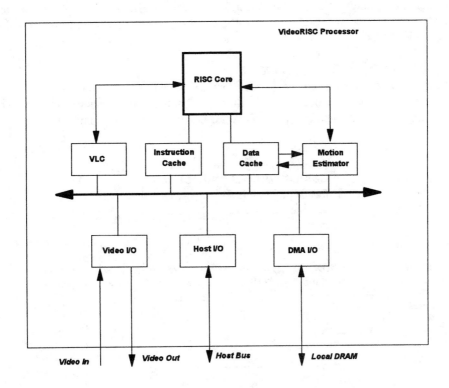

Figure 7. Block diagram of the C-Cube's VideoRISC processor, which applies an adapted programmable architecture.

Table 2. Programmable Multimedia Processors

Multimedia Processor	Clock [MHz]	GOPS	Key Characteristics
TI MVP (TMS320C80)	50	2	Flexible programmable MPEG-1 encoder/decoder MPEG-2 decoder H.261 codec
IIT VCP	80	2	Flexible programmable MPEG-1 encoder/decoder MPEG-2 decoder H.261 codec
NEC VSP3	300	1.5	Adapted programmable H.261 codec
C-Cube VideoRISC2	60	2.5	Adapted programmable MPEG-1 encoder/decoder
Matsushita VDSP2	100	2	Adapted programmable MPEG-2 encoder (requires external motion estimation)
Array Microsystems VideoFlow	50	1	Adapted programmable MPEG-1 encoder (requires External motion estimation and Huffman encoder) MPEG-2 decoder

Comparison of these two programmable architectures in terms of silicon area and frame rate, for a variety of codec implementations reported in the literature, is performed in [1]. Adapted processor design can achieve an efficiency gain in terms of the AT criterion by a factor 6-7 compared to flexible architectures. According to this study, 100mm²/GOPS for flexible architectures and 15 mm²/GOPS for adapted programmable architectures are needed for a typical video codec.

3.3 NEW ARCHITECTURAL TRENDS

The advanced dedicated multimedia processors use SIMD and VLIW architectural schemes and their variations to achieve very high parallelism. Figure 8 shows the architectural models applied in contemporary multimedia processors and several promising approaches.

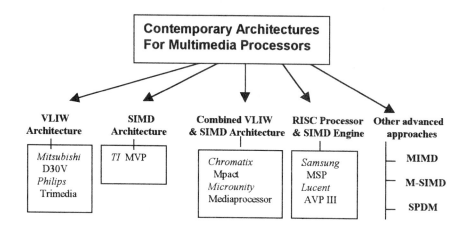

Figure 8. The architectural models applied in advanced multimedia processors.

Two commonly used parallel schemes, the SIMD and the VLIW, are described next.   The SIMD parallel computer organization, applied in multimedia processors, typically uses a single control unit (or master processor), a number of processing elements (PEs), and shared memory among the PEs, as shown in Figure 9 [11]. An interconnection network, such as crossbar switch, is used to interconnect the control processor, all PEs, and shared memory. The control processor evaluates every instruction. If it is a scalar or program control operation, a master processor will directly execute it. If the instruction is a vector operation, it will be broadcast to all the PEs for parallel execution. Partitioned data sets are distributed to the shared memory modules before starting the program execution. Then, the same instruction is executed by all the PEs in the same cycle, but on different data elements.

The VLIW architectural model is used in the latest dedicated multimedia processors. A typical VLIW architecture uses long instruction words with more than hundreds of bits in length. The idea behind VLIW concept is to reduce the number of cycles per instruction required for execution of highly complex and parallel algorithms by the use of multiple independent functional units that are directly controlled by long instruction words. This concept is illustrated in Figure 10, where multiple functional units operate in parallel under control of a long instruction. All functional units share a common large register file [11]. Different fields of the long instruction word contain opcodes to activate different functional units. Programs written for conventional 32-bit instruction word computers must be compacted to fit the VLIW instructions. This code compaction is typically done by a special compiler, which can predict branch outcomes by applying an algorithm known as trace scheduling.

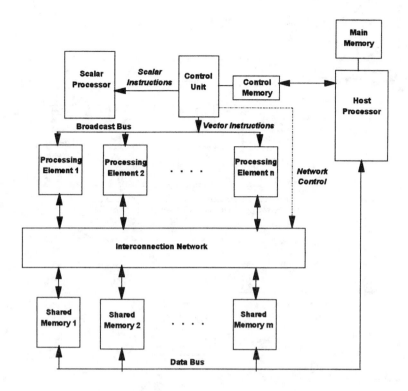

Figure 9. A general SIMD architectural model applied in multimedia processors.

SIMD and VLIW approaches require a giant routing network of buses and crossbar switches. VLIW machines fetch one large instruction per clock cycle and execute all operations on different ALUs. The advantage of this approach is that the ALUs can be specialized to fit the requirements of a given set of applications. However, these architectures' use of silicon is inefficient, because of the area required by the huge interconnection network and hundreds of pipeline data paths.

Another approach consists of combining a RISC processor with a SIMD machine that operates as a vector processor. A SIMD engine simply executes a conventional 32-bit instruction per clock cycle. This instruction processes a single vector of data points, which execute on a set of identical ALUs of a single pipeline. The data vector is treated as a single number for operand access and memory references. The advantage of this approach includes an efficient use of silicon, because only one pipeline has to be implemented, rather than hundreds.

The next generation of programmable multimedia processors incorporates increased parallelism by combining SIMD, VLIW, and some other hybrid architectural schemes. For example, the Mitsubishi D30V and Philips Semiconductor's Trimedia use the VLIW architecture to boost the performance of their video processors. The Chromatix Mpact multimedia processor combines both VLIW and SIMD concepts. The Lucent's AVP III uses a RISC processor and an SIMD engine for highly parallel operations, and has dedicated functional units for motion estimation and variable-length encoding and decoding.

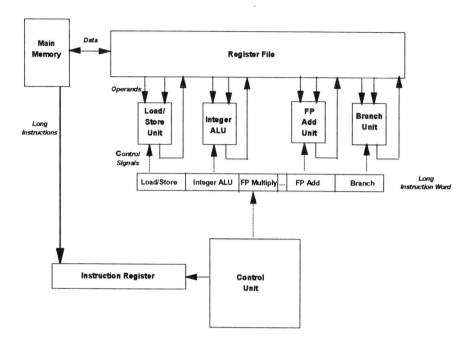

Figure 10. The very-long-instruction-word (VLIW) architectural model applied in
dedicated multimedia processors.

Samsung's Multimedia Signal Processor (MSP) combines a traditional RISC controller with
SIMD vector processor (VP) and special-purpose hardware engines. The RISC processor
runs the RTOS, performs overall system management and control, and some scalar media
processing. The VP processor performs high-performance signal processing. Special-purpose
hardware units handle some other functions that cannot be performed efficiently in the other
two units.

The Mediaprocessor from Microunity Systems Engineering (Sunnyvale, CA) combines a
128-bit load-and-store RISC engine (VLIW concept) with an SIMD-like variation, called
single-instruction-group-data (SIGD) parallelism. The architecture also includes a large
register file allowing tens of instructions to be executed in parallel. In addition, it also has an
execution pipeline that can be either deep (superpipelined), wide (superscalar), or both [7].

Promising Approaches
For the performance and functionality that will be required in next five years, several new
approaches are evolving (see Figure 8).

Multiple-instruction, multiple-data (MIMD) architectures offer 10 to 100 times more
throughput than existing VLIW and SIMD architectures. In the MIMD approach, multiple
instructions are executed in parallel on multiple data, requiring a control unit for each data
path. This requires a significant increase in silicon area to implement a control unit for each
data path. In addition, a major practical limitation of the MIMD approach is that its implicit
asynchronous nature increases the complexity of software development.

Due to these limitations, other hybrid solutions are being studied. One approach is referred to as *multiple single-instruction, multiple-data (M-SIMD)* or SIMD clustering. In this approach, several SIMD clusters are used, each of which consists of a specific number of data paths and an associated control unit. The data paths within each cluster operate as a SIMD array, while the clusters operate in the MIMD mode.

Another promising approach, referred to as *single-program, multiple-data (SPDM)*, combines SIMD and MIMD architectural features. The SIMD nature of this architecture is that it executes a single program or a task at a time, while the MIMD feature is that the data paths operate asynchronously.

4. GENERAL-PURPOSE PROCESSORS AND THEIR SUPPORT FOR MULTIMEDIA

The real-time multimedia processing on PCs and workstations is still handled by dedicated multimedia processors. However, the advanced GP processors provide an efficient support for certain multimedia applications. These processors can provide software-only solutions for many multimedia functions, which may significantly reduce the cost of the system.

GP processors apply the SIMD approach, described in previous section, by sharing their existing integer or floating-point data paths with a SIMD coprocessor. All leading processor vendors have recently designed GP processors that support multimedia, as shown in Figure 1. The main differences among these processors are in the way they reconfigure the internal register file structure to accommodate SIMD operations, and the multimedia instructions they choose to add.

4.1 GENERIC OPERATIONS IN MULTIMEDIA PROCESSING

The instruction mix of multimedia extensions of GP processors varies depending on their application focus. Table 3, adapted from [5], shows typical arithmetic operations required for the main functional blocks of the image and video compression standards, their complexity, inherent parallelism, and the speed-up achieved by current GP processors based on the SIMD approach.

The following conclusions drawn from Table 3 can be used as the main guidelines when specifying multimedia extensions for GP processors [5]:

- Input data and coefficients are typically 8-bit and 16-bit data elements.
- There is no need for floating-point operations.
- The multiply-accumulate operation is very common, but most of multiplications are with constants.
- Saturation arithmetic, where the result is clipped to the maximum or minimum value of a predefined range, is common in many operations.

With the exception of the Huffman (variable length) encoder and decoder, all other operations can be parallelized. Therefore, contemporary GP processors take advantage of this fact by applying the SIMD approach to these operations. A SIMD coprocessor typically performs up to four identical arithmetic or logic operations on different integer-type data. This approach can significantly boost the performance of the GP processors in handling multimedia applications with inherent parallelism (video compression and decompression, image filtering, etc.).

In addition to the arithmetic operations, video processing requires efficient data addressing and I/O processing, which is implemented in some GP processors.

Several contemporary GP processors with multimedia extensions are described in the following sections.

Table 3. Generic Operations Needed for Multimedia Compression

Function	Operations	Complexity	Parallelism
Color transformation (RGB-YUV) Preprocessing and Postprocessing	ΣC_iX_i, *clip()* $(X_i+X_j)/2$ $(1/4)\Sigma X_i$	Constant for every pixel	Highly parallel
FDCT and IDCT	$ax+b$ ΣC_iX_i	Either constant or a function of the average number of non-zero DCT coefficients	Depends on the implementation of FDCT or IDCT
Quantization	X_i/C_i	Constant for every pixel	Highly parallel
Dequantization	X_iC_i	Function of the average number of non-zero DCT coefficients	Highly parallel
Motion estimation (Encoder)	$\Sigma \mid X_i-Y_i \mid$ or $\Sigma(X_i-Y_i)^2$ $min(a,b)$	Depends on the selected motion estimation algorithm	Highly parallel both data-intensive and instruction-intensive processing
Motion compensation (Decoder)	X_i+cX_j Block copies Pixel interpolations	Block copies with pixel interpolations	Highly parallel
VLC (Huffman) Encoding/Decoding	Data shifts Comparisons	Function of the average number of symbols in the bitstream	Fully sequential

4.2 INTEL MMX TECHNOLOGY

Intel MMX technology for Intel Pentium processors is targeted to accelerate multimedia and communications applications, especially on the Internet. The fundamental architectural concept in the MMX system consists of the parallel, SIMD-like operation on small data elements (8 and 16 bits). The MMX system extends the basic integer instructions: *add, subtract, multiply, compare, and shift* into SIMD versions. These instructions perform parallel operations on multiple data elements packed into new 64-bit data types (8x8 bit, 4x16 bit, or 2x32 bit fixed-point elements). The MMX instructions also support saturation arithmetic, described in Section 4.1, which is important for multimedia applications.

The following example of *image composition* illustrates how the SIMD concept has been implemented in the Intel MMX system [12]. In this example, fade-in-fade-out effect in video production is performed between two images, A and B, to produce the final image, R, as a weighted average of A and B:

$$R = A*fade + B*(1-fade) = fade*(A-B)+B \tag{3}$$

where *fade* is gradually changing from 1 to 0 across a few video frames, thus producing a fade-in-fade-out effect. Let's assume that the frames are in RGB format, where R, G, and B components are not interleaved. In that case, the MMX processor can access four elements of both A and B frames in a single memory access, subtract them in parallel, and then multiply the result with the fade factor in parallel, as illustrated in Figure 11. The MMX code performing this operation is shown in Figure 12.

Performance results for the Pentium processor with MMX technology, reported in [12], show the improvement between 65% to 370% over the same Pentium processor without MMX technology. For example, MPEG-1 video decompression speed up with MMX is about 80%, while some other applications, such as image filtering speed up to 370%.

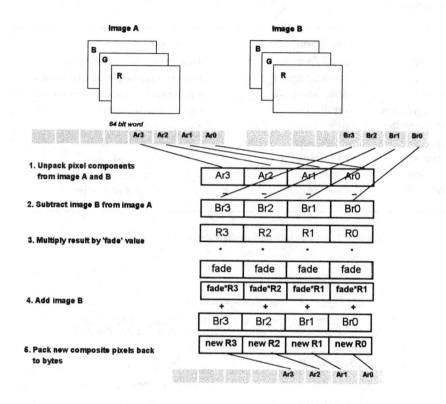

Figure 11. Image composition – fade-in-fade-out effect performed by the MMX system [12].

4.3 SUN'S VISUAL INSTRUCTION SET

Sun has developed Visual Instruction Set (VIS) for its UltraSPARC processors, which provides graphics and image processing capabilities needed for multimedia applications [13],[14]. The VIS supports new data types used for video processing pixels and fixed data. Pixels consist of four 8-bit unsigned integers contained in a 32-bit word, while fixed data consist of either four 16-bit fixed point components or two 32-bit fixed point components both contained in a 64-bit word. The SIMD concept has also been applied for some arithmetic and logic instructions (multiplication, addition, subtraction, and logical evaluations), providing parallel operation on four pixels. An innovative concept, applied in the UltraSPARC, is the *motion estimation instruction* (PDIST), implemented in hardware rather than software. The hardware-implemented instruction PDIST computes the sum of the absolute differences between two 8 pixel vectors, which would require about 48 operations on most processors. Accumulating the error for a 16x16 block requires only 32 PDIST instructions; this operation typically requires 1500 conventional instructions. The hardware implementation of the PDIST (pixel distance) instruction is shown in Figure 13. The circuitry consists of three 4:2 adders, two 11-bit adders, and a 53-bit incrementer. It operates on 8-bit pixels, stored in a pair of double-precision registers, and produces the result in a single-cycle operation.

As reported in [2],[14], the VIS provides four times or greater speedup for most of the time-critical computations for video decompression, including IDCT, motion estimation, and color conversion. According to an analysis, reported in [2], a 200-MHz UltraSPARC processor is capable of decoding MPEG-2 video of 720x480 pixels resolution at 30 fps entirely in software.

pxor	mm7,mm7	; zero out mm7
movq	mm3,fade_val	; load 4 times replicated fade value
movd	mm0,image A	; load 4 red pixel components from image A
movd	mm1,image B	; load 4 red pixel components from image B
punpcklbw	mm0,mm7	; unpack 4 pixels to 16 bits
punpcklbw	mm1,mm7	; unpack 4 pixels to 16 bits
psubw	mm0,mm1	; subtract image B from A
pmulhw	mm0,mm3	; multiply result by *fade* values
paddw	mm0,mm1	; add result to image B
packuswb	mm0,mm7	; pack 16-bit result back to bytes

Figure 12. MMX code performing fade-in-fade-out effect [12].

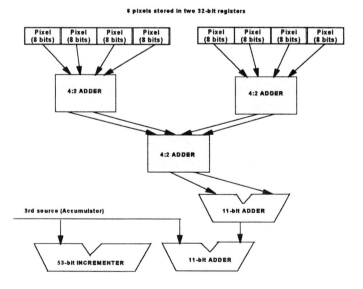

Figure 13. The implementation of the motion estimation instruction in UltraSPARC processor.

4.4 OTHER GENERAL-PURPOSE PROCESSORS

The majority of contemporary general-purpose processors also support multimedia applications (Figure 1). They all apply similar concepts, such as support for new data types and SIMD-like parallel execution of arithmetic and logic operations.

4.4.1 HP PA7100LC Processor

Hewlett-Packard has introduced the PA7100LC processor and its successor HP-PA RISC2 [15]. The processor has two ALU units, which allows a parallelism of four 16-bit operations per cycle. Implementing the color conversation step together with the color recovery step has enhanced the graphics subsystem. Color conversation converts between YCbCr and the RGB color formats, while color recovery allows 24-bit RGB color that had been "color compressed" into 8 bits to be converted back to 24-bit color before being displayed (dithering operation). This enhancement reduces the display operation in MPEG decoding. The memory controller and the I/O controller have been integrated, which significantly reduces the overhead in the memory to frame buffer bandwidth.

4.4.2 DEC Alpha 21164 Processor and MVI Extensions

The Alpha architecture has been enhanced with Motion Video Instruction (MVI) extensions [16]. The MVI consists of three classes of instructions: pixel-error instruction (PERR), Max/Min, and Pack/Unpack instructions. The PERR motion estimation instruction computes the sum of absolute value of differences of eight pairs of bytes. It replaces nine traditional operations. The Max and Min instructions allow efficient clamping of pixel values to the maximum or minimum values, which is convenient for image and video processing applications. The Pack and Unpack instructions expand and contract the data width on bytes and words. Initial results indicate that MVI improves MPEG-2 compression performance more than 400%, compared to the Alpha 21164 processor without MVI [16].

4.4.3 MIPS V Processor and SGI MDMX Extensions

MIPS V processor supports multimedia applications through its instruction-set architecture (ISA) extensions and MIPS Digital Media Extensions (MDMX). Similar to other processors, ISA extensions use new data types (8 bits and 16 bits) and a SIMD approach to perform some arithmetic and logical operations in parallel. MIPS ISA extensions, unlike other processors, also provide support for single-precision floating point operations, which are useful for front end image and video synthesis. MDMX extensions, nicknamed Mad Max, use the innovation from the DSP world, by providing an accumulator with extra precision to support the width required by intermediate calculations. Unlike DSPs, MDMX implements a vector accumulator to take advantage of the SIMD aspect of the instruction set.

4.5 PERFORMANCE ANALYSIS

In summary, GP processors that support multimedia apply new integer data types, well suited for multimedia, new multimedia instructions, and an SIMD architecture for parallel execution of identical instructions on different data.

An example, adapted from [2], shows how a GP processor with an SIMD coprocessor can speedup the MPEG-2 decoding. In the example in Section 2, we calculated the complexity of a typical MPEG-2 decoder, and the obtained results were in the range 609-740 MOPS. However, in most GP processors integer multiplication has a higher complexity than other instructions and, therefore, we will assume that one multiplication is equivalent to 4 generic operations. In this case, the complexity of the MPEG-2 decoder becomes 735 to 876 MOPS for a bit rate of 4 Mbps.

As indicated earlier, the block 1 bit stream parsing and Huffman decoder, cannot be paralellized, and its complexity remains the same – 12 MOPS. However, operations in all the other blocks can be parallelized by a factor 4, assuming a SIMD coprocessor that executes four identical parallel operations on different data. The complexity of the MPEG-2 decoder, implemented on such GP processor, becomes in the 194 to 227 MOPS range, as illustrated in Table 4.

Similarly, for an increased bit rate of 8 Mbps, the total MPEG-2 complexity on a GP processor with an SIMD coprocessor becomes 220-250 MOPS, and for 16 Mbps, is in the 320-352 MOPS range [2].

Table 4. The Complexity of the MPEG-2 Decoder and Its Implementation on a GP Processor with an SIMD Coprocessor

MPEG-2 Functions	Complexity [MOPS]	Parallel Implementation on a GP Processor Using a SIMD coprocessor
Parser & VLC	12	12
Dequantization	14	4
IDCT	206	52
Motion Compensation	143-274	36-69
YUV to RGB Conversion	360	90
TOTAL COMPLEXITY	735-876	194-227

Contemporary GP processors use superscalar RISC architectures, in which the number of executed instructions is at least 2 x Clock Frequency. Therefore, a 200 MHz processor can execute about 400 MOPS, which suggests that a software-only MPEG-2 decoder can be easily implemented. However, according to Table 1, MPEG encoders require 3,000 to 22,000 MOPS, and even their parallel implementation using a SIMD approach, will require around 1,000 MOPS. This still cannot be achieved with GP processors and dedicated multimedia processors must be used.

5. CONCLUSIONS

In summary, general-purpose designers have recently realized that they should begin investing some of the available chip real estate to support multimedia. We should expect that new generations of GP processors would devote more and more transistors to multimedia. How far and how fast this process will go will be determined by the market demand. By the end of this decade we may see a complete MPEG decoder, large frame buffers, a variety of functional units for video, image, and audio processing, and much more, all packed within a single processor chip.

On the other hand, computationally intensive multimedia functions, such as MPEG encoding, HDTV codecs, 3D processing, and virtual reality, will still require dedicated processors for a long time to come. Therefore, we can expect that general-purpose processors that support multimedia and dedicated multimedia processors will coexist for some time.

REFERENCES

1. Pirsch, P., Demassieux, N., and Gehrke, W., "VLSI Architectures for Video Compression – A Survey," *Proceedings of the IEEE*, 83(2), 220-246, February 1995.
2. Zhou, C-G., Kohn, L., Rice, D., Kabir, I., Jabbi, A., and Hu, X-P., "MPEG Video Decoding with the UltraSPARC Visual Instruction Set," *Proceedings of the IEEE Compcon*, San Francisco, CA, March 1995, pp. 470-475.
3. Pennenbaker, W.B. and Mitchell, J.L., "JPEG Still Image Data Compression Standard," Van Nostrand Reinhold, New York, 1993.
4. Fujiwara, H., Liou, M.L., Sun, M-T., Yang, K-M., Maruyama, M., Shomura, K., and Ohyama, K., "An All-ASCI Implementation of a Low Bit-rate Video Codec," *IEEE Trans. On Circuits and Systems for Video Technology*, 2(2), 123-134, June 1992.
5. Bhaskaran, V. and Konstantinides, K., "Image and Video Compression Standards – Algorithms and Architectures," Kluwer Academic Publishers, Boston, MA, 1995.
6. Guttag, K., Gove, R.J., and Van Aken, J.R., "A Single-Chip Multiprocessor For Multimedia: The MVP," *IEEE Computer Graphics & Applications*, 53-64, November 1992.
7. Cole, B., "New Processors Up Multimedia's Punch," *Electronic Engineering Times*, 71, February 3, 1997.
8. Lee, W., Kim, Y., Gove, R.J., and Reed, C.J., "MediaStation 5000: Integrating Video and Audio," *IEEE MultiMedia*, 1(2), 50-61, Summer 1994.
9. Ackland, B., "The Role of VLSI in Multimedia," *IEEE J. Solid-State Circuits*, 29, 1886-1893, December 1992.
10. Akari, T. et al., "Video DSP Architecture for MPEG2 Codec," *Proceedings of ICASSP*, Vol. 2, IEEE Press, 417-420, 1994.
11. Hwang, K., "Advanced Computer Architecture with Parallel Programming," McGraw-Hill, 1993.
12. Peleg, A., Wilkie, S., and Weiser, U., "Intel MMX for Multimedia PCs," *Communications of the ACM*, 40(1), 25-38, January 1997.
13. Tremblay, M., O'Connor, J.M., Narayanan, V., and Liang, H., "VIS Speeds New Media Processing," *IEEE Micro*, 16(4), 10-20, August 1996.
14. Kohn, L., Maturana, G., Tremblay, M., Prabhu, A., and Zyner, G., "The Visual Instruction Set (VIS) in UltraSPARC," *Proceedings of the IEEE Compcon*, San Francisco, CA, 462-469, March 1995.
15. Lee, R.B. "Realtime MPEG Video via Software Decompression on a PA-RISC Processor," *Proceedings of the IEEE Compcon*, San Francisco, CA, 186-192, March 1995.
16. Bannon, P. and Jain, A., "MVI Instructions Boost Alpha Processor," *Electronic Engineering Times*, 74, February 3, 1997.

22

AUTHORING TECHNIQUES FOR TEMPORAL SCENARIOS OF MULTIMEDIA DOCUMENTS

Muriel Jourdan, Nabil Layaïda, and Cécile Roisin
OPERA Project, INRIA Rhône-Alpes
655 Avenue de l'Europe,
38330 Montbonnot, France
e-mail: [Muriel.Jourdan, Nabil.Layaida, Cecile.Roisin]@inrialpes.fr
http://opera.inrialpes.fr/OPERA/

1. **INTRODUCTION**..470
2. **AN EXAMPLE OF A MULTIMEDIA DOCUMENT** 471
3. **MULTIMEDIA AUTHORING REQUIREMENTS**.................................472
    3.1 EXPRESSIVE POWER..472
    3.2 AUTHORING CAPABILITIES 476
4. **STATE OF THE ART THROUGH TWO CLASSES OF APPROACHES** 477
    4.1 OPERATIONAL APPROACHES...478
    4.2 CONSTRAINT-BASED APPROACHES 482
5. **SYNTHESIS**...486
    REFERENCES 488

Abstract. This chapter presents a survey on authoring techniques for the creation of temporal scenarios for multimedia documents. We classify existing techniques by comparing them against two kinds of requirements: expressive power and authoring capabilities. These two sets of requirements lead to grouping multimedia authoring systems into two classes: operational and constraint-based. Both approaches provide synchronization facilities allowing the construction of temporal scenarios. But, the in-depth analysis achieved in this chapter shows that they do not fulfill the same requirements. This analysis is illustrated by a document example that is specified using each presented system.

1. INTRODUCTION

In traditional text oriented document systems, the communication mode is characterized by the spatial nature of information layout and the eye's ability to actively browse parts of the display. The reader is active while the rendering itself is passive. This active-passive role is reversed in audio-video communications; information flows actively to a passive listener or viewer. Interactive multimedia documents combine both of these roles as they contain both spatial and temporal types of information. In addition, they allow the reader to interact with the document presentation. For example, hypermedia links can be used to navigate inside the same document and/or between different documents.

Multimedia documents combine different types of elements in time and space like video, audio, still-picture, text, synthesized image, etc. Compared to classical documents, multimedia documents are characterized by inherent temporal dimension. Basic media objects, like video, have intrinsic duration. Furthermore, they can be temporally organized by the author, which adds to the document a temporal structure called the **temporal scenario**.

Due to this temporal dimension, building an authoring tool is a challenging task because the **Wysiwyg** paradigm, used for classical documents, is not relevant any more; it is not possible to specify a dynamic behavior and to immediately see its result. Edition and presentation operations are carried out at different times and by different users; the first being performed by the authors, the second by the readers. So we must distinguish between the specification phase (or editing phase) of the temporal scenario and its presentation phase (or execution phase).

An authoring system for multimedia documents must handle these two phases, because it is essential for an author to easily skip from the editing phase to the execution phase in order to gradually test and improve the document presentation. Within the past decade, numerous research papers (Cmifed [26], Firefly [3], HTSPN [23], HPAS [29], Interval Expressions [13], Isis [24], Madeus [9]), have presented various ways of specifying temporal scenarios, focusing on a particular understanding of temporal synchronization. The purpose of this chapter is to classify and discuss the relevance of these proposals. Compared with other surveys on multimedia synchronization [2], [7], [15], [19], [21] and [28], this study is characterized by the twofold step:

- We distinguish between two kinds of requirements: expressive power and authoring capabilities.

- We classify the various ways of specifying temporal scenarios into two broad classes: operational and constraint-based approaches.

This allows a clearer framework for classifying and comparing existing authoring environments from the temporal dimension point of view.

Moreover, we clarify what often becomes confusing when dealing with temporal scenario specifications, i.e., the various semantics that are associated with the Allen's operators [1]. It is an important point, since it is very common in multimedia authoring that expressive power is considered as equivalent to the ability to express all the Allen's operators. In this chapter, we give more precise definitions of expressive power requirements for multimedia specifications. As a result, this allows a more rigorous basis for comparing the different approaches.

The chapter is organized into four sections. In the first, we present a working example containing interesting challenges as far as both expressiveness and authoring capabilities needs are concerned. In the second section, we define and detail these two kinds of requirements. The third section defines the two classes of approaches (operational and constraint based) and presents some well-known authoring environments for each class and check if they fulfill the requirements. The last section concludes this overview. In particular, like in [7], a table summarizes the results for the environments covered in this study.

2. AN EXAMPLE OF A MULTIMEDIA DOCUMENT

Before getting to the main purpose of the chapter, we present a multimedia document example. In this example, we cover some relevant cases that can be required when composing multimedia documents (see Section 3). Its specification is (partially) given through the different systems that we analyze in Section 4.

"BestCom" is a communication company that answers a call of the International Football Organization for the design of a mascot. In order to provide an attractive and complete response, BestCom has created a multimedia document to be presented to its client.

The scenario is organized into two parts: (1) a presentation of the company (called Company) and (2) a presentation of the mascot proposal (called Mascot). These two parts of the scenario can be read sequentially but hypermedia links allow the reader to jump at any time from one part of the document to the other.

The Company part should globally last about 3 minutes. It is composed of a sequence of three objects: an audio clip (History) which gives the history of the company, followed by a textual message displaying the name of the company on the screen (Name), and ends with a graphic listing its main achievements (PressBook). History audio lasts for approximately 1 minute, Name and PressBook must each be one displayed for at least 45 seconds. In addition to this first specification, the author added a 2-minute movie that gives an overview of the company together with its geographical localization (called Geography). This movie must be started so that the mapping of the Name on the screen is synchronized with the period of the Geography movie when the company building appears (approximately 20 seconds from its beginning).

The Mascot part is composed mainly of a virtual animation of the proposal (Animated Proposal). This animation ends with a last picture of the mascot (Proposal). This last frame remains displayed on the screen during 30 seconds together with a balloon (Balloon) on the right of the mascot mouth, which contains its name. In addition, in order to see the mascot name faster, the reader is asked by an audio message (Message) to click on a button (Button) during the presentation of the Animated Proposal. When the reader clicks on the button, the audio message stops and the balloon appears at the top of the screen and moves until it reaches its final position (near the mouth of the mascot) exactly when the animation ends. Figure 1 gives a possible execution of this document in which the reader of the document has interacted twice. At second 140, after the beginning of the document, he jumped to the Mascot part (cropping the presentation of the Company Press-book) and, at the 180th second, he activated the button to see the mascot Name faster. As a consequence, the name appears on a balloon at the top of the screen and moves during such a period of time that it stops exactly when the animated proposal ends.

We will show in Section 4 how some parts of this example could be specified in various approaches (see Figures 5 to 11).

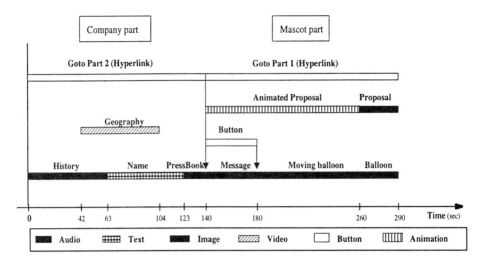

Figure 1. A possible execution for the Mascot presentation.

3. MULTIMEDIA AUTHORING REQUIREMENTS

The variety of multimedia approaches reflects the large number of requirements that have to be covered by a multimedia authoring system, but these needs are only partially fulfilled by existing applications. In order to give a structured and readable analysis, we focus only on authoring requirements and group them in two main classes (expressive power and authoring capabilities).

3.1. EXPRESSIVE POWER

The expressive power of an authoring system is related to the ability of the system to cover a broad range of temporal scenarios required by the author. This criterion is hard to measure since defining an acceptable level of expressive power is strongly dependent on author practice and experience. Furthermore, we still have limited knowledge about the authoring process of time-based documents. So far, expressive power has been mainly considered mainly from an informal point of view. In this chapter, we try a more formal approach.

We consider a document presented by an authoring system as a state machine (see Figure 2) characterized by:
A set of objects O.
A set of inputs IN (clock tics and events on the objects).
A set of outputs OUT (start, stop, ... on the objects).
An execution loop defined as getting some inputs, producing some outputs, and updating some state variables.

This state machine can be modeled by a Mealy automata where each state is a node and each arc is labeled by an input vector and an output vector that reflect the state transitions representing the document behavior.

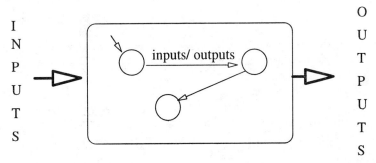

Figure 2. State machine of a document.

With this description, the expressive power of a specification language can be evaluated by its ability to describe any state machine from a given set of objects and their related events. In the remaining part of this chapter, we will refine this model and use it to obtain a comparison criteria.

We have classified authoring requirements into three sets: (a) the needs arising from the intrinsic nature of the objects composing multimedia documents, (b) those arising from their composition, and, finally, (c) those related to hypermedia navigation. Our analysis is independent from the underlying method used by the author to build these documents (programming language, constraint operators, tree structure, etc.).

(a) Multimedia objects

Authoring environments must provide the author with:

A wide variety of basic objects (issue 1): Objects like text, video, audio, still pictures, virtual animations, programs, or applets are good examples of what must be supported. These objects differ in nature, as they can be discrete: their content is delivered instantaneously such as text and still picture; or continuous: their content is delivered progressively such as video or audio.

Therefore, the set O of objects is composed of DO (Discrete Objects) and CO (Continuous Objects).

A presentation system must allow distinction between mapping (and unmapping) of objects and execution or playtime of continuous objects. For example, a video can be mapped onto the screen (the first image is displayed) but its execution can be run at a different instant. Therefore, presenting objects to a reader requires the following outputs of the state machine:

map(o), unmap(o) for displayed objects,
start(co), stop(co), pause(co), and resume(co) for continuous objects.

- **The possibility to control the delivery of continuous objects (issue 2):** The author must be able to express that the content of a continuous object is to be completely delivered (i.e., it will not be interrupted or cropped) even if its end has to be synchronized with other time points. For instance, in our example, the virtual animation (Animated Proposal) has to be delivered entirely; otherwise, the spatial synchronization required between the Balloon and the Mascot picture cannot be met.

- **Interactivity capabilities (issue 3):** The author must be able to make any kind of objects activable (called buttons) during a given period of time with which the reader can interact during the presentation of the document.

  Therefore, objects are set (unset) activable by the two following outputs of the state machine: activable(o) and disactivable(o). A user activation on such an object o is defined by the click(o) input.

- **Temporal style definitions (issue 4):** motion effects or audio with variation of volume are examples of temporal styles. They can be associated at any temporal interval with any discrete or continuous object o by the two outputs of the state machine: styleon(o, s) and styleoff(o, s).

- **A support for unpredictable objects (issue 5):** Java applets or some videos are examples of such kinds of objects. They are either continuous objects or objects transformed into buttons.

  - Continuous objects are unpredictable if their duration is not known beforehand or statically [3], because their effective duration at presentation time can be affected by external factors (resource limitations like machine load for instance). Therefore, it is impossible to assign them a static duration if their content must be completely delivered.

  - Buttons are by nature always unpredictable since their effective duration is defined by the interaction of the reader during the presentation phase (and may change at every execution).

The distinction between predictable an unpredictable objects depends not only on the nature of the objects (video, audio) but also on their internal coding and the semantics of their content. For example, to recover a network delay, the duration of a video coded in MPEG can be controlled by dropping some of its frames [18]. Similarly, the duration of a synthetic audio should be easier to control than a recorded speech. Thus, some objects can become predictable in authoring systems with powerful object access, manipulation, and rendering techniques, while they can be considered as unpredictable in less advanced systems. For this reason we give the following definition:

*An object is **predictable** in a particular environment if and only if the presentation system guarantees its duration without semantic loss.*

Therefore, the set CO of continuous objects contains the set UCO of unpredictable continuous objects and the state machine can receive another kind of inputs: end(uco) which is the event related to the normal termination of an UCO object.

In our example, the three sensible areas (the two hyperlinks and the Button) are unpredictable. Moreover, audio and video are considered as unpredictable objects while the Animated Proposal is considered as predictable since it is a synthesized animation (in animated gif).

(b) Temporal Composition (issue 6)

As far as expressive power is concerned, temporal composition aims at expressing any arbitrary ordering between temporal intervals corresponding to the different objects. In terms of the state machine model, this is equivalent to the ability to describe any significant state machines for a given set of objects and their related events as identified.

A state machine is said to be not significant when it contains some executions (sequences of transitions from an initial state) which are inconsistent. For instance, a sequence in which an object is stopped before it begins running is irrelevant. Taking into account the different requirements listed above, the input and output sets of the state machine model of a document can be more precisely defined:

$IN = \{tic, click(o), end(uco)\}$, see issues 3 and 5.
$OUT = \{map(o), unmap(o), start(co), stop(co), pause(co), resume(co), styleon(o,s),$
$styleoff(o,s), activable(o), disactivable(o)\}$, see issues 1, 3 and 4.

Let O, IN, OUT be the set of objects, inputs, and outputs; MS(O, IN, OUT) be the set of significant state machines that can be defined upon O, IN, and OUT by a specification language S. The comparison of the expressive power between two specification languages S1 and S2 can be done by comparing the sets of objects (O1, O2), of inputs (IN1, IN2), of outputs (OUT1, OUT2), and the state machines (MS1(O1, IN1, OUT1), MS2(O2, IN2, OUT2)) of the languages.

(c) Interactions (issue 7)

Two kinds of interactions can be distinguished

- Temporal Access Control (TAC) such as pause, resume, fast-forward, etc., which provide the reader with a way to control the document rendering. TAC does not depend on the document and, therefore, it does not appear in the specification of the temporal scenario.

- Document interactions through buttons (see issue 3) whose semantics are specified in the document specification.

Document interactions can be classified into two classes according to their associated semantics. If the interaction involves all the active objects of the document at the presentation time, it is named a **global interaction**; if only a subpart of this set is concerned by the interaction, it is **a local interaction**. It is obvious that both kinds of interaction appear in a multimedia specification as:

- A usual hypertext link (allowing navigation facilities) is a global interaction since it interrupts or freezes the execution of all the active objects of the document. This results in starting other objects in another part of either the same document or another document. The hypermedia links between the two parts of the example are global interactions.

- On the contrary, a local button involving only a sub-part of a scenario is a local interaction; the button of the Mascot part interrupts the audio message and starts the balloon movement while the Animated Proposal is not affected.

A global interaction can be seen as a special case of local interaction, but we prefer to consider it separate, as their management is different (local ones are much more difficult to handle for synchronization reasons) and most of the existing systems do not provide local interactions but only global ones.

3.2 AUTHORING CAPABILITIES

At this point, the relevant question is how long it takes for an author to design a scenario. We specified seven criteria to measure the efficiency of a given approach regarding the issue of authoring capabilities. These are:

- **Adaptability to computer illiterate people (issue 8):** The idea is to evaluate how a system can be used efficiently by a large community of authors, in particular, those having no particular skills in computer programming.

- **Straightforward design (issue 9):** The author has a temporal organization of objects in his mind which is expressed mainly in terms of relative temporal placements between objects, i.e., temporal information (duration or ending/beginning instants) is given by reference to objects.[1] An authoring system must allow the user to specify the temporal relations in any order.

  For instance, in the Company part (Figure 1), the author would first specify a sequence between three objects (History, Name and Pressbook) and then synchronization of a 20 s of shift between the beginning of Name and the beginning of the Geography Video. The ease of translating these placements in terms of a given authoring approach is the whole question.

- **Indeterministic scenario authoring capabilities (issue 10):** A scenario can specify multiple presentations of the same document due to the presence of unpredictable objects. Thus the authoring system must help the author get a global perception of his document, since he cannot manually explore all the possible solutions. This can be done by visualization tools and by static checking techniques which can inform the author about some global properties of the scenario, as, for instance, the mutual exclusion of two audios.

- **Adaptability to the incremental nature of the editing process:** Building an interactive multimedia document is a cyclic "specify, test, and modify" process; one never reaches the right temporal layout at the first stage. Two requirements follow this observation:

  1. **Ease of local modifications (issue 11):** It must be easy for the author to make a local change in the specification. In particular, the authoring system must undertake the global consequences of a local change into the document specification, both from the structural and temporal points of view. This feature depends heavily on the used authoring approach and, therefore, it will be illustrated later for each presented method.

  2. **Fast editing/presentation cycle (issue 12):** It should be fast to switch between the specification phase of a document and its presentation.

---

[1] By contrast with an absolute placement which supposes that temporal information of an object is defined without taking into account the other objects.

- **Abstraction capabilities (issue 13):** A multimedia authoring system must help the author compose large documents by providing the means to abstract and reuse parts of documents.

- **Multimedia document models (issue 14):** Generic models such as SGML [12] or XML [30] of textual documents have improved document manipulation technologies. Similarly, the ability to define classes of multimedia documents will ease the author's task and will enhance multimedia environments by providing automatic document processing,

- **Multigrids reading support (issue 15):** A multimedia document should be understandable by different categories of readers. Categories can be defined by the native language of the readers or the level of the students in a course. An authoring tool must help the author while designing such kind of documents by allowing sharing of common parts which can be objects as well as temporal scenarios.

4. STATE OF THE ART THROUGH TWO CLASSES OF APPROACHES

In this chapter, we distinguish between two classes of authoring approaches, operational and constraint-based. They have been defined depending on how close the document description is to the presentation level. Unlike other classifications, we do not consider imperative against declarative approaches that allow only separating programming or script-based paradigms from other paradigms. Instead, we have chosen to discuss constraint-based and operational approaches since they allow a better identification of common properties with respect to the requirements previously mentioned.

The two classes of approaches are defined as follows:

- Operational approaches are based on the direct specification of the state machine, which defines the temporal scenario of the document (see Section 1.1). The author specifies how a scenario must be executed based on either a script language or an operational structure (tree or Petri-nets are good examples). Therefore, the presentation phase directly implements the operational semantics provided by the used structure.[2]

- Constraint-based approaches set the specification outside this operational scheme (see Figure 3). They are based on constraint programming and are characterized by a formatting phase that computes starting times and duration, as required by the scenario. This formatting phase can be seen as a compilation of a declarative specification into an operational structure, which can be interpreted by the presentation phase. Thus, the author specifies what scenario he needs without involvement of how to get the result in terms of operational actions, in a declarative way.

The end of the section is devoted to the presentation of main multimedia authoring systems in light of the requirements and classification previously stated.

---

[2] Some operational approaches (like tree structures) also have this declarative property, but their formalism is closer to the operational structure than to the constraint-based one.

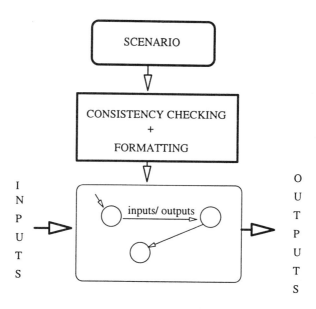

Figure 3. The state machine for the constraint-based approach.

4.1. OPERATIONAL APPROACHES

We present operational approaches through three classes: absolute temporal axis, script languages, and graphical structures. The authoring process of these approaches is mainly characterized by the fact that authors have to usually give more temporal information as necessary.

Let's take the following example. The author wants to synchronize (both their beginning and ending) a video with a sequence of one still picture and another video. Assume that the duration of the two videos is predictable. With an operational approach (other than scripts), the author has two solutions: either he defines duration of the three objects, or he only defines the duration of the still picture and specifies that the shorter video interrupts the longer one. In the first solution, the author must assign duration values and as a result we obtain a scenario that is not easy to modify. In the second solution, the end of one video is not delivered entirely to the reader. This abnormal ending of one video may not satisfy the author.

4.1.1. Absolute Temporal Axis

The most intuitive way to identify a temporal specification is to place objects on a temporal axis. Doing so, the author gives absolute values for the beginning instant and the duration of each object. In such approaches, the corresponding state machine has only tics as inputs (see Figure 4); it does not take into account either unpredictable objects (issue 5) or buttons (issue 3).

Authoring capabilities of such approaches are poor. Issue 8 is met, thanks to the simplicity of the metaphor, while the others are far from being fulfilled. For instance, the author has to translate each relative placement into absolute ones (issue 9) preventing him from any easy modifications (issue 11).

In fact, such a paradigm is always used together with another kind of approach. For instance, Macromedia Director [20] uses both an absolute temporal axis and a script language.

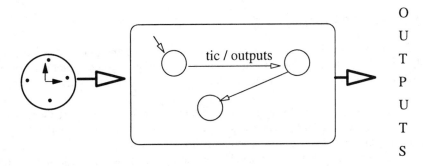

Figure 4. Input of the state machine associated with a absolute temporal axis.

4.1.2. Script Languages

The most widespread approaches for specifying multimedia documents are based on the programming paradigm Lingo [20], IconAuthor [11], MHEG [22]. It is obvious that these approaches are the most expressive as they are capable of implementing scenarios with any arbitrary complexity. In MHEG, for example, a temporal behavior can be associated to any composite object by means of a "link object" composed of a set of "event & conditions -> actions" statements. Thus, as far as the expressive power requirements are concerned, these approaches are very satisfactory (issues 1 to 7), even if most existing languages do not fit all of them. As an example, the Company part is given in Figure 5 in terms of the inputs (end(o)) and the outputs (start, map, unmap) of the state machine model previously defined.

Start audio "History.au";

Wait (40);

Start video "Geography.mpeg" ;

When end(History)

 Map text "Name.doc";

Wait (45);

Unmap text "Name.doc" ;

Map picture "PressBook.pic" ;

Wait (45);

Unmap picture "PressBook" ;

Figure 5. The Company part scenario in script language.

The weak side of these approaches is their poor authoring capabilities. Except for the abstraction and multi-grids abilities provided with the object-oriented design and macro facilities in MHEG (issues 13 and 15), they cannot perfectly meet the authoring requirements previously listed. First of all, authors are assumed to have programming skills (issue 8). Moreover, it is difficult to achieve a temporal placement by using a script language and to modify an existing script in order to get a new temporal organization (issues 9 and 11).

In some languages like MHEG, the temporal composition is spread among the objects behavior programs, preventing the author from getting a global view of his scenario.

4.1.3. Graphical Structures

In order to provide higher level specification interfaces and to give a better perception of the structure of the temporal composition, some tools propose to use graphical structures such as trees and Petri-nets in order to specify the organization of the document.

As far as expressive power is concerned, the common problem of these approaches is that some scenarios cannot be expressed due to the necessity of handling variables to dynamically compute some duration (combination of issues 5 and 6). This is the case with the Mascot part of our example. We need a variable to compute the duration of the balloon movement (or its speed), which depends on the activation instant of the button, in order to respect the termination constraint (Balloon near the Mascot mouth). Indeed, the specification is not met if the speed of that movement is statically computed. The resulting execution would interrupt either the balloon movement or the animation (depending on which one terminates first).

The other common limit is the restriction of issue 11 and, more precisely, about the partial support of automatic adjustment of duration during the editing process. Indeed, it is the author's responsibility and not the authoring tool to compute object duration values. These values have to be recomputed by the author when the scenario is changed. This situation will be detailed below for each approach.

Tree structures

Tree structures are well known in the area of structured documents (like in SGML standard [12]) to express hierarchical decomposition and they have numerous algorithms associated to them. In the multimedia document context, the tree structure may be used to represent temporal composition. Each node is associated with a temporal operator and each leaf represents a basic object.

The set of temporal operators depends on the system. CMIFed [26] proposes both sequential and parallel operators. The semantics of the parallel operator is to start its operands simultaneously without any constraint on the operand termination; SRT [15] has the sequential and the equal operators (the operands start simultaneously and must have the same duration). Let us note that in SRT a static checking phase is used to verify that the operands of an equal operator have the same duration. As a consequence, it is not possible to integrate in the SRT formalism either unpredictable objects or local interactions issues. Interval Expressions [13] and SMIL [31] have a more advanced set of operators to express interruptions like Par_min. This last operator is defined as follows: A Par_min B expresses that the two operands start together and the shortest one stops the other.

As far as authoring requirements are concerned, one important limitation of these approaches involves the straightforward and structural edition criterion (issue 9) which is illustrated by the Company part of the working example. The only way to get a tree structure of this scenario is to fix the delay between the beginning of History and that of Geography, see Figure 5(a). Thus, the temporal information between Geography and Name is lost and modifying the duration of History implies reconsidering the specification (issue 11).

In order to cope with this problem, CMIFed introduces the notion of Synchronization Arcs, which breaks the tree structure by allowing additional temporal information between any pair of nodes of the tree. In our example, a synchronization Arc is set between Geography and Name which expresses the delay (20 seconds) between their beginnings, see Figure 6(b).

The semantics of such synchronization arcs is unclear, as far as a potential conflict with the tree structure. For instance, considering the specification given in Figure 6(c), if A is longer than 20 seconds, what is the resulting scenario execution? Moreover, it is possible to generate deadlocks by using such arcs, but nothing is said about their detection.

Synchronization Arcs are also used to express local and global interactions (issue 7). These two kinds of interactions have been integrated into a uniform model, the Amsterdam Hypertext Model (AHM) [6]. As far as multigrids reading support (issue 15) is concerned, the channel view of the CMIFed environment provides the author with a way to share temporal scenarios among multiple versions of documents.

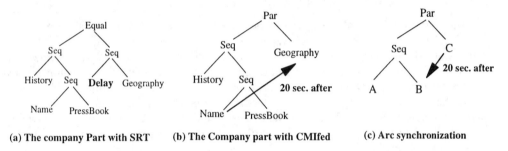

(a) The company Part with SRT   (b) The Company part with CMIfed   (c) Arc synchronization

Figure 6. Company scenario with SRT and CMIFed.

Petri-net Structure

Petri-nets are well known in the area of parallel computing to express temporal synchronization and to perform static checking of properties such as safety and liveness. In the context of multimedia authoring, it has been used both in OCPN [19] and HTSPN [23] to model temporal scenario. Objects are modeled by places. Temporal information is either associated with places (duration in OCPN) or with arcs (validity interval in HTSPN) and transitions are labeled with temporal operators (sequentiality and equality in OCPN and a richer set of possibilities, with Par_min for instance, in HTSPN). HTSPN provides the author with a way of abstracting some behaviors by a hierarchical organization through abstract places representing sub-networks (issue 13). They also provide the reader with global and local interactions (issue 7).

Petri-nets are more appropriate than tree approaches to capture the temporal structure of the scenarios (issue 9). The Company part of our example can be expressed in OCPN as shown in Figure 7. The synchronization between Name and Geography is not lost (Delay2 in Figure 7). Nevertheless, if the author changes the duration of History from 60 s to 30 s, other duration must be manually updated (Delay1 in the figure). In fact, OCPN is close to SRT; the equal operator implies a static checking of operands duration and both systems do not handle unpredictable objects (issue 5).

In addition to the previous remark about the need of explicit delay definitions, Petri-nets miss author's skills and straightforward design requirements (issues 8 and 9). Translating a scenario into a graph structure of places and arcs is definitively not an end-user activity despite the graphical nature of Petri-nets.

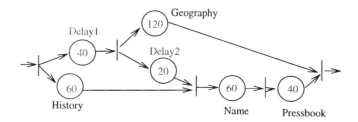

Figure 7. Company scenario using Timed Petri-Nets.

4.2. CONSTRAINT-BASED APPROACHES

The starting point of all these approaches is the constraint theory. The idea is that the author declares a set of relations between either instants ($=$, $>$, $<$) or intervals (thirteen relations of Allen's algebra [1]). Each multimedia object can also be associated with a minimum, a maximum, and an optimal duration, either chosen by the author or automatically fixed by the authoring system depending on the nature of the object (text, image. video, etc.). This is the Elastic time model first introduced in TemporalGlue [5] and Firefly [3]. For instance, the Company part of our example can be described by the Allen's relations given in Figure 8. The DelayGlob object is a fictive object (without content) which fixes the global duration of the Company part.

Set of objects with their possible durations		*Set of constraints*
History	[55,65]	History meets Name
Name	[45, 80]	Name meets Pressbook
Pressbook	[45,80]	Delay2 starts Geography
Delay2	[20,20]	Delay2 meets Name
Geography	[115,125]	History starts DelayGlob
DelayGlob	[170,190]	Pressbook finishes DelayGlob

Figure 8. Company part described with Allen's relations.

The main point of constraint-based approaches is that the aim of the temporal formatter (see Figure 3) is, first, to check the temporal consistency of this set (there are no contradictory requests) and, second, to compute one solution, possibly an optimal one, which satisfies all the relations (see Figure 3). Algorithms used for these two phases are issued from either the temporal constraint satisfaction area [4] or linear programming [8].

These approaches are very interesting as far as authoring capabilities are concerned. Indeed, it is an intuitive way of expression (issue 8) which can easily capture the temporal information of multimedia documents (issue 6) by using the thirteen relations of Allen's algebra. Modifications of the scenario are made easier since the author does not have to reconsider the whole structure of his document but only add or delete a relation.

For instance, if the author decides to complete the Company part by adding a Music after the Geography video in such a way that the Music ends simultaneously with the end of the PressBook, he just has to add the two following relations: Geography meets Music; Music finishes PressBook. Moreover, when he modifies an object, he does not change the rest of the specification (issue 11). In the same part of the example, the author can replace the History object by a shorter one without modifying any other objects duration. This feature is very interesting to cope with the incremental nature of the editing process and also when the author wants to reuse his document in another context, for instance, to translate it into another language. The counterpart of these advantages is the necessity to provide a formatting phase that produces an executable form of the scenario. One challenge is to make such systems with good time performances. Another is to handle local interactions and unpredictable objects (issues 5 and 7). Therefore, the temporal consistency checking phase must take into account uncertainty and, thus, the formatting phase becomes partially dynamic.

More precisely, it should be possible to express any relative placement between intervals [1] together with interruption operators (issue 6). In order to take into account issue 2 (controlling the delivery of continuous objects), it is necessary to distinguish two cases of the equal relation. Either the termination of one of the objects causes the termination or cropping of the other one, or the duration of the two objects are constrained to start and end at the same time, provided that their content is not cropped.

As an example, let's take two objects, A and B, that are, respectively, a video and an audio. Consider the two following specifications:

A and B start together and the shortest interrupts the longest one.
A and B start together and have the same duration.

The difference between the two scenarios is that in the first case, the content of one object is not fully delivered to the reader of the document, while the second case expresses that both objects deliver their whole content. We distinguish these two temporal compositions as Par_min for the first specification and equal for the second one. A large number of misunderstandings in the field of temporal synchronization comes from the unclear distinction between these two behaviors.

In the rest of this section, we present the main features of three systems belonging to this category: Isis, Firefly and Madeus. Let us note that another more recent work, namely HPAS [29], also proposes a constraint-based multimedia editing system, which is close to these.

4.2.1. Isis

In Isis [16], the set of relations between objects contains the four basic relations of the Allen's Algebra (meets, equals, starts, finishes). The others can be built from this set by introducing appropriate delays. All the objects durations are considered as predictable (issue 5 is not taken into account). Great effort has been devoted to compute the optimal solution taking into account fairness considerations (fair time dispatching among objects). Algorithms used for this computation are issued from linear programming.

In order to get better time performances, Isis designers studied how to benefit from incremental methods [25], resulting in the use of temporal constraint networks (Dechter's algorithm [4]) and to adapt the shortest path algorithm of Dijkstra. One of their other challenges is to help the author when a temporal inconsistency is found in a set of relations (issue 10).

We are not aware of Isis experiments in introducing unpredictable duration in their framework. Moreover they do not provide the author with a Par_min relation. As a consequence, it is not possible to describe the Mascot part of our example. Isis provides the author with an interactive graphical interface, which uses a graphical syntax equivalent to the set of relations. Figure 9 shows the view associated with the Company part. This graphical view of the temporal scenario presents flexibility of objects by means of a spring metaphor (issues 8 and 10).

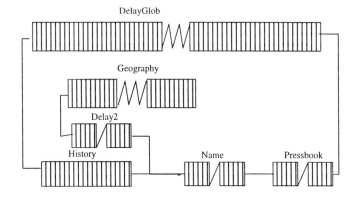

Figure 9. Company scenario with Isis.

In order to offer abstraction functions (issue 13), they provide the user with structuring capabilities in terms of a timed Petri-net in which each place is a component described by a set of relations and each arc models a global user interaction [24]. From the authors' point of view, the use of Petri-nets seems to be in contradiction with the authoring advantages (mainly issues 8 and 9) gained by the constraint-based approach.

4.2.2. Firefly

In Firefly [3], temporal composition is expressed in terms of relations between instants (beginning and ending of objects and user interactions). The equal relation between instants is not oriented, so, if the author wants to start and end two objects simultaneously, he cannot decide whether the ending synchronization is due to an interruption or not (distinction between equal and Par_min). In fact, the two semantics are supported, but the Firefly scheduler makes this choice: unpredictable objects imply a Par_min composition.

This is the first work in the constraint-based area that has considered the unpredictable nature of some multimedia objects (like user interactions) (issue 5). In order to provide a static formatting process handling this kind of objects, the Firefly scheduler partitions the temporal scenario at compile time by grouping connected components (i.e., instants related by a temporal relation or a predictable duration). Figure 10 shows the Firefly description of the Mascot scenario; there are two sets of connected components and two unpredictable objects (Button and Message) which appear with a dotted line.

The simplex algorithm is used to independently find the optimal solution of each partition. An event-driven scheduler dynamically handles the integration of the partitions. Unfortunately, the time performances of this batch process is not good enough [3] in an interactive and incremental context (issue 12). This is the most important drawback of the Firefly approach. Another weak point of Firefly is that it does not provide the user with any abstraction capabilities (issue 13).

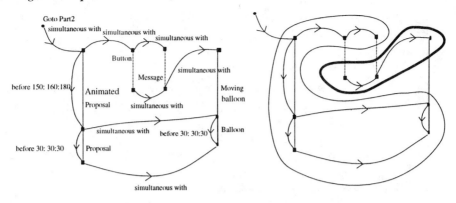

Figure 10. Mascot scenario with Firefly.

4.2.3 Madeus

The set of temporal relations in Madeus is composed of the quantified Allen operators together with two additional interruption operators, Par_min and Par_master (only the first operand called master can interrupt the other one). Object duration can be predictable or not (issue 5). Abstraction capabilities (issue 13) are provided by hierarchical decomposition of the scenario, which gives a framework to set temporal relations; two objects can be related if and only if they have the same parent in the tree structure. This located placement of the relations usually fits well with author's needs and does not show the disadvantage of the approaches which set a temporal operator on each node of the tree structure (see Section 3.1.3). However, it may induce the same drawback of tree structures when the author wants to apply some modifications that break down the current structure of the document (issue 11).

The hierarchical structure of our example is very simple (left part of Figure 11). The root is composed of two parts (Company and Mascot), two hyperlinks (GotoPart1 and GotoPart2) and the delay DelayGlob. The relations associated with the root (Company part and Mascot part) are given in the right part of Figure 11.

Madeus uses temporal constraint networks algorithms to incrementally detect temporal inconsistencies (issues 11 and 12). Difficulties arise when integrating unpredictable durations and interruption operators in such algorithms [17]. As far as we know, the only theoretical work that deals with the integration of interruption in the temporal constraint networks context, is [27].

Madeus is a real running application [9], which partially implements the formatting phase, providing the user with easy and rapid switches between the specification phase, and the presentation phase (issue 12). Currently, the editing phase is based mainly on an integrated textual editor, although it is possible to modify the temporal scenario by direct manipulation on objects and by the use of a palette of temporal operators (issue 8). However, the design of a valuable interface for a constraint-based authoring system is more complex since, as stated in issue 10, the difficulty is to provide the author with a global perception of the set of solutions [10]. Algorithms to manage unpredictable objects are being studied and currently bring partial results.

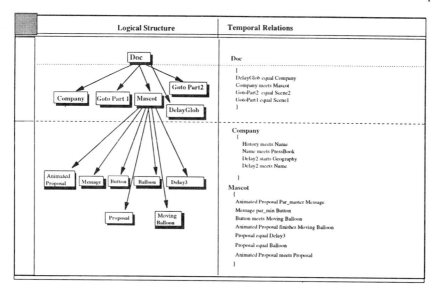

Figure 11. The complete example with Madeus.

5. SYNTHESIS

In this chapter, we analyzed how different approaches for the specification of multimedia documents can meet the requirements for expressive power and authoring capabilities.

This work is summarized in the table of Figure 12 where we tried to compare the different systems according to the different issues (1 to 15) in spite of the difficulty of this exercise. The fifteen issues, identified throughout this work, are recalled below:

A wide variety of basic objects and a rich set of operations on them (issue 1)
The possibility to control the delivery of continuous objects (issue 2)
Interactivity capabilities attached to objects (issue 3)
Temporal style definitions (issue 4)
A support for unpredictable objects (issue 5)
Temporal Composition (issue 6)
Interactions (issue 7)
Adaptability to computer-illiterate people (issue 8)
Straightforward design (issue 9)
Indeterministic scenario authoring capabilities (issue 10)
Ease of local modifications (issue 11)
Fast editing/presentation cycle (issue 12)
Abstraction capabilities (issue 13)
Multimedia document models (issue 14)
Multigrids reading support (issue 15)

We use a three-levels notation for that table: "-" the issue is not addressed, "+" the issue is a major concern of the system and "+/-" the issue is partially supported. When we have no information, we use a "?".

Issue \ Authoring tool	1	2	3	4	5	6	7	8	9	10	11	12	13	14	15
CMIFed	+/-	-	+/-	-	+	+/-	+	+/-	-	-	-	+	+	-	+/-
ISIS	+/-	-	?	-	-	+/-	+/-	+	+	-	+	+	+	-	-
Firefly	+/-	-	?	-	+/-	+/-	+/-	+	+	-	+	-	-	-	-
Madeus	+/-	+/-	+	+	+/-	+/-	+/-	+	+	+/-	+	+	+	-	+/-
MHEG	+/-	-	+	-	+	+/-	+								
SMIL	+/-	-	+	-	+/-	-	+/-								

Figure 12. Comparative table.

Let us note that for MHEG and SMIL languages, we have not filled the authoring issues since currently there is no associated authoring tool for them.

We can draw the following main remarks from this table:

Each system/language partially fits the first issue but none of them is able to provide fine temporal operations on objects: no distinction between mapping (respectively unmapping) and starting (respectively stopping) of objects and no pause and resume actions.

Temporal style definition issue (issue 4) has not been fairly taken care of, although it is an essential feature to build attractive multimedia documents (see, for example, the numerous programmed animations on the Web).

It is difficult to compare the temporal composition feature (issue 6) of the studied systems because this issue is clearly related to the inputs and outputs taken into account by the system (see issues 1 to 5). As we have stated in Section 2.2, even if Allen's relations can be expressed by all of them, they are not equivalent when considering their ability to control the delivery of continuous objects.

Except in CMIFed, the interaction issue (7) is weakly addressed, mainly because local interactions raise difficulties in a constraint-based context.

Constraint-based approaches are better adapted for satisfying author needs (issues 9 and 11) thanks to the relative approach they allow.

Document modeling has not yet been considered for multimedia documents (issue 14), but it is clear that it will become a main issue when such documents become widely used.

Finally, we want to focus on the two following conclusions:

1. Constraint-based approaches seem to be more adapted for building powerful authoring tools and they can offer equivalent or higher expressive power capabilities than operational techniques. The author is not required to give the duration of all the objects involved in his document (as formulated in the description of our example in Section 2). A temporal formatter, removing the burden of this task from the author and allowing him to obtain reusable scenarios, computes the durations.

However, this formatting has to be time efficient and must provide the solutions desired by the author. Firefly chooses a linear programming technique to perform its formatting phase, while incremental considerations motivate the use of constraint networks techniques in Isis and Madeus. Unpredictable objects, partially handled by Firefly and Madeus, overcome time performance difficulties in the formatting phase.

2. Constraint-based approaches can also provide a better support for the presentation phase in a distributed environment. In such context, the presentation system must deal with network delays that can affect the timing of other objects in the presentation leading to an out-of-synchronization situation. A global supervision of the timing during the presentation scheduling is therefore required in order to ensure that the author's specifications are met. During the presentation, temporal supervision can be seen as the process of adjusting the scenario in order to meet the timing constraints. In a constraint-based system, the temporal formatter can dynamically achieve this adjustment while it is not possible in an operational system in which some durations are statically fixed.

The multimedia authoring domain is still in its infancy but let's bet that it will expand considerably very soon. New standards such as SMIL [31] should give a new boost to this domain because users are eager to get new multimedia authoring tools. Taking into account the distribution of multimedia objects will become the great challenge in the years to come.

REFERENCES

1. Allen J.F., "Maintaining Knowledge about Temporal Intervals," Communications of the ACM, Vol. 26, No. 11, pp. 832-843, November 1983.

2. Blakowski G. and Steinmetz R.A., "Media Synchronization Survey: Reference Model, Specification, and Case Studies," IEEE Journal Of Selected Areas In Communications", Vol. 14, No. 1, pp. 5-34, January 1996.

3. Buchanan M.C. and Zellweger P.T., "Automatic Temporal Layout Mechanisms," Proceedings of the First ACM International Conference on Multimedia, pp. 341-350, Anaheim, California, August 1993.

4. Dechter R., Meiri I., and Pearl J., "Temporal constraint networks," Artificial Intelligence, Vol. 49, pp. 61-95, 1991.

5. Hamakawa R. and Reikimoto J. "Object Composition and Playback Models for Handling Multimedia Data," Proceedings of the First ACM International Conference on Multimedia, pp. 273-281, ACM Press, Anaheim, California, August 1993.

6. Hardman L., Bulterman D.C.A., and van Rossum G., "The Amsterdam Hypermedia Model: Adding Time and Context to the Dexter Model," CACM, Vol. 37, No. 2, pp. 50-62, February 1994.

7. Erfle R. "Specification of temporal constraints in multimedia documents using HyTime," Electronic Publishing, Vol. 6, No. 4, pp. 397-411, December 1993.

8. Hillier F.S. and Lieberman G.J., Operations research, Holden-Day, San Francisco, CA, 1974.

9. Jourdan M., Layaïda N., and Sabry-Ismail L, "Time Representation and Management in Madeus: an Authoring Environment for Multimedia Documents," in Proceedings of Multimedia Computing and Networking '97, SPIE Vol. 3020, San Jose, CA, February 1997.

10. Jourdan M., Roisin C., and Tardif L., "User interface of a new generation of authoring environment of multimedia documents," Proceeding of the Third ERCIM Workshop on User Interfaces for All, Strasbourg (France), November 1997.

11. IconAuthor 6.0, User's Guide, Aim Tech.

12. International Standard ISO 8879, "Information Processing - Text and Office Systems - Standard Generalized Markup Language (SGML)," International Standard Organization, 1986.

13. Keramane C. and Duda A., "Interval Expressions," Proc. of IEEE International Conference Multimedia Computing Systems, November 1996.

14. Koegel Buford J. F., "Multimedia Systems," ACM Press, Addison Wesley, 1994.

15. Kim W., Kenchammana-Hosekote D., and Srivasta J., "Synchronization Relation Tree: A model for Temporal Synchronization in Multimedia Presentation," Technical Report TR92-42, Dept. of Computer Science, Univ. of Minnesota, 1992.

16. Kim M. Y. and Song J., "Multimedia Documents with Elastic Time," Proceedings of the Third ACM International Conference on Multimedia, ACM Press, pp. 143-154, San Francisco, CA, November 1995.

17. Layaïda N. and Sabry-Ismail L., "Maintaining Temporal Consistency of Multimedia Documents Using Constraint Networks," Multimedia Computing and Networking '96, M. Freeman, P. Jardetzky, H. M. Vin, Eds., pp. 124-135, SPIE Vol. 2667, San-Jose, CA, February 1996.

18. Legall D., "MPEG: A Video Compression Standard for Multimedia Applications," Communications of the ACM, Vol. 34, No. 4, pp. 45-68, April 1991.

19. Little T.D.C. and Ghafoor A., "Synchronization and Storage Models for Multimedia Objects," IEEE Journal on Selected Areas in Communications, Vol. 8, No. 3, pp. 413-426, April 1990.

20. Macromedia Director, User's Guide, Macromedia Inc., 1995.

21. Perez-Luque, M. J. and Little, T.D.C., "A Temporal Reference Framework for Multimedia Synchronization," IEEE Journal on Selected Areas in Communications, Vol. 14, No. 1, pp. 36-51, January 1996.

22. Price R., "MHEG: An Introduction to the Future International Standard for Hypermedia Object Interchange," Proceedings of the First ACM Conference on Multimedia, pp. 121-128, ACM Press, Anaheim, California, August 1993.

23. Sénac P., Diaz M., Léger A., and de Saqui-Sannes P., "Modeling Logical and Temporal Synchronization in Hypermedia Systems," IEEE Journal of Selected Areas on Communications, Vol. 14, No. 1, pp. 84-103, 1996.

24. Song J., Doganata Y, Kim M., and Tantawi A., "Modeling Timed User-Interactions in Multimedia Documents," Proceedings of the IEEE International Conference on Multimedia Computing and Systems, November 1996.

25. Song J., Kim M., Ramalingam G., and Miller R., Interactive Authoring Multimedia Documents, Visual Language, 1996.

26. Van Rossum G., Jansen J., Mullender K., and Bulterman D., "CMIFed: A Presentation Environment for Portable Hypermedia Documents," Proceedings of the ACM Multimedia Conference, Anaheim, CA, 1993.

27. Vidal, T. and Fargier, H., "Contingent duration in temporal CSP: from consistency to controllabilities," 4th Int. Workshop on Temporal Representation and Reasoning (TIME97), Daytona Beach, FL, May 1997.

28. Wahl T. and Rothermel K., "Representing Time in Multimedia Systems," Proceedings of the IEEE International Conference on Multimedia Computing and Systems, pp. 538-543, IEEE Computer Society Press, Boston, MA, May 1994.

29. Yu, J. and Xiang Y., "Hypermedia Presentation and Authoring System," Sixth Int. World Wide Web Conference, Hyper Proceedings, California, April 1997.

30. W3C. "Working draft specification of XML (Extensible Markup Language)," W3C: http://www.w3.org/TR/WD-xml-lang, August 1997.

31. W3C. "Working draft specification of SMIL (Synchronized Multimedia Integration Language)," W3C: http://www.w3.org/TR/WD-smil, November 1997.

23

SCHEDULING FOR INTEGRATED SERVICE IN MULTIMEDIA SYSTEMS

A. L. Narasimha Reddy and Ravi Wijayaratne
Texas A & M University
214 Zachary
College Station, TX 77843-3128
reddy@ee.tamu.edu

1. **INTRODUCTION**..492
2. **MULTIPLE LEVELS OF QOS** 493
3. **DISK SCHEDULING** 494
    3.1   DETERMINISTIC GUARANTEES FOR VBR STREAMS...................494
    3.2   LATENCY AND BANDWIDTH GUARANTEES 498
    3.3   SCHEDULING FOR MULTIPLE QOS LEVELS 498
    3.4   OTHER ISSUES IN DISK SCHEDULING.................................501
4. **CPU SCHEDULING**..502
5. **NETWORK SCHEDULING** 503
6. **SUMMARY**..504
    REFERENCES 504

Abstract. The recent dramatic advances in computer and communications technology has led to a demand to support multimedia data (digitized video and audio) across data networks. Storage, processor, memory and network subsystems have to be appropriately scheduled to meet the requirements imposed by the continuous media. Proposed techniques for scheduling resources in a multimedia system are discussed. Integrated service for different levels of quality of service is studied with an emphasis on the disk subsystem.

0-8493-1825-4/99/$0.00+$.50
© 1999 by CRC Press LLC

1. INTRODUCTION

System level support of continuous media has been receiving wide attention. Continuous media impose timing requirements on the retrieval and delivery of data unlike traditional data such as text and images. Timely retrieval and delivery of data requires that the system and network pay attention to notions of time and deadlines. Data retrieval is handled by the I/O system (File system, disk drivers, disks, etc.) and the delivery is handled by the network system (network software and the network). Without appropriate CPU scheduling, the requests may experience delays that interrupt processing and scheduling of other resources in the system.

Different levels of service can be provided for continuous media. *Deterministic service* provides guarantees that the required data will be retrieved in time. *Statistical service* provides statistical guarantees about data retrieval, e.g., 99% of the requested blocks will be retrieved in time. Data streams can be classified as Constant Bit Rate (CBR) or Variable Bit Rate (VBR) depending on whether the stream requests the same amount of data in an interval.

System requirements of a multimedia stream can be characterized by a vector of the CPU load, the disk load, and the network load of that stream. Each of the resources, CPU, disk, and network have to be appropriately scheduled to meet the performance guarantees of the stream. A video-on-demand stream may require minimal CPU processing while it imposes a large load on the disk and the network. A video capture stream may require large CPU power for compressing the video as it is being captured while requiring little disk bandwidth and no network bandwidth. An uncompressed stream, such as in production quality TV broadcasting, may stress the disk and network bandwidth. Each subsystem has to deal with the allocation and scheduling of available resources to meet the performance requirements of individual streams.

Providing deterministic service at the disk is complicated by the random service time costs involved in disk transfers (because of the random seek and latency overheads). This problem has been addressed effectively by suitable disk scheduling policies [1,2]. These scheduling policies group a number of requests into rounds or batches and service the requests in a round using a disk seek optimizing policy such as SCAN. Then the service time for the entire round can be bounded to provide guarantees. This strategy works well with CBR streams. However, with VBR streams, the workload changes from round to round and hence such an approach will have to consider the variations in load for providing guarantees.

Providing deterministic guarantees for data delivery has received considerable attention in the networking community [3,4,5]. A VBR stream is characterized by its worst-case demand on the network over any period of time. This characterization of the stream's behavior is used to calculate the worst-case delays possible through a switch when multiple streams pass through a switch. Network infrastructure has to be modified to enable an application to request and reserve resources [6] for these guarantees to be provided. Protocols have been developed to support best-effort delivery of multimedia data over existing networks [7,8]. These protocols adapt to the availability of network bandwidth to deliver as high quality data as possible on existing network infrastructure.

The multimedia streams require a processor for servicing the interrupts and scheduling of other resources in the system. Without appropriate scheduling, the requests may experience long delays in queues defeating the scheduling in other resources. CPU processing may be required for compressing or decompressing a stream or for network protocol processing for delivery purposes. Strict real-time scheduling of resources or priority-based schemes may not be suited for the various levels of support required by the multimedia data. Lottery scheduling [9] and hierarchical scheduling [10] have recently been proposed as flexible algorithms for scheduling CPU resources for multimedia.

In this chapter, we will look at the disk scheduling problem in detail and give a brief overview of work done in processor and network scheduling. Continuous media applications may require deterministic performance guarantees, i.e., guarantee that a requested block will be continuously available within a specified amount of time during the application's execution. A request from an interactive game or a request to change the sequence of frames in a continuous media application may require that the request have low response time, i.e., may require a latency guarantee. A regular file request may require only best-effort service but also that a certain number of requests be served in a given time, i.e., may require a throughput guarantee. It may be desirable to provide both deterministic service and statistical service to VBR streams in the same system. Deterministic service may be too demanding on the system's resources. A user may request statistical service when a request for deterministic service is denied due to lack of resources. There is a clear need for supporting multiple levels of performance guarantees within the system.

Several interesting questions need to be addressed when multiple levels of QOS need to be supported in the same system: (a) how to allocate and balance resources for the different QOS levels, (b) how to control and limit the usage of resources to allocated levels, (c) how to schedule different requests to meet the desired performance goals, and (d) how do system level parameters and design decisions affect the different types of requests?

Section 2 discusses an approach for providing different levels of QOS in a single system. Section 3 discusses a scheduling algorithm for providing integrated service at the disk. Section 4 discusses CPU scheduling algorithms and Section 5 looks at approaches for network scheduling. Since it is difficult to discuss all aspects of scheduling in a short chapter, more emphasis is put on disk scheduling and a brief overview of CPU scheduling and network scheduling policies is provided.

2. MULTIPLE LEVELS OF QOS

Three different categories of requests are considered here. *Periodic* requests require service at regular intervals of time. Periodic requests model the behavior of video playback where data is retrieved at regular intervals of time. Periodic requests can be either CBR or VBR. *Interactive* requests require quick response from the I/O system. Interactive requests can be used to model the behavior of change-of-sequence requests in an interactive video playback application or the requests in an interactive video game. These requests arrive at irregular intervals of time. *Aperiodic* requests are regular file requests. The following performance goals are considered: (a) deterministic or statistical guarantees for periodic requests, (b) low response times for interactive requests, and (c) guaranteed minimum level of service or bandwidth guarantees for aperiodic requests.

Integrated service is provided by allocating bandwidth to classes of requests and then appropriately scheduling the requests at the disk. Bandwidth allocation and rate controls are used to ensure that a class of applications does not interfere with the performance objectives of other classes of applications. Disk bandwidth is allocated appropriately among the three different types of requests. Periodic requests and interactive requests employ admission controllers to limit the disk utilization to the allocated level for these requests as shown in Figure 1. To provide throughput guarantees for aperiodic requests, we limit the allocated bandwidth for periodic and interactive requests to less than 100% through admission control. Aperiodic requests utilize the remaining disk bandwidth. This guarantees that the aperiodic requests are not ignored and receive some minimum level of service.

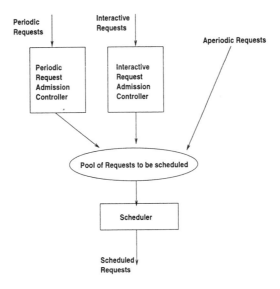

Figure 1. Supporting multiple QOS levels.

The admission controllers employed for periodic and interactive requests depend on the service provided for these requests. In the next section, we discuss how to provide deterministic service for periodic requests. The proposed approach can be modified to implement statistical guarantees for periodic requests as well. Interactive requests are treated as high-priority aperiodic requests. The scheduler and the admission controller are designed to provide low response times for these requests. A leaky-bucket controller is used for interactive requests.

A leaky bucket controller controls the burstiness of interactive requests (by allowing only a specified number of requests in a given window of time) and thus limits the impact it may have on other requests. Similar bandwidth allocation approaches have been adopted in CPU scheduling [10] and network scheduling [3]. However, the scheduling policies employed in each subsystem are different. The scheduling policies exploit the different characteristics of the resources being scheduled.

3. DISK SCHEDULING

3.1 DETERMINISTIC GUARANTEES FOR VBR STREAMS
Providing deterministic service for VBR streams is complicated by the following factors: (i) the load of a stream on the system varies from one round to the next, (ii) scheduling the first block doesn't guarantee that the following blocks of the stream can be scheduled. To ensure that all the blocks required by a stream can be retrieved, the peak rate of a stream can be computed and enough disk bandwidth can be reserved to satisfy the peak requirements. However, this approach results in a considerable overestimate of required resources and fewer supporting streams.

Resource allocation based on the peak demands of the stream will underutilize the disk bandwidth since the peak demand is observed only for short duration compared to the length of the duration of the stream. However, when many streams are served in the system, the peaks do not necessarily overlap each other and it may be possible to serve more steams than allowed by the peak-rate allocation. Can this statistical multiplexing be exploited to increase the deterministic service provided by the system? An approach is presented here that allows the system to exploit statistical multiplexing while providing deterministic service.

Disk service is broken into fixed size time units called rounds or batches. Each round may span 0.25-1 seconds of time [1]. An application requiring service for a VBR stream supplies the I/O system with a trace of its I/O demand. This data could be based on frame rate, i.e., given on a frame-to-frame basis or could be more closely tied to the I/O system. Specifying the load on a frame basis is more flexible and the application doesn't have to be aware of how the I/O system is organized (block size or round size). If the I/O system's block size is known and the duration of each round is known, then the trace can be compacted by specifying the I/O load on a round-by-round basis in terms of the blocks. For example, a frame-by-frame trace may look like 83,888, 9,960, 10,008, 27,044, etc., which indicates the number of bits of data needed to display each frame. If the round size is, say, 2 frames, i.e., 1/12th of a second, and the I/O system uses a block size of 4KB, then the compacted trace would have $\lceil (83888+9960)/(4*1024*8) \rceil = 3$ in the first entry. The second entry would have $\lceil (10008+27044)-(3*1024*8 \ -83888-9960)/(4*1024*8) \rceil = 1$ block. Hence, the equivalent compacted trace for the stream would be 3, 1, ... A 40,000 frame trace of the movie "Silence of the Lambs" (24 frames/second) requires 203,285 bytes on a frame by frame basis compared to a 3,333 byte description of the same movie when compacted with the knowledge of the round size of 0.5 seconds and a block size of 8KB. It is assumed that this information, the *demand trace*, is available to the I/O system in either description.

The I/O system itself keeps track of the worst-case time committed for service in each round at each of its disks in the form of a *load trace*. Before a stream is admitted, its demand trace is combined with the load trace of the appropriate disks to see if the load on any one of the disks exceeds the capacity (committed time greater than the length of the round). The load trace of a system consists of load traces of all the disks over a sufficient period of time. This requires knowledge of the placement of blocks of the requesting stream. This information can be obtained from the storage volume manager.

A stream is admitted if its demand can be accommodated by the system. It is possible that the stream cannot be supported in the round the request arrives. The *stream scheduling* policy will look for a round in which this stream can be scheduled. We will assume that a stream will wait for a maximum amount of time, given by *latency target*, for admittance. (The impact of stream scheduling policies has been studied in [11].) Let $load[i][j]$ denote the load on disk i in round j. Let the demand of a stream be given by $demand[j]$ indicating the number of blocks to be retrieved by that stream in round j. Then, a stream can be admitted if a k exists such that $(load[i][j+k] + serv\_time(demand[j])) \leq$ round time, for all j, where i = disk storing data for round j, and k is the startup latency $\leq$ *latency target*. If multiple disks can store the data required by a stream in a round, the above check needs to be appropriately modified to verify that these disks can support the retrieval of needed data. The function *serv_time()* estimates the worst-case service time required for retrieving a given number of blocks from a disk given the current load of the disk. This function utilizes the current load of the disk (number of requests and blocks) and the load of the arriving request to estimate the worst-case time required to serve the new request along with the already scheduled requests. A similar check can be applied against buffer resources when needed.

Data layout plays a significant role on the performance of disk access. It has been suggested by many researchers [12,13,14] that video data should be striped [15] across the disks for load balancing and to improve throughput available for a single data stream. Data for a VBR stream can be stored in (i) Constant Data Length (CDL) units or (ii) Constant Time Length (CTL) units. In CDL, data is distributed in some fixed size units across the disks, say, 64KB blocks. In BCTL (block-constrained CTL, a variant of CTL considered here), data is distributed in some constant time units, say, 0.5 seconds of display time rounded to the closest block (4KB). In CDL, a stream may require service from several disks in a round and in BCTL, a stream will require service from, at most, one disk.

Figure 2 shows the impact of block size and data layout strategy on the stream throughput. The workload consisted of an equal number of 27-minute streams of a cartoon *Asterix*, two movies *Silence of the Lambs* and *Terminator,* and a news clip *News* [16].

It is observed that peak rate based allocation leads to significantly less throughput than the proposed approach. The proposed approach achieves 130% to 195% more stream throughput than the peak rate allocation. This improvement is primarily achieved by exploiting the statistical multiplexing of different streams. When requests arrive at the same time, flexible starting times (through latency targets) allow the peaks in demand to be spread over time to improve the throughput.

As the block size is increased, a stream fetches less number of blocks in a round and, hence, CDL tends to be more efficient at larger block sizes (due to smaller seek and rotational latency costs). The stream throughput for CDL improves significantly for all the data streams as the block size is increased from 32 KB to 256 KB. The stream throughput drops slowly for BCTL as the block size is increased. This is due to effects of larger quantization of service allocation for a request. For the block sizes considered, the BCTL data layout performs better than the CDL data layout. CDL performs worse than BCTL due to paying a rotational latency penalty for each block compared to each time slice in BCTL.

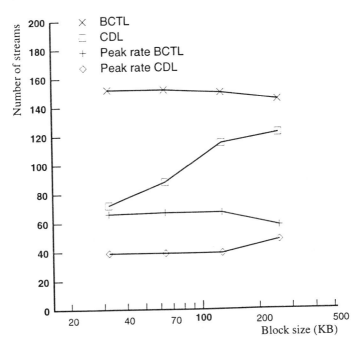

Figure 2. Impact of data layout and block size on VBR streams.

Figure 3 shows the impact of statistical guarantees on stream throughput. Instead of requiring that every block of data be retrieved in time, a fraction of the blocks for each stream were allowed to miss deadlines or not be provided service. This fraction is varied among 0.1%, 0.2%, 0.5%, 1.0%, 2.0%, and 5.0% at various latency targets. It is observed that, as more blocks are allowed to be dropped, it is possible to achieve more throughput compared to deterministic guarantees. Stream throughput can be improved by up to 20% by allowing 5% of the blocks to be dropped. Dropping blocks is more effective at lower latency targets than at higher latency targets. For example, dropping up to 2% of the blocks improves the stream throughput by 14.5% at a latency target of 100 rounds compared to an improvement of 6% at a latency target of 1000 rounds. Stream throughput can also be improved by relaxing the latency targets.

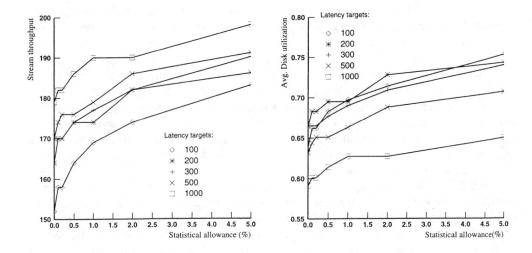

Figure 3. Effect of statistical allowances.

Figure 3 also shows the tradeoffs possible between latency targets and the number of blocks allowed to be dropped. At a latency target of 100 rounds, 152 streams can be provided deterministic service. To achieve higher stream throughput, latency targets can be increased or blocks can be dropped. For example, when the latency target is increased to 1000 rounds, 179 streams could be scheduled without dropping any blocks. However, to achieve the same throughput at a latency target of 100 rounds, more than 2% of the blocks have to be dropped. Hence, desired throughput can be achieved either by allowing larger latency targets or by allowing a fraction of the blocks to be denied service.

Figure 3 also shows the impact on the average disk utilizations as a function of the statistical allowances and latency targets. As higher statistical allowances are made, the disk utilizations are improved as more streams are supported. As latency targets are increased from 100 rounds, average disk utilizations first increase and then decrease to lower levels. As latency targets are increased, an arriving stream finds more choices for a suitable starting spot to utilize the available bandwidth. However, as the latency targets are increased further, the streams are scheduled farther and farther into the future resulting in decreasing disk utilizations.

Usually considered statistical guarantees of 99% (i.e., dropping 1% of blocks) did not provide significant improvements in stream throughput compared to deterministic guarantees. In our measurements, the improvements were less than 6% for all latency targets except 100, which achieved an improvement of 11%. Most of the dropped blocks tended to be dropped in a small range of time. Even though a 30 minute movie drops only a few blocks during its playback, the dropped blocks tended to be clustered over a 2 minute window instead of over the entire movie. This suggests that storing the data during the peak demands of popular movies in memory (not the entire movie) can lead to considerable improvement in performance.

3.2 LATENCY AND BANDWIDTH GUARANTEES

Aperiodic requests are provided bandwidth guarantees by restricting the periodic and interactive requests to a certain fraction of the available bandwidth. The admission controller for periodic and interactive requests enforces the bandwidth allocations. Aperiodic requests utilize the remaining I/O bandwidth. If periodic and interactive requests cannot utilize the allocated bandwidths, aperiodic requests are allowed to utilize the available bandwidth to improve the response times for aperiodic requests. In our system, bandwidths are allocated statically to different types of requests.

Latency guarantees are provided by the disk scheduler. The next section provides a description of the scheduler and how it provides low response times for interactive requests. The arrival behavior of interactive requests was modeled by a random exponential arrival process. When requests arrive randomly, a burst of requests can possibly disturb the guarantees provided to the periodic requests. To avoid this possibility, interactive requests are controlled by a leaky-bucket controller which controls the burstiness by allowing only a certain maximum number of interactive requests to be served in a given time window. For example, when interactive request service is limited to, say, 5 per second, the leaky-bucket controller will ensure that no more than 5 requests are released to the scheduler, irrespective of the request arrival behavior. Hence, an interactive request can experience delay for service in the controller as well as at the scheduler. If sufficient bandwidth is allocated for these requests, the waiting time at the controller will be limited to periods when requests arrive in a burst.

3.3 SCHEDULING FOR MULTIPLE QOS LEVELS

Disks typically employ seek optimization techniques to minimize the seek costs in serving requests. Deadline scheduling and similar real-time requests provide real-time guarantees but may not be efficient because of associated higher seek costs. Disk scheduling strategies have been proposed that allow seek optimizations while providing delivery guarantees for continuous media applications [1,2,17,18]. Most of this work considered seek optimizing policies that can provide delivery guarantees required by continuous media in Video-on-demand (VOD) and similar servers. A few of these studies [1,18] have considered scheduling policies for multiple levels of service within the same system.

Since the requests do not have strict priorities over each other, priority scheduling is not feasible. Periodic requests have to be given priority over others if they are close to missing deadlines. But, if there is sufficient slack time, interactive requests have higher priority such that they can receive lower latencies. Periodic requests are available at the beginning of the round and interactive and aperiodic requests arrive asynchronously at the disk. If periodic requests are given higher priority and served first, aperiodic and interactive requests will experience long response times at the beginning of a round until periodic requests are served. Moreover, it may be possible to better optimize seeks if all the available requests are considered at once.

It is assumed that the requests are identified by their service type at the scheduler or provided different queues for different request types. The scheduler is designed to be independent of the bandwidth allocations. The bandwidth allocation parameters or the admission controllers can be changed without modifying the scheduler. To enable this, the aperiodic requests are queued into two separate queues. The first queue holds requests, based on the minimum throughput guarantee, provided for these requests. The second queue holds any other requests waiting to be served. The scheduler considers the requests from the second queue after periodic requests and interactive requests are served so that these requests can utilize the unused disk bandwidth.

The scheduler merges the periodic requests and aperiodic requests (from queue 1) into a SCAN order at the beginning of a round. These requests are then grouped into a number of subgroups based on their location on the disk surface. The scheduler serves one subgroup of requests at a time and considers serving interactive requests only at the beginning of a subgroup, i.e., the disk SCAN order is not disturbed within a subgroup. If an interactive request is to be served, the scheduler groups this request into the closest subgroup and serves that group next. An interactive request gets a quick response. Interactive requests are served by a first-come first-serve policy to limit the maximum response time of a single request. Since an interactive request (if waiting for service) is served by every subgroup, the response time for an interactive request is $<(n+2)$ (time for serving a subgroup), where n is the number of interactive requests waiting in front of an arriving request. Hence, the response times for interactive requests are determined by the burstiness of the interactive requests and the size of the subgroup. The size of the subgroup can be decreased if tighter latency guarantees are required. If aperiodic requests are considered only at the beginning of the round, it is likely that requests arriving later will suffer long response times. To avoid this problem, aperiodic requests (of queue 1) are considered and merged into one of the subgroups on their arrival. Admission controllers are designed such that the total time for serving the requests seen by the scheduler in the periodic, interactive and the first aperiodic queue takes less time than a round. Requests in the second aperiodic queue are served when no periodic and interactive requests are waiting for service. The requests in this queue use the unutilized bandwidth of aperiodic and interactive requests.

Figure 4 shows the average disk utilization when periodic requests are allocated 50% bandwidth, and aperiodic and interactive requests are each allocated 25% bandwidth. A scheduling round of 0.5 seconds and a subgroup of 62.5 milliseconds were considered.

The number of periodic request streams was maintained at the maximum that the system can support. Aperiodic request rate is varied while maintaining the interactive request rate at 50 requests/sec (request rates are measured over the entire system of 8 disks). It is observed that the average utilization of the periodic streams stays below 50%.

Because of variations in demand over time, more periodic streams could not be admitted. The utilizations of periodic and interactive requests are unaffected by the aperiodic request rate. It is also observed that as the aperiodic request rate is increased, aperiodic requests take up more and more bandwidth and eventually utilize more than the allocated 25% bandwidth. When periodic and interactive requests don't make use of the allocated bandwidth, aperiodic requests make use of any available bandwidth (25% is the minimum available) and hence can achieve more than the allocated 25% utilization of the disk. This shows that disks are not left idle when aperiodic requests are waiting to be served.

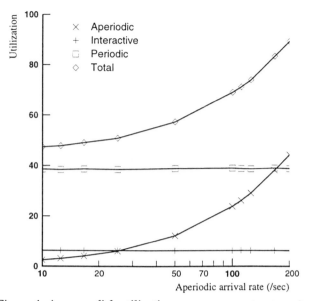

Figure 4. Average disk utilizations across request categories.

Figure 5 shows the average and maximum response times of aperiodic and interactive requests as a function of the aperiodic request rate. The number of streams is kept at the maximum allowed by the system and the interactive arrival rate is kept at 50 requests/sec. Interactive response times are not considerably affected by the aperiodic arrival rate and the maximum interactive response time stays relatively independent of the aperiodic arrival rate. It is also observed that the interactive requests achieve considerably better response times than aperiodic requests (260ms maximum interactive response time compared to 1600ms for aperiodic requests both at 50 reqs/sec). Both average and maximum response times are better for interactive requests than for aperiodic requests even at lower aperiodic arrival rates. It was observed that the maximum interactive response times are only dependent on the burstiness of arrival of interactive requests and the bandwidth allocated to them. Zero percentage of periodic requests missed deadlines as aperiodic request rate is varied.

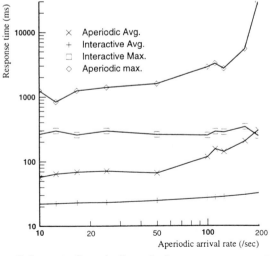

Figure 5. Impact of aperiodic arrival rate on response times.

Figure 6 shows the response times of aperiodic requests and interactive requests (both at 25 requests/sec) as the number of requested streams in the system is varied from 5 to 100. With the considered allocation of bandwidths, the system could support a maximum of 33 streams. Hence, even when more streams are requested, the system admits only 33 streams. This shows that the periodic request rate is contained to allow aperiodic requests and interactive requests to achieve their performance goals. We observe that the maximum response times of interactive requests are not considerably impacted by the number of requested streams in the system.

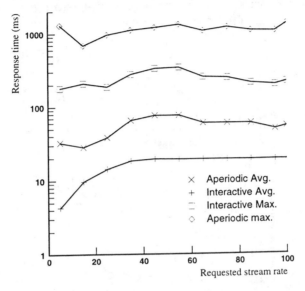

Figure 6. Impact of requested stream rate on response times.

Figure 7 shows the performance of interactive requests when interactive arrival rate is varied. It is observed that the response times of interactive requests stay bounded at the scheduler irrespective of the arrival rate. Beyond the supported rate, the interactive requests are forced to wait longer in the leaky-bucket controller. Hence, beyond the supported rate, the total delay experienced by an interactive request can exceed the desired latency bound. If a higher interactive request rate needs to be supported, these requests have to be allocated a higher bandwidth to limit the delays at the leaky-bucket controller. We observed that the maximum number of streams supported by the system stayed constant (at 33) irrespective of the arrival rate of the interactive requests and zero percentage of these requests missed deadlines as interactive request rate is varied.

3.4 OTHER ISSUES IN DISK SCHEDULING

Data striping increases the need for protecting against failures since the failure of any disk can render service unavailable for all the streams. Parity protection such as RAID [15] or data duplication can provide data availability guarantees after a failure, but these techniques cannot guarantee availability of the necessary I/O bandwidth for timely delivery of data after a failure. Scheduling data delivery after a component failure is a difficult problem. Much work needs to be done in this area. Overdesigning the system is one of the possible options so that, even after a failure, the data can be delivered in a timely fashion. Dynamic resource allocation for tolerating failures is another possible option. In certain cases, only statistical guarantees may be provided after a failure.

Providing a VCR-like capability of pause/resume, fast-forward/reverse requires that sufficient resources be available at the server to absorb the variations in bandwidth demands due to such operations [19]. Pause operation may reduce the bandwidth demand at the server and other operations may increase the bandwidth requirements. To support such operations, the server has to determine that these bandwidth variations do not affect the delivery of other scheduled streams. It is also possible to keep the bandwidth requirements at the server constant by serving alternate copies of video streams that have less quality encoding at the higher frame rates required by the fast-forward and reverse operations [20]. Then the server can serve the alternate copies of video data during fast-forward and reverse operations without altering the schedule of the scheduled streams.

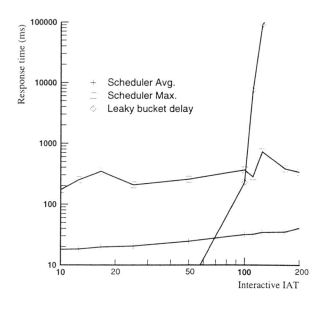

Figure 7. Impact of interactive arrival rate on response times.

4. CPU SCHEDULING

Most existing operating systems use priority-based schemes for scheduling processes with different performance requirements. Priority based schemes however do not provide a convenient mechanism for dividing bandwidth among multiple classes of applications. To satisfy the conflicting demands of different multimedia applications, it may be necessary to give different priorities for the same process depending on the nature of the competing processes at that time. It has been observed that the assignment of priorities and the dynamic adjustment of priorities are often ad hoc [21]. Fair share schedulers [22] have been proposed for distributing CPU resources fairly over long periods of time (several minutes). Techniques also exist for achieving service rate objectives using decay-usage scheduling [23]. These schemes monitor the CPU usage and dynamically alter the priorities to achieve the service objectives. These techniques work over long periods of time and cannot provide any service guarantees over shorter durations. Microeconomic and market-based approaches for resource allocation have been studied [24]. In these schemes, processes bid for resources based on their "funds" or allocations and unsuccessful processes are allowed to increase their bids to improve chances of acquiring the resources in the future.

Lottery scheduler [9] assigns the CPU based on a randomized fair algorithm to achieve proportional CPU allocation. Because of the inherent randomness, this algorithm achieves fairness over long periods of time. Hierarchical scheduling algorithm makes a distinction between CPU allocation among different request types and the scheduling of CPU resources among multiple threads of a request type. Hierarchical scheduler uses static resource allocation and the recent CPU usage information to decide the next process to schedule. The threads within a request type or a process can be scheduled differently based on the application requirements, for example, hard real-time requests could use EDF and soft real-time requests could use a fair scheduler.

5. NETWORK SCHEDULING

Traditionally, the network scheduling is done on a best-effort basis, i.e., provide as small a delay as possible and as large throughput as possible but without any guarantees on the delivered performance. Best-effort protocols for multimedia delivery follow this approach with an aim to utilizing the existing network resources. These protocols typically adapt delivery to the available bandwidth. The multimedia application may adjust the compression such that lower quality data is received when network congestion reduces available bandwidth. For example, video frame rate or the bit rate in each frame can be adjusted to suit the available network bandwidth. Transport protocols such as TCP adjust the sending rates based on the available bandwidth. However, TCP is designed for reliable delivery of data without regard to the delays experienced by individual packets in a transmission and hence not quite suitable for video delivery. Another popular transport protocol UDP does not adapt to network resources.

Buffering can be used to ameliorate network congestion problems. However, buffering increases the delay between the time of transmission and the time of consumption of delivered data. Long delays may be acceptable when delivering stored media such as prerecorded video and audio. In such cases, buffering delay will result in a longer startup delay at the receiver. Long delays (due to buffering or network) are, however, unacceptable in live media transmissions such as in teleconferencing. Packets lost in the network due to congestion or buffer overflow may have to be retransmitted. In compressed video, not all the packets contain the same quality data and hence it is important that some packets be given more priority over others during delivery. It has been shown that prioritized transmission of data can deliver better quality [8]. Protocols can be designed to give priority to certain packets over others at the sender during transmission to achieve better quality data delivery [7]. Feedback can be exchanged between the sender and receiver to adapt the delivery to the current network conditions. The feedback can be in the form of measured delay [7] or in the form of available bandwidth. Feedback can also be exchanged between routers and switches in the network [8]. Adaptation can be in the form of adjusting the frame rate or the bit rate [25] or in the form of delivering only higher quality frames [7] while dropping the lower quality frames.

The other approach to delivery is based on reserving resources in the network based on the application needs [6]. In this connection-oriented approach, each application characterizes its requirements and passes them on to the network at the time of connection establishment. These requirements are processed by the network switches to estimate the possible guarantees that can be provided. When this negotiation process between application requirements and the network guarantees is completed, it is expected that if the application limits its resource usage to its requirements, the network will be able to meet the promised performance guarantees. To make this possible, the switches in the network have to schedule packets appropriately. Much work has been done in characterizing the application requirements and the bounds that can be provided under various scheduling policies [3,4,5,26,27]. Statistical and deterministic guarantees are considered in these scheduling policies.

A scheduling policy is termed *non-work-conserving* if the switch can be idle even when there are packets to be switched and *work-conserving* otherwise. Non-work-conserving policies can waste network bandwidth, but simplify network resource control significantly by restricting the output traffic rate at each switch. To ensure that the user limits network resource consumption to the stated demands, the network switches may adopt *rate control* or per-connection queuing. RCSP [3], and Stop-and-go [26] are examples of non-work-conserving scheduling policies. Fair queuing [27] and general processor sharing [4] are examples of work-conserving scheduling policies.

6. SUMMARY

Multimedia applications can be provided different levels of service depending on the nature of the application and the availability of resources. An application requires service from the CPU, disks, memory, and network to meet the performance goals. Bandwidth allocation and rate controls can be used to ensure that applications do not interfere with a different class of applications in the system. Appropriate scheduling policies can provide the performance guarantees required by the applications.

In this chapter, we provided a comprehensive view of the disk scheduling problem in providing integrated service. A method has been presented that allows exploitation of statistical multiplexing while providing deterministic service for VBR streams. Through bandwidth allocations and round-based seek optimization scheduling, performance goals have been achieved for different classes of applications. Similarities in CPU scheduling and network scheduling strategies have been pointed out.

REFERENCES

1. L. N. Reddy and J. Wyllie, "I/O issues in a multimedia system," *IEEE Computer*, March 1994.
2. P. S. Yu, M. S. Chen, and D. D. Kandlur, "Grouped sweeping scheduling for DASD-based multimedia, *Multimedia Systems*, Vol. 1, pp. 99-109, 1993.
3. H. Zhang and D. Ferrari, "Rate-controlled static-priority queueing," *Proc. IEEE INFOCOM*, April 1993.
4. A. Parekh and R. Gallager, "A generalized processor sharing approach to flow control in integrated service networks: The multiple node case," *Proc. IEEE INFOCOMM'93*, pp. 521-530, March 1993.
5. R. Cruz, "A Calculus for Network Delay, Part I: Network elements in isolation," *IEEE Trans. on Information Theory*, Vol. 37, No.1, pp. 114-131, January 1991.
6. L. Zhang, S. Deering, D. Estrin, S. Shenker, and D. Zappala. "RSVP: A new resource reservation protocol," *IEEE Network Magazine*, September 1993.
7. Smith, "Cyclic-UDP: A priority-driven best-effort protocol," Tech. Report, Cornell University, 1996.

8. H. Kanakia, P. Mishra, and A. Reibman, "An adaptive congestion control scheme for real-time packet video transport," *Proc. of ACM SIGCOMM*, October 1993.

9. R. Waldspurger and W. Weihl, "Lottery Scheduling: Flexible proportional-share resource management," *Proc. of Symp. on Operating System Design and Implementation*, November 1994.

10. P. Goyal, X. Guo, and H. Vin, "A hierarchical CPU scheduler for multimedia operating systems," *Proc. of Symp. on Operating System Design and Implementation*, 1996.

11. L. Narasimha Reddy and R. Wijayaratne, "On providing deterministic guarantees for VBR streams," *Tech. Report TAMU-ECE-9701*, Texas A&M University, April 1997.

12. R. Haskin, "The shark continuous-media file server," *Proc. of IEEE COMPCON*, February 1993.

13. Microsoft, "The tiger video server," *Microsoft Press Release*, April 1994.

14. B. Laursen, J. Olkin, and M. Porter, "Oracle media server: providing consumer based interactive access to multimedia data," *Proc. of SIGMOD*, pp. 470-477, 1994.

15. D. Patterson, G. Gibson, and R. H. Katz, "A case for redundant arrays of inexpensive disks (RAID)," *ACM SIGMOD Conference*, June 1988.

16. O. Rose, "Mpeg trace data sets," *ftp-info3.informatik.uni-wuerzburg.de*, 1995.

17. J. Gemmell and S. Christodoulakis, "Principles of delay-sensitive multimedia storage and retrieval," *ACM Trans. on Info. Systems*, pp. 51-90, 1992.

18. C. Martin, P. Narayanan, B. Ozden, R. Rastogi, and A. Silberschatz, "The Fellini multimedia storage server," *In Multimedia Information Storage and Management*, Ed: S. Chung, Kluwer Academic Publishers, 1996.

19. K. D. Jayanta, J. D. Salehi, J. F. Kurose, and D. Towsley, "Providing VCR capabilities in large-scale video server," *Proc. of ACM Multimedia Conf.*, pp. 25-32, October 1994.

20. M. S. Chen, D. Kandlur, and P. S. Yu, "Support for fully interactive playout in a disk-array-based video server," *Proc. of ACM Multimedia Conf.*, pp. 391-398, October 1994.

21. H. Deitel, "Operating systems," *Addison Wesley*, 1990.

22. J. Kay and P. Lauder, "A fair share scheduler," *Comm. of ACM*, January 1988.

23. J. Hellerstein, "Achieving service rate objectives with decay usage scheduling," *IEEE Trans. on Software Eng.*, August 1993.

24. D. Ferguson, Y. Yemini, and C. Nikolau, "Microeconomic algorithms for load-balancing in distributed computer systems," *Int. Conf. on Distributed Computer Systems*, 1988.

25. K. Jeffay, D. Stone, T. Talley, and F. Smith, "Adaptive, best-effort delivery of digital audio and video across packet-switched networks," *Proc. Network and Operating System support for Digital Audio and Video*, 1993.

26. S. Golestani, "Duration limited statistical multiplexing of delay-sensitive traffic," *Proc. of INFOCOMM*, pp. 12-20, 1991.

27. K. Demers, S. Keshav, and S. Shenker, "Analysis and simulations of a fair queuing algorithm," *Proc. of ACM SIGCOMM*, pp. 3-12, 1989.

24

STORAGE ORGANIZATIONS FOR MULTIMEDIA DATA

Clement H. C. Leung and Philip K.C. Tse
Victoria University of Technology
Department of Computer and Mathematical Sciences
Ballarat Road, P.O. Box 14428, MCMC
Melbourne, Victoria 8001, Australia

1.   **INTRODUCTION**..508
2.   **BASIC PERFORMANCE PARAMETERS** 509
     2.1   VARIABLE DENSITY RECORDING DISKS 509
     2.2   CONSTANT DENSITY RECORDING DISKS 511
3.   **OPTIMIZATION CONSIDERATIONS**..512
4.   **DATA PLACEMENT** 513
     4.1   INTERLEAVED CONTIGUOUS PLACEMENT 513
     4.2   FREQUENCY BASED PLACEMENT 516
     4.3   LOAD BALANCED PLACEMENT 516
5.   **DATA PLACEMENT AMONG MULTIPLE DISKS** 516
     5.1   DISK STRIPING 517
6.   **DATA PLACEMENT ON HIERARCHICAL STORAGE SYSTEMS** 520
     6.1   REDUCING THE COST 521
     6.2   SELECTING THE FREE DISKS...521
     6.3   REDUCING DISK SPACE AND STAGING TIME 522
7.   **CONCLUDING REMARKS**..523
     REFERENCES 523

Abstract. Multimedia data exhibit significantly different characteristics compared with conventional data in terms of storage requirements, access structure, usage pattern, and response time constraints. The disk has always been recognized as a performance bottleneck in conventional systems due the huge speed gap between disk storage and other parts of the computer system, which is typically of the order of 10^6. Such performance mismatch is made much more pronounced in multimedia applications. In this chapter, different storage organizations for multimedia data are evaluated and optimization procedures for speeding up access are presented. Both hardware-oriented and software-oriented solutions are discussed. The benefits of using hierarchical tertiary storage and optimal data placement strategies are evaluated.

1. INTRODUCTION

There is a substantial performance gap between disk storage and other parts of the computer system. Main memory access time is of the order of 10^{-8} seconds while current disk technology supports an access time of only 10^{-2} seconds. Such problems already exist for conventional structured data and text-based applications, but they are made much worse in multimedia applications.

Table 1. Characteristics of Multimedia Data

Large data size	Video and audio data are very large in size. Their storage requirements in main and secondary memories are vast, necessitating huge storage capacity on all types of storage devices.
Compressed data	Multimedia data are always kept in compressed format because of the large data size. Existing compression standards like JPEG and MPEG standards can compress multimedia data to a smaller size without much noticeable effects on novice users. Typically, the JPEG (Joint Photographic Experts Group) standard can compress images in the ratio of 15:1 and the MPEG (Motion Picture Experts Group) standard can compress videos in the ratio of 50:1.
Multiple data streams	A multimedia object often consists of several media components. These media components are separate at input and arrive at the storage devices as different media streams. These media components are usually retrieved from the storage devices at similar time and merged together before display.
Synchronous retrieval	The data streams that are merged on output are often required to be synchronized before display. Otherwise, artifacts such as video of a talking person without lip synchronization may result.
Frequent read, seldom write	Multimedia data are more often retrieved than modified. This is also inherent to the nature of multimedia production that professional expertise is necessary to generate quality product, while retrieval can be done by novice users.
Continuous and periodic requests	Multimedia data are stored and retrieved using a stream of data requests. These data requests are applied until all data in the objects are accessed. The requests are periodic and uniform in nature, but each request may retrieve a different amount of data.
Tight real time constraints	The storage server must guarantee that their recording and retrieval can be finished within tight real-time constraints. Otherwise, delays would be incurred in the display stream and *jitters* and *hiccups* would appear to users.

Conventional databases focus mainly on Online Transaction Processing (OLTP) applications and these typically require no more than a handful of rows from a relational table. Online Analytic Processing (OLAP), data warehouses, decision support applications, and data mining admittedly require a higher level of data intensity, but their performance constraint is much less stringent than that for real-time multimedia applications.

In general, multimedia data exhibit characteristics, which are different from conventional data. These are listed in Table 1.

A multimedia file system stores a pool of multimedia objects, and is different from a conventional file system due to the support required for continuous retrieval of the multimedia streams and for efficient browsing and indexing for interactive access of the data [1]. A multimedia object can consist of data from several media streams such as audio and video. Stored information of a multimedia object may consist of compressed media streams, length of each block, the inter-media synchronization information, the real-time access bandwidth, the display bandwidth, and the resolution of the objects, which must be stored and maintained by the system [2].

2. BASIC PERFORMANCE PARAMETERS

The performance of traditional computer systems is often calibrated by their disk I/O throughput. The performance of multimedia systems is, however, determined by their response time. Several kinds of delays exist in a multimedia system:

1.   the disk request service time,
2.   the network delays,
3.   the copying time when data are migrated from tertiary storage devices to disks,
4.   the initial setup time to fill the disk buffers.

These delays must be taken into consideration in designing systems that will provide good quality of service to users. Reducing individual delay and system optimization are required to achieve the best overall response time. Disk organizations may be distinguished into (i) variable density recording (VDR), and (ii) constant density recording (CDR). The former is exemplified by the conventional disks, while the latter has greater potential for efficiently supporting multimedia data storage and retrieval. Disk performance depends on a number of parameters. Table 2 summarizes the main notations used for the different parameters used throughout this chapter.

2.1 VARIABLE DENSITY RECORDING DISKS

In accessing data, the disk arm travels through a number of tracks to the required one. The traveling distance is commonly referred to as the *seek distance*. If all the seek destinations are random, the average seek distance would be $(b-a)/3$, where a and b are the radii of the innermost and outermost tracks, respectively [7]. Frequently, the seek time is taken to be a linear function of the seek distance. In reality, the seek time is the time required for the following motions:

1.   accelerate the disk arm until it reaches the maximum speed;
2.   move the arm at the maximum speed;
3.   decelerate the arm until it stops;
4.   settle the disk head on the required track.

Table 2. Notations Used in This Chapter

T	time for one disk revolution
a	radius of the innermost track
b	radius of the outermost track
ε	recording density of the innermost track
d	seek distance
s	seek time
l	rotational latency
ρ	data transfer rate of disks
γ	data transfer rate of tertiary storage library
τ	data transfer time
β	disk bandwidth
δ	display time of a media block
ω	queue time in tertiary store
χ	media exchange and reposition time of tertiary store
η	network bandwidth
D	number of bytes in a data block
M	number of data blocks in a media block
G	gap size between two media blocks in number of data blocks
V	number of data blocks in a media object
B	total used bandwidth of a device after allocation
S	total used space of a device after allocation
L	available load on video file server
L_{cache}	fraction of free disk space
L_{stream}	fraction of free disk bandwidth
L_{net}	fraction of free network bandwidth

Using motion dynamics of the disk arm, the seek time is shown in [3] to be

$$s = \begin{cases} a_1 + a_2 d, & d > a_5 \\ a_3 + a_4 \sqrt{d}, & d \le a_5 \end{cases}, \tag{1}$$

where a_1, a_2, a_3, a_4, a_5 are fixed parameters and d is the seek distance.

Rotational latency is the time required for the starting position of the desired data block to rotate under the read/write head. This is often estimated as half of a disk revolution time that is $T/2$. However, the rotational latency for fixed block size is not uniformly distributed. This is because data transfer can begin only at fixed block starting positions and fixed angular positions. The sum of seek time plus rotational latency, hence, must necessarily be in integral multiples of basic block duration for consecutive access in busy conditions [4].

After the I/O path is established and the desired data come under the head, the disk can start transferring data. The head sends data over a bit-serial wire to the I/O controller. The speed of transferring data must be the same as the speed of data coming under the head. The speed of data transfer is directly proportional to the recording density and rotation speed of the disk. The *data transfer time* is the time required for the required data within the current track to be read. The data transfer time τ for a data block for a VDR disk can be shown to be

$$\tau = \frac{D \cdot T}{2\pi a \cdot \varepsilon},$$

(2)

where a and ε are the radius and recording density of the innermost track, respectively. The data transfer rate ρ is

$$\rho = \frac{2\pi a \cdot \varepsilon}{T}.$$

(3)

The disk bandwidth is given by

$$\beta = \frac{D}{s + l + \tau}.$$

(4)

2.2 CONSTANT DENSITY RECORDING DISKS

A disk format now gaining increasing acceptance is *constant density recording* or *zoned-bit-recording*. This is done by dividing each disk into several concentric zones by grouping tracks of similar radii together (Figure 1). Recording densities in each zone are optimized and are nearly equal. Because outer zones are larger in diameter, they can contain more bits and sectors. As the disk rotates at constant angular velocity, the read/write head traverses more bits in the outer zones than in the inner zones within the same period of time. Hence, the data transfer rate is higher in the outer zones. Optical disks use a similar approach to increase their storage capacities, but they rotate at variable speed to maintain a constant linear velocity. Hence, their data transfer rates are the same while their track capacity varies [5]. The performance of constant density recording disks can be shown to be superior to that of conventional disks. If all seek actions are random, the average seek distance is shown in [6] to be

$$\bar{d} = \frac{4(b-a)(a^2 + 3ab + b^2)}{15(a+b)^2}.$$

(5)

Equation 1 can then be used to find the average seek time.

The average rotational latency is the same as that for variable density recording disks and is equal to $T/2$. The average data transfer time depends on the number of zones on the disk. The smallest average data transfer time is achieved when there is only one track in each zone, in which case, the average data transfer time τ for a data block is shown in [6] to be

$$\bar{\tau} = \frac{D \cdot T}{\pi(a+b)\varepsilon}.$$

(6)

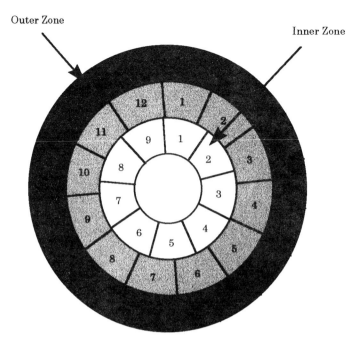

Figure 1. Constant density recording disk.

The average data transfer rate of the disk is then

$$\bar{\rho} = \frac{\pi(a+b) \cdot \varepsilon}{T}. \tag{7}$$

The disk bandwidth is then calculated as

$$\beta = \frac{D}{\bar{s} + \bar{l} + \bar{\tau}}. \tag{8}$$

3. OPTIMIZATION CONSIDERATIONS

The performance of disk storage depends on many parameters, such as the disk size, recording density, rotational speed, and others as shown in Table 2. A slight change in one parameter may affect the disk performance significantly. In order to achieve the optimal performance in accessing data from disks, performance behavior must be quantitatively modeled [7].

Apart from the parameters that are fixed by the manufacturer, disk performance is also significantly influenced by the usage pattern. For example, consider two data objects that are always retrieved together as consecutive data requests. If these two objects are placed at two extreme ends of a disk, the disk arm will need to move a long distance to retrieve both objects. The seek time and rotational latency involved are very long and can be of the order of a hundred milliseconds. However, if these two objects are placed at consecutive physical locations on the disk, the second data request can be serviced instantly without additional seek actions. The two objects can then be retrieved in a much shorter time in the order of milliseconds. Therefore, efficient data placement can be a critical factor in disk performance.

Different techniques may improve different components of disk performance. However, choosing one technique may affect or limit the effectiveness of other techniques. There is often a tradeoff between different techniques in determining the disk performance. For example, a frequency based placement method would place the hottest objects at the center of the tracks to reduce disk seek time. A balanced placement approach would, however, place the hottest objects at the outermost zone in a constant density recording disk to reduce data transfer time. A tradeoff or optimization is then required to reduce the overall data access time.

Many techniques can be used to obtain optimum performance from disks. The techniques to place multimedia data within a single disk are described in Section 4. Several techniques to place multimedia data among multiple disks are presented in Section 5. The techniques to place multimedia data in the hierarchical storage system are described in Section 6.

4. DATA PLACEMENT

Intra-disk data placement is the most important component in all data placement strategies. Success of any other data placement strategies, such as inter-disk data placement and hierarchical storage placement, all depend on an efficient intra-disk placement technique. An efficient placement technique should take into account the data and their access characteristics in multimedia systems. While reducing the response time, the system should provide a guarantee on the maximum response time, which is important to the choice of placement technique.

Several placement strategies are traditionally used to place data within a disk in computer systems. The random placement strategy places data at random locations on the disk. This approach produces the worst performance and can be used as a reference for comparison. The contiguous placement strategy places data at contiguous locations on the disk. This placement strategy is most suitable for sequential data processing. When the whole data object is accessed with consecutive data requests, all the data requests can be serviced with only one seek action. The data access time can be minimal only when no other data are being accessed within the time period. Interleaved contiguous placement, load balanced placement, and frequency based placement techniques are described in the reminder of this section.

4.1 INTERLEAVED CONTIGUOUS PLACEMENT

Multimedia data are recorded and retrieved using aperiodic request streams. An approach, called *interleaved contiguous* placement, is used to mix several streams together [8] so that

1. data of each stream are separated into a number of data blocks based on the disk block size;
2. a number of data blocks are grouped together to form one media block;
3. consecutive media blocks of one stream are separated, leaving some gaps, the size of which is determined by the time available before the next media block is required during retrieval, and these gaps can be filled with data of another stream;
4. consecutive media blocks are also placed close enough together in the storage device so that sequential access can be finished within real-time constraint.

Therefore, each data stream is characterized by a storage pattern composed of two parameters M and G, where M is the number of data blocks in each media block, and G is the number of data blocks between two consecutive media blocks. The storage pattern can satisfy the continuous retrieval requirement if

$$\frac{M + G}{\rho} \leq \delta. \tag{9}$$

That is, the time to skip over the gap and retrieve the next successive media block from the storage device is less than the time to display a media block. Since the left-hand side of the inequality is the time to skip over a gap and read the next media block from the device, and this is less than the display time of one media block, there is enough time to retrieve the next successive media block while the current media block is displayed. Continuing likewise, the whole data stream can be retrieved and displayed without delay.

> **Example 1**: Consider a video stream of 640x480 pixels/frame, 24-bit color, 30 frames/second compressed at 50:1. Here,
>
> 1 frame/block = 0.147 Mbit,
> $\delta = 1/30 = 0.0333$ seconds,
> $\rho = 50$ Mbit/sec.
>
> The maximum gap, G, is = 50 x 0.0333 – 0.147 = 1.33 Mbit.   ■

Let M_i be the number of data blocks in the ith data stream and G_i be the number of space blocks in the ith data stream. In the following two subsections, we consider the condition to merge data streams (M_1, G_1), (M_2, G_2), ..., (M_k, G_k) while maintaining the continuous retrieval requirement. Two or more data streams may be placed together by a process of *merging* (Figure 2). Two policies, the Storage Pattern Preserving Policy (SPP policy) and the Storage Pattern Altering Policy (SPA policy) are used to decide the feasibility conditions of merging. The SPP policy maintains the storage pattern of each data stream unchanged after merging. The SPA policy may change the storage pattern during merging but maintains the average storage pattern during the merging.

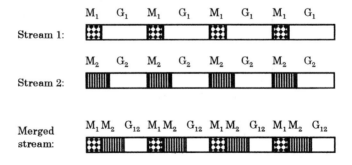

Figure 2. Interleaved contiguous placement.

4.1.1 Storage pattern preserving policy

When two media streams are merged together, the continuous retrieval requirement of each individual media stream remains valid if the storage pattern of each media stream is unchanged; i.e., every M_i and G_i are unchanged.

It is shown in [8] that two media streams can be merged using the SPP policy if and only if their greatest common divisor satisfies the condition

$$M_1 + M_2 \leq \text{GCD}(M_1 + G_1, M_2 + G_2), \tag{10}$$

where GCD denotes the greatest common divisor of the list of numbers enclosed in brackets.

Example 2: Let $M_1 = 2$, $G_1 = 8$, $M_2 = 2$, $G_2 = 13$. Then

$$M_1 + M_2 = 2 + 2 = 4$$
$$m = \text{GCD}(2+8, 2+13) = \text{GCD}(10, 15) = 5 > 4 = M_1 + M_2.$$

Hence, these two streams can be merged under the SPP policy. ∎

Example 3: Let $M_1 = 1$, $G_1 = 1$, $M_2 = 2$, $G_2 = 3$. Then

$$M_1 + M_2 = 1 + 2 = 3$$
$$m = \text{GCD}(1+1, 2+3) = \text{GCD}(2, 5) = 1 < 3 = M_1 + M_2.$$

Hence, these two streams cannot be merged under the SPP policy. ∎

The SPP policy can maintain the continuous retrieval conditions with memory buffer and retrieval time unaltered by the merging for every component media stream. However, the merged stream no longer fulfills the requirements of the original individual media stream in terms of the media and gap regularity conditions. Thus, the feasibility condition for merging more than two streams cannot be easily generalized.

4.1.2 Storage pattern altering policy

The SPA policy allows change of the storage pattern during the merging process. If the storage pattern is altered, the continuous retrieval requirement may be violated. While maintaining the average gap size over a number of media blocks, the continuous retrieval requirement could still remain valid. This is achieved by using more memory buffers to keep the extra media blocks in memory before they are consumed. It is shown in [9] that a number of data streams (M_1, G_1), (M_2, G_2), ... , (M_k, G_k) can be merged if and only if

$$\frac{M_1}{M_1 + G_1} + \frac{M_2}{M_2 + G_2} + \ldots + \frac{M_k}{M_k + G_k} \leq 1. \tag{11}$$

The following examples illustrate the usefulness of this inequality.

Example 4: Let $M_1 = 1$, $G_1 = 1$, $M_2 = 1$, $G_2 = 3$. Then

$$\frac{M_1}{M_1 + G_1} + \frac{M_2}{M_2 + G_2} = \frac{1}{2} + \frac{1}{4} = 0.75 < 1$$

Hence, these two streams can be merged under the SPA policy. ∎

Example 5: Let $M_1 = 1$, $G_1 = 1$, $M_2 = 2$, $G_2 = 1$. Then

$$\frac{M_1}{M_1 + G_1} + \frac{M_2}{M_2 + G_2} = \frac{1}{2} + \frac{2}{3} = \frac{7}{6} > 1$$

Hence, these two streams cannot be merged under the SPA policy. ∎

Example 6: Using the same parameters as in Example 3, that is $M_1 = 1$, $G_1 = 1$, $M_2 = 2$, $G_2 = 3$, we have

$$\frac{M_1}{M_1 + G_1} + \frac{M_2}{M_2 + G_2} = \frac{1}{2} + \frac{2}{5} = \frac{9}{10} < 1$$

We saw in Example 3 that these two streams, which cannot be merged under the SPP policy, can now be merged under the SPA policy. ∎

4.2 FREQUENCY BASED PLACEMENT

The magnitude of average seek time on constant density recording disks are different from conventional disks because of the difference in data transfer rate. Hence, the order of placement for constant density recording disks follows a different pattern (Figure 3). The hottest objects V_1, V_2, and V_3 are placed at the sub-outer zone and the next hottest objects V_4 and V_5 are placed in the next zone [10].

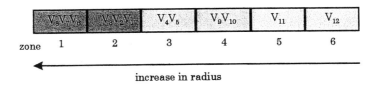

Figure 3. Frequency based placement.

4.3 LOAD BALANCED PLACEMENT

Multimedia objects have various bandwidth and size characteristics. Each zone in a constant density recording disk has a different data transfer rate. If high bandwidth data are placed in low bandwidth inner zones, the retrieval time of these data objects are very long and the disk requests will respond slowly. The queuing time of all the waiting requests would increase significantly, leading to poor disk performance.

Load balanced placement is a method that reduces the variation in disk access time, and excessive variation (large variance and second moment) could have a detrimental effect on response time [7]. This placement method stores data according to the necessary bandwidth. Thus, high bandwidth multimedia data are placed in outer zones while low bandwidth multimedia data are placed in inner zones. Disk requests would have a much shorter wait and they could respond faster [6].

5. DATA PLACEMENT AMONG MULTIPLE DISKS

RAID disks (Redundant Array of Inexpensive Disks) have been widely accepted in recent years. A limitation of RAID is its lack of control on the placement of data in multimedia systems. The data bandwidth cannot be effectively controlled and the memory buffer can easily overflow.

When placing data among multiple disks, several aspects must be considered. This includes load balancing, fast response time, and small memory buffer. If disk load is not balanced, one disk may receive all the requests and limits the disk array performance. The data request response time is still the determining factor in comparing various placement algorithms. The memory buffer consumption, if too large, would also limit the efficiency and effectiveness of an algorithm.

5.1 DISK STRIPING

The main strategy to place data among multiple disks is *disk striping* (Figure 4). The algorithm for disk striping [11,12,13] consists of: if the data blocks are striped across N disks, then the first data block is placed on disk 1, the second data block is placed on disk 2, and so on. In general, the ith data block is placed on disk i mod N.

When data are accessed, a number of disk requests are sent to the disks at the same time. While the first disk is repositioning its read/write head to the desired location, the second to the last disks are also repositioning their read/write heads to the appropriate locations. One block of data is then transferred from the disk to the memory buffer in each disk. Hence, the time required to retrieve N data blocks from N identical disks takes about the same amount of time as retrieving only one data block from one disk. In this way, the bandwidths of all N disks are used together to provide sufficient bandwidth for the multimedia data. When data blocks are distributed to N disks, the bandwidth of data retrieval becomes $N\beta$, where β is the bandwidth of a single disk.

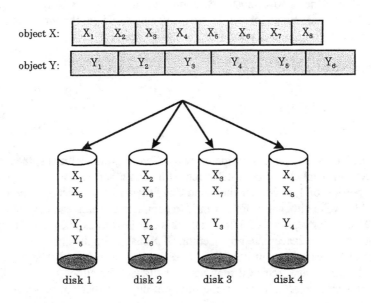

Figure 4. Disk striping.

However, the amount of data buffers in memory is also increased [11]. In order to retrieve a data stream from the disks, buffer for $N+1$ data blocks are required. Initially, N data blocks are fetched from the disks to the N buffers. The $(N+1)$th buffer is starting to fill from the disk while data in the first buffer is being consumed. When the first buffer is exhausted, the $(N+2)$th data block is started to fill and the second block is consumed. After the kth data block is exhausted, the $(N+k)$th data block is then started to fill and the $(k+1)$th data block is consumed. The buffers are used in a cyclic manner. Thus, the whole stream can be retrieved using $N+1$ buffers and the initial latency is the time to fill N buffers.

In order to support real-time display of the media stream, the retrieval time of one media block must be less than the display time of N media block. Hence, the constraint for a single stream is

$$s + l + M\rho < N\delta. \tag{12}$$

Similarly, the constraint for r streams of request is

$$r(s+l) + \rho \sum_{j=1}^{r} M_j \le N \min_{j=1,\Lambda,r} (\delta_j). \tag{13}$$

If the maximum values for seek and latency are used, this constraint provides a *hard guarantee* for multiple streams. It is most conservative using the worst case estimates, and the data retrieval time can be 100% guaranteed. Disk bandwidth is, however, wasted and the disks are under-utilized since maximum seek is rarely incurred. Another way to provide guarantee for multiple streams is through *soft guarantee*. The requests are queued for disk accesses. The waiting requests are chosen according to the disk scheduling policy. The disks may achieve higher utilization, but the quality of the stream is reduced.

5.1.1 Data replication and user delays

In order to maintain the disk retrieval bandwidth at a level similar to the display level, the number of disks to decluster each multimedia stream is limited. The degree of declustering for a multimedia object is first calculated. Then the multimedia object is declustered across a group of disks according to the degree [14].

Letting m to be the degree of declustering, we have

$$m = \left\lceil \frac{\delta}{\beta} \right\rceil. \tag{14}$$

If two multimedia objects X and Y reside on two different groups of disks, these two objects can be retrieved in parallel without interfering with each other. However, if some portion of X and some portion of Y reside on the same disk, then while object X is being retrieved, object Y would have to either wait for object X to complete or share the disk bandwidth with object X. If Y waits for requests of X to finish, this can lead to expensive waiting time. The response time would be exacerbated by queuing. If Y shares the disk bandwidth with X, this increases the disk seek time significantly. The disk bandwidth would then be reduced, and the total bandwidth of disk retrieval may not be sufficient for either X or Y. One approach would be to replicate object Y across some different disks so that object Y can be retrieved from other disks (Figure 5).

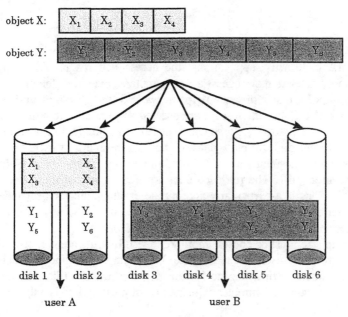

Figure 5. Data replication.

5.1.2 Staggered striping

Another approach that can be used is *staggered striping* [15]. A multimedia object is partitioned into a two-dimensional (m x n) matrix of sub-object X_{ij}. These sub-objects are then placed in different disks in a staggered manner (Figure 6). While object X is being retrieved, the disks are used in a rotating manner. As long as each disk has some free time period, object Y can be retrieved within the time gap. The staggered striping method provides effective support for multiple users accessing different objects from a group of striped disks, and it balances the loading on individual disks.

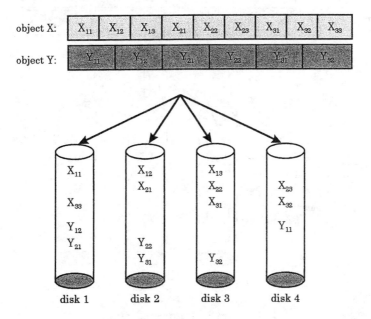

Figure 6. Staggered striping.

5.1.3 Phase-based striping

In some multimedia applications, the access patterns of videos are very much skewed. A number of users may request a very popular movie at different times. A video is organized as a (*m* x *n*) matrix of video strips in *phase-based striping* and these video strips are placed on *m* disks. Consecutive strips are ordered sequentially from disk 1 to disk *m* and so on. Each column of *n* strips is stored consecutively on a single disk or a single node. The whole video file is thus divided into *n* phases, and up to *n* groups of users can view different phases of the same video simultaneously. All users viewing the same phase of the movie are serviced as one user [16]. The retrieved data are then broadcast to all users of the same phase (Figure 7). This is a particularly appropriate organization for near video-on-demand applications. Here, the phase delay is given by V/m. If the access pattern is uniformly distributed, the average waiting time of new users is $V/(2m)$.

The strip size must be chosen appropriately so that the amount of waiting time and the number of groups of users are reasonable. For example, consider a 2-hour long movie divided into 10 minutes strips; the movie can be placed on 12 disks. The average waiting time of a new user would be 5 minutes. The maximum waiting time is only 10 minutes.

6. DATA PLACEMENT ON HIERARCHICAL STORAGE SYSTEMS

Large multimedia systems may need data storage of the order of petabytes. This often makes the inexpensive magnetic disks neither economical nor practical. Tertiary storage devices can provide storage of the order of terabytes, but they cannot provide adequate bandwidth for real-time display. Therefore, a hierarchical storage system combining both tertiary storage devices and disks may be used to meet large size and bandwidth demands for multimedia data.

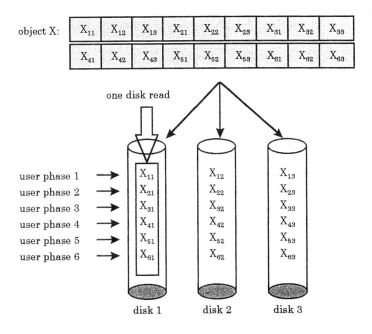

Figure 7. Phase based striping.

A hierarchical storage system consists of two levels of storage devices. In the first level, secondary storage devices provide fast data retrieval and smaller retrieval size at higher media storage cost. In the second level, tertiary storage library provides cheap media storage at a slower data retrieval rate. The secondary storage devices can be magnetic disks, solid state disks, WORM disks, and other direct access storage devices. The tertiary storage library may consist of automatic disk changers, optical jukeboxes, or tape libraries.

Tertiary storage devices provide permanent storage of all multimedia data objects at the lowest cost. Frequently accessed multimedia objects may reside permanently in the disks. Using a process of *staging*, infrequently accessed objects are copied temporarily to the disks when required; these disk images are then displayed to users and can be deleted afterward. An efficient hierarchical storage technique needs to

1. reduce the total system cost;
2. select the appropriate disks to store the staged data;
3. maintain the balance of space and bandwidth; and
4. minimize disk space consumption and user response time.

6.1 REDUCING THE COST

The cost of a multimedia storage server consists of the data storage cost and the bandwidth cost. If tertiary storage is not used, then all the data have to be stored in the more expensive magnetic disks. Hence, tertiary storage is an essential component of a multimedia server due to its inexpensive storage capacity. Although tertiary storage devices can store data cheaper than disks, their bandwidth cost is higher than that of magnetic disk arrays [17]. Increasing the number of streams from the tertiary storage would increase the cost of disk buffers substantially, resulting in higher overall cost of the system [18]. Therefore, the number of streams from tertiary storage should be kept low and the disk buffers should be used as little as possible.

In a distributed environment, the cost per stream can be reduced by increasing the number of subsystems. A multimedia storage server can be built in a cost-effective way by coupling several smaller subsystems together [18].

6.2 SELECTING THE FREE DISKS

The disk that is selected to hold the staged data should, of course, have sufficient space to contain the data. The bandwidth constraint in Equation 4 should also be valid. In order to balance the loading on the disks, the appropriate disk should be chosen while maintaining the balance of disk load. Disk striping techniques can also be used in hierarchical storage systems to store data from a tertiary storage library.

6.2.1 Bandwidth-to-space ratio

When a large cold object is placed on a fast device, there is little disk space left to store other objects. This would erode disk bandwidth due to limitations on the disk space constraint. Likewise, when a small hot object is placed on a slow device, there is little bandwidth left to service other objects. This would then erode disk space due to the limitations on the disk bandwidth constraint [19].

Therefore, the placement of objects should consider the balance of space and bandwidth of objects already on the disk. A bandwidth-to-space ratio (BSR) policy should be used to select the storage device. This BSR policy should attempt to balance the loading and storage space in each storage device. The bandwidth-to-space ratio of the video objects on a device is defined as $BSR = B/S$.

It is recommended in [19] that the following rule be followed. If the video object placed on that device will lower the BSR, then this device is chosen; otherwise, the device causing minimum increase in BSR is selected.

6.2.2 Distributed cache techniques

A distributed system includes one or more archive servers (AS) and one or more video file servers (VFS) connected together via a network of limited bandwidth. The archive servers contain the permanent store of videos. The video file servers contain the staged videos from the archive. All videos are displayed from the video file servers [20,21]. Consider the performance of staging a video in such a situation. The available load on VFS is defined as $L = L_{cache} L_{stream} L_{net}$ and $0 \leq L \leq 1$.

The VFS with the minimum load, if storage is sufficient, would then be chosen to store the staged video. The staging time or request response time is given in [21] as

$$\omega + \chi + \max(\frac{V}{\gamma}, \frac{V}{\eta}),\qquad(15)$$

where ω is the queuing time in tertiary store, χ is the media exchange and reposition time of tertiary store, V is the length of the video, γ is the data transfer rate of the tertiary store, and η is the network bandwidth.

6.3 REDUCING DISK SPACE AND STAGING TIME

The staging process has three problems. First, users have to wait for the staging process, which takes a long time to complete. Second, the disk space containing these infrequently accessed objects is reserved until the multimedia data is no longer required. Third, the disk bandwidth is wasted as both writing and reading on the disks are required for each staging. The pipeline methods are often proposed to rectify some of these problems.

6.3.1 Pipeline method

For certain applications such as display on demand systems, users can only request to view video from start to finish. Since the time to stage multimedia objects from tertiary store to secondary storage devices can be very long, the system may start to display the data to users before the whole object is completely copied to disks. This *pipelining* technique can reduce the waiting time before the user can start to view the multimedia objects [22].

An object X is divided into a number of blocks. The pipelining technique groups the blocks of X into s logical slices $(X_1, X_2, \ldots, X_s)$ such that the display time of X_1 is longer than the retrieval time of X_2, the display time of $(X_1 + X_2)$ is longer than the retrieval time of $(X_2 + X_3)$, and so on.

The Production Consumption Ratio, PCR, is defined as

$$\text{PCR} = \frac{\gamma}{\delta}.\qquad(16)$$

It is shown in [22] that if PCR < 1, then the waiting time would be minimal when the last slice consists of a single block. In this case, the size of the first slice is given by $V - \lfloor \text{PCR}(V-1) \rfloor$, with the initial setup time given by

$$\omega + \chi + \frac{\left(V - \lfloor \text{PCR}(V-1) \rfloor\right)}{\gamma}.\qquad(17)$$

6.3.2 Space efficient pipeline method

In the space efficient pipeline method, the HEAD portion or the first slice of objects are cached to disks. The TAIL portion or the rest of objects are loaded on demand. A circular buffer can be used to retrieve and display the TAIL portion. This staging buffer size may shrink when the size of the slices of the objects decrease [23]. The maximum buffer space required for an object of size V is estimated as $(1 - PCR^2)V$.

7. CONCLUDING REMARKS

The ability to deliver a vast selection of multimedia data in an efficient and flexible manner will remain a key challenge in the design and construction of multimedia data storage systems. System performance is mostly determined by two factors:

1.   The technology constraints, hardware parameters, and storage organizations governing the different types of storage devices.
2.   The data placement and access algorithms used to store and obtain data from these storage devices.

The technology will no doubt continue to advance, giving, in particular, lower access times and higher storage capacities. The data placement techniques described in this chapter all help to reduce the data access time in the retrieval of multimedia data from storage devices. Intra-disk data placement helps to decide where to place the objects within a disk, and inter-disk data placement shows how to partition a multimedia object to achieve efficient parallelism. The hierarchical storage techniques take into consideration the feasibility, economy, and efficiency factors in utilizing storage resources for multimedia data usage.

The storage organization of CDR disks is particularly promising for multimedia data retrieval as it eliminates the erosion in both bandwidth and storage capacities of conventional VDR disks. With the amount of multimedia data reaching petabyte magnitude, there is no question that storage devices other than disks will have to be employed. Here, careful data placement, parallelization, and staging considerations will play a key role in determining the overall performance of a multimedia system.

REFERENCES

1.   Terry, D.B. and Swinehart, D.C., "Managing stored voice in the etherphone system," *ACM Transactions on Computer Systems*, 6(1), 3-27, 1988.

2.   Kunii, T.L., Shinagawa, Y., Paul, R.M., Khan, M.F., and Khokhar, A.A., "Issues in storage and retrieval of multimedia data," *Multimedia Systems*, 3, 298-304, 1995.

3.   Ruemmler, C. and Wilkes, J., "An introduction to disk drive modeling," *IEEE Computer*, 17-28, March 1994.

4.   Leung, C.H.C. and Choo, Q.H., "The effect of fixed-length record implementation on file system response," *Acta Informatica*, 17, 399-409, 1982.

5.   Steinmetz R., "Analyzing the multimedia operating system," *IEEE Multimedia*, 68-84, Spring 1995.

6.   Tse, P.K.C. and Leung, C.H.C., "Improving multimedia systems performance using constant density recording disks," *Technical Report*, Department of Computer and Mathematical Sciences, Victoria University of Technology, 1997.

7. Leung, C.H.C., *Quantitative Analysis of Computer Systems*. John Wiley & Sons, 1988.

8. Yu, C., Sun W., Bitton, D., Yang, Q., Bruno, R., and Tullis, J., "Efficient placement of audio data on optical disks for real-time applications," *Communications of the ACM*, 32(7), 862-871, July 1989.

9. Rangan, P.V. and Vin, H.M., "Efficient storage techniques for digital continuous multimedia," *IEEE Transactions on Knowledge and Data Engineering*, 5(4), 564-573, August 1993.

10. Chen, S. and Thapar, M., "Zone-bit-recording-enhanced video data layout strategies," *Proceedings of MASCOTS*, IEEE, 29-35, 1996.

11. Lougher, P. and Shepherd, D., "The design of a storage server for continuous media," *The Computer Journal*, 36(1), 32-42, 1993.

12. Hsieh, J., Lin, M., Liu, J.C.L., Du, D.H.C., and Ruwart, T.M., "Performance of a mass storage system for video-on-demand," *Proceedings of the Fourteenth Annual Joint Conference of the IEEE Computer and Communications Societies*, 2, IEEE, 771-778, 1995.

13. Oyang, Y.J., Lee, M.H., Wen, C.H., and Cheng, C.Y., "Design of multimedia storage systems for on-demand playback," *Proceedings of the Eleventh International Conference on Data Engineering*, IEEE, 457-465, 1995.

14. Ghandeharizadeh, S. and Ramos, L., "Continuous retrieval of multimedia data using parallelism," *IEEE Transactions on Knowledge and Data Engineering*, 5(4), 658-669, August 1993.

15. Berson, S., Ghandeharizadeh, S., Muntz, R., and Ju, X., "Staggered striping in multimedia information systems," *Proceedings of SIGMOD*, ACM, 79-90, 1994.

16. Chua, T.S., Li, J., Ooi, B.C., and Tan, K.L., "Disk striping strategies for large video-on-demand servers," *Proceedings of Multimedia '96*, ACM, 297-306, 1996.

17. Chervenak, A.L., Patterson, D.A., and Katz, R.H., "Storage systems for movies-on-demand video servers," *Proceedings of the Fourteenth IEEE Symposium on Mass Storage Systems*, IEEE, 246-256, 1995.

18. Doganata, Y.N. and Tantawi, A.N., "A cost/performance study of video servers with hierarchical storage," *Proceedings of the International Conference on Multimedia Computing and Systems*, 393-402, 1994.

19. Dan, A. and Sitaram, D., "An online video placement policy based on bandwidth to space ratio (BSR)," *Proceedings of SIGMOD*, ACM, 376-385, 1995.

20. Rowe, L.A., Boreczky, J.S., and Berger, D.A., "A distributed hierarchical video-on-demand system," *Proceedings of IEEE International Conference on Image Processing*, IEEE, 334-337, 1995.

21. Brubeck, D.W. and Rowe, L.A., "Hierarchical storage management in a distributed VOD system," *IEEE Multimedia*, 37-47, Fall 1996.

22. Ghandeharizadeh, S. and Shahabi, C., "On multimedia repositories, personal computers, and hierarchical storage systems," *Proceedings of Multimedia '94*, ACM, 407-416, October 1994.

23. Wang, J.Z., Hua, D.A., and Young, H.C., "SEP: a space efficient pipelining technique for managing disk buffers in multimedia servers," *Proceedings of the International IEEE Conference on Multimedia Computing and Systems*, 598-607, 1996.

25

MULTIMEDIA SYNCHRONIZATION

B. Prabhakaran

Department of Information Systems & Computer Science
National University of Singapore
Singapore 119620
prabha@iscs.nus.edu.sg

1. **INTRODUCTION**..526
    1.1   MODELING TEMPORAL RELATIONS..527
2. **PETRI NETS BASED MODELS** 528
    2.1   HYPERTEXT MODELS USING TIMED PETRI NETS 530
    2.2   THE OBJECT COMPOSITION PETRI NETS 532
    2.3   DYNAMIC TIMED PETRI NETS...532
3. **TIME-FLOW GRAPH MODEL** 535
4. **FLEXIBLE TEMPORAL MODELS** 537
    4.1   DIFFERENCE CONSTRAINTS APPROACH...537
    4.2   FLIPS MODEL...538
5. **MULTIMEDIA SYNCHRONIZATION AND OBJECT RETRIEVAL SCHEDULE**........539
6. **MULTIMEDIA SYNCHRONIZATION AND COMMUNICATION REQUIREMENTS**.540
    6.1   QOS REQUIREMENTS OF AN ORCHESTRATED PRESENTATION.....................541
    6.2   TRAFFIC SOURCE MODELING...542
7. **SUMMARY AND CONCLUSION**..542
    REFERENCES 543

Abstract. Multimedia information comprises different media streams such as text, images, audio, and video. Presentation of multimedia information to the user involves spatial organization, temporal organization, delivery of the components composing the multimedia objects, and allowing the user to interact with the presentation sequence. Presentation of objects in the various media streams has to be ordered in time. Multimedia synchronization refers to the task of coordinating this ordering of presentation of various objects in the time domain. In multimedia databases, ordering of presentation is explicitly formulated and stored along with the multimedia objects. Ordering of multimedia objects presentation is specified by parameters such as time instant, duration, and synchronization of an object presentation with those of others. The above parameters can be specified either in a hard or flexible manner. In this chapter, we present both hard and flexible synchronization models for multimedia databases. We also discuss the advantages and disadvantages of the various synchronization models.

1   INTRODUCTION

Multimedia information comprises of different media streams such as text, images, audio, and video. The presentation of multimedia information to the user involves spatial organization, temporal organization, delivery of the components composing the multimedia objects, and allowing the user to interact with the presentation sequence. The presentation of multimedia information can be either *live* or *orchestrated*. In live presentation, multimedia objects are acquired in realtime from devices such as video cameras and microphones. In orchestrated presentation, the multimedia objects are typically acquired from stored databases. The presentation of objects in the various media streams have to be ordered in time. *Multimedia synchronization* refers to the task of coordinating this ordering of presentation of various objects in the time domain. In a live multimedia presentation, the ordering of objects in the time domain is implied and is dynamically formulated. In an orchestrated presentation, this ordering is explicitly formulated and stored along with the multimedia objects.

The objects composing an orchestrated multimedia presentation have associated temporal characteristics. These characteristics specify the following parameters:

- Time instant of an object presentation.

- Duration of presentation.

- Synchronization of an object presentation with those of others.

The above parameters can be specified either in a hard or flexible manner. In the case of hard temporal specification, the parameters such as time instants and durations of presentation of objects are fixed. In the case of flexible specification, these parameters are allowed to vary as long as they preserve certain specified relationships. As an example, consider the following temporal specifications:

a. Show the video of the movie *JFK* AT 11 pm FOR 20 minutes.

b. Show the video of the movie *JFK* SOMETIME BETWEEN 10:58 pm and 11:03 pm, until the audio is played out.

The first choice, (a), is a hard temporal specification with the time instant and duration of presentation fixed at 11 pm and for 20 minutes, respectively, whereas specification (b) is flexible, allowing the presentation start time to vary within a range of 5 minutes and the duration of video presentation until the corresponding audio is played out.

The temporal specification, apart from describing the parameters for an individual object presentation, also needs to describe the synchronization among the composing objects. This synchronization description brings out the temporal dependencies among the individual object presentations. For example, in the temporal specification (b), video has to be presented until the audio object is presented. Hence, a temporal specification needs to describe individual object presentation characteristics (time instant and duration of presentation) as well as the relationships among the composing objects.

The points of synchronization in a multimedia presentation can be modified by the user going through the presentation. In an orchestrated presentation, for example, a

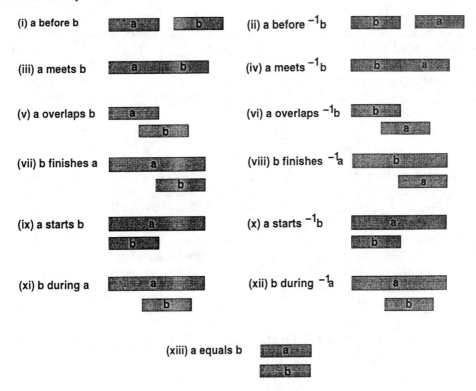

Figure 1: **13 Possible Temporal Relations**

user may interact by giving inputs such as skip event(s), reverse presentation, navigate in time, scale the speed of presentation, scale the spatial requirements, handle spatial clash, freeze and restart of a presentation. User inputs such as skip, reverse presentation, and navigate time modify the sequence of objects that are being presented. User inputs such as scaling the speed of presentation modify the presentation duration of the objects. User inputs such as handling spatial clash on the display screen make the corresponding media stream *active* or *passive* depending on whether the window is in the foreground or background. Similarly, while the freeze user input suspends the activities on all streams, restart input resumes the activities on all streams. In the presence of non-sequential storage of multimedia objects, data compression, data distribution, and random communication delays, supporting these user operations can be very difficult.

1.1 Modeling Temporal Relations

Given any two multimedia object presentations, the temporal requirements of one object can be related to that of another in thirteen possible ways, as shown in Figure 1. These thirteen relationships describe how the time instants and presentation durations of two multimedia objects are related. These relationships, however, do not quantify the temporal parameters, time instants, and duration of presentations. Many models have been proposed to describe the temporal relationships among the multimedia objects.

One approach to the specification of multimedia synchronization is to use parallel language paradigms that can be parsed during presentation to the user. Here, the presentation of individual media streams are assigned to executable processes and these processes synchronize via inherent language constructs. Language based schemes for multimedia synchronization have been proposed in [8, 10, 11]. Another approach is to use graphical models. Graphical models have the additional advantage of providing a visual representation of the synchronization specification. Graphical models for synchronization specification have been based on Petri nets [1] and Time-flow Graphs [17].

Outline of this Chapter: In this chapter, we discuss the various methodologies used for describing multimedia synchronization in an orchestrated multimedia presentation. In Sections 2 and 3, we discuss graphical models based on Petri nets and Time-flow Graphs. Next, we present flexible temporal specification models, in Section 4. We then consider distributed orchestrated multimedia presentations where objects have to be retrieved over a computer network before their delivery to the user. In Sections 5 and 6, we describe how a multimedia synchronization specification can be applied to derive schedules for object retrieval over computer networks and to derive the communication requirements of an orchestrated presentation.

2   PETRI NETS BASED MODELS

Petri Nets, as a modeling tool, have the ability to describe real-time process requirements as well as interprocess timing relationships, as required for multimedia presentations [1, 2]. A Petri net is a bipartite graph consisting of 'place' nodes and 'transition' nodes. Places, represented by circles, are used to represent conditions; transitions, drawn as bars, are used to represent events. A *Petri net structure P* is a triple,

$P = \{ T, P, A \}$ where

$\mathbf{T} = \{ t_1, t_2, \ldots \}$ represents a set of transitions (bars)

$\mathbf{P} = \{ p_1, p_2, \ldots \}$ represents a set of places (circles)

$\mathbf{A} : \{ \mathbf{T} * \mathbf{P} \} \mathbf{U} \{ \mathbf{P} * \mathbf{T} \} - \mathbf{I}, \mathbf{I} = \{ \mathbf{1, 2, } \ldots \}$ represents a set of integers

The arcs represented by A describe the *pre-* and *post*-relations for places and transitions. The set of places that are incident on a transition t is termed the *input places* of the transition. The set of places that follow a transition t is termed the *output places* of the transition. A Marked Petri Net is one in which a set of 'tokens' is assigned to the places of the net. Tokens, represented by small dots inside the places, are used to define the execution of the Petri net, and their number and position change during execution. The marking (M) of a Petri net is a function from the set of places P to the set of nonnegative integers I, $M : P \rightarrow I$. A marking is generally written as a vector $(m_1, m_2, \ldots, m_n)$ in which $m_i = M(p_i)$. Each integer in a marking indicates the number of tokens residing in the corresponding place (say, p_i).

Figure 2: **Timed Petri Nets Model**

Execution of a Petri net implies *firing* of a transition. In a Marked Petri net, a transition t is enabled for firing iff each of its input places contains at least one token, i.e., $\forall(p \in InputPlace(t)) : M(p) \geq 1$. Firing t consists of removing one token from each of its input places and adding one token to each of its output places, and this operation defines a new marking. An execution of a Petri net is described by a sequence of markings, beginning with an initial marking M_o and ending in some final marking M_f. Marking of a Petri net defines the *state* of the net. During the execution, Petri net moves from a marked state M_i to another state M_j by firing any transition t that are enabled in the state M_i.

For the purpose of modeling time-driven systems, the notion of time was introduced in Petri nets, calling them Timed Petri Nets (TPN) [3]. In TPN models, the basic Petri net model is augmented by attaching an execution time variable to each node in the net. The node in the Petri net can be either the place or the transition. In a marked TPN, a set of tokens are assigned to places. A TPN N is defined as:

$$N = \{ \text{T, P, A, D, M} \} \text{ where}$$

M : P $\rightarrow$ I represents marking M which assigns tokens (dots) to each place in the net

D : P $\rightarrow$ R represents durations as a mapping from the set of places to the set of real numbers

Other descriptions *T, P, A* are the same as those of the *normal* Petri net.

A transition is enabled for execution iff each of its input places contain at least one token. The firing of a transition causes a token to be held in a locked state for a specified time interval in the output place of the transition, if the time intervals are assigned to places. If time intervals are assigned to transitions, the token is in a transition state for the assigned duration. The execution of a Petri net process might have to be interrupted in order to carry out another higher priority activity. Pre-emption of the on-going execution of a Petri net process can be modeled using escape arcs to interrupt the execution of a process [5]. In this section, we examine Petri nets-based models for the purpose of describing the synchronization characteristics of the multimedia components.

The TPN model can be used for modeling the temporal requirements of multimedia database applications. Figure 2 shows the TPN model for a temporal relation: object a *meeting* b. The objects have the same presentation durations, d1 = d2, and a start time, t1. The object presentations are denoted by *places* (circles) and the presentation

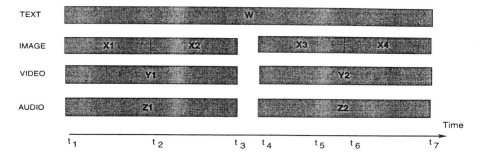

Figure 3: **Timeline Model**

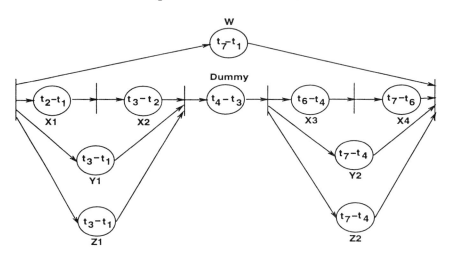

Figure 4: **TPN Model For Figure 3**

durations are represented as values assigned to places. The transitions represent the synchronization of the start and the completion of presentation of the objects a and b.

Figure 3 shows an example of a multimedia presentation. This example describes the timing requirements of objects composing a presentation. For instance, the time instant and duration of presentation of the text object W are t_1 and $t_7 - t_1$. A synchronization model should be able, apart from modeling the time requirements of individual objects, to describe dependencies among object presentations. For example, in Figure 3, video object $Y1$ and audio object $Z1$ have to be presented simultaneously. This dependency has to be explicitly brought out in a synchronization model. Figure 4 shows the TPN model for describing the synchronization characteristics of the example described in Figure 3. Here, the transitions associated with each object presentation describe the synchronization among their presentations.

2.1   Hypertext Models Using Timed Petri Nets

The TPN concept has been used to specify the browsing semantics in the Trellis Hypertext System [6, 9]. This Petri nets-based Hypertext model allows browsing events to be initiated by the reader or by the document itself. A synchronous hypertext H is defined as a 7-tuple H $= < $ N, M_o, C, W, B, P_l, $P_d >$ in which

N is a timed Petri net structure

M_o is an initial state (or initial marking) for N

C is a set of document contents

W is a set of windows

B is a set of buttons

P_l is a logical projection for the document

P_d is a display projection for the document.

In the above definition, the structure of the timed Petri net specifies the structure of the hypertext document. A marking in the hypertext represents the possible paths through a hyperdocument from the browsing point it represents. The initial marking of a synchronous hypertext therefore describes a particular browsing pattern. The definition also includes several sets of components *(contents, windows,* and *buttons)* to be presented to the user going through the document. Two collections of mappings or *projections* are also defined: one from the Petri net to the user components and another from the user components to the display mechanism.

The content elements from the set C can be text, graphics, still image, motion video, audio information or *another hypertext.* A *button* is an action selected from the set B. A *window* is defined as a logically distinct locus of information and is selected from the set W. P_l, the logical projection, provides a mapping from the components of a Petri net (place and transitions) to the *human-consumable* portions of a hypertext (contents, windows, and buttons). A content element from the set C and a window element for the abstract display of the content from the set W, are mapped to each place in the Petri net. A logical button from set B is mapped to each transition in the Petri net. P_d, the display projection, provides a mapping from the logical components of the hypertext to the tangible representations, such as screen layouts, sound generation, video, etc. The layout of the windows and the way text information and buttons are displayed are determined by P_d.

2.1.1 Trellis Hypertext: An Example

We shall consider the guided tour example discussed in [6]. In a guided tour, a set of related display windows is created by an author. All the windows in a set are displayed concurrently. A tour is constructed by linking such sets to form a directed graph. The graph can be cyclic as well. From any one set of display windows, there may be several alternative paths. Figure 5 shows a representation of guided tour using the Trellis hypertext. Here, the set of windows to be displayed at any instant of time is described by a Petri net place. A place is connected by a transition to as many places as there are sets of windows to be displayed. A token is placed in the place(s) representing the first set of windows to be displayed. The actual path of browsing is determined by the user going through the information. For example, when the token is in *p1*, the information contents associated with *p1* are displayed and the buttons for the transitions *t1* and *t2* are selectable by the user.

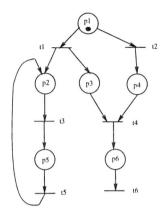

Figure 5: Guided Tour Using Trellis Hypertext

2.2   The Object Composition Petri Nets

The Object Composition Petri Net (OCPN) model has been proposed in [7, 12] for describing multimedia synchronization. The OCPN is an augmented Timed Petri Nets (TPN) model with values of time represented as durations and resource utilization being associated with each place in the net. An OCPN is defined as

$$C_{OCPN} = \{ \ T, P, A, D, R, M \ \} \ \text{where}$$

R : **P** $\rightarrow$ { $r_1, r_2, \ldots$ }   represents the mapping from a set of places to a set of resources.

Other descriptions are the same as those in the TPN model.

It has been shown in [7, 12], that the OCPN can represent all possible thirteen different temporal relationships between any two object presentations. The Petri nets have hierarchical modeling property that states that *subnets* of a Petri net can be replaced by equivalent abstract places and this property is applicable to the OCPN as well. Using the subnet replacement, an arbitrarily complex process model composed of temporal relations can be constructed with the OCPN by choosing pairwise, temporal relationships between process entities [7]. The OCPNs are also proved to be deterministic since no conflicts are modeled, transitions are instantaneous, and tokens remain at places for known, finite durations. OCPNs are also demonstrated to be *live* and *safe*, following the Petri nets definitions for these properties. Modeling multimedia presentations using OCPN is very similar to using TPN, as discussed in the previous Section.

2.3   Dynamic Timed Petri Nets

A *Dynamic Timed Petri Nets* (DTPN) model has been suggested in [14] by allowing user-defined 'interrupts' to pre-empt the Petri net execution sequence and modify the time duration associated with the pre-empted Petri net process. In the DTPN model, nonnegative execution times are assigned to each place in the net and the notion of

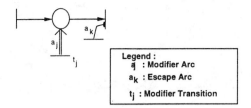

Figure 6: **Dynamic Timed Petri Nets Structure**

instantaneous firing of transitions is preserved. Basically, the following types of modifications of execution time after preemption are allowed:

1. Deference of execution.
   For the operation of preemption with deference of execution, the remaining duration associated with the preempted Petri net place is changed considering the time spent until its preemption.

2. Termination of execution.
   The operation of preemption with termination is like premature ending of the execution.

3. Temporary modification of remaining time duration.
   The operation of preemption with modification of execution time is like 'setting' the time duration associated with the preempted Petri net *place* to a 'new value,' as appropriately determined by the type of user input. For temporary modification of execution time, the *remaining time duration* associated with the place is modified.

4. Permanent modification of execution time duration.
   For permanent modification, the *execution time duration* associated with the place is modified.

In the DTPN model, preemption is modeled by using *escape arcs*. Escape arcs are marked by dots instead of arrow heads and they can *interrupt* an *active* Petri net place. Modification of execution time duration (temporary or permanent) associated with a place is modeled by *modifier arc*. Modifier arcs are denoted by double-lined arcs with arrow heads, as shown in Figure 6.

2.3.1 Synchronization Models Using DTPN

The proposed DTPN can be effectively used in synchronization models for flexible multimedia presentation with user participation. DTPN constructions for describing handling of user inputs such as reverse presentation, freeze and restart to a *single object presentation* is the simplest case. These DTPN constructions for handling user inputs on single object presentations can be used in full multimedia presentation.

A skip operation can be modeled as shown in Figure 7. Execution of p_i is preempted and terminated, and the transition to enable next object presentation is fired. In a similar manner, freeze and restart operation can be modeled as shown in Figure 7. The type of interrupt to be applied to the execution sequence is preemption with deference of execution. The remaining time duration associated with p_i is modified to reflect the

Modeling Pause Operation :

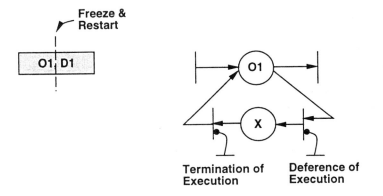

Modeling (Simple) Skip Operation :

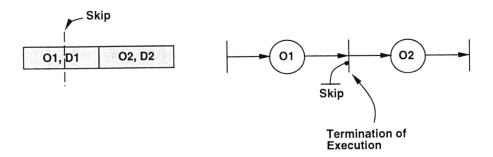

Figure 7: **Modeling Using DTPN**

time spent until its preemption and the locked token in p_i is removed. A token is added to the output place p_j of the preempting transition. A large time duration is associated with p_j and its execution is preempted only upon the receipt of *restart* signal from the user. Preemption of p_j causes the token to be 'returned' to the place p_i.

3 TIME-FLOW GRAPH MODEL

In [17], multimedia synchronization involving independent sources for teleorchestra applications (remote multimedia presentation) has been considered. In the teleorchestra application, a user creates multimedia presentations using data objects stored in a distributed system. The distributed nature of the data objects may result in the non-availability of precise temporal relationships among the objects. However, *relative* or *fuzzy* temporal relationships can be specified among the objects to be presented. A Time-flow Graph (TFG) model for describing fuzzy temporal relationships has been proposed in [17] where *temporal interval* is taken as a primitive. The terms *object X* and *interval X* are considered synonymous. One temporal interval may contain several objects in different media, i.e., several concurrent multimedia intervals.

There are thirteen relations (seven relations and their inverses) that are considered between any two temporal intervals [4]. The relations are 'meets,' 'before,' 'equal,' 'overlap,' 'during,' 'start,' and 'finish.' The other relations are their inverse, e.g., 'di' is the inverse of the relation 'd' (during). The following set R describes all thirteen possible temporal relations.
$R = \{b, e, m, o, d, s, f, bi, mi, di, oi, si, fi\}$.
The temporal relationships among the involved objects can be parallel or sequential.

Sequential Relations in TFG: The sequential relation between any two intervals can be either 'meets' (**m**) or 'before' (**b**). In teleorchestra applications, multiple intervals can be involved in the sequential relation requirement. Hence, the sequential relation specification provided in TFG are

1. $A\{B\}$: Interval(s) in B will start after all the intervals in A are finished.

2. $< A > B$: Interval(s) in B will start when one of the intervals (the first) in A is finished.

Parallel Relations in TFG: A subset R_f ($R_f \in R$) is defined as:
$R = \{e, o, d, s, f, oi, di, si, fi\}$.
Considering two object intervals X and Y, X(r)Y describes the temporal relationship between the two intervals. When r = 's' the relation X(s)Y specifies that object X and Y are to be displayed with the same start time. In a teleorchestra application scenario, the temporal relationships have to be specified despite the lack of duration information of the involved intervals. The presentation semantics are hence defined in TFG models as follows [17]:

1. X(d)Y(d)Z: All the other objects are displayed during the presentation of the object with the longest presentation duration.

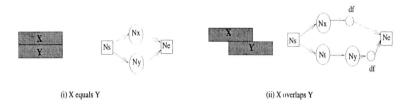

(i) X equals Y   (ii) X overlaps Y

Figure 8: TFG Synchronization Models

2. X(e)Y(e)Z: The display of all the objects are started simultaneously. The presentation of all the other objects will be cut off when one of the objects (first) is finished.

3. ch(X,Y,Z) = Y: The presentation duration of all the involved objects should equal the one chosen. Objects are displayed according to the relations $r \in R_f$ specified between every two of them. Presentation of some of the objects might be cut off to equal the chosen duration.

Therefore, three duration specifications $r \in R_m = \{d, e, ch\}$ can be applied to presentations involving concurrent multiple intervals.

Using the above sequential and parallel relationship specification, multimedia presentation scenarios can be described. In TFG, the notation $\mathbf{N}$ is used to denote all the intervals contained in a scenario. The temporal relationship of an object interval N_x with other intervals is represented by the interval vector n_x. The interval vector n_x is defined as $n_x = (S_r, O_{id}, F_s, F_e)$ where S_r denotes the *source* (or the owner) of the interval, O_{id} the object identifier, and F_s and F_e the presentation semantics chosen for the start and end of the display of the object. An interval vector can represent an object presentation or an intermission. The intermission vector, represented by n_τ, describes a presentation interval that is not mapped to any multimedia object. Intermissions are used to specify *gaps* in the multimedia presentation.

For describing multimedia presentations, the model of interval vectors and the involved temporal information are maintained in a Flow Graph (TFG). In TFG, intervals are described by nodes. A TFG is defined by the tuple $TFG = \{\Delta_N, N_t, E_d\}$ where Δ_N is a set of nodes for the interval vectors, N_t is a set of transit nodes, and E_d is a set of directed edges. The model Δ_x of an interval vector n_x is composed of an interval node N_x, representing the interval of n_x, and δ node(s), representing its parallel relation to other intervals. N_x may associate none, one, or two δ nodes. An intermission node has no δ nodes. The sequential specifications $\{A\}B$ and $< A > B$ are represented by the transit nodes in N_t, the *sq-node* and the *tri-node*, respectively.

Synchronization Specification Using TFG: An Example The TFG specifications for the relations A *ends* B and A *overlaps* B are shown in Figure 8(i) and (ii). The square nodes N_s and N_e are the *sq-nodes* representing the sequential relation $\{A\}B$. Figure 8(ii) has intermission node N_τ to describe the time lag between the event A and B. The δ nodes are used in Figure 8(ii) to signify the end of the concurrent presentation.

4   FLEXIBLE TEMPORAL MODELS

These models represent the temporal requirements in a *soft* manner. Here, the start time, duration of presentation, and the synchronization among different objects are described with a range of values (in contrast to a single value in hard temporal specification). Figure 9 describes a flexible temporal specification for the temporal relation: object a *before* object b. The values for the durations of presentations of the objects, $d1$ and $d2$, have ranges, $x_6 - x_5$ and $x_8 - x_7$, respectively. Similarly, the presentation start times of the objects a and b are related by the range specified by the relation, $x_3 < t2 - t1 < x_4$. This type of range specification gives flexibility to the temporal parameters.

4.1   Difference Constraints Approach

Difference constraints can be used to describe this flexibility in multimedia presentation [15, 21, 22]. The difference constraints specifications are similar to the value range specifications described above; however, the difference constraints specifications have a particular structure for describing the range of values. As an example, the difference constraints specification for the presentation start times $t1$ and $t2$ of objects a and b in Figure 9 will be represented as $t2 - t1 \geq u$ (u being a positive real number).

a do b	(i) $x1 < d0 < x2$
d1 ---- d2	(ii) $x_3 < t2 - t1 < x_4$
t1 t2	(iii) $x_5 < d1 < x_6$
Temporal Relation : a before b	(iv) $x_7 < d2 < x_8$
	Flexible Temporal Specification

Figure 9: **Flexible Temporal Specification**

In a similar manner, relations between other temporal parameters can be represented as difference constraints. These difference constraints specifications have to be *solved* to *select* values for the temporal parameters. For example, a solution for the value $d0$ (in Figure 9) has to lie within $x1$ and $x2$. Thus, difference constraints are a special case of linear constraints where

1. There are only two variables, and

2. One variable has coefficient 1 while the other has coefficient -1.

With each object O in a multimedia document D, one can associate a set, T_O, of temporal constraints. Constraints are constructed from *variables*. In the case of multimedia documents, the following *temporal variables* are associated with each multimedia object O in the document:

- $st(O)$: Denotes the start time of the display of the object O

- $et(O)$: Denotes the end time of the display of the object O

There are four types of temporal presentation constraints.

$$\boxed{\begin{array}{ll} \bullet \ \mathcal{T}(o) - t \le \delta t & \bullet \ \mathcal{T}(o) - t \ge \delta t \\ \bullet \ t - \mathcal{T}(o) \le \delta t & \bullet \ t - \mathcal{T}(o) \ge \delta t \end{array}}$$

where:

1. $\mathcal{T}(o) \in \{st(o), st(o)\}$,

2. $t \in \bigcup_j \{et(o_j), et(o_j)\} \bigcup \{st_p, et_p\}$, and

3. st_p and et_p denote the start and end of the presentation, respectively.

Example 4.1 Let us assume that there exist two objects o_1 and o_2 that we want to display simultaneously, i.e., we want them to start and finish simultaneously. This requirement can be described using the following constraints:

$$\begin{aligned} st(o_1) - st(o_2) &\le 0 \\ st(o_2) - st(o_1) &\le 0 \\ et(o_1) - et(o_2) &\le 0 \\ et(o_2) - et(o_1) &\le 0 \end{aligned}$$

Using these constraints, Allen's 13 temporal relationships [4] between events can be modeled. Suppose D is any document and T_D is the set of temporal constraints associated with D. With this set of difference constraints, a graph $G = (V, E)$ can be defined as follows:

1. **Vertices:** For each constraint variable τ_i occurring in the set of difference constraints T_D, V contains a vertex v_i representing that variable. In addition, V contains two special vertices v_s (document "start" node) and v_e (document "end" node).

2. **Edges:** If $\tau_j - \tau_i \le \delta t$ is a constraint in the set of difference constraints being considered, then E contains an edge from v_i to v_j and the weight associated with this edge is δt. Furthermore, for each node v_i, there is an edge from v_i to v_s with weight 0 and from v_e to v_i with weight 0.

Thus, for given any multimedia document D, one graph is associated with its temporal specifications. The shortest path solution of this graph (from the end of presentation node to the start of presentation node) results in a schedule that satisfies the temporal specification. Variations of shortest-path algorithm for generating a flexible presentation schedule are presented in [21, 22]. Linear programming approaches have also been used for solving difference constraints [15].

4.2 FLIPS Model

A concept of *barriers* and *enablers* has been used for describing temporal requirements [19]. The model, called *Flexible Interactive Presentation Synchronization* (FLIPS), describes the synchronization of multimedia objects using relationships between the presentation events. The presentation events considered by FLIPS are *Begin* and *End* of an

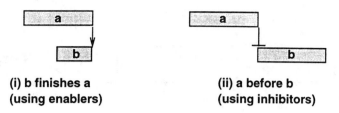

(i) b finishes a   (ii) a before b
(using enablers)   (using inhibitors)

Figure 10: **Enablers and Inhibitors in FLIPS Model**

object presentation. FLIPS employ two types of relationships, *enabling* and *inhibitive*. For example, the *End* of an object presentation can *enable* the *Begin* of another object presentation, or an object presentation can be forced to end when another object finishes. Figure 10 (i) shows an enabling relationship for the temporal relation, b finishes a. Here, b is forced to end when a ends. In a similar manner, the *inhibitive* relationship prevents an event from occurring until another one has occurred. Figure 10 (ii) describes the inhibitive relationship for the temporal relation, a before b. Here, the start of presentation of object b is inhibited until the end of a.

5   MULTIMEDIA SYNCHRONIZATION AND OBJECT RETRIEVAL SCHEDULES

Orchestrated multimedia presentations might be carried out over a computer network thereby rendering the application distributed. In such distributed presentations, the required multimedia objects have to be retrieved from the server(s) and transferred over the computer network to the client. The communication network can introduce delays in transferring the required multimedia objects. Other conditions such as congestion of a database server at a given time and locking of the data objects by some other application also have to be considered. Retrieval of the multimedia objects have to be made keeping in mind these delays that might be introduced during the presentation. A retrieval scheduling algorithm has to be designed based on the synchronization characteristics of the orchestrated presentation incorporating features for allowing the delays that might be encountered during the presentation.

The retrieval schedule specifies when a client should retrieve an object from its server so that the object can be delivered according to its presentation schedule. As an example, in the temporal specification for the movie *JFK*, if we know that the delay for retrieving the video object from its server is 3 minutes, then the retrieval schedule can be fixed at 10.56 pm (so that the movie presentation can be started according to its presentation schedule at 10.59 pm). The derivation of retrieval schedule is constrained by the following factors:

- Throughput (or the bandwidth) of the communication channel between the server and the client (i.e., the amount of data that will be sent through the network per unit time. It is specified in terms of bits per second).

- Buffer availability in the client for retrieved objects

- Size(s) of the object(s), in terms of bytes, that is(are) to be retrieved from the server

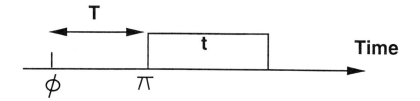

Figure 11: Delay Factors in Object Retrieval

- Time duration available for retrieval.

In [12, 13], a multimedia object retrieval scheduling algorithm has been presented based on the synchronization characteristics represented by the OCPN. Characterizing the properties of the multimedia objects and the communication channel, the total end-to-end delay for a packet can consist of the following components:

- Propagation delay, D_p

- Transfer delay, D_t, proportional to the packet size

- Variable delay, D_v, a function of the end-to-end network traffic.

The multimedia objects can be very large and hence can consist of many packets. If an object consists of r packets, the end-to-end delay for the object is :
$D_e = D_p + rD_t + \sum_{j=1}^{r} D_{v_j}$.
Control time T_i is defined as the skew between putting an object i onto the communication channel and playing it out. Considering the end-to-end delay, D_e, the control time T_i should be greater than D_e. The various timing parameters, the playout time (π), the control time (T), and the *retrieval time* (ϕ) are as shown in Figure 11. The retrieval time for an object i (ϕ_i) or the object production time at the server is defined as $\phi_i = \pi_i - T_i$.

In the TFG model, the playout instances (π) for the multimedia objects are described in a *fuzzy* or relative manner. These fuzzy temporal relations have to be converted into absolute schedules for retrieving the objects from a server. In [17], retrieval scheduling algorithms have been designed for the TFG specification of the synchronization characteristics; [21, 22] describes a flexible retrieval scheduling algorithm based on difference constraints specification.

6   MULTIMEDIA SYNCHRONIZATION AND COMMUNICATION REQUIREMENTS

In a distributed orchestrated multimedia presentation, the communication network provides support for transfer of data in realtime. The synchronization characteristics of an orchestrated presentation define a *predictable* sequence of events that happen in the time domain. This sequence of events can be used by the network service provider to understand the behavior of the orchestrated application in terms of the Quality of

Service (QoS) requirements and the network load that might be generated [16, 18, 20]. The QoS parameters are characterized by a set of parameters such as the end-to-end throughput, the end-to-end delay, and packet loss probabilities. The offered network load is characterized by the traffic that might be generated by the application.

6.1 QoS Requirements of an Orchestrated Presentation

In a distributed orchestrated presentation, it is essential that the object is available at the client before the presentation. In general, the client can adopt two different strategies for buffering the multimedia objects: minimum buffering strategy (B1) and maximum buffering strategy (B2). The B1 strategy tries to minimize the buffer requirements by buffering, at most, one object or a frame as the case may be, before its presentation. In the B2 strategy, the approach is to buffer up to a certain limit (say, B_{max}) for each media stream on the client side, before the presentation. This implies that more than one object in a media stream will be buffered by the client during the presentation sequence.

The B1 strategy minimizes the buffer space requirements of the client and the QoS derived based on this strategy gives the *preferred* values for the client. The QoS requirements derived, based on the B2 strategy, specifies the *acceptable* values for the client. In a distributed orchestrated presentation, multimedia objects composing the presentation are retrieved from the server. The retrieval of objects do not impose any real-time demands from the network service provider. Hence, for orchestrated presentations, it is sufficient if the network service provider guarantees the required throughput.

Computation of Preferred Throughput: For objects such as still images, we can determine the average throughput required by the application with the B1 buffering strategy, assuming that, at most, one object in each multimedia stream is buffered by the application on the client system before the presentation. For objects such as video that consists of a set of frames to be presented at regular intervals, the application following the B1 strategy can buffer, at most, one frame of the video object. Let us consider a multimedia stream with an object O_i at a playout time instant t_i and let the object size be Z_{O_i}. Since only one object is assumed to be buffered before the playout time instant for the stream, the retrieval of objects can be started only after the immediately preceding playout time instant t_{i-1} and has to be completed before t_i. Hence, the preferred throughput C_{app}^{pref} is [20] :

$$C_{app}^{pref}[t_{i-1}, t_i] \geq \frac{Z_{O_i}}{t_i - t_{i-1}}$$

Computation of Acceptable Throughput: For calculating the *acceptable* QoS parameters, we should find out the minimum values that are required by the application. A minimum value of throughput (C_{app}^{acc}) implies that the application will be following the B2 buffering strategy of buffering more than one object (in the stream for which throughput is being calculated) before its presentation. When more than one object in a stream is buffered by the application, the start of the presentation is delayed by the time required for retrieving B_{max} bits using the acceptable throughput of C_{app}^{acc}. If B_{max} is the maximum buffer space available and $\sum_{i=1}^{n} Z_{O_i}$ is the total size of all objects to be retrieved, then the acceptable throughput is [20] :

$$C_{app}^{acc} \geq \frac{(\sum_{i=1}^{n} Z_{O_i} - B_{max})}{t_{final} - t_{initial}}$$

6.2   Traffic Source Modeling

The synchronization characteristics of an orchestrated presentation describes a sequence of objects with an associated duration of presentation, to be presented at different time instants. This sequence gives an implicit description of the traffic associated with the orchestrated presentation [20]. However, the traffic generated by an orchestrated presentation server also *depends on the object retrieval schedule* adopted by the client going through the presentation. This retrieval schedule basically determines the time instant(s) at which the client wants to receive the object(s). This schedule depends on the buffering that can be done at the client side. With the minimum buffering strategy (B_1), the delivery time of an object (or a frame, in case of video objects) is the *presentation time* of the previous object. As an example, object O_i will be delivered from the server at t_{i-1} just after the presentation time instant t_{i-1} of the object O_{i-1}. With maximum buffering strategy B_2, the delivery schedule at the server is such that B_{max} bits will be delivered from the server every Γ seconds, where $\Gamma = B_{max}/C_{app}^{acc}$. C_{app}^{acc} is the minimum acceptable throughput that should be offered by the network for a multimedia stream with the B_2 buffering strategy.

7   SUMMARY AND CONCLUSION

Distributed orchestrated multimedia presentation applications such as multimedia lecture presentations, multimedia databases, and on-demand multimedia servers are becoming increasingly popular. An orchestrated application has synchronization characteristics that specifies the time instants at which the presentation of objects in the media streams must synchronize. These synchronization characteristics are specified in the form of pre-defined temporal relations and are stored along with the multimedia database. In this chapter, we presented the problem of specifying the synchronization characteristics of an orchestrated multimedia presentation. We discussed the methodologies that have been proposed in the literature for describing the synchronization characteristics.

The synchronization characteristics of the presentation describe a *predictable* pattern of events that happen in the time domain. In a distributed orchestrated presentation, this pattern of events can be used to determine the object retrieval schedule that is to be adopted by a client. It can also be used by the network service provider to understand the QoS requirements of orchestrated applications and its network traffic generation characteristics. In [18, 20], an approach based on the Probabilistic Attributed Context Free Grammar (PACFG) has been proposed for deriving the QoS requirements and the network traffic generation characteristics of orchestrated multimedia presentation based on its synchronization characteristics. Based on these studies, protocols have been specified for multimedia synchronization [12] and for handling QoS negotiations in orchestrated presentations [20].

References

[1] J.L. Peterson, *Petri Net Theory and The Modeling of Systems*, Prentice-Hall Inc., 1981.

[2] W. Reisig, *Petri Nets: An Introduction*, Springer-Verlag Publication, 1982.

[3] J.E. Coolahan. Jr. and N. Roussopoulos, "Timing requirements for Time-Driven Systems Using Augmented Petri Nets," IEEE Trans. Software Eng., Vol. SE-9, Sept. 1983, pp 603-616

[4] J.F. Allen, "Maintaining Knowledge about Temporal Intervals," Communications of the ACM, November 1983, Vol. 26, no. 11, pp. 832-843.

[5] W.M. Zuberek, "M-Timed Petri nets, Priorities, Pre-Emptions and Performance Evaluation of Systems," Advances in Petri nets 1985, Lecture Notes in Computer Science (LNCS 222), Springer-Verlag, 1985.

[6] P.D. Stotts and R. Frutta, "Petri-Net-Based Hypertext : Document Structure With Browsing Semantics," ACM Trans. on Office Information Systems, Vol. 7, no. 1, Jan 1989, pp. 3-29.

[7] T.D.C. Little and A Ghafoor, "Synchronization and Storage Models for Multimedia Objects," IEEE Journal on Selected Areas of Communication, Vol. 8, no. 3, April 1990, pp. 413-427.

[8] R. Steinmetz, "Synchronization Properties in Multimedia Systems," IEEE J. on Selected Areas of Communication, Vol. 8, no. 3, April 1990, pp. 401-412.

[9] P.D. Stotts and R. Frutta, "Temporal Hyperprogramming," Journal of Visual Languages and Computing, Sept. 1990, pp. 237-253.

[10] S. Gibbs, "Composite Multimedia and Active Objects," Proc. OOPSLA '91, pp. 97-112.

[11] J. Stefani, L. Hazard and F. Horn, "Computational model for distributed multimedia applications based on a synchronous programming language," Computer Communication, Butterworth-Hienmann Ltd., Vol. 15, no. 2, March 1992, pp.114-128.

[12] T.D.C. Little, *Synchronization For Distributed Multimedia Database Systems*, Ph.D. Dissertation, Syracuse University, August 1991.

[13] T.D.C. Little and A. Ghafoor, "Scheduling of Bandwidth-Constrained Multimedia Traffic," Computer Communication, Butterworth-Heinemann, July/August 1992, pp. 381-388.

[14] B. Prabhakaran and S.V. Raghavan, "Synchronization Models For Multimedia Presentation With User Participation," ACM/Springer-Verlag Journal of Multimedia Systems, Vol.2, no. 2, August 1994, pp. 53-62. Also in the Proceedings of the First ACM Conference on MultiMedia Systems, Anaheim, California, August 1993, pp.157-166.

[15] M.C. Buchanan and P.T. Zellweger, "Automatically Generating Consistent Schedules for Multimedia Documents," ACM/Springer-Verlag Journal of Multimedia Systems, Vol. 1, No. 2, 1993.

[16] S.V. Raghavan, B. Prabhakaran and S.K. Tripathi, "Quality of Service Negotiation For Orchestrated MultiMedia Presentation," Proceedings of High Performance Networking Conference HPN 94, Grenoble, France, June 1994, pp.217-238.

[17] L. Li, A. Karmouch and N.D. Georganas, "Multimedia Teleorchestra With Independent Sources : Parts 1 & 2," ACM/Springer-Verlag Journal of Multimedia Systems, Vol. 1, No. 4, February 1994, pp.143-165.

[18] S.V. Raghavan, B. Prabhakaran and S.K. Tripathi, "Synchronization Representation and Traffic Source Modeling in Orchestrated Presentation," IEEE Journal on Selected Areas in Communication, special issue on Multimedia Synchronization, Vol. 14, No. 1, January 1996.

[19] J. Schnepf, J.A. Konstan and D.H.-C. Du, "Doing FLIPS: Flexible Interactive Presentation Synchronization," IEEE Journal on Selected Areas in Communications, Vol. 14, No. 1, January 1996.

[20] S.V. Raghavan, B. Prabhakaran and S.K. Tripathi, "Handling QoS Negotiations In Orchestrated Multimedia Presentation," Journal of High Speed Networking, Vol. 5, No. 3, 1996, pp. 277-292.

[21] K.S. Candan, B. Prabhakaran and V.S. Subrahmanian, "CHIMP : A Framework for Supporting Multimedia Document Authoring and Presentation," Proceedings of ACM Multimedia '96 Conference, Boston, November 1996.

[22] K.S. Candan, B. Prabhakaran and V.S. Subrahmanian, "Retrieval Schedules Based on Resource Availability and Flexible Presentation Specifications," ACM Multimedia Systems Journal, Vol. 6, No. 4, pp. 232–250.

26

HIGH-PRECISION TEMPORAL SYNCHRONIZATION IN MULTIMEDIA SYSTEMS

Wolfgang A. Halang, Markus Wannemacher, and Reiner Lichtenecker
FernUniversität Hagen
Faculty of Electrical Engineering
D-58084 Hagen, Germany

Phillip A. Laplante
BCC/NJIT Technology Education Center, County Route 530
Pemberton, NJ 08068-1599, U.S.A.

Alexander D. Stoyen
Department of Computer and Information Sciences
New Jersey Institute of Technology
Newark, NJ 07102, U.S.A.

1. INTRODUCTION..546
2. TIMING AND CLOCK SYNCHRONIZATION 547
3. TIME STANDARDS...547
4. TERRESTRIAL TIME SIGNAL STATIONS 547
5. SATELLITE-BASED TIME BROADCASTING...550
6. A HIGH PRECISION TIMER..551
7. PREDICTABLE SYNCHRONOUS DATA EXCHANGE 554
8. CONCLUSION...555
   REFERENCES 555

Abstract. The relatively new technology of multimedia computing represents complex real-time applications in which it can be argued that synchronization of processes is more important than deadline satisfaction. In this chapter, we discuss synchronization techniques – and specifically their implementation in hardware – that can be used to achieve deadline satisfaction. In particular, it is shown that by endowing computers with high-precision timers supporting the use of exact time specifications, synchronization and deadline satisfaction can both be achieved at the same time – and without any jitter.

Continuous multimedia applications require accurate synchronization of the clocks in different processors. This problem is particularly evident in widely distributed multimedia networks. Such networks are required for all interactive services like video-on-demand, audio-on-demand, or pay-per-view. The available solutions have, among other drawbacks, poor accuracy, limited applicability (e.g., to computers distributed over rather small geographical areas only), or require additional cabling. Local clock synchronization by radio-transmitted time information turns out to be the only general-purpose and high-accuracy technique that is applicable with reasonable effort.

1. INTRODUCTION

Multimedia computing generally involves microcomputer systems equipped with high-resolution graphics, CD-ROM drives, mice, high-performance sound cards, and multi-tasking operating systems which support these devices. Applications for multimedia computing are largely found in:

- education and training,

- entertainment and recreation,

- sales and marketing.

Like any other real-time systems, multimedia systems must fulfill the following two fundamental real-time requirements under any circumstances, i.e., even under extreme load or so-called worst-case conditions:

- timeliness and

- simultaneity.

Multimedia applications involve concurrent programs and processors, shared peripherals, and the important notion that synchronization is at least as important as timeliness. For example, in virtual-reality-type flight simulators, even a slight skew in the synchronization of a pilot's commands and the resultant display update (e.g., a turn is made) can cause nausea [PIM]. Similarly, in multimedia applications, it is clear that audio speech output must be in synchrony with the image of a person speaking (this problem, we argue, can in fact be addressed in the hardware, operating system, and language implementation).

Modern interactive multimedia services like video-on-demand, audio-on-demand, or pay-per-view require data transmissions in widely distributed networks. In such networks the transfer time of data packets is not known. Data packets may even be received in reversed order. To restore the original data stream, the receiving node needs to know not only the information of the correct sequence of the data packets; it is also essential to know at which time the data packet was sent and received. Timeliness and simultaneity can be achieved only if this information is available.

In this chapter, it will be shown that the above stated problems can be solved most easily and with highest precision by making use of exact time specifications and by employing radio-transmitted absolute time information for clock synchronization purposes. This approach differs from that in other distributed real-time systems, such as Mars [KDK], in that all data entering or leaving a computer are either time-stamped or are transferred at pre-defined instants, whereas in Mars, for instance, only system-internal messages are time-stamped and all peripherals are polled by the clock interrupt service routine.

2. TIMING AND CLOCK SYNCHRONIZATION

Timeliness and simultaneity rely heavily on the availability of precise timing information. Their application in distributed systems therefore necessitates the synchronous operation of all local clocks. Clock synchronization in distributed environments is assumed to be a serious problem by many researchers, and is usually approached with rather complicated software (with accuracy usually worse than 1 ms) or combined hardware and software methods. An example for the latter was described in [KO]. From an engineering point of view, however, clock synchronization is rather easy because, as shown in this chapter, in a computer a reliable, globally consistent time base of highest precision can be provided in form of a radio receiver for standard date and time signals, which are derived from the official – and only legal – atomic time and which are being broadcast by official agencies such as the National Institute of Standards and Technology. Furthermore, the use of radio clocks also enables the accurate synchronization of widely distributed and even non-stationary systems, which cannot be achieved by any other method.

3. TIME STANDARDS

Although the following discussion is rather lengthy, we feel that the subject of access to accurate, standardized international time has not been adequately covered in the computer science literature. Consequently, we feel it is important to explain how this idea works, as part of our advocating the use of such time – transmitted by radio signals – for synchronization purposes, not only in multimedia, but generally in any kind of distributed systems.

Over the past century different time standards were developed. Usually new systems were introduced to increase the accuracy of the international time scale. Universal time (UT), also known as Greenwich Mean Time (GMT), is based on the mean angular velocity of the earth's rotation in relation to the sun. Since there are many irregularities in the earth's rotation, the second was redefined in 1967 based on the 9.2 GHz frequency of an atomic transition in the cesium atom. The Bureau International des Poids et Messures calculates "temps atomique international" (TAI) from a weighted average of the measurements of about 100 cesium clocks that are operated at different institutes in the world. The UT time scale and TAI will drift apart more and more, because of the reducing rotational speed of the earth. Especially for navigation purposes, a time scale is required that is proportional to the rotation angle of the earth, like Universal Time. Therefore, Coordinated Universal Time (UTC) was introduced as another time scale, which is derived from TAI by adding an integral number of so-called leap-seconds, i.e., UTC = TAI + N seconds. Following an international agreement, the absolute time information that is broadcast by radio stations is based on UTC. Leap-seconds are regularly introduced, coordinated by the Bureau International de l'Heure (BIH) in Paris. Whenever a leap-second is introduced, the corresponding minute has a length of 59 or 61 seconds, respectively.

4. TERRESTRIAL TIME SIGNAL STATIONS

First systems for the synchronization of clocks by radio signals were already developed in 1905. On a regular basis, time signals have been transmitted since 1960. The original goal was to distribute normalized frequencies for calibration purposes or to support navigation. Soon after, some stations started to code absolute time in broadcast signals, as, for example, WWV (1961) and WWVH (1965) in the U.S.A. [LOM] and DCF 77 (1973) of Physikalisch-Technische Bundesanstalt in Germany. Currently, some 12 radio stations in the world distribute absolute time information [KLA,LIC,REP].

Although there is an international agreement to base transmitted absolute times on UTC, no general agreement exists on the way of coding and the protocols to use for transmission of this information. However, there are two main groups of stations that use similar protocols. The first one uses a slightly modified version of the IRIG-H code, which is one of the protocols for transmission of time information that were standardized in the Interrange-Instrumentation-Group. Different from IRIG-H, the European stations transmit month of the year, day of month, and day of week. These protocols also contain a number of parity bits (P1-P3) that enable the detection of single-bit errors. In addition to the coding protocol, the kind of modulation that is used to transmit information differs between radio stations. Simple amplitude modulation as well as pulse width modulation and phase keying are used. Some radio stations even provide a combination of two methods. The difference is mainly in the susceptibility to perturbations and the effort required to demodulate the signal.

While AM is very simple to decode, it can be easily disturbed by electric or electronic devices. Phase keying is generally the most stable modulation method, but it requires a higher transmission bandwidth of one or several kilohertz. IRIG-H, like most European radio stations that broadcast time, uses pulse width modulation, i.e., a logical 0 is, for example, encoded as a 100 ms pulse of amplitude reduction of the carrier wave, while the reduction has a length of 200 ms for a logical 1. To give an impression of the transmitted information, Figure 1 shows a one-minute time frame as it is broadcast by DCF77.

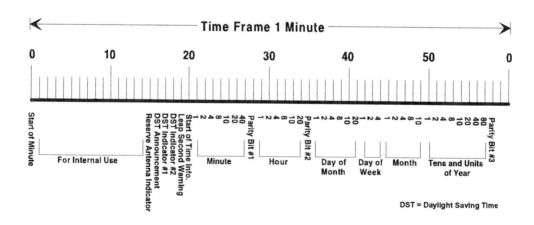

Figure 1. DCF77 coding plan.

First of all synchronization of different clocks requires the unambiguous and accurate detection of a single event and, second, an agreement on the absolute time that should be assigned to that event. To estimate the accuracy of absolute time synchronization of different clocks, the accuracy of event detection and, additionally, the variation of the time it takes to transmit the event to different recipients has to be taken into account. These requirements are the same for any method of clock synchronization, implemented in software as well as hardware.

With radio-transmitted time signals, the single event that has to be detected is the start of a minute, which is specially marked in each protocol. After that, the absolute time of that minute is decoded from the received data. Since data are transmitted at a rate of one bit per second, it takes about two minutes to synchronize a clock, if one assumes that no transmission errors occur.

Terrestrial time signal stations usually broadcast in the long-wave frequency range between 30–300 kHz and use amplitude modulation. The exact instant of the start of a minute as well as the start of a second is marked by an increase or reduction of the carrier amplitude. The accuracy of detecting this event depends on the carrier amplitude's slope of change. Simple radio-driven clocks which only use amplitude modulation for synchronization provide typical accuracy of about 1–10 ms between different clocks. An increase of the accuracy is achieved by synchronizing a clock's internal crystal-oscillator with the received signal by a phase-locked loop with a long time constant. A relatively slow reaction of the clock's oscillator to changes in the received signal reduces the effect of random noise. In order to increase absolute accuracy with a relatively low additional effort, the DCF 77 signal is modulated with a pseudo-random phase-shifting since 1983. The random sequence is repeated every second. It can be decoded and cross-correlated with the same sequence that is reproduced in the receiving clock. This technique makes clock synchronization less sensitive to perturbations in comparison to simple AM, although it requires a bandwidth of 1 kHz. Clocks using this method achieve a synchronization accuracy of 50–20 µs between different clocks.

Another effect that influences absolute synchronization of clocks apart from the accuracy of event detection is the signal propagation delay and its variation. Long-wave radio transmission provides a very stable propagation for ranges of up to several thousand kilometers distance from the broadcasting station in comparison to other frequencies. Therefore, synchronization errors due to propagation delay can be estimated with sufficient accuracy from the speed of light and the distance between the clock and the radio station, which amount to a value of about 1 ms per 300 km. As this is a systematic error, it may even be compensated if the distance is known.

Generally, radio signals in the LF and VLF frequency range propagate via two different paths from the senders to the receivers' antenna. While part of the signal is transmitted on a "straight line" between the two antennas within the so-called "ground wave," transmission also occurs via the "space wave," which is a reflection of the signal at the ionosphere layers of the atmosphere. A radio clock will always receive a signal, which is a composition of the space wave and the ground wave, independent of the distance between sender and receiver. Because ground and space waves are transmitted via different paths, they have different amplitude and phase angles at the receiver's site. Variations of the composed signal are primarily caused by variations in the transmission delay of the space wave.

At distances of up to approximately 500 km, the ground wave will be significantly stronger than the space wave, so the revived signal exhibits a stable transmission delay. This delay can easily be compensated by a receiving radio clock if the distance is known and clocks for improved accuracy requirements generally provide such compensation.

At larger distances in the range of approximately 500 to 1100 km both signals may be equally strong. Depending on their relative phase angles, destructive interference (fading), which can even annihilate the composed signal, may occur. Consequently a radio clock will lose synchronization during these times. On the other hand, it may also happen that the composed signal is stronger than each of its components. Such effects have, for example, been observed in measurements of the German PTB in Sicily. Because phase angle and amplitude of the received space wave vary with the height of the atmospheric D-layer they are also time dependent. In general these effects are relatively slow with time constants of about 15 minutes. They may nevertheless produce absolute synchronization errors of up to 200 µs.

Safety of radio clocks, first of all, depends on the continuous availability of time signals. As the broadcasting stations are supported by national standardization institutes, they are usually equipped with auxiliary antennas and redundant clocks in order to provide continuous broadcasting even during maintenance phases.

Every radio clock also contains its own crystal oscillator. This increases the accuracy of synchronization and insures the availability of a correct time even if the radio signal cannot be correctly received due to perturbations. The relative frequency stability of crystal oscillators ranges from 10^{-5} to 10^{-8}, where the first value refers to simple quartzes, as they are usually employed in computers, and the latter to oven-controlled oscillators. These oscillators reduce the increase of asynchronicity to less than about 36 ms–36 µs per hour, even if a synchronizing signal is not available.

Second, the detection and correction of errors in the received information has to be considered. From the point of view of coding theory, a single time telegram is relatively unsafe, as it usually contains only a few additional parity bits, which enable single error detection but no error correction. But there are a number of redundancies in the transmitted information, which is often used by commercial clocks to detect errors in a single protocol. For example, the number of minutes and hours has to be in the range of 0-59 and 0-23, respectively. Additionally, a sequence of transmitted telegrams contains a very high degree of redundancy, as consecutively received time information always has to differ by one minute. Thus, the analysis of sequences of telegrams enables safe reception even if only a low signal-to-noise-ratio is available. The use of this information in radio clocks is one of the reasons why changes from standard to daylight-saving time and the introduction of leap-seconds are announced in advance by special bits in the protocols, as these discontinuities have to be considered when checking the correctness of received data.

A wide variety of radio clocks for the synchronization of computer systems and even wristwatches with integrated receivers is already on the market. As receivers of time signals, a large number of plug-in boards are commercially available for various computer systems and a wide range of communication media as, for example, serial RS-232-C data transmission, VME/VXI-bus, Ethernet, etc. These clocks usually consist of a single Euro-size board, but much higher integration is possible using specialized hardware components and new integration technologies.

Prices for long-wave receivers that can be used as time servers in personal computer networks start at about $30.

5. SATELLITE-BASED TIME BROADCASTING

In addition to terrestrial radio stations, time information is also distributed by a number of satellite systems, the most popular one being the Global Positioning System (GPS). In mid 1993, it became fully operational with the launch of the last of 24 satellites, which are stationed in six orbits at a height of approximately 20,169 km. The signals from four satellites may be received simultaneously anywhere on earth, which enables the continuous calculation of absolute position and time.

Each of the satellites carries two cesium-beam-normals and two rubidium atomic clocks. The clock with the best performance is used as time standard. The satellites are supervised by a ground control station at Falcon Air Force Base in Colorado, which calculates their exact tracks from the measurements taken at five monitoring stations (Hawaii, Kwajalein, Ascension Island, Diego Garcia, Colorado Springs), as well as the deviation of a satellite's local clocks with respect to GPS system time. GPS time differs from coordinated universal time UTC broadcast by terrestrial stations, because it does not include leap-seconds. However, in order to allow for a reconstruction of UTC from GPS system time, data transmitted by the satellites also contains information on the difference between the two time scales. This difference, together with the deviation of the local clock and exact track information, is sent to each of the satellites once a day and is made available to the users in the information broadcast by the satellites.

GPS includes a Standard Positioning Service (SPS), available to all (civilian) GPS users on a continuous, worldwide basis with no direct charge. SPS provides the capability to achieve a horizontal positioning accuracy within 100 m and to obtain time information with a precision of better than nominally 100 ns, while (U.S.) military users can achieve accuracy of even 10 ns [DAN,DP,LEI].

A GPS message contains, among other data, an identification of the received satellite, a time-stamp that indicates the instant of broadcasting the message, and a pseudo-range correction that allows compensation of delays which are caused by influences of the atmosphere on signal propagation. Full information, i.e., position and time, may be calculated from the data received from four satellites. If the receiver's position is known, which can be easily achieved for stationary receivers, the reception of a single satellite's signals suffices to determine time. The advantage of clock synchronization using GPS is the high accuracy and availability provided. Apart from the higher complexity of the receiver, the main disadvantage in comparison to long-wave radio transmission is that signals at GHz-frequencies behave almost like light and, therefore, cannot be received inside buildings, i.e., a receiver requires an antenna that is mounted outside a building and has "visual contact" to the satellites.

GPS satellite receivers are available from several vendors. The GPS Receiver module Micro-Tracker made by Rockwell, for instance, measures only 72 x 51 x 14 mm and is available for less than $400. A wide variety of GPS antennas are also offered. They can be configured as either passive or active with different amplifiers. The connection from an antenna to a receiver is made by thin RG316 cable of required length. The micro-strip patch antenna from MicroPulse measures 40 x 40 x 11 mm and costs less than $100.

6. A HIGH-PRECISION TIMER

Since data delays due to processing and communication between the various nodes of distributed systems are not fixed, they must at least be known. This establishes the need for local clocks synchronized with high accuracy. With the advent of the satellite-based GPS and the commercial availability of GPS-receivers, this accuracy can be achieved very easily. In [HW] we already presented a GPS-based high-precision timer. If all nodes in a distributed multimedia system are furnished with such a timer, then all clock synchronizations become superfluous, since all clocks show the only official and legal UTC.

In order to ensure simultaneity and exact timing and to provide for efficient handling of time instances and fostering behavioural predictability, we developed the concept of alarm jobs and a high-precision timer handling them. Once instants become known, by any kind of program execution or external events, they are transferred as alarm jobs to an external high-precision timer. An alarm job consists of an alarm time and a unique alarm number identifying an associated activity. The timer keeps track of all alarm jobs and can always receive new alarm jobs. Thus, a corresponding computer system can transfer alarm jobs to its timer without any delay. Since time passes in a strictly linear fashion, alarm jobs can be sorted in ascending order. The timer simply needs to keep a sorted list of alarm jobs and to compare the alarm time of the earliest alarm job with its real-time clock. When this alarm time is reached, the timer sends an alarm signal to the processor of the node and provides the alarm number.

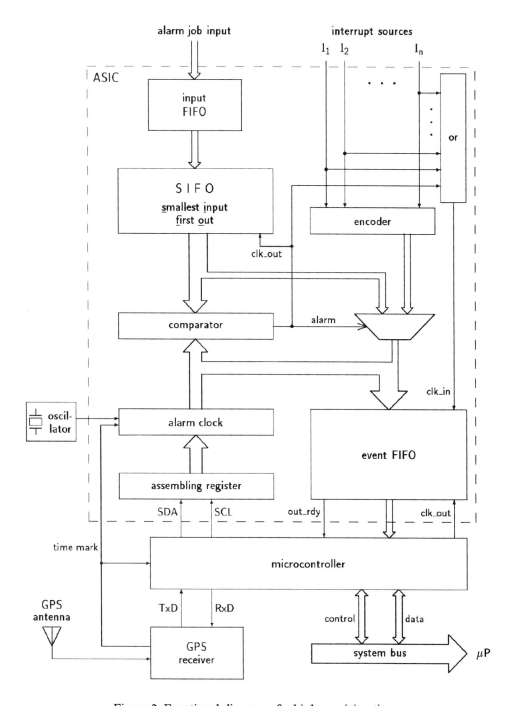

Figure 2. Functional diagram of a high-precision timer.

In order to perform the required time-stamping, we extended our timer by an interrupt receptacle (Figure 2). When a signal arrives at one of the interrupt lines I_1 ... I_n, a corresponding time-stamp is formed by the interrupt's arrival time and the encoded interrupt line number. The time-stamp descriptor is latched in the event FIFO and then transferred via the microcontroller to the processor of the node.

The high-precision timer consists of an ASIC implementing an alarm job handler and the time-stamping unit, a GPS-receiver with attached antenna, and a microcontroller interfacing the GPS-receiver to the counter of an alarm clock. The information obtained by the GPS receiver includes, among others, UTC time and date, position, and GPS-status and is transmitted via a serial data interface to the microcontroller. Every second the time information is transferred into the alarm clock. To this end, first the information is assembled in a corresponding register and then transferred to the alarm clock. Thus, the alarm clock keeps track with leap-seconds. Our alarm clock prototype has a resolution of 100 μs. It is driven by a free running oscillator and synchronized with UTC using the time mark signal as provided by the GPS receiver, which has an accuracy of 1 μs. The microcontroller is also used to interpret the GPS status information, which is made available to the event processor together with the time information. The presented timer is a working prototype, which was developed to carry out a feasibility study. It was implemented as an application specific integrated circuit (ASIC) by using the ES2 1.5 μm CMOS standard cell technology. With this n-well single poly, double metal technology, the chip has an area of 64 mm^2 and fits into a standard 40 pin package. The ASIC was fabricated by ES2, using EUROCHIP's MPW prototyping service. EUROCHIP is part of the VLSI Design Action within the ESPRIT program of the European Union.

The design can be easily enhanced and extended: other interfaces (e.g., bus width), higher resolutions (down to the accuracy of 1 μs), or the use of GPS time instead of UTC (GPS time has no leap seconds). In our prototype we do not make use of the accuracy as provided by the receiver. Since we use an external free running oscillator to increment the alarm clock, we reach only the absolute accuracy

$$t_{abs} = t_{rel, OSC} \times 1\,s = 100\,ppm \times 1\,s = 100\,\mu s.$$

To avoid this error, it is much better to use the synchronized frequency inside the GPS receiver. With the use of digital temperature compensated crystal oscillators (DTCXO) and by applying a closed loop control, it is possible to obtain very high accuracy. Only a short time of continuous reception is required to synchronize this internal frequency with the UTC time information of GPS. Even a low cost quartz can be used, since long term stability of the quartz becomes negligible.

Temporary disturbances of the GPS reception cause no serious problems. In the sense of graceful degradation, the synchronized DTCXO inside the GPS receiver serves as a very good back-up system until a reception problem has disappeared. With the new two-chip GPS receiver Zodiac of Rockwell Semiconductor Systems it is possible to use the internal frequency as described above. This receiver also contains an embedded microcontroller that can be used instead of the separate microcontroller in Figure 2. The chip set is available for $70.

In order to drive multimedia output devices, it is also necessary to generate precisely timed signals to trigger the output data stream. To this end, the timer can be extended with output generators, one for each output line. The multimedia processor launches special alarm jobs to control these lines. The match register of each output generator can be loaded with the alarm number of such an alarm job. When an alarm occurs, all output generators holding the corresponding alarm number will toggle their output signal, cp. Figure 3. A similar technique is used in the time processing unit (TPU) of the Motorola MC68332 processor.

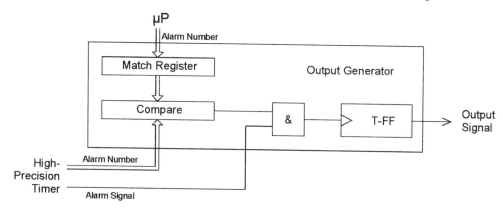

Figure 3. Output generator.

7. PREDICTABLE SYNCHRONOUS DATA EXCHANGE

To enable observability and to establish information consistency, distributed real-time systems require a common time base to measure the absolute time of event occurrences. This feature is particularly important for interactive multimedia services where data packets of audio and visual information are transferred. Since data delays due to processing and communication between the various nodes are not fixed, they must at least be known.

As an example, consider a multimedia system consisting of a satellite feed of visual and audio information, a local feed of visual and audio information of a reporter, and local computer generated graphics. Clearly, the local feed of the reporter and his or her voice must be synchronized together, as well as being synchronized with the satellite feed of, say, Somalia. Both the remote and local feeds are digitized and processed by a computer before recombination. Local computer generated graphics are added to the combined images. Using Warnier-Orr notation (a set-like notation where sequence is indicated from top to bottom and hierarchy is indicated from left to right), we can describe this multimedia scenario (see Figure 4). Here][is used to indicate parallelism.

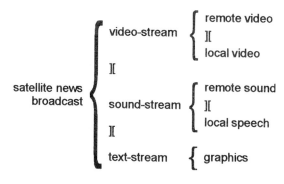

Figure 4. A multimedia news broadcast combining remote and local media using global synchronization.

If all data packets entering or leaving the local and remote computers are time-stamped, the correct timing as well as temporal and causal order of all transferred data can be determined and, therefore, the necessary timeliness and simultaneity can be achieved. This holds in particular for simultaneously occurring events whose simultaneity will, of course, be recognized only at a later stage when they will be (sequentially) processed.

To achieve the objective, the times for every data exchange are pre-determined. Moreover, the input/output units need to be equipped with additional hardware to carry through time-related functions. Like device addresses, the instants of external data exchanges become part of the control information sent to I/O controllers by the driver software. The advantage of this design is the predictability it provides.

8. CONCLUSION

Synchronization through time-stamping of input/output operations opens a new way of synchronizing the data streams in distributed continuous multimedia applications. While such situations arise in many (distributed) applications, they are prevalent in multimedia environments. Thus, hardware, programming languages, and operating systems that support these applications will need to be equipped with time-stamping facilities of the kind presented here.

It was shown that the problems of unpredictable transmission delays and response times of non-negligible length can easily be solved by endowing real-time computers with high-precision timers to make use of exact time specifications. The advantage of this feature is the predictability it provides.

The current state-of-the-art in clock synchronization on the basis of radio-transmitted signals shows that this technique can be – and is already being – applied to technical synchronization problems. The high degree of redundancy of the transmitted information, which stems from the fact that, after correct synchronization, the time-stamps of subsequently received protocol frames can be predicted by the receiver, enables safe decoding of time protocols even if only a low signal-to-noise-ratio is available. Therefore, radio clocks ought to become a standard component of computers and multimedia systems, especially in distributed systems.

While in this chapter we have discussed what we feel is a good engineering solution to the real-time problems of distributed multimedia applications, we would like to highlight the fact that there are fundamental problems of real-time synchronization in multimedia systems which have to be addressed at the application level (algorithmically or otherwise). These problems are, not surprisingly, inherent to the multimedia applications themselves.

REFERENCES

[PIM]   K. Pimental, *Through the New Looking Glass*. Blue-Ridge Summit, Windcrest/ McGraw-Hill, 1993.

[KDK]   H. Kopetz, A. Damm, C. Koza, M. Mulazzani, W. Schabl, C. Senft, and R. Zainlinger, "Distributed Fault-Tolerant Real-Time Systems: The Mars Approach," *IEEE Micro* 9, 1, 25–40, 1989.

[KO]   H. Kopetz and W. Ochsenreiter, "Clock Synchronization in Distributed Real-Time Systems," *IEEE Transactions on Computers* C-36, 8, 933-940, 1987.

[LOM]   M.A. Lombardi, *How to Get NIST-Traceable Time on Your Computer*, Publication of the National Institute of Standard and Technology, Physics Laboratory, Time and Frequency Division.

[KLA]   G. Klawitter, *Time Signal Stations*, 11th Edition. Meckenheim, Germany: Siebel Verlag, 1988.

[LIC]   R. Lichtenecker, "Terrestrial Time Signal Dissemination," *Real-Time Systems,* 12, 1, 41– 61, 1997

[REP]   *Standard Frequency and Time Signals*, Rep. 580-3, in: Reports of the CCIR, International Telecommunication Union, 1990.

[HW]   W.A. Halang and M. Wannemacher, "A High-Precision Time Processor for Distributed Real-Time Systems," Proc. *12th IFAC Workshop on Distributed Computer Control Systems*, Toledo, September 1994.

[DP]   P. Dana and B. Penrod, "The Role of GPS in Precise Time and Frequency Dissemination," *GPS World*, July/August 1990.

[DAN]   P. Dana, "Global Positioning System (GPS) Time Dissemination for Real-Time Applications," *Real-Time Systems*, 12, 1, 1997.

[LEI]   A. Leick, *GPS Satellite Surveying*, John Wiley & Sons, 1990.

[HW]   W.A. Halang and M. Wannemacher, "High Accuracy Concurrent Event Processing in Hard Real-Time Systems," *Real-Time Systems,* 12, 1, 77– 94, 1997

27

DESIGN AND IMPLEMENTATION OF MULTIMEDIA SERVERS

Shahram Ghandeharizadeh
Department of Computer Science
University of Southern California
Los Angeles, California 90089
shahram@perspolis.usc.edu

1.	**INTRODUCTION**	558
	1.1 CONTINUOUS MEDIA	559
2.	**STREAM-BASED PRESENTATION**	560
	2.1 CONTINUOUS DISPLAY	562
	2.2 PIPELINING TO MINIMIZE LATENCY TIME	568
	2.3 HIGH BANDWIDTH OBJECTS AND SCALABLE SERVERS	569
	2.4 CHALLENGES	570
3.	**STRUCTURED PRESENTATION**	570
	3.1 ATOMIC OBJECT LAYER	572
	3.2 COMPOSED OBJECT LAYER	573
	3.3 CHALLENGES	574
4.	**CONCLUSION**	576
	REFERENCES	576

Abstract. Information management systems that support both traditional and next generation data types, e.g., continuous media, are expected to play a major role in many applications such as education, health-care, entertainment, scientific applications, etc. These systems are termed multimedia. This chapter describes the issues, solutions, and challenges of designing multimedia servers. In particular, we focus on continuous media (audio and video) and how a system can support its display. We describe two alternative approaches to representing video objects (stream-based and structured) and how a system can support their hiccup-free display. For each approach, we describe the existing solutions and the future research directions from a database system perspective.

0-8493-1825-4/99/$0.00+$.50

1   Introduction

Advances in computer processing, storage, and communication has facilitated servers in support of multimedia data. In addition to traditional data types such as text and record based information, a multimedia server manages still images and continuous media data types, i.e., audio and video clips. Management of continuous media has introduced a number of challenges to be addressed by the scientific community. The focus of this chapter is on the requirements of this media type, several existing solutions in support of these requirement, and challenges that remain to be addressed. We start with an application to motivate the role of continuous media in a multimedia server. Subsequently, we analyze the technical solutions and challenges of this media type.

As an example application, news is a multimedia content. To illustrate, consider the tragic crash of TWA flight 800. This event consists of many newspaper articles, a large number of still images taken from the crash site itself and the items recovered from there, video footage of the crash site and investigators describing the day-to-day progress of their activities, and audio recording from the conversation between the pilot and the air traffic control tower along with eye-witnesses' description of the event, list of passengers and their related statistics, etc. This content is diverse and requires careful organization. For example, there are still images in support of the hypotheses that a missile shot down the airplane. There are still images and video interviews with officials in support of this claim. There are other hypotheses with their own supporting evidence. The organization of this material for efficient retrieval is a challenge in itself.

Broadcasters have long recognized the need for a multimedia server to manage content, facilitate its sharing, and to render it accessible in support of breaking news. A multimedia server can be deployed for news archiving, browsing, querying, and editing. Such a server becomes a library that might be accessed by different editors to produce a variety of programs. For example, an editor can use the system to author a one-hour documentary on the different hypotheses about the crash of TWA Flight 800. Alternatively, one could use the library to compare this tragedy with other plane crashes this century (assuming that the other crashes are digitized as multimedia content and stored in the server).

From a technical perspective, such servers raise a number of challenging topics; here are a few (we have already seen that the organization of information is a challenge):

- System functionality and performance: A multimedia server must support continuous display of audio and video clips (in addition to timely retrieval of other data types). With audio and video clips, the data must be retrieved at a pre-specified rate; otherwise, the display will suffer from frequent disruptions and delays that become annoying and, over time, render a system useless.

  A server in support of editing must meet a certain level of performance: number of simultaneous clients (throughput) that it can support and the average wait time (startup latency) for a client to be serviced. The operating system literature has demonstrated that a startup latency longer than one tenth of a second is noticeable and intolerable [12]. Ideally, the startup latency to display audio and video clips should fall below this threshold.

- Effective querying techniques: As a multimedia server grows to store additional content, techniques that allow a user to retrieve the relevant information become challenging. For example, an editor should be able to author a query that interrogates the content to retrieve all the video footage of Bosnia acquired during December 1993.

- Knowledge discovery: A multimedia server in support of news editing contains a large amount of content acquired over a period of time. A system that can discover interesting facts and bring them to the attention of an editor would be extremely valuable. For example, the New York Times recently printed an article that reports 2% of the engineers at the Long Island railroad are responsible for 95% of the accidents at that organization. Assuming that a server has the necessary tables and statistical tools, it would be useful for it to discover such a trend. Of course, to serve a wide variety of applications, the knowledge discovery tools should be general purpose and include tailoring tools that enable an application to specialize them for their specific requirements.

Continuous media is one of the novelties of a multimedia server. This chapter focuses on this media type and its storage and retrieval requirements. We analyze two alternative representations for this media: structured and stream-based. We briefly discuss the tradeoff associated with querying each representation.

1.1 Continuous Media

Unlike traditional data types, continuous media consists of a sequence of information components that convey meaning when presented at the right time relative to the start of a presentation. Continuous media servers are expected to play a major role in many applications including library information systems, entertainment industry, educational applications, etc. Without loss of generality and in order to simplify the discussion, in this chapter, we focus on video objects and their requirements as representative of continuous media.

A server may employ two alternative approaches to represent a video clip.

1. **Stream-based**: A video clip consists of a sequence of pictures (commonly termed two dimensional frames) that are displayed at a pre-specified rate, e.g., 30 frames a second for TV shows; 24 frames a second for most movies shown in a theater, due to the dim lighting. If an object is displayed at a rate lower than its pre-specified bandwidth, its display will suffer from frequent disruptions and delays, termed hiccups.

2. **Structured**: A video clip consists of a sequence of scenes. Each scene consists of a collection of background objects, actors (e.g., 3-dimensional representation of Mickey Mouse, dinosaurs, lions), light sources that define shading, and the audience's viewpoint. Spatial constructs are used to place objects that constitute a scene in a rendering space while temporal constructs describe how the objects and their relationship evolve as a function of time. The rendering of a structured presentation is hiccup-free when it satisfies the temporal constraints imposed on the display of each object. "Reboot" [2] is an animated Saturday morning children's show created using this approach.

Each approach has its own advantages and disadvantages. The stream-based approach benefits from more than a century of research and development on devices that generate high resolution frames; however, it suffers from the following limitations. First, while humans are capable of reasoning about the contents of a stream-based presentation, it is difficult to design techniques to process the contents of a movie for query processing (e.g., select all scenes of those clips that contain a plane crash). Second, it is difficult to extract the contents of one stream-based presentation to be re-used into another. To illustrate, with animation, it is difficult to extract Mickey Mouse from one animated sequence to be incorporated in another; typically Mickey Mouse is re-drawn from scratch for the new animation. However, this is not to imply that this task is impossible. For example, the movie "Forrest Gump" incorporates Tom Hanks (the main actor) with different presidents (J. F. Kennedy, L. B. Johnson, and R. Nixon). This was a tedious, time-consuming task that required the efforts of: 1) a creative director choosing from among the old news clips available on different presidents and selecting those that fit the movie's plot, 2) a skilled actor imagining the chosen scene and acting against a blue background,[1] and 3)

---

[1] A blue background is used because it can be easily eliminated once overlaid with the old news clip.

knowledgeable engineers who incorporated this footage with the old news clips on the different presidents.

A structured video clip eliminates the disadvantages of the stream-based approach because it provides adequate information to support query processing techniques and re-usability of information. It enables the system to retrieve and manipulate the individual objects that constitute a scene. While structured video is directly usable in both animation and video games that employ animated characters, their use in video clips is limited. This is because there are no devices equivalent to a camcorder that can analyze a scene to compute either its individual objects or the temporal and spatial relationships that exist among these objects. Perhaps another century of research and development is required before such devices become commercially available. However, it is important to note that once a repository of objects is constructed, the potential to re-use information to construct different scenarios and stories is almost limitless.

In this chapter, we describe each of these two approaches in detail (Sections 2 and 3). For each approach, we describe some of the existing solutions, and challenges that remain to be investigated. From a systems perspective, the structured approach has received little attention and requires further investigation. Brief conclusions are offered in Section 4.

2 Stream-based Presentation

A server may process requests for stream-based presentations using either a demand driven or a data driven paradigm. With the demand driven paradigm, the system waits for the arrival of a request to reference an object prior to retrieving it. With the data driven paradigm, the system retrieves and displays data items periodically (similar to how a broadcasting company such as HBO transmits movies at a certain time). The clients referencing an object wait for the onset of a display; at which point, the system transmits the referenced stream to all waiting clients. Each paradigm has its own tradeoffs. With the demand driven paradigm, each request observes a relatively low latency time as long as the number of active displays is lower than the maximum number of displays supported by a system (its throughput). When the number of active displays is larger than the throughput of the system, the wait time for a queue depends on the status of the active requests, the average service time of a request, and the length of the queue of pending requests.

The data driven paradigm is appropriate when the number of active requests is expected to far exceed the throughput of the system (a technique based on this paradigm is described in [18, 29]). However, with this paradigm, the system must decide: 1) what objects should it broadcast? 2) how frequently should each object be broadcast? 3) when is an object broadcast? and 4) what is the interval of time between two broadcasts of a single object? The answers to these questions are based on expectations. In the worst case, a stream might be broadcast with no client expressing interest in its display. A limitation of this paradigm is starvation: requests referencing unpopular video clips might wait for a long time before the referenced clip is broadcast. Moreover, with this paradigm, multiple clients that share a stream of data may fall out of synchronization with each other every time a user invokes a pause or fast-forward functionality. The system might either disallow such functionalities (as is done with the current broadcasting companies) or implement sophisticated techniques based on resource reservation to accommodate such operations. The focus of this chapter is on demand-driven display of continuous media.

Stream-based video clips exhibit two characteristics:

1. They require a continuous retrieval rate for a hiccup-free display. Stream-based objects should be retrieved at a pre-specified bandwidth. This bandwidth is defined by the object's

media type. For example, the bandwidth required by NTSC[2] for "network-quality" video is approximately 45 megabits per second (mbps) [24]. Recommendation 601 of the International Radio Consultative Committee (CCIR) calls for a 216 mbps bandwidth for video objects [16]. A video object based on HDTV requires a bandwidth of approximately 800 mbps.

2. They are large in size: A 30 minute uncompressed object based on NTSC is 10 gigabytes in size. With a compression technique that reduces the bandwidth requirement of this object to 1.5 mbps, this object is 337 megabytes in size. A repository (e.g., corresponding to an encyclopedia) that contains hundreds of such clips is potentially terabytes in size.

One may employ a lossy compression techniques (e.g., MPEG [17]) in order to reduce both the size and the bandwidth requirement of an object. These techniques encode data into a form that consumes a relatively small amount of space; however, when the data is decoded, it yields a representation similar to the original (some loss of data). Most of the compression schemes are Constant Bit Rate (CBR) but some are Variable Bit Rate (VBR). With both techniques, the data must be delivered at a pre-specified rate. Typically CBR schemes allow some bounded variation of this rate based on some amount of memory at the display. With VBR, this variation is not bounded. The VBR schemes have the advantage that, for the same average bandwidth as CBR, they can maintain a more constant quality in the delivered image by utilizing more megabits per second when needed, e.g., when there is more action in a scene.

Even with a lossy compression technique, the size of a stream-based video repository is typically very large. For example, the USC instructional TV program tapes approximately 1700 hours of video per semester. With MPEG-1 compression technique that reduces the bandwidth of each video object to 1.5 mbps (unacceptably low resolution), this center produces approximately 1.1 terabytes of data per semester. (A semester is approximately fifteen weeks long.) The large size of these databases motivates the use of hierarchical storage structures primarily by dollars and cents. Storing terabytes of data using DRAM would be very expensive. Moreover, it would be wasteful because only a small fraction of the data is referenced at any given instant in time (i.e., some tapes corresponding to particular classes are more frequently accessed than the others; there exists locality of reference). A similar argument applies to other devices, i.e., magnetic disks. The most practical choice would be to employ a combination of fast and slow devices, where the system controls the placement of the data in order to hide the high latency of slow devices using fast devices.

Assume a hierarchical storage structure consisting of random access memory (DRAM), magnetic disk drives, and a tape library [7]. As the different strata of the hierarchy are traversed starting with memory, both the density of the medium (the amount of data it can store) and its latency increases, while its cost per megabyte of storage decreases. At the time of this writing, these costs vary from $4/megabyte of DRAM to $0.05/megabyte of disk storage to less than $0.001/megabyte of tape storage. An application referencing an object that is disk resident observes both the average latency time and the delivery rate of a magnetic disk drive (which is superior to that of the tape library). An application would observe the best performance when its working set becomes resident at the highest level of the hierarchy: memory. However, in our assumed environment, the magnetic disk drives are the more likely staging area for this working set due to the large size of objects. As described below, the memory is used to stage a small fraction of an object for immediate processing and display. We define the working set [12] of an application as a collection of objects that are repeatedly referenced. For example, in existing video stores, a few titles are expected to be accessed frequently and a store maintains several (sometimes many) copies of these titles to satisfy the expected demand. These movies constitute the working set of a database system whose application provides a video-on-demand service.

---

[2]The U.S. standard established by the National Television System Committee.

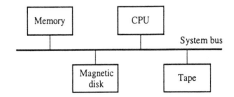

Figure 1: Architecture.

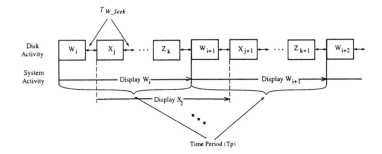

Figure 2: Time period

To simplify the discussion, we assume the architecture of Figure 1 for the rest of this section. Using this platform, we describe: 1) a technique to support a hiccup-free display of stream-based objects, and 2) a pipelining mechanism to minimize the latency time of the system.

2.1   Continuous Display

This study assumes that a disk drive provides a constant bandwidth, R_D. Moreover, all objects have the same display rate R_C. To support continuous display of an object X, it is partitioned into n equi-sized blocks: $X_0, X_1, ..., X_{n-1}$, where n is a function of the block size ($\mathcal{B}$) and the size of X. We assume a block is laid out contiguously on the disk and is the unit of transfer from disk to main memory. The time required to display a block is defined as a time period (T_p).

$$T_p = \frac{\mathcal{B}}{R_C} \tag{1}$$

This section describes four alternative techniques to support the continuous display of multiple objects. The size of a block, and hence the memory requirement, is different with each technique. Moreover, the maximum observed startup latency varies per technique.

2.1.1   A Simple Technique

With this technique, when an object X is referenced, the system stages X_0 in memory and initiates its display. Prior to completion of a time period, it initiates the retrieval of X_1 into memory in order to ensure a continuous display. This process is repeated until all blocks of an object have been displayed.

To support simultaneous displays of several objects, a time period is partitioned into fixed-size slots, with each slot corresponding to the retrieval time of a block from the disk drive. The number of slots in a time period defines the number of simultaneous displays that can be supported by the system ($\mathcal{N}$). For example, a block size of 1 MB corresponding to a MPEG-2 compressed movie ($R_C = 4$ Mb/s) has a 2 second display time ($T_p = 2$). Assuming a typical magnetic disk with a transfer rate of 68 Mb/s ($R_D = 68$ Mb/s) and maximum seek time of 17 milliseconds, 14 such blocks can be retrieved in 2 seconds. Therefore, a single disk supports 14 simultaneous displays. Figure 2 demonstrates the concept of a time period and a time slot. Each box represents a time slot. Assuming that each block is stored contiguously on the surface of the disk, the disk incurs a seek every time it switches from one block of an object to another. We denote this as T_{W_Seek} and assume that it includes the average rotational latency time of the disk drive. We will not discuss rotational latency further because it is a constant added to every seek time.

The seek time is a function of the distance traveled by the disk arm [5, 23, 30]. Several studies have introduced analytical models to estimate seek time as a function of this distance. To be independent from any specific equation, this study assumes a general seek function. Thus, let $Seek(d)$ denote the time required for the disk arm to travel d cylinders to reposition itself from cylinder i to cylinder $i + d$ (or $i - d$). Hence, $Seek(1)$ denotes the time required to reposition the disk arm between two adjacent cylinders, while $Seek(\#cyl)$ denotes a complete stroke from the first to the last cylinder of a disk (with $\#cyl$ cylinders). Typically, seek is a linear function of distance except for small values of d [5, 30]. For example, [20] employed the following seek function:

$$Seek(d) = \begin{cases} 3.24 + (0.4 \times \sqrt{d}) & \text{if } d < 383 \\ 8.0 + (0.008 \times d) & \text{otherwise} \end{cases} \qquad (2)$$

Since the blocks of different objects are scattered across the disk surface, the simple technique should assume the maximum seek time (i.e., $Seek(\#cyl)$) when multiplexing the bandwidth of the disk among multiple displays. Otherwise, a continuous display of each object cannot be guaranteed.

Seek is a wasteful operation that minimizes the number of simultaneous displays supported by the disk. In the worst case, disk performs $\mathcal{N}$ seeks during a time period. Hence, the percentage of time that the disk performs wasteful work can be quantified as $\frac{\mathcal{N} \times Seek(d)}{T_p} \times 100$, where d is the maximum distance between two blocks retrieved consecutively ($d = \#cyl$ with simple). By substituting T_p from Eq. 1, we obtain the percentage of wasted disk bandwidth.

$$wasteful = \frac{\mathcal{N} \times Seek(d) \times R_C}{B} \times 100 \qquad (3)$$

By reducing this percentage, the system can support a higher number of simultaneous displays. We can manipulate two factors to reduce this percentage: 1) decrease the distance traversed by a seek (d), and/or 2) increase the block size (B). A limitation of increasing the block size is that it results in a higher memory requirement. In this chapter, we investigate display techniques that reduce the first factor. An alternative aspect is that by manipulating d and fixing the throughput, one can decrease the block size and benefit from a system with a lower memory requirement for staging the blocks. The following paragraphs elaborate more on this aspect.

Suppose $\mathcal{N}$ blocks are retrieved during a time period, then $T_p = \frac{\mathcal{N}B}{R_D} + \mathcal{N} \times Seek(\#cyl)$. By substituting T_p from Eq. 1, we solve for B to obtain

$$B_{simple} = \frac{R_C \times R_D}{R_D - \mathcal{N} \times R_C} \times \mathcal{N} \times Seek(\#cyl) \qquad (4)$$

From Eq. 4, for a given $\mathcal{N}$, the size of a block is proportional to $Seek(\#cyl)$. Hence, if one can decrease the duration of the seek time, then the same number of simultaneous displays can be supported with smaller block sizes. This will save some memory. Briefly, for a fixed number of simultaneous displays, as the duration of the worst seek time decreases (increases) the size of the blocks shrinks (grows) proportionally with no impact on throughput. This impacts the amount of memory required to support $\mathcal{N}$ displays. For example assume: $Seek(\#cyl) = 17$ msec, $R_D = 68$ Mb/s, $R_C = 4$ Mb/s, and $\mathcal{N} = 15$. From Eq. 4, we compute a block size of 1.08 MB that wastes 12% of the disk bandwidth. If a display technique reduces the worst seek time by a factor of two, then the same throughput can be maintained with a block size of 0.54 MB, reducing the amount of required memory by a factor of two and maintaining the percentage of wasted disk bandwidth at 12%. This observation will be used repeatedly in this chapter.

The maximum startup latency observed by a request with this technique is

$$\ell_{simple} = T_p \tag{5}$$

This is because a request might arrive a little too late to employ the empty slot in the current time period. Note that ℓ is the maximum startup latency (the average latency is $\frac{\ell}{2}$) when the number of active users is $\mathcal{N} - 1$. If the number of active displays exceeds $\mathcal{N}$ then Eq. 5 should be extended with appropriate queuing models. This discussion holds true for the maximum startup latencies computed for other techniques in this chapter.

In the following sections we investigate two general techniques to reduce the duration of the worst seek time. While the first technique schedules the order of block retrieval from the disk, the second controls the placement of the blocks across the disk surface. These two techniques are orthogonal and we investigate a technique that incorporates both approaches.

2.1.2 Disk Scheduling

One approach to reduce the worst seek time is Grouped Sweeping Scheme [34], GSS. GSS groups $\mathcal{N}$ active requests of a time period into g groups. This divides a time period into g subcycles, each corresponding to the retrieval of $\lceil \frac{\mathcal{N}}{g} \rceil$ blocks. The movement of the disk head to retrieve the blocks within a group abides by the SCAN algorithm, in order to reduce the incurred seek time in a group. Across the groups there is no constraint on the disk head movement. To support the SCAN policy within a group, GSS shuffles the order that the blocks are retrieved. For example, assuming X, Y, and Z belong to a single group, the sequence of the block retrieval might be X_1 followed by Y_4 and Z_6 (denoted as $X_1 \to Y_4 \to Z_6$) during one time period, while during the next time period it might change to $Z_7 \to X_2 \to Y_5$. In this case, the display of, say, X might suffer from hiccups because the time elapsed between the retrievals of X_1 and X_2 is greater than one time period. To eliminate this possibility, [34] suggests the following display mechanism: the displays of all the blocks retrieved during subcycle i start at the beginning of subcycle $i + 1$.

The maximum startup latency observed with this technique is the summation of one time period (if the request arrives when the empty slot is missed) and the duration of a subcycle ($\frac{T_p}{g}$):

$$\ell_{gss} = T_p + \frac{T_p}{g} \tag{6}$$

By comparing Eq. 6 with Eq. 5, it may appear that GSS results in a higher latency than simple. However, this is not necessarily true because the duration of the time period is different with these two techniques due to a choice of different block size. This can be observed from Eq. 1 where the duration of a time period is a function of the block size.

To compute the block size with GSS, we first compute the total duration of time contributed to seek times during a time period. Assuming $\lceil \frac{\mathcal{N}}{g} \rceil$ blocks retrieved during a subcycle are distributed uniformly across the disk surface, the disk incurs a seek time of $Seek(\frac{\#cyl}{\frac{\mathcal{N}}{g}})$ between every two consecutive block retrievals. This assumption maximizes the seek time according to the square root model, providing the worst case scenario. Since $\mathcal{N}$ blocks are retrieved during a time period, the system incurs $\mathcal{N}$ seek times in addition to $\mathcal{N}$ block retrievals during a period, i.e., $T_p = \frac{\mathcal{N}B}{R_D} + \mathcal{N} \times Seek(\frac{\#cyl \times g}{\mathcal{N}})$. By substituting T_p from Eq. 1 and solving for $\mathcal{B}$, we obtain

$$\mathcal{B}_{gss} = \frac{R_C \times R_D}{R_D - \mathcal{N} \times R_C} \times \mathcal{N} \times Seek(\frac{\#cyl \times g}{\mathcal{N}}) \tag{7}$$

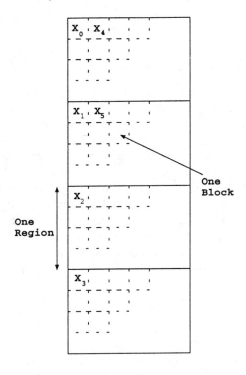

Figure 3: OREO

By comparing Eq. 7 with Eq. 4, observe that the bound on the distance between two blocks retrieved consecutively is reduced by a factor of $\frac{g}{N}$, noting that $g \leq N$.

Observe that $g = N$ simulates the simple technique of Section 2.1.1. (By substituting g with N in Eq. 7, it reduces to Eq. 4.)

2.1.3 Constrained Data Placement

An alternative approach to reduce the worst seek time is to control the placement of the blocks across the disk surface [6, 8, 10, 20]. OREO[3] reduces the worst seek time by bounding the distance between any two blocks that are retrieved consecutively. This is achieved by partitioning the disk space into $\mathcal{R}$ regions. Next, successive blocks of an object X are assigned to the regions in a round-robin manner as shown in Figure 3. The round-robin assignment follows the efficient movement of disk head as in the scan algorithm. To display an object, the disk head moves *inward* until it reaches the innermost region and then it repositions itself to the outermost region to start another scan. This minimizes the movement of the disk head required to simultaneously retrieve N objects because the display of each object abides by the following rules:

1. The disk head moves in one direction (either *inward* or *outward*) depending on the placement of data. Without loss of generality and to simplify the discussion, assume that the data is placed in a round-robin manner starting from the outermost region of the disk drive. Thus, the disk head moves in an inward direction.

2. For a given time period, the disk services those displays that correspond to a single region (termed active region, R_{active}).

3. In the next time period, the disk services requests corresponding to region ($active + 1$) $mod \, \mathcal{R}$.

---

[3]OREO is the name of an optimized version of the REBECA technique as originally described in [20].

4. Upon the arrival of a request referencing object X, it is assigned to the region containing X_0 (termed S_{X_0}).

5. The display of X does not start until the active region reaches S_{X_0}.

When retrieving the blocks of a region during a time period, to compute the maximum seek time incurred with OREO, note that the distance between two blocks retrieved consecutively is bounded by the length of a region[4] (i.e., $\frac{\#cyl}{\mathcal{R}}$). However, the system observes a long seek, seek(#cyl), every $\mathcal{R}$ regions (to reposition the head to the outermost cylinder). To compensate for this, the system must ensure that after every $\mathcal{R}$ block retrievals, enough data has been prefetched on behalf of each display to eclipse a delay equivalent to seek(#cyl). There are several ways of achieving this effect. One might force the first block along with every $\mathcal{R}$ other blocks to be slightly larger than the other blocks. We describe OREO based on a fix-sized block approach that renders all blocks to be equi-sized. With this approach, every block is padded so that after every $\mathcal{R}$ block retrievals, the system has enough data to eclipse the seek(#cyl) delay. Thus, the duration of a time period is $T_p = \frac{\mathcal{N}B}{R_D} + \mathcal{N} \times Seek(\frac{\#cyl}{\mathcal{R}}) + \frac{Seek(\#cyl)}{\mathcal{R}}$. By substituting T_p from Eq. 1, we solve for B to obtain

$$\mathcal{B}_{oreo} = \frac{R_C \times R_D}{R_D - \mathcal{N} \times R_C} \times [\mathcal{N} \times Seek(\frac{\#cyl}{\mathcal{R}}) + \frac{Seek(\#cyl)}{\mathcal{R}}] \tag{8}$$

Introducing regions to reduce the seek time increases the average latency observed by a request. This is because during each time period the system can initiate the display of only those objects that correspond to the active region and whose assignment direction corresponds to that of the current direction of the disk head. With OREO, the maximum startup latency is

$$\ell_{oreo} = \begin{cases} (\mathcal{R}+1) \times T_p & \text{if } \mathcal{R} > 2 \\ (2 \times T_p) & \text{if } \mathcal{R} = 2 \\ T_p & \text{if } \mathcal{R} = 1 \end{cases} \tag{9}$$

An interesting observation is that the computed startup latency does not apply for **recording** of live objects.[5] That is, if $\mathcal{N}$ sessions of multimedia objects are recorded live, the transfer of each stream from memory to the disk can start immediately. This is because the first block of an object X can be stored starting with any region. Hence, it is possible to start its storage from the active region (i.e., $R_{active} \leftarrow R_X$).

In summary, partitioning the disk space into regions using OREO is a tradeoff between throughput and latency.

2.1.4   Disk Scheduling + Constrained Data Placement

In order to cover a wide spectrum of applications, GSS and OREO can be combined. Recall that with OREO the placement of objects within a region is un-constrained. Hence, the distance between two blocks retrieved consecutively is bounded by the length of a region. However, one can introduce the concept of grouping the retrieval of blocks within a region. In this case, assuming a uniform distribution of blocks across a region surface, the distance between every two blocks retrieved consecutively is bounded by $\frac{\#cyl \times g}{\mathcal{N}\mathcal{R}}$. Hence, $T_p = \frac{\mathcal{N}B}{R_D} + \mathcal{N} \times Seek(\frac{\#cyl \times g}{\mathcal{N}\mathcal{R}}) + \frac{Seek(\#cyl)}{\mathcal{R}}$. By substituting T_p from Eq. 1, we solve for $\mathcal{B}_{combined}$ to obtain:

$$\frac{R_C \times R_D}{R_D - \mathcal{N} \times R_C} \times [\mathcal{N} \times Seek(\frac{\#cyl \times g}{\mathcal{N}\mathcal{R}}) + \frac{Seek(\#cyl)}{\mathcal{R}}] \tag{10}$$

---

[4]This distance is bounded by $2 \times \frac{\#cyl}{\mathcal{R}}$ when the blocks belong to two different regions. This occurs only for the last block retrieved during time period i and the first block retrieved during time period $i + 1$. To simplify the discussions, we eliminated this factor from the equations (see [20] for precise equations). However, the precise equations were employed by the experiments of Section 2.1.6.

[5]Recording a live session is similar to taping a live football game. In this case, a video camera or a compression algorithm is the producer and the disk drive is the consumer.

Table 1: Disk parameters used in the experiments (Seagate ST12450W)

Minimum Transfer Rate (R_D)	68.6 Mb/s
Minimum Seek Time (track-to-track)	0.6 msec
Maximum Seek Time	17.0 msec
Rotation Time	8.33 msec
Average Rotational Latency	4.17 msec

Observe that with OREO+GSS, both reduction factors of GSS and OREO are applied to the upper bound on the distance between any two consecutively retrieved blocks (compare Eq. 10 with both Eqs. 7 and 8).

The maximum startup latency observed with OREO+GSS is identical to OREO when $\mathcal{R} > 1$ (see Eq. 9). When $\mathcal{R} = 1$, its startup latency is identical to GSS.

2.1.5 Memory Requirements

The technique employed to manage memory impacts the amount of memory required to support $\mathcal{N}$ simultaneous displays. A simple approach to manage memory is to assign each user two dedicated blocks of memory: one for retrieval of data from disk to memory and the other for delivery of data from memory to the display station. Trivially, the data is retrieved into one block while it is consumed from the other. Subsequently, the role of these two blocks is switched. The amount of memory required with this technique is:

$$M_{unshared} = 2 \times \mathcal{N} \times \mathcal{B} \tag{11}$$

Note that $\mathcal{B}$ is different for alternative display techniques: $\mathcal{B}_{gss}$ with GSS, $\mathcal{B}_{oreo}$ with OREO, and $\mathcal{B}_{combined}$ with OREO+GSS.

The total amount of memory required by a display technique that employs both GSS and coarse-grain memory sharing is

$$M_{coarse} = (\mathcal{N} + \lceil \frac{\mathcal{N}}{g} \rceil) \times \mathcal{B} \tag{12}$$

To support $\mathcal{N}$ simultaneous displays, the system employs $\mathcal{N}$ blocks for $\mathcal{N}$ displays and $\lceil \frac{\mathcal{N}}{g} \rceil$ blocks for data retrieval on behalf of the group that reads its block from disk.

OREO and OREO + GSS can employ Eq. 12. This is because the memory requirement of OREO is a special case of GSS where $g = \mathcal{N}$. However, the block size ($\mathcal{B}$) computed for each approach is different: $\mathcal{B}_{gss}$ with GSS, $\mathcal{B}_{oreo}$ with OREO, and $\mathcal{B}_{combined}$ with OREO+GSS.

2.1.6 Performance Comparison

We verified our experimental model of GSS by performing experiments using the disk characteristics and consumption rate reported in [34]. First, we compared the memory requirement and the maximum startup latency of GSS with those of OREO by employing coarse-grain memory sharing (Table 2). GSS is superior to OREO when $\mathcal{R} = 2$. As the number of regions ($\mathcal{R}$) increases, OREO results in a lower memory requirement and a higher startup latency when compared with GSS.

We also compared the memory requirement and the maximum startup latency of GSS with those of OREO+GSS (Table 3). OREO+GSS simulates GSS when configured with a single region ($\mathcal{R} = 1$). As we increase the number of regions with OREO+GSS, its memory requirement decreases and the maximum startup latency increases. For example, when $\mathcal{R} = 4$, OREO+GSS reduces the total memory requirement of 16 simultaneous displays from 18.05 to

Table 2: GSS vs. OREO

| $\mathcal{N}$ | Memory Requirement (MB) | | | Startup Latency Time (sec) | | |
| | GSS | OREO | | GSS | OREO | |
		$\mathcal{R} = 2$	$\mathcal{R} = 4$		$\mathcal{R} = 2$	$\mathcal{R} = 4$
8	0.71	0.81	0.44	0.19	0.34	0.62
9	1.00	1.12	0.62	0.21	0.43	0.78
10	1.30	1.55	0.86	0.36	0.55	0.99
11	1.83	2.15	1.20	0.39	0.70	1.26
12	2.45	3.02	1.68	0.42	0.91	1.63
13	3.57	4.34	2.43	0.62	1.22	2.19
14	5.22	6.57	3.69	0.84	1.73	3.10
15	8.64	10.97	6.17	1.31	2.72	4.85
16	18.05	23.16	13.05	2.35	5.43	9.65
17	154.87	199.2	112.4	18.06	44.24	78.50

Table 3: GSS vs. OREO+GSS

| $\mathcal{N}$ | Memory Requirement (MB) | | | Startup Latency Time (sec) | | |
| | GSS | OREO+GSS | | GSS | OREO+GSS | |
		$\mathcal{R} = 2$	$\mathcal{R} = 4$		$\mathcal{R} = 2$	$\mathcal{R} = 4$
8	0.71	0.67	0.44	0.19	0.26	0.51
9	1.00	0.88	0.61	0.21	0.32	0.59
10	1.30	1.24	0.83	0.36	0.39	0.80
11	1.83	1.66	1.16	0.39	0.54	1.04
12	2.45	2.24	1.60	0.42	0.63	1.23
13	3.57	3.31	2.32	0.62	0.97	1.94
14	5.22	4.84	3.47	0.84	1.25	2.52
15	8.64	7.85	5.83	1.31	1.81	3.63
16	18.05	16.30	12.17	2.35	3.65	6.92
17	154.87	141.92	105.33	18.06	30.47	62.76

13.85 MB for $\mathcal{N} = 16$ (a 23% saving in memory as compared to GSS). However, the maximum startup latency is increased from 2.35 to 6.92 seconds (a factor of 3 increase). Varying the number of regions with OREO+GSS is a tradeoff between memory requirement and startup latency. Thus, OREO+GSS provides a wider range of configuration choices including those of GSS.

2.2 Pipelining to Minimize Latency Time

With a hierarchical storage organization, when a request references an object that is not resident on the disk drive(s), the system may service the request using the bandwidth of the tertiary storage device as long as: 1) the tertiary storage device is free, and 2) the bandwidth required to support a hiccup-free display of the referenced object (R_C) is lower than the bandwidth of the tertiary storage device (R_T). Indeed, one may envision multiplexing a tertiary storage device that provides a high transfer rate (e.g., Ampex DST [25] with a 116 mbps sustained transfer rate) among several active devices using the paradigm of Section 2.1. However, this might be wasteful due to the significant seek time of these devices (in the order of seconds).

If R_C is higher than R_T (i.e., the tertiary cannot support a hiccup-free display of the referenced object) then the object must first be staged on the disk drive prior to its display. One approach might materialize the object on the disk drives in its entirety before initiating its display. In this case, the latency time of the system is determined by the bandwidth of the tertiary storage device and the size of the referenced object. Stream-based video objects require a sequential retrieval to support their display, hence, a better alternative is to use a pipelining mechanism that overlaps the display of an object with its materialization, in order to minimize the latency time.

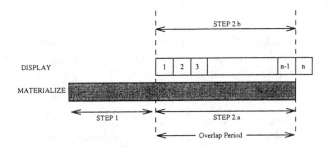

Figure 4: The pipelining mechanism.

With pipelining, a portion of the time required to materialize X can be overlapped with its display. This is achieved by grouping the subobjects of X into s logical slices ($S_{X,1}$, $S_{X,2}$, $S_{X,3}$, ..., $S_{X,s}$), such that the display time of $S_{X,1}$, $T_{Display}(S_{X,1})$, overlaps the time required to materialize $S_{X,2}$; $T_{Display}(S_{X,2})$ overlaps $T_{Materialize}(S_{X,3})$, etc. Thus

$$T_{Display}(S_{X,i}) \geq T_{Materialize}(S_{X,i+1}) \; for \; 1 \leq i < s \qquad (13)$$

Upon the retrieval of a tertiary resident object X, the pipelining mechanism is as follows:

1. Materialize the subobject(s) that constitute $S_{X,1}$ on the disk drive.

2. For $i = 2$ to s

   a. Initiate the materialization of $S_{X,i}$ from tertiary onto the disk.

   b. Initiate the display of $S_{X,i-1}$.

3. Display the last slice ($S_{X,s}$).

The duration of Step 1 determines the latency time of the system. Its duration is equivalent to $T_{Materialize}(X) - T_{Display}(X) +$ (one Time Period). Step 3 displays the last slice materialized on the disk drive. In order to minimize the latency time,[6] $S_{X,s}$ should consist of a single subobject. To illustrate this, consider Figure 4. If the last slice consists of more than one subobject then the duration of the overlap is minimized, elongating duration of Step 1.

2.3 High Bandwidth Objects and Scalable Servers

There are applications that cannot tolerate the use of a lossy compression technique (e.g., video signals collected from space by NASA [13]). Clearly, a technique that can support the display of an object for both application types is desirable. Assuming a multi-disk architecture, staggered striping [3] is such a technique. It is flexible enough to support those objects whose bandwidth requires either the aggregate bandwidth of multiple disks or fraction of the bandwidth of a single disk. Using the declustering technique of [21], it employs the aggregate bandwidth of multiple disk drives to support a hiccup-free display of those objects whose bandwidth exceeds the bandwidth of a single disk drive. Hence, it provides effective support for a database that consists of a mix of media types, each with a different bandwidth requirement. Moreover, its design enables the system to scale to thousands of disk drives because its overhead does not increase prohibitively as a function of additional resources.

Several studies have investigated extensions of the pipelining mechanism in support of on time delivery from tertiary in support of continuous display [19, 33]. Hiccup-free display in the presence of disk failures is investigated in [4].

---

[6]Maximize the length of the pipeline.

2.4 Challenges

A number of challanging issues remain to be addressed with continuous media servers: buffer pool management [26, 31], heterogeneous disk subsystems [11, 35], dead-line driven approaches [1, 28], inter-operability between the different data formats and platforms, VCR functionalities [22], networking issues, etc. We describe two (chosen arbitrarily) in order to be brief.

First, while the focus thus far has been on a demand-driven approach to display presentations, the design of a system that can switch between data-driven and demand-driven paradigms (or support both simultaneously) depending on the number of requests requiring service, the throughput of the system, the pattern of reference to the objects, and the quality of service desired by the clients. The precise definition of quality of service is application dependent. For video servers, it may refer to either the functionality provided to a client (e.g., fast-forward, pause) or the resolution of the display.[7]

Second, both the news broadcasters and post-production facilities of studios have produced a strong demand for digital non-linear editing systems. To illustrate, consider the role of such a system in a news orgnaization, e.g., CNN. With sports, a producer tailors a presentation based on highlights of different clips, e.g., events at the Olympics. Moreover, the producer might add an audio narration to logically tie these highlights together. Upon the display of the presentation, the system is required to display: (1) the audio naration in synchrony with video, and (2) the highlights in sequence, one after another, with no delay between two consecutive highlight; If the system treats the display of each highlight as a request for a stream then the startup latency must be minimized between each stream to provide the desired effects, [9] presents a framework in support of this requirement. In addition to the synchronization and retrieval issues, these systems must be able to: 1) accept satellite input from remote sources to populate the server with new video clips, and 2) be able to broadcast data [1]. With a satellite input, a clip might be written to the server at four times the regular display rates. In addition, the server must manage the multiplexing of disk bandwidth between: 1) the different editors accessing the server, and 2) the broadcasted stream that has the highest priority. It must also manage the disk space to prevent its fragmentation and ensure availability of enough space (by writing old data to disk). These requirements require further extensions to the solutions described in this chapter.

3 Structured Presentation

As an alternative to a stream-based presentation, a video object can be represented as a collection of objects, spatial and temporal constructs, and rendering features (termed structured presentation). The spatial and temporal constructs define where in the rendering space and when in the temporal space the component objects are displayed. The rendering features define how the objects are displayed.

A Rendering Space is a coordinate system defined by n orthogonal vectors, where n is the number of dimensions (i.e., $n = 3$ for 3D, $n = 2$ for 2D). A spatial construct specifies the placement of a component in the rendering space. Analogously, different components are rendered within a time interval, termed Temporal Space. For example, if a movie has 30 scenes of 3 minutes each, then the temporal space of the movie is $[0, 90]$. Moreover there is a temporal construct specifying the subinterval within the temporal space that should render each scene. For example, a temporal construct for the first scene will specify the subinterval $[0, 3]$.

To illustrate the use of both constructs simultaneously, consider the motion of a rolling ball.

---

[7]The resolution of a display dictates the bandwidth required to support that display. A system may maintain multiple copies of a video object based on different resolutions and service the different clients using a different copy based on how much they pay.

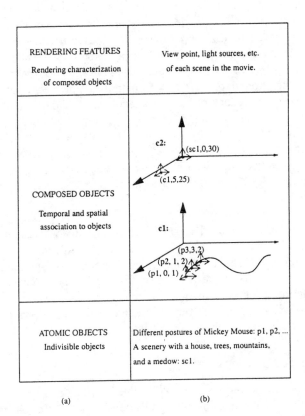

RENDERING FEATURES Rendering characterization of composed objects	View point, light sources, etc. of each scene in the movie.
COMPOSED OBJECTS Temporal and spatial association to objects	
ATOMIC OBJECTS Indivisible objects	Different postures of Mickey Mouse: p1, p2, ... A scenery with a house, trees, mountains, and a medow: sc1.

(a)　　　　　　　　　　　(b)

Figure 5: Three levels of abstraction.

The motion is captured by a sequence of snapshots, represented by a sequence of triplets: (the object, i.e., the ball, its positioning, subinterval). Each triplet specifies a spatial and a temporal constraint. In this section, we partition the information associated with a structured video into three layers:

1. Atomic objects that define indivisible entities (e.g., the 3D representation of a ball).

2. Composed objects that consist of objects constrained using temporal and spatial constructs, e.g., a triplet: (the ball, a position, a subinterval).

3. The rendering features (e.g., viewpoint, light sources, etc.).

Figure 5 shows the different levels of abstraction of a media object and an example of the representation of a scene. Assume that the objective is to describe a character (e.g., Mickey Mouse) walking along a path in the scene. The atomic object layer contains the 3D representations of different postures of Mickey Mouse, denoted by p1, p2, etc. For example, his posture when he starts to walk, his posture one second later, etc. These postures might have been originals composed by an artist or generated using interpolation. We also include the 3D representation of the background (denoted by sc1) in the atomic object layer.

To represent the walking motion, the author specifies spatial and temporal constructs among the different postures of Mickey Mouse. The result is a composed object. The curve labeled **c1** specifies the path followed by Mickey Mouse (i.e., the different positions reached). Each of the coordinate systems describe the direction of a posture of the character. For each posture, a temporal construct specifies the time when the object appears in the temporal space. For example, the point labeled by (p1, 0, 1) indicates that posture p1 appears at time 0 and lasts for 1 second.

The spatial and temporal constructs in the composed objects layer (**c2**) associate the motion of Mickey Mouse to the background. The spatial constructs define where in the rendering space the motion and the background are placed. The temporal constructs define the timing of the appearances of the background and the motion. In this example, the background sc1 appears at the beginning of the scene while Mickey Mouse starts to walk (c1) at the 5th second.

Finally, the rendering features are assigned by specifying the view point, the light sources, etc., for the time interval at which the scene is rendered. In the following two sections, we describe each of the atomic and composed objects layers in more detail.

3.1   Atomic Object Layer

This layer contains objects that are considered indivisible (i.e., they are rendered in their entirety). The exact representation of an atomic object is application dependent. In animation, as described in [32], the alternative representations include

1. Wire-frame representation: an object is represented by a set of segment lines.

2. Surface representation: an object is represented by a set of primitive surfaces, typically triangles, polygons, equations of algebraic surfaces or patches.

3. Solid representation: an object is a set of primitive volumes.

From a physical perspective, these physical representations are considered as an unstructured unit, termed a BLOB. These objects can also be described as

1. A procedure that consumes a number of parameters to compute a BLOB that represents an object. For example, a geometric object can be represented by its dimensions (i.e., the radius, the length of a side of a square, etc.), a value for these dimensions, and a procedure that consumes these values to compute a bitmap representation of the object. This type of representation is termed Parametric.

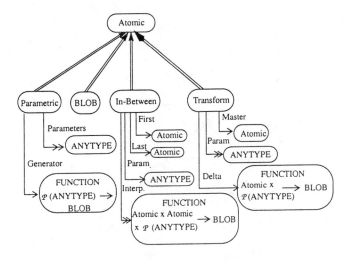

Figure 6: Atomic object schema.

2. An interpolation of two other atomic objects. For example, in animation, the motion of a character can be represented as postures at selected times and the postures in between can be obtained by interpolation. In animation, this representation is termed In-Between.

3. A transformation applied to another atomic object. For example the representation of a posture of Mickey Mouse can be obtained by applying some transformation to a master representation. This representation is termed Transform.

Figure 6 presents the schema of the type atomic that describes these alternative representations. The conventions employed in this schema representation as well as others presented in this chapter are as follows: The names of built-in types (i.e., strings, integers, etc.) are in capital letters as opposed to defined types that use lower case letters. ANYTYPE refers to strings, integers, characters, and complex data structures. A type is represented by its name surrounded by an oval. The attributes of a type are denoted by arrows with single line tails. The name of the attribute labels the arrow and the type is given at the head of the arrow. Multivalued attributes are denoted by arrows with two heads and single value attributes by arrows with a single head. For multivalued attributes, an S overlapping the arrow is used to denote a sequence instead of a set. The type/subtype relationship is denoted by an arrow with a double line tail. The type at the tail is the subtype and the type at the head is the supertype.

For example, in Figure 6 Parametric is a subtype of Atomic, and it has two attributes, Parameters and Generator. Parameters is a set of elements of any type and Generator is a function that maps a set of elements of any type (i.e., Parameters) into a BLOB.

3.2 Composed Object Layer

This layer contains the representation of temporal and spatial constructs. In addition to specifying positioning and timing of objects, these constructs define objects as composed by other objects. The composition might be recursive (i.e., a composed object may consist of a collection of other composed objects). For example, Mickey Mouse might be represented as a composed object consisting of 3D representation of a head, two ears, a tail, two legs, etc. The spatial relationship between these atomic objects would define Mickey Mouse.

Spatial constructs place objects in the rendering space and implicitly define spatial relationships between objects. The placement of an object defines its position and direction in the rendering space. For example, consider a path from a house to a pond. The placement of a

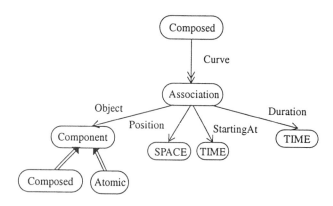

Figure 7: Composed object schema.

character on the path must include, in addition to its position, the direction of the character (e.g., heading toward the pond or heading toward the house).

A coordinate system defined by n orthogonal vectors defines unambiguously the position and direction of an object in the rendering space. Formally, a Spatial Construct of a component object o is a bijection that maps n orthogonal vectors in o into n orthogonal vectors in the rendering space, where n is the number of dimensions. Let the coordinate system of o and the mapped coordinate system be defined by the n orthogonal vectors in o and the mapped vectors, respectively. The placement of a component object o in the rendering space is the translation of o from its coordinate system to the mapped coordinate system, such that its relative position with respect to both coordinate systems does not change. Note that there is a unique placement for a given spatial construct.

Temporal constructs define the rendering time of objects and implicitly establish temporal relationships among the objects. They are always defined with respect to a temporal space. Given a temporal space $[0, t]$, a Temporal Construct of a component o of duration d, maps o to a subinterval $[i, j]$ such that $0 \leq i \leq j \leq t$ and $j - i = d$.

A composed object C is represented by the set

$$\{(e_i, p_i, s_i, d_i) \mid \quad e_i \text{ is a component of } C,$$
$$p_i \text{ is the mapped coordinate system in } C\text{'s rendering}$$
$$\text{space defined by the spatial construct on } e_i, \text{ and}$$
$$[s_i, d_i] \text{ is the subinterval defined by a temporal}$$
$$\text{construct on } e_i\}$$

A composed object may have more than one occurrence of the same component. For example, a character may appear and disappear in a scene. Then, the description of the scene includes one 4-tuple for each appearance of the character. Each tuple specifies the character's position in the scene and a subinterval when the character appears.

The definition of composed objects establishes a hierarchy among the different components of an object. This hierarchy can be represented as a tree. Each node in the tree represents an object with spatial and temporal constructs (i.e., the 4-tuple in the composed object representation (component, position, starting time, duration)), and each arch represents the component of relation between objects.

3.3   Challenges

The presented data model is not necessarily complete and may need additional constructs. A target application (e.g., animation) and its users can evaluate a final data model and refine (or tailor) it to obtain the desired functionality. Assuming that a data model is defined, the following research topics require further investigation. First, a final system requires authoring packages to populate the database and tools to display the captured data. These tools should be as effective and friendly as their currently available stream-based siblings. An analogy is the archive of stream-based collections maintained by most owners of a camcorder. The camcorder is a friendly yet effective tool to capture the desired data. The VCR is another effective tool to display the captured data. A VCR can also record broadcast stream-based video objects.

Tools to author 3-D objects are starting to emerge from disciplines such as CAD/CAM, scientific visualization, and geometrical modeling (see [27] for a list of available commercial packages). There are packages that can generate a 3-D object as a list of triangles. For example, one can draw 2-D objects using either AutoCAD or MacDraw. Subsequently, a user can interact with these tools to convert a 2-D object into 3-D. Finally, this 3-D object is saved in a file as a list of triangles. At the time of this writing, there are two other approaches to author 3-D objects. If the actual object is available, then it can be scanned using a Cyberware scanner that outputs a triangle list. The second method employs volume based point sample techniques to extract triangle lists. With this method, a point sample indicates whether the point is inside or outside of a surface or object (like a CT or MRI might).

Tools to display structured video are grouped into two categories, compilers and interpreters. A compiler consumes a structured video clip to produce its corresponding stream-based video to be stored in the database and displayed at a later time. An interpreter, on the other hand, renders a structured video either statically or interactively. A static interpreter [15] displays a structure without accepting input. An interactive interpreter accepts input, allowing a user to navigate the environment described by a structured object (e.g., video games, virtual reality applications that either visualize a data set for a scientist or trains an individual on a specific task). A challenging task when designing an interpreter is to ensure a hiccup-free display of the referenced scene. This task is guided by the structure of the complex object that describes a scenario.

For static interpreters, this structure dictates a schedule for what objects should be retrieved at what time. An intelligent scheduler should take advantage of this information to minimize the amount of resources required to support a display. At times, adequate resources (memory and disk bandwidth) may not be available to support a hiccup-free display. In this case, the interpreter might pursue two alternative paths. First, it may compute a hybrid representation by compiling the temporal constructs that exists among different objects to compute streams for these objects. In essence, it would compute an intermediate representation of a structured video clip that consists of a collection of: 1) streams that must be displayed simultaneously, and 2) certain objects that should be interpreted and displayed with the streams. We speculate that this would minimize the number of constraints imposed on the display, simplifying the scheduling task. As an alternative, the interpreter may elect to prefetch certain objects (those with a high frequency of access) into memory in order to simplify the scheduling task [14, 15].

Unlike the interpreter, the compiler is not required to support a continuous display. However, this is not to imply a lack of research topics in this area. Below, we list several of them. First, the compiler must compress the final output in order to reduce both its size and the bandwidth requirements. Traditional compression techniques that manipulate a stream-based presentation (e.g., MPEG) cannot take advantage of the contents of the video clip because none is available. With a structured presentation, the compiler should employ new algorithms that take advantage of the available content information during compression. We speculate that a content-based compression technique can outperform the traditional heuristic based technique (e.g., MPEG) by providing a higher resolution, a lower size, and a lower average bandwidth to support a hiccup-free display. Second, the compiler should minimize the amount of time required to produce a stream-based video object. It may create the frames in a non-sequential manner in order to achieve this objective (by computing the different postures of an object only once and reusing it in all the frames that reference it).

If the term "object-oriented" was the buzz word of the 1980s, "content-based retrieval" is almost certainly emerging as the catch phrase of the 1990s. A structured video clip has the ability to support content-based queries. Its temporal and spatial primitives can be used to author more complex relationships that exist among objects (e.g., hugging, chasing, hitting). This raises a host of research topics. What are the specifications of a query language that interrogates these relationships? What techniques would be employed by a system that executes queries? What indexing techniques can be designed to speed up the retrieval time of a query? How is the data presented at a physical level? How should the system represent temporal and spatial constructs to enable a user to author more complex relationships? Each of these topics deserves further investigation. Hopefully, a host of agreed upon concepts will emerge from this activity.

Finally, the system will almost certainly be required to support multiple users. This is because its data (e.g., 3-dimensional postures of characters, structured scenes, etc.,) is valuable and, similar to software engineering, several users might want to share and re-use each other's objects in different scenes. Minimizing the amount of resources required to support the above functionality in the presence of multiple users is an important topic. A challenging task is to support interpreted display of different objects to several users simultaneously. This is due to the hiccup-free requirement of an interpreted structured video.

4   Conclusion

Multimedia servers in support of stream-based and structured continuous media are shaping the frontiers of the computer technology (both hardware and software). Each approach provides its own set of solutions and challenges. We believe that in the near future, the structured approach will gain increased popularity because it facilitates for effective user interactions. It can support virtual worlds where a user becomes an active participant (instead of a passive recipient of information). It will almost certainly have a tremendous impact on educational, scientific, and entertainment applications. Virtual reality environments currently employ this approach for their target application. However, their primary focus has been on graphics (i.e., rendering aspects) and tools to interact with a user. For this paradigm to become useful on a day-to-day basis, a significant amount of research and development is required on: 1) its storage and retrieval of data to support user queries and a hiccup-free display, and 2) tools to populate and query a database.

References

[1] W. Aref, I. Kamel, S. Niranjan, and S. Ghandeharizadeh. Disk scheduling for Displaying and Recording Video in Non-Linear News Editing Systems. Multimedia Computing and Networking, February 1997.

[2] S. Bernstein. Techno-Artists 'Tooning Up. Los Angeles Times, Section F, November 10 1994.

[3] S. Berson, S. Ghandeharizadeh, R. Muntz, and X. Ju. Staggered Striping in Multimedia Information Systems. In Proceedings of ACM-SIGMOD, pages 79–89, 1994.

[4] S. Berson, L. Golubchik, and R. R. Muntz. A Fault Tolerant Design of a Multimedia Server. In Proceedings of ACM-SIGMOD, 1995.

[5] D. Bitton and J. Gray. Disk shadowing. In Proceedings of Very Large Databases, pages 331–338, September 1988.

[6] P. Bocheck, H. Meadows, and S. Chang. Disk Partitioning Technique for Reducing Multimedia Access Delay. In ISMM Distributed Systems and Multimedia Applications, August 1994.

[7] M. Carey, L. Haas, and M. Livny. Tapes hold data, too: Challenges of tuples on tertiary storage. In Proceedings of ACM-SIGMOD, pages 413–417, 1993.

[8] E. Chang and H. Garcia-Molina. Reducing Initial Latency in Media Servers. IEEE Multimedia Magazine, 4(3):50–62, September 1997.

[9] S. Chaudhuri, S. Ghandeharizadeh, and C. Shahabi. Retrieval of Composite Multimedia Objects. In Proceedings of Very Large Databases, September 1995.

[10] A. Cohen, W. Burkhard, and P.V. Rangan. Pipelined Disk Arrays for Digital Movie Retrieval. In Proceedings of IEEE ICMCS'95, 1995.

[11] A. Dan and D. Sitaram. An Online Video Placement Policy based on Bandwidth to Space Ratio (BSR). In Proceedings of ACM-SIGMOD, pages 376–385, San Jose, May 1995.

[12] P. J. Denning. The Working Set Model for Program Behavior. Communications of the ACM, 11(5):323–333, 1968.

[13] J. Dozier. Access to data in NASA's Earth observing system (Keynote Address). In Proceedings of ACM-SIGMOD, pages 1–1, June 1992.

[14] M. L. Escobar-Molano and S. Ghandeharizadeh. On Coordinated Display of Structured Video. IEEE Multimedia Magazine, 4(3):62–76, September 1997.

[15] M. L. Escobar-Molano, S. Ghandeharizadeh, and D. Ierardi. An Optimal Resource Scheduler for Continuous Display of Structured Video Objects. IEEE Transactions on Knowledge and Data Engineering, 5(3):508–511, June 1996.

[16] E. A. Fox. Advances in Interactive Digital Multimedia Sytems. IEEE Computer, pages 9–21, October 1991.

[17] D. Le Gall. MPEG: a video compression standard for multimedia applications. Communications of the ACM, April 1991.

[18] M. Garofalakis, B. Ozden, and A. Silberschatz. Resource Scheduling in Enhanced Pay-Per-View Continuous Media Databases. In Proceedings of Very Large Databases, 1997.

[19] S. Ghandeharizadeh, A. Dashti, and C. Shahabi. Object Materialization with Staggered Striping. Computer Communications, March 1995.

[20] S. Ghandeharizadeh, S. H. Kim, and C. Shahabi. On Configuring a Single Disk Continuous Media Server. In Proceedings of the ACM SIGMETRICS/PERFORMANCE, May 1995.

[21] S. Ghandeharizadeh and L. Ramos. Continuous Retrieval of Multimedia Data Using Parallelism. IEEE Transactions on Knowledge and Data Engineering, 5(4):658–669, August 1993.

[22] S. Ghandeharizadeh, R. Zimmermann, S. Kim, W. Shi, and J. Al-Marri. Scalable Video Browsing Techniques for Intranet Video Servers. In Workshop on Information Technologies and Systems, December 1997.

[23] J. Gray, B. Host, and M. Walker. Parity striping of disc arrays: Low-cost reliable storage with acceptable throughput. In Proceedings of Very Large Databases, pages 148–162, August 1990.

[24] B. Haskell. International standards activities in image data compression. In Proceedings of Scientific Data Compression Workshop, pages 439–449, 1989. NASA conference Publication 3025, NASA Office of Management, Scientific and Technical Information Division.

[25] C. Johnson. Architectural Constructs of AMPEX DST. Third NASA GSFC Conference on Mass Storage Systems and Technologies, pages 153–162, 1993.

[26] M. Kamath, K. Ramamritham, and D. Towsley. Continuous Media Sharing in Multimedia Servers. In Proceedings of the Fourth International Conference on Database Systems for Advanced Applications, pages 79–86, 1995.

[27] K. Kornbluh. Active data analysis: Advanced software for the '90s. IEEE Spectrum, 31(11):57–83, November 1994.

[28] R. Muntz, J. Renato Santos, and S. Berson. RIO: A Real-time Multimedia Object Server. ACM Performance Evaluation Review, 25(2):29–36, September 1997.

[29] B. Ozden, A. Biliris, R. Rastogi, and A. Silberschatz. A Low-Cost Storage Server for Movie on Demand Databases. In Proceedings of Very Large Databases, 1994.

[30] C. Ruemmler and J. Wilkes. An Introduction to Disk Drive Modeling. IEEE Computer, pages 17–28, March 1994.

[31] W. Shi and S. Ghandeharizadeh. Buffer Sharing in Video-On-Demand Servers. ACM Performance Evaluation Review, 25(2):13–21, September 1997.

[32] Nadia Magnenat Thalmann and Daniel Thalmann, Editors. Computer Animation Theory and Practice. Springer-Verlag, 1990.

[33] P Triantafillou and T. Papadakis. On Demand Data Elevation in a Hierarchical Multimedia Storage Server. In Proceedings of Very Large Databases, 1997.

[34] P. S. Yu, M. S. Chen, and D. D. Kandlur. Design and Analysis of a Grouped Sweeping Scheme for Multimedia Storage Management. In Proceedings of the Third International Workshop on Network and Operating System Support for Digital Audio and Video, November 1992.

[35] R. Zimmermann and S. Ghandeharizadeh. Continuous Display using Heterogeneous Disk Systems. In ACM International Multimedia Conference, November 1997.

28

MULTIMEDIA DATABASE MANAGEMENT SYSTEMS

K. Aberer, H. Thimm, and E.J. Neuhold
GMD-IPSI
Dolivostr. 15, 64293 Darmstadt, Germany

1. **INTRODUCTION**..580
2. **DATABASE SUPPORT FOR MULTIMEDIA APPLICATIONS** 581
    2.1   SAMPLE APPLICATIONS 581
    2.2   TRADITIONAL DATABASE TECHNOLOGIES 582
    2.3   MULTIMEDIA SPECIFIC SUPPORT EXPECTED FROM MMDBMS 583
3. **DATA MODELING IN MMDBMS**..584
    3.1   MEDIA AND DOCUMENTS 584
    3.2   STRUCTURAL AND BEHAVIORAL MODELING OF MEDIA DATA 586
    3.3   DOCUMENT MODELING...588
    3.4   DATA INDEPENDENCE..589
    3.5   METADATA 590
4. **IMPLEMENTATION OF MMDBMS**..592
    4.1   BUILDING BLOCKS AND PRINCIPLE DESIGN CONSIDERATIONS............................592
    4.2   SPECIFIC IMPLEMENTATION ISSUES 596
5. **CONCLUSION** 599
    REFERENCES 599

Abstract. Many multimedia applications require the use of database technology. Traditionally, database technology has been developed for managing large volumes of highly structured (alphanumerical) data with requirements that are different from those of multimedia applications. Therefore, traditional database technology is currently extended by multimedia-specific components and language primitives that enable MMDBMSs to handle multimedia data efficiently and thus to support multimedia applications adequately. In particular, this concerns extensions that allow the interpretation of media data contents for manipulation and retrieval and that take into account specific properties of media data such as large data volume, or synchronization and real-time constraints in processing. Furthermore, multimedia applications demand specific support for composite interactive multimedia presentations. In this chapter, we give an overview of the main issues in the field of Multimedia Database Management Systems (MMDBMSs). We discuss sample applications and the specific support they are expected to offer. Then, we discuss the data modeling issue and the implementation of MMDBMS demonstrating the AMOS system developed at GMD-IPSI.

1. INTRODUCTION

Multimedia data is playing a more and more central role in today's communication and information systems as a consequence of the rapid technological development in the available platforms for telecommunication and computation. This leads consequently to the creation of large collections of multimedia data and, thus, to the need to manage this data properly. In this chapter, we outline the specific characteristics of multimedia data management, which differ from conventional data management. New concepts and solutions have been suggested and more are developing in the context MMDBMSs.

MMDBMSs are characterized by their ability to manage *databases* that contain *multiple media*. More precisely, MMDBMSs support the management of *perception media* [88] in addition to the management of conventional, alphanumeric data. Perception media convey information over sensory channels, mostly seeing and hearing. Other types of perceptions may be included, such as measurements from physical experiments. This is an important difference with regard to conventional data, where the information is explicitly structured according to a given data model, e.g., the relational data model or the object-oriented data model.

This principal difference between conventional data and media data also reflects in the kind of data management systems needed. A conventional, e.g., relational, DBMS is designed to support the manipulation of data structured according to the given data model; thus, the data model drives the available operations. For example, a formally well defined language (SQL), backed by strong mathematical foundation (relational algebra), describes the possible operations for data definition and manipulation in a RDMBS. In a MMDBMS the situation is somewhat converse. Depending on what type of operations are supported by the MMDBMS, different data models are required.

Some users and researchers see the role of MMDBMS as a repository for multimedia data based on conventional database technology, with no media specific processing support. Such a repository would contain references to the raw, i.e., uninterpreted, media data and some administrative information related to it. Actual processing of media data is then performed within different applications.

In this chapter we take a different view, which also reflects current developments in multimedia data management very well. MMDBMSs provide specific support for the management of media data while preserving basic properties that are already well established in conventional database management systems. In addition to traditional database services, like persistency or multi-user access, the different paradigm of information representation with digital media leads to a number of problem types that need to be specifically tackled by MMDBMSs.

- For the efficient and effective management of media data it is required that the internal structure and information content of the media data is interpreted, at least partially. This is true both for the internal processing (or *physical level)* and the data modeling (or *logical level)*. At the physical level, for example, the sequential structure of time-dependent media data is exploited for storage or buffer management, or the spatial structure of visual data is exploited for efficient access structures. At the logical level, for example, the information content of media data is modeled for supporting retrieval.
- From a functional viewpoint, MMDBMSs have to support the presentation of the media contents to the user, a functionality that is called *playout management* [95]. Perception is a time-dependent process and thus most media data is inherently time-dependent or is presented in a time-dependent manner. Compared to conventional database systems, this requires genuine functional extensions to support media presentations for the issues of time-dependency and interactivity.
- From a technical perspective, the characteristic properties of multimedia data [49] lead to a number of specific data processing requirements that are quite different from those of

conventional database systems. Media data is highly voluminous and thus processing is data intensive. Data distribution is a highly relevant issue, since it is advantageous to move media data close to applications. Handling of continuous media streams and mechanisms for supporting synchronization and interaction are required.

The realization of a MMDBMSs is not only challenging because of the required rich functionality, as described above, but also because of the framework in which this functionality has to be implemented. We mention some of these more external factors that need to be taken into account.

- The bandwidth of requirements from applications is extremely broad. Therefore, a MMDBMS must be open to changing requirements.
- External tools for handling and processing media data play a much more prominent role than in conventional database management systems. The integration of the functionality of external tools with the database management functionality poses severe integration problems.
- The interfaces of MMDBMSs to applications and tools are more complex to design and implement, since they have to consider not only the functional but also the temporal aspects of multimedia data access.

In this chapter we will outline several general technical and conceptual issues in MMDBMSs. More background material on detailed technical issues and concrete systems can be found in different surveys, e.g. [7,11,31,34,59,67,68,77,78,92].

2. DATABASE SUPPORT FOR MULTIMEDIA APPLICATIONS

In this section we first describe typical multimedia applications where the use of database technology is especially appealing. Then, we show the general data management services found in traditional database technology and identify multimedia-specific functionality.

2.1 SAMPLE APPLICATIONS

Employing database technology for multimedia applications is especially appealing in areas with certain characteristics. In particular, it is recommended for areas where groups of (multimedia) information producers create complexly structured multimedia information that has to be kept and manipulated/updated over a long period of time, and that will be accessed by different information consumers who typically look for "individualized" information. In such environments, multiple concurrent producers and consumers have to handle the system. Therefore, from the viewpoint of concurrency control, both the isolation of different users as well as cooperative access, e.g., for editing and design, are required. Below, we describe four sample applications where these characteristics can be found. Telemedicine, entertainment, engineering, and digital libraries are further example applications that exhibit the above mentioned characteristics.

2.1.1 Information and News Services.

Typically, in information and news services [74,98,99], conventional alphanumerical data and multimedia data are usually "glued together" in multimedia documents. A large collection of such multimedia documents that users want to access by different means is stored. Access via Web Browsers and access from other dedicated application-specific interfaces are often supported at the same time. The document collections are mostly retrieved in a browsing mode by the information consumers. Only rarely are the documents updated by the providers. As an example, consider a sport news service where documents about the Tour de France can be found. The documents may contain multimedia stage reports, portraits of competitors and teams, and background of technology of racing bikes. A sample stage report may comprise videos from a helicopter camera, a motorcycle camera following the leader, and others that keep track of the crowd, interviews with the winner, images showing the route of the day, and so on. Such a service may be provided within a Metropolitan Area Network together with other services such as a tourist information service.

2.1.2   Multimedia Publishing

Similar to the print media industry, efficient electronic publishing or, as a synonymous term, multimedia publishing is performed according to a clearly defined publication process. In general, this process has an underlying publication model that usually makes use of dedicated publication environments as described in [93]. A publication environment supports both the editing process where the different participants (layouter, texter, authors, graphical artists, etc.) cooperatively (and gradually) produce multimedia documents and provide them to readers. Normally, multimedia publishing requires publication environments to provide strong support for managing structured documents such as SGML [44]and support for cooperative editing of documents [100] where several versions of documents and document components usually have to be administered.

2.1.3   Video Archives

Large collections of videos are found in areas where the costs and reuse potential encourage the use of video archiving technology. For example, video archives are frequently used in the broadcast and advertisement or in news agencies. Users of video archives typically want to search and retrieve videos based on access mechanisms that go beyond the typical exact match paradigm. Rather, they want to submit content-oriented queries involving similarity-based predicates. In order to facilitate such access, a dedicated video data model is usually used. In particular, video data models have been proposed (e.g., in [25]) where the specific structural properties of videos are addressed (e.g., segmentation into clips, scene shots, video frames), which may be used to accommodate proper indices over large video collections. These indices are normally generated automatically or semi-automatically because a fully manual video indexing is too expensive and prone to errors. Semi-automatic video indexing methods often overcome ambiguity by exploiting application specific ontologies.

2.1.4   Education and Training

Today, computer technology is rapidly penetrating educational and training applications in the public and industrial sectors. In general, computer-based education and training applications are often centered on collections of interactive teaching documents that embody student lessons. Such teaching documents are often referred to as "active documents" due to the fact that they incorporate components that adapt the flow of a teaching lesson to the users' individual needs and interests. For example, when a mechanical engineering student who executes a lesson on car engines is interested in particular details, he may "zoom into" a respective graphical model by clicking on the corresponding model parts. Furthermore, teaching documents are usually adaptable to the capabilities of the end-user environments and the (possibly different) network capabilities. Education and training applications are not only aimed at non-moderated asynchronous teaching scenarios where students either isolatedly share or use different teaching documents. One can also think of other scenarios where a group of students do a lesson together in a synchronized manner, thereby employing video conferencing technology.

2.2 TRADITIONAL DATABASE TECHNOLOGY

Traditionally, a database is viewed as a controlled collection of data related to a specific universe of discourse. A database management system (DBMS) is regarded as a collection of such interrelated data together with the sets of programs and operations used to define, create, store, access, manage, query, and present the information in the database. In general, a DBMS can be characterized by two aspects, namely, the data model and the functional components that implement operations made available by the data model.

While in Section 3 we concentrate on data modeling issues, in the following, we summarize the key functional properties of database systems.

Persistency. The primary purpose of a DBMS is to store data exceeding the life cycle of an application program. This property of the system is generally referred to as persistency.

Decoupling of applications. One of the central ideas of a DBMS is to modularize functionality that is generally required in the context of persistent data storage and to make it available in an application-independent way. That is, different applications that use the data need not reimplement these basic services.

Database system interface. The deployment of DBMSs is usually based on appropriate interfaces to applications (or users). These interfaces need to support the operations that are provided with the data model. The use of the interface must guarantee the consistency constraints that are imposed by the data model and database schemas.

Multi-user access. Multiple users must be able to simultaneously access the database through its interface. Maintaining the consistency constraints imposed by the data model and database schemas while data is shared by concurrent users is a key feature of a DBMS.

Recovery. When a data operation that is called by an application or the DBMS itself is performed with an error, an inconsistent database state will appear. Therefore, to ensure consistent database states, DBMSs incorporate mechanisms that perform error recovery, e.g., by restoring the latest consistent database state.

Apart from the features listed above, data distribution, authorization, versioning, and interoperability are further properties supported by most DBMS.

2.3 MULTIMEDIA SPECIFIC SUPPORT EXPECTED FROM MMDBMS

In Section 2.2, we described traditional properties that most prevalent DBMSs provide. As a matter of fact, one may realize certain aspects of multimedia applications based on these properties. However, as shown in the context of several different DBMS research prototypes (e.g., the projects described in [29,60,61,63,67,108]) multimedia-specific extensions and refinements may result in quantitatively and qualitatively better support of multimedia applications. The MMDBMS is commonly used to refer to a DBMS that accommodates such multimedia-specific improvements. Although a widely accepted definition of the particular multimedia-specific support to be available does not exist, a consensus can be observed with respect to several capabilities expected from MMDBMSs in addition to those of the preceding section.

2.3.1 Multimedia data types

Obviously, MMDBMSs are expected to provide new language primitives to model database schemas of multimedia applications [1] and to query the contents of a multimedia database [39, 53, 72]. In particular, they are required to provide new data types for video, audio [58], image, text, and digital animation [102]. These new data types need to support media type specific operations and they must isolate users from the details of storage device management and storage structures.

2.3.2 Information retrieval capabilities and multimedia query support.

In general, methods developed in the area of information retrieval [65, 104] are more suited for multimedia applications as opposed to traditional query capabilities of DBMS. This is because, in multimedia applications, users often need to browse through a database or query a multimedia database by referring to the contents of media data (e.g., objects shown in an image [9, 41]). Furthermore, matches in MMDBMSs are usually not exact matches. Namely, when comparing two multimedia data items the resulting matches are often approximate or similarity matches. Therefore, MMDBMSs are expected to implement such methods in addition to traditionally supported query facilities, which are restricted to exact matches. This also includes support of a Query-by-Example method extended for multimedia databases, especially for image and video databases.

2.3.3 Multimedia interface and interactivity

When multimedia data is stored in a database, it will be most frequently accessed and retrieved later for presentation to end users and not for the data processing tasks of application programs. Therefore, MMDBMSs support multimedia specific interfaces that allow users to search for multimedia data (see above) and present the data according to the specific nature of the media types and the wishes of the user [8]. In particular, the multimedia interface must allow interactive presentation control [21,95] such as those found in VCR control panels, but with new features.

2.3.4   Multimedia playout management

A MMDBMS offers a presentation mechanism for composite multimedia presentations that is useful for many multimedia applications [30,50,84] and regarded as playout management service [95, 96]. A generic presentation engine enables this mechanism to perform on demand by users such composite multimedia presentations in a synchronized manner [56]. In fact, a playout management service enables a MMDBMS to provide playout independence [87].

2.3.5   Continuous data management and delivery

Continuous data differ from discrete data in several aspects. The data volume of continuous data and time-dependency are key differences. As a result, continuous data cannot be handled like discrete data, and special mechanisms must be developed for them. MMDBMSs incorporate special mechanisms especially for storing [62,79,105], buffering [40,71,64], and transferring [55] and presenting continuous data [86].

3.   DATA MODELING IN MMDBMS

Multimedia data modeling can be differentiated into three main aspects. The modeling of the implicit temporal and spatial properties of media data, the use of documents to describe media compositions, and the role of metadata to provide additional information on the media data contents.

3.1 MEDIA AND DOCUMENTS

Media data, as described earlier, consist of digital representations of physical processes that are perceived by humans or are measured/processed by tools. In many cases media data is artificially created or composed by means of a specification. Such specifications of synthetic media are normally called documents. Though documents are managed in many cases within MMDBMSs in a way similar to media data, we have to clearly distinguish the two notions of media data and documents. In the following we discuss the specific properties of media and documents with respect to their impact on data modeling in MMDBMSs.

3.1.1   Media

At a logical level media data always consist of samples of measurements for a specified domain in a discrete multidimensional space. The actual information content of media data is encoded at a subsymbolic level, thus it is represented implicitly and (often) redundantly. At a physical level, the raw media data are represented in a media type specific format as a binary sequence, where the representation format often involves complex compression and preprocessing steps. Transformations between different representations of the same media and between media types are possible. We also explicitly include into our definition of media natural symbolic information representation mechanisms, like natural language or genetic codes, since a computer system can observe only the symbol sequence as a physical phenomenon without being able to interpret it (considering the current state-of-the-art). We give a number of frequently occurring examples of media types in Table 1. This table can be easily extended particularly by including more specialized types of media. For example, such types often occur as experimental data in natural sciences and engineering. The example of video shows that the same media type can be interpreted or represented in different ways, depending on how the coordinate spaces and sample types are chosen.

Table 1. Media Types

Media type	Coordinate Space	Samples	Formats	Compression methods
Audio	1 temporal dim	Audio samples	Digital Audio	e.g., ADPCM
Image	2 spatial dim	Pixels	JPEG	e.g., DCT
Video	1 temporal dim	Image	Motion JPEG	
Video	2 spatial dim + 1 temporal dim	Pixels	MPEG	differential compression
Text	1 discrete dim	Alphabet	ASCII	e.g., Huffman
Ink [12]	1 discrete dim	(x,y,t)		
Genetic sequence	1 discrete dim	A,C,G,T		
3D spatial data	3 spatial dim	Voxels		

3.1.2 Documents

Documents describe synthetic media data by using a formal, computer processable language. The specification of media compositions by documents may include natural media data, either by reference or by value. For each document type there exists a transformation method to convert the document into media data for the purposes of presentation or further processing. This conversion might be either trivial or unique. Examples of document types are given in Table 2.

Table 2. Document Types

Document Type	Language (Example)	Media represented	Media included
Textual document	SGML	Text	Text
Music	MIDI	Audio	None
Virtual reality	VRML	3D spatial data	Image
Animation		Video	Image, Video
Graphic	GFK	Image	Image, Text
Multimedia document	HTML, Hytime, MPEG4	Audio/Video	All
Interactive documents	MHEG, Java, Toolbook	All	All

The role of documents within MMDBMSs is twofold. On one hand, document data in binary representation is treated by the DBMS similar to raw media data. For efficiency reasons often only part of the internal structure of document data is interpreted, as far as required for efficient processing of the document within the DBMS. On the other side, document types are based on the same abstractions that are used for structural models of media data. For the design and implementation of MMDBMSs, these two roles of documents need to be clearly distinguished. Thus, whenever we talk about a structural representation for media data, we will refer to *multimedia objects*. The description of media objects within a document language will be called document, while the structural representation of documents will be called *document objects*.

3.2 STRUCTURAL AND BEHAVIORAL MODELING OF MEDIA DATA

Structural models for multimedia data provide a framework for the structural *interpretation* of existing media data and for the structural *manipulation* of media data. They are (ideally) characterized by the following properties:

- They provide identification mechanisms. This requires a *localization mechanism* for the automatic identification of multimedia objects as portions within raw media data, and an identification mechanism for composite multimedia objects.
- They provide a *structural representation* of multimedia objects, including attributes and relationships to other multimedia objects, that can be automatically derived for existing multimedia objects from the raw media data and can be created, accessed, and updated by *multimedia data manipulation operations*.
- They provide a *materialization mechanism* for the creation of new raw media data for multimedia objects by manipulating the structural representation of multimedia objects.

All other data related to multimedia objects are considered as *metadata*, which will be discussed in Section 3.5. Structural models for multimedia data correspond to data models of conventional databases systems, given by DDL and DML. A main difference is the tight coupling between the structural media data representation and the raw media data.

The most important type of structural models for multimedia data are spatio-temporal models. Spatio-temporal data models are one fundamental building block in multimedia data modeling. While spatial data modeling has a long tradition in the area of image [27] and geographical databases, temporal modeling has attracted substantial attention recently in the context of MMDBMSs supporting continuous media data.

3.2.1   Temporal data models

Objects can be identified in temporal models by basic time units, which can be either time intervals or time points. Qualitative relationships between temporal media objects are described within *temporal algebras* [28]. The qualitative relationships allow definition of constraints on temporal media objects as well as to formulate search conditions on temporal media objects. Depending on the type of time units used, this leads to the distinction of point-based and interval-based temporal algebras. There are 3 basic point relations ($<$, $=$, $>$) and 13 basic interval relations. By including indefinite relations, which are the possible disjunctions of the basic relations, one obtains more expressive temporal algebras.

Quantitative relationships of temporal media objects are required particularly for the composition of new media objects. In the simplest case, the *time-line-model* is employed, where each temporal media object is aligned with the temporal coordinate space. The time-line-model is, however, a rather inflexible specification model for temporal compositions, since it does not support the relative positioning of objects. For that purpose, several data models have been proposed based on the qualitative temporal relationships extended by quantitative specifications. One popular example are OCPNs, an extended Petri net model [54]. Locations in the Petri net are used to represent the durations or delays of temporal media objects, while the transitions serve as synchronization points. Temporal relations can be specified in these models before the precise presentation times are known. In order to support the modular specification of temporal compositions of media objects, different temporal data models also offer the hierarchical structuring of composite temporal media objects. One example is hierarchically nested OCPNs where single places can contain complex OCPNs. Another example, where hierarchical composition is the algebraic video model [107], will be used in the following as a running example for multimedia data modeling.

Example. We chose the algebraic video data model for the illustration of multimedia data modeling concepts, since it is a relatively compact model that still captures a number of different aspects and possess an intuitive semantics. It includes operations for the interpretation of the raw video data, for temporal composition, for spatial composition of video objects, for supporting interactivity, and for the annotation with metadata. We give an overview of the most important operators of the algebra in Table 3.

Video objects are created by means of interpretation by assigning them to intervals on the raw video data using the **create** operator. Temporal composition is supported by the union, intersection, concatenation and parallel operators. The model allows for hierarchical composition of media objects by means of functional composition. The structure of composite media objects can be accessed by using the query operator **contains**. The other operators of the algebra will be discussed in subsequent sections

Table 3. Algebraic Video Model

Operation	Description	Type
Create name begin end	Creates a presentation from the range within identified raw video segment	Interpretation
$E_1 \bullet E_2$ (concatenation)	Defines the presentation where E_2 follows E_1	temporal manipulation
$E_1 \cup E_2$ (union)	Defines the presentation where E_2 follows E_1 and common footage is not repeated	temporal manipulation
$E_1 \cap E_2$ (intersection)	Defines the presentation where only footage of E_2 follows E_1	temporal manipulation
E_1 7 E_2 (parallel)	Defines the presentation where E_1 and E_2 are played concurrently and start simultaneously	temporal manipulation
Test ? E_1 : ... : E_n	Defines the presentation where E_i is played if test evaluates to i	interactivity
Stretch E_1 factor	The duration of the presentation is equal to factor times the duration of E_1. This is achieved by changing the playback speed of the video expression	media manipulation
Contains E_1 query	Defines the presentation that contains component expressions of E_1 that match query	access
Window E_1 (x_1,y_1) — (x_2,y_2)	Specifies that E_1 will be displayed in the window defined by (x_1,y_1) as the bottom left corner and (x_2,y_2) as the top-right corner	spatial manipulation
Description E_1 content	Specifies that E_1 is described by content	metadata

3.2.2 Spatial data models

Data modeling for spatial data has a long history in computer graphics, image database systems, and geographic information systems. The basic means of identification of objects within media data are generalizations of intervals to multiple dimensions, like rectangles and volume areas. More complex units of manipulation are, for example, regions, that consist of arbitrary sets of rectangles or volume areas. Regions can be efficiently represented by using space filling curves, e.g., Hilbert or Peano curves [13]. Complex objects within spatial data are then approximated by those basic units, e.g., so-called minimum bounding rectangles or regions.

Spatial relationships of media objects extend the temporal relationships. In [52], 12 directional relationships and 5 topological relationships have been identified for minimum bounding rectangles in two dimensional space. The 5 topological relationships are also applicable for regions, and are used, for example, in the implementation of the QBISM system [13]. The composition of new spatial media objects in 2D or 3D spaces is a core issue in computer graphics. Similarly, for temporal modeling, one can distinguish models that allow the specification of spatial compositions in terms of absolute coordinates or by relative positioning, e.g., by using distances and angles. In addition, advanced models also allow the hierarchical composition of spatial media objects. A good example of this type of model is the data model used by VRML [25]. For modeling video data, spatial and temporal aspects are combined to describe media objects both in space and time, e.g., to capture movements of objects. In the algebraic video model, spatial composition is described by means of the **window** operator.

3.2.3   Active multimedia objects

Several of the models that have been discussed for the composition of temporal media capture not only structural but also behavioral aspects of media data. In this sense, they play a dual role. For example, an algebraic video expression or an OCPN may be understood as a structural composition of temporal media objects, resulting in a new temporal media object. This is the structural view, but at the same time this description can be understood as a process description. The process that is described is a *media presentation* composed of different media objects. Due to this duality of temporal models, they play a special role within multimedia data modeling as compared to spatial models.

A presentation contains typically, in addition to media presentation actions, also interactions with the user. In addition to graph-oriented methods to specify presentations, like OCPNs extended with interactive events [21] or other graph-based temporal synchronization models that have been proposed [28], mechanisms based on event-condition-action rules [1,102,103] are frequently used. In the algebraic video model, the **test** operator is foreseen to incorporate interactivity.

3.3 DOCUMENT MODELING

Document languages, like SGML [44], VRML, or MHEG [45], play an important role in the context of multimedia data management. One aspect, that has already been mentioned in the previous section, is that many structural models for multimedia objects actually emerged from document languages, which have been proposed for data exchange or multimedia data processing, e.g., in publication environments. The second aspect is the management of document data itself, which we discuss now.

Within the logical structure of a document, two components can be distinguished. Its *primary structure* corresponds to the hierarchical structuring of document parts that is given by the grammatical structure of the document language. This structure can be extracted by parsing and explicitly represented in a structured data model. An explicit representation and storage of the primary document structure can be useful for different reasons.

- It supports the effective and consistent update of existing documents, according to the grammar of the document language.
- In many cases document models are used for the representation of metadata (see Section 3.5), where the document model typically is used as a semi-structured data model [3]. Then the primary document structure can be used for accessing and manipulating this information.
- For certain media types, the primary document structure corresponds to the logical structure of the media data. This is particularly true for text documents where the hierarchical and sequential composition of the text is directly described by the parse tree.

Examples, where the primary structure of a document is explicitly modeled in a MMDBMS, can be found in [1,3,5,16,17,73].

The *secondary structure* of a document refers to the information on media data that can be extracted only by interpreting the document content beyond parsing. This includes, in particular, structural and behavioral features, i.e., the temporal and spatial relationships and active media presentation specifications. Typical examples are hypertext links and spatio-temporal compositions, that are expressed within the SGML document language using the language constructs given by the HyTime [46] standard. The structural features represented within the secondary structure of documents are mapped into the structural representation of media objects, as discussed in Section 3.2. Examples of an explicit representation of the secondary structure of documents can be found in [18,73].

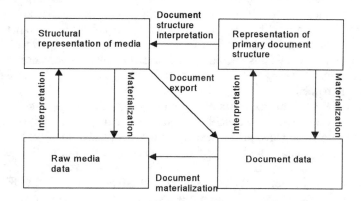

Figure 1. Relationships of media, documents, and structured models.

In Figure 1, we describe the different relationships between media data, documents, and structural data models that have been discussed so far. Additionally, the figure reflects that documents can be generated from a structural media representation. This document export is often used to exchange data among media specific processing tools.

3.4 DATA INDEPENDENCE

Access to and operations on media data are expressed in terms of the structural model given for the media data. In principle, every operation on the media data specified in terms of the structural model can be executed directly on the media data itself, by interpretation and materialization. For example, when defining within an extensible DBMS a new media type, like image, the object type includes typically the definition of methods to directly manipulate the raw image data in terms of the corresponding, e.g., 2D spatial, structural model. Typical operations would be "replace a rectangle by another bitmap image" or "access the pixel at position (x,y)." For efficient management of media data, however, an explicit physical representation of the structural model is often used and stored in the database. The existence of such a redundant representation for the media data leads to a data independence notion. The raw media data level can be understood as the physical level, while the structural representation can be understood as the logical level. The physical execution of the operations on the media data can then be decoupled from their execution at the logical level. Two things can happen:

1. With regard to interpretation, it is possible to perform the extraction of the associated structural data of selected media objects in advance, in case the frequent usage of the object is expected and the access is expensive.
2. With regard to materialization of composite media objects, it is possible to postpone the creation of the associated raw media data until it is needed for further processing.

We illustrate both cases with the following examples.

Example 1 – Interpretation. Recently a number of approaches have been proposed in the context of text document management, providing an explicit structural representation of the primary document structure within a database management system. For example, in the context of SGML document management [3,73], several approaches are described that generate document type specific databases schemas for object-oriented database systems. These provide an explicit structural representation of the complete document by mapping each document element to a database object. This corresponds to the method of interpreting the complete document in advance. However, in many cases only selected elements of a document will be accessed frequently. In this case, it is advantageous to provide an explicit structural representation of a document element only for those accessed frequently. This approach is described in [16,17], where a specification can be given which determines the SGML elements that are to be represented explicitly in advance. All other elements are accessed by parsing on-demand. The other extreme is described in [5], where textual data is accessed only by parsing. In this approach, there exists no alternative, since the grammatical structure used for accessing the document is given dynamically by means of regular expressions within queries.

Example 2 - Materialization: The effect of the **create** operator in the algebraic video model can realized by explicitly generating a new logical video object. Several operators in the algebraic video model, namely, join, union, and difference, create new objects from several existing ones. The raw media representation does not need to be materialized immediately; in fact, the materialization as raw video data can even be delegated to external tools, i.e., presentation engines. Another example of this type is given in the DB2 system [26], which provides a mechanism allowing the decoupling of the manipulation of binary large objects and the instantiation of a new binary large object values.

3.5 METADATA

Metadata is any kind of data that is related to structural media objects modeled within one of the structural data models discussed in Section 3.2. In contrast to the structural media objects, that enable the manipulation of the media data, metadata is required to support the processing, in particular, the administration, retrieval, or presentation of the media data. For example, in the algebraic video data model, the generic operator **description** is provided to describe any type of metadata of media objects. Metadata can be structured data but may as well include media data. Metadata can be directly attributed to media objects and indirectly to other metadata.

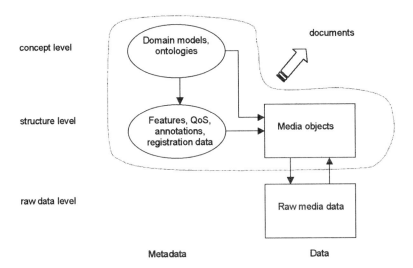

Figure 2. Abstraction levels for media data and metadata.

Although the notion of metadata plays an important role for conventional databases, it is much more important for multimedia data management for different reasons:

- For the search on media data, the structural access mechanisms are of only limited use. Content-based retrieval requires information about the media contents that goes beyond the pure structural properties.
- Multimedia data is processed not only within the database management system but also in a number of accompanying applications. These applications require metadata on the stored media data for proper processing.
- An inherent property of perception media is redundancy in the implicit representation of information. As a consequence, degradation of the media data can be acceptable. The acceptable degradations are described by a special kind of metadata, namely, quality of service (QoS) parameters.

There exist many features that are discussed in literature to characterize metadata [19,20,47]. For classification of metadata from a content-oriented point of view, which is especially relevant to retrieval, the following criteria can be considered:

- Content-dependency: refers to the property on which the metadata depends for media content. In other words the metadata is functionally dependent on the media contents (which is also called media-driven metadata).
- Domain-dependency: certain types of metadata are applicable only for specific application domains or makes use of domain-specific models (which is also called domain-driven metadata).

More technical considerations lead to the following criteria for metadata:

- Automatic computability: metadata can be either computationally derived or purely intellectually or semiautomatically annotated.
- Global/local properties [104]: metadata attributed to a certain media object can either describe a global property of the media object or refer to the property of a subobject of the media object.

Domain-dependent metadata is often not directly related to media objects, but defined indirectly as a function of features, i.e., automatically derived from domain-independent and content-dependent metadata. The domain dependent metadata is then used to perform reasoning over the media data.

In Figure 2 we present the different relationships of metadata and media data. The distinction of a structure and concept level is strongly in line with models proposed for retrieval, e.g., the Hermes reference model [43] or the VIMSYS model [41]. The figure also indicates that documents in general capture not only the structural features of media objects, but also the corresponding metadata. A detailed classification of metadata is given in Table 4.

In the following we discuss sample aspects of metadata (more examples are found in [47,77]). Extensive use of registration data is made in satellite image management applications [10]. This data includes the grid structure of satellite images, the geographical coordinates, the time the image was taken, and the processing history of the image. Image and video features are often based on statistical properties, like color histograms. Image segmentation techniques [27], like boundary detection or region growing, are used to locate media objects within an image that have a specific geometric property. Properties that are identified by these methods are, for example, edges, shapes, or textures. Note that the feature is not the media object, but the particular information on the geometric property of the media object. Similarly, video cut detection is an important method to identify the basic feature of shots in videos. Domain objects are automatically derived from features. Knowledge bases, which can be, for example, a semantic network, a concept lattice, or a rule base [65], establish domain specific relationships between the domain objects and enable reasoning. For example, in facial image analysis, the domain objects correspond to the different parts of the human face, like hair, eyes, nose, or mouth. The knowledge base contains knowledge on the spatial relationships of the different parts of a face. Domain specific descriptors are manually annotated and are based on controlled vocabularies and ontologies. Ontologies provide semantic relationships between the terms of a vocabulary [47]. These relationships are used, for example, to establish relationships between media objects of different types.

Table 4. Classification of Metadata

Metadata	Description	Content dependent			Purpose
Registration and identification data	Format, coding, compression scheme, processing history, location, version history, status, authors	No			Processing administration
Presentation data	Quality of Service parameters: resolution, delay, jitter, Layout information	No			Presentation
			Domain dependent	Automatically derived	
Features	Any information which is efficient to compute, organizable in a data structure	Yes	No	Yes	search
Domain objects	Domain concepts that can be translated into features	Yes	Yes	Yes	search
Annotations	Uncontrolled textual and structural descriptions	Yes	No	No	search
Domain-specific descriptors	Controlled vocabularies, classifications, ontologies	Yes	Yes	No	search

4. IMPLEMENTATION OF MMDBMS

In this section, we discuss implementation issues of MMDBMSs. First, we describe building blocks and general design considerations. Then, we discuss specific issues that have received special attention in the research community.

4. 1 BUILDING BLOCKS AND PRINCIPLE DESIGN CONSIDERATIONS

MMDBMSs are distributed multimedia systems for which a general purpose computing environment does not exist. However, most implementations of MMDBMSs such as the AMOS System of GMD-IPSI [80], Informix Universal Server [14], and the MMDBMS developed at the University of Alberta [73] make use of the following complementary building blocks: i) a platform for structural data management that is provided by existing database technology, ii) dedicated media servers that enable efficient storage management and buffer management for media objects of all media types but especially for continuous media objects, and iii) multimedia delivery components that provide specialized mechanisms for distribution transparent delivery of multimedia data.

These building blocks and possibly other multimedia-specific services provided by operating systems and high speed networks need to be integrated with each other so that multimedia data handling can be efficiently performed. Note that a major success factor for efficient multimedia data handling is the number of duplicates of media objects maintained by the MMDBMS to serve an application request.

Figure 3 illustrates a high-level architecture of a MMDBMS composed of these building blocks. This abstract architecture may be instantiated into different concrete implementation architectures. Most current implementations of MMDBMSs demonstrate a best-effort architecture where guarantees for multimedia processes (especially for delivering continuous data) through resource allocation [89] is not attempted. In contrast, guarantees according to the QoS requirements of the users [66, 106] may be given by deployment of mechanisms generally existing in real-time systems and especially in distributed multimedia platforms [85,89].

Different implementation architectures can also be distinguished according to the way that multimedia data delivery between clients and the server (particularly media servers) is organized. In client-pull architectures, the data delivery is globally controlled by clients who drive the continuous data retrieval and network-based delivery by subsequent requests. That is, according to a dedicated protocol, a client repeatedly issues explicit requests triggering the server to transfer next data units. In server-push architectures, clients usually do not issue these explicit requests and only notify the server about user interactions to be reflected in the data delivery [83].

To achieve efficient data delivery in MMDBMSs, it seems a proper solution to directly connect the physical storage device that stores the bulk multimedia data to the network (i.e., the network adapter). As a result, the data delivery bypasses the DBS's special object buffer that would otherwise (unnecessarily) reduce the delivery throughput [97]. For example, this is the approach of the Oracle video server [51].

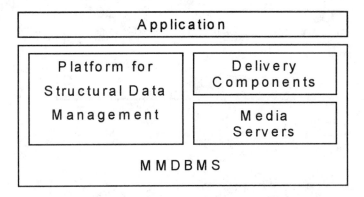

Figure 3. High-level architecture of MMDBMS.

Before we generally discuss the building blocks mentioned above in more detail, let us describe a sample implementation architecture of a MMDBMS. In particular, we demonstrate the AMOS System, a research MMDBMS prototype developed at GMD-IPSI that went through several revision steps [78,80]. Figure 4 illustrates the AMOS architecture composed of the basic building blocks identified above.

An extensible DBMS is used as a platform for structural data management. In particular, we make use of the INFORMIX Universal Server (IUS) that manages application-specific data, metadata, and discrete media objects. The EOS system (Extensible Storage Management System) [BP94] developed at Bell Labs is used as a media server for the persistent storage of continuous data. Buffer management for continuous data is performed by the Continuous Object Manager upon request by clients. When data is delivered to a client, a Transport Manager at the server and a Transport Manager at the client control the continuous transfer of the data from the object buffer at the server to the client's object buffer. The latter is managed by a local Continuous Object Manager. Data available in this buffer may be either directly processed by the application or is presented to the user by the Playout Manager [95]. The Playout Manager provides a service for playout management that coordinates the retrieval of media objects and interactive presentation scenarios from the server. Furthermore, it coordinates the respective playout devices according to the synchronization constraints and user interactions. Data that is stored in the structural database is transferred based on the conventional distribution mechanism of the IUS DBMS. Clients also include special functionality useful for structured document handling and content-based retrieval of multimedia data.

Note that the shaded graphical connections between the components in Figure 4 represent control relationships. For example, the Media Server is under global control of the IUS.

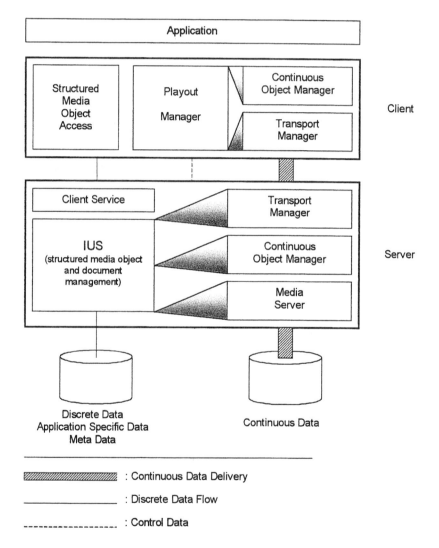

Figure 4. AMOS architecture.

4.1.1 Platform for structural data management

The platform for structural data management has to implement the structural data models for temporal and spatial modeling, modeling of active media objects, and structured document modeling. It has to support the management of the metadata associated with media data and application specific alphanumeric data. By "structural data management" we generally mean data management particularly for these structured alphanumeric data and object references. Using existing database technology for the management of the structural data, typical database services, multi-user operation by a supporting concurrency control, and query support by means of access mechanisms and optimization are utilized.

There are basically two ways to implement a new data model. Either a new database language is designed or a data model is extended with new structures. By the first approach, an existing language should be modified and the code for its implementation embedded into a database system. By the second method special structures suitable for multimedia data management are constructed and added as extensions to an extensible DBMS. To what extent the database system can provide specific processing support depends strongly on what kind of hooks the extensible DBMS provides to extend its functionality.

With the first approach, advantages are higher type safety in the database language since many constraints of the model are implicit and a more efficient and direct implementation can be achieved. Examples for this approach (in experimental systems) are mostly found in specialized query languages (e.g., MOQL [53]). This more direct approach is however, at the expense of high implementation effort due to little reuse of existing technology and inflexibility with regard to changes in requirements. These observations advocate for the second approach. With regard to the implementation effort, as soon as industrial strength platforms are required, there is always a strong motivation to reuse the technology developed over many years, particularly in the area of relational database management systems.

Since no consensus exists – or a consensus might not be possible – on a general data model to provide optimal support for multimedia applications, the data model supported must be open for extensions. Conventional data management is driven by the structured data types that are managed, e.g., tabular data in relational databases. This clearly determines what kind of operations are needed to manipulate the data and what system design can efficiently support them. For multimedia data management the situation is somewhat converse. It is not the structured data itself that drives the design of the MMDBMS, but, in the first place, it is the media data and their processing requirements. Applications determine which kind of operations are needed, i.e., how this media data is to be structurally interpreted to make effective use of this data. These requirements determine what data structures are used to support an efficient implementation of these operations. This explains why it is difficult to design a general multimedia data model.

Therefore, most commercial and research-oriented implementations of MMDBMSs use object-oriented or object-relational database technology in different ways. It has to be noted that this approach still suffers from the fact that extending internal processing capabilities is, in general, limited to extensions by new access structures and simple modifications of the query optimization component. Examples of concrete system implementations based on this approach are the AMOS prototype [80], the STORM system [6], the DISIMA database [69], the QBISM medical database [13], and the image retrieval system VIMSYS [41], just to name a few. Also most of the large database vendors provide database extensions to support media asset management, e.g., the VIRAGE system based on Informix and Oracle, IUS DataBlades, or IBM DB2 extenders.

4.1.2 Media Servers

Traditional file systems and storage servers are designed to handle the storage and retrieval of conventional data that do not have rate requirements (e.g., text, binary files). Such systems store and retrieve continuous media data in a fashion similar to conventional data. As a result, they do not provide rate guarantees for the storage and retrieval of continuous media data. Furthermore, when laying out data on disks, replacing pages in the buffer cache, and prefetching data into the buffer cache, they do not exploit the sequential structure of accesses to continuous media data. Media servers, in general, explicitly address these aspects of dealing with media data, especially continuous data. Hence, they render an important component for MMDBMSs that complement traditional database technology. In particular, in MMDBMSs they are devoted to the storage and buffer management for the data objects that consist of bulk media data.

In numerous multimedia storage projects, technology for media servers has been developed such as in Swift [22], Shark [41], and Fellini [62], to only name a few.

Special attention in the field of media servers has been paid to the deployment of RAID technology (Redundant Arrays of Inexpensive Disks). In this technology, a file server manages a rack of disks, and data blocks are split up and written to several disks in parallel [76].

Media servers often deploy admission control to ensure proper resource allocation and hence restrict the number of requests that can be served concurrently. Furthermore, they make use of dedicated real-time scheduling techniques and they support the notion of Quality-of-Service.

4.1.3   Multimedia Delivery Components

In MMDBMS, distribution transparent delivery of multimedia data is performed by specific delivery components. We regard these components as a further building block of MMDBMS that is required due to the fact that distribution mechanisms in traditional database technology have been developed only for conventional alphanumerical data and the requirements of multimedia data delivery cannot be met. That is, MMDBMSs should accommodate both the traditional distribution multimedia specific delivery mechanisms.

In general, the delivery components must enable the DBS to exchange all types of multimedia data back and forth on demand in various network environments. Particularly crucial is the delivery of continuous data from the storage device to the receiving machine of the user due to the real-time nature of continuous data and the fact that the data is usually delivered to a remote machine for subsequent presentation to a user, i.e., playout deadlines must be met. Delivering continuous data as required for the insertion of media objects is less crucial because there are no playout deadlines to be met.

The multimedia delivery components have to allow multimedia transfer by employing emerging new technologies developed in the area of multimedia communication such as multimedia transport systems and multimedia protocols [23,37,91]. Using these technologies, they must enable the DBMS to transfer multimedia data to client machines in a synchronized manner, thereby offering streaming support for continuous data QoS guarantees [36]. By buffering the data at the receiving clients in a dedicated data cache, typical problems of multimedia communication such as jitter delay and enforcement of intermedia synchronization constraints can be resolved.

4.2 SPECIFIC IMPLEMENTATION ISSUES

For MMDBMSs, several specific implementation issues can be identified that require new implementation methods. Below we discuss some of the issues which have received special attention.

4.2.3   Hierarchical storage management

Storage systems for multimedia data generally need to provide huge storage capacities to accommodate the high-volume multimedia data found in applications. By a hierarchical organization, a multimedia storage system provides unique features that facilitate efficient storage management [33]. In a hierarchical storage system, the multimedia objects are placed in a four-layer hierarchy of devices [7] as shown in Figure 5. More specifically, the highest level provides the highest cost but the smallest storage capacity and least permanence. Cost and performance (in terms of access time) decrease as we go down the hierarchy, while storage capacity and permanence increase. Typically, in most multimedia storage systems the highest level of storage is (volatile) random access memory, followed by magnetic disk drives which provide online services. Optical storage devices are used at the next level of storage which provides near-line services in most cases (e.g., services of jukeboxes); but in some cases online services will also be offered. The lowest level in the storage hierarchy are offline storage devices, including among others magnetic tapes and optical disks. They provide the highest storage capacity and permanence but the least performance in terms of access time.

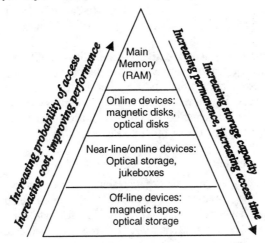

Figure 5. Hierarchical storage management for multimedia databases [7].

Using a hierarchical storage system requires the MMDBMS to manage and organize multimedia data at any level in the hierarchy. In particular, it must accommodate mechanisms for automatically migrating multimedia data objects from one storage level to another. Migration policies such as popularity based placement allow the optimization of performance parameters such as access time.

4.2.4 Continuous Data Management

Among other properties, continuous media data are usually high-volume and delay-sensitive data [38]. In particular, the delay-sensitivity of continuous data streams imposes real-time constraints that need to be taken care of when data is stored, retrieved, transferred, and presented to users [71]. MMDBMSs need to reflect these properties by incorporating specialized mechanisms aimed toward multimedia data. In the following, we take a closer look at main issues of continuous buffer management and continuous data retrieval in more detail, because these two mechanisms play important roles in MMDBMSs.

Continuous buffer management refers to a mechanism that allocates data buffers and performs buffer replacement [40,64,71] according to the data demand of applications. The calculation of the buffer size is a crucial task due to the multitude and dynamics of parameters and environment specific details. Note that the dynamics has to be considered because continuous buffer management needs to reflect resource fluctuations such as variable network or disk bandwidth. Furthermore, it needs to reflect user interactions such as pause and resume. Apart from the allocation of buffers, continuous buffer management must maintain a buffer fill level according to the data requirements of the applications. It is important that the different parameters described above are observed by use of specialized buffer replacement algorithms [64].

By continuous data retrieval we refer to a mechanism for continuous retrieval of multimedia data from the storage device(s). The performance of such a mechanism is mainly governed by the fragmentation of continuous data into storage data units and the placement of these units on the storage device(s). For efficient continuous retrieval of the data units from the storage devices(s) the mechanism makes use of specialized disk scheduling algorithms.

4.2.5   Delivery Scheduling

Multimedia delivery mechanisms in MMDBMS can be implemented based on delivery scheduling [55,57,82]. However, because of the multitude of different resources along the data delivery path such as disk bandwidth, CPU, network bandwidth, and buffers at the server and receivers, a respective integrated end-to-end scheduling framework is needed. In such a framework, QoS parameters according to the users' needs are exchanged between the different scheduling components [89].

Apart from the issues above, delivery scheduling in MMDBMSs is also concerned with retrieval schedules. In general, retrieval schedules specify several multimedia objects to be retrieved and their temporal relationships, i.e., their intermedia synchronization constraints. A MMDBMS may deploy a retrieval schedule for the delivery of the media objects. Some researchers have investigated dynamic schedule modifications to overcome unpredictable bandwidth limitations in the network or other bottlenecks [24].

4.2.6   Playout Management

Playout management is regarded as a presentation mechanism that provides a generic presentation engine for composite pre-orchestrated multimedia presentations [94]. SGML/HyTime and MHEG are sample representation formats supporting spatio-temporal composition of such multimedia presentations. In order to provide accordingly coordinated playout for arbitrary multimedia presentations, a playout management mechanism needs to address several issues. In particular, the coordination of possibly parallel playout devices needs to be considered according to the intermedia and intramedia synchronization constraints [90] and random user interactions.

Obviously, a dedicated management protocol is required for the cooperation between the playout management mechanism and the delivery mechanism because they need to perform actions that are well coordinated with each other. For example, when the presentation mechanism receives a request to pause a video presentation due to a respective user interaction, the transfer of the corresponding video data should be suspended. Some researchers even go so far in this protocol that the coordination of QoS parameters is also included to overcome resource fluctuations using an embedded QoS control system [101].

4.2.7   Access mechanisms

Traditional storage and access structures can only partially support the complex and multimedia-specific types of queries, since they are based on the concept of exact matching. A typical multimedia query may not specify an exact criterion for the existence of a multimedia object in the database but rather specifies an example and asks for the ordering of objects with respect to their similarity according to a given criterion. In particular, the index structures for multidimensional spaces, like K-d-tress, Quad-Trees, multidimensional hashing, or grid files, play a more prominent role among the traditional, match-based techniques for indexing, as compared to traditional database systems. For specific data, like spatial or temporal data, exact match search is not common, but rather intersection searches need to be supported. For spatial data an intersection search would be, given a query region, find all objects that intersect it. Index structures that support this type of search are R-Trees and 2D strings. For text data, PAT trees are an important index structure, supporting different types of queries, like prefix searching or proximity searching. To support content oriented types of search, similarity indexing mechanisms become increasingly significant for multimedia databases [35]. Different types of index structures are proposed for this type of search, including different types of metric trees, like GNAT trees, VP-trees, and M-trees [32].

In order to exploit the different indexing mechanisms, the corresponding query processors of the platform for structural data management should be extensible [2]. Another aspect of optimization of query access is the use of query transformations, which utilize the semantics of the structural multimedia model or the application semantics. Examples for this in the realm of document querying can be found in [103]. Examples for transformation rules that can be applied to spatial queries are given in [52].

5. CONCLUSION

In recent years, database technology has rapidly advanced toward MMDBMSs that provide an important platform for many multimedia applications. Apart from the traditional data management functionality, MMDBMSs offer multimedia-specific language extensions and system components. In particular, they provide new language primitives that are required for efficiently modeling and accessing a multimedia database. New system components, such as dedicated media servers and delivery mechanisms, reflect the specific properties of media objects and enable the performance to meet requirements of multimedia applications.

In this chapter, we have discussed central issues of MMDBMSs from the viewpoint of current state-of-the-art. We have described sample applications and a functional view on MMDBMS. Then, an overview of data modeling in MMDBMSs was given and implementation issues were described. As sample architecture of a MMDBMS, we demonstrated the AMOS system that has been developed at GMD-IPSI. Apart from our own efforts, numerous other groups are also developing research prototypes for MMDBMSs. Recently, commercial products have become available into which various proposals from the research community have been incorporated.

Questions that need further attention are, among others, the role of transaction management services within MMDBMS, the tighter integration of retrieval with data management techniques, and the languages and optimization for multimedia queries. In addition, more work is required on the incorporation of technologies developed in the areas of real-time operating systems, middleware, and high-speed networking.

REFERENCES

1. Aberer, K. and Klas, K., "Supporting Temporal Multimedia Operations in Object-oriented Database Systems," IEEE International Conference on Multimedia Computing Systems, May 14-19, 1994, Boston, USA.
2. Aberer, K. and Fischer, G., "Semantic Query Optimization for Methods in Object-Oriented Database Systems," Proceedings of ICDE, 1995, pp. 70-79.
3. Abiteboul, S., "Querying Semi-Structured Data," Proceedings of ICDT, 1997, pp. 1-18.
4. Abiteboul, S., Cluet, S., Chrisophides, V., Milo, T., Moerkotte, G., and Simeon, J, "Querying documents in object databases," International Journal on Digital Libraries, pp. 5-19, 1997.
5. Abiteboul, S., Cluet, S., and Milo. T., "Querying and updating the file," Proc. VLDB, 1993.
6. Adiba, M., "STORM: An Object-Oriented Multimedia DBMS, MMDBMSs, Design and Implementation Strategies," in K. C. Nwosu, B. Thuraisingham, P.B. Berra (Eds.), Kluwer Academic Publishers, Boston/Dortrecht/London, 1996.
7. Adjeroh, D. and Nwosu, K., "Multimedia Database Management-Requirements and Issues," IEEE Multimedia, July-September 1997, pp.24-33, IEEE Computer Society Press.
8. Adjeroh, D.A. and Lee, M.C., "Synchronization and User Interaction," in Distributed Multimedia Presentation Systems, in K. Nwosu and B. Berra and B. Thuraisingham (Ed.) Design and Implementation of MMDBMSs, Kluwer Academic Publishers, 1996.

9. Analyti, A. and Christodoulakis, S., "Content-Based Querying, Multimedia Databases in Perspective," P.M.G. Apers, H.M. Blanken, M.A.W. Houtsma (Eds.), Springer-Verlag London, 1997.

10. Anderson, J. and Stonebraker, M., "Sequioa 2000 Metadata Schema for Satellite Images," in: Klaus, W., Sheth, A. (Eds.), SIGMOD Record, Special issue on Metadata for digital media, 23 (4), Dec. 1994.

11. Apers, P.M.G., Blanken, H.M., and Houtsma, M.A.W. (Eds.), Multimedia Databases in Perspective, Springer-Verlag London, 1997.

12. Aref, W.G., Barbara, D., and Lopresti, D., "Ink as a First-Class Datatype in Multimedia Databases MMDBMSs," in Issues and Research Directions, V.S. Subrahmanian and S. Jajodia (Eds.), Springer-Verlag, Berlin-Heidelberg, 1996.

13. Arya, M., Cody, W., Faloutsos, C., Richardson, J., and Toga, A., "The QBISM Medical Image DBMS," in Issues and Research Directions, V.S. Subrahmanian and S. Jajodia (Eds.), Springer-Verlag, Berlin-Heidelberg, 1996.

14. Bloor Research Group, Illustra and Informix, Bloor Research Group, 1996-1.0, 1996.

15. Böhm, K., Aberer, K., and Klas, K., "Building a Hybrid Database Application for Structured Documents," Multimedia Tools and Applications, 1997.

16. Böhm, K., Aberer, K., and Neuhold, E.J., "Administering Structured Documents in Digital Libraries Advances in Digital Libraries," Lecture Notes in Computer Science, Vol. 916, Springer Verlag, 1995 .

17. Böhm, K., Aberer, K., Neuhold, E.J., and Yang, X., "Structured Document Storage and Refined Declarative and Navigational Access Mechanisms in HyperStorM," VLDB Journal, Vol. 6, 1997.

18. Böhm, K. and Aberer, K., "An Object-Oriented Database Application for HyTime Document Structure," Proceedings of Third International Conference on Information and Knowledge Management, Nov. 29 - Dec. 1, 1994, Gaithersburg, MD.

19. Böhm, K. and Rakow, T., "Metadata for Multimedia Documents," ACM SIGMOD Record Special Issue on Metadata for Digital Media, Vol. 23(4), Dec. 1994, pp. 21 - 26.

20. Böhm, K., "Metadata Handling," in HyperStorM, Managing Multimedia Data: Using Metadata to Integrate and Apply Digital Data, W. Klas and A. Shet (Eds.), 1997.

21. Boll, S., Klas,W., and Löhr, M., "Integrated Database Services for Multimedia Presentations," S. M. Chung (Ed.): Multimedia Information Storage and Management, Kluwer Academic Publishers, 1996.

22. Cabrera, L.F. and Long, D.D.E., "Swift: Using Distributed Disk Striping to Provide High I/O Data Rates," Computer Systems, 4(4): 405-436, Fall 1991.

23. Campbell, G. , Coulson, F., Garcia, D., and Hutchinson R., "A Continuous Media Transport and Orchestration Service," Computer Communication Review, 22(4):99-110, October 1992.

24. Candan, S.K., Prabhakaran, B., and Subrahmanian, V.S., "Retrieval Schedules Based on Resource Availability and Flexible Presentation Specifications," University of Maryland, CSTR 3616/UMIACS TR96-21, Department of Computer Science, University of Maryland, College Park, February 1996.

25. Carey, R. and Bell, G., The annotated VRML 2.0 Reference Manual, Addison-Wesley, 1997.

26. Chamberlain, D., Using the New DB2, Morgan Kaufmann, 1996.

27. Chang, S.-K., Jungert, E., and Tortora, S.-K., Intelligent Image DataBase Systems, World Scientific, 1996.

28. Chang. H.J. and Chang, S.K., "Temporal Modelling and Intermedia Synchronization for Presentation of Multimedia Streams," in S. M. Chung (Ed.): Multimedia Information Storage and Management, Kluwer Academic Publishers, 1996.

29. Chen, C.Y.R. et al., "Design of a Multimedia Object-Oriented DBMS," Multimedia Systems, Vol. 3, No. 5-6, 1995, pp. 217-227.

30. Christodoulakis, S., Ho, F., and Theodoridou, M., "The Multimedia Object Presentation Manager of MINOS: A Symmetric Approach," Proc. Int. Conf. on Management of Data, Washington, 1986, pp. 295-310.
31. Chung, S.M. (Ed.), Multimedia Information Storage and Management, 1996, Kluwer Academic Publishers.
32. Ciaccia, P., Patella, M., and Zezula, P., "M-tree: An Efficient Access Method for Similarity Search in Metric Spaces," VLDB 1997, 426-435.
33. Doganata, Y. and Tanawi, A., "Storage Hierarchy in Multimedia Servers," in Multimedia Information Storage and Management, S. Chung (Ed.), Kluwer Academic Publishers, 1996, pp. 61-94.,
34. Elmagarmid, A.K., Jiang, H., Helal, A.A., Joshi, A., and Ahmed, M., Video Database Systems, Issues, Products, and Applications, Kluwer Academic Publishers, Boston/Dortrecht/London, 1997.
35. Faloutsos, C. et al., "Index Organization for MMDBMSs," ACM Computing Surveys, Special Issue on Multimedia Systems - Symposium on Multimedia, Vol. 27(4), 1995, pp. 607-608.
36. Ferrari, D., Banerjea, A., and Zhang, H., "Network Support for Multimedia," Technical Report TR-92-072, International Computer Science Institute, Berkeley, CA, November 1992.
37. Ferrari, D., "Real-Time Communication in an Internetwork," Journal of High Speed Networks, 1(1): 79-103, 1992.
38. Gemmel, J. and Christodoulakis, S., "Principles of Delay Sensitive Data Storage and Retrieval," ACM Trans. Inf. Syst., Vol. 10(1), 1992.
39. Ghandi, M., Robertson, E., and Gucht, D., "Modelling and Querying Primitives for Digital Media," IEEE Int. Workshop on MMDBMSs, IEEE Computer Society Press, Los Alamitos, CA, 1995, pp. 82-89.
40. Gollapudi, S. and Zhang, A., "Buffer Management in MMDBMSs, " Proc. IEEE Int. Conf. Multimedia Computing and Systems, Hiroshima, Japan, 1996.
41. Gupta, A., Weymouth, T., and Jain, R., "Semantic queries with pictures: the VIMSYS model, " Proc. of Int. Conf. Very Large Data Bases Barcelona, Spain, 1991.
42. Haskin, R., "The Shark Continuous-Media File Server," Proc. of IEEE COMPCON, Feb. 1993.
43. Hermes Consortium: ESPRIT Long Term Research Project No. 9141.
44. ISO: Information Processing – Text and Office Systems – Standardized Generalized Markup Language (SGML), ISO 8879-1986 (E), International Organization for Standardization, 1986.
45. ISO: Information Technology – Coded Representation of Multimedia and Hpermedia Information Objects (MHEG), ISO/IEC JTC 1/SC 29, International Organization for Standardization, 1993.
46. ISO: Information Technology – Hypermedia/Time-based Structuring Language (HyTime), ISO/IEC 10744, 1992 (E), International Organization for Standardization, 1992.
47. Kashyap, V., Shah, K., and Sheth, A., "Metadata for Building the Multimedia Patch Quilt MMDBMSs," in Issues and Research Directions, V.S. Subrahmanian and S. Jajodia (Eds.), Springer-Verlag, Berlin-Heidelberg, 1996.
48. Kerherve, B. et al., "On Distributed Multimedia Presentational Applications: Functional and Computational Architecture and QoS Negotiation, " Proc. Conf. on Protocols for High Speed Networks, pp. 21-37, Vancouver, 1994.
49. Klas, W. and Aberer, K., "Multimedia and its Impact on Database Systems Architectures," in Multimedia Databases in Perspective, P.M.G. Apers, H.M. Blanken, and M.A.W. Houtsma (Eds.), Springer-Verlag London, 1997.
50. Klas, W., de Vries, A., and Breiteneder, C., "Current and Emerging Applications," in Multimedia Databases in Perspective, P.M.G. Apers, H.M. Blanken, and M.A.W. Houtsma (Eds.), Springer-Verlag, London, 1997.

51. Laursen, A., Olkin, J., and Porter, M., "Oracle Media Server: Providing Consumer Based Interactive Access to Multimedia Data," Proc. ACM SIGMOD 1994, Minneapolis, May 1994, pp. 470-477.

52. Li, J. Z., Özsu, M.T., and Szafron, D., "Spatial Reasoning Rules in Multimedia Management System," Proceedings of International Conference on Multimedia Modelling, Toulouse, France, November 1996, pp. 119-133.

53. Li, J. Z., Özsu, M.T., Szafron, D., and Oria, V., "MOQL: A Multimedia Object Query Language," Proceedings of Third International Workshop on Multimedia Information Systems, Como, Italy, September 1997, pp. 19-28.

54. Little, T.D.C. and Ghafoor, A., "Interval-Based Conceptual Models for Time Dependent Multimedia Data," IEEE Transactions on Knowledge and Data Engineering, 1993.

55. Little, T.D.C. and Ghafoor, A., "Scheduling of bandwidth constrained multimedia traffic," Computer Communications Vol. 15(6), 1992, pp. 381-387.

56. Little, T.D.C. and Ghafoor, A., "Synchronization and Storage Models for Multimedia Objects," IEEE J. on Selected Areas in Communications, Vol. 8(3), 1990, pp. 413—427.

57. Little, T.D.C., "A Framework for Synchronous Delivery of Time Dependent Multimedia Data," Multimedia Systems, Vol. 1(2), 1993, pp. 87-94.

58. Löhr, M. and Rakow, T.C., "Audio Support for an Object-Oriented Database Management System," Multimedia Systems Journal, Special Issue on MMDBMSs, Vol. 3, 1995.

59. Marcus, S. and Subrahmanian, V.S.: Foundations of MMDBMSs, J. ACM, Vol. 43(3), May 1995, pp. 474-523.

60. Marcus, S., and Subrahmanian, V.S., "Towards a Theory of MMDBMSs," in Issues and Research Directions, V.S. Subrahmanian and S. Jajodia (Eds.), Springer-Verlag, Berlin-Heidelberg, 1996.

61. Marder, U. and Robbert, G., "The KANGAROO Project," Proc. 3rd Int. Workshop on Multimedia Information Systems, pp. 54-57, 1997, Como, Italy.

62. Martin, C., Narayan, P., Oezden, B., Rastogi, R. and Silberschatz, A.: The Fellini Multimedia Storage Server, S.M. Chung (Ed.), Multimedia Information Storage and Management, 1996, Kluwer Academic Publishers, pp. 117-146.

63. Masunaga, Y., "Multimedia Databases: A Formal Framework," Proc. IEEE CS Office Automation Symp., IEEE Computer Society Press, Los Alamitos, CA, April, 1987, pp. 36-45.

64. Moser, F., Kraiss, A. and Klas, W., "L/MRP: A Buffer Management Strategy for Interactive Continuous Data Flows in a Multimedia Database Management System," Proc. of the VLDB '95, Zurich, Switzerland, 1995, pp. 275-286.

65. Müller, M. and Everts, A., "Interactive Image Retrieval by Means of Abductive Inference," Proc. of the 5th Conference: Computer-Assisted Information Searching on Internet (RIAO'97), pp. 450-466, Montreal, Canada, June 25-27, 1997.

66. Nahrstedt, K. and Smith, J., "The QoS Broker," IEEE Multimedia Magazine, Vol. 2(1), 1995, pp. 53-67.

67. Narasimhalu, A., "Multimedia Databases," Multimedia Systems, Vol. 5, No. 4, Oct 1996, pp. 226-249.

68. Nwosu, K. C., Thuraisingham, B., Berra, P.B. (Eds), MMDBMSs, Design and Implementation Strategies, Kluwer Academic Publishers, Boston/Dortrecht/London, 1996.

69. Oria, V., Özsu, M.T., Liu, L., Li, X., Li, J.Z., Niu, Y., and Iglinski, P., "Modelling Images for Content-Based Queries: The DISIMA Approach," Proc. Second International Conference on Visual Information Systems, San Diego, CA, December 1995.

70. Ott, M. et al., "Heidi-II: A Software Architecture for ATM Network Based Distributed Multimedia Systems," Proc. of European Workshop on Interactive Distributed Multimedia Systems and Telecommunication Services, Springer, Berlin, Germany, 1996.

71. Özden, B., Rastogi, R. and Silberschatz, A., "Buffer Replacement Algorithms for Multimedia Databases," in S. Chung (Ed.), Multimedia Information Storage and Management, 1996, Kluwer Academic Publishers, pp. 162-182.

72. Özsoyoglu, G., Hakkoymaz, V., and Kraft, J.D., "Automating the Assembly of Presentations from Multimedia Databases," Proc. 12th IEEE Int. Conf. on Data Engineering, New Orleans, LA, 1996, pp. 593-601.

73. Özsu, M. T., Iglinski, P., Szafron, D., El-Medani, S., and Junghanns, M., "An Object-Oriented SGML/HYTIME Compliant Multimedia Database Management System," Proc. Fifth ACM International Multimedia Conference, ACM Multimedia '97, Seattle, WA, November 1997, pp. 239-249.

74. Özsu, M.T., Szafron, D., El-Medani, G., and Vittal, C., "An object-oriented multimedia database system for a news-on-demand," IEEE Multimedia, No. 3, 1995, pp. 182-203.

75. Özsu, T. et al., "An Object-Oriented Multimedia Database System for a News-on-Demand Application," Multimedia Systems, Vol. 3, No. 5-6, 1995, pp. 182-203.

76. Patterson, D.A., Gobson, G., and Kats, R.H., "A Case for Redundant Arrays of Inexpensive Disks (RAID)," Proc. of the ACM Conf. on Management of Data, pp. 109-116, June 1988.

77. Prabhakaran, B., Multimedia Database Management Systems, Kluwer Academic Publishers, Boston/Dortrecht/London, 1997.

78. Rakow, T.C. , Löhr, M. and Neuhold, E.J., Multimedia Databases - The Notions and the Issues, GI-Fachtagung Datenbanksysteme in Buro, Technik und Wissenschaft BTW 95, Dresden, Germany, pp. 1-29, 1995.

79. Rakow, T.C. and Muth, P., "The V^3 Video Server-Managing Analog and Digital Video Clips," Proceedings ACM SIGMOD'93, Washington D.C., 1993, pp. 556-557.

80. Rakow, T.C., Klas, W., and Neuhold, E.J., "Research on MMDBMSs at GMD-IPSI," IEEE Multimedia Newsletter, Vol. 4(1), 1996, pp. 40-45.

81. Rakow, T.C., Klas, W., and Neuhold, E. J., "Abstractions for MMDBMSs," Proceedings 2nd Int. Workshop on Multimedia Information Systems, Sept. 26-28, 1996. West Point, New York.

82. Rangan, P.V., Ramanathan, S., and Sampathkumar, S., "Feedback Techniques for Continuity and Synchronization in Multimedia Information Retrieval," ACM Transactions on Information Systems, Vol. 13(2), 1995, pp. 145-176.

83. Roa, S., Vin, H., and Tarafdar, A., "Comparative Evaluation of Server-push and Client-pull Architectures for Multimedia Servers," Proc. of the Fifth International Workshop on Network and Operating System Support of Digital Audio and Video (NOSSDAV'96), Springer, 1996, pp. 45-48.

84. Rody, J.A. and Karmouch, A., "A Remote Presentation Agent for Multimedia Databases," Proc. of the IEEE Int. Conference on Multimedia Computing Systems `95, Washington D.C., 1995, pp. 223-230.

85. Rothermel, K., Dermler, G., and Fiederer, W., "QoS Negotiation and Resource Reservation for Distributed Multimedia Applications," Proc. 4th IEEE Int. Conf. on Multimedia Computing and Systems, Ottawa, Ontario, Canada, 1997, pp. 319-325.

86. Rowe, L.A. and Smith, B.C., "A Continuous Media Player," Proc. of the Third Int. Workshop on Network and Operating System Support for Digital Audio and Video, La Jolla, CA, 1992, pp. 237-249.

87. Staehli, R., Maier, D., and Walpole, J., "Device and Data Independence for Multimedia Presentations," ACM Computing Surveys, Special Issue on Multimedia Systems - Symposium on Multimedia, Vol. 27(4), 1995, pp. 640-642.

88. Steinmetz, R., and Nahrstedt, K., Multimedia: Computing, Communications & Applications, Prentice Hall, 1995.

89. Steinmetz, R., and Nahrstedt, K., "Resource Management in Networked Multimedia Systems," IEEE Computer, 1995, pp. 52-63.

90. Steinmetz, R., "Synchronization Properties in Multimedia Systems," IEEE Journal on Selected Areas in Communications, Vol. 8(3), 1990, pp. 401-412.

91. Stuettgen, B., "Network Evolution and Multimedia Communication," IEEE Multimedia, Vol. 2, No. 3, Fall 1995, pp. 42-59.

92. Subrahmanian, V.S. and Jajodia, S. (Eds.), Multimedia Database Systems: Issues and Research Directions, Springer-Verlag, Berlin-Heidelberg, 1996.

93. Süllow et al., "Multimedia Forum: An Interactive Online Journal," Proc. of the Int. Conf. on Electronic Publishing, Document Manipulation, and Typography, EP'94, Darmstadt, Germany, John Wiley & Sons, Ltd., 1994.

94. Thimm, H. and Rakow, T.C., "A DBMS Based Multimedia Archiving Teleservice Incorporating Mail," Proc. of the 1st Int. Conf. on Applications of Databases, LCNCS 819, pp. 281-298, 1994, Vadstena, Sweden.

95. Thimm, H. and Klas, W., "Playout Management in MMDBMSs," in Design and Implementation Strategies, K. C. Nwosu, B. Thuraisingham, and P.B. Berra (Eds.), Kluwer Academic Publishers, Boston/Dortrecht/London, 1996.

96. Thimm, H. and Klas, W., "δ-Sets for Optimized Reactive Adaptive Playout Management in Distributed MMDBMSs," Proc. 12th IEEE Int. Conf. on Data Engineering, New Orleans, LO, 1996, pp. 584-592.

97. Thimm, H., Klas, W., Walpole, J., Pu, C., and Cowan, C., "Managing Adaptive Presentation Executions in Distributed MMDBMSs," Proc. IEEE Int. Workshop on MMDBMSs, Blue Mountain Lake, NY, 1996, pp. 152-159.

98. Thimm, H., Rakow, T.C., and Neuhold, E.J., "Using Multimedia Archives for Hypermedia Applications in Open Networks," in J. Eberspacher (Ed.), New Markets with Multimedia, Telecommunications, pp. 153-176, Springer, Berlin, 1995.

99. Thimm, H., Roehr, K, and Rakow, T.C., "A Mail Based Teleservice Architecture for Archiving and Retrieving Dynamically Composable Multimedia Documents," Proc. of the Int. Workshop on Multimedia Transport and Teleservices, pp. 14-34, 1994.

100. Thimm, H., "A Multimedia Enhanced CSCW Teleservice for Wide Area Cooperative Authoring of Multimedia Documents," ACM SIGOIS Bulletin, Vol. 15(2), 1994, pp. 49-57.

101. Thimm, H., Optimal Quality of Service under Dynamic Resource Constraints in MMDBMSs, Ph.D. Dissertation, Darmstadt University of Technology, 1998.

102. Vazirgiannis, M. and Boll, S., "Events in Interactive Multimedia Applications: Modelling and Implementation Design," IEEE International Conference on Multimedia Computing and Systems, June 3-6, Ottawa, Ontario, Canada, 1997.

103. Vazirgiannis, M., "An Object-Oriented Modelling of Multimedia Database Objects and Applications," in MMDBMSs: Design and Implementation Strategies, K. C. Nwosu, B. Thuraisingham, and P.B. Berra (Eds.), Kluwer Academic Publishers, Boston 1996.

104. Venkat N. G., Vijay, V., Raghavan, and Vanapipat, K., "A Unified Approach to Data Modelling and Retrieval for a Class of Image Database," in Issues and Research Directions, V.S. Subrahmanian and S. Jajodia (Eds.), Springer-Verlag, Berlin-Heidelberg, 1996.

105. Vin, H. and Rangan, V., "Multimedia Storage Systems," in B. Furht (Ed.), Multimedia Systems and Techniques, 1996, Kluwer Academic Publishers, pp. 123-144.

106. Vogel, A., Kerherve, B., Bochmann, G., and Gecsei, J., "Distributed Multimedia and QOS: A Survey," IEEE Multimedia Systems Journal, 1995, pp. 10-19.

107. Weiss, R., Duda, A., and Gifford, D., "Composition and Search with a Video Algebra," IEEE MultiMedia, Vol. 2, No. 1, Spring 1995 .

108. Woelk, D. and Kim, W., "Multimedia Information Management in an Object Oriented Database System," Proc. of the 13th VLDB Conference, pp. 319-329, 1987.

29

MULTIMEDIA SUPPORT IN JAVA

Joseph Celi[1] and Borko Furht[2]
[1]Internet Development Group
IBM, Boca Raton, Florida
[2]Department of Computer Science and Engineering
Florida Atlantic University, Boca Raton, Florida 33431

1.	**INTRODUCTION**	606
2.	**ANIMATION SUPPORT IN JAVA**	607
	2.1 FRAME-BASED ANIMATION	607
	2.2 SPRITE-BASED ANIMATION	614
3.	**AUDIO SUPPORT IN JAVA**	620
	3.1 PLAYING AN AUDIO CLIP FROM A JAVA APPLET	620
	3.2 PLAYING AN AUDIO CLIP USING A MORE SOPHISTICATED APPROACH	620
	3.3 PLAYING AND STOPPING AN AUDIO CLIP	622
4.	**VIDEO SUPPORT IN JAVA**	622
	4.1 STANDARD VIDEO	622
	4.2 STREAMING VIDEO	623
5.	**JAVA MEDIA API**	624
6.	**CONCLUSION**	625
	REFERENCES	626

Abstract. In this chapter, we discuss multimedia support in Java. The object-oriented paradigm, applied in Java, allows software developers to build upon the available class libraries in order to create new custom class libraries, thus extending the language. We present Java support for animation and audio, and we also create working Java applets, which can accomplish various animation and audio tasks. The current Java class libraries do not provide support for MIDI, streaming audio, or any form of video. However, a new Java Media Application Programming Interface (API), which is briefly introduced in the chapter, defines a set of multimedia classes to support interactive media, including audio and video.

1. INTRODUCTION

Java is an exciting new technology that has hit the computer industry by storm. This technology, developed by Sun Microsystems, is gaining widespread acceptance at an unprecedented pace. What makes the Java programming language stand out from the others?

To answer this and other questions about Java, one must first understand exactly what Java is. Java is an object oriented programming language that allows developers to create platform independent applications [1]. The language borrows its syntax and style from C++ but does not carry the extra baggage of having to be backward compatible with a predecessor language. Java is a clear, concise language that adheres closely to the object-oriented design principles of information hiding, encapsulation, data abstraction, inheritance, and polymorphism. These features promote code reuse, which is a highly desirable feature for most software development shops. Java provides support for exceptions, which aid programs to become more reliable since they are better equipped to handle error conditions.

Java is an interpreted language requiring a Java interpreter to be present on the machine running the Java program. The Java interpreter is often called the Java Virtual Machine or JVM for short. The Java compiler compiles a Java program into byte codes that reside in a .CLASS file. The .CLASS file is fed to the JVM for execution. Figure 1 depicts the areas described in this section.

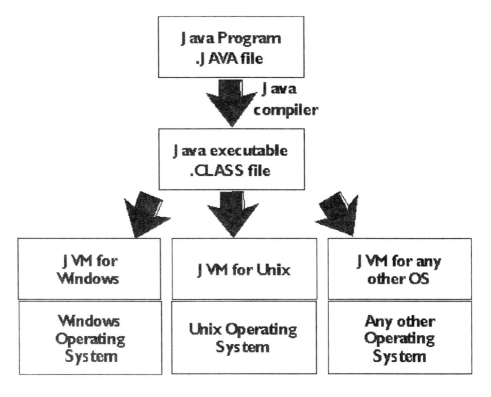

Figure 1. Java environment.

The Java program is machine independent. The machine dependencies are contained within the JVM [2]. Currently there are JVMs written for all of the popular operating systems. Java applications can be run under any operating system that supplies a JVM.

Java applets are similar to Java applications in that they define an executable entity. Java applets are typically located on a Web server and run remotely on a client machine. For security reasons, Java applets have limited access to the API at run time. The built-in security features of Java make it a very attractive solution for distributed programming. Most Web browsers available today support Java applets.

The portable nature of the Java language is the key element driving the industry toward this new technology [3]. The "write once, run many" philosophy that Java presents has attracted many programming organizations to this new and exciting language.

2. ANIMATION SUPPORT IN JAVA

Displaying a sequence of pre-drawn images one after another creates an animation. Each image or frame in the animation is carefully drawn with respect to a previous frame to simulate movement. If the system rendering the animation is capable of displaying the images at a rate of approximately 15 frames per second, the transitions from frame to frame will seem fluid, hence simulating real movement.

The Java application programming interface (API) provides support for animation by allowing users to load and manipulate images using classes and methods are included in the Java Development Kit (JDK). Java distributes the task of retrieving, decoding, and rendering images over several classes and packages. The Applet, Image, Graphics, and Toolkit classes all play a part in producing the finished product.

Other classes provide additional support. Network support is provided by the URL and URL Connection classes. The MediaTracker class and the ImageObserver interface provide a means to monitor the image loading progress. These capabilities are integrated into the Java runtime system and perform their respective roles in the background. The following sections concentrate on the direct support classes and the methods that can be used to build image animations.

2.1 FRAME-BASED ANIMATION
Frame-based animation, as described above, is an animation sequence, which is produced by displaying a set of frames in some predefined sequence. In the simplest case, the images are all of the same size so that each frame simply overlays the previous one. The key issues to be tackled here are performance and picture clarity. The following example demonstrates the techniques used to ensure the best possible frame-based animations.

The *FrameAnimation* example loads three images and displays them in sequence to produce a simple animation. The animation frames are displayed in Figure 2.

The frames are displayed in the following order {1, 2, 3, 2, 1}. This frame sequence, when played over in a continuous manner gives the illusion of the famous "let your fingers do the walking" animation that is often used in commercials used to advertise the yellow pages telephone book.

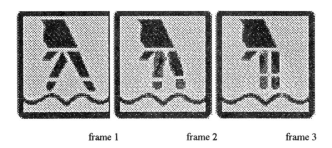

frame 1   frame 2   frame 3

Figure 2. Frames uses for animation sequence.

The *FrameAnimation* example is in the form of a Java applet, which executes within a Java enabled browser or within the applet viewer utility. The two most popular Internet browsers in use today, from Netscape and Microsoft, both support Java applets. The applet viewer utility comes as part of the JDK from Sun. The code for this applet is shown in Figure 3.

The *FrameAnimation* applet loads the three images from its *init* method. The browser or applet viewer informs the applet that it has been loaded into the system and calls the init method of an applet. It is always called before the first time the *start* method is called.

The *getImage* method returns an Image object that can then be painted on the screen. This method requires the caller to specify a URL pointing to the location of the image. The image name is also required to be provided as a parameter. This method will always return immediately even if the image cannot be located. For this reason one should always check for a valid return from the *getImage* method. The Java libraries will load the actual image data, asynchronously, under the execution of another thread. If an attempt is made to draw an image before all of the data has been transmitted, only the portion of the image that has been loaded at that point in time will be displayed.

In order to reduce the initial image flickering caused by partially loaded images, the FrameAnimation applet prepares each image that it uses for the animation. The *prepareImage* method, contained in the Component class, will return *false* if the image is not fully prepared for rendering. Prepared, in this context, means that all of the bits of the image have been transmitted across the Internet and the image has been scaled to the height and width specified. In this example, no dimension parameters were provided to the *prepareImage* method so the image will not be scaled.

Once all of the images in the animation sequence have been prepared, the program is ready to start displaying the animation. To create animation, a series of images or frames are displayed in some logical order. A pause or sleep between the rendering of consecutive images is necessary to provide the illusion of movement. The amount of time to sleep between frames must be carefully chosen. If the time interval is too short, the motion will be too fast.

```
import java.awt.*;
import java.applet.*;

public class FrameAnimation extends Applet implements Runnable
{
 Thread    runner;
 Image     img1, img2, img3, curImg;
 boolean   fOkToPaint = false;

 public void init()
 {
    System.out.println("In init method");

    img1 = getImage(getDocumentBase(), "fingers1.gif");
    if(img1 == null)
       System.out.println("getImage failed to obtain fingers1.gif");

    img2 = getImage(getDocumentBase(), "fingers2.gif");
    if(img2 == null)
       System.out.println("getImage failed to obtain fingers2.gif");

    img3 = getImage(getDocumentBase(), "fingers3.gif");
    if(img3 == null)
       System.out.println("getImage failed to obtain fingers3.gif");

    while(!prepareImage(img1, this))
    {
       // System.out.println("Sleeping while preparing img1");
       mySleep(10);
    }
    // System.out.println("Finished preparing img1");
    // System.out.println("img1 = " + img1);
    curImg = img1;

    while(!prepareImage(img2, this))
    {
       // System.out.println("Sleeping while preparing img2");
       mySleep(10);
    }

     // System.out.println("Finished preparing img2");
    // System.out.println("img2 = " + img2);

    while(!prepareImage(img3, this))
    {
       // System.out.println("Sleeping while preparing img3");
       mySleep(10);
    }
    // System.out.println("Finished preparing img3");
    // System.out.println("img3 = " + img3);
    fOkToPaint = true;
 }

 public void start()
 {
    System.out.println("In start method");
    if(runner == null)
    {
       runner = new Thread(this);
       runner.start();
    }
 }
```

Figure 3. Java applet for frame animation.

```
public void stop()
{
    System.out.println("In stop method");
    if(runner != null)
    {
        runner.stop();
        runner = null;
    }
}

public void run()
{
    System.out.println("In run method");
    while(true)
    {
        if(curImg == img1)
            curImg = img2;
        else if(curImg == img2)
            curImg = img3;
        else
            curImg = img1;
        repaint();
        mySleep(100);
    }
}

//
// We will override the update method in order to
// get rid of the flicker.  The default update
// method will always fill in the area with the
// background color and then call the paint
// method.
//
public void update(Graphics g)
{
    paint(g);
}
public void paint(Graphics g)
{
    // System.out.println("In paint method");
    if(fOkToPaint)
        g.drawImage(curImg, 0, 0, this);
}

public void mySleep(long millis)
{
    try
    {
        Thread.sleep(millis);
    }
    catch(InterruptedException e) {}
}
}
```

Figure 3 (cont.) Java applet for frame animation.

The motion could also appear jerky if there is not sufficient time for the eye to keep up with the frames. If the time interval chosen is too long, the output will look more like a slide show than animation. The sample animation applet uses a 100-millisecond sleep time between frames.

support in Java allows programmers the ability to build sophisticated programs and games that can accept user input while performing some other complex task [4].

Overall, using multiple threads often reduces program execution time. This is depicted in Figure 4. Referring to the figure, three systems are displayed: a single threaded system, a multi-threaded system running under a single CPU, and a multi-threaded system utilizing multiple CPUs. On the single threaded system, a task runs to completion before the next task is executed. If a task performs an expensive I/O operation, the CPU will remain idle until the operation has completed.

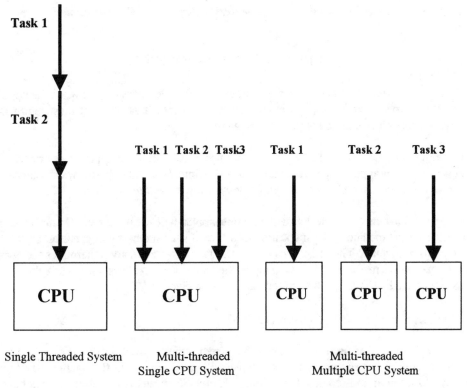

Figure 4. Single vs. multiple threading environments.

Of the three, the single threaded system will often yield the worst performance. The second system shows a multi-threaded system running under a single CPU. In this system the tasks are allowed to run for an interval of time called a time slice. When the time slice expires, the next task is given the CPU and the state of the previous task is saved. This system often yields better overall CPU utilization than the first, since the CPU does not have to sit idle during I/O requests. In this system, since there is only one CPU, each task may take a bit longer to run, due to time-slicing, but the overall time to execute all tasks is almost always shorter then the single threaded counterpart. The third system shows a multi-threaded system running under multiple CPUs. This system will almost always yield the best overall performance for the obvious fact that adding more CPUs will boost system performance.

It is important to understand the execution process of a Java applet when writing applets, which require multiple thread support. Figure 5 shows the execution cycle of a Java applet.

The arrows show the events that take place in the browser; the circles represent the corresponding functions in the Java applet class called to handle those events.

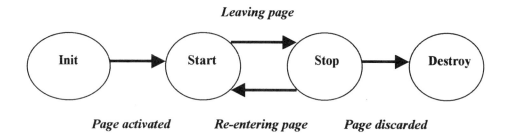

Leaving page

Page activated   *Re-entering page*   *Page discarded*

Figure 5. Life cycle of a Java applet.

A Java applets' *init* and *start* method are automatically called by the JVM when the applet is started. In order to keep the Java environment responsive, a Java applet must return from the invocation of these methods in a timely manner.

The animation sequence in this example continues to play until the applet is destroyed. The FrameAnimation applet implements the *Runnable* interface. Any class whose instances are intended to be executed by a thread can implement the *Runnable* interface.

During the *start* method, the FrameAnimation applet will create a new *Thread* class and execute its *start* method. The invocation of a thread *start* method will cause an objects *run* method to be invoked. The class, provided to the Threads constructor, determines the owning object of the run method. In this example, the *"this"* keyword was used when the *Thread* was constructed. The actual line of code is displayed below:

```
runner = new Thread(this);
```

The *"this"* keyword is used to represent the current object, which in this case is the applet itself. Therefore, the *run* method of this applet will gain control. In that method, the images are cycled through and repainted in a loop. The *mySleep* method is used to sleep between the rendering of consecutive frames.

The animation thread is halted when the *stop* method is invoked. The *stop* method of an applet is invoked when user leaves the page that contains the applet. Although the applet is still running, the *stop* method provides the applet writer with a means to perform some action when the applet is no longer in view. In this case, the CPU intensive animation sequence is halted. An applet will receive a *destroy* method before it is actually terminated by the JVM.

2.1.2 Eliminating Flicker

The FrameAnimation applet employed a technique to eliminate flicker. Flicker, in this context, is an annoying visual side effect caused by the introduction of unnecessary insertion of blank frames in the animation sequence. Figure 6 graphically displays an animation sequence that produces screen flicker.

Figure 6. Animation frame sequence when default *update* method is being used.

A good understanding of the Java painting protocol allows developers the ability to produce flicker-free animation sequences [5]. Figure 7 graphically displays the final frame sequence of a flicker free animation. In order to produce this sequence, the FrameAnimation applet subclasses the *update* method.

Figure 7. Animation frame sequence when default *update* method is subclassed.

In this example, the *repaint* method is called from within the animation thread to signal the painting of the next frame in the animation sequence. When the *repaint* method is invoked, the JVM will call the corresponding *update* method for that object. The default *update* method, as contained in the Java 1.0 release is displayed below:

```
public void update(Graphics g)
{
      g.setColor(getBackground());
      g.fillRect(0, 0, width, height);
      g.setColor(getForeground());
      paint(g);
}
```

The *update* method clears the graphics area with the background color before calling the paint method. In this example the *update* method is subclassed and simply calls the paint method. The code for this method is displayed below:

```
public void update(Graphics g)
      {
      paint(g);
      }
```

Referring to Figure 5, the default *update* method is causing a black rectangle to be displayed between each of the consecutive animation frames. Although this black frame is only displayed for a few milliseconds, it will cause the animation to flicker. By subclassing the *update* method we eliminate the flicker since the black frames will no longer be displayed between each of the consecutive animation frames. This technique works fine for this application since it is drawing the images at the same location over and over. If the images were moving or other graphics were being rendered onto the screen, then a more sophisticated version of the *update* method would need to be employed.

2.2 SPRITE-BASED ANIMATION

In the first animation example the animation frames were simply overlayed on top of the previous one in the exact same location. The applet was able to optimize things based on the characteristics of that type of animation. Although simple frame-based animations are frequently used, a more powerful type of animation is required for applications such as computer games. A sprite is an image that has a transparent background. In computer games the sprites are moved about the game while the background scenery is preserved. How is this accomplished in Java?

There are other issues involved in sprite-based animation. For example, how is the background restored when the sprite is moved across the screen? The next example will demonstrate techniques that allow programmers to build programs using sprite-based animations. The *SpriteAnimation* example, presented in Figure 8, draws a red bouncing ball on a blue background. The ball bounces off the edges of the applet as a real ball bounces off a wall. The source code for the SpriteAnimation applet is given in Figure 9.

Figure 8. Output of the SpriteAnimation Java applet.

2.2.1 Transparency

Java supports the GIF89a image file format. In this format an RGB color value is assigned within the GIF file to represent the transparent color [6]. When the GIF is rendered to the screen, all pixels in the GIF matching this assigned RGB color value are not drawn, hence yielding the transparent effect. Java programmers can create images with the proper transparency settings using any image editor, which supports the GIF89a image file format. The Java programmer simply uses these special images to create transparent effects. This is an improvement upon previous windowing systems, such as Windows, where the programmer must perform special instructions to draw transparent images onto the screen.

2.2.2 Double Buffering

The SpriteAnimation applet uses a technique called "double buffering" to render the sprite across the screen in a fast manner. Double buffering tackles two problems inherit in sprite-based animation. These problems are avoiding flicker and preserving the background.

In double buffering, an application draws to memory before updating the screen. By first drawing into memory, all flicker can be eliminated since only the finished frame is rendered to the screen. This is demonstrated in Figure 10.

```
import java.awt.*;
import java.applet.*;

public class SpriteAnimation extends Applet implements Runnable
{
 Thread    runner;
 Image     ball, offImg;
 int       x = 0;
 int       xInc = 1;
 int       yInc = 1;
 int       y = 0;
 int       imgX, imgY;
 Graphics offG;

 public void init()
 {
    System.out.println("In init method");

    ball = getImage(getDocumentBase(), "Ball.gif");
    if(ball == null)
       System.out.println("getImage failed to obtain Ball.gif");

    while(!prepareImage(ball, this))
    {
       // System.out.println("Sleeping while preparing ball");
       mySleep(10);
    }

    imgX = ball.getWidth(this);
    System.out.println("imgX = " + imgX);

    imgY = ball.getHeight(this);
    System.out.println("imgY = " + imgY);
 }
 public void start()
 {
    System.out.println("In start method");
    if(runner == null)
    {
       runner = new Thread(this);
       runner.start();
    }
 }
 public void stop()
 {
    System.out.println("In stop method");
    if(runner != null)
    {
       runner.stop();
       runner = null;
    }
 }
 public void run()
 {
    System.out.println("In run method");
    while(true)
    {
       repaint();
       mySleep(32);
    }
  {
```

Figure 9. The Java applet for sprite animation.

```
public void update(Graphics g)
{
    Dimension d = size();

    if(offG == null)
    {
        offImg = createImage(d.width, d.height);
        offG = offImg.getGraphics();
    }

    offG.setColor(Color.blue);
    offG.fillRect(0, 0, d.width, d.height);
    offG.drawImage(ball, x, y, this);

    //
    // Now test to see if the ball hit the right or left wall.
    //
    if((x + imgX) >= d.width)
    {
        xInc = -1;
    }
    else if(x <= 0)
    {
        xInc = 1;
    }
    x += xInc;

    //
    // Now test to see if the ball hit the bottom or top wall.
    //
    if((y + imgY) >= d.height)
    {
        yInc = -1;
    }
    else if(y <= 0)
    {
        yInc = 1;
    }
    y += yInc;

    g.drawImage(offImg, 0, 0, this);
}

public void paint(Graphics g)
{
}

public void mySleep(long millis)
{
    try
    {
        Thread.sleep(millis);
    }
    catch(InterruptedException e) {}
}
}
```

Figure 9 (cont.) The Java applet for sprite animation.

Double buffer in system memory   **Video memory**

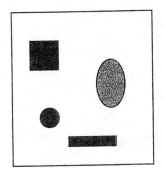 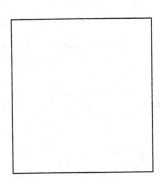

(a) Instead of drawing to video memory, a double buffer is used.

Double buffer in system memory   **Video memory**

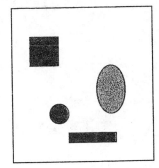 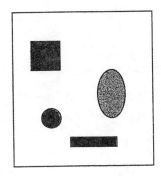

(b) When finished drawing, the double buffer is copied to video memory.

Figure 10. Double buffering concept.

Double buffering is handled in the *update* method of the SpriteAnimation applet. The *update* method is shown in Figure 11.

An off-screen memory image is created using the *createImage* method. The *createImage* method takes the width and height of the image as parameters. In this example, the size of the applets client area is used. Once a memory image is created, a corresponding *Graphics* instance is obtained using the *getGraphics* method.

In the SpriteAnimation example, the background is always blue. This makes it easy for the applet to preserve the background pixels. In applications with sophisticated background scenery, the applet would typically keep a copy of the area under the sprite so that it can be restored when the sprite is moved.

```
public void update(Graphics g)
{
 Dimension d = size();

 if(offG == null)
 {
    offImg = createImage(d.width, d.height);
    offG = offImg.getGraphics();
 }

 offG.setColor(Color.blue);
 offG.fillRect(0, 0, d.width, d.height);
 offG.drawImage(ball, x, y, this);

 //
 // Now test to see if the ball hit the right or left wall.
 //
 if((x + imgX) >= d.width)
 {
    xInc = -1;
 }
 else if(x <= 0)
 {
    xInc = 1;
 }
 x += xInc;

 //
 // Now test to see if the ball hit the bottom or top wall.
 //
 if((y + imgY) >= d.height)
 {
    yInc = -1;
 }
 else if(y <= 0)
 {
    yInc = 1;
 }
 y += yInc;

 g.drawImage(offImg, 0, 0, this);
}
```

Figure 11. The "update" method for sprite animation.

2.2.3 Collision Areas

Most computer games that use sprite animation also maintain "collision areas." The collision areas are regions on the screen that cause an event when the sprite intersects it. The SpriteAnimation example uses trivial collision detection, which is graphically depicted in Figure 12.

When the sprite hits one of the boundaries of the applet's viewable area, the direction of the sprite is changed. This gives the effect of a ball bouncing against a wall. The code for the collision detection is shown in Figure 13.

Figure 12. Collision area detection diagram.

```
offG.drawImage(ball, x, y, this);

//
// Now test to see if the ball hit the right or left wall.
//
if((x + imgX) >= d.width)
{
    xInc = -1;
}
else if(x <= 0)
{
    xInc = 1;
}
x += xInc;

//
// Now test to see if the ball hit the bottom or top wall.
//
if((y + imgY) >= d.height)
{
    yInc = -1;
}
else if(y <= 0)
{
    yInc = 1;
}
y += yInc;
```

Figure 13. The Java code for collision detection.

If the ball hits the right boundary, then the x incriminator value (xInc) is set to -1. This will start the ball moving to the left on the next pass. Similarly, if the ball hits the left boundary, then xInc is set to 1, causing the ball to go toward the right on the next pass. The tests are made for the Y-axis. The origin of the ball is with respect to the upper left-hand corner of the screen, so the size of the image must be used when testing for a right or bottom wall hit test.

3. AUDIO SUPPORT IN JAVA

An essential element to any multimedia experience is the inclusion of sounds. The Java Applet class provides the necessary methods, which allow programmers to load and play sound files [7]. The current level of the JDK supports only the Sun ".AU" audio file format. This limitation can be evaded by using utilities to convert audio files from some other format to the AU format.

In most cases, this evasion seems to be sufficient except for the MIDI (Musical Instrument Digital Interface) file format. A MIDI audio file is sufficiently different than the others in that it is not an actual recording as AU or WAV files are. MIDI files are computer programs, which instruct a synthesizer to produce sounds. Therefore, one cannot rely on utility programs to convert MIDI files to AU files. JavaSoft has addressed MIDI in its recently released Java Media API. The Java Media API defines a new and exciting set of multimedia classes. The Java Media API is covered in more detail later in this chapter.

3.1 PLAYING AN AUDIO CLIP FROM A JAVA

The first audio-enabled Java applet presented here will play an audio clip. The source code for this applet is presented below. It takes only one line of Java code to create a simple Java applet, which plays a predefined audio clip. Although this is an oversimplified example, it provides a compelling reason for programmers to investigate Java for multimedia programming.

```
import java.applet.*;
import java.awt.*;

public class Sound1 extends Applet
{
    public void init()
    {
        play(getCodeBase(),"spacemusic.au");
    }
}
```

3.2 PLAYING AN AUDIO CLIP USING A MORE SOPHISTICATED APPROACH

In the first Java audio example, the program loaded and played the audio clip using the *play* method of the applet class. Although that applet was trivial to write, it is not very useful for a practical solution since it does not provide a means to replay the audio clip. It simply plays the audio clip once and does nothing after that.

Most applications that utilize audio provide the user with a mechanism to play the audio clip when they are ready to hear it. They also allow the user to replay the audio clip if they want to hear it again. The second Java audio example adds a "play" button to the applet. The output screen for the *Sound2* applet is displayed in Figure 14. The audio clip is played whenever the "play" button is clicked on. The source code for the *Sound2* Java applet is shown in Figure 15.

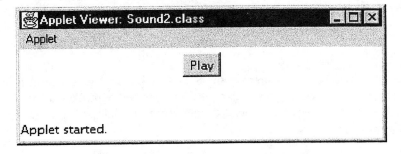

Figure 14. Output of the Sound2 Java applet.

```java
import java.applet.*;
import java.awt.*;

public class Sound2 extends Applet
{

    Button    play;
    AudioClip aclip;

    public void init( )
    {
        aclip = getAudioClip(getCodeBase( ), "spacemusic.au");

        play = new Button("Play");
        add(play);
    }

    public boolean action(Event evt, Object arg)
    {
        if(evt.target instanceof Button)
        {
            if(arg.equals("Play"))
            {
                if(aclip == null)
                {
                    System.out.println("Sound2: Err audio clip not
loaded.");
                }
                if(aclip != null)
                {
                    aclip.play();
                }
                return true;
            }
        }
        return false;

    } // end of action
}
```

Figure 15. The source code for Sound2 Java applet.

The audio clip is loaded at initialization time using the following Java statement:

```
aclip = getAudioClip(getCodeBase( ), "spacemusic.au");
```

When the "play" pushbutton is pressed, the Sound2 applet will gain control in its *action* method. The audio clip will be played using the *play* method of the AudioClip class. If the audio clip has not been successfully loaded, the *action* method will print a message out accordingly.

3.3 PLAYING AND STOPPING AN AUDIO CLIP

In the next audio example, Sound3, the program allows the user to start and stop playing the audio clip via the user interface. The output screen from the Sound3 Java applet is displayed in Figure 16.

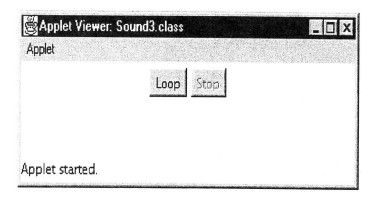

Figure 16. Output of the Sound3 Java applet.

Two pushbuttons are provided. When the user presses the "Loop" pushbutton, the audio clip is played using the *loop* method of the AudioClip class. This method differs from the *play* method in that it will continuously play the audio clip in a loop. The *stop* method of the AudioClip class is used to stop playing the clip. The source code for this final Java audio example is given in Figure 17.

4. VIDEO SUPPORT IN JAVA

Similar to MIDI support, the base Java classes in the latest level of the JDK do not support video playback. This is most probably due to the fact that there are numerous non-Java video solutions available for the Internet today.

There are two primary approaches to delivering video on the Internet: downloading stored files vs. "streaming" video (and audio). Each presents special challenges and opportunities for bandwidth allocation.

4.1 STANDARD VIDEO

Downloading and playing stored video files over the Internet is the older of the two available video playback approaches. Here, digital video files are stored on a server (typically in MPEG1 or QuickTime Movie format) and, when someone wants to access the video, they must download it in full before viewing it. The time it takes to download the file largely depends on two things: first, how large the file is (i.e., the larger the file, the longer it takes to download) and, second, how much bandwidth is available, both on the server and client sides of the network.

```java
import java.applet.*;
import java.awt.*;

public class Sound3 extends Applet
{

    Button    loop;       // Starts playing loop
    Button    stop;       // Stops playing loop
    AudioClip loopClip;   // Audio clip

    public void init( )
    {
        loopClip = getAudioClip(getCodeBase( ),"spacemusic.au");

        loop = new Button("Loop");
        loop.enable();
        add(loop);

        stop = new Button("Stop");
        stop.disable();
        add(stop);
    }

    public boolean action(Event evt, Object arg)
    {
        if(evt.target instanceof Button)
        {
            if(arg.equals("Loop"))
            {
                if(loopClip != null)
                {
                    loopClip.loop();
                    stop.enable();
                    loop.disable();
                }
                return true;
            }
            else if(arg.equals("Stop"))
            {
                loopClip.stop();
                loop.enable();
                stop.disable();
                return true;
            }
        }
        return false;

    } // end of action
}
```

Figure 17. Java applet for playing and stopping an audio clip.

4.2 STREAMING VIDEO

Streaming video (and audio) represents a second and more complex area of video on the Internet. Streaming involves the delivery of video or audio "in real time" through a number of techniques, including some that place several frames of video into a buffer on the client's hard drive, and then begin playing the video, as more files are placed into the buffer. To the viewer, the video plays in approximately real time, without having to wait for an entire large video file to download.

Each streaming video solution defines its own proprietary movie file format with a corresponding encoder utility that converts a standard movie file such as AVI or MPEG to their own native format. These streaming video providers usually give away the streaming player and sell the encoder.

Providing support for video in Java requires the selection of some standard movie file format such as the selection of AU files for audio. Since most users are accessing the Internet via modem, one would assume that a streaming video solution would be provided.

In trying to obtain all available information on this subject, it appears that JavaSoft's future support for video and all multimedia support will be defined by the Java Media API. JavaSoft has been working with a group of industry-leading companies to establish the standards for Java Media: Adobe®, Apple, Intel, Macromedia, Netscape, SGI, and Sun Microsystems. The Java Media API is briefly described in the next section.

5. JAVA MEDIA API

The Java Media API defines a set of multimedia classes which support a wide range of rich, interactive media on and off the Web, including audio, video, 2D, 3D, animation, telephony, and collaboration [8]. An extensible Media Framework provides common control and synchronization of all time-based media (audio, video, animation, video teleconferencing) as well as filters and processors.

The Java Media API is composed of several distinct components, each associated with either a specific type of media (audio, video, 2D, 3D), or a media-related activity (animation, collaboration, telephony). Collectively, these interfaces provide Java Language programmers with the ability to handle a wide variety of different media types within their applications and applets.

The Java Media API is highly extensible. The API accommodates today's large and ever-changing suite of media transports, containers, and encoding formats, and allows the addition of new media-related functionality as they become available.

The components of the Java Media APIs are as follows:

- Java 2D API - Provides graphics and imaging capabilities beyond those available with the Java Applet API. The 2D API allows the creation of high quality, platform-independent graphics including line art, text, and images in a single model that uniformly addresses color, spatial transforms and compositing. It also provides an extension mechanism to support a wide array of different presentation devices (such as displays and printers), image formats, image encoding, color spaces, and compositors.

- Java Media Framework API - Handles traditional time-critical media, such as audio, video, and MIDI. The framework provides a common model for timing, synchronization, and composition, which can be applied to media components to allow them to interoperate. It is designed to handle streaming data, live or stored, compressed or raw, as well as from sampled audio and video streams.

- Video API - Accommodates both streaming and stored video sources. It defines basic data formats and control interfaces.

- Audio API - Supports sampled and synthesized audio. It includes a specification for 3D spatial audio, and accommodates both streaming and stored audio sources.

- MIDI API - Provides support for timed-event streams. It uses the Media Framework for synchronization with other activities, and for an extensibility mechanism for new synthesizers and effects.

- Java Animation API - Supports traditional 2D animation of sprites, with stacking order control. It makes use of 2D interfaces for compositing and the Media Framework for synchronization, composition, and timing.

- Java Share API - Provides the basic abstraction for live, two-way, multi-party communication between objects over a variety of networks and transport protocols. The API enables synchronization and session management, and allows sharing of both "collaboration-aware" and "collaboration-unaware" applets.

- Java Telephony API - Unifies computer/telephony integration. It provides basic functionality for control of phone calls: 1st-party call control (simple desktop phone), 3rd-party call control (phone call distribution center), teleconferencing, call transfer, caller ID, and DTMF decode/encode.

- Java 3D API - Provides high-performance, interactive, 3D graphics support. It supports VRML, and has a high-level specification of behavior and control of 3D objects. The 3D API simplifies 3D-application programming and provides access to lower level interfaces for performance. The 3D API is closely integrated with Audio, Video, MIDI, and Animation areas.

6. CONCLUSION

Programming in any object-oriented language requires a good understanding of the tools and class libraries. The class libraries define the set of functions that are available to the Java programmer. The more robust the class libraries are, the less work will be required to be completed by the Java programmer. The object-oriented paradigm allows software developers to build upon the available class libraries to create new custom class libraries, thus extending the language.

The Java class libraries available today provide enough support to allow developers to write Java programs that do simple animations and play audio clips. This chapter presented working Java applets that accomplished these tasks. The current Java class libraries did not provide support for MIDI, streaming audio or any form of video playback.

Language extensions via custom classes can be used to add addition multimedia support to Java [9]. The sheer size and complexity of the code required to extend Java's multimedia support are the main reasons why these extensions are not available today. This problem is magnified by the fact that playing audio or video will eventually require low level programming, which is, at the least, operating system dependent.

Java provides an interface for this type of low level coding called the "native method" interface. Native methods are code fragments that can be written in some other programming language. In most cases, the native methods are written in "C" and interface directly with the operating system. Native methods are platform dependent and must be re-written for every operating system that one chooses to support. Any custom multimedia classes would require native methods.

The shortcomings of Java in the multi-media arena appear to be temporary. The Java Media Framework (JMF) API is on the horizon. This API offers a robust set of multi-media services that provide support for almost any current audio or video format by building upon an established media playback framework. Current research in multimedia, based on object models [10], appears to be a direct match for the flexible object-oriented Java language.

REFERENCES

[1]   J. Lam, "Java and Java Tools: Waking Up the Web," *PC Magazine*, June 11, 1996.

[2]   T. Cramer, R. Friedman, T. Miller, D. Seberger, R. Wilson, and M. Wolczko, "Compiling Java Just In Time," *IEEE Micro*, Vol. 17, No. 3, pp. 36-43, May - June 1997.

[3]   S. Ritchie, "Systems Programming in Java," *IEEE Micro*, Vol. 17, No. 2, pp. 30-35, May - June 1997.

[4]   B. Lewis and D. J. Berg, "How to Program with Threads (An Introduction to Multi-threaded Programming)," *Sun World*, Vol. 10, No. 2, February 1996.

[5]   P. Buchheit, "Flicker-free Animation Using Java," *Linux Journal*, October 1996.

[6]   Graphics Interchange Format (sm) - Version 89a (c) 1987,1988,1989,1990. Copyright CompuServe Incorporated Columbus, Ohio, 31 July 1990.

[7]   C. S. Wah and J. D. Mitchell, "How to Play Audio in Applications," *Java World*, February 1997.

[8]   B. M. Day, Jr., "Java Media Framework Player API," *Java World*, April 1997.

[9]   J. Begole, C. A. Strumble, and C. A. Shaffer, "Leveraging Java Applets: Toward Collaboration Transparency in Java," *IEEE Micro*, Vol. 17, No. 2, March - April 1997.

[10]   V.M. Bove, Jr., "Multimedia Based on Object Models: Some Whys and Hows," *IBM Systems Journal*, Vol. 35, Nos. 3&4, pp. 337-348, 1996.

[11]   B.R. Montague, "JN: OS for an Embedded Java Network Computer," *IEEE Micro*, Vol. 17, No. 2, pp. 54-61, May-June 1997.

[12]   E. Yourdan, "Java, the Web, and Software Development," *IEEE Computer*, Vol. 29, No. 8, pp. 25-30, August 1996.

[13]   E. Evans and D. Rogers, "Using Java Applets and CORBA for Multi-User Distributed Applications," *IEEE Internet Computing*, Vol. 1, No. 3, pp. 43-55, May/June 1997.

30

OPERATING SYSTEM ISSUES FOR CONTINUOUS MEDIA

Henning Schulzrinne
Columbia University
Department of Computer Science
New York, NY 10027

1.	**INTRODUCTION**	628
	1.1 CHARACTERISTICS OF CONTINUOUS MEDIA	631
	1.2 WORKLOAD CHARACTERIZATION AND ADMISSION CONTROL	631
	1.3 EXISTING SYSTEMS	633
	1.4 STATIC PRIORITY FOR REAL-TIME PROCESSES AND THREADS	634
	1.5 PRIORITY INVERSION	635
	1.6 DEADLINE-BASED SCHEDULING	635
	1.7 IMPRECISE COMPUTATION AND ADAPTIVE APPLICATIONS	636
2.	**MEMORY ALLOCATION, PAGING, AND SWAPPING**	637
3.	**PERFORMANCE ENHANCEMENTS**	637
	3.1 CLOCKS AND TIMERS	637
	3.2 INTERRUPT HANDLING	638
	3.3 MEMORY ACCESS AND COPYING	638
4.	**NETWORK INTERFACE AND PROTOCOL PROCESSING**	639
5.	**LIBRARIES, TOOLKITS, AND APPLICATION ENVIRONMENTS**	639
	5.1 AUDIO	639
	5.2 VIDEO	641
	5.3 MULTIMEDIA CONTROL AND SCRIPTING	641
6.	**SECURITY**	641
7.	**CONCLUSION**	642
	REFERENCES	642

Abstract. Continuous media, such as audio and video, pose new challenges to all parts of multipurpose operating systems. In this chapter, we discuss issues related to CPU scheduling, memory allocation, system support and application environments, and summarize some of the solutions proposed in the literature.

0-8493-1825-4/99/$0.00+$.50

1. INTRODUCTION

Operating systems play a crucial role in supporting multimedia applications. Here we investigate the problems that are introduced by multimedia and some approaches to their solution. General introductions to operating systems can be found in [1, 2], with specific surveys of the UNIX operating system in [3,4]. Although only a combination of network and operating system design can guarantee performance, network issues seem to have required far more attention in the past. As higher-speed LANs touting integrated services are becoming available, operating system deficiencies are becoming more apparent. These and some attempted approaches are the subject of this chapter, with a strong emphasis on implementation-related work rather than on theoretical results from scheduling theory.

First, it is helpful to distinguish between *continuous media* [5] and *multimedia*, where the latter includes the former. Continuous media are characterized by a timing relationship between source and sink, that is, the sink must reproduce the timing relationship that existed at the source. The most common examples of continuous media include audio and motion video, but MIDI commands also belong in this category [6]. Continuous media can be *real-time (interactive)*, where there is a "tight" timing relationship between source and sink, or *playback*, where the relationship is less strict. For simplicity, we also include "recording," as for a tape recorder when using the term "playback." Video conferencing is the stereotypical application for interactive continuous media. For interactive continuous media, the acceptable delay is often governed by human reaction time or issues of echo for audio. These delays are in the order of no more than a few hundred milliseconds. The tightest delay constraints are imposed by bidirectional audio. If (currently rather expensive) hardware echo cancellation is to be avoided, delays of no more than around 40 ms are tolerable. For playback applications, the delay is limited mostly by the amount of buffering that can be supported. In addition, for some playback applications, the total delay, including network delays, is limited by the desired reaction time for control commands. For example, a video-on-demand playback application should be able to react to a "reverse" command within no more than about half a second.

In the operating system context, multimedia indicates the integration of various media within the same system, some of which may well be continuous media of both playback and interactive types, but can also be still images, text, or graphics. One specific problem is the coordination in time (synchronization) of these media.

Because their characteristics differ most markedly from traditional data types supported within operating systems, we focus largely on *continuous media*. It is often assumed that continuous media are challenging because they impose the highest data rates or processing on the system. This is not necessarily so; graphics or transaction processing may well impose larger loads on a larger range of system components, but the timing requirements and the guaranteed throughput required for continuous media force specific consideration in designing operating systems.

The design of multimedia operating systems is fundamentally determined by how the media data are handled within the computer system. We can distinguish a control-only approach from a fully integrated approach. In a control-only approach, the continuous media data do not touch the operating system or main memory, but rather use a separate infrastructure. For the case of video, the control-only approach simply connects analog video to a separate monitor or uses analog picture-in-picture techniques. The earliest experiments in integrating analog video such as those in [7] had the workstation control a VCR or laser disk player, with video either displayed on a separate monitor or fed through an analog mixer. For a monochrome system, a simple control plane can be used, while for a color system, chromakeying is a traditional technique long used for TV production. Analog mixing makes it difficult to integrate video into, say, the windowing system, so the user perceives it as an attachment rather than an integral part of the system. There is also likely to be a rather low upper bound on the number of concurrent video windows. Audio control functionality, like talker indication or on-screen volume unit (VU) display, cannot be readily supported. While this architecture imposes some mild control timing constraints on the operating system, it is not likely to require fundamental changes. The Etherphone [8], VOX [9], DVI [10] and IMAL [11] systems are examples of the separation of control and data for audio.

Instead of analog mixing, the Pandora system [12] integrates digital video streams. This is done through a separate video processor and a pixel switch that decides for each pixel whether to display the workstation graphics stream or the external live video source. This allows almost seamless integration into the windowing system, but with a separate data path and the inability, for example, to capture screen dumps of live video. The combined multimedia workstation also requires two separate network interfaces. A more integrated approach has live video and workstation graphics share the same frame buffer, as is done for many workstation-based video boards [13].

A more recent, fully digital version of separate or separable data paths for continuous media is found in the idea of desk-area networks [14–17] that extend cell-based communication into the workstation, with a cell switch replacing a traditional bus or the path through memory. However, this approach offers the choice of treating continuous media as data to be either processed or simply switched from, say, network device to display device. If data do not touch the CPU on their path through the system, operating system requirements are relaxed. Thus, for our purposes, we will not discuss this mode further.

Given that many continuous media applications need not pass media data through the CPU, (with one of the approaches outlined), the reader may ask why integration is desirable at all, given the complexity.

Naturally, AI-like functions like image categorization require CPU intervention, but other, lower-level operations like encoding and decoding, scaling, or sampling rate conversion can be done either in hardware or software. Software generally has a price advantage. In particular, the incremental cost of adding video to an existing workstation can be close to zero if only decoding is desired. Except for switch-based backplane architectures, there is also another pragmatic reason to involve the CPU in that most workstation architectures are simply not designed to allow adapter-to-adapter communication. With evolving standards in the area of network protocols and media compression, software-intensive approaches offer far more flexibility. The type of advanced media functionality described in [18] is likely difficult to achieve when continuous media bypass the operating system and the CPU.

There are other advantages as well, in particular, scalable performance. Software decoding, for example, can display several windows of live video simultaneously (depending on workstation performance), while most hardware decoders support only a single output window. Examples include the decoding of video [19, 20], both encoding and decoding of video [21–23], audio [24], and the processing of MIDI data [6]. The integration of standard continuous media I/O devices on the motherboard is at least as important as the necessary processing power. Currently, devices for high-quality audio are integrated, with video likely to follow soon. The integration of these devices in workstations has had the salutary effect of accelerating integration of continuous-media support in the vendor-supplied operating systems. It should be noted, however, that many multimedia PCs, despite featuring a CD-quality audio interface, are unsuitable for *interactive* continuous media because they cannot handle concurrent reading and writing of data, i.e., they are half duplex. Also, their DMA mechanism is designed for playback of sounds, not low-latency interaction.

While the increasing computational power of workstations should enable fairly extensive manipulation of continuous media, a number of factors reduce the ability of workstations to deal with continuous media below what might be expected from pure MIPS or SPECmark benchmark numbers. Continuous media stress a number of architectural areas poorly covered by traditional CPU-oriented benchmarks and areas in which performance has not increased with raw CPU MIPS performance; in particular, interrupt latencies, context switching overhead, and data movement. Audio, for example, is often handled in small chunks to reduce packetization delays. (A 20 ms audio packet sampled at 8 kHz and coded as μ-law consists of 160 bytes.) These small packets cause a large interrupt load for network devices and frequent context switches for applications. (In the example, potentially 100 context switches per second.) MIDI has a low data rate of 31 kb/s, but extremely tight latency requirements of around 1 ms.

Other continuous media types produce large data rates. CD-quality audio, for example, generates samples at rates of around 1.5 Mb/s. Video exacerbates the demands by requiring data rates of about 1.2 Mb/s for MPEG-compressed, VHS-quality video [25], 20 Mb/s for compressed HDTV, up to 200 Mb/s for 24-bit (RGB) uncompressed video at 30 frames/s (640 by 480 pixels) or 1.2 Gb/s for uncompressed HDTV. While networks and file servers rarely carry uncompressed video, operating systems may have to handle these if decompression is done in software.

Unfortunately, as observed by Ousterhout [26], both memory bandwidth and operating system functions, such as context switches or interrupt handling, have not improved at the same rate as CPU instruction cycles per second. Even though basic DRAM memory speeds have not increased much in the last decade, workstation designers have been able to improve benchmarked performance by enlarging and speeding up static RAM-based cache memory. Cache helps with some continuous media tasks, such as software compression and decompression, but the large amounts of data flowing through the CPU and memory system will likely decrease overall cache hit ratios, with system performance dominated by slower main memory and I/O accesses. This memory bottleneck was observed, for example, for a software MPEG decoder [19], where memory bandwidth, not the processing for the inverse cosine transform, limited the achievable frame rate. Disk access speeds have not improved dramatically either. Disk caches are of limited use since most continuous media are accessed sequentially and only once, with the exception of large video-on-demand servers.

In general, the relationship of system resources to requirements can be depicted in a graph as in Figure 1. In the upper left region, resources are insufficient even for a single stream, with no other system activity. As we move into the region of scarce resources, a limited number of continuous media streams can be handled, as long as they and any non-real-time processes are controlled carefully, i.e., appropriately scheduled and possibly denied concurrent access. As we move further to the labeled abundance of resources on the right, we may have enough resources on average for all comers, but may still have to maintain local control to avoid missing deadlines for individual streams. Note that this division corresponds with those in communication resources. There, the window of scarcity reflects the region in which admission control is needed.

The data points shown naturally reflect only "typical" usage. In particular, the mixing of several audio or video streams, their manipulation (special effects), or higher spatiotemporal resolution can extend the window of scarcity almost indefinitely.

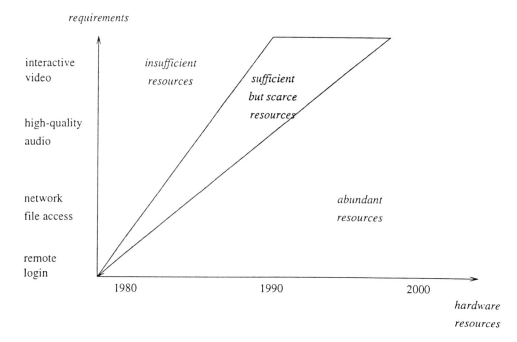

Figure 1. The window of scarcity [27].

We have indicated some of the challenges faced by system designers when integrating continuous media into a general-purpose operating system. However, the basic functionality required of a general-purpose, continuous media-enabled operating system remains similar. It must arbitrate resource demands, protect processes against each other, and provide abstractions of low-level physical devices. The protection of processes, however, now encompasses not just protection against external memory accesses, but also of their negotiated slice of CPU time, I/O bandwidth, and other resources. In addition to these "kernel" functions, such enhanced operating systems may also support multimedia applications by offering security measures and protocols for data sharing and by orchestrating multimedia data.

In the following sections, we discuss two of the major bottleneck system resources, CPU and disk. Then we look at higher-level system support through libraries and at security issues. Finally we discuss some systems explicitly designed for continuous media applications. We discover that many of the resource issues faced by the operating system have counterparts within integrated services networks, while the possible design approaches are somewhat more flexible, due principally to the reduced latencies within an operating system compared to those of a distributed network. Furthermore, an operating system can usually obtain a global view of the system, unlike a distributed network.

1.1. CHARACTERISTICS OF CONTINUOUS MEDIA

The characteristics of multimedia and collaborative data sources on networks and operating systems can be roughly divided as in Figure 2, adapted from [28]. Traditional (hard) real-time events occur periodically; if an event is not processed or not processed by its deadline, this is considered a catastrophic failure [29], e.g., a chemical plant explodes. Interactive audio and video typically also arrive periodically from input devices and roughly so from the network, but with far less stringent reliability constraints. Other system events, such as mouse movements, keystrokes, or window events, must be processed reliably within a few hundred milliseconds, but do not have predictable arrival patterns.

1.2. WORKLOAD CHARACTERIZATION AND ADMISSION CONTROL

Current time-sharing operating systems do not expect CPU time commitments from processes and, in turn, cannot make commitments of response times. Process creation requests are rejected only when some other resource, such as process slots or swap space, is insufficient. This behavior is analogous to a datagram network.

Just as networks have difficulties making quality-of-service (QOS) guarantees unless the traffic is bounded in burstiness and the packet scheduling isolates streams from each other, a process scheduler needs to do the same. Unfortunately, applications generally do not know their resource requirements, except perhaps by historical statistics. The difficulty is even worse than for estimating network requirements (e.g., cell-rate statistics), as subtle configuration changes or hardware upgrades can drastically alter the execution time required for the continuous media task. To confound matters further, execution times can depend upon the behavior of other processes. Generally, the busier a system is, the more per-process CPU time is required as CPU and memory management unit (MMU) caches are flushed more frequently. There are likely to be more involuntary context switches, run queues to be searched by the scheduler are longer, and so on. This pattern of increased resource consumption just when the system is busy has no analogue in the communication realm, except perhaps for overloaded routers.

Despite these dependencies, it appears that most continuous media processes could provide reasonable upper bounds on their resource usage, at least as long as their repertoire of operations is limited to simple combinations of frame retrieval, compression/decompression, dithering, and the like. Attempts at estimation based on prior execution have been made, e.g., by Jones [30]. However, as pointed out in [31], upper or pessimistic bounds may lead to poor resource utilization and unnecessary denials of service. However, incomplete resource utilization by continuous media processes may also provide the necessary head room to non-real-time applications, so that a larger fraction of the system's capacity can be reserved for real-time tasks. In computer-supported cooperative work (CSCW) applications, for example, it appears

Interval

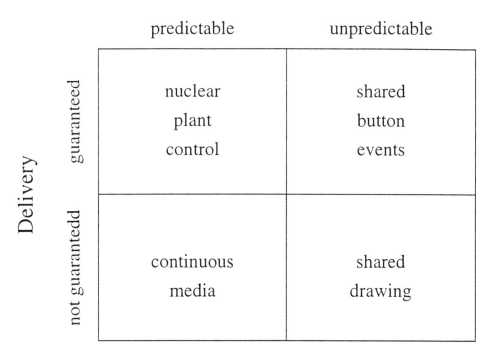

Figure 2. Characteristics of time-critical data [28].

to be common to have a mix of interactive, continuous media applications and more traditional data applications like shared windowing systems, whiteboards, and conference control. Another approach, optimistic bounds, reserves only the bare minimum of resources for a real-time task and allows for occasional glitches and service degradations, things we have come to tolerate in analog telephony and over-the-air television.

Many interactive, continuous media applications are characterized by a cycle, occurring at frame rate or audio packet rate, and consisting of waiting for available data either from the network, an audio input device, or framegrabber, followed by CPU and memory-intensive processing. While the media input-device events occur at regular intervals, network arrivals can be quite bursty, particularly if an application receives packets from a number of sources. For audio and intraframe-coded video, each such round requires a fairly constant amount of processing, while, for example, the processing and memory accesses required for MPEG I frames are likely to be much larger than for B and P frames, with a strong dependency on image content and frame size. Thus, audio input follows a traditional real-time model of periodic, predictable needs for CPU time, while all other tasks have either unpredictable arrival instances or widely varying processing requirements. The application is likely to have no notion how much processing is required for each set of images and for the particular processor architecture it happens to be running on.

This periodic resource requirement is actually not too far removed from the characteristic pattern of hard real-time applications, as they might be found on a factory floor, sampling sensors at a fixed rate and computing control responses. Playback applications tend to be much burstier in that they may read a number of frames from disk, decompress until the process is preempted, and continue.

One simple model for continuous media requirements is the linear bounded arrival process (LBAP), originally developed by Cruz [32, 33] and suggested by Anderson [5, 27, 34–36] as a model for both communication networks and operating systems. In the LBAP, the message arrival rate in any interval t may not exceed $B + Rt$, where B is the maximum burst size and R is the average arrival rate. Instead of messages, other units like required CPU seconds or number of bytes to be read from disk could be used.

For scheduling, we can distinguish between *critical* and *workahead* processes. First, we define the logical arrival time of a message as the time it would have arrived had the generating process strictly obeyed its maximum message rate. More formally, the logical arrival time $l(m_i)$ is defined as

$$l(m_i) = a_i + \frac{w(m_i)}{R},$$

where a_i is the arrival time. The workahead $w(m_i)$ is defined as $\max(0, w(m_{i-1}) - R(a_i - a_{i-1}) + 1) = \max_{t_0 < a_i}(0, N(t_0, a_i) - R|a_i - t_0|)$. The workahead (or backlog) measures how much the process is "ahead of schedule" relative to its long-term rate R. Note that with this measure, a single message arriving late can delay the logical arrival time of all subsequent messages and thus their processing. Also, the burst size B does not enter into the computation of the logical arrival time. A message arriving after its logical arrival time is termed *critical*, while one arriving before is termed *workahead*. An example is shown in Figure 3.

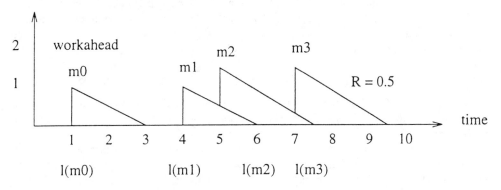

Figure 3. Example of workahead function [5].

Any of the scheduling algorithms discussed in this section apply to both processes and threads. (Threads are schedulable entities without their own address space.) Indeed, Govindan and Anderson argue, in their split-level scheduling proposal [37], that both real-time threads and processes should be supported. Scheduling within threads, if implemented at the user level rather than in the kernel, has the advantage of avoiding some of the frequent context switches and user-kernel interactions.

1.3. EXISTING SYSTEMS

Before addressing the issue of CPU scheduling and (implicitly) resource reservation, it helps to establish that current practice in general-purpose *and* real-time operating systems cannot provide the desired quality of delivery of continuous media. On the positive side, most current UNIX-based workstations can keep up with a single audio or video stream as long as there are no other applications and the continuous media stream is only piped through the system with moderate processing. (This accounts for the success of multimedia demos at trade shows.) However, even for a quiescent system, there can be significant variation in the interdeparture and application-visible interarrival times caused by system demons or process rescheduling, as measured in [38].

The reasons for these variations are found in the properties of kernels and process schedulers. Both System-V [4] and Berkeley software distribution (BSD)-derived schedulers [3] use a multilevel feedback queue, where processes are served in round robin fashion within a priority level, but moved from one level to another based on CPU time accumulated and a preference for I/O-intensive processes. The priority level is adjusted only if a process exhausts its CPU time slice of (typically) 100 ms or if it has been sleeping longer than a second. Thus, typical continuous media applications should maintain their priority throughout, but other processes could preempt it when starting or if they can "convince" the kernel that they are more I/O intensive. (Process priority is highest at the time the process is created, unless it is manually changed by the superuser.) A process is only preempted after using its time-slice or when returning from a system call. Thus, even after raising the priority of the continuous media process, it can suffer delays of up to 100 ms until a lower-priority process that was scheduled during the wait period resurfaces from the kernel or exhausts its time slice. Residence time in the kernel is not bounded at all, regardless of the priority of the process. The problems with this time-sharing scheduling discipline have been empirically evaluated by Nieh et al. [39]. They discuss how a video application, a typing simulator, the X server, and a compiler-like computing job that continuously spawns new short-lived processes compete for resources. Simply adjusting priorities (known as "nice" values in UNIX) may help, but often has counterintuitive effects, in that *lowering* the priority of a process may, say, increase frame rates.

As noted, UNIX process scheduling decreases the process priority with accumulated CPU usage. However, for periodic processes, sampling aliasing can dramatically skew the estimate so that each video or audio frame is charged the full CPU tick or nothing at all [40], leading to periodic oscillations in process priority as application intervals and measurement intervals drift with respect to one another. Random sampling intervals solve this particular problem.

Real-time UNIX systems [41,42] generally implement fixed priority, preemptive schedulers and are thus not suited for a general-purpose system shared by real-time (continuous media) interactive and batch applications.

1.4. STATIC PRIORITY FOR REAL-TIME PROCESSES AND THREADS

There are a number of conceptually simple ways of improving the behaviour of standard operating systems like UNIX for continuous media applications without giving up on a general-purpose operating system.

One problem noted in the preceding section was the unbound kernel-residence time. Newer versions of UNIX SVR4 [43] and the Mach operating system implement a thread-based, fully-preemptible kernel, so that low-priority processes executing kernel code cannot prevent higher-priority processes from running. This change reduced dispatch latencies from 100 ms to about 2 ms on a standard workstation. Another approach to reducing maximum kernel residence time is by introducing preemption points [44], where system routines such as fork, execution, or exit, check whether any high-priority user processes are ready to run. It should be noted that the interruptability of kernel code comes at a price in overall performance, as threads must execute semaphores and the run queue must be checked at every preemption point.

UNIX SVR4 also introduced installable scheduling classes [6, 43], including a real-time class with fixed priorities (which are always higher than those of processes within the time-sharing class). Processes in the real-time class can execute until either blocked or finished, or a time limit can be associated with the process. Since the priority of the real-time class must be higher than that for system processes like the swapper in order to guarantee delay bounds, use of this class can obviously have dire consequences for system behavior. (Not surprisingly, use of this class requires superuser privileges.) This is documented in [39] through the example of a video display process that can cause the whole system to become unresponsive. However, the example chosen in [39] is clearly inappropriate for the real-time class as it is a CPU-bound process that will dominate the CPU if given a chance. A high-priority real-time class can work only if the processes in that class relinquish the processor so that lower-priority processes are not starved. Nieh et al. [39] present a new time-sharing class that provides a better balance among interactive, real-time, and batch applications.

It should be noted that running a continuous media application within an elevated priority real-time scheduling class by itself may not be sufficient, if this application must rely on other system services that are likely to execute as time-sharing or system processes. Examples include the X-window server for video output and the stream handler for audio input and output. To avoid wholesale priority elevation of all system services, they must be be threaded, with only those threads operating on behalf of real-time applications getting improved service. Indeed, even within a real-time application, there may be significant non-real-time components, particularly the user interface or logging. Again, only separate threads of control with separate system-level scheduling, can avoid these problems. Threads within most thread libraries, however, are scheduled only within the time slice of the overall process.

To allocate CPU cycles to interactive continuous media processes, results from the scheduling of hard real-time processes can be used. (A hard real-time system suffers catastrophic failure if a process is not completed before the assigned deadline. Examples include air-traffic control, process control, and embedded systems [45].) A simple, static priority policy that is widely used in such systems is the *rate-monotonic* scheduler [46]. The policy is preemptive and assigns scheduling priorities according to the rate of arrival for a particular kind of process, with higher priorities for more frequent processes. For processes to meet their deadlines, the schedulability must be tested prior to allowing a new process to use CPU resources. For processes that are periodic, independent, and have a deadline equal to their period, there are necessary and sufficient conditions that ensure this.

Liu and Layland show that, for periodic, non-communicating processes with constant computation times and zero context switch overheads, a set of processes can be scheduled successfully if

$$\sum_{i=1}^{n} \frac{C_i}{T_i} \leq n(2^{1/n} - 1),$$

where n is the number of periodic programs, with program i requiring C_i of computation at a period of T_i. For a large n, this bounds the utilization from below to about 69%. However, Lehoczky et al. [47] show that, on average, a utilization of 88% can be reached. Others [48, 49] have provided bounds requiring fewer assumptions, though they may be harder to compute.

While the Liu/Layland assumptions are onerous for many hard real-time systems, they reflect the processing of continuouis media reasonably well. If anything, the delay bound of a single period is probably excessive, as audio and video can typically tolerate delay jitter higher than that if the output device provides sufficient buffering. A generalization of the rate-monotonic policy is the *deadline- monotonic* [50] scheduler, with priorities assigned according to process deadlines. These deadlines do not have to be equal to the period. Both are optimal static priority policies because if any static priority policy can schedule a set of processes, the rate and deadline-monotonic ones can as well. A schedulability test is presented in [45], while a general survey of scheduling algorithms is presented by Audsley and Burns [51].

1.5. PRIORITY INVERSION

Simple priority inversion occurs if a high-priority process has to wait for a resource held by a low-priority process. *Unbounded priority inversion* occurs if this low-priority process, while holding the resource, is preempted by a medium-priority process, delaying release of the resource and blocking the high-priority process for an indeterminate time [52]. There are a number of remedies [48], the simplest of which is the basic priority-inheritance protocol. The basic priority-inheritance protocol attempts to bound the duration of priority inversion during resource blocking by having the high-priority thread propagate its priority to all lower-priority threads that block it [43].

1.6. DEADLINE-BASED SCHEDULING

If several concurrent continuous media streams are to be handled by the operating system, higher priorities need to be assigned to processes with closer deadlines. However, this preemptive priority may lead to processes with lower priorities missing their deadlines, even though the system could have scheduled both high and low priority processes on time.

To avoid this difficulty and the problem of having to assign priorities manually, we can schedule processes with the earliest deadline first (EDF) [46]. EDF scheduling does not require processes to be periodic; it also has nice optimality properties in that it yields a schedule that avoids missed deadlines, if at all possible. EDF scheduling is also used in communication networks, but for CPU scheduling, the preemptive variety is appropriate, with the readiness of a new process with a closer deadline preempting the currently executing process. Liu and

Layland showed that, for periodic tasks,

$$\sum_{i=1}^{n} \frac{C_i}{T_i} \leq 1$$

is sufficient for schedulability.

EDF scheduling within the UNIX operating system has been implemented by Hagsand and Sjödin [44], for Mach by Tokuda et al. [42] and Nakajima et al. [53]. A more sophisticated version of EDF scheduling, called processor-capacity reserves [54,55], was added to real-time Mach [42]. Here, programs are assigned a periodic processor capacity, with programs that have not yet consumed their allocation taking precedence over unreserved programs. In a micro kernel environment, particular care must be taken to ensure that all user-level server threads invoked by the kernel thread are "charged" to the invoking thread.

In [44], a process starts towards its deadline if one of the designed file descriptors becomes ready, triggered, for example, by the arrival of a video frame from a framegrabber or the network interface. Real-time processes are designated by waiting on a file descriptor passed to a variation of the standard `select` system call. There is no schedulability test, however, so real-time processes are not protected from each other.

The Yet Another Real-Time Operating System (YARTOS) [56,57] uses a related approach. Here, the deadline clock starts to tick with the arrival of messages (events), a generalization of the file-descriptor approach already mentioned. Events have associated deadlines and a defined minimum interarrival time. With this and the specification of resources needed and available, the kernel can offer guarantees to tasks.

Another approach to deadline-based scheduling is the deadline-workahead scheduler (DWS) [35,36]. With the LBAP workload characterization described in Section 1.2, a simple policy can be formulated: critical processes are scheduled with the EDF, regular interactive (non-real-time) processes have priority over workahead processes, but are preempted when such processes become critical. Finally, the scheme defines background processes as those executing when the system would otherwise be idle. The approach is thus seen as a refinement of the pure EDF approach, with a built-in bound on the resource consumption of individual message streams.

Either priority classes or deadline scheduling offer a tempting target for application writers to "improve" the performance of their application while penalizing other users or applications, leading, in the worst case, to an "arms race" between applications and defeating kernel scheduling altogether [58]. Making class assignments accessible to the superuser only on a per-process basis makes them basically unusable for normal user applications.

1.7. IMPRECISE COMPUTATION AND ADAPTIVE APPLICATIONS

Some CPU-intensive continuous media tasks are characterized by the fact that they can be carried to different degrees of precision. As an example, consider a video encoder in which the motion estimation search can be more or less exhaustive. If a process runs out of time, it can terminate before completion with a useful, but less precise result [59]. The system could signal to the process that "times's up," causing it to terminate that round of processing and avoiding missing its own deadline or endangering that of another message. These tasks are labeled as *imprecise computations* or are said to give increasing reward with increasing service (IRIS). In principle, imprecise computation offers a graceful degradation of the media quality within a continuous media system as system load increases.

This seemingly straightforward and appealing approach has a practical problem. The typical continuous media computation consists of a CPU-intensive task that can be varied in length and is followed by "packaging" (e.g., Huffman coding for JPEG, or generating MPEG frames) and any system overhead needed to render or transfer the processed data. While there are theoretical investigations in the properties of imprecise computation [60,61], there does not seem to be any practical experience with actually using such algorithms for codecs.

A slightly different adaptation algorithm works on a longer time scale. Instead of rejecting new real-time tasks, the system detects overload and then renegotiates resource requirements with these tasks [62]. A real-time thread package for Mach [63] supports both periodic and aperiodic execution with deadline bounds. It uses timing-fault notification for threads serving adaptive applications to self-stabilize. A timing-fault occurs if a thread misses its deadline. The timing fault handler can then reduce the requested frequency of thread execution to self-stabilize the system. With the right control loop, this ensures smooth display of video sequences, although at a reduced rate, under the conditions of a heavy load. An alternate approach explored by the authors has a QOS manager control the frame rate within bounds specified by the thread.

Unlike most computational (batch) applications that are useful over a range of execution durations from milliseconds to hours, most continuous media applications have a fairly narrow range of adaptability. Video frame rates can perhaps be varied by a factor of 2 (from 30 to 15 frames per second, say) without fundamentally being altered in usability (from moving video to changing still images). It should also be noted that adaptation of continuous media for the network could either cooperate with or defeat operating system-induced adjustments. Frame rate reductions would relieve load both on the network and the end system, while changing to a lower-bitrate coding would likely be more computationally intensive. Thus, network-motivated adjustments must be carefully coordinated with local system resources.

2. MEMORY ALLOCATION, PAGING, AND SWAPPING

In the past, increased swapping and paging was a concern for system performance, but it appears that increased memory has largely eliminated swapping, except in dormant applications. In any event, given the ever larger ratio of CPU speeds to disk speeds, reasonable system performance cannot be obtained if processes have to retrieve memory pages after the initial load during startup.

However, with increasing availability on workstations, demands on memory have grown from caches for disks and network information retrieval systems, to temporary file systems, to speed up compilations [58]. Instead of the relatively small number of active processes when user interaction was through terminals, each user now typically has sets of mostly inactive applications. Typical per-user process counts are probably fairly close to a busy time sharing system of some years ago. Any of these processes, when awakened, will grab pages from other processes, including those with real-time constraints. Least-recently-used (LRU) policies offer some protection to periodically executing processes, but there are likely parts of an interactive application that are executed only infrequently, e.g., to update statistics. For single threaded applications, paging in these parts of the continuous media application could then delay all real-time handling within the same application. Memory access is typically not tied to scheduling priority so that a low-priority batch job can easily interfere with a high-priority continuous media task.

Simple tools like a process telling linker to colocate certain memory segments could lead to decreased working sets [58], but are generally not supported.

3. PERFORMANCE ENHANCEMENTS

In this section, we investigate approaches to streamline processing for high data rate, low-latency applications. We also mention special requirements on common functionality found within current operating systems, e.g., high-resolution clocks and clock synchronization.

3.1. CLOCKS AND TIMERS

High-resolution clocks and timers are required for low-latency, event-driven applications. Typical UNIX clocks have a resolution of only 10 ms or lower, while resolutions less than a millisecond are probably required for applications like MIDI. Timers may have large cumulative errors; that is, if a timer is rescheduled periodically, the total accumulated time may be significantly greater than the sum of the timer values. For intermedia synchronization, it is important that the system clock can be read with low overhead and without the possibility of pre-emption at the end of the system call.

Generally, the system timer is ill-suited to clock the gathering of continuous media data, as it likely runs at a slightly different frequency than the sampling clock on the audio/video data acquisition hardware, leading to buffer overflows or starvation both for input and output. It appears best to use the hardware to clock both data acquisition and playback.

Since the notion of time is central for continuous media, operating systems for multimedia should also provide basic support for synchronization of media streams. Synchronization between media streams has been the topic of a large body of research [64–67]. It appears, however, that once synchronized clocks are available with clock differences of a few milliseconds [68], the problem is largely solved. Explicit synchronization algorithms appear to provide special case, multi-party clock synchronization. Some further experimental work on playout synchronization in different networks is useful, although the need for sophisticated algorithms arises primarily in lower-speed packet networks like the Internet [69].

3.2. INTERRUPT HANDLING

As mentioned in Section 1, some continuous media types may cause high system load, due not to their bandwidth, but rather to their high interrupt and context-switching frequency. It has been observed elsewhere that both have come to dominate actual protocol processing, particularly if they cause caches to be flushed and MMU tables to be invalidated. Because of their relatively low interrupt and context switch overhead, operating systems that do not offer pre-emptive multitasking and separate address spaces (e.g., Microsoft Windows 3.1 or Apple System 7) may perform significantly better in real time than UNIX derivatives. Because of the lack of separation of a kernel and user space, processing is often done within interrupt handlers, offering low latency, but clearly at the cost of higher, nonpredictable delays for other processes [6]. One approach for System-V-derived kernels may be the use of modules pushed onto the streams-processing stack [70], either as pseudo-code or as compiled modules. However, like upcalls from kernel to user space, they pose protection problems and may contravene attempts to limit kernel-residence times. The Berkeley packet filter [71] provides one example (in the somewhat different domain of selecting and processing network packets for debugging) of how to construct a simple, restricted, interpreted language that is downloaded into the kernel and then executed for every arriving packet.

In a BSD-derived operating system, interrupts triggered by hardware, so-called "hard interrupts," preempt any other system activity (except other interrupts of higher priority). Therefore, handlers for these interrupts commonly attend to only the hardware-related tasks, leaving the actual work to be done (e.g., the copying of data) to a so-called "soft" interrupt of lower priority than that of all other interrupt handlers, but still pre-empting other user processes. Some such interrupt handling (e.g., for background network traffic) is typically of lower priority than real-time processes and, given sufficient background load, it may pay to defer them [44]. However, deciding whether, for example, a packet belongs to a network association deserving high-priority treatment may not be trivial at hard interrupt time and could outweigh any gains. As is the case with assigning processes to scheduling classes, what looks like a low-priority packet arrival may actually be in the critical path for a real-time application.

3.3. MEMORY ACCESS AND COPYING

As mentioned earlier, continuous media applications often need to move data continuously and at high rates from one I/O device to another, e.g., from framegrabber to network interface. In a standard UNIX kernel with DMA-capable devices, the data is copied three or four times: via DMA to a device-driver managed buffer in RAM, then by the CPU to internal data structures like *mbufs*, back into the output device's DMA buffer, and finally via DMA into the output device [72]. If no further processing is required, direct driver-to-driver data transfers could off-load the CPU, although the competition for bus cycles may still reduce system performance unless the peripherals can use a dedicated I/O bus as in the microchannel architecture.

Another approach, used also by the Mach operating system, is to avoid copying by remapping pages from one process to another. However, the attendant overhead in updating kernel tables and remapping pointers may approach the cost of copying for all but the largest messages. Anderson [5] introduces a restricted remapping in the context of the DASH message-based operating system for continuous media, in which only a special memory region can be remapped and only between the same virtual addresses in sender and receiver address spaces. A related approach presented in [37] emphasizes shared memory for synchronizing data transfer between the user and the kernel space rather than (necessarily) for the actual data transfer.

4. NETWORK INTERFACE AND PROTOCOL PROCESSING

High-rate continuous media pose some of the same performance problems as volume data applications. Solutions include the elimination of copying between network adapter [73] and operating system buffers, or kernel and user space, or combining copying and checksumming [74]. For continuous media, the User Datagram Protocol (UDP) is used as a transport protocol rather than the Transmission Control Protocol (TCP), as the reliability and flow control offered by TCP interfere with the delay requirements and inherent rate of continuous media. However, UDP checksumming still imposes unnecessary processing costs. Measurements [74] have shown that, for large packets as would be found in video transmission, the sender latency is dominated by checksumming and, if used, any software fragmentation into ATM cells. For example, for 1400-byte packets, a BSD 4.4 sender implementation spends 39% of its time on the TCP checksum (which is the same as the UDP checksum). For audio and video, bit errors are usually preferable to dropping packets. For video, even if the bit error corrupts the frame encoding structure, at least the part of the video frame preceeding the bit error can be used by the receiver. Unfortunately, most existing network stacks do not allow checksumming to be turned off for an individual network association. (Turning off UDP checksums in general can lead to corrupted data in the network file system.)

For the small packets typically found for low-bit-rate voice, processing costs are more evenly distributed among copies, checksum, protocol processing, operating system-priority management, the network-interface driver, and interrupt handling [75]. For low-latency voice, packets arrive at a frequency of at least 50 packets a second. Thus, efficient interrupt handling and process scheduling is particularly important (see also Section 3.2). Even with a relatively slow workstation, however, per-packet processing delay was measured at less than 500 μs per packet for TCP and should be significantly less for UDP.

Protocols like ST-II [76] claim to be particularly optimized for multimedia streams, offering both facilities for resource reservation, and, less importantly, a reduced per-packet handling overhead. However, it appears [77] that the performance gains are modest.

5. LIBRARIES, TOOLKITS, AND APPLICATION ENVIRONMENTS

While the libraries described in this section are typically implemented in user space rather than the operating system kernel, they provide the necessary isolation of applications from details of the hardware and from the behavior of other processes. In general, the audio and video extensions, servers, and libraries would also be natural places to locate admission control.

5.1. AUDIO

While POSIX and X11 allow reasonably quick cross-platform development on UNIX systems for many interactive applications, every vendor seems to have his own audio and video programming interface. Generally, both audio and video are sequential devices, so that the basic UNIX device or streams model is appropriate, enhanced with the necessary control functionality for adjusting parameters such as the sampling rate, volume for audio and brightness, and frame rate for video. This device model makes it relatively straightforward to incorporate reading from an audio device and reading an audio clip stored in a disk file.

SGI Irix extends the device model by offering up to four logically independent audio streams with mixing performed by the audio hardware. Solaris has a single, non-shareable audio device, but allows several processes to control audio parameters that do not affect the encoding of the audio stream. Audio device abstractions should provide for variable triggering depths on input, i.e., the amount of data resident in the low-level first-in, first-out (FIFO) before the kernel signals to the application that a new chunk of audio data is ready for reading. This would mean that interactive applications could trade low delay for occasional audio glitches, while playback and recording applications could incur a higher delay and fewer context switches. Furthermore, it is currently difficult to ascertain with any accuracy when a particular audio sample was acquired (for audio input) and when it is going to be played (for audio output). Both of these times are important for synchronizing streams and echo cancellation.

The principal deficiency of these audio-as-device models is the lack of resource sharing, i.e., only a single application has access to the audio device until this application explicitly relinquishes control (a kind of cooperative multitasking). System sounds and other background sounds [78] are difficult to implement this way.

An audio API (or engine) should allow serveral applications to share the single speaker by either mixing at various volumes or priority pre-emption. External applications like VU meters [79], recorders, or automatic gain control should be attachable to the audio input and output, without having to be replicated for every application. The audio engine should transparently translate encoding, sampling rates, and channel counts to the desired output format. It may provide for synchronization between several audio streams or, if possible, between an audio stream and a video or MIDI stream. Separating the audio source and sink by a network requires sophisticated playout adjustment at the receiver, particularly if the solution is to be usable beyond an uncongested LAN. Thus, a general system solution seems preferable to every application having to develop its own solution. Design complexities remain; for example, indicating the current talker is more complicated for a system library, as is the compensation for losses or other interventions by the application. Thus, the audio library must provide either almost all the desirable audio services or very few beyond mixing, volume control, and the like.

Existing implementations such as those discussed in [38] favor the client-server model, following the approach taken by the X-window system. Applications contain a clientside library, which transfers audio data to a server running at the workstation with the physical audio input and output devices. The server integrates output requests onto a single physical device either by alternating between them according to some priority order or by mixing them in some user-determined weighting.

The Alib client-server library [80] allows components to be tied together by logical "wires." Such components include telephones, audio input and output devices, speech synthesizers and recognizers, recorders, and playback devices. Commands, sent through a separate command pipeline, are automatically sequentialized, so that a playback operation can be followed immediately by recording audio.

Some attempts have been made at cross-platform APIs with enhanced functionality [81], but these appear to have a number of shortcomings. Most audio APIs seem to be designed mainly for playing back and recording audio clips rather than for real-time use. Netaudio [82] and AudioFile [83, 84] also abandon the UNIX device-as-file model, requiring separate hooks into event handlers, separate read/write routines, and so on. This appears to be a step backward and makes it difficult to use the same code to read from an interactive audio device and a file containing audio data.

Unlike windowing systems, these libraries have separate control and data streams. This makes it difficult to change audio parameters at precisely defined points, e.g., to change the audio encoding when switching between two streams. With the current control structure, this is inherently difficult since devices are controlled asynchronously, causing data in the internal operating systems buffers to be misinterpreted. Some kind of marking of the audio stream is required so that the physical device can be switched at the appropriate instant.

From these discussions, we can identify the following requirements for future work:

- The abstraction should be suitable for high-packet-rate, low-latency, interactive use as well as playback and recording.

- It should support a variety of encodings transparently, with in-line switching between encodings.

- It should be possible either to place the client and server within the same LAN, with low latency and delay jitter, or to spread them across a wide area network (WAN), with large delay jitter and packet loss. In other words, the transport mechanism cannot be a traditional data transport protocol; adaptive compensation of playout delay needs to be handled.

- Streams should be able to share physical audio devices, by pre-emption, mixing, or a combination (lowering volume of other streams).

- Servers should cache sound clips for repeated play.

- Resource reservation may be needed to ensure that decoding and mixing does not exceed the available system capacity.

An operating system enhancement fulfilling these requirements makes it possible to add interactive and playback audio to applications quickly without having to reimplement relatively complicated media handling in every application.

5.2. VIDEO

There seem to be relatively few windowing system extensions that directly integrate motion video. Schnorf [85] describes an extension of the ET++ windowing toolkit, in which motion video, generated by a hardware or software decoder, becomes a first class object that can be clipped and moved like other windowing objects. The XIL [86] toolkit attempts to shield the user from the complexities of video manipulation, frame grabbing, scaling, and compression. In particular, the library automatically composes several operations into a single "molecule," linking, say, frame grabbing and scaling and avoiding unnecessary data copying and normalization. The library automatically downloads the necessary code into the video processor chip on the framegrabber board. However, because of restrictions on what operations can be combined, it is easy to generate sequences for which every other frame is scaled and then dropped. Operations that would appear to be associative are not.

5.3. MULTIMEDIA CONTROL AND SCRIPTING

Apple QuickTime and the MuX multimedia I/O server [87] are examples of operating system extensions that attempt to integrate multimedia objects. QuickTime is limited to a single host, while MuX has a similar architecture as the X-window system, with clients and servers potentially distributed among hosts. Both follow a video production model, with the ability to compose multimedia objects from tracks of audio and video. Lacking are the ability to integrate real-time video and sophisticated user interaction such as hypertext-like linking, as well the integration of graphics.

Another form of simple integration is offered by Microsoft Windows: system events like executing a file can be associated with multimedia objects.

6. SECURITY

Continuous media data poses particular security concerns. For most data, the concern was whether an unauthorized user could read or modify a user's file or process space. If multimedia devices are attached to a workstation, the workstation can become a remotely controlled monitoring device [28]. For example, some workstations were delivered with the audio input device set world-readable, allowing remote listening to whomever attached a process to that device [88, 89]. Some operating systems have added the facility that ownership of these devices follows that of the console, which avoids monitoring of the one sitting in front of the workstation by remote parties, but does not solve the problem of superuser access or "forgetting" to shut off video and audio applications when leaving a group office. Tang [90] suggests enforcing mutual viewing, so that if A can see B, B can also see A, but admits that this is hardly practical in a distributed system. In general, the use of receiver-oriented multicasting for efficiency will make encryption the only viable means of protecting privacy. Zimmermann [88] suggests a capability-based protection system for multimedia operating systems.

If continuous media data are encrypted and decrypted within the application, traditional user-kernel boundaries and attendant copying across that boundary are no longer needed. Buffers can be mapped directly into a number of user memory spaces, shared between user processes. For compressed video, it may be possible to encrypt only parts of the frame or of a frame sequence (I frames for MPEG) to save processing time, as long as the remainder of the frame or frame sequence cannot be displayed at reasonable quality without those encoded parts.

7. CONCLUSION

We have attempted to offer an overview of the challenges of providing integrated continuous media on general-purpose workstations, focusing on issues of CPU scheduling, memory access, and general operating system enhancements, with a brief overview of network implementation issues. The survey has ignored issues of storage scheduling [91] and management [92], as they are generally of less importance for end-user workstations. These issues dominate, however, for video-on-demand servers [93]. It is also not yet clear whether general-purpose workstations and operating systems are the most suitable for large-scale servers, particularly if they are to generate constant rate, synchronous streams for set-top boxes. However, many of the approaches used by the network file system (NFS) and web servers might also be applicable here. Video-on-demand servers are likely to have somewhat different requirements in that their workload is more predictable, primarily because they are mainly dispensing bits rather than processing them.

General purpose, multiuser operating systems can still deliver only relatively small amounts of video information, with very limited processing, even though raw CPU and bus performance would seem to allow much better capabilities. The theoretical issues seem well understood, but implementations need to follow suit.

References

1. A. S. Tanenbaum, *Operating systems: design and implementation.* Englewood Cliffs, New Jersey: Prentice-Hall, 1987.

2. J. L. Peterson and A. Silberschatz, *Operating System Principles.* Reading, Massachusetts: Addison-Wesley, 1983.

3. S. J. Leffler, M. K. McKusick, M. J. Karels, and J. S. Quarterman, *The Design and Implementation of the 4.3BSD UNIX Operating System.* Reading, Massachusetts: Addison-Wesley, 1988.

4. M. J. Bach, *The Design of the Unix Operating System.* Englewood Cliffs, New Jersey: Prentice-Hall, 1986.

5. D. P. Anderson, S.-Y. Tzou, R. Wahbe, R. Govindan, and M. Andrews, "Support for continuous media in the DASH system," Technical Report CSD 89/537, University of California, Berkeley, Oct. 1989.

6. R. Schaufler, "Realtime workstation performance for MIDI," in *Proc. of Usenix Winter Conference,* (San Francisco, California), pp. 139–151, Usenix, Jan. 1992.

7. P. G. Milazzo, "Shared video under Unix," in *Proc. of Usenix Summer Conference,* (Nashville, Tennessee), pp. 369–383, June 1991.

8. D. B. Terry and D. C. Swinehart, "Managing stored voice in the Etherphone system," *ACM Transactions on Computer Systems,* Vol. 6, pp. 3–27, Feb. 1988.

9. B. Arons, C. Binding, K. Lantz, and C. Schmandt, "The VOX audio server," in *Multimedia '89: 2nd IEEE COMSOC International Multimedia Communications Workshop,* (Ottawa, Ontario), Apr. 1989.

10. G. D. Ripley, "DVI – a digital multimedia technology," *Communications ACM*, Vol. 32, pp. 811–822, July 1989.

11. L. F. Ludwig and D. F. Dunn, "Laboratory for the emulation and study of integrated and coordinated media communication," in *SIGCOMM Symposium on Communications Architectures and Protocols*, (Stowe, Vermont), pp. 283–291, ACM, Aug. 1987.

12. A. Hopper, "Pandora – an experimental system for multimedia applications," *ACM Operating Systems Review*, Vol. 24, pp. 19–34, Apr. 1990. also as Olivetti Technical Report.

13. Parallax Graphics, "The Parallax 1280 series videographic processor," technical report, Parallax Graphics, 1987.

14. I. M. Leslie, D. R. McAuley, and D. L. Tennenhouse, "ATM everywhere?" *IEEE Network*, Vol. 7, pp. 40–46, Mar. 1993.

15. D. R. McAuley, "Operating system support for the Desk Area Network," in *Proceedings of the 4th International Workshop on Network and Operating System Support for Digital Audio and Video*, (Lancaster, U.K.), pp. 13–20, Lancaster University, Springer Verlag, Nov. 1993. Lecture Notes in Computer Science 846.

16. M. Hayter and D. McAuley, "The desk area network," *ACM Operating Systems Review*, Vol. 25, pp. 14–21, May 1991.

17. I. M. Leslie, D. R. McAuley, and S. J. Mullender, "Pegasus — operating system support for distributed multimedia systems," *ACM Operating Systems Review*, Vol. 27, pp. 69–78, Jan. 1993.

18. C. J. Lindblad, D. J. Wetherall, W. F. Stasior, J. F. Adam, H. H. Houh, M. Ismert, D. R. Bacher, B. M. Philips, and D. L. Tennenhouse, "Distributed video applications – a software oriented approach," in *Gigabit Networking Workshop (GBN)*, (Toronto, Canada), IEEE, June 1994.

19. K. Patel, B. C. Smith, and L. A. Rowe, "Performance of a software MPEG video decoder," in *Proceedings of ACM Multimedia 93*, (Anaheim, California), ACM, Aug. 1993.

20. Sun Microsystems, *SunVideo User's Guide*. Sun Microsystems, Mountain View, California, Aug. 1994.

21. R. Frederick, "Experiences with real-time software video compression," in *Sixth International Workshop on Packet Video*, (Portland, Oregon), Sept. 1994.

22. T. Turletti, "The INRIA videoconferencing system IVS," *Connexions*, Vol. 8, pp. 20–24, Oct. 1994.

23. H.-C. Huang, J.-H. Huang, and J.-L. Wu, "Real-time software-based video coder for multimedia communication systems," in *Proceedings of ACM Multimedia '93*, (Anaheim, California), pp. 65–73, Aug. 1993.

24. H. Schulzrinne, "Voice communication across the Internet: A network voice terminal," Technical Report TR 92-50, Dept. of Computer Science, University of Massachusetts, Amherst, Massachusetts, July 1992.

25. W. Tawbi, F. Horn, E. Horlait, and J.-B. Stéfani, "Video compression standards and quality of service," *Computer Journal*, Vol. 36, pp. 43–54, Feb. 1994.

26. J. K. Ousterhout, "Why aren't operating systems getting faster as fast as hardware?" in *Proc. of Usenix Summer Conference*, (Anaheim, California), pp. 247–256, June 1990. Code archived at http://ftp.digital.com/pub/BSD/UCB/bench.tar.Z and ftp://ftp.cs.berkeley.edu/ucb/sprite/bench.tar.Z.

27. D. P. Anderson and R. Wahbe, "A framework for multimedia communication in a general-purpose distributed system," Tech. Rep. UCB/CSD 89/498, University of California at Berkeley, CS Division, Berkeley, California, Mar. 1989.

28. A. Pearl, "System support for integrated desktop video conferencing," Technical Report TR-92-4, Sun Microsystems Laboratories, Mountain View, California, Dec. 1992.

29. Ç. M. Aras, J. F. Kurose, D. S. Reeves, and H. Schulzrinne, "Real-time communications in packet-switched networks," *Proceedings of the IEEE*, Vol. 82, pp. 122–139, Jan. 1994.

30. M. B. Jones, "Adaptive real-time resource management supporting modular composition of digital multimedia services," in *Proceedings of the 4th International Workshop on Network and Operating System Support for Digital Audio and Video*, (Lancaster, U.K.), pp. 21–28, Lancaster University, Nov. 1993. Lecture Notes in Computer Science 846.

31. R. G. Herrtwich, "The role of performance, scheduling, and resource reservation in multi-media systems," in *Operating Systems of the 90s and Beyond* (A. Karshmer and J. Nehmer, eds.), (Dagstuhl Castle, Wadern, Germany), pp. 279–284, July 1994. Springer Lecture Notes in Computer Science 563.

32. R. L. Cruz, "A calculus for network delay, part I: Network elements in isolation," *IEEE Transactions on Information Theory*, Vol. 37, pp. 114–131, Jan. 1991.

33. R. L. Cruz, "A calculus for network delay, part II: Network analysis," *IEEE Transactions on Information Theory*, Vol. 37, pp. 132–141, Jan. 1991.

34. D. P. Anderson, "Meta-scheduling for distributed continuous media," Technical Report UCB/CSD 90/599, University of California, Berkeley, Oct. 1990.

35. R. Govindan, "Operating systems mechanisms for continuous media," Tech. Rep. UCB/CSD 92/697, University of California, Berkeley, July 1992.

36. D. P. Anderson, "Metascheduling for continuous media," *ACM Transactions on Computer Systems*, Vol. 11, pp. 226–252, Aug. 1993.

37. R. Govindan and D. P. Anderson, "Scheduling and IPC mechanisms for continuous media," Technical Report CSD-91-622, University of California at Berkeley, Berkeley, California, Mar. 1991.

38. R. Terek and J. Pasquale, "Experiences with audio conferencing using the X window system, UNIX, and TCP/IP," in *Proc. of Usenix Summer Conference*, (Nashville, Tennessee), pp. 405–418, June 1991.

39. J. Nieh, J. G. Hanko, J. D. Northcutt, and G. A. Wall, "SVR4 UNIX scheduler unacceptable for multimedia applications," in *Proceedings of the 4th International Workshop on Network and Operating System Support for Digital Audio and Video*, (Lancaster, U.K.), pp. 41–53, Lancaster University, Nov. 1993. Lecture Notes in Computer Science 846.

40. S. McCanne and C. Torek, "A randomized sampling clock for CPU utilization estimation and code profiling," in *Proc. of Usenix Winter Conference*, (San Diego, California), pp. 387–394, Jan. 1993.

41. T. Sanderson, S. Ho, N. Heijden, E. Jabs, and J. L. Green, "Near-realtime data transmission during the ICE comet Giacobini-Zinner encounter," *ESA Bulletin*, Vol. 45, pp. 21–23, Feb. 1986.

42. H. Tokuda, T. Nakajima, and P. Rao, "Real-time Mach: Towards a predictable real-time system," in *Proc. of USENIX Mach Workshop*, (Burlington, Vermont), pp. 73–82, Oct. 1990.

43. S. Khanna, M. Sebrée, and J. Zolnowsky, "Realtime scheduling in SunOS 5.0," in *Proc. of Usenix Winter Conference*, pp. 375–390, 1992.

44. O. Hagsand and P. Sjdin, "Workstation support for real-time multimedia communication," in *Proc. of Usenix Winter Conference*, (San Francisco, California), pp. 133–142, Usenix, Jan. 1994.

45. N. C. Audsley, A. Burns, M. F. Richardson, and A. J. Wellings, "Hard real-time scheduling: The deadline monotonic approach," in *Proceedings 8th IEEE Workshop on Real-Time Operating Systems and Software*, (Atlanta, Georgia), pp. 127–132, IEEE, May 1991.

46. C. L. Liu and J. W. Layland, "Scheduling algorithms for multiprogramming in a hard real-time environment," *Journal of the ACM*, Vol. 20, pp. 46–61, Jan. 1973.

47. J. Lehoczky, L. Sha, and Y. Ding, "The rate monotonic scheduling algorithm: Exact characterization and average case behavior," in *IEEE Real-Time Systems Symposium*, (Santa Monica, California), pp. 166–171, IEEE, Dec. 1989.

48. L. Sha, R. Rajkumar, and J. P. Lehoczky, "Priority inheritance protocols: an approach to real-time synchronization," *IEEE Transactions on Computers*, Vol. 39, pp. 1175–1185, Sept. 1990.

49. B. Sprunt, L. Sha, and J. P. Lehoczky, "Aperiodic task scheduling for hard real-time systems," *The Journal of Real-Time Systems*, Vol. 1, pp. 27–60, June 1989.

50. J. Y.-T. Leung and J. Whitehead, "On the complexity of fixed-priority scheduling of periodic, real-time tasks," *Performance Evaluation*, Vol. 2, pp. 237–250, 1982.

51. N. Audsley and A. Burns, "Real-time system scheduling," Tech. Rep. YCS 134, University of York, 1990. First year report, ESPRIT BRA Project (3092).

52. R. Rajkumar, L. Sha, and J. P. Lehoczky, "Real-time synchronization protocols for multiprocessors," in *Proceedings of the IEEE Real-Time Systems Symposium*, (Huntsville, Alabama), IEEE, Dec. 1988.

53. J. Nakajima, M. Yazaki, and H. Matsumoto, "Multimedia/realtime extensions for the Mach operating system," in *Proc. of Usenix Summer Conference*, (Nashville, Tennessee), pp. 183–198, June 1991.

54. C. W. Mercer, S. Savage, and H. Tokuda, "Processor capacity reserves: An abstraction for managing processing usage," in *4th Workshop on Workstation Operating Systems (WWOS-IV)*, (Napa, California), pp. 129–134, IEEE Computer Society, Oct. 1993.

55. C. W. Mercer, S. Savage, and H. Tokuda, "Processor capacity reserves: Operating system support for multimedia applications," in *Proceedings of the IEEE International Conference on Multimedia Computing and Systems*, (Boston, Massachusetts), pp. 90–99, May 1994. (This is a condensed version of tech report CMU-CS-93-157.).

56. K. Jeffay, "On kernel support for real-time multimedia applications," in *Proceedings Third IEEE Workshop on Workstation Operating Systems*, (Key Biscayne, Florida), pp. 39–46, Apr. 1992.

57. K. Jeffay, D. Stone, and D. Poirier, "Yartos: kernel support for efficient, predictable real-time systems," in *Real-Time Programming* (W. A. Halang and K. Ramamritham, eds.), pp. 7–12, Pergamon Press, 1992.

58. S. Evans, K. Clarke, D. Singleton, and B. Smaalders, "Optimizing Unix resource scheduling for Unix interaction," in *Proc. of Usenix Summer Conference*, (Cincinnati, Ohio), pp. 205–218, June 1993.

59. K.-J. Lin, S. Natarajan, and J. W.-S. Liu, "Imprecise results: utilizing partial computations in real-time systems," in *Proc. of the Eighth IEEE Real-Time Systems Symposium*, (San Jose, California), pp. 210–217, Dec. 1987.

60. J. K. Dey Sircar, J. F. Kurose, and D. Towsley, "On-line scheduling policies for a class of IRIS (increasing reward with increasing service) real-time tasks," *IEEE Transactions on Computers*, Vol. 45, pp. 802–812, July 1996.

61. J. K. Dey, J. F. Kurose, D. Towsley, and M. Girkar, "Efficient on-line processor scheduling for a class of IRIS (increasing reward with increasing service) real-time tasks," in *Proc. of ACM Sigmetrics Conference*, pp. 217–228, May 1993.

62. J. G. Hanko, E. M. Kuerner, J. D. Northcutt, and G. A. Wall, "Workstation support for time-critical applications," in *Proc. 2nd International Workshop on Network and Operating System Support for Digital Audio and Video (NOSSDAV)*, (Heidelberg, Germany), pp. 4–9, Springer, Nov. 1991. Lecture Notes in Computer Science 614.

63. H. Tokuda and T. Kitayama, "Dynamic QoS control based on real-time threads," in *Proceedings of the 4th International Workshop on Network and Operating System Support for Digital Audio and Video*, (Lancaster, U.K.), pp. 114–123, Lancaster University, Nov. 1993. Lecture Notes in Computer Science 846.

64. S. Ramanathan and P. V. Rangan, "Feedback techniques for intra-media continuity and inter-media synchronization in distributed multimedia systems," *Computer Journal*, Vol. 36, pp. 19–31, Feb. 1993.

65. S. Ramanathan and V. P. Rangan, "Adaptive feedback techniques for synchronized multimedia retrieval over integrated networks," *IEEE/ACM Transactions on Networking*, Vol. 1, pp. 246–260, Apr. 1993.

66. D. C. A. Bulterman, "Synchronization of multi-sourced multimedia data for heterogeneous target systems," in *Third International Workshop on network and operating system support for digital audio and video*, (San Diego, California), pp. 110–120, IEEE Communications Society, Nov. 1992.

67. T. D. C. Little, A. Ghafoor, C. Y. R. Chen, C. S. Chang, and P. B. Berra, "Multimedia synchronization," *The Quarterly Bulletin of the IEEE Computer Society Technical Committe on Data Engineering*, Vol. 14, pp. 26–35, Sept. 1991.

68. D. L. Mills, "Internet time synchronization: the network time protocol," *IEEE Transactions on Communications*, Vol. 39, pp. 1482–1493, Oct. 1991.

69. R. Ramjee, J. Kurose, D. Towsley, and H. Schulzrinne, "Adaptive playout mechanisms for packetized audio applications in wide-area networks," in *Proceedings of the Conference on Computer Communications (IEEE Infocom)*, (Toronto, Canada), pp. 680–688, IEEE Computer Society Press, Los Alamitos, California, June 1994.

70. AT&T, *Streams Programmers Guide and Streams Primer*. Englewood Cliffs, New Jersey: Prentice Hall, 1987.

71. S. McCanne and V. Jacobson, "A BSD packet filter: A new architecture for user-level packet capture," in *Proc. of Usenix Winter Conference*, (San Diego, California), pp. 259–269, Usenix, Jan. 1993.

72. M. Pasieka, P. Crumley, A. Marks, and A. Infortuna, "Distributed multimedia: how can the necessary data rates be supported?" in *Proc. of Usenix Summer Conference*, (Nashville, Tennessee), pp. 169–182, June 1991.

73. D. Clark, V. Jacobson, J. Romkey, and M. Salwen, "An analysis of TCP processing overhead," *IEEE Communications Magazine*, Vol. 27, pp. 23–29, June 1989.

74. A. Wolman, G. Voelker, and C. A. Thekkath, "Latency analysis of TCP on ATM network," in *Proc. of Usenix Winter Conference*, (San Francisco, California), pp. 167–179, Usenix, Jan. 1994.

75. C. Partridge and S. Pink, "A faster UDP," *IEEE/ACM Transactions on Networking*, Vol. 1, pp. 429–440, Aug. 1993.

76. C. Topolcic, "Experimental internet stream protocol, version 2 (ST-II)," Request for Comments (Experimental) 1190, Internet Engineering Task Force, Oct. 1990. (Obsoleted by RFC1819).

77. L. Delgrossi, R. G. Herrtwich, and F. O. Hoffmann, "An implementation of ST-II for the Heidelberg transport system," *Internetworking: Research and Experience*, Vol. 5, pp. 43–69, June 19943.

78. W. W. Gaver, "Sound support for collaboration," in *Proceedings of the Second European Conference on Computer-Supported Cooperative Work (ECSCW'91)* (L. Bannon, M. Robinson, and K. Schmidt, eds.), (Amsterdam, The Netherlands), pp. 293–308, Amsterdam, Sept. 1991.

79. H. A. Chinn, D. K. Gannett, and R. M. Morris, "A new standard volume indicator and reference level," *Bell System Technical Journal*, Vol. 19, pp. 94–137, Jan. 1940.

80. S. Angebranndt, R. L. Hyde, D. H. Luong, N. Siravara, and C. Schmandt, "Integrating audio and telephony in a distributed workstation environment," in *Proc. of Usenix Summer Conference*, (Nashville, Tennessee), pp. 419–435, June 1991.

81. G. V. Neville-Neil, "Current efforts in client/server audio," *X Resource*, Vol. 8, pp. 69–86, 1992.

82. J. Fulton and G. Renda, "The network audio system," in *X Technical Conference*, X Consortium, Cambridge, Massachusetts, 1994. also in *X Resource: A Practical Journal of the X Window System*, O'Reilly, Issue 9, pp. 181–194.

83. T. M. Levergood, A. C. Payne, J. Gettys, W. G. Treese, and L. C. Stewart, "Audiofile: a network-transparent system for distributed audio applications," in *Proc. of Usenix Summer Conference*, (Cincinnati, Ohio), pp. 219–236, June 1993.

84. T. M. Levergood, A. C. Payne, G. James, G. W. Treese, and L. C. Stewart, "AudioFile: A network-transparent system for distributed audio applications," Technical Report 93/8, Digital Equipment Corporation, Cambridge Research Lab, Cambridge, Massachusetts, June 1993.

85. P. Schnorf, "Integrating video into an application framework," in *Proc. of ACM Multimedia*, (Anaheim, California), pp. 411–417, Aug. 1993.

86. Sun Microsystems, *XIL Programmer's Guide*. Sun Microsystems, Mountain View, California, Aug. 1994.

87. E. Rennison, R. Baker, D. D. Kim, and Y.-H. Lim, "MuX: an X co-existent time-based multimedia I/O server," *The X Resource*, Vol. 1, pp. 213–233, Winter 1992.

88. C. Zimmermann, "Making distributed multimedia systems secure: the switchboard approach," *ACM Operating Systems Review*, Vol. 28, pp. 88–100, Jan. 1994.

89. C. C. Center, "Cert advisory ca-93:15: /usr/lib/sendmail, /bin/tar, and /dev/audio vulnerabilities," Oct. 1993.

90. J. C. Tang and E. A. Isaacs, "Why do users like video? Studies of multimedia-supported collaboration," Technical Report TR-92-5, Sun Microsystems Laboratories, Mountain View, California, Dec. 1992.

91. A. L. N. Reddy and J. Wyllie, "Disk scheduling in a multimedia I/O system," in *Proc. of ACM Multimedia*, (Anaheim, California), pp. 225–233, Aug. 1993.

92. C. Yu, W. Sun, D. Bitton, Q. Yang, R. Bruno, and J. Yus, "Efficient placement of audio data on optical disks for real-time applications," *Communications ACM*, Vol. 7, pp. 862–871, July 1989.

93. K. Ramakrishnan, L. Vaitzblit, C. Gray, U. Vahalia, D. Ting, P. Tzelnic, S. Glaser, and W. Duso, "Operating system support for a video-on-demand file service," in *Proceedings of the 4th International Workshop on Network and Operating System Support for Digital Audio and Video*, (Lancaster, U.K.), pp. 216–227, Lancaster University, Nov. 1993. Lecture Notes in Computer Science 846.

31

HYPERMEDIA TECHNIQUES FOR DISTRIBUTED SYSTEMS

Mark Kessler[1] and Borko Furht[2]
[1]Motorola, Inc., Boynton Beach, Florida
[2]Florida Atlantic University, Boca Raton, Florida

1. **INTRODUCTION**..650
2. **HYPERTEXT** 652
    2.1 BASIC APPROACHES TO HYPERTEXT 652
    2.2 THE DEXTER HYPERTEXT REFERENCE MODEL 653
3. **HYPERMEDIA RELATED STANDARDS**...................................655
    3.1 STANDARD GENERALIZED MARKUP LANGUAGE (SGML) 656
    3.2 HYTIME..658
    3.3 MHEG 660
4. **EXTENDING HYPERTEXT TO HYPERMEDIA** 660
    4.1 HYPERMEDIA USING A WORD PROCESSING PARADIGM................660
    4.2 MOSAIC 662
    4.3 THE DEVISE HYPERMEDIA MODEL...666
    4.4 THE AMSTERDAM HYPERMEDIA MODEL 669
5. **COMPARISON OF DIFFERENT APPROACHES** 675
6. **CONCLUSION AND FUTURE WORK**.....................................676
    REFERENCES 679

Abstract. This chapter is a survey of research issues for hypermedia in distributed systems. The chapter begins by describing the assumptions made in reference to the environment and high level functions that a distributed hypermedia system needs to support. A state-of-the-art model for hypertext systems is presented, and then relevant standards efforts that impact the hypermedia landscape are described. Three projects that are focused on extending hypertext technologies to support hypermedia are reviewed and compared. Finally, conclusions based on this survey and opportunities for future work are presented.

1. INTRODUCTION

Hypermedia is a hypertext information system where the components of information are not constrained to be text. Hypertext is a system of text management that facilitates nonlinear text traversal. In general, the scope of hypermedia is focused not only on the components of information in a document(s) but on the space and relationships between them. Hypermedia systems inherently support compound documents with multimedia components. Compound documents refer to digital formats that contain multiple media types. A document with text, bitmapped images, spreadsheets, audio, and video is an example of such a document. One aspect of a compound document that distinguishes it from a more traditional document type is that the notion of active concurrent execution is embedded into the document. For example, "reading" audio data implies running a program that will use the audio data as input; it would make sense "reads audio concurrently with other activities." Hypermedia can be summarized as a technology used to connect, link, organize and exploit the relationships between information in various formats. Distributed systems are defined to mean loosely coupled computers, each with an autonomous memory, clock, CPU and file system but supporting a high degree of resource sharing and high rates of information exchange. Distributed systems are also implicitly multi-user by nature. Consequently, hypermedia documents in distributed systems may have components that support a variety of digital media, are decentralized across a network, and provide the opportunity for concurrent access by multiple users.

Hypermedia is, in some sense, an extension of traditional hypertext technology to include support for multimedia components. The fundamental differences between hypertext, multimedia, and hypermedia are illustrated in Figure 1. The VanDam article [39] is an excellent first person summary of the important threads in early hypertext research and outlines challenges that are still pertinent for current hypermedia systems. Some of the more successful applications of hypertext/hypermedia include training, on-line help, and network based information retrieval and navigation. In general, hypertext tools have provided powerful methods for informally categorizing and managing information. There are literally hundreds of systems available in both research and commercial settings that are designed to provide this capability and there is substantial interest in the extension of these systems to support the rapidly evolving multimedia environment. However, there are significant challenges.

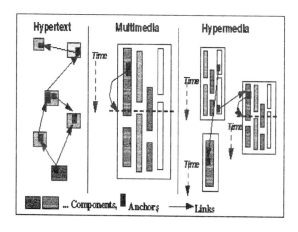

Figure 1. Timing issues in hypertext, multimedia, and hypermedia.

Virtually all of the computing environments in widespread use today are heavily influenced by architectural decisions made over the past several decades. Since multimedia applications are relatively new, the majority of these environments were not designed with the demands of multimedia in mind. It is often true that these demands are more stringent but in many cases they are simply different. Network traffic for "traditional" data, such as file transfers or remote execution of binary files, is bursty, not very time sensitive (in the sense of real-time constraints), and has an extremely low tolerance to error. By contrast, multimedia traffic often has real-time constraints with synchronization requirements, and it is high volume long duration data that has a greater tolerance to errors. The pattern that most current systems used as guidelines for determining design parameters is not always appropriate. For example, if the data being transmitted is encoded video and audio data with real-time playback requirements on a remote system, not only are the files huge but the transfer requirements are quite different than a traditional file transfer.

A reasonable approach is to buffer a portion of the data at the receiving end and begin playback when a sufficient amount of data has been received. The design constraints introduced by this situation are very different than transferring any size data or locally executing a remote file across a network.

In addition, there is an absence of formal foundations for the hypertext models as compared to other systems for managing and cataloging information. An interesting point of reference is the relational model for database systems. Both systems fundamentally allow the reuse or viewing of existing data in new ways without the overhead of recreating or redefining data, and they both do it in a way that guarantees its integrity. As data becomes more complex, including the huge files that are required for digital video and audio, creative navigation and reuse without duplication become increasingly important issues. However, the underlying models for accessing and creating a database are at a much more mature level than they are for hypertext systems.

The introduction of multimedia material into this setting presents a unique set of challenges for extending the informal but well understood technology of hypertext systems to the relatively new environment of multimedia documents and hypermedia applications.

This situation, of a shifting paradigm and more challenging requirements, spans user interface development, networking, operating systems, and computer architectures. It is clear to most researchers that substantial convergence of technology will be required to effectively support broad-based hypermedia applications. This includes technology that is currently in an evolving state, which makes a detailed projection of computing environments a hazardous endeavor. However, it is clear what some underlying characteristics of a state-of-the-art environment for the next few years are likely to be.

These include exploitation of scaleable display technology, powerful graphical user interface and system navigation tools, heterogeneous distributed environments, and tightly integrated networking technologies that may extend into a wireless domain. It is also reasonable to expect that the development tools will require a sophisticated understanding of this environment but will probably shield the developer from some of the implementation details. This is currently evidenced by cross platform development tools that encapsulate abstractions for a graphical interface, an operating system interface (with a model for distributed memory and/or messaging), a networking interface, and a database management system interface. The assumptions made here are that these trends will continue and accelerate.

2. HYPERTEXT

In order to understand the issues associated with hypermedia, one approach is to analyze the fundamental technologies implemented in hypertext systems and then to evaluate opportunities for extending those technologies to include multimedia support. This section provides a brief overview of the hypertext technology and some of the issues that need to be addressed in order to effectively support hypermedia.

2.1 BASIC APPROACHES TO HYPERTEXT

Fundamentally, a hypertext system provides its users with the ability to create, manipulate, and examine a network of information containing components interconnected by relational links. Hypertext software allows an author to annotate a document by creating links to other components within the document or other documents in their entirety. Traversing this network of links provides a method to navigate within and between nodes (documents) in an extremely powerful fashion. In practice nodes have most often been text components. In its simplest form, this could be used to allow a reference to another document to have a link attribute to the actual information so the user could see the referenced information in its entirety by simply invoking the reference (for example, with a mouse click).

To illustrate the difference between this and a database, consider the example of a collection of movies both cataloged by a relational database and annotated by a hypertext system. The database would support information retrieval not explicitly predetermined, such as all the movies directed by "x." On the other hand, the hypertext system would allow users to explicitly construct or follow references, such as if you liked "x"'s work in movie "y," you might also be interested in movie "z," without formally classifying the relationship between x, y and z.

Just like the characteristics of a relational model are at the heart of supporting and manipulating a relational database, the collection and properties of these "links" in a hypertext system are at the heart of its capabilities. In essence, the hypertext system allows you to add a dynamic aspect to information that was not previously possible and traverse it in an extremely flexible fashion, but it does not support new combinations of data based on ad hoc criteria (such as queries).

There are a number of issues that immediately arise in the design of a hypertext system. They include:

- the fundamental choice of altering a document's structure to include hypertext information or storing the information externally,
- the basic unit of reference for links,
- the presentation of links to the user,
- the management of internal and external links,
- attributes of links,
- the management of unresolved link properties, and
- link formats and support for dual modes of interaction (i.e., authoring or navigation only).

Unfortunately, there does not exist a universally accepted theoretical model for describing the behavior of hypertext systems and there are a wide variety of design decisions, which are made during implementation. For example, Intermedia [10,41] and NoteCards [11] provide users with a universe of arbitrary-length documents while KMS [1] and HyperCard [2,17] are built around a model of a fixed-size canvas onto which items such as text and graphics can be placed. This situation makes it difficult to separate the fundamental characteristics of a hypertext system from specific applications. However, there has been some recent work in this area as represented by the Dexter model.

3.2 THE DEXTER HYPERTEXT REFERENCE MODEL

This model is an effort to formally capture the important characteristics and abstractions of current hypertext systems. This work was initiated at two small workshops on hypertext with representation from many of the major hypertext systems and researchers. The first workshop was held in 1988 at the Dexter Inn in New Hampshire—hence the name. The goal of this effort has been to provide a principled method for comparing hypertext systems and to form a basis for developing interchange and interoperability standards. The discussion here is intended to illustrate some of the more important technical aspects of hypertext and to put the issues of hypermedia in context. A more detailed presentation can be found in the article by Halasz and Schwartz [12], and a formal specification in the Z language is available from NIST [13].

The Dexter model is divided into three layers: run-time, storage, and within component layers. The run-time layer describes the mechanisms supporting the user interaction with the hypertext. The storage layer describes the network of nodes and links that are the heart of a hypertext system. The within component layer ascribes the content and structure within hypertext nodes. The main emphasis of the Dexter model is on the basic node-link network structure as outlined in the storage layer. The architecture of the Dexter model is illustrated by Figure 2.

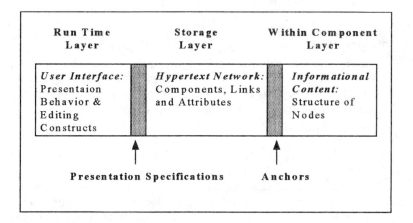

Figure 2. Dexter architecture.

The storage layer describes the structure of a hypertext as a finite set of components together with *a resolver* and *an accessor* function. These two functions are jointly responsible for retrieving components, which are the fundamental unit of addressability in the storage layer. A component is an atom, a link, or a composite entity made from other components. Atomic components are primitives in this layer of the model and they are often referred to as nodes in the literature. Atoms are an attempt at abstracting the properties of nodes as represented by many different hypertext systems (such as cards, frames, documents, and statements in NoteCards, KMS Intermedia, and Augment, respectively).

The internal structure of the component is not specified in this layer of the model but is in the domain of the within-component layer. Links are entities that represent relations between other components. They are a sequence of two or more endpoint specifications, each of which refers to a component of the hypertext. Link attributes are used to specify information about the link that may not be inherent in the component. For example, link attributes may contain the information for invoking the target of a link in a view only or an editable mode. Composite components, as their name indicates, are constructed out of other components.

The composite component hierarchy, created by a container relationship of composite components, is restricted to be a directed acyclic graph (DAG), i.e., a component can be a subcomponent of multiple composites but it may not contain itself either directly or indirectly. Composite components are relatively scarce in the current generation of hypertext systems. Every component has a globally unique identity, which is represented by a unique identifier (UID). Utilizing UIDs provides a mechanism for addressing any component in the hypertext but it is too restrictive in a general sense. Specifically, it is very desirable to support access to components using a more indirect form of addressing. This is the role of the resolver function. For example, to create a link to a statement, which contains some specific attribute (such as containing the word "links to"). The statement may not exist at the time the link is generated or it may change over time as the text is manipulated. In either case, the choice of a hard-coded UID to reference the link is a poor one.

The resolver function is responsible for taking a component specification (or attribute) and returning a UID or set of UIDs that the accessor function can then use to obtain the desired component(s). This mechanism is intended to solve the problem of dangling links, which are implicitly avoided in Dexter, and links that change over time. UIDs are primitive in the model, but they are assumed to be uniquely assigned across the entire universe of interest, i.e., the model specifically supports a scope of interest that spans more than one hypertext while preserving the uniqueness of component identifiers (UIDs).

The interface between the hypertext network and the within-component structure is handled by a mechanism known as anchoring. This mechanism is required to support links between multiple documents as well as between a span of characters in one document and a span of characters in another document. The requirement implies that a link can specify or point to a substructure within a component while at the same time preserving the independence of the storage and within component layers of the model. As a result, the mechanism used cannot depend in any way on knowledge of the internal structure of components.

To achieve this goal, an anchor has two components: an anchor id and a value. The anchor value is an arbitrary value that specifies some location, region, item, or substructure of a component. This anchor value is treated as a primitive by the hypertext system; it is used and maintained only by the application responsible for handling the content structure of the component. The *anchor id* is a component that uniquely identifies an anchor within the scope of its component, and hence anchors can be uniquely identified across the universe with a (component UID, anchor id) tuple. Anchors provide the primary mechanism for interface between the storage layer and the within component layer. In summary, an anchor provides a fixed point of reference that is used by the storage layer and a variable field for use by the within-component layer.

There is an additional entity called a specifier that extends the concept of an anchor by encapsulating two additional fields, a direction and a presentation specification. The specifier entity describes fully the end points of a link as a sequence of two or more specifiers. It is important to note that this definition allows links to multiple targets, even though most current systems do not support links to multiple targets. Multiple targets would have a natural application in hypermedia settings where traversing a link might result in the initiation of multiple activities such as audio, video, or still images being displayed concurrently with text.

The storage layer also has an associated set of operations that can be used to access and/or modify a hypertext. Access operations include retrieving a component given its UID, or any specifier that can be resolved to its UID, and determining the interconnectivity of the network structure (LinksTo and LinksToAnchor). *The modify* operations include adding a component to a hypertext, deleting a component from the hypertext, and modifying the contents or ancillary information (such as anchors or attributes) of a component. This must all be accomplished while maintaining the invariants of the hypertext. The invariants of a Dexter hypertext are equivalent to maintaining the following set of constraints:

- The accessor function must be an invertible mapping from UIDs to components
- The resolver function must be able to produce all possible valid UIDs
- The acyclic nature (DAG) of the component relationship is preserved

The anchor ids of a component must equal the anchor ids of the specifiers resolving to the component.

The hypertext must be link-consistent: the component specifiers of every link must resolve to extant components, i.e., this requires that when deleting a component, any links whose specifiers resolve to that link must be deleted as well.

The key concept of the run time layer is the instantiation of a component. This is best thought of as the presentation of a component to the user and the user interaction with the information contained within the component. In the Dexter model, a copy of the component is presented to the user, the user interacts with the component, and the altered copy is written back into the storage layer, if desired. Each instantiation is assigned a unique identifier (IID) and there is nothing in the model to prohibit multiple instantiations of the same component. At any given moment, a user may be viewing and editing any number of component instantiations. The run-time layer includes an entity called a session, which serves to keep track of the moment-by-moment mapping between components and their instantiation. If a user deletes a component through one of its instantiations, all other instantiations are automatically removed.

The use of Dexter as a basis for formal exchange of hypertext documents is based on a Structured General Markup Language (SGML) rendering of the entities. SGML and other pertinent standards referenced in this chapter are described in the next section. Dexter provides a more comprehensive model than those used by most current hypertext systems. As a consequence, any practical SGML rendering for exchanging data would require some form of graceful degradation, but they have been successfully demonstrated as an interchange format with proof of concept software for existing hypermedia systems [21].

In summary, Dexter represents a state-of-the-art attempt at modeling and standards for hypertext systems. It is described here as a reference point for extending hypertext to hypermedia. However, before beginning that discussion, there are a number of other pertinent standards efforts that need to be identified.

3. HYPERMEDIA RELATED STANDARDS

The role of standards in an environment that is under transition is critical, not only because of the interoperability that can be achieved by developing standard conformant products, but also because they capture the essence of current thought in a nonproduct specific manner. There are two general approaches to the standardization efforts in hypermedia. One set of efforts is focused on the contents of the information chunks contained in a hypermedia document. Content data can be classified as static or dynamic. Static content types include text, computer graphics, and still (raster) images. Specifications for these content types are relatively mature (GIF, XBM, JPEG, etc.).

Digital forms of dynamic content types include moving raster images, animated computer graphics, recorded audio, MIDI music, and synthetic speech. Specifications for data in these formats are relatively new and still evolving (MPEG, MPEG2, SQL/MM, etc.). The relationship between the content chunks document composition and exchange of content chunks is the general focus of the second type of standards efforts. A brief summary of these standards is presented in this section to facilitate a better understanding of the subsequent discussion.

3.1 STANDARD GENERALIZED MARKUP LANGUAGE (SGML)

SGML is an international standard for document exchange [19]. SGML standardizes the syntax for "tagging" the constituent pieces of information for a composite set of data elements. A set of data elements and their tags constitutes a document. SGML documents are not conceptually limited to traditional printed documents and could include "documents" like spreadsheets with all the implicit (hidden) formulas, a multimedia presentation, or a collection of hypermedia documents. The tags in an SGML document are collectively referred to as markup. Tags constitute a "wrapper" that is universally parsable and provides some indication of the content and the intent for management purposes. SGML is based on the concept of generic markup as opposed to procedural markup.

Procedural markup is focused on how a thing is to be formatted and, in contrast, generic markup is focused on what kind of object is being processed. The benefit of procedural markup is that it can provide rich medium specific formatting. The benefit of SGML documents is that they can be used in multiple contexts by mapping objects to presentation attributes in a specific setting. In essence, SGML is object oriented and captures attributes (like presentation intent, among others) for instantiation at run time. This has the added benefit of being able to manage document components as objects and also to create hierarchies of document components.

The features of definable components and methods for document exchange make SGML an important standard for hypermedia work. Consequently, SGML merits a closer look at some of its components.

3.1.1 SGML Internal Components

Figure 3 illustrates the basic internal components of the SGML architecture for a simple conceptual model of a book. Conceptual components are marked or delineated by tags that, together with the data it contains, constitute an element of the document. The Document Type Definitions (DTDs) describe the formal rules of containment, occurrence, and sequence for the components of a class of documents. Each element type has a content model with notation that is similar to productions using standard BNF conventions.

In Figure 3, the DTD specifies that a book must contain one or more chapters, a chapter contains exactly one title and one or more paragraphs, and so on. Every document represented in SGML consists of a DTD (or a reference to a standard public DTD) and a "document instance set" – the actual marked up information of the document. SGML also provides a mechanism to represent essential non-structural information about an element. This is done with constructs called "attributes." Attributes are associated with elements; each attribute consists of an "attribute name, attribute value." Attribute names and values appear as part of the start-tags; i.e., they are part of the markup and not part of the data. Attributes are similar to variables in a programming language and like a programming language can be strongly or weakly typed. The possible attribute names and value types of particular elements are declared in the governing DTD.

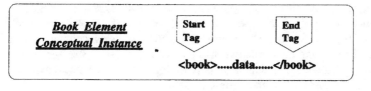

<!ELEMENT book   – – (author,chapter+) >
<!ATTLIST book author CDATA #REQUIRED >
<!ELEMENT chapter   – – (title, para+)>
<!ELEMENT (title|para) – – CDATA >

Book DTD

Book Structure Satisfying DTD

```
<book ...data>
    <chapter>
        <title> ... data... </title>
        <para> ... data ... </para>
    </chapter>
    <chapter>
        <title> ... data ... </title>
        <para> ... data ... </para>
        <para> ... data ... </para>
    </chapter>
<... /book>
```

A Very Simple Book

```
<book author="mgk"><chapter><title>
This is a title</title><para>And a paragraph
</para></chapter></book>
```

Figure 3. Example of SGML.

The "Book" DTD in Figure 3 has "author" as a required attribute of type character data (the weakest and most general data type). There are two special types of attribute values that are routinely used by SGML-based hypertext systems for intra-document links. They are ID and IDREF. If an element has an ID-type attribute, the value of the attribute must be a unique name for that element. If, for any reason, another element makes reference to a uniquely named element, one of its attributes of type IDREF can use that unique name as its value. This unique identifier referencing facility implicitly supports a directed graph style of structure for SGML documents.

There is an additional structure supported in SGML that references any source of data, including a file, a hardware subsystem, a memory buffer, etc. This structure is an entity. If an entire SGML document is contained in a single file, that file is the only entity that the SGML system needs to consult. However, within a more complex document, multiple entity references can occur. These references act in principle like C-language #include "filename" preprocessor directives. The mechanism it uses is an SGML "entity reference open" character, followed by the local name that was associated with some system address in an "<!ENTITY .... >" declaration in the prolog of the document. For example, within a document instance, the appearance of the string "&yourentity" would cause the SGML system to refer to an already-encountered entity declaration and use that as the source of input. This mechanism is extremely beneficial for two reasons. The obvious benefit is using entities as containers of non-SGML data. The second benefit is that it separates the physical structure (entities) from its logical structure (elements) which is important for both distributed environments and documents that may be instantiated in multiple contexts.

3.2 HyTime

HyTime (Hypermedia Time-Based Structuring Language) is a standardized infrastructure for the representation of integrated, open hypermedia documents. It is an international standard that was developed principally by the ANSI committee X3V1.8M and subsequently adopted by ISO [18]. HyTime is an SGML-based standard for hypermedia documents. The standard specifies how concepts common to all hypermedia documents can be represented using SGML and adds mechanisms for modeling time-based structures. These concepts include:

- Association of objects within documents containing hyperlinks
- Placement and interrelation of objects in space and time
- Logical Structure of the document
- Inclusion of non-textual data in the document

An object in HyTime is part of a document that is unrestricted in form – it may be video, audio, text, a program, graphics, or something additional. HyTime is not itself an SGML Data Type Definition (DTD) but it provides the constructs and guidelines for making DTDs that describe hypermedia documents; in essence, it is a meta-DTD. There are six modules that comprise the HyTime specification. They are

Base:
> Provides facilities required by other modules, including formats for specifying applications defined expressions and identification of policies for coping with changes to a document.

Finite Coordinate Space (FCS):
> This allows an object to be scheduled in time and/or space within a bounding box called an event.

Location Address:
> Specifies how to identify locations of document objects by name, coordinate location, or semantic construct.

Hyperlinks:
> Five different types of hyperlinks are provided.

Event Projection:
> Specifies how events in source FCSs are to be mapped onto a target FCS.

Object Modification:
> Facilitates the modification of objects before rendering, in an object specific way.

There are three logical structures supported by SGML/HyTime (see Figure 4). The first can be regarded as a tree of nodes and is referred to as SGML hierarchical element structure. (In SGML syntax, parent elements contain all of their children recursively.) The HyTime hyperlinked structures support arbitrary relationships between nodes to be expressed. For example, a link end need not be an element or an entity, a link can have any number of link ends, each with its own semantic load, and complex traversal semantics can be represented. This is a significant extension to the concept of links supported in SGML using the IDREF pointer to an ID facility as described in the previous section.

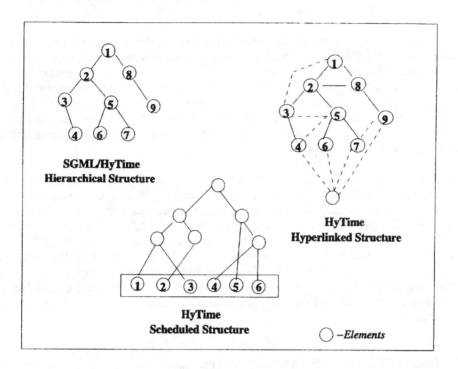

Figure 4. SGML/HyTime structure types.

HyTime scheduled structures is another significant contribution of the HyTime model. Schedule structures are built on the concept of finite coordinate spaces (FCSs) for both events and objects. FCSs can be used to represent any number of different associative lists containing the same data to appear in the document without repeating the data. The semantics of adjacency, co-location, remoteness, etc. of information objects in these lists or schedules is application defined. FCSs can be regarded as

- application-neutral instructions for the temporal and spatial rendition of information intended for human perception,

- application-neutral representations of n-dimensional relational databases, and

- application-neutral means of interchanging dependency data including time dependencies and model information.

HyTime also provides a convention, called "SBENTO," that allows the structure of interleaved data entities to be expressed in an internationally standard fashion and still accessed as independent streams at various points within the data other than the beginning. This is particularly useful since interleaved digital streams for the audio and video components of hypermedia data are fairly common in some formats but need to be separate in others. For example, interleaving might be required to minimize the movement of a head on a CD-ROM, but there may be instances within an application where it is not desirable to access them jointly or work strictly from beginning to end. It is possible that run time capabilities may dictate audio only, or a hypermedia presentation may provide a link into the middle of an audio or visual sequence, or both.

Additional details on the HyTime standard can be found in the references [26, 27].

3.3 MHEG

Multimedia and Hypermedia Information Coding Experts Group (MHEG) refers to both the working group and the draft proposal for hypermedia document representation. This effort is an emerging standard and is focused on two aspects of hypermedia documents, object representation and inter object linking. MHEG represents objects in a non-revisable form and is not intended as an input form. Consequently, MHEG would not be suitable as a format for supporting hypermedia authoring environments. However, it could be used as a common output format for hypermedia authoring tools and, as a result, provide for interoperability of MHEG compliant presentation software.

There are four types of objects currently identified by the standard. These are input objects (i.e., user control like a button or mouse), output objects (graphics, audio, visual display, etc.), interactive objects (both input and output) and hyperobjects (i.e., a composite object consisting of other objects with links between them). MHEG supports a number of synchronization modes for modeling objects and their relationships. While MHEG is not a multimedia document format, it does provide rules for the structure of multimedia objects that support an extensible representation in convenient form. For example, video could be represented as an MPEG [25] data stream. The intent of MHEG is to provide a mechanism for characterizing and standardizing the data structuring activity associated with hypermedia environments.

3.4 MIME

The Multiple Internet Mail Extensions (MIME) are a proposed Internet standard (RFC1341) sponsored by the Internet Architecture Board. MIME is focused primarily on extending the Internet mail specification to multimedia messages, but does it in a way to support user defined types and actions based on the message [20]. This facility makes it useful as a process for exchanging data between programs or using it to support file transfer mechanisms in a manner that is transparent to the end user. MIME also supports several pre-defined types of non-textual message contents, such 8-bit audio, GIF image files, and PostScript programs.

MIME is designed to

- provide facilities to include multiple objects in a single message,
- represent body text in character sets other than US-ASCII,
- represent formatted multi-font text messages,
- represent non-textual material such as images and audio fragments, and
- facilitate extensions defining new types of Internet mail for use by co-operating agents.

4. EXPENDING HYPERTEXT TO HYPERMEDIA

The next issue to be addressed is extending a technology that has been primarily developed for text-based applications to support multimedia components.

4.1 HYPERMEDIA USING A WORD PROCESSING PARADIGM

A "natural" extension of hypertext to hypermedia is accomplished by modifying the underlying text system to include multimedia components. This is generally referred to as including multimedia based on the word processing paradigm. The approach has shortcomings, but it does support multimedia components with dynamic behavior in a hypertext system, and it is a useful mechanism to illustrate the issues. The approach is "natural" in the sense that virtually all of the existing hypertext systems provide a paradigm for tightly integrated support of an underlying text editor/viewer. Adding multimedia support to hypertext is realized by including support for images, video, and audio in the underlying text manipulation mechanism and using the paradigm of a text editor to create and manipulate the data. This is nothing new or unusual; in fact, the inclusion of graphics, video, and audio is becoming more common in a number of word processing programs.

This word processing approach to hypermedia would, in Dexter terms, pushes the multimedia information into the within-component layer and leaves the interpretation of the content entirely up to the application that works on it. This approach fits nicely within most existing hypertext frameworks. A principal issue becomes where to manage the timing relationships of the multimedia components (see Figure 5). Since timing constraints are not actually part of the model there are fundamentally two choices.

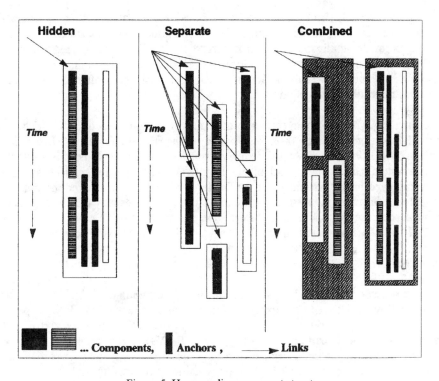

Figure 5. Hypermedia component structure.

One choice is to support applications that hide these complexities from the user. In this instance the user has no choice in the granularity of timing within these applications. The second choice is to provide completely separate structures for the timing of each multimedia component, in effect, providing a level of granularity in the other extreme. There is a synthetic third choice by supporting both of these and providing a combined structure. Much of the literature available on the Dexter model makes no distinction between hypertext and hypermedia with implicit assumptions that hypermedia can be readily addressed with these types of extensions. This is a useful tool for improved understanding, but it does not address the issue that there is a fundamental lack of support for timing constraints within existing hypertext systems and the Dexter model. Recent research and experimental systems indicate that this approach may not scale well and general mechanisms for modeling sophisticated timing relationships are required for advanced applications.

In essence, there are two main problems with the word processing approach to hypermedia. First is the issue of context. In a hypermedia setting, one would like to be able to control some attributes at a global level that provide a context for the multimedia components of a hypermedia application. A simple example would be settings for sound volume. It would often be appropriate to set it as an environment variable (i.e., a context) that all applications using sound could implement as a default.

In addition, there are many behaviors that would be useful to control at a global level, such as

- the initialization of devices,
- identifying capabilities of the environment to support multimedia attributes like video quality, playback rates, and
- support for multiple sessions or the locking of resources by one application to the exclusion of others.

Existing hypertext models simply do not address this set of issues and each atomic component is responsible for managing its own context. The second issue is the robustness of the timing model for hypermedia applications. When hypertext is extended to hypermedia as outlined above, there is no concept in the authoring model that includes timing as part of its composition technique. The resulting fidelity of the timing model is often not adequate for sophisticated applications interactions.

The extension of hypertext to hypermedia continues to be an area of active debate and research. This section describes three recent efforts, the Mosaic Project [44], the DeVise Hypermedia Model [9], and the Amsterdam Hypermedia Model [15]. Mosaic is a distributed hypermedia system that is widely available on the Internet. The other two projects are focused on developing hypermedia systems based on Dexter or a synthesis of Dexter and multimedia methods. These efforts are interesting in the contrasting approaches they take to extending the underlying model, the way they highlight the state of the art, and the contributions that the Dexter model and the related standards efforts have made to the growing body of hypermedia technology.

4.2 MOSAIC

Mosaic was developed at the National Center for Supercomputing Applications at the University of Illinois, Urbana-Champaign. Mosaic is an Internet based global hypermedia browser that supports the discovery, retrieval, and display of documents and data from Internet sources. Mosaic is part of the World Wide Web (W3) project originally developed at CERN and it represents the collaboration of a large informal design and development team that is distributed throughout the globe. Mosaic is uniquely interesting in the sense that it is the Visicalc of distributed hypermedia applications. It has a number of attributes that may, in retrospect, seem primitive in future applications, but it illustrates the power and possibilities of distributed hypermedia systems in a way that has not been previously accomplished and it does it in a truly eye opening way.

Mosaic is best understood in the context of the W3 project components and supporting software (see Figure 6). This includes the Wide Area Information Server (WAIS), the HyperText Markup Language (HTML), the Uniform Resource Loader (URI) and the HyperText Transmission Protocol (HTTP).

The W3 project is a distributed global web of hyperlinks intended to support the navigation of information available on the Internet. This project has focused on developing conventions for hyperlinks, addressing, lookup, and registry technologies for information access and implementation of the conceptual system. Much of the documentation available is in the form

Internet Engineering Task Force documents and is available on line [20]. W3 can be thought of as a truly distributed global hypermedia network of information, where the information content is contained in the files available on the internet and the "links" are the W3 pointers to them. The WAIS software is a registry and resolver mechanism used on the Internet to locate information by providing a logical reference and resolving it to a physical reference. It is not the only mechanism used to find information on the Internet, but it is the preferred method directly supported by Mosaic.

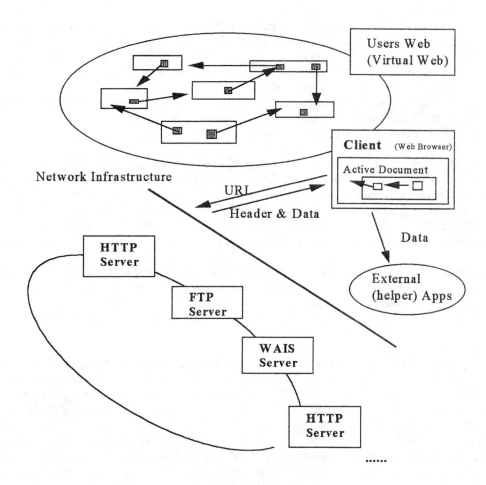

Figure 6. Mosaic in context.

This brief summary clearly glosses over a tremendous amount of information, but W3 is not the focus of this chapter. The essential point is that there exists a web of hyperlink information with a mechanism for resolving symbolic references (names) to accessible physical devices, without *a priori* knowledge of the data content or account management on remote machines. Consequently there is a mechanism for building hyperlink data sets and referencing data independently of the physical location or even the existence of the data. This provides a test bed for the building and active execution of distributed hypermedia documents that can be developed independently of the multimedia components they reference. This is built on a model with few, if any, assumptions about the timing constraints of applications, network speeds, and the content or structure of the information nodes. However, it was designed with implicit assumptions of typical Internet connectivity such as high speed LANs interconnected with dedicated lines and remote access by modem.

The Mosaic software is focused on navigating this web of information (links) and can be thought of as a visual front end to W3. This environment provides a high level of networking integration as well as support for dangling links and autonomous systems that are loosely coupled in the extreme. Within this context some of the most important concepts of Mosaic are viewers, hyperlink authoring, resource loading, and transport mechanism.

4.2.1 Mosaic Viewers
Mosaic is a client/server application that separates the viewing of web data from the navigation, downloading, and network queries for information about the web. Viewing the data runs on a client machine and is relatively autonomous from the other operations. Mosaic has the concept of viewers as resources that are invoked to display or act on the data that is the target of a link. Although it is transparent to the end user, this is a two-step process of downloading the data and then acting on it. There is some limited end user control over this process as the user can specify the viewing program that is invoked or suppress it altogether and save the data in a file for later operations.

Different viewers can be invoked by setting default operations based on file types using methods very similar to most desktop managers for specifying defaults of opening or printing files. One of the strengths of this approach is that Mosaic documents can leverage existing multimedia programs and data. The default Mosaic resources utilize widely available Internet software based on emerging standards including JPEG[40] and MPEG[25] based viewers. It is support for these resources that differentiates Mosaic from other HTML document browsers.

However, the W3 model does not address the fine grained synchronization of multimedia components and it does not provide the opportunity to act directly on data across the network. Consequently, it does not address synchronization issues that are network dependent, and Mosaic does not provide multiple concurrent views of a document on the client side.

4.2.2 Hyper-Text-Markup Language
The goal of HTML is to provide one simple format for describing linked information within all W3 compatible programs. W3 references of the Multipurpose Internet Mail Extensions (MIMES RFC13413) are used to allow objects to be transmitted in an open variety of representations. W3 uses the Hypertext Transfer Protocol, (HTTP), which allows transfer representations to be negotiated between client and server, the result being returned in an extended MIME message. HTML is therefore one of the potentially many representations used with W3. HTML is proposed as a MIME content type and it is a Structured General Markup Language (SGML) Document Type definition (DTD). HTML documents are in plain text format and can be created using any text editor, although there are several rudimentary HTML editors such as tkWWW that hide the HTML details from users with a WYSIWYG interface to documents.

HTML uses case-insensitive tags to tell the W3 viewer (for example, Mosaic) how to display the text. The chief power of HTML is derived from its ability to link regions of text and images to another document. HTML's single hypertext related directive is A, which stands for anchor. For example, a hypertext reference could be specified as follows:

<a href="HockeyStats.html">Hockey</a>

The HTML viewer would interpret "Hockey" as a link to the document "HockeyStats.html."

Anchors can also be used to move to a particular area within a document. Suppose it was desirable to set a link from document A to a specific section in document B. First, what is called a named anchor is set up in document B to serve as a target for the link. For example, to add an anchor named "my_ref" to document B, one would insert

Here's <a name="my_ref">some text</a>

somewhere in document B. Now when a link is created in document A, it includes not only the filename, but also the named anchor, separated with a hash mark (#)

This is my <a href="documentB.html#my_ref>link<a>.

Now clicking on the word "link" in document A would send the reader directly to the words "some text" in document B. Anchors to specific sections within the current document work exactly the same as above, but the file name is omitted.

Image manipulation is an extension of the HTML specification by Mosaic and it is used to support X Bitmap (XBM) or GIF format images inside documents. Images can be aligned with the surrounding text and displayed inline or in all external windows. This can be used to facilitate performance issues. For example, it would be possible to display a low resolution postage stamp image that is used as a hyperlink to the full size image that is displayed in an external window when the link is followed.

4.2.3 URLs and HTTP

A Uniform Resource Locator (URL) is an extension of the standard filename concept for networked environments. Using a URL, it is possible to point to a file in a directory. This file and the directory can exist on any machine on the network, and it can be served via any of several different methods. It might not even be something as simple as a file. URLs can point to queries, documents stored within databases, the results of a finger, or an *archie* command. The URL concept is built on the premise that, if it is on the network somewhere, it can be referenced by a pointer mechanism.

A complete URL consists of a naming scheme specifier followed by a string whose format is a function of the naming scheme. The format of a URL using the REP scheme would be

http://host.domain[:port]/pathname.

The same conventions are appropriate to other schemes. Suppose, for example, that there is a document called "foobar.txt;" it sits on an anonymous ftp server called "ftp.yoyodyne.edu" in a directory "/pub/files." The URL for this file is then in the form:

ftp://ftp.yoyodyne.edu/pub/files/foobar.txt

URL support extends to directories in a direct manner, i.e.,

ftp://ftp.yoyodyne.edu/

The most commonly supported schemes for URLs include file, ftp, gopher, and WAIS. The underlying support for resolving URLs relies on the availability of a message-based system for exchanging information with a service provider of the appropriate type. This is the mechanism that translates references pointed to by URLs into real things in the document. A complete BNF description of URLs is available as an IETF working draft [20].

The final component of the environment is the Hypertext Transfer Protocol. HTTP is a protocol designed specifically for a distributed collaborative hypermedia information system. It is a generic, stateless, object-oriented protocol, which may be used for many similar tasks, such as name servers and distributed object-oriented systems, by extending the commands or "methods" used. An important feature of HTTP is the negotiation of data representation, allowing systems to be built independently of the development of new or advanced representations.

The protocol is built on a message based transaction that consists of establishing a connection, exchanging requests and responses, and then closing the session. The motivation for HTTP is that information systems require more functionality than simple retrieval. The protocol is designed for support that would include performing an index search, implementing front-end update, such as uncompressing or preprocessing a file, annotation, and the ability to refer a client to another server. The HTTP protocol messages themselves are encoded in HTML and, as a result, allow an open-ended set of methods to be used. This is also the mechanism that allows browsers to encapsulate existing resources and separate the presentation of data on the web from the navigation of the web. Additional information on HTTP message types and contents can be found in the IETF working drafts [20].

4.2.4 Mosaic/W3 Summary

Mosaic/W3 has made a substantial contribution by providing a widely available hypermedia technology to a large number of people. The model that it is built on is sophisticated in terms of network integration, message-based transfer protocols, distributed architecture, and adaptation of structured markup techniques. It has also created an opportunity for authoring hypermedia applications at a very sophisticated level to anyone capable of authoring HTML documents. In using Mosaic to research this chapter, it rapidly became apparent that the sophistication is extraordinary for a public domain application. This is a significant contribution to the research community and Mosaic has often been described as the "tour de force" application for illustrating the power of the Internet.

The W3 system, and its ongoing evolution is an important achievement; however, from the view point of hypermedia, it is clearly an early prototype. The concept that Mosaic uses for hyperlinks correlates closely to some of the advanced concepts of linking and anchoring. The components of the URN correspond fairly close to the resolver/specifier functions in spirit and the viewers are effective tools for managing the loosely coupled data that would correspond to the within component layer; but the model (from a hypertext point of view) is relatively simple.

4.3 THE DeVise HYPERMEDIA MODEL (DHM)

The DeVise project, at Aarhus University, Denmark, is writing general purpose tools to support experimental system development and cooperative design in a variety of application areas including large engineering projects [9]. Because the demands of this environment, including a shared database, access from multiple platforms, portability, extensibility, and customization are not met by commercially available systems, the principle investigators of the DeVise project undertook to build their own system based on the Dexter hypertext model. The Devise project turned the Dexter model into an object-oriented design for their prototype system and implemented it on the Apple MacIntosh platform using the BETA programming language. Their implementation includes support for the following:

- persistent objects (an object-oriented database) in which they stored their hypermedia structures,
- text graphics and QuickTime videos at atomic component level, and
- component and link configuration browsing and editing.

Their conclusion is that they were largely successful in taking the approach of a direct implementation of the Dexter model. The issues of links anchors, composites, and cross-layer interfaces are reviewed in some detail to provide insight into the design issues addressed.

Dexter's notion of a link component is heralded as a unifying concept for many hypertext systems. Recall that Dexter can model multithreaded links and, because links are components, they can be the end points of other links as well. The model also supports computed as well as static links through the use of specifier's resolver functions. Simple typing for links is supported by the use of link attributes. The model semantics of Dexter prohibits links with fewer than two end pints (i.e., no dangling links other than the indirect references with the resolver accessor function described earlier). The implementers of DHM found issues primarily with Dexter's presentation of link directionality and dangling links.

DHM advocates support dangling links for several reasons. First, they allow lazy updating and garbage collection following component and anchor deletion. This is particularly useful in a distributor environment when the link to be deleted may be locked by another user or exist on a different machine. Another related issue involves data objects outside the control of the hypermedia For example, the component data may actually be a file that is managed (moved/deleted/edited) by tools independent of the hypermedia. This issue is substantially more important in a distributed heterogeneous multimedia environment than it is in a dedicated homogenous hypertext system. The third reason is that the dangling end points can be a useful tool for editing links. This can be used to avoid the modal start/link end/link creation of most systems and, consequently, create a more robust interface for the user. Dangling links could be created as placeholders to information that may not yet be available (which would be typical in a collaborative distributed work environment), and then be completed as the reference was created at a later time. In addition, it can also be used from a system perspective to gain efficiency in building links by simply reconnecting a dangling link to another component or anchor without having to rebuild the entire link.

The DHM project has identified four situations that were the source of their decision to support dangling links. The end point of a component has been deleted, its anchor has been deleted, relevant objects referred to by the components content are unavailable, and, finally, an anchor value is invalid. The first two cases can be detected within the context of the hypermedia model and presented to the user for resolution. DHM has successfully implemented this strategy for the first case. The last two situations generally result from actions outside the control of the hypermedia. For example, if the component content is a file identifier and the file has been renamed independently of the hypermedia application, this situation could be caught and acted upon by the software.

The followLink operation should catch the file access exception from the operating system, resolve it if possible and, if not, pass it along as a dangling link to the user. In reference to case four, recall that an anchor has two parts, one aced on bar the hypertext and one acted on by the application. If the application is operated independently of the hypermedia, the within component information referenced by the anchor may be modified by an editor outside of the control of the hypermedia and the modifications may invalidate the anchor reference.

Without some facility to update the hypertext model (i.e., some form of messaging between the application and the hypermedia system), this situation is generally impossible to detect and act upon because the invalid anchor information may simply be out of date and not raise an exception. Consider a simple example of a two-minute video clip that is referenced many times at time zero and once 60 seconds from the beginning of clip. If for some reason the first 30 seconds of the video are deemed to be inappropriate and edited out without updating the hypermedia, most references continue to work fine, but one now starts 30 seconds after it should and there is no way of detecting it programmatically.

Anchors are a controlled means of referring to information in the within component layer without relying on intimate knowledge of the component structure. It allows the designer to provide a finer granularity for interacting with the components of a hypermedia without embedding application dependent information within the supporting web of hypermedia nodes and links. Anchors were viewed as a major contribution of the Dexter model because they clearly describe the "glue" connecting network states to the contents of particular components. However, the implementers of DHM encountered difficulties with the relation of anchors to composite components in the Dexter Model.

The basic criticism is that Dexter does not clearly specify how anchors should refer to base components within a parent composite and this ambiguity provides unnecessary latitude of design alternatives with a significant impact on implementation methods. For example, it is not clear whether an anchor should be allowed to indirectly address through a composite component to its base component, i.e., should an anchor in a parent component be allowed to resolve to one of its member component anchors?

The general issue of sharing vs. multiplying anchors is left open in Dexter. DBI extended Dexter's model of anchors in several ways. First, they used dynamic references ("pointers") instead of anchor ids. This has the effect that links the specifier's point directly to component anchors, which eliminates the need for an accessor function. DHM also distinguishes three high level anchor types, which are independent of the enclosing component, while component anchors support a degenerate case of link end points not anchored within a component's contents. A marked anchor is one for which the object is directly embedded in the component's contents. This object is called a link maker in Dexter nomenclature. In addition, unmarked anchors are supported.

The fundamental difference between a marked and an unmarked anchor is that an unsnarled anchor location within a component is not known *a priori* and must normally be computed. This can be useful for determining anchors at run time, for example, based on keyword references for a text component or scene, changes in a video clip component based on some property that could be computed. However, the disadvantage is that the reference requires an inordinate amount of computation and does not run in constant time as does the anchor. The DHN group supports the belief that both techniques should be part of the model.

A similar issue relates to the dynamic aspect of structures that have some unique behavior described at run time. The contribution of the Dexter model in this area is twofold. First, it provides a clean separation of the run time environment and the storage environment. Virtual composites can then be implemented as a simple variant to mature some of this dynamic behavior in the model. Second, the notion that a composite component provides a mechanism for the overall structure of a hypertext into a single node is not possible in a purely link-based system. The DHM project needed to extend these ideas as follow: support of virtual component types for any component, not just composites. Such components resemble normal components but are only saved in the Base if pointed at by anther component.

Virtual components resemble objects in a dynamic computing environment. If they are not pointed at, they can be reclaimed by garbage collection mechanisms during active sessions and lost at the end of a session. Support of computed components for any component type was also added. A typical behavior supported by this extension is a component created on the basis of executing a query. The component contents can later be computed, either automatically or on demand. Computed components in DHM typically reflect the contents or structure of part of the network and are extremely useful for inspecting the network relationships. They may be recomputed periodically or triggered by a change to the status of the network. The final extension is that support for component contents is also advocated. The criticism of the Dexter model in this regard is that it makes assumptions that the components are basically a container mechanism and the contents of components are static and relatively flat. In a hypermedia application, this is generally not the case. The contents are often highly structured and can include external data objects or references to other components as well as behavior.

The issue of an extendible model for component content is of increasing importance when hypermedia is used in a general setting. In the last few years developers have tried to use hypermedia types of links as an integration tool for multimedia applications. There are a number of reasons for this, but they all revolve around the fact that the probability of working within an all encompassing hypermedia system, i.e., one providing an environment for navigation, system interaction, and the application software itself, is actually quite small.

The argument is that, rather than build hypermedia systems that include all of the applications required in a work setting, one should focus on hypermedia as a linking architecture to connect the world and not own it. The Dexter model makes an important contribution to this approach by distinguishing clearly what is in the domain of the application, what is in the domain of the hypertext, and defining a mechanism for interfacing between them. However, Dexter falls short in this area in two ways. First, it does not distinguish between components whose contents are managed by the hypermedia and those whose contents are managed by third party applications. The second, and related problem, is that there is no mechanism for managing documents with a robust internal structure. The sophistication of the Dexter model is limited to embedding these documents in a "Wrapper." The DHM model does not directly address this issue either, but the implementers were confronted with the problem in trying to adopt the Dexter paradigm and describe the issues in some detail [3]. However, this chapter addresses the issues in the context of The Amsterdam Hypermedia Model.

4.4 THE AMSTERDAM HYPERMEDIA MODEL (AHM)

The approach used by The Amsterdam Hypermedia Model developed at CWI (Centrum voor Wiskunde en informatica) is a synthesis of the hypertext and multimedia environments [15]. This work at CWI was an outgrowth of the Multimedia Kernel Systems project, which focused on developing solutions for hypermedia systems that combine the notions of structured documents, flexible runtime scheduling, and hyperlink support. The goal of the project was to attack the problems caused by the use of multimedia in a distributed heterogeneous environment, especially synchronization between data streams originating from different remote sources. One of the expected derivatives is to make multimedia presentations more portable between platforms and easier to change.

This approach represents a significant difference to the one used in the Devise Hype text Model. DHM attempts to directly implement the Dexter Model with extensions as necessary for effective multimedia support. In contrast, AHM fundamentally modifies the Dexter Model by adding to it the motions of time, high-level presentation attributes, and link context. The components of the AHM model axe derived from the Dexter model with extensions to support these issues (see Figure 7). Significant sources of ideas for these extensions are derived from the CMIP (CWI Multimedia-Interchange Format) document model and the CMIF Editor developed to support it [16][42]. As a consequence, it represents a synthesis of hypertext and multimedia techniques by using the CMIF model for the presentation of multimedia documents and the Dexter model to support the user interaction with the presentation.

The synthesis type of approach used in the AHM model is motivated in large part by two issues. First is the issue of collecting and synchronizing components in execution (events). The developers of AHM looked to the Dexter model and composite components to facilitate this activity but came to the conclusion that, without some mechanism to control the relative execution of components within a collection, the model would not be robust enough for their needs. The other issue is link attributes and their management.

If one considers for a moment the nature links in a hypertext model and contrast that with the nature of links in a hypermedia model, it is clear that something has fundamentally changed. First the links used in a text model can be decomposed to virtually any desired granularity and as a result they constitute a relatively flat model.

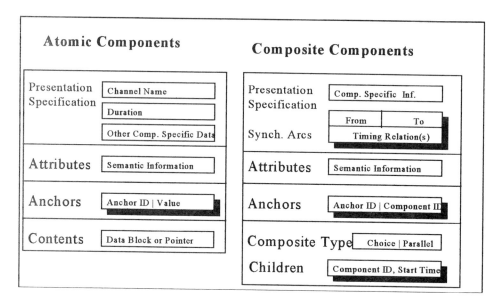

Figure 7. Components of the Amsterdam hypermedia model.

For example, it would be reasonable to have a link that pointed to a document, a paragraph, a sentence, a word, or a character. The granularity of link components directly supports a reference to any desired level of a component within a document. Furthermore, there is a strong synergy between character references and file location, which can facilitate navigation algorithms.

Other media types tend to be very different in the following sense. Links don't have the same level of component granularity, they tend not to have much synergy with file formats, and they are used inherently (even in atomic components) in a new way. For example, consider a video clip as the component referenced by a link. The video clip components are scenes and images (that don't line up well on any particular file boundaries) and may require the support of multiple synchronized links of audio tools and links may be used internally to provide a fast forward reference within the content. Links have the potential to appear within atomic components in a way that is not addressed by the Dexter model and they may have an interpretation that is context sensitive. In addition, there is a context issue regarding what should happen when a link is initiated and when the target is reached.

For example, if the link references an audio target, it may make sense to terminate any audio that is in progress and replace it with the target of the link. However, if the link references a video, it may be more appropriate to start a new process and let it run independently of whatever is currently active, depending on the capabilities of the system and the perceptual model of the viewer. The model needs some mechanism to capture this type of behavior that is not part of the Dexter paradigm.

The primary contribution of ideas from CMIF is in the implementation-independent behavioral model of multimedia and the development and implementation of a paradigm for editing hypermedia applications. These contributions address the problems described above and provide advanced mechanisms for authoring and changing hypermedia presentations. Prior to summarizing the modifications from Dexter that are represented in AMH, a brief outline of the CMIF model and the CMIP editor are presented.

4.4.1 CMIF Model

There are two dominant paradigms currently used in creating multimedia presentations; one is scripting and the other is a timeline. Scripting supports a program-like metaphor, with added constraints on data structures and decision mechanisms, for putting together multimedia presentations. It is particularly useful for small documents but, for larger documents, it is a cumbersome method without well-defined mechanisms for structuring and manipulating components. The timeline paradigm is built around synchronization of components relative to a timing sequence. The problems inherent in this approach are maintaining complex timing mechanisms with reference to editing and manipulating the components of the presentation. The CMIF metaphor creates an alternative that presents the user with a collection of events and timing constraints among those events that can be manipulated. The CMIF editor was implemented in Python, a high level interpreted object oriented prototyping language on the Silicon Graphics UNIX workstations. This initial target environment was chosen because of the rich diversity of multimedia support and the robust development environment. The underlying model includes tree structured documents, events, channels, timing constraints, hyperlinks, and attributes. It is described in the following paragraphs.

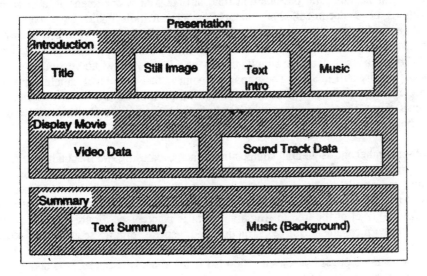

Figure 8. Hierarchy tree map view of CMIF presentation.

The CMIF model describes a document as a tree, which specifies the presentation in an abstract, machine independent way (see Figure 8). The specification is created and edited using an authoring system and it is mapped to particular platform by a viewing system. This implies that a presentation could be overly specified with the viewing system responsible for a graceful degradation of the specification when it is presented. This is considered a feature of the system. This is in sharp contrast to methods that try to implement performance constraints at creation time, such as the approach used for QuickTime video. The fundamental structure of a CMIF document is achieved by recursively building a presentation from a number of sub-presentations. In general, a presentation is either a composite (containing other presentations) or an atomic presentation (not containing others). Consequently a CMIF document is structured like a tree graph whose leaf nodes are atomic presentations.

An atomic presentation is a collection of events. An event is the smallest fragment of media data that is manipulated within the system. It is usually a small fragment of video, audio, image, or text data. The model does not address the contents of this data, but does address certain media specific properties such as width, height, duration, and markers within the data. These are used as reference points for hyperlink access and also for timing constraints in the case of dynamic media. Events refer to the actual data via pointers. These pointers can be filenames or other kinds of reference. Pointers are used to facilitate reusing the same data multiple times without increasing the storage requirements. The media specific property and markers are stored tags with the data. Presentation specific properties are stored with the event. In general there are three levels used for this purpose. The event description describes the event as it occurs in a presentation, a data descriptor describes the static properties of the data, and the data file holds the raw information. The data file specifies where it is in the presentation, attributes about the data format, and the raw data

A channel is an abstraction for a group of properties shared by some events of the same media type. Each event is tied to exactly one channel. Each channel has a media type, which must match the media type of the events assigned to it. Other properties of a channel depend on its media type. For example, an audio channel might specify a playback volume, a text channel might specify a font name, etc. Several channels can have the same media type. This structure is left up to the author at creation time and mapped onto available resources at presentation time, which is consistent with the design philosophy described earlier. Channels provide the mechanism for handling the presentation time attributes of a document as well as parallel presentations of a document. For example, a presentation could have parallel audio explanations in different languages available on multiple channels with the user activating the appropriate one. Similarly, it may be useful to have a parallel visual presentation from multiple perspectives – all active simultaneously or a lower bandwidth version as a sequence of reduced quality still images. The important point is that the model should support all of these presentations and not introduce artificial constraints on the use of the hypermedia. The constraints, if any, should be imposed by run time limitations of the playback device or active design choices.

Support for parallel and sequential composition is achieved using two mechanisms. First order synchronization is accomplished by placing the events in a tree whose nodes specify sequential and parallel compositions. The location in the tree describes a coarse sequencing. Events at the same level can happen in parallel and a coarse grained sequential timing is implied by the level of the tree in which an event is placed (see Figure 8). This provides a relatively easy mechanism for constructing the general timing sequence of document presentation and is outlined in more detail in the user interface description of the hierarchy view. When a more precise synchronization between events is required, it is obtained by the use of synchronization arcs.

A sync arc is a relation between two events in the same atomic presentation (i.e., at the same level of the tree), by specifying a desired delay and the allowed deviations from the desired delay. For example, a video tour combined with an audio narration from a different source may require the audio to start five seconds after the video and tolerate a one second variation in its starting time. Sync arcs would be used to accomplish this. However, sync arcs are not powerful enough to accomplish synchronization between a visual and audio presentation of a dialog from different sources, unless one is willing to tolerate the addition of markers and corresponding sync arcs at numerous reference points within the raw data. This type of synchronization is addressed by a continuous sync arc, which conveys to the presentation that the delay specified is to be maintained throughout the concurrent presentation of the data.

Hyperlinks form the basis for interactive presentations. These are the presentations that allow the user some form of control over the path that is to be followed through to presentation or the pace that is to be followed. This is accomplished with the use of links and anchors. The model conforms fairly closely to the Dexter model's implementation of links and anchors with anchors as part of the media type and a link as a directed connection between two anchors. The destination of a link may also be a composite node within an atomic presentation. The source and destination of a link need not be in the same document.

Attributes are used to specify properties like file names, duration, user options, and similar aspects. The model supports the general notion of an attribute list. Presentations, events, channels composite nodes, sync arcs, anchors, and links all have an attribute list. This is maintained as a table mapping names to values. The type of value depends only on the attribute name. The meaning of an attribute depends on what kind of object it belongs to and on its media type. Attributes with unrecognized names are ignored. They are maintained for the benefit of other applications that might support CMIFed files or components of CMIFed files.

5.4.2 CMIF User Interface

Considering the model in terms of the prototype user interface can add to our understanding. The CMIF user interface provides three views on a presentation. Each of these three views highlights some principle aspect of a presentation. They are also used to reconcile the sometimes conflicting goals of a WYS[WYG approach to editing and the design objective of accommodating a variation in capabilities between the specification content (determined at creation time) and presentation (determined at run time) environments. These views are the hierarchy view, the channel view, and the presentation view. They are tightly coupled to the model and present the user with the mechanisms for interaction with it.

The hierarchy view is the principle mechanism for editing presentations. It is used for both viewing the main tree as well as the trees within an atomic component. There is a marking procedure at the branch level to support parallel or sequential execution of sub-branches. The principle mechanism for editing and manipulating the tree is to present the information as a geometrical relationship in a tree map (Figure 8). The diagram represents branches as boxes with sub-branches as boxes contained in the larger ones. A box can contain parallel or sequentially executed contents and is marked as parallel or choice (for making a choice of sequential execution among its children) to indicate the desired property. For example, a schema might consist sequentially of an introduction, a video scene, and a summary. Within the introduction section, several events could happen in parallel, such as a drawing a title, presenting a still image, popping up a window with descriptive text, and starting some background music.

The subsequent video scene might consist of a video clip, sound background, and so on. Note that the CMIFed is not a comprehensive editor for the components. Instead it is focused on providing a framework for the interaction of the various components and it is not tightly integrated with the behavior of the component editors, which are likely to be loosely coupled third party editors.

The channel view describes the contextual behavior of the components and presents a more traditional (time line) sequence of extents. The layout of the channel view (see Figure 9) is as follows. Time is expressed as a linear sequence moving from the top to the bottom of the view. Each column represents a channel with global attributes and specific events that occur at discrete points in time, with a derived relationship between the start and stop time of the event and the size of the rectangle representing it. Sync arcs are presented as directed arrows between boxes. The channel view can be used to edit the attributes of a channel, suppress it from a presentation, or add a new one. It can also be used to change the relationship of components to each other through manipulation of the sync arcs. However, it cannot be used to alter the structure of a presentation. Consequently the channel view, the hierarchy view, and the presentation view are used in concert.

The presentation view (or player) is used to show the effect of mapping the abstract document to a specific platform and editing the layout specific attributes (screen location, etc.) of a document. The paradigm for the player is to present the user with the type of control interface that is common on most CD players, with the addition of popup facilities to manage channels and option attributes. It is the implementation of the player view that is most interesting. The model for implementing all views is an event driven object oriented model. This is a fairly standard approach for current state-of-the-art interface development and is well understood when the paradigm of user interaction is based around editing, like it is in the hierarchy and channel views.

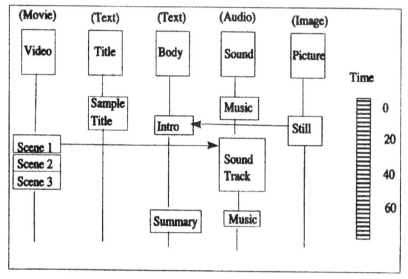

Figure 9. Channel view of CMIF presentation.

In the hierarchy view example, one would reasonably expect support for operations like cloning a presentation to create a view that starts at a different level, cutting and pasting components displaying/editing attributes of a presentation, and similar types of operations. However, the player has a somewhat different orientation. It is responsible for interaction centered on presenting the individual media events in a timely fashion and it has to satisfy constraints (timing) specified by the author within the limits supported by the hardware platform and operating system. The player also needs to support the desired hypermedia style of navigation throughout the document. These operations would include stop, reset, fast forward, skipping, and de-referencing types of functions.

The CWI player implements an event dispatching mechanism, a timer and scheduling queue to support the timing model. The algorithm to satisfy timing constraints is designed to address all but the maximum delays and fine grained timing between applications. These would require a model that has *a priori* knowledge or hard guarantees from the operating system and a communication facility between applications. The algorithm is multiphase and it operates on a graph representing the presentations and timing relationships between them. The player begins by building a graph of timing dependencies.

The nodes in the graph corresponds to begin and end points of the interior and leaf nodes in the atomic presentation being played and the edges represent timing relations between two nodes. The graph is initialized with the edges that represent the timing constraints implied by the tree structure, i.e., the end of each child must precede the beginning of the next. Edges are also added to represent the duration of events gathered by inspection of the data descriptors (or file headers). The graph is then extended with edges representing the sync arcs. When interior markers are used to attach sync arcs, new nodes are created and new edges are added to link them to the begin/end and other markers of the same event. The player then traverses this graph to execute the presentation.

The timing of the traversal is controlled by marking the nodes and edges of the graph. Initially a special start node is marked. When a node is marked, an event (presentation) is typically triggered and all of its outgoing edges are labeled with the current value of the clock. When the current clock value minus the edge clock value is greater than the delay value of the edge, the edge is also marked. When all of a nodes incoming edges are marked, the node is also marked. When the end node is marked, the presentation is over. The timing mechanism thus becomes a mixture of real time and virtual time. For example, the timer could be two times the real clock to represent fast forward.

Similarly, events can be scheduled, presentations paused or restarted, and the general paradigm of the player supported by traversing this graph consistent with the timing status; i.e., it could address questions like running the presentation from the state it would be in after executing for ten minutes. There are, of course, variations due to non-deterministic timing between different executions of the same document in a distributed heterogeneous environment, alternate paths that could have been be result of hyperlink transversal, and limitations implicit in the level of integration between the multimedia components and the CMIF environment.

Open issues for future research, identified by the CWI project, include:

- the adaptation of a general specification for sync arcs (ideal, max, min delays),
- more user control over interpretation of link traversal,
- adding a more dynamic aspect to document presentation by presenting the results of a data base query in hypermedia form, and
- implementing a truly distributed system.

5. COMPARISON OF DIFFERENT APPROACHES

In summary, a state-of-the-art model for hypertext technology has been reviewed and three systems that represent a range of approaches for extending Hypertext to Hypermedia have been presented. The Internet based World Wide Web and the Mosaic interface demonstrates the power and flexibility of a straightforward hypertext model in a sophisticated environment. The environment this web browser operates in has a network based name space, a message passing protocol between client/server software, and it includes techniques for a purposeful decoupling of the hyperlink, data, and the application resources that operate on the data.

Mosaic effectively transfers much of the responsibility for issues addressed by more advanced models to the end user. It does this by exploiting the sophisticated networked environment, by providing tools that give the user considerable opportunity for extending the system, and also by requiring a significant amount of decision making on the end user's part. This approach also provides the opportunity for end user authoring of application and in a dramatic fashion demonstrates the concept of distributed hypermedia as a development platform in a context of its own.

The Devise Hypertext Model demonstrated the extent to which you can accomplish a powerful Hypermedia system using extensions to the hypertext model based on a word processing paradigm. This approach treats the multimedia components of compound documents as atomic entities. In essence it pushes all of the control for their behavior and interaction into the component level, which provides a mechanism for implementing hypermedia but has implications for managing the structure of components and for authoring in terms of both context and time issues.

The Amsterdam Hypertext Model made contributions by recasting the Dexter Model as a synthesis of Hypertext and Multimedia models to address the issues of context and time. These included the introduction of a tree-map for authoring and sequencing events, and synchronization relationships for higher fidelity timing models. Execution of documents by translating links components and sync arcs into a graph model that can be used to for traversal, synchronization, and validation of the hypermedia documents integrity are a unique contribution of this work. AHM also provides a model that allows for a clear separation of issues into the realm of design (addressed at creation time) and run time execution of the document, which may be system dependent. In addition, concepts for grouping attributes and mapping them to channels for global management of system related attributes, structured methodologies for authoring documents including multiple integrated (hierarchy, channel, and player) views for document creation, editing, and playback were all contributions of the Amsterdam Model.

6. CONCLUSION AND FUTURE WORK

As this chapter indicates, there is active research in the area of distributed hypermedia. This survey has touched on several areas of work, including reference models, standards, timing and synchronization issues, strategies for distributed system support, the exchange of hypermedia docents and representative implementations of current research ideas. The opportunities for further work include these areas but it should also be possible to extend and build on them. Examples of this category include critical analysis of distributed vs. local models, development of hypermedia authoring models, integration of hypermedia systems and hypermedia components, hypermedia as a tool for rapid prototyping, and leveraging hypermedia navigation with other disciplines.

Analysis of distributed vs. local models
The extension of the Dexter Model to include time and context is a significant improvement, but it still does not address issues in a hypermedia model that would be inherent in a truly distributed heterogeneous system. To state the obvious, there are fundamental differences between distributed and centralized systems, and there are inherent strengths and weaknesses in each design alternative. Strengths of a distributed multi-user system include scalability and improved resource sharing, but change control, concurrency, and integration is more difficult. In addition, many of the systems components have indeterminate behavior. For example, the timing model for network based applications may be indeterminate, or the links in a distributed system may be so dynamic that important properties, like the transitive closure, behave in a non-tractable manner from a computability standpoint. Strengths of a centralized system include a more deterministic behavioral model, a uniform address space, and the potential for tight integration at the system level, but they require a redundancy of resources. The same characteristic is true of the information content in hypermedia models – dedicated systems require dedicated information.

These issues may seem obvious, but architectural assumptions creep into the models in subtle ways. For example, in order to achieve greater performance, the DeVise implementation of the Dexter reference model uses memory pointers to bypass the accessor function and consequently makes conclusions about the accessor component of the model that would be disastrous in a distributed environment like the W3 project and Mosaic. Conversely, the web is extremely decentralized, but in one important sense, due to the copy and operate model, it behaves very much like a centralized system with a sophisticated capability for collecting resources from remote sites for local operations. This has shortcomings due in large part to the indeterminate characteristics of acquiring network based resources. Traditionally hypertext/hypermedia systems have been designed with one paradigm or the other in mind and the approaches have been mutually exclusive; i.e., the paradigms are dedicated closed systems like personal note cards or worldwide collaboration. However, modern hardware systems have a combination of characteristics; powerful local capabilities with integrated access to distributed resources. Perhaps the best software system would also embody a synthesis of approaches. There is very little work that has been done to formally take these characteristics into account in the modeling, analysis, and design of hypermedia systems.

Integration of hypermedia components with hypermedia systems

In order to preserve the integrity of a system that utilizes discrete components, which may change over time, it is important for the system, have access to information about the components and to be notified in some way when that information changes. This is particularly important for input for a hypermedia system that utilizes components which it does not directly manage (i.e., virtually all current systems). Implementing mechanisms for notifying the hypermedia system or enabling the hypermedia system to discover when attributes of the component change is a difficult task. The W3 project has made some progress in this area with the implementation of the HTTP protocol, URL specification, and the various registry schemes (WAIS, Gopher etc.) for a distributed heterogeneous system.

The universal file registry mechanism used by Apple and exploited by DeVise also illustrates the utility of this mechanism. It is clear that this would be a very useful concept to exploit, but it is not clear what the implementation strategies should be or how to quantify and articulate the benefits. Models that identify the required information content to be maintained and simulations that quantify the benefits of these extensions have not yet been undertaken. Mechanisms for dealing with this issue are fundamental to the use of hypermedia as a tool for system or desktop integration. These integration issues are summarized in [36].

Hypermedia-based rapid prototyping

The concept of active execution for a hypermedia document provides a unique opportunity for simulating some models of behavior. This could be used to simulate the potential behavior of some rather complex systems and it would be particularly useful in areas where it was desirable to simulate the interaction dynamics of people and machinery. Consider designing a user interface for a stereo receiver. The controls of the system, the information panels a user is confronted with, and their relationship to each other could be modeled as a collection of hypermedia components and links that would simulate the appropriate behavior. For example, invoking a link to program the receiver could execute a "document" that takes over a portion of the display with appropriate information for programming the receiver and its own embedded links. The system simulation would be somewhat primitive (there is no actual antenna, power source amplifier, or microprocessors) but it would provide an interesting test bed to discover how people interact with the system. Many users of hypertext systems are quick to identify and exploit this type of capability but there has been a minimal amount of formal analysis and research. It may be possible to analyze and develop domain specific SGML DTDs and viewers similar to the Mosaic system for use in these areas.

Developing hypermedia authoring models

The success of multimedia applications depends in large part on the availability of high quality data. A candid assessment of the current generation of authoring tools indicates that there is considerable opportunity for improvement. This could be due in large part to the strategy of extending traditional word processing paradigms for authoring to include multimedia components. They simply do not address the issues of active documents with a temporal component. Addressing this issue is the most significant contribution of the HyTime standard. However, the model would still require authors to take the approach of scripting a document; in essence, they would have to be programmers and authors. In addition, these approaches do not address the issues of presentation, navigation, and managing a collection of documents. The AHM model and the CMIFed it uses present novel ways of thinking about and managing some of these issues (presentation capabilities, course grained parallelism, and fine grained timing). In addition, they are modeled in a way that supports incremental execution, quick revisions in a non-programmatic manner, and they are analogous to a generic markup strategy (modeled on object based abstractions and then realized by system capabilities at run time). The synthesis of editing models that support WEB visualization and editing, HyTime concepts and CMIFed concepts, is an area that merits further investigation.

Leveraging hypermedia navigation with other disciplines

Leveraging hypermedia navigation is a two-way proposition. There is potentially significant benefit that hypermedia could obtain from other disciplines and vice versa. A long standing research issue for the hypermedia community is how to improve the search and retrieval mechanisms of hypermedia navigation; i.e., how to solve the lost-in-hyperspace problem. Models that use techniques from other disciplines for creating starting points of hypermedia navigation have been identified in the literature but seldom explored. Hybrid systems that build a relational data base of WEB components (links) and use SQL queries to obtain links of interest in addition to traditional link traversal have been suggested but not investigated. There are numerous other methods that may also be of research interest and provide practical benefits. For example, a collection of hyperlink references to a video sequence based on automatically detecting scene changes in a video sequence would be extremely useful.

The pliability of generic hypermedia systems makes them a powerful tool for this type of investigation. Conversely, hypermedia technology could be employed in many more settings than the traditional on line help facility. Software engineering systems generally create a number of artifacts that developers exploit to document or discover the design intent and behavior of a system. They are traditionally very good at presenting a static view of the system and managing a hierarchy of information, but they do not capture the dynamic behavior of the system. Adaptation of hypermedia viewing technology could potentially capture the essence of more dynamic behavior and non-hierarchical relationships.

In closing, it is widely recognized that software can be severely limited by the robustness and integrity of underlying data models, the interoperability with other tools in the application domain, and, of course, an unsophisticated user interface. But in some important sense, the real measure of any system is how effectively it enhances a user ability to reason, remember, and communicate. Hypermedia presents complex issues that have been the subject of discussion for almost 50 years [4,38,28]. There are at least two additional aspects that should be considered in the context of this chapter. First is the impact of the software on the application domain itself. Some tools create a dynamic interaction with organizations that use them and consequently introduce additional complexities for understanding and developing software systems. This situation can often be identified with a paradigm shift in the way we use the technology and supporting tools. Technology in this state is very difficult to manage and definitive solutions are hard to articulate while evolutionary progress is under way. The second issue is that software that spans multiple application domains often takes longer to emerge as a mature discipline. This point is addressed by Legget and Schnase [24] in the criticism of Dexter as being too quick to standardize a technology that is still evolving.

Hypermedia tools have tremendous potential to augment our capabilities. However, hypermedia presents a paradigm shift in document processing and hypermedia definitely spans multiple disciplines, both of which combine to make it an interesting and challenging domain.

REFERENCES

1. Akscyn, R., McCracken, D., and Yoder, E., "KMS: A Distributed Hypermedia System for Managing Knowledge in Organizations." *Communications of the ACM*, Vol. 31, No. 7, pp. 820-835, July 1988.
2. Apple Computer, "HyperCard™ Script Language Guide: The Hypertalk Language," Addison-Wesley, Reading MA, 1988.
3. Barret, E., "The Society of Text: Hypertext Hypermedia, and the Social Construction of Information," Cambridge, MA: The MIT Press, 1989.
4. Bush, V., "As we may think," Atlantic Monthly, Vol. 176, pp. 100-108, 1945 (Reprinted in CDROM: The New Papyrus, Lambert S., Ropiequet, S. (Editors), pp. 3-20, Microsoft Press 1986.
5. Colaitis, F. and Kretz, F., "Standardizing Hypermedia Information Objects," *IEEE Communications*, pp. 60-70, May 1992
6. Conklin, J., "Hypertext: An introduction and survey," *IEEE Computer*, Vol. 20, No. 9, pp. 17-41, September 1987.
7. Drapeau, G., "Synchronization in the MAEstro Multimedia Authoring Environment," *Proceedings of the ACM Multimedia '93,* Anaheim, CA, August 1-6, 1993.
8. Gaines, B., Shaw, M., "Open Architecture Multimedia Documents," *Proceedings of ACM Multimedia '93*, Anaheim, CA, August 1-6, 1993, pp. 137-146
9. Gronbaek, K. and Trigg, R., "Design Issues for a Dexter-Based Hypermedia System," *Communications of the ACM*, 37(2), pp. 41-49, February 1994.
10. Haan, B., Kahn., P., Riley, A., Coombs, and Meyrowitz, N, "IRIS Hypermedia Service," (Intermedia), *Communications of the ACM*, 35 (1), 36-51, January 1992.
11. Halasz, F., Moran, T., and Trigg, R., "NoteCards in a Nutshell," *Proceedings of the CHI 87, Conference on Human Factors in Computing Systems.* ACM, pp. 5-52, April 1987.
12. Halasz, F. and Schwartz, M., "The Dexter Hypertext Reference Model," NIST Hypertext Standardization Workshop, Gaithersburg, MD, January 16-18, 1990.
13. Halasz, F. and Schwartz, M., "The Dexter Hypertext Reference Model," *Communications of the ACM*, 37 (2), 30-39, February 1994.
14. Halasz, F., "Reflections on Note-Cards: Seven Issues for the Next Generation of Hypermedia Systems," *Communications of the ACM*, Vol. 31, No 7, 836-852, July 1988.
15. Hardman, L., Bulterman, D., and van Rossum, G., "The Amsterdam Hypermedia Model: Adding Time and Context to the Dexter Model," *Communications of the ACM*, 37 (2), 50-62, February 1994.
16. Hardman, L., Bulterman, D., and van Rossum, G., "Structured Multimedia Authoring," *Proceedings of ACM Multimedia '93*, Anaheim, August 1-6, 1993.
17. Harvey, G., "Understanding HyperCard" Alameda," CA: SYBEX, Inc. 1988.
18. ISO 10744:1992, Information Technology – Hypermedia/Time-based Structuring Language (HyTime), ANSI, 13th Floor, 11 West 42nd Street, NY, 10036, 1992.
19. ISO 8879:1986, Information processing - Text and office systems - Standard Generalized Markup Language (SGML), ANSI, 13th Floor, 11 West 42nd Street, NY, 10036, 1986.
20. Internet Drafts: Available on line @ cnri.reston.va.us/internet-drafts, unless noted:
    MIME (Multipurpose Internet Mail Extensions) Part One: Mechanisms for Specifying and Describing the Format of Internet Message Bodies, 06/15/1994, <draft-ietf-822ext-mime-imb-00.ps
    HyperText Markup Language, Version 1.2, proposed to be registered as a MIME (RFC1341) content type, Available at http://info.cern.ch/hypertext/WWW/MarkUp
    HTML+ (Hypertext markup format), 11/08/1993, <draft-raggett-www-html-00.ps>
    Uniform Resource Locators (URL) A Syntax for the Expression of Access Information of Objects on the Network, 04/05/1994, <draft-ietf-uri-url-03.ps>

Hypertext Transfer Protocol (HTTP) A Stateless Search, Retrieve and Manipulation Protocol, 11/16/1993, <draft-ietf-iiir-http-00.ps>

21. Killough, R. and Leggett, J., "Hypertext Interchange with the Dexter Model: Intermedia to KMS.," Dept of Computer Science Tech. Rep. TAMU-HRL 90-002, Texas A&M University, College Station, Texas, 1990.

22. Koegel, J., Rutledge, L., Rutledge J., and Keskin, C., "HYOCTANE: A HyTime Engine for an MMIS," *Proceedings of ACM Multimedia '93* Anaheim, August 1-6, 1993.

23. Kappe F., "Aspects of a Modern Multimedia Information System," Ph.D. Dissertation, Technical University Graz Austria, June 1991, (also IIG Report 308).

24. Leggett, J. and Schnase, J., "Viewing Dexter With Open Eyes," *Communications of the ACM*, 37 (2), 77-86, February 1994.

25. Gall, L., "MPEG: A Video Compression Standard for Multimedia Applications" *Communication of the ACM*, April 1991 34(4), pp. 77-86.

26. Newcomb, S., "Multimedia Interchange using SGML: The ISO "HyTime" Standard," Course notes – Survey of Formal Standards for Multimedia Systems, *ACM Multimedia '93* Anaheim, CA, August 1-6, 1993.

27. Newcomb, S., "The HyTime Hypermedia/Time based Document Structuring Language," *Communications of the ACM*, 67-83, November 1991.

28. Nielsen, J., "Hypertext and Hypermedia," Academic Press, San Diego, Calif., 1990

29. Nielsen, J., "The Art of Navigating Through HyperText," *Communications of the ACM*, 33 (3), 296-310, March 1990.

30. Price, R., "MHEG: An Introduction to the future International Standard for Hypermedia Object Interchange," *Proceedings of ACM Multimedia* '93, Anaheim, August 1-6, 1993.

31. Rare Project OBR(92)046v2, "A Survey of Distributed Multimedia Research, Standards and Products," Adie, C. Ed.
Available Electronically from ftp.edinburgh.cac.uk:/pub/mmsurvey/

32. Shneiderman, B. and Kearsley, G., Hypertext Hands-On!, Addison-Wesley, Reading, MA, 1989.

33. Smith, J. and Weiss, S., "An Overview of Hypertext," *Communications of the ACM*, Vol. 31, No. 7, July 1988.

34. Stotts, P. and Furuta, R., "Petri-Net-Based Hypertext: Document Structure with Browsing Semantics", ACM Transactions on Information Systems, Vol. 7, No. 1, January 1989.

35. Thomas et al., "Diamond: A Multimedia Message System Built on a Distributed Architecture," *IEEE Computer*, December 1985.

36. Thomas, I. and Nejmeh, B., "Definitions of Tool Integration for Environments," *IEEE Software*, March 1992.

37. Tompa, F., "A Data Model for Flexible Hypertext Database Systems," *ACM Transactions on Information Systems*, Vol. 7, No 1, January 1989.

38. Trehan, R., Sawashima, N., Yamaguchi, K., and Hasebe, K., "Toolkit for Shared Hypermedia on a Distributed Object Oriented Architecture," *Proceedings of ACM Multimedia '93*, Anaheim, CA, August 1-6, 1993.

39. Van Dam, A., "Hypertext '87 Keynote Address," Communications of the ACM, Vol. 31, No. 7, 887-895, July 1988.

40. Wallace, G., "The JPEG Still Picture Compression Standard," *Communications of the ACM*, 34 (2), 30-44, April 1991.

41. Yankelovich, N., Hann, J., and Meyrowitz, N., "Intermedia: The Concept and the Construction of a Seamless Information Environment," *IEEE Computer*, January 1988.

42. Van Rossum, G., Jansen, J. Mullender, and K., Bulterman, D., "CMIFed: A Presentation Environment for Portable Hypermedia Documents," *Proceedings of ACM Multimedia '93*, Anaheim, CA, August 1-6, 1993.

43. NCSA, "A Beginner's Guide to HTML," available online in pubs@ncsa.uiuc.edu.

44. University of Illinois, National Center for Supercomputing, "NCSA Mosaic," available online in mosaic@ncsa.uiuc.edu.

32

DISTRIBUTED MULTIMEDIA SYSTEMS

Victor O. K. Li[1] and Wanjiun Liao[2]
[1]Department of Electrical and Electronic Engineering
The University of Hong Kong, Hong Kong, China
[2]Department of Electrical Engineering
National Taiwan University, Taipei, Taiwan

1.	**INTRODUCTION**	682
2.	**DIGITAL MEDIA FUNDAMENTALS**	684
2.1	DIGITAL IMAGE	684
2.2	DIGITAL VIDEO	684
2.3	DIGITAL AUDIO	685
3.	**ENABLING TECHNOLOGIES**	685
3.1	DATA COMPRESSION	685
3.2	RESOURCE MANAGEMENT	689
3.3	NETWORKING	691
3.4	MULTIMEDIA OPERATING SYSTEM	694
3.5	SYNCHRONIZATION	694
3.6	MULTIMEDIA INFORMATION SYSTEM	696
4.	**CONCLUSIONS**	699
	REFERENCES	699

Abstract. A distributed multimedia system (DMS) is an integrated communication, computing, and information system which enables the processing, management, delivery, and presentation of synchronized multimedia information with quality-of-service guarantees. Multimedia information may include time-independent media such as text, data, and images, and time-dependent media such as video and audio. Such a system enhances human communications by exploiting both visual and aural senses, and provides the ultimate flexibility in work and entertainment, allowing one to collaborate with remote participants, view movies on demand, access on-line digital libraries from the desktop, and so forth. In this chapter, we present a technical survey of a DMS. We give an overview of distributed multimedia systems, examine the fundamental concepts of digital media, identify the applications, and survey the important enabling technologies.

1. INTRODUCTION

Distributed multimedia systems (DMS) [1] will revolutionize current lifestyles, especially those aspects associated with human communications. Such systems create an electronic world in which people are allowed to shop, work, or learn at home electronically, watch digital video programs on demand, access online digital libraries from the desktop, and so forth. Technological advances in computers, communications, consumer electronics, and information technologies, coupled with the availability of multimedia resources, mechanisms, and manipulation tools, the development of the relevant standards, and the convergence of the computer, telecommunication, and cable TV industries, are accelerating the realization of such systems.

A multimedia system is an interactive digital media system. It seamlessly integrates multimedia information via computers, and allows users to interact with such information according to their preferences. Multimedia information includes video, audio, and other time dependent (or continuous) media in addition to time-independent (or discrete) media such as text, data, and still images. Time-independent media data are often displayed as one presentation unit, while time-dependent media data is composed of a series of consecutive units of equal presentation duration [2]. The ability to accommodate time-dependent media as well as time-independent media in an integrated system is the distinguishing feature of multimedia systems. A DMS augments stand-alone multimedia systems with a real-time network (real time here refers to timely delivery with acceptable quality).

According to application needs, the system provides services in an interactive (e.g., video phone) or distributive (e.g., broadcast video) mode, and in a timely (e.g., video browsing) or messaging (e.g., multimedia email) manner. Internet today, and Next Generation Internet (NGI) tomorrow, coupled with a number of multimedia personal computers (PCs), workstations, Web servers, and continuous media servers, is evolving towards a global DMS. Such networked multimedia systems not only dramatically enhance the existing CD-ROM based multimedia applications, but also encourage newly emerging broadband applications, at the expense of more complexity due to the requirement of quality-of-service (QoS) guarantees. Such QoS guarantees include constraints on bit error rates, packet loss probabilities, and delivery delays required in a traditional point-to-point information delivery system. Additional constraints, introduced due to the orchestration of distributed media in a DMS, include the synchronization among multiple media streams from distributed sources to achieve a meaningful presentation. We formally define a DMS as follows.

A distributed multimedia system is an integrated communication, computing, and information system which enables the processing, management, delivery and presentation of synchronized multimedia information with quality-of-service guarantees.

Figure 1 summarizes a DMS. The inputs of the system consist of the important factors which drive a DMS from concept to reality and the outputs consist of a wide range of distributed multimedia applications. The system inputs can be divided into three orthogonal dimensions. The inputs from the left-hand side are the major contribution industries, including the computer, telecommunication, cable TV, entertainment, and consumer electronics industries. The inputs from the right-hand side are the important issues in the development of a DMS, including the technical, standardization, regulation, copyright, market, and social and human factors. The inputs from the top are a collection of the enabling technologies of the information subsystem (for storage), the communication subsystem (for transmission), and the computing subsystem (for processing).

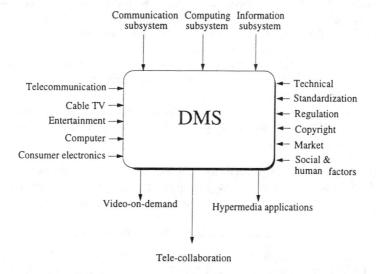

Figure 1. A distributed multimedia system.

The information subsystem consists of the multimedia servers, information archives, and multimedia database systems. It stores and retrieves multimedia information, serves a large number of simultaneous user requests with QoS guarantees, and manages the data for consistency, security, and reliability. The communication subsystem consists of the transmission medium and transport protocols. It connects the users with distributed multimedia resources, and delivers multimedia materials with QoS guarantees, such as real-time delivery for video or audio data, and error-free delivery for text data. The computing subsystem consists of a multimedia platform (ranging from a high-end graphics workstation to a multimedia PC equipped with CD-ROM drives, speaker, sound card, and video card), operating system (OS), presentation and authoring tool, and multimedia manipulation software. It allows users to manipulate the multimedia data.

The outputs of the system can be broadly classified into three different types of distributed multimedia applications: interactive TV (ITV), tele-cooperation, and hypermedia applications. ITV allows subscribers to access video programs when they want and to interact with them. Services include home shopping, interactive video games, financial transactions, movie-on-demand, news-on-demand, or CD-on-demand. Tele-cooperation allows remote participants to join a group activity without time and location restrictions. Services include remote learning, telecommuting, tele-servicing, tele-operation, multimedia email, videophone, desktop conferencing, electronic meeting room, joint editing, or group drawing. A hypermedia document is a multimedia document with "links" to other multimedia documents, and allows users to browse multimedia information in a non-sequential manner. Services include digital libraries, electronic encyclopedia, multimedia magazine, multimedia document, information kiosk, computer-aided learning tools, and World Wide Web surfing. The main features of a DMS are then summarized as follows [3,4,5,6,7,8,9,10]:

1. Technology integration: integrates information, communication, and computing systems to form a unified digital processing environment.
2. Multimedia integration: accommodates time-independent data as well as time-dependent data in an integrated environment.
3. Real-time performance: requires the storage systems, processing systems, and the transmission systems to have real-time performance. Hence, huge storage volume, high I/O rate, high network transmission rate, and high CPU processing rate are required.

4. System-wide QoS support: supports diverse QoS requirements on an end-to-end basis, along the data path from the sender, through the transport network, to the receiver.
5. Interactivity: requires duplex communication between the user and the system, and allows each user to control the information.
6. Multimedia synchronization support: preserves the playback continuity of media frames within a single continuous media stream, and the temporal relationships among multiple related data objects.
7. Standardization support: allows interoperability despite heterogeneity in the information content, presentation format, user interfaces, network protocols, and consumer electronics.

The rest of the chapter is organized as follows. Section 2 overviews digital media fundamentals. Section 3 addresses the technical aspects of the information, telecommunication, and the computing subsystems. Finally, we conclude in Section 4.

2. DIGITAL MEDIA FUNDAMENTALS

A medium is something through which information is carried or transferred. Examples of electronic media include computer disks, CD-ROMs, videotapes, and cables. Information can be represented as analog or digital signals. Analog signals exhibit continuous tone of smooth fluctuations, while digital signals are composed of discrete values represented by numbers. The transformation from analog to digital signals is achieved by digitizing. Digitization is composed of sampling and quantizing. Sampling snapshots the analog waveform at certain points in time, and the sampling rate determines how often the analog signal is digitized. According to the Nyquist Theorem, the sampling rate must be at least twice the highest frequency component of the analog waveform to optimally reproduce the signal. Quantization determines the digital measured value of the analog waveform at the sampling time. The larger the range of numbers used for the quantization, the more gradations the digitally sampled waveform can present. Generally speaking, digital signals are superior to analog counterpart in terms of their robustness, seamless integration, reusability, and ease of distribution potential.

2.1 DIGITAL IMAGE

Digital images are composed of two-dimensional pixels, which further consist of the red (R), the green (G), and the blue (B) components. This two-dimensional (or spatial) representation is called the image resolution. The number of bits to represent a pixel is called the color depth, which decides the actual number of colors available to represent a pixel. The resolution and the color depth determine the presentation quality and the size of image storage. The more pixels and the more colors, the better the quality, and the larger the volume. For example, a 640-by-480 image with 24-bit color requires 640x480x24 = 7.4 Mbits of storage. To reduce the storage requirement, three different approaches may be applied. (1) *Indexed color* which reduces the file size by a limited number of bits with a color look-up table (or color palette) to represent a pixel. The value associated with the pixel, instead of direct color information, represents the index of the color table. (2) *Color sub-sampling* which shrinks the file size by downsampling the chrominance (or color difference) component (i.e., using less bits to represent the chrominance component), while leaving the luminance (or brightness) component unchanged. This approach takes advantage of the deficiency that human vision is more sensitive to variation in the luminance than in the chrominance. (3) *Spatial compression* which reduces the size by throwing away the spatial redundancy within the images.

2.2 DIGITAL VIDEO

Video is composed of a series of still image frames, and produces the illusion of movement via quickly displaying frames one after another. The biggest challenges posed by digital video are the massive volume of data involved and how to meet the real-time constraints on retrieval, delivery, and display. The possible solutions entail the following. (1) *Compromise in the presentation quality*: instead of video with full-frame (i.e., images filling the complete screen), full-fidelity (i.e., millions of colors at screen resolution), and full motion (i.e., equal to or greater than 30 fps), one may reduce the image size, or use less bits to represent colors, or reduce the frame rate. (For a frame rate less than 16 fps, the illusion of motion is replaced by the perception of a series of frames.) (2) *Video compression*: to reduce the massive volume of digital video data, a compression technique with high compression ratio is required. In addition to throwing away the spatial and color similarities of individual images, the temporal redundancies between adjacent video frames are eliminated. (3) *Layered (or scalable) video*: to adapt to various conditions, such as different transmission, storage, and application requirements, by encoding video as a range of layers that contains different video components.

2.3 DIGITAL AUDIO
Digital audio systems are designed to make use of the range of human hearing (20 to 20k Hz). The quality of digital audio is characterized by the sampling rate, the sampling resolution, and the number of channels. The sampling rate (which is determined by Nyquist Theorem) determines the frequency response of a digital audio system; here frequency response refers to the range of frequencies that a medium can reproduce accurately. For example, the sampling rate of CD-quality audio is 44.1 kHz (which can accommodate the highest frequency of human hearing, namely, 20 kHz), while telephone-quality sound adopts an 8kHz sampling rate (which can accommodate the most sensitive frequency of human hearing, up to 4 kHz).

The sampling resolution, i.e., the number of bits per sample, determines the dynamic range, which describes the spectrum of the softest to the loudest sound amplitude levels that a medium can reproduce. One bit yields 6 dB of dynamic range. For example, 16-bit audio contributes 96 dB of dynamic range found in CD-grade audio, nearly the dynamic range of human hearing. Different systems have different number of channels. For example, mono systems have single channels, stereo systems have two channels (left and right), and Dolby surround sound systems have 5.1 channels, corresponding to five full range channels of audio, including three front channels (i.e., left, center, right), plus two surrounds, and a low frequency bass effect channel called the subwoofer. (Note that because the subwoofer has only limited frequency response, about 100 Hz, it is sometimes referred to as the ".1" channel). With the higher sampling rate, the more bits per sample, and the more channels, it renders higher quality of the digital audio, and therefore higher storage and bandwidth requirements. For example, 44.1 kHz sampling rate, 16-bit sampling resolution, and stereo audio reception produce CD quality audio, but require a bandwidth of 44,100x16x2 = 1.4 Mbits per second (Mbps). Telephone quality audio, with a sampling rate of 8 kHz, 8-bit sampling resolution, and mono audio reception, needs only a data throughput of 8000x8x1 = 64 Kbps. Again, digital audio compression, or a compromise in quality can be applied to reduce the file size.

3. ENABLING TECHNOLOGIES

3.1 DATA COMPRESSION
Continuous media data are typically large in volume. Without compression, existing computer platforms, storage devices, and networks are unable to satisfy the requirements of the massive storage space, high data transfer rate, and huge transmission bandwidth typical of multimedia data. For example, the transmission bandwidth requirement for digital video with a resolution of 640 by 480, 24-bit colors, and 30 fps is 640x480x24 = 7.4 Mbits per frame, and 7.4 Mbits per frame x 30 frames per sec = 221 Mbps. Currently available bandwidth is much smaller. For example, CD-ROM drives currently have the range of 1.5 Mbps to 48 Mbps, T1 lines 1.5 Mbps, T3 lines around 45 Mbps, coaxial cables around 40 Mbps, and OC-3 optical fibers 155 Mbps. Without data compression, current technologies are inadequate for supporting today's video, and certainly inadequate for the High Definition TV (HDTV) quality video in the future.

Compression schemes exploit and eliminate any redundancies within each frame (i.e., spatial redundancy, including space and color similarities) and between sequential frames (i.e., temporal redundancy), resulting in the reduction of data being stored and transmitted. The former is called *intra-frame* compression, and the latter *inter-frame* compression. Note that squeezing the color similarities exploits the artifacts of human vision, which is more sensitive to luminance than to chrominance. Compression techniques can be categorized based on the following considerations. (1) *Lossless* or *lossy*: if the decompressed data is identical to the original, it is referred to as lossless compression; otherwise, lossy compression. (2) *Entropy* encoding or *source* encoding: entropy compression does not differentiate the types of data, but analyzes the statistical properties of data to reduce the size, while source compression deals with the contents of the source material and makes use of their semantic and special characteristics to achieve data reduction. (3) *Symmetrical* or *asymmetrical*: if the time required to compress and to decompress is roughly the same, it is referred to as symmetrical compression. In asymmetrical compression, the time taken for compression is usually much longer than decompression. (4) *Software* or *hardware*: the compression may be performed by software or hardware. In the following, we will examine some important techniques widely used for digital image, video, and audio compression.

3.1.1 Still image
A still image compression scheme throws away the spatial and/or color redundancies. It can be based on coding techniques, such as run-length coding, Huffman coding, and Lempel-Ziv-Welch (LZW), or spatial transformation, such as DCT, Fractal, and Wavelet.

GIF (Graphic Interchange Format) and JPEG (Joint Picture Experts Group) are two image formats widely used in the WWW. GIF was developed by CompuServe for displaying and transmitting on-line graphics. Each image in a GIF file is associated with a 8-bit color map (i.e., indexed color), with the data compressed according to LZW algorithm. It also supports interleaved representation of images so that, with a four-pass process, a rough image loads and displays quickly, and has more resolution with time.

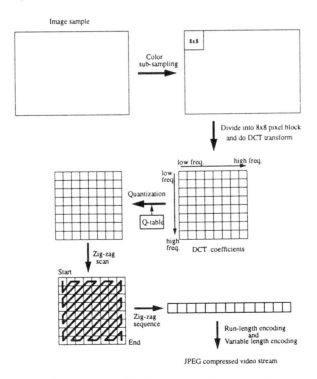

Figure 2. The block diagram of JPEG codec.

JPEG [11,12] standard, developed by International Standards Organization (ISO) and CCITT, is designed for arbitrary still images (i.e., continuous-tone images). The basic processing steps are summarized as follows. (1) Transforms RBG to YUV color space, and downsamples chrominance to exploit color redundancy. (2) Applies DCT transform on pixel blocks to exploit spatial redundancy. Images are divided into a series of blocks of 8x8 pixels before entering the DCT engine. (3) Quantizes the 64 frequency components in each block with higher quantization values on the high frequencies. (4) Zig-zag ordering to order the 2D output of quantization, creating a bit stream with zero value coefficients close to the end, since the low-frequency components (most likely non-zero) are placed in front of the high-frequency components (most likely zero). (5) Entropy encoding applied to pack the resulting zeros. and further reduced coded streams. The block diagram for JPEG codec is depicted as in Figure 2.

3.1.2. Digital video
Digital video compression may either apply intra-frame compression to each individual frame of the video (e.g., Motion-JPEG) or combines both intra-frame compression and inter-frame compression (e.g., H.26x, MPEG-x Video). The former scheme yields a lower compression ratio than the latter, due to the absence of exploiting temporal redundancy between adjacent frames. Motion estimation along with motion compensation is a promising technique for inter-frame compression. It compares the current frame with the previous one, and encodes the motion vectors (i.e., the change in coordinate values due to the motion) and pixel differences after motion.

Motion-JPEG. Motion-JPEG is an intra-frame compression technique, and applies JPEG to each individual frame of the video. Since it does not exploit the interframe redundancy, it produces lower compression ratio. It is widely used for nonlinearly editing.

H.26x. ITU-T Recommendation H.261 (or px64) [13] is part of the H.320 group of standards which describes the various standard components of a videoconferencing system. H.261 was developed to provide audiovisual services at integral multiples of 64 Kbps for videophones and video conferencing over ISDN telephone lines. Only two image resolutions are supported: CIF and QCIF. The bitstreams produced by H.261 encoders have the hierarchical structure as follows: Picture, Groups of Block (GOB), Macro Block (MB), and Block. H.261 has two modes for compression. In the intra-frame mode, every 8x8 block in a picture is DCT transformed thereby eliminating spatial redundancy. In the inter-frame mode, motion compensation with DCT is applied. A comparison of the current frame with the previous one is made. If the difference is higher than a certain threshold, the difference is sent to be DCT transformed; otherwise, no data is sent.

H.263 is an extension and enhancement of H.261. With a number of improvements, it is intended to produce a higher quality of video at low bit rate so that video conferencing over the Public Switched Telephone Network (PSTN) can be supported.

MPEG Video. Unlike H.261 which is optimized for teleconferencing where motion is naturally limited, the ISO MPEG Video standard was devised for a wide range of video and motion pictures [14,15]. MPEG compression is lossy and asymmetric, with the encoding more expensive than the decoding. It defines the structure of coded video bit streams transmitted to the decoder and the decoder architecture, but leaves the encoder architecture undefined. The structure of an MPEG video bit stream includes Sequence, Group of Picture (GOP), Picture, Slice, and Macroblock.

Three main types of encoded frames are defined in MPEG: I (Intra-frame) frame, P (Predicted) frame, and B (Bidirectional) frame. An I frame contains all the necessary information to reproduce a complete frame, and thus is independent of any other frames in the video sequence. It basically applies the intra-frame compression of the basic JPEG DCT algorithm. A P frame is predicted from the differences from the previous I or P frame in the sequence. A B frame is bidirectional interpolated by the preceding and the subsequent I or P frames. Figure 3 depicts the relationship among these three types of encoded frames. The inter-frame dependency of P and B frames implies that a current P frame can be decoded only if the preceding I or P frame has been presented to be decoded. Similarly, without both the preceding and subsequent I or P frames in the decoder, it is impossible to generate a B frame. For example, if the presentation order of a video sequence is {IBBPBBPBBI}, then the actual input sequence of MPEG frames to a decoder should be {IPBBPBBIBB}. Therefore, the patterns of video frame sequence in storage and during transmission is different from that for presentation.

There are different versions of MPEG, denoted by MPEG-x. MPEG-1 was targeted at CD-ROM and applications at bit rate of about 1.5 Mbps. The video is strictly progressive (i.e., non-interlaced), and picture quality is approximately equivalent to VHS. MPEG-2 is an extension of MPEG-1. It addresses high quality coding for all digital transmission of broadcast TV quality video at data rates of between 2 and 15 Mbps. The major applications include digital storage media, and digital television (including HDTV). Note that originally HDTV applications were addressed by MPEG-3, but it got folded into MPEG-2. The primary enhancement is centered on the addition of interlaced video. Thus MPEG-2 supports two coding structures: field and frame. A range of profiles and levels are specified in MPEG-2 for the support of a wide range of applications. MPEG-4 originally aimed to address generic coding standard to support low bit rate applications. Now the focus is changed to support a wide range of applications that are not fully addressed by existing standards.

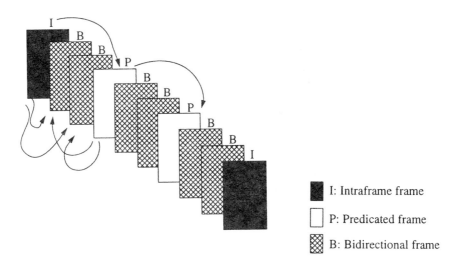

Figure 3. The relationship among I, P, and B frames.

3.1.3. Digital Audio

Compression of entertainment quality audio signals has been widely studied, ranging from μ-law companding, ADPCM, to the more recent MPEG Audio standard and Dolby AC-3 with high fidelity and surround sound effect.

1. μ-law companding: μ-law is widely used to encode speech over the telephone line in the U.S. and Japan. A similar approach called A-law is used in Europe. The basic idea is to use quantization steps of different sizes that increase logarithmically with the signal levels to compress the signal, and to use the inverse function to expand the signal. As a result, the

quantization levels are spaced far apart when the signal is louder, and closer together when the signal is quieter [16]. G.711 supports μ-law companding.

2. ADPCM: ADPCM takes advantage of the fact that consecutive audio samples are generally similar, and employs predictive coding for data reduction. Instead of quantizing each audio sample independently as in PCM, an ADPCM encoder calculates the difference between each audio sample and its predicted value, and outputs the quantized difference (i.e., the PCM value of the differential). The performance is improved by employing adaptive prediction and quantization, so that the predictor and difference quantizer adapt to the characteristics of the audio signal by changing the step size. The decoder reconstructs the audio sample by using the identical quantization step size to obtain a linear difference plus possibly adding 1/2 for the correction of truncation errors, and then adding the quantized difference to its predicted value. G.721, G.723, and G.726 implement ADPCM schemes with different data rates.

3. Perceptual coding: perceptual coding takes advantage of the psycho-acoustic phenomena and exploits human auditory masking to squeeze out the acoustically irrelevant parts of audio signals [17]. Audio masking is a perceptual weakness of human ears. Whenever a strong audio signal is present, the spectral neighborhood of weaker audio signals becomes imperceptible. Measurements of human hearing sensitivity have shown that the ear integrates audio signals, which are very close in frequency, and treats them as a group. Only when the signals are sufficiently different in frequencies, will the ear perceive the loudness of each signal individually. In perceptual coding, the audio spectrum is divided into a set of a narrow frequency bands, corresponding to the critical bands to reflect the frequency selectivity of human hearing. Then, it is possible to sharply filter coding noise to force it to stay close to the frequency of the frequency components of the audio signal being coded, thereby masking out the noise. By reducing the coding noise when no audio is present, and allowing strong audio to mask the noise at other times, the sound fidelity of the original signals can be perceptually preserved. Two famous examples of multi-channel perceptual coding techniques include Dolby AC-3 and MPEG Audio, both of which have 5.1 channels.

3.2 RESOURCE MANAGEMENT

Without proper management of shared system resources, such as CPU, memory, network bandwidth, and disk I/O bandwidth, it is difficult to commit the desired QoS level for a diversity of distributed multimedia applications. Such QoS commitment requires (1) quantitative specification rather than qualitative description to flexibly accommodate a wide range of applications with diverse QoS requirements in an unified system, (2) system-wide resource management, because the multimedia server, network, or host system alone cannot guarantee end-to-end QoS, and (3) dynamic management, i.e., QoS dynamically adjusted, to adapt to the resource consumption by the set of statistically multiplexed flows.

QoS, in the context of DMSs, is thus defined as the quantitative description of whether the services provided by the system satisfy the application needs, and is expressed as a set of parameter-value pairs [18]. The parametric definition of QoS requirements provides flexible and customized services to the diversity of performance requirements from different applications in a unified system. These QoS parameters are negotiated between the users and the service providers, and between the users and the users. The service agreement with the negotiated QoS and the call characteristics (such as mean data rate, peak data rate) is called the service contract. With QoS translation between different system layers, QoS requirements can be mapped into desired resources in the corresponding system components, and then can be managed by the corresponding resource managers to maintain QoS commitment with respect to the negotiated service contracts.

Three levels of QoS commitment supported by the system: (1) *deterministic*, which guarantees the performance is the same as the negotiated service contract, (2) *statistical*, which guarantees the performance with some probability, and (3) *best effort*, which offers no service guarantee.

System-wide resource management aims to the coordination between system components to achieve end-to-end QoS guarantees. Under such coordination, the major functions are summarized as follows: (1) negotiate, control, and manage the service contracts, and (2) reserve, allocate, manage, adapt, and release system resources according to the negotiated values. Once the service contract has been negotiated, it will be preserved throughout the lifetime of the connection. It is also possible, through proper notification and renegotiation, to dynamically tune the QoS level [19,20]. Admission control protects and maintains the performance of existing users in the system, with the principle that new requests can be accepted so long as the performance guarantees of existing connections are not violated. Example prototypes of system-wide resource management include the QoS-A model of the University of Lancaster [19] and the QoS broker of the University of Pennsylvania [21].

3.2.1. QoS Protocol Reference Model

The QoS reference model provides a generic framework to integrate, coordinate, and manage system components to provide end-to-end, guaranteed QoS for a wide range of applications. Figure 4 illustrates our proposed QoS protocol reference model. The layer architecture consists of the application layer, the orchestration layer, and the communication layer. The communication layer is further divided into two different parts: network part and multimedia host-system part. The application layer corresponds to the generic application platform. The orchestration layer is responsible for maintaining playback continuity in single streams, and the coordination across multiple related multimedia streams. The communication layer provides real-time scheduling via the operating system (OS) at the host system and real-time delivery via the network.

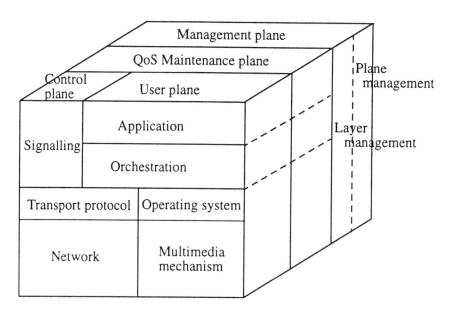

Figure 4. QoS reference model.

Four planes in the reference model include user plane, control plane, QoS maintenance plane, and management plane. The user plane is for the transport of multimedia data from the source to the destination. The control plane is for the signaling of multimedia call establishment, maintenance, and disconnection. The QoS maintenance plane guarantees contracted QoS levels to multimedia applications on an end-to-end basis.

The main functions performed on this plane include QoS management, connection management, and admission control. The QoS managers span all system layers, and each is responsible for QoS negotiation, QoS translation between the adjacent layers, and interaction with the corresponding layer (e.g., to gather status messages about QoS from that layer). The connection manager is responsible for the connection establishment, maintenance, and disconnection. The connection manager also has to adapt dynamically to QoS degradation. Admission control is responsible for performing the admissibility test. Such tests include the schedulability test, bandwidth allocation test, and buffer allocation test. The connection manager is required to closely interact with the QoS manager and with admission control to achieve guaranteed performance. The management plane, including layer management and plane management, is responsible for Operation, Administration, Maintenance, and Provision (OAM&P) services. Layer management and plane management provide intra-plane and inter-plane management for seamless communication.

3.3 NETWORKING
The multimedia network, encompassing the transmission media and the transport protocols, delivers multimedia traffic with QoS guarantee. According to application requirements, the transmission media may be wired (twisted pair, coaxial cable, fiber optics) or wireless (radio channels, satellite channels), and the transport protocols may provide connection-oriented or connectionless services, and best effort or service guaranteed performance commitment. General speaking, the complexity of transport protocols is determined by the mismatch between the QoS requirements of the applications and the QoS support of the underlying networks.

To support multimedia applications, the network must satisfy the requirements of multimedia traffic with diverse characteristics and various QoS requirements. Discrete media traffic (e.g., file transfer, image retrieval) requires error-free services, but is tolerant of delay. Continuous media traffic (e.g., video or audio playback), on the other hand, requires real-time, high-speed transmission, and is connection-oriented. It is sensitive to delay and delay jitter, or the packet delay variations between consecutive packets, but is tolerant of occasional packet losses. In addition, the network has to support application specific requirements. For example, video conferencing needs multicast service for group distribution, and ITV requires switched, point-to-point services, and asymmetric bandwidth for the downstream (video server to user) and the upstream (user to video server) directions. The Internet has rapidly evolved into a significant network infrastructure for communication. It runs the Internet protocol (IP) with its best-effort delivery service, and enjoys a large user base.

Another promising technique, Asynchronous Transfer Mode (ATM), is rapidly appearing in the market, due to the extensive support of telephone companies. It allows bandwidth-on-demand and guaranteed QoS, and is expected to be the best candidate for high-quality, broadband media delivery. In the following, we will examine the Internet effort toward the support of multimedia transmission, the elegant properties of ATM, which make it especially suited for distributed multimedia applications, and the issues of integrating ATM networks with the emerging Integrated Services Internet.

3.3.1. Internet
Internet refers to the global network to which a large percentage of existing networks are now interconnected by routers or gateways. It runs the TCP/IP protocol suite. IP is the key to success for the Internet. It provides point-to-point and datagram delivery (best effort, connectionless) service, and leaves the reliability issues (delay, out of order delivery, packet losses, misdelivery) to the end-systems. It uses a global addressing scheme for a vast range of services. Each datagram, in addition to data, carries routing information in the header to be independently forwarded to the destination.

The primitive service model of the Internet promises only point-to-point and best-effort services. Such services are particularly suited for traditional applications such as file transfer, WWW browsing, and remote login. It performs well for real-time media traffic (e.g., video, audio) only under lightly loaded networks. The development of IP multicast, resource reservation, and higher-level real-time transport protocols are the major efforts on the Internet geared toward the support of multimedia applications. We will examine these three issues next.

(1) IP Multicast

Multicast refers to the ability to send a single packet to multiple destinations. Applications that require multicast capability include teleconferencing, email multicast, Usenet news, remote learning, and group communication. Traditional protocols such as TCP or User Data Protocol (UDP) provide only unicast transmission. The provision of multicast service with unicast transmission requires the delivery of replicated unicast packets to each recipient. To avoid sending multiple replicated unicast copies, thereby increasing network utilization, multicast transmission is required. Figure 5 shows the difference between unicasting and multicasting. With IP multicast, each data source sends an IP packet to a multicast address, and lets the network forward a copy of the packet to each of a group of hosts. The basic transport service of IP multicast is unreliable multicast transmission of datagrams, which is suitable for applications geared more toward performance than reliability. A reliable protocol for IP multicast, called Multicast Transport Protocol (MTP) [22], has been developed to ensure atomicity and reliability.

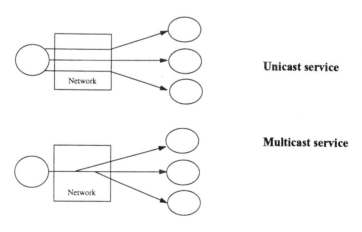

Figure 5. Unicast vs. multicast.

Multicast routing protocols provide a mechanism that enables routers to propagate multicast datagrams a way that minimizes the number of excess copies transmitted to any particular subnet. In addition, they must be flexible to allow participants to join and leave the system without affecting others. The key is to determine which hosts on which subnet will participate in the group. Multicast routing protocols are either the extension of the existing unicast routing protocols, such as Distance Vector Multicast Routing Protocol (DVMRP) [23] and Multicast Open Shortest Path First (MOSPF) [24], or the design from scratch, such as Core Base Tree (CBT) [25] and Protocol Independent Multicast (PIM) [26].

IP multicast services in the Internet were realized with the development of MBone (Multicast Backbone). It was first used to deliver live audio conference sessions of an Internet Engineering Task Force (IETF) meeting in the Internet in 1992. MBone is a virtual network implementing class D addressing and tunneling on top of the physical Internet [27]. The network consists of subnet that can directly support IP multicast, such as Ethernet or FDDI, connected by virtual point-to-point tunnels. Tunnel-connected endpoints are multicast-enhanced routers (i.e., mrouters), that encapsulate multicast IP packets within regular IP datagrams for transmission through the existing Internet. Since they look like normal unicast packets, no special treatment by any regular routers and subnets is necessary. When an mrouter receives a packet through a tunnel, it strips off the header and multicasts the packet as appropriate. The multicast routing protocol adopted by the MBone is DVMRP. MBone supports many applications such as multi-party video-conferencing and entertainment. The most popular MBone tools include network video (nv), visual audio tool (vat), and shared drawing whiteboard (wb).

(2) ReSerVation Protocol (RSVP)

RSVP is a IP-based resource reservation protocol developed for the support of the desired QoS level for real-time traffic, such as audiovisual conferencing. Datagram delivery essentially provides best effort services. RSVP supports the concept of flow, which is the network traffic stream from the sender to one or more receivers and is one important step toward the support of a new service model. It serves as a vehicle to communicate with the network for the requirements of applications. Strictly speaking, it can be treated as a signaling protocol in the sense that its primary purpose is to set up the "state" in the network routers for the establishment, maintenance, and teardown of the flow. Three important features of reservation principles of RSVP are: receiver-initiated, soft state, and merging and reservation style. RSVP is receiver-initiated so that it can (1) accommodate heterogeneous receivers with diverse requirements of the service quality, and (2) allow group members to dynamically join and leave without disturbing the sender and the other participants. RSVP supports the soft state and therefore periodic updates to the states at the intermediate routers are required, where the soft state refers to "a state maintained at network switches which, when lost, will be automatically reinstated by RSVP soon thereafter" [28]. It enables (1) the flexibility of dynamic group membership management, and (2) the robustness of the adaptive to the changes of flow routes. Finally, the merging and different reservation styles are designed to share the resources among different applications with different QoS requirements.

RSVP supports two types of messages: Path and Reservation (Resv). Each sender sends a Path message to the one or more receivers in the routing direction. When a router receives a Path message, it records the relevant information and sends a Resv message in the reverse direction of the Path message back to the sender. Multiple receivers in the same multicast group may send Resv messages toward the same sender. These Resv messages are merged as they travel back up in the multicast tree, and only the merged Resv is forwarded toward the sender. These two types of messages are sent periodically to refresh the states in the intermediate nodes. In this way, when a new participant requests to join, it informs the local LAN of its existence and may incur a slight change of the mutlicast tree. It waits for the Path message from the sender and then sends back the Resv message; then, it officially joins the corresponding session. From the sender and the others perspective, such join, or leave, makes no difference for their operations: the sender sends the Path message and the receivers send the Resv message periodically to refresh their states in the routers.

(3) Real-time Transport Protocol (RTP)

RTP provides end-to-end data transport services for the delivery of real-time data (e.g., video, audio) over unicast or multicast networks [29]. The data transport is augmented by the RTP Control Protocol (RTCP) to monitor QoS and provide minimal control, management, and identification. RTP and RTCP make no assumption on transport protocols and the underlying network, although they are typically run on top of UDP/IP and IP multicast. Except for framing, RTP makes no specific assumptions on the capabilities of the lower layers. It does not perform resource reservation, and no QoS guarantees are made. In addition, no mechanisms are defined for flow control and reliability. Timely delivery relies only on the support of lower-layer services such as RSVP that have control over the resources in networks. The functions supported by RTP include time-stamping, sequence numbering, translator, and mixer. Based on the timing information and sequence number carried in the RTP header, receivers are allowed to reconstruct and play audio and video sequences, despite occasional loss or misdelivery of packets.

3.3.2. B-ISDN and Asynchronous Transfer Mode (ATM)

ATM is basically virtual circuit switching, enhanced by the virtual path concept. It uses small, fixed-size (53 bytes, 5 for header and 48 for payload) cells and simple communication protocols to reduce per-cell processing and to speed up switching. The ATM network has a layered structure allowing multimedia traffic to be mixed in the network. It includes the upper layer, ATM Adaptation layer (AAL), ATM layer, and physical layer.

1. The upper layer includes higher layer protocols such as TCP, RTP, and Xpress Transport Protocol (XTP).
2. The AAL layer adapts the upper layer protocols to the ATM format. It inserts or extracts user information as 48-byte payloads. The AAL layer consists of two sub-layers: the convergence sub-layer (CS) and the segmentation and reassembly (SAR) sub-layer. CS converges different types of user traffic, and encapsulates/decapsulates data flow to and from the SAR sub-layer. The SAR sub-layer, in the sender, segments data into a series of 48-byte cells, and in the receiver, reassembles cell sequences back to the original data.
2   The ATM layer adds or strips the 5-byte header to or from the payload. For the sender, it takes 48-byte data from the AAL, and adds the 5-byte header that contains routing information to ensure the cell is sent on the right connection; for the receiver, it strips the 5-byte header and passes the 48-byte payload to the corresponding AAL.
3   The physical layer defines the electrical characteristics and network interfaces, and places ATM cells into the transmission medium. The ATM network is not tied to a specific type of physical medium, but is optimized to work with the Synchronous Optical Network (SONET).

3.3.3. The Integration of IP and ATM

The two major contenders as the protocol for global internetworking are IP and ATM. For either to succeed, there are major obstacles. The strength of IP is the large installed base. It is the protocol used in the Internet, which is the biggest and fastest-growing computer network in the world. The Internet is a packet-switched network and basically provides connectionless and best-effort transport services. The major problem is that the best-effort delivery of messages does not support the various QoS required in a truly integrated service network. In addition, the existing Internet has very limited bandwidth, although there are plans to upgrade to higher bandwidth. The development of IP multicast, resource reservation protocols, and real-time transport protocols allows the Internet to provide limited forms of multimedia services. Even with the upgraded bandwidth, the Internet will be inadequate for many multimedia applications, such as VOD. On the other hand, the ATM network is connection-oriented. The strength of ATM lies in the possibility to set up connections with a class of service, which matches the requirements of the application involved. The planned bit rates and bit error rates also meet the requirements of real-time transmission of audio and video streams. However, ATM works best in an environment where every one uses ATM, and the major obstacle is the large installed base of non-ATM equipment. The Internet community is developing resource reservation protocols, such as RSVP, which give QoS guarantees. In addition, IP over ATM has been successfully deployed. The future global internetworking protocol will likely be one that supports QoS guarantees, and may include both ATM and IP technologies.

3.4 MULTIMEDIA OPERATING SYSTEM

Operating systems (OS) manage computer resources (e.g., CPU, memory, I/O devices, etc.), hide the physical characteristics of the underlying hardware, and provide an efficient and convenient environment for end-users. A multimedia operating system extends the functionalities of traditional OS to accommodate multimedia data manipulation to provide an environment for real-time support and QoS-based resource management while simultaneously running traditional applications efficiently. Together they ensure that QoS requirements of multimedia applications are met, and provide intelligent overload control for transient misses of playback deadlines. A multimedia OS may be developed as an extension of traditional OS, or constructed from scratch such as by using the micro-kernel architecture (e.g.,Chorus [30], Real-Time Mach [31]). In any case, it should provide the following functions: (1) conventional OS functionalities such as CPU scheduling, memory management, device management, I/O management, and file management, and (2) QoS-based resource management, and temporal and synchronization support.

3.5 SYNCHRONIZATION

Multimedia synchronization attempts to ensure the desired temporal ordering among a set of multimedia objects in a multimedia scenario, where multimedia scenario denotes the temporal semantics of a multimedia session [32,33]. Multimedia synchronization mechanisms aim at preserving the playback continuity of media frames within single continuous media, and the desired temporal dependencies among multiple related data objects, given that user interactions are allowed. Temporal dependency may either be *implicit* or *explicit*. For implicit dependency, the timing relationship is captured at the time of media acquisition. One such example is lip synchronization, which refers to the requirement that the voice should match the movement of the lips of the speaker. Explicit dependency means that the time relationship is created explicitly. A slide show with pictures and annotated text is an example.

Multimedia synchronization differs from traditional synchronization mechanisms, such as monitor or semaphore, in that it imposes real-time constraints (i.e., deadlines) on the event, and differs from real-time systems in that such deadlines are predetermined, periodic, and soft (i.e., no disaster is caused if the deadlines are missed). Missing deadlines in multimedia presentation may annoy users with synchronization anomalies, such as hiccups in audio or jerkiness in video. The correction of such synchronization anomalies includes dropping, blocking, duplicating, or re-sampling frames at the presentation site to resynchronize the playback. For example, restricted blocking [34] repeats the display of the last frame or takes alternative action (such as playing some music) to fill up the time, in order to resynchronize the presentation. It has been shown that human beings are less tolerant of audio than of video errors. Therefore, in an integrated service network in which the audio stream is competing with the video stream for network resources, higher priority should be accorded the audio stream.

In a distributed system, the enforcement of such coordinated presentation becomes more complicated, because, for each stream, random delays may be incurred along the data path: data retrieval in the storage system, data transmission in the network, and data processing in the host computer. Media sources are widely distributed, and different media located in remote sites may be required to be played back in a coordinated fashion at the same time or at multiple sites on the network. Without proper orchestration, the existence of random delays among multiple related streams may result in synchronization anomalies, such as loss of lip synchronization. Another associated problem is the synchronization accuracy between the clocks of the sender and the receiver when global timing knowledge is used. Currently, the Internet uses the Network Time Protocol (NTP) [35] to solve this problem. Ramanathan and Rangan [36] proposed a protocol, which employs adaptive feedback techniques, to synchronize multimedia presentation of distributed sources in the absence of a global clock.

According to the granularity, there are three levels of synchronization. (1) *Intra-media* synchronization preserves the temporal relationship between consecutive frames, and the continuity of playback within a single media stream. The basic idea is to satisfy the latency and throughput constraints of the media and to smooth the delay jitters experienced in the storage system, the network, and the host system, by using real-time protocols (including real-time retrieval, real-time transport, and real-time processing) and providing sufficient buffers along the data path. (2) *Inter-media* synchronization coordinates the different media streams to achieve the desired temporal relationships among them. It can further be categorized as *continuous* synchronization (or *live* synchronization), which preserves the implicit temporal relationships, and *event-driven* synchronization (or *synthetic* synchronization), which maintains the explicit specified temporal relationships. Inter-media synchronization is provided by the orchestration layer (shown in Figure 4) of the QoS reference model, which performs end-to-end orchestration to achieve inter-stream coordination for a meaningful presentation. (3) *Inter-party* synchronization maintains the intra-media and/or inter-media synchronization among different participants at distributed locations.

In general, multimedia synchronization can be divided into two levels of treatment: temporal specification and temporal synchronization. *Temporal specification* sits on the upper level. It models the temporal relationships among the set of related abstract multimedia objects of a presentation scenario, where an abstract object denotes a logical unit of media data, such as a video object or a text object. Temporal relationships among different objects can be represented by either graphical-based (e.g., Timed Petri Net [37] or flow graph [38]), language-based [39], or a hybrid [40] description. Graphics-based specification takes advantage of pictorial visualization. Language-based methodology exploits the power of flexible expression of language, which enables ease of inclusion of user interactions. *Temporal synchronization* locates at the lower level. It translates the temporal specification of a presentation scenario into the desired presentation scheduling sequences, and enforces the playback deadlines, despite the indeterministic delays due to the server, the network, and the host system.

3.6 MULTIMEDIA INFORMATION SYSTEM

A multimedia information system manages the exponentially growing multimedia information generated by various applications, ranging from desktop multimedia interactive services to distributed, collaborative, hypermedia systems. It can be a multimedia database system (MDBS) or a media server. An MDBS differs from a multimedia server in that the MDBS provides all users a common interface, high-level query support, and management services for data handling; while the media server leaves the responsibilities of formatting, organizing, and managing multimedia data to the users. An MDBS is composed of multimedia databases (MDB) and a database management system (DBMS). The inclusion of multimedia data introduces more challenges into the design of DBMS for the MDBS. Such challenges come from the new application needs and the nature of multimedia data which coexist in the system, including (1) time-dependent and time-independent media, (2) structured and uninterpreted (or raw) data content, (3) single data type and composite document, (4) one-dimensional (e.g., text, audio), two-dimensional (e.g., image), and three-dimensional (e.g., video) media, (5) a wide range of data volume, (6) short duration and long duration transaction, (7) passive and interactive presentation, and (8) single user and multiple participant collaboration. These call for new supports such as QoS guarantee, efficient storage management, content-based access plus indexing and browsing, presentation and authoring, and media integration and composition.

In essence, an MDBS is an intelligent, integrated object repository. It supports the various media types and provides the facilities for data handling and presentation. Typical design approaches may come from the direct extension of the existing database systems or from the development of new systems from scratch. The extension approach develops a multimedia extension on top of the existing data model or database system. The object-oriented database systems designed for news-on-demand at the University of Alberta [41] is one such example. This approach is ease of development. However, the inherent restrictions and lack of multimedia capabilities of the underlying DBMS may introduce inefficiencies and inflexibility in the management and manipulation of multimedia information. The development-from-scratch approach allows multimedia features to be embedded into the core of the data model. Figure 6 shows the functional components of a generic architecture of the multimedia database system. The standard alphanumeric database contains non-multimedia, real-world application entities. The multimedia database contains information about multimedia objects, and their properties and relationships. The metadatabase stores content-dependent metadata extracted by the feature processing module and used for content-based retrieval. With the support of processing modules, the database system allows complex content-based queries, and acts as an intelligent agent.

3.6.1. Multimedia Data Modeling

The data model sits at the heart of the multimedia database system. It must be able to model the structure and semantics of multimedia documents flexibly and efficiently, allow the temporal and spatial compositions to support the presentation task, coordinate the sharing of multimedia information among multiple users, and support the fundamental functions for digital media handling, including content-based retrieval, indexing, browsing, and other media specific operations. No restriction should be placed on the creation and modeling of how the data is actually used, and users should be allowed to compose data in an arbitrary manner. Finally, it should be efficient at managing complex data and long computing time media functions. The simple node and link model in hypermedia system, and the flat relational data model were proven not to be rich and flexible enough to satisfy the productivity and performance requirements of multimedia application development [42]. The object-oriented data model, on the other hand, enables rich semantic relationships among objects thereby providing the modeling flexibility of arbitrary data type, data size, data structure, and supporting content-based access and media presentation interactivity as well. This model has been considered to be the best candidate for the multimedia DBMS by some researchers [43]. Another promising alternative is the object-relational data model, which in essence is a hybrid of the relational and the object-oriented data models. It combines the rich modeling power of the object-oriented model with the Structured Query Language (SQL) support of the relational model. One notable commercial product of the object-relational model is *Illustra*.

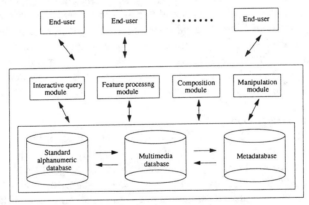

Figure 6. The generic architecture of a multimedia database system.

3.6.2. Representation, Manipulation, and Presentation of Data

A multimedia database system provides mechanisms to define and manipulate multimedia information. The data definition language (DDL) allows users to specify (both structured and uninterpreted) content, QoS parameters, and integration of multimedia data objects with arbitrary data types, object structures, and arbitrary data sizes. The data manipulation language (DML) allows users to (1) manipulate data objects with such media specific functions as play, fast-forward, and pause for video or audio, or blur, sharpen, condense, warp, and morph for image, (2) share and integrate multimedia information, (3) perform non-linear editing, and (4) query support. Multimedia query support is an important topic for MDBS. Keyword indexing for raw data is more difficult because of its unstructured nature. The content-based, or visual and/or aural supported query is more desirable for multimedia information. Such query may be in the form of query language, or query by example. In addition, browsing may be used to search for multimedia information when one only has incomplete information on what one is looking for, especially in hypermedia applications. Typically one alternates between two steps: browsing the material to narrow the searching range, and then precisely searching for a particular target. During browsing, one just glances over the data. Therefore, the representative features of objects can be extracted to facilitate browsing. The temporal and spatial composition is key for the meaningful presentation of multimedia documents. The spatial structure describes the spatial relationship of multimedia information for display, including the logical and layout structures of the multimedia document, the width and height of an image for display, etc. The temporal composition describes the timing relationship among the related objects.

3.6.3. Metadata Management
Metadata is the data about data. It contains concise information about the characteristics, location, QoS parameters, and content of data. Metadata play a more important role in the multimedia database system than in the traditional structured text-oriented system. Multimedia information, in addition to text, contains a large portion of visual (e.g., images and video) and aural (e.g., speech and music) data. It is usually very hard to perform exact match via content-based searches, and even if it is possible, it is very time-consuming. Therefore, additional information along with the information content, such as semantics and composition among the related data, derived or interpreted data, and content irrelevant data (e.g., attributes of data, creation date, author), are required. Such information is metadata. Metadata help and ease the management of large volumes of data, information query and retrieval, material sharing, and directory services. According to the functionality, metadata may be classified in the following categories. (1) *Descriptive* metadata, which specify the content irrelevant information about data, such as data type, attribute, material title, file size, program type, author name, creation or modification date, storage location, and other related information. (2) *Content-based* metadata, which specify content dependent features, and are generated automatically or semi-automatically from the information content. This type of metadata is used to assist in content-based query and retrieval. For example, the eigenvalues and eigenvectors extracted from images via the user impression and image content [44] can be used as content-based metadata. (3) *Structural* metadata, which specify the temporal and/or spatial compositions of data. The metadata generation methods are media dependent, with the rule of thumb that automatic (rather than manual) generation is more desirable.

3.6.4. Transaction Management
Transaction management ensures reliable storage of multimedia information and consistent concurrent accesses to these data. Multimedia data size and structure may be arbitrary. The unit of data in a transaction, therefore, should be flexible enough to represent all data objects. In addition, multimedia data in a transaction may be time-dependent and time-independent. The concurrency control manager should satisfy the real-time constraints of the time-dependent transactions, while preventing the time-independent transactions from starvation. Multimedia transaction should be able to model the characteristic of long-duration and interactive database access of multimedia applications. Traditional concurrency control mechanisms, such as two-phase locking and time-stamp ordering, strictly enforce the serializability of transaction executions, and are appropriate for short duration transactions. With such exclusive, serialized access, intolerably long waiting time will be incurred, and a large amount of work will be lost when transactions are aborted before being committed. In multimedia transactions, temporary violation of the serializability in execution will not result in big errors as in traditional business transactions, but may allow flexibility of interactions among cooperative users. This calls for relaxing serializability as the consistency criteria, and devising new correctness criteria.

4. CONCLUSIONS

Distributed multimedia applications emerge from advances in a variety of technologies, spawning new applications which in turn push such technologies to their limits and demand fundamental changes to satisfy a diversity of new requirements. With the rapid development of the Internet, distributed multimedia applications are accelerating the realization of the information superhighway, creating gigantic potential new markets, and ushering in a new era in human communications. Up-to-the-minute information, computer simulated immersive experience (virtual reality), on-demand services, telecommuting, etc., will be the way of life in the future.

This chapter gives an overview of distributed multimedia systems, identifies the applications, and surveys the enabling technologies. Much effort has been made in various areas by both the academic and the industrial communities. However, many research issues still need to be resolved before distributed multimedia applications can be widely deployed. Such applications consume considerable system resources, require system-wide QoS guarantees to ensure their correct delivery and presentation, and must be provided with friendly user interfaces. More user control and interactivity are desired. Faster processors and hardware, higher network bandwidths and data compression ratios, and improvements in a variety of related technologies are necessary. Standardization is also important to accommodate the heterogeneity of techniques, and to provide portability of applications. The intellectual property rights of the creators of multimedia works must be protected to encourage the creation of such works. Deregulation will accelerate the convergence of the telecommunications, cable TV, entertainment, and consumer electronics industries. Social and human factors should be considered in the development and deployment of new applications. Finally, for these applications to be commercially viable, costs will be an important consideration.

REFERENCES

1. V. O. K. Li and W. J. Liao. "Distributed Multimedia Systems," *Proceedings of the IEEE*, Vol. 85, No. 7, July 1997.
2. G. Blakowski and R. Steinmetz. "A Media Synchronization Survey: Reference Model, Specification, and Case Studies," *IEEE Journal on Selected Areas in Communications*, Vol. 14, No. 1, pp. 5-35, January 1996.
3. B. Furht. "Multimedia Systems: an Overview," *IEEE Multimedia*, pp. 47-59, Spring 1994.
4. N. Williams and G. S. Blair. "Distributed Multimedia Applications: a Review," *Computer Communications*, Vol. 17, No. 2, pp. 199-132, 1994.
5. Special Issue on Multimedia Communications, *IEEE Journal on Selected Areas in Communications*, Vol. 8, No. 3, 1990.
6. Special Issue on Multimedia Information Systems, *IEEE Computer*, Vol. 24, No. 10, 1991.
7. Special Issue on Multimedia Communications, *IEEE Communications Magazine*, Vol. 30, No. 5, May 1992.
8. Special Issue on Distributed Multimedia Systems, *Computer Journal*, Vol. 36, No. 1, 1993.
9. Special Issue on Multimedia Information Systems, *IEEE Transactions on Knowledge and Data Engineering*, Vol. 5, No. 4, August 1993.
10. Special Issue on Multimedia, *IEEE Computer*, Vol. 28, No. 5, May 1995.
11. G. K. Wallace. "The JPEG Still Picture Compression Standard," *Communications of the ACM*, Vol. 34, No. 4, pp. 30-44, 1991.
12. ISO IEC JTC 1 "Information Technology - Digital Compression and Coding of Continuous-Tone Still Images," International Standard ISO/IEC IS 10918, 1993
13. M. Liou. "Overview of the px64 Kbit/s Video Coding Standard," *Communications of the ACM*, Vol. 34, No. 4, pp. 59-63, 1991.
14. D. L. Gall. "MPEG: a Video Compression Standard for Multimedia Applications," *Communications of the ACM*, Vol. 34, No. 4, pp. 46-58, 1991.
15. ISO IEC JTC 1 "Information Technology - Coding of Moving Pictures and Associated Audio for Digital Storage Media Up to About 1.5 Mbit/s," International Standard ISO/IEC IS 11 172, 1993.
16. K. C. Pohlmann, Principles of Digital Audio, *Mc-Graw Hill*, 1995.

17. D. Y. Pan. "A Tutorial MPEG/Audio Compression," *IEEE Multimedia*, pp. 60-74, Spring 1995.
18. A. Vogel, B. Kerherve, G. V. Bockmann, and J. Gecsei. "Distributed Multimedia and QOS: A Survey," *IEEE Multimedia*, pp. 10-19, Summer 1995.
19. A. Campell, G. Coulson, and D. Hutchison. "A Quality of Service Architecture," *Computer Communication Review*, Vol. 24, No. 2, pp. 6-27, April 1994.
20. K. Nahrsted and R. Steinmetz. "Resource Management in Networked Multimedia Systems," *IEEE Computer*, Vol. 28, No. 5, pp. 52-63, May 1995.
21. K. Nahrstedt and J. M. Smith. "The QOS Broker," *IEEE Multimedia*, pp. 53-67, Spring 1995.
22. S. Armstrong, A. Freier, and K. Marzullo. "Multicast Transport Protocol," Internet RFC 1301, 1992.
23. D. Waitzman, C. Partridge, and S. Deering. "Distance Vector Multicast Routing Protocol," RFC 1075, November 1988.
24. J. Moy. " Multicast Extensions to OSPF," RFC 1584, March 1994.
25. A. Ballardie. "Core Based Tree (CBT) Multicast Routing Architecture," RFC 2201, September 1997.
26. S. Deering, D. Estrin, D. Farinacci, V. Jacobson, Ching-Gung Liu, and Liming Wei. "An Architecture for Wide-Area Multicast Routing," *ACM SIGCOMM*, pp.126-135, 1994.
27. M. R. Macedonia and D. P. Brutzman. "MBone Provides Audio and Video Across the Internet," *IEEE Computer*, pp. 30-36, April 1994.
28. L. Zhang, S. Deering, D. Estrin, S. Shenker, and D. Zappala. "RSVP: a New Resource ReSerVation Protocol," *IEEE Network*, pp. 8-18, September 1993.
29. H. Schulzrinne, S. Casner, R. Frederick, and V. Jacobson. "RTP: A Transport Protocol for Real-time Applications," Internet RFC 1889, January 1996.
30. G. Coulson, G. S. Blair, and P. Robin. "Micro-Kernel Support for Continuous Media in Distributed Systems," *Computer Networks and ISDN Systems*, Vol. 26, pp. 1323-1341, 1994.
31. H. Tokuda, T. Nakajima, and P. Rao. "Real-Time Mach: Towards a Predictable Real-Time System, " *Proc. Usenix Mach Workshop*, 1990.
32. Synchronization Issues in Multimedia Communications, *IEEE Journal on Selected Areas in Communications*, Vol. 14, No. 1, January 1996.
33. M. J. Perez-Luque and T. D. C. Little. "A Temporal Reference Framework for Multimedia Synchronization," *IEEE Journal on Selected Areas in Communications*, Vol. 14, No. 1, pp. 36-51, January 1996.
34. R. Steinmetz. "Synchronization Properties in Multimedia Systems," *IEEE Journal on Selected Areas in Communications*, Vol. 8, No. 3, pp. 401-412, April 1990.
35. D. L. Mills. "Internet Time Synchronization: The Network Time Protocol," *IEEE Trans. on Communications*, Vol. 39, No.10, pp. 1482-1493, October 1991.
36. S. Ramanathan and P.V. Rangan. "Adaptive Feedback Techniques for Synchronized Multimedia Retrieval over Integrated Networks," *IEEE/ACM Transactions on Networking*, Vol. 1, No. 2, pp. 246-260, April 1993.
37. T. D.C. Little and A. Ghafoor. "Synchronization and Storage Models for Multimedia Objects," *IEEE Journal on Selected Areas in Communications*, Vol. 8, No. 3, pp. 413-427, April 1990.
38. L. Li, A. Karmouch, and N.D. Georganas. "Multimedia Teleorchestra with Independent Sources: Part 1 - Temporal Modeling of Collaborative Multimedia Scenarios," *Multimedia Systems*, Vol. 1, No. 4, pp.143-153, 1994.
39. G. S. Blair, G. Coulson, M. Papathomas, P. Robin, J. B. Stefani, F. Horn, and L. Hazard. "A Programming Model and System Infrastructure for Real-Time Synchronization in Distributed Multimedia systems," *Journal on Selected Areas in Communications*, Vol. 14, No. 1, pp. 249-263, 1996.
40. C. M. Huang and C. M. Lo. "An EFSM-based Multimedia Synchronization Model and the Authoring System," *IEEE Journal on Selected Areas in Communications*, Vol. 14, No. 1, pp. 138-152, January 1996.
41. M. T. Ozsu, D. Szafron, G. Elmedani, and C. Vittal. "An Object-Oriented Multimedia Database System for a News-on-Demand Application," *Multimedia Systems*, Vol. 3, No. 5/6, pp. 217-227, 1995.
42. W. Klas, E. J. Neuhold, and M. Schrefl. "Using an Object-Oriented Approach to Model Multimedia Data," *Computer Communications*, Vol. 13, No. 4, pp. 204-216, 1990.
43. K. C. Nwosu, B. Thuraisingham, and P. B. Berra. "Multimedia Database Systems – A New Frontier," *IEEE Multimedia*, pp. 24-32, July-September 1997.
44. Y. Kiyoki, T. Kitagawa, and T. Hayama. "A Metadatabase System for Semantic Image Search by a Mathematical Model of Meaning," *ACM SIGMOD Records*, Vol. 23, No. 4, pp. 34-41, 1994.

33

INTERACTIVE MOVIES

Ryohei Nakatsu and Naoko Tosa
ATR Media Integration & Communications Research Laboratories
2-2, Hikaridai, Seika-cho, Soraku-gun, Kyoto, 619-02 Japan

1.   **INTRODUCTION**..702
2.   **POSITIONING OF INTERACTIVE MOVIES**.................................702
    2.1   CONCEPT...702
    2.2   EXAMINATION OF CONVENTIONAL MEDIA................................702
    2.3   INTERACTIVE MOVIES AS A NEW TYPE OF MEDIA.....................703
3.   **STORY GENERATION**...704
4.   **SCENE GENERATION**..705
5.   **CHARACTER GENERATION**...705
6.   **INTERACTIONS**...706
7.   **EXAMPLE OF SYSTEM CONFIGURATION**.................................706
    7.1   MAIN FEATURES 706
    7.2   SOFTWARE CONFIGURATION..707
    7.3   HARDWARE CONFIGURATION 709
8.   **EXAMPLE OF INTERACTIVE STORY PRODUCTION**.................710
9.   **CONCLUSION** 711
    REFERENCES 712

Abstract. It is highly desirable for new types of media to emerge based on multimedia technologies, virtual reality technologies, and AI technologies. As an example of a new type of media, 'interactive movies' are proposed which will be created by the integration of conventional media such as movies, telecommunications, and video games. Interactive movies have the capability of creating a virtual world with various kinds of realistic/hyper-realistic scenes and computer characters. In addition, it can give people the ability to interact within this virtual world using speech and gestures. Therefore, people can experience stories in the virtual world through interactions with the characters and the environments of the world. In this chapter, the basic concept of such a new media will be described along with an experimental system we have developed.

1. INTRODUCTION

It is highly desirable for new types of media to emerge based on multimedia technologies, virtual reality technologies, and AI technologies. The concepts of such new media are expected to be extensions of present trends in the areas of telecommunications, entertainment, and amusement. In this field, significant changes are now taking place. A single statement can describe these changes: a new technology is bringing cyberspace to telecommunications, entertainment, and amusement.

For example, in the field of telecommunications, the Internet is creating new communication sites. The Internet can be regarded as a huge cyberspace that links people all over the world. In the movie industry, which forms a huge entertainment market, digital technology and computer graphics give moviemakers the power to create hyper-realities – cyberspaces – on the screen. Video games, particularly role-playing games (RPGs) allow players to participate in the games as the main character and experience virtual reality, or cyberspace.

There is a high possibility that a new dream media will be created by combining these new currents of technology that are tiding over the fields of telecommunications, movies, and games. As one example of this dream media. we propose "Interactive Movies." Interactive movies produce a cyberspace that offers hyper-realistic images and scenes, and enables people to "enter" that virtual reality world. In cyberspace, people can interact with the human-like characters, animals, and plants in the story. This function enables an individual to create his or her own unique cyberspace, in which the person can act out the leading role.

In this chapter, we describe the positioning of interactive movies, and then we examine the requirements for constructing them. We will also introduce the details of an interactive movie project that we are currently working on.

2. POSITIONING OF INTERACTIVE MOVIES

2.1 CONCEPT

Interactive movies are a new type of media that integrates conventional media such as movies, novels, video games, and telecommunications. The closest description of interactive movies, in relation to conventional media, is "movies or theaters that allow the audience to 'experience' the story through participation." Interactive movies consist of the following elements:

(1) Interactive stories that allow the participants to interact.
(2) Participants who can individually "experience" the virtual reality created by the interactive story as the main character.
(3) Characters that interact with the main character in the story development.

2.2 EXAMINATION OF CONVENTIONAL MEDIA

For a medium to gain popularity, it must attract the interest of people and draw their attention. Conventional media use various methods to draw readers or audiences into the realities created by them and to affect their emotions. The following are representative types of conventional media.

(1) Novels and poems

Novels and poems draw on the power of words to lure readers into the world depicted by the writers so that the readers can "experience" what the writers intended to provide to them. The main factor that allows this is the imaginative power of people. People can envision an image in their minds from a verbal or written description.

(2) Movies

In a movie, visual images are shown on a large screen, and loud sounds accompany the images. Therefore, a movie appeals to both the visual and auditory senses of people, and draws them into the imaginary world shown on the screen. The rapid advancement of computer graphics technology in recent years has enabled the creation of imaginary situations and impossible events on the screen as if they were real. A movie pulls its audience into an imaginary world by feeding overwhelming visual and audio information to the audience, rather than stimulating their imagination.

(3) Video games

Video games, especially role-playing games (RPGs), present stories similar to those of novels in a game format. A player controls the story development by manipulating the main character. Although a variety of elements are incorporated, RPGs can be considered a new type of media that brings interaction into the stories of novels. It not only gives pleasant stimulation to people's senses, but also affects the players' emotions.

2.3 INTERACTIVE MOVIES AS A NEW TYPE OF MEDIA

We have examined the possibility of creating a new type of media by combining the story development capability of movies with visual and audio information, the power of novels to appeal to people's imaginations through a simple media form that uses words (language), and the interactive features of video games. Various attempts have been made in the past to create a virtual reality environment that interacts with its audience. These efforts include the creation of computer-generated characters [1][2] that can interact with people on behavioral and emotional levels, and interactive art [3]. However, in these achievements, the interactions were short-lived, and there was no story involved. The movie industry has long cherished the idea of audience-participating movies, but the actual application has been limited to primitive levels. RPGs are the closest in concept to interactive movies, but the essential difference is that RPGs require button operations for interactions while interactive movies aim to enable "person-to-person" interactions. Interactive movies have the following main features.

(1) Establishment of a cyberspace with images and sound

The use of CG, the mixing of CG images and actual footage, and the application of three-dimensional image and sound technologies enable the creation of a virtual reality environment that could not be offered by any other media in the past. This cyberspace provides an unprecedented level of stimulation to the imaginations of people.

(2) Immersion in the cyberspace

The cyberspace created by interactive movies does not exist separately from the audience, but the audience can enter this virtual reality environment.

(3) Experiencing the story in cyberspace

In an interactive movie cyberspace, the participant is more than an observer; the participant is the main character in the environment and experiences the story that takes place in that world. This is expected to provide a new realm of experience to people.

(4) Interactions in cyberspace

People can interact with other "residents" in a cyberspace – in the case of a movie, characters surrounding the main character – by talking and gesturing in the story.

The creation of these functions requires combined efforts in both technical and artistic areas. In many of the successful media such as movies and RPGs, creative efforts by technical and artistic people have been indispensable. Hollywood movies once entered a period of decline. However, the industry emerged from that dark age by successfully combining advanced CG technologies with know-how in artistic image rendering accumulated through many years of movie production. Like movies, RPGs are also acquiring artistic elements. For instance, the story setting and development in RPGs are well planned, and original music is produced and inserted effectively to match the story. In developing the interactive movie, creating "advanced" interactions should not be the main focus of using the latest sound and image processing technologies. Instead, the interaction technology should be regarded as a means of enabling the audience to participate in the story interactively and to experience the virtual reality. For this reason, the technical features of interactions must be in balance with other elements. Artistic aspects are also important in interactive stories. Therefore, the use of artistic talents (script writers, visual artists, music composers, etc.) must be maximized in interactive movie production, so that the story takes full advantage of interactive features, the visual images captivate the viewers, and the music enhances the visual images.

Figure 1 shows how an interactive movie is related to each type of conventional media described above. Of all the basic elements in an interactive movie, the most important are the cyberspace generating functions and interaction functions. The cyberspace generating functions include the story generating function, the scene generating function, and the cyberspace character generating function. The following describes these basic functions in detail.

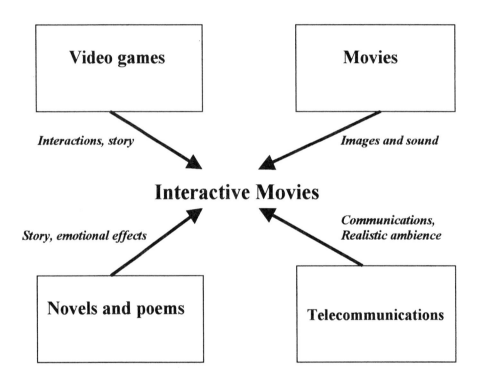

Figure 1. Interactive movies in comparison with conventional media.

3. STORY GENERATION

This section focuses on the details of the methods for designing and producing a story that develops through interaction with the audience. The following shows the systems of story development that can be applied to the construction of an interactive story.

(1) Semi-fixed story type
In the semi-fixed story type, the main plot of the story is predetermined. In this sense, it is similar to the fixed story type that novels and movies are based on. The semi-fixed story type,

however, provides a certain degree of flexibility during the progress of the story. This allows the participant to enjoy limited variations of story development through interactions. Current RPGs are categorized as this type. One advantage of the semi-fixed story type is that the accumulated know-how in story writing and movie making can be directly applied.

(2) Free development type
A story of the free development type has no scenario, and the story develops in a variety of ways depending on the interactions of the participant. Since it is impossible to predict what actions the participant will take in the story, the production group must consider all possibilities in designing the virtual reality environment. In a sense, this is similar to creating one whole isolated world; accomplishing this is close to impossible. At the same time, having free reign over the story development often puts the participant in a state of confusion, thus in some cases disabling him/her from making decisions.

Therefore, a story of the completely free development type is not expected to be created, at least in the foreseeable future. Considering these story development styles, the semi-fixed story type is deemed the most feasible.

4. SCENE GENERATION

To generate scenes in cyberspace, it is necessary to review the scene generating methods used in various media. The conventional scene generating methods can be roughly divided into the following two systems.

(1) Systems used in novels and poems
Novels and poems must draw on the power of words to communicate to readers. Illustrations are sometimes used in books, but their function is only supplementary. Writing conveys minimal information, and this is the very reason why novels and poems can appeal to the imaginations of people. In other words, novels and poems effectively use the power of written words to generate cyberspace scenes in the minds of readers.

(2) Systems used in movies
Movies use overwhelming images and sounds to generate scenes that the audience can see and hear. Their realistic images and sounds provide so much sensory input to the audience that the viewers can enjoy true-to-life experiences. This, however, may sometimes limit the range of human imagination.

The scene generation method used in recent years is based on a system used in movies, and applies advanced techniques to make the scenes more realistic. Nevertheless, no matter how innovative the images become, people soon grow accustomed to them. On the other hand, properly stimulated, the imaginative faculty of humans is capable of creating a cyberspace that no visual image or sound can match. In other words, virtual reality technology by itself has its limitations in the creation of cyberspaces. For the successful establishment of cyberspaces, the key point is to arrange a condition that works on people's imaginative power and appeals to their emotional faculty.

5. CHARACTER GENERATION

The most important but the most difficult task in producing an interactive movie is the creation of characters that interact with participants and draw them into the world of cyberspace. The following are important points for the generation of characters.

(1) Resemblance to humans
Creating human-like characters does not necessarily mean imitating the appearance of humans. Characters in animation movies do not always look identical to real humans; their

proportions and appearances are deformed to a large extent in many cases. People also instill their feelings into animal characters such as Walt Disney's creations. This is because those characters display a likeness to humans, not in appearance but through actions and behaviors, thereby reinforcing believability [5][6][7]. The characters in the interactive movie must also possess these qualities.

(2) Autonomous characters vs. animated characters
There are two methods of preparing character reaction patterns and the sequences of their motions. In one method, all of the patterns and sequences are prearranged as animated images, while, in the other method, the characters are given an autonomous function that enables them to automatically react and behave on their own to a certain degree. Extensive studies have been conducted on autonomous characters [5][8], but fully autonomous characters have not been developed yet. For this reason, the best approach to take at this time is to use animators for the creation of animated characters, and to gradually equip those characters with an autonomous function.

6. INTERACTIONS

The following describes the key points in achieving smooth interactions between the characters and the participants.

(1) Multi-modal interactions
Communications between people are based on multi-modal interactions. More concretely, in person-to-person communications, we use facial expressions and gestures in addition to verbal expressions. Interactions in interactive movies should also be based on more than one mode of communications, and use the combination of speech and gestures. This not only helps provide for more natural interactions, but also leads to deeper emotional involvement and the infusion of feelings by the participant.

(2) Non-verbal interactions
In person-to-person communications, information is conveyed by spoken words (verbal) and by other means (non-verbal). Non-verbal information includes personal information, emotions, and sensibilities [9]. Unfortunately, previous research activities in communications technology focused on developing a technology that supports verbal information exchange. However, the exchange of emotional and sensory information also serves a vital function in communications. To enable the characters in a virtual reality environment to carry out non-verbal communications with people, it is necessary to equip the characters with functions that recognize and express emotions [2].

7. EXAMPLE OF SYSTEM CONFIGURATION

Based on the above concept and considerations, we are currently developing an interactive movie system.

7.1 MAIN FEATURES
The main features of the interactive movie under development are summarized as follows:

(1) Collaborative work between artists and engineers
As stated in Section 2.3, it is essential to have artistic tastes in creating interactive movies, which are able to catch the heat of people and let them feel empathy. In our project, therefore, in such areas as the creation of an interactive story, music, and CG characters, artists played the main role. On the other hand, in the area of software and hardware system production as well as the interaction technologies, engineers are the key persons.

(2) Adoption of virtual reality technologies
Three-dimensional images projected on an arched screen recreate a true-to-life scene setting. These virtual reality technologies help draw the audience into the world created by the interactive movie.

(3) Natural interactions including non-verbal interactions
Speech recognition and gesture recognition functions are used to achieve natural interactions through verbal communications and gestures. In addition, to make non-verbal interaction possible, recognition of emotions involved in speech is introduced.

(4) Two types of interactions
Two types of interactions are introduced in the process of interactive stories to increase the chances of interactions between a participant and the movie world.

a) Interactions at points where the story development branches off into different directions. The results of the interactions at these points have major effects in the ensuing story development.
b) Interactions that have no effect on the story development. These actions allow the participant to enjoy communications and interactions with other characters in the story.

(5) Multi-story CG animation
Because an interactive story results in a complicated story development, a huge amount of animated images must be prepared for each and every story developing possibility. Although the amount of necessary images can be greatly reduced by equipping the CG characters with an autonomous function, taking that approach can result in unnatural animation as indicated in Section 5. In our research, therefore, we have placed our priorities on achieving the highest level of animation quality, and have prepared all the necessary animated images in advance.

7.2 SOFTWARE CONFIGURATION
Figure 2 shows the software configuration of our system.

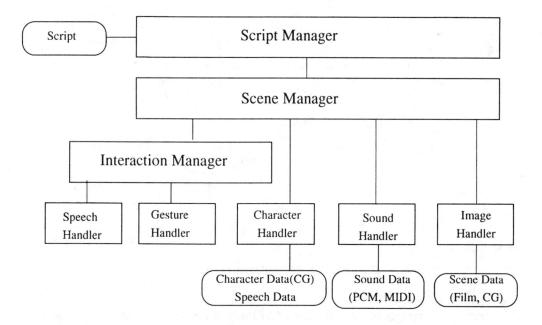

Figure 2. Software configuration.

(1) Script manager

The script manager controls the overall development of the story based on the interactive scenario produced from the script and scenario prepared by the storywriter. An interactive story consists of various kinds of scenes and transitions among scenes. Each scene also consists of various kinds of 'shots' and the transitions among these shots. The functions of the script manager are to define the composing elements of each scene and to control scene transitions based on an infinite automaton, as shown in Figure 3. The transition from a scene to one of possible consecutive scenes is decided based on the interaction result sent from the scene manager.

(2) Scene manager

The scene manager receives the definition of each scene from the script manager and controls the creation of the scenes. Each scene consists of the following factors.

a) Background scene and background music.
b) Character animations and their utterances including the timing for each utterance.
c) The kinds of interactions between a participant and these characters including the timing for the interactions.

The background scenes are made by mixing CG-generated scenarios and actual footage. At the beginning of each scene, the scene manager starts the output of the scene image and background music by sending commands to the appropriate handlers. The characters are generated by CG. Using the information of b), the scene manager starts the animation of each character by controlling the character handler and, at the appropriate time, lets them speak utterances. Additionally, at the predetermined time, the scene manager starts the interactions by sending commands to the interaction manager.

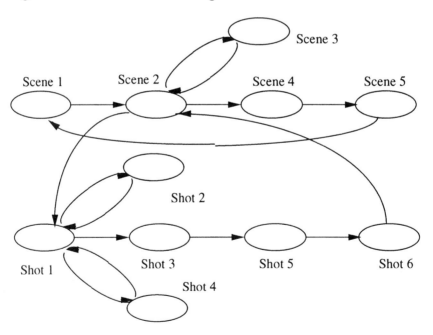

Figure 3. Scene and short transition.

(3) Interaction manager

The interaction manager is under the control of the script manager and the scene manager. The interaction manager controls the interactions that take place in each scene. The interactions are based on speeches and gestures. We use voice recognition, emotion recognition, and image recognition functions as the means of interaction. By receiving commands from the scene manager that indicate the types and timings of the interactions, the interaction manager starts the speech recognition, emotion recognition, and gesture recognition by controlling the appropriate handlers. After receiving multiple recognition results, the interaction manager combines these recognition results, obtains the interaction result and sends it to the script manager through the scene manager, thus achieving a multi-modal interaction function (Figure 4).

(4) Handlers

The handlers are under the control of either the scene manager or the interaction manager. Their functions are to control the various input and output devices. We use the following handlers in our system.

a) Speech handler

The speech handler controls the speech recognition function and emotion recognition function. The speech recognition algorithm is based on an HMM while the emotion recognition algorithm is based on a Neural Network architecture.

b) Gesture handler
c) Character handler
d) Sound handler
e)   Image handler

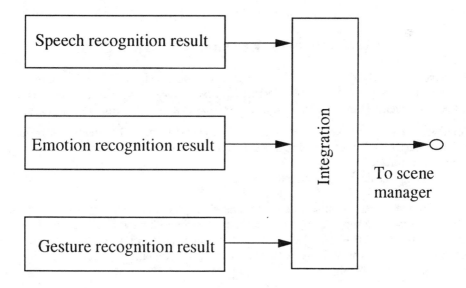

Figure 4. Function of the interaction manager.

7.3 HARDWARE CONFIGURATION

Figure 5 illustrates the hardware configuration. With a high-speed CG generating WS (Onyx Infinite Reality) serving the core function, the system also includes a speech recognition WS, a motion recognition WS, and voice and sound output WS. The visual outputs are projected onto the arched screen by two projectors.

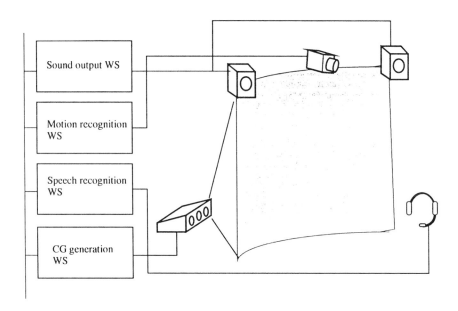

Figure 5. Hardware configuration.

8. EXAMPLE OF INTERACTIVE STORY PRODUCTION

We have produced an interactive story based on the previously described concepts and systems. We selected " Alice in Wonderland," a very famous story, and "Urashima Taro," one of the representative fairy tales in Japan, as the base stories for the following reasons:

a) These stories are familiar to everyone, so they can easily attract the attention of people.
b) These stories are simple, yet have a profound impact. Because they are simple, they can be easily reconstructed.
c) The stories contain visually attractive scenes.

The integrated interactive story is called "Wonderland." A brief summary of Wonderland is as follows. First, let's suppose you are a participant and will act the role of the main actor (or actress) in the interactive story. In a fairyland, you see a rabbit being cruelly treated by several gangsters. Upon sympathizing with and helping the rabbit, you are led to an electric pheromone castle – Wonderland.

The Muse, who is the princess and ruler of the Wonderland castle, warmly welcomes you. You experience various kinds of wonderful things such as musical entertainment, interactive poems, and so on. After having a good time, you finally decide to go back. Muse gives you, as a gift, a treasure box with a message not to open the box. After returning home from the castle, you find it difficult to keep your word to Muse not to open the box and finally open the box.

To make the story interactive, several branching points are included in the story. Examples of the branching points are as follows:

a) Whether or not to help the rabbit that is being cruelly treated by gangsters.
b) Whether or not to stay at the castle.
c) Whether or not to open the treasure box.

The participant must stand in front of the screen wearing a 3-D LCD-shutter glass and holding a microphone. The participant follows the story presented in images and sound, and participates in, and experiences, the story development through interactions with the characters in the story. Figures 6 and 7 show a participant interacting in the story.

9. CONCLUSION

This chapter proposes the concept of interactive movies, which are considered to be a new type of media that integrates various media types including telecommunications, novels, movies, and video games. In interactive movies, people enter cyberspace and enjoy the development of a story there by interacting with the characters in the story. In the chapter, we also tried to explain the relationships between this new media type and conventional media, as well as the technologies and systems necessary to achieve interactive movies. We also described the configuration of the system we are currently developing as an example of interactive movie application, and the context of the adopted interactive story based on famous fairy tales. We constructed a first-stage system, and are now evaluating this system. We plan to describe the details and evaluation results of the system in a separate report.

Figure 6. Example of interaction (1).

Figure 7. Example of interaction (2).

REFERENCES

1. P. Maes et al., "The ALIVE system: Full-body Interaction with Autonomous Agents," *Proceedings of the Computer Animation '95 Conference* (1995).

2. N. Tosa and R. Nakatsu, "Life-like Communication Agent – Emotion Sensing Character 'MIC' and Feeling Session Character 'MUSE'," *Proceedings of the International Conference on Multimedia Computing and Systems*, pp. 12-19 (1996).

3. C. Sommerer and L. Mignonneau, " Intro Act & MIC Exploration Space," *Visual Proceedings of SIGGRAPH '96*, pp. 17 (1996).

4. R. Nakatsu, "Integration of Art and Technology for Realizing Life-like Computer Characters," *Proceedings of Life-Like Computer Characters '96*, pp. 62 (1996).

5. J. Bates et al., "An Architecture for Action, Emotion, and Social Behavior," *Proceedings of the Fourth European Workshop on Modeling Autonomous Agents in a Multi-Agent World,* (1992).

6. K. Perlin, "Real Time Responsive Animation with Personality," *IEEE Trans. on Visualization and Computer Graphics*, Vol. 1, No. 1, pp. 5-15 (1995).

7. Proceedings of Life-like Computer Characters '96 (1996).

8. A. Bruderlin and T. Calvert, "Knowledge-driven, Interactive Animation of Human Running, " *Graphics Interface '96*, pp. 213-221 (1996).

9. S. Wertz, "Nonverbal Communication," New York: Oxford Univ. Press (1974).

34

VIRTUAL REALITY SYSTEMS FOR BROWSING MULTIMEDIA

Antonio Massari
*Autorità per l'Informatica nella
Pubblica Amministrazione
Via Po 14 00198 Roma, Italy*

Lorenzo Saladini
*Integra Sistemi srl.
Via Fara Sabina 2 00199
Roma, Italy*

**Fabio Sisinni
Walter Napolitano**
*Università di Roma "La Sapienza"
Dipartimento di Informatica e
Sistemistica, Via Salaria 113
00198 Roma, Italy*

**Matthias Hemmje
Aldo Paradiso
Martin Leissler**
*GMD - German National Research
Center for Information Technology
Integrated Publication and
Information Systems Institute (IPSI)
Dolivostrasse 15 D-64293
Darmstadt, Germany*

1. **INTRODUCTION**..714
2. **MOTIVATION AND RELATED WORKS**...............................715
3. **BASIC NOTIONS**...717
    3.1 STRUCTURE TREE 718
    3.2 VIRTUAL WORLD OBJECTS 719
    3.3 METAPHORS 722
4. **ARCHITECTURE OF VIRGILIO** 725
    4.1 SYSTEM ADMINISTRATOR TASKS 726
    4.2 SCENE CONSTRUCTOR...728
5. **PROTOTYPE AND WORKING EXAMPLE** 728
    5.1 WORKING EXAMPLE..729
6. **CONCLUSIONS AND FUTURE WORK**................................734
    REFERENCES 735

0-8493-1825-4/99/$0.00+$.50

Abstract. In this chapter we introduce the main features and propose the architecture of a system, which supports the construction of Virtual Reality-based visualizations of complex data objects representing the result of a query performed on a multimedia database. Such a system takes as input the dataset resulting from a query on a generic database, displays attribute values of the dataset on virtual world objects according to the capability of these objects to represent the proper type of data, represents semantic relationships among the objects in the dataset using the containment relationship, and creates a corresponding visual representation composed of a collection of Virtual Reality Modeling Language scenes.

1. INTRODUCTION

The potential of a database system as an information source for naive end-users can only be fully exploited if it is possible to easily formulate proper queries expressing the users' information need towards the database and if the results of such queries can be presented to users in a cognitively effective manner. Visual query interfaces [3][26] may help inexperienced users easily express queries, but may possibly return large amounts of complex or highly structured information. In this case, the problem that the complexity of the query result could confuse users, remains.

Taking the user's point of view, two types of critical situations can appear:

1. When the underlying database schema contains many semantic relationships and constraints, the dataset representing the whole query result can be composed of many objects arranged in different levels of nested structural relationships.
2. Users often have only a rough idea about the information required. To solve their information need, therefore, they tend to favour browsing-oriented retrieval strategies, which cannot be supported by access mechanisms of traditional information systems, like visual query systems and matching paradigm oriented IR systems [4][18][21][23].

These basic problems can be solved utilizing advanced graphics technology to lower the cost of finding information and accessing it once it has been found. Increasing masses of information confronting a business unit or an individual have created a demand for graphic information management applications. While in the 1980s, text-editing tasks forced the shaping of the desktop metaphor and many graphic user interfaces which are the state of the art today, in the next years, following the manifold of multimedia information resources provided by the Web, information management, retrieval and access will be a primary force in shaping the successor to the desktop metaphor [31].

In this chapter, we present Virgilio, a system which explores a user interface paradigm that goes beyond the desktop metaphor. It aims at exploiting the capabilities offered by 3D visualization and Virtual Reality techniques. Virgilio generates 3D visualizations of complex data objects. It takes the dataset resulting from a query on a generic multimedia database as input and creates a visual representation composed of a collection of scenes described in VRML (Virtual Reality Modeling Language) [29].

In order to generate VRML scenes to represent the results of queries, Virgilio supports the definition of an information visualization mapping, or *metaphor* [16], among the objects of the dataset and the objects of a virtual world. In order to allow a proper visualization of data items, the construction of such a mapping is constrained by the following requirements:

1. The structure of the query result must be preserved; i.e., the aggregations (tuples, sets, sequences) derived from the database schema must be maintained in the virtual scenes;

2. Virtual objects must be suitable for supporting the type of data to be displayed, (e.g., an object "portrait case" is suitable for an image data type, a virtual TV is suitable for a video data type);

3. Visualization issues, concerning whether or not discriminating attributes are displayed in the "right" place to allow an effective browsing, must also be considered.

The chapter is organized as follows: we will first discuss basic motivations and related works. Then, basic notions and concepts underlying the Virgilio system design are introduced and an overview of the system architecture is provided. Furthermore, we describe the currently existent prototypical implementation of the system and a working example. Finally, conclusions are drawn and future developments are outlined.

2. MOTIVATIONS AND RELATED WORKS

With the increasing hardware performance of PCs and workstations, computer graphics is assuming an important role for multimedia data presentation. It is possible to display structural relationships among data and its context by applying visualizations. Such relationships would be more difficult to detect by a succession of individual search requests, and traditional, mostly list-oriented presentations.

A proper data presentation system has to face some important issues [13]:

- Visualization of large sets of objects;
- Control of the intra-object complexity in the way to generate meaningful visualizations of single objects;
- Control of the inter-object complexity in the way to generate meaningful visualizations of collections of objects;
- User interaction to allow users to define areas of interest dynamically and to develop task specific visualizations of their own.

Until recently, visualization methods and metaphors were limited to 2D graphics, but now hardware and software performances allow visualizing static as well as dynamic 3D scenes [34]. 3D display methods can be usefully adopted for managing large sets of objects because they take advantage of natural human skills for spatial perception, orientation and spatial memories in the process of perceiving information spaces by means of spatial metaphors [5][17]. 3D visualization enables making the screen space "larger" and "denser" [31], thus allowing visualization of large sets of objects. The screen space becomes larger because the user can get to a larger amount of ready-to-use information in short time and becomes denser because the same amount of screen can hold more objects, which the user can zoom into or animate into view in a short time. By means of perspective visualization, users are provided with a simple type of fish-eye view [33] and can focus on a small part of the whole dataset.

The addition of user interaction to the 3D display techniques can provide solutions for controlling the intra-object complexity and defining areas of interest dynamically. By manipulating objects or moving in the space, the user will be able to disambiguate images, reveal hidden information, or zoom in for more detail, quickly accessing more information. Furthermore, 3D environments can easily accommodate standard as well as multimedia attributes of the information objects, like pictures and videos. Indeed, recent works in scientific visualization showed that by exploring the data graphically, the users can understand and realize the internal structure of data of large datasets [25][32].

In regard to inter-object complexity, the semantic relationships among the objects in the dataset can be represented using the containment relationship among 3D objects. The three-dimensional perspective "naturally" organizes the information spatially into a global context and local areas of interest. Furthermore, 3D visualizations for some of the classical data organizations have already been explored: Hierarchical (Cone Tree) [30], Linear (Perspective Wall) [24], Spatial [31].

Virtual reality techniques allow combining the advantages of 3D visualization with the power of metaphorical representations. The power of virtual reality is that it makes a part of the interface invisible: the user no longer has to manipulate the interface to manipulate the data: the user only needs to manipulate the data directly [11]. VR permits shifting cognitive processing load to the perceptual system more than other visual abstraction. By arranging the data of the query result into VR scenes, users are able to explore data more easily since they interact with familiar objects. Both the behavior of the system, i.e., the way in which the system reacts to the input of the user, and the structural and dynamic properties of the objects in a virtual world, i.e., the way in which objects can be composed and can act themselves, are completely known because they belong to the users' general backgrounds. As a consequence, no particular learning should be required to interact with and explore the dataset and in this way, it is possible to reduce significantly the learning overhead of naive users in the process of accessing information. Moreover, since VR scenes can be enriched with many details (e.g., a painting in a room or a flower vase) users can easily locate the database objects within a certain context; in other words, stay oriented, thus reducing the risk of getting lost in the VR space and in the explored information space as well.

Until now, our interest focused on metaphorical capabilities offered by non-immersive VR techniques. The interface problems of immersive environments have not been solved yet. In fact some studies revealed the visual disorders and the binocular deficits caused by head-mounted systems [37][36][28]. Others, highlighted the user problems related to the headgear's heaviness and the glove device's inaccuracy of measurement [11]. Moreover, other studies have shown that lag in immersive environments greatly affects the accuracy of positioning tasks [7]. However, when these problems are solved, immersive environments could enrich metaphorical capabilities with a stronger sense of spatial presence involving the entire sensorial system of the users.

Various studies on database visualization systems have been conducted, but they usually do not determine a flexible approach to the problem. Some systems provide users with interface tools to explore datasets in a specific application domain (e.g., statistical data [27], medical data, document databases [18][20][38][10]).

An interesting development is the Dynamic Query paradigm tightly coupled with the Starfield Display [1][35] to allow rapid, incremental and reversible navigations by querying over data resident in main memory. Range selections can be easily made on attributes via graphical user interface sliders. For every slider adjustment, a scatterplot display is updated to show the new query conditions. This method is useful for rapid exploration and detection of patterns and exceptions of data, but is limited to simple queries like conjunctions or disjunctions.

Some systems (e.g., LyberWorld [18] and Cone trees [30]) use 3D visualization techniques to represent information by means of abstract metaphors, where objects from an abstract world (e.g., cones, spheres) are used to compose visual representation of the explored dataset.

The SemNet [12] system is an early example of 3D visualization of information structures. The structures visualized were mostly large knowledge bases, and were often arbitrary graphs. The results tended to be cluttered, and the cognitive task of understanding the structure was still quite difficult.

The n-Vision system [14] exploits 3D to visualize n-dimensional business data. Multivariate functions are displayed in nested coordinates systems, using a metaphor called worlds-within-worlds. Although n-Vision focuses on continuous multivariate functions, it does exploit the human 3D perceptual apparatus to visualize abstract data.

The Xerox PARC Cone Tree and Perspective Wall both focus on the visualization of linear and hierarchical information structures. For linear information, the perspective wall arranges information left to right on a virtual wall. For hierarchical information, the cone tree view is used. In the cone tree, hierarchies are laid out uniformly in three dimensions. The problem of intra-object complexity is not addressed by either visualization. A general mechanism for navigation within the information of a single node is not suggested.

As opposed to the previous systems, Virgilio has been specifically thought to be a general-purpose exploration tool for highly structured multimedia data where both the domain of interest and the user requests are considered as external parameters. It exploits the capabilities offered by 3D graphics to face the visualization of large sets of objects, the intra-object and inter-object complexity and the user interaction, but Virgilio also utilizes Virtual Reality techniques and their metaphorical potentialities to reduce the cognitive load in the process of information assimilation. Moreover, Virgilio is based on concrete metaphors (i.e., metaphors where the visual domain is composed of objects from every-day experience) in order to take advantage of common knowledge about real world objects.

3. BASIC NOTIONS

In the following subsections, we will describe the internal representation models which have been adopted to support Virgilio's components. More specifically:

- we will describe the notion of STRUCTURE TREE that will be used to represent the way in which objects in the query result are aggregated;
- we will provide an abstract description of the objects (VIRTUAL WORLD OBJECTS) used to build the visual representation of data returned by the query;
- we will introduce the notion of Metaphor as a correspondence among Virtual World Objects and data in the query result.

In order to better explain the internal models, we will refer to a specific database. Its Entity-Relationship schema is shown in Figure 1.

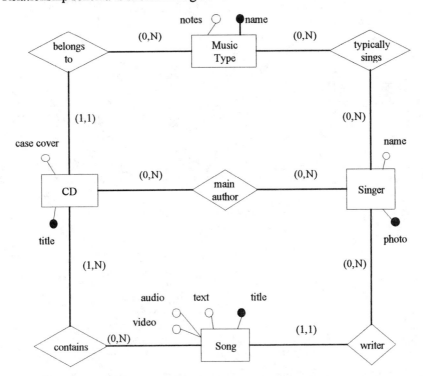

Figure 1. E-R schema of the example database.

The database chosen as an example contains information about CD records, singers, music types and songs. Note that a considerable part of the information stored in our CD database is multimedia, for example, the database contains a photograph for each singer, the cover picture for each CD, the audio and video file for each song.

3.1 STRUCTURE TREE

An important notion of the Virgilio framework is the model used to represent the structure of the information to visualize. We will assume the portion of database returned by the user query to be organized according to a hierarchical structure. In particular, we will use the notion of *nested relation* [2] (informally, a set of tuples such that the values of attributes are allowed to be nested relations themselves) to represent the way in which the information to explore is organized. In such a context, we can state that Virgilio is a VR system for the visualization and the exploration of nested relations.

We will call *structure tree* the structure of a nested relation, which can be described by recursively composing the two constructs **set_of** and **record**.

Referring to our example database schema reported in Figure 1 consider the following query:

α   Retrieve all the names and notes of a specific music type. For each music type, retrieve the name and the photo of the singers typically singing such music type. For each singer display:

     β   information about all the CDs of which the singer is the main author. In particular, for each CD, display titles, texts, audio and video files of all the songs.

     γ   all titles, texts, audio and video files of the songs written by the singer.

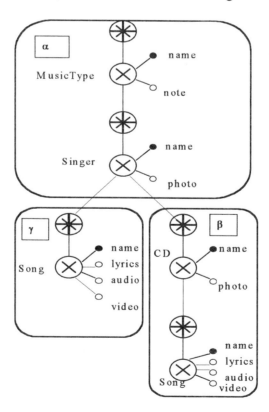

Figure 2. A structure tree representing a query on the musical CD database.

The structure tree associated with the previous query is shown in Figure 2, where the **set_of** and **record** constructs are displayed respectively with the symbols ⊗ and ⊛ The circles attached to **record** symbols represent the atomic attributes.

In a structure tree, we will define a *key* attribute as an attribute whose value identifies at most, one tuple in the immediately preceding **set_of** construct. Key attributes are displayed as black circles. The complete mapping among symbols and structure tree nodes is represented in Table 1.

Table 1. Mapping Among Symbols and Structure Nodes

Structure Tree node	Symbol
Set of node	⊗
Record node	⊛
Attribute node	○
Key Attribute node	●

In a formal way, a structure tree can be recursively defined as:
1. D, where D is an atomic domain of values;
2. **set of** (T), where T is a structure tree;
3. **record** $A_1{:}T_1,...A_n{:}T_n$ **end**, where the A_i are distinct symbols, and the T_i are structure trees.

A *result object* is an instance of a structure tree that can be recursively defined following its definition. Let T be a structure tree;
1. if T is an atomic domain D, then each element of D is an instance of T;
2. if T has the form **set of** (T'), then an instance of T is a finite set of instances of T';
3. if T has the form **record** $A_1{:}T_1,...A_n{:}T_n$ **end**, then an instance of T is a tuple t over $A_1,...A_n$ such that $t[A_i]$ is an instance of T_i, for $1{\leq}i{\leq}n$.

Consider the following structure tree:
- T : set of
- record
- $A_1{:}T_1,...A_k{:}T_k,...A_n{:}T_n$
- end

If we say that the attribute A_k is a **key**, it implies that for each pair of tuples t' t'' in the set $t'[Ak] \neq t''[Ak]$.

3.2 VIRTUAL WORLD OBJECTS

Virtual World Objects (VWO) represent the building blocks for the construction of 3D visualizations. In order to allow a proper visualization of the data items, virtual world objects must have the following properties:
- they must be able to display the different domains of data (e.g., text, images, etc.);

- they have to properly represent data aggregations (tuples, sets) composing the query result structure.

In order to exploit the advantages of metaphorical representations, data aggregations must be presented to the user in a familiar way, i.e., by clustering together VWO which, according to common knowledge, are known to be grouped together. Our basic assumption is that of considering the *natural containment relation* (e.g., a room is contained in a corridor) among VWO as the grouping relation which is part of each user background. As a consequence, we claim, that by choosing an appropriate mapping among VWO and database objects, we are able to make use of the natural containment relation existing among VWOs, to "carry," and properly visualize, structural relationships among objects of the database. This assumption will be formalized, and better defined, by means of the notion of *metaphor* introduced in the following section.

Beyond their visual aspects, which can, of course, be more or less rich of details and realism, VWOs must be characterized, first of all, by the role they play in the representation of database objects and logical aggregations among them. It is necessary to clearly identify which VWO can contain which other VWO, which is the modality of containment (i.e., whether or not a VWO can contain only homogeneous objects) and which is the capability of the VWO to display information of the database. Moreover, in order to define a proper visualization for supporting the user's browsing activity, a number of issues concerning visibility and hiding of VWO must also be addressed.

In the Virgilio system, all information regarding VWO are represented in a repository. Its E-R schema is displayed in Figure 3.

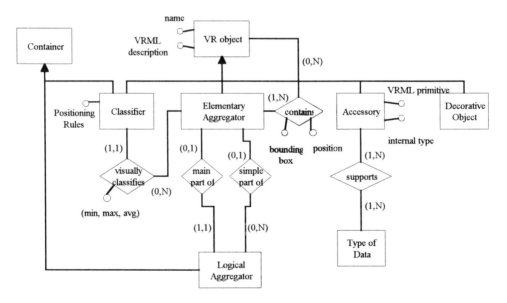

Figure 3. Virtual World Objects.

A Virtual World (VW) is simply a set of VWOs, which are typically placed in the same context (e.g., the VW of a Ship will include the VWO cabin, rescue boat, etc). VWO is described by means of a **name** and a **VRML description** (a visual representation of **VWO** is shown in Table 2). VWO may be partitioned into: `Containers` and `Accessories.`

A container is an object related to other objects according to a containment relation. The containment relation can be of two forms, **classification** and **aggregation**. A container can classify a set of aggregators of the same type (for example, an object *file cabinet* classifies objects of type *folder*). In this case, we will say that the container is a **classifier**.

Conversely, a container can aggregate a set of objects of different types (for example, a *desk* aggregates an object of type *book* and an object of type *portrait case*). In this case, we will say that the container is an **aggregator**.

An aggregator is associated with a (possibly empty) set of **accessories**, each accessory representing a support where one or more types of data (e.g., texts, strings, and pictures) can be displayed.

Table 2. Examples of Virtual World Objects

Aggregator	Classifier	Accessories	
desk	drawer-case	label with text	photo-frame with image

Note that the notions of *classifier, aggregator* and *accessory*, map, respectively, into the structure tree primitives: *set_of, record* and *attribute*.

Continuing the repository description, relationship **classifies** relates each classifier object to the aggregator it classifies. Such a relationship has three attributes, **min, avg, max** representing the minimum, average and maximum number of objects contained in the classifier. At the base of the Virgilio system is the idea of using metaphorical power of Virtual Reality to effectively represent information of a database. Therefore, the naturalness of a scene is a critical factor for the success of such an approach; in other words, there should be a minimal distance of the synthesized environment to what the user considers a "normal" situation. Distributions of real world objects are typically constrained into well defined boundaries, for example, a book will typically be composed of more than 10-20 pages and less than 2000, or a building can have a number of floors ranging from 1 to 150. By means of this information, it will be possible to avoid the generation of "unnatural" scenes with either too many or too few virtual world objects (e.g., a building with 1000 floors and a book with only one page).

The entity **accessory** represents the set of the virtual world objects that pertain to some aggregator. The relationship **supports** relates an accessory to the set of **type of data** it can display.

The attribute **visible inside** of the entity accessory and the relationship **visible from** represent visual characteristics to be considered for allowing the user to effectively browse the dataset. Information on visibility has to be considered in order to avoid the generation of scenes where the objects either remain hidden or indistinguishable from each other.

In particular, the attribute **visible inside** represents, for each accessory, whether or not it can be seen in the same scene in which the corresponding aggregator object is visible. The relationship **visible from** identifies, for each accessory *a*, the set of classifiers which *do not hide a*.

an accessory suitable for representing a string data type, it is not visible from inside (i.e., it is not visible in the same scene in which the object ROOM is displayed, see Figure 11), while it is visible from CORRIDOR (i.e., it can be seen from the scene where the object CORRIDOR is visible, see Figure 10). As a result, standing in the corridor and observing the label on the doors, the user will be able to distinguish the different database objects, which will result mapped on the virtual objects rooms.

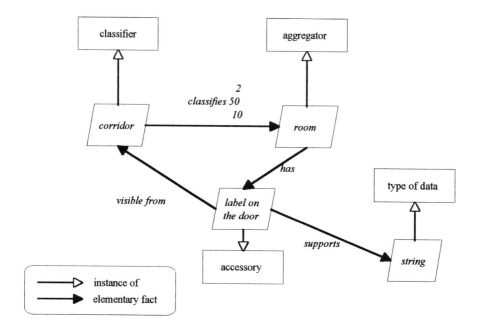

Figure 4. Relationships among virtual world objects.

3.3 METAPHORS

We define a metaphor to be a mapping between VWO and nodes of the structure tree corresponding to the user query (see Table 3 for an example of metaphor).

Table 3. An Example of a Metaphor

VW Object	Kind	Structure Tree
Corridor	Classifier	set of singers
Room	Aggregator	singer
Label on the	Accessory	name of the singer
Photo frame	Accessory	image of the singer
....	....	....

In order to make the visualization of the final data an effective one, the metaphor should be carefully designed by following some general guidelines, more specifically:

In order to make the visualization of the final data an effective one, the metaphor should be carefully designed by following some general guidelines, more specifically:

- The aggregation structure of the query result must be preserved.
- Each data item of the query result must be provided with a physical support for its visualization.
- The user must be able to see in the scenes the appropriate data in order to perform browsing.

In the following paragraph we define the notion of **structurally sound metaphor** as a formal way of modeling a legitimate mapping with respect to the previous guidelines.

3.3.1 Structurally sound metaphors

Let T be the structure tree of the query. We define a metaphor to be structurally sound if the following conditions are satisfied:

- Each set of construct S in T is mapped into a VWO of kind classifier. The number of VWO, which the classifier naturally classifies, must be in the same range of the cardinality of the instance of S.
- Each record R in T is mapped into an aggregator having enough accessories to display the attributes of R and containing a set of classifiers each for every set of construct in R.
- Let r be a record construct in T; if Agg is the aggregator chosen for displaying r, a key attribute of r must be mapped in both an accessory that is visible from the classifier classifying Agg and an accessory visible from inside Agg.

3.3.2 Metaphor example

Following the introduced guidelines, it is now possible to build a *sound* visual representation, composed of objects of the Virtual World, for the α part of the previously specified query (see Figure 5); the correspondence between Virtual World objects and structure tree nodes is shown inside the VW tree representation itself. In Table 4 the graphic symbols used to indicate different object types are shown.

Table 4. Graph Symbols Indicating Different Object Types

Represented Object	Node Symbols
Aggregator	
Classifier	
Accessory	
Accessory visible from outside	
Mapping	

Note that, according to the rules expressed in previous sections, classifiers have been used to represent SetOf nodes, e.g., a Button Table represents the Set of Music Types and a Corridor represents the Set of Singers; conversely, aggregators have been used to represent Record nodes, e.g., a Floor represents the Music Type node and a Room represents the Singer node. Moreover proper accessories, capable of supporting Key Attributes with correct visibility properties, have been chosen, in order to guarantee the structural soundness of the metaphor.

As an example, let us consider the Button Table and the Floor objects, which represent the Set of Music Types and the Music Type nodes of the structure tree, respectively; the Key Attribute Name of the Music Type has been mapped both on the Button Label accessory and on the Poster on the Floor accessory. They are both accessories of the Floor object but the former is visible from the Button Table, i.e., the object classifying the Floor, while the latter is visible inside the Floor itself.

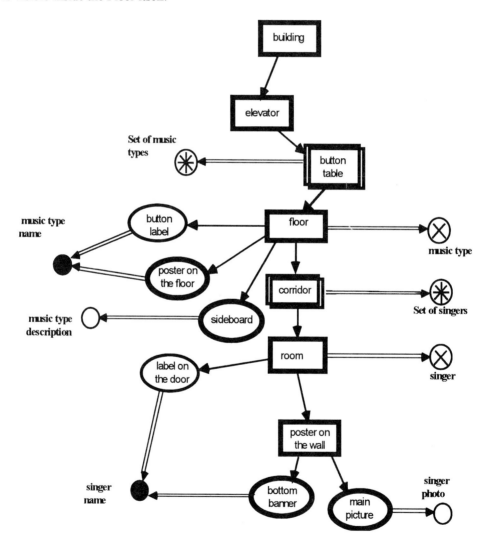

Figure 5. Virtual World Objects tree representing a metaphor.

It is worth noting that each of the Virtual World objects represents, at most, one node from the structure tree, but it is possible to have VW objects which are not bound to any structure tree node (e.g., the elevator node).

4. ARCHITECTURE OF VIRGILIO

In Figure 6, Virgilio system architecture is displayed. The main components of Virgilio are:

- a set of modules, called System Administrator Tools,
- a global repository of information, and
- a Scene Construction server.

The rest of the items displayed in Figure 6, namely a DBMS a Web browser and an unspecified web network connection, will be considered external to Virgilio; we will assume the database to be a generic one with a structure composed of different kinds of objects, many semantic relationships and possibly containing multimedia data.

As we have already stated, Virgilio has been thought of as a visualization system suitable whenever the information to explore is composed of a lot of highly structured data items. The strategy adopted in Virgilio is to present data resulting from query execution embedded in a 3D virtual scenario composed of virtual world objects. Such objects, due to their structural characteristics, can hide other objects or, simply make their visualization in the current scene unnecessary (For example, in a scene with a corridor of closed and opaque rooms, it will be not necessary to display the set of data items contained in the rooms.) Therefore, in order to completely define a VR scene, not all data items of the query need to be retrieved at once. As a consequence, in order to avoid heavy load to the database server and unnecessary disk space allocation for storing the whole query result, it makes sense to adopt a client-server architecture where database access is broken up into small query/result transactions returning only the information necessary to display the scene currently explored by the user. If an object-oriented database engine is available, it will furthermore make sense to capture metaphor's mapping and scene construction methods in the DB functionalities by providing appropriate methods on information and meta information objects.

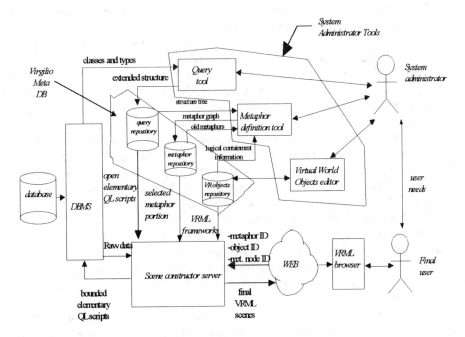

Figure 6. Architecture of Virgilio system.

Users interacting with Virgilio belong to two different stereotypes:

- system administrators (expert users)
- final users (inexperienced users)

We assume each of the two user stereotypes interact with Virgilio according to specific roles. System administrators will collect specific needs of the final user and, in response, define queries which are of interest specifying "nice" and effective VR visualization of data resulting from the execution of the queries. Final users interact with the Virgilio system by retrieving 3D scenes and browsing embedded information by means of a VRML browser. Also, they may communicate with system administrators in order to request new queries and metaphors to be built.

Similar to a standard client-server application running on the Web, a typical interaction between Virgilio and a final user will have the following framework:

- users ask for browsing a VR object (e.g., a building).
- Virgilio builds the corresponding first scene retrieving the necessary information from the database (raw data).
- users explore the scene. When a user decides to navigate to another scene of the virtual world, a message is sent back to Virgilio, which, in response, will generate a new scene.
- client application reads and displays the new scene, and so on.

In the following, a description of the tasks carried out by a System Administrator user is introduced and a brief explanation of the **Scene Constructor Server** is provided.

4.1 SYSTEM ADMINISTRATOR TASKS

As previously stated, the role of a system administrator user is to customize Virgilio in order to allow final users to access data through VR scenes exploration.

Three tasks have to be performed by the system administrator:

- defining queries in response to the user's needs.
- defining new virtual world objects, specifying both their visual aspects and the containment relationships with other objects.
- specifying a set of proper VR visualizations of such queries by defining a mapping (or metaphor) among database objects and objects of a virtual world.

In order to carry out these tasks, a system administrator user is provided with a *set of tools*. In general, such tools will access the database only for retrieving information about the schema of the database and some statistical information about the distribution of the data items. This information (*metadata*) will be used to express the queries which the final user will be interested in, and to determine an abstract structure of the data resulting from such queries (see the **Structure Tree** section). Some tools will be used to create the Virtual World objects which will be used to accommodate the query result, while others will be used to define how database objects will result mapped in the objects of the virtual world. In both cases, the activity carried out by a system administrator using these tools will result in updating the different repositories of information, depicted in Figure 6.

The task of defining a query over the existing databases will be performed by means of a module that is called **Query Tool**. Such a tool can be any general purpose query system which allows expression of a generic query over a structured database; many examples of query tools useful for such a task can be found in the literature, and in this chapter we will not refer to a specific one.

Eventually, the query specification task will result in storing a set of data items in the **Query repository**. Such data items will represent a *Structure Tree* plus a set of *database language scripts* associated with the Structure Tree nodes. The scripts are useful for executing those transactions on the database which retrieve the instances of the structure tree nodes.

Administrator users will define new VR objects, e.g., tables or drawers, by means of the **Virtual World Object Editor**. This tool will allow the user to specify the object type, according to the **VR object repository** classification, and its VRML description. Also, according to the type of object defined, it will be necessary to specify all the logical relations among the newly created object and the VR objects already present in the repository, i.e., containment and visibility relationships with respect to other objects.

4.1.1 Metaphor definition task

The main task of the system administrator is to specify an appropriate VR visualization for the result of the queries. In order to do that, the system administrator has at his/her disposal:

- the structure tree of the query, i.e., the way in which the data resulting from the query is aggregated, and
- a set of virtual world objects, which are related to each other by means of containment and visibility relationships.

The definition of a metaphor must be made according to the general guidelines presented in the *Structurally Sound Metaphors* section. First of all, one or more metaphors which are structurally sound with respect to the query are to be found out, then the system administrator can select the most appropriate one and enrich it by adding decorative objects or refining the mapping.

In order to find out the set of structurally sound metaphors, the system administrator can take advantage of the **metaphor generator**, a specific component of the **Metaphor Definition Tool** that are not displayed in Figure 6. Given a particular Structure Tree, the **metaphor generator** is able to select a set of Virtual Worlds, which can be used to *soundly map* the structure tree. We can assume the metaphor generator to work in the following way: given a set of virtual world objects stored in the VR object repository, the metaphor generator is able to extract the logical containment information and to find out one or more configurations which are structurally sound with respect to the given query. In order to simplify the search of metaphors, we can assume that the system administrator will specify the virtual world object, which must be the starting point of the first scene.

Besides the aforementioned issues, other considerations have to be taken into account, in order to allow the definition of a "good" metaphor:

- Familiarity of the user with the VR object chosen. For example, a user belonging to the class of sailors will be familiar with the world of a ship, while, on the contrary, he may be unfamiliar with the world of a skyscraper.
- Previous history of interaction of users with other metaphors. Important to the definition of a suitable metaphor will be the consistency of a mapping with respect to the metaphor previously learned by a user. In order to cope with this issue, the tools for defining a metaphor must maintain an internal history of interaction with final users.
- Constraints derived from a particular cultural background of a user. In the virtual world of a school building, for example, mapping the attribute "case cover of a CD" into the virtual world object "board of a classroom" would not be accepted by a teacher, who considers the board as an object designated to hold "serious kind of information." On the contrary, a student, who has a less respectful conception of the board usage, would more likely accept the same mapping.

The expected next query the user may want to see on the system. It will also be important to try to foresee the future user requests in order to allow, in the future, the addition of new objects into the scenes without having to rebuild a completely new world.

Thus, it is evident that the role of the system administrator in defining a metaphor is a central one: from the set of all the structurally sound metaphors chosen by the metaphor generator tool, the system administrator has to find out which is the most appropriate one and to improve it by adding or removing virtual objects in the scenes. Even this task will eventually result in storing an appropriate data structure (*a metaphor graph*) in the **Metaphor Repository**.

4.2 SCENE CONSTRUCTOR

The scene constructor is one of the most important modules of the Virgilio architecture. It executes the process of generating a scene in response to client requests produced by an end user during the exploration of a virtual world. Note that VRML directly supports the definition of a 3D scene as a tree of nested 3D objects, therefore each time an end user requests further information, Scene Constructor traverses a subtree of the metaphor tree currently used and builds the corresponding 3D scene.

When an end user interacts with the VRML browser, each user action, like clicking on a VR object or issuing a shortcut command, is translated into a request sent to the server with the following parameters:

- identifier of the query whose result has to be displayed;
- identifier of the metaphor used to display information;
- identifier of the metaphor node to be displayed;
- identifier of the database object for which a visualization is requested.

All this information has been previously enclosed in the actually browsed VRML scene, when such a scene has been built by the Scene Constructor. As a consequence, one of the tasks of the scene constructor will be embedding proper information in the result VRML scene, in order to allow further navigation to other subportions of the retrieved information.

In response to end user input, Scene Constructor has to perform the following tasks:

- retrieve a subportion of the actual metaphor;
- retrieve the Virtual World Objects corresponding to the traversed nodes;
- retrieve data from the database;
- position Virtual World Objects and include data according to specific layout rules.

The algorithm used by the Scene Constructor is a recursive one and it is driven by the metaphor currently selected, i.e., the scene construction algorithm will traverse in a recursive manner a portion of the metaphor graph, starting from the metaphor node provided as an input in the user request. For each metaphor node N traversed, the visual information (VRML frameworks, positioning rules) corresponding to the VR object associated with N will be considered for the scene construction. If the node N is also associated with a node of the structure tree, say T, then the query associated with T will be first bound to the current Oid and then executed against the database.

Thus, the scene constructor has to access the metaphor repository in order to retrieve a subportion of the metaphor graph, the VW repository in order to retrieve the proper VRML frameworks, the Query repository to get the query language expressions associated with the structure tree nodes and the database server actually storing the data which have to be bound in the final scene.

5. PROTOTYPE AND WORKING EXAMPLE

Two prototypes of the Virgilio system exist. Both the prototypes use DBMS functionalities to deal with the aforementioned repositories. The former uses Illustra™ DBMS and is parametrical with respect to the database extension, but query, VW objects description and metaphor are still hardcoded in the Scene Constructor.

The latter uses Access™ as DBMS and the actual Scene Constructor is now parametrical with respect to all parameters: database extension, query, VW objects description and metaphors.

New development efforts will take more advantage of the new ORDB technology. Such technology allows dealing more easily with complex objects as virtual and multimedia objects are. Most of the complexity will be transferred from the Scene Constructor to ORDBMS Server increasing in this way the system performance.

The tool we have chosen to describe the final scenes representing the dataset embedded in a virtual scenario is VRML [10], an advanced language for describing interactive simulations and virtual worlds. Based on SGI Open Inventor ASCII format, it allows the specification of 3D scenes with rendered objects, lighting, materials, ambient properties and realism effects; it also supports extensions for networking and linking among different scene graphs allowing users to seamlessly navigate in 3D scenes distributed all over the Internet. Although its current version supports only a subset of the interactive behaviors offered by Open Inventor language, its standardization effort represents the most important single step to put VR on the Web and VRML promises to be an open and extensible language for distributed virtual world representations. The used external VRML browser is Cosmo Player™.

5.1 WORKING EXAMPLE

We consider the multimedia database whose schema is depicted in Figure 1. On a such database, we formulate the following query:

α   Retrieve all the names and notes of a specific music type. For each music type, retrieve the names and the photos of the singers typically singing that music type.

For each singer display:

β   information about all the CDs of which the singer is the main author. In particular, for each CD, display titles, texts, audio and video files of all the songs.

γ   all titles, texts, audio and video files of the songs written by the singer.

The corresponding structure tree is depicted in Figure 2.

5.1.1 The "Palace World" metaphor

Our prototype makes possible display of the same query resulting dataset using two different metaphors. The first metaphor used is called "Palace World" and is represented in Figure 7.

The first object in the scene graph represents a building: it contains the whole dataset, returned as the result of the query, and is the starting point for the exploration. Inside the building, the entrance hall (Figure 8) aggregates different decorative objects and one classifier, the elevator (Figure 9); it classifies different kinds of music, providing an access to the next level of aggregation in the structure tree.

Stepping out of the elevator, users may see a poster reminding them which floor had been chosen. The poster has been automatically chosen from the metaphor generator, since the elevator buttons are no longer visible in the scene. The notes of the music type have been mapped into a floorboard while the corridor in front of the entrance provides access to the different singers (Figure 10).

Walking through the corridor, it is possible to choose singers by means of labels beside each door (Figure 11). Note that a label on the door is an accessory of room that is visible from corridor, therefore it is suitable for mapping a key attribute of singer.

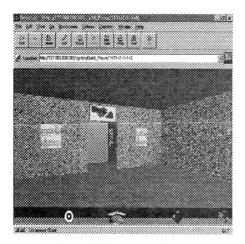

Figure 7. The entrance hall.

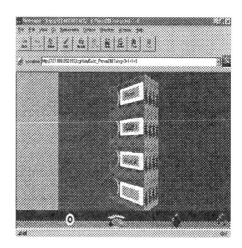

Figure 8. The elevator.

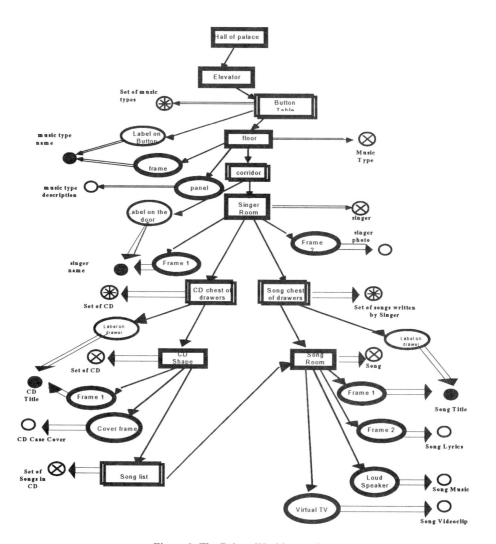

Figure 9. The Palace World metaphor.

Inside the room (Figure 12), users can see different objects representing the information related to the singer (in this case a band). Inside the room, there are two drawer-cases, both contain different drawers; in the first one, each drawer contains one CD and its related information; in the latter, each drawer is related to each song passing over a level of data aggregation according to the left branch of the structure tree of Figure 2.

On the first drawer-case, both the title of the CD and its cover photo are used here to identify the content of each drawer (Figure 13).

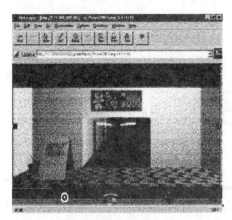

Figure 10. The Pop floor.

Figure 11. The corridor.

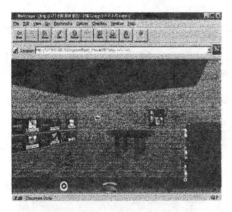

Figure 12. The Beatles' room.

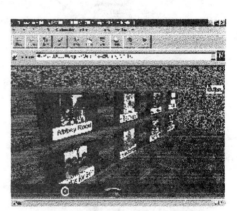

Figure 13. The drawer-case, a classifier of CDs.

Figure 14. CD information.

Figure 15. The song room.

By clicking on a drawer, users access to another scene representing the CD related information: cover photo, CD title and the list of the songs (Figure14).

By selecting a song from the list, users can be "teletransported" in a new virtual scene representing the lowest level of data aggregation in the aforementioned structure tree. In such a scene, information requested about the selected song, title, text, audio and video files, are respectively mapped on a label, a wallboard, a speaker and a TV (Figure 15).

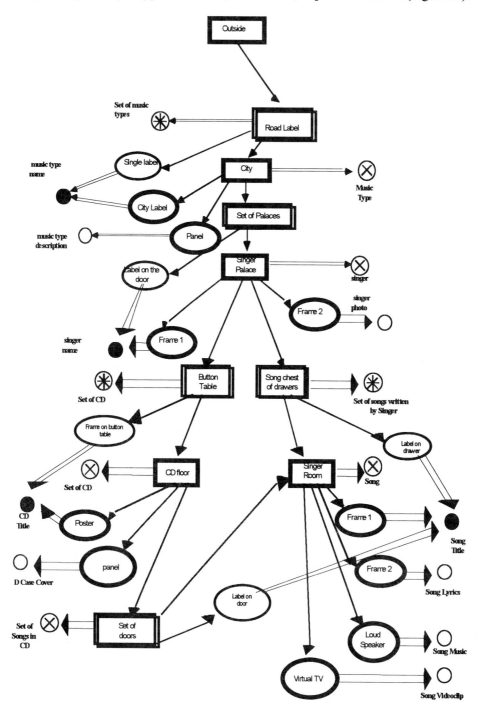

Figure 16. The City World metaphor.

As soon as users get in the virtual room, TV and speaker start playing the videoclip and the song.

5.1.2 The "City World" metaphor

The second used metaphor is called "City World" and is represented in Figure 16 below.

The starting scene represents an external environment in which a traffic sign classifies different cities according to first level of data aggregation in the structure tree (Figure 17).

Clicking on the city sign, users access the related music type information.

Figure 17. The traffic sign, a classifier of cities.   Figure 18. The city's welcome sign.

A sign and a board, representing the name and the notes of the music type selected, welcome users to the city (Figure 18). After bringing themselves near the buildings, users can choose the palace's singer in which to go in by clicking on the main door. An accessory like a label on the main door maps the singer's name (Figure 19).

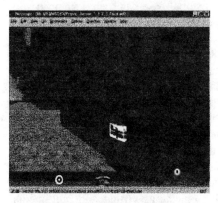 

Figure 19. The Beatles' main door.   Figure 20. The palace hall.

Inside the palace hall, singer related information is mapped on different accessories (Figure 20). A classifier like a drawer-case classifies all the songs where the singer is the main author. Such a classifier provides access to the lowest level of data aggregation "teletransporting" users inside the song room, according to the previous used metaphor.

In the elevator, the classifier button table maps CD titles (Figure 21). By selecting a button, users access to the related CD floor.

Walking through the corridor, users can choose the "song room" to go in by means of the accessory "label on the door" (Figure 22). The lowest level of data regarding aggregation of the relevant metaphor sub-portion coincides with the previously used metaphor, so users access to the same scene of Figure 15.

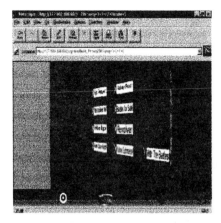

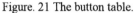

Figure. 21 The button table.   Figure 22. The corridor

6. CONCLUSIONS AND FUTURE WORK

We have presented a system which explores an UI paradigm that goes beyond the desktop metaphor to exploit the capabilities offered by 3D visualization and Virtual Reality techniques. It is able to handle important data visualization issues like visualization of large sets of objects, control of the intra-object complexity and the inter-object complexity, but Virgilio also utilizes Virtual Reality techniques and their "concrete" metaphorical potentialities to reduce the cognitive load in the process of information assimilation .

Virgilio's underlying model for flexibly encoding the mapping from the semantic space of information objects to the virtual space of visualization has been described.

A prototype with parametricity limited to the extensional base has been developed and first informal usability test has been conducted with end-users. The next development efforts will be addressed to reach the total parametricity in order to have a general-purpose visualization tool. Future works will focus on various development directions.

VRML 2.0 new features [29] coupled with the capability to manage local interactions by means of Java enhance the user interaction with data. These features will allow the user to control the visualization of the data interactively and to highlight similar characteristics of the data by means of the object movements and animations.

Another important development direction follows the way of optimization resources in order to fit the different technical network infrastructures (ISDN, INTRANET) possibilities with the requested bandwidth of the multimedia attributes of the DB and the VR.

New development efforts will take more advantage of the new ORDB technology. Such a technology allows dealing more easily with complex objects as virtual and multimedia objects are. Most of the complexity will be transferred from the Scene Constructor to ORDBMS Server, increasing the system performance in this way.

Last, we hope to put our theories of VR-concrete metaphors mapping information to a more complex test in which it will possibly compare the utility and learning support provided by several different information access scenarios. These will include the printed page, hypermedia documents, 2D metaphors, 3D-concrete metaphors, 3D abstract metaphors, and immersive VR.

REFERENCES

1. Ahlberg, C. and Shneidermann, B., "Visual Information Seeking: Tight Coupling of Dynamic Query Filters with Starfield Displays," *Proc. CHI`94 Human Factors in Computing Systems*, ACM Press, 1994, pp. 313-317.
2. Atzeni, P. and de Antonellis, V., "Relational Database Theory," Benjamin Cummings, 1993.
3. Batini, C., Catarci, T., Costabile, M. F., and Levialdi S., "On Visual Representation for Database Query Systems," *Proc. of the Interface to Real and Virtual Worlds Conference*, Montpellier, France, March 1993, pp. 273-283.
4. Belkin, N. J., "Interaction with texts: Information Retrieval As Information-Seeking Behavior," *Information Retrieval '93: Von derModellierung zu Anwendung*, 1993, pp. 55-66.
5. Bolter, J., Hodges, L., Meyer, T., and Nichols, A., "Integrating Perceptual and Symbolic Information in VR," *IEEE Computer Graphics and Applications*, Vol. 15, No. 4, July 1995, pp. 8-11.
6. Bolter, J., Bowman, D. A., and Hodges, L. F., "The Virtual Venue: User-Computer Interaction In Information-Rich Virtual Environments."
7. Bryson, S., "Effects of lag and frame rate on various tracking tasks."
8. Bryson, S., "Virtual Reality in Scientific Visualization," *Communications of the ACM*, Vol. 39, No. 5, May 1996, pp. 62-76.
9. Canter, D., Rivers, R, and Storrs, G., "Characterizing User Navigation Through Complex Data Structures," *Behaviour and Information Technology*, Vol. 4, No. 2, 1985, pp. 93-102.
10. Chalmers, M. and Chitson, P., "Bead: Explorations in Information Exploration," *Proc. SIGIR'92*, published as a special issue of SIGIR Forum, ACM Press, pp. 330-337.
11. Erickson, T., "Artificial Realities as Data Visualization Environments: Problems and Prospects," *Virtual Reality Applications and Explorations*, Ed. A.Wexelblat, Academic Press, 1993.
12. Fairchild, K. M., Poltrock, S. E., and Furnas G. W., "Sem net: Three-dimensional graphic representations of large knowledge bases," *Cognitive Science and its Applications for Human Computer Interaction*, Guindon, R. Ed., Lawrence Erlbaum, 1988.
13. Fairchild K. M., "Information Management Using Virtual Reality-Based Visualization," *Virtual Reality Applications and Explorations*, Ed A.Wexelblat, Academic Press, 1993.
14. Feiner, S. and Beshers, C., "World within worlds: Metaphors for exploring n-dimensional virtual worlds," *Proceedings of the UIST'90*, 1990, pp. 76-83.
15. Goldstein, J. and Roth, S.F., "Using Aggregation and Dynamic Queries for Exploring Large Data Sets," *Proc. CHI`94 Human Factors in Computing Systems*, ACM Press 1994, pp. 23-29.
16. Haber, E. M., Ioannidis, Y. E., and Livny, M., "Foundations of Visual Metaphors for Schema Display," *Journal of Intelligent information Systems*, Special Issue on the Management of Visual Information, 1994.
17. Hemmje, M., "A 3D Based User Interface for Information Retrieval Systems," *Proceedings IEEE Workshop on Database Issues for Data Visualization*, J.P.Lee, G.G. Grinstein (eds), Springer Verlag LNCS, Vol. 871, Oct. 1994, pp. 194-207.
18. Hemmje, M., Kunkel, C., and Willet A., "Lyberworld - A Visualisation User Interface Supporting Full Text Retrieval," *Proceedings of ACM SIGIR`94*, July 3-6, Dublin, 1994.
19. Javener, M. K., "Virtual Reality - What Will It Do to You?" *Computer Graphics*, November 1994, Vol. 28, No. 4, pp. 244-245.

20. Krohn, U., "VINETA: Navigation through Virtual Information Spaces," *Proc. Workshop on Advanced Visual Interfaces 1996*, pp. 49-58.

21. Lashkari, Y., "Domain Independent Disambiguation of Vague Query Specifications," Univ. of Wisconsin (*CS-TR-93-1181*).

22. Lee, J. P. and Grinstein, G.G, "An Architecture for Retaining and Analyzing Visual Explorations of Databases," *Proceedings of Visualization '95*, pp. 101-108.

23. Lee, J. P., "Data Exploration Interactions and the ExBase System," *Proceedings IEEE Workshop on Database Issues for Data Visualization*, J.P.Lee, G.G. Grinstein (Eds.), Springer Verlag LNCS Vol. 871, October 1994, pp. 118-137.

24. Mackinlay, J. D., Robertson, G. G., and Card, S. K., "Perspective wall: Detail and context smoothly integrated," *Proceedings of SIGCHI'91*, pp. 173-179

25. McCormick, B., DeFanti, T. A., and Brown, M. D., Eds. "Visualization in scientific computing" *Comput. Graphics 21*, 6 (1987).

26. Massari, A., Pavani, S.,. Saladini, L., and Chrysanthis P.K., "QBI: Query By Icons," *Proceedings of the International Conference ACM-SIGMOD*, San Jose, California, 1995.

27. Meo-Evoli, L., Rafanelli, M., and Ricci, F.L., "An Interface for the Direct Manipulation of Statistical Data," *Journal of Visual Languages and Computing*, 1994, 5, pp. 175-202.

28. Oman, C. M., "Sensory conflict in motion sickness: an Observery Theory approach," *Pictorial Communication in Virtual and Real Environments*, S.R.Ellis, M.K. Kaiser, A.C. Grunwald (eds.), London: Taylor and Francis, 1991, pp. 362-376.

29. *The Virtual Reality Modeling Language*, Version 2.0 Spec.http://vag.vrml.org/VRML2.0/FINAL/spec/.

30. Robertson, G. G., Mackinlay, J. D., and Card, S. K., "Cone Trees: Animated 3D Visualizations of Hierarchical Information," *Proc. CHI'91 Human Factors in Computing Systems*, ACM Press 1991, pp. 189-194.

31. Robertson, G. G., Card, S. K., and Mackinlay, J.D., "Information Visualization Using 3D Interactive Animation," *Communications of the ACM*, Vol. 36, No. 4, April 1993.

32. Rosemblum, L., et al., Eds., "Scientific Visualization: Advances and Challenges," 1995, Academic Press.

33. Sarkar, M., and Brown, M.H., "Graphical Fisheye Views," *Communications of the ACM*, December 1994, Vol. 37, No. 12, pp. 73-83.

34. Seligmann, D. D. and Feiner S., "Automated Generation of Intent-Based 3D Illustrations," *Computer Graphics 25* (4), 1991, pp. 123-132

35. Shneiderman, B., "Dynamic Queries: A Step Beyond Database Languages," University of Maryland Technical Report CS-TR-3022, 1993.

36. Strong, G. W and O'Neil S. K. E., "Visual guidance for information navigation: a computer-human interface design principle derived from the cognitive neuroscience," *Interacting with computers: the interdisciplinary Journal of HCI*, Vol. 3, No. 2, Butterworth-Heinemann, 1991, pp. 217-231.

37. Travis, D., Watson, T., and Atyeo, M., "Human Psychology in Virtual Environments," *Interacting with Virtual Environments*, L.MacDonald, J.Vince (Eds.), John Wiley & Sons Ltd., 1994, pp. 43-59.

38. Wilson, B. A., Fowler, R. H., and Fowler, W. A. L., "Integrating Query, Thesaurus, and Documents through a Common Visual Representation," *Proc. of the 14th Annual International ACM SIGIR Conference on Research and Development in Information Retrieval*, 1991, pp. 249-259.

35

MULTIMEDIA VIRTUAL REALITY SYSTEMS

Tsuneo Ikedo
The University of Aizu
Graduate Department of Information Systems
Aizuwakamatsu-city, Fukushima, Japan

1. INTRODUCTION...738
2. SYSTEM ORGANIZATION..740
3. MULTIMEDIA ACCELERATOR...741
4. GRAPHICS RENDERER..744
5. VIDEO DATA CAPTURE AND SYNTHESIS OF COMPUTER GRAPHICS.................746
6. AUDIO RENDERER 748
7. CODECS..749
8. INTERACTION...750
    REFERENCES 750

Abstract. This chapter describes trends in the architecture of multimedia virtual reality systems that may be predicted on the basis of the availability of ULSI with 10s of millions of gates. Multimedia processing comprised of multi-granular parallelism for diverse media requires supercomputing power for multi-threaded, process-level execution. Due to the appearance of large-scale integration for what has been termed system on silicon, a new scheme for building multimedia-centric architecture will be realized. This chapter discusses advanced implementation technologies for multimedia virtual reality systems employing a reconfigurable architecture and using hundreds of processing elements embedded within an ULSI.

1. INTRODUCTION

A Virtual Reality system is a computer-aided modeling system designed to simulate and express nature or estimated physical phenomena involving human interaction. Such a system ultimately strives for expressive power to provoke human emotion with an intensity rivaling that of nature. Conventional VR systems can be classified into the following applications:

- **Simulation:** Flight, driving, etc.
- **Design and Modeling:** Architecture, viewing, science, etc.
- **Relaxation:** Games, entertainment, etc.

A VR subsystem can be thought of as a component of a general multimedia system, an example of which is shown in Figure 1 (as established at the University of Aizu in 1995). This system is configured with multimedia component technologies such as broadband communication; multimedia file systems and databases; multi-modal human interfaces; audio and video compression; sound and MIDI synthesis; computer-aided training and education; image processing and 3D rendering; multimedia conferencing, internet telephony, and electronic mail; authoring systems; and virtual shopping.

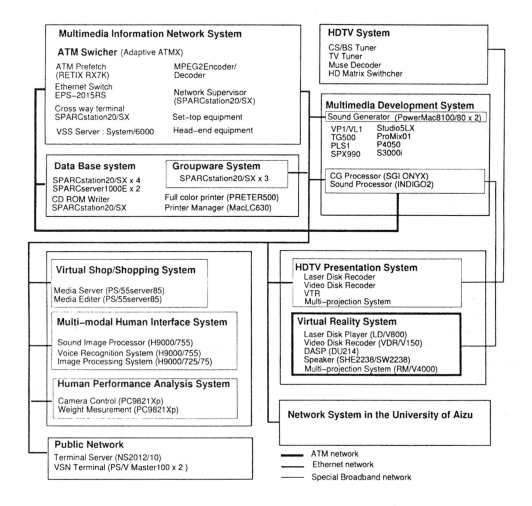

Figure 1. Multimedia system.

The system shown in Figure 1 seems very large. However, projections of future multimedia technology suggest that the many functions and processes in Figure 1 might be implemented in a portable computer. Such functionality might include the following applications:

- *Live broadcast and teleconferences,*
- *Fax/Voice telephony,*
- *Realtime VR games with remote friends,*
- *Virtual shopping and teleconversation with friends, and*
- *Satellite schools or virtual universities and hypermedia.*

In such applications, graphics, video, audio, codecs, networking and invisible large-scale multigranular computation is required. A multimedia VR system is a target of such dynamic component technologies, and has the following common and indispensable features:

- *Audio and Visual Computing (including codecs for buffering and transmission),*
- *Realism,*
- *Realtime response (both high throughput and low latency), and*
- *Interaction.*

Distinguishing multimedia VR systems from related conventional systems such as audio systems for music appreciation, movies, simulators, or games is difficult. Mixed media, bi-directionality, interactivity, digital processing, and transmission of diverse data types in a unified network are indicated as fundamentals of a multimedia system. However, the relationship of the media and the processing depends on the applications and environments. In the near future, many applications related to human interface will be developed and called "multimedia VR systems."

Multimedia VR applications are generally implemented by multigranular processing combined uniformly with four major media--- fonts, computer graphics, video, and audio--- and supported by fundamental technologies--- multimedia file and database management, codecs, network, and interactive control of machinery, as shown in Figure 2. Such integration brings quite new technologies into the realm of media processing, e.g., synchronization between audio and graphics, synthesis of graphics and video images in 3-space, and amphibious (combining hardware and micro-programming) codecs in network communication and buffering, which problems are not yet completely solved. This chapter shows an architecture to implement a multimedia VR system that satisfies the above requirements.

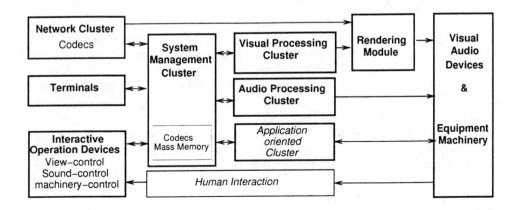

Figure 2. Multimedia virtual reality system.

2. SYSTEM ORGANIZATION

In a multimedia system, multigranular and interactive operations are required in realtime for diverse and continuous media---such as animated graphics, video, and audio---[1][2] which must be manipulated without frame or phrase reduction. The system shown in Figure 2 is implemented with multiple processors (including software functions) to achieve multigranular parallelism for graphics, audio, and codecs. These processors comprise the following:

1. Multimedia Accelerator
   Multimedia operating system processor
   Geometric and audio accelerator
   User interactive processing manager
2. Graphics Renderer
   Rendering (outline) processor
   Vector processor
   Span processor
   Phong-shading processors
   Texture-mapping (and video image-mapping) processor
   Bump-mapping processor
   Shadow-casting processor
   Image processing processor with 7 x 7 convolution
   Gaseous-object renderer
   BitBlt (bit-block transfer) processor
   Vector/polygon anti-alias processor
   Outline-font generator
   HDTV (high-definition TV) controller
   Programmable DRAM (frame buffer) controller
   Triple 256 x 8-bit video refresh shift register
   NTSC/HDTV video output
3. Audio Renderer
   Sound synthesizer (wavetable, physical models, etc.)
   Geometric acoustic accelerator (3D localization, reverberation, chorus, etc.)
   Post-processor (mixer, equalizer, compressor, loudspeaker crosstalk compensation, etc.)
4. Communication and Buffer Codec Processor
   Codecs processor (J/MPEG, PCM, etc.)
   Cryptograph processor

The success of any multimedia VR system depends on how well these functions can be implemented toward getting realtime audio and visual processing with realistic sound and images, respectively. These requirements suggest the need for dynamic systems with media-specific computing power. Table 1 estimates the computational cost, for each function, of generating realistic images in a VR scene where graphics rendering performance is around 10 million polygons (100 pixels)/sec. It will be impossible to achieve media-specific arithmetic operations of Tera-order performance in a single general-purpose computer in the next 10 years. One realistic solution is a hybrid configuration of hardware and processing elements (or general-purpose computers) as follows:

Graphics accelerator: multiple processing elements
Graphics renderer: hardware
Audio and codecs: amphibious logic (combining hardware and microprogramming)

Table 1.Computational Cost Estimation for Multimedia Processing

FUNCTION	ARITHEMTIC POWER	REMARK
Geometric Accelerator	30 GFlops	10 million polygon/sec
Graphics Renderer	1-3 Tera (integer/s)	Refelection with texture
Acoustic Accelerator	10 GFlops	Ray-tracing method
MPEG2 Video Encoder/Decoder	5/0.35 Giga operation/s	MP@ML (NTSC)
MPEG2 Audio	0.1-0.5 Giga operation/s	

Configurations of this kind will be realized in a single chip sometime within 5--7 years through development of VLSI technology. Table 2, summarizing data provided by the Semiconductor Industry Association, projects VLSI and ASIC (Application-Specific Integrated Circuit) development. According to these estimates, in the year 2001, an ASIC with 26 million gates will be produced, with a switching speed of 1 GHz (practical 300 MHz) and an available pin number greater than a thousand. This gate number is twenty times current numbers and the pin number is twice current capacity. Such a scale will be equivalent to the implementation of two thousand floating point processors on a single chip (considering that a 200 Flops extended single precision arithmetic unit can be implemented by about 40,000 gates at 100 MHz on-chip frequency. On-chip frequency in Table 2 shows a toggle switching of flip-flop, so that the practical operating frequency will be about 1/3 in ASIC), having an estimated total performance of 130 GFlops at 2001. ASIC will be a key technology for multimedia computing and systems.

Table 2. History and Projections of VLSI Development

FEATURE	1995	1998	2001	2004	2007
ASIC (gates per chip)	5M	14M	26M	50M	210M
Microprocessor (transistor/chip)	12M	28M	64M	150M	350M
Micron rules m	0.35	0.25	0.18	0.13	0.10
Number of package pins	750	1100	1700	2200	3000
On-chip frequency (MHz)	300	450	600	800	1000
Off-chip frequency (MHz)	150	200	300	350	
Voltage (v)	3.3	2.5	1.8	1.5	1.2
Cost/transistor	1	0.5	0.2	0.1	0.05

There are two approaches for overviewing multimedia VR systems, surveying current technologies and environments and forecasting future technologies. According to the road map shown in Table 2 for development of semiconductors, multimedia applications will rapidly change the nature of system design, and current technologies, especially in computer architecture, will soon fade away.

3. MULTIMEDIA ACCELERATOR

A multimedia accelerator performs multimedia operating system functions: memory and file management; resource and process management for media-dependent parallelism; coarse-grained processing for graphics, audio, codecs and interaction; and network I/O management.

Independent of the success of microcomputers with uniprocessor architecture for general applications, massively parallel processing architectures have been proposed for high-performance graphics processors [3][4][5]. This situation probably will not be changed for the next ten years, since single-chip performance improves by a factor of only about three every four years. Such an improvement rate is insufficient to achieve realtime rendering for virtual reality applications in the near future. Around three to four GFlops of performance are needed for coarse-grained processing, and ten times more performance for fine-grained processing, in order to reach the much-sought million polygons/sec. milestone. A performance of one million polygons/sec., however, is still insufficient (by a factor of 10) for walk-through virtual reality systems.

Over the last 15 years, torus, matrix, and pipeline topologies have been considered as interconnection networks for parallel processing. SIMD or MIMD architectures can achieve high performance for specialized geometric models, defined by particular, unique algorithms (e.g., mathematical models). However, for multimedia applications in which diverse data with asynchronous events must be processed, such special-purpose architectures may offer less advantage than those platformed on uniprocessors with no intra-connection overhead and easier compilation. To resolve this dilemma, architectures with a complete-graph or similar network enabling reconfigurable processing may be indispensable. The wiring for a complete-graph network for massively deployed PEs (Processing Elements) has never been considered practical, due to the estimated increase in the demand made on the communication bus. The revolution signaled by the appearance of ASICs with millions of gates will abolish such conventional prejudice, due to the possible layout of millions of intra-connections on a chip. A complete graph network has the following significant features:

(1) Memory-mapped node addressing with software-less protocol
(2) Completely reconfigurable architecture, dependent upon data types
(3) Time- and space-shared processing with asynchronization/synchronization
(4) Bus conflict-free local and global shared memory structure

Feature 1 provides for an accelerator with a unique computing environment–a common addressing system and dynamic parallelism in time and space for multi-granular processing of continuous media streams with minimum overhead. This structure potentially removes the need for software protocol, and makes intra-communication possible with only load and store instructions[6]. Thus, data transmission is performed with the same efficiency as a pipeline network. Features 2 and 3 offer more remarkable capabilities for a parallel processing system. In coarse-grained execution for media streams, executive routines classify any finite types. These routines are implemented at every event by configuring a temporal multiscalar processor with specified numbers of PEs. The physical size (usable PE) of task processing is dynamically changed according to the operation rate in the total task schedule. Thus, such a system allows multithread and process-level parallelism. In conventional schemes, heavy processes are partitioned and shared across a fixed number of PEs in order to achieve equal load-balance. Such an instruction-level architecture, in the case of deep pipeline-level, incurs a large overhead at process switching, and provides less flexibility for concurrent and multimedia data. In a complete-graph system, the scale of parallelism can be configured depending on the process size by dynamic routing of intra-connection between PEs, and not by the overlapping of the instructions. Figure 3 shows the architecture of a multimedia VR system, and Figure 4 shows an example of a complete-graph network which configures the geometry, audio, and codec cluster of Figure 3.

In Figure 3, a cluster is configured with multiple PEs, which are intra-connected through routers. The architecture, number of PEs, and function of each cluster must be reconfigurable to handle different type of media processing. These processes are carried out by router control and a writable stored program of PE. Considering both practical circuit scale and layout capability, a complete-graph interconnection can be designed with a single ASIC of 10 million gates with a single cluster (on physical base) consisting of 128 processing elements (IEEE 754) extended single precision; 32-bit mantissa, 10-bit exponent to operate at 40 GFlops. Each PE carries on rather coarse-grained operations, and consists of a floating point multiplier, adder/subtracter, FIFO, a register file, writable stored program memory, arithmetic function table, local memory, and router. These PEs are used for coordinate transformations in polygon rendering, computation of intersection/reflection, and detection of intersection of objects with a cast ray in a multiple-reflection model for shading or for audio DSP. According to our evaluation, 32 PEs structured by 12 level pipelines can calculate an intersected point between the cast ray and a quadratic surface within a single clock cycle (at 10ns/intersection). This metric measures the time between input of the receiving surface and ray parameters and output of the intersection point. The number of gates used for processing element is 40,000--50,000, so that the total number of gates for the graphics accelerator can be estimated at approximately 6 million gates. By the year 2001, this number will be doubled, and configured with two clusters/chip.

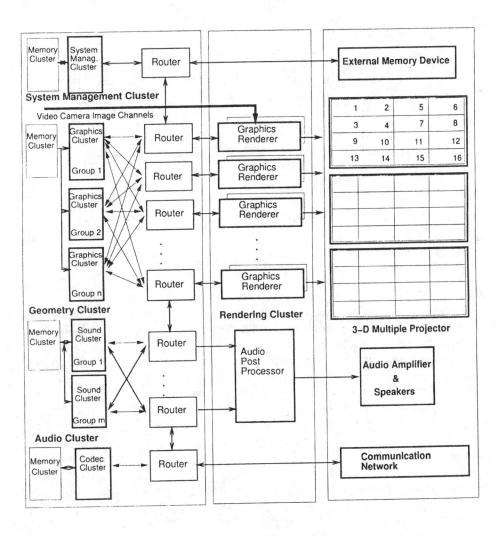

Figure 3. Multimedia VR architecture.

For audio processing, the multimedia accelerator can be used to implement common DSP functions, as well as less common advanced effects processing, based upon rendering methods sharing calculation with the ray-tracing required for concurrent graphic rendering. Common DSP functions require a floating-point processor (multiplier and adder) and memory for delay-buffers simulating the propagation times for sound transmission. Thus, specialized hardware may not be needed; rather, the writable stored program on the multimedia accelerator can play an important role in allocating resources for a variety of rendering tasks.

The above-described architecture is one of the examples of multimedia processors that can be considered likely. By around 2005, such multimedia functions will also be developed with conventional structures of personal computers and workstations (general-purpose processors will try to keep multimedia workloads for a while). However, such development may be diversified into two types: hybrid structures in silicon of general-purpose processors and specific hardware (parts of graphic processors and codecs); and massively parallel processing structures with multiple PEs and graphics hardware. In either case, graphics processing must be carried out by specific circuits, due to the load indicated by Table 1.

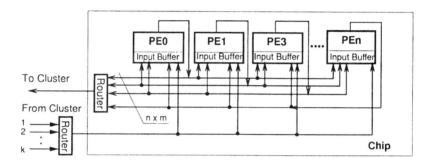

Figure 4. Example of reconfigurable architecture.

4. GRAPHICS RENDERER

Despite the fact that multimedia systems manipulate various kinds of data and functions, implementation of graphics and video processing on silicon is a key technology for the successful commercial production of a multimedia system (that satisfies the functions described in the introduction) with reasonable cost/performance. This is because the workload for visual processing is much bigger than for other modalities. A realtime rendering scheme based on ray-tracing or radiosity can be partially realized in an age of millions of gates; nevertheless, polygon rendering may continue to play a major role for graphics. In polygon rendering, graphics processing is divided into two components, acceleration and rendering. Figure 3 shows the layout of these components. The geometry cluster performs coarse-grained parallelism while the rendering cluster performs fine-grained processing. In consideration of future extensions of the multimedia processors graphics functions, the architecture has been designed with a modular structure that allows for the selection of functions of greatest leverage to the specified application. In fine-grained graphics processing (e.g., pixel shading, color blending, hidden surface removal, and texture mapping), it is more efficient to design a specialized circuit than to use the PEs, since operational speeds must meet one pixel per clock-cycle for realtime rendering. This performance cannot be obtained by PE architecture, even in a billion-transistor era. Figure 3 shows the block diagram for the multimedia processor architecture, including graphics, audio, and codecs clusters. Fine-grained processing for graphics is carried out in the graphics renderer shown in Figure 5.

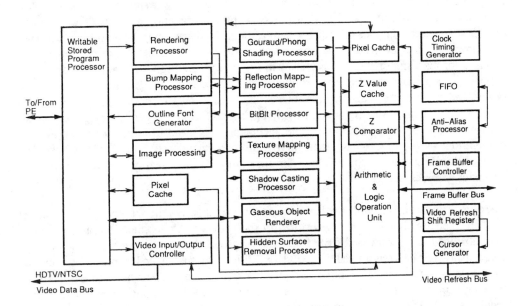

Figure 5. Graphics renderer.

A graphics renderer with the various functions described in section 2 must be implemented together with a multimedia accelerator in a single chip. These graphics functions may be designed with modular structure in the age of millions gates[7], and modules do not share common hardware resources. Attaining high-performance rendering with small numbers of gates is not difficult, as long as unlimited parallel expansion of frame-buffer fragments is allowed. However, such an approach is not practical for deployment on personal computer systems, because large-sized DRAM cannot be used effectively.

Graphics performance is not limited by gate scale, but by the bandwidth of frame buffer bus (which is restricted by the pin number of the chip). For a graphics renderer, a new type of pixel cache configuration or frame buffer interface to improve I/O bandwidth is necessary until the entire frame buffer can be embedded within a single chip. In the case of a configurable pixel cache architecture of 32-pixels, 100 MHz synchronous DRAM, and 256 pins for the frame-buffer bus, the maximum attainable speed (e.g., write- or read-only) is 1.875ns/24-bit pixel, which is equivalent to 1.6 GHz/byte in a single chip architecture. This is 15 times faster than sequential bit-mapping access. The pixel cache system uses 16 synchronous DRAMs of 16 or 64 Mbit for the frame-buffer system, so that the frame buffer size must be at least 4K x 4K x 24 bits. Since there is no additional hardware cost, this feature is useful for double-buffering of pixels, z-buffering, shadow casting buffering, alpha blending, video capture, texture pattern memory, overlay plane, etc. By the time the entire frame buffer is embedded within a single chip, the pixel cache may be kept as a useful architectural component.

5. VIDEO DATA CAPTURE AND SYNTHESIS OF COMPUTER GRAPHICS

The synthesis of computer graphics and video images in 3-space is a key technology in the production of realistic visual effects. This hybrid reality operation is performed by the video image processor. The video image processor in a multimedia VR system has two main roles: video capture (buffering) combined with codec processing and mapping. The mapping operation generates static or refreshed video (camera) images to map onto multiple windows at appropriate sizes or onto 3D surface-defined objects in realtime. There are three basic schemes for mapping of images, as shown in Figure 6: mapping video camera images onto windows or surface-defined objects, synthesis of video camera images and surface-defined object, and synthesis of video camera images in 3-space. This mapping technology is used for all image composition. 2D window mapping is used for ordinary video image display for teleconferences or live broadcasts. The technology required in this processing is 2D convolution for scaling of original images in correspondence with the window size. Meanwhile, 3D spatial mapping is used for generating a virtual reality scene combined with computer graphics images.

The application of this technology is similar to texture mapping, the difference being that not only are predefined or static images stored in the pattern RAM applied, but also refreshed images from the network or BitBlt from memory. In either case, transmitted or buffered video data may be compressed in JPEG or MPEG, so that a codec processor must be interfaced between the video processor and network or buffer. Further, various kinds of filtering must be applied selectively, depending on the quality of video images. The driving requirement for this function is realtime rendering; the mapped images must be rendered at a rate of several millions of polygons (100 pixels/polygon) per second, which performance had not previously been practically developed.

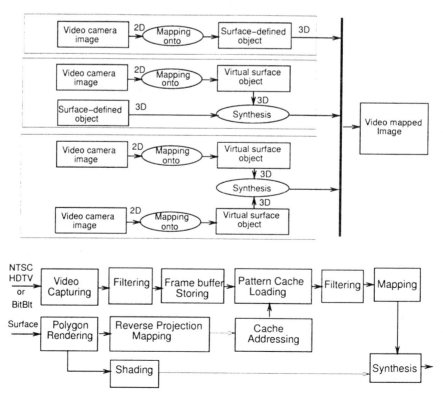

Figure 6. Video mapping scheme.

The mapping of video images onto polygon surfaces has the following distinguishing features, compared to direct-transformation of a pixel array: (1) easier definition and modification of video images by mapping onto the polygon vertex (allowing linear interpolation), (2) allocation of video data in 3-space that allows overlap (hidden surface removal) of images and synthesis with surface-defined object, and (3) easier computation of shading and transparency effects via only definition of attributes on polygon vertices.

Video image mapping requires the following procedures: (1) capturing video data such as HDTV or BitBlt from external devices, and storing them into the frame buffer, (2) defining a mapping area and loading them into a video pattern cache, and (3) mapping patterns onto a surface with scaling and filtering.

The refreshed video image mapping processor consists of seven major circuits: video input controller, polygon renderer, reverse projection processor, video pattern cache and pattern scaler, shading processor, and pixel cache. As shown in Figure 7, the mapped data are buffered at the video input port first (1-2) and stored into the frame buffer via pixel cache FIFO (3). The data are stored into a specified area of the frame buffer with a specified size by applying a scale with filtering and read out to the pattern cache (4) according to cache management embedded in the reverse projection processor. The surface is rendered in the rendering processor, which outputs the coordinates and attributes of polygon edges to interpolate at the shading processor. The interpolated pixels (5) are mapped by the pattern from pattern cache. When the pattern is mapped onto the surface, selective filtering is applied. The shaded texture pattern surface is then cached (6) and transferred to the frame buffer (7). The system must perform all of these processes at about 100 million pixels/sec. without reduction of the video frame rate, which refresh might be 30 Hz.

Video capture without any decrease in performance of other simultaneously applied functions may be an essential condition for many multimedia applications (i.e., those involving simultaneous operations of computer graphic [CG] image synthesis and video data processing). Multiple buffers for video data and wide bandwidth for the frame buffer are required. If an application calls for realtime rendering with video mapping (e.g., combining a natural scene with a CG image), then synchronization between polygon rendering and video capture is also required.

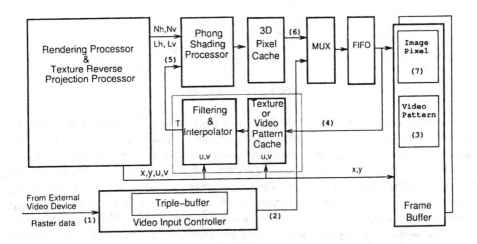

Figure 7. Video mapping processor.

6. AUDIO RENDERER

The term "audio renderer" implies a level of sophistication in audio signal processing that is akin to that involved in 3D graphics rendering. In fact, the comprehensive "rendering equation" for audio is quite similar to that proposed for graphics [8]. The sound synthesis and geometric acoustic processing components shown in Figure 8 are intended to provide a type of realism for a multimedia system's audio that would deserve to be recognized as "sonorealism," by analogy to photorealism. Similarly, sonorealism requires both the simulation of dry sound sources with natural physical properties, and the simulation of natural environmental effects. In the terminology of VR, these two audio signal-processing components, synthesis and effects processing, address the need for creating virtual sound sources and placing those sources into virtual acoustical spaces (including distance and direction effects). Realistically simulating the sound of such spaces has been termed "auralization" [9]. A third audio processor is required to code and decode audio signals, so that streamed audio may be handled efficiently. An audio cluster must also handle the mixing of audio signals from multiple origins to multiple destinations, including conventional post-production processes such as equalization and compression. Processing at this stage is not expected to be modulated over time, and so it is well suited for implementing stationary functions, such as compensation for loudspeaker crosstalk, which can enhance spatial sound imagery [10].

All sound synthesis functions for creating dry sources can be carried out by a DSP implementing various IIR (Infinite Impulse Response) filtering algorithms and inter-polating multi-tap delay lines. The possibility of including convolution- and FFT-based processing is included in the proposed architecture. Physical models of musical instruments, phase-vocoder-based manipulations, and granular synthesis are also achievable. Conventional MIDI-based controls of wavetable synthesis are supported, as are the extensions proposed in the recently released "Level 1 Specification" for downloadable sounds (DLS1).

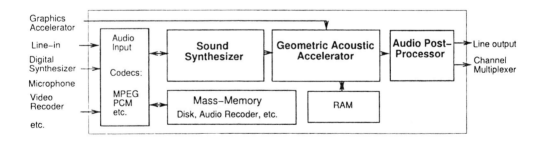

Figure 8. Audio cluster.

The geometric acoustic accelerator responds to data sent from the graphics renderer, which performs many calculations that can be used to configure audio signal processing as well as image synthesis. If, for example, a VR application requires tight coupling between 3D graphics and spatial audio, significant computational efficiency can be gained by sharing multiple-reflection intersection points between graphic and audio rendering. The key to a successful solution to the general rendering problem is to include in the architectural design a mechanism for switching between various levels-of-detail (LODs). This is as appropriate in audio rendering as it is in graphics rendering. Regardless of how many GFlops of arithmetic performance the ASIC provides, there will always be a need to compromise between the quality and the computational efficiency of audio rendering. The most important sound sources, typically those that are closest to the observer's position in space, will be rendered at higher quality than those in the distance. Of course, an audio renderer with hundreds of pseudo-DSPs can be configured in a parallel-processing architecture to provide excellent rendering quality for many sound sources; however, it is most prudent to plan for optimal use of computational resources, and for dynamic reallocation of those resources presented with the changing demands by a given application.

The multimedia accelerator described in Section 3 performs various DSP functions by a writable stored program and specified intra-connection structures. One PE has a performance of 200 MFlops with extended single precision (32-bit mantissa). This performance is roughly 5-10 times faster than what is available on a common commercial DSP. The audio processing threads are configured (shared) within a cluster of PEs. Note that the most significant difference between the geometric acoustic accelerator and the graphics accelerator is that the audio processes need a relatively large amount of memory for delay buffers, which may not be implemented on chips. To cope with this problem, some of the PEs can be specially assigned to manage external RAM access.

7. CODECS

JPEG/MPEG video and audio codecs, proposed as international standards by ISO-IEC, are indispensable functions embedded within an ASIC for a multimedia processor. Since the algorithms are standardized, no special architectural technology is required for them; rather, such modules are generally provided as a standard macro library by semiconductor manufacturers. However, in addition to hardware implementation of these standard libraries, software codecs are needed to handle future extensions. Some standards (such as MPEG4) are still being developed. This system implements both codec macro library (hardware function) and software codecs, consisting of DSP (described in Section 3) and amphibious logic. The latter uses multiple PEs for DSP and stored programs. Figure 9 shows the interface for codecs in this system. Encoded video and audio data from the interconnection network are stored directly to mass-memory or decoded in realtime for display. These coding operations are carried out by a codec cluster composed of multiple PEs and memory clusters, which are located between mass-memory or the interconnection network and the geometry clusters. The software codecs can be reorganized as needed. The memory cluster is one of the aforementioned specialized PEs which are assigned a large address space.

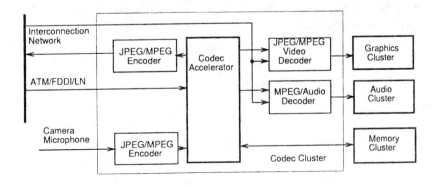

Figure 9. Codec cluster.

8. INTERACTION

Quick response time for interaction is essential, and comprises two factors, through-put and latency. Latency is usually a more serious problem than throughput in a VR system. If a system cannot synchronize rendering of image and sound with an operator's eye- or head-movement, disorientation and/or nausea ("VR sickness") can result. The implication is that unlimited pipeline delay-time in pursuit of high throughput is not always acceptable. Meanwhile, interactive procedures are tightly coupled to data structures of graphics and sound.   In the system shown in Figure 2, specific PEs are assigned to interactive file management, combining with memory clusters. Thus, interaction is defined by application-dependent software installed in specified PEs.

REFERENCES

1. Escalante Hardware Overview, Talisman Graphics and Multimedia Systems, Microsoft Corporation. Version 3, (July 12,1996).
2. Diefendorff K., and Dubey P.K., "How Multimedia Workloads Will Change Processor Design." *IEEE Computer*, Vol. 30, No. 8, September 1997, pp. 43-45.
3. Jayasinghe J. and Herrmann O., "Two level pipeline of systolic array graphics engines," in Advances in computer graphics and CAD, Springer, Berlin Heidelberg, 1991.
4. Gharachorloo N., Gupta S., et al., "Sub-nanosecond Pixel Rendering with Million Transistor Chips," *Proc. of Siggraph '88*, 22, 4, August 1988, pp. 41-49.
5. Akeley K., "Reality Engine Graphics," *ACM Computer Graphics (Siggraph '93 Proceedings)*, August 1993, pp. 109-116.
6. Ikedo T., Yamada J., et al., "An Architecture Based on the Memory Mapped Node Addressing in Reconfigurable Interconnection Network," The Second Aizu International Symposium on Parallel Algorithms/Architecture Synthesis, IEEE Press, March 1997, pp. 50-57.
7. Ikedo T. and Ma J., "The Truga001: A Scalable Rendering Processor," *Journal of IEEE Computer Graphics and Applications*, March 1998, pp. 61-81.
8. Kajiya T., "The Rendering Equation," *Siggraph '86 Proceedings*, Aug. 1986, pp. 143-150.
9. Kleiner M., Dalenback B.I., et al., "Auralization-An Overview," Journal of Audio Eng. *Soc.*, 44, 1993, pp. 861-875.
10. Cooper D. and Bauck J., "Prospects for transaural recording," *Journal of Audio Eng. Soc.*, Vol. 37, 1989, pp. 3-19.

36

MULTIMEDIA EDUCATION

Roy Rada
Washington State University
Pullman, WA 99164-2752
Email: rada@eecs.wsu.edu

1. **INTRODUCTION**..752
2. **LEARNING AND COURSEWARE** 753
    2.1   Historical Snapshot 753
    2.2   Intelligent Tutoring..754
    2.3   Tutoring Shells 756
    2.4   Standards 757
    2.5   Virtual Reality Tutoring..759
    2.6   Meta-analysis..761
3. TEACHING AND CLASSROOMS..762
    3.1   Communication Channels..762
    3.2   Asynchronous Classrooms 765
    3.3   Studio Course 766
4. **ADMINISTERING SCHOOLS** 767
    4.1   Schools..767
    4.2   Commercial System 769
    4.3   A Common Architecture 769
5. **AUTHORING COURSEWARE**..771
    5.1   One Company's Approach..771
    5.2   Courseware Life Cycle..771
    5.3   Delivery Platforms..774
    5.4   Reuse..775
6. **CONCLUSION** 776
      REFERENCES 777

Abstract. The use of multimedia in the educational enterprise can be viewed from many perspectives. The common view is that of the student learning by interacting with a computer. The courseware on the computer contains multiple media and guides the student through a learning experience. In this chapter we address this learning and courseware aspect of interactive educational multimedia but we also go beyond that.

Education involves classrooms and schools and the generation of content. In the classroom, students might interact with one another across telecommunications channels as one component of the multimedia experience. The school needs to support libraries of information and continuity for students across courses. Finally, the role of publishers or content providers is crucial in multimedia education. Multiple experts must be brought together in a sophisticated, production life-cycle in order that educational multimedia is adequately produced. All of these views are systematically addressed in this chapter.

1. INTRODUCTION

Audiovideo is a kind of multimedia in that it connects images in time with sound. Video was considered early in the 20th century to potentially be an enormous influence on education. We note in a textbook from that time (Duggan, 1936):

> Two new kinds of equipment which have already influenced teaching and are likely to influence it further are the radio and the motion picture. ..... The motion picture as an aid to teaching began to attract attention early, but the expense, the lack of suitable films and of an efficient manner of using them long prevented their introduction into schools. The matter of expense has become less burdensome by the development in recent years of a standard narrow (16 mm.) film which produces pictures large enough for class use at a greatly reduced cost and which can be shown by means of a portable projector and without fire hazard.

In 1936, people predicted great impacts of new advances in *audiovideo technology* on the classroom use of audiovideo tapes, but these predictions were not realized.

The introduction of computers and networking has changed the complexion of educational technology and allowed multimedia to assume a new importance. Multimedia for us will mean more than synchronized media. Our use of the term emphasizes computer-supported interactive multimedia. Such emphasis might be more rightly called a hypermedia emphasis than a multimedia emphasis (Rada, 1995b).

This rather all-embracing perspective of the educational enterprise and its relationship to new information technology and multimedia is extensively documented in the textbook *Virtual Education Manifesto* (Rada, 1997). There the educational enterprise is viewed as involving learning and courseware, teaching and the virtual classroom, administering and the virtual school, and the production of content. All four of these aspects of multimedia education are addressed in this chapter with a section devoted to each aspect.

Education is one of the most vital concerns of a society for it fundamentally addresses the perpetuation of a society. All children go through a typically state-financed educational experience. However, companies and other organizations are also concerned with their perpetuation, and the education of their employees and customers is vital to their long-term success. While this practical education may be often called training, for our purposes, the terms 'education' and 'training' mean the same thing. As organizations extend their global reach and as the needs for education grow, the potential for hypermedia-supported education becomes increasingly important. After studying this chapter, the reader should have a good sense of the major issues facing society as it attempts to extend the use of hypermedia in education.

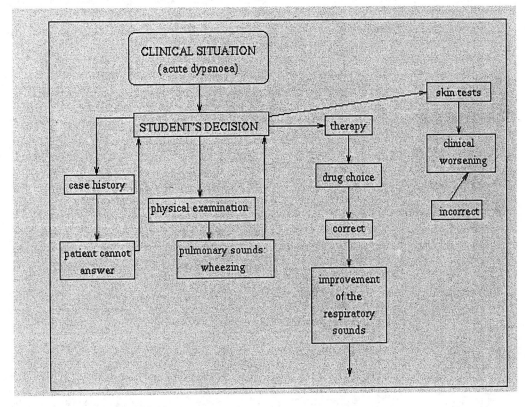

Figure 1. Flowchart describing all routes that the student may follow managing the simulated patients affected by allergic asthma (Corvetta et al., 1991).

2. LEARNING AND COURSEWARE

Courseware is the embodiment of educational material in a computer system. The dream of courseware developers is that students can interact with the computer in ways that would have otherwise been restricted to the interaction between the student and the teacher.

A courseware system that behaves like a teacher is sometimes called an intelligent tutoring system (Rada, 1991). What are the basic components that such systems must have to be effective? Developing intelligent tutoring systems is very costly. Are there tools that facilitate the creation of intelligent tutors?

As the knowledge of students, the domain, and teaching are incorporated into intelligent tutoring systems, where else can such systems go for heightened features? One direction is the incorporation of further hypermedia features to give the student the sense of being embedded in a real-world situation despite only being on the computer. Such virtual reality systems have what future in education?

2.1 HISTORICAL SNAPSHOT

For several decades using computers to support education has been popular. The early years of traditional *computer-assisted instruction* were revealing along many dimensions. First, we learned that courseware as a stand-alone tool can be effective under certain circumstances. Second, the development of pre-planned, tutorials proved far more difficult than we had thought it would when the movement hit its stride in the late 1960s and early '70s. Third, students often became frustrated with non-interactive linear or lockstep instruction over which they had very little control. Even so, some of the early computer-aided instruction was effective, and the lessons from it are worth remembering. The technology-aided instruction of today is taking on a decidedly different pedagogical flavor from these earlier efforts (Cartwright, 1993).

We describe one medical school example from the 1980s that integrates several tools and methods. In 1985, the Cornell School of Medicine began experimenting with the idea of using computers to make the learning process more efficient (Diaz 1991). As a result, students taking the course *Introductory Pathology* could enroll in an electronic version PathMac of the course. Macintosh computers tied into the PathMac database were scattered throughout the campus for student access. Students could study online textbooks, run simulated laboratories, or test their mastery of physiology by viewing online dissections.

PathMac provided online access to approximately seven gigabytes of images and bibliographical material that can be searched intelligently, cross-referenced, and printed. A selection of materials was available for biochemistry, anatomy, neuroscience, parasitology, physiology, radiology, and pathology.

One online application was an electronic pathology text called *HyperPath*, which included large portions of a version of a well-known book textbook. Professors could add text and graphics. A visual archive called Carousel included thousands of images. Carousel images could be paired with questions.

Another program was used to perform *simulated laboratory experiments* that otherwise would be performed on live cats. The system could be set up to test the response of various drugs on simulated cat muscle. The students chose which drug to inject, in what quantity, and then electrically stimulated the muscle and recorded the results on a simulated strip chart. Much more control over the results could be achieved than is possible with live muscle. One kind of simulation uses *flowchart logic*. For instance, in one courseware, a young man is presented who had a severe asthmatic attack after a walk (see Figure 1 "Flowchart"). The season is spring and the walk was in the countryside, both facts suggesting an allergic etiology of the disease. If the student's choice is to perform the case history or the skin tests, the computerized tutor comments that the choice is wrong given that the priority is to relieve the patient's symptoms. An essential physical examination and appropriate treatment should be immediately performed. Once the prescription of the correct medication results in normalization of the respiratory sound and congratulations from the tutor, a case history may be taken. The tutor emphasizes the key questions that should be asked in order to determine the possible allergic origin of a respiratory disease. The student performs the skin tests and evaluates the reactions. Diagnosis of the allergy pollens may be made and a correct hyposensitizing treatment planned. After usage with medical students, the teachers concluded that hypermedia was an effective and powerful learning environment that could be used to supplement, but not replace, traditional methods.

2.2 INTELLIGENT TUTORING

In terms of generally powerful intelligent tutoring systems, a set of basic *components* is needed. In general, all intelligent tutoring systems have a similar architecture comprised of an expert or domain module, a student module and an instructional or pedagogical module (Vasandani and Govindaraj, 1995; Murray, 1997). The domain module contains the domain expertise which is also the knowledge to be taught to the student. The student module contains a model of the student's current level of competence. The pedagogy module is designed to sequence instructions and tasks based on the information provided by the domain and student models (see Figure 2 "Intelligent Tutoring System").

The *student module* in an intelligent tutoring system maintains a model of the student's current understanding of the domain. It stores actions taken by the student and has some means of representing the student's knowledge derived from recorded actions. Representation of data in such a student model must facilitate its comparison with the domain model of the task to enable evaluation of misconceptions in the student (Van Marcke, 1995).

The *pedagogy module* of an intelligent tutoring system is responsible for several activities. Its primary function is to control the curriculum, that is, select the material to be presented and its form of presentation. In addition, the pedagogy module evaluates student's misconceptions based on observed actions. The pedagogy module makes use of rules pertaining to presentation methods, query response, and conditions for tutorial intervention.

An intelligent tutoring system models a student's understanding of a topic as she progresses through tasks, and compares this against a model of what an expert in that domain understands. If there is a mismatch, it can use its domain model to generate an *explanation* in that domain that will help the student understand. Broad actions considered by the pedagogy module include:

- Give help,

- Motivate learners,

- Give exercise,

- Guide with explanation, and

- Assess student progress.

As evidenced from an extract of a taxonomy of intelligent tutoring systems (Mizoguchi et al., 1996), the interactions between the tutoring system and the learner must specify the mode of interaction, communication roles, and content type (see Figure 3 "Learner-system Interactions").

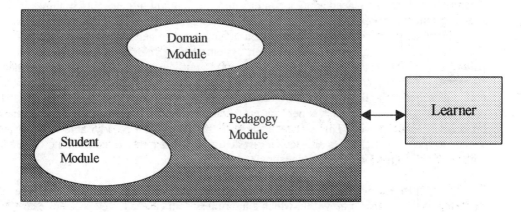

Figure 2. Intelligent tutoring system and learner.

```
Learner-system interaction
 Mode of interaction
    Menu
    Text
    Speech
    Virtual reality
+Communication roles
    Teacher-Learner
    Master-Apprentice
    Collaborative partners
+Content types
    Problem
    Question
    Example
+Control
    In-turn
    Free dialogue
    Case-oriented
```

Figure 3. Learner-system interactions. A part of the taxonomy with just 3 bottom-level children.

2.3 TUTORING SHELLS

While the inherent complexity of intelligent tutoring system applications results in many benefits over those found in more traditional computer-aided instruction approaches, these benefits have historically come at the expense of undesirably high development, delivery, and maintenance *costs*. A reasonable approach to reducing development costs is through the use of a tutoring shell, a specialized construction tool. The generality of such shells can vary greatly and there may be different types of generality. The shell might attempt to be very general, or it might restrict the resulting tutoring systems to a particular domain (e.g., electronics) or it might restrict the tutoring systems to a particular type of task (e.g., conversing with another human over the phone).

A *tutoring shell* can be placed along a continuum of the amount of generality it allows in the resulting systems. An excellent opportunity for understanding the difficulties associated with very general tutoring system shells can be seen in the history of general purpose expert system shells. As with tutoring system shells, expert system shell development has been driven, in part, by the need to reduce system development costs. Early expert system shell development attempted to follow the 'more is better' approach and incorporated many features within one tool. This approach allows a shell to meet the needs of more users, but often at the expense of any particular user. In later expert system shells, many of these features were deemed unnecessary and removed. This evidence suggests that it may not be advisable to construct general purpose, "one-size fits all," tutoring system shells, but rather to concentrate on shells with general features for a specific domain or type of task.

With shells that restrict the type of tutoring system that they can produce, one type of restriction is the *domain area* within which a tutoring system can be developed. For example, a shell might be developed that includes a great deal of domain knowledge about electronics and allows instructional designers to develop a variety of intelligent tutoring systems within that domain. The resulting systems could vary according to the age and background of the target learners and also according to type of learning environment best suited for the particular aspects of the domain being addressed.

Another way to use limitations on the generality of a shell (to produce higher quality resulting systems) is by restricting not by domain area but by the *type of task* that the learner is asked to perform. For example, a system can be used to produce a variety of intelligent tutoring systems, but each will be centered around the task of a learner conversing with another human over the phone. The learner might be someone training to be a customer sales, service or repair representative, a travel agent or a human resources specialist.

While end-users (students) may not need to know the linkage between the "upper models" and implementation details, the tutor developers do (Yum and Crawford, 1996). The trouble with conventional development of tutoring systems is that their abstraction layers are mainly for internal (largely computer science based) consumption. As a result, the abstraction is too involved for use by other experts who are not in the computing field. To overcome such barriers for generic tutoring system development, tools are needed to provide handles for the developers to input their *upper model specifications*. For example, if the purpose is to support the specifications of a tutorial strategy, the collaborative development system may need to provide three major functionalities:

- a simple database front-end interface for the instructional designers to input or import their tutorial rules;

- a dialogue box to allow the developer to select from a list of tutorial rule firing strategies; and

- a rule invocation tracer to track the firing of rules.

The remainder of the system may be hidden away from the instructional designer. Some intelligent tutoring systems already have some of these capabilities (Yum et al., 1995).

2.4 STANDARDS

The extent to which common practice in the world has produced intelligent tutoring systems that have interchangeable components is minimal. This means that intelligent tutoring courseware prepared in one toolset is typically not *compatible* with courseware produced from a different toolset. Teachers are reduced to worrying even about whether simple matters such as image format will be compatible. To address these needs the aviation industry, which heavily invests in courseware, has produced some standards (AICC, 1995).

2.4.1　Importing and Exporting

The aviation standards for courseware recommend guidelines for the interchange of the elements that occur in courseware. These elements include:

- Text,

- Graphics,

- Video,

- Audio, and

- Logic.

The standard recommends the use of authoring systems able to export and import courseware elements in standard formats. Specifically, the authoring system must be able to:

- Export and import all basic elements to individual files in standard industry formats

- Export and import lesson logic to a text representation

The *recommended formats* for courseware elements emphasize the common ones. As this book has not discussed the specifics of graphics, video, or audio formats, we will not repeat here the details from the standard as to which media format is most suitable. A little example for the advanced reader would say that images can be in bitmap format and audio in *wav* format. We will however render next the specifics about courseware logic.

Logic elements can be stored in one or more plain text files per lesson. The text files may contain programming language code, a scripting language, or standard generalized markup language tagged text. The content, in whatever format, must be comprehensive and clear enough to enable a person with a good understanding (of the scripting or markup language) to reproduce (without any other information) the exported courseware completely.

We shall specify some rather simple but nevertheless potent criteria for the description of the *components* of a piece of courseware. A course may be as simple as a few lessons to be viewed sequentially, or it may be as complex as hundreds of lessons, some of which are prerequisites to others and some of which may be experienced in any order.

In the aviation standard, courses have *pedagogical and structure components*. The pedagogical elements are all the lessons, tests, and other assignable units in the course. Frequently, these elements also include all of the objectives to be mastered in the course. In defining a structure, the developer frequently groups lessons for assignment. In other cases, the designer defines complex lesson hierarchies.

Files can be used to describe a course's content and structure. The level of complexity determines the number of files required and the amount of information required in each file. The following list briefly describes the contents or purpose of several of the files:

- Course Description File: Information about the course as a whole including a textual description of the course, and general makeup of the course – the number and type of elements.

- Course Structure File: The basic data on the structure of the course, including how the elements are organized.

- Objectives Relationships File: Objectives have complex and variable relationships to other elements of a course. This file defines all of these relationships.

Files are the most common data structure in computer science and by asking that the courseware structure is represented in files, the standards developers have reached to the lowest common denominator among the target audience, as standards developers are expected to do.

In addition to the aviation industry, other organizations are concerned about the standardization of educational technology. Educom is an association of higher education institutions that tries to improve the use of technology in education. Educom has produced a standard called the Instructional Management Systems (IMS) *Metadata Specification* (Educom, 1997). This specification is directed toward describing learning resources that are accessible, or perhaps just catalogued, online. The IMS Metadata Specification consists of three primary parts: a dictionary of terms, a description of learning resource types, and a system for managing the Specification. The IMS Dictionary identifies the terms that constitute IMS Metadata. These are the terms that are used to label the learning resources. IMS Metadata is broken down into fields and corresponding values. All of the proposed available fields are defined in the dictionary and their values are enumerated. These fields include author, credits, interactivity level, learning level, objectives, platform, prerequisites, price code, user rights, and user support. The hope of Educom is that all higher education institutions will use this metadata format to characterize their online educational material. Educom is working with the World Wide Web Consortium in the introduction of metadata information into the specification of the World Wide Web itself so that this metadata standard is conformant with other efforts at standardizing metadata formats across all web content.

2.4.2 Implications

Authoring systems can have different levels of *compliance* with the standard. We mention here the minimal and the most comprehensive levels. At a minimum, an authoring system must be able to export, in an automated fashion, all graphic, audio, and text elements from a lesson. For comprehensive compliance, in addition to meeting all compliance criteria of the minimal level, an authoring system must be able to import, in an automated fashion, the logic contained in text files and all accompanying graphic, audio, and text elements. The logic description must include the course description, the course structure, and the objectives relationships files (AICC, 1997).

The purpose of the aviation courseware standards is to facilitate the movement of courseware content from one environment to another. This ability enables the courseware owner to:

- *Reuse* elements of an existing program that were developed in one authoring system in a new program being developed in a different authoring system.

- Reduce *maintenance costs* by moving all courseware into one authoring system so that a staff with expertise in multiple authoring systems is not required to maintain an organization's courseware.

Obtaining these goals of reuse and reduced maintenance costs are noble but only reachable when the standard is widely followed.

To what extent are these aviation-industry courseware standards being followed by the developers of courseware authoring tools and of courseware itself? Since the advent of the *World Wide Web* the standardization of text, graphics, audio, and video has become more widespread. Now there is such a large marketplace of information that contains these different media types that the limited types commonly supported by web browsers have effectively led to market-type enforcement of a standard in this area.

2.5 VIRTUAL REALITY TUTORING

We have been emphasizing the abstract aspects of courseware. Intelligent tutoring systems require student models, domain models, and pedagogy models that are expressed as computer algorithms and data structures – very precise and abstract. For the student to learn effectively, the student must feel engaged, and the tutor can increase that sense of engagement with the appropriate use of *media* and of simulations that involve the media.

Multimedia engages the student through communication channels. Virtual reality enables the real world to be simulated and manipulated in realistic ways without, necessarily, the danger, inconvenience, or cost consequences of action in the real world. An early example of artificially representing the world is flight simulation used for training pilots. Computer-generated graphics rather than actual video often provide the visual aspect of the virtual reality world. The user knows that the virtual reality world is simulated but can accept its objects such as landscapes, rooms and corridors as representations of the real world. Some tactile sensation is also being offered in some virtual reality systems by the use of touch sensitive pressure pads. Hand gloves may be used to manipulate objects in this way. Movement in this artificial world is commonly synchronized with the user's actual bodily movements of walking, jumping, and running. The *virtual environment* can be defined as a multidimensional experience which is totally or partially computer-generated and can be accepted as cognitively valid (Jense and Kuijper, 1993).

In virtual reality group applications, individuals directly interact and collaborate within a simulated world. The virtual office gives teleworkers an impression of being in a familiar place in the presence of co-workers and with access to the usual office equipment. Trainee surgeons may acquire some of the skills required to perform *keyhole surgery* by practicing on virtual patients. Keyhole surgery is already performed remotely, by means of microscopic cameras which can be connected to monitors displaying close-up images of the patient's tissue. The keyhole method of surgery is beneficial to patients in terms of minimizing surgical intervention and improving recovery rates but it is difficult to teach. Real patients may not be used for practice. A virtual reality patient displayed on the monitor can, however, provide a good simulation, enabling the surgeon to learn the required techniques by doing surgery.

By way of further illustration, we describe a virtual reality tutoring system that supports students inside a three-dimensional setting derived from a ship's engine room, to train on maintenance and operation tasks using simulations (Stiles et al., 1996). There are several benefits associated with an immersive *ship-board training simulation*. The software-based simulator could replace most of what is accomplished in mockups. Maintenance training procedures could be done without bringing down systems and allow training on other ship-variants before change in duty. If the system uses Internet standards, it could enable effective distribution of training revisions, bypassing delays in printing, training instructors, and distribution.

One or more students, each with an associated viewer, are immersed in this ship engine room environment (see Figure 4 "Virtual Reality Environment"). Objects in the environment, such as control systems, actuators, and other equipment, are simulated for training. Other team members, or an instructor, are also simulated. As students select and manipulate objects in the virtual environment, they cause simulations to change the state of the world, and these changes are sensed by *agent systems*, which can intervene, explain, or demonstrate tasks for the student. The computer manages all the changes caused by the student, the objects being simulated, and the agents representing other people.

The costs of developing an intelligent tutoring system are high. The *costs* of developing an intelligent virtual reality tutoring system are even higher. The examples given of successful applications in ship board engine maintenance and keyhole surgery are examples were the costs of traditional training are very high. Thus the expense of the intelligent virtual reality tutor is willingly born by the organization that otherwise has to pay for the regular teachers and equipment. Based on these examples alone, one might suspect that relatively few situations are appropriate for such high-end tutoring systems. What other considerations might effect the cost-benefit analysis?

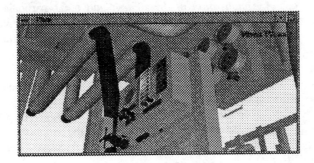

Figure 4. Virtual Reality Environment. The screen from Virtual Reality Tutor (Stiles et al., 1996) is part of what students see.

With large audiences, the *per student cost* of a virtual reality tutor declines. A science class for children may not be expensive to teach to a few students, and thus the school is not willing to spend millions to have a virtual reality tutor. However, given that millions of children every day are studying science, a successful intelligent virtual reality tutoring system could cost millions of dollars to develop but still cost each school only a few dollars. However, another challenge is whether the student will have access to the necessary computers to run the system. Currently, most schools are not well equipped to support intelligent virtual reality tutoring systems. As the technological infrastructure of the society continues to advance, the extent to which even children in school will have equipment that supports virtual reality systems will increase.

2.6 META-ANALYSIS

Many studies have been done on the efficacy of intelligent tutoring systems or courseware on the learning of students. The area is so complex that very differing conclusions are possible to draw. One approach to collecting the results from many different investigations is to use a *meta-analysis*. To do a meta-analysis, one first identifies dozens of studies on the same phenomenon. For our interest, the phenomenon is the efficacy of courseware. Then one identifies common variables across all the studies. Finally, one analyses and interprets the results of the different studies on the common variables. For instance, if 25 studies showed a significant improvement in student performance when using courseware versus when learning in the traditional way and only 5 studies showed a decrease in performance, then we could conclude that the use of courseware corresponds with improved student performance. The meta-analysis technique is particularly popular in the health care area where one needs to know whether a particular treatment that has been studied many times but with different results is truly a helpful treatment or not. Some meta-analysis has also been done in the realm of the efficacy of courseware.

Some meta-analyses have shown that computer-assisted instruction is equal or superior to conventional instruction on the following *variables*:

- student achievement, covering both immediate and long-term retention;

- attitude toward the subject matter and the instructor; and

- time to complete the task.

The generalization is that students taught via courseware realize *higher achievement* in significantly less time than the conventionally instructed students (Cartwright, 1993).

However, other meta-analyses have yielded different results. What has been surprising is the dominating influence of the *motivation of the student* and other particulars of the student situation that are quite independent of the courseware per se. Highly motivated students responded well to material presented on the computer and less highly motivated students responded less well (Chen and Rada, 1996).

The challenge is to be clear about the specifics of the student situation, the learning objectives, and the attributes of the courseware being used. We have not yet well established what the language should be to describe the different attributes of students, learning objectives, and courseware. We do know, however, that the *mapping* among these three entities is very complex. For any given students or learning objectives, the tools that will be appropriate may be different.

3. TEACHING AND CLASSROOMS

In one-to-one computer-based tutoring, the system interacts with one student and attempts to personalize the tutoring to the needs of the student. On the other hand, in a one-to-many collaborative learning environment, the system interacts with a group of students, imparting the subject knowledge using a classroom strategy. In principle, we could take the most sophisticated intelligent tutoring system designed for a one-to-one interaction and augment it for the group setting or classroom setting. However, *intelligent tutoring systems* are generally not available and certainly not ones that also account for group interactions.

What we will emphasize in the *virtual classroom* are means for students to interact with one another or with the teacher (Rada et al., 1989). How might computer networks support these interactions? What kinds of interactions do we specifically want? What is the evidence that student-student and student-teacher interactions are beneficial for learning?

During *student-student interactions*, high-ability students tend to assume a teacher's role. They summarize and explain the material to peers and answer peers' questions about the information. Low-ability students, on the other hand, tend to assume the role of learner. They listen to peers' summaries of the information, compare what they know with the information being presented by peers, and ask questions about parts of the material that are initially unclear. In this way, students are able to interact, collaborate, and learn from each other (Miyake, 1986).

3.1 COMMUNICATION CHANNELS

Telephone conferences are simpler and initially more engaging than computer conferences. For students, the most successful and popular element of a class is often the part that is technologically simplest: the use of a speakerphone to enliven class sessions with outside guests. This is done by plugging a speakerphone into a regular phone jack and making a pre-arranged, long-distance call.

In this section on communication channels, we are emphasizing some of the functionality that can be achieved with various technologies. We should hasten to remind ourselves, however, of the fundamental theme of the overall document – namely that a technology must fit into the work flow of those who are to use it. Despite the many ways in which a successful telephone conference could be used in a classroom, the fact remains that most classrooms do not use telephones. Yet, telephones are extensively used in most homes and offices. Why does the telephone not fit into the *workflow* of most classrooms?

An analysis of the culture of classrooms indicates that they are very importantly conveying the hierarchical structure of organizations with teachers having supreme authority and in turn reporting directly to some supervisor of a set of teachers. The technologies that succeed in this environment are those which support the *hierarchical relationships*, such as whiteboards which allow the teacher to further control the dissemination of information. Hodas (1995) says:

> We might also consider the school intercom system. Ideally suited to the purposes of centralized authority and the one-way flow of information, it is as ubiquitous in classrooms as its polar opposite, the direct-dial telephone, is rare. ... In general, resources that can be administered, that can be made subject to central control and organization, will find more favor from both administrators and teachers than those that cannot.

So while one teacher in one classroom might report positive results with the use of phones or phone conferencing, the evidence is meager that such approaches are popular. The explanation for the failure of the phone to make large inroads into traditional classrooms might be this interpretation of the *culture of the classroom*.

3.1.1 Video Conferencing

We've talked about students and teachers engaging in telephone conferences, but from the technological perspective a richer mode of synchronous interaction would include a video link. If we could reproduce the sense of physical presence that a traditional classroom gives through quality *audiovideo connections*, what else would we need to make the virtual classroom as good as the real classroom?

Research results indicate that video conferencing could be adequate in situations involving giving or receiving information, asking questions, exchanging opinions, solving problems, and generating ideas. In addition, the video may allow users to have a sense of presence of other people. The *sense of presence* is an important factor that may affect individual performance within the group. The sense of presence depends on the size of the video screen. The feeling of 'presence' is low for normal television screens. A large projection display increases the feeling of presence.

Nevertheless, compared with face-to-face interaction, *video has limitations*, mainly affecting the coordination of interaction (Isaacs and Tang, 1993). Interacting remotely through video makes it difficult for participants to control the floor through body position and eye gaze (it is not possible to ascertain exactly at whom other participants are looking when all the other participants appear on each participant's screen). By the same token, users have difficulty pointing at things in each other's space.

To promote interactivity in a video-conference arrangement for classrooms, *guidelines for teachers* have been designed as follows (Woodruff and Mosby, 1997):

- Include the participants in the conference within the first 5 minutes. Involve them early so they don't turn away. Try a name game, or ask a compelling question that taps their affective domain.

- For group work, select individuals at each site to participate on inter-site teams.

- Using the pre-obtained roster, call on students at both sites by name. Encourage discussion.

- Take as many questions from the distant site as you take from the local site and encourage students at distant sites to answer.

- Devote 30%-65% of each hour to student activity.

Asking a question can be daunting for students, especially if it means they must get the attention of a remote teacher and talk to a television screen. Teachers can help by noting the body language of remote students and taking the time to query when students seem puzzled or disinterested. Eye contact and use of names both help make students feel more comfortable. These people skills are obvious and natural in a "live" classroom, but may seem awkward in a distance learning situation. "Eye contact" means looking at the camera and the monitor rather than local students, and teachers might have to make a special effort to attend to remote learners.

3.1.2   Multiple Channel

Three groups of students at geographically distinct locations were asked to solve an engineering design problem using a rich, multimodal, groupware system (Geri and Lentini, 1995). Students were given two hours to design a windmill which would produce two volts under the forced air from a hair dryer. The groups were given tasks analogous to those of a main contractor and two subcontractors, but the specific tasks of each group were left ambiguous to force the students to negotiate the boundaries of their tasks.

The groupware system consisted of *multiple communication technologies* and multimedia databases. The communication resources were all three-way, and each channel was active throughout the session. The resources were as follows:

- a three-way, closed circuit video-conferencing system which allowed all groups to see and hear all of the activities in the other groups,

- a terminal-conferencing system which allowed students to type messages on their computer and send them to their collaborators, and

- another part of the terminal-conferencing system which allowed the students to draw a design on one screen and have it appear on the other two.

The multimedia databases included:

- an interactive multimedia database of engineering information which contained information on each of the subject areas the students would need to address in their design: gears, structures, aerodynamics, power, and generators, and

- scanned engineering textbooks, which also covered the subject areas that would need to be addressed by the students.

There was a link between *student activity and technological resource* used, and this was a critical part of how the students used the system. The multiple channels were used by the students to either increase the depth of the discussion or increase the breadth of the discussion. Using multiple channels to increase depth involved using more than one channel to converse about one topic, while using multiple channels to increase breadth involved conversation on multiple topics, with each topic on one channel.

The ability to use multiple representations allowed the students to supplement a mental and video representation of the design artifact with a drawing that showed details not immediately obvious from looking at the assembled design. Increasing the depth of the interactions allowed students to more effectively communicate their meanings and create much richer representations of the designs. The use of multiple channels to increase breadth proved especially useful when one group member was engaged in a time-consuming activity on one channel. Using the breadth available via multiple channels also became important near the end of the session when the groups had to transmit a great deal of information in very little time. Thus, we see again that the *mapping* between the technology that is appropriate and the student learning objective is a complex mapping. No one technology is right for all learning objectives.

3.2 ASYNCHRONOUS CLASSROOMS

An *asynchronous classroom* is one in which the students and teacher interact without needing to be synchronized. Thus the teacher might put an assignment on the web one day, a student read it anytime later, and answer it yet later. Typically, there is a broad time schedule in that course starts at some date and over some weeks students must submit certain exercises and take certain tests. A correspondence course handled by paper mail could be an example of an asynchronous classroom but students in such a course might not have any interaction with other students.

Studies of the effectiveness of distance education courses have been ongoing for many years. In 1928, R. E. Crump published "Correspondence and Class Extension Work in Oklahoma." In the work of the 20s and 30s the emphasis was on correspondence courses and moved later into television and radio. Of course, contemporary emphasis tends to be on Internet-supported courses. In one listing of hundreds of studies done since the 1920s, the fundamental conclusion is that no fundamental differences in quality between face-to-face classrooms and virtual classrooms has been demonstrated (Russell, 1997).

We will next describe the New Jersey Institute of Technology *Virtual Classroom*™. The special software structures incorporated in the system were specifically designed to support collaborative learning, including discussions, student presentations, joint projects, debates, and role-playing games (Turroff, 1995). Participation is generally asynchronous and participants may dial-in from any telephone system. Students can study a complete B.A. in Information Systems or B.S. in Computer Science via the virtual classroom.

A Virtual Classroom environment can be used in many different *media mixes*:

- Face-to-Face plus Virtual Classroom: This can vary from adding system use to enrich on-campus courses conducted by traditional means; to distance courses where system use is supplemented by one or two face-to-face meetings.

- Virtual Classroom as the sole means of delivery: with the use of print media in the form of textbooks or course notes, in addition.

- Multimedia: Virtual Classroom plus Videocassette; or Virtual Classroom plus CD-ROM.

The Virtual Classroom in each of these modes requires different management than a traditional course requires.

The Virtual Classroom has been used in teaching many courses. One of the salient conclusions is that students must be *actively guided*. It does not 'work' to simply make the Virtual Classroom available and tell students that they can use it to ask questions about the readings or discuss aspects of the course at any time (Hiltz,1995). If it is not a 'required' and graded, integral part of the course, the majority of the students will never use it at all; and those who start to use it, will generally decide that 'nothing is going on there' and will stop using it.

Some of the courses use standard public television courses, such as "Discovering Psychology," produced by the Public Broadcasting System. However, most video segments are filmed by New Jersey Institute of Technology in its "candid classroom" and then distributed to remote students on videotape, or via broadcast on a cable channel or satellite. In all *video variations*, the Virtual Classroom is used for all assignments and additional discussions.

Numerous studies have been done of the reaction of students to the Virtual Classroom. One can conclude that

- mastery of course material in the Virtual Classroom is equal or superior to that in the traditional classroom, and

- Virtual Classroom students report higher subjective satisfaction with the Virtual Classroom than the traditional classroom on a number of dimensions, including improved overall quality.

On post-course questionnaire, students were asked a series of questions about their course, the instructor, and their experiences. Most of the items showed *no significant differences* among modes. The differences in course and instructor ratings are evidently more affected by factors other than mode.

What are the *costs of teaching* with the Virtual Classroom? Teaching with the Virtual Classroom and videotapes can be more demanding than traditional face-to-face lectures. The first time one prepares the materials for weekly Virtual Classroom modules and moderates the conferences, this is much more work than just delivering lectures face-to-face.

Once the course has had its basic delivery materials and videotapes developed:

- If the class has less than 25 students, the actual amount of work to conduct it is about the same as for a traditional class.

- The amount of work is directly proportional to the number of students, since there is no limit to the amount of time each student can ask questions.

- For more than about 30 students, class conferences have to be divided to be manageable, thus increasing the faculty workload substantially.

Institutions may initially think that virtual classrooms are a "cheap" way to deliver education. If done right, with full-time faculty conducting courses, it is actually *more expensive*. There is much to be done in discovering which tasks can be offloaded from faculty to lower priced teaching assistants, without substantially decreasing the quality of the product delivered.

3.3 STUDIO COURSE

In some disciplines, particularly the science and engineering disciplines, a course will often require students to meet in different types of rooms for different types of work at different times. The lecture may include hundreds of students at one time. A laboratory session may occur one afternoon each week, and students would work under loose supervision in this laboratory to explore hands-on some aspect of the course. A recitation session may additionally be held each week in which students meet as a small group with a teaching assistant to discuss problems with the reading material or textbook assignments. When these three course activities are combined and students always meet in the same room at the same time and face in the one meeting a combination of lecture, recitation, and lab, then we have a *studio course.* What's important about studio courses for us? With the addition of courseware, the studio course method has been shown to have very impressive educational results.

LearnLinc™ is a *commercial, virtual studio course toolset* that is designed to support Studio Courses (ILINC, 1997). LearnLinc provides desktop videoconferencing, application sharing, scalable class size, enhanced multimedia authoring tools, and multimedia resource management tools.

At the top of the *LearnLinc screen* are a variety of tools that instructors and students can use to launch applications, content books and multimedia presentations, and join live, interactive sessions. Students have tools that allow them to open courseware, register for and join interactive sessions, and launch applications that are registered with LearnLinc. Instructors have all of the student tools, as well as the ability to schedule and edit sessions. Authors and administrators have additional tools that allow them to work with authoring tools, add multimedia resources to the system, and perform system administration tasks. Teachers can author material with popular commercial courseware authoring tools.

A *Synchronization Agent* is designed for a specific application. Essentially, the Synchronization Agent shows the floor holder's actions within a synchronous application. The floor holder can navigate through multimedia content, move a shared pointer, highlight significant text, or launch multimedia clips embedded in course material – and all of these actions are shown in real-time on each participant's workstation.

QNA is one of LearnLinc's application that heightens the interactivity of a session by allowing the teacher to anonymously *poll the session participants.* QNA allows the teacher to ask a question with up to five multiple choice answers. As the participants enter their answers, the teacher can view their responses immediately, in the form of percentages. The teacher can also ask a question verbally, and request a show of electronic hands. That way the teacher can get a rough idea of how well the class is following the course material.

LearnLinc allows students to meet *across distances* at the same time and still interact with one another through various means. The students may also go into courseware to explore the specifics of the content of the particular course. However, the teacher can monitor what every student is doing continually. Thus some students can be in the same room with the teacher but other students could be at arbitrary distances and the general features of the studio course should still attain.

4. ADMINISTERING SCHOOLS

We've looked at how students learn and how courseware can support learning. Then we moved to the classroom as the first step in institutionalizing learning. Given that teaching and learning occur, one of the next concerns is the *administering* of the virtual school.

4.1 SCHOOLS

Different schools have different *requirements.* The Education Network of Maine does distance learning with no residential students and needs support for such distant students. The Maricopa Community Colleges have a commuter base with diverse needs. The University of Texas at Austin has a large, residential student population. These different schools have different information technology needs.

There are eight academic units in the University of Maine System, seven traditional campuses and the *Education Network of Maine* (ENM). ENM supports the distance learning programs

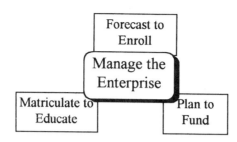

Figure 5. Education business practices. To manage
the enterprise, SCT includes focuses on the three
functions depicted in the plain rectangles.

of the University System. To understand the needs of a distant student, the university developed scenarios for a student enrolling in courses from separate University of Maine System campuses. Several scenarios for that fictional student followed her progress through a maze of campus procedures. The conclusion was that unless enrollment and administrative services are reconfigured for ENM students, the process will remain discouraging. Telecommunications and technology have done more than link people together at a distance; they have also revealed that traditional processes for serving them are not particularly suited to an integrated, virtual mode of operation.

The *Maricopa County Community College District* (MCCCD) in Arizona is the United States' second-largest system of its kind, exceeded only by the Los Angeles system. It offers 6,000 courses to a population of commuter students. MCCCD has problems not unrelated to those identified by ENM – namely, MCCCD needs to facilitate the movement of students to and from its various operations. To develop the information technology infrastructure to support its educational mission, MCCCD contracted with a major software company to develop a Learner Centered System. This Learner Centered System replaced, integrated, and expanded the functionality of MCCCD's previous systems that impacted learners, such as the Student Information System, the Monitoring Academic Progress System, the Course Program Register, the Course Inventory Audit, the tutor management system, and the on-line grading system.

The *University of Texas at Austin* has evolved its computing system over several decades, adding technological innovations as appropriate. The university licenses software from established companies that service the education sector. However, the university's systems are generally programmed in-house. The university employs about 400 full-time computer programmers.

The computational needs and costs are radically different depending on the type and size of a school. The University of Texas at Austin has 50,000 students and its information systems are not applicable to a smaller school. For a small school, such as the *University of Texas at Permian Basin* with 1,000 students, the school's accounting needs can be adequately handled with a spreadsheet package on a personal computer. The *University of Vermont* with its 10,000 students is intermediate in size between the University of Texas at Austin and the University of Texas at Permian Basin. The University of Vermont employs 50 full-time information technology staff and licenses its main information system from a commercial vendor.

The *Tennessee Board of Regents* serves approximately 200,000 students and is committed to connecting students and services so that every student is assured online, immediate access to admissions, registration, and grading information. The Tennessee Board of Regents has contracted with one software house for all its software needs and that software house is described next (SCT, 1997b).

4.2 COMMERCIAL SYSTEM

A school that wants an integrated information technology system faces a large challenge when it wants to implement this system from scratch in-house. Why not purchase a system from a company with expertise in providing such solutions for schools? In the preceding description of higher education school systems, we mentioned repeatedly that schools had acquired software from a commercial vendor. In many cases, this vendor is *Systems & Computer Technology Corporation* (SCT).

The University of Texas at Austin uses SCT software. The University of Vermont paid SCT one million dollars for a license to its major university information system and assigns five full-time staff in-house to maintain the operation of that SCT system. The multi-year contract that the Tennessee Board of Regents has signed with a commercial vendor is a contract with SCT for installation of SCT software throughout the state of Tennessee.

One of SCT's major products for higher education is called Banner and the latest version of that is *Banner2000*. Banner2000 enables (SCT, 1997a) an educational enterprise to operate based on a common set of business practices: Manage the Enterprise, Forecast to Enroll, Matriculate to Educate, and Plan to Fund (see Figure 5 "Education Business Practices"). University users manage revenue and costs with processing designed specifically for the higher education environment. Managing the workforce goes beyond payroll, employment, compensation, and benefits. Position control, tenure, deferred pay, work study, and regulatory requirements further define the information needs. Banner2000's enterprise model supports core financial and human resources business processes with built-in workflow, centralized or distributed information processing, decision support, and employee self-service. Potential students access the institution's information, apply, and research financial aid by themselves across the Internet. With Banner2000, faculty and students can advise, register, grade, and locate financial aid sources by themselves.

4.3 A COMMON ARCHITECTURE

In Figure 6 "Modular Environment," a *structural/functional view of an education information system* is presented. Students go through a student management module to teachers, administration, library, and other services. Teachers manage teaching assistants who in turn interact with students through the student management module and have access to library and ancillary services. The model does not address some important concerns, such as marketing, finance, or course production. The simple model addresses principally *the teaching function*:

- The course material is stored in the library as lessons. Lessons are grouped into courses, which are in turn linked into certificate and degree programs. These are one of the resource modules in the common architecture suggested earlier in this chapter.

- The student has a record that identifies the student and points to lesson accomplishments that are recorded separately for each student and each lesson.

- Teachers each have identification records, too. Additionally, a record of transactions by the teacher with the student management and teaching assistants is maintained.

- Administration collects student evaluations of teacher performance and manages the assignment of teachers to courses and curricular management.

With such extensive recording of teaching-related activities, quality control of teaching is facilitated.

An indication of the breadth of possible *support services* in a virtual school notes these four categories of such support (Lawrence and Service, 1977):

- Academic Support

- Student Service

- Institutional Support

- Student Access

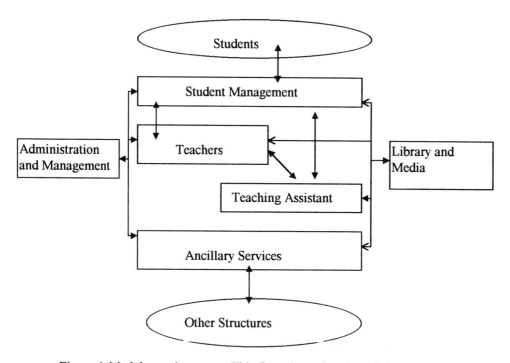

Figure 6. Modular environment. This flow chart of a school information system is based on student information and focused on professional activities.

Academic support is further decomposed into Computing, Course Development, and Academic Personnel Development. Student Service is basically counseling and depending on the student body may involve support for students to advance in their job. Institutional Support includes logistics, administrative computing, faculty services, and public relations. Student Access includes student recruitment and financial aid administration.

Extending our information system model for a virtual school, we further address the *roles* of student, teacher, librarian, administrator, marketer, budgeter, personnel manager, and course developer. The librarians acquire course material from third parties. The marketer develops relationships with organizations representing students and sells the course. The budgeter distributes revenue from student tuition fees to cost centers. Each role can be implemented in different ways but should have a well specified interface that allows other roles to communicate with it.

5.   AUTHORING COURSEWARE

We have emphasized the delivery of education in virtual mode, but before this can occur, there must be content to be delivered. The development effort required to produce courseware is substantial (McDonough, et al., 1994). In the aerospace training sector, one company spends about 400 hours in developing each hour of training material. The inclusion of high quality sound, animation, or video can mean that developing a course from which students gain 1 hour of training time will require 800 hours. Who can possibly afford such *production costs* and what methods of production are used? We give one example of how a company that specializes in the production of aerospace courseware operates.

5.1 ONE COMPANY'S APPROACH

AMTECH is a subsidiary of Gruppo Agusta. Gruppo Agusta is an organization of about 10,000 employees that designs and manufacturers helicopters. In order to better approach the application of new technologies to education and training, Gruppo Agusta established AMTECH solely to make courseware and particularly for the aerospace manufacturing sector. AMTECH employs 100 full-time courseware specialists that follow well-defined courseware life cycles (Rada, 1995a).

A course developed by Agusta AMTECH has a *standard structure*. Each course is split into modules which identify one or more subject areas. A module is split into one or more lessons. Each of them will describe one topic. The topic will be provided to the trainee during a teaching session. A teaching session should be 45 minutes in duration. Between two teaching sessions, a break has to be allowed.

Recurrent parts are present in each *lesson*, which have the aim to describe contents and give general information about a lesson. These parts are: lesson title, lesson description, and lesson conclusion. The lesson title is a standard format frame containing the title of the lesson. The lesson description is a standard format frame, or a series of frames, stating:

- lesson objective;

- what the trainee will be able to achieve at the end of the lesson;

- pre-requisite background necessary to reach the lesson;

- lesson length.

The lesson conclusion is a standard format frame which reports general information when the trainee has completed the lesson and the next lesson to perform.

5.2 COURSEWARE LIFE-CYCLE

In the following paragraphs, the procedures for the implementation of a *courseware project* are listed, and the different phases in which the project will be articulated are identified. All the different working groups involved in the project are identified together with the tasks, activities, and documentation they have to produce.

The *courseware life-cycle* at AMTECH has eight phases (see Figure 7 "The AMTECH Courseware Life-Cycle"). In each phases, there are strictly interconnected intermediate phases. All the phases are subject to quality control in order to establish conformity to the relevant specifications. The quality control is performed on both the result and the methodology used to generate it. Active customer involvement in the process is a must for the project success. This is similar to a software life-cycle but with additional courseware-specific steps, such as "storyboard production."

PHASE	DOCUMENTS
Requirements and Planning	Requirements Specification; Development Plan; Quality Assurance Plan
Preliminary Design	Design Specification
Storyboard Production	Storyboard Collection; Storyboard Test Report; Audiovideo Specification
Implementation	Frame Listing; Lesson Test Report
Integration	Trainee Manual; Instruction Manual
Delivery	Configuration List Item Data; Acceptance Test Report

Figure 7. AMTECH courseware life-cycle. The documents, which result from a phase, are listed in the right-hand side of the box describing the phase. The final two phases not listed here are "guarantee" and "maintenance."

Courseware product development originates from a *customer training request*. The customer training request, which is rendered official with the issue of a system document, is the basis for generating a development contract. Starting from the customer training request, the project group performs the following activities:

- it identifies the training goals of the courseware and the target population;

- it defines how the training goals will be met;

- it plans the activities needed to develop the courseware.

In the *Requirements and Planning phase,* the project group issues the Courseware Requirement Specification document, which includes hardware and software architecture, applicable teaching strategy, and interconnection between the different components of the courseware. At the same time, the Courseware Development Plan document is issued containing the planning of activities, the employed resources, and the time schedule. In addition, the Courseware Test Plan document is produced which describes the testing methodology. At the same time, the Quality Assurance group issues the Courseware Quality Assurance Plan document.

The *Review of Requirements* is held to verify the completeness of the requirements and to approve the testing criteria. The following staff take part in the Requirements Review:

- The Didactic Systems Office Manager (President);

- The Software Project Quality Representative (Secretary);

- One or More Customer Representatives;

- The Configuration Management Representative;

- The Training Systems Technical Manager;

- The Quality Assurance Manager;

- The Project Technical Manager; and

- Current Documentation Authors.

At the end of the meeting, a report is issued describing the discussed topics, the problems encountered, the corrective actions to be performed, and the time necessary to complete them.

During the *Design phase*, the customer is allowed to analyze a sample lesson showing the training strategy and the courseware graphic, audio, and video. This phase is completed once the Design Review is held. The staff that take part in the Design Review are basically the same as those who take part in the Requirements Review.

For any single lesson, a *storyboard* will be drafted on paper, containing one or more graphic images (drawing or pictures) to describe a particular item inside a section. These images describe what will be implemented on the computer in terms of:

- objects to be drawn on the screen;

- interaction with the trainee;

- text layout;

- audio sentences; and

- flow-charts to describe the logical links among the blocks of frames constituting a particular topic in the section.

The storyboards allow the simulation of the lesson before its implementation on the computer.

The Courseware Designer, with the possible help of the Subject Matter Expert, issues the storyboards of the current module, on the basis of agreed standards which are contained in the documents issued during the previous activities. The storyboards, together with the relevant flow-charts, are gathered in the *Storyboard Collection document*.

In the *Implementation phase*, the storyboards are implemented on the computer. All the graphics, texts, and logical links of the lesson are developed. At the same time, the visual and audio material is implemented in a preliminary way. Each module is composed of one or more lessons. Each lesson is to verify the correctness of logical structure and adherence of the lesson content to the storyboards.

In the *Integration phase*, graphics and text are integrated with the final audio and video. At the same time, the Courseware Usage Manuals are produced. Those manuals will contain an exhaustive summary of the contents in each lesson in the course. In particular the Manual for the Instructor will contain a list of all tests. A Final System Review is held to analyze and approve the issued documentation, and to examine and approve the courseware produced. In this phase, the final version of the course is officially delivered to the Customer.

The hardware and the software are guaranteed by the contract. The *Courseware Guarantee* starts after the Delivery Review, and lasts for the period provided by contract. The guarantee covers the eventual technical problems which have not been found during the testing phase or which have manifested themselves during the effective usage of the courseware.

Errors have to be signaled with a document written by the Customer containing:

- complete courseware identifier;

- description of the frame where the error has occurred;

- error description; and

- description of the conditions in which the error has occurred.

The *error report* will be assessed by the producer in order to guarantee a quick action. Any modifications to the produced courseware involves an update of the whole documentation and configuration. The corrected courseware will be submitted to all the tests provided for the integration phase. The Customer can request modifications involving substantial variations to the delivered courseware, but pursuing such modifications will give rise to a dedicated contract.

5.3 DELIVERY PLATFORMS

Training is for people distributed in classrooms. The AMTECH *delivery platform* is controlled by main computers which manage the trainee stations in the classroom. Each classroom is equipped with an instructor station and a large screen system connected to the instructor station. Both the trainee station and the instructor station support multimedia.

The *station* has a high resolution color graphics board. The effectiveness of the training session is enhanced by means of videodisc real images and digitized audio. Touch screen and mouse allow a natural interaction with the system.

The software elements of the training system fall into four categories:

- Operating System,

- Authoring System,

- Audio Edit System, and

- Management System.

All *software packages are proprietary*. The training system operates under a multiuser operating system. The authoring system can be summarized as having two distinct functions that are courseware creation and courseware delivery. The authoring system provides an integrated graphics editor to develop displays in terms of graphics, text, video, and animation. The authoring system also provides an easy tool to develop the lesson branching logic. The audio edit system supports digitizing audio sentences and storing them on the main computer hard disk. A Management System provides the instructor with numerous facilities, including selection of the most suitable instruction for a student at a particular time and automatic testing of students both before and after instruction. The Management System creates a data base to store information on the trainee learning process for each course and lesson.

5.4 REUSE

For many years, courseware authors have tried to determine the factors which influence the efficiency of courseware development. Reusable, instructional templates were identified as contributing to *efficient courseware authoring* over fifteen years ago (Avner 1979). As the availability of courseware components has increased, the attractiveness of building and exploiting libraries of these components has grown.

Reusable information can take many forms, such as a library of software routines included in a computer program, or a standard letter used by a company to offer the same services to a number of customers. Approaches to courseware reuse center on multiple access points into libraries of teaching material and the ability to reassemble components (Rada, 1990).

For libraries of textual material, good methods of indexing and retrieving information are relatively well known. For other media, the story is less simple. For instance, the University of Bristol has produced a videodisc with 36,000 biomedical images. Copyright of the images remains with the donors of the images. The images can, however, be freely reused for non-profit making purposes. A text catalogue of the material is available and can be searched with a free text retrieval system (Williams and Hammond, 1994).

The production of a single frame of film often costs over $300. Amazingly this ultra-expensive footage is only used once. The million dollar scene has its place in the movie, and that is the only place it will be seen. Several efforts have been made to build *video libraries* which could be reused. The MIT Media Laboratory experimented with repurposing footage from the soap opera "Dallas" for interactive replay. The experiment failed because this apparently multithreaded soap opera was too tightly structured to be repurposed (Pentland et al., 1993).

As we might have expected, the more complex media types are more difficult to effectively reuse. However, on further study, we would find that the real bottleneck to reuse is not something peculiar to the content to be reused so much as the ethos of the teams doing the authoring. Reuse is not typically much encouraged. When people author, their primary objective is to produce a document. Contributing to a reuse library is typically not a part of this task. Reuse must be part of an *organization-wide commitment* for it to succeed. Libraries must be built or acquired and authors must be rewarded for contributing to or taking from the reuse library. One advantage to formalizing the model of courseware authoring, as done in the preceding subsections, is that the modelers now have further opportunities to try to institutionalize reuse by entering it into the model.

6. CONCLUSION

Education is achieved through learning. Learning is, in turn, achieved through the modification of a model in the student's mind. Rote memorization is a crude learning task, while synthetic reasoning accomplishes more sophisticated learning. Through *courseware* the computer supports learning tasks. At its simplest, courseware holds linked text that gives the student a different kind of flexibility with browsing the information for memorizing content. For different learning tasks, different presentations of information are appropriate. The book printed on paper remains a valuable tool for some understanding tasks and is likely to remain so for the foreseeable future. On the other hand, the new technologies offer new possibilities. An intelligent tutoring system uses domain, pedagogy, and student models in ways that human teachers do. These models can help guide rich multimedia interactions in the form of virtual realities. However, the cost of building intelligent, virtual reality tutoring systems is currently prohibitively high for most occasions. Standards for the components of these intelligent, virtual reality tutors do not exist. The paucity of courseware standards interferes with the perpetuation of courseware.

Courseware may be used by a lone student or in the context of a classroom. In classroom learning, the student interacts with other students and the teacher in order to gain further insights. The *virtual classroom* exists on the information superhighway. Groupware technologies are particularly apropos to the classroom. Groupware supports the activities of a group in synchronous or asynchronous mode. The simplest way to do this is to provide for online submission of exercise answers and electronic bulletin boards for discussion of those answers. Groupware may be used for courses that still have regular face-to-face meetings, or all meetings might occur via the groupware and none in face-to-face mode. In the Studio Course, groupware complements lectures and courseware. The Studio Course has been shown to reduce the cost of traditional teaching and to improve quality. The virtual classroom allows teachers to manage the submission of work and student-student interactions in ways that would be impractical without the computer support.

A classroom exists within a school. The *virtual school* is a type of virtual organization. In a successful virtual organization, the technology fits into the workflow of the people. To place a school onto the information superhighway, one needs a model of the school. This model must accommodate students, teachers, administrators, marketers, and more. Information systems are commercially available which implement the standard model of a school and which can be tailored to any particular school's needs. One of the impediments to progress in this arena is the idiosyncratic character of individual schools and the corresponding high cost of tailoring an information system to a particular school. Standards for schools and their information systems reduce the costs of individual school information systems. Standards for operation also facilitate quality control. Furthermore, with computer networks, one can monitor many of the transactions within a school and automatically give feedback about the quality of performance of individuals within the school.

The production of sophisticated courseware may require specialist teams. This is not for the lone teacher to do, as is too often the case in universities. Instead a manufacturing process may be applied to courseware production. Different people play highly specialized roles in keeping to a precise schedule of sequentially linked deliverables that form the courseware life cycle. People involved in *courseware production* require substantial organizational support.

While the automation of schools systems was seen as unlikely in the five year forecast, the educational organization will have become, in thirty years, more *effective and efficient* through the proper use of information technology. The judicious use of technology under inspired leadership can help a school separate content production, from delivery, from assessment. Students, teachers, and administrators will better share information in ways that improve quality control.

The detailed shape of information technology thirty years hence is *difficult to predict*. Wireless computers the size of a credit card will receive data or multimedia information anywhere and anytime for some people. Artificial intelligence techniques will allow some roles in the organization to be performed by computers. To the extent that these or very different technologies become prevalent, they will be implemented first in non-educational organizations. For instance, the financial sector will use multimedia information and artificial intelligence before the education sector does. Nevertheless, in thirty years time some educational organizations should be significantly different from those we know today, while some will be little changed from their current situation.

REFERENCES

AICC (1995) "Courseware Interchange Guidelines and Recommendations" from *Aviation Industry CBT Committee Courseware Interchange, AGR 007, Version 1.0* by Courseware Technology Subcommittee at *http://www.aicc.org/ agr007.htm*.

AICC (1997) "Computer Managed Instruction Guidelines and Recommendations," from *Aviation Industry CBT Committee Computer Managed Instruction, AGR 006, Version 1.1* by CMI Subcommittee at *http://www.aicc.org/agr006.htm*.

Avner, A. (1979) "Production of Computer-Based Instructional Materials," *Issues in Instructional Systems Development*, Ed. H. F. O'Neil, Jr., pp. 133-180, Academic Press: New York.

Cartwright, P. (1993) "Teaching with Dynamic Technologies: Part I," *Change Magazine* Nov/Dec. also at *http://contract.kent.edu/change/ articles/novdec93.html*.

Chen, C. and Rada, R. (1996) Interacting with hypertext: A meta-analysis of experimental studies. *Human-Computer Interaction*, 11, 2, pp. 125-156.

Corvetta, A., Pomponio, G., Salvi, A., and Luchetti, M.M. (1991) "Teaching Medicine Using Hypertext: Three Years of Experience at the Ancona Medical School," *Artificial Intelligence in Medicine*, 3, pp. 203-209.

Diaz, L. (1991) "PathMAC: An Alternative Approach to Medical School Education at Cornell School of Medicine," in *Hypertext/Hypermedia Handbook*, Ed. E. Berk and J. Devlin, pp. 488-492, McGraw-Hill: New York.

Duggan, S. (1936) *A Student's Textbook in the History of Education*, Appleton-Century: New York.

Educom (1997) "IMS Metadata Executive Summary," *IMS Metadata*, http://www.imsproject .org/metadata/MDexec.html.

Gay, G. and Lentini, M. (1995) "Use of Communication Resources in a Networked Collaborative Design Environment," at *http://www.osu.edu/units/jcmc/IMG_JCMC/ ResourceUse.html*.

Hiltz, S. R. (1995) "Teaching in a Virtual Classroom," *1995 International Conference on Computer Assisted Instruction ICCAI'95*, March 7-10, 1995 National Chiao Tung University, Hsinchu, Taiwan, also available at *http://it.njit.edu/njIT/ Department/CCCC/ VC/Papers/Teaching.html*.

Hodas, S. (1995) "Technology Refusal and The Organizational Culture of Schools, Version 2," at *http://homepage.seas.upenn.edu/~cpage/*, Version 1 appeared in *Education Policy Analysis Archives*, 1, 10, September 1993 an electronic journal.

ILINC (1997) "Welcome to ILINC," at *http://www.ilinc.com/*, Interactive Learning International Corporation.

Isaacs, E. A. and Tang, J. C. (1993) "What video can and can't do for collaboration: a cast study," *Proceedings of ACM Multimedia '93*, pp. 199-206, ACM Press: New York.

Jense, G. J. and Kuijper, F. (1993) "Applying Virtual Environments to Training and Simulation," *Annual Meeting of the Applied Vision Association*, University of Bristol, England.

Lawrence, G. and Service, A., Editors (1977) *Quantitative Approaches to Higher Education Management: Potential, Limits, and Challenges*, American Association for Higher Education.

McDonough, D., Strivens J., and Rada, R. (1994) "University Courseware Development: Differences between Computer-Based Teaching Users and Non-Users," *Computers and Education*, 23, 3, pp. 211-220.

Miyake, N. (1986) "Constructive interaction and the iterative process of understanding," *Cognitive Science*, 10, pp. 151-177.

Mizoguchi, R., Sinitsa, K., and Ikeda, M. (1996) "Task Ontology Design for Intelligent Educational/Training Systems," *ITS'96 Workshop on Architectures and Methods for Designing Cost-Effective and Reusable ITSs*, Montreal, June 10, 1996, *http://advlearn.lrdc.pitt.edu/its-arch/papers/mizoguchi.html*.

Murray, T. (1997) "Toward a Conceptual Vocabulary for Intelligent Tutoring Systems," *http://www.cs.umass.edu/~ckc/*.

Pentland, A., Picard, R., Davenport, G., and Welsh, R. (1993) "The BT/MIT Project on Advanced Image Tools for Telecommunications: An Overview," *Proceedings of 2nd International Conference on Image Communications*.

Rada, R., Keith, B., Burgoine, M., George, S., and Reid, D. (1989) "Collaborative Writing of Text and Hypertext," *Hypermedia*, 1(2), 1989, 93-110.

Rada, R. (1990) "Hypertext Writing and Document Reuse: The Role of a Semantic Net," *Electronic Publishing*, 3, 3, pp. 3-13.

Rada, R. (1991) *Hypertext: from Text to Expertext*, McGraw-Hill: London.

Rada, R. (1995a) *Developing Educational Hypermedia: Coordination and Reuse*, Ablex Publishing: Norwood, New Jersey, 1995a.

Rada, R. (1995b) *Interactive Media*, Springer Verlag, New York.

Rada, R. (1997) *Virtual Education Manifesto*, Hypermedia Solutions Limited, *http://hsl.gnacademy.org/gnacademy/hsl/*.

Russell, T. L. (1997) *The 'No Significant Difference' Phenomenon as reported in 248 Research Reports, Summaries, and Papers, Fourth Edition*, North Carolina State University, *http://tenb.mta.ca/phenom/ nsd.txt*.

SCT (1977a) "Banner2000 Overview," *http://www.sctcorp.com/ses/ban2000.html*, Systems and Computer Technology Incorporated.

SCT (1997b) "Tennessee Board of Regents," *http://www.sctcorp.com/news87.htm*, Systems and Computer Technology Incorporated.

Stiles, R., McCarthy, L., Munro, A., Pizzini, Q., Johnson, L., and Rickel, J. (1996) "Virtual Environments for Shipboard Training," Printed in the *Proceedings of the Intelligent Ships Symposium*, American Society of Naval Engineers, Nov. 1996, Philadelphia, PA also available at *http://vet.parl.com/~vet/iships/iships.html*.

Turroff, M. (1995) "Designing a Virtual Classroom," *1995 International Conference on Computer Assisted Instruction ICCAI'95* March 7-10, 1995 National Chiao Tung University Hsinchu, Taiwan available at *http://it.njit.edu/njIT/ Department/CCCC/VC /Papers/Design.html*.

Van Marcke, K. et al. (1995) "Learner adaptivity in generic instructional strategies," *Proc. of AIED'95*, pp.323-333.

Vasandani, V. and Govindaraj, T. (1995) "Knowledge Organization in Intelligent Tutoring Systems for Problem Solving in Complex Dynamic Domains," *IEEE Transactions on Systems, Man, and Cybernetics*, SMC-25, and available at *http://www.isye.gatech.edu/ chmsr/T_Govindaraj/papers/knowledge.ps*

Williams, P. J. and Hammond, P. (1994) "The Creation of Electronic Visual Archives for Teaching and Learning," *Proceedings of the 12 UK Eurographics Conference.*

Woodruff, M. and Mosby, J. (1997) *A Brief Description of VideoConferencing http://www.kn.pacbell.com/wired/vidconf/description.html.*

Yum, K.-K. and Crawford, J. R. (1996) "On the Feasibility of an Interoperable Tutorial Machine to Support the Development and Delivery of Teaching," *ITS'96 Workshop on Architectures and Methods for Designing Cost-Effective and Reusable ITSs*, Montreal, June 10th available at *http://advlearn.lrdc.pitt.edu/its-arch/papers/yum.html.*

IV

MULTIMEDIA COMMUNICATIONS AND NETWORKING

37

MULTIMEDIA NETWORKS

Nalin Sharda
Victoria University of Technology
Melbourne, Australia
nalin@matilda.vut.edu.au

1. **PERFORMANCE PARAMETERS** 784
    1.1 SYNCHRONIZATION ACCURACY SPECIFICATION (SAS) FACTORS 785
    1.2 TRAFFIC CHARACTERIZATION PARAMETERS 787
    1.3 NETWORK PERFORMANCE PARAMETERS 787
2. **QUALITY OF SERVICE** 789
3. **MULTIMEDIA TRANSMISSION REQUIREMENTS** 790
4. **MULTIMEDIA TRANSMISSION OVER WANS** 794
    4.1 CIRCUIT SWITCHED SERVICES 794
    4.2 INTEGRATED SERVICES DIGITAL NETWORK – ISDN 796
    4.3 PACKET SWITCHED AND RESIDENTIAL SERVICES 797
    4.4 THE INTERNET 799
    4.5 IP MULTICAST, MBONE, ST-II, RTP, AND RSVP 802
    4.6 THE INTERNET2 INITIATIVE 804
5. **MULTIMEDIA TRANSMISSION OVER LANS** 804
    5.1 ETHERNET LANS 804
    5.2 RING NETWORKS 806
6. **MULTIMEDIA TRANSMISSION WITH ATM** 807
    6.1 ATM: THE MULTIMEDIA NETWORKING TECHNOLOGY 807
    6.2 FEATURES OF THE ATM TECHNOLOGY 810
    6.3 ATM ARCHITECTURE 810
    6.4 APPLICATION OF ATM IN LANS 813
7. **CONCLUSIONS** 813
    REFERENCES 814

Abstract. The focus of this chapter is networks and their ability to carry multimedia information. A network that is suitable for carrying multimedia information can be called a *multimedia network*. In general, it is not possible to give a simple Yes/No answer to the question of if a network is a multimedia network or not. Many legacy networks are still in operation. It is important to understand the ability of these networks to carry multimedia traffic. This ability is evaluated by comparing multimedia application's characteristics, and the network's performance parameters.

The main characteristic of real-time multimedia applications are high throughput, bursty traffic, low end-to-end delay, and very low delay variance. Networking technologies that can satisfy these requirements can be used for carrying multimedia traffic. Most of the legacy WAN and LAN technologies were not designed to carry multimedia traffic. Enhancements to these technologies have been developed in an effort to make them capable of carrying multimedia information. Switched Ethernet, Isochronous Ethernet, Fast Ethernet, 100VGAnyLAN, FDDI-II, and Synchronous FDDI are some such efforts for LAN systems. Digital leased lines and ISDN are WAN options for multimedia networking.

To make it possible to carry real-time multimedia traffic over the Internet, new protocols such as M-Bone, ST-II, RTP, and RSVP have been developed. A new initiative called Internet2 aims to overcome the problems of throughput, delay and jitter encountered on the original Internet. The Asynchronous Transfer Mode (ATM) technology has been developed with multimedia networking as one of its main applications. ATM technology can be used for multimedia networking in the WAN as well as LAN environments.

1. PERFORMANCE PARAMETERS

How can it be decided if a network will be able to carry multimedia traffic or not? The following procedure can be used. First, a set of parameters should be used to state clearly what the application needs from the network. Then, a similar set of parameters should be used to specify what the network could provide. By comparing what the application needs, and what the network provides, it can be decided if the network can carry the multimedia traffic or not.

Multimedia traffic consists of a stream of multimedia objects. The needs of an application depend upon the type of objects contained in the multimedia stream. These needs are characterized mainly by four factors, namely:

- **Delay,**
- **Delay jitter,**
- **Delay skew, and**
- **Error rate.**

These factors specify the level of synchronization required between the various objects in a multimedia stream. These factors are therefore called the synchronization accuracy specification (SAS) factors.

Two traffic characterization parameters are used to characterize the traffic generated by an application. These are:

- **Throughput, and**
- **Burstiness.**

A set of parameters similar to the SAS factors are used to characterize the performance of a network. These are called Network Performance Parameters (NPPs). The NPPs are:

- **Network throughput**
- **Networking delay**
- **Delay variance**
- **Error rate**

Note that three of the parameters in the NPP set are similar to those included in the SAS factors. These parameters are used to describe the ability of various networking systems to carry multimedia traffic.

1.1 SYNCHRONIZATION ACCURACY SPECIFICATION (SAS) FACTORS

Before considering the SAS factors, we need to understand the various types of synchronization required in multimedia streams. Any multimedia presentation requires composition of object streams. This composition has two aspects:

- **Spatial composition, and**
- **Temporal composition**

Spatial composition relates to the placement of multimedia objects in space at any point in time. Temporal composition takes care of synchronization between object streams. Two kinds of temporal synchronization may be required:

- **Point synchronization**
- **Stream synchronization.**

Point synchronization is used when a single object in one stream needs to be synchronized with an object in another stream at one point in time. Stream synchronization is done continuously over a period of time, as in the case of a video presentation. Stream synchronization is also called continuous synchronization [Furht, 94].

Multimedia systems can be classified based on the level of synchrony between the various object streams in the system. The term synchronous is derived from Greek, meaning 'together in time.' Based on the level of synchronization, three types of systems can be considered, namely:

- **Asynchronous media**
- **Synchronous media**
- **Isochronous media**

Asynchronous Media

In an *asynchronous system,* **there is no well-defined timing relationship between the objects of one or more object stream(s).** This synchrony can either be intrastream or interstream. A well-known example of intrastream asynchronous communication is a user typing text on a keyboard. Since no user can type at a constant rate, the time gaps between consecutive characters vary.

Synchronous and Isochronous Multimedia

In synchronous and isochronous multimedia, well-defined temporal relationships exist between the objects. The term isochronous is also derived from Greek, meaning, 'equal time,' whereas the term synchronous means 'same time.' The term isochronous is applicable when one stream is considered at a time; that is, it is an intramedia concept. The term synchronous is applicable mainly to the temporal relationship between two different media streams [Agnew, 96, pp. 34]; it is therefore an intermedia concept. Synchronous and isochronous temporal relationships are specified for multimedia object streams, as they are captured, stored, retrieved, transmitted, received and played back.

Isochronous streams: An *isochronous* **stream has equal time gaps between consecutive objects.** This time is equal to the period of the stream. A video clip when played without sound is an isochronous media. If it was stored at 24 fps, then it must be played back at 24 fps. It is not acceptable to play the video at 20 fps in one second and then compensate by playing it at 28 fps in the next.

Synchronous streams: For interstream synchrony, two (or more) object streams need to be considered. Interstream synchrony implies that time gaps between related objects are equal to a constant called $T_{constant}$. The most often used meaning of synchrony is that the corresponding objects of the two streams occur at the same time, that is $T_{constant} = 0$. A video clip, when played along with audio, is a synchronous media. Not only must the sound and video streams play isochronously – that is, at the correct rate – they must also be synchronized to each other.

Delay Factor

The *delay factor* **is used to measure the end-to-end time delay encountered in multimedia applications.** The details of the delay encountered depend upon the type of application. In an interactive application, the delay refers to the response time delay. In a streamed multimedia application, the delay refers to the total time taken by each object to go from the source to the destination.

Delay Jitter

Due to variations in delay factors encountered especially on networked multimedia systems, the temporal relationships can deviate from their desired values. In packet switching networks, different packets may take different paths through the network, leading to variation in the end-to-end delay. This variation is described by a factor called jitter.

Jitter **is the instantaneous difference between the desired presentation times and the actual presentation times of streamed multimedia objects.** Jitter can occur as intramedia as well as intermedia jitter.

Intramedia Jitter: Intramedia jitter occurs in a single object stream, in which the expected presentation instants are determined by a reference clock. The deviations in the presentation time are instantaneous, and not cumulative. **Thus,** *intramedia jitter* **refers to instantaneous asynchrony in isochronous object streams.** The consequence of intramedia jitter in an animation clip will be shaky picture. Intramedia jitter in an audio stream will lead to quivering voice.

Intermedia Jitter: Intermedia jitter occurs between two object streams. **The instantaneous deviations in the presentation times of the related objects in the two streams lead to** *intermedia jitter.* The consequence of intermedia jitter between video and audio streams in a video clip will be loss of lip-synchronization, on top of a shaky picture.

Delay Skew

Skew (in the delay factor) is also caused by variations in the end-to-end delay in object streams. In a skewed presentation, the average rate of object delivery deviates from the desired average rate. *Skew* **is the average difference between the desired presentation times and the actual presentation times of streamed multimedia objects.** Skew occurs as intramedia as well as intermedia skew.

Intramedia Skew: *Intramedia skew* **refers to continuous asynchrony in isochronous object streams.** The consequence of intramedia skew in an animation clip will be either slow or fast moving picture. Intramedia skew in an audio stream will lead to the voice at lower or higher pitch than the normal.

Intermedia Skew: Intermedia skew occurs between two (or more) object streams. The expected presentation times may be determined either by a reference clock, or the two streams may be viewed relative to each other. The average deviation in the presentation times of the related objects in the two streams leads to intermedia skew. The consequence of intermedia skew between video and audio streams in a video clip will be complete loss of lip-synchronization, after some time.

Error Rate

Errors can occur in any digital transmission. The acceptable level of errors differs from one media type to another. A few single bit errors may be acceptable in text transmission. Whereas, in an executable code, even a single bit error can be fatal. If a remote multimedia presentation is transmitted as executable JAVA byte code, all code bytes must be received without any error. The level of errors encountered on a communication channel is specified as its bit error rate (BER). BER is also called BERT [Beyda, 89]. It is defined as the ratio of the number of bit errors detected to the total number of bits transmitted over a given period.

Since data is transmitted as packets, the error rate of packets is a more useful measure. A packet is considered corrupted irrespective of the number of bits in error. The ratio of the number of packets corrupted to the total number of packets transmitted is called the packet error rate (PER). PER is also called block error rate (BLERT).

In data transmission systems, most communication protocols are designed to request for retransmission of corrupted packets. In networked multimedia systems, retransmission of the corrupted packets is not necessarily the best option. Retransmission can lead to severe disruption of intramedia and intermedia synchronization. It is sometimes more appropriate to discard the corrupted packet(s) so that synchrony can be maintained for the uncorrupted packets.

1.2 TRAFFIC CHARACTERIZATION PARAMETERS

Throughput
The overall capacity of any system to process its inputs and generate the required output is called the system's throughput. For example, the throughput of a car factory is the number of cars produced, specified as cars produced per day, per month, or per year.

The input to any network is the stream of data bits that carry the information. The output of a network is the error free delivery of these information bits to the destination. Generally, the ability of a network to carry data bits is specified as the bit rate. But this bit rate does not translate directly into the overall rate at which information bits are transported. For most of the networks, the bit rate of the physical medium is specified. The bit rate is called by many other names as well, such as, data rate, transfer rate and (digital) bandwidth. But, this transmission rate is not always achieved in practice. A number of factors hamper the transmission of information at this maximum rate.

The bit rate that an application requires of the network is the rate at which the application generates information, plus overhead bits. This bit rate can be either constant or variable, which gives two types of applications, namely:

- **Constant bit rate (CBR) applications**
- **Variable bit rate (VBR) applications**

An application such as digital voice transmission is a CBR application. Digital transmission of voice generally uses 8 K sampling rate and 8-bit sample resolution. This generates a constant traffic at the rate of 64 Kbps. Thus, uncompressed digital voice transmission generates CBR traffic, but when it is subjected to compression, it generates VBR traffic. In fact, most multimedia applications – such as, video transmission using MPEG compression – generate VBR traffic.

Traffic Burstiness
In an application with VBR traffic, the variation in the traffic volume over time is called its *burstiness*. Burstiness implies that the traffic is generated in bursts; where the size and duration of the traffic bursts vary. The burstiness of a data stream is specified in terms of peak bit rate (PBR), and mean bit rate (MBR). A measure of burstiness is specified as the burstiness ratio, defined as follows [Fluckiger, 95]:

Burstiness Ratio = MBR / PBR

1.3 NETWORK PERFORMANCE PARAMETERS

Network Throughput
Consider the example of an Ethernet network. The bit rate for a 10BaseT Ethernet is specified as 10 Mbps. Now the question is, can information be transmitted at 10 Mbps, i.e., will a 10 Mbit file transfer over an Ethernet network in 1 second? In an Ethernet system, the

CSMA/CD protocol used at the MAC layer is a contention protocol. Therefore, every attempt to transmit a packet is not successful. There are many packet collisions on the bus medium. After each collision, the transmitter has to back off and wait for some time before attempting retransmission. Also, the transmission protocols require headers and tails to be added to the information bits. Collisions and protocol overhead reduce the effective rate at which information bits are transmitted. The bit rate specified for a packet-based network is the maximum transmission rate of the interface card, not the network throughput. Thus, the 10 Mbps rate of the Ethernet system is the maximum rate at which the NIC (network interface card) can communicate, and not the average rate at which the information is transferred.

The effective rate of transmission of information bits is called the network *throughput*. Throughput is also called the net bandwidth. Throughput is the average number of information bits transmitted in one second. On LANs and packet switching WANs, the throughput is also affected by the other traffic on the network. The throughput of a transmission system is affected by all the hardware and software components through which the data has to pass. The factors that can reduce the throughput on a network are:

- **Low bit rate of a component in the path of transmission**
- **Protocol processing overhead**
- **Other traffic on the network**
- **Queuing delays**
- **Congestion**
- **Errors**

Networking Delay

Networking delay is the time taken by a bit to traverse the network, i.e., the time difference between the instant when it is ready for transmission over the network and the instant when it is ready for use at the other end of the network. Networking delay consists of the following three components:

- **Packetization delay**
- **Transmission delay**
- **Propagation delay**

Large delays are unacceptable for most multimedia applications. The maximum acceptable delay for voice and video is 250ms. Overall delay includes the delays encountered on the transmitting and the receiving stations also.

Delay Variance

While delay is bad for multimedia traffic, delay variations are worse. Delay variance refers to the fact that different packets experience different delays on the network. Delay variance can take the form of delay jitter and delay skew. Up to 10 ms of delay can be tolerated for voice and TV quality video signals. For compressed video and high quality stereo music, the jitter should be less than 1 ms.

Error rate

There are three types of error rates used to specify the level of errors expected on a network, namely:

- **Bit Error Rate:** It is the number of bits that get corrupted per unit time.
- **Packet/Cell Error Rate:** The packet/cell error rate (PER/CER) is the number of packets/cells corrupted per unit time.
- **Packet/Cell Loss Rate:** The number of packets/cells lost per unit time is called the packet loss rate (PLR)/cell loss rate (CLR).

2. QUALITY OF SERVICE

The need to define a quality of service (QoS) arises from the realization that the users require different quality presentations at different times. The different quality presentations map onto different parameter values. When a multimedia presentation is transmitted via a network, it translates into some requirements of the network, in terms of the Network Performance Parameters.

To be able to specify QoS aspects concisely and to request these of a network, it must be specified as a set of parameters that can be assigned numerical values. In a multimedia presentation, the ultimate user of the system is a human being. Thus, the quality of the presentation is a matter of the user's perception, which is limited by the response of the human vision and auditory senses. This perceptive nature of QoS makes it subjective, and difficult to quantify precisely. Thus, it is easier to specify a range of values, rather than a single value.

The concept of quality of service has evolved over the years. It was originally developed by ISO in the 1980s. The QoS concept developed by ISO had a rather restricted perspective. It focused mainly on the SAS factors for the application, and the NPPs for the network. More recently, a wider view has been developed to describe QoS for multimedia applications.

QoS Perspectives

A complete QoS specification must consider all aspects of presentation, hardware and software components in the system. The various aspects of QoS are usually grouped under some well-defined categories. In [Vogel, 95] QoS parameters are grouped under five categories. These five categories and their examples, as listed in [Vogel, 95], are given in Table 1.

Vogel's categorization is not a standard. Nonetheless, it gives a general idea of how categorization can be done. The International Telecommunications Union-Telecommunications Sector (ITU-T) defined QoS and NPPs in its recommendations E.800 [ITU-T, 88] as well as in recommendation I.350 [ITU-T, 92]. The manner in which QoS and NPPs are defined in these recommendations creates some problems [Jung, 96-1]. One of the main problems pointed out by Jung is that, as per the ITU-T recommendations, a QoS parameter can have different interpretations. Therefore, work on defining QoS parameters continues. Many projects in this area have given different interpretations to the QoS parameters and recommended procedures for using the QoS parameters to request the desired service of the network.

Table 1. Five categories of QoS parameters

Category	Example Parameters
Performance-oriented	End-to-end delay and bit rate.
Format-oriented	Video resolution, frame rate, storage format, and compression scheme.
Synchronization-oriented	Skew between the beginning of audio and video sequences.
Cost-oriented	Connection and data transmission charges and copyright fees.
User-oriented	Subjective image and sound quality.

3. MULTIMEDIA TRANSMISSION REQUIREMENTS

The two most demanding types of multimedia object streams are audio and video. This section explores the ability of various networks to carry audio and video traffic. The requirements for transmitting digital audio and video over networks depend upon the media levity, i.e., is it captured in real-time or retrieved from a storage device. These requirements depend even more upon the type of receiver. If the receiver is a human being, then the requirements are geared toward making a good quality presentation, as perceived by this observer. If the receiver is a computer, then the requirements are geared toward ensuring that the information is received and stored with maximum possible fidelity.

Qualitative Requirements

The qualitative and quantitative requirements for audio and video transmission depend upon the ability of the human senses. Surprisingly, auditory senses and vision work in quite different ways. Human auditory senses are more sensitive to variations than human vision.

Response of the Human Ear: The human ear can detect audio frequencies in the range of 20 Hz to 20 KHz. Normal human voice is restricted to a 10 KHz bandwidth, higher frequencies are present mostly in music. The human ear is very sensitive to change in signal levels. The behavior of the human ear can be modeled as a differentiator [Fluckiger, 95]. Suppression, or distortion, of frequencies by as little as 10%, for a period as short as 40 ms, can be detected when introduced in a high fidelity audio presentation. In other words, the response of the human ear accentuates variations.

Response of the Human Eye: The human vision system - the eye and the associated vision perception faculty - smooth out variations in the images projected on the eye. In this sense, the vision system acts like an integrator [Fluckiger, 95]. The viewer may not even notice small variations in the intensity and the color. Larger variations may be noticed, but still be acceptable to the viewer.

Tolerance to Errors: Tolerance to errors depends upon the level of compression of the original signal. In uncompressed signals, much higher error rate can be tolerated than in compressed signals. In many compression techniques, the transmitted signal is a relative value, sent as a variation to the previously transmitted signal(s). Thus, error in one signal value may effect many subsequent signal values. Because of the properties explained above, the audio signal is relatively sensitive to errors, being a differentiator, whereas a video signal can tolerate relatively higher error levels, being an integrator.

Tolerance to Delay and Jitter: Sensitivity to delay and delay jitter depends upon the type of the receiver. If the signals are received by a computer, and stored for future use, then delay and delay jitter do not cause any problem. If the signals are being sensed by a human being, then the delay must be small, especially for live conferencing types of applications. Interactive applications, especially virtual reality systems, require very small delays. For a steady presentation, the delay jitter needs to be an order of magnitude lower than the delay.

Lip Synchronization: One of the most critical aspects of any video presentation is lip-synchronization. This requires tight intermedia synchronization, i.e., synchronization between the voice signal and the live picture of the lip movement associated with this voice.

Quantitative Requirements – Audio

Qualitative specifications, discussed above, are good for building an overall understanding of what the application requires from the network. But it is difficult to use qualitative specifications for carrying out QoS negotiations. To ask for the required service, quantitative specifications are required. The quantitative requirements for the important parameters for audio and video transmission are given in this section.

Audio Bandwidth: The bandwidth required for various types of audio signals are given in Table 2. These are listed under two categories: uncompressed and compressed audio. The bandwidth **BWbps** of an audio signal is given by the following formula: Bandwidth = No of Channels (**NC**) x Sampling Frequency (**SFHz**) x Amplitude Resolution (**ARbit**).

Phone quality audio: Telephone quality audio uses one channel and 8000 Hz sampling frequency. The amplitude resolution can be either 8-bit or 7-bit. The choice of the amplitude resolution depends upon the available channel bandwidth. Uncompressed audio signals with 8-bit resolution require 64 Kbps bandwidth. By using compression, the bandwidth requirement can be reduced to 32 Kbps.

The bit rate required for audio transmission can be lowered further, by using a compression technique called Adaptive Pulse Code Modulation (ADPCM). With ADPCM, the bit rate can be reduced down to 4 Kbps. But, this reduction in the bandwidth is accompanied by some reduction in the quality of the reproduced audio; generally, lower bandwidth leads to lower quality signals.

Compact Disk (CD) Quality Audio: CD quality audio uses two channels, and 44.1 KHz sampling rate, and 16-bit sampling resolution. Uncompressed CD quality signals require 1.411 Mbps bandwidth. By using the compression technique specified in a scheme called MUSICAM, the bandwidth requirement can be reduced to 192 Kbps for stereophonic music. The MPEG (motion pictures expert group) audio compression standard gives a layered architecture for compression. The higher layers give higher level of compression. By using the higher layer MPEG compression techniques, the bandwidth required for a monophonic CD quality channel can be reduced to as low as 64 Kbps.

Table 2. Bandwidth Requirements – Audio

Audio Quality	No. of Channels NC	Sampling freq.-SFHz	Amplitude res.-ARbit	Bandwidth BWbps
Phone - Uncompressed	1	8 KHz	7-bit	56 Kbps
Phone - Uncompressed	1	8 KHz	8-bit	64 Kbps
Phone - Compressed	1	8 KHz	8-bit	4 - 32 Kbps
CD - Uncompressed	2	44.1 KHz	16-bit	1.411 Mbps
CD - Compressed	2	44.1 KHz	16-bit	64 - 192 Kbps

SAS Factors for Audio

Delay: The value for acceptable delay depends upon the application. In an application involving conversation between two people, the one-way delay should be in the 100 ms to 500 ms range. Higher than 24 ms delay requires echo cancellation. In virtual reality applications, the delay should be in the range of 40 ms to 100 ms.

Jitter: Delay jitter must be an order of magnitude better than the delay value. Thus, if a delay must be less than 100 ms, then the delay jitter must be less than 10 ms. Delay equalization is achieved by adding an intentional delay to every packet on the receiver. This technique requires large buffers on the receiving end.

Lip synchronization: The intermedia synchronization required between the audio and video for lip synchronization should be better than 100 ms; i.e., the sound and its related lip movement video frames must be presented within 100 ms of each other.

Error rate: The bit error rate (BER) on a telephone quality audio stream should be less than 0.01. This figure implies that less than one in every 100 bits should be corrupted to get an acceptable sound quality when the signal is played out. For uncompressed CD quality audio, the error rate should be less than 0.001 (i.e., 1 in 1000). The acceptable error rate for compressed data streams is an order of magnitude less than that acceptable for uncompressed data streams. Thus, a compressed audio stream carrying CD quality sound must use a channel with error rate less than 0.0001 (i.e., 1 in 10,000).

Quantitative Requirements -Video

The quantitative requirements for transmitting video are not the same as those for audio transmission. The bandwidth required for video is much higher then the bandwidth required for audio. The delay and jitter requirements for video are similar to those for audio. The acceptable channel error rate depends upon the quality of the video being transmitted.

Video Bandwidth: The bandwidth required for various types of video signals are given in Table 3. The bandwidth (BW) of an video signal depends upon the following screen parameters:

- **Horizontal Resolution (HR = pixels per line)**
- **Vertical Resolution (VR = lines per frame)**
- **Color Resolution (CR = bits per pixel)**
- **Frame Rate (FR in fps)**

Table 3. Bandwidth Requirements -Video

Video quality	HR	VR	CR	FR	Uncompressed BWbps	Compressed BWbps	Standard
Television							
HDTV	1920	1080	24	60	2000 Mbps	25-34 Mbps	MPEG-2
Broadcast TV	720	576	24	25	150 Mbps	3-6 Mbps	MPEG-2
VCR	640	480	24	25	92 Mbps	1.5 Mbps	MPEG-1
Video Conference							
CIF format}	352	288	8	15	N.A.	112 Kbps	px64 or
QCIF format}	176	144	8	5-10	N.A.	4.8-64 Kbps	MPEG-4

HDTV Quality Video: The best quality high-resolution TV (HDTV) uses a screen resolution of 1920 x 1080. The color resolution is 24 bits per pixel, at 60 frame per second. Such uncompressed video signal will require a 2 Gbps bandwidth channel for transmission. Therefore, in practice, HDTV signals are transmitted only after compression. The current MPEG-2 standard includes an option of compressing HDTV signals. By using the MPEG-2 standard for compression, the bandwidth requirement can be reduced to 25–34 Mbps range [Fluckiger, 95]. This is given in the first row of Table 2.

Broadcast Quality TV: The bandwidth requirements for PAL and SECAM quality TV signals are given in the second row of Table 3. Uncompressed TV quality video will generate about 150 Mbps data rate. When compressed with the MPEG-2 standard, the data rate can be reduced to 3–6 Mbps range. The bandwidth requirements for the NTSC TV signals are similar.

Video Cassette Recorder (VCR) Quality Picture: The bandwidth requirements for the VCR picture quality is about half of the bandwidth required for the broadcast quality TV picture. Uncompressed VCR quality video will require about 92 Mbps data rate. By using MPEG-1 compression the data rate can be reduced to about 1.5 Mbps.

Video Conference Quality Picture: Video conference does not require picture quality as good as that for broadcast TV or VCR. Two picture formats are commonly used:

Common Intermedia Format (CIF), and Quarter-CIF (QCIF). The most important parameter for successful video conferencing is the end-to-end delay. To lower the data rate, and therefore the cost and delay values, image compression is almost always used in video conferencing.

Two commonly used compression standards for video conferencing are Px64 and MPEG-4. The Px64 standard is also called H.261 standard. To keep the data rate down, the frame rate is also reduced in a videoconference. Data rates possible for video conferencing are given in the last two rows of Table 3. The larger frame size combined with the higher frame rate (15 fps) gives a data rate of about 112 Kbps after compression. With the smaller (quarter size) frame and lower frame rate (giving a jerky picture), the data rate can be reduced to 64 Kbps. The lowest possible data rate used for video conferencing is about 4.8 Kbps.

SAS Factors for Video

Delay and jitter: The SAS factors applicable to a video presentation are similar to those for audio transmission. The delay and delay jitter values are dictated by the audio component of the presentation. In a good quality video presentation, the need for lip synchronization demands that the delay and jitter values used for audio be applied to the video stream as well. Therefore, the delay should be less than 50 ms for HDTV and less than 100 ms for broadcast quality TV. These figures are at the lower end of the range specified for audio. In a video conference, the low frame rate and the associated jerky picture can mask the effect of high values of SAS factors. Therefore, delay of the order of 500 ms can be tolerated in a video conference.

Error Rate: To derive the values of the acceptable error rates for video transmission, the effect of these errors must be understood. In an uncompressed video stream, relatively high error rates can be tolerated. But, uncompressed video requires such high bandwidth (2 Gbps for HDTV and 150 Mbps for TV quality), that it is seldom used.

Most of the data communication systems use error detection and retransmission protocols to overcome the effect of errors. Retransmission of erroneous frames is not useful for real-time video transmission, because the retransmitted frames will arrive out-of-sequence. And, out-of-sequence frames are useless in the case of a video stream. Thus, frames with errors have to be dropped.

In most cases, error detection is not even carried out during the transmission of a video stream. Therefore, the channel error rate must be low enough so as not to corrupt too many frames. Specific values for the acceptable error rates are given below. As will be seen in the following calculations, the error rates have been chosen to cause just a few (or less) corrupted bits in every frame.

HDTV: The bit error rate (BER) for HDTV should be less than 10^{-6} [Fluckiger, 95]. A BER of 10^{-6} will lead to about 24 bits corrupted in every second, given a transmission rate of 24 Mbps. Since 60 frames are transmitted in every second, this translates to, on average, four bits corrupted in every tenth frame.

Broadcast TV: The BER for broadcast quality TV should be less than 10^{-5}. At a transmission rate of 5 Mbps, a BER of 10^{-5} will lead to about 50 bits corrupted in every second. With 25 frames transmitted in each second, this error rate is equivalent to two bits being corrupted in every frame.

Video conference: The BER for video conference connection should be less than 10^{-4}. Over a 100 Kbps video conferencing connection, a BER of 10^{-4} translates into about ten bits being corrupted in every second. The frame rate of around 15 fps implies that one bit is corrupted every 1.5 frames, or, on average, two bits corrupted in every third frame.

Improving Channel Error Rate

What can be done if the available channel has higher error rate than that required for a good quality audio or video transmission? Forward error correction can be used to reduce the effective end-to-end error rate. But forward error correction techniques reduce the channel throughput, because of the additional bits used for error correction. Therefore, the raw bandwidth of the channel must be sufficiently higher than the transmission rate required for the audio and video transmission.

4. MULTIMEDIA TRANSMISSION OVER WANS

The ability of the various traditional WAN technologies to carry multimedia traffic, in particular audio and video traffic, is discussed in this section.

4.1 CIRCUIT SWITCHED SERVICES

The bandwidths of the various circuit switched services are listed in Table 4. It starts with the low bandwidth POTS connections and lists the various WAN services in ascending order, with respect to their bandwidths. The ability of these services to carry multimedia traffic is discussed in the following sub-sections. This ability is discussed with respect to the requirements described in Section 3.

Plain Old Telephone Service (POTS)

The telephone network is the world's most wide-spread electronic network, and is called the Public Switched Telephone Network (PSTN). Part of the PSTN that looks after simple phone connections is called the Plain Old Telephone Service (POTS). Many local and national POTS networks are spread out widely across the globe, and are also connected to each other. Before the proliferation of the digital networks, the POTS provided the only readily available electronic network.

Table 4. Bandwidths of Circuit Switched WAN Technologies

Type of Service	Bandwidth		Application, standard, advantages, limitations
POTS			{ **Plain Old Telephone Service**
Using V.32 modem	4.8	Kbps	{ Limited by the 3-4 KHz bandwidth, Low cost
Using V.34 modem	28.8	Kbps	{ Widely available, TCM modulation
Using V.42bis "	38.4	Kbps	{ Not very reliable on higher data rates
LEASED LINES			{ **Low delay, jitter, and error rate**
Switched 56	56	Kbps	Low resolution video conference
ISDN			{ **Integrated Services Digital Network**
Basic-rate interface	144-192	Kbps	Digitized voice and video conference
Primary-rate "	1.54- 2	Mbps	Compressed VCR quality video
DIGITAL LEASED LINES			{ **Good for transmitting following video**
Fractional T-1	384	Kbps	Video conference. Also called switched 384
T-1 (DS-1)	1.544	Mbps	VCR quality compressed video
T-2 (DS-2)	6.312	Mbps	Broadcast TV quality compressed video
T-3 (DS-3)	44.736	Mbps	HDTV quality compressed video
T-4 (DS-4)	274.176	Mbps	Multiple video channels
SONET			{**Synchronous Optical Network**
OC-1	51.84	Mbps	Available in multiples of 51.84 Mbps
OC-48	2.488	Gbps	

Note: Common aspects are preceded by braces, i.e., {

The data transmission rate that can be obtained over a POTS connection is always less than 64 Kbps. Modems that can transmit at 28.8 Kbps and 38.4 Kbps are now commonly available. Even when stretched to their limit, data rates over a POTS connection cannot be expected to go beyond 57.6 Kbps. These rates are adequate for text and audio transmission, but fall short of the bandwidth required for good quality video transmission in real-time, though, video telephones that work over POTS connects are available. These video phones use low frame rate and small picture size, in conjunction with image compression.

Leased Lines

When the dial-up POTS network is not adequate for the application at hand, then the next step is to look at leased lines. The charges for a leased connection are in terms of installation cost, and monthly fee. A leased line can be an analog line or a digital line.

Analog leased line

An *analog leased* **line is like a phone connection that never hangs up**. A leased line does not require any dial-up procedure to establish a connection between two sites. Another advantage of a leased phone line is that it provides better quality than that of a dial-up connection. Because of the better line quality, a higher signal to noise ratio (SNR) is obtained. Higher SNR values provide higher data transmission rates over leased lines, as compared to those on a dial-up line of the same bandwidth.

Switched 56 Service: The *switched 56 service* **provides a bandwidth of 56 Kbps over switched lines** [Szuprowicz, 95]. This service can be used for low resolution video conferencing as an alternative to the POTS network. It can be used for multi-point conferencing as well. As it is billed based on connection time, it can be more economical than a leased connection for low volume data traffic.

Digital Leased Line

Time Division Multiplexed lines have been used as the inter-exchange trunks on the telephone networks since the 1950s. These lines have become available for leasing since the early 1980s [Szuprowicz, 95]. These trunk lines are called T-1, T-2, T-3 and T-4 in the U.S., Japan and Korea. The bandwidth and the multimedia application of these lines are listed in table 5.

Table 5. Digital Lease Lines and their Multimedia Applications

Speed Mbps	Line Type	Applications and Comments
0.384	FT-1	Video conferencing. Also called switched 384.
1.544	T-1	Equivalent standard in Europe, Australia, and Asia: E-1 at 2.048 Mbps.
6.312	T-2	Equivalent to 96 voice channels on a single line.
44.70	T-3	TV-quality video transmission.
274.00	T-4	Highest bandwidth leased line.

T-1 and Fractional T-1 Leased Lines: The T-1 line was developed to carry 24 voice channels at 64 Kbps with 8 Kbps of synchronization and framing information. This adds up to 1544 (= 64 x 24 + 8) Kbps data rate. Full-screen video at 30 fps, after compression requires around 1.544 Mbps bandwidth. Therefore, a T-1 can be used for high quality compressed video transmission. The T-1 leased line can also be used for connecting LANs.

Since the late 1980s, fractional T-1 (FT-1) lines have also become available. The bit rates available on these fractional T-1 lines are multiples of 56 or 64 Kbps. The switched 384 line is a fractional T-1 line with a 384 Kbps bandwidth. Fractional T-1 lines can be used for video conferencing by using compression standards such as Px64 (also called H.261) and MPEG-4.

T-2/3/4 Lease Lines: The T-2 leased line provides a bandwidth of 6.312 Mbps. It is equivalent to 96 voice channels. It can be used for LAN to LAN connectivity and other similar high-speed applications. It can sustain multiple video conferencing connections depending upon the quality, and thus the bandwidth, required for each of the video streams. The T-3 leased line is equivalent to 28 T-1 lines giving a bandwidth of nearly 45 Mbps. The T-3 lines are the main trunk lines used in telephone networks. Even the T-3 line falls short of the 90 Mbps bandwidth required for transmitting high quality uncompressed video signals. It is suitable for high-end applications such as 3-D visualization on a high resolution workstation connected to a remotely located super computer. The T-4 line is the highest bandwidth leased line available. It is equivalent to 4032 voice channels, giving a bandwidth of 273 Mbps.

QoS and Cost of Digital Leased Lines

Leased lines are excellent for providing the required QoS for the transmission of multimedia information. Because of the end-to-end connection, the SAS factors can be controlled very well. But the cost of leased lines can make them uneconomical for many application areas. To mitigate the high cost associated with digital leased lines, the ISDN concept was developed to provide end-to-end digital transmission over dial-up connections.

4.2 INTEGRATED SERVICES DIGITAL NETWORK – ISDN

The Integrated Services Digital Network (ISDN) started in the 1980s as an alternative to digital leased lines. It was designed to provide data rates in the range of Kbps to Mbps. To provide higher data rates, Mbps to Gbps over ATM and SONET systems, the original ISDN was extended to Broadband-ISDN (B-ISDN). The original ISDN can thus be called Narrowband-ISDN to distinguish it from the B-ISDN; but in practice, the older, Narrowband-ISDN is referred to as ISDN.

There are two key aspects of the Integrated Services Digital Network: integrated services, and digital networking. The principal underpinning the development of the ISDN concept was to provide an end-to-end digital network that can integrate all types of services. The services to be integrated include voice, digital data, text, and video. Thus, the ISDN networking technology was designed to be multimedia enabled from its very inception.

ISDN Channels

ISDN channels, their bandwidths, and application areas are listed in Table 6 [Beyda, 96]. These channels are combined to provide standard interfaces called: Basic Rate Interface (BRI), Primary Rate Interface (PRI), and Hybrid Interface. A description of the various ISDN channels and interfaces follows.

Table 6. ISDN Channels

Channel Designation	Channel Type	Bandwidth	Application area
A	Analog	3- 4 KHz	Analog voice
B	Digital	64 Kbps	Digitized voice or data
C	Digital	< 16 Kbps	Low speed data
D	Digital	16 or 64 Kbps	Signaling or data

The A-channel is an analog channel included to make ISDN connections upward compatible with the current analog POTS based telephone machines. The B-channel is also called the *bearer* channel. It is expected to 'bear,' or carry high volume traffic such as digitized voice, video and data. It provides a 64 Kbps bandwidth. Clearly, a single B-channel is not adequate for high quality video traffic. A number of B channels are used in a single user interface. The C-channel is used for low-speed digital data transfer. It was designed to work with older style, dumb terminals requiring a bandwidth of less than 16 Kbps. The D-channel is also called the data channel. It is used for 'out-of-band-signaling.' In out-of-band-signaling, the control signals are not mixed with the data stream, but carried on a separate circuit.

ISDN Interfaces

ISDN services are provided to the user as ISDN interfaces. Each ISDN interface comprises a few ISDN channels. The more widely used interfaces in ISDN are the Basic Rate Interface (BRI), and the Primary Rate Interface (PRI). Both BRI and PRI are fully digital interfaces. The Hybrid Interface allows connections that use a hybrid of analog and digital communication. The various ISDN interfaces are listed in Table 7.

Basic Rate Interface – BRI: The BRI interface is aimed at providing a simple interface to the desk-top, that includes a phone connection and a digital interface for the desk-top computer. The D-channel is used for signaling; and the two B-channels provide a bandwidth of 128 Kbps for data transmission. The bandwidth of the BRI interface falls short for any serious multimedia application. The 144 to 192 Kbps bandwidth of the ISDN-BRI interface is barely enough for low-end video conferencing.

Primary Rate Interface – PRI: In the PRI interface 23 or 30 B channels are combined. The D-channel in the PRI is used for out-of-band signaling. The 1.544 to 2.048 Mbps bandwidth provided by PRI is adequate for video transmission at VCR quality, apart from other multimedia applications.

Table 7. ISDN Interfaces

Interface Name	Channels Included	Combined Bandwidth	Application area
Basic-rate interface	2B+D	144-192 Kbps	Digitized voice and data
Primary-rate interface	23B + D	1.544 Mbps	{High volume data
	or 30B + D	2.048 Mbps	{e.g., LAN to LAN connection
Hybrid interface	A + C	Analog voice	{For a hybrid connection
		+ 16 Kbps data	{to be used for transition period

4.3 PACKET SWITCHED AND RESIDENTIAL SERVICES

This section explores the suitability of packet switching networks (PSNs) for multimedia information transmission. Packet switching is based on transmitting the information as independent packets over the network. Two transmission options in the packet switching scheme are virtual circuit (VC) and datagram (DG) approaches. **In the *datagram* approach, each packet is treated as an independent entity and transmitted through the network;** i.e., no end-to-end dedicated connection is established between the two communicating nodes. **In the v*irtual circuit* technique, an end-to-end path is selected and a virtual circuit is established before any data packets are transmitted,** though there is no end-to-end physical connection, as in the circuit switching technique. All packets take the same path over the network. This path works virtually like a circuit. In a packet switching network, the transmission approach, and some other factors, determine the end-to-end delay, jitter, and throughput. Variations in end-to-end delay can be experienced from one packet to another. Therefore, isochronous data streams cannot be transmitted successfully over a packet switching network without introducing large buffering delays. In this regard, the performance of a VC-based connection is better than that of a DG connection.

The transmission rates over the various packet switched and residential services are listed in Table 8. The ability of these services to carry multimedia traffic is discussed in the following sub-sections.

X.25 Service

The X.25 service standard provides specifications for connecting to a PSN that can provide connection-oriented packet switching services. The X.25 standard does not concern itself with the internal working of the network. This standard has been used for wide area networking since the 1970s. Because of its original design limitations, it is not suitable for most multimedia applications. The X.25 protocol includes error detection and correction over every hop. This slows the transmission process considerably, leading to delays that are not acceptable for real-time traffic. The bandwidth available on an X.25 connection is generally limited to 2 Mbps, though some 8 Mbps connections are also available. Bandwidth reservation is not readily available, nor is the facility of multicasting. Most X.25 implementations cannot provide bit rate guarantees, neither deterministic guarantees nor statistical guarantees. Thus, multimedia applications such as video conferencing cannot be run over X.25 networks.

Table 8. Bandwidth of Packet Switching Networks and Residential Technologies

Type of Service	Bandwidth	Properties and Application
PACKET SWITCHING		{ Large delay and, jitter
X.25 older	9.6–56 Kbps	{ Not suitable for isochronous traffic
X.25 newer	2–8 Mbps	{ such as audio and video
Frame Relay	56 Kbps to 1.544 Mbps	{ Better suited for multimedia than { packet switching
SMDS	1.544 Mbps to 46 Mbps	{ Can carry multimedia traffic, though not a { true multimedia network technology
Internet	Depends upon the implementation	{ TCP/IP protocol suite not suitable for { multimedia traffic. It requires new { protocols such as RTP, ST-II, and RSVP
RESIDENTIAL		
ADSL	1.544 Mbps to 6.1 Mbps	{ VoD and Internet access type of { applications

Frame Relay

Frame relay can be considered as an enhancement to the packet switching concept. While both X.25 and frame relay are connection oriented, they have some significant differences. In the traditional packet switching networks, such as the X.25 based networks, error control and flow control is applied over each hop. **In frame relay, the packet is sent from the source node to the destination node without any node-to-node error and flow**

control. Packet acknowledgment is sent only from the destination node, and is relayed back without any processing on the intermediate nodes. The data packets and their acknowledgments are sent like the baton in a relay race, hence the name.

By eliminating hop-by-hop processing, frame relay provides throughput that is an order of magnitude higher than in packet switching networks. Bandwidth in the range of 56 Kbps – 1.544 Mbps is available. The capability of the service to carry multimedia traffic will depend upon the details of the underlying networking technology. Some service providers implement their frame relay service by using special frame relay switches. These switches are designed to minimize processing delays and can provide guaranteed average throughput [Fluckiger, 95]. Some service providers can even guarantee packet delay jitter. Thus, the type of multimedia traffic can be carried over a frame relay service will depend upon the detailed specifications of the service. In any case, the frame relay service is much more suitable for multimedia information networking than the X.25 service.

Switched Multimegabit Data Service (SMDS)

Switched Multimegabit Data Service (SMDS) is designed primarily for interconnecting high speed LANs. Like frame relay, it is a service definition that can use existing high speed communication links. Unlike X.25 and frame relay, the SMDS service is a connection-less service. This is because it is designed to connect LANs that use connection-less communication. SMDS uses variable length datagrams with a maximum length of 9188 octets (bytes). Large and variable packet size is useful, for it can encapsulate the native packets of different LANs, such as Ethernet, FDDI, and Token Ring.

SMDS provides various speed connections starting with T-1 speed of 1.54 Mbps, going up to 34 or 45 Mbps. Services providing data rates of up to 155 Mbps, using ATM as the underlying technology, may also be available. SMDS is designed primarily for interconnecting high speed LANs. It is a service definition that can use existing high speed communication links. SMDS provides high data rates and thus can be suitable for some multimedia applications. On a 45 Mbps SMDS channel up to six broadcast-quality TV signals can be transmitted. The end-to-end delay is less than 10 ms [Fluckiger, 95]. SMDS provides multicasting facility, which makes it suitable for video broadcasting and near video-on-demand applications. But, SMDS was not designed to provide QoS guarantees required of a true multimedia network. The delay jitter depends upon the underlying technology. Thus, the ability of SMDS to carry real-time video or audio transmission is a function of the carrier technology used for providing the service.

Asymmetric Digital Subscriber Loop (ADSL)

The ADSL technology has been developed to deliver multimedia information to the home. Over good quality local loops, shorter than 5.5 Km, the ADSL technology can carry 1.544 Mbps data. This is the data rate of a T-1 line. If the length of the local loop is restricted to less than about 3 Km, then the data rate can be increased to 6.1 Mbps. VoD is one of the main applications of the ADSL technology. Access to the Internet, and other computer services is also promising application of ADSL.

Synchronous Optical Network (SONET)

Synchronous optical network (SONET) **is a data transmission service based on optical transmission.** The media used in SONET is optical fiber, therefore it provides a much higher bandwidths than the copper based circuits. SONET is a transport service that can be used for advanced network services such as Broadband-ISDN (B-ISDN), Fiber Distributed Data Interface (FDDI), and High-Definition Television (HDTV) transmission.

SONET is used in conjunction with the Asynchronous Transmission Mode (ATM) for the B-ISDN systems. The bandwidths available in the SONET's Optical Carrier (OC) standards are given in Table 4. OC-1 service provides a bandwidth of 51.48 Mbps. Higher services provide bandwidths that are multiples of 51.48 Mbps. The OC-48 service provides 2.488 Gigabit bandwidth.

4.4 THE INTERNET

The Internet is a network that spans the globe. It is a collection of a large number of disparate networks. Development of technologies and protocols used over the Internet were initiated by the U.S. Defense Advanced Research Projects Agency (DARPA) under the ARPANet project. Its importance has increased with the inclusion of the World Wide Web (WWW) as a mechanism for information dissemination. Information repositories called Web sites are used to store the information. Much of the information stored on Web sites includes multimedia content. Other possible multimedia applications of Internet include audio and video information transmission. How well does the Internet handle multimedia information? This question can be answered by studying the communication protocols used over the Internet. This section presents the fundamentals of the communication protocols used over the Internet. The multimedia capability of these protocols and their enhancements are also discussed. The Internet has seen exponential growth in the number of users in the recent years. This has put too much demand on its bandwidth, making it almost impossible to transmit any real-time multimedia information successfully. A new initiative called the Internet2 (I2) was initiated in 1996-97. A brief description of the I2 initiative is also given.

TCP/IP Protocol Suite

The communications protocols used over the Internet are called the TCP/IP suite of protocols. The two main protocols in the TCP/IP suite are the Transmission Control Protocol (TCP), and the Internet Protocol (IP). These protocols have seen many enhancements over the years. The latest enhancements aim to make these protocols capable of carrying multimedia information.

Architecture of TCP/IP

The architecture of the TCP/IP protocol stack is not as well defined as that of the OSI model. Nonetheless, its functions can be viewed in a layered architecture against the OSI model. The TCP/IP protocol stack consists of five layers [Stalling, 97]:

- **Application Layer,**
- **Host-to-host, or Transport Layer,**
- **Internet Layer,**
- **Network Access Layer, and**
- **Physical Layer.**

Application Layer

The application layer contains the logic required to interface the communication system with user applications. It is implemented in software. The TCP-application layer covers functions similar to those of the OSI-application layer, the OSI-presentation layer, and some of the functions of the OSI-session layer. Many application layer protocols have been developed for specific functions. Some of the most commonly used TCP-application layer protocols include: Simple Mail Transfer Protocol (SMTP), Multipurpose Internet Mail Extension (MIME), File Transfer Protocol (FTP), TELNET protocol for remote login, Hyper-Text Transfer Protocol (HTTP), and Simple Network Management Protocol (SNMP).

Host-to-Host, or Transport Layer

The transport layer, also called the host-to-host layer, is responsible for the end-to-end data transfer. This transport layer performs some of the functions of the OSI-session layer, and the functions of the OSI-transport layer. There are two protocols used at this layer: TCP and UDP. Each one of these is briefly described next.

TCP: The Transmission Control Protocol (TCP) is the main protocol used at this layer. TCP is a connection oriented transport protocol. It includes mechanisms for establishing a connection between the two end-systems, and for data transmission. The TCP protocol ensures that the receiver is ready to receive data before any transmission begins. The TCP protocol includes error control and flow control procedures. Thus, the data received by the application layer is error free, and the receiver cannot be flooded with data if it is not ready to receive the same. It is defined in the Internet standard RFC 793.

UDP: The User Datagram Protocol (UDP) is a connection-less transport protocol. It does not seek permission from the destination station before sending the data. It includes options for multicasting as well as broadcasting. It is defined in RFC 768.

Internet Layer

The Internet layer performs data routing over the Internet. It performs some of the functions performed by the OSI-network layer. The Internet layer protocol is called the Internet Protocol (IP). It is a connection-less protocol. IP protocol (version 4) is also called a 'best-effort' protocol, because it does not guarantee any average or minimum bit rate [Fluckiger, 95]. It is defined by the Internet standard RFC 791. Various IP implementations suitable for different network access mechanisms, and physical layers are available. Different IP routing protocols exist, some with static and some with dynamic routing capability. Devices called IP routers are also used to handle the routing function.

Network Access Layer

The Network Access Layer is responsible for routing data between two end-systems attached to the same network. Of course, when a data packet has to go from one network to another, then it must make use of the Internet layer for routing. Different implementations of the Network Access Layer exist for different types of networks. The individual network may be a circuit switched network, a packet switched network or a LAN.

Physical Layer

The physical layer is similar to the OSI-physical layer. The physical layer standards are derived from existing network implementations, and their physical layer standards.

Multimedia Capability of the Internet

The Internet, like many other older technologies, was not designed to carry multimedia traffic. The (version 4) IP protocol is a 'best-effort' protocol. It does not guarantee SAS parameters such as bandwidth, delay, and delay jitter. The TCP protocol builds a reliable transmission service over the IP protocol by including error control and flow control. These aspects make the protocol 'heavy' and fundamentally unsuitable for multimedia traffic. New Internet protocols such as the Real-time Transport Protocol (RTP) and extensions to the IP protocol, such as ST-II and RSVP can support real-time multimedia traffic.

The overall data transmission rate between two end-systems depends upon all the links, nodes, subnets, routers, and WAN connections that the data has to pass through. Users do not have control over all the devices, communication links and services that the data has to traverse. Thus, only applications that do not demand strict bounds on SAS parameters can be used successfully over the Internet. Some typical multimedia applications and their likelihood of success on the Internet are discussed in the following sections.

Multimedia E-mail

Electronic mail does not require time-bound delivery. Therefore, the Internet is good enough for carrying multimedia mail. The MIME protocol specifies the storage format for multimedia E-mail. Thus, it is possible to send multimedia E-mail over the Internet as MIME attachments to the SMTP protocol-based messages.

Isochronous and Real-Time Multimedia under TCP

One of the main problems with the TCP protocol is that it is a connection-oriented protocol, with full error and flow control. It is therefore not well suited for isochronous and real-time streamed traffic. Use of UDP protocol at the Transport layer is better for multimedia transmission [Fluckiger, 95]. This is because the UDP protocol is a connection-less protocol. More importantly, UDP is a light weight protocol, i.e., it can neglect error control. Because of the reduced processing, UDP protocol can deliver real-time data if errors can be tolerated, as is the case with uncompressed audio and video.

Many IP WANs provide data rates in the range of 45 - 100 Mbps, and IP routers can switch packets in milliseconds. Such IP-based WANs can be used for multimedia traffic [Fluckiger, 95].

In conclusion, the multimedia capability of the Internet depends upon many factors and must be evaluated for specific sites and applications. In the past, the Internet could not be used for real-time or isochronous multimedia traffic. Enhancements to the existing network infrastructure, and development of new protocols are making it possible to use the Internet for multimedia information networking. Some of new Internet protocols, designed to make it (the Internet) multimedia capable are discussed in the following section.

4.5 IP MULTICAST, MBONE, ST-II, RTP, AND RSVP

The original Internet protocols (i.e., the TCP/IP suite) were not designed for supporting bounded values of key SAS factors (e.g., delay, delay jitter, bandwidth) required for isochronous multimedia traffic. To make the Internet capable of carrying multimedia traffic, either the older communication protocols have to be enhanced, or new protocols have to be developed. Efforts in this direction have been made since the late 1980s. These efforts include enhancements to the original IP protocol and new protocols for supporting the following features:

- **Multicasting**
- **Real-time delivery**
- **Integrated services and QoS**

The need for each of these features, and the protocols developed to meet these needs, are described in the following sub-sections.

Multicasting
Many multimedia applications, such as audio and video conferencing, require the ability to multicast the traffic from one transmitter to multiple receivers. The original IP protocol did not include facility for this. An extension to the IP protocol called IP Multicast has been developed. The IP multicast protocol is used in another protocol called the Virtual Internet Backbone for Multicast IP, or Multicast Backbone (MBone) for the Internet.

Real-time delivery
To provide support for real-time delivery of packets, the network must be able to provide bounded values of SAS factors, such as delay, and delay jitter. Efforts in this direction led to the development of Internet Stream Protocol ST, in 1979. This protocol was enhanced in the early 90s and called the ST protocol version 2, or ST-II. It is described in RFC 1190. The ST-II effort has not been widely used. Subsequently, another transport protocol has been developed for real-time applications. This protocol is called Real-Time Protocol (RTP), and is described in RFC 1889.

Integrated services and QoS on Internet
A model for providing integrated services over the Internet has also been proposed. This model is called the Integrated Services (IS) model. It includes support for best-effort services, real-time services, and controlled link sharing. The IS model is described in RFC 1633. To provide a variety of service levels over the Internet, it is essential to be able to specify QoS parameters and reservation of resources. The resource ReSerVation Protocol (RSVP) has been designed for this purpose.

Most of the above introduced protocols are in a state of flux, some of these are still being researched and tested. Nonetheless, a brief description of each one of these, based on their initial development, is given below.

IP Multicast
The original layer-3 protocol used over the Internet is called the IP protocol. This IP

protocol was designed as a best-effort, unicast transmission protocol. Unicast implies that a message or its constituent packets can be sent from one source node to only one destination node at a time. Best-effort implies that there is no guarantee of delivery or any bounds on parameters such as delay and delay jitter. To be able to use the Internet for the delivery of real-time multimedia traffic, these limitations have to be removed. It is always possible to emulate multicast transmission by using multiple unicast transmissions. But this adds undesirable processing overhead on the transmitter and additional traffic on the network. Techniques for efficient multicast transmission over the Internet have been incorporated as extensions to the original IP protocol and called IP multicast. IP multicast supports the following features [Fluckiger, 95]:

- **Dynamic and distributed group membership:** Physically distributed end-nodes may join or leave groups dynamically. There is no central node that controls group membership.
- **Multiple group membership:** An end-node may belong to several groups at the same time.
- **Multiple send / receive modes:** An end-node may use any of the following three transmission modes: 1) send only, 2) receive only, and 3) send and receive data.

The best possible implementation of IP multicast routing is based on special multicast IP routers, though the standard IP routers can also play a part in the transmission. The IP multicast extensions are included in the IP version 6 protocol (IPv6), also called IP Next Generation (IPng) protocol.

Multicast Backbone – MBone

The *MBone* **(Virtual Internet Backbone for Multicast IP, or Multicast Backbone) is a real-world implementation of the IP multicast protocol.** The MBone system started in 1992; since then it has seen exponential growth. MBone can be used for group communication applications such as video conferencing and collaborative conferencing.

Stream Protocol ST-II

Stream Protocol *ST-II* **was developed as an Internet-layer (layer-3) protocol for end-to-end guaranteed packet delivery service across the Internet.** It is therefore a protocol that replaces the IP protocol at layer-3. ST-II supports delivery of streams of packets delivered to either a single destination, or to multiple destinations with controlled delay characteristics. Every node through which ST traffic passes maintains state information about the stream. ST-II includes facility for resource reservation to support the real-time traffic. Transport protocols that can use the ST protocol include TCP, packet video, and voice protocols. The ST-II protocol is described in RFC 1190.

The ST-II protocol uses a fixed route to establish a virtual link before starting transmission. Resources such as buffers, and bandwidth are allocated at every node on the route to give some QoS guarantees. The fixed route becomes a drawback in case of any node or link failure on the route. A new virtual link must be established before transmission can resume. In a group communication situation, a new end-node must get the transmitter's permission to join the group. This is different from the more flexible facility given in the IP multicast protocol. The ST-II protocol has been demonstrated to perform satisfactorily [Elliot, 93]. But the level of isochronism is not as good as in a circuit-switched network.

Real-time Transport Protocol – RTP

Another protocol developed for supporting real-time applications is the Real-time Transport Protocol (RTP). This protocol is described in RFC 1889. This is an Application-layer (Internet layer-5) protocol. *RTP* **provides end-to-end transport service to real-time data such as audio stream, video stream, and simulation data.** It works over unicast or multicast network-layer services. It does not provide QoS guarantees or facilities for resource reservation. RTP often runs over the IP and the UDP protocols.

Resource ReSerVation Protocol – RSVP

The main aim of the resource *ReSerVation Protocol (RSVP)* is to provide QoS guarantees for multimedia traffic over the Internet. RSVP protocol is used by the end-nodes to request QoS from the network. On each network node on the transmission path, the RSVP protocol attempts to reserve required sources to be able to provide the requested QoS. RSVP is highly scalable, i.e., it can scale to very large multicast groups, because it uses receiver initiated reservation requests. It is aimed primarily at multicast communications; though it can work with unicast communication as well. RSVP can run over IPv4 and IPv6. RSVP allows dynamic group memberships, and can adapt to routing changes.

4.6 THE INTERNET2 INITIATIVE

The Internet2 is an initiative designed to overcome the fundamental problems of throughput, delay and delay jitter encountered on the original Internet. It was announced in October 1996. By November 1997, it had grown from 34 universities to over 100 academic and commercial participants in the United States of America [Internet2].

The original Internet provides unrestricted access to all those who wish to use it. Despite the various enhancements to the TCP/IP protocol described above, the original Internet cannot be used for real-time multimedia transmission with any level of certainty. The main reason is the extremely loose control over its use and management. There is no single body that controls the (original) Internet's operation. Internet2 is a well-managed, Giga-bit network, serving the academic and the research communities. Education-on-demand, video conferencing, and virtual classrooms will be some of its main applications.

5. MULTIMEDIA TRANSMISSION OVER LANS

The ability of LAN technologies to carry multimedia traffic is discussed in this section. The original LAN technologies were not designed to carry multimedia traffic. Some of the current enhancements to these LAN technologies enable them to transmit real-time multimedia traffic.

The hallmark of LAN systems is their ability to share the transmission medium. Special access protocols are used to be able to share the media between many tens of stations. Each media access protocol is designed to work with specific network topologies. For example, contention protocols are used over bus and tree topologies. Token passing is used mainly over ring topology (though it can be used over any topology).

The media sharing aspect of the older LANs makes then unsuitable for carrying multimedia traffic. The effect of media sharing is discussed in the following sub-sections, followed by the techniques used in the current enhancements to make LANs capable of carrying multimedia traffic.

Speed, throughput, and the ability of various LAN technologies to carry multimedia traffic are listed in Table 9.

5.1 ETHERNET LANS

Ethernet is one of the most widely used networking technology. The maximum bit rate specified for Ethernet LANs is in the range of 10 to 100 Mbps. But the throughput is well below the maximum bit rate. There have been many efforts in making it capable of carrying multimedia traffic. Enhancements to the Ethernet technology include Switched Ethernet, IsoENET, Fast Ethernet, and 100VGAnyLAN.

Standard Ethernet

The Ethernet LANs are based on the bus topology and the CSMA/CD protocol. The raw speed of the physical layer components used in the Ethernet technology is 10 Mbps. The best possible scenario is that of only two stations connected to one segment. In this case, the chances of collisions are eliminated, especially if one station is transmitting and the other station is receiving the information. Even with this best case scenario, the maximum throughput is about 9 Mbps [Fluckiger, 95], and not the 10 Mbps raw transmission rate.

Table 9. Multimedia Capability of LAN Technologies

LAN TYPE	Speed	Throughput	Multimedia capability
ETHERNET			{ Undeterministic delay
Ethernet	10 Mbps	3–9 Mbps	Not suitable for multimedia.
Switched Ethernet	9 Mbps		Can be used for stored multimedia
Isochronous	6.144 Mbps		Suitable for videoconference.
Fast Ethernet	100 Mbps	40–90 Mbps	Can be used for stored and live multimedia.
100VGAnyLAN	100 Mbps		Deterministic delay. Suitable for interactive multimedia and video conferencing.
TOKEN RING			{ Deterministic delay
Token Ring at	4 Mbps	3.8 Mbps	Not adequate throughput per station.
Token Ring at	16 Mbps	15.5 Mbps	Can carry such as audio and video.
FDDI			{ Guaranteed delay and throughput
FDDI / CDDI	100 Mbps	50–60 Mbps	
Synchronous FDDI		As allocated	Can carry multimedia traffic.
FDDI-II	6.144 Mbps		Wideband channels carry multimedia traffic.
ATM	34–155 Mbps		Designed to carry multimedia traffic

Note: Common aspects are preceded by braces, i.e., {

As more stations are added to the network, causing more collisions, the throughput drops dramatically. If the maximum number of stations allowed are connected on an Ethernet segment, then the aggregate throughput may drop to around 3.6 Mbps. From this figure, it may appear that VCR and Broadcast quality video can be transmitted over an Ethernet network, because these require only 1.5 Mbps and 3 Mbps transmission rates, respectively. But, the aggregate throughput is the sum of the individual throughputs of all the stations on the network. If a hundred stations are connected to the network, then the nominal throughput of each station will be 3600/100 = 36 Kbps only. Moreover, because of the collisions in the Ethernet system, the delays encountered by the individual packets can vary beyond the jitter limits specified for acceptable quality audio and video. Thus, a network based on the standard Ethernet technology is not suitable for multimedia traffic.

Switched Ethernet

One enhancement used to make the conventional Ethernet technology suitable for multimedia is the Switched Ethernet system. This system uses the star topology. Each of the workstations, server(s), printer(s), and other devices is connected to a central hub via a point-to-point link, using the Ethernet physical layer standard. The hub is a switching system capable of looking at the MAC layer packets on an incoming link and switching them, in hardware, to the destination link. 9 Mbps throughput is theoretically possible for each link. The overall throughput will depend upon switching speed and architecture of the hub. But without explicit support for isochronous traffic, a switched Ethernet system cannot be used for live audio and video transmissions.

Isochronous Ethernet

Isochronous Ethernet (IsoENET) can transmit isochronous traffic over switched Ethernet LANs. It adds an isochronous channel of 6.144 Mbps capacity to the standard 10 Mbps Ethernet capacity. This capacity can be broken into 96 sub-channels of 64 Kbps each. These channels work as circuit switched channels with low transmission delay. IsoENET can support multimedia applications such as video conferencing. National Semiconductors and IBM designed special video compression chips, so that up to six video calls could be transmitted simultaneously over an IsoENET network. While IsoENET provides a solution for carrying isochronous multimedia traffic, it has a number of disadvantages. It is not a real Ethernet solution, making internetworking complex and expensive. The original 10 Mbps channel cannot be used for isochronous traffic even if it is idle.

Fast Ethernet

Fast Ethernet is a physical layer standard designed for 100 Mbps transmission rate. There are further options in the Fast Ethernet range, called 100BaseX and 100BaseT4. The 100BaseX networks use separate links for data transmission and reception. 100BaseTX works over shielded twisted pair (STP) copper wires, or category-5 unshielded twisted pair (UTP-5) wires. 100BaseFX works with a pair of optical fibers. The 100BaseT4 specification allows the use of voice grade UTP-3 cables. Even though the bit rate is 100 Mbps on a Fast Ethernet, due to collisions on a network with many (up to 100) stations, the effective throughput drops to about 40 Mbps. This throughput is adequate for transmitting non-live multimedia information, such as VoD. But, what about live multimedia? Because of the delay variance experienced by the CSMA/CD protocol even the Fast Ethernet system is not suitable for real-time isochronous traffic.

Switched Fast Ethernet

If collisions are avoided by using a 100 Mbps switch as the hub of a switched Ethernet system, then the network can be used to carry real-time multimedia traffic. A switched Ethernet system using a hybrid of 100 Mbps and 10 Mbps Ethernet links is a cost-effective solution for building a multimedia LAN. End systems requiring high throughput are connected to the hub via 100 Mbps links, while most workstations are connected to the hub via less expensive 10 Mbps links.

100VG-AnyLAN

A standard called 100VG-AnyLAN is designed to support 100 Mbps transmission over voice grade lines, and multiple MAC layer frame types. It uses a hierarchical Star topology.

The media access protocol for the 100VGAnyLAN uses a round-robin scheme. Two priority levels are available, normal and high. Any station wishing to transmit data sends a request to the hub. Only on receiving permission from the hub does the station transmit data. Real-time traffic can be transmitted with minimum delay, by using its demand priority scheme. Interactive multimedia and video conferencing traffic can be supported by the 100VGAnyLAN technology.

5.2 RING NETWORKS

Ring topology networks use a deterministic media access scheme called token passing. This gives a definite edge to such networks over the Ethernet networks in terms of delay and delay variance. The token-based media access schemes include priority and reservation mechanisms. These priority mechanisms make it possible to allocate high priority to real-time multimedia traffic.

Token Ring

The original ring technology is based on the IEEE 802.5 Token passing MAC protocol. It can be operated at either 4 Mbps or 16 Mbps. At the 4 Mbps rate, the system's aggregate throughput can be around 3.6 Mbps for a hundred station ring. This reduction in the throughput is much smaller on a token ring network (from 4 to 3.6 Mbps) than on an Ethernet network (from 10 to 3.6 Mbps). If a hundred stations were sharing the 3.6 Mbps aggregate throughput almost equally, then each station will get only 3600/100 = 36 Kbps throughput. This is barely adequate for transmitting even compressed telephone quality voice, even though the delays are deterministic. Thus, a 4 Mbps token ring network cannot support live video transmission, even for the lowest quality video.

The 16 Mbps operating speed helps by increasing the throughput allocated to individual stations. The priority and reservation features of the 802.5 protocol facilitate successful transmission of isochronous traffic. Up to ten simultaneous sessions of VCR quality audio and video have been demonstrated on the 16 Mbps Priority Token Ring [Fluckiger, 95] by reserving 80% of the bandwidth for the real-time multimedia traffic.

FDDI and CDDI

The fiber distributed data interface (FDDI) uses optical fibers to form a LAN or a MAN. The FDDI standard is based on a dual ring topology. The current version of the standard can use either optical fiber (FDDI) or twisted pair copper wires (CDDI). The FDDI protocol uses a capacity allocation scheme that breaks traffic into synchronous and asynchronous components. A finite transmission capacity is allocated to each station. The traffic that makes use of the reserved capacity is called synchronous traffic. The remaining capacity is used for asynchronous traffic. By keeping the volume of asynchronous traffic low, the synchronous traffic allocation can be used for transmitting multimedia information.

FDDI provides deterministic guarantee for delay and a statistical guarantee for bandwidth. Thus, FDDI is suitable for multimedia information networking.

FDDI-II

This enhancement to the fiber based networking technology aims to carry isochronous traffic with guarantee of delay and delay jitter values. Thus, it is also called isochronous FDDI. The 100 Mbps bandwidth is broken into 16 channels, called wideband channels (WBC), each capable of carrying traffic at 6.144 Mbps. These channels behave like circuit switched channels, and can be divided into sub-channels of 8 Kbps each, or multiples of this value. These channels are suitable for carrying traffic at a constant bit rate (CBR). FDDI-II is capable of carrying broadcast TV quality video traffic.

6. MULTIMEDIA TRANSMISSION WITH ATM

The Asynchronous Transfer Mode (ATM) technology was conceived as a service that can support multimedia traffic. ATM is based on the principle of cell switching. Data is transmitted as small (53 byte) fixed size cells. Switching of small cells in hardware allows the traffic to be transmitted with low delay and delay jitter. ATM technology allows bandwidths generally ranging from 34 to 155 Mbps, and going up to 622 Mbps.

6.1 ATM: THE MULTIMEDIA NETWORKING TECHNOLOGY

The idea of developing large-scale networks based on the Asynchronous Transfer Mode (ATM) emerged in the middle of 1980s. ATM was chosen as the technique that could be used to implement networks for all types of applications: applications requiring low bandwidth, applications requiring high bandwidth, applications requiring low delay and jitter, as well as applications with no restrictions on delay and jitter.

The Need

The need for developing a universal networking technology was felt because of the problems encountered in combining disparate networks to form large corporate networks that can carry multimedia traffic.

Many WAN and LAN technologies were developed in the 1980s. Different networking technologies can differ considerably in their operation. It is not possible to simply join two networks that use different technologies when there is a need to build a larger network. To combine a number of networks into a single corporate network, various internetworking devices are used. While internetworking provides a means for combining different networks, it suffers from the following disadvantages [Goralski, 94]:

- Internetworking adds to the **complexity** of the network.
- **Mismatching speed** and characteristics of the connected networks cause additional protocol processing delays.
- A single **low performance** link on an end-to-end path reduces the performance of the entire communication path.

Also, multimedia technology started developing into viable systems by late 1980s. The need to transmit multimedia traffic over networks was recognized even before that. Most of the original networks were not designed to carry multimedia traffic. Therefore, the need to develop a single technology that could carry multimedia traffic over networks of varying spans was felt. The main objectives set for this new technology were:

- **Carry multimedia traffic:** The aim was to develop a technology that could carry multimedia traffic, i.e., provide the required transmission rate, and low delay for voice and video streams. It had to be able to deliver isochronous traffic without unacceptable levels of degradation to the intramedia and intermedia synchronization.
- **Be scalable:** This technology had to be scalable in terms of distance as well as speed. That is, a single technology had to work for local area, as well as for wide area networks, and had to provide a wide range of transmission speeds, so that the same network could be used for low speed as well as for high-speed traffic.
- **Be adaptable:** This technology had to be adaptable, so that it could interface with existing networks. This would make it possible to use this technology as an internetworking technology before it could become the universal technology for end-to-end connections.
- **Be economical:** It is easy to provide an adequate, or more than adequate, networking service for any application if the cost is not a limiting factor. In real-life, the consumers use a service only if it is economical. This new networking technology had to provide a fair means of charging the customer. Low charge for low bandwidth and low priority traffic, and high charge for high bandwidth and high priority traffic.

The above requirements can be summed up by saying that the *ideal* networking technology to be developed had to provide service-on-demand. That is, the user had to have the freedom to specify the desired network performance parameters, such as bandwidth, delay, jitter, etc., and expect the network to provide them. This does not happen in the traditional networks. For example, in an Ethernet LAN, the bandwidth cannot exceed 10 Mbps. In fact, the real transmission rate is much lower due to packet collisions.

The concept on which the chosen ideal networking technology is based is covered in the next section.

The Concept

The ATM technology is based on the concept of asynchronous data transfer. The implementation of this concept is based on using the virtual circuit mode of packet switching, with fixed size packets, called *cells*.

What is asynchronous transfer, and why is asynchronous transfer suitable for the ideal networking technology? To understand what is asynchronous transfer, and why is it suitable for providing service-on-demand, we need to revisit the circuit switching and packet switching concepts. The best possible end-to-end circuit that can be provided for any application is a dedicated connection. But it is not possible to provide dedicated connections between a large number of sites. As the number of sites grows, the number of connections grows exponentially.

A solution to this problem was found for building the telephone networks. This solution is the circuit switching concept. In circuit switching, a dedicated circuit is established between the two sites as and when required. But once a circuit is established its properties, such as bandwidth and delay, are fixed.

Synchronous Multiplexing: Large networks are often built by sharing high-speed links among many low speed end users; this sharing is done by using various multiplexing techniques. In the telephone network, the inter-exchange trunk lines are high-speed connections carrying the traffic for many individual POTS circuits. These high-speed trunk lines are shared by using pure time division multiplexing, which is also called synchronous multiplexing.

Synchronous multiplexing uses the synchronous transfer mode, in which each POTS circuit is allocated a time slot on the high-speed trunk line. Synchronous multiplexing works efficiently only for constant traffic. For variable traffic, many time slots go unused. For example, in a telephone conversation, during the periods of silence, there is no signal to be transmitted. The time slots allocated to a POTS connection will go to waste whenever no one is talking on that line.

Asynchronous Multiplexing: Statistical time division multiplexing overcomes the above described disadvantage. **Statistical time division multiplexing uses the asynchronous transfer mode.** The asynchrony in the asynchronous transfer mode refers to the fact that the useful data packets arrive asynchronously. That is, the time gap between consecutive data packets in not constant. Each user is allocated time slots on the high-speed link only when required. This is the basis for developing the service-on-demand networking technology. The flexibility of the asynchronous transfer mode makes service-on-demand possible.

Packet Switching

Even greater level of flexibility is accorded by the packet switching systems. In a packet switching system, each data packet is treated as an independent entity by the network. The packets can arrive asynchronously, and be processed as they arrive. Thus, a packet switching system is an asynchronous time division multiplexing system.

Connectionless Mode: The maximum possible flexibility is achieved in the connectionless mode of operation of packet switching. In this mode, each packet is treated as a completely independent entity, i.e., as if, it has no relationship with the packets that come before it or those that follow it. The connectionless mode is not able to carry isochronous traffic because of the different delays encountered by the different packets. Also, packets can arrive out-of-sequence on the destination node; this is not acceptable for transferring streams of live information, such as audio and video.

Connection-oriented Mode: The connection-oriented mode of packet switching provides the flexibility of getting service-on-demand, along with the ability to carry isochronous traffic. In the connection-oriented mode, packets arrive in the correct sequence and do not experience highly varying delays. **Thus, the connection-oriented mode of packet switching was chosen as the basis for the ATM technology.** Connectionless service is also available in the ATM protocols for applications in which the order of cells is not important.

Packet Size

The question of packet size still remains to be answered. Should the packet size be fixed or variable, small or large. These questions are explored in the following section. The concept of breaking large data files into packets has been used in data communications for a long time. In general, different protocols use different size packets. Even the internal structure of these packets differ from one protocol to another. One of the main causes of delay and delay jitter in packet switching networks is the packet processing time. As packets hop from node to node on a packet switching network, these packets get queued on the input ports, waiting to be processed. Once processed, these packets get queued on the output port buffers, waiting to be transmitted to the next node on the path.

On a network that uses a protocol of variable packet size, it is quite possible for small packets to get stuck behind large packets. The small packets may be carrying real-time audio or video traffic, whereas the large packets may be carrying text data. In this case, the large delay-insensitive packet will delay the small delay-sensitive packets. The solution to this problem is to use small fixed size packets for every type of data. Small, fixed size packets can be switched in hardware reducing the queuing delays encountered on the switching nodes. Hardware switches can operate many times faster than (microprocessor based) software switches. This is the basis for selecting a small fixed size cell for the ATM technology. Having chosen the asynchronous transfer mode and fixed size cell is just the beginning. There are many more desirable features built into the ATM technology.

6.2 FEATURES OF THE ATM TECHNOLOGY

The key features of the ATM technology are described in this section. The structure of the ATM cell is designed to support these features.

Virtual Paths and Channels: In an ATM network, end-to-end paths are called virtual paths. Each virtual path can have multiple virtual channels. Because cells travel over virtual channels, they always arrive at the destination in the correct order.

Hardware Switching: Routing of the cells is done by switching nodes built around hardware switches. At high transmission rates, only a few microseconds are available for switching the packets. For example, on a link operating at 1 Gbps, the time available to process one cell, **t_p,** is given by:

$$t_p = \text{No. of bits in a cell / Bit rate}$$
$$= 53 \times 8 / 10^9 = 0.424 \text{ microsecond}$$

Such fast switching cannot be performed by microprocessor based switches. Therefore, the switching logic for ATM systems is built in hardware. Cells are stored in buffers as they arrive on an input port of an ATM switch, and switched to the correct output port by the hardware logic. Fixed size cells facilitate the design of efficient buffering and switching hardware.

Relaxed Error Control: ATM does not perform hop-by-hop error detection and correction. Error detection is performed on the header independent of the payload. A cell with a corrupted header is simply discarded. Corrupted packets are not retransmitted. This is done to minimize cell delay and delay jitter. This relaxed error control ensures that the packets that do arrive at the destination are in the correct sequence. This aspect is important for carrying multimedia traffic. If complete error control is required, it can be performed by the higher layer protocols.

Flow Control: ATM was originally expected to have no flow and congestion control mechanisms. Input rate control mechanisms were expected to take care of the rate at which data is delivered to the network. In the current versions of ATM implementations flow and congestion control are being included, but in a form quite different from that used in the traditional networks.

Congestion control: Congestion occurs when a switching node cannot process the packets as they arrive. ATM performs congestion control by simply discarding packets that cannot be processed within the required time bound. Recovery of lost packets has to be done by the higher layer protocols, if required and possible. In most real-time applications, there is no use of recovering lost packets. For example, in a live video conference, a few lost packets will cause some interruption to the image being transmitted. But, recovering and displaying the lost packets some time later will only make the conversation more confusing. If the disruption to the transmission was long enough to interrupt the conversation, the receiving party will in any case say something like, "Please, come again," until the message is fully conveyed.

6.3 ATM ARCHITECTURE

The architecture of the ATM technology is based on a layered model, like all other networking technologies. The three main layers of an ATM system are listed below. Two of these layers, namely the physical and the adaptation layers are further divided into two sub-layers each.

1. **Physical Layer**
2. **ATM Layer**
3. **ATM Adaptation Layer**

Physical Layer

The physical layer deals with the issues related to the media and the signals carried on the media. This layer is divided into two sub-layers:

- **Physical Media (PM) sub-layer, and**
- **Transmission Convergence (TC) sub-layer.**

Physical Media sub-layer: The physical media sub-layer includes options for a variety of media, such as UTP, Coax, and optical fiber. In the original proposal (CCITT 1988 Blue Book), the ATM physical media was closely related to the long-distance fiber optic networks. To provide greater flexibility for implementation, the ATM Forum has included the other media types in the ATM Physical Layer. The physical media sub-layer includes specification of the signal encoding; which is often tied to the specific media. Providing clocking information, by using self clocking encoding schemes such as Manchester encoding, is also done by the PM sub-layer.

Transmission Convergence sub-layer: The *Transmission convergence (TC) sub-layer* provides the ability to use the ATM cells over a variety of physical media.

ATM Layer

The core functions of ATM networking are performed by the ATM Layer. The fundamental concepts of ATM described earlier are implemented at this layer. ATM provides many logical connections, called virtual paths and virtual channels, over the physical paths. Some knowledge of these concepts is required for understanding the functions of the ATM layer.

Virtual Paths and Channels

In ATM, a logical connection is created by a two level abstraction. The first level of abstraction is used to create virtual paths (VPs) by combining a series of physical links. A VP is identified by a VP identifier (VPI). Each VP can carry many virtual channels (VCs). A VC works as an end-to-end conduit for carrying data. A VC is identified by a VC identifier (VCI). The purpose of this two level abstraction for creating logical connections, is to have the ability to define one of these statically, and allocate the other one dynamically. VPs are defined statically and VCs are allocated dynamically.

ATM Adaptation Layer

In the past, communication protocols were designed to suite specific types of applications. ATM has been designed as a generic protocol, and not for any specific application. The *ATM adaptation layer (AAL)* **provides a means of adapting the traffic generated by different applications to the ATM layer protocol.** The main services provided by the AAL are:

- **Segmentation of large data blocks to fit ATM cells**
- **Handling of transmission errors**
- **Handling lost and misinserted cells**
- **Flow control and timing control**

Classification of AAL services

Instead of defining a separate AAL protocol for each application, four types of AAL protocols have been defined. These AAL protocols are used for four classes of applications, simply called class-A, B, C, and D applications, as listed in Table 10 [Stalling, 97].

Class A applications: Class A applications require a constant bit rate connection-oriented service. A timing relationship is required, to cater to isochronous and synchronous traffic. Uncompressed voice is such an application. Class A applications are serviced by the adaptation layer protocol called AAL 1. The service, provided by AAL 1, is very similar to that of a circuit switched link. Therefore, it is also called (switched) circuit emulation service.

Table 10. AAL Service Classes

APPLICATION TYPE>>>	Class A	Class B	Class C	Class D
AAL protocol >>>>>>>>	AAL 1	AAL 2	AAL 3/4	AAL 5
Bit rate >>>>>>>>>>>>	Constant	<---------------------- Variable ---------------->		
Timing relationship >>>>	<--------- Required ---------->		<------- Not Required ------->	
Connection mode >>>>>>	<--- Connection-oriented ---->		<---------Connectionless ----->	
Application example >>>>	Voice	Comp. Video	Data	Data

Class B applications: Class B applications differ from class A applications only in the type of bit rate required. Class B applications require a variable bit rate, over a connection-oriented service. Timing relationship must be maintained during the transmission. Compressed video is a class B application. Class B applications are serviced by the adaptation layer called AAL 2.

Class C and Class D applications: Originally, AAL 3 was designed to service connection-oriented applications called Class C applications; and AAL 4 was designed to service connectionless applications called Class D applications. Later, the AAL 3 and AAL 4 AAL protocols were merged into AAL 3/4 protocol for serving Class C or D applications with a connectionless transmission mode. A new protocol called the AAL 5 protocol has also been designed to eliminate some of the overhead introduced in the AAL 3 protocol, and carried over to the AAL 3/4 protocol.

Class C and Class D applications differ from Class B applications in terms of the required timing relationship. Class C/D applications do not require any timing relationship. The service provided is connectionless, and includes the facility to carry variable bit rate. Text and other data transmission applications fall under this class. Class C or D applications can be serviced by the AAL 3/4 as well as the AAL 5 protocol.

Convergence Sublayer

The ATM technology derives its ability to support multimedia traffic because of the convergence facility provided by the ATM adaptation layer. The convergence sublayer (CS) provides the facility to interface the ATM layer to the various higher layer protocols used for carrying the application data. Here interfacing refers to the creation of the proper protocol data units (PDUs). There is a CS sublayer protocol for each service type. These protocols use a *service access point* (SAP) as the address for each block of information submitted by a higher layer. This information block - submitted by the higher layer - is called a *service data unit* (SDU).

For AAL 1 and AAL 2, the function of the CS sublayer is to add protocol information suitable for timing and cell loss recovery. For AAL 3/4 and AAL 5, the function of the CS sublayer is to add protocol information suitable for cell loss detection only.

Segmentation and Reassembly Sublayer

The segmentation and assembly sublayer (SAR) is responsible for converting the data received from the CS sublayer into PDUs suitable for the ATM layer. The ATM cell structure uses a 5 byte header and a 48 byte payload. Thus, the SAR protocols break up the data received from the CS sublayer into 48 byte units. There are four SAR protocols for the four different AAL protocols.

The simplicity of the AAL5 protocol is making it one of the most widely used AAL protocol. It is used for:

- **LAN applications,**
- **Multimedia applications, and**
- **Signaling applications.**

6.4 APPLICATION OF ATM IN LANS

One of the main benefits of the ATM technology is that it can be used for WANs as well as for LANs. ATM is used in LANs in two different modes:

- **ATM switch based LANs**
- **LAN emulation**

Switch-Based ATM LAN

ATM switches can also be used for creating a LAN. In this case, the stations are connected directly to the ATM switches, and the individual stations transmit and receive data under the ATM protocol. Therefore, sessions involving multimedia traffic can be established between any two stations.

In another LAN scenario, ATM switches are used to form a backbone for a multi-segment network. The individual LAN segments connected to the ATM backbone can be Ethernet, Token Ring, or others. These segments connect to the ATM switches through bridges. The ability to transmit multimedia information between two stations now depends upon the capability of the LANs to which each of these are connected.

LAN Emulation

ATM can also be used for building LANs in a mode called LAN emulation (LANE). In this mode, the ATM network transports the conventional LAN frames. LAN emulation for various conventional LAN technologies, such as Ethernet and Token Ring, are available. LAN emulation provides a migration path from the current LAN technology to fully ATM based networks. The multimedia capability of a LAN emulation system depends upon the LAN being emulated.

7. CONCLUSIONS

Multimedia traffic requires high throughput, low delay and very low delay variance for real-time delivery. Most legacy networking systems were not designed for multimedia traffic. This chapter presented the limitations of the legacy networks, and the fundamentals of advanced networks that can carry real-time multimedia traffic.

The various wide area networking options for multimedia networking include the POTS connection, leased lines, and ISDN. Being able to use the Internet for transmitting real-time multimedia traffic is a very attractive proposition. But the original Internet, like many other older technologies, was not designed to carry multimedia traffic. Multimedia enabling protocols, such as RTP and RSVP, have been developed to carry multimedia traffic over the Internet. A new effort called Internet2 aims to overcome the problems of throughput and delay by using Gigabit technologies as its backbone.

Enhancements to existing LAN technologies have been developed in an effort to make them capable of carrying multimedia information. Switched Ethernet, Isochronous Ethernet, Fast Ethernet, 100VGAnyLAN, FDDI-II, and Synchronous FDDI are some such enhancements for LAN systems.

One technology that was designed to carry multimedia traffic is the ATM technology. The future of multimedia information networking is ATM networks using fiber-based physical media, such as SONET.

REFERENCES

[Agnew, 96]   P. W. Agnew and A. S. Kellerman, *Distributed Multimedia,* Addison Wesley, 1996.

[Beyda, 89]   W. J. Beyda, *Basic Data Communications: A Comprehensive Overview,* Beyda, Prentice Hall, 1989.

[Elliot, 93]   C. Elliot, "High Quality Multimedia Conferencing Through Long-Haul Packet Networks," ACM Multimedia 93, Conference Proceedings, Anaheim, California, 1993.

[Fluckiger, 95]   F. Fluckiger *Understanding Networked Multimedia: Applications and Technology,* Prentice Hall, 1995.

[Furht, 94]   B. Furht, "Multimedia Systems: An Overview," *IEEE Multimedia,* Vol. 1, Spring 1994, pp. 47-59.

[Goralski, 94]   ATM: The Future of High Speed Networking, Walter Goralski, Computer Technology Research Corp., 1994.

[Internet2]   http://www.internet2.edu

[ITU-T, 88]   ITU-T Rec. E.800, "Terms and Definitions Related to the Quality of Telecommunication Services," Blue Book, 1988.

[ITU-T, 92]   Draft Rec. I.350, "General Aspects of Quality of Service and Network Performance in Digital Networks, Including ISDN," April 1992.

[Jung, 96-1]   J. Jung, "Quality of Service in Telecommunications Part-I: Proposition of a Quality of Service framework and its applications to B-ISDN," IEEE Communications Magazine, August 1996, pp. 108-111.

[Jung, 96-2]   J. Jung, "Quality of Service in Telecommunications Part-2: Translation of a Quality of Service parameters into ATM Performance Parameters in B-ISDN," IEEE Communications Magazine, August 1996.

[Stalling, 97]   W. Stalling, *Data and Computer Communications,* Fifth edition, Prentice Hall, 1997.

[Szuprowicz, 95] B. O. Szuprowicz, *Multimedia Networking,* McGraw-Hill, 1995.

[Vogel, 95]   A. Vogel et al., "Distributed Multimedia and QOS: a Survey," *IEEE Multimedia,* Vol. 2, No. 2, pp. 10-19, Summer 1995.

38

VIDEO TRANSPORT IN ATM NETWORKS:
A SYSTEM VIEW

D. Raychaudhuri, D. Reininger, and R. Siracusa
NEC USA, C&C Research Laboratories
4, Independence Way, Princeton, NJ 08540
ray@ccrl.nj.nec.com

1. **INTRODUCTION** 816
2. **SYSTEM ARCHITECTURE CONSIDERATIONS** 817
3. **SELECTED RESEARCH RESULTS** 821
    3.1   VBR/ATM INTERFACE 821
    3.2   NETWORK QoS WITH VBR+ 826
    3.3   CELL-LOSS CONCEALMENT FOR ATM 828
    3.4   TRANSPORT PROTOCOLS FOR VIDEO 831
4. **CONCLUDING REMARKS** 835
    REFERENCES 835

Abstract. This chapter presents a system view of video transport issues in ATM networks. Since video is a critical component of future distributed multimedia applications, we consider technical approaches necessary to realize a flexible, robust and efficient ATM framework for video delivery. The overall system design problem is discussed for a general distributed multimedia computing scenario, and key video-related design issues are identified. This is followed by a more detailed discussion of selected ATM video topics, including: (1) Variable bit-rate (VBR) statistical multiplexing and dynamic usage parameter control (VBR+); (2) Dynamic Quality-of-Service with VBR+; (3) ATM cell loss concealment in MPEG decoders; (4) Transport protocols for video and multimedia. Supporting simulation or experimental results from ongoing research are given where available.

This chapter is based on the paper with the same title that appeared in Multimedia Systems Journal, Volume 4:305-315, published by Springer-Verlag in 1996. Reproduced with permission of Springer Verlag.

1. INTRODUCTION

Core technologies for both high-speed networking and digital video have matured significantly during the last few years. MPEG standards [1] for video compression in several important application scenarios have recently been issued with broad industry consensus. In parallel, the ATM Forum has issued an initial specification [2] for local area ATM products with similarly wide industry support. Based on these specifications, VLSI for both MPEG and ATM processing have become available since 1992, and are currently being applied to the development of early broadband network-based digital TV and multimedia applications.

Although "video over ATM" has been an active R&D topic for over five years (see for example [3]), a clear consensus on the technical approach is still lacking. It is difficult to develop a uniform technical approach for video over ATM because of the wide range of application scenarios supported by these technologies. Each application scenario (e.g., TV broadcasting, videoconferencing, VoD, multimedia computing, etc.) will tend to have different design criteria, as summarized in Table 1 below. As a result, it is unlikely that a single video over ATM solution can be developed in the near future. The likely evolution is towards two or three system design approaches aimed at different application regimes.

Table 1. Application Scenarios and Key Design Criteria for Video on ATM

Application Scenario	Key Design Criteria
(1) TV or HDTV broadcasting	• high picture quality • high cell loss resilience • low cost receiver
(2) Videoconferencing	• low interactive delay • high bandwidth efficiency • low cost encoder/decoder
(3) Video on-Demand (VoD)	• high bandwidth efficiency • service flexibility • low cost decoder
(4) Distributed multimedia computing (MoD, PC services, etc.)	• low interactive delay • service flexibility & scalability • software integration

Currently, there is a de-facto MPEG over ATM solution for the TV broadcasting scenario [4], and to some extent, this approach may also be used in simple video-on-demand (VoD) applications. The early specification calls for constant bit-rate (CBR) MPEG with MPEG-2 systems [5] on the codec side, with CBR/ATM service via an existing AAL protocol (such as AAL5) on the network side. While this method may be acceptable for broadcasting and certain VoD applications, further work is required to identify a more flexible and efficient video transport framework for multimedia computing over ATM.

In the remainder of this chapter, we discuss video-related design issues for a general ATM-based multimedia computing scenario (i.e., item 4 in Table 1). The video transport approach, discussed here, is composed of the following elements:

(1) Variable bit-rate (VBR) video with usage parameter control (UPC) based encoder rate control,
(2) Quality-of-Service (QoS) based ATM services, including a dynamic renegotiation VBR mode (VBR+) and a reserved burst transfer mode (ABR+),
(3) New multimedia transport protocol with a choice of error and flow control options for video,
(4) Efficient integration of network video into computing hardware and software framework.

Overall system architecture considerations are first presented in Section 2, followed by a more detailed coverage of key subsystems in Section 3. Concluding remarks and references are given in Sections 4 and 5, respectively.

2. SYSTEM ARCHITECTURE CONSIDERATIONS

A typical multimedia computing and communication ("C&C") scenario is shown in Figure 1.

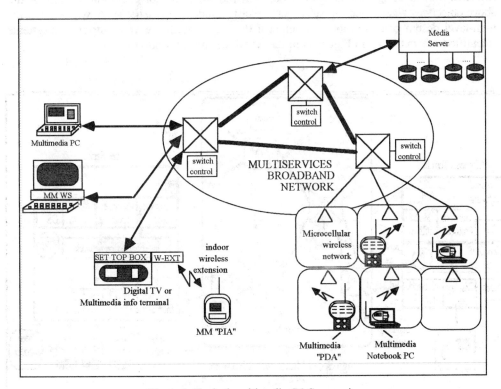

Figure 1. Typical multimedia C&C scenario.

In this scenario, a variety of general purpose computing platforms (both wired and wireless) exchange multimedia information via a high-speed (ATM) multiservices network. Applications will often be of the "client-server" type involving access of video, image and data information from media servers that is attached to the network. The same framework should also support peer-to-peer communicative applications such as multimedia groupware or simple teleconferencing. For both types of applications, video support in the network, terminal or server hardware/software is a key consideration that tends to dominate multimedia system design.

A number of system design criteria must be considered for video integration into the multimedia networking architecture outlined in Figure 1. Some of the important design objectives include:

- Video quality vs. bit-rate characteristics necessary for cost-effective applications;
- High overall network efficiency for integrated services including video;
- Low end-to-end application delay, particularly for interactive applications;
- Hardware and software throughputs appropriate for full-quality and/or multi-stream video;
- Integration of video into software framework, including quality-of-service (QoS) support;
- Scaleable system capable of working with different bandwidth/QoS, CPU speeds, displays;
- Graceful degradation during network congestion or processing overload.

Effective system design for network video will require prior consideration of each of the above objectives when selecting subsystem level technical approaches. We will summarize high-level design considerations for some of the major hardware and software subsystems (identified schematically in Figure 2) in the remainder of this section.

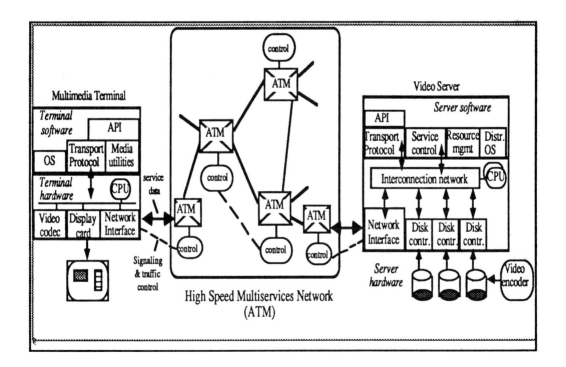

Figure 2. Typical hardware/software components of ATM-based distributed multimedia system.

(1) <u>Video compression</u>: MPEG video coding standards (MPEG-1 and MPEG-2) are likely to be used in all four application scenarios outlined in the previous section. At present, the emphasis in most R&D work tends to be on utilizing the recently specified MPEG standard rather than on defining alternative solutions for video compression. While the MPEG video coding syntax itself is completely specified, several design issues arise in connection with specific application scenarios. For the ATM scenario, an important open issue is that of encoder rate control for variable bit-rate (VBR) ATM transport, taking into account usage parameter control (UPC) requirements at the UNI [6]. Also, mechanisms for incorporating feedback about ATM network congestion into video rate control have been investigated [7]. On the video decoder side, a basic issue is that of error concealment for amelioration of occasional cell loss in shared bandwidth ATM services [8]. While error concealment of conventional one-layer MPEG video should be sufficient for many scenarios, several groups have also investigated the use of layered coding and prioritized transport over ATM for additional cell loss robustness [9]. Multiresolution / scaleable implementations of MPEG for various multi-tier application scenarios also remains an open design issue in video coding. For multimedia terminals based on general purpose processors, scalability of picture size and decoder processing requirements are important for realization of useful and robust systems. This is particularly true for the wireless terminal scenario in which video decoding and display capabilities may be CPU limited. Support for scaleable video is limited in the current MPEG standards, motivating consideration of more general video coding syntax as the successor to current MPEG specifications [10].

(2) <u>Multimedia/video transport protocol</u>: A suitable transport protocol (such as TCP used in current Internet services) is necessary for reliable end-to-end delivery of media between software-based devices. Since TCP was designed for packet data without time deadlines, it is generally accepted that alternative stream-oriented protocols will be required for video support. For example, an experimental protocol "PVP" has been used on an experimental basis in Internet [11]. More recently, RTP has been used for multicasted video delivery in Internet [12]. In ATM, the framework for transport protocols is to first use a lightweight, hardware-based adaptation layer (AAL) protocol for basic segmentation / reassembly, etc. and then add a variable length packet data unit (PDU) transport layer above it. Recently developed broadcast oriented protocols such as MPEG++ [13] and MPEG-2 Systems layer [5] may be used in place of a more general transport protocol in certain scenarios, generally at the expense of flexibility and additional processing cost. It is our view that with the exception of TV broadcasting and derivative applications (e.g., simple VoD), it is preferable to define a video-specific AAL (traditionally known as "AAL2") and apply a lightweight PDU-level protocol above it to support video as well as other media required by the application in an integrated manner. In designing such a protocol stack, considerations include hardware implementability of the AAL layer, efficient software processing of higher layers, low total overhead, options for error recovery and receiver flow control, etc.

(3) <u>Multimedia-capable software</u>: Software design is an important issue for both terminal and server, and includes selection of operating system (OS), media support middleware, network interface/API, application programs/scripts, etc. A fair amount of work has been done on real-time OS schedulers, capable of supporting time-critical media types such as video [14,15]. While video integration into commercial OSs is feasible at limited bit-rates (~10–20 Mbps, depending on processor speed), higher speed/quality video generally requires real-time OS capabilities. The related network API issue also has to be addressed for new multimedia systems, as current TCP does not provide a lightweight stream mode necessary for video delivery. In our view, the high-level software API should provide the application programmer with access to a choice of high-speed transport protocols, AAL and ATM services (with selectable quality-of-service), but in a relatively simple manner. This can potentially be accomplished by developing a new middleware layer ("ATM service manager" [16]) responsible for mapping application communication requirements to available

transport and ATM services. In general, the functions of this layer may include adaptation to network congestion conditions via renegotiation of QoS, service type, etc. and/or source rate control. At the higher software layers, a suitable distributed object service needs to be implemented for flexible and modular application development [17]. Application programs for many network-based multimedia applications can be efficiently developed in a platform-independent manner using an interpreted language approach such as the Java language [18].

(4) Multimedia capable hardware: There are several hardware design issues that need to be addressed for effective video support in both the video/media server and the terminal device. Video support in conventional PC or workstation architectures may face CPU, bus, disk I/O or network interface bottlenecks associated with transport protocol termination and media routing functions. At the video/media server, a suitable combination of distributed processor, fast interconnection network/bus, RAID disk arrays and high-speed ATM network interface hardware will generally be required to support a large number of simultaneous video channels. Architectures for video servers [19,20] are still evolving, and most will require new hardware modules and parallel processing to overcome existing performance bottlenecks. On the terminal side, multimedia PCs using microprocessors with special instructions [21,22] are capable of MPEG-2 video playback without an add-on board with dedicated hardware decoders [23]. As applications evolve towards higher video quality (e.g., HDTV at 15 Mbps+) and/or multiple video streams, it becomes necessary to move towards distributed terminal architectures [24,25] with hardware support for communications, routing and media processing functions. Distributed hardware options include ATM interface cards with on-board processing, dual bus, media routing switch, video processing accelerators, etc. In terms of the MPEG video decoder itself, a good design should provide for multiresolution /multistream operation (needed for most typical window-based user interfaces), as well as error concealment functions necessary to deal with occasional ATM cell loss events.

(5) Multiservices ATM Network: Efficient support of the general multimedia networking scenario requires an ATM network with multiple service types and quality-of-service (QoS) control. Specific services currently defined for ATM are ABR (available bit-rate), VBR (variable bit-rate) and CBR (constant bit-rate). Each of these service types is potentially applicable to video delivery, depending on the desired cost/quality trade-off. Traditional CBR service is the simplest solution for video in many applications (e.g., broadcasting or VoD), but it suffers from disadvantages of variable video quality, high end-to-end delay and relatively high transmission cost. Connectionless ABR service is likely to be the least expensive mode, and can usually provide constant quality and low delay. However, since ABR provides no numerical performance guarantees, its use may be limited to certain classes of loss/delay insensitive video applications (e.g., browsing). When quality-of-service (QoS) guarantees are needed along with a relatively constant video quality and/or low interaction delay, VBR is generally viewed as the appropriate ATM traffic class [26,27]. The VBR service mode allows for efficient utilization using statistical multiplexing, but with QoS-based call admission controls. VBR video connections are characterized by a set of three parameters, peak rate, sustained rate and burst length that constitutes the UPC (usage parameter control) specification for video. This UPC is used to shape and monitor traffic on the network via a dual-leaky bucket algorithm, which has been specified by the ATM Forum [2]. The design issue here is to achieve reasonably high statistical multiplexing gain with VBR video within the framework of UPC controls, etc. Typically, such VBR operation involves encoder rate control based on leaky bucket occupancies, in order to stay within the specified peak and average bit-rate limits [28]. The concept of "VBR+," in which the UPC parameter may be dynamically negotiated between the encoder and the network depending on current requirements is now under investigation [29]. Experimental results with this type of operation have been shown to facilitate efficient statistical multiplexing within the ATM

network while maintaining nominally constant video quality over a wide range of material [30].

3. SELECTED RESEARCH RESULTS

Recognizing that detailed consideration of all the design issues discussed in Section 2 is beyond the scope of a single chapter, we now narrow the focus and present selected results on a few important problems. Specific topics considered in this section are: (1) VBR/ATM interface; (2) Cell-loss concealment in ATM; (3) Transport protocols for video delivery.

3.1 VBR/ATM INTERFACE

In this section, we examine the interface between a VBR video codec and the ATM network. Potential problems with conventional usage parameter control (UPC)-based VBR approaches are discussed. A new scheme (VBR+) in which UPC parameters may be varied dynamically by the encoder or the network is proposed as a solution, and preliminary simulation results are given.

The VBR/ATM network interface adapts the VBR video bitstream for ATM transport. In computer-based applications, the video encoder places the data on a buffer defined in user-memory. The network interface card (NIC) pulls data from the buffer, segments it into ATM cells, adds the ATM adaptation headers and sends ATM cells to the network. The rate at which the NIC sends data to the network is regulated by a traffic shaper compliant with UPC parameters specified at call-set up. The VBR video codec and the NIC can interface in either open-loop or closed-loop modes. In open-loop mode, encoder quantization and UPC parameters are selected such that peak encoder bit-rates can be accepted by the network with an acceptably low probability of data loss. Typically, a multi-frame smoothing buffer is used to reduce the peak-to-average ratio of the video process before it enters the network interface. In closed-loop mode (as shown in Figure 3), the traffic shaper is supplemented with source quantization control to ensure that the encoding rate and transfer rate are appropriate for the display frame rate and delay tolerance of the application.

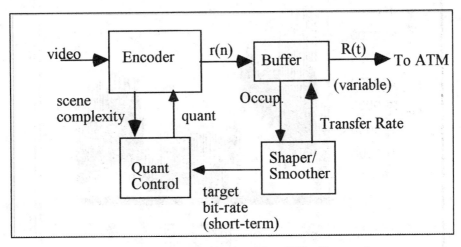

Figure 3. Implementation of a closed-loop VBR video encoder.

The conventional ATM VBR service class supports connections with a static traffic profile (established at call set-up) defined as a set of UPC traffic descriptors such as peak rate (R_P), sustained rate (R_S), and burst length (B_L). The network admits (or rejects) a VBR connection based on its declared UPC. The network will enforce the declared UPC using a leaky-bucket based network policer [31]. The traffic shaper at the NIC is then also implemented with a leaky-bucket that mirrors the shaper within the network. Each time a cell passes through the leaky-bucket a counter is incremented and it is constantly decremented at the sustained rate. A source complies with its UPC if it produces up to B_L consecutive cells with inter-cell spacing of up to $\dfrac{1}{R_P}$ and, until the cell counter is cleared, all the remaining cells arrive at inter-cell spacing of up to $\dfrac{1}{R_S}$.

The main problem with the conventional static UPC VBR approach is the selection of a single UPC value for non-stationary video. Figure 4 shows a typical sample path for the bit-rate per frame of a VBR MPEG encoder. In this example, three activity regions are easily identified. Each region corresponds to video scenes with different bit-rate requirements for uniform picture quality.

The non-stationary behavior due to scene changes implies that a short-term scene-by-scene assignment of traffic descriptors is more appropriate than a long-term static descriptor. Previous studies on VBR video transmission under static UPC [32] have confirmed that the size of the leaky bucket counter must be quite long (possibly as long as several seconds, which may be excessive from a network designer's point of view) to allow uniform picture quality over the duration of a video connection. Thus, when the static UPC based VBR mode is used for video, it tends to require a high degree of smoothing (which adds delay) along with intentional overdimensioning of the bit-rate parameters (corresponding to the most stressful video sequences). This tends to limit the achievable statistical multiplexing gain achieved with VBR (relative to conventional CBR video) to relatively modest values (e.g., ~25%).

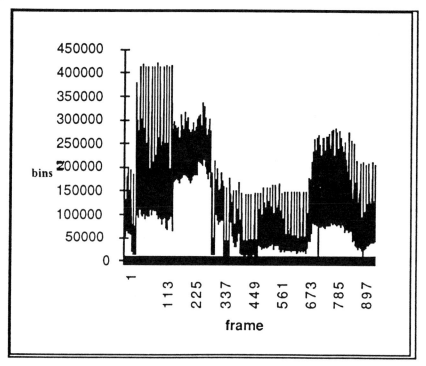

Figure 4. VBR MPEG bit-rate sample path shows the non-stationary behavior.

In view of these limitations of conventional VBR, we are currently investigating dynamic renegotiation of UPC parameters as a means of obtaining high statistical multiplexing gain with quality-of-service (QoS) control. In this scheme (called VBR+), the NIC and network can rapidly renegotiate UPC parameters to meet current video encoder and network needs. For example, when a video encoder changes scene, new UPC values can be established within a relatively short time (~10-100 ms, depending on the propagation and processing speed scenario). Similarly, a network experiencing congestion can optionally initiate UPC renegotiation in order to maintain a reasonable service level for all users. Dynamic UPC can work as a preventive network congestion control scheme where the network[1] can accept or block a UPC request depending on its current utilization, bandwidth reservation and QoS contracts. The user does not need to specify exactly its UPC at connection set-up since it will be dynamically adjusted according to its bandwidth requirements as the call progresses. Source rate control is used to adjust the encoder bit-rate during periods of congestion on which the network may reject a UPC request from the encoder. For the scheme to work, the source must release reserved resources when it is able to sustain its QoS using a lower UPC.

Figure 5 shows a model of a VBR+ video encoder with dynamic UPC renegotiation. The *VBR Encoder* generates an MPEG [1] compressed bitstream from the incoming raw digital video. Each frame is segmented into macroblocks and DCT coded. The resulting DCT coefficients are quantized with a uniform quantizer with quantization step-size *mquant*. The quantized coefficients are variable-length coded and the VBR bitstream is placed in a buffer. The *Quant Control* block on the encoder selects the corresponding *mquant* based on the *target rate* specified by the *UPC control*; in addition, it sends the average *mquant* over a frame, *Q*, to the *UPC control*. The *UPC control* runs a feedback algorithm that triggers the UPC renegotiation request based on the status of the buffer and the value of *Q*. The algorithm also estimates the necessary UPC for the encoder to operate at Q_{target}. The *Traffic Shaper* clocks the data out of the buffer and into the packetizer at a rate specified dynamically by the *UPC control*. The ATM I/F prepares the compressed data for ATM transport and sends it to the ATM network.

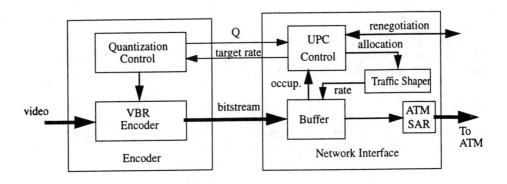

Figure 5. VBR+ ATM network interface.

---

[1]The VBR+ dynamic UPC renegotiation is currently envisioned to be only between the user's VBR/ATM and the access switch at the edge of the network.

<u>Simulation Results</u>: MPEG-compressed digital video was obtained by encoding 7300 frames (4 minutes @ 30 fps) of raw video captured from D-1 format.[2] The video contains 10 sequences including scenes from movies (e.g., The Mask, Maverick, and Wyatt-Earpl), commercials (e.g., NEC Oregon Plant), and a concatenated sequence obtained from a number of short (30 sec.) test sequences with a wide range of traffic characteristics (e.g., Flower-garden, Table Tennis, Mobi, etc.,) to simulate rapid scene changes. The encoding was done using the MPEG software Simulation Group [33] modified for VBR operation. The MPEG parameters used are N=12, M=3,[3] and $Q_{target} = (Q_I, Q_P, Q_B) = (3, 4, 6)$.

Table 2 gives the bit-rate statistics observed for some of the open-loop (constant Q) VBR encoded sequences. Observe that to select *a priori* a single UPC to sustain the desired picture quality on all sequences, one would need to select the worst case traffic descriptor, i.e., average bit-rate of sequence 6 and the peak-rate of sequence 2. Selecting the average overall sequences for peak and average bit-rate will result in quantization adjustments on sequences with larger than average traffic descriptor.

Table 2. Traffic Statistics for Some Open-Loop Encoded Sequences

Sequence	Name	Length (frames)	Average bit-rate (Mbps)	Peak to average ratio
1	The Mask	1680	1.8	5
2	Maverick	1530	2.0	7
3	NEC Oregon	1800	2.0	4
4	Flower-garden	150	3.0	3
5	Mobi	150	5.0	3
6	Bus	150	6.0	1.7

When the VBR+ mode is adopted, Figure 6 shows a trace of the dynamic UPC requested by the NIC to the ATM switch corresponding to the stressful segment of the open-loop VBR video shown in Figure 4. In this example, three UPC levels are used, corresponding to a high activity scene (frames 1 – 400), a low activity scene (frames 400 – 800) and a medium activity scene (frame 800 – 1000).

It is observed from the above results that dynamic renegotiation of UPCs at the VBR interface can provide a more uniform video quality (based on a more uniform PSNR trace), while using only the necessary network resources during each epoch.

Experimental results with real-time VBR+ encoding using NEC's VisuaLink 7000 MPEG-2 codec are described in [30]. Extensive subjective and objective evaluation (based on quantizer statistics) indicate that VBR+ video quality is more uniform and remains closer to the target level longer than the one obtained with traditional VBR coding.

---

[2] 4:2:0 YUV SIF (360x240) video was obtained by filtering the original D-1 4:2:2 720x480 source.

[3] In MPEG, a Group-of-Pictures (GOP) is defined by two parameters, N and M. N is the GOP length as well as the distance, in frames, between intra-coded frames. M is the distance between anchor frames used to derive the predicted frames.

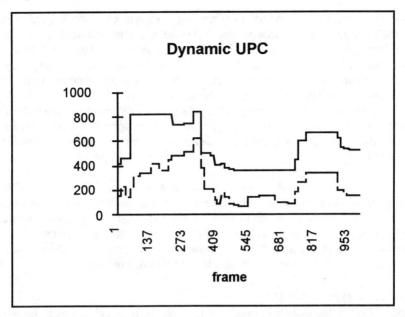

Figure 6. Peak (top curve) & sustained (bottom curve) rate for MPEG video with dynamic UPC.

Figure 7 shows the corresponding trace for peak signal-to-noise ratio (PSNR) and compares it to the PSNR curve obtained from a static UPC assignment (set to the long-term average UPC value).

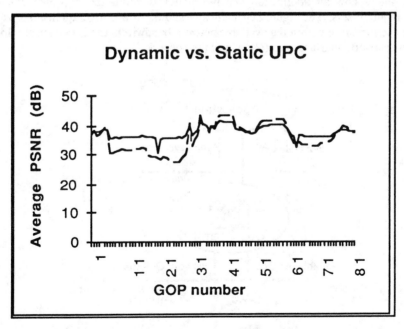

Figure 7. Peak signal-to-noise ratio for dynamic (top curve) and static (bottom curve) UPC.

These results have been obtained assuming the ideal case where the network has capacity available to satisfy the sources' renegotiation requests. However, when the network is congested, more extensive use of source rate control may be necessary. In [34], a connection admission control (CAC) algorithm that efficiently handles renegotiation is presented to evaluate the performance of VBR+ under more realistic network conditions. Simulation results show that the CAC is robust in admitting a variety of video sources with widely different traffic burstiness. By distributing bandwidth among contending connections to achieve uniform quality, the CAC allows high video quality and bandwidth utilization. In [35], additional performance metrics besides PSNR and multiplexing gains, such as local buffer requirements, are considered. The trade-off among renegotiation frequency, renegotiation policy, and buffering delay is studied when VBR+ is used for video delivery to the home. A methodology for selecting traffic descriptor parameters dynamically is given in [36]. The methodology computes the UPC parameters from transport-level statistics, instead of network level statistics, significantly reducing the processing requirements of the renegotiation algorithm.

Finally, [37] describes the use of VBR+ in the wireless ATM scenario. In particular, the role of VBR+ in improving the allocation efficiency on the medium access is studied with simulations. An algorithm for medium access control (MAC) slot allocation that combines the VBR+ dynamic UPC with rapid MAC level estimates of the requirements for each VBR virtual circuit is implemented. Results show that the proposed scheme can achieve throughputs in the 60-70% range while maintaining reasonable QoS.

3.2 NETWORK QoS WITH VBR+

The notion of QoS in the distributed multimedia scenario is associated with the provision of adequate network resources for *acceptable* application performance. From the network perspective, efficient QoS support requires the use of dynamic renegotiation to match the network bandwidth to the application requirements. From the user perspective, dynamic renegotiation allows an operating point with suitable cost/performance.

Figure 8 shows how an application can use VBR+ to tailor the network service to its dynamic requirements. The figure schematically shows an adaptive application capable of scaling its performance within the available network bandwidth, the QoS control middleware around the network interface card (NIC), and the network.

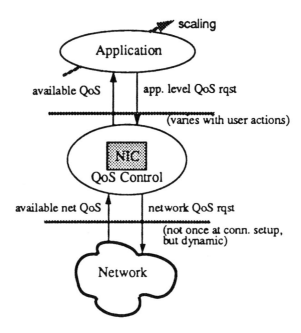

Figure 8. System model for dynamic QoS control with VBR+.

The application program interface (API) between the application and the QoS control allows renegotiation of application-level QoS. The parameters of this API describe, in abstract terms, the desired video quality; for example, a QoS-aware multi-window video browser described in [17] uses the notion of a service contract object that specifies the desired level-of-detail (LoD) and importance-of-presence (IoP) of the video. The QoS control software uses the application's service contract and the video traffic characteristics to request an appropriate traffic descriptor. The network API allows dynamic QoS renegotiation. When the network is congested, the application needs to scale its performance to the available QoS.

The support of VBR+ in ATM networks requires extensions to the Q.2931 UNI connection set-up model [38]. The ATM Forum signaling group is discussing the addition of new messages to support in-call renegotiation by extending the ideas adopted in the ITU recommendation Q.2963 [39]. Figure 9 shows how a server uses this signaling extension to support client-initiated QoS renegotiation. The signaling daemon at each switch controller extracts the requested QoS parameters from received MODIFY_REQ messages and passes them to the QoS controller. The controller replies using the MODIFY_AVAIL message.

A proof-of-concept implementation of the system in Figure 9 is presented in [17]. The prototype implements a media-on-demand service with scalable QoS control. Users can dynamically change their QoS contracts and receive feedback on QoS status, network usage and cost. The client terminals host a multimedia browser. The software modules executing on the server consist of a *Scalable Media Server* that sets the video frame-rate, and compression level based on the application QoS contract. The server can scale the bit-stream by selecting among multiple tracks with different quantizations and resolutions. Currently, the server uses ten JPEG-encoded tracks per movie. The tracks are obtained by encoding the movie using five quantization levels, and two resolutions, (640x480) and (320x240). Video tracks can be switched at video frame boundaries. The Media Server also interacts with the ATM driver using extensions to support QoS control and bandwidth renegotiation. Through these extensions, the server can set water-mark levels on the ATM driver's buffer. The driver reports the buffer state when these water-mark levels are crossed. The server computes a traffic descriptor for the video bit-stream and renegotiates with the network when the computed traffic descriptor significantly differs from the one currently negotiated with the network.

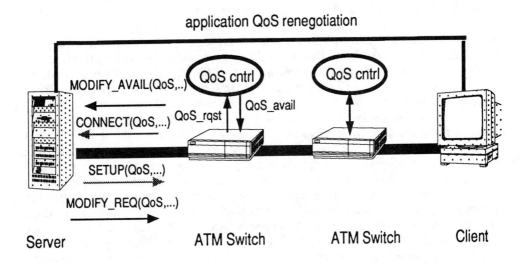

Figure 9. ATM signaling extensions for VBR+ support.

The QoS controller at each switch processes the renegotiation request and allocates a new bandwidth and traffic descriptor to the connection. The server receives the newly allocated descriptor and sets the NIC's shaper parameters via the extensions provided by our ATM driver. While the renegotiation is in progress, the server uses source rate control to maintain the driver's buffer level. Rate control changes the video quality by first, increasing the compression level of the stream and keeping the frame-rate and resolution fixed to the level specified in the service contract. The frame-rate and, eventually the resolution, could be reduced if additional source rate control is needed beyond the range achievable with quantization level alone.

The server sends feedback on the status of the service contract to the browser. For example, the prototype sends the connection's bit-rate, its cost and service alerts. The connection's bit-rate is updated with each bandwidth renegotiation. The cost is derived from the current traffic descriptor. Service alerts are used to indicate compliance with the service contract. More details on the experiences with this prototype can be found in [17].

3.3 CELL-LOSS CONCEALMENT FOR ATM

Receiver-based cell-loss (error) concealment algorithms are essential for efficient video transmission over ATM. Error concealment techniques are intended to ameliorate the impact of cell-loss experienced by statistically multiplexed VBR virtual circuits during occasional periods of network congestion. The impact of such cell losses on decoded video quality can be quite serious for MPEG video, since resulting artifacts tend to persist and disperse spatially due to motion compensated interframe prediction. When ATM was originally being planned, it was anticipated that video would require a relatively low cell-loss rate ($\sim 10^{-9}$), but recently developed decoder concealment algorithms for MPEG video [8] now make it possible to operate at cell-loss rate levels as high as $10^{-2} - 10^{-3}$. This means that VBR or VBR+ statistically multiplexed call admission control (CAC) procedures (corresponding to earlier discussions in Section 3.1) can be designed for significantly higher efficiencies.

In general, cell loss resilience can be provided by a combination of transport-layer/AAL functions for reliable identification of lost video data and receiver error concealment for mitigating the subjective impact on displayed video presented to the user. We focus here on the latter problem of error concealment, assuming the existence of an appropriate transport structure (which will be addressed in the Section 3.3). Figure 10 schematically shows a video decoder for ATM with cell loss detection and error concealment.

The ATM cells that arrive at the receiver contain compressed video data with a video AAL that has an appropriate error detection field such as a continuity counter for identification of lost data. The AAL information is extracted at the SAR/AAL block. When a cell-loss is detected, an appropriate "error token" is passed to the video decoder, which will then initiate concealment operations as needed. Once the temporal and spatial location(s) corresponding to lost cells is determined by the decoder, it will execute an error concealment procedure to replace lost picture areas with subjectively acceptable material estimated from available picture regions. In general, two basic approaches are used: temporal replacement and spatial interpolation. In temporal replacement, damaged blocks in the current frame are replaced by the spatially corresponding ones in the previously decoded data (decoder anchor frame) with motion compensation if motion information is available. In spatial interpolation, lost blocks are interpolated with data from spatially adjacent blocks (typically vertically adjacent, since a cell loss tends to affect a sequence of horizontal blocks). The Adaptive Spatio-temporal concealment block, shown in Figure 8, decides which concealment method (temporal replacement or spatial interpolation) should be used based on easily obtained measures of image activity from the neighboring (i.e., top and bottom) macroblocks. If local motion (indicated by the motion vectors), is smaller than spatial detail (computed from the pixel-domain variance), temporal replacement is used; when local motion is greater than local spatial detail, spatial interpolation is used. The algorithm first uses temporal replacement and then spatial interpolation since after temporal replacement it is more likely that spatially interpolated blocks will be surrounded by valid image blocks resulting in less blurring.

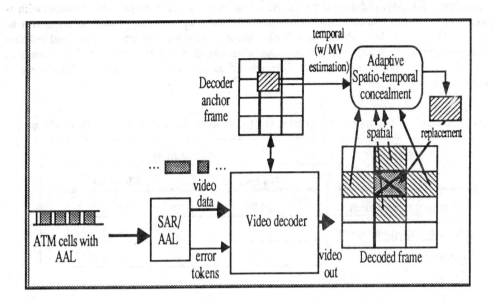

Figure 10. Receiver with cell-loss detection and decoder concealment.

In MPEG, I-frame errors, which are imperfectly concealed, tend to propagate through all frames in the Group of Pictures (GOP). Therefore, it is desirable to develop an enhancement to the basic spatio-temporal concealment to further improve the accuracy with which missing I-frame pixels are replaced. An enhancement to the adaptive spatio-temporal concealment has been proposed by H. Sun et al., [8]. Specifically, I-frame pseudo motion vectors are added in the encoder because motion information is very useful in concealing losses in P and B frames, but is not available for I-frames. It has been shown [8], that if motion vectors are made available for all MPEG frames (including intra-coded ones) as an aid for error concealment, the subjective picture quality is noticeably superior to conventional temporal replacement, and that the overhead for transmitting the additional motion vectors is less than 0.7% of the total bit-rate.

Simulation Results: We summarize some recent MPEG cell-loss concealment results from [8], which describes detailed simulation experiments for a number of alternative schemes. A 150 frame CCIR 601 test sequence was encoded using MPEG-1 (plus extensions where noted) with N=12, M=3 at 7 Mbps with slice size=15 MB. The MPEG-1 bit stream may either be transmitted with a single transmission quality, or be split into high priority (HP) and low priority (LP) streams with a 20%:80% bit-rate ratio. Video data is packed into fixed length cells with AAL headers for one- or two-tier transport, as appropriate. Cell losses are induced at the appropriate rate using a random, independent channel model.[4] In the two-tier case, the total cell loss rate is maintained constant with HP CLR=0 and LP cell loss rate=CLR/r (where r<1 is the fraction of LP data). Cell-loss rates (CLR) in the region of 10^{-1}

---

[4] The actual distribution of cell losses in ATM depends on link utilization. At high utilization, cell losses appear to be clustered [28]. However, the random model tends to be pessimistic if the cell loss run length is short enough to be confined to one or two MPEG slices.

to 10^{-3} have been considered, since lower CLR values cannot easily be evaluated due to relatively infrequent error events.

Table 3 compares the peak signal-to-noise ratio (PSNR) performance for the three basic concealment algorithms outlined above. Note that in the given example, concealment with I-motion vectors outperforms temporal replacement and adaptive spatio-temporal concealment by approximately 1 dB. Tables 4 and 5 also show comparisons of PSNR with and without (spatio-temporal) concealment in one-tier and two-tier MPEG transmission scenarios respectively. A more comprehensive comparison among these concealment algorithms is given in [8].

Table 3. Concealment Performance for Different Algorithms at High Cell-Loss Rate (Bus Sequence).

Method	PSNR (dB)	
	No loss	CLR of 10^{-2}
Temporal replacement	30.79	25.19
Adaptive spatio-temporal	30.79	25.67
I-motion vectors	30.75	26.84

Table 4. Concealment Performance for a One-Tier System at Different CLR Values
(Flower-Garden Sequence Encoded at 33.8 dB)

CLR	PSNR with concealment (dB)	PSNR without concealment (dB)
0.1	26.1	10.0
0.01	31.7	17.8
0.001	33.3	29.3

Table 5. Concealment Performance for a Two-Tier System at Different CLR Values
(Flower-Garden Sequence Encoded at 33.8 dB)

CLR	PSNR with concealment (dB)	PSNR without concealment (dB)
0.1	28.0	17.2
0.01	31.5	27.2
0.001	33.0	31.3

From the above simulation results, some observations can be made: first, in all cases cell-loss concealment provides significant PSNR improvement in decoded video relative to no concealment . At a cell loss rate of 0.1%, the typical concealment error in a one-tier system is quite small (<0.5 dB), with a maximum of 2 dB in certain isolated regions of the picture. The subjectively observed level of degradation at 0.1% CLR is probably acceptable for many applications. At 1% (10^{-2}) cell loss, degradations in the one-tier case are somewhat higher, and can be expected to produce visible picture impairments. Given that CLR is unlikely to exceed 0.1% in the majority of ATM scenarios (including statistically multiplexed VBR), one-tier MPEG video with decoder concealment should provide adequate robustness at the application level. Layered coding methods may be considered for ABR scenarios (without QoS guarantees), particularly in applications benefiting from multiresolution processing and display formats.

3.4 TRANSPORT PROTOCOLS FOR VIDEO

As discussed in Section 2, software based network multimedia applications will require a new generation of transport protocols capable of supporting video effectively. TCP, which was originally developed for packet switching scenarios, may be carried over to the ATM environment, but is limited in its applicability to stream-oriented and/or high-speed media transfers. The window-based retransmission mechanism in TCP may not be appropriate for video, which is more tolerant to errors than to delay variations. For example, if cell-loss concealment mechanisms similar to those discussed in Section 3.2 are available, then it may be acceptable to just pass the received packet stream to the video decoder along with suitable error tokens for data loss events. Also, in the high-speed network scenario, it may be preferable to decouple the error recovery process from receiver flow control and network congestion control mechanisms. Requirements such as these motivate new transport protocols capable of providing various error recovery modes and alternative receiver flow controls [40,41]. For example, it may be desirable to provide selective-reject packet retransmission with a maximum time limit on retransmissions of real-time media. Also, rate-based flow control may be better suited for connection-oriented services than the window flow control used in TCP. Another important transport layer issue is that of maintaining high terminal (host) i/o throughputs corresponding to peak ATM rates of 100 Mbps or more, thus motivating a lightweight protocol design with appropriate hardware support options.

The above considerations motivated us to develop the "multimedia transport protocol (MTP)" prototype for video and multimedia applications over ATM. This software prototype was experimentally evaluated on the ATM testbed at NEC USA's C&C Research Laboratories in Princeton, NJ. MTP is a lightweight stream-oriented transport protocol with a flexible, modular and lightweight implementation based on the use of a hardware ATM AAL. Table 6 compares the features of MTP with TCP and IP.

Table 6. Comparison of MTP Features with TCP and IP

Protocol Features	MTP	TCP	IP
Connection oriented	Yes	Yes	No
Message boundaries	optional	No	Yes
Data checksum	Yes[1]	Yes	No
Positive ACK	optional	Yes	No
Timeout & Retransmit	optional	Yes	No
Duplicate Detection	optional	Yes	No
SAR	optional	Yes	No
Flow Control	optional	Yes	No

1: CRC on TPDU Header bytes, optional CRC on entire payload.

Some of the major features of MTP include:

SELECTABLE RESPONSE TO CELL LOSS DUE TO CONGESTION OR ERRORS
*   Detect single cell losses.
*   Replace loss with single application supplied error token.
*   Report cell-loss-list for each PDU.
*   Optionally deliver corrupted PDU payload data to the application.
*   If a specified timeout hasn't expired, request retransmission of PDU segment.

The MTP and supporting AAL facilitate error control after detecting the loss of one or more cells on the channel. Depending upon the error characteristics of the losses due to statistical multiplexing, a standard AAL may not provide optimal error recovery. By identifying specific transport bundling information, the MTP can identify losses with cell-level resolution, and then select from appropriate recovery options including retransmission, retransmission with time-limit, delivery with error token, etc. To detect single cell losses, the MTP-AAL provides a continuity counter for loss detection over all cells within a PDU. A map of data loss is optionally provided to the upper layer software so that it can apply appropriate concealment algorithms to the missing data. Also provided is a means to segment an application PDU into a number of Transport PDUs (TPDU), and a means of reassembling TPDUs at the decoder. To support decoder concealment in an MPEG video decoder, MTP can emit an error token when a loss is detected.

WHERE SUPPORTED, DIRECT TO USER-SPACE COPY FOR TRANSMIT AND RECEIVE
Implementation of MTP under UNIX explores techniques for zero-copy transfers between kernel and user space. In some non-Unix systems without the distinction of kernel/user space, this feature is provided by default.

OPTIONALLY PROVIDE RATE-BASED FLOW CONTROL
Where flow control is a transport protocol requirement, MTP provides a side-channel signaling method to control the server transmission rate to a client. The flow control algorithms are experimental and are instrumented to study their performance. Both rate-based and window-based flow control methods are examined.

MTP AND AAL SYNTAX SPECIFICATIONS:
The MTP objectives require the detection of a single cell loss which is not possible using AAL5 and which is poorly supported in AAL1 through AAL4 (only a four-bit Sequence Number (SN) is available to detect loses). Also, the number of bytes used to define the AAL2 through AAL4 syntax is an unjustified overhead for the low error rate on ATM. Therefore, a custom AAL has been designed for MTP. PDU encapsulation is accomplished by segmenting the PDU into multiple transport units (TPDU), each with a header to define its place in the PDU. The MTP-AAL supports cell-level detection with a larger and more meaningful SN field than provided by AAL1 through AAL4; labeled the continuity counter (CC). Figure 11 shows how a PDU is segmented into multiple TPDU components.

TPDU HEADER COMPONENT DEFINITION
Each MTP packet (one TPDU) will contain the Base_MTP header followed by optional headers, dependent upon which modules were pushed on the MTP Streams stack. Decoding these headers assumes the receiver is configured with the same MTP modules, pushed on the stack in the same order, as the transmitter. Therefore, the header identification is not derived from the header data itself; the header definition is implied by the ordering of the selected MTP modules on the Streams stack. As shown in Figure 12, if the Start_of_TPDU flag is set in the MTP ALL Header, then one or more TPDU header fields exist in the TPDU header.

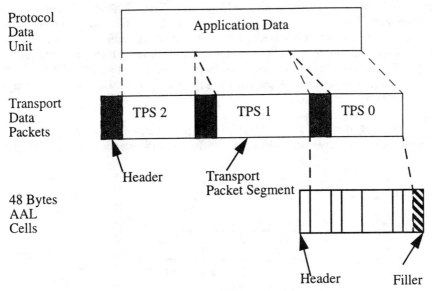

Figure 11. MTP PDU encapsulation.

UNIX STREAMS IMPLEMENTATION:

The Unix STREAMS programming model is used to support run-time configuration of the protocol stack. STREAMS is a collection of system calls, kernel resources and utilities that can create, use, and dismantle a "stream." A stream is a full-duplex processing and data transfer path between a process in user space and a device driver in kernel space. Each stream has three parts: a stream head, module(s), and a device driver. The user process typically interfaces with just the stream head. Any number of modules can be pushed on the stream, in last-in/first-out fashion. The modules, which reside in kernel space, operate on the data as it moves down to the driver or up to the user process. Using the STREAMS facility, a flexible protocol stack can be configured at run-time when connections are opened. Multiple MTP stacks would exist to meet the needs of each application, as illustrated in Figure 13.

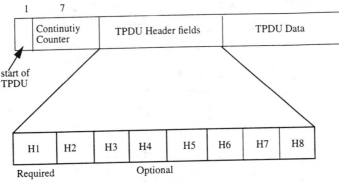

H1 : Base MTP Header
H2 : Rate-based Flow Control
H3 : Data CRC
H4 : Encryption
H5 : Window-based Flow Control
H6 : Error Recovery
H7 : TPDU SAR
H8 : N-Tier Sequencing

Figure 12. TPDU header fields in MTP.

Available MTP modules include: Cap MTP, Multi-Tier Sequencing Mux, transport Segmentation and Reassembly (SAR), Error Replacement/Identification, Error Recovery, Window-based Flow Control, Encryption, Data CRC, Rate-based Flow Control, Base MTP, and Rate & Error Measurement. Most of these modules have transport protocol header components. Future modules can be added to support application specific TP header bytes, and time stamping. Cell-level error detection is supported using a modified version of AAL 1 called the MTP-AAL or MAAL.

Preliminary throughput results for the MTP Streams stack running on an i960 processor with pSOS operating system have been obtained. Example performance numbers are given in Table 7.

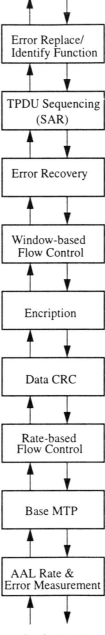

Figure 13. Example of MTP STREAMS stack.

Table 7. Preliminary Experimental Results for MTP on i960 Processor / pSOS / Streams

Experimental configuration	Throughput (RX)	Throughput (TX)
MTP= Cap, SAR, Base, Rate & Error Meas. Avg. PDU length = 64 KB, fixed Hardware AAL(2)	38 Mbps	75 Mbps
MTP= Cap, Base, Rate & Error Meas. Avg. PDU length = 64 KB, fixed Hardware AAL(2)	87 Mbps	105 Mbps

Concurrent with our development of MTP, a transport protocol for real-time applications, called RTP was proposed in the Internet community [42]. RTP provides end-to-end network transport functions. The data transport is augmented by a control protocol (RTCP) to allow monitoring of the data delivery in a manner scalable to large multicast networks, and to provide minimal control and identification functionality. RTP and RTCP are designed to be independent of the underlying transport and network layers. Since [42], RTP has matured and gained wide acceptance in the Internet [12]. For example, RTP payloads formats for MPEG video have been proposed in [43].

We are currently consolidating the functionality provided by MTP and RTP and evaluating the resulting performance in the context of adaptive multimedia applications.

4. CONCLUDING REMARKS

In this chapter, we have provided a system design perspective for integration of video into a network-based multimedia computing scenario. An overall system architecture was presented and key subsystems were identified and discussed in the context of video support. Selected research results on specific design issues including VBR/ATM interface, dynamic QoS, cell loss concealment and multimedia/video transport protocol were given. While progress has been made on a number of technical issues, further work on ATM, network interface and terminal/video server hardware and software will be required to reach a highly functional and efficient system design.

REFERENCES

[1] International Organization for Standardization, Generic Coding of Moving Pictures and Associated Audio, ISO/IEC/JTC1/SC29/WG11, March 1993.

[2] ATM Forum, ATM User-Network Interface Specification, Version 3.0. Prentice-Hall, 1993.

[3] IEEE Journal on Selected Areas in Communications, Special Issue on Packet Video and Voice, SAC-7 (No.5), June 1989.

[4] ATM Forum, Technical Working Group, SAA Audio-visual Multimedia Service (AMS) Implementation Agreement, Contribution 95-0012, Burlingame, California, February 1995.

[5] MPEG-2 Systems Committee, MPEG-2 Systems Working Draft, ISO/IEC/JTC1/SC29/WG11-N0501, Seoul, July 1993.

[6] D. Reininger, G. Ramamurthy, and D. Raychaudhuri, "Feedback Enhanced Multimedia Communications over ATM," IEEE Workshop on Visual Signal Processing & Communications, Rutgers University, New Jersey, Sept. 1994.

[7] H. Kanakia, P. Mishra, and A. Reibman, "An Adaptive Congestion Control Scheme for Real-Time Packet Video Transport," in Proceedings of SIGCOMM'93, Ithaca, N.Y., ACM, New York, September 1993, pp. 20-31

[8] H. Sun, W. Kwok, J. Zdepski, and D. Raychaudhuri, "Concealment of damaged block transform coded images using projection onto convex sets," IEEE Trans. on Image Processing, Vol. 4, 1993, pp. 470-474.

[9] M. Ghanbari, "Two-layer Coding of Video signals for VBR networks," IEEE Journal on Selected Areas in Communications, June 1989, SAC-7 (No 5), pp. 771-781.

[10] T. Sikora and L. Chiariglione, "MPEG-4 video and its potential for future multimedia services," Proceedings of 1997 IEEE International Symposium on Circuits and Systems. Circuits and Systems in the Information Age, ISCAS'97, pp. 1468-1471, Hong Kong, June 1997.

[11] C. Topolcic, "Experimental Internet Stream Protocol, Version 2 (ST-II)," RFC 1190, University of Southern California, USC Information Sciences Institute, October 1990.

[12] H. Schulzrinne, S. Casner, R. Frederick, and V. Jacobson, "RTP: A Transport Protocol for Real-Time Applications," IETF Network Working Group RFC 1889, January 1996.

[13] R. Siracusa, K. Joseph, J. Zdepski, and D. Raychaudhuri, "Flexible and Robust Packet Transport for Digital HDTV," *IEEE J. Selected Areas in Comm.*, January 1993, pp. 88-98.

[14] J.D. Northcutt, "Mechanisms for Reliable Distributed Real-Time Operating Systems: The Alpha Kernel," Academic Press, Boston, MA, 1987.

[15] C. Mercer, "Operating System Support for Multimedia Applications," in Proceedings of Multimedia '94, San Francisco, California, October 1994.

[16] V. Bansal, R. Siracusa, J. Hern, G. Ramamurthy, and D. Raychaudhuri, "Adaptive QoS-based API for ATM Networking," in Proceedings of 5th International Workshop on Network and Operating System Support for Digital Audio and Video (NOSSDAV'95), Durham N.H, April 1995, ACM, New York, pp. 299-302.

[17] M. Ott, G. Michelitsch, D. Reininger, and G. Welling, "An Architecture for Adaptive QoS and its Application to Multimedia System Design," the Special Issue of Computer Communications on Building Quality of Service into Distributed Systems.

[18] D. Flanagan, "Java in a Nutshell," O'Reilly & Associates, Inc., 1996.

[19] H. Ghafir and H. Chadwick, "Multimedia Servers – Design and Performance," in Proceedings of 1994 IEEE Globecom, San Francisco, November 1994.

[20] J. Hui, J. Zhang, J. Li, "Quality of Service Control in GRAMS for ATM Local Area Network," to appear, IEEE J. Selected Areas of Communications, 1995.

[21] M. Trembley, "The Visual Instruction Set (VIS) in UltraSPARC," Compcon 95, 5-9, 1995.

[22] O. Lempel, A. Peleg, and U. Weiser, "Intel's MMX Technology - A New Instruction Set Extension," Compcon Spring 97 Forty-Second IEEE Computer Society International Conference Proceedings, pp. 255-259, 1997.

[23] M. Ikekawa, D. Ishii, E. Murata, K. Numata, Y. Takamizawa, and M. Tanaka, "A Real-time Software MPEG-2 Decoder for Multimedia PCs," 1997 IEEE International Conference on Consumer Electronics, Chicago, IL, pp. 2-3, April 97.

[24] J. D. Northcutt, "A High Resolution Video Workstation," Sun Microsystems Laboratories, Technical Report SMLI-92-0056, 1992.

[25] S. Wray, T. Galuert, and A. Hopper, "Networked Multimedia: The Medusa Environment," IEEE Multimedia Magazine, Winter 1994, pp. 54-63.

[26] W. Verbiest, L. Pinnoo, and B. Voeten, "The Impact of the ATM Concept on Video Coding," IEEE J. Selected Areas in Communications, SAC-6, (No 9), pp. 1623-1632, December 1988.

[27] F. Kishino and K. Manabe, "Variable bitrate coding of video signals for ATM networks," IEEE J. Selected Areas in Communications, SAC-7, (No 5), pp. 801-806, June 1989.

[28] D. Reininger, D. Raychaudhuri, B. Melamed, and B. Sengupta, "Statistical Multiplexing of VBR MPEG Compressed Video on ATM Networks," Proceedings of INFOCOM'93, San Francisco, March 1993.

[29] D. Reininger, G. Ramamurthy, and D. Raychaudhuri, "VBR MPEG Video Coding with Dynamic Bandwidth Renegotiation," in Proceedings of 1995 IEEE International Conference on Communications, ICC'95, June 1995, Seattle, WA.

[30] D. Reininger, Y. Senda, and H. Harasaki, "VBR MPEG-2 encoder for ATM networks with UPC renegotiation," in Proceedings of the 7th International Workshop on Packet Video, Brisbane, Australia, March 1996.

[31] CCITT, "Traffic control and congestion control in B-ISDN," Recommendation I.371, Geneva, June 1992.

[32] H. Harasaki and M. Yano, "A Study on VBR Coder Control Under Usage Parameter Control," in Proceedings of Fifth International Packet Video Workshop, Berlin, Germany, March 1993.

[33] MPEG Software Simulation Group, MPEG-L@netcom.com.

[34] S. Mukherjee, D. Reininger, and B. Sengupta, "An Adaptive Connection Admission Control Policy for VBR+ Service Class," Proceedings of IEEE INFOCOM'98, March 1998.

[35] D. Reininger, D. Raychaudhuri, and J. Hui, "Dynamic Bandwidth Allocation for VBR Video over ATM networks," IEEE Journal on Selected Areas in Communications, 14(6):1076-1086, August 1996.

[36] G. Ramamurthy, D. Raychaudhuri, and D. Reininger, "VBR MPEG Video Encoder for ATM Networks with Dynamic Bandwidth Renegotiation," United States Patent 5,675,384, October 1997.

[37] S. Biswas, D. Reininger, and D. Raychaudhuri, "Bandwidth Allocation for VBR Video in Wireless ATM Links," in Proceeding of IEEE International Conference on Communications, ICC'97, Montreal, Canada, June 1997.

[38] The ATM Forum, "ATM User-Network Interface (UNI) signaling specification," ATM Forum/95-1434R11, February 1996.

[39] ITU-T, "Peak cell rate modification by the connection owner," ITU-T Q.2963.1, July 1996.

[40] A. Feldmeier, "An Overview of the TP++ Transport Protocol Project," High Performance Networks - Frontiers and Experience, Kluwer Academic Publishers, pp. 157-176, 1993.

[41] B. Cheriton, "VMTP: A transport protocol for the next generation of computer systems," Proceedings of ACM SIGCOMM '86 Symposium, 1986.

[42] H. Schulzrinne, S. Casner, R. Frederick, and V. Jacobson, "RTP: A Transport Protocol for Real-Time Applications," Internet Draft, March 21st, 1995.

[43] D. Hoffman and V. Goyal, "RTP Payload Format for MPEG1/MPEG2 Video," Internet Draft, June 1995.

39

QUALITY OF SERVICE IN NETWORKED MULTIMEDIA SYSTEMS

Klara Nahrstedt
Department of Computer Science
University of Illinois at Urbana-Champaign
Urbana, Illinois 61801

1. **INTRODUCTION**...840
    1.1 REQUIREMENTS AND CONSTRAINTS 840
    1.2 PROCESSING AND COMMUNICATION CONSTRAINTS 841
    1.3 QUALITY OF SERVICE DEFINITION...................................841
    1.4 RESOURCE...846
    1.5 RESOURCE MANAGEMENT ARCHITECTURE............................846
    1.6 RELATION BETWEEN QoS AND RESOURCES 847
2. **QOS SERVICES DURING ESTABLISHMENT OF A MULTIMEDIA CALL** 848
    2.1 QoS NEGOTIATION 848
    2.2 TRANSLATION..851
    2.3 SCALING..853
    2.4 ADMISSION CONTROL..854
    2.5 RESERVATION/ALLOCATION ACCORDING TO QoS REQUIREMENTS.............856
3. **QOS ENFORCEMENT SERVICES DURING MULTIMEDIA
    TRANSMISSION**..859
    3.1 TRAFFIC SHAPING...859
    3.2 RATE CONTROL 861
    3.3 END-TO-END ERROR CONTROL 863
    3.4 QoS AND RESOURCE MONITORING....................................866
    3.5 QoS RENEGOTIATION AND ADAPTATION..............................867
4. **QOS ARCHITECTURES**...870
5. **CONCLUSION** 871
    REFERENCES 871

Abstract. Currently, the telecommunication industry undergoes fundamental changes due to challenges to support multimedia communication. These challenges come from new media such as audio, video, haptic data that have very different temporal and spatial requirements from traditional data and text information. Particularly, their requirements for quality of service (QoS) and guarantees in end-to-end fashion will need to be satisfied. The reason is that the quality of multimedia delivery over data networks competes with the quality of radio and television services which the users already know and are used to their quality.

In this chapter we present QoS-based services and protocols, and concepts and algorithms for provision of end-to-end QoS guarantees in multimedia networked systems. We present frameworks and possible solutions for the above-described challenges.

1. INTRODUCTION

1.1 REQUIREMENTS AND CONSTRAINTS

The users/applications utilizing Networked Multimedia Systems (NMS) put heterogeneous requirements on their services and protocols.

The requirements span from (1) **time-sensitive requests**, (2) **high data throughput**, (3) **service guarantees**, (4) **high or partial reliability** requests with timing constraints, to (5) **cost-based fairness** decision.

The **time-sensitive requirements** are important because the audio/video communication needs to be bounded by deadlines or even defined by a time interval. This requirement then implies that end-to-end jitter must be bounded, synchronization skews among dependent streams must be bounded, or end-to-end delay for conversational applications must be bounded.

High data throughput requirement comes from the video representation of images and its stream-like behavior. This behavior can represent a long-lived requirement in case of applications such as video-on-demand or video conferencing. Even in compressed form, audio-visual streams demand high throughput from a workstation or a network.

The **service guarantees requirement** means that processing and communication services must provide guarantees during the whole time the audio-visual media are processed and communicated within applications. This means that the time-sensitive requirements and the high-throughput might be provided and sustained over a long period of time, which is very different from previous data applications. Furthermore, different shapes of the network traffic produced by heterogeneous multimedia applications cause difficulties. The applications require that the NMS accommodates the bursty shape of the audio-visual streams and provides in addition to CBR (constant bit rate) traffic guarantees, also VBR (variable bit rate) traffic service provision.

High or partial reliability requirement with timing constraints is an important request on the NMS because the traditional systems until now supported either unreliable or highly reliable processing and communication without any timing constraints. However, the various multimedia applications require mostly at least a partial reliability to provide a good service quality and some high-quality video applications require high-reliability with timing constraints.

Cost-based fairness requirement is triggered by the request for quality and resources allocated to provide timing and throughput service guarantees. The applications may request that if they pay the corresponding resource cost for its requested quality, then the quality of the audio-visual streams should be delivered to the applications. This means that the fairness principle to let every application process and communicate through FIFO queues will not apply here because in this case the timing requirements of the audio-visual streams could be violated. However, some fairness should be enforced between the sharing of the resources between the time-sensitive and no time-sensitive applications so that the communication of discrete data does not starve.

1.2 PROCESSING AND COMMUNICATION CONSTRAINTS
Due to the layered communication architectures, processing and communication services and protocols, have on the contrary, several constraints which need to be considered when we want to match user/application requirements onto the system and communication platform. The constraints span from (1) **limitations in data movement**, (2) **segmentation and reassembly**, to (3) **retransmission error-recovery** mechanisms.

The **data movement constraint** needs to be considered because protocols involve a lot of data movements through the layered communication architecture. However, copying is expensive and has become a bottleneck, therefore new mechanisms for buffer management must be found.

Due to the layered architecture, different layers of the communication system may have different PDUs (Protocol Data Unit) sizes, therefore a **segmentation and reassembly** must occur. This phase must be done quickly and efficiently.

Some parts of protocols may use **retransmission error-recovery** mechanism, which imposes requirements on buffer space for queues at the expense of larger end-to-end delays. This constraint must be considered when requesting the granularity of end-to-end timing guarantees.

1.3 QUALITY OF SERVICE DEFINITION
The user/application requirements on the NMS need to be mapped into services, which then make the effort to satisfy the requirements. Because of the heterogeneity of the requirements, coming from different distributed multimedia applications, the services in the NMS must be *parametrized*. Parameterization of requirements as well as of underlying services allows for flexibility, and customization of the services, resulting in quality-controllable services so that classes of system and communication services can be developed and each application does not result in implementing of a new set of service providers.

Parameterization of the services was defined in ISO (International Standard Organization) standards through the notion of Quality of Service (**QoS**). The ISO standard defined QoS as a concept for specifying how ``good'' the offered networking services are. This concept was further developed and several new QoS considerations emerged: (1) **layering of QoS**, (2) **service objects parameterized by QoS**, (3) **QoS description**, (4) **QoS parameter values and types of service**, and (5) **relation between QoS, resources and their management**.

1.3.1. QoS Layering
Traditional QoS (ISO standards) was provided by the network layer of the communication system. An enhancement of QoS was achieved through inducing QoS into transport services. For NMS, the QoS concept must be extended because many services in other layers than just network and transport services contribute to the end-to-end service quality. Therefore, we need a *layered* QoS model, which aligns with the layered communication architecture of NMS. We assume throughout this section that our NMS and QoS models comply with the layered architecture shown in Figure 1.

The NMS consists of four layers: *user, application, system* (including communication services and operating system services), and *devices* (network and MultiMedia (MM) devices). Note that individual layers can have sublayers and with them connected QoS parameters, if necessary. However, as the requirements above suggest, too many layers in communication architecture impose a large performance overhead, hence low end-to-end quality, and violation of user/application requirements on multimedia processing and communication. Above the application may or may not reside a human user.

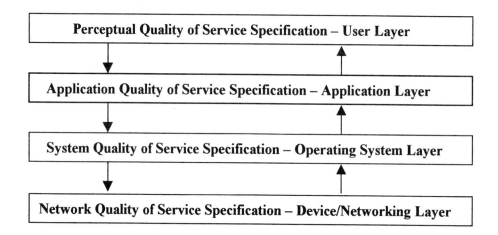

Figure 1. Layered QoS Model for the NMS.

In our further discussion, we will concentrate on the application, system and device layers and with them connected QoS parameters. This means that we will consider *application* QoS, system QoS, and network QoS parameters. In the case of having a human user, the NMS may also have a *perceptual* QoS specification. We concentrate in the network layer on the network device and its QoS because it is of interest to us in the NMS. The MM devices find their representation in application QoS.

1.3.2 Service Objects

Services are performed on different objects, for example, media sources, media sinks, tasks, connections and Virtual Circuits (VCs); hence, the QoS parameterization reflects these *service objects*. In ISO standards, the QoS description is meant to be for services, processing a transport/network connection. In Tenet protocol suite, the services operate over a **real-time channel** of a packet switched network [FeVe90]. In Lancaster's Multimedia Enhanced Transport System (METS), a QoS parameter specification is given for **call, connection and VC** objects [CaCoHu93]. In Resource Reservation Protocol (RSVP), a flow specification is given for parameterization of the **packet scheduling mechanism** in the routers or hosts [ZDESZ93]. At higher layers in communication systems, the service objects, for example, **media** [NaSm95] or streams [Stei93b] may be specified. In operating systems (OS), which are integral parts in provision of the end-to-end quality guarantees, the QoS objects such as **tasks** [LeRaMe96, ChuNa97], or **memory chunks** [NChN97] must be characterized to control the CPU bandwidth and pinned memory availability.

1.3.3 QoS Specification

The set of chosen parameters for the particular service determines what will be measured as the QoS. Most of the current QoS parameters differ from the parameters described in ISO because of the heterogeneity of (1) applications, (2) media, (3) networks, and (4) end-systems. The traditional ISO network layer QoS parameters included the **throughput, delay, error rate, secrecy** and **cost**. The transport layer QoS parameters included **connection establishment delay, connection establishment failure, throughput, transit delay, residual error rate, transfer failure probability, connection release delay, connection release failure probability, protection, priority** and **resilience**. These parameters were expanded according to the layered model and led to many different QoS parameterizations in the literature. We give here one possible set of QoS parameters for each layer of NMS.

The *application QoS parameters* describe requirements for the application services possibly specified in terms of (1) media **quality**, which includes the media characteristics and their transmission characteristics, such as end-to-end delay, frame rate, jitter, and (2) **media relations**, which specify the relations among media, such as media conversion or inter/intra stream synchronization [NaSm95, KiNa97].

System QoS parameters describe requirements on the communication services and OS services resulting from the application QoS. They may be specified in terms of both **quantitative** and **qualitative** criteria. *Quantitative criteria* are those which can be evaluated in terms of concrete measures, such as bits per second, number of errors, task processing time, task period, PDU size, etc. The QoS parameters include throughput, delay, response time, rate, data corruption at the system level, and task and buffer specification [NaSm96, KiNa97]. *Qualitative criteria* specify the expected functions needed for provision of QoS, such as interstream synchronization, ordered delivery of data, error-recovery mechanism, scheduling mechanism, etc. The expected services can be associated with specific parameters. For example, the interstream synchronization can be defined through an acceptable synchronization skew within the particular data stream [Stei93b]. Qualitative criteria can be used by the **coordination control** to invoke proper services for particular applications.

Network QoS parameters describe requirements on low level network services. They may be specified in terms of: (1) **network load**, describing the ongoing network traffic and characterized through *average/minimal interarrival* time on the network connection, *burstiness, packet/cell size* and *service time* in the node for the connection's packet/cell [FeVe90}] and (2) **network performance**, describing the requirements which the network services must guarantee. Performance might be expressed through a source-to-destination delay bound for the connection's packet and packet loss rate [FeVe90]. Generally, performance bounds are chosen for QoS parameters, such as latency, bandwidth, or delay-jitter, where delay jitter is the maximum difference between end-to-end delays experienced by any two packets [ZhKe91], but also other parameters for control of QoS (e.g., priority). Note that network services depend on a **traffic model** (arrival of connection requests) and perform according to **traffic envelope** with parameters, such as average and peak data rate or burst length. Hence, calculated traffic parameters are dependent on network QoS parameters and specified in a **traffic contract**.

Device QoS parameters typically specify timing and throughput demands for media data units given by audio/video devices such as audio speakers, or video capture board.

As a concrete example for a layered QoS model, we will discuss application and system QoS parameters for MPEG compressed video streams [KiNa97] (see Table 1). Note, that the application QoS is quite complex to express the source coding and to capture the compression algorithm behavior, which produces the input and output to and from the system and network layers. In Table 1, we provide the symbol description of the QoS parameters because later on we will use this example to illustrate QoS translation and other relations in the overall QoS management.

Note that the classification of the QoS specification as described above happens due to our layered NMS model. However, there is also another aspect which one has to considered when specifying QoS parameters: Individual quality parameters need to be classified into

input and **output QoS** parameters. Most of the APIs (Application Programming Interfaces) require inputting, as a quality parameter, the requested output QoS value, but do not consider the actual input quality. However, it is important what is the input QoS, so that the service can react and achieve the requested output QoS. For example, if a *display task* receives from a digitizer only 10 frames per second as the input sample rate, it is not semantically possible and feasible to display 30 frames per second as the output sample rate. The relation between the input and output QoS might be defined through a **service curve** [Cruz97] or a **reward profile** [Liu97]. This relation then allows for decisions on how to reach output quality starting from the input quality.

Table 1. Application and System QoS Parameters for MPEG Video Stream

QoS type	Specification	QoS parameter	Symbol
Application QoS	*Processing requirements*	Sample Size	M_A
		Different Sample Sizes for I, P, B Frames	M_A^I , M_A^P , M_A^B
		Sample Rate	R_A
		Number of Frames Per GOP	G
		Compression Pattern	G_I , G_P , G_I
		Original Size of GOP	M_G
		Processing Size of GOP	M'_G
		Degradation Factor	D
	Communication requirements	End-to-end Delay	E_A
		Synchronization Skew	$Sync_A$
System QoS	*CPU requirements*	Processing Time	C
		Cycle Time	T
		CPU Utilization	U
	Memory requirements	Memory Space Request	Mem_{req}
	Communication requirements	Packet Size	M_N
		Packet Rate	R_N
		Bandwidth	B_N
		End-to-end Delay	E_N

1.3.4 QoS Parameter Values and Types Service

The specification of QoS parameter values determines the types of service. There are at least three types of service distinguished: *guaranteed, predictive* and *best-effort* services.

Guaranteed services provide QoS guarantees, as specified through the QoS parameter values (bounds) either in **deterministic** or **statistical** representation. The **deterministic** QoS parameters can be represented by a real number at certain time, it means:

$$QoS \; : T \; \rightarrow \; R$$

where T is a time domain representing the lifetime of a service, during which QoS should hold, and R is the domain of real numbers representing the value of the QoS parameter. The overall QoS deterministic bounds can be specified either by a **single value** (e.g., average value, contractual value, threshold value, target value), a **pair of values** $[QoS_{min}$, $QoS_{max}]$(e.g., minimum and average value, lowest quality and target quality) which can represent an **interval of values** with lower bound as the minimum value and upper bound as the maximum value ($QoS_{min} \leq QoS(t) \leq QoS_{max}$). For example, ATM Fore network allows specifying a pair of values for bandwidth requirement (B) with $B_N^{min} \leq B \leq B_N^{max}$. The pair value specification divides the QoS range into **acceptable quality regions** $QoS^{min} \leq QoS(t) \leq QoS^{max}$ and **unacceptable quality regions** $QoS(t) < QoS^{min}$ as shown in Figure 2. The overall QoS can be also specified by a **triple of values** such as best value QOS_{max}, average value QoS_{ave}, and worst value QoS_{min} with $QoS_{min} \leq QoS_{ave} \leq QoS_{max}$.

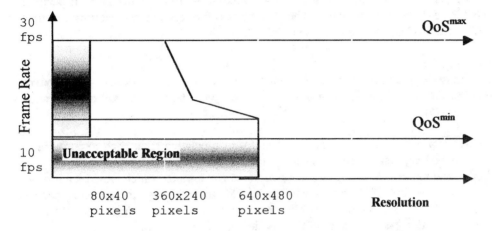

Figure 2. Range representation of QoS parameters.

Guaranteed services may also deal with **statistical** bounds of QoS parameters [FeVe90], such as statistical bound on error rate, bandwidth and other QoS parameters. For example, the requirement for bandwidth parameter value might be represented as $P(B \leq B_N^{max}) = p$.

A *predictable service* (historical service) is based on past network behavior, hence the QoS parameter bounds are estimates of past behavior which the service tries to match [CSZ92]. For example, if bandwidth $B_N^{predict}$ was calculated as an average of the bandwidth which the service provided in the past, i.e., $B_N^{predict} = 1/n \ (\sum B_N^I)$, where I=1,...,n, B_N^I are previous (history) values, then the predictable service could promise to provide bandwidth B_N with $B_N \leq B_N^{predict}$.

In this example, the history values taken into account of $B_N^{predict}$ are from the start of the communication. One also could predict the QoS values based on a recent history. For example, if L is the length of the sliding bandwidth history window, then

$$B_N^{predict} = 1/L(\sum_{i=0}^{L} B_N^{n-i})$$

Best-effort services are services based on either no guarantees, or on partial guarantees. There is either no specification of QoS parameters required, or a bound in deterministic or statistical forms is given. Most of the current network protocols have best effort services.

In our further discussion about the QoS guarantees, we will concentrate on *guaranteed services*.

Note that various systems may provide different classifications of services:

- An example is the classification of **integrated services** in the current proposal of the **modified Internet architecture** [BCS94]. The Internet integrated services consider in addition to **best-effort** and **real-time services** (guaranteed service), also a service such as the **controlled link sharing** as a part of the service model.
- Another example is the classification of ATM (Asynchronous Transfer Mode) services [Ke97]. The ATM communication architecture considers currently the **Constant Bit Rate** (CBR), **Variable Bit Rate** (VBR), **Available Bit Rate** (ABR), and **Unspecified Bit Rate** (UBR) service classes. The VBR class is further refined supporting real-time VBR traffic class and non-real-time VBR traffic class.

1.4 RESOURCE

When discussing provision of QoS, one must consider **resources** because the **resource availability** determines the actual quality of service which the network, OS or application deliver [NaSt95].

A *resource* is a system entity required by tasks for manipulating data. Each resource has a set of distinguishing characteristics [StNa95] and they can be classified as follows:
- **active** and **passive** resources. An active resource is a resource which provides a service. Examples are the CPU or the network adapter for protocol processing. A passive resource denotes system capability required by active resources. Examples are the main memory (buffer space) or bandwidth (link throughput).
- **exclusive** and **shared** resources. An exclusive resource is allocated to only one task. An example is a speaker. A shared resource is allocated to multiple tasks and is shared among them. An example is network bandwidth, which is shared among various network tasks.
- **single** and **multiple** resource. A single resource exists only once in a computer system. An example is a video digitizer card in a PC. A multiple resource has multiple copies of itself in a computer system. An example is the CPU in a transputer-based multiprocessor system.

Services for networked multimedia applications need resources to perform their functions. Of special interest are resources, which are single in an end-system of the NMS, and shared among application, system and network, such as CPU cycles, or network bandwidth. The considered resource can be passive or active. It is important to point out that individual resources used in each layer of the NMS (application, system, network) can be mapped into four main system resources such as the **bandwidth of communication channels**, **disk bandwidth**, **memory space** and **CPU bandwidth**.

1.5 RESOURCE MANAGEMENT ARCHITECTURE

Resources are managed by various components of a resource management subsystem in a networked multimedia system. The main goal of resource management in NMS is to provide the requested end-to-end output QoS which means for the NMS to provide guaranteed delivery of multimedia data. The guaranteed service and the provision of end-to-end QoS require from the resource management at least three main actions:

1. **reserve** and **allocate** resources (end-to-end) during a multimedia call establishment so that traffic can flow according to the QoS specification, which means distribution and negotiation of the QoS specification to system components involved in the data transfer from the source(s) to the sink(s);
2. **provide** and **enforce** resources reserved according to the QoS specification, which means adhering to resource allocation during multimedia delivery, using traffic shaping and proper scheduling service disciplines; and
3. **adapt** to resource changes during on-going multimedia data processing.

Resources are managed by various components of the resource management subsystem in the NMS. Figure 3 shows possible design architecture. The resource management subsystem includes **resource managers** called *resource brokers* at the hosts as well as the network nodes such as the communication broker, disk broker, memory broker and CPU broker [NChN97]. The resource brokers with their resource servers provide individual QoS guarantees over shared resources such as bandwidth disk, memory and CPU. **Resource management protocols** are used to exchange information about resources among the resource management components and coordinate the resource among each other. The **QoS broker** entities between the underlying resource management and the applications allow for QoS translation, QoS negotiation, and coordination among various resources. The specific tasks of the resource brokers, QoS brokers and their protocols are discussed in the next subsections.

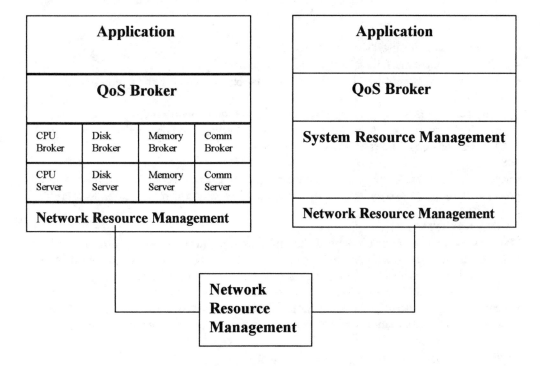

Figure 3. Resource management architecture for NMS.

1.6 RELATION BETWEEN QoS AND RESOURCES

The requested output QoS parameters are dependent on the input quality and the resource quantity allocated to the services, as well as on the service disciplines managing the shared resource in NMS. According to the requested output QoS parameters, we can determine how many resources are required to achieve it. For example, the requested end-to-end delay QoS parameter determines the behavior of transmission services along the path between media source and sink with respect to packet scheduling (bandwidth allocation), queuing (buffer allocation) and task scheduling (CPU processing time allocation).

The above described relation between QoS and resources is embedded in the form of different mappings, service curves and profiles between QoS parameters and their corresponding resources in the resource management. The below-described protocol shows the QoS and resource relations. Consider an application client, which requests a resource allocation by specifying its requirements through an application QoS specification. This QoS specification is translated by a **QoS broker** entity into the system QoS and their required resources. The required resources are equivalent to a reservation request. The **resource broker** checks its own resource utilization and decides if the reservation request can be served or not. All existing reservations are stored. This way their share in terms of the respective resource capacity is guaranteed. Moreover, the QoS broker component negotiates and coordinates the reservation request with other resource brokers, if necessary. Once the resource reservation/allocation is performed, another set of QoS services and protocols is needed to enforce the QoS-based reservation.

2. QoS SERVICES DURING ESTABLISHMENT OF A MULTIMEDIA CALL

Before any transmission with QoS guarantees in NMS can be performed, several steps must be executed:

- the application (or user) defines the required application QoS;
- QoS parameters must be distributed and negotiated;
- QoS parameters between different layers must be translated if their representation is different;
- QoS parameters must be mapped to the resource requirements; and
- required resources must be admitted/reserved/allocated and coordinated along the path between sender(s) and receiver(s).

These steps are performed during **multimedia call establishment**. The *close-down procedure*, from the resource management point of view, concerns resource **deallocation**.

2.1 QoS NEGOTIATION

If we assume that the user has defined the multimedia application QoS requirements, these requirements must be distributed to the resource management entities of all involved system components. The distribution of QoS parameters requires two major services: **negotiation of QoS parameters** and **translation of QoS parameters** (if different QoS specification of system components occurs). To characterize an actual negotiation, we specify the *parties* who participate in negotiation and the *protocols* of how the parties negotiate.

There are really two parties to any QoS negotiation. We will consider **peer-to-peer negotiation**, which can be, for example, application-to-application negotiation, and **layer-to-layer communication**, which might be, for example, application-to-system negotiation or human-user-to-application negotiation.

The purpose of the negotiation is to establish common QoS parameter values among the service users (peers) and service providers (underlying layers). We present negotiation of QoS parameters where the QoS parameter values are specified with single or pair deterministic bounds (minimal value QoS_{min} and average value QoS_{ave}). Note, that in some systems when user cannot specify QoS parameters immediately, negotiation protocols can apply **probing service** [NHK96] first, to learn what kind of bounds the system can provide at all, and then, use the learned quality values to start real negotiation. Probing service allows sending a probe message, which does not have any QoS specification through the measured system and as the probe gets processed, it captures its resource requirements which can be further translated to QoS requirements. The probe returns to the sender with suggested (estimated) QoS requirements, which can be used in the negotiation and reservation process.

There are several possibilities of negotiation among the peers (caller, callee) and the service provider:

- **Bilateral Peer-to-Peer Negotiation**

This type of negotiation takes place between two peers, and the service provider is not allowed to modify the QoS value proposed by the service user. Only the receiving service user can modify the requested QoS value (QoS_{ave}^{req}) and suggest a lower bound ($QoS_{ave}^{confirm} \leq QoS_{ave}^{req}$) which should be in the acceptable range of the application.

- **Bilateral Layer-to-Layer Negotiation**

This type of negotiation takes place only between the service user and service provider. This negotiation covers two possible communications: (1) between local service users and providers, (e.g., negotiation between application and OS services), and (2) between host-sender and the network, (e.g., negotiation between host-sender and the network provider when the sender wants to broadcast multimedia streams).

- **Unilateral Negotiation**

In this negotiation, the service provider, as well as the called service user, are not allowed to change the QoS parameters proposed by the calling user. This negotiation is reduced to "take it or leave it" [DaBo93]. Further, this negotiation allows the case in which the receiver may take the proposed QoS and, although may not have the capability to accommodate the QoS parameters, it can modify the host-receiver and participate with lower quality on the communication. A similar case occurs in TV broadcasting. The color TV signal broadcasts the signal uniformly to every user, but users with black and white TVs can still watch the TV program, i.e., the control of the quality is done at the receiver device.

- **Hybrid Negotiation**

In the case of broadcast/multicast communication, every participating host-receiver may have different capabilities from the host-sender, but still wants to participate in the communication (e.g., conference). Hence, between host-sender and network, the QoS parameter values can be negotiated using bilateral layer-to-layer negotiation. The unilateral negotiation occurs between network and host-receiver as described above.

- **Triangular Negotiation for Information Exchange**

In this type of negotiation, the calling user requests the average value of a QoS parameter(QoS_{ave}^{req}). This value can be changed by the service provider (QoS_{ave}^{sp})/callee (QoS_{ave}^{ca}) along the path through an indication/response primitive before presenting the final value ($QoS_{ave}^{confirm} \leq QoS_{ave}^{ca} \leq QoS_{ave}^{sp} \leq QoS_{ave}^{req}$)in the confirm primitive to the caller. At the end of the negotiation, all parties have the same QoS parameter value.

- **Triangular Negotiation for a Bounded Target**

This is the same type of negotiation as the previous one, only the values of a QoS parameter are represented through two bounds: target (average value QoS_{ave}^{req}), and the lowest quality acceptable (minimal value QoS_{min}). The goal is to negotiate the target value $QoS^{target} = QoS_{ave}^{confirm} \geq QoS_{min}$, i.e., the service provider (*sp*) is not allowed to change the value of the lowest quality (if it cannot provide at least the lowest quality, then the connection request is immediately rejected), but it is free to modify the target value ($QoS^{sp}=QoS^{target}$): $QoS_{min} \leq QoS_{ave}^{sp} \leq QoS_{ave}^{req}$. The callee will make the final decision concerning the selected value of the target $QoS_{min} \leq QoS_{ave}^{target} \leq QoS_{ave}^{sp}$. This selected value of the QoS will be returned to the caller by the confirm primitive [DaBo93] ($QoS^{target} = QoS_{ave}^{confirm}$).

- **Triangular Negotiation for a Contractual Value**

In this case, the QoS parameters are specified through a minimal requested value QoS_{min}^{req} and bound of strengthening $QoS_{bound} > QoS_{min}^{req}$. The goal of this negotiation is to agree on a contractual value $QoS_{contract}$, which in this case is the minimal request QoS parameter value ($QoS_{min}^{req} \leq QoS^{contract} = QoS_{min}^{confirm} \leq QoS_{bound}$). The service provider can modify the minimal request value towards the strengthening bound value. The callee makes the final decision and reports with a response/confirm primitive to the caller. The contractual value can also be the maximal QoS parameter value, or threshold [DaBo93] values, which the service user wants to achieve as a contract value.

There already exist several **multimedia call establishment**   protocols which have negotiation mechanisms built in. The call establishment protocols include several levels of negotiation. The negotiation can be done at the networking level, at the system level or at the application level. We present some protocol examples, which have the notion of negotiation in them.

The **ST-II protocol** is a network protocol and provides end-to-end guaranteed service across the Internet network [WoHe94]. The parameters related to the throughput are negotiated with a triangular negotiation for a bounded target. For parameters related to delay,   there is no negotiation. The calling user specifies the maximum transit delay in the connect request. During the establishment of the connection, each ST-agent participating in the stream will have to estimate the average transit delay that it will provide for this stream and the average variance of this delay. The provider presents in the connect indication the total estimated average delay and average variance of delay. The called user decides if the (expected) average delay and delay jitter are sufficient before accepting the connection. The parameters related to the error control are not negotiated.

The **ATM Signaling Protocol** (UNI 3.0) includes the bilateral peer-to-peer negotiation for the CBR (Constant Bit Rate) traffic parameter *peak cell rate*(PCR) as well as the triangular negotiation for bounded target which is applied to the real-time VBR (Variable Bit Rate) traffic. In this ATM class, the minimum bandwidth – *sustainable cell rate* (SCR) is requested and the PCR is negotiable. CBR and VBR traffic allow also negotiation for delay guarantees such as the cell delay and its variation [Ke97].

Other network establishment protocols such as **RCAP (Real-time Channel Administration Protocol** [BaMa91]), **RSVP (Resource Reservation Protocol** [ZDESZ93]), and others use triangular negotiation for different network QoS parameter values such as bandwidth, or end-to-end delay.

The QoS broker provides negotiation at a higher level of the communication architecture [NaSm96] than the network level negotiation (see Figure 3). It includes bilateral negotiation to negotiate as the representative of the application level between peers, unilateral negotiation with the CPU server and the memory server, and triangular negotiation with the transport subsystem layer using the underlying ATM signaling network protocol as the service provider.

2.2 TRANSLATION

It is widely accepted that different NMS components require different QoS parameters, for example, the mean loss rate, known from packet networks, has no meaning as a QoS video capture device. Likewise, frame quality is of little use to a link layer service provider because the frame quality in terms of number of pixels in both axes is a QoS value to initialize frame capture buffers.

We distinguish between user, application, system and network with different QoS parameters as discussed in Section 1.3.1. However, in future systems, there may be even more *'layers'* or there may be a hierarchy of layers, where some QoS values are inherited and others are specific to certain components. In any case, it should always be possible to derive QoS requirement values at the lower system/network level from the user and application QoS requirement values. This derivation – known as **translation** – may require `additional knowledge'* stored together with the specific component. The additional knowledge might be a rule or a preference specified by the user or application if the translation mapping are not *unambiguous*. Overall, translation is an additional service for layer-to-layer communication during the call establishment phase. In general, translations are known and used in layered systems for functions such as naming for long time. For example, in file systems the high-level user file name is translated into file identifier and block number where the file physically starts. In our layered networked multimedia system, we will concentrate on translation between the QoS requirements in individual layers. Due to the layering, shown in Figure 1, the split of parameters requires translation functions as follows:

- **Human Interface –Application QoS**

The service, which may implement the translation between a human user and application QoS parameters is called a **tuning service**. A tuning service provides a user with a *Graphical User Interface* (GUI) for input of application QoS, as well as output of the negotiated application QoS. The translation is represented through video and audio clips (in the case of audio-visual media), which will run at the negotiated quality corresponding, for example, to the video frame resolution that end-system and the network can support. The tuning service can also use sliders, meters and other animated GUI elements to ease the input of perceptual QoS parameters. If both perceptual and application QoS are available at the GUI, then it is important to guarantee corresponding translation between those parameters. For example, if a user views a video clip, and corresponding frame rate and frame resolution are shown as well, then it is important to show the correct frame rate and resolution numbers. The user could use a slider to change the frame rates, which will immediately show in the playback of the viewed video clip. Several current NMSs offer these kinds of GUIs for input and output of application and perceptual QoS parameters [NaSm96,NaQi96].

- **Application QoS – System QoS**

Here, the translation must map the application requirements into the system QoS parameters, which may lead to translation such as from ``high quality'' synchronization user requirement to a small (milliseconds) synchronization skew QoS parameter [Stei93b], or from video frame size to transport packet size. It may also be connected with possible segmentation/reassembly functions. We will present some examples of possible translations between the application QoS and communication, CPU and memory QoS parameters in Table 2. The semantics of individual symbols are given in Table 1.

Table 2. Translation Between Application and Communication Quality Requirements

Relations	Affects	Affected By	Additional Notes
$\lceil M_A/M_N \rceil > 1$	Fragmentation and C_A	Size of M_A and M_N	
$R_N = \lceil M_A/M_N \rceil * R_A$	Traffic Shaping	M_A, R_A	
$B_N = R_N * M_N$	B_N	R_N , M_N	After computation of R_N
$E_N = (E_A - C_A^S - C_A^R)\lceil M_A/M_N \rceil$	E_N	$E_A, C_A^S, C_A^R, \lceil M_A/M_N \rceil$	Appl. Proc. Times C_A^S(sender), C_A^R (receiver)
$R_N' = B_N' / M_N$	R_N	$B_N' < B_N$ - changed bandwidth parameter	After negotiation response
$M_A' = \lfloor R_N'/R_A \rfloor * M_N$	M_A'	B_N'	R_A is fixed
$R_A' = R_N'/\lceil M_A/M_N \rceil$	R_A'	B_N'	M_A is fixed
$C_A^F = \max(C(M_A^I), C(M_A^P), C(M_A^B))$	C_A^F estimated processing time per frame	Processing times C of messages and their sizes $M_A^I M_A^P M_A^B$	C_A^F is resulting time for frame-based scheduling of MPEG video
$C_A^G = C(M_G)$	C_A^G estimated processing time per GOP	$C(M_G) = G_I * C(M_G^I) + G_P * C(M_G^P) + G_B * C(M_G^B)$	C_A^G is resulting time for GOP-based scheduling of MPEG video
$Mem_{req} = k * M_A$	Mem_{req}	Size of the requested buffer to accommodate $k * M_A$	

The translation relations show examples of mappings between application protocol data units (APDU) sizes M_A and the transport PDU (TPDU) sizes M_N, their rates R_A, R_N and bandwidth dependencies B_N as well as processing times C_A^F, C_A^G for MPEG video applications and their dependencies from scheduling decisions (frame-based scheduling versus group-of-picture-based scheduling). Note, that the translation from the communication QoS requirements to the application QoS requirements after the negotiation response from the remote site is not unambiguous. It means we can get either R_A' or M_A' depending on which parameter (M_A or R_A) we fix when translating from bandwidth B_N' to application rate R_A' and the APDU size M_A'. To resolve this ambiguity, the translation service will need additional information from the application/user which translation relation to take. This means in our case that the application/user must decide, in case of degradation of bandwidth ($B_N > B_N'$) during the negotiation, if the user will decrease the rate of displayed APDUs or resolution of displayed APDUs.

- **System QoS – Network QoS**

This translation maps the system QoS (e.g., transport packet end-to-end delay) into the underlying network QoS parameters (e.g., in ATM, the end-to-end delay of cells) and vice versa. The translations between system and network QoS are similar to the translation between APDU and TPDU messages as shown in Table 2 because this level of translation has to translate between TPDU and lower level PDU messages.

The important property of a translation service is that it be a **bidirectional translation** [NaSm95]. This can cause problems because, when, for example, two application QoS parameters, such as the video rate and video frame size, together map into one system QoS parameter, such as the throughput parameter, for the communication channel. Now, if the throughput bound has to be relaxed, the new throughput value may translate into either lowering the quality of the image or lowering the video frame rate as mentioned in the application-system translation paragraph. At this point, using the previously mentioned "*additional knowledge,*" a bidirectional translation is possible. In the above mentioned example, such a rule may be: (1) to reduce the frame size (always keeping the same ratio between horizontal and vertical resolution) until we encounter 112 pixels in the horizontal direction, (2) to reduce the frame rate until we have one frame per second; and, (3) to provide an indication that no further reduction is possible and the connection must be closed.

The reverse translation results in **media scaling**. In general, media scaling methods perform different degrees of media quality degradation if resources are not available. The dynamic QoS change (translation, negotiation, renegotiation of QoS) is used in conjunction with scaling techniques [To92].

2.3 SCALING
Scaling means to subsample a data stream and only present a fraction of its original contents. In general, scaling can be done either at the source or at the receiver. Scaling methods, used in a NMS, can be classified as follows [Del93]:

- **Transparent scaling** methods can be applied independently from the upper protocol and application layers. This means that the transport system scales the media down. Transparent scaling is usually achieved by *dropping mechanisms* where insignificant parts of the multimedia stream will be dropped. These portions need to be identifiable by the transport system. For example, in case of MPEG video, the compressed data stream consists of basic layer (I frames) and enhancement layers (P and B frames) which can be labeled with different priority bits. In case of resource availability degradation, enhancement layers should be dropped first to scale down the resource utilization and resolve resource contention. This kind of property can be expressed with the degradation QoS parameter D (see Table 1) and considered in translation relations when computing system QoS [KiNa97] (e.g., processing time for a GOP(group of pictures) in case of a GOP-based scheduling will be : $C_G = C(M_G') = C(M_G*D)$, where D is the degradation ratio).
- **Non-transparent scaling** methods require an interaction of the transport system with the upper layers. This kind of scaling implies a modification of the media stream before it is presented to the transport layer. Non-transparent scaling typically requires modification of some parameters in the coding algorithms, or even re-coding of a stream that was previously encoded in a different format. For example, if a video stream will scale down due to the change of its frame resolution, then this change must be done at the video encoding side and not in the transport subsystem level because this level does

not have any internal semantic information about the PDU payload nor services to process the internal payload information.

In a NMS, scaling can be applied to both audio and video data:

* For **audio**, transparent scaling is difficult because presenting a fraction of the original data is easily noticed by the human listener. Dropping a channel of a stereo stream is an example. Hence, non-transparent scaling must be used for audio streams. For example, a change of the sampling rate or sample bit resolution (audio sample quantization) at the audio encoding source achieves an audio scaling.
* For **video** streams, the applicability of a specific scaling method depends strongly on the underlying compression technique. There are several domains to which scaling can be applied [Del93]:

    * **Temporal scaling** reduces the resolution of the video stream in the time domain. This means that the number of video frames transmitted within a time interval decreases. Temporal scaling is best suited for video streams in which individual frames are self-contained and can be accessed independently. An example is the Motion JPEG-encoded(MJPEG) video where individual I frames are self-contained and can be accessed independently. Hence, we can drop different frames within the stream if the frame rate needs to be reduced.
    * **Spatial scaling** reduces the number of pixels of each image in a video stream. For spatial scaling, hierarchical arrangement is ideal because it has the advantage that the compressed video is immediately available in various resolutions. Several MJPEG video compression cards provide this capability which allows the NMS to serve video clients with different resolutions (e.g., Lucent Technology MJEP compression card).
    * **Frequency scaling** reduces the number of DCT coefficients applied to the compression of an image.
    * **Amplitude scaling** reduces the color depth for each image pixel. This can be achieved by introducing a coarser quantization of the DCT coefficients, hence requiring a control of the scaling algorithm over the compression procedure.
    * **Color space scaling** reduces the number of entries in the color space. One way to realize color space scaling is to switch from color to gray-scale presentation.

A combination of these scaling methods is possible. In the case of non-transparent scaling, frequency, amplitude and color space scaling are applied at the source during the encoding of the video. Transparent scaling may use temporal scaling or spatial scaling. This type of scaling can be applied at the source or at the destination.

2.4. ADMISSION CONTROL

The next step, after every layer inquires or gets its own QoS specification through negotiation and translation, is **resource admission control**. The admission service is an important service at every shared resource such as network, CPU and/or buffers along the path between source (sender) and sink (receiver) to check resources for availability. For example, in **networks**, admission control is a mechanism used to accept, modified or reject new connections. Note, that if an admission value of a connection is modified, then the admission service suggests a new lower value QoS^{target} with $QoS^{req} \geq QoS^{target} \geq QoS_{min}$ depending on which negotiation protocol is running.

The admission service checks availability of shared resources using availability tests in the broker's entities (see Figure 3). The resource availability tests are called **admission tests**. Based on the results of the admission tests, the *negotiation* protocol creates either a "*reserve*" message with admitted or modified QoS values, or a "*reject*" message when the minimal bound of QoS values (QoS_{min}) cannot be satisfied. The admitted QoS values QoS^{target} may be lower than the requested value QoS^{req}, but they must still be above the minimal value QoS_{min}.

There are at least three types of tests which admission control should perform:

(1)   a **schedulability test** of shared resources such as CPU schedulability, packet schedulability at the entrance to the network and at each network node to provide delay, jitter, throughput and reliability guarantees;

(2)   a **spatial test** for buffer allocation to provide delay and reliability guarantees; and,

(3)   a **link bandwidth test** to provide throughput guarantees.

Table 3 shows some examples of admission tests for the CPU, buffer and network bandwidth availability [NaSm96, KiNa97].

Table 3. Examples of Admission Tests

Admitted Resources	Admission Tests
CPU admission test	$\sum_{i=1}^{n} (C_i/T_i) \leq 1$, i is number of tasks sharing the CPU
Spatial test	$\sum_{j=1}^{k} (Mem^j_{alloc}) + Mem_{req} \leq Mem_{global}$, where Mem^j_{alloc} is already allocated/pinned buffer space, and Mem_{global} is the overall space available.
Bandwidth test	$\sum_j (B_N^j) + B_N^{req} \leq B_N^{global}$

The admission tests, as mentioned above, depend on the implementation of control (e.g., rate control) mechanisms in the multimedia processing and communication protocols. There is extensive research in the area of admission control [HLP93, Ke92, NaSm96, An97], etc. At this point, it is important to emphasize that any QoS negotiation, and therefore resource admission must be closely related to a {\em cost function}, expressed in terms of pricing to differentiate between various **QoS classes** of these services [VeNa97]. If no differentiation with respect to cost/pricing exists, users will always request more resources than needed (over-provisioning) which will decrease the number of users using guaranteed services.

As one example, let us assume we have a *video-on-demand* service running in a community. We can save resources if we allow the video clip to be moved to a server "nearby" the respective client. This can be done more easily if we have prior knowledge of the required demand. Hence, a user who "orders" a video clip for a certain future time (e.g., 1 hour ahead) may pay less than another user who chooses some video clip and immediately wants to access it. If the client is not forced to pay, he/she will always demand the best available QoS. In this case, some other clients may end up with a reduction in quality or not using this service at all because this is the only result they get through any QoS negotiation. With the introduction of appropriate pricing, QoS negotiation may well become a real negotiation [VeNa97].

2.5. RESERVATION/ALLOCATION ACCORDING TO QoS REQUIREMENTS

For the provision of guaranteed QoS in NMS, **reservation and allocation of resources** is necessary. Without resource reservation and management in end-systems and routers/switches, transmission of multimedia data leads to lost (dropped or delayed) packets. The reservation and allocation of resources in most systems is **simplex**, i.e., the resources are reserved only in one direction on a link, which implies that the senders are logically distinct from receivers.

Reservation/allocation of resources can be made either in a **pessimistic** or in an **optimistic** way:

- The **pessimistic approach** avoids resource conflicts by making reservations for the worst case, for example, a reservation for the longest processing time of the CPU or the highest bandwidth needed by a task. For example, in case of MPEG-encoded video pessimistic reservation for frame-based scheduling reserves for each frame (I, P, and B frames) $C(M_A^I)$ processing time, although $C(M_A^I) > C(M_A^P) > C(M_A^B)$. In case of bandwidth B_N, the pessimistic bandwidth reservation reserves $B_N = M_A^I * R_A$, although there might be a request for only $B_N = G_I * M_A^I + G_P * M_A^P + G_B * M_A^B$ (G_I, G_P, G_B represent number of I, P, B frames per second). Resource conflicts are therefore avoided. This leads potentially to an under-utilization of resources. This method results in a guaranteed QoS.
- The **optimistic approach** reserves resources according to an average workload. In the case of the above-mentioned example, CPU is only allocated for the average processing time per frame, i.e., $C_A^{ave} = (G_I * M_A^I + G_P * M_A^P + G_B * M_A^B)/G$. This approach may overload resources when unpredictable behavior occurs. QoS parameters are met as far as possible. Resources are highly utilized, though an overload situation may result in failure. A **monitor function** to detect overload and to solve the problem should be implemented. This function is connected with a **dispatching function**, which then preempts processes according to their importance and deadline if overrun/overload is notified.

Both approaches represent points in a continuum because the process requires a resource in a stochastic fashion. This requirement has both an average QoS_{ave} and a peak value QoS_{max}. One can assign to it any value between the average and the peak value ($QoS_{ave} \leq QoS \leq QoS_{max}$). The closer the assignment is to the peak value, the lower the probability that the process will be denied the use of the resource at a certain time. Hence, the assignment represents a tradeoff between the peak rate multiplexing (pessimistic approach) and the statistical multiplexing (optimistic approach).

Additional mechanisms to detect and solve resource conflicts must be implemented. The resource brokers (e.g., HeiRAT [WoHe94], QualMan [NChN97]) may support the following data structures and functions for resource reservation:

- **Resource Table**: A resource table located in resource brokers contains information about the managed resources. This might include static information like the total resource capacity available (e.g., $CPU^{avail} = CPU^{global} - C_A^{alloc}$ means available bandwidth which remains after other reservation requests C_A^{alloc} were satisfied), the maximum allowable resource capacity (e.g., CPU^{global} which equals to the CPU bandwidth we want to use for reservations. Note that not all bandwidths have to be allocated for reservation and guaranteed services), the scheduling algorithm used (e.g., Rate Monotonic), dynamic information like pointers to the connections currently using the resource, and the total capacity currently reserved.

- **Reservation Table**: A reservation table (e.g., dispatch table [ChuNa97]) provides information about the connections/tasks for which portions of the managed resources are currently reserved (C_A^{alloc}). This information includes the QoS guarantees given to the connections and the fractions of resource capacities reserved for these connections.
- **Reservation Function**: A reservation function in the resource broker calculates the QoS guarantees via admission control that can be given to the new connection/task and reserves the corresponding resource capacities.

The reservation and allocation of network resources along the end-to-end path depends on the **reservation model, negotiation/reservation protocols** and a set of **resource administration functions**, such as admission, allocation, monitoring and de-allocation, of individual resources.

2.5.1 Reservation Model
There are three types of reservation models in the communication architecture of a NMS:

(1) Single Sender/Single Receiver (e.g., RCAP protocol);
(2) Single Sender/Multiple Receivers (e.g., ST-II protocol);
(3) Multiple Senders/Multiple Receivers (e.g., Internet's RSVP protocol).

The reservation model is determined by its **reservation direction and style** [ZDESZ93]. The reservation direction can be **sender-oriented** (e.g., ST-II protocol) or **receiver-oriented** (e.g., RSVP protocol).

Sender-oriented reservation means that the sender transmits a QoS specification (e.g., flow specification) to the targets. The intermediate routers and switches may adjust the QoS specification according to corresponding negotiation strategies where the QoS adjustment depends on available resources. The reservation protocol carries and reserves resources according to the admitted QoS value(s) from the sender to the receiver, and the resulting confirmed QoS value(s) enforce allocation of resources on the way from the receiver to the sender.

Receiver-oriented reservation means that the receiver describes its resource requirements in a QoS specification and sends it to the sender in a **reservation** message [ZDESZ93]. It is assumed that a sender has issued a **path** message before, providing information about outgoing data. On the way from the sender to the receiver, the resources will be allocated.

The **reservation style** represents a creation of a path reservation and time when the senders and receivers perform the QoS negotiation and resource reservation. The style for sender-oriented reservation may be either that the sender creates a **single reservation** along the link to the receiver, or the sender creates a **multicast reservation** to several targets. The reservation style for receiver-oriented reservation is defined in RSVP as follows [ZDESZ93]:

- **Wildcard-Filter style** where a receiver creates a single reservation, or resource **pipe**, along each link, shared among all senders for the given session.
- **Fixed Filter style** where each receiver selects the particular sender whose data packets it wants to receive.

- **Dynamic Filter (DF) style** where each receiver creates N distinct reservations to carry flows from up to N different senders. A later DF reservation from the same receiver may specify the same value of N and the same common flow specification, but a different selection of particular senders, without a new admission control check. This is known as **channel switching**, which is analogous to a television set. If a receiver, using DF reservation style, changes the number of distinct reservations N or the common flow specification, this is treated as a new reservation that is subject to admission control and may fail.

The reservation style can also be divided with respect to time when actual resource allocation occurs: (1) **immediate reservation**, and (2) **advanced reservation**.

The **advanced reservation service** is essential in multi-party multimedia applications. There are two possible approaches to the advanced reservation: a **centralized** approach, where an advanced reservation server exists, and a **distributed** approach, where each node on the channel's path *"remembers"* the reservations.

2.5.2 Resource Reservation/Allocation Protocols

A resource reservation protocol performs no reservation or allocation of required resources itself; it is only a vehicle to transfer information about resource requirements and to negotiate QoS values, which users desire for their end-to-end applications. Resource reservation protocols are control protocols embedded in a multimedia call establishment protocol. The resource reservation protocol implies that every node and host has **resource brokers** which are responsible for sending and receiving the control messages, and invoking the resource administration functions (such as admission control, QoS translation, mapping between QoS and resources, QoS routing, and other QoS management services) needed to make the proper decision for establishing a multimedia call between senders and receivers with QoS guarantees. It means that the resource brokers work closely with network management agents for proper reservation and administration decisions in the networks.

The resource reservation protocols work generally as follows: the initiator of the connection (e.g., sender) sends QoS specifications in a **reservation** message (connect request); at each router/switch along the path, the reservation protocol passes a new resource reservation request to the resource manager, which may consist of several components (for example, in RSVP, this kind of manager is called a "traffic controller" and consists of an admission control routine, packet scheduler and packet classifier); after the admission decision, the resource manager reserves the resources and updates the particular service information for QoS provision (e.g., packet scheduler in RSVP). On the way back from the initiate to the initiator, an **allocation** message (connect confirm) enforces to change the reservation state to allocation state of individual resources.

2.5.3 Resource De-allocation

After the transmission of media, resources must be de-allocated, which means, the CPU, network bandwidth and buffer space must be freed and the connections through which the media flow must be torn down. The tear down process must be done without disruption of other flows in the network. Further, the tear down process implies updating the resource and reservation tables to reflect the resource availability by the resource broker. The resource de-allocation is divided with respect to the direction of the request:

(1) **Sender** requests closing of the multimedia call. This implies that the resources for all connections corresponding to the multimedia call along the path between sender and receiver(s) must be de-allocated and the resource availability must be updated at every node;

(2) **Receiver** requests closing of the multimedia call. This request is sent to the sender and during the traversing of the path, the resources are de-allocated.

De-allocation depends on the mechanisms of resource management at the nodes and on the tear down protocols.

3. QoS ENFORCEMENT SERVICES DURING MULTIMEDIA TRANSMISSION

QoS guarantees must be met in the application, system and network (see Figure 1) to get the acceptance of the users of NMS. There are several QoS constraints, which must be enforced to provide guarantees during multimedia transmission:

(1)   **time constraints** which include delays;
(2)   **space constraints** such as system buffers;
(3)   **device constraints** such as frame grabbers allocation;
(4)   **frequency constraints** which include network bandwidth and system bandwidth for data transmission; and,
(5)   **reliability constraints**.

These constraints can be enforced if proper QoS and resource management are available at the end-points, as well as in the network. However, these five constraints are related to each other in such a way that one parameter may imply choosing another. For example, time constraints for the scheduling of video frame data imply a corresponding bandwidth allocation. We will concentrate in the following section on QoS enforcement services for network resources and discuss network traffic shaping mechanisms, rate control scheduling services for delay, delay-jitter and throughput (bandwidth) provision, as well as error control for reliability provision.

We assume at this point that proper resource reservation and allocation have occurred as described in the previous sections.

3.1 TRAFFIC SHAPING
One of the important components of QoS enforcement is **traffic shaping**. The reasons for traffic shaping are as follows: The resource reservation algorithm needs to analyze the QoS specification associated with all connections utilizing the shared resource in order to determine the service quality that can be offered to individual connections. Since the number of connections sharing the common network resource can be very large, it is important that the QoS specification per connection be simple for easy management. Unfortunately, traffic generated in NMS is very bursty due to compressed multimedia streams, and often difficult to model and specify. To alleviate the problem, traffic generated by multimedia sources is passed through a **traffic shaper**. Traffic shaping should allow (1) a simple way for a connection to describe its traffic so that the network knows what kind of traffic to expect (note that the QoS specification for traffic, called *traffic envelope*, should be able to capture a wide range of traffic characteristics), (2) the network to perform an admission control, and (3) the network to monitor the connection's traffic and to police/confirm that the connection is behaving as it promised [Pa94, RaTr98]. We will examine various shaping schemes, which fit different types of traffic.

The simplest traffic shaping schemes try to shape all traffic into **isochronous flows**, with regular amounts of data being emitted at regular time intervals between samples as they are sent into the network. We will mention here two shaping schemes:

- **Leaky Bucket**: In this scheme each connection has its own leaky bucket [Tu86]. When data is to be sent, the sending host places the connection's cells/packets into a bucket. Cells drain out of the bottom of the bucket and are sent into the network at the rate R_N. The rate is enforced by a regulator at the bottom of the bucket. The bucket size, β, limits how much data may build up waiting for the network. If the connection presents more data than the size of bucket allows, then the excess data is discarded. In this scheme, shaped data characteristic equals to equally spaced cells, each cell being emitted $1/R_N$ units of time after the last one. The effect of the bucket size β is both to bound the amount of delay a cell can incur before getting into the network and limit the maximum burst size the sender can try to send.

- **(r,T)-Smooth Algorithm:** In an *(r,T)*- smooth traffic system, a connection is permitted to inject no more than *r* bits of data into the network in any *T* bit times, where T is a fixed constant through the network [Go90]. '*r*' varies on a per-connection basis. If the next packet to be sent would cause the connection to use more than *r* bits in the current frame, then the connection must hold the packet until the next frame starts. If we compare the *(r,T)*-smooth algorithm with the leaky bucket scheme, then this algorithm, rather than sending one cell of size M_N every $1/R_N$ time units, allows the connection to send $T x M_N/R_N$ bits of data every *T* bit times. This shaping algorithm is part of the scheduling service discipline, stop-and-go described in the next subsection.

Overall, *isochronous* shaping schemes are easy to implement, however, the range of behaviors they describe is limited to fixed-rate data flows.

Another class of shaping algorithms consists of schemes, which integrate **isochronous schemes with priority schemes**. The basic idea is that every packet is tagged with a bit pattern that tells the network how important the packet is to the connection's application. If the network finds itself congested at some point, it discards some or all of the traffic that are marked as less important. ATM supports a two-priority scheme using the CLP bit [Ke97]. This class of shaping schemes has two main problems: (1) the amount of traffic that can be guaranteed is rather low, typically no more than 50% of the total bandwidth of a link [Pa94]; (2) discarding selective packets when communication devices use FIFO queues. The issue is that when the device is overloaded, and needs to discard some low-priority packets, it is unable to look inside its FIFO queues. The implication is that such devices employ the policy of discarding the low-priority packets as they arrive (e.g., ATM CISCO switch uses early discard policy).

In order to support a richer range of traffic characteristics, a class of **shaping algorithms** was developed which support **bursty traffic patterns**. We will describe two such algorithms:

- **Token Bucket**: In a token bucket system, R_N is the rate at which tokens are placed in the *token bucket*. The bucket has the occupancy β. If the bucket fills, newly arriving tokens are discarded. When a packet is sent, it is placed in a *separate data buffer queue*. To transmit the packet, the regulator must remove a number of tokens equal to the packet size from the bucket. Token bucket permits burstiness but bounds it. This scheme guarantees that the burstiness is bounded so that the connection never sends more than

$\beta + \tau/R_N$ tokens worth of data in an interval τ and that the long-term transmission rate will not exceed R_N.

- **Token Bucket with Leaky Bucket Rate Control**: This scheme has a token bucket of size β, and data buffer queue sending the data with regulator rate of R_N. When the regulator lets data through, the data is then placed in a simple leaky bucket (also of size β), from which the data is drained at rate $C > R_N$. This scheme permits bursty traffic but regulates it so that the maximum transmission rate at any time is C and the long-term average has an upper bound of R_N.

This class of shaping schemes has more complexity in terms of policing or implementation. Token bucket algorithm has a policing problem when the connection is allowed to exceed rate R_N by β tokens because if the network tries to police connections by simply measuring their traffic over time interval τ, a connection can cheat[1] by sending $\beta + \tau/R_N$ tokens of data in every interval. The token bucket with leaky bucket requires more complex implementation than token bucket and complex policing.

3.2 RATE CONTROL

If we assume a NMS to be a tightly coupled system, which has a central process managing all system components, then this central instance can impose a synchronous data handling over all resources; in effect, we encounter a fixed, imposed data rate. However, a NMS usually comprises loosely coupled end-systems, which communicate over networks. In such a setup, rates must be imposed. Here, we make use of all available strategies in the communications environment.

High-speed networking provides opportunities for multimedia applications to have stringent performance requirements in terms of throughput, delay, delay-jitter and loss rate. Conventional packet switching data networks with window-based flow control and FCFS cannot provide services with strict performance guarantees. Hence, for NMS, new **rate-based flow control** and **rate-based scheduling service disciplines** are being introduced. These control mechanisms are connected with a connection-oriented network architecture, which supports explicit resource allocation and admission control policies.

A **rate-based service discipline** is one that provides a client with a minimum service rate independent of the traffic characteristics of other clients. Such a discipline, operating at a switch, manages the following resources: **bandwidth, service time (priority)** and **buffer space**. Together with proper admission policies, such disciplines provide throughput, delay, delay-jitter and loss rate guarantees. Several rate-based scheduling disciplines have been developed [ZhKe91]:

- **Fair Queuing:** If N channels share an output trunk, then each one should get $1/N$th of the bandwidth. If any channel uses less bandwidth than its share, then this portion is shared among the rest equally. This mechanism can be achieved by the *Bit-by-bit Round Robin* (BR) service among the channels. The BR discipline serves N queues in the round robin service, sending one bit from each queue that has a packet in it. Clearly, this scheme is not efficient; hence, fair queuing emulates BR as follows: each packet is

---

[1] Over the interval of 2τ, the connection would send data equal to $2\beta + 2\tau/R_N$ tokens. However, it is supposed to send at most $\beta + 2\tau/R_N$.

given a finish number, which is the round number at which the packet would have received service, if the server had been doing BR. The packets are served in the order of the finish number. Channels can be given different fractions of the bandwidth by assigning them weights, where weight corresponds to the number of bits of service the channel receives per round of BR service.

- **Virtual Clock:** This discipline emulates *Time Division Multiplexing (TDM)*. A virtual transmission time is allocated to each packet. It is the time at which the packet would have been transmitted, if the server would actually be doing TDM[Zh90].

- **Delay Earliest-Due-Date (Delay EDD):** Delay EDD [FeVe90] is an extension of EDF scheduling (Earliest Deadline First) where the server negotiates a service contract with each source. The contract states that if a source obeys a peak and average sending rate, then the server provides bounded delay. The key then lies in the assignment of deadlines to packets. The server sets a packet's deadline to the time at which it should be sent, if it had been received according to the contract. This actually is the expected arrival time added to the delay bound at the server. By reserving bandwidth at the peak rate (B_N^{peak}), Delay EDD can assure each channel a guaranteed delay bound.

- **Jitter Earliest-Due-Date (Jitter EDD)**: Jitter EDD extends Delay EDD to provide delay-jitter bounds. After a packet has been served at each server, it is stamped with the difference between its deadline and actual finishing time. A regulator at the entrance of the next switch holds the packet for this period before it is made eligible to be scheduled. This provides the minimum and maximum delay guarantees.

- **Stop-and-Go:** This discipline preserves the *"smoothness"* property of the traffic as it traverses through the network. The main idea is to treat all traffic as frames of fixed length T bits, meaning the time is divided into frames. At each frame time, only packets that have arrived at the server in the previous frame time are sent. It can be shown that the delay and delay-jitter are bounded, although the jitter bound does not come free. The reason is that under Stop-and-Go rules, packets arriving at the start of an incoming frame must be held by full time T before being forwarded. So, all the packets that would arrive quickly are instead being delayed. Further, since the delay and delay-jitter bounds are linked to the length of the frame time, improvement of Stop-and-Go can be achieved using multiple frame sizes, which means it may operate with various frame sizes.

- **Hierarchical Round Robin (HRR)**: A HRR server has several service levels where each level provides round robin service to a fixed number of slots. Some number of slots at a selected level are allocated to a channel and the server cycles through the slots at each level. The time a server takes to service all the slots at a level is called the *frame time* at the level. The key of HRR is that it gives each level a constant share of the bandwidth. "Higher" levels get more bandwidth than "lower" levels, so the frame time at a higher level is smaller than the frame time at a lower level. Since a server always completes one round through its slots once every frame time, it can provide a maximum delay bound to the channels allocated to that level.

Some other disciplines, suitable for providing guaranteed services, are schemes such as the **Weighted Fair Queueing (WFQ)** algorithm [CSZ92]. In WFQ, each packet is stamped with a time-stamp as it arrives and then it is transmitted in increasing order of the time-stamps.

Rate-based disciplines are divided depending on the policy they adopt: the **work-conserving discipline** serves packets at the higher rate as long as it does not affect the performance guarantees of other channels which also means a server is never idle when there is a packet to be sent (e.g., Delay EDD, Virtual Clock, Fair Queuing); and the **non-work-conserving discipline** does not serve packets at a higher rate under any circumstances, which also means that each packet is assigned, explicitly or implicitly, an *eligibility time*. Even when the server is idle, if no packets are eligible, none will be transmitted (e.g., Stop-and-Go, HRR, Jitter EDD).

Rate-based service disciplines need to allocate resources per client, hence the clients need to specify their traffic (using QoS parameters). The traffic specification for Virtual Clock, HRR and Stop-and-Go are: a **transmission rate (R_N)** averaged over an *interval*. Delay EDD and Jitter EDD have three parameters: **minimal packet inter-arrival time, average packet inter-arrival time** and *interval* over which the average packet inter-arrival time was computed. Fair Queuing was described for datagram networks, so no traffic specification was proposed.

The buffer space requirements for the three non-work-conserving disciplines are almost constant for each node traversed by the channel [ZhKe91]. The buffer space requirement for work-conserving Delay EDD increases linearly for each node along the path. Throughput guarantees are provided by all rate-based services. Delay guarantees are provided only by Delay EDD and all non-work-conserving services (also by Weighted Fair Queueing). Jitter guarantees are provided by Stop-and-Go and Jitter EDD.

3.3 END-TO-END ERROR CONTROL
Multimedia extensions to existing operating systems provide a fast and efficient data transport between sources and destinations located at the same computer. Glitches on video streams may (but should not) occur, but audio is always conveyed in a reliable way. The solution becomes different if we take into account networks. In the past, several multimedia communication systems have been proposed which usually offer unreliable transport. For example, the UDP/IP protocol was used for experiments to transmit digital audio over the Internet. Other examples are the Tenet protocol suite's transport protocols RMPT (Real-time Message Transport Protocol) and CMTP (Continuous Media Transport Protocol) which provide unreliable but timely delivery for multimedia communication.

A substantive degree of reliability in NMSs is necessary because of the following:
- **Decompression Technology:** Most audio and video compression schemes cannot tolerate loss; they are unable to resynchronize themselves after a packet loss or at least visible and/or other perceptual errors are introduced. For example, the current MPEG players must receive a full frame with no bit/byte losses if it should be decompressed and displayed.
- **Human Perception:** Loss of digital audio, for example, is detected by a human ear very quickly and results in lower acceptance of the multimedia system. Even in video case when temporal resolution is too low, users reject this quality of video. Losses also impact strongly the inter-stream synchronization and cause out of sync behavior [QiNa97].
- **Data Integrity**: For example, in a recording application, one cannot recover from an error that is induced in the first recording of data. Fortunately, in this type of application, where multimedia data is written to disk, there are often less stringent real-time requirements for the receiver.

To ensure required reliability of NMSs, end-to-end error control consists of two steps, **error detection** and **error correction**.

3.3.1 Error Detection
Reliability should be enforced, although there is some error tolerance in the multimedia systems. This works only if the application is able to isolate the errors. For example, some

wrong colors within a video frame may not matter because they are hardly visible to the human user as they appear for only a short fraction of a second, but if the frame boundaries are destroyed, there is no way to recover from the error. This means that structural information within a data stream needs to be protected, but not always content. This also implies that existing error detection mechanisms, such as **checksumming** and **PDU sequencing**, must be extended toward conveying further information. These existing mechanisms allow detection of data corruption, loss, duplication and misorder at the lower levels (e.g., packets in the transport layer), but on the application PDU level, where the decision should actually be made, if the packet is lost or not, error detection is left out.

Another example for enforcing error detection at a higher layer (above the transport layer) is MPEG-2 encoded video. This compression produces three types of frames in the video streams. The most important frame type is the I-frame, which contains the structural information of the video stream for a certain time interval. The two other types of video frames (P-frame and B-frame) follow the I-frame with supporting information. Hence, it is important for the multimedia communication system not to lose the I-frame (strict reliability requirements on the sequence of I-frames), but there is a certain tolerance towards losses of P-frames or B-frames.

In the transport and lower layers, the error detection mechanisms must be extended too because of the "**lateness**" concept. It means that if a PDU arrives too late at the receiver, this information is useless for an application and should be detected as an error. To identify late data, it is necessary to determine the lifetime of PDUs expected arrival time. The latest expected arrival time can be derived from the traffic model (throughput and rate) associated with a connection. This means that for continuous streams, the expiration time can be calculated from the PDU rate. Therefore, only the first PDU has to carry a time stamp, although this is not an ideal solution because error detection is forced to start with the first PDU, and no interruption of the service is possible. With a time stamp in every PDU, the error detection can start at any point during the media transmission. This mechanism requires a synchronized system clock at the sender **and** receiver to allow an accurate determination of the end-to-end delay. A possible protocol for this kind of synchronization is Mill's **Network Time Protocol (NTP)** [Mills93].

3.3.2 Error Correction
The traditional mechanism for reliability provision is **retransmission** (e.g., TCP protocol uses this mechanism), which uses an acknowledgment principle after receiving data or window-based flow control. If the acknowledgment is negative, the data are re-sent by the sender. The traditional reliable transfer strategies are not suitable for multimedia communication because:

(1)   with explicit acknowledgment the amount of data to be stored at the sender for potential retransmission can become very large (e.g., in the case of video);

(2)   with the traditional window-based flow control, the sender may be forced to suspend transmission while a continuous data flow is required;

(3)   the retransmitted data might be received "*too late*" to be consumed in real-time; and,

(4)   traditional mechanisms also do not scale to multiple-target communication – they are not designed for multicasting communication, only for point-to-point communication.

We will outline some error correction schemes for NMS currently discussed in the research:

- **Go-back-N Retransmission**: This method is the most rigid error correction scheme. The mechanism is as follows: if PDU i is lost, the sender will go back to i and restart transmission from i. The successive PDUs after i are dropped at the receiver. The lost PDU is recovered only if $i \leq n$, where n is specified at the beginning of the transmission. This means it is specified (n) how far back the data should be retransmitted if a packet is lost. This is a simple protocol where no buffering or resequencing of the PDUs at the receiver are necessary. The receiver only sends a negative acknowledgment if PDU i is lost. The problem is that if after that $i'th$ PDU the packets were transmitted successfully, they are dropped too, which may lead to several implications: **gap introduction** and **violation of throughput guarantees**. The retransmission introduces gaps because the receiver has to wait at least $2 * E_A$ to get the proper PDU i. Also, for a multimedia connection where throughput guarantees are provided through rate control, the retransmitted data must be sent either ``on top'' of the guaranteed throughput or the retransmitted PDU will fall under the rate control. This again leads to a gap in the stream presentation, which needs to be handled properly through a mechanism such as freezing the video, or turning down the audio.

- **Selective Retransmission**: Selective retransmission provides better channel utilization. The receiver sends a negative acknowledgment to the sender if PDU $i \leq n$ is lost. The sender retransmits only those PDUs which have been reported missing, not the consecutive packets, too. The disadvantage of this mechanism is its complicated implementation. At the receiver, every successfully received PDU must be stored until all previous PDUs have been received correctly. It has been shown that this resequencing is worthwhile only if the receiver is able to store at least two times the data corresponding to the bandwidth-delay product.

- **Partially Reliable Streams**: Partially reliable streams introduce a weak concept of reliability. This mechanism limits the number of packets to be retransmitted. Only the last n packets of the stream in a certain time interval will be retransmitted. The value n can be calculated from the timing constraint of the multimedia application, taking into account the reliability of the underlying network. The possible n can be negotiated during the call setup between the sender and receiver.

- **Forward Error Correction (FEC)**: In this mechanism, the sender adds additional information to the original data such that the receiver can locate and correct bits or bit sequences. FEC for ATM networks is discussed in [Bie93]. A given FEC mechanism can be specified by its code rate R (code efficiency), which can be computed: $R = S/(S+N)$; S represents the number of bits to be sent, N represents the number of added check bits. The redundancy introduced by the mechanism is $(1-R)$ and it must be determined by the transport system. The transport system needs two pieces of information: the **error probability** of the network between the sender and receiver; and the **reliability** required from the application. FEC results in a low end-to-end delay and there is no need for exclusive buffering of data before play-out. It also does not require a control channel from the receiver to the sender. The disadvantage of FEC is that it works only for error detection and correction within a packet but not for complete packet loss, i.e., FEC cannot guarantee that corrupted or lost packets can always be recovered. Further, FEC increases the demand on throughput significantly. The negative effects of added congestion on a network due to FEC overhead can more than offset the benefits of FEC recovery [Bie93]. FEC requires hardware support at end-systems to encode and decode the redundant information with sufficient speed. FEC is also used for storing audio data at Compact Disc (CD) devices.

- **Priority Channel Coding**: Priority channel coding refers to a class of approaches that separates the medium (e.g., voice) into multiple data streams with different priorities. These priorities are then used to tag voice packets so that during periods of congestion, the network is more likely to discard low-priority packets which carry information less important for reconstructing the original media stream. This scheme enables multiple priority channels to maintain a higher QoS over larger loss ranges than channels using a single priority for all voice packets. Channel coding requires that the network be able to control packet loss during congestion through a priority mechanism. The use of different streams for different priorities requires synchronization at a per-packet granularity to reconstruct the voice signal. Another example where prioritized transmission can be used is for MPEG-2 encoded video. Here, I and P frames could be sent at high priority and B frames could be sent at low priority. Network switches drop lower-priority cells or provide a lower grade of service during periods of network congestion.

- **Slack Automatic Repeat ReQuest (S-ARQ):** S-ARQ is an error control scheme based on retransmission of lost voice packets in high-speed LANs. The packets are subject to delay-jitter, hence the receiver observes **gaps**, which result in interruptions of continuous playback of the voice stream. Delay-jitter in packetized voice transmission is commonly addressed through a control time at the receiver. The first packet is artificially delayed at the receiver for the period of the control time to buffer sufficient packets to provide for continuous playback in the presence of jitter. The voice data consists of talk spurts and periods of silence. Since talk spurts are generally isolated from each other by relatively long silence periods, voice protocols typically impose the control time on the first packet of each talk spurt. The **slack time** of a packet is defined as the difference between its arrival time at the receiver and its playback time, which is the point in time at which playback of the packet must begin at the receiver to achieve a zero-gap playback schedule for the talk spurt. Due to delay-jitter, a packet may arrive before or after its playback time. In the former case, the packet is placed in a **packet voice receiver** queue until it is due for playback. In the latter case, a gap has occurred and the packet is played immediately. The principle of S-ARQ is to extend the control time at the beginning of a talk spurt and to use it so that the slack time of arriving packets is lengthened [DLW93].

The error control/correction schemes for multimedia communication systems, as described above, can be divided into two classes: **partial retransmission mechanisms** (e.g., Go-Back-N, Selective Retransmission, Partially Reliable streams, S-ARQ); and **preventive mechanisms** (e.g., FEC, Priority Channel Coding). All partial retransmission schemes lack the possibility of introducing a discontinuity or of working properly if we introduce large end-to-end delays with large buffers. Hence, preventive schemes should be used.

3.4 QoS AND RESOURCE MONITORING

Resource monitoring is an important part of QoS enforcement in networks, as well as at the end-points. Resource monitoring functionality is embedded in the resource manager/broker and is closely connected to the network management agent. To use network management for QoS enforcement, the MIBs (Management Information Bases) of the network management must be extended for multimedia communication with the QoS parameters. Further, network management may be enhanced with functions for QoS supervision and problem resolving functions.

Monitoring in networks can add overhead during multimedia transmission, which should not cause a violation of QoS guarantees. Hence, monitoring should be flexible, which means that most of the monitoring variables should be optional; and, monitoring should be able to be turned on and off [WoHe94]. There are two possible modes to operate resource monitoring: **end-user mode** and **network mode**. The former requests a status report about the resources; the latter regularly reports the resource status on different nodes along the path between communicating end-users.

Monitoring at end-systems includes a *supervisor function* to continuously observe that the processed QoS parameters do not exceed their negotiated values. As an example, a compression component may allow delivery at a peak rate of 6 Mbits/s over a duration of at most three frame lengths. However, at some point in time the system starts to deliver a continuous bit rate of 10 Mbits/s. The monitoring function will detect this behavior by being called from an exception handler of the rate control component: a buffer overflow occurred at the sender – something which should never happen. The monitoring function finds out that the origin of the exceeded QoS value is an erroneous compressing component. It should be pointed out that the design and implementation of such a monitoring function is a non-trivial task and that a clearly defined notion of the QoS is a prerequisite.

3.5 QoS RENEGOTIATION AND ADAPTATION

In continuous media communication, it is important to support a framework capable of dynamically changing the resource capacity of each session. Hence, it is important for the NMS architecture to support dynamic change of QoS parameters so that they can be balanced to reach an optimal value for all sessions in a predictable manner.

There are two important factors which must be provided to achieve this goal: **notification and renegotiation of QoS parameters**, i.e., a protocol for reporting the QoS changes and modifying QoS parameters of existing connections (may be done by resource administration protocols); and, **QoS adaptation** to respond to and accommodate the changes either in the network, the hosts or both.

During multimedia transmission, change of QoS parameters and associated resources can occur. The changes can be two-fold: (1) changes **violating the minimal negotiated bound** QoS_{min} or **modifying the negotiated range**; (2) changes **within the negotiated range** $[QoS_{min}, QoS_{max}]$. If violation/modification changes occur, then **renegotiation of QoS parameters** must begin. If fluctuation changes within the negotiated range occur, then **QoS adaptation** must be performed.

3.5.1 QoS Renegotiation

QoS renegotiation is a process of QoS negotiation when a call is already setup. The renegotiation request can come either from the user, who wants to change the quality of service, from the host system due to overload of the workstation (multi-user, multi-process environment) or from the network due to overload and congestion. The renegotiation request is sent to the resource broker.

- **User Request for Renegotiation**: If the *sender* requires a change of QoS, this implies change in reservation of multimedia sources, host system resources, and network resources. The resource manager must check if local resources are available. Further, the resource reservation/renegotiation protocol must be invoked to check the availability of network resources if the change of QoS requires change of network resources. If resources are available, resource reservation and allocation is performed. If the *receiver* requires change of QoS for the receiving media, first the resource manager checks the local resource and reserves it. Then, the sender is notified via a resource reservation protocol and the same admission procedure follows as in the case of a sender requiring QoS changes. At the end, the receiver must be notified to change the local resource allocation. In a broadcast or multicast communication structure, different QoS values may be applied for the same connection to different end-systems.

- **Host System Request for Renegotiation:** This request may come from a QoS-aware operating system [NChN97] in a multi-user environment. In this case, several users are admitted and some of the users violated their admitted application requirements. Then, a notification about the degradation of the QoS performance is issued to the application client. The degradation of one's QoS performance may also result in degradation of performance for other users of the workstation. The response is either dispatching of the misbehaved user/application to the admitted level, or a renegotiation request for new QoS bounds. If host QoS changes result in renegotiation of new QoS bounds, then the host resource broker will need to invoke the resource reservation/renegotiation protocol to renegotiate the QoS parameters in the network between the sender and receiver as well.

- **Network Request for Renegotiation:** Overload of the network at some nodes can cause a renegotiation request for QoS change. This request comes as a notification from the resource renegotiation protocol to the host, reporting that the reservation/allocation of host resources might change. There are two possibilities: **the network can adapt** to the overload; or, **the network cannot adapt** to the overload. In the former case, the network still needs to notify the host because some degradation may occur during the modification of resources (e.g., if the network tears down a connection and establishes a new connection). This actually may interrupt the media flow, so the host must react to this change. In the latter case, the source/application must adapt [Si97].

3.5.2 QoS Adaptation

We describe several mechanisms for QoS adaptation when the resource availability fluctuation is monitored. The adaptation mechanisms implicitly offer partial solutions for cases when the adaptation request comes from the user or the host system.

- **Network Adaptation:** The fixed routing and resource reservation for only lower QoS bounds (e.g., QoS_{min}), combined with load fluctuations in the range $[QoS_{min}, QoS_{max}]$, introduce possible problems of network unavailability for QoS > QoS_{min}. Thus, a proper balancing of the network load is desirable and necessary to: (1) increase network availability; (2) allow network administrators to reclaim resources; and, (3) reduce the impact of unscheduled, run-time maintenance on clients with guaranteed services. Efficient routing and resource allocation decisions, made for previous clients which made requests for QoS guarantees, reduce the probability that a new client's request will be refused by the admission scheme. The more efficient the routing and resource allocation, the more guaranteed connection requests are accepted. One possibility for implementing a **load balancing policy** is to employ the following mechanisms: *QoS routing, performance monitoring* (detecting load changes), *dynamic re-routing* (changing the route) and *load balancing control* (making a decision to re-route a channel [PZF92]. The routing mechanism implements the routing algorithm, which selects a route in adherence to QoS requirements [MaSt97, CheNa97]. The performance monitoring mechanism monitors the appropriate network performance and reports it to the load balancing control. The dynamic re-routing mechanism is needed to establish the alternative route and to perform a transparent transition from the primary route to the alternative route. The load balancing control mechanism receives information from the performance monitoring mechanism and determines whether load balancing can be attempted using a load balancing algorithm defined by the policy. If load balancing can be attempted, the routing mechanism provides an alternative route and the transition from the primary route to the alternative route is accomplished using the dynamic re-routing mechanism. The adaptive resource scheme in this protocol is the **dynamic re-**

routing mechanism. When channel i is to be re-routed, the source tries to establish a new channel that has the same traffic and performance parameters and shares the same source and destination as channel i, but takes a different route. The new channel is called **shadow channel** [PZF92] of channel i. After the shadow channel has been established, the source can switch from channel i to the shadow channel and start sending packets on it. After waiting for the maximum end-to-end delay time of channel i, the source initiates a tear-down message for channel i. If the shadow channel shares part of the route with the old channel, it is desirable to let the two channels share resources. This further implies that the establishment and tear-down procedures are aware of this situation, so that the establishment does not request the new resource and the tear-down procedure does not free the old resource.

- **Source/Application Adaptation**: Another alternative reaction to changes in the network load is to adapt the source rate according to the currently available network resources. This approach requires **feedback** information from the network to the source , which results in graceful degradation in the media quality during periods of congestion. For example, in [KMR93], the feedback control mechanism is based on predicting the evolution of the system state over time. The predicted system state is used to compute the target sending rate for each frame of video data. The adaptation policy strives to keep the bottleneck queue size for each connection at a constant level. Each switch monitors the buffer occupancy and service rate per connection. The buffer occupancy information is a count of the number of queued packets for the connection at the instant when the feedback message is sent. The rate information is the number of packets transmitted for the connection in the time interval between two feedback messages. There are two possibilities to implement the feedback transmission mechanism.

1. The per-connection state information is periodically appended to a data packet for the corresponding connection. At the destination, this information is extracted and sent back to the source. A switch updates the information fields in a packet only if the local service rate is lower than that reported by a previous switch along the path.

2. The feedback message is sent in a separate control packet, which is sent back along the path of the connection towards the source.

Other source adaptation schemes (for video traffic) may control the overload:

- **Rate Control using Network Feedback**: In this approach, each source adapts to changes in network conditions caused by an increase or decrease in the number of connections or by sudden changes in the sending rates of existing connections. Changes in the traffic conditions are detected by explicit or implicit feedback from the network. Explicit feedback is in the form of information about the traffic loads or buffer occupancy levels. Implicit feedback information about packet losses and round robin delay is available from acknowledgments.

- **Traffic Shaping at Source**: Another way to control congestion is to smooth out traffic at the source. Typically, most of the burstiness reduction can be obtained by smoothing over an interval of 1–4 frames [KMR93].

- **Hierarchical Coding**: Hierarchical coding describes algorithms, which produce two or more types of cells describing the same block of pixels with different degrees of detail. However, these coders are more complex and use a greater amount of bandwidth to transmit images than single-layer coders [KMR93].

4. QoS ARCHITECTURES

QoS specification, distribution, provision and connected resource admission, reservation, allocation and provision must be embedded in different components of the end-to-end multimedia communication architecture (see Figure 3). This means that proper services and protocols discussed in this section must be provided in the end-to-end architecture of the NMS.

Some examples of architectural choices where QoS and resource management are designed and implemented include the following:

- The **OSI architecture** provides QoS in the network layer and some enhancements in the transport layer. The OSI 95 project considers *integrated   QoS   specification* and *negotiation* in the transport protocols [DaBo93].
- **Lancaster's QoS-Architecture** (QoS-A) [CaCoHu93] offers a framework to specify and implement the required performance properties of multimedia applications over high-performance ATM-based networks. QoS-A incorporates the notions of *flow*}, *service contract* and *flow management*. The **Multimedia Enhanced Transport Service** (METS) provides the functionality to contract QoS.
- The **Heidelberg Transport System** (HeiTS) [WoHe94] together with HeiRAT OS support, is based on the ST-II network protocol, provides continuous-media exchange with QoS guarantees, upcall structure, resource management and real-time mechanisms. HeiTS transfers continuous media data streams from one origin to one or multiple targets via multicast. HeiTS nodes negotiate QoS values by exchanging flow specification to determine the resources required – delay, jitter, throughput and reliability.
- The **UC Berkeley's Tenet Protocol Suite** with protocol set RCAP, RTIP, RMTP and CMTP provides network QoS negotiation, reservation and resource administration through the RCAP control and management protocol.
- The **Internet protocol stack**, based on IP protocol, provides soft QoS guarantees using soft resource reservations if the RSVP control protocol [ZDESZ93] is used. Internet is an example of a connectionless network where QoS is introduced on a packet basis (every IP packet carries type of service parameters because the Internet does not have a service notion yet).
- QoS handling and management is provided in UPenn's end-point architecture (**OMEGA Architecture**) at the application and transport subsystems [NaSm96], where the *QoS Broker*, as the end-to-end control and management protocol, implements QoS handling over both subsystems and relies on control and management in ATM networks.
- The **Native-Mode ATM Protocol Stack** [Ke95], developed in the IDLInet (IIT Delhi Low-cost Integrated Network) testbed at the Indian Institute of technology, provides network QoS guarantees.
- The **UIUC QualMan System** [NChN97] provides a QoS-aware resource management architecture at the end-points, in concert with ATM QoS provision it delivers application end-to-end QoS guarantees.

4. CONCLUSION

Provision of end-to-end QoS guarantees is a challenging goal in NMS. It is a challenging goal due to:

- user *expectations* of multimedia processing and communication in a digital distributed environments, which are always compared with cable TV and radio quality networks.
- large *heterogeneity of OS services* (Windows NT, UNIX) running on different platforms (workstations, PCs).
- large *heterogeneity of network protocols* (Internet RSVP, IPv6, RTP, RTSP, HTTP, ST-II, TCP/IP, UDP/IP) running on different high-speed networks (ATM, Fast Ethernet).
- large differences in QoS awareness of OS and network services.
- increasing *application varieties* and requirements.
- incoming *new media* transmitted over high-bandwidth (ATM) and low-bandwidth networks (wireless networks).

To achieve this goal, QoS and resource management, based on QoS requirements, as discussed in this section, must become an important and integral part of networked multimedia systems across all end-to-end system components.

REFERENCES

[An97] O. Angin, A. Campbell, L.-T. Cheok, R. Liao, K.-S. Lim, and K. Nahrstedt, "Report on the 5th IFIP International Workshop on Quality of Service," ACM SIGCOMM Computer Communication Review, July 1997.

[BaMa91] A. Banerjea and B. Mah, "The Real-Time Channel Administration Protocol," 2nd International Workshop on Network and Operating System Support for Digital Video and Audio, Heidelberg, Germany, November 1991.

[Bie93] E. Biersack, "Performance Evaluation of Forward Error Correction in an ATM Environment," IEEE Journal on Selected Areas in Communications, 11(4), May 1993, pp. 631-640.

[BCS94] B. Braden, D. Clark, and S. Shenker, "Integrated Services in the Internet Architecture: An Overview," Internet Draft, RFC 1633, June 1994.

[CaCoHu93] A. Campbell, G. Coulson, and D. Hutchison, "A Multimedia Enhanced Transport Service in Quality of Service Architecture," Workshop on Network and Operating System Support for Digital Video and Audio, Lancaster, England, November 1993.

[CheNa97] S. Chen and K. Nahrstedt, "Distributed QoS Routing," Technical Report UIUCDCS-R-97-2017, University of Illinois at Urbana-Champaign, July 1997.

[ChuNa97] H.-H. Chu and K Nahrstedt, "A Soft Real Time Server in UNIX Operating System," IDMS'97 (European Workshop on Interactive Multimedia Systems), Darmstadt, Germany, September 1997.

[CSZ92] D. D. Clark, S. Shenker, and L. Zhang, "Supporting Real-Time Applications in an Integrated Services Packet Network: Architecture and Mechanism," ACM SIGCOMM'92, Baltimore, MD, August 1992, pp. 14-22.

[Cruz97] R. Cruz, "SCED: Efficient Management of Quality of Service Guarantees," Technical Report 9713, Center for Wireless Communications, UCSD, 1997.

[DaBo93] A. Danthine, O. Bonaventura, Y. Baguette, G. Leduc, and L. Leonard, "QoS Enhancements and the New Transport Services," in 'Local Network Interconnections,' Raleigh, NC, October 1993, pp. 1-22.

[Del93] L. Delgrossi, C. Halstrick, D. Hehmann, and R.G. Herrtwich, "Media Scaling for Audiovisual Communication with the Heidelberg Transport System," Technical Report 43.9305, IBM European Networking Center, Heidelberg, Germany, 1993.

[DLW93] B.J. Dempsey, J. Lieberherr, and A.C. Weaver, "A New Error Control Scheme for Packetized Voice over High-Speed Local Area Networks," 18th Conference on Local Computer Networks, Minneapolis, MN, September 1993.

[FeVe90] D. Ferrari and D.C. Verma, "A Scheme for Real-Time Channel Establishment in Wide-Area Networks," IEEE Journal on Selected Areas in Communications, 8(3), April 1990, pp. 368-379.

[Go90] S.J. Golestani, "A Stop-and-Go Queueing Framework for Congestion Management," ACM SIGCOMM'90, 20(4), September 1990, pp. 8-18.

[HLP93] J.M. Hyman, A. A. Lazar, and G. Pacifici, "A Separation Principle Between Scheduling and Admission Control for Broadband Switching," IEEE Journal on Selected Areas in Communications, 11(4), May 1993, pp. 605-616.

[KMR93] H. Kanakia, P.P. Mishra, and A. Reibman, "An Adaptive Congestion Control Scheme for Real-Time Packet Video Transport," ACM SIGCOMM'93, Baltimore, MD, August 1993.

[Ke97] J. Kenney, "Intermediate Traffic Management," CSE seminar/talk at University of Illinois at Urbana-Champaign, November 17, 1997.

[Ke92] S. Keshav, "Report on Workshop on QoS Issues in High-Speed Networks," Computer Communications Review, 22(5), October 1992, pp. 74-85.

[Ke95] S. Keshav and H. Saran, "Semantics and Implementation of a Native-Mode ATM Protocol Stack," Internal Technical Report, AT&T Bell Laboratories, Murray Hill, January 1995.

[KiNa97] K. Kim and K. Nahrstedt, "QoS Translation and Admission Control for MPEG Video," 5th International IFIP Workshop on Quality of Service, New York, NY, May 1997, pp. 359-362.

[LeRaMe96] Ch. Lee, R. Rajkumar, and C. Mercer, "Experiences with Processor Reservation and Dynamic QoS in Real-Time Mach," IEEE Multimedia Computing and Systems, Hiroshima, Japan, June 1996.

[Liu97] J. Liu, K. Nahrstedt, D. Hull, S. Chen, and B. Li, "EPIQ QoS Characterization," ARPA Technical Report, Quorum Meeting, July 1997.

[MaSt97] Q. Ma and P. Steenkiste, "Quality of Service Routing for Traffic with Performance Guarantees," 5th International IFIP Workshop on Quality of Service, New York, NY, May 1997, pp. 115-126.

[Mills93] D.M. Mills, "Precision Synchronization of Computer Network Clocks," ACM Computer Communication Review, 24(2), April 1993, pp. 28-43.

[NChN97] K. Nahrstedt. H, Chu, and S. Narayan, "QoS-aware Resource Management," Technical Report UIUCDCS-R-97-2030, University of Illinois at Urbana-Champaign, October 1997.

[NaSm95] K. Nahrstedt and J. Smith, "The QoS Broker," IEEE Multimedia, 2(1), Spring 1995, pp. 53-67.

[NaSm96] K. Nahrstedt and J. Smith, "Design, Implementation and Experiences of the OMEGA End-Point Architecture," IEEE JSAC, Special Issue on Distributed Multimedia Systems and Technology, 14(7), September 1997, pp. 1263-1279.

[NaSt95] K. Nahrstedt and R. Steinmetz, "Resource Management in Networked Multimedia Systems," IEEE Computer, May 1995, pp. 52-63.

[NaQi96] K. Nahrstedt and L. Qiao, "A Tuning System for Distributed Multimedia Applications," Technical Report UIUCDCS-R-96-1958, University of Illinois at Urbana-Champaign, July 1996.

[PZF92] C. Parris, H. Zhang, and D. Ferrari, "A Mechanism for Dynamic Re-Routing of Real-Time Services on Packet Networks," Technical Report TR-92-05, ICSI/UC Berkeley, August 1992.

[Pa94] C. Partridge, "Gigabit Networking," Addison-Wesley , 1994.

[QiNa97] L. Qiao and K. Nahrstedt, "Lip Synchronization within an Adaptive VOD System," SPIE Multimedia Computing and Networking, San Jose, CA, February 1997, pp. 170-181.

[RaTr98] S.V. Raghavan, S.K. Tripathi, "Networked Multimedia Systems," Prentice Hall, 1998.

[Si97] D. Sisalem, "End-to-End Quality of Service Control Using Adaptive Applications," 5th IFIP International Workshop on QoS, May 1997, pp. 381-391.

[Stei93b] R. Steinmetz, "Human Perception of Media Synchronization," Technical Report 43.9310, IBM European Networking Center, Heidelberg, Germany, 1993.

[StNa95] R. Steinmetz and K. Nahrstedt, "Multimedia: Computing, Communications and Applications," Prentice Hall, 1995.

[To92] H. Tokuda, Y. Tobe, S.T.C. Chou, and J.M.F. Moura, "Continuous Media Communication with Dynamic QoS Control Using ARTS with an FDDI Network," ACM SIGCOMM'92, Baltimore, MD, September 1992, pp. 88-98.

[Tu86] J.S. Turner, "New Directions in Communications (or Which Way to the Information Age)," IEEE Communications, 24(10), October 1986, pp. 8-15.

[VeNa97] N. Venkatasubriamanian and K. Nahrstedt, "An Integrated Metric for Video QoS," ACM Multimedia Conference, November 1997, Seattle, WA.

[WoHe94] L. Wolf and R. G. Herrtwich, "The System Architecture of the Heidelberg Transport System," ACM Operating Systems Review, 28(2), April 1994, pp. 51-64.

[ZhKe91] H. Zhang and S. Keshav, "Comparison of Rate-Based Service Disciplines," ACM SIGCOMM'91, Zurich, Switzerland, September 1991, pp. 113-122.

[Zh90] L. Zhang, "Virtual Clock: A New Traffic Control Algorithm for Packet Switching Networks," ACM SIGCOM'90, Philadelphia, PA, September 1990.

[ZDESZ93] L. Zhang, S. Deering, D. Estrin, S. Shenker, and D. Zappala, "RSVP: A New Resource Reservation Protocol," IEEE Computer, September 1993.

40

END-TO-END QUALITY IN MULTIMEDIA APPLICATIONS

Mark Claypool[1] and John Riedl[2]
*[1]Worcester Polytechnic Institute
Computer Science Department
claypool@cs.wpi.edu
[2]University of Minnesota
Computer Science Department
riedl@cs.umn.edu*

1.   **INTRODUCTION**...876
2.   **PERCEPTUAL QUALITY OF MULTIMEDIA** 878
3.   **AN EXAMPLE: END-TO-END QUALITY FOR VIDEOCONFERENCES**...................880
   3.1   THE REGION OF ACCEPTABLE VIDEOCONFERENCE QUALITY 880
   3.2   DETERMINING JITTER 881
   3.3   DETERMINING LATENCY 881
   3.4   DETERMINING DATA LOSS...882
   3.5   DETERMINING END-TO-END QUALITY...882
   3.6   HIGH-PERFORMANCE PROCESSORS AND HIGH-SPEED NETWORKS...................883
   3.7   USERS..884
   3.8   PROCESSOR AND NETWORK LOAD 885
4.   **SUMMARY**..885
   REFERENCES 887

Abstract. The tremendous power and low price of today's computer systems have created the opportunity for exciting applications rich with graphics, audio and video. In order to live up to their potential, these multimedia applications must meet the performance needs of the users they support. In particular, multimedia performance is dependent upon delay, jitter and data loss. In this chapter, we present end-to-end methods for determining delay, jitter and data loss. Furthermore, we tie delay, jitter and data loss into a perceptual quality metric that quantitatively evaluates application performance from the user perspective. As an example, we work through the application of our performance metric to a videoconference.

1. INTRODUCTION

The tremendous power and low price of today's computer systems have created the opportunity for exciting applications rich with graphics, audio and video. These new multimedia applications promise to support and even enhance the work we do in teams by allowing users to collaborate across both time and space. In order to live up to their potential, these multimedia applications must meet the performance needs of the users they support.

Thus far, research in multimedia performance has been targeted mostly at the systems-level characteristics of performance. These characteristics, called Quality of Service (QoS), represent the set of quantitative and qualitative characteristics of a distributed multimedia system necessary to achieve the required functionality of an application. Typical QoS parameters deal with system-level requirements, such as a bound on network delay. Resource reservation schemes are also tied to system-level capacities, such as guaranteed network throughput [ZDE93].

Application performance should strive to meet user-level requirements in addition to system level requirements. Users do not necessarily care about the throughput of the network or delay on network packet arrival times. Instead, users want defined image resolutions and audio clarity, a smooth playout of audio and video, and an upper bound on response time for interactive applications. Kalkbrenner had this in mind when he developed an interface to map user choices into system parameters [Kal94]. Users chose image size, resolution, and color for video and speech of telephone or CD quality for audio. These choices were then mapped into lower-level system parameters. Conversely, a measure of multimedia application performance should reflect how well the user choices are met by the system. From a user's point of view, what is needed is a performance metric that accounts for user-level requirements and gives them a measure of end-to-end quality.

"End-to-end" refers to the performance from the source of a multimedia conversation (often a microphone, video codec or disk) to the destination (often a speaker or monitor). An end-to-end measure of quality accounts for all the system components between the source and the destination that affect the performance of the application. For example, the end-to-end quality of a video-on-demand system on the Internet would be determined by the server workstation (codec, disk, bus, processor, ram, etc.), network (protocol, bandwidth, routers, etc.), and client workstation (processor, ram, video card, monitor, etc.). Acceptable performance of one component may result in poor application quality if the performance bottleneck is in another component. For example, determining that a network is supplying the required bits/second for a video display does not guarantee that the user workstation is displaying those frames smoothly or even that it is displaying them at all. An end-to-end measure of quality must take into account all system components that affect the media.

Different media place different constraints on computer systems. For instance, human eyes can smooth over occasional glitches in a video stream more readily than human ears can smooth over breaks in an audio stream [Cor97]. Having the computer system place greater emphasis on preserving audio data than on preserving video data might be important for user satisfaction. What is needed is a performance metric that accounts for performance effects from different media.

In addition, the constraints for each type of media can vary from application to application. For example, the acceptable delay for an audio broadcast application such as a radio program may be far more than the acceptable delay for an audioconference. In an audioconference, users require low latencies so that the conversation is as life-like as possible. However, in an audio broadcast program, the users do not interact, allowing a larger delay to go unnoticed. You could imagine a user downloading an entire radio program overnight and then playing it back in the morning. In this case, a delay of over eight hours might be quite acceptable. What is needed is a performance metric that accounts for user perceptions of different media.

Although we often think of a multimedia application as a continuous stream of data, computer systems handle multimedia in discrete events. An event may be receiving an update packet or displaying a rendered video frame on the screen. The quantity and timing of these events give us measures that affect application quality. Based on previous multimedia application research [SW93, AFKN95, Roy94, IKK93, PSR93, RS94, MS94, Fer92, KN82, TJ94, Par94, FM76], we have identified three measures that determine quality for most multimedia applications:

Latency. The time it takes information to move from the server through the client to the user we call latency. Latency decreases the effectiveness of applications by making them less like real-life interaction [Zeb93, IKK93, Roy94, DCJ93].

Jitter. Distributed applications usually run on non-dedicated systems. The underlying networks are often packet-switched and the workstations are often running multiple processes. These non-dedicated systems cause variance in the latency, which we call jitter. Jitter can cause gaps in the playout of a stream such as in an audioconference, or a choppy appearance to a video display [JSTS92, RS94, JVS91].

Data Loss. Any data less than the amount determined by the user requirements we call data loss. Data loss takes many forms such as reduced bits of color, pixel groups, smaller images, dropped frames and lossy compression [AFKN95, OOM95, MS94, SW93]. Data loss may be done voluntarily by either the client or the server in order to reduce load or to reduce jitter and/or latency. When any component in the end-to-end link does not have sufficient capacity to transmit data at the rate required by the application, data loss occurs. For example, if the network has a maximum bandwidth of 5 Mbps and a videoconference requires 10 Mbps, there will be 50% data loss.

The effects of latency on a user's perception of an application are well understood and well researched [Zeb93, IKK93, Roy94, DCJ93]. Human perception of latency is around 150 milliseconds. Generally, for interactive applications, latency must be under 500 milliseconds, often as low as 200 milliseconds.

Similarly, there is a clear relationship between data loss and application performance deterioration [AFKN95, OOM95, MS94, SW93]. Audio rates of 64 Kbits/second are acceptable for human voice. CD-quality sound requires around 1.5 Mbits/second. Frame rates of at least 3 frames per second have been found to be minimal for doing effective work. The human eye blends discrete images into motion at about 12 frames per second. Motion picture quality video is about 30 frames per second.

Methods to ameliorate the effects of jitter have been explored by many researchers [SJ95, RS94, Fer92, CHR97]. The tradeoff between buffering and jitter has also been explored [KN82, SR95].

There is no "one-size fits all" method for determining end-to-end multimedia performance. Previous research has defined metrics for components fundamental to most multimedia applications [WS95]. However, while there are fundamental requirements for most multimedia applications, some applications have unique user-level requirements. For example, a video display with audio has a user synchronization requirement for the sound and the display. Multimedia applications that have only audio or only video do not have a synchronization requirement. An end-to-end measure of quality must be flexible enough to incorporate application specific requirements in addition to the fundamental multimedia requirements.

The rest of this chapter is laid out as follows:

In Section 2, we present a performance metric for determining the end-to-end quality of multimedia applications. We describe the fundamental properties of a multimedia quality metric and propose our metric that satisfies these properties.

In Section 3, we present an example detailing the application of our quality metric to videoconferences. We introduce videoconferences, apply our metric and predict videoconference performance under a variety of system configurations, including faster processors and networks, increasing users and increasing system load.

In Section 4, we summarize the conclusions from this chapter. We also describe possibilities for future research including other quality metrics, media scaling and applications with changing requirements.

2. PERCEPTUAL QUALITY OF MULTIMEDIA

Perceptual quality is a measure of the performance of a multimedia application based on the requirements expected by the user. If the user performance requirements are met, application quality will be acceptable. If the user performance requirements are not met, application quality will be unacceptable. A multimedia performance metric must account for components fundamental to multimedia applications. As described in the beginning of the chapter, we have identified three fundamental measures that determine quality for most distributed multimedia applications: latency, jitter and data loss.

Ideally, we would like there to be no latency, jitter or data loss. Unfortunately, on a variable delay network and non-dedicated computer, this can never be achieved. To compute the perceptual quality of the multimedia application, we use the above quality components in a process depicted in Figure 1. The user requirements for the application define the acceptable latency, jitter and data loss. The end-to-end system determines the actual latency, jitter and data loss. Acceptable and actual data are fed into a *quality metric* for the application. The quality metric is a function, based on the acceptable components and dependent upon the actual components, that computes the application quality.

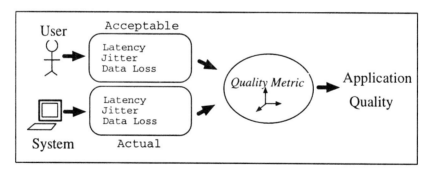

Figure 1. The Process for computing application quality.

The user defines the acceptable latency, jitter and data loss and the end-to-end system determines the actual values. Based on the acceptable values specified in the user requirements, a quality metric computes the application quality from the actual values.

In order to quantitatively evaluate application quality, we need a reasonable quality metric.[1] In the mathematical sense, given a space S with at least 3 elements (x, y, z), a metric is a real function of 2 variables $D(x,y)$ such that:

$D(x,y) >= 0$ (non-negative)

$D(x,y) = 0$ iff x=y (x and y are the same elements)

---

[1] A metric is sometimes called a measure of the distance between 2 points in any space.

D(x,y) = D(y,x) (symmetry)

D(x,y) + D(y,z) >= D(x,z) (triangle inequality, which says you cannot gain by going through an intermediate point)

We further define a perceptual quality metric for multimedia as having several other important properties:

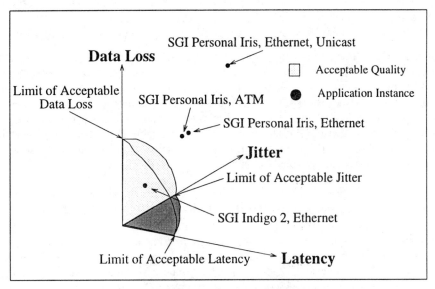

Figure 2. A perceptual quality space for multimedia applications.

The user defines the acceptable latency, jitter and data loss. These values determine a region of acceptable application quality, depicted by the shaded region. All points inside the shaded region have acceptable quality, while those outside the region do not. An instantiation of the application and the underlying computer system lies at one point in this space. Four application configuration instantiations are shown.

It incorporates the three fundamental multimedia perceptual quality components: latency, jitter and data loss.

It treats the fundamental components equally, which seems appropriate in the absence of user studies to the contrary.

It produces a convex region of acceptable quality. This fits our intuition about changes in quality: the measure increases total quality with any increase in quality along one axis. There are no pockets of unacceptable quality within the acceptable quality region, nor can you move from unacceptable to acceptable by any combinations of increase along the axes.

We propose a quality metric extended from the work of Naylor and Kleinrock [KN82]. Naylor and Kleinrock developed a model for measuring the quality of an audioconference based on the amount of dropped frames and client-side buffering. We extend this model by using each quality component as one axis, creating a multi-dimensional quality space. We place the best quality value for each axis at the origin and normalize each axis so that the user-defined minimum acceptable values have an equal weight. An instantiation of the application lies at one point in this space. The location of the point is determined by our predictions of the amount of latency, jitter and data loss that would occur with the given system configuration. In order to satisfy the mathematical properties of a metric, we compute the application quality by taking the Euclidean distance from the point to the origin. All points inside the region defined by the user-defined minimums have acceptable quality while points outside do not. Figure 2 depicts an example 3-D perceptual quality space for multimedia applications.

Our metric attains all of the mathematical metric properties and multimedia metric properties listed above. There can be many possible quality metrics for a given application. In fact, there may be many quality metrics that agree with a user's perception of the application. Mean opinion score (MOS) testing can be used to determine if a metric agrees with users' perceptions. The MOS is a five-point scale where a MOS of 5 indicates perfect quality and a score of 4 or more represents high quality. MOS has been used extensively in determining the acceptability of coded speech. MOS testing has been beyond the scope of our research, so we cannot be certain our quality metric fits users' perceptions. However, if new metrics are developed and validated with MOS testing, they can be used in place of our quality metric.

One limitation to multimedia perceptual quality metrics is that after scaling, the upper limits on the axes have different characteristics. The "data loss" axis has a finite upper-limit of 100%, while the "latency" and "jitter" axes each have an infinite bound. Comparing application quality for two different configurations at the upper-limit of any of the axes may not match user perception. Fortunately, this limitation usually arises when comparing two very unacceptable configurations. The metric is most valuable for determining whether a configuration provides "acceptable" or "unacceptable" application quality and comparing configurations within the "acceptable" region.

3. AN EXAMPLE: END-TO-END QUALITY FOR VIDEOCONFERENCES

In this section, we show how our perceptual quality metric for multimedia can be used to study the performance of videoconferences. We can learn a lot from videoconferences. Videoconferences incorporate both audio and video. Interactive videoconferences can have from two to tens of users, while videoconference broadcasts can have hundreds or perhaps even thousands of viewers. In addition, videoconferences are often integrated into larger multimedia applications. Determining end-to-end quality for various system configurations to support videoconferences is valuable for businesses wishing to invest in videoconference technology.

In order to apply our quality metric to a videoconference under various system configurations, we must: 1) determine the region of acceptable videoconference quality; 2) determine jitter; 3) determine latency; and 4) determine data loss.

3.1 THE REGION OF ACCEPTABLE VIDEOCONFERENCE QUALITY
To determine the region of acceptable videoconference quality, we need to define acceptable limits for videoconferences along each of the latency, jitter, and data loss axes. According to Jeffay and Stone, delays of 230 milliseconds or under are acceptable for a videoconference [JSS92]. For data loss, research in remote teleoperator performance has found that task performance is virtually impossible below a threshold of 3 frames per second [MS94]. We use 3 frames per second as the minimum acceptable frame rate.

The presence of jitter often presents an opportunity for a tradeoff among latency and data loss. Buffering, an application-level technique for ameliorating the effects of jitter, can compensate for jitter at the expense of latency. Transmitted frames are buffered in memory by the receiver for a period of time. Then, the receiver plays out each frame with a constant latency, achieving a steady stream. If the buffer is made sufficiently large so that it can hold all arriving data for a period of time as long as the tardiest frame, then the user receives a complete, steady stream. However, the added latency from buffering can be disturbing [Par94], so minimizing the amount of delay compensation is desirable.

Another buffering technique to compensate for jitter is to discard any late frame at the expense of data loss. Discarding frames causes a temporal gap in the play-out of the stream. Discarding frames can keep play-out latency low and constant, but as little as 6% gaps in the playout stream can also be disturbing [KN82]. In the case of audio speech, the listener would experience an annoying pause during this period. In the case of video, the viewer would see the frozen image of the most recently delivered frame.

Naylor and Kleinrock describe two policies that make use of these buffering techniques: the E-Policy (for Expanded time) and the I-Policy (for late data Ignored) [KN82]. Under the E-policy, frames are never dropped. Under the I-policy, frames later than a given amount are dropped. Since it has been observed that using a strict E-Policy tends to cause the playout latency to grow excessively and that dropping frames occasionally is tolerable [CSZ92, SJ95], we use the I-Policy as a means of examining needed jitter compensation for a multimedia stream.

The I-policy leads to a useful way to view the effects of jitter on a multimedia stream. Figure 3 depicts the tradeoff between dropped frames and buffering as a result of jitter. We generated the graph by first recording a trace of video frame interarrival times. We then fixed a delay buffer for the receiver and computed the percentage of frames that would be dropped. This represents one point in the graph. We repeated this computation with buffers ranging from 0 to 250 milliseconds to generate the curved line. The graph can be read in two ways. In the first, we choose a tolerable amount of dropped frames (the horizontal axis), then follow that point up to the line to determine how many milliseconds of buffering are required. In the second, we choose a fixed buffer size (the vertical axis), then follow that point over to the line to determine what percent of frames are dropped. If we wish to restrict the amount of buffering to 100 milliseconds, then we must drop about 2% of the frames since that is how many will be more than 100 milliseconds late, on average. For a 2 Mbps video stream consisting of 33 6-Kbyte frames per second, this equates to dropping one frame every 1.5 seconds. On the other hand, if we wish to not drop any frames, we have to buffer for over 200 milliseconds.

3.2 DETERMINING JITTER
Previous experiments measuring the effectiveness of several jitter reduction techniques give us the relationship between load and jitter for faster processors and networks [CHR97]. We also know the reduction in jitter due to real-time operating system priorities [CHR97]. We use these results as the basis for determining the jitter in the videoconference under various system configurations.

3.3 DETERMINING LATENCY
We can predict the amount of latency from the jitter compensation buffer by using predictions on the amount of jitter. In addition to the buffering latency, there is the additional latency from the sender processing, the network transmitting and the receiver processing. In previous experiments, we measured the latency from recording and playing video [CR96]. From other previous experiments, we measured the latency attributed to sending and receiving packets [CR94]. We can compute the latency from the network based on the frame size and network bandwidth. To predict the total latency, we add the latencies from: recording the video frame; sending the video frame to the client; receiving the video frame from the receiver; buffering in the jitter compensation curve; and playing the video frame.

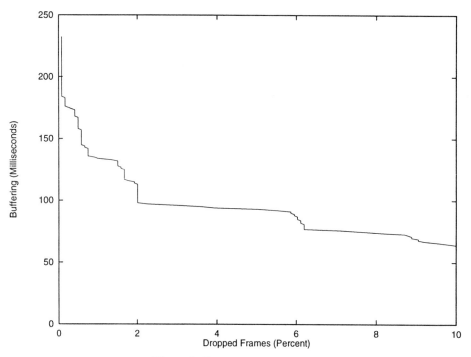

Figure 3. Jitter compensation.
This picture depicts the amount of buffering needed for a given number of dropped frames. The horizontal axis is the percentage of dropped frames. The vertical axis is the number of milliseconds of buffering needed.

3.4 DETERMINING DATA LOSS

In order to predict data loss, we need to identify what form data loss may take and when data loss may occur. In general, data loss can take many forms such as reduced bits of color, jumbo pixels, smaller images, dropped frames and lossy compression. For a videoconference, we assume data loss only in the form of dropped frames or reduced frame rate. For a videoconference, we assume data loss under three conditions:

- *Voluntary.* As described in Section 3.1, an application may choose to discard late frames in order to keep playout latency low and constant. We assume the videoconference chooses to discard enough frames to achieve the best quality.

- *Saturation.* When either the network or the processor do not have sufficient capacity to transmit data at the required frame rate, data loss occurs. For example, if the network has a maximum bandwidth of 5 Mbps and the videoconference required 10 Mbps, there will be a 50% data loss. We can compute when systems reach capacity based on our previous work measuring processor capacities [CR94, CR96] and theoretical network bandwidths.

- *Transmission Loss.* In previous experiments, we found that typically about 0.5% packets on the average are lost when the network is running under maximum load [CR96]. We assume a maximum lost data rate of about 0.5% due to network transmission.

3.5 DETERMINING END-TO-END QUALITY

We can now use our metric to explore end-to-end videoconference quality under different system configurations. We can quantify how effectively today's computer systems support multi-person videoconferences. We can determine when today's systems will fail due to too many users or too much load on the processors or networks. We can see how using real-time priorities will help videoconference quality. We can evaluate the benefits of expensive high-performance processors and high-speed networks before installing them. We can even investigate possible performance benefits from networks and processors that have not yet been built. Let's go exploring!

We determine application quality for three scenarios: 1) high-performance processors and high-speed networks; 2) increasing users; and 3) increasing system load.

For all of our videoconference quality predictions we assume:

- *Multicast.* Our previous work has found that multicast is crucial for many-person multimedia applications [CR96]. Using unicast routing, multi-person multimedia applications saturate existing networks for even a few participants. Multicast routing dramatically increases the user scalability of multi-person applications.

- *Specialized Hardware.* The processor load for processing video frames can be substantial [CRC+95]. We assume specialized hardware that does most of the computation required for video frame processing.

3.6 HIGH-PERFORMANCE PROCESSORS AND HIGH-SPEED NETWORKS
Our previous experimental results showed that both high-performance processors and high-speed networks reduce jitter [CHR97]. However, which reduces jitter more? And more importantly, which improves application quality more?

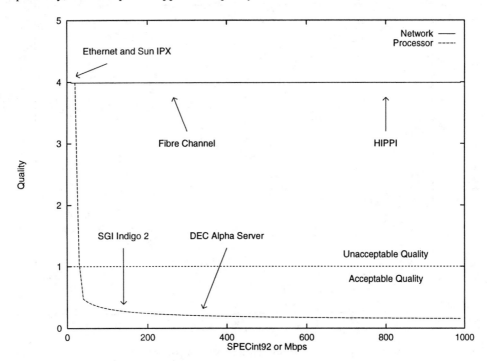

Figure 4. Videoconference quality versus processor or network increase.

The horizontal axis is the SPECint92 power of the workstation or the network Mbps. The vertical axis is the predicted quality. There are two scenarios depicted. In the first, the processor power is constant, equivalent to a Sun IPX (SPECint92 = 22), while the network bandwidth increases. This is depicted by the solid curve. In the second scenario, the network bandwidth is constant, equivalent to an Ethernet (10 Mbps), while the processor power increases. This is depicted by the dashed curve. The horizontal line marks the limit between acceptable and unacceptable videoconference quality.

We assume we have five videoconference participants. In Subsection 3.7, we use our model to evaluate quality for a variable number of users, but here we evaluate a likely videoconference configuration that has interesting quality predictions. We compute quality under two different scenarios. In the first, processor load remains constant while the network bandwidth increases. In the second, network bandwidth remains constant while processor power increases. We use the Standard Performance Evaluation Corporation (SPEC) benchmarks to make predictions about end-to-end quality on more powerful workstations [Cor94]. Figure 4 shows these predictions. For five users, increasing the processor power to a SPECint92 of 40 or greater results in acceptable videoconference quality. At no time does increasing the network bandwidth result in an acceptable quality. In this scenario, we conclude that processor power influences videoconference quality more than does network bandwidth.

3.7 USERS

While today's computer systems may struggle to support even five videoconference participants, tomorrow's processor improvements promise to support more and more users. But how many more? How do more and more videoconference users affect application quality? Figure 5 depicts the predicted effects of increasing users on videoconference quality.

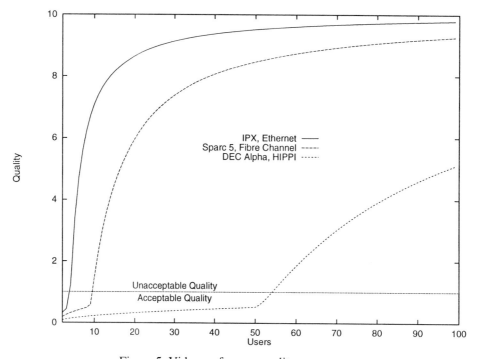

Figure 5. Videoconference quality versus users.

The horizontal axis is the number of users. The vertical axis is the predicted quality. There are three scenarios depicted. In the first, the processors is a Sun IPXs connected by an Ethernet. In the second, the processors is a Sun Sparc 5s connected by a Fibre Channel. In the third, the processors are DEC Alphas connected by a HIPPI. The horizontal line marks the limit between acceptable and unacceptable videoconference quality.

We predict videoconference quality for three different videoconference configurations: a low-end workstation with a typical network (Sun IPX and Ethernet), a mid-range workstation with a fast network (Sun Sparc 5 and Fibre Channel), and a high-performance workstation with a high-speed network (DEC Alpha and HIPPI). As we saw in Subsection 3.6, today's low-end workstation and typical Ethernet network cannot support even five videoconference participants. However, workstations such as Sun Sparc 5s connected by fast networks such as a Fibre Channel can support up to 10 users. Very high-performance workstations such as DEC Alphas connected by a high-speed network such as a HIPPI can support over 50 users.

3.8 PROCESSOR AND NETWORK LOAD

Videoconferences are resource intensive, forcing processors and networks to run at heavy loads. In addition, videoconference streams are often integrated into larger distributed multimedia applications. In the past, applications have tended to expand to fill (or surpass) available system capacity. As system capacities increase, videoconference users will demand higher frame rates and better resolution, making heavy-load conditions likely in the future. We predict the effects of increasing load on videoconference quality.

Figure 6 depicts the predicted effects of load on videoconference quality (remember, we are assuming specialized hardware for video processing and multicast routing). There are three classes of systems depicted. A traditional system has Sun IPXs connected by an Ethernet. A mid-range system has Sun Sparc 5 connected by a Fibre Channel. A high-end system has DEC Alphas connected by a HIPPI. The predictions for videoconference quality are almost identical for the three systems. We saw in Subsection 3.6 that the processor is more crucial than network for videoconference quality. Increasing processor load has a larger effect on decreasing videoconference quality than does improving the network speed and processor power.

Figure 6 also depicts Sun IPXs connected by an Ethernet but using real-time priorities instead of default priorities, shown by the bottom line. With real-time priorities, videoconference quality does not suffer from increased jitter from the processor as processor load increases. For conditions of increasing load, real-time priorities have a greater effect on improving quality than do faster processors and faster networks.

4. SUMMARY

Today's explosive growth in fast networks and powerful workstations has provided the potential to support and even enhance group work through multimedia applications. Before realizing the real and potential benefits of multimedia, we must overcome several obstacles in designing multimedia applications and systems. Multimedia and multi-user applications are more resource intensive than traditional text-based, single-user applications. In addition, multimedia applications have different performance requirements than do text-based applications. Text-based applications are sensitive to latency and loss, while multimedia applications are sensitive to latency and jitter. The bottlenecks to text-based application performance might lie in those components that induce latency, while the bottlenecks to multimedia applications might lie in those components that induce the jitter. New techniques must be developed to identify bottlenecks in the end-to-end perceptual quality of multimedia applications.

A measure of end-to-end quality must take into account the components fundamental to multimedia applications: latency, jitter and data loss. In addition, such a measure should allow the investigation of bottlenecks in quality by being adjustable to number of users, applications, different quality metrics and alternate hardware and architectures. In this chapter, we present one such measure of multimedia application quality from the user perspective.

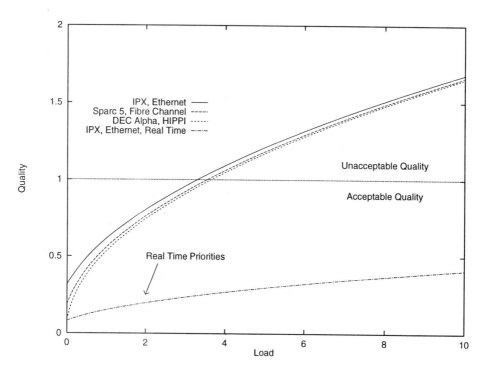

Figure 6. Videoconference quality versus load.

The horizontal axis is the processor load. The vertical axis is the quality prediction. There are four system configurations depicted. In the first, the processors are Sun IPXs connected by an Ethernet. In the second, the processors are Sun Sparc 5s connected by a Fibre Channel. In the third, the processors are DEC Alphas connected by a HIPPI. In the fourth, the processors are again Sun IPXs connected by an Ethernet, but they are using real-time priorities instead of default priorities. The upper horizontal line marks the limit between acceptable and unacceptable videoconference quality.

There are still many exciting areas for future work. As presented in this chapter, the fundamental perceptual quality component of "data loss" can be expanded upon. We have described the "percent" of lost data as if all bytes in a multimedia stream were equivalent. In reality, some parts of the stream are more important that others. For example, the silent parts between words in speech are less important for user intelligibility than the words themselves. Likewise, movie frames that have very little scene change from the previous frames are likely less important to the user than are frames which vary a lot. On the systems level, too, there may be bytes that are more important than other bytes. For example, the I frames in an MPEG video stream are more important to the system than the P frames since you cannot reconstruct subsequent P frames without the I frames. If possible, the data loss axis should be weighted to reflect the import of the bytes that are actually lost.

For some applications, there is potential for interaction effects among the quality events. For example, 3-D graphics applications have multiple factors affecting users' perception of objects and different combinations of requirements may yield satisfactory results. Such applications may even have a non-convex region of acceptable quality. Future research into new quality metrics appropriate for these applications may be required.

Applications that have changing user requirements present another challenge. For example, users doing remote problem solving via a video link may want to maximize frame rate at the expense of frame resolution while they are identifying the location of the problem. Once the problem is located, they may want to maximize frame resolution at the expense of frame rate (perhaps even wanting a still image) to best identify the problem. As presented, our metric does not allow specification of dynamic user requirements. One possible solution would be to apply a separate quality metric to each set of user requirements specified. The metric that had the poorest quality for a given system configuration could then be examined more closely to determine the application quality bottleneck within.

REFERENCES

[AFKN95]   R. T. Apteker, J. A. Fisher, V. S. Kismov, and H. Neishlos. Video acceptability and frame rate. *IEEE Multimedia,* pp. 32–40, Fall 1995.

[CHR97]   M. Claypool, J. Habermann, and J. Riedl. The effects of high-performance processors, real-time priorities and high-speed networks on jitter in a multimedia stream. Technical Report TR-97-023, University of Minnesota, Department of Computer Science, June 1997.

[Cor94]   Standard Performance Evaluation Corporation. SPEC primer. July 1994. The SPEC primer is frequently posted to the newsgroup comp.benchmarks. SPEC questions can also be sent to spec-ncga@cup.portal.com.

[Cor97]   American Technology Corporation. *HyperSonic Sound System (HSS) – (A New Method of Sound Reproduction).* July 1997. The URL for this document can be found at http://www.atcsd.com/HTML/sound2.html.

[CR94]   M. Claypool and J. Riedl. Silence is golden? The effects of silence deletion on the CPU load of an audio conference. *Proceedings of IEEE Multimedia,* Boston, May 1994.

[CR96]   M. Claypool and J. Riedl. A quality planning model for distributed multimedia in the virtual cockpit. *Proceedings of ACM Multimedia,* pp. 253-264, November 1996.

[CRC⁺95]   M. Claypool, J. Riedl, J. Carlis, G. Wilcox, R. Elde, E. Retzel, A. Georgopoulos, J. Pardo, K. Ugurbil, B. Miller, and C. Honda. Network requirements for 3D flying in a zoomable brain database. *IEEE JSAC Special Issue on Gigabit Networking,* 13(5), June 1995.

[CSZ92]   D. Clark, S. Shenker, and L. Zhang. Supporting real-time applications in integrated services packet network: Architecture and mechanism. *Computer Communication Review,* 22(4), July 1992.

[DCJ93]   S. Dimolitsas, F. L. Corcoran, and J. G. Philips Jr. Impact of transmission delay on ISDN videotelephony. *Proceedings of Globecom '93 – IEEE Telecommunications Conference,* pp. 376–379, Houston, TX, November 1993.

[Fer92]   D. Ferrari. Delay jitter control scheme for packet-switching internetworks. *Computer Communications,* 15(6): 367 – 373, July 1992.

[FM76]   J.W. Forgie and C.W. McElwain. Some comments on NSC note 78' effects of lost packets on speech intelligibility. Technical Report Network Speech Compression Note 92, M. I. T., Lincoln Laboratory, March 1976.

[IKK93]   S. Iai, T. Kurita, and N. Kitawaki. Quality requirements for multimedia communication services and terminals – interaction of speech and video delays. *Proceedings of Globecom '93 – IEEE Telecommunications Conference,* pp. 394–398, Houston, TX, November 1993.

[JSS92]   K. Jeffay, D. Stone, and F. Smith. Kernel support for live digital audio and video. *Computer Communications,* 15(6), 1992.

[JSTS92]   K. Jeffay, D. L. Stone, T. Talley, and F. D. Smith. Adaptive, best-effort, delivery of audio and video data across packet-switched networks. *Proc. of 3rd International Workshop on Network and Operating System Support for Digital Audio and Video,* November 1992.

[JVS91]   S. Jin, D. R. Vaman, and D. Sina. A performance management framework to provide bounded packet delay and variance in packet switched networks. *Computer networks and ISDN Systems,* pp. 249 – 264, September 1991.

[Kal94]   B. Kalkbrenner. Quality of Service (QoS) in distributed hypermedia systems. *Proceedings of the 2nd International Workshop on Principles of Document Processing,* 1994.

[KN82]   R. Kleinrock and A. Naylor. Stream traffic communication in packet switched networks: Destination buffering considerations. *IEEE Transactions on Communication,* COM-30(12):252-2534, December 1982.

[MS94]   M. J. Massimino and T. B. Sheridan. Teleoperator performance with varying force and visual feedback. *Human Factors,* pp. 145-157, March 1994.

[OOM95]   J. S. Olson, G. M. Olson, and D. K. Meader. What mix of video and audio is useful for real-time work? *Proceedings of CHI'95 – Proceedings of the Conference in Human Factors in Computing Systems,* pp. 362 – 368, 1995.

[Par94]   C. Partridge. Gigabit Networking. Addison-Wesley, 1994.

[PSR93]   K. Patel, B. C. Smith, and L. A. Rowe. Performance of a software MPEG video decoder. *Proceedings of ACM Multimedia,* Anaheim, CA, 1993.

[Roy94]   R. R. Roy. Networking constraints in multimedia conferencing and the role of ATM networks. *AT&T Technical Journal,* July/August 1994.

[RS94]   R. Ramjee, J. Kurose, D. Towsley, and H. Schulzrinne. Adaptive playout mechanisms for packetized audio applications in wide-area networks. *Proceedings of the 13th Annual Joint Conference of the IEEE Computer and Communications Societies on Networking for Global Communication.* Vol. 2, pp. 680-688, Los Alamitos, CA, 1994. IEEE Computer Society Press.

[SJ95]   D. Stone and K. Jeffay. An empirical study of delay jitter management policies. *Multimedia Systems,* 1995.

[SR95]   M. V. Stein and J. T. Riedl. The effects of transport method on the quality of audioconferences with silence deletion. Technical Report, University of Minnesota, Department of Computer Science, June 1995.

[SW93]   M. Swartz and D. Wallace. Effects of frame rate and resolution reduction on human performance. *Proceedings of IS&T's 46th Annual Conference,* Munich, Germany, 1993.

[TJ94]   T. Talley and K. Jeffay. Two-dimensional scaling techniques for adaptive, rate-based transmission control of live audio and video streams. *Proceedings of the 2nd ACM International Conference on Multimedia,* pp. 247-254, October 1994.

[WS95]   D. Wijesekera and J. Srivastava. Quality of service metrics for continuous media. *Protocols for Multimedia Systems,* pp. 269-289, 1995.

[ZDE93]   L. Zhang, S. Deering, and D. Estrin. RSVP: A new resource ReSerVation Protocol. Novel design features lead to an internet protocol that is flexible and scalable. *IEEE Network,* 7(5), September 1993.

[Zeb93]   J. A. Zebarth. Let me be me. *Proceedings of Globecom '93 – IEEE Telecommunications Conference,* pp. 389–393, Houston, TX, November 1993.

41

RESOURCE MANAGEMENT IN MULTIMEDIA SYSTEMS

Lars C. Wolf
Darmstadt University of Technology
Department of Electrical Engineering & Information Technology
Industrial Process and System Communications
Merckstr. 25 · D-64283 Darmstadt · Germany

1. **INTRODUCTION** 892
2. **RESOURCES AND RESOURCE MANAGEMENT** 893
   2.1 RESOURCES 893
   2.2 RESOURCE CAPACITY 894
   2.3 RESOURCE MANAGEMENT FUNCTIONALITY 895
   2.4 RESOURCE RESERVATION PROTOCOLS 897
   2.5 RESOURCE MANAGEMENT SYSTEM STRUCTURE 898
3. **PROCESSOR MANAGEMENT** 899
   3.1 REQUIREMENTS 900
   3.2 COMMON METHODS 900
   3.3 LIMITATIONS AND EXTENSIONS 902
   3.4 TASK DEPENDENCIES 902
4. **MEMORY MANAGEMENT** 903
5. **ADAPTIVE RESOURCE MANAGEMENT** 905
6. **FURTHER ISSUES** 908
   6.1 RESOURCE ACCOUNTING 908
   6.2 RESOURCE MANAGEMENT IN FUTURE OPERATING SYSTEMS 909
   6.3 RESERVATION IN ADVANCE 909
7. **SUMMARY** 910
   REFERENCES 911

Abstract. Multimedia systems must be able to support a certain Quality of Service (QoS) to satisfy the stringent real-time performance requirements of their applications. Resource management systems contain mechanisms to administer and schedule system resources to give time-critical multimedia applications access to all necessary resources when needed so that their QoS requirements can be met. Static resource management systems use and extend techniques developed in the field of real-time systems. They perform QoS calculation and resource reservation based on the requirement specifications given by applications during their setup, and schedule the resources in such a way that processing deadlines are met.

While this approach can offer strong guarantees for the application's performance, it has the drawback that it is difficult to determine the amount of resources needed in advance and that it cannot easily cope with a change in the set of running applications during the run-time of an application. Dynamic schemes, also called adaptive resource management, extend the static approach by methods for resource usage monitoring and renegotiation. They gain more flexibility in exchange to the firmness of the reachable QoS. In this chapter, we describe the purpose of resource management systems and give an overview about the principles.

1. INTRODUCTION

Multimedia applications integrating audio and video data into distributed computer systems have become possible due to the advances in computer and communication technology such as increased processing speed, network bandwidth, and storage size.

In comparison to media traditionally handled in computers, e.g., text and graphics, audio and video have different characteristics. Humans perceive audio and video as continuously changing, therefore, they are also called continuous media. This contrasts with discrete media such as text and graphics. Since audiovisual information is time critical, the processing requirements of such continuous media data are different from discrete media data because the value of the applications processing depends not only on the accuracy of the computations, but also on the time when this processing has finished. In addition to the time criticality, the processing demands of digital audio and video data are typically large. The treatment and finally, the display of audiovisual data must be done with a certain quality in order to provide for a satisfying overall presentation.

An application must operate with a certain Quality of Service (QoS) to fulfill its task. The required QoS depends on various issues, for example, the used media (video, audio, etc.), the coding format used to encode the data, the application, and the type of the application. For instance, the QoS of a video conference is different from that of a video retrieval application, since the dialogue-mode communication of a conference requires a short delay which is not as important for playback applications.

Processing within multimedia systems is performed in various layers: in application-layer code, in the operating system, in the communication system, etc. And each of these layers can be constructed by layering. In each of these several layers, a different notion of QoS exists, e.g., QoS at the application layer is usually described at a higher level than QoS at the network layer of a communication system and different terms are used. However, the QoS parameters, bandwidth, delay, and loss are used in all layers, sometimes in conjunction with other parameters. The applications specify their requirements in higher layer QoS terms. These are potentially translated in several steps towards more system-oriented parameters, which are used to control the system parameters.

A resource management system (e.g., [17]) provides the means to offer QoS to multimedia applications, e.g., so that the participants in a video conference do not experience large delays or low video frame rates during their interaction. These mechanisms administer and schedule system resources to give time-critical multimedia applications access to all necessary resources when needed, so that their QoS requirements can be met. These mechanisms must address the following issues:

.

- QoS calculation - to check whether the QoS demands of an application can be satisfied.
- Resource reservation - to reserve an amount of resources according to the given QoS guarantee.
- Resource scheduling - to enforce that the given QoS guarantees are satisfied by appropriate scheduling of resource access.

In addition to such static functionality, adaptive resource management systems (such as, e.g., [7]) also offer mechanisms which help the applications to adapt their behavior and their resource demands in case the available resource capacity changes or the reserved resources are insufficient. The former case can occur if the user decides to execute an additional application, the latter case can be due to an incorrect specification of resource requirements. We will discuss adaptive resource management in Section 5.

Multimedia applications have to deal with the processing of time-critical, large volume, audiovisual data on one hand, and on the other hand, they have to provide a nice looking, easy to use interface to the user. To ease the task of application programmers, the processing of the continuous media streams can be encapsulated in specific software modules, as has been proposed by several research groups (e.g., [5], [6]). This allows for code reuse and simplified application development. Examples for such building blocks are modules for decompression, for mixing streams, etc. An application specifies which modules are needed and how they have to be connected, forming a directed (not necessarily linear) graph of modules. As an example, Figure 1 shows an application consisting of three modules. If such an approach is used, the resource management must be devised for such a module-based system.

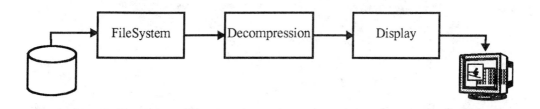

Figure 1. Application containing three modules.

2. RESOURCES AND RESOURCE MANAGEMENT

2.1 RESOURCES

Resources are all the entities, which participate in the overall task of the application, i.e., all parts which are required for processing, for transmitting, and for presenting the data. This comprises resources on the path from source(s) via networks including routers and switches to sink(s), both in the local systems and the network.

Resources can be classified whether they are (1) active or passive, e.g., CPU vs. memory, (2) exclusive or shared by several processes at a time, and (3) single or multiple, e.g., how many instances of a resource are available in the system.

Each resource has a certain capacity, which can be used by applications to perform their task. The capacity of a resource is administered by the resource management system.

A resource management system manages all the resources, which are critical for the execution of the continuous media data processing of an application, e.g., CPU time, network bandwidth, and memory. This comprises all resources, which are involved in the overall task of the application, i.e., those used by the application for local processing, those to move the data to or from the transport system interface, and those needed by the transport system to transfer the messages across the network (illustrated in Figure 2). This, therefore, includes all the limited system resources through which a media stream passes which are:

- bus (resp. switch) bandwidth, e.g., for the movement of data from memory to network adapter,
- I/O devices, e.g., special (de-)compression boards,
- external storage, e.g., hard disks, with file systems,
- network adapters and network resources to transfer packets from one node to another,
- processors to execute application and system software,
- main memory to hold the application and system code and buffer space for the data.

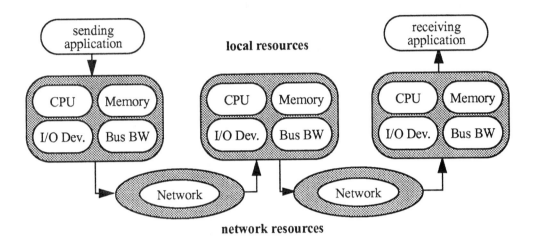

Figure 2. Resources to be managed.

Most work deals with the management of the processors, the network resources, and the file systems, while little work has been done on the management of the bus bandwidth. Within this chapter we will illustrate general methods of resource management and discuss mechanisms for processors and the main memory as examples for resource managers, which administer a particular resource.

2.2 RESOURCE CAPACITY

To deliver a particular level of QoS to an application, the system must possess resource capacities, which are at least as large as the requirements. In addition to the overall available capacity, these resources must be scheduled in such a way that they are available for the application when needed. Many of today's communication and computer systems offer sufficient resources to handle some continuous media streams, but the quantity and quality of such streams is still limited since the resources are limited. The "window of scarcity" postulated by Anderson, et al., in [1] illustrates this (Figure 3 shows an adapted version).

The available resources are insufficient to provide acceptable service at a specific time and for certain application types (left side, Figure 3). Due to ongoing improvements in technology, system resources become sufficient for new applications, however, the available resources are scarce, i.e., they must be administrated and scheduled carefully to offer the desired QoS (middle, Figure 3). After further technology advances, resources are abundant with respect to a particular application, i.e., the service can be offered without specific management mechanisms (right side, Figure 3).

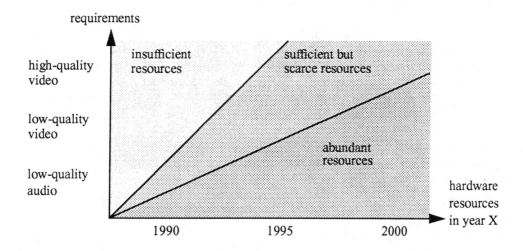

Figure 3. "Window of Scarcity" (adapted from [1]).

Depending on the particular notion of 'quality', the number of concurrent users and the number of concurrent continuous media streams of one user, the areas are reached at a different point in time. Nevertheless, at least in the near future, distributed computer systems will have only sufficient but scarce system resources available for, e.g., the processing of multiple continuous media streams. Due to increased user expectations, e.g., larger video frame sizes, etc., it takes more time until the region of abundant resources is reached, if ever. Furthermore, also in the future, when large system resources might be available for processing and transmitting of data, a time-critical application must be `shielded' against non-real-time and other real-time applications so that they cannot inhibit its real-time processing. And for shared systems offering services to several users simultaneously, e.g., video-on-demand servers, means to manage the available system resources are needed in the future as well because providers of such systems want as efficient resource use as possible, i.e., to serve as many clients using as few systems as possible.

The mechanisms for QoS calculation, resource reservation and scheduling rely on the knowledge of the amount of resources required for the execution of a particular multimedia application. Therefore, methods to determine the resource requirements are needed to successfully apply the resource management mechanisms mentioned above. Because resource requirements depend on the particular computer system and its configuration, the techniques to find out the resource demands of an application must allow for flexible and automatic measurements, e.g., at installation time or even at run-time but without delaying the application start-up which would be annoying to most users. If the application has been constructed using a module-based system as mentioned above, its resource requirements consist of the requirements of each single module. These demands must be collected and combined by according mechanisms.

2.3 RESOURCE MANAGEMENT FUNCTIONALITY
A multimedia application, which desires to get support from the resource management system, specifies the overall QoS demands it has which, in turn, result in requirements on the various resources. The resource management system, for instance HeiRAT (Heidelberg Resource Administration Technique) [15], [16], checks whether this additional workload can

be handled and what kind of service it can offer. Furthermore, it reserves the required resources and schedules incoming processing requests accordingly. After the handling of the workload has ended, the reserved resources are released. Hence, it offers the following functionality for both active and passive resources:

- Admission test: When a new multimedia stream shall be established, it is checked whether enough free resource capacity is available to handle it. This decision is influenced by the QoS guarantees already given to other streams; with static resource management, these guarantees must not be violated by adding the new stream.
- QoS calculation: Every resource computes the QoS it can provide for the new stream.
- Resource reservation: The resource capacity is reserved that is required to provide the QoS guarantee.
- Resource scheduling: Resource access is coordinated so that the respective QoS guarantees of all streams are satisfied.
- Resource deallocation: The reserved resources are released.

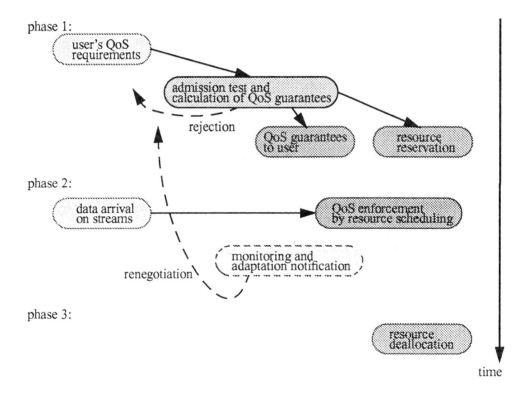

Figure 4. Resource management phases.

As illustrated in Figure 4, these functions can be grouped into three phases. The first three functions belong to the set-up or QoS negotiation phase. In that phase, applications specify their QoS requirements which are used for the admission test (e.g., the schedulability test for the CPU) and the QoS calculation. This results either in a resource reservation or in the rejection of the request in case the QoS cannot be met. The second phase is the transmission or QoS enforcement phase. In this phase, after the successful establishment of a stream, the resources are scheduled with respect to the given QoS guarantees. The usage of the resources is monitored and, if necessary, the necessity to change the behavior is indicated to the applications. In order to perform these last two steps, functions are necessary during the processing of a stream for

- Resource monitoring: observe the resource usage of the applications, and monitor the overall load put onto the resource,
- Adaptation: inform applications that their resource usage must change and that they should renegotiate their resource reservations.

These functions are especially needed if an adaptive resource management system is used. Finally, in the deallocation phase, the reserved resources are released.

In the set-up phase, resource management systems typically offer several options by which applications can specify their QoS requirements. For instance, QoS values can be given in terms of maximum end-to-end delay, minimum throughput needed, and reliability class defining how the loss of data shall be treated. An application can select one of the QoS parameters for optimization by specifying an interval from desired to worst acceptable values. For example, a video application might request a throughput between 15 and 30 video frames per second, indicating that video quality would not be acceptable with less than 15 frames, but that more than 30 frames are never needed. The resource management system will then return the best QoS it can guarantee within this interval and make the corresponding reservation. If even the lower bound cannot be supported, the request is rejected in a static resource management system. In an adaptive system, the resource management may ask already running applications to reduce their resource requirements and reservations to provide sufficient spare capacity to serve this additional, new application.

In the transmission phase, data are processed and transmitted according to their urgency. Schedulers handle time-critical multimedia streams prior to time-independent data. They exploit properties of the underlying resources, for example, they are based on the operating system priority scheme for CPU scheduling or the MAC priority scheme of the network.

In the deallocation phase, after the transmission has finished, the allocated resources such as CPU or buffer space must be released. This can be initiated by the application, which performed the reservation or by the system, e.g., due to a system failure or a permanent mismatch between negotiated and delivered QoS or resource usage.

The reservation can be made in different ways. One possibility is to distinguish between a pessimistic and an optimistic manner. With the pessimistic approach, the resource capacities are reserved for the worst case, i.e., the maximum demand a stream may have during its lifetime. The advantage of this scheme is that it avoids conflicts and offers deterministic guarantees. However, reserving extensive amounts of capacities for such peak requirements can be rather costly and leads to the underutilization of resources if there is a significant difference between peak and average data rate of a stream. A cheaper alternative is followed by the optimistic approach where resources are reserved on average workload, i.e., they can be slightly overbooked. This implies that while QoS requirements will be met most of the time, occasional QoS violations may occur. Applications, which perform optimistic reservations, must be aware of temporary resource conflicts, hence, they must be ready to cope with them. This can, therefore, already be considered as a (simple) adaptive scheme.

2.4 RESOURCE RESERVATION PROTOCOLS
In distributed multimedia systems, continuous media streams are transmitted across a multi-hop network. On their way, they are handled by multiple system resources. To obtain an end-to-end QoS guarantee, from source to destination, reservations on all the individual resources handling the stream must be made and the according guarantees must be aggregated. This requires a resource reservation protocol such as RSVP [3] to exchange and negotiate QoS requirements across system boundaries. The fact that the network is one of the resources to be

managed makes it necessary to integrate the resource reservation protocol with the network layer of the transport system; higher layers have no information about the different resources in the network.

Depending on the reservation protocol, the reservation can be made in a receiver- or a sender-oriented way. In both cases, several entities participate in the end-to-end QoS negotiation: sending and receiving applications, agents executing the resource reservation protocol, and local resource managers (Figure 5).

Applications specify their QoS requirements, which are possibly mapped by the transport layer on a QoS request in terms of network layer units due to packet segmentation. This request becomes part of a reservation message. Each local resource manager on the path receiving the message checks whether its available resource capacities can serve this request and reserve the resource capacities needed.

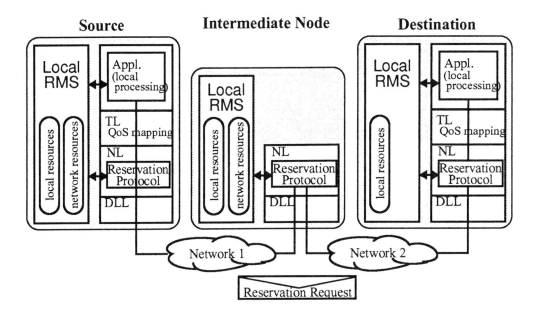

Figure 5. Distributed resource reservation.

2.5 RESOURCE MANAGEMENT SYSTEM STRUCTURE

The resource management contains components used in the enforcement phase, i.e., to schedule the access to the system resources and to monitor their usage, and modules needed in the negotiation phase, i.e., to perform the throughput test, the QoS computation, and the resource reservation. To be able to perform the scheduling, the enforcement components must be located near the affected resources. The components used during the negotiation must be structured in such a way that the data structures of the resource management system are protected all of the time. To avoid any inconsistencies due to malfunctioning programs, the resource management system must be structured as a daemon, which offers the management functions via an IPC interface.

Using IPC mechanisms, which can handle remote IPC as well, clients may also reserve resources at a non-local resource management agent, either for all resources or for specified resources only, while other resources are reserved at the local agent. It can be useful to reserve all resources of one kind at one agent because this leads to better system knowledge and therefore to better resource allocation decisions. For instance, systems on a shared medium network such as Token Ring can use their local agent to reserve the local resources (CPU and memory) but reserve network bandwidth for the Token Ring only at one central agent which leads to global knowledge at that agent. Drawbacks of this centralized approach are that it is not scalable and that it represents a single point of failure.

The overall resource management consists of a 'System Resource Manager' which controls the single 'Resource Managers' for the various resources within the particular system (Figure 6). It contains algorithms for admission control and policy control – to ensure that sufficient resources are available to handle the data stream and that the particular data stream (and the user associated with this) is permitted to use the resources, respectively. Each resource manager keeps information about the characteristics of the resource and its actual reservations. The scheduler selects which packet gets access to the resource. The monitor observes the resource usage by the applications and the overall load of the resource.

At least parts of a resource manager are either directly located inside the operating system or interact tightly with it. For instance, the CPU resource manager cooperates closely with the CPU scheduler of the operating system, e.g., by using the real-time priorities the latter may offer.

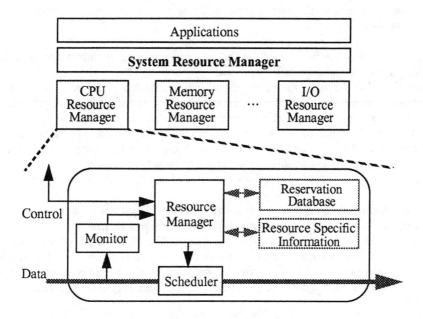

Figure 6. Resource Manager.

3. PROCESSOR MANAGEMENT

To ensure that applications are indeed served with the promised QoS, it must be controlled which work item is processed by a certain resource at a given time. Otherwise, it cannot be guaranteed that deadlines can be met. Using resource management techniques, scheduling mechanisms are applied which ensure that an application task gets access to the resource when needed. In case not all applications can be served, decisions based on importance or criticality are made.

3.1 REQUIREMENTS
The processing of audio and video data is usually performed in a periodical manner due to the periodicity of these continuous media data. These operations must be finished within certain deadlines to serve the real-time characteristics of these media. Sometimes, multimedia systems for single-user (and especially for single tasking) machines provide only simple mechanisms to provide time-based operations, e.g., for delaying program execution, but no real-time support. For these systems, it is often argued that this is sufficient since the CPU is used mostly for the multimedia application during its run time and if the user has another time-consuming application running, it is easy for the user to abandon that application. This approach is not satisfying even for single-user systems and falls short for multi-user and server systems such as video-on-demand servers. For such systems, the assumption that bothering applications can simply be stopped is already not valid. Other user applications can disturb multimedia applications in such a way that the QoS falls below an acceptable level.

Real-time CPU scheduling techniques, which serve multimedia application processing with respect to their time-criticality, provide a solution to these problems. However, the purpose of multimedia systems is the integration of continuous media and discrete-media data into computer systems, hence, multimedia applications rely as much on the processing of media like text and graphics as on that of audio and video. Thus, operations on continuous media data should not lead to a starvation of the processing of discrete media. Neither should priority inversion occur, i.e., where the handling of discrete-media data disturbs the processing of continuous media data (in a more general way: a low-priority application should not block a high-priority task).

If the real-time processing is achieved by the usage of preferred operating system priorities, an incorrect implemented application may use 100% of the CPU and stop the system from doing anything else. To avoid this, commercial workstation operating systems, which offer such priorities, do not allow arbitrary users to run their applications with such a priority. Instead, only a privileged system administrator is able to use them. In order to give users the ability to execute continuous media applications with appropriate processor scheduling, specific real-time scheduling and monitoring servers can be implemented which control the usage of these priorities by performing admission control, perhaps policy control, and by checking that no process uses (substantially) more CPU than it has reserved.

Traditional real-time methods used in command and control systems in areas such as factory automation, plant and aircraft control, etc. have often-stringent demands, e.g., that deadlines are met and that fault tolerance and security are ensured. For most multimedia systems (unless they are used in similar mission-critical scenarios), the requirements towards these issues are less critical. For instance, for many multimedia applications, it is not a severe failure to miss a deadline as long as it doesn't occur often. Therefore, multimedia systems are often considered as soft real time.

3.2 COMMON METHODS
The processor scheduling mechanisms used for multimedia systems are often similar to the methods derived within the real-time systems field, perhaps modified to provide for adaptive behavior. Especially the well known rate monotonic (RM) and earliest deadline first (EDF) algorithms [11] are often used to schedule the processing of periodic, continuous media data. EDF scheduling assumes each task to have a deadline at which its processing must be finished. The task with the earliest deadline among the waiting tasks is executed first. RM scheduling is defined in the context of tasks that require CPU processing periodically. Here, the task with the highest rate (i.e., the smallest period) is given the highest priority.

RM is an optimal static technique. As a static scheme, it assigns the priorities to each task of the considered task set once at the beginning of the processing of the set. Priorities are not changed dynamically during application lifetime but only when the task set changes, e.g., due to a newly arriving application with its associated task(s). RM is optimal in the sense that if a task set can be scheduled by any static algorithm, it can also be scheduled by RM.

EDF is an optimal, dynamic scheme. Dynamic means that it schedules every instance of each incoming task independently according to its demands. Hence, the processing order between the various tasks may change permanently during the lifetime of the tasks. If a scheduler, which follows the EDF scheme, is implemented by mapping deadlines on operating system priorities, the task priorities may be rearranged frequently, inducing some additional load into the system. EDF is optimal in the sense that if a set of tasks can be scheduled by any priority assignment scheme, it can also be scheduled by EDF.

For both schemes exist a simple schedulability test, which decides whether a set of tasks can be scheduled, i.e., whether the processing of these tasks can always finish within the deadlines. As has been shown in the classical work from Liu and Layland [11], a new task can be accepted (i.e., no overload condition occurs) if the following inequality holds:

$$\sum_{i=1}^{n} R_i \bullet P_i \leq U_n$$

In this inequality, the index i runs through the task set {T1, ..., Tn} containing all existing real-time tasks and also the new task. Ri denotes the rate of task i, Pi its processing time per period, and Un is a non-negative real number representing a schedulability bound. This means that if the sum on the left-hand side, i.e., the load generated by all real-time tasks, does not exceed Un, the processing of all instances of all tasks is guaranteed to terminate within their respective deadlines 1/Ri. If the sum is greater, this may still be the case, but no guarantees can be given with this test.

For EDF scheduling, the limit for Un is 1, i.e., as long as the total workload is less than the overall capacity of the processor, it can be guaranteed that all deadlines will be met. For RM scheduling, the limit for Un for any task set (with arbitrary rates) is

$$U_n = n(2^{\frac{1}{n}} - 1)$$

which approaches ln(2) ($\approx$ 0.69). It should be noticed here that the schedulability boundary U for RM scheduling can be relaxed in certain cases. If the periods of the tasks have a certain ratio, U can be larger than ln(2): e.g., if the periods are (integer) multiples of the smallest period in the task set, then U = 1 can be chosen. Also, it has been shown in [9] that the maximum CPU load which can be accepted for RM scheduling is, in the average case, notably larger than ln(2).

However, the restriction of the maximum CPU utilization U for multimedia processing scheduled by the RM algorithm to a value smaller than 1 is not such a strong limitation as it might seem. It is a limit for the real-time task set only and not for the total CPU utilization (as the sum of real-time and non-real-time processing). And in most cases, some CPU capacity has to be left for tasks performing other than multimedia related processing anyway, e.g., for control operations, to avoid starvation of such non-real-time tasks. Thus, in general, also for EDF it is advisable to restrict the utilization U to values smaller than 1 in order to provide some residual CPU capacity to other non-multimedia tasks.

3.3 LIMITATIONS AND EXTENSIONS

The discussion above assumed that the processing of the tasks can be preempted, i.e., that the currently executed task is suspended if a task with higher priority becomes 'ready to run'. Nowadays, for most operating systems, this assumption is true for processor scheduling. This is, however, not always the case for the scheduling of other resources, e.g., network access, because there the processing cannot be suspended for a while and resumed later without changing the semantics of the operation. A non-preemptive scheduling algorithm can be used in such a case, e.g., as discussed in [14]. But, unfortunately, the achieved processor utilization is much lower in comparison to a preemptive scheme.

The rates R_i and the processing time requirements P_i are needed for the schedulability test. While the rates can be usually derived directly from the properties of the application, the processing times have to be measured. For a module-based application, the processing requirements can be determined for any single software module and these values can be gathered and combined to calculate the overall P_i value [17]. For applications which are not built in this way, the processing times can be measured by executing the application several times with varying input data. The measurement of these processing times is not trivial because they depend, e.g., on the used hardware platform, the installed system software, and the input data. Additionally, they are influenced by other concurrently executing applications. Moreover, these times can vary significantly, e.g., consider the processing requirements for an MPEG compression which encodes an I-frame in period k followed by a B-frame in period k+1 where significant time is needed for the determination of motion vectors.

Algorithms such as RM need the time requirements P_i for the worst case to ensure the schedulability. If the average execution time is significantly lower than the worst-case time, the resulting CPU utilization is low. Furthermore, as said above, it is difficult to determine the processing times in general and the maximum of that in particular. Hence, it might happen that more time is needed than specified. To handle such situations, extensions to this algorithm have been developed. One approach is the division of the overall task into a mandatory part and an optional part [12]. After the processing of the mandatory part has been finished, an acceptable result has been gained which can be refined by processing the optional part. The mandatory part can be scheduled by RM, various policies can be applied to the scheduling of the optional part.

Real-time systems which contain not only periodic but also aperiodic tasks must be able to schedule both types of tasks. One approach is to apply a sporadic server for the processing of aperiodic requests. This server has a budget of computation time which is refreshed a specified time after it has been exhausted. This budget is used to process aperiodic requests with a certain, specified priority; if the budget is exhausted, the processing is done with a background priority.

Nevertheless, the rate-monotonic algorithm is often used for the scheduling of multimedia applications because it is a simple method, it avoids large administrative overheads, and it provides a controlled system behavior in case of (unforeseen) overload, the tasks with higher rates will be served first. Additionally, if rates are mapped to operating system priorities, a classification method can be introduced which distinguishes the tasks not only with respect to their rates but also among a further 'importance' scheme. Tasks which perform reservations based on worst-case assumptions (needing deterministic guarantees) get a higher priority than tasks with weaker reservations followed by non-time-critical tasks.

3.4 TASK DEPENDENCIES

It occurs often that a task which finishes its periodic processing of time-critical data gives its results to another task to perform further operations on these data or that the task uses the services provided by another task during its own processing of the data. This second task can be an application specific task, e.g., the total application has been split into parts, or a system provided task. Problems can occur if no coordination among the priorities of the participating tasks is done, e.g., if the follow-on task is executed without an according priority, the real-time characteristics of the first task are discarded. Such a situation can occur especially within microkernel systems, but also with other systems, where much of the processing is performed in user-level server tasks (e.g., a server to process incoming network packets).

One example is the X Windows System - here, the X server task displays the images which it receives from a video playback application to present them to the user. Even if shared memory between server and client is used, a non-real-time X server can introduce deadline violations, especially if it is single threaded and several requests from other applications have to be executed as well. For simple scenarios, tests showed that just increasing the priority of the X server slightly (e.g., via UNIX `nice' mechanism) can be sufficient. A better solution would be the provision of a real-time X server which allows the specification of processing requirements for requests.

For the problem of displaying video data via the X server, a special solution can be devised, i.e., a mechanism which allows a user program to bypass the X server by writing directly to a specific area on the screen (the display adapter memory). This could be implemented in a way that the window manager allows the user program to write to the particular memory area where its window is mapped by attaching the memory to the program's address space via a special system call, other memory areas may still be protected. Any change in the visibility, size, or location of the window is known inside the window manager which can change or withdraw the memory from the program's address space accordingly.

A more general approach is the `transfer' of a CPU reservation and the according priority to the server process as suggested in [13].

4. MEMORY MANAGEMENT

Memory has always been a scarce resource. Virtual memory mechanisms (swapping and paging) have been applied successfully to give applications the illusion that they are working in a world not constrained by memory sizes. These mechanisms swap parts of the data (which has not been used for a while) from main memory to an external storage device, typically a disk. Into this empty area other data, which has been requested by an application, is swapped in from the external storage. If the data which has been swapped out is needed again, the application which tried to access that data generates a 'page fault' and this data is swapped in again. Nowadays, not only applications but also parts of the operating system kernel can be swapped. Swapping operations take some time, depending on the used disks, interfaces, etc.; yet, this is acceptable for non-time-critical applications - their run time is increased but their semantics are not changed.

Within multimedia systems, as in other systems as well, main memory is needed for several purposes:

- to store the code of the applications and the system components such as the operating system kernel,
- to store data structures used to hold, e.g., the state of this software,
- to store the data on which the processing is done, e.g., a video frame.

In opposite to non-time-critical applications, swapping operations should not be applied to memory areas used by continuous media applications. If a page fault occurs (due to an application accessing a swapped out data area), it takes too much time to transfer this data from an external storage device such as a disk to main memory. Furthermore, such delays introduce large variations into the processing times of applications which must be avoided as well. To avoid swapping operations on memory areas touched by the processing of continuous media data, these data areas can be locked or pinned into memory. A problem is that the amount of memory which must be pinned can be quite large because not only the application code performing, say, the video decompression, but the functions used by it inside libraries, operating system kernel, etc. – everything which is used by that code – must be pinned as well. This is not always possible and also has the drawback that pinning large memory areas reduces overall system performance. Further, it is also contrary to the trend in workstation operating systems to provide for the swapping of kernel code.

Continuous media data has typically large space requirements which also implies large data movement costs. Therefore, it is important to handle continuous media data carefully and avoid unnecessary physical data movements. Similar to protocol processing, where headers are prepended by the sender to the actual data before transmission which are removed by the receiver, multimedia systems require operations for concatenation and segmentation of data, etc. To handle the data efficiently, without copy operations, buffer management schemes can be applied which use, e.g., scatter/gather techniques.

Such approaches have been developed already over a couple of years as support infrastructure for the implementation of communication systems. Examples are the mechanisms used in the x-kernel and mbuf scheme used in BSD UNIX operating systems. The latter is widely used in kernel space protocol implementations. Messages are stored in one or multiple chained mbufs. Each mbuf consists of offset fields, pointers, and a small data area internal to the mbuf. To store larger messages, a memory block of fixed size can be attached to the mbuf. Additionally, mbufs can be chained together using another pointer. This way, headers can be prepended to data without copying the data.

These management schemes have been designed for kernel level implementations only. This means that data must be copied between kernel and user level to exchange the data with applications. Alternatively, the memory areas holding the data areas may be remapped by virtual memory operations, e.g., from the kernel into the applications address space. Another issue is that such systems do not provide for the reservation of buffer space areas for certain streams but serve all requests (non-real-time and real-time) from the same pool.

In traditional, discrete-media data processing applications, the application executes a system call to read data, the kernel performs the actual steps to get the data from the device, and copies (or remaps) the data to the application's address space; then the application operates on the data, and finally writes it via the kernel (potentially copying the data again) to the output device. This structure applies for many multimedia applications which perform operations on the continuous media data as well. However, for several multimedia systems, especially for video servers, there are no data manipulation operations or other 'application' steps performed on the audiovisual information. Instead of this, a more simplified model applies where the application reads the data from one device, e.g., disk, and writes it to another device, e.g., the network, without performing any modifications to the data, the application adds no value. The performance of this continuous media data stream and the system as a whole is degraded due to the necessary context switches and the (potentially) needed copy operations. Future systems will improve this by offering a different 'streaming mode,' several approaches have been suggested by researchers, see e.g., [4].

Hereby, the data flows directly from the source device to the sink device in an application specified manner. This can be achieved in two different ways. One approach is that new system calls (read_stream, write_stream) are used which read the data from a device into a kernel buffer (and leave the data inside the kernel) and write it from that buffer to a device respectively, the application is responsible for the timing of these I/O operations. The other approach, 'kernel streaming', is to create a new kernel thread per stream which performs the read and write operations; the application specifies the timing of the stream and the thread ensures that this is met. The role of the application is mainly to control the thread. Figure 7 illustrates the different styles.

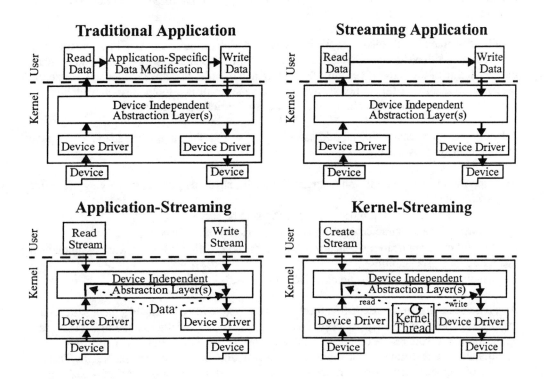

Figure 7. Data movement styles.

5. ADAPTIVE RESOURCE MANAGEMENT

Static resource management can provide reliable QoS in principle, i.e., it ensures that all resource requirements of multimedia applications can be met. For this, information about the resource demands of applications must be available and these requirements must be relatively constant. These two conditions can be satisfied for certain application classes, for instance, for most video server architectures.

However, for several (end system) multimedia applications, these demands are not known or they do not have this characteristic but require a varying amount of resources over time. For example, a video playback application which performs software decompression of the audiovisual data needs a varying number of CPU cycles over time, e.g., to decode the various types of MPEG frames and also due to scene changes.

With static resource management, a change in the set of running applications is only possible if the total amount of required resources is less than the overall available capacities. Hence, if the spare capacity is less than needed for an additional application, it can only be started if another application is terminated. Yet, several scenarios exist in which a user would like to start an additional application and keep all others running, perhaps with reduced quality. For instance, a user watches some news stories and receives a videophone call; she would like to keep the news stories running (probably with a reduced video size and without audio) and talk to the caller. Yet, the system resources are not sufficient to serve all these applications with unchanged quality (e.g., there might be enough spare resources to serve the videophone application with low quality). With static resource management, the user may stop the news story or accept the videophone connection with low quality – which is different or even opposite to the intention of the user (low quality news, high quality videophone) because the videophone will receive most attention.

Finally, distributed multimedia applications use several resources, e.g., CPU, memory and network. As we have seen in Section 3.4, to resolve access interdependencies among them, the scheduling of these resources must be coordinated in order to achieve an overall satisfying presentation quality. If this is not always possible, the result is a temporary unavailability of required resources which potentially leads to a missed deadline.

Adaptive resource management addresses these issues. The goals of adaptive resource management systems are, e.g.,

- support of variable-bit rate streams which have dynamically varying resource requirements,
- adaptation to changes in the set of applications to be served,
- allowing for a dynamic change in the relative priority of applications,
- serving more applications concurrently as is possible with hard (worst-case assumptions) based QoS provisioning,
- handling of changes in resource availability.

As a drawback, due to the adaptation mechanisms, adaptive resource management systems are usually not able to provide guaranteed, constant QoS. They typically assume that multimedia applications are soft real-time and are tolerant to graceful adaptations, which differs from traditional hard real-time applications. This assumption is usually acceptable for desktop multimedia applications. However, for some recording and production scenarios and special applications, used in, e.g., telesurgery or other mission-critical scenarios, this is, of course, not the case.

While multimedia applications executing under a static resource management system may assume that their resource requirements will be fulfilled all of the time and that they always have access to the resources when needed, this is not the case with adaptive resource management systems. Here, applications must be prepared that the amount of resources available for them varies over time, due to:

- changes in the size and mixture of the application set,
- modifications in the priority among applications,
- varying resource requirements because of inexact resource specifications.

To limit the changes in accessible resource capacities, the adaptive resource management system can provide applications with the ability to specify their requirements as a range [min, max], i.e., the minimum amount of resources needed for proper operation is min.

The basic scheme applied by adaptive resource management systems involves the system resource manager and resource monitor components and the applications (as illustrated in Figure 8).

- The resource monitor is a part of the resource manager for a particular resource. It observes the resource usage of applications and the overall load of the considered resource. It delivers state information according to the system resource manager.

- The system resource manager gathers the state information from the resource monitors. This component is also responsible for the negotiations with the application (at the beginning and during run-time for renegotiations); thus, it has information about the QoS requirements and resource demands of all applications. Based on this information about system state and application characteristics, it can decide which application should adapt its resource usage and to what extent.

- The applications receive adaptation notifications from the system resource manager. Based on that, they decide how they change their behavior to adapt their resource demands. Additionally, they monitor the QoS they can achieve, if this becomes too low or too high, they start a QoS (and hence resource requirements) renegotiation with the system resource manager.

Instead of choosing just one application for adaptation, the system resource manager can balance the need for adaptation over several or even all applications. This way, it can provide for fairness among the applications or it can ensure that applications which are critical for the whole system or important for the user are preferred, i.e., they do not have to reduce their resource requirements. In collaboration with the applications and their QoS requirements, the system resource manager can also perform a balancing among various resources, e.g., trading network bandwidth vs. CPU.

Adaptations do not always have to be towards lower resource usage. For instance, if an application finishes, the resources used by it so far are deallocated. Hence, they become available for other applications, either for the running applications which can then execute with better quality or for new applications which will be started in the future. To support the former case, the system resource manager can perform a QoS renegotiation with the applications (indicating the amount of resources available for them). Again, the adaptations can be balanced, to increase the quality of all applications or only a subset.

Various architectures have been designed for adaptive resource management. One example is AQUA (Adaptive Quality of service Architecture) [8].

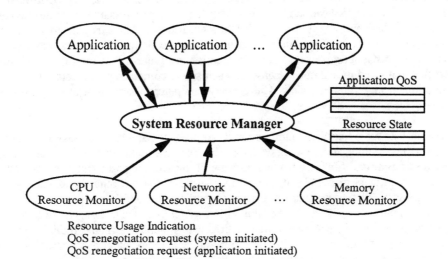

Figure 8. Basic adaptation scheme.

A cooperative model of resource management is applied by AQUA where the application and the resource management cooperate to manage the resources. For CPU scheduling, AQUA uses a 'rate-based adjustable priority' policy. This extension of the simple rate-monotonic scheduling method accounts for unknown and varying compute times and global adaptation across many applications. An application, which starts its operations, gives only a partial specification of its resource requirements. For example, the application specifies the execution rate but not the compute requirements. The resource manager allocates resources for this application based on an estimate of the available capacity. A regulator ensures that a task does not execute more often than specified by that initial rate.

During the execution of the application, the application estimates its resource requirements and the QoS it receives. The resource management performs similar operations, monitoring is performed inside the system (by the scheduler) to detect the resource usage. Based on the gained information about resource usage, the resource management potentially requests a reduction of the execution rate from the application. Changes in the measured QoS occur if the requirements of the application vary or if the resource availability alters. Then renegotiations are performed between the application and the resource management; further, according adaptations in the processing steps performed by the application are made to ensure that a predictable service is provided.

6. FURTHER ISSUES

6.1 RESOURCE ACCOUNTING

Knowledge about resource usage is necessary for several issues. It is required for the admission control, for instance, for the rate-monotonic schedulability test the processing times and rates are needed. And it is needed to 'charge' the user for its consumption of resources. Additionally, having exact information about current resource usage with fine granularity allows for better resource allocation and also scheduling decisions (mostly with adaptive schemes) and enables the resource management to detect misbehaving applications. (i.e., which use much more resources than originally specified).

The determination of the requirements used for admission control can be performed in advance, i.e., before the application is actually executed. Yet, the measurements must be done on the system, which will execute the application because the demands depend on several issues such as hardware platform and operating system version. Such estimations may be performed in an installation phase of the application. Nevertheless, bounding the application requirements to a fixed measurement phase on each single computer complicates the system administration in large environments where many computers share applications stored on central file servers.

To charge the user for resource consumption and especially to use resource usage information for allocation, scheduling, and policing decisions, on-line measurements must be made during the applications run-time. Since such a measurement influences the performance of the system permanently, it must be possible with very low overhead. On the other hand, the yielded values must also be of fine granularity. Current operating systems do not provide sufficient support for this purpose. At best, it is possible to see when a particular task started and when it stopped its execution in a period (often with coarse granularity in the order of several milliseconds only) but not how long it used the resource. These values can be quite different because other tasks or system activities might have been executing in the meantime.

This could be simplified if the operating system would provide appropriate and better support mechanisms. One relatively simple and cheap approach is to introduce a task state variable D_i that contains the run-time of the task i. It can be implemented in the following way:

- A system-wide variable E holds the time stamp of the last context switch or interrupt.
- As part of the creation of a new task j, the variable Dj is set to 0.
- If the operating system dispatcher deactivates a task k and activates a task l, thus, while performing a context switch, the time elapsed since the last interrupt respectively context switch is added to Dk and E is set to current_time.

While such a method can help to determine the processing time requirements of tasks and to check whether they stay (reasonably) within their specifications, it does not provide support to accumulate the resource amount used in summary for a particular application. For this, the resource usage of server tasks which are executing on behalf of this application must also be taken into account (see also Section 3.4 where we noticed that such a system structure leads to difficulties due to task dependencies).

Support for the processing of time-critical multimedia applications in an existing operating system is often restricted by the basic design and structure of that system. While enhancements can be made, there are often limitations, which cannot be relieved without major changes in the base system. A more radical but also more general approach is to develop a new operating system where support for continuous media data is incorporated in the design from the beginning.

6.2 RESOURCE MANAGEMENT IN FUTURE OPERATING SYSTEMS

With today's operating systems, resource management for multimedia processing is mostly an add-on feature but not fully integrated. Therefore, several limitations exist with respect to the ability to handle concurrently several high-performance, high-quality continuous media streams.

Future operating systems, where the requirements of multimedia applications are taken into consideration already from the very beginning of the design, may offer enhanced capabilities. With them, more efficient resource management support and, hence, simpler and better handling of continuous media data can be provided. And fewer limitations will exist for the distributed multimedia systems based on them.

Such operating systems and the according resource management mechanisms within them will offer the ability to perform exact accounting of resource consumption, avoid dependencies among tasks, and will be able to circumvent the interference between multimedia applications.

Nemesis [10] is an operating system, which has been designed to support, and distributed multimedia applications. Nemesis takes a revolutionary approach of starting the operating system design from scratch and to not just make incremental changes. It offers facilities for the dynamic allocation of resources to applications, it ensures that resource consumption is accounted to the correct application, and it allows that applications avoid the use of shared server tasks - as much processing as possible is done within the application itself, whereby protection among applications and security is nevertheless given.

6.3 RESERVATION IN ADVANCE

For several application scenarios, the model of 'immediate reservations' applied so far is not fully appropriate. As in our daily lives, it must be possible to perform a reservation in advance to ensure that our application can be executed with sufficient QoS. If there is a noticeable blocking probability for immediate reservations, it must be possible to reserve in advance specified start time and duration. This means that Resource Reservation in Advance (ReRA) [18] mechanisms are needed, but now, only preliminary results are available on this topic. There are subtle problems to be solved, besides a more complex resource management, some of the problems occurring in ReRA systems are state maintenance and failure handling.

ReRA must be performed on an end-to-end basis. Appropriate resource requirement information must be exchanged in advance among the participating systems by extending the Flow Specifications distributed via the reservation protocols. The resource management on each node needs extended admission control tests, which check whether the required resources can be provided during the requested time interval. And the data structures used to store the reservation information must contain time values (beginning and duration of a reservation).

The state associated with an advance reservation must be kept on all the participating systems for a potentially long time. It must either be stored in non-volatile memory to survive system failures and regular shutdowns, e.g., due to system maintenance, or a soft-state approach must be used where the reservation is refreshed from time-to-time: the closer the actual usage time comes, the higher the frequency of the refresh messages. The handling of failures, which occur between the reservation setup and its use, must differ from the steps taken to resolve errors of running applications. The reason is that the application, which had lost its reservation, is not running. So, it is not immediately clear which entity is to be notified and by which means. Further, potentially the failure situation can be cleared already before the resources are needed.

7. SUMMARY

Multimedia applications need the integrated treatment of continuous media and discrete-media data in distributed computer systems. The handling of continuous media data such as audio and video places requirements on the multimedia computing and communication infrastructure which are uncommon for workstations and most other computer systems. To deal with the timing demands of these applications, new mechanisms must be used.

Resource management has the goal to provide reliable QoS to distributed multimedia applications. It uses admission control and scheduling mechanisms to manage the resources needed during the processing and transmitting of the audiovisual data. For that, resource management has to interact in a tight manner with operating system and communication system mechanisms to achieve its goals. Furthermore, according services must be available in the end systems and the networks.

Resource management has been an area of active research for several years and it is still a field where research and development is proceeding. Various mechanisms have been designed over time, both for static and for adaptive resource management, and several example systems have been designed, implemented, and evaluated.

Increased processing speeds, higher network bandwidth, larger memories, and other hardware improvements might reduce the need for resource management techniques in future systems. However, it is likely that application demands will increase as well. Additionally, for systems and components shared by several users, resource management mechanisms will be an important piece of future multimedia infrastructures to provide a reliable QoS.

Resource management designed within the context of current operating systems is somewhat limited in the functionality it can provide. Future operating systems, which are designed for the handling of multimedia applications, will be able to relieve these limitations.

REFERENCES

1. Anderson, D. P., Tzou, S., Wahbe, R., Govindan, R., and Andrews, M., "Support for Continuous Media in the DASH System," Proceedings of the 10th ICDCS, Paris, France, May 1990.

2. Anderson, D. P., "Metascheduling for Continuous Media," ACM Transactions on Computer Systems, Vol. 11, No. 3, 1993.

3. Braden, R., Zhang, L. Berson, S., Herzog, S., and Jamin, S., "Resource Reservation Protocol (RSVP) - Version 1 Functional Specification," RFC 2205, September 1997.

4. Fall, K. and Pasquale, J., "Improving Continuous media Playback Performance with In-Kernel Data Paths," Proceedings of the IEEE ICMCS, Boston, MA, USA, May 1994.

5. Herrtwich, R. G. and Wolf, L.C., "A System Software Structure for Distributed Multimedia Systems," Proceedings of the ACM SIGOPS European Workshop, Le Mont Saint-Michel, France, September 1992.

6. Huang, J., Kenchammana-Hosekote, D., Agrawal, M., and Richardson, J., "Presto - A System for Mission-Critical Multimedia Applications," Journal of Real-Time Systems, July 1997.

7. Jones, M., "Adaptive Real-Time Resource Management Supporting Modular Composition of Digital Multimedia Services," Proceedings of the NOSSDAV Workshop, Lancaster, UK, 1993.

8. Lakshman, K., Yavatkar, R., and Finkel, R., "Integrated CPU and Network-I/O QoS Management in an Endsystem," Proceedings of IWQoS, New York, NY, May 1997.

9. Lehoczky, J., Sha, L., and Ding, Y., "The Rate Monotonic Scheduling Algorithm: Exact Characterization and Average Case Behavior," Proceedings of the IEEE Real-Time Systems Symposium, Santa Monica, CA, USA, 1989.

10. Leslie, I., McAuley, D., Black, R., Roscoe, T., Barham, P., Evers, D., Fairbairns, R., and Hyden, E., "The Design and Implementation of an Operating System to Support Distributed Multimedia Applications," IEEE Journal on Selected Areas in Communications, Vol. 14, No. 7, September 1996.

11. Liu, C. L. and Layland, J. W., "Scheduling Algorithms for Multiprogramming in a Hard Real-Time Environment," Journal of the ACM, Vol. 20, No. 1, 1973.

12. Liu, J. W. S., Lin, K.-J., Shih, W.-K., Yu, A. C., Chung, J.-Y., and Zhao, W, "Algorithms for Scheduling Imprecise Computations," IEEE Computer, Vol. 24, No. 5, May 1991.

13. Mercer, C. M., Savage, S., and Tokuda, H., "Processor Capacity Reserves: Operating System Support for Multimedia Applications," Proceedings of the IEEE ICMCS, Boston, MA, May 1994.

14. Nagarajan, R. and Vogt, C., "Guaranteed-Performance Transport of Multimedia Traffic over the Token Ring," IBM Tech. Rep. No. 43.9201, IBM ENC, Heidelberg, 1992.

15. Vogt, C., Herrtwich, R.G., and Nagarajan, R., "HeiRAT: The Heidelberg Resource Administration Technique – Design Philosophy and Goals," Proceedings of Kommunikation in Verteilten Systemen, Munich, Springer-Verlag, 1993.

16. Vogt, C., Wolf, L. C., Herrtwich, R.G., and Wittig, H., "HeiRAT - Quality-of-Service Management for Distributed Multimedia Systems," ACM Multimedia Systems Journal - Special Issue on QoS Systems, 1998.

17. Wolf, L.C., "Resource Management for Distributed Multimedia Systems," Kluwer, Boston, MA, 1996.

18. Wolf, L.C. and Steinmetz, R., "Concepts for Resource Reservation in Advance," Multimedia Tools and Applications, May 1997.

42

A FRAMEWORK FOR BUILDING ADAPTIVE CONTINUOUS MEDIA APPLICATIONS USING SERVICE PROXIES

Tatsuo Nakajima

Japan Advanced Institute of Science and Technology
1-1 Asahidai, Tatsunokuchi, Ishikawa, 923-12, Japan
tatsuo@jaist.ac.jp

1. **INTRODUCTION**..914
2. **ISSUES IN DESIGNING MOBILE APPLICATIONS** 915
    2.1   LIMITED RESOURCES OF MOBILE COMPUTERS...............................915
    2.2   APPLICATION-AWARE ADAPTATION 916
3. **OVERVIEW OF SERVICE PROXY** 916
4. **TOOLKIT FOR IMPLEMENTING MOBILE APPLICATIONS USING SERVICE PROXIES**...918
    4.1   TOOLKIT STRUCTURE 918
    4.2   INTERFACE 920
    4.3   SERVICE PROXY AND OBJECT GRAPH...921
5. **VIDEO VIEWER ON MBONE USING SERVICE PROXY** 923
6. **HOST MOBILITY SUPPORT** 925
    6.1   HANDOFF PROTOCOL AND OBJECT MIGRATION 926
    6.2   ROBUSTNESS OF HANDOFF PROTOCOL 927
    6.3   ADAPTABLE OBJECT MIGRATION IN MOBILE SUPPORTS 929
7. **RELATED WORK**...930
8. **CONCLUSION** 932
    REFERENCES 932

Abstract. Portable computers used in today's mobile computing environments may change machine configurations dynamically by replacing I/O and memory devices while executing applications. Applications on such computers are required to deal with drastic changes of network bandwidth and machine configurations caused by these replaceable devices. However, traditional applications on mobile computers are not aware of the replacement of the devices. The applications also do not reconfigure their structures according to these drastic changes. Therefore, performances may be degraded significantly since these changes are not taken into account.

913

This chapter presents a new framework for building continuous media applications in mobile computing environments. In mobile computing environments, network bandwidth and machine configurations may be dramatically changed, and mobile applications should be adapted to various operational environments for being executed efficiently.

In our framework, an application is partitioned into two fragments. One fragment runs on a mobile computer such as a notebook computer and a PDA, and another fragment runs on a stationary computer. They are connected by several types of wireless networks that can be replaced at any time while applications run. The fragment on a stationary computer is called a *service proxy*. The service proxy filters or caches data from servers on the Internet before transmitting the data to the fragment on a mobile computer. These two fragments are constructed by composing small objects. The composition of objects can be dynamically reconfigured by adding or removing replaceable devices transparently from users.

1. INTRODUCTION

In a mobile computing environment [Forman94, Marsh93], where wireless networks connect mobile computers and powerful stationary computers, various problems caused by drastic changes of machine configurations and network bandwidth should be taken into consideration. These applications may run in a wide variety of operating conditions. Mobile computers may be attached to high-speed wireless networks at one moment and to low-speed cellular networks the next. Also, applications on mobile computers are required to be implemented carefully due to limited resources of mobile computers such as display size, amount of memory, CPU power, and battery energy.

Since the PC Card Interface (formerly called PCMCIA interface) is now widely used in portable computers [Bender93], the configuration of a mobile computer can be dynamically changed by replacing such devices while executing applications. These replaceable devices introduce a new requirement that applications need to adapt to various unexpected environments. However, applications cannot adapt to such changes if operating systems are not notified of the changes to the applications. This kind of adaptation is called application-aware adaptation [Noble95]. For example, an application can change its cache replacement policy if it is notified that a memory card has been inserted.

Since this approach does not hide drastic changes of mobile computers from applications, it may allow us to adopt more aggressive solutions. For example, Weiser proposed a number of algorithms by which the operating system scheduler could attempt to optimize system power by monitoring and minimizing idle time by reducing clock speed [Weiser94]. A more aggressive strategy that shortens computation time of an application can be adopted by reconfiguring the structure of an application, and decreasing the precision of the computation if the application is aware of the current CPU energy and utilization.

This chapter proposes a new framework for constructing mobile applications using the notion of *service proxies*. Our framework makes application-aware adaptation possible, and provides a toolkit for developing adaptive applications easily on Real-Time Mach [Tokuda90]. Our approach provides a systematic way for supporting application-aware adaptation in various operating conditions. The toolkit makes our work novel since previous work does not focus on systematic programming support for building adaptive applications. In our framework, mobile applications are also divided into two fragments. We call the fragment that resides on a powerful stationary computer connected to the Internet *a service proxy*. The service proxy communicates with servers on the Internet. Our framework especially focuses on applications that access information on the Internet such as WWW browsers and MBONE conference tools. Applications and service proxies can reconfigure their structures dynamically according to the changes of network bandwidth and machine configurations.

The role of a service proxy depends on applications. For instance, a service proxy reduces the bandwidth of data from the Internet according to the properties of the wireless network that is currently used by a mobile computer. Also, a caching policy in a service proxy may be replaced when a memory card is inserted in a mobile computer.

For building such adaptable applications systematically, our toolkit provides a framework for building an application by composing small objects. The composition can be dynamically reconfigured due to the changes in operating environment where the application is running.

The remainder of this chapter is structured as follows. In Section 2, we describe several issues for building applications in mobile computing environments, and propose service proxies in Section 3. Section 4 presents a toolkit for implementing applications using service proxies. In Section 5, we show how to build applications using *service proxies* by using a video viewer on MBONE, and describe the mobility supports for our framework in Section 6. In Section 7, related work is presented, and we summarize the chapter in Section 8.

2. ISSUES IN DESIGNING MOBILE APPLICATIONS

An application in a mobile computing environment must take into account the following two issues for efficient execution even when the configurations of computers and network bandwidth dramatically change.

- A mobile computer is more resource poor than a traditional stationary computer, and the properties of wireless networks are different from wired networks.

- An operating environment of mobile computers may change drastically caused by replacement of PC Card devices during the execution of applications.

The following subsections discuss why the above issues are difficult to solve in detail.

2.1 LIMITED RESOURCES OF MOBILE COMPUTERS

A mobile computer is equipped with less powerful CPU, small amount of memory, low bandwidth network, small display due to limited size, and limited power supply compared to a desktop. Thus, traditional applications that consume a large amount of resources do not run efficiently on mobile computers. An approach to solve this problem is to partition the application into two fragments. One fragment consuming a small amount of resources runs on the mobile computer, and another fragment that executes resource-consuming computation resides on the stationary computer. The technique can solve the problem caused by limited resources of mobile computers.

The properties of networks such as error rate, bandwidth, and latency are dramatically different in wired and wireless networks. Therefore, it is difficult to use the same protocol for both networks. However, if applications are partitioned into two fragments, a fragment on a stationary computer can filter data received from servers on the Internet before sending the data to a mobile computer since wireless networks may not have enough bandwidth to transmit the entire data in a timely manner. Also, each application can select a suitable communication protocol for transmitting data on a wireless network according to the properties of applications.

For example, it takes a long time to transmit an HTML page with several large color images on a low bandwidth wireless network. In this case, the fragment of the application on the stationary computer fetches color images from a server, and reduces the size of the color images, or converts the color images to monochrome images to decrease data size. Also, a large audio file is cached on the stationary computer, and only the necessary portions of the audio file are sent to the mobile computer without violating timing constraints of respective audio samples for decreasing the buffer size in a mobile computer.

However, if the structures of these fragments are static, the solution cannot take into account drastic changes in machine configurations. When the machine configurations change, it may not be necessary to consider limitation of resources. For instance, if a network protocol between two fragments is optimized for a low speed network, the protocol cannot be used for a high-speed network.

2.2 APPLICATION-AWARE ADAPTATION

The machine configuration of a mobile computer changes when replaceable devices such as PC Card devices are inserted and removed, and an application must be notified of these changes for efficient execution. Let us consider that an application may send too much data when the bandwidth of a wireless network becomes low. If the response time of the application becomes slow, users may become frustrated. In this case, the application should reduce the data rate for improving the response time. Many similar situations occur when applications are not aware of the changes in machine configurations.

The following two issues are important for realizing application-aware adaptation. The first issue is that operating systems should support mechanisms to notify changes of machine configurations to applications, and applications configure their structures when the notifications are received. The second issue is to provide a systematic way for building adaptive applications.

3. OVERVIEW OF SERVICE PROXY

Our framework provides a uniform solution for answering the problems in the previous section. The central concept in our framework is the service proxy. An application is divided into two fragments, one fragment on a mobile computer, and another fragment on a stationary computer. The fragment of an application, which resides on an intermediate stationary computer is called a service proxy. The service proxy communicates with servers on the Internet using standard Internet protocols as shown in Figure 1. The two fragments communicate using protocols suitable for wireless networks. The architecture enables a fragment of the application on the mobile computer to be executed efficiently even when the computer is resource poor.

A typical use of the service proxy is as follows.

- A service proxy filters data received from the Internet, and sends them to a mobile computer. For example, color video streams are converted to monochrome video streams if the bandwidth of a wireless network is low.

- A service proxy fetches an entire file from a server, and sends only the necessary data from the file to the mobile host according to the bandwidth of the wireless network. The method reduces the buffer size used by the fragment of the application on the mobile computer since the computer may not need to store the entire file.

- An application and its corresponding service proxy reconfigure their structures when the machine configuration of a mobile computer changes. For example, if a memory card is removed, the size of a buffer in an application on the mobile computer may be reduced. This may require a change in the buffer management policy (prefetch or on-demand) on the service proxy.

- A part of the program, which requires heavy-weighted computation, is executed by the service proxy since it is executed on a powerful stationary computer. Thus, a mobile computer executes only lightweight computation. As a result, a mobile computer can be small and cheap.

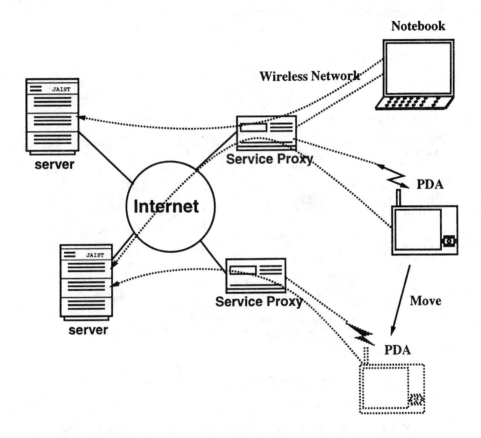

Figure 1. Service proxy.

For solving the issues in the previous section, a mobile application is developed by composing objects that contain small functions. We call the composition of objects, an *object graph*. In other words, a mobile application consists of two *object graphs*. One graph is on the mobile computer, and the other graph is on the service proxy.

Figure 2 illustrates *object graphs* for a mobile application. In our framework, an application consists of a control script and two *object graphs*. The control script is written in Tcl [Ousterhout94]. The script contains code for composing objects on both a mobile computer and a stationary computer. An object included in an *object graph* contains code for filtering or caching data.

When an operating system notifies an application that a PC Card device has been inserted or removed on a mobile computer, the application reconfigures its *object graphs* for adapting to the new condition. The idea enables us to build adaptive applications systematically.

Let us assume that the *object graphs* in Figure 2 represent a video conference application. When a network device is switched from a low speed cellular network to a high-speed wireless LAN, the script program receives a notification from the operating system that the network device changed. The service proxy of the videoconference application replaces the object that converts the color video stream to a monochrome video stream to an object that reduces the depth of the color. Also, an object for dithering the video stream is inserted on the mobile computer as shown in Figure 2. The example shows that our framework can solve the issues described in Section 2.1 and 2.2 by providing a framework that enables the structure of an application to be changed systematically.

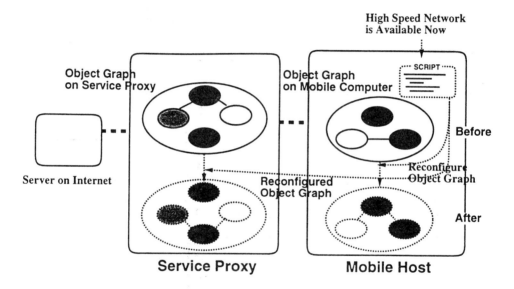

Figure 2. Application structuring using object graphs.

4. TOOLKIT FOR IMPLEMENTING MOBILE APPLICATIONS USING SERVICE PROXIES

In this section, we describe the structure and the interface of our toolkit, then show how a mobile application runs using our toolkit.

4.1 TOOLKIT STRUCTURE

Figure 3 shows the structure of a mobile application using our framework. The fragment of the application executed on a mobile computer is called a mobile *object graph*. The proxy *object graph* is the fragment of the mobile application on a stationary computer. A mobile application consists of these two *object graphs*.

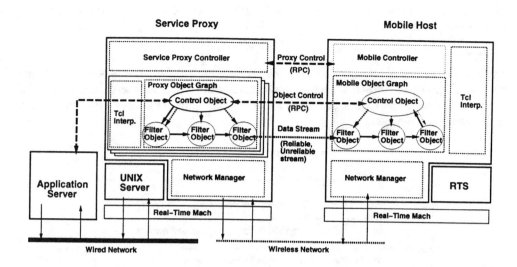

Figure 3. Structure of a mobile application using service proxy.

A mobile controller, that controls the mobile application on a mobile computer, provides three functions. The first function is to select a stationary computer for executing a service proxy. The second function is to send a request for creating the service proxy on the stationary station. The last function is to manage the movement of the service proxy when a handoff occurs. A service proxy controller manages creation and deletion of proxy *object graphs* according to requests from the *mobile controller*. Also, it manages the movement of service proxies between two stationary computers when a handoff occurs. A mobile controller contains a Tcl Interpreter, and a service proxy controller creates a new Tcl interpreter whenever a new proxy *object graph* is created. The interpreters execute Tcl scripts for configuring object graphs of a mobile application upon initialization, and reconfigure the object graphs when a mobile machine configuration changes.

In this chapter, we focus on the configuration of objects graphs, thus we do not describe a detailed protocol and interface for managing the selection of a stationary computer for executing a service proxy and the movement of a service proxy between stationary computers.

The network managers run on both the mobile computer and the stationary computer, and manage communication between them. The network manager provides several protocols suitable for wireless networks. Currently, it provides three network protocols, RPC protocol, reliable stream protocol, and unreliable stream protocol. The RPC protocol is used to send requests from a mobile object graph to a proxy object graph. Also, the mobile controller and the service proxy controller communicate using the RPC protocol. The reliable stream protocol is used for sending texts and images, and the unreliable protocol is used to send timing critical video and audio streams. The network manager adopts the x-kernel [Hutchinson91] as the infrastructure for implementing the protocols.

We adopt two operating system servers running on Real-Time Mach for executing the above components. A mobile computer requires a small operating system for executing applications. We choose RTS [Nakajima93], which is a small operating system server suitable for small computers. RTS supports process management, a memory-based file system, device management, and a simple command interpreter. On the other hand, the service proxy runs on the Lites server [Helander94] that emulates Unix system calls. The service proxy communicates with servers on the Internet using the socket interface provided by the Lites server.

4.2 INTERFACE

Table 1 and Table 2 shows interfaces provided by our toolkit. The functions in Table 1 are used in C programs. When a mobile application starts on a mobile computer, it calls *CreateProxyGraph* that requests to create a proxy object graph to a service proxy controller in the stationary computer.

Table 1. C Interface of Toolkit

Proxy* CreateProxyGraph(Object* proxy, char* name)
int DeleteProxyGraph(Object* proxy, char* name)
int MsgPush(Object* object, char* buffer, int size)

Several objects are connected linearly for processing multimedia data such as text, images, video streams, and audio streams. *MsgPush* is called for sending media data to the next object. Since all objects that need to be connected in an object graph provide *MsgPush*, an object can send the media data to any object using this function.

Object graphs are configured by a Tcl script including Tcl commands shown in Table 2. The commands are classified into three categories. The first category includes commands for creating an object graph. *mCreate* creates an object, and *mConnect* connects two objects. The connected objects transfer data using *MsgPush*.

Table 2. Tcl Interface for Toolkit

EventRegister -event 'event-name' -callback 'proc name'
EventCancel -event 'event-name'
mEval controller ``script-name''
mCreate 'object-name' -type 'type'
mDelete 'object-name'
mConnect 'object-name1' -with 'object-name2'
mDisconnect 'object-name'
mSetStatus 'object-name' -name 'variable-name' -value 'value'
mGetStatus 'object-name' -name 'variable-name' -value 'value'

The second category includes the command: *mEval* that is called on a mobile computer for requesting the execution of a Tcl command on a stationary computer. The first argument specifies a controller. If the controller is a mobile controller, the command specified as the second argument is called on the mobile computer. However, if the first argument is a service *proxy controller*, the command specified as the second argument is executed as a remote command on the service proxy.

The third category includes commands for detecting events that result from changes in machine configuration. The mechanism enables a mobile application to be adapted to various operating conditions. *EventRegister* specifies two arguments "event-name" and "proc-name." "event-name" indicates an event in which an application requests a notification. For example, inserting or removing PC Card devices, and replacing network devices can be specified as "event-name." Also, an event indicating that battery level is low can be specified. "proc-name" is a command name executed when an event is detected. The command specified in "proc-name" reconfigures object graphs for adapting an application to a new machine configuration.

4.3 SERVICE PROXY AND OBJECT GRAPH

In this section, we describe how each component works together when a mobile application is executed. Also, we show a sample Tcl script that shows how to configure object graphs, and how to manage events notified by the operating systems.

Each object graph contains two types of objects, control objects and filter objects. A control object is a body of the mobile application. The control object in the mobile object graph sends a request to the control object in the proxy object graph when the application needs to access servers on the Internet. The control object of the proxy object graph fetches data from the servers. The filter object manipulates received data, and sends the data to the next filter object. Each filter object contains small codes for manipulating data.

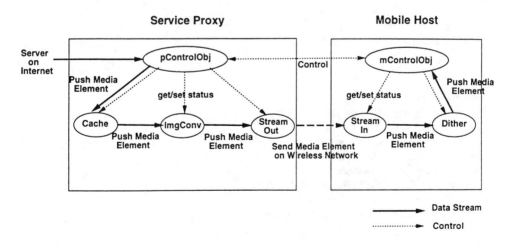

Figure 4. A mobile application.

In the example shown in Figure 4, a control object, *pControlObj* in a proxy object graph receives data from a server on the Internet. Let us assume that the application fetches a color video file from a WWW server, and displays the stream on the mobile computer's display. *pControlObj* fetches the entire video file from the WWW server, and sends the entire stream to Cache. Cache stores the entire data in the buffer, and sends each video frame periodically to *ImgConv*. The object converts the color depth of the video frame, and sends it to *StreamOut*. *StreamOut* transmits the video frame to *StreamIn* in the mobile proxy using the network manager. Next, *StreamIn* sends the frame to *Dither*, and finally the frame is delivered to *mControlObj*, which is a control object in the mobile object graph, then the object displays the frame to the window.

In our framework, a mobile application is written as a Tcl script. A mobile controller sends a copy of the Tcl script to the service proxy controller using the RPC protocol provided by the network manager after the mobile controller sends a request that creates a new proxy object graph to the service proxy controller. The mobile controller executes the Tcl script for creating a mobile object graph and waiting for events from a user. When the user inputs an event, a command provided by the control object of the mobile object graph is called. The command may send a request to the control object of the proxy object graph.

After receiving the Tcl script, the service proxy controller executes the Tcl script for creating the proxy object graph when it receives a request for creating a new proxy object graph from the mobile controller. Then, it calls a command provided by the control object that waits for a request from the control object of the mobile object graph.

The following script shows a fragment of a typical script used by a mobile application. A mobile controller executes the *MobileStartup* command for creating a mobile object graph. A service proxy controller also executes the *ProxyStartup* command for creating a proxy object graph.

```
proc ProxyStartup {} {
  mCreate .pobjectCtr -type pControlObj
  mCreate .cache -type Cache
  mCreate .imgconv -type ImgConv
  mCreate .streamout -type StreamOut
  mConnect .pobjectCtr -with .cache
  mConnect .cache -with .imgconv
  mConnect .imgconv -with .streamout
  ....
}

proc MobileStartup {} {
  mCreate .mobjectCtr -type mControlObj
  mCreate .dither -type Dither
  mCreate .streamin -type Streamin
  mConnect .streamin -with .dither
  mConnect .dither -with .mobjectCtr
  mSetStatus .dither -name BufferSize -value 1024
  EventRegister -event MemoryCardInsert \
          -callback MemoryCardInsertHandler
  ....
}

proc MemoryCardInsertHandler {attribute} {
  ....
  mSetStatus .dither -name BufferSize -value 20480
  ....
}
```

ProxyStartup creates four objects: *pControlObj* object, *Cache* object, *ImgConv* object, and *StreamOut* object using *mCreate*, then connects these objects using *mConnect*. *MobileStartup* creates three objects, *mControlObj* object, *StreamIn* object, and *Dither* object, then these objects are connected. When a command provided by *mControlObj* is executed, the object sends a request to *pControlObj* object using the RPC protocol. *pControlObj* object fetches a video file from a WWW server, and sends it to *Cache* object. The data is finally delivered to *mControlObj* object, after which the object displays the data to a window.

When a notification of a change in the machine configuration of a mobile computer is required, *EventRegister* is called. In the above example, *MobileStartup* calls *EventRegister* for requesting a notification when a memory card is inserted. *MemoryInsertHandler* specified as an argument of *EventRegister* is called when inserting a memory card to a mobile computer. Before inserting the memory card, the application cannot allocate a large amount of memory for executing *Dither* object, so a small buffer is allocated for *Dither* object by calling *mSetStatus*. However, inserting the memory card enables *Dither* object to allocate a large buffer. Therefore, the application increases the buffer size by calling *mSetStatus* in *MemoryInsertHandler*.

5. VIDEO VIEWER ON MBONE USING SERVICE PROXY

In this section, we show an example program that handles continuous media using the service proxy. An application's TCL script controls object graphs on a mobile host and a service proxy dynamically. When an application is started on a mobile computer, it requests to create a new service proxy on a stationary computer, and sends a TCL script to the computer. The script configures object graphs both on the mobile computer and the stationary computer executing the service proxy. Also, the script registers a callback for notifying the changes of the machine configuration of the mobile computer.

Figure 5 shows a program playing back video streams on MBONE [Eriksson94] using the service proxy.

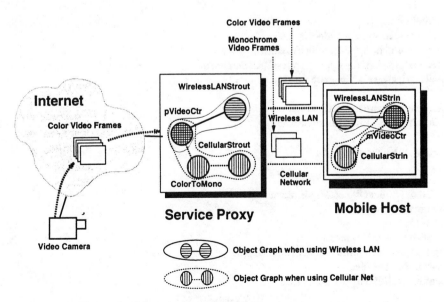

Figure 5. Video viewer on MBONE using the service proxy.

In the figure, a computer connecting a video camera transmits a high quality video stream to a service proxy to which a mobile computer connects with a wireless LAN or a cellular network. The mobile computer can communicate with the service proxy by the wireless LAN when the mobile computer is used in the campus of a university, but the mobile computer communicates with the service proxy by using a cellular network when the mobile computer is used in a town.

The following script shows a part of a control script for a simple video viewer application on MBONE using our framework. In the application, a service proxy receives a video stream on MBONE, and filters the stream to a mobile computer according to the bandwidth of wireless networks before sending the media stream to the mobile computer.

```
proc ProxyStartup {} {
  mCreate .pVideo -type pVideoControl
  mCreate .cellularout -type CellularStreamOut
  mCreate .wirelessLANout -type WirelessLANStreamOut
  mCreate .tomono -type ColorToMono
  mConnect .pVideo -with .wirelessLANout
  ....
}

proc pMBONEVideoCellularGraph {} {
  mDisconnect .pVideo
  mConnect .tomono -with .cellularout
  mConnect .pVideo -with .tomono
  mSetStatus .pVideo -name FrameRate -value 10
}

proc pMBONEVideoWirelessLANGraph {} {
  mDisconnect .pVideo
  mConnect .pVideo -with .wirelessLANout
  mSetStatus .pVideo -name FrameRate -value 30
}

proc MobileStartup {} {
  mCreate .mVideo -type mVideoControl
  mCreate .cellularin -type CellularStreamIn
  mCreate .wirelessLANin -type WirelessLANStreamIn
  mConnect .wirelessLANin -with .mVideo
  ...
  EventRegister -event InsertCard \
  -callback mMBONEVideoInsertCard
  ...
  mSetStatus .mVideo -color
}

proc mMBONEVideoObjectGraph {device} {
  switch $device {
    Cellular {
      mSetStatus .mVideo -mono
      mEval .pSimVideo pSimVideoCellularGraph
      mDisconnect .mVideo
      mConnect .cellularin -with .mVideo
    }
    WirelessLAN {
      mSetStatus .mVideo -color
```

```
    mEval .pSimVideo pSimVideoWirelessLANGraph
    mDisconnect .mVideo
    mConnect .wirelessLANin -with .mVideo
  }
  ....
  }
}

proc mMBONEVideoInsertCard {name slot} {
  ....
  mMBONEVideoObjectGraph $name
  ....
}
```

On the mobile computer, the application executes *MobileStartup* command after the new service proxy is created on a stationary computer. The command creates three objects, *mVideoControl*, *CellularStreamIn* and *WirelessLANStreamIn* object by using *mcreate* primitive. The application assumes that the mobile computer is connected to the stationary computer on which the service proxy runs with a wireless LAN. *WirelessLANStreamIn* are connected with *mVideoControl* for displaying video frames received from a wireless LAN by using *mConnect* primitive. Also, the command calls *EventRegister* command for registering *mMBONEVideoInsertCard* command as a callback command, which is called when *InsertCard* event occurs. The event is generated when a new PC card is inserted in the mobile computer. The last command in *mSetStatus* command initializes a window in order to playback a color video stream.

The newly created service proxy executes *ProxyStartup* command after the above TCL script is received from the mobile computer. The script is transmitted by the mobile computer when the execution of *MobileStartup* is completed. The command creates the following four objects, *pVideoControl*, *CellularStreamOut*, *WirelessLANStreamOut* and *ColorToMono* object, then *pVideoControl* are connected with *WirelessLANStreamOut* since we assume that the mobile computer and the stationary computer running the service proxy can communicate by using the wireless LAN when the application is started in this example.

When the mobile computer removes the wireless LAN card and inserts a cellular network card, a kernel generates *InsertCard* event, and *mMBONEVideoInsertCard* command is called on the mobile computer. For changing object graphs on the service proxy and the mobile computer, *mMBONEVideoInsertCard* command calls *mMBONEVideoObjectGraph* command. The command requests to execute *pMBONEVideoCellularGraph* on the service proxy using mEval command. *PMBONEVideoCellularGraph* command inserts *ColorToMono* object in the current object graph of the service proxy for converting respective color video frames to monochrome video frames for reducing the bandwidth of the video stream. Also, *pSimVideoCellularGraph* command changes the frame rate from 30 fps to 10 fps using *mSetStatus* command by sending the request to *mVideoControl*. When a wireless LAN card is inserted again, the object graphs are recovered to the original object graphs with a similar sequence.

6. HOST MOBILITY SUPPORT

Supporting host mobility is one of the most important topics in mobile computing environment. In Mobile-IP [Ioannisdis91,Teraoka91], a router connected by a mobile host should be changed when the mobile host is moved and it cannot communicate with the router when the mobile computer goes away from the range where the router communicates with the mobile computer. In this case, the mobile host selects a new router that can communicate with the mobile host for accessing servers on the Internet without reconnecting sessions. The movement of routing entities between servers and the mobile computers is called handoff.

Similarly, host mobility in our framework requires changing stationary computers executing the service proxy. Let us assume that a user goes out of his campus with the mobile host. In the campus, a wireless LAN can be used to connect to servers on the Internet, but the wireless LAN is not available out of the campus. However, a cellular network can be used for connecting to the Internet when the mobile computer is out of the campus. Figure 6 shows how the mobile computer continues to connect to the Internet using the service proxy. While the user is within the campus, the mobile computer is connected to SVP0 using the wireless LAN. However, when the user goes out of the campus, the service proxy which communicates with the user's mobile computer should be moved to SVP1 since SVP0 does not have an interface device for the cellular network. Their object graphs are also changed according to the bandwidth of the cellular network. In this example, an object that reduces the frame rate of a video stream is inserted in the object graph of the service proxy when the service proxy is moved to SVP1. When object graphs are recreated, the states of objects of the old service proxy are moved to the objects of the new service proxy.

However, if the states of the object graph of the old service proxy are not necessary for building an object graph of the new service proxy, SVP1 may need not to communicate with SVP0 since the object graph of the new service proxy can be created by sending a script from the mobile computer.

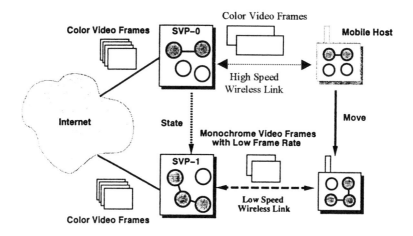

Figure 6. Host mobility.

6.1 HANDOFF PROTOCOL AND OBJECT MIGRATION

When a handoff occurs, the service proxy of a mobile application should be moved to another stationary host. In this case, the objects in the service proxy's object graph should be moved to the new stationary host.

Figure 7 shows the actual protocol for migrating a service proxy from a stationary host to another stationary host. The following shows the sequence of the protocol.

1. Mobile host MH sends a handoff request message to the new intermediate stationary host SP(n). If SP(n) can accept the request, SP(n) returns a handoff accept message to MH. If a proxy move complete message is not returned to the mobile host before a specified time, a timeout occurs and the mobile host sends a handoff request message again.

2. SP(n) sends an object transfer request message to SP(n-1). SP(n-1) transfers the states of objects in its object graph to SP(n). If SP(n) finishes to receive the states of objects from SP(n-1) for creating a new service proxy on SP(n), it returns a proxy move complete message to MH.

3. MH sends a data transfer request message to SP(n). After receiving the request, the packets received by SP(n-1) are forwarded to SP(n) until routing information are updated and no packet from the servers are delivered to SP(n-1).

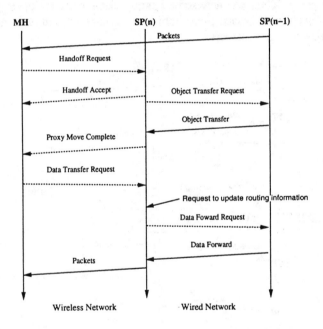

Figure 7. Handoff protocol (1).

The handoff protocol is very suitable for handling the crash of service proxies since an application can recover its service proxy using the control script kept in the mobile host as described in the next section.

The approach also has another advantage. Traditional protocols require keeping the communication with an old service proxy until the handoff is completed. However, our approach communicates with an only new service proxy. Thus, the handoff protocol needs not to be completed before the mobile host cannot communicate with the old service proxy.

6.2 ROBUSTNESS OF HANDOFF PROTOCOL
The protocol described in the previous section may cause a problem when SP(n-1) is crashed while a mobile host accesses servers. This section describes how to recover a mobile application when its corresponding service proxy is crashed. The robustness of the service

proxy framework is achieved by keeping important states in the mobile application so that the service proxy can be reconstructed using the states in the mobile application. However, all states of the application cannot be kept in the mobile application. For example, the recovered application may degrade the performance due to the loss of cached data in the objects of the crashed service proxy.

Our approach allows a new service proxy to be reconstructed without the states of objects in the old service proxy. The approach may not recover the application completely, but it allows the application to be executed if the mobile application can use another stationary host for executing a new service proxy.

Figure 8 shows the sequence for recovering a mobile application when a service proxy is crashed. First, a handoff request message is sent to a new service proxy. If the proxy cannot communicate with the old service proxy, a "could not found old proxy" message is returned. In this case, the mobile host sends a reconstruct request message with the control script to the new service proxy. Thus, the new service proxy reconstructs an object graph using the control script. Lastly, the service proxy returns a reconstruct complete message, and the application resumes to access servers.

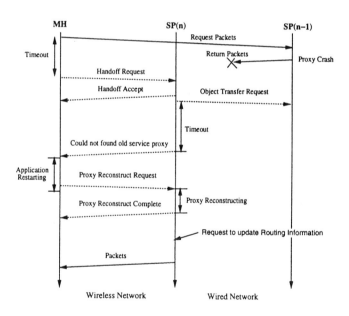

Figure 8. Handoff protocol (2).

MH cannot distinguish the crash of a service proxy from the loss of connectivity between MH and the service proxy. Thus, when a handoff request is received by a service proxy, the service proxy needs to identify the crash of the old service proxy by using timeout.

Also, a similar approach can be adopted for making the handoff protocol that is described in the previous section robust (Figure 9). The following is the handoff sequence when an old service proxy has crashed.

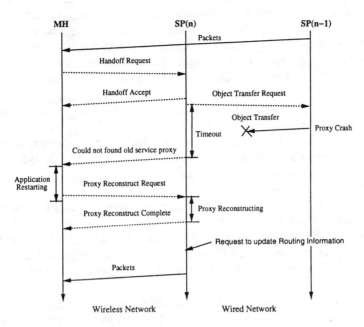

Figure 9. Handoff protocol (3).

1. MH sends a handoff request message to the new intermediate stationary host SP(n). If SP(n) can accept the handoff of MH, SP(n) returns a handoff accept message to MH.

2. SP(n) sends an object transfer request message to the SP(n-1). If SP(n) can not complete the transfer of the states from the old service proxy due to the crash of the old service proxy, a timeout occurs, and it sends a proxy move timeout message to MH.

3. An application on MH sends a proxy reconstruct request message with a control script for creating the new service proxy to SP(n). If the application on MH fails to recover its service proxy on SP(n), the application will be restarted. Otherwise, the reconstruction of the object graph on SP(n) can be allowed without the states of the old service proxy, and a proxy reconstruct complete message is returned to MH.

Since the approach can recover service proxies that have crashed, the reliability of a mobile application is dramatically improved.

6.3 ADAPTABLE OBJECT MIGRATION IN MOBILE SUPPORTS
As described in the previous sections, the objects in an old service proxy are migrated to a new service proxy when a handoff occurs. However, the transmission time may take a long time if the states of object are big. In this case, some states that are not important to reconstruct the new service proxy need not be transferred for making a handoff time short.

For example, a Web service proxy cache received files from servers. When a handoff occurs, the Web service proxy is migrated to the new intermediate stationary host. In this case, cached files may not need to be transferred for reconstructing the new service proxy. The strategy makes the handoff time short since only a few states should be transferred during the handoff.

However, it may be a clever approach to send all cached data when the cached files can be quickly transferred using high bandwidth networks. In our approach, each object specifies the importance of states, and a system determines which states should be transferred during a handoff according to the sizes of states and the bandwidth of a network between the service proxies. Thus, a mobile application can take into account the tradeoff between the time required to the handoff and the completeness of the object's reconstruction.

For example, if the application specifies that the quick handoff time is important, no cached files are transferred. Thus, it may be a long time to fetch HTML files that are previously accessed. On the other hand, if the application specifies that the completeness of the object's reconstruction is important, all cached files are transferred, and the application fetches HTML files that are previously accessed quickly.

Our framework makes the above adaptive object migration possible by defining multiple state transfer methods for respective objects. Each method transfers a different amount of states between two objects, and specifies the condition of operational environments such as CPU and network load for invoking the methods. The system selects and invokes a suitable state transfer method according to the current condition of operational environments.

For realizing an adaptable object migration, multiple methods for state transfer are defined for each object graph. The method is the polymorphic function. To select a suitable method for operational environments, the environments are presented using a lattice. The higher rank of the lattice is high quality services and the lower rank is low quality services. The methods for state transfer are corresponded to the lattice. The rank of the lattice is transited by changing operational environments. If the quality level of an operational environment is high, the service of state transfer is the higher rank of the lattice. On the other hand, if the quality level is low, the service is the low rank of the lattice.

7. RELATED WORK

Some researchers have developed several extensions to the IP protocol for mobile computing [Ioannisdis91,Teraoka91]. Since their extensions provide mobility transparency to applications, mobile computers can be moved anywhere without the application noticing. Moreover, existing network applications can be used without modifying applications. However, the applications cannot deal with drastic changes of network bandwidth. Also, the effect of mobility to reliable transport protocols such as TCP may decrease the throughput of applications [Caceres94].

I-TCP [Bakre95] solves the problem of TCP for dividing a stream into two connections. One connection connects a mobile computer and an intermediate stationary computer with a low speed network, and another connection connects the intermediate computer and a stationary computer executing an application with a high-speed network. Since each connection performs flow control and congestion control independently, each connection can select parameters suitable for its underlying network. Also, the approach does not require modifications of existing network applications.

Another approach proposed in [Balakrishnan95] solves the problem of TCP by snooping TCP packets in routers. The approach recovers lost packets on wireless networks by caching the packets at the routers before the transmission, and retransmitting the packets when a packet loss is detected by routers by snooping TCP packets.

I-TCP and TCP snooping take into account the respective properties of wireless and wired networks, but they do not take into account drastic changes in network bandwidth.

A more aggressive approach was proposed in [Kojo95, Zenel95]. In their approach, a stream is decomposed into two connections, and an intermediate computer connects the two connections. When the bandwidth of the wireless network becomes low, an intermediate stationary computer filters data from the high-speed network before sending the data to the mobile computer. The intermediate computer filters the data according to the content. For instance, reducing the size of each video frame may degrade video data. This solution answers the problem caused by drastic changes of network bandwidth, but it does not solve the problem due to changes in machine configurations. Also, the system does not provide programming support for creating intermediate filters systematically.

Mobile computers usually do not have enough resources for executing sophisticated applications. Some researchers focus on the structures of mobile applications for solving this problem. Wit [Watson94] and ParcTab [Want95] divide applications into two fragments. One of the fragments is executed on a mobile computer, and another is executed on a stationary computer, while these computers communicate over a wireless network. These approaches solve problems caused by resource limitations of mobile computers since lightweight computation requiring less computational power and less amount of memory is executed on the mobile computer, and more resource hungry computation is executed on the powerful stationary computer. However, these systems do not take into account drastic changes of configurations of mobile computers.

Multimedia researchers proposed several solutions for delivering video streams on multicast channels connecting heterogeneous machines [Amir95, Pasquale93]. In these proposals, continuous media streams can be filtered on intermediate routers or application-level gateways since a workstation connected by a multicast channel does not have a power for processing the original video frames. Also, the approach may change the formats of continuous media streams. For example, JPEG streams are converted into H.261 streams on an applications level gateway since a destination workstation may have no sophisticated compression hardware. However, their approaches may solve problems caused by the difference of network bandwidth between wired and wireless networks, but they do not provide any programming supports for creating filters systematically, and their approaches do not take into account drastic changes of machine configurations.

Recently, there are several systems that share many common themes with the work presented in the paper. The new version of Wit [Watson94b] allows mobile applications to determine which portion of data should be cached, prefetched, and reduced dynamically by using the access patterns on the application's typed data structures. Since these policies can be changed according to the configuration of mobile computers, the approach makes mobile applications adaptive.

Rover toolkit [Joseph95] provides relocatable dynamic objects and queued remote procedure calls for building mobile applications that are partitioned into two fragments easily. The focus of the toolkit is to build mobile applications that support disconnected operation although the relocatable dynamic objects allow dynamic configuration of data filters that enables mobile applications to be adapted to drastic changes of configurations of mobile computers.

The above two systems make mobile applications adaptive by changing policies for caching, prefetching, and reducing data according to the configuration of machines. On the other hand, our approach changes the structure of mobile applications when the execution environment is changed. Thus, our approach allows more aggressive adaptation than these two approaches.

8. CONCLUSION

In this chapter, we proposed a new framework for constructing adaptive continuous media mobile applications. Our approach enables us to build adaptive applications that can deal with drastic changes in the operating environment. In our framework, applications are structured using object graphs. Applications can adapt to various operating environments by reconfiguring object graphs.

We also implemented a toolkit for constructing such adaptive applications on real-time Mach, and showed the effectiveness of our framework by constructing a video viewer on MBONE using our toolkit.

Acknowledgments
The author would like to thank Dr. Atsushi Shionozaki for proof reading the draft. This project is funded by the Advanced Information Technology Program (AITP) of Information-technology Promotion Agency (IPA), Japan.

REFERENCES

1.   E. Amir, S. McCanne, and H. Zhang, "An Application Level Video Gateway," ACM Multimedia '95, 1995.

2.   A. Bakre and B.R. Badrinath, "I-TCP: Indirect TCP for Mobile Hosts," In the Proceedings of the 15th International Conference on Distributed Computing Systems, 1995.

3.   H. Balakrishnan, et al., "Improving TCP/IP Performance over Wireless Networks," International Conference on Mobile Computing and Networking, 1995.

4.   M. Bender, et al., "Unix for Normads: Making Unix Support Mobile Computing," USENIX Mobile and Location Independent Computing Symposium, 1993.

5.   R. Caceres and L. Iftode, "The Effects of Mobility on Reliable Transport Protocols," The 14th International Conference on Distributed Computing Systems, 1994.

6.   H. Eriksson, "MBONE: The Multicast Backbone," Communications of the ACM, Vol. 37, No. 8, 1994.

7.   G. H. Forman and J. Zahorjan, "The Challenges of Mobile Computing," IEEE Computer, Vol. 27, No. 4, 1994.

8.   J. Helander, "Unix under Mach: The Lites Server," Helsinki University of Technology, Master's Thesis, 1994.

9.   N. Hutchinson and L. Peterson, "The x-Kernel: An Architecture for Implementing Network Protocols," IEEE Transactions on Software Engineering, Vol. 17, No. 1, 1991.

10. J. Ioannidis, D. Duchamp, and G. Maguire, "IP-based Protocols for Mobile Internetworking," ACM SIGCOMM'91, September 1991.

11. A. D. Joseph, A. F. deLespinnasse, J. A. Tauber, D. K. Gifford, and M. F. Kaashoek, "Rover: A Toolkit for Mobile Information Access," Proceedings of Fifteenth ACM Symposium on Operating Systems Principles, 1995.

12. M. Kojo, T. Alanko, M. Liljeberg, and K. Raaticainen, "Enhanced Communication Services for Mobile TCP/IP Networking," Technical Report C-1995-15, University of Helsinki, April 1995.

13. B. Marsh, "System Issues on Mobile Computing," Matsushita Information Technology Laboratory, Technical Report MITL-TR-50-93, 1993.

14. T. Nakajima, T. Kitayama, and H. Tokuda, "Experiments with Real-Time Servers in Real-Time Mach," USENIX 3rd Mach Symposium, 1993.

15. B. D. Noble, M. Price, and M. Satyanarayanan, "A Programming Interface for Application-Aware Adaptation in Mobile Computing," The 2nd Usenix Symposium on Mobile and Location-Independent Computing, 1995.

16. J. J. Ousterhout, "Tcl and the Tk Toolkit," Addison-Wesley, 1994.

17. J. C. Pasquale, G. C. Polyzos, E. W. Anderson, and V.P.Lompella, "Filter Propagation in Dissemination Trees: Trading Off Bandwidth and Processing in Continuous Media Networks," The 4th International Workshop on NOSSDAV, November 1993.

18. S. Seshan, H. Balakrishnan, and R. H. Katz, Handoffs in Cellular Wireless Networks: The Daedalus Implementation and Experience, Technical Report, University of California, Berkeley, 1995.

19. F. Teraoka, Y. Yokote, and M. Tokoro, "A Network Architecture Providing Host Migration Transparency," ACM SIGCOMM'91, 1991.

20. H. Tokuda, T. Nakajima, and P. Rao, "Real-Time Mach: Towards a Predictable Real-Time System," USENIX Mach Workshop, October 1990.

21. R. Want, B. N. Schilit, N. I. Adams, R. Gold, K. Petersen, D. Goldberg, J. R. Ellis, and M. Weiser, "The PARCTAB Ubiquitous Computing Experiment," Technical Report CSL-95-1, Xerox PARC, 1995.

22. T. Watson, "Wit: An Infrastructure for Wireless Palmtop Computing," Washington University, Technical Report, UW-CSE-94-11-01, 1994.

23. T. Watson, "Effective Wireless Communication through Application Partitioning," Proceedings of the Fifth Workshop on Hot Topics in Operating Systems, 1995.

24. M. Weiser, B. Welch, A. Demers, and S. Shenker, "Scheduling for Reduced CPU Energy," USENIX 1st Symposium on Operating Systems Design and Implementation, 1994.

25. B. Zenel and D.Duchamp, "General Purpose Proxies: Solved and unsolved problems," 6th Workshop on Hot Topics in Operating Systems, 1997.

43

CONFERENCING AND COLLABORATIVE COMPUTING

Eve M. Schooler
University of Southern California
Information Sciences Institute
Marina Del Rey, CA 90292

1. **INTRODUCTION**..936
    1.1   GROUPWARE AND TELECOLLABORATION DEFINED................................936
    1.2   SYNERGY AMONG DISCIPLINES...936
    1.3   COLLABORATION DIMENSION..937
    1.4   VENUE AGILITY...938
2. **SURVEY: SEMINAL WORK TO STATE OF THE ART**.............................938
    2.1   SHARED COMPUTER-BASED WORKSPACES...939
    2.2   AUDIO CONFERENCING..942
    2.3   VIDEO CONFERENCING...944
3. **APPLICATION DOMAINS**...945
    3.1   TELEMEDICINE 946
    3.2   TELESCIENCE 946
    3.3   TELEINSTRUCTION 946
    3.4   CYBER ART...946
    3.5   VIRTUAL COLLABORATIVE SPACES 946
    3.6   DISTRIBUTED SIMULATION 947
4. **ARCHITECTURAL CONSIDERATIONS**...947
    4.1   COMMUNICATION UNDERPINNINGS 947
    4.2   MODELS FOR WIDESPREAD COLLABORATION...948
    4.3   COLLABORATION POLICIES 949
    4.4   LIGHT-WEIGHT SESSIONS 950
    4.5   DISTRIBUTED MESSAGING 951
    4.6   HETEROGENITY...951
    4.7   SYNCHRONIZATION..952
    4.8   FLOOR CONTROL REVISITED...953
    4.9   GROUP RENDEZVOUS 953
5. **CONCLUSIONS**..955
       REFERENCES 956

Abstract. Conferencing and collaborative computing have emerged as new styles of communication. They emphasize using the computer directly to facilitate human-to-human interaction, as well as multi-user communication. In this chapter, we present an overview of the field, first characterizing multimedia conferencing systems, then focusing on the architectural requirements for collaborative computing, and concluding with research directions for the future.

1. INTRODUCTION

With the confluence of computers, televisions and telephones, conferencing and collaborative computing have emerged as new styles of communication. The interactions that were once supported using several different technologies, over several disparate networks, are beginning to be integrated within one framework; the computer. This field is distinguished from traditional computer endeavors in two ways: it emphasizes using the computer directly to facilitate *human-to-human interaction*, as well as *multi-user communication*.

After a brief characterization of multimedia conferencing systems, an historical overview of the field will be given, as well as an assessment of its evolutionary progress. We follow this with an in-depth discussion of the architectural requirements for collaborative computing. Finally, this chapter takes both a look back and a look forward to describe research directions for this important multimedia application area.

1.1 GROUPWARE AND TELECOLLABORATION DEFINED

Broadly defined, the field of collaborative computing, otherwise known as computer-supported cooperative work (CSCW), encompasses the use of computers to support coordination and cooperation of two or more people who attempt to perform a task or solve a problem together [Borenstein 1992]. Not surprisingly, systems that have been honed to support group work are referred to as *groupware*. The essence of groupware is the creation of shared workspaces among collaborators.

Conferencing is simply one form of collaborative computing. It is a term most often used to describe synchronous *telecollaboration*, where shared computer-based applications (e.g., shared editors, whiteboards) are supported in real-time. Often conferencing systems combine shared workspaces with live media, such as audio and/or video. In those instances, the notion of a shared computer-based workspace is enhanced by an element of shared presence in multiple media.

1.2 SYNERGY AMONG DISCIPLINES

Collaborative computing sits at the crossroads of many different disciplines: multimedia, distributed systems, networking, and human factors, to name just a few.

Conferencing is reliant on multimedia solutions, because at some level, conferencing is the management of multiple users in multiple media. As such, it requires low latency for user interactivity and high bandwidth for potentially data-intensive media. However, these problems are compounded by the fact that media is now being distributed among multiple end-users. Thus, there is even more of an urgency to adopt techniques to optimize data delivery.

Collaborative environments are inherently distributed. Whether data sharing is at the level of the graphical user interface (GUI) or the network, conferencing relies on distributed messaging for the dissemination of data and/or control information. Furthermore, the shared nature of groupware leads to issues in data consistency as well as fault tolerance.

Networking plays an increasingly important role for widespread conferencing. With the migration of collaborative software out of local-area testbeds and into more wide-area venues, networking substrates, like multicast [Deering 1988], are needed to provide efficient multiway communication (*1-to-N*, *N-to-1*, and *N-to-N*). In addition, protocol abstractions, such as distributed session control, are needed to shield users from the complexities of multiparty, multimedia coordination.

It is important to stress that conferencing is as much about human factors as it is about the underlying technology. As a result, we, as researchers in CSCW, must embrace the interdisciplinary nature of the field [Malone and Crowston 1994, Ellis et al. 1991]. It is crucial to devise collaborative systems with an understanding of how sociological and psychological factors impact group work, especially since mismatched expectations in group-oriented systems have resulted in serious groupware failures [Grudin 1990].

1.3 COLLABORATION DIMENSIONS

There are several differentiating features among conferencing and collaborative systems. The design space is most frequently categorized according to the attributes that appear in Figure 1: synchrony, locality and scale. One may think of these variables as forming a multidimensional space with each system falling somewhere in that space (admittedly, some points within the space are more interesting than others). See [Ellis et al. 1991, Grudin 1994, Nunamaker 1991, Rangan and Vin 1991, Schooler et al. 1991, Szyperski and Ventre 1993, Watabe et al. 1991] for related categorizations of collaboration attributes.

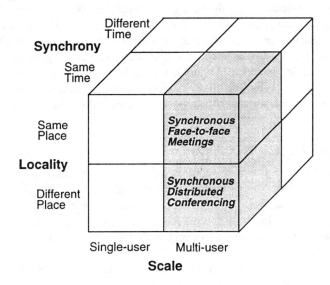

Figure 1. Collaboration matrix.

1.3.1   Synchrony

Perhaps the most basic division is between synchronous and asynchronous conferencing. While both forms of conferencing cater to multiple users, synchronous conferencing is intended for simultaneous users who have real-time interactions, while asynchronous conferencing systems, such as structured messaging systems [Lai and Malone 1988], multimedia electronic mail [Borenstein 1993], and multiparty calendar services [Beard et al. 1990] provide non-real-time communication. In this chapter, we concentrate on synchronous multimedia collaborative systems and therefore will use the terms conferencing and collaborative computing interchangeably.

1.3.2   Locality

Another fundamental distinction is local face-to-face computer-augmented meetings [Mantei 1988, Stefik et al. 1987a, Nunamaker 1991], versus remote meetings for which a real-time voice and/or video channel is required [Crowley et al 1990, Craighill et al. 1993, Chen et al. 1992, Vin et al. 1991, Casner and Deering 1992]. These live media may be carried in digital [Casner and Deering 1992, Elliott 1993] or analog [Arango et al. 1992, Root 1988, Ahuja et al. 1988] form. Another contrasting feature is that some remote conferencing systems are designed for inter-office collaboration [Root 1988, Arango et al. 1992] while others are for conferences between special meeting rooms [Elliott 1993, Casner et al. 1990]. In addition, some remote systems have been optimized to operate with the low delays seen across a local area network (LAN) [Swinehart 1991, Arango et al. 1992], whereas others have been designed to tolerate the longer delays of a more geographically dispersed wide area network (WAN) [Casner et al. 1990, Macedonia and Brutzman 1994, Handley and Wilbur 1992, Elliott 1993].

1.3.3   Scale

A third axis of the state space is the extent to which a system is able to scale up to support growing numbers of collaborators [Schooler 1993a, Szyperski and Ventre 1993], or groups of collaborators [Nunamaker 1991, Rangan and Vin 1991]. A criticism frequently lodged at specialized groupware systems is that they are often completely disjointed from the software ordinarily used by individuals when working alone. Thus, there is impetus to create solutions that offer familiar single-user tools in group settings. There is also a critical need to seamlessly bridge the gap between applications designed to support single-user mode, point-to-point mode, and multipoint mode. Although we are beginning to see systems that have better support for multi-user modes, they frequently have implementation-related upper bounds on the number of collaborators they are able to support [Schooler 1993a].

1.4 VENUE AGILITY

As conferencing systems become more sophisticated, they may support *venue-agility* [Gust 1989]. That is, they may allow users to operate in multiple points of the multidimensional space. Such a system may support a move between synchronous modes (e.g., collaborative editing) and asynchronous modes (e.g., electronic mailings of these edits), or allow the transition from working stand-alone, to working with one other person, to working with a group of people.

The complication of providing venue agility is that selecting a point in the design space has often been intimately tied to an underlying architectural model (see the discussion in Section 4, Architectural Considerations). However, there are several ongoing efforts to understand what is needed to provide more fluidity between the collaboration attributes and the underlying architecture choices [Schooler 1993a, Shenker et al. 1994, Roseman and Greenberg 1994, Crowley et al. 1990, Schulzrinne 1995, Handley et al. 1995]. One promising approach is to supply adaptive mechanisms that are semi-transparent to end-users [Ellis et al. 1991].

2.   SURVEY: SEMINAL WORK TO STATE OF THE ART

Having laid the groundwork for the taxonomy behind collaborative systems, we are ready to discuss the evolution of this field, and to detail the technological and sociological trends behind it. If we look historically at the field of multimedia collaborative systems, we see that it is an outgrowth of several disparate efforts; shared computer-based workspaces, real-time audio and live video spaces. We begin with an introduction to each of these components, describing sample research that has contributed to the maturation of each venue. We highlight the variations in media capabilities and requirements, and present results gleaned from studies of systems in use.

2.1 SHARED COMPUTER-BASED WORKSPACES

Collaborative computing has its roots in the development of computer-based shared workspaces. The idea of group collaboration via computer was inspired first by the seminal ideas of Bush [Bush 1945], who introduced the notion of Memex, a group hypertext system, and also has been broadly influenced by Engelbart, whose NLS/AUGMENT [Engelbart 1968] was one of the first systems implemented that used computers for asynchronous, as well as synchronous group interaction. Both of these efforts represent extremely forward-thinking research, since the computer was barely capable of such tasks when these ideas first appeared.

Since then, there has been an explosion of interest and development of groupware systems ranging from multi-user text editors [Crowley et al 1990, Ellis et al. 1991], to annotation systems [Neuwirth et al. 1990, Cavalier et al. 1991], sketching programs [Minneman and Bly 1991, Stefik et al. 1987a, Ishii 1990, Ishii et al. 1993, Jacobson and McCanne 1993b], and group support systems [Nunamaker 1991].

Originally designed for computer-equipped meeting rooms that allowed small groups to focus on problem solving in face-to-face meetings [Stefik et al. 1987a, Mantei 1988, Gibbs 1989], shared workspaces subsequently have been introduced into larger electronic classrooms [Nunamaker 1991], and into inter-meeting-room and inter-office conferencing. When groupware applications are used among geographically distributed individuals, a voice channel substitutes for face-to-face speech. Typically, audio is supplied either by conventional telephone conference calls, or packet-based networks [Vin et al. 1991, Schooler 1993b, Elliott 1993].

Part of the motivation behind computer-enhanced meeting rooms were studies that suggest considerable amounts of time are spent in meetings, that the presence of computers in meetings is still quite minimal even though they are used with increasing frequency outside of meetings, and that software that runs on computers is typically geared toward individuals rather than groups. Finally, tasks regularly found in meetings are ideally suited to computers (display, manipulation, storage and redisplay of data).

However, by integrating computers into group endeavors, a different set of user challenges arises. For instance, how will the system:

- support concurrency control
- provide the necessary visual cues that online data is part of a shared interaction
- preserve some separation between public and private workspaces
- optimize user interactivity yet maintain data consistency
- establish some continuity between the applications used when working alone and those used in meetings.

These issues are addressed in the sections below, through a discussion of floor control, GUI enhancements, and workspace architecture trade-offs.

2.1.1 Floor Control

Within shared workspaces, *floor policies* are employed to control access to the shared workspace. Each system must decide the level of simultaneity to support (i.e., numbers of active users at once) and granularity at which to enforce access control (e.g., at the level of character entry or paragraph entry). In the simplest form of floor control, applications use *gavel passing*; only one participant has the floor at any given time and the floor is handed off when requested. To obtain the floor, one may be required to take an explicit action, like the selection of a special function key, whereas less restrictive systems allow any keyboard or mouse activity to signal a floor change. More recently, some systems are providing a range of policies to fit the different types of meetings that arise [Altenhofen et al. 1993, Craighill et al. 1993, Crowley et al. 1990, Roseman and Greenberg 1992], allowing participants to play a range of *roles* (e.g., meeting chairperson).

Note that floor control policy is differentiated from floor control mechanism [Crowley et al. 1990]. The distinction is that floor policies describe how participants request the floor and how it is assigned and released, whereas floor mechanisms are low-level means used to implement floor policies [Reinhard et al. 1994]. A variety of mechanisms exist to maintain data consistency among group members, including centralized locks, token passing schemes, and dependency detection. For a more detailed discussion on groupware data consistency mechanisms see [Ellis et al. 1991].

2.1.2   GUI Enhancements

A continued theme has been how to visually display shared simultaneously accessible workspaces. One solution is to enforce a *strict* What-You-See-Is-What-I-See (WYSIWIS) policy for the display [Stefik et al. 1987a]. However, a simple mapping of an application's GUI from a single-user mode to a group-oriented mode is not always effective, e.g., multiple cursors on the screen (one for each participant) may lead to confusion.

Essentially, multi-user interfaces require some sense of shared context, but they also should preserve some degree of private control over the fate of the workspace. This has led to *relaxed* WYSIWIS, or What-You-See-Is-Not-What-I-See (WYSINWIS), which allows a mixture of public and private windows, and personalized window layouts [Stefik et al. 1987b]. However, personalized views of public windows may also cause confusion if one participant points to data that does not appear in another participant's view, causing sudden context switches.

Furthermore, users may want to know about changes being made by other users (e.g., to avoid contention over the same data, to be appraised of workspace modifications), regardless of the degree of private control over the workspace. However, notification of other users' activities should not be exceedingly distracting. For example, techniques to display data sharing include graying out portions of the screen to provide a busy signal for data being modified by another group member, and using color to *age* text modifications (transitioning them through a series of colors, such as yellow, orange, red, brown, black) to indicate regions of recent and not-so-recent activity [Stefik et al. 1987b, Ellis et al. 1991].

In synchronous group meeting systems, designers also can take advantage of the availability of a verbal channel to mediate data contention among a small numbers of users. While race conditions can be mitigated by the use of visual GUI cues, the participants also can rely on verbal negotiation with other group members before altering shared data. As a result, strict distributed database concurrency methods often have been avoided and changes to shared data can be installed by merely broadcasting modifications without any synchronization. These techniques have been effective in supporting a floor mechanism that is light-weight and a floor policy that gives all users simultaneous access to the shared workspace.

2.1.3   Workspace Architectures

There is ongoing debate about the optimal underlying architecture for computer-based shared workspaces. The architectural choices are classified as *centralized* [Garfinkel 1989, Lauwers and Lantz 1990, Patterson et al. 1990], *replicated* [Crowley et al. 1990, Dabous and Kiss 1993, Jacobson and McCanne 1993b] or *hybrid* [Bentley et al. 1994]. As illustrated in Figure 2, the centralized model is based on the execution of the application at one site. Input is forwarded from whichever site has the floor to the site where the application executes and all output broadcast to the other sites. By comparison, a fully replicated architecture runs a copy of the application at each site in the conference. Input from the site with the floor is broadcast to the other participating sites and output is generated locally at each site.

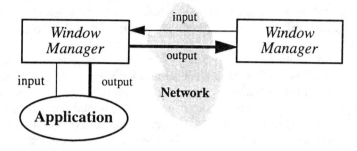

a) Centralized Architecture.

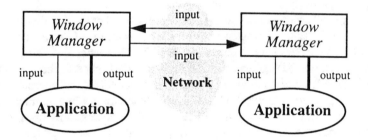

b) Replicated Architecture.

Figure 2. Architecture for computer-based shared workspaces.

One of the reasons why centralized approaches are advocated over replicated ones is that it is often straightforward to take existing single-user applications and make them group-oriented without modification [Garfinkel 1989]. This conversion is referred to as making applications *collaboration-transparent* since the application is unaware of the new mode of operation. Thus users can continue to use familiar applications. A program that uses simple character input/output is especially easy to import into centralized schemes in this fashion.

Because of the potential that an arbitrary window management facility is not available across a wide range of platforms, sometimes graphically oriented programs cannot be incorporated in a straightforward fashion. In addition, if only one copy of an application runs, but the output is duplicated to all sites, it is impossible to support display policies other than WYSIWIS, which results in an inability to tailor the public workspace to individual needs or preferences. For these reasons, although Lauwers and Lantz lobby for centralized computer conferencing architectures, they conclude that modern window systems make this task very difficult to achieve [Lauwers and Lantz 1990]. However, emerging groupware toolkits make it possible to adapt single-user applications to collaborative settings with only a few changes aimed to combat these shortcomings [Knister and Prakash 1990, Jeffay et al.

1992, Roseman and Greenberg 1992, Bentley et al. 1994, Patterson et al. 1990, Patel and Kalter 1993]. The resulting application is thus *collaboration-aware*.

With the migration to wide-area environs, centralized workspace architectures are often supplanted by distributed ones. Although it might be easier to take a centralized approach, in a geographically distributed environment, the choice may result in unacceptable communication delays. Centralized architectures may provide poor interactive response to the conferee with the floor when accessing an application running at a different site. In addition, they may impose a heavier level of network traffic than replicated architectures because output, rather than input, must be distributed to all sites. In LANs, these disadvantages are masked, due to low delays, but they are exacerbated by the large distances involved in transcontinental WANs. Because of this, the replicated strategy seems more suited to the WAN setting.

However, with replicated architectures, applications must avoid operations that are dependent on the timing of input (e.g., holding down a mouse key to scroll a window). To avoid nondeterminism, applications are often specifically designed, or converted, to be collaboration-aware. Additionally, tools that use a replicated architecture [Crowley et al. 1990, Jacobson and McCanne 1993b] require each site to have its own copy of all files, be they data or executables. A valid concern is how and when to orchestrate file distribution; pre-stage [SunSoft 1992, DeSchon and Braden 1988], at startup [Jacobson and McCanne 1993b, Crowley et al. 1990], and/or on-demand. Once in session, there is the added burden to maintain synchronization among copies of the shared workspace, and to facilitate late joiners who may need the latest session context.

Hybrid approaches attempt to mix the best of these schemes; for example, [Bentley et al. 1994] maintains data consistency through a centralized data store, but supports individualized views by creating replicated graphical front-ends.

Whether a centralized, replicated or hybrid approach is chosen, there are other difficulties that arise in large, diverse communication environments like the Internet. For example, the Internet may at times provide highly variable delays or routing failures that create brief service outages. Resynchronization after such a failure is considerably easier for centralized architectures, because there is only one copy of the data [Lauwers and Lantz 1990].

2.2 AUDIO CONFERENCING

Audio has been incorporated into conferencing systems in two forms. First, audio data, like other media, may be embedded in the computer-based workspace. Second, audio may be used to supplement the conferencing context when conferees are not meeting face-to-face.

2.2.1   Audio as Data

Although audio is not yet considered a standard data type for computers, there have been many research projects aimed at understanding how to make it so [Swinehart et al. 1983, Buchanan and Zellweger 1993, Borenstein 1993, Resnick 1993]. The challenge for audio in groupware workspaces is to store efficiently and to smoothly play out the audio stream. Other issues must also be dealt with. For example, in face-to-face conferencing, unless close synchrony can be achieved, the audio component of a multimedia document should only get played out through one set of speakers in the room. This contrasts with the treatment of the textual or graphical data that are part of the shared workspace and that are displayed at each user's workstation. This simple example implies that the groupware application would need to know the context of usage to behave properly.

In those cases where conference participants are dispersed, the choice of data architecture (centralized or replicated) will influence the behavior of the system. When the architecture is centralized, then audio originating at the central archive site will need to be sent over the network to each of the other participants and smooth playout requires each site to buffer for potential WAN delays. In the case of replicated groupware, the audio is likely to be stored locally at each site, avoiding network problems. In either case, there may be a desire to synchronize playout of the audio streams at all of the remote sites.

There are also storage concerns, since digital audio consumes considerably more storage than ASCII text. An indirect pointer technique called ropes has been used to efficiently re-use replicated audio segments [Vin et al. 1991]. See [Steinmetz 1994a, Steinmetz 1994b] for further discussion of compression schemes.

2.2.2 Audio as Communication Channel

Because bidirectional audio has often conjured up images of telephones, some of the early work on audio integration reflects this influence. [Resnick 1993, Schmandt and Casner 1989, Watabe et al. 1991, Schmandt 1993, Hoshi et al. 1992, Clark 1992] are examples of computers coupled with telephony. This has been achieved through use of ISDN signaling, as well as through computer-controlled telephones. Using the computer as an alternate device to control advanced telephone functionality makes perfect sense when we consider the interface to the telephone. Anyone who has ever been lost in a voicemail selection maze knows that the telephone's keypad is far from optimal! Fortunately, there are efforts to improve the interface to the telephone, in part through more standard integration with computers and fax machines [Resnick 1993, Schmandt 1993].

There also have been attempts to carry not only audio control, but also the speech data itself over computer networks, bypassing the telephone altogether [Swinehart 1991, Chen et al. 1992, Elliott 1993, Casner and Deering 1992]. Whereas early experiments targeted transmission of packet audio over local Ethernets but reverted to telephony for long-distance calls [Vin et al. 1991], subsequent work has aimed to transmit audio data over the wide-area, first in testbeds [Casner et al. 1990] and more recently over the general Internet [Jacobson and McCanne 1992, Schulzrinne 1992a, Casner and Deering 1992]. A fundamental challenge for conversational audio in the packet realm is not only jitter-free playback, but also the need to meet delay thresholds for interactivity. Reasonable delays for interactive audio hover in the 40 to 100 millisecond (msec) range; delay is generally undetectable when under 20 msec, can cause trouble when significant echo is present if between 40 and 80 msec, and begins to effect normal conversation when greater than 100 msec [Swinehart 1991]. An added concern for wide-area packet audio conferencing, where packet loss is more likely due to routing mishaps and queueing delays, is that the ear can tolerate only a certain percentage of packet loss, typically in the 5-10% range.

For remote conferencing, the audio component is unquestionably the most important media stream, not only because audio carries important intonation cues with regard to people's reactions, but also it is typically the stream that carries the critical content for group discussion. In implicit floor control schemes, it has been observed that the conferences audio channel is often used to negotiate who should next take the floor and that without verbal agreement, a flurry of retries sometimes results. With explicit floor control schemes, the audio channel is often used to verify that the mechanics of electronically-mediated floor control are working.

A related observation is that full-duplex audio is important for recreating face-to-face group protocols. Telephone conference calls typically do not support this feature. For *N*-way multiparty conferences on computer-based systems, it is possible to achieve the full-duplex analogue by performing audio mixing in software at the end systems [Casner et al. 1990, Jacobson and McCanne 1992, Schulzrinne 1992a]. This technique allows multiple users to talk at once if desired, although when more than a few people speak at once, it renders mixed audio unintelligible.

Ergonomic considerations, such as audio equipment quality and unobtrusiveness, also influence the acceptance and regular usage of audio conferencing. For instance, now that workstations and PCs have built-in audio capabilities, it is easy to sit at one's desk and conduct conversations via the computer instead of the telephone. Nonetheless, the problem of acoustic feedback must be addressed by either using headphones or employing echo cancellation technology.

2.3 VIDEO CONFERENCING

Like audio, video has begun to appear in shared workspaces. It has many of the same storage and distribution concerns as audio. Yet, the increased demands made by video on the display technology, bus architecture, CPU, and network fabric, dictate when and where to include video in distributed environments.

Video is also being used as an additional communication channel in telecollaborations. Experimentation with live video has moved beyond specialized meeting rooms and meeting places to individualized desktop solutions. Although some systems are targeted to supply analog video and others offer video in digital form, in both cases there is a trend toward integration with computer-based workspaces.

2.3.1   Video as Data

As part of shared workspaces, video has been used predominantly to capture shared drawings. [Tan92] supplies a group drawing surface via live video, whereby individual architects could simultaneously share drawings as if co-located. In [Ishii et al. 1993], the idea of a video-based whiteboard is extended by merging drawn pictures with camera images of the participants (the effect is similar to having a clear or see-through drawing surface), capturing gestures and reactions to the video space. Similarly, the objective in [Ishii 1990] is to incorporate non-computer-based materials, such as calligraphy drawn on paper, to support seamless transitions from computer collaborations to non-computer collaborations. In [Milazzo 1991], video appears as a data type alongside other media in structured documents, and in distributed teleconferences, participants who are outfitted with identical video databases may view identical video clips via a hierarchy of VCR or laserdisc servers.

2.3.2   Video Walls

Important trial implementations of video teleconferencing include the video wall experiments conducted by Xerox Corporation between Palo Alto and Portland, and the VideoWindow project at Bellcore. Each experiment linked two research facilities, with connections that operated continuously 24 hours a day. To encourage unplanned interactions across the two sites, the video walls were placed in common areas. Preliminary data from the Xerox experiment indicated that 70% of all communications were of a casual, drop-in nature, with users reporting that most probably would not have occurred in the absence of the video link [Goodman and Abel 1986]. Roughly two-thirds of all VideoWindow interactions were primarily technical in nature, the remainder being social [Root 1988]. It was observed that despite mediocre quality of both audio and video, users reported that the system was moderately useful for sharing culture and maintaining relationships across the two sites. However, the 56 Kbps digital video channel was considered insufficient for crucial aspects of joint work, such as detailed collaboration or delicate negotiation [Kraut et al. 1988].

The motivation behind these projects was to provide impromptu access to colleagues and to provide a sense of proximity, thus fostering scientific discovery [Kraut et al. 1988]. Although VideoWindow made spontaneous conversation possible, the rate of impromptu interaction was less than half that of face-to-face communication [Cool et al. 1992]. This was attributed to the somewhat false sense of symmetry of video windows (e.g., if you can be seen, you can be heard; if I can see you, you can see me), and to the problems of placing the window where it would be the most accessible to the most people. Competition for use of the window was also noted as a factor in its mixed reception, as was the extra effort one had to undertake to meet somewhere other than one's office.

2.3.3 Video Windows

Nonetheless, these experiments served as precursors to other forms of shared virtual spaces and have led to several natural extensions. First, there has been the impetus to supply inter-meeting room conferencing, which has less of the continuous 24-hour connection flavor and more of a set-up-as-needed approach [Elliott 1993, Casner et al. 1990, Snell 1994].

A second extension for video walls has been the move toward inter-office rendezvous, where video is displayed on monitors separate from the workspace computers. Initial implementations catered to computer-controlled solutions, with real-time media carried over switched analog networks [Root 1988, Ahuja and Ensor 1988, Arango et al. 1992]. The initial audience for these systems were colleagues distributed throughout a building, whose computers were accessible across a LAN. Predominantly catering to small groups of local individuals, remote users were reachable via codec bridges.

Although some studies [Egido 1988] indicate a preference for inter-office conferencing, meeting-room-style conferencing does have its place; it has been noted that meeting rooms better accommodate groups of more than three conferees and that they typically provide higher audio quality. The distinction between these two types of collaborations may also be a function of economy, since high-end equipment can be expensive, and it is easier to equip a small number of conference rooms than all participants.

A third trend has been the expectation that video, like its audio counterpart, can be carried in digital form and transmitted across computer networks as a standard data type. As a result, packet video conferencing systems have been developed, not only for LAN-based conferencing [Vin et al. 1991], but also for wide-area collaborations [Casner et al. 1990, Turletti 1993, Fredericks 1994, Elliott 1993, Macedonia and Brutzman 1994, McCanne and Jacobson 1994] with video-in-a-window becoming a standard commodity.

A problem that is frequently cited with digital video is the tremendous amount of data that is generated by a single stream [Steinmetz 1994a, Steinmetz 1994b]. A conservative estimate for a rudimentary system would be that each site generates 64 Kbps of audio, 128 Kbps of video, and shared workspace data (of a non-real-time nature) that is a negligible amount of data relative to the other media. The resultant per site data rate is approximately 200 Kbps. Multiply that by the number of participants in a conference and it becomes clear that one N-way conference alone is likely to consume a large amount of bandwidth. Fortunately, this news is tempered by the realization that in face-to-face meetings not all participants are always viewing all other participants, so it is not necessary in distributed electronic sessions to provide such a feature. Nonetheless, the entire capacity of a T3 backbone link (45 Mbps) could be consumed by 225 sites sending data simultaneously.

3. APPLICATION DOMAINS

Although computer-based shared workspaces, real-time audio and real-time video have matured as separate system entities, the usage of these media is converging. So much so that collaborative computing is moving away from the notion of conferencing for conferencing's sake and into richer application domains. Medicine, science, education, and art are just a few of the areas in which conferencing has been adopted, and each new discipline places new demands on the collaboration infrastructure.

3.1 TELEMEDICINE

Telemedicine has made collaborative radiology, neurology and surgery a reality [Krieger et al. 1991, Anupam and Bajaj 1993, Mulvihill et al. 1993, Sauer and Mansur 1994]. System prototypes mix real-time teleconsultation with online medical records. Shared workspaces therefore must combine radiographic material with 3D magnetic resonance images, stored audio records, and written text. The critical nature of the information requires high-quality display technology above and beyond standard CRTs and reliable delivery is required for **both** images and real-time visualizations. In addition, privacy of medical information places a new and somewhat conflicting demand on the otherwise open infrastructure needed for group collaboration.

3.2 TELESCIENCE

Telescience, such as marine biology and global atmospheric studies, are being conducted by dispersed collectives of scientists in a distributed fashion [Macedonia and Brutzman 1994, Banerjea et al. 1994]. Scientists who were once isolated in remote settings are now given the opportunity to remain connected, albeit electronically. With steady improvements to virtual collaborative spaces, the importance of co-location is decreasing and roving experts, with affiliations across several institutions, are becoming more common. As a result, electronic communities or consortia are giving new meaning to the notion of the Collaboratory, an early vision of electronic telecollaboration to facilitate scientific discovery [Lederberg 1988].

3.3 TELEINSRUCTION

Teleinstruction via networks (e.g., Silicon Valley's BAGnet, NSF's Supercomputing consortium, the European Mice project, the electronically based National University in the U.S.) is rapidly changing the way we view education. Because educational teleconferencing runs the gamut from formal seminar-style presentations to interactive student discussions, there is a high demand for flexible floor policies to reflect the spread of social protocols that exist in the classroom. For an institution offering teleservices, there are additional concerns, such as tracking remote student registration and payment, not to mention student authentication at exam time!

3.4 CYBER ART

Artists are also capitalizing on the opportunity of telecollaboration and teleperformance. Distributed performance [Fields-Meyer 1994, Escobar et al. 1994], networked film-making [Ramirez 1993] and synchronous CD-mastering [Anderson et al. 1994] are fast becoming realities. Organizations such as the International Interactive Communication Society (IICS), regularly host teleperformances between the Electronic Cafe, located in Los Angeles, CA, and other Electronic Cafes around the world, allowing musicians, dancers and artists to perform together synchronously over the network [Fields-Meyer 1994]. A frequently cited caveat is the insurmountable time zone differences; it is challenging to schedule collaborations among communities that span the globe.

3.5 VIRTUAL COLLABORATIVE SPACES

Although many systems have been designed to simulate the existence of real meeting places, and thus to evoke a sense of familiarity, designers more and more are turning their efforts to convene people in virtual conferencing environments [BacIntyre and Feiner 1994]. [Donath 1994, Morgan et al. 1994] are experiments with visual spaces that allow configurable meeting spaces and that capture gesturing and interaction patterns through real-time data interpolation. For example, in [Donath 1994] individual bitmap images of conference participants are arranged around a local representation of the virtual meeting space and as a conferee talk, the other conferees appear to be looking in his or her direction. Experimentation with the audio equivalent for this scheme is also underway [Smith 1994]; audio is processed to sound as though it is coming from different spatial locations depending on who is speaking and where they are seated in the local depiction of the virtual space.

3.6 DISTRIBUTED SIMULATION

A related effort is the creation of the distributed simulation Internet (DSInet) that provides online wargaming exercises for the U.S. government [DSI Newsletter 1994]. What normally entails physically transplanting hundreds of troops and equipment (fighter jets, tanks, aircraft carriers) is now simulated on the computer via remote collaboration software. Exercises conducted in November 1993 relied on the successful cooperation of several hundred individuals/entities across the DSInet testbed, and the aim is to scale eventually to 100,000. The simulation may be thought of as a shared workspace to which many individuals have access and which they are able to modify simultaneously. The notification strategy in this realm is somewhat different than a distributed shared workspace, in that modifications to the workspace are only of importance to individuals who are within range to see and hear them. Similar issues will eventually need to be addressed by commercial multi-user games, such as Doom from Id Software.

4. ARCHITECTURAL CONSIDERATIONS

As shown by the diversity in application domains, collaborative computing has made enormous strides in recent years. Yet, the infrastructure to support collaboration is far from complete. Widespread conferencing relies on interoperable solutions. There are at least two thrusts behind the search for interoperability. First, there is the promise that common building blocks will simplify the development process for groupware through re-useable components. Second, as collaborations span more dispersed and larger communities, the likelihood of heterogeneity increases; shared abstractions and standard interfaces are needed to better accommodate heterogeneity.

At what level do we devise mechanisms to supply interoperation? In this section, we present an overview of several outstanding issues that are integral to constructing an architectural foundation for interoperable collaborative computing.

4.1 COMMUNICATION UNDERPINNINGS

Multiple media associated with a particular conference session may have varied network transmission requirements. As such, a variety of underlying communication services are needed to carry conference data to other members. And, for interoperability, these protocols require standardization. Several protocol suites have been developed that cater to the varied needs of remote conferencing [Ferrari et al. 1992, Wolf and Herrtwich 1994, Schooler 1993b]. Several standards setting organizations (IETF, CCITT/ITU) as well as a number of consortia [Snell 1994] also are concentrating on this area. What differentiates these communities are their assumptions about operating environments. The Internet Engineering Task Force (IETF) has traditionally concentrated on teleconferencing solutions for the computer packet-switched realm, whereas the International Telecommunications Union

(ITU) has evolved from a more circuit-switched perspective. Nonetheless, the shared focus has been on extensions to support real-time and group-modes of communication.

4.1.1   Interactivity

Because collaboration is a human-to-human endeavor, there is a concern about minimizing communication delays. Delays seem to come in two flavors: delays for collaborative tools to propagate updates to all sites, and end-to-end delay of real-time media. Minimizing interaction delay is at the root of the centralized versus replicated debate for computer conferencing architectures. Delays may be noticed during information updates, as well as during floor changes. End-to-end delay of real-time audio has the potential to affect normal conversation, as seen in early satellite implementations. Consequently, the development of real-time transport protocols for time-sensitive data are equally critical [Schulzrinne et al. 1995].

4.1.2   Scaling and Efficient Distribution

As teleconferences scale up in numbers of users, multicast distribution [Deering 1988] becomes essential for bandwidth reduction, considering that there is an $N \times N$ bandwidth explosion for media such as video that normally transmit continuously. Management of these group addresses also becomes more difficult. One complication is that there is a fixed number of multicast addresses. Because most telecollaborations will be transient, address assignment and reassignment will be highly dynamic. A global scheme is required to avoid unwanted address collisions and to promote reasonable address space sharing [Pejhan et al. 1994, Deering et al. 1994, Braudes and Zabele 1993, Schulzrinne 1992b], by partitioning the address space either randomly or among a hierarchy of multicast address servers. To offload dynamic addressing mechanisms, we can make use of fixed multicast addresses for static conferences, such as regularly held conferences or task force meetings, and use unicast addressing in point-to-point calls.

4.1 3 QoS: Quality of Service

Even though teleconferencing is presently possible on lightly loaded networks, conferencing in the large requires network resource management mechanisms to avoid congestion [Topolcic 1987, Zhang et al. 1993, Clark et al. 1992, Wolf and Herrtwich 1994]. Those mechanisms will have to scale to track many connections or flows at once, perhaps using some form of data aggregation. Although resource management pertains to the usage of the network bandwidth, there are several layers of abstraction needed to convey QoS information from users to the network. Specifically, conference operating parameters from the user interface will need to be collected and delivered to these lower-level mechanisms for translation into flow specifications [Partridge 1992].

4.2 MODELS FOR WIDESPREAD COLLABORATION

Increasingly, there have been efforts to develop abstractions to model synchronous conferencing systems [Vin et al. 1991, Chen et al. 1992, Garcia-Luna-Aceves 1988, Chang and Whaley 1992, Roseman and Greenberg 1992, Rangan and Vin 1991, Schooler 1993a]. These models serve a variety of purposes. At the most basic level, they introduce a common taxonomy [Szyperski and Ventre 1993, Rangan and Vin 1991], but they also aim to compartmentalize system functionality [Schooler 1993b, Bentley et al. 1994, Vin et al.

1991], to identify information flow [Craighill et al. 1993], and to specify component interfaces [Interactive Multimedia Association 1993, Arango et al. 1992, Leung et al. 1990].

The difficulty in the goal to model several disparate media types (shared workspace, audio and video) under one simplifying scheme is that each media has different requirements and different usage patterns. Nonetheless, there appears to be a growing consensus in terms of architectural modularity. In particular, many groupware control issues are similar across all media, whether or not the media is computer-based. This is evidenced by the enormous spread of research from ISDN-based conferencing solutions [Clark 1992] to packet-based equivalents [Casner et al. 1990, Altenhofen et al. 1993, Macedonia and Brutzman 1994]. Thus, the idea of a separable session control component has appeared both in audio/video based conferencing systems [Vin et al. 1991, Schooler 1993a, Ahuja and Ensor 1992, Arango et al. 1992, Schulzrinne 1995, Handley et al. 1995], as well as groupware-driven developments [Roseman and Greenberg 1992, Crowley et al. 1990]. As shown in Figure 3, the idea of a session manager is at the core of the architecture, which separates media control from media transport.

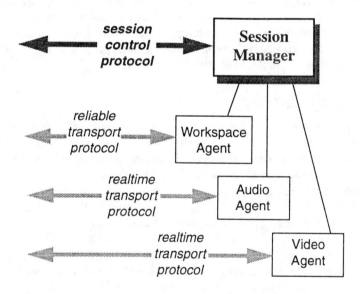

Figure 3. Session control architecture.

By creating a re-usable *session manager*, which is separate from the user interface, conference-oriented tools avoid duplication of effort. Session control encompasses the management of participation, authentication and presentation of coordinated user interfaces. Yet, the session manager is also separate from underlying *media agents*, which are responsible for decisions specific to each type of shared media. This modularity promotes the development of replaceable agents to cater to diverse hardware capabilities and user preferences.

Finally, the session manager provides a conduit for control. Locally, it facilitates inter-communication among media agents; such as exchanges that pertain to interrelated QoS, floor control or synchronization. Remotely it acts to facilitate inter-site communication among peer session managers.

4.3 COLLABORATION POLICIES

Even if all media are unified under one control scheme, not all sessions have the exact same control needs. For instance, the control flow for a design group meeting might be highly unstructured with no particular chairperson, whereas a seminar-type conference might require a professor at the helm who decides the order in which participants speak.

A first step to accommodate session diversity has been to try to identify the range of collaboration styles that exist [Szyperski and Ventre 1993]. In part, this is accomplished by cataloguing what we observe socially and by recognizing the various roles played by participants in group interactions. However, a closer examination of the problem has revealed that sessions are characterized not only as a collection of participants and the media being used among them, but also by a collection of *policies* which govern their interactions [Arango et al. 1992, MMusic 1993, Roseman and Greenberg 1992]. These policies impact everything from who may join a session, when and how a session may be modified, to who may learn of information pertaining to the session.

To experiment further with policy trade-offs, [Roseman and Greenberg 1994, Jacobson et al. 1993] have proposed policy modules that are dynamically bound to a session at run-time, when policy choices are selected. Trial implementations have focused on floor control policies. The Internet Engineering Task Force (IETF) working group on Multiparty Multimedia Session Control (MMusic) has approached session policies through protocol design. The focus is on the specification of a distributed session control protocol, which is built on a common message substrate for multiparty agreement [Shenker et al. 1994] and a flexible language to describe policy and policy combinations [Roseman and Greenberg 1992, Handley and Wilbur 1992, Handley et al. 1995].

4.4 LIGHT-WEIGHT SESSIONS

Not surprisingly, there is ongoing discussion about the trade-offs of distributed versus centralized control models, which very much resemble the issues in shared workspace architectures. However, in shared workspaces, the debate surrounds data distribution. Here, the arguments are centered around the flow of control information. With the movement of collaborative systems out into the general Internet, the conveniences of a centralized session manager [Craighill et al. 1993, Vin et al. 1991, Handley and Wilbur 1992, Arango et al. 1992] are outweighed by the improved response time and resiliency of distributed session control [MMusic 1994, Schooler 1993a, Chang and Whaley 1992].

Yet, even within distributed control architectures, there is debate over the management of session state. At some level, conferences are a collection of shared state (who is participating in the session, what is the session name, when did the session start, what are the policies associated with the session). The degree to which state is private (only known locally) or shared (among multiple entities), and the degree to which it must be identical across participating sites dictates the scheme chosen to disseminate state information.

The fundamental trade-off is between using reliable messaging to disseminate shared session information for immediate synchrony, or using unreliable messaging with periodic refreshes for eventual consistency. Within a WAN context, the former is harder to guarantee. The latter approach, which has come to be known as *light-weight sessions*, may also be advantageous in sessions with a high degree of dynamics (e.g., many membership changes) [Jacobson et al. 1993]. However, for static sessions where it would be redundant to send state refreshes or sessions requiring a tighter control loop, light-weight sessions are less appropriate.

The success of light-weight sessions can be seen in the Multicast Backbone (MBone), a multicast-capable segment of the Internet. A principle behind several of the most popular tools [Jacobson and McCanne 1992, Fredericks 1994, Turletti 1993, Schulzrinne 1992a, McCanne and Jacobson 1994] is that multicast is used to disseminate local information (the local user's address and alias) to other participants tuned in to the same multicast address. Each site distributes its own participation status to other conferees, but there is no global notion of the group membership (who are the recipients of this information), and thus no guarantees that all users will have the same view of the state space (the participant list). This approach of loose-control, where there is little to no shared state and no strict dissemination requirements, has worked quite well for large sessions with little need for coordinated control.

In addition, loose-control sessions are easy to implement because there is no one locale responsible for coordinating session state – each site is responsible for multicasting its own status. An added benefit is the inherent fault tolerance. If the network partitions mid-conference, but eventually is repaired, it is easier to re-establish state, since there are no strict consistency requirements. Finally, the scaling properties of loose-control sessions are quite good, though at some point the refresh periodicity needs to be adaptive to the size and scope of the session, otherwise, the session may be in danger of flooding itself with session reports.

4.5 DISTRIBUTED MESSAGING

There are scenarios where conferees do want assurances that their views of the session are virtually identical to each other, and really do want to exert more control over dissemination and reception of all conference-related activity. For example, it may be important to know the actual membership of a conference, both to decide whether or not to join in the first place, and to know if it is appropriate to discuss certain matters based on who is part of the discussion. This requires stricter multiway distribution mechanisms to maintain global synchrony of shared state. This is exactly the problem that shared workspace applications face.

Although there have been mechanisms similar to remote procedure call to accommodate distributed control among objects, one of their premises is that the relationship between the objects is of a client-server nature [Srinivasan 1994]. This is not necessarily desirable in multimedia collaborative environments, where individual system components are frequently peers and have equal access to and control over the session. The very impressive collection of distribution protocols provided by the ISIS toolkit have the same drawback, although ISIS has gone to great lengths to analyze and provide a range of group-oriented messaging for atomic and causal services [Birman 1993]. As a result, there are several efforts to support more suitable (scalable, decentralized) multiway protocols at both the transport and the application levels. A key aspect is the ability to provide reliable group-oriented communication through the use of negative acknowledgments [Dabous and Kiss 1993, Whetten and Kaplan 1994, Freier and Marzullo 1990, Floyd et al. 1995].

Yet, depending on how session policies have been established, it is very possible that not all conference-related functions require the same degree of reliable delivery. For example, periodic update messages may not require reliable delivery at all. On the other hand, for a floor change request, it may be critical to know that the update was received by all participants, since, if not, multiple video channels may result and may overextend the capacity of the network. [Handley et al. 1995] have even noted that different conferees may care differently about the delivery of the same message; a low-bandwidth link cares more about the news of a floor change than a high bandwidth link that can sustain multiple streams until the floor gavel is passed correctly.

4.6 HETEROGENITY

Standard protocols and modular plug-and-play architectures are not complete without self-describing media agents [Nicolaou 1990, Schooler 1993a, MMusic 1994]. The implication is that a descriptive language is needed to characterize groupware capabilities and requirements. In turn, these descriptions must be exported (e.g., catalogued in a configuration resource directory) to allow selection among them.

Furthermore, multiway interactions may require pairwise translations among of conference participants, such as those required to bridge different media encoding schemes. *Combination nodes* [Schooler 1993a, Pasquale 1992, Lukacs 1994] have been proposed as a general solution to work in conjunction with participant sources and sinks. They would act to combine media streams as they head toward the receivers. These include software or hardware modules that embed functions for: mixing, as with audio streams; compositing, or assembling the interesting pieces of several video flows into a single flow; selection, by a sender (chairperson) or receiver (individually tailored); translation, between encodings; reduction, when scalable coding is used; and combinations of these operations along the path from senders to receiver. These functions may reside at users' end-systems, or in the network. In the latter case, they may be operated as a community resource [Lukacs 1994].

Combination nodes not only are applicable to the translation problem for heterogeneity, but also may be used to avoid wasting network bandwidth by deferring reduction decisions until data arrives at the receiver. For example, to circumvent bandwidth limitations that would otherwise prohibit or restrict conference participation, a mixer would be located upstream from a slow link, then used to combine several streams into one.

4.7 SYNCHRONIZATION

As multiple media are brought together under one control framework, a range of synchronization schemes become possible. Although schemes exist that achieve synchronization by bundling all media together in a single flow, synchronization also has been achieved with separate flows, via timestamping and adaptive synchronization mechanisms [Escobar et al. 1994, Little and Kao 1992]. Although these approaches may not be particular to conferencing, they are further stressed by the multiway nature of collaboration.

A motivating factor behind same-stream transport for the different media is *inter-stream* synchronization. Typical examples of inter-stream synchronization that might occur at each user site include lip-synch (synchrony between audio and video streams) and the correlation between audio and workspace activity (e.g., telepointer). These are trivial to achieve using a shared transport scheme.

However, in certain circumstances, inter-stream synchronization may be more detrimental than it is helpful. If it takes a few hundred milliseconds to encode and compress video data before it is ready for transport across the network (an estimate based on a commercially available video codecs), then audio data would also be delayed by that amount, resulting in undesirably large delays for interactivity. Thus, decoupling the media may work better in this case. In addition, if the video resolution is too low to be able to detect lip-synchrony, it is certainly not worth delaying audio delivery.

In addition, it may be important to take advantage of inherent differences of the media. From a bandwidth and quality of service perspective, a conferencing system may opt to route media across different segments of the network, or across different networks altogether. From a user preference perspective, each user may opt to receive different media streams, which may necessitate unbundling media to provide the needed flexibility. From a heterogeneity perspective, not all of the media generated might be deliverable to all sites. If the media travel over different networks, each may experience different delays along the route between source and destination. Therefore, resynchronization at the endpoints may be necessary.

Because collaboration may occur among multiple users at multiple sites, synchronization in the form of *inter-site* coordination may also be required. For instance, a conferencing system or distributed simulation may require that all workspace events are delivered at the same time to all participating sites, so that some degree of equity is achieved in terms of information sharing. Because the network is a dynamic entity, both inter-site and intermedia delays may fluctuate throughout the lifetime of a session. Thus [Escobar et al. 1994] has created an algorithm to dynamically adapt to the network, while continuing to achieve synchronization among media and sites. This technique was used to achieve synchronization for a teleperformance of a distributed Haydn trio across the Internet.

4.8 FLOOR CONTROL REVISITED

As collaborative sessions grow in size, there is more of a need for floor control – at least in those situations where high user participation is expected. This is true in the non-electronic realm as well, and usually results in hand raising or resorting to chaired sessions with rules of order. A unified architecture has the ability to allow flexible floor control policies across the different media associated with a collaborative session. Certain scenarios call for an integrated floor control approach, whereas others demand separate treatment of the individual media.

Floor control in shared workspaces is as often used to maintain data consistency as it is to institute social protocol. With real-time audio, there is no notion of data consistency; instead floor control is typically used in more formal settings to promote turn taking (e.g., the distributed classroom). But, for more life-like audio interactions, minimal floor control may be optimal; all participants should be able to speak at any time, with audio from simultaneous speakers being mixed together as they would be if co-located. However, audio is a self-moderating channel because realistically only a small number of people can speak at once. Also, in a large conference, most users probably will be silent at any given time. This is not necessarily the case with video. As a result, floor control for real-time video is frequently used to control bandwidth usage.

Consider systems with no floor control. All sites send video to all other sites. In N-way conferencing that means the receiver is faced with a bandwidth N times that of the sender. While multicasting reduces bandwidth usage by senders, mechanisms are also needed for reductions at receivers. A receiver may only want to process M of the N streams that are sent to it. Thus, at the end-systems, each user decides individually which of the video streams is most important to display, either as video-in-a-window [Fredericks 1994], or captured via external codecs that support customized views [Lukacs 1994, Elliott 1993, Casner et al. 1990].

With floor control, a session-wide floor holder typically is selected by a chairperson. For those sites that do not hold the floor, control messages propagate back to senders and avoid wasting bandwidth by sending video that subsequently is not displayed at the receivers. This approach accommodates low-bandwidth links that do not have the resources to handle multiple streams at once. However, more lenient floor policies have also been instituted, such as allowing the last N floor holders to continue to send video [Schooler 1993b].

Even if there is enough bandwidth to support N-way conferencing, there may also be problems decoding and/or presenting all the information at once. Upper bounds in the numbers of streams that may be viewed simultaneously may be hardware-related, in the case of external codecs; they may be CPU-related, in the number of video streams that can be decoded and displayed to the frame buffer at the same time; or may simply be bounded by the amount of screen real estate that a local user wants to invest in viewing remote users.

More interestingly, there is a need to couple the floor control of different media with each other. For instance, policies of video-to-follow-audio or video-to-follow-groupware tie the selection of the video floor holder to activities that are more pertinent to the group activity.

4.9 GROUP RENDEZVOUS

How does one initiate a rendezvous with users or groups of users electronically? Both synchronous and asynchronous rendezvous techniques have been proposed and are presently in use across the network.

4.9.1   Directories and Explicit Invitations

Within the MBone, the session directory tool, *sd*, is used as a TV guide to announce open conferences to which users may join [Jacobson and McCanne 1993a]. Sd resides at a known address and port on each user's workstation, listening at that address for announcements, and posting its own sessions there as well [Handley and Jacobson 1995]. These session announcements are distributed via periodic multicasting. The tool relies on the time-to-live (ttl) feature of multicast to control the scope of the announcements; the ttl is an upper bound for the number of hops the message is allowed to traverse before it no longer is forwarded. Although this is sufficient for now, in the future, as more sessions are announced in this fashion, other schemes with more granularity for scoping may be needed.

In contrast, the session orchestration tool, mmcc, aims to support rendezvous via explicit invitation [Schooler 1993b]. These collaborations may be point-to-point or multipoint in nature. Mmcc also is intended to reside at a well known address and port on users' machines. Although this seems straightforward, there are problems with boot strapping, since calling others requires knowing where users reside. Schemes to register users include creating a registry for end-user addresses and aliases [Arango et al. 1992], leveraging off of the X.500 or DNS infrastructure [Mockapetris 1989, Weider and Reynolds 1992], and creating a multicast solution much like the sd tool, which would dynamically track users as they 'tune' into a well-known registry channel [MMusic 1994].

Another complication is that, for security measures, sites typically have gone to great lengths to hide information about host names. While e-mail addresses are readily available, they usually place users behind a domain name, e.g., username@isi.edu, which gives no notion of where users physically reside. In other words, information is typically not included regarding the particular host machine(s) with which a user is affiliated. While it may be beneficial to promote a naming scheme that hides the details of user locale, it may add a level of complexity not only to the control model for user rendezvous, but also to the routing and delivery of audio and/or video to the actual end-systems.

4.9.2   E-mail and WWW

Prototype e-mail rendezvous mechanisms also exist [Borenstein 1992, Kumar 1994]. Even though e-mail is asynchronous in nature, Borenstein suggests we use e-mail as a platform from which synchronous applications can be launched among groups of individuals. Sufficient information is contained in the message body for group session establishment.

The beauty of this scheme is that it builds on the already existing e-mail infrastructure both to disseminate information and to address end users. E-mail also combats the user buy-in problem [Borenstein 1992], which is basically the technical equivalent of the chicken and egg problem; to create a community of users means enticing them to use the software regularly, yet to entice users to use the software means creating a community of users with whom others can rendezvous. E-mail already has a large user following.

In a similar vein, the WWW infrastructure is also beginning to be used to support synchronous rendezvous [MMusic 1994]. Researchers at Naval Research Laboratory are using the WWW to capture and to dynamically update public session announcements for ongoing or upcoming open teleconferences, while work underway at Stanford Research Institute is designed to provide synchronous rendezvous with authors over documents that appear as hyper-text pages in the web.

5. CONCLUSIONS

Teleconferencing is hardly a novel concept. The idea of video conferencing debuted in the 1920's [Bell Systems Research Labs 1971], AT&T introduced its PicturePhone at the World's Fair in the 1960's, and marketing forecasts of the 70's, 80's and 90's have continued to promise a teleconferencing revolution [Snell 1994]. It would seem that videoconferencing has been touted perpetually as a revolutionary concept on the brink of success [Egido 1988].

Yet, conferencing and collaborative computing have often fallen short of expectations as effective means of communication. Grudin [Grudin 1990] attributes this to the technologically driven nature of the pursuit and paraphrases a colleague who sees this shortcoming as technology searching for a need. Egido's articulate discussion of its failures points to factors lying beyond the scope of technology, such as psychological and sociological ones, and argues that the casting of electronic communication in the image of face-to-face meetings has stood in the way of developing multimedia conferencing technology to its fullest potential [Egido 1988]. Others have lobbied for systems more attuned to group processes, taking the stance that system builders must consider the tools and technology already in place, as well as individual preferences.

Clearly, the mission of conferencing and collaborative computing is not only to bring individuals together in space and time, but also to make groups more effective at their work. This requires an awareness of the interplay between technology and group productivity. Successful conferencing projects have had discoveries of seemingly unimportant human factors that flew in the face of technology – small modifications of either psychological or sociological import that created a good match between the capabilities of the systems and the tolerance, expectations, and needs of their user communities [Mantei 1988, Goodman and Abel 1986, Elliott 1993, Macedonia and Brutzman 1994, Root 1988].

Recurring themes have also emerged. Simple considerations, such as accommodating a variety of conferencing scenarios, guarding against cognitive overload, and catering to a sense of familiarity, have repeatedly been cited as guidelines used by system builders. The necessity and quality of real-time media also figure into a system's effectiveness, as do the simplicity of groupware interfaces and the impact of communication delays. These realizations reaffirm that collaborative computing is not only a multidisciplinary field, but an interdisciplinary one that must create synergies among its varied components [Ellis et al. 1991, Malone and Crowston 1994].

The idea that collaborative technology is an activity in search of a need no longer holds. Increasingly, the world is digitally connected. As a result, conferencing becomes critical among individuals who spend most of their time in group endeavors, who use computers to do their work, and for whom potential collaboration has been impaired by a lack of geographic proximity. It is especially well suited for the kinds of scientific collaborations envisioned for the Collaboratory, a virtual scientific laboratory without walls. The growing acceptance of multimedia conferencing also reflects a change in the way conferencing is promoted; it is a supplement to, not a replica of, face-to-face collaboration.

A testament to the staying power of the concept of conferencing is the emergence of commercial products that have actually made inroads in the market; Silicon Graphics' InPerson, ShowMe from Sun Microsystems, Intel's ProShare, and publicly available tools that are in widespread use on the Internet and MBone [Jacobson and McCanne 1992, Schulzrinne 1992a, Schooler 1993b, Jacobson and McCanne 1993a, Turletti and Huitima 1992, Fredericks 1994, Jacobson and McCanne 1993b, Mcanne and Jacobson 1994]. In particular, these developments are a result of the emergence of standards for interoperability. Windowing systems, such as the X window system [Scheifler et al. 1988], configurable graphical user interfaces, like the Tk/Tcl toolkit [Ousterhout 1990, Ousterhout 1991], and widely available network application programming interfaces (APIs), such as Unix sockets [Sun Microsystems 1988], all have given rise to more generalized software platforms on top of which interoperable systems can be built. Additionally, the increased speed of processors, disks and networks have contributed to the more rapid adoption of distributed solutions and the move to include various real-time media as standard data types.

Nonetheless, there are still many aspects about computer architectures that make it difficult to achieve widespread availability of these services, from the need for communication standards to seamless techniques to accommodate multi-user GUIs. There is the continued challenge to support not only small groups or moderate sized organizations [Grudin 1994], which have traditionally been the focus of most groupware systems, but much larger scale telecollaborations [Schooler 1993a]. The expectation is that integrated solutions, combining audio, video and shared workspaces, will eventually make it as easy to rendezvous electronically as it is physically. More importantly, telecollaborations must support not one, but many real-world interaction protocols. Finally, an integral part of the coming-of-age process will be the continued attention to issues beyond the scope of technology itself.

Acknowledgments

This research was sponsored in part by the National Science Foundation (NSF) Center for Research in Parallel Computation, the Advanced Research Projects Agency (ARPA) under Fort Huachuca contract number DABT63-91-C-0001, the Airforce Office of Scientific Research (AFOSR) grant AFOSR-91-0070, and a grant from the American Association of University Women (AAUW) Educational Foundation. The views and conclusions in this document are those of the author and should not be interpreted as representing the official policies, either expressed or implied, of NSF, ARPA, AFOSR, AAUW or the U.S. government.

REFERENCES

1. Ahuja, S. R., Ensor, J. R., and Horn, D. N. 1988. The Rapport Multimedia Conferencing Systems, *Proc. ACM Conf. on Office Inf. Sys.*, 1-8.

2. Ahuja, S.R., Ensor, J. R. 1992. Coordination and Control of Multimedia Conferencing, *IEEE Comm., 20*, 5, 38-43.

3. Altenhofen, M., Dittrich, J., Hammerschmidt, R., Kappner, T. Kruschel, C., Kuckes, A., and Steinig, T. 1993. The BERKOM Multimedia Collaboration Service, *Proc. 1st ACM Conf. on MM.*, Los Angeles, CA, 457-463.

4. Anderson, D., Doris, R., and Moorer, J. 1994. A Distributed Computer System for Professional Audio, *Proc. 2nd ACM Conf. on MM.*, San Francisco, CA.

5. Anupam, V. and Bajaj, C.L. 1993. Collaborative Multimedia Scientific Design in SHASTRA, *Proc. 1st ACM Conf. on MM.*, Los Angeles, CA, 447-456.

6. Arango, M. et al. 1992. Touring Machine: A Software Platform for Distributed Multimedia Applications, *Proc. IFIP International Conf. on Upper Layer Protocols, Architectures and Applications*, Vancouver, Canada.

7. Banerjea, A., Knightly, E., Templin, F., and Zhang, H. 1994. Experiments with the Tenet Real-Time Protocol Suite on the Sequoia 2000 Wide Area Network, *Proc. 2nd ACM Conf. on MM.*, San Francisco, CA.

8. Beard, D., Palaniappan, M., Humm, A., Banks, D., Nair, and A., Shan, Y. 1990. A Visual Calendar for Scheduling Group Meetings, *Proc. ACM Conf. on CSCW*, Los Angeles, CA, 279-290.

9. Bell Systems Research Labs 1971. The Picturephone System, *Bell Sys. Tech. J.*

10. Bentley, R., Rodden, T., Sawyer, P., and Sommerville, I. 1994. Architectural Support for Cooperative Multiuser Interfaces, *IEEE Computer, 27*, 5, 37-46.

11. Birman, K. P. 1993. The Process Group Approach to Reliable Distributed Computing, *Comm. ACM, 36*, 12.

12. Borenstein, N.S. 1992. Computational Mail as Network Infrastructure for Computer-Supported Cooperative Work, *Proc. ACM Conf. on CSCW*, Toronto, Canada, 67-73.

13. Borenstein, N.S. 1993. MIME: a portable and robust multimedia format for Internet mail, *J. MM. Sys., 1*, 1, 29-36.

14. Braudes and R., Zabele, S. 1993. Requirements for Multicast Protocols, RFC 1458.

15. Buchanan, M. C. and Zellweger, P.T. 1993. Automatic Temporal Layout Mechanisms, *Proc. 1st ACM Conf. on MM.*, Los Angeles, CA, 341-350.

16. Bush, V. 1945. As We May Think, *Atlantic Monthly, 176*, 1, 101-108.

17. Casner, S., Seo, K., and Edmond, W. 1990. N-Way Conferencing with Packet Video, *Proc. 3rd International Workshop on Packet Video*, Morristown, NJ.

18. Casner, S. and Deering, S. 1992. First IETF Internet Audiocast, *ACM Comp. Comm. Review, 22*, 3.

19. Cavalier, T., Chandhok, R., Morris, J., Kaufer, D. and Neuwirth, C. 1991. A Visual Design for Collaborative Work: Columns for Commenting and Annotation, *Proc. 24th Annual Hawaii International Conf. on Sys. Sci., 3*, 729-738.

20. Chang, Y. and Whaley, J. 1992. Remote Conferencing Architecture, *Proc. 24th IETF*, Teleconferencing Architecture BOF, Boston, MA.

21. Chen, M., Barzilai, T., and Vin, H. M. 1992. Software Architecture of DiCE: A Distributed Collaboration Environment, *Proc. 4th IEEE ComSoc International Workshop on MM. Comm.*, Monterey, CA, 172-185.

22. Clark, W. J. 1992. The European ÒMIASÓ System for ISDN Multimedia Conferencing, *Proc. 4th IEEE ComSoc International Workshop on MM. Comm.*, Monterey, CA,14-27.

23. Clark, D., Shenker S., and Zhang, L. 1992. Supporting Real-Time Applications in an Integrated Services Packet Network: Architecture and Mechanism, *Proc. ACM Conf. SIGCOMM*, Baltimore, MD.

24. Cool, C., Fish, R. S., Kraut, R. E., and Lowery, C. M. 1992. Iterative Design of Video Communication Systems, *Proc. ACM Conf. on CSCW*, Toronto, Canada.

25. Craighill, E., Lang, R., Skinner, K., and Fong, M. 1993. CECED: A System for Informal Multimedia Collaboration, *Proc. 1st ACM Conf. on MM.*, Los Angeles, CA.

26. Crowley, T. et al. 1990. MMConf: An Infrastructure for Building Shared Multimedia Applications, *Proc. ACM Conf. on CSCW*, Los Angeles, CA.

27. Dabous, W. and Kiss, B. 1993. A Reliable Multicast Protocol for a White Board Application, Tech. Rep., INRIA Centre de Sophia Antipolis, France.

28. Deering, S. 1988. Host Extensions for IP Multicasting, RFC 1054, Stanford University, Stanford, CA.

29. Deering, S., Estrin, D., Farinacci, D., Jacobson, V., Liu, C.-G., and Wei, L. 1994. An Architecture for Wide-Area Multicast Routing, *Proc. ACM Conf. SIGCOMM*, 126-135.

30. DeSchon and A., Braden, R. 1988. Background File Transfer Program BFTP, RFC 1068, USC/Information Sciences Institute, Marina del Rey, CA.

31. Donath, J. S. 1994, Casual Collaboration, *Proc. of the IEEE International Conf. on MM. Comput. and Sys.*

32. DSI Newsletter, BBN Systems and Technologies, Cambridge, MA, 1, 6, 2.

33. Egido, C. 1988. Video Conferencing as a Technology to Support Group Work: A Review of its Failures, *Proc. ACM Conf. on CSCW*, Portland, OR, 13-24.

34. Ellis, C. A., Gibbs, S. J., and Rein, G. L., 1991. Groupware: Some Issues and Experiences, *Comm. ACM, 34*, 1, 39-58.

35. Elliott, C. 1993. High-Quality Multimedia Conferencing Through a Long-Haul Packet Network, *Proc. 1st ACM Conf. on MM.*, Los Angeles, CA, 91-98.

36. Engelbart, D. C. 1968. A Research Center for Augmenting Human Intellect, Proc. of FJCC, 33, 1, 395-410, AFIPS Press, Montvale, NY.

37. Escobar, J., Deutsch, D., and Partridge, C. 1994. Flow Synchronization Protocol, *IEEE/ACM Trans. on Net.*, 2, 2, 111-121.

38. Ferrari, D., Banerjea, A, and Zhang, H. 1992. Network Support for Multimedia: A Discussion of the Tenet Approach, Tech. Rep. TR-92-072, Comp. Sci. Div., UC Berkeley.

39. Fields-Meyer, T. 1994. Artists Get a Lift Onto Info Superhighway, Los Angeles Times, p. W6, May 1.

40. Floyd, S., Jacobson, V., McCanne, S., Zhang, L., and Liu, C.-G. 1995. A Reliable Multicast Framework for Light-weight Sessions and Application Level Framing, *Proc. ACM Conf. SIGCOMM.*

41. Freier, A. O. and Marzullo, K. 1990. MTP: An Atomic Multicast Transport Protocol, Tech. Rep., No. 90-1141, CS Dept., Cornell Univ.

42. Fredericks, R. 1994. Experiences with real-time software video compression, Xerox PARC.

43. Garcia-Luna-Aceves, J. J., Craighill, E. J., and Lang, R. 1988. An Open-Systems Model for Computer-Supported Collaboration, *Proc. 2nd IEEE Conf. on Workstations.*

44. Garfinkel, D., Gust, P., Lemon, M., and Lowder, S. 1989. The SharedX Multi-user Interface User's Guide, version 2.0, HP Res. Rep., STL-TM-89-07, Palo Alto, CA.

45. Goodman, G. O. and Abel, M. J. 1986. Collaboration Research in SCL, *Proc. ACM Conf. on CSCW*, Austin, TX.

46. Gibbs, S. J. 1989. LIZA: An Extensible Groupware Toolkit, *Proc. ACM SIGCHI.*

47. Grudin, J. 1990. Why CSCW Applications Fail: Problems in the Design and Evaluation of Organizational Interfaces, *Proc. ACM Conf. on CSCW*, Portland, OR, 85-93.

48. Grudin, J. 1994. Computer-Supported Cooperative Work: History and Focus, *IEEE Comp., 27*, 5, 19-26.

49. Gust, P. 1989. Multi-user Interfaces for Extended Group Collaboration, Groupware Tech. Workshop, IFIP 8.4 WG, Palo Alto, CA.

50. Handley, M. J., Wilbur, S. 1992. Multimedia Conferencing: From Prototype to National Pilot, Proc. INET, Internet Society, Reston, VA, 483-390.

51. Handley, M. J., Wakeman, I., and Crowcroft, J. 1995. CCCP: Conference Control Channel Protocol: A Scalable Base for Building Conference Control Applications, Proc. ACM Conf. SIGCOMM.

52. Handley, M. and Jacobson, V., 1995. SDP: Session Description Protocol, IETF MMusic Working Group, Internet Draft.

53. Hoshi, T., Takahashi, Y., and Mori, K. 1992. An Integrated Multimedia Desktop Communication and Collaboration Platform for B-ISDN, *Proc. 4th IEEE ComSoc International Workshop on MM. Comm.*, Monterey, CA, 28-38.

54. Huang, H., Huang, J., and Wu, J. 1993. Real-Time Software-Based Video Coder for Multimedia Communication Systems, *ACM J. MM. Sys., 1*, 3, 110-119.

55. Interactive Multimedia Association 1993. Submission and Response to the Multimedia System Services RFT, Network FoG.

56. Ishii, H. 1990. TeamWorkStation: Towards a Seamless Shared Workspace, *Proc. ACM Conf. on CSCW*, Los Angeles, CA, 13-26.

57. Ishii, H., Kobayashi, M., and Grudin, J. 1993. Integration of Interpersonal Space and Shared Workspace: ClearBoard Design and Experiments, *ACM Trans. on Inf. Sys., 11*, 4, 349-375.

58. Jacobson, V. and McCanne, S. 1992. vat, Video Audio tool, Unix Manual Page.

59. Jacobson, V. and McCanne, S. 1993a. sd, Session Directory tool, Unix Manual Page.

60. Jacobson, V. and McCanne, S. 1993b. wb, Whiteboard, Unix Manual Page.

61. Jacobson, V., McCanne, S., and Floyd, S. 1993c. A Conferencing Architecture for Light-Weight Sessions, Mice Seminar Series, Univ. College London, UK.

62. Jeffay, K., Lin, J. K., Menges, J., Smith, F. D., and Smith, J. B. 1992. Architecture of the Artifact-Based Collaboration System Matrix, *Proc ACM Conf. on CSCW*, Toronto, Canada, 195-202.

63. Knister, M. J. and Prakash, A. 1990. DistEdit: A Distributed Toolkit for Supporting Multiple Group Editors, *Proc. ACM Conf. on CSCW*, Los Angeles, CA.

64. Kraut, R. Egido, C., and Galegher, J. 1988. Patterns of Contact and Communication in Scientific research Collaboration, *Proc. ACM Conf. on CSCW*, 1-12.

65. Krieger, D., Burk, G., and Sclabassi, R. J. 1991. NeuroNet: A Distributed Real-Time System for Monitoring Neurophysiologic Function in the Medical Environment, *IEEE Comp.*

66. V. Kumar 1994. mmphone, e-mail correspondence.

67. Lai, K. Y. and Malone, T. W. 1988. Object Lens: A Spreadsheet for Cooperative Work, *Proc. ACM Conf. on CSCW*, Portland, OR, 115-124.

68. Lauwers, J. C. and Lantz, K. A. 1990. Collaboration Awareness in Support of Collaboration Transparency: Requirements for the Next Generation of Shared Window Systems, *Proc. ACM Conf. on CHI*.

69. Lederberg, J. and Uncapher, K. 1988. Towards a National Collaboratory, Report of an Invitational Workshop at the Rockefeller Univ., NY, NY.

70. Leung, W. H., Baumgartner, T. J., Hwang, Y. H., Morgan, M. J., and Tu, S. C. 1990. A Software Architecture for Workstations Supporting Multimedia Conferencing in Packet Switching Networks, *IEEE J. on Selected Areas in Comm., 8*, 3.

71. Little, T. D. C. and Kao, F. 1992. An Intermedia Skew Control System for Multimedia Data Presentation, *Proc. 3rd International Workshop on Net. and O.S. Support for Digital Audio and Video*, San Diego, CA.

72. Lukacs, M. E. 1994. The Personal Presence System - Hardware Architecture, *Proc. 2nd ACM Conf. on MM*.

73. Macedonia, M. R. and Brutzman, D. P. 1994. MBone Provides Audio and Video Across the Internet, *IEEE Comp., 27*, 4, 30-36.

74. MacIntyre, B. and Feiner, S. 1994. Future Multimedia User Interfaces, *Proc. Dagstuhl International Workshop on Fundamentals and Perspectives on Multimedia Systems*, Dagstuhl, German, 209-249.

75. Malone, T. W., Crowston, K. 1994. The Interdisciplinary Study of Coordination, *ACM Comput. Surv., 26*, 1, 87-120.

76. Mantei, M. 1988. Capturing the Capture Lab Concepts: A Case Study in the Design of a Computer Supported Meeting Environment, *Proc. ACM CSCW*, Portland, OR, 257-270.

77. McCanne, S. and Jacobson, V. 1994. vic, Video Conferencing tool, Unix Manual Page.

78. Milazzo, P. 1991. Shared Video under UNIX, *Proc. Summer USENIX Conf.*

79. Minneman, S. L. and Bly, S. A. 1991. Managing a Trois: A Study of a Multi-user Drawing Tool in Distributed Design Work, Proc. ACM Conf. on CHI,217-224.

80. Mockapetris, P. V. 1989. DNS Encoding of Network Names and Other Types, RFC 1035.

81. Morgan, B., Mankin, A., and Landwebber, L. L. 1994. Observations of Internet Video Conferencing: Towards a Virtual Reality Based Conferencing Environment, *Journal of Internetworking: Res. and Experience*.

82. Minutes of the Multiparty Multimedia Session Control Working Group (MMusic) 1993. *Proc. 28th IETF*, Houston, TX, 523-542.

83. Minutes of the Multiparty Multimedia Session Control Working Group (MMusic) 1994. *Proc. 29th IETF*, Seattle, WA, 545-572.

84. Mulvihill, C., McDermott, G., and Patel, A. 1993. Cooperative Decision Support for Medical Diagnosis, *ACM Comp. Comm. Review, 16*, 9.

85. Neuwirth, C. M., Kaufer, D. S., Chandhok, R., and Morriss, J. H. 1990. Issues in the Design of Computer Support for Co-Authoring and Commenting, *Proc. ACM Conf. on CSCW*, Los Angeles, CA.

86. Nicolaou, C. 1990. An Architecture for Real-Time Multimedia Communications Systems, *IEEE J. on Selected Areas in Comm.*, 8, 3, 391-400.

87. Nunamaker, J. F., Dennis, A. R., Valacich, J. S., Vogel, D. R., and George, J. F. 1991. Electronic Meeting Systems to Support Group Work, *Comm. ACM, 34*, 7, 40-61.

88. Ousterhout, J. K. 1990. Tcl: An Embeddable Command Language, *Proc. Winter USENIX Conf.*

89. Ousterhout, J. K. 1991. An X11 Toolkit Based on the Tcl Language, *Proc. Winter USENIX Conf.*

90. Partridge, C. 1992. A Proposed Flow Specification, RFC 1363.

91. Pasquale, J. C., Polyzos, G. C., Anderson, E. W., and Kompella, V. P. 1992. The Multimedia Multicast Channel, *Proc. 3rd International Workshop on Net. and O.S. Support for Digital Audio and Video*, San Diego, CA, 185-195.

92. Patterson, J. F., Hill, R. D., and Rohall, S. L. 1990. Rendezvous: An Architecture for Synchronous Multi-User Applications, *Proc. ACM Conf. on CSCW*, Los Angeles, CA, 317-328.

93. Patel, D. and Kalter, S. D. 1993. A UNIX Toolkit for Distributed Synchronous Collaborative Applications, *J. Computi. Sys.*, 6, 2, 105-134.

94. Patel, K., Smith, B. C., and Rowe, L. A. 1993. Performance of a Software MPEG Video Decoder, *Proc. 1st ACM Conf. on MM.*, 83-90.

95. Pejhan, S., Eleftheriadis, A., and Anastassiou, D. 1994. Distributed Multicast Address Management in the Global Internet, Columbia Univ., New York, NY, 1994.

96. Rangan, P. V. and Vin, H. M. 1991. Multimedia Conferencing as a Universal Paradigm for Collaboration, Proc. Eurographics Workshop on MM. Sys., Applications, and Interactions, Stockholm, Sweden.

97. Ramirez, A. 1993. A Major Record Album: Only a Phone Call Away, New York Times, p.C17, Oct 7.

98. Reinhard, W., Schweitzer, J., and Volksen, G. 1994. CSCW Tools: Concepts and Architectures, *Comm. ACM, 27*, 5, 28-36.

99. Resnick, P. 1993. Phone-Based CSCW: Tools and Trials, *Trans. Inf. Sys., 11*, 4, 401-424.

100. Root, R. W. 1988. Design of a Multi-Media Vehicle for Social Browsing, *Proc. ACM Conf. on CSCW*, Portland, OR, 25-38.

101. Roseman, M. and Greenberg, S. 1992. Groupkit: A Groupware Toolkit for Building Real-Time Conferencing Applications, *Proc. ACM Conf. on CSCW*, Toronto, CA.

102. Roseman, M. and Greenberg, S. 1994. Submitted to ACM Conf. on CSCW.

103. Sauer, F. and Mansur, K. 1994. Multimedia Technology in the Radiology Department, Proc. 2nd ACM Conf. on MM., San Francisco, CA.

104. Scheifler, R., Gettys, J., and Newman, R. 1988. The X Window System: C Library and Protocol Reference, DEC Press.

105. Schmandt, C. and Casner, S. 1989. Phonetool: Integrating Telephones and Workstations, *Proc. IEEE Globecom*.

106. Schmandt, C. 1993. Phoneshell: The Telephone as Computer Terminal, *Proc. 1st ACM Conf. on MM.*, 373-382.

107. Schooler, E.M., Casner, S. L., and Postel, P. 1991. Multimedia Conferencing: Has it come of age?, *Proc. 24th Annual Hawaii International Conf. on Sys. Sci., 3*, 707-716.

108. Schooler, E. M. 1993a. The Impact of Scale on a Multimedia Connection Architecture, *ACM J. MM. Sys.*, 1, 1, 2-9.

109. Schooler, E. M. 1993b. Case Study: Multimedia Conference Control in a Packet-switched Teleconferencing System, *J. Internetworking: Res. and Experience*, 99-120.

110. Schulzrinne, H. 1995. Dynamic Configuration of Conferencing Applications using Pattern-Matching Multicast, *Proc. 5th International Workshop on Net. and O.S. Support for Digital Audio and Video*, Durham, New Hampshire, 231-242.

111. Schulzrinne, H. 1992a. Voice Communication Across the Internet: A Network Voice Terminal, Dept of Elec. and Comp. Eng., Dept. of C.S., Univ. of Mass., Amherst, MA.

112. Schulzrinne, H. 1992b. Issues in Designing a Transport Protocol for Audio and Video Conferences and other Multiparticipant Real-Time Applications, IETF AVT Working Group, Working Draft.

113. Schulzrinne, H., Casner, S., Fredericks, R., and Jacobson, V. 1995. RTP: A Transport Protocol for Real-Time Applications, IETF AVT Working Group, Internet Draft.

114. Shenker, S., Weinrib, A., and Schooler, E. 1994. Managing Shared Ephemeral Teleconferencing State: Policy and Mechanism, *Proc. International COST237 Workshop on MM. Transport and Teleservices*, Vienna, Austria.

115. Smith, B. e-mail correspondence, Comp. Sci. Dept., Cornell Univ., Cornell, NY.

116. Snell, M. 1994. Picture This: Videoconferencing, *IEEE Computer*, 27, 5, 8-10.

117. Srinivasan, R. 1994. RPC: A Remote Procedure Call Protocol Specification Version 2, Internet Draft.

118. Stefik, M., Foster, G., Bobrow, D. G., Kahn, K., Lanning, S., and Suchman; L. 1987a. Beyond the Chalkboard: Computer Support for Collaboration and Problem Solving in Meetings, *Comm. ACM, 30*, 1, 32-47.

119. Stefik, M., Bobrow, D. G., Foster, G., Lanning, S., and Tatar, D. 1987b. WYSIWIS revised: Early Experiences with Multi-user Interfaces, *ACM Trans. Office Inf. Sys., 5*, 2, 147-167.

120. Steinmetz, R. 1994a. Data Compression in Multimedia Computing: Principles and Techniques, *ACM J. MM. Sys.*, 1, 4, 166-172.

121. Steinmetz. R. 1994b. Data Compression in Multimedia Computing: Standards and Systems, *ACM J. MM. Sys.*, 1, 5, 187-204.

122. Sun Microsystems 1988. A Socket-based Interprocess Communications Tutorial, Network Programming Document, Sun Microsystems, Inc., Mountain View, CA.

123. SunSoft 1992. Forum teleconferencing software.

124. Szyperski, C. and Ventre, G. 1993. A Characterization of Multi-Party Interactive Multimedia Applications, Tech. Rep. TR-93-006, International Comp. Sci. Inst., Berkeley, CA.

125. Swinehart, D. C., Stewart, L. C., Ornstein, S. M. 1983. Adding Voice to an Office Computer Network, *Proc. IEEE GlobeCom Conf.*

126. Swinehart, D. 1991. The Connection Architecture for the Etherphone System, Tech. Rep. CSL 91-8, Xerox PARC, Palo Alto, CA.

127. Topolcic, C. 1987. Experimental Internet Stream Protocol, RFC 1190, IETF CIP Working Group.

128. Turletti, T. 1993. H.261 Software Codec for Videoconferencing over the Internet, Res. Rep. 1834, Institut National de Recherche en Informatique et en Automatique, Sophia-Antipolis, France.

129. Vin, H. M., Zellweger, P. T., Swinehart, D. C., and Rangan, P. V. 1991. Multimedia Conferencing in the Etherphone Environment, *IEEE Comp.*, 24, 10, .

130. Watabe, K. et al. 1991. Distributed Desktop Conferencing System with Multi-user Multimedia Interface, *IEEE J. Selected Areas in Comm.*, 9, 4, 531-539.

131. Weider, C. and Reynolds, J. 1992. Technical Overview of Directory Services Using the X.500 Protocol, RFC 1309.

132. Whetten, B. and Kaplan, S. 1994. A High Performance Totally Ordered Multicast Protocol, Univ. CA, Berkeley.

133. Wolf, L. C. and Herrtwich, R. G. 1994. The System Architecture of the Heidelberg Transport System, ACM Op. Sys. Rev., 28, 2, 51-64.

INDEX

A

abstraction 3, 5-9, 12
access mechanisms 598
access time 508, 513, 516, 523
acoustic features 217, 219, 221
active multimedia objects 588
A/D conversion 136
adaptive continuous media applications 913
Adaptive Differential Pulse Code Modulation (ADPCM) 142, 147
adaptive resource management 905
admission control 631, 854
Aesthetics 3, 10-11
algebraic video model 586-588, 590
allocation protocol 858
Amsterdam hypermedia model 669-670
animation 5-6, 9, 15
animation sequence 608, 613
application quality 878
approximate substring matching 438
Asymmetric Digital Subscriber Line (ADSL) 799
asynchronous classroom 765
asynchronous multimedia 785
Asynchronous Transfer Mode (ATM) 693-694, 807-811, 815-823, 850
atomic object layer 572
audience 3, 5, 10-12, 14
audio
  bandwidth 211
  brightness 211
  class 22
  classification 224
  clip 620, 622
  cluster 748
  conferencing 942
  cuts 369
  databases 220
  discrimination 214
  encoding 349
  events 369
  feature analysis 209
  feature extraction 210
  feature vector 369
  file systems 220
  loudness 210
  pitch 210
  query by example 213
  renderer 748
  segmentation 224
authoring capabilities 476
authoring courseware 771
authoring tool 470
automatic video manipulation 317

B

bandwidth guarantees 498
bandwidth-to-space ratio 521
beat detection 216
binary facts 48
Binary Large Object (BLOB) 44, 406, 590
broadcast automation 386
browsing schemes 274
buffer management 580, 592-593, 595, 597
buffer replacement algorithms 597
bulk media data 595

C

camera model 326
camera motion 325
camera work 263
canonical description 47-48
card-based querying 397
casual media 406-407
cell loss 831
  concealment 828
character generation 705
circuit switched services 794
class hierarchy 19-22, 24-25, 33
client-pull architecture 593
clip assembly 372
clip class 23
clip selection 371
clock synchronization 547
closed-captioned video 404
cluster tree 330
CMIF model 671-674
codec cluster 749

cognitive 5, 7, 9-10, 14
collaboration matrix 937
collaboration policies 949
collaborative computing 935
collision area detection 619
collision areas 618
color content features 230
   color coherence vector 233, 246, 365,
     438
   color correlogram 234
   color histogram 230, 246, 365, 392
   color moments 232, 246
commercial block 426-427
commercial detection system, self-
   learning 442
commercial detection, performance 442
commercials, legal regulations 428
commercials, list of technical features 427
comparative testing 5
complexity 4, 10, 449, 466
composed object layer 573
composite class 22-23
composite multimedia presentation 584
composite object 22-23, 25-31
compression measures 160
compression ratio 140-144, 146-147, 160
computed synchronization 412-413
computer-assisted instruction 753, 761
conceptual clustering 318-319, 327, 331
conferencing system 58
Constant Bit Rate (CBR) 492-493, 787
constant density recording 511-512
constraint-based specification 482
constrained data placement 565-566
content-based indexing 43
content-based retrieval 227-229, 590, 594
content-based search 335
content-based video sampling 346-347
context-dependent retrieval 333-334
context-free retrieval 333, 335
continuous buffer management 597
continuous data management 584, 597
continuous data retrieval 593, 597
continuous display 562
continuous media 302, 559
  stream-based 559
  structured 559
continuous object manager 593
continuous retrieval requirement 514-515
copy prevention 301
courseware life cycle 771
cover image escrow 306
CPU scheduling 502, 633
cross-modal information retrieval 403-

404, 408
cryptography 301-302, 307-308
cryptolopes 301
cut detection 390
cyber art 946

D

D/A converter 148
database language 595
database management 44
database of commercials 441
data independence 589
data loss 877, 879, 882
data model 43-48, 52-53
data modeling 43-47, 52-53, 579-580,
   583-584, 586-588
data placement 507, 512-513, 516, 520,
   523
data replication 518-519
data transfer rate 510-512, 516, 522
data transfer time 510-511, 513
DAVIC (Digital Audio Visual Council)
   89-90
DAVIC,
   1.0 90
   1.1 90
   1.2 98
   1.3 102
   1.4 105
   audio-visual session 93
   base specification 92-93
DC coefficients 155-157
deadline-based scheduler 635
deadline monotonic scheduler 635
decision tree 215
declustering 518
decoration 6
delay jitter 786
delay skew 786
delivery scheduling 598
delivery system 96
   evolution 90
   functionalities 90, 107
   information flows 91
   Internet access 95
   interoperability 92
   reference decoder model 96
   service consumer system 93
   service provider system 97
   set top unit (STU) 93-94
   tools 107

detectability 6-8
deterministic service 492
DeVice hypermedia model 666-668
Dexter hypermedia model 653
dialog detection 367
dialog frame sequence 367
difference constraints approach 537
Differential Pulse Code Modulation (DPCM) 141-143
digital watermarks 299-300
  destination-based watermarks 300
  detection of watermarks 306
  insertion of watermarks 303
  linear watermarks 303
  non-linear watermarks 303
  source-based watermarks 300
  statistically encoded watermarks 305
directional average speed 270
Discrete Cosine Transform (DCT) 144-145
disk bandwidth 510-512, 518, 521-522, 597-598
disk scheduling 494, 501, 564, 566, 597
disk striping 517
disk utilization 500
distance measures 209-211, 213-214, 217-218, 224, 244
distributed cache technique 522
distributed messaging 951
distributed multimedia application 56-57, 59
distributed multimedia system 681-683, 818
distributed server 102
distributed simulation 947
document dependency 305
document languages 585, 588
document modeling 588
document objects 585
domain-driven metadata 591
dominant frequency 144
double buffering 614, 617
dynamic video manipulation 317

E

earcons 6
Earliest Deadline First (EDF) scheduler 635-636, 900-901
Edge Change Ratio (ECR) 434
education and training 582
educational software 4
eliminating flicker 612

end-to-end error control 863
end-to-end quality 875, 880, 882
entity-relationship model 46
erroneously inserted clips 442
error correction 864
error detection 863
error rate 786, 788
escrow techniques 307
Ethernet network 804-806
evaluation protocols 4, 8, 10, 12-13, 15
event-based authoring 78
event-driven control 59
event-driven programming 62, 78
expressive power 472

F

face detectors 366
facial expression 120
fades 432
feature-based commercial detection 428, 435
features of TV commercials 426
Fiber Distributed Data Interface (FDDI) 807
field evaluations 10
film introduction 427
Firefly 484
Flexible Interactive Presentation Synchronization (FLIPS) 538-539
flexible temporal model 537
formative 10, 13-14, 16
Forward Discrete Cosine Transform (FDCT) 155
frame-based animation 607-608
frame relay 798
frequency-based placement 516
functional magnetic resonance imagery 411

G

global motion 269
granularity 6-8
graphics renderer 744-745
group of objects 84
group rendezvous 953
Grouped Sweeping Scheme (GSS) 564
groupware 936
GUI object 17, 19, 24

H

H.261/263 standard 177-181, 687
  video codecs 177
handoff protocol 926-929
hard cut 430, 433
hard guarantee 518
hierarchical abstraction 53
hierarchical browser 274-277
hierarchical storage 520
hierarchical storage management 596-597
high bandwidth objects 569
High Definition Television (HDTV) 172-173
high level content abstraction 45
high-precision timer 551-553
histogram model 214
Hoffman coding 158-159
home entertainment 362
host mobility support 925
HTTP 665
human-computer interactions 4
human input/output modalities 114
hypermedia document 58, 349
hypermedia standards 655
hypermedia techniques 649
hypertext 650, 652
Hyper-Text Markup language (HTML) 664
HyTime 584, 589, 598, 658-659

I

icon 5-7, 9, 12-14
image compression 149
image database 228-229
image indexing 227, 245
image presentation 149
image similarity 248, 251
  Euclidean distance 231, 244-245
  histogram intersection 244
  L_1-distance 244
  L_2-distance 244
  Mahalonobis distance 244-245
  search 355
imperceptible watermarking 300
imprecise computation 636
indexing 43-47, 50, 53, 217, 227, 245, 281-286, 292, 294-295, 297
information and news services 581
information retrieval system 421, 583

inherent synchronization 412
instrument identification 217
Intel MMX technology 462
intelligent tutoring 754-755
interaction 475
  global 475
  local 475
interactive manager 708-709
interactive movies 701-703
interactive multimedia interfaces 111-112
interactive story 710
interactivity 3-4, 10-11, 13-14, 16
inter-disk data placement 513, 523
interface agents 121
Integrated Services Digital Network (ISDN) 796-797
interleaved contiguous placement 513-514
Internet 800, 804
interrupt handling 638
interviews 10
intradisk data placement 513, 523
Inverse Discrete Cosine Transform (IDCT) 159, 450
IP multicast 691, 802
Isis 483

J

JAVA 605
  animation support 607
  applet 609-610, 612, 615-616, 621, 623
  audio support 616
  environment 606
  media API 624
  multimedia support 605
  video support 622
jitter 877, 879, 881
JPEG 154-155, 261, 749
  decoder 169
  encoder 155
  hierarchical 169
  interactive progressive 168
  lossless 169-170
  progressive 164-165
  sequential 155,161

K

key frame 257, 264-267, 269, 271, 273-277, 322-324

key frame clustering 324
key frame selection 323-324
key-object 266, 271-274
knowledge-based system 51

L

latency 877, 879, 881
latency guarantees 498
latency time 568
learning and courseware 753
least-significant bit encoding 305
level 1 gateway 93
level 2 gateway 93
light table 274
light-weight sessions 950
linear insertion 303-305
Linear Predictive Coding (LPC) 143-145
load balanced placement 516
local average speed 270
logarithmic encoding 139-140, 142
Logical Time System (LTS) 36-37
lossless compression 154
lossy compression 154

M

Madeus 485-486
manual synchronization 406, 413
media composition 584-585
media correlation 413
media redundancy 408
media server 595
media taxonomy 3-16
memory access 638
memory allocation 637
memory copying 638
memory management 903
meta-analysis 761
meta data 380, 382, 384, 584, 586-588,
   590-592, 594
   management 398, 698
metaphor 3, 5-6, 11-12, 722-724, 727,
   730, 732-733
MHEG 32-33, 585, 588, 598, 660
MHEG-5 32-35
micon (motion icon) 267
mobile applications 915, 918, 921
   toolkit 918
mobile computers 915

mobile computing 127
mobile multimedia 59, 72
modeling temporal relations 527
monochrome frames 429
Mosaic 662-664
motion 3, 5-6, 8-10, 12-13
motion compensation 186, 450
motion estimation 186
motion estimation instruction 464
motion JPEG 687
motion vector 188
motion vector length 435
movie marketing 362
MPEG video compression standard 181,
   261-264, 272, 466, 687, 749, 816, 822,
   829
   audio encoder and decoder 194
   data stream 184
   frame structure 182
   interleaved A/V data stream 195
   video decoder 183, 449
   video encoder 183, 435
multidimensional access structure (MAS)
   283-284
multimedia accelerator 741
multimedia agents 59
multimedia archiving 362, 379-380, 386,
   398
multimedia authoring 472
multimedia content retrieval 396
multimedia databases 281-283, 404, 579
multimedia data modeling 43-44, 62, 73,
   86, 696
multimedia data objects 74, 86
multimedia data port 98
multimedia document 469-471
multimedia education 751, 755
multimedia indices 388
multimedia information retrieval 282, 345
   content-based 282
multimedia information systems 696
multimedia logging 379-380, 386
multimedia networks 783
multimedia object 17-20, 23-29, 31-32,
   36, 39-40, 62, 74, 77-78, 84, 86, 388,
   473, 585-586, 588, 596
multimedia operating systems 627, 694
multimedia processing 741
multimedia processors 448, 458
   adapted programmable 456
   dedicated 452
   function specific 453
   programmable dedicated 454
multimedia publishing 582

multimedia retrieval 379-380
multimedia scripting 641
multimedia servers 557
multimedia synchronization 525, 694-695
multimedia transmission 790, 794
Multimedia Transport Protocol (MTP)
    831-835
multimedia virtual reality architecture 743
multimodal interaction 706
multimodality 114
Multiple Internet mail Extensions
    (MIME) 660
multiple QOS levels 493-494, 498
multiple threading environment 611
multiple threads 611
multi-story animation 707
multi-user access 583
music 4-6, 9, 16
music analysis 215
music compression 135-136
musical CD database 718
Musical Instrument Digital Interface
    (MIDI) 217

N

natural language processing 117
navigation mechanism 353
navigational 13
    browsing 333
network load 885
network performance 787
network scheduling 503
network throughput 787
networked multimedia system 839
non-linear insertion 304
non-verbal interaction 706
nonspeech audio interfaces 118
NTSC 172-173
Nyquist frequency 138

O

object authoring approaches 62
object class hierarchy 68
object composition 27-28, 31, 39
object graph 921
object hierarchy 28, 31
object migration 926, 929
object motion analysis 263
object retrieval schedule 539

observations 4, 10
orchestrated presentation 541

P

packet switched services 797
paging 637
pen technology 116
perceptible watermarking 300
perceptual capacity 309-310
perceptual modeling 304
perceptual quality 878-879
Petri nets 481, 528
    Dynamic Timed Petri Nets (DTPN)
        532-534
    Object Composition Petri Nets (OCPN)
        532
    Timed Petri Nets (TPN) 529-530
phase-based striping 520
pictorial index 355-356
pictorial transcript 345, 350, 352
picture quality 160
Plain Old Telephone Service (POTS) 794
playback model 27, 31
playout management 580, 598
point of view (POV) 286, 288-289
precision rate 381-382, 384
predictable service 845
presentation engine 584, 590, 598
presentation functions 60, 62, 67-69
presentation objects 62-80, 86
priority inversion 635
processor load 885
processor management 899
Production Consumption Ratio (PCR) 522
psychoacoustic model 136
Pulse Code Modulation (PCM) 136-137

Q

Quality of Service (QoS) 59, 789, 826-
    827, 839-870, 892, 897
    adaptation 866, 868
    architecture 869
    constraints 840
    definition 841
    guarantees 596, 631
    layering 841
    negotiation 848
    parameters 598

protocol reference model 690
renegotiation 866-867
requirements 541, 593, 840, 856
specification 842
quantization 137-143, 145-146, 156-157
quantization error 138
quantization tables 156
query 44-45, 52
query functionality 381, 384-385
query media 408
query vector 249

R

rate control 861
rate guarantees 595
rate monotonic scheduler 635
Real-time Transport Protocol (RTP) 693,
    803, 834
recall rate 381-382, 384
recognition-based commercial detection
    437, 439-440
reconfigurable architecture 744
recording density 510-512
Redundant Arrays of Inexpensive Disks
    (RAID) 596
relevance feedback 228-230, 248
    architecture 249
reservation in advance 909
reservation model 857
ReSerVation Protocol (RSVP) 693
resource accounting 908
resource capacity 894
resource management 689, 891
    architecture 846-847
    functionality 895
    phases 896
    system structure 898
resource manager 899
resource monitoring 866
resource reservation 858, 897
    protocol 897
retrieval 43-47, 50, 52
RGB representation 150-151, 451
rhythm analysis 216
ring networks 806
role tree 330
Root Mean Square (RMS) error 160
rotational latency 510-512

S

salient stills 263, 267, 274
sampled media 302
satellite-based time broadcasting 550
scaling 853
scalable server 569
scene break 430
scene construction 728
scene determination 370
scene generation 705
scene manager 707
scene transition viewgraph 276
script-free transcript 405
script language 62, 65, 479
script-less content 405
script-light 405
script manager 707
script-tight 405
security tools 99
seek distance 509-511
seek time 509-513, 516, 518
semantic content retrieval 396
semantic network 591
service objects 842
service proxies 913, 916-917, 921, 923
shape features 240-243
    circularity 242
    eccentricity 242
    Fourier shape features 240
    major axis orientation 242
    moment invariants 242
    turning angle 241
shot boundary detection 369
shot clustering 272, 370
shot detection 258
    block comparison 259
    compression-based 261
    DCT-based 261
    editing model fitting 260
    histogram comparison 259
    hybrid algorithm 262
    motion-based 263
shot grouping 391
shot similarity 273
similarity-based retrieval 281
single threading environment 611
slide-and-lecture presentation 410
soft guarantee 518
sound 3, 5-6, 8-10, 12-14
sound effects 212, 218, 221

sound effects browser 221-222
spatial composition 22-23
spatial data model 587
spatial orientation graph 285
spatial query 243, 284
spatial representation 285-286
speech-based media 410
speech feature recognition 417
speech to text 217
sprite-based animation 614, 618
staggered striping 519
staging 522
static media 302
static priority 634
statistic motion features 270
statistical service 492
steganography 301
storage organization 507
storage pattern altering policy 515
storage pattern preserve policy 514
storyboard 772-774
story generation 704
stream-based presentation 560
streaming delivery 357-358
structural data management 592-594, 598
structure of commercial block 426
structure tree 718
structured document modeling 594
Structured General Markup Language
    (SGML) 582, 585, 588-590, 598, 655-
    657
structured logging 387, 393
structured presentation 570
structured video content 268
surveillance 223
swapping 637
Switched Multimegabit Data Service
    (SMDS) 799
synchronized computation 417
synchronous multimedia 785
Synchronous Optical Network (SONET)
    799
synthesis of computer graphics 745
system testing 10

T

target media 408
telecollaboration 936
teleinstruction 946

telemedicine 946
telescience 946
television commercials 425-426
temporal algebra 586
temporal composition 23, 39, 474
temporal data model 586
temporal media 302, 407
temporal modeling 586-588
temporal relations 527
temporal scenario 470
temporal synchronization 405, 408-410,
    413-415, 417, 421-422, 545
temporal transformation 26
temporal variance 269
terrestrial time signal stations 547-549
tertiary storage devices 507, 509-510,
    520-522
text processing 348
text recognition 368
text segmentation 368
texture features 234, 247
    coarseness 235
    contrast 236
    directionality 236
    Gabor features 238
    orientation 237
    shape 239
    Tamura features 235
    wavelet 239
time-driven presentation 58
timed streams 406
time-flow graph 535-536
time-line display 274
time-line model 530, 586
timelines 79, 87
time standards 547
title extraction 368
token ring 806
traffic characterization 787
traffic shaping 859
traffic source modeling 542
trailer generation 370
trailer production 361
transaction management 698
transcription graph 415-416
transform-based audio compression 144-
    147
transition detection 260
translation synchronization 412
transport protocols for video 830
tutoring shell 756

U

Uniform Resource Locator (URL) 665
unpredictable objects 474
usability 8, 10
usefulness 3, 8, 10-12
user controls 14

V

Variable Bit Rate (VBR) 492-494, 787,
  817-818, 821-822
variable density recording 509
vector quantization 143
video abstract 363, 365
video abstraction 264
video archives 582
video browsing 255, 257, 266, 271, 274,
  277
video class 21-22
video classification 318-319, 323
video compression techniques 175
videoconference quality 880, 883-886
videoconferencing 178, 763, 944
video content representation 267
video cut 591
video data capture 745
video data model 582, 586, 590
video fingerprint 438
video formats 172
  computer 172
  television 172
video games 703
video icon (3-D icon) 266
video indexing 267
video information manipulation system
  (VIMS) 318-320, 330, 338-340
video information units 174
video mapping 746
  processor 747
  scheme 746
video mosaic 266-267
video object 21-22, 24, 26, 30, 39
video-on-demand 45
video parsing 257
  panning 259, 263, 265
  scene detection 262
  shot detection 258
  zooming 263, 265
video partitioning 323
videophone 178
video production 323
video program 323, 348

video representation 172
video retrieval 255-257
video segmentation 369
video skimming 267
video trailer 363
video transport 815
video transport protocol 819
video viewer 923
virtual classroom 765-766
virtual collaborative spaces 946
virtual reality environment 760-761
Virtual Reality Markup Language
  (VRML) 585, 588, 714
virtual realty school 752, 767, 770, 776
virtual reality system 713, 737-739
virtual reality technique 716
virtual reality tutoring 759
virtual world object 719-722, 724
visual information systems 52
Visual Instruction Set (VIS) 463
visual searching 353
voice compression 136
voice recognition 117

W

waiting time 518, 520, 522
wavelets 135, 144-145
window-based user interfaces 113
workload characterization 631
workspace architectures 940

X

X.25 service 798
XYZ video compression 195
  decoder 200
  encoder 196

Y

YUV representation 150-151, 451

Z

zoned-bit recording 511